The Middle Ages • SIMPSON

The Sixteenth Century • GREENBLATT / LOGAN

The Early Seventeenth Century
MAUS

The Restoration and the Eighteenth Century
NOGGLE

The Romantic Period • LYNCH

The Victorian Age • ROBSON

The Twentieth and Twenty-First Centuries
RAMAZANI

THE NORTON ANTHOLOGY OF

ENGLISH LITERATURE

TENTH EDITION

VOLUME D

THE ROMANTIC PERIOD

THE NORTON ANTHOLOGY OF

ENGLISH

LITERATURE

TENTH EDITION

Stephen Greenblatt, *General Editor*

COGAN UNIVERSITY PROFESSOR OF THE HUMANITIES

HARVARD UNIVERSITY

VOLUME D

THE ROMANTIC PERIOD

Deidre Shauna Lynch

W·W·NORTON & COMPANY

NEW YORK · LONDON

W. W. Norton & Company has been independent since its founding in 1923, when William Warder Norton and Mary D. Herter Norton first published lectures delivered at the People's Institute, the adult education division of New York City's Cooper Union. The firm soon expanded its program beyond the Institute, publishing books by celebrated academics from America and abroad. By midcentury, the two major pillars of Norton's publishing program— trade books and college texts—were firmly established. In the 1950s, the Norton family transferred control of the company to its employees, and today—with a staff of four hundred and a comparable number of trade, college, and professional titles published each year—W. W. Norton & Company stands as the largest and oldest publishing house owned wholly by its employees.

Editors: Julia Reidhead and Marian Johnson
Assistant Editor, Print: Rachel Taylor
Manuscript Editors: Michael Fleming, Katharine Ings, Candace Levy
Media Editor: Carly Fraser Doria
Assistant Editor, Media: Ava Bramson
Marketing Manager, Literature: Kimberly Bowers
Managing Editor, College Digital Media: Kim Yi
Production Manager: Sean Mintus
Text design: Jo Anne Metsch
Art director: Rubina Yeh
Photo Editor: Nelson Colon
Permissions Manager: Megan Jackson Schindel
Permissions Clearing: Nancy J. Rodwan
Cartographer: Adrian Kitzinger
Composition: Westchester Book Company
Manufacturing: LSC Crawfordsville

ISBN: 978-0-393-60305-7

W. W. Norton & Company, Inc., 500 Fifth Avenue, New York, NY 10110
wwnorton.com

W. W. Norton & Company Ltd., 15 Carlisle Street, London W1D 3BS

6 7 8 9 0

Contents*

The Romantic Period (1785–1832)

* Additional readings are available on the NAEL Archive (digital.wwnorton.com/englishlit10def).

THE ROMANTIC IMAGINATION AND THE
"ORIENTAL NATIONS"   922

_____

Preface to the Tenth Edition

For centuries the study of literature has occupied a central place in the Humanities curriculum. The power of great literature to reach across time and space, its exploration of the expressive potential of language, and its ability to capture the whole range of experiences from the most exalted to the everyday have made it an essential part of education. But there are significant challenges to any attempt to derive the full measure of enlightenment and pleasure from this precious resource. In a world in which distraction reigns, savoring works of literature requires quiet focus. In a society in which new media clamor for attention, attending to words on the page can prove difficult. And in a period obsessed with the present at its most instantaneous, it takes a certain effort to look at anything penned earlier than late last night.

The Norton Anthology of English Literature is designed to meet these challenges. It is deeply rewarding to enter the sensibility of a different place, to hear a new voice, to be touched by an unfamiliar era. It is critically important to escape the narrow boundaries of our immediate preoccupations and to respond with empathy to lives other than our own. It is moving, even astonishing, to feel that someone you never met is speaking directly to you. But for any of this to happen requires help. The overarching goal of the Norton Anthology—as it has been for over fifty-five years and ten editions—is to help instructors energize their classrooms, engage their students, and bring literature to life.* At a time when the Humanities are under great pressure, we are committed to facilitating the special joy that comes with encountering significant works of art.

The works anthologized in these six volumes generally form the core of courses designed to introduce students to English literature. The selections reach back to the earliest moments of literary creativity in English, when the language itself was still molten, and extend to some of the most recent experiments, when, once again, English seems remarkably fluid and open. That openness—a recurrent characteristic of a language that has never been officially regulated and that has constantly renewed itself—helps to account for the sense of freshness that characterizes the works brought together here.

One of the joys of literature in English is its spectacular abundance. Even within the geographical confines of England, Scotland, Wales, and

---

* For more on the help we offer and how to access it, see "Additional Resources for Instructors and Students," p. xxvi.

Ireland, where the majority of texts in this collection originated, one can find more than enough distinguished and exciting works to fill the pages of this anthology many times over. But English literature is not confined to the British Isles; it is a global phenomenon. This border-crossing is not a consequence of modernity alone. It is fitting that among the first works here is *Beowulf*, a powerful epic written in the Germanic language known as Old English about a singularly restless Scandinavian hero. *Beowulf*'s remarkable translator in *The Norton Anthology of English Literature*, Seamus Heaney, was one of the great contemporary masters of English literature—he was awarded the Nobel Prize for Literature in 1995—but it would be potentially misleading to call him an "English poet" for he was born in Northern Ireland and was not in fact English. It would be still more misleading to call him a "British poet," as if the British Empire were the most salient fact about the language he spoke and wrote in or the culture by which he was shaped. What matters is that the language in which Heaney wrote is English, and this fact links him powerfully with the authors assembled in these volumes, a linguistic community that stubbornly refuses to fit comfortably within any firm geographical or ethnic or national boundaries. So too, to glance at other authors and writings in the anthology, in the twelfth century, the noblewoman Marie de France wrote her short stories in an Anglo-Norman dialect at home on both sides of the channel; in the sixteenth century William Tyndale, in exile in the Low Countries and inspired by German religious reformers, translated the New Testament from Greek and thereby changed the course of the English language; in the seventeenth century Aphra Behn touched readers with a story that moves from Africa, where its hero is born, to South America, where Behn herself may have witnessed some of the tragic events she describes; and early in the twentieth century Joseph Conrad, born in Ukraine of Polish parents, wrote in eloquent English a celebrated novella whose ironic vision of European empire gave way by the century's end to the voices of those over whom the empire, now in ruins, had once hoped to rule: the Caribbean-born Claude McKay, Louise Bennett, Derek Walcott, Kamau Brathwaite, V. S. Naipaul, and Grace Nichols; the African-born Chinua Achebe, J. M. Coetzee, Ngũgĩ Wa Thiong'o, and Chimamanda Ngozi Adichie; and the Indian-born A. K. Ramanujan and Salman Rushdie.

A vital literary culture is always on the move. This principle was the watchword of M. H. Abrams, the distinguished literary critic who first conceived *The Norton Anthology of English Literature,* brought together the original team of editors, and, with characteristic insight, diplomacy, and humor, oversaw seven editions. Abrams wisely understood that new scholarly discoveries and the shifting interests of readers constantly alter the landscape of literary history. To stay vital, the anthology, therefore, would need to undergo a process of periodic revision, guided by advice from teachers, as well as students, who view the anthology with a loyal but critical eye. As with past editions, we have benefited from detailed information on the works actually assigned and suggestions for improvements from 273 reviewers. Their participation has been crucial as the editors grapple with the task of strengthening the selection of more traditional texts while adding texts that reflect the expansion of the field of English studies.

With each edition, *The Norton Anthology of English Literature* has offered a broadened canon without sacrificing major writers and a selection of complete longer texts in which readers can immerse themselves. Perhaps the most emblematic of these great texts are the epics *Beowulf* and *Paradise Lost*. Among the many other complete longer works in the Tenth Edition are *Sir Gawain and the Green Knight* (in Simon Armitage's spectacular translation), Sir Thomas More's *Utopia*, Sir Philip Sidney's *Defense of Poesy*, William Shakespeare's *Twelfth Night* and *Othello*, Samuel Johnson's *Rasselas*, Aphra Behn's *Oroonoko*, Jonathan Swift's *Gulliver's Travels*, Laurence Sterne's *A Sentimental Journey through France and Italy*, Charles Dickens's *A Christmas Carol*, Robert Louis Stevenson's *The Strange Case of Dr. Jekyll and Mr. Hyde*, Rudyard Kipling's *The Man Who Would Be King*, Joseph Conrad's *Heart of Darkness*, Virginia Woolf's *Mrs. Dalloway*, James Joyce's *Portrait of the Artist as a Young Man*, Samuel Beckett's *Waiting for Godot*, Harold Pinter's *The Dumb Waiter*, and Tom Stoppard's *Arcadia*. To augment the number of complete longer works instructors can assign, and—a special concern—better to represent the achievements of novelists, the publisher is making available the full list of Norton Critical Editions, more than 240 titles, including such frequently assigned novels as Jane Austen's *Pride and Prejudice*, Mary Shelley's *Frankenstein*, Charles Dickens's *Hard Times*, and Chinua Achebe's *Things Fall Apart*. A Norton Critical Edition may be included with either package (volumes A, B, C and volumes D, E, F) or any individual volume at a discounted price (contact your Norton representative for details).

We have in this edition continued to expand the selection of writing by women in several historical periods. The sustained work of scholars in recent years has recovered dozens of significant authors who had been marginalized or neglected by a male-dominated literary tradition and has deepened our understanding of those women writers who had managed, against considerable odds, to claim a place in that tradition. The First Edition of the Norton Anthology included 6 women writers; this Tenth Edition includes 84, of whom 13 are newly added and 10 are reselected or expanded. Poets and dramatists whose names were scarcely mentioned even in the specialized literary histories of earlier generations—Aemilia Lanyer, Lady Mary Wroth, Margaret Cavendish, Mary Leapor, Anna Letitia Barbauld, Charlotte Smith, Letitia Elizabeth Landon, Mary Elizabeth Coleridge, Mina Loy, and many others—now appear in the company of their male contemporaries. There are in addition four complete long prose works by women— Aphra Behn's *Oroonoko*, Eliza Haywood's *Fantomina*, Jane Austen's *Love and Friendship,* and Virginia Woolf's *Mrs. Dalloway*—along with selections from such celebrated fiction writers as Maria Edgeworth, Jean Rhys, Katherine Mansfield, Doris Lessing, Margaret Atwood, Kiran Desai, Zadie Smith, and new authors Hilary Mantel and Chimamanda Ngozi Adichie.

Building on an innovation introduced in the First Edition, the editors have expanded the array of topical clusters that gather together short texts illuminating the cultural, historical, intellectual, and literary concerns of each of the periods. We have designed these clusters with three aims: to make them lively and accessible, to ensure that they can be taught effectively in a class meeting or two, and to make clear their relevance to the surrounding works of literature. Hence, for example, in the Sixteenth Century, a new cluster, "The Wider World," showcases the English fascination with narratives of adventure, exploration, trade, and reconnaissance. New in the Eighteenth Century, "Print Culture and the Rise of the Novel" offers statements on the emergence of what would become English literature's most popular form as well as excerpts from *Robinson Crusoe* and *Evelina*. And in the Romantic Period, a new cluster on "The Romantic Imagination and the 'Oriental Nations'" joins contemporary discussion of the literature of those nations with selections from William Beckford's *Vathek* and Byron's *The Giaour*, among other texts. Across the volumes the clusters provide an exciting way to broaden the field of the literary and to set masterpieces in a wider cultural, social, and historical framework

Now, as in the past, cultures define themselves by the songs they sing and the stories they tell. But the central importance of visual media in contemporary culture has heightened our awareness of the ways in which songs and stories have always been closely linked to the images that societies have fashioned and viewed. The Tenth Edition of *The Norton Anthology of English Literature* features fifty-six pages of color plates (in seven color inserts) and more than 120 black-and-white illustrations throughout the volumes, including six new maps. In selecting visual material—from the Sutton Hoo treasure of the seventh century to Yinka Shonibare's *Nelson's Ship in a Bottle* in the twenty-first century—the editors sought to provide images that conjure up, whether directly or indirectly, the individual writers in each section; that relate specifically to individual works in the anthology; and that shape and illuminate the culture of a particular literary period. We have tried to choose visually striking images that will interest students and provoke discussion, and our captions draw attention to important details and cross-reference related texts in the anthology.

Period-by-Period Revisions

The Middle Ages. Edited by James Simpson, this period, huge in its scope and immensely varied in its voices, continues to offer exciting surprises. The heart of the Anglo-Saxon portion is the great epic *Beowulf*, in the acclaimed translation by Seamus Heaney. Now accompanied by a map of England at the time, the Anglo-Saxon texts include the haunting poems "Wulf and Eadwacer" and "The Ruin" as well as an intriguing collection of Anglo-Saxon riddles. These new works join verse translations of the *Dream of the Rood*, the *Wanderer*, and *The Wife's Lament*. An Irish Literature selection features a tale from *The Tain* and a group of ninth-century lyrics. The Anglo-Norman section—a key bridge between the Anglo-Saxon period and the time of Chaucer—offers a new pairing of texts about the tragic story of Tristan and Ysolt; an illuminating cluster on the Romance, with three stories by Marie de France (in award-winning translations); and *Sir Orfeo*, a comic version of the Orpheus and Eurydice story. The Middle English section centers, as always, on Chaucer, with a generous selection of tales and poems glossed and annotated so as to heighten their accessibility. Simon Armitage's brilliant verse translation of *Sir Gawain and the Green Knight* appears once again, and we offer newly modernized versions both of Thomas Hoccleve's *My Complaint*, a startlingly personal account of the speaker's attempt to reenter society after a period of mental instability, and of the playfully ironic and spiritually moving *Second Shepherds' Play*. "Talking Animals," a delightful new cluster, presents texts by Marie de France, Chaucer, and Robert Henryson that show how medieval writers used animals in stories that reveal much about humankind.

The Sixteenth Century, edited by Stephen Greenblatt and George Logan, features eight extraordinary longer texts in their entirety: More's *Utopia* (with two letters from More to Peter Giles); Book 1 of Spenser's *Faerie Queene* and, new to this edition, the posthumously published *Mutabilitie Cantos*, which arguably offer some of Spenser's finest poetry; Marlowe's *Hero and Leander* and *Doctor Faustus*, Sidney's *Defense of Poesy*; and Shakespeare's *Twelfth Night* and *Othello,* which has been added to the Tenth Edition by instructor request. Two exciting new topical clusters join the section. "An Elizabethan Miscellany" is a full, richly teachable grouping of sixteenth-century poems in English, by writers from George Gascoigne to Michael Drayton to Thomas Campion, among others, and provides access the period's explosion of lyric genius. "The Wider World" showcases the English Renaissance fascination with narratives of adventure, exploration, trade, and reconnaissance. Ranging from Africa to the Muslim East to the New World, the texts are compelling reading in our contemporary global context and offer particularly suggestive insights into the world of Shakespeare's *Othello*.

The Early Seventeenth Century. At the heart of this period, edited by Katharine Eisaman Maus, is John Milton's *Paradise Lost,* presented in its entirety. New to the Tenth Edition are the Arguments to each book, which are especially helpful for students first reading this magnificent, compelling epic. Along with Milton's "Lycidas" and *Samson Agonistes,* which is new to this edition, other complete longer works include John Donne's *Satire 3* and *The Anatomy of the World: The First Anniversary;* Aemilia Lanyer's country-house poem "The Description of Cookham"; Ben Jonson's *Volpone* and the moving Cary-Morison ode; and John Webster's tragedy *The Duchess of Malfi.* Generous selections from Donne, Mary Wroth, George Herbert, Katherine Philips, Andrew Marvell, and others, as well as the clusters "Inquiry and Experience," "Gender Relations," and "Crisis of Authority," together make for an exciting and thorough representation of the period.

The Restoration and the Eighteenth Century. The impressive array of complete longer texts in this period, edited by James Noggle, includes Dryden's *Absalom and Achitophel* and *MacFlecknoe;* Aphra Behn's *Oroonoko* (now with its dedicatory epistle); Congreve's comedy *The Way of the World;* Swift's *Gulliver's Travels* (newly complete, with illustrations from the first edition); Pope's *Essay on Criticism, The Rape of the Lock,* and *Epistle to Dr. Arbuthnot;* Gay's *Beggar's Opera;* Eliza Haywood's novella of sexual role-playing, *Fantomina;* Hogarth's graphic satire "Marriage A-la-Mode"; Johnson's *Vanity of Human Wishes* and *Rasselas;* Laurence Sterne's *A Sentimental Journey through France and Italy* (new to this edition); Gray's "Elegy Written in a Country Churchyard"; and Goldsmith's "The Deserted Village." An exciting new topical cluster, "Print Culture and the Rise of the Novel," with selections by Daniel Defoe, Henry Fielding, Samuel Richardson, Frances Burney, Clara Reeve, and others, enables readers to explore the origins of English literature's most popular form.

The Romantic Period. Edited by Deidre Shauna Lynch, this period again offers many remarkable additions. Chief among them are two topical clusters: "Romantic Literature and Wartime," which, through texts by Godwin, Wordsworth, Coleridge, Barbauld, Byron, De Quincey, and others, explores the varied ways in which war's violence came home to English literature; and "The Romantic Imagination and the 'Oriental Nations,'" which shows how English writers of the late eighteenth and early nineteenth centuries looked eastward for new, often contradictory themes of cultural identity and difference and for "exotic" subjects that were novel and enticing to the English audience. Also new to this period are poems by Barbauld, Robinson, Charlotte Smith, Wordsworth, Shelley, Hemans, and Landon. We are excited to include an excerpt from *The History of Mary Prince, a West Indian Slave*—the first slave narrative by a woman. John Clare, the increasingly appreciated "natural poet," receives four new texts.

The Victorian Age, edited by Catherine Robson, offers an impressive array of complete longer works. New to the prose selections is Charles Dickens's *A Christmas Carol,* complete with its original illustrations. Dickens's celebrated tale, which entertains at the same time that it deals brilliantly with matters social, economic, and spiritual, joins Robert Louis Stevenson's *The Strange Case of Dr. Jekyll and Mr. Hyde,* Arthur Conan Doyle's *The Speckled Band,* Elizabeth Gaskell's *The Old Nurse's Story,* and Rudyard Kipling's *The Man Who Would Be King.* Authors with significant longer poems include Elizabeth Barrett Browning, Alfred, Lord Tennyson, Robert Browning, Dante Gabriel Rossetti, Christina Rossetti, Algernon Charles Swinburne, and Gerard Manley Hopkins. Plays include Oscar Wilde's *The Importance of Being Earnest* and George Bernard Shaw's controversial drama on prostitution, *Mrs Warren's Profession.* And, continuing the tradition of enabling readers to grapple with the period's most resonant and often fiercely contentious issues, the Tenth Edition offers an exciting new cluster, "Beacons of the Future? Education in Victorian Britain," which brings together powerful reflections by John Stuart Mill and others, government reports on the nature of education, and illuminating excerpts from *Hard Times, Alice's Adventures in Wonderland, Tom Brown's School Days,* and *Jude the Obscure.*

The Twentieth and Twenty-First Centuries. The editor, Jahan Ramazani, continues his careful revision of this, the most rapidly changing period in the anthology. Once again its core is three modernist masterpieces: Virginia Woolf's *Mrs. Dalloway,* James Joyce's *Portrait of the Artist as a Young Man,* and Samuel Beckett's *Waiting for Godot,* all complete. These works are surrounded by a dazzling array of other fiction and drama. New to the Tenth Edition are the recent recipient of the Nobel Prize for Literature, Kazuo Ishiguro, along with Hilary Mantel, Caryl Phillips, and Chimamanda Ngozi Adichie. Their works join Joseph Conrad's *Heart of Darkness,* Harold Pinter's *The Dumb Waiter,* Tom Stoppard's *Arcadia,* and stories by D. H. Lawrence,

Katherine Mansfield, Jean Rhys, Doris Lessing, Nadine Gordimer, Kiran Desai, and Zadie Smith. A generous representation of poetry centers on substantial selections from Thomas Hardy, William Butler Yeats, and T. S. Eliot, and extends out to a wide range of other poets, from A. E. Housman, Wilfred Owen, and W. H. Auden to Philip Larkin, Derek Walcott, and Seamus Heaney. Two new poets, frequently requested by our readers, join the anthology: Anne Carson and Simon Armitage; and there are new poems by Yeats, Heaney, Geoffrey Hill, and Carol Ann Duffy. Visual aids have proved very helpful in teaching this period, and new ones include facsimile manuscript pages of poems by Isaac Rosenberg and Wilfred Owen, plus five new maps, which illustrate, among other things, the dramatic changes in the British Empire from 1891 to the late twentieth century, the movement of peoples to and from England during this time, and the journeys around London of the central characters in Woolf's *Mrs. Dalloway*. Linton Kwesi Johnson, Bernardine Evaristo, Patience Agbabi, and Dajlit Nagra join Claude McKay, Louise Bennett, Kamau Brathwaite, Ngũgĩ Wa Thiong'o, M. NourbeSe Philip, Salman Rushdie, and Grace Nichols in the much-praised cluster "Nation, Race, and Language"—together they bear witness to the global diffusion of English, the urgency of issues of nation and identity, and the rich complexity of literary history.

Editorial Procedures and Format

The Tenth Edition adheres to the principles that have always characterized *The Norton Anthology of English Literature*. Period introductions, head-notes, and annotations are designed to enhance students' reading and, without imposing an interpretation, to give students the information they need to understand each text. The aim of these editorial materials is to make the anthology self-sufficient, so that it can be read anywhere—in a coffeeshop, on a bus, under a tree.

The Norton Anthology of English Literature prides itself on both the scholarly accuracy and the readability of its texts. To ease students' encounter with some works, we have normalized spelling and capitalization in texts up to and including the Romantic period—for the most part they now follow the conventions of modern English. We leave unaltered, however, texts in which such modernizing would change semantic or metrical qualities. From the Victorian period onward, we have used the original spelling and punctuation. We continue other editorial procedures that have proved useful in the past. After each work, we cite the date of first publication on the right; in some instances, this date is followed by the date of a revised edition for which the author was responsible. Dates of composition, when they differ from those of publication and when they are known, are provided on the left. We use square brackets to indicate titles supplied by the editors for the convenience of readers. Whenever a portion of a text is omitted, we indicate that omission with three asterisks. If the omitted portion is important for following the plot or argument, we provide a brief summary within the text or in a footnote. Finally, we have reconsidered annotations throughout and increased the number of marginal glosses for archaic, dialect, or unfamiliar words.

The Tenth Edition includes the useful "Literary Terminology" appendix, a quick-reference alphabetical glossary with examples from works in the anthology. We have also updated the General Bibliography that appears in the print volumes, as well as the period and author bibliographies, which appear online, where they can be easily searched and updated.

Additional Resources for Instructors and Students

The idea that a vital literary culture is always on the move applies not only to the print anthology but also to the resources that accompany it. For the Tenth Edition, we have added exciting new resources and improved and updated existing resources to make them more useful and easy to find.

We are pleased to launch the new NAEL Archive site, found at digital. wwnorton.com/englishlit10abc (for volumes A, B, C) and digital.wwnorton .com/englishlit10def (for volumes D, E, F). This searchable and sortable site contains thousands of resources for students and instructors in one centralized place at no additional cost. Following are some highlights:

- A series of twenty brand-new video modules designed to enhance classroom presentation of the literary works. These videos, conceived of and narrated by the anthology editors, bring various texts from the anthology to life by providing a closer look at a rarely seen manuscript, visiting a place of literary significance, or offering a conversation with a living writer.
- Over 1,000 additional readings from the Middle Ages to the turn of the twentieth century, edited, glossed, and annotated to the scholarly standards and with the sensitivity to classroom use for which the Norton Anthology is renowned. Teachers who wish to add to the selections in the print anthology will find numerous exciting works, including Wycherley's *The Country Wife*, Joanna Baillie's "A Mother to Her Waking Infant," and Edward Lear's "The Jumblies." In addition, there are many fascinating topical clusters—"The First Crusade: Sanctifying War," "Genius," and "The Satanic and Byronic Hero," to name only a few—all designed to draw readers into larger cultural contexts and to expose them to a wide spectrum of voices.
- Hundreds of images—maps, author portraits, literary places, and manuscripts—available for student browsing or instructor download for in-class presentation.
- Several hours of audio recordings.
- Annotated bibliographies for all periods and authors in the anthology.

The NAEL Archive also provides a wealth of teaching resources that are unlocked on instructor log-in:

- "Quick read" summaries, teaching notes, and discussion questions for every work in the anthology, from the much-praised *Teaching with The Norton Anthology of English Literature: A Guide for Instructors* by Naomi Howell (University of Exeter), Philip Schwyzer (University of Exeter), Judyta Frodyma (University of Northern British Columbia), and Sondra Archimedes (University of California–Santa Cruz).

- Downloadable PowerPoints featuring images and audio for in-class presentation

In addition to the wealth of resources in the NAEL Archive, Norton offers a downloadable coursepack that allows instructors to easily add high-quality Norton digital media to online, hybrid, or lecture courses—all at no cost. Norton Coursepacks work within existing learning management systems; there's no new system to learn, and access is free and easy. Content is customizable and includes over seventy-four reading-comprehension quizzes, short-answer questions with suggested answers, links to the video modules, and more.

The editors are deeply grateful to the hundreds of teachers worldwide who have helped us to improve *The Norton Anthology of English Literature*. A list of the instructors who replied to a detailed questionnaire follows, under Acknowledgments. The editors would like to express appreciation for their assistance to Jessica Berman (University of Maryland Baltimore County), Lara Bovilsky (University of Oregon), Gordon Braden (University of Virginia), Bruce Bradley (Clongowes Wood College), Dympna Callaghan (Syracuse University), Ariel Churchill (Harvard University), Joseph Connors (Harvard University), Taylor Cowdery (University of North Carolina at Chapel Hill), Maria Devlin (Harvard University), Lars Engel (University of Tulsa), James Engell (Harvard University), Aubrey Everett (Harvard University), Anne Fernald (Fordham University), Kevis Goodman (University of California, Berkeley), Alexander Gourlay (Rhode Island School of Design), John Hale (University of Otago), Stephen Hequembourg (University of Virginia), Seth Herbst (United States Military Academy, West Point), Rhema Hokama (Singapore University of Technology and Design), Jean Howard (Columbia University), Robert Irvine (University of Edinburgh), Thomas Keirstead (University of Toronto), Margaret Kelleher (University College Dublin), Cara Lewis (Indiana University Northwest), Mario Menendez (Harvard University), Tara Menon (New York University), John Miller (University of Virginia), Peter Miller (University of Virginia), A. J. Odasso (Wellesley College), Declan O'Keeffe (Clongowes Wood College), Juan Christian Pellicer (University of Oslo), Robert Pinsky (Boston University), Will Porter (Harvard University), Mark Rankin (James Madison University), Josephine Reece (Harvard University), Jessica Rosenberg (University of Miami), Suparna Roychoudhury (Mount Holyoke College), Peter Sacks (Harvard University), Ray Siemens (University of Victoria), Kim Simpson (University of Southampton), Bailey Sincox (Harvard University), Ramie Targoff (Brandeis University), Misha Teramura (Reed College), Gordon Teskey (Harvard University), Katie Trumpener (Yale University), Paul Westover (Brigham Young University), Katy Woodring (Harvard University), and Faye Zhang (Harvard University).

We also thank the many people at Norton, an employee-owned publishing house with a commitment to excellence, who contributed to the Tenth Edition. In planning this edition, Julia Reidhead served, as she has done in the past, as our wise and effective collaborator. In addition, we are now working with Marian Johnson, literature editor and managing editor for college books, a splendid new collaborator who has helped us bring the

Tenth Edition to fruition. With admirable equanimity and skill, Carly Frasier Doria, electronic media editor and course guide editor, fashioned the new video modules and brought together the dazzling array of web resources and other pedagogical aids. We also have debts of gratitude to Katharine Ings, Candace Levy, and Michael Fleming, manuscript editors; Sean Mintus, senior production manager; Kimberly Bowers, marketing manager for literature; Megan Jackson Schindel and Nancy Rodwan, permissions; Jo Anne Metsch, designer; Nelson Colon, photo editor; and Rachel Taylor and Ava Bramson, assistant editor and assistant media editor, respectively. All these friends provided the editors with indispensable help in meeting the challenge of representing the unparalleled range and variety of English literature.

STEPHEN GREENBLATT

Acknowledgments

The editors would like to express appreciation and thanks to the hundreds of teachers who provided reviews:

Michel Aaij (Auburn University at Montgomery), Jerry J. Alexander (Presbyterian College), Sarah Alexander (The University of Vermont), Marshall N. Armintor (University of North Texas), Marilyn Judith Atlas (Ohio University), Alison Baker (California State Polytechnic University, Pomona), Reid Barbour (University of North Carolina, Chapel Hill), Jessica Barnes-Pietruszynski (West Virginia State University), Jessica Barr (Eureka College), Chris Barrett (Louisiana State University), Craig Barrette (Brescia University), Carol Beran (St. Mary's College), Peter Berek (Amherst College), David Bergman (Towson University), Scott Black (University of Utah), William R. "Beau" Black III (Weatherford College), Justin Blessinger (Dakota State University), William E. Bolton (La Salle University), Wyatt Bonikowski (Suffolk University), Rebecca Bossie (University of Texas at El Paso), Bruce Brandt (South Dakota State University), Heather Braun (University of Akron), Mark Brown (University of Jamestown), Logan D. Browning (Rice University), Monica Brzezinski Potkay (College of William and Mary), Rebecca Bushnell (University of Pennsylvania), Claire Busse (La Salle University), Thomas Butler (Eastern Kentucky University), Jim Casey (Arcadia University), Susan P. Cerasano (Colgate University), Maria Chappell (University of Georgia), Brinda Charry (Keene State College), Susannah Chewning (Union County College), Lin Chih-hsin (National Chengchi University), Kathryn Chittick (Trent University), Rita Colanzi (Immaculata University), Nora Corrigan (Mississippi University for Women), David Cowart (University of South Carolina), Catherine Craft-Fairchild (University of St. Thomas), Susan Crisafulli (Franklin College), Jenny Crisp (Dalton State College), Ashley Cross (Manhattan College), James P. Crowley (Bridgewater State University), Susie Crowson (Del Mar College), Rebecca Crump (Louisiana State University), Cyrus Mulready (SUNY New Paltz), Lisa Darien (Hartwick College), Sean Dempsey (University of Arkansas), Anthony Ding (Grossmont Community College), Lorraine Eadie (Hillsdale College), Schuyler Eastin (San Diego Christian College), Gary Eddy (Winona State University), J. Craig Eller (Louisburg College), Robert Ellison (Marshall University), Nikolai Endres (Western Kentucky University), Robert Epstein (Fairfield University), Richard Erable (Franklin College), Simon C. Estok (Sungkyunkwan University), Michael Faitell (Mohawk Valley Community College), Jonathan Farina (Seton Hall University), Tyler Farrell (Marquette

University), Jennifer Feather (The University of North Carolina Greensboro), Annette Federico (James Madison University), Kerstin Feindert (Cosumnes River College), Maryanne Felter (Cayuga Community College), Benjamin Fischer (Northwest Nazarene University), Matthew Fisher (University of California, Los Angeles), Chris Fletcher (North Central University), Michael J. Flynn (The University of North Dakota), James E. Foley (Worcester State University), Walter C. Foreman (University of Kentucky), Ann Frank Wake (Elmhurst College), Michael D. Friedman (University of Scranton), Lee Garver (Butler University), Paul L. Gaston (Kent State University), Sara E. Gerend (Aurora University), Avilah Getzler (Grand View University), Edward Gieskes (University of South Carolina), Elaine Glanz (Immaculata University), Adam Golaski (Brown University), Rachel Goldberg (Northeastern CPS), Augusta Gooch (University of Alabama–Huntsville), Nathan Gorelick (Utah Valley University), Robert Gorsch (Saint Mary's College of California), Carey Goyette (Clinton Community College), Richard J. Grande (Pennsylvania State University–Abington), David A. Grant (Columbus State Community College), Sian Griffiths (Weber State University), Ann H. Guess (Alvin Community College), Audley Hall (NorthWest Arkansas Community College), Jenni Halpin (Savannah State University), Brian Harries (Concordia University Wisconsin), Samantha Harvey (Boise State University), Raychel Haugrud Reiff (University of Wisconsin–Superior), Erica Haugtvedt (The Ohio State University), Mary Hayes (University of Mississippi), Joshua R. Held (Indiana University, Bloomington), Roze Hentschell (Colorado State University), Erich Hertz (Siena College), Natalie Hewitt (Hope International University), Lisa Hinrichsen (University of Arkansas), Lorretta Holloway (Framingham State University), Catherine Howard (University of Houston), Chia-Yin Huang (Chinese Culture University), Sister Marie Hubert Kealy (Immaculata University), Elizabeth Hutcheon (Huntingdon College), Peter Hyland (Huron University College, Western University), Eileen Jankowski (Chapman University), Alan Johnson (Idaho State University), Brian Jukes (Yuba College), Kari Kalve (Earlham College), Parmita Kapadia (Northern Kentucky University), Deborah Kennedy (Saint Mary's University), Mark Kipperman (Northern Illinois University), Cindy Klestinec (Miami University–Ohio), Neal W. Kramer (Brigham Young University), Kathryn Laity (College of Saint Rose), Jameela Lares (University of Southern Mississippi), Caroline Levine (University of Wisconsin–Madison), Melinda Linscott (Idaho State University), Janet Madden (El Camino College), Gerald Margolis (Temple University), Elizabeth Mazzola (The City College of New York), Keely McCarthy (Chestnut Hill College), Cathryn McCarthy Donahue (College of Mount Saint Vincent), Mary H. McMurran (University of Western Ontario), Josephine A. McQuail (Tennessee Technological University), Brett Mertins (Metropolitan Community College), Christian Michener (Saint Mary's University), Brook Miller (University of Minnesota, Morris), Kristine Miller (Utah State University), Jacqueline T. Miller (Rutgers University), Richard J. Moll (University of Western Ontario), Lorne Mook (Taylor University), Rod Moore (Los Angeles Valley College), Rory Moore (University of California, Riverside), Grant Moss (Utah Valley University), Nicholas D. Nace (Hampden-Sydney College), Jonathan Naito (St. Olaf College), Mary Nelson (Dallas Baptist University), Mary Anne Nunn (Central Connecticut State University), John O'Brien (University of Virginia),

Onno Oerlemans (Hamilton College), Michael Oishi (Leeward Community College), Sylvia Pamboukian (Robert Morris University), Adam Parkes (University of Georgia), Michelle Parkinson (University of Wisconsin–River Falls), Geoffrey Payne (Macquarie University), Anna Peak (Temple University), Dan Pearce (Brigham Young University–Idaho), Christopher Penna (University of Delaware), Zina Petersen (Brigham Young University), Kaara L. Peterson (Miami University of Ohio), Keith Peterson (Brigham Young University–Hawaii), Professor Maggie Piccolo (Rowan University), Ann Pleiss Morris (Ripon College), Michael Pogach (Northampton Community College), Matthew Potolsky (The University of Utah), Miguel Powers (Fullerton College), Gregory Priebe (Harford Community College), Jonathan Purkiss (Pulaski Technical College), Kevin A. Quarmby (Oxford College of Emory University), Mark Rankin (James Madison University), Tawnya Ravy (The George Washington University), Joan Ray (University of Colorado, Colorado Springs), Helaine Razovsky (Northwestern State University of Louisiana), Vince Redder (Dakota Wesleyan University), Elizabeth Rich (Saginaw Valley State University), Patricia Rigg (Acadia University), Albert J. Rivero (Marquette University), Phillip Ronald Stormer (Culver-Stockton College), Kenneth Rooney (University College Cork, Ireland), David Ruiter (University of Texas at El Paso), Kathryn Rummell (California Polytechnic State University), Richard Ruppel (Chapman University), Jonathan Sachs (Concordia University), David A. Salomon (Russell Sage College), Abigail Scherer (Nicholls State University), Roger Schmidt (Idaho State University), William Sheldon (Hutchinson Community College), Christian Sheridan (Bridgewater College), Nicole Sidhu (East Carolina University), Lisa Siefker Bailey (Indiana University–Purdue University Columbus), Samuel Smith (Messiah College), Cindy Soldan (Lakehead University), Diana Solomon (Simon Fraser University), Vivasvan Soni (Northwestern University), Timothy Spurgin (Lawrence University), Felicia Jean Steele (The College of New Jersey), Carole Lynn Stewart (Brock University), Judy Suh (Duquesne University), Dean Swinford (Fayetteville State University), Allison Symonds (Cecil College), Brenda Tuberville (Rogers State University), Verne Underwood (Rogue Community College), Janine Utell (Widener University), Paul Varner (Abilene Christian University), Deborah Vause (York College of Pennsylvania), Nicholas Wallerstein (Black Hills State University), Rod Waterman (Central Connecticut State University), Eleanor Welsh (Chesapeake College), Paul Westover (Brigham Young University), Christopher Wheatley (The Catholic University of America), Miranda Wilcox (Brigham Young University), Brett D. Wilson (College of William & Mary), Lorraine Wood (Brigham Young University), Nicholas A. Wright (Marist College), Michael Wutz (Weber State University).

THE NORTON ANTHOLOGY OF

ENGLISH

LITERATURE

TENTH EDITION

VOLUME D

THE ROMANTIC PERIOD

The Romantic Period
1785–1832

1787:	Establishment of the Society for Effecting the Abolition of the Trade in Slaves
1789–1815:	Revolutionary and Napoleonic period in France.—1789: Revolution begins with the assembly of the Estates General in May and the storming of the Bastille on July 14.—1793: King Louis XVI executed; England joins the alliance against France.—1793–94: Reign of Terror under Robespierre. 1804: Napoleon crowned emperor.—1815: Napoleon defeated at Waterloo
1807:	British slave trade outlawed (slavery abolished throughout the empire, the West Indies included, twenty-six years later)
1811–20:	The Regency—George, Prince of Wales, acts as regent for George III, who has been declared incurably insane
1819:	Peterloo Massacre
1820:	Accession of George IV
1830:	Accession of William IV
1832:	Passage of the Reform Bill in Parliament

T he Romantic period, though by far the shortest, is at least as complex and diverse as any other period in British literary history, and it is, tellingly, demarcated differently than any of the other eras that literary historians and anthologists include in their timelines. By convention, the boundaries delimiting those other epochs are either set by the reigns of monarchs (so that we have the "Elizabethan" and "Victorian" ages named for two long-reigning queens) or conceptualized as coinciding with the openings and closings of centuries (as with the volume of this Norton Anthology titled "The Twentieth and Twenty-First Centuries"). The date usually serving as the terminus of the Romantic age, 1832, represents a

Sir Brooke Boothby, by Joseph Wright. For more information about this image, see the color insert in this volume.

3

contrast to this pattern, strongly associated as it is with a signal political event, the first major reform of the British Parliament. A diverse range of dates have been identified as marking off the beginning of the Romantic period, but, almost always, each of these too is associated with an event of tremendous political and social impact. As some scholars tell it, the new era began in 1776, the year Americans declared their independence; others single out 1783, when shattering military defeat at the hands of those Americans dealt a blow to the credibility of Britain's ruling elites; and many settle on 1789, the year that launched democratic revolution in France, ushered in decades of fierce political unrest in Britain in its turn, and laid the ground for a war between the British and French Empires and their allies that would envelop an entire generation and take almost the whole of the globe as its theater.

Although politics has often provided a framework for the Romantic period, as such arrangements for periodization suggest, the fascination and provocation that this moment of cultural watershed presents for students of literary history have equally to do with another peculiarity in its construction: the Romantic is also the sole period that is named after a literary form, the romance. A great scholarly achievement of the later eighteenth century had been the recovery from obscurity of the medieval romances, previously ignored by literary historians more concerned with classical influences, and the Romantic period witnessed a reevaluation of those wild verse-tales of adventure, chivalry, and love. Exactly the traits—their barbarous deviations from probability and rationality, their unabashed fictionality, the fantasies they induced in their readers—that once justified medieval romances' fall into oblivion were seen anew, as commentators moved from lauding the room for idealization and visionary imagination that romance had afforded premodern writers to proposing that *modern* literature should follow suit and become, in one sense, more romantic, too. At a moment when real political events themselves seemed to entail improbabilities and impossibilities (for example the common people proclaiming independence from their rulers), that rehabilitation of romance was, in addition, spurred by the period's probing of the relation between what William Godwin in a subtitle to his 1794 novel *Caleb Williams* called "Things as They Are" and the alternative worlds that imagination could summon into being. "What is now proved was once, only imagin'd," William Blake declared in *The Marriage of Heaven and Hell* in 1790. His declaration is imbued with the new sense of power that poets, those professional imaginers, were inclined to claim at this moment, when the literary imagination appeared in new ways both to speak to and to guide historical change, and when political philosophy gained a new authority in and through poetry and fiction.

About a hundred years ago, *The Cambridge History of English Literature* segmented the era that this volume covers into two parts, tidily divvying off the "Period of the French Revolution" (1789–1815) from a subsequent period of "Romance Revival" that filled in the years between the defeat of Napoleonic France and the ascent of Queen Victoria. The messier option of treating the era as a single entity equips us better to do justice to its complex multiplicity. In refraining from the attempt to disentangle romance from history and literary from political change, we can better see how this period, in confronting their entanglement, originated the questions about the relations of art and activism, aesthetics and politics, that trouble us still. We can better see too how the notions of poetic autonomy that were involved in the rehabilitation of romance's extravagant, untrammelled fictionality were likewise forged under the pressure of political events, and how the reconception of the relation of the present to the past at stake in this recovery of a lost literary tradition often entailed as well imagining a new political future.

Since the days of the old *Cambridge History*, we have likewise begun to engage with a greater range of literary accomplishments, thereby recognizing the centrifugal energies and the eclecticism distinguishing this era, even as its authors firmly believed themselves to be participating in a common temporal period. Recent scholarship has expanded, or reexpanded, a canon formerly centered on introspective lyric poems inspired by poets' encounters with objects in or features of the natural world. Abolitionist songs, ballads and ballad imitations, Turkish tales (favorite forms of Byron's), versified fairy tales (Letitia Landon's "Fairy of the Fountains"), poems in which nature does not prompt a human speaker's meditation but rather speaks itself (John Clare's "Swordy Well"; Anna Barbauld's "Mouse's Petition"), and, in prose, travelogues, "table talk," Gothic novels, and historical romances—all now get numbered among the forms of Romantic literature, a more capacious category than it was in the past. And whereas earlier criticism, especially during the third quarter of the twentieth century, developed accounts of a unified Romanticism by extrapolating from the writings of the six male poets that it had singled out for attention (Blake, Wordsworth, and Coleridge in the first generation, and Byron, Shelley, and Keats in the second), we are readier to stress the friction among these figures, whose poetic and social aspirations divided as well as united them. We are also readier to accept that the work of women writers helped make this exciting period what it was. The conspicuous presence on the literary scene of a new "female literature" and the "poetesses" producing it (to use the quaint phraseology of the male reviewers)—and the fact, more generally, that this was the most prolific age of literary production ever seen in European history—attracted much commentary and some lament. The learned lady or Bluestocking, one critic complained in 1823, "is a creature of modern growth, and capable of existing only in such times as the present."

REVOLUTION AND REACTION

During these times, England was experiencing the ordeal of change from a primarily agricultural society, where wealth and power had been concentrated in the landholding aristocracy, to a modern industrial nation. And this change occurred, as mentioned earlier, in a context of revolution—in America, then France, then Haiti—of counterrevolution, of war, of economic cycles of inflation and depression, and of the constant threat to the social structure from imported revolutionary ideologies to which the ruling classes responded by the repression of traditional liberties.

The early period of the French Revolution, marked by the Declaration of the Rights of Man and the storming of the Bastille, evoked enthusiastic support from English liberals and radicals alike. Three important books epitomize the radical social thinking stimulated by the Revolution. Mary Wollstonecraft's *A Vindication of the Rights of Men* (1790) justified the Revolution against Edmund Burke's attack in his *Reflections on the Revolution in France* (1790). Thomas Paine's *Rights of Man* (1791–92) also advocated for England a democratic republic that was to be achieved, if lesser pressures failed, by popular revolution. More important as an influence on Wordsworth and Percy Shelley was Godwin's *Enquiry Concerning Political Justice* (1793), which foretold an inevitable but peaceful evolution of society to a final stage in which property would be equally distributed and government would wither away. But English sympathizers dropped off as the Revolution followed its increasingly grim course: the accession to power by Jacobin extremists, intent on purifying their new republic by purging it of its enemies; the "September Massacres" of the imprisoned nobility in 1792, followed by the execution of the king and queen; the new French Republic's invasion of the Rhineland and the Netherlands, which brought England into the war against France; the guillotining of thousands in the Reign of Terror under Robespierre; and, after the execution in their turn of the men who had directed the Terror, the emergence of Napoleon, first as dictator then as emperor of France. As Wordsworth wrote in *The Prelude*,

> become Oppressors in their turn,
> Frenchmen had changed a war of self-defence
> For one of Conquest, losing sight of all
> Which they had struggled for. . . . (11.206–09)

Napoleon, the brilliant tactician whose rise through the ranks of the army had seemed to epitomize the egalitarian principles of the Revolution, had become an arch-aggressor, a despot, and would-be founder of a new imperial dynasty. By 1800 liberals found they had no side they could wholeheartedly espouse. Napoleon's defeat at Waterloo in 1815 proved to be the triumph, not of progress and reform, but of reactionary despotisms throughout continental Europe. In this year, accordingly, the debates about the legitimacy of the ruling class and about patrician degeneracy that figures such as Godwin, Paine, and Wollstonecraft had launched in the early 1790s returned with a vengeance.

From start to finish, this was a period of harsh, repressive measures. Public meetings were prohibited in 1795, the right of habeas corpus (the legal principle protecting individuals from arbitrary imprisonment) was suspended for the first time in over a hundred years, and advocates of even moderate political change were charged with treason. Efforts during these war years to repeal the laws that barred Protestants who did not conform to the Anglican Church from the universities and government came to nothing: in the new climate of counterrevolutionary alarm, it was easy to portray even a slight abridgement of the privileges of the established Church as a measure that, validating the Jacobins' campaigns to de-Christianize France, would aid the enemy cause. Another early casualty of this counterrevolution was the movement to abolish the slave trade, a cause supported initially by a wide cross-section of English society. In the 1780s and 1790s numerous writers, both white (Anna Letitia Barbauld, Coleridge, and Hannah More) and black (Ottobah Cugoano and Olaudah Equiano), attacked the greed of the owners of the West Indian sugar plantations and detailed the horrors of the traffic in African flesh that provided them with their labor power. But the bloodshed that accompanied political change in France strengthened the hand of apologists for slavery, by making any manner of reform seem the prelude to violent insurrection. Parliament rejected a bill abolishing the trade in 1791, and sixteen years—marked by slave rebellions and by the planters' brutal reprisals—elapsed before it passed a new version of the bill.

The frustration of the abolitionist cause is an emblematic chapter in the larger story of how a reactionary government sacrificed hopes of reform while it mobilized the nation's resources for war. Yet this was the very time when economic and social changes were creating a desperate need for corresponding changes in political arrangements. For one thing, new classes inside England—manufacturing rather than agricultural—were beginning to demand a voice in government proportionate to their wealth. The "Industrial Revolution"—the shift in manufacturing that resulted from the invention of power-driven machinery to replace hand labor—had begun in the mid-eighteenth century with improvements in machines for processing textiles, and was given immense impetus when James Watt perfected the steam engine in 1765. In the succeeding decades steam replaced wind and water as the primary source of power for all sorts of manufacturing processes, beginning that dynamic of ever-accelerating economic expansion and technological development that we still identify as the hallmark of the modern age. A new laboring population massed in sprawling mill towns such as Manchester, whose population increased by a factor of five in fifty years. In agricultural communities the destruction of home industry was accompanied by the acceleration of the process of enclosing open fields and wastelands (usually, in fact, "commons" that had provided the means of subsistence for entire communities) and incorporating them into larger, privately owned holdings. Enclosure was by and large necessary for the more efficient methods of agriculture required to feed the nation's growing population (although some of the land that the wealthy acquired through parliamentary acts of enclosure they in fact incorporated into their private estates). But enclosure was socially destructive, breaking up villages, creating a landless class who either migrated to the industrial towns or remained as farm laborers, subsisting on starvation wages and the little they could obtain from parish charity. The landscape of England began to take on its modern appearance—the hitherto open rural areas subdivided into a checkerboard of fields enclosed by hedges and stone walls, with the factories of the cities casting a pall of smoke over vast areas of cheaply built houses and slum tenements. Meanwhile, the population was increasingly polarized into what Benjamin Disraeli later called the "Two Nations"—the two classes of capital and labor, the rich and the poor.

No attempt was made to regulate this shift from the old economic world to the new, since even liberal reformers were committed to the philosophy of laissez-faire. This theory of "let alone," set out in Adam Smith's *The Wealth of Nations* in 1776, holds that the general welfare can be ensured only by the free operation of economic laws; the government should maintain a policy of strict noninterference and leave people to pursue, unfettered, their private interests. On the one hand, laissez-faire thinking might have helped pave the way for the long-postponed emancipation of the slave population of the West Indies; by 1833, when Parliament finally ended slavery, the anomaly that their unfree labor represented for the new economic and social orthodoxies evidently had become intolerable. But for the great majority of the laboring class at home, the results of laissez-faire and the "freedom" of contract it secured were inadequate wages and long hours of work under harsh discipline and in sordid conditions. Investigators' reports on the coal mines, where male and female children of ten or even five years of age were harnessed to heavy coal-sledges that they dragged by crawling on their hands and knees, read like scenes from Dante's *Inferno*. With the end of the war in 1815, the nation's workforce was enlarged by demobilized troops at the very moment when demand for manufactured goods, until now augmented by the needs of the military, fell dramatically. The result was an unemployment crisis that persisted through the 1820s. Because the workers had no vote and were prevented by law from unionizing, their only recourses were petitions, protest meetings, and riots, to which the ruling class responded with even more repressive measures. The introduction of new machinery into the mills resulted in further loss of jobs, provoking sporadic attempts by the displaced workers to destroy the machines. After one such outbreak of "Luddite" machine breaking, the House of Lords—despite Byron's eloquent protest—passed a bill (1812) making death the penalty for destroying the frames used for weaving in the stocking industry. In 1819 hundreds of thousands of workers organized meetings to demand parliamentary reform. In August of that year, a huge but orderly assembly at St. Peter's Fields, Manchester, was charged by saber-wielding troops, who killed nine and injured hundreds more; this was the notorious "Peterloo Massacre," so named with sardonic reference to the Battle of Waterloo.

Suffering was largely confined to the poor, however, while the landed classes and industrialists prospered. So did many merchants, who profited from the new markets opened up as the British Empire expanded aggressively, compensating with victories against the French for the traumatic loss of America in 1783. England's merchants profited, too, thanks to the marketing successes that, over time, converted once-exotic imports from these colonies into everyday fare for the English. In the eighteenth century tea and sugar had been transformed in this way, and in the nineteenth century other commodities followed suit: the Indian muslin, for instance, that was the fabric of choice for gentlemen's cravats and fashionable ladies' gowns, and the laudanum (Indian opium dissolved in alcohol) that so many ailing writers of the period appear to have found irresistible. The West End of London and new seaside resorts like Brighton became in the early nineteenth century consumers' paradises, sites where West Indian planters and nabobs (a Hindi word that entered English as a name for those who owed their fortunes to Indian gain) could be glimpsed displaying their purchasing power in a manner that made them moralists' favorite examples of nouveau riche vulgarity. The word *shopping* came into English usage in this era. Luxury villas sprang up in London, and the prince regent, who in 1820 became George IV, built himself palaces and pleasure domes, retreats from his not very onerous public responsibilities.

But even, or especially, in private life at home, the prosperous could not escape being touched by the great events of this period. French revolutionary principles were feared by English conservatives almost as much for their challenge to the "proper" ordering of the relations between men and women as for their challenge to traditional political arrangements. Yet the account of what it meant to be English that developed in reaction to this challenge—an account emphasizing the special virtues of the English sense of home and family—was in its way equally revolutionary. In an unprecedented way, the war that the English waged almost without intermission between 1793 and 1815 had a "home front." The menaced sanctuary of the domestic fireside became the symbol of what the nation's military might was safeguarding. What popularity the monarchy held on to during this turbulent period was thus a function not of the two King Georges' traditional exercise of a monarch's sovereign powers but instead of the publicity, tailored to suit this nationalist rhetoric, that emphasized each one's domestic bliss within a "royal family." Conceptions of proper femininity altered as well under the influence of this new idealization and nationalization of the home, this project (as Burke put it) of "binding up the constitution of our country with our dearest domestic ties."

And that alteration both put new pressures on women and granted them new opportunities. As in earlier English history, women in the Romantic period were provided only limited schooling, were subjected to a rigid code of sexual behavior, and (especially after marriage) were bereft of legal rights. In this period women began, as well, to be deluged by books, sermons, and magazine articles that insisted vehemently on the physical and mental differences between the sexes and instructed women that, because of these differences, they should accept that their roles in life involved child rearing, housekeeping, and nothing more. (Of course, in tendering this advice promoters of female domesticity conveniently ignored the definitions of duty that industrialists imposed on the poor women who worked in their mills.) Yet a paradoxical byproduct of the connections that the new nationalist rhetoric forged between the well-being of the state and domestic life was that the identity of the patriot became one a woman might attempt, with some legitimacy, to claim. Within the framework created by the new accounts of English national identity, a woman's private virtues now had a public relevance. They had to be seen as crucial to the nation's welfare. Those virtues might well be manifested in the work of raising patriotic sons, but, as the thousands of women in this period who made their ostensibly natural feminine feelings of pity their alibi for participation in abolitionism demonstrated, they could be turned to nontraditional uses as well.

The new idea that, as the historian Linda Colley has put it, a woman's place was not simply in the home but also in the nation could also justify or at least extenuate the affront to proper feminine modesty represented by publication—by a woman's entry into the public sphere of authorship. "Bluestockings"—educated women—remained targets of masculine scorn, as we have seen. This became, nonetheless, the first era in literary history in which women writers began to compete with men in their numbers, sales, and literary reputations. These female authors had to tread carefully, to be sure, to avoid suggesting that (as one male critic fulminated) they wished the nation's "affectionate wives, kind mothers, and lovely daughters" to be metamorphosed into "studious philosophers" and "busy politicians." And figures like Wollstonecraft, who in the *Vindication of the Rights of Woman* grafted a radical proposal about gender equality onto a more orthodox argument about the education women needed to be proper mothers, remained exceptional. Later women writers tended cautiously to either ignore her example or define themselves against it.

Only in the Victorian period would Wollstonecraft's cause of women's rights rally enough support for substantial legal reform to begin, and that process would not be completed until the twentieth century. In the early nineteenth century the pressures for political reform focused on the rights of men, as distinct from women. From 1785 on, the year in which Prime Minister William Pitt (who would soon shift his political allegiances) proposed in vain a bill for parliamentary reform, middle-class and working-class men, entering into strategic and short-lived alliances, made the restructuring of the British electoral system their common cause. Finally, at a time of acute economic distress, the first Reform Bill was passed in 1832. It did away with the rotten boroughs (depopulated areas whose seats in the House of Commons were at the disposal of a few noblemen), redistributed parliamentary representation to include the industrial cities, and extended the franchise. Although about half the middle class, almost all the working class, and all women remained without a vote, the principle of the peaceful adjustment of conflicting interests by parliamentary majority had been firmly established. Reform was to go on, by stages, until Britain acquired universal adult suffrage in 1928.

THE NEW POETRIES: THEORY AND PRACTICE

Writers working in this period, from 1785 to 1832, did not think of themselves as constituting a group of "Romantic" authors. It was Victorian critics who first wrote of the previous generation as the Romantics and promoted the term as a description for a period of recent, modern rather than premodern, history. Contemporaries, by contrast, treated these writers as independent individuals or else grouped them (usually maliciously, but with some basis in fact) into a number of separate "schools" or "sects": the "Lake School" of Wordsworth, Coleridge, and Robert Southey (a "sect of poets," the critic Francis Jeffrey sniped, determined to be "*dissenters* from the established systems in poetry and criticism" and valuing themselves highly "for having broken loose from the bondage of ancient authority"); the "Cockney School," a derogatory term for vulgar Londoners Leigh Hunt, William Hazlitt, and associated writers who had pretensions beyond their station, including Keats; and the impious "Satanic School" of Leigh Hunt (again), Percy Shelley, and Byron. At the start of the period, the satirist Richard Polwhele also practiced this name-calling as he cataloged the sphere of "female literature": the aim of his 1797 *The Unsex'd Females* was, by naming and shaming, to firmly distinguish the virtuous lady writers of his moment from the "Amazonian band" formed by Wollstonecraft and her followers, a group who, so Polwhele complained, had sacrificed their feminine charms for lead roles in revolutionary polemicizing.

The proliferation of schools and sects suggests the fault lines running through this fractious literary world. Where agreement could be found was around the proposition that this was a watershed moment in literary history. "Literature, well or ill conducted," the satirist Thomas James Mathias proclaimed in the book that inspired Polwhele's, "is the great engine by which . . . all civilized states must ultimately be supported or overthrown." Radicals concurred with conservatives like Mathias in this conviction that literature was where the action was—that literature in effect *was* action—even as they disagreed on the meaning to be ascribed to that very term (a term formerly synonymous with learning in general, only in this period did *literature* begin to settle down into that modern meaning that confines it exclusively to artistic expression, works of the imagination particularly). Introducing *The New Cambridge History of the English Romantic Period*, James Chandler highlights, as a defining characteristic of the Romantic age, how often this era's most talented men gravitated to poetry in particular. They confirmed poetry's elevated cultural status by abandoning other careers, the ministry in Coleridge's case, the law in Sir Walter Scott's, medicine in Keats's. Even George Canning, Tory leader of Britain's House of Commons, published in 1823 a *Collected Poems*. In his 1802 Preface to *Lyrical Ballads* Wordsworth unfavorably contrasted what the "Man of Science" could do as a benefactor of humanity with what the "Poet" could, whose vocation it was to "bind together by passion and knowledge the vast empire of human society, as it is spread over the whole earth and over all time." "The most unfailing herald, companion, and follower of the awakening of a great people to work a beneficial change in opinion or institution, is Poetry," Percy Shelley declared.

The "most eccentric feature of this entire culture," literary historian Stuart Curran suggests, was that it was "simply mad for poetry." To a degree inconceivable in the twenty-first century, poetry back then penetrated everyday life, as something appearing in daily papers alongside news stories and notices of bankruptcies, deaths, and marriages, and as something to be memorized, sung, transcribed into commonplace books, and made the basis of parlor games on long winters' evenings. The calling of poet beckoned to many: among those hordes of devoted readers, many were eager—too eager, their reviewers complained—to become authors in turn, imagining that verse might provide their springboard to fame. If those enthusiasms laid the ground for confident declarations like Shelley's and Wordsworth's, they also, inevitably, generated a backlash, the more so as the new poetries of the Romantic period rode to this cultural prominence on the back of a media culture that at this moment was reaching increasing numbers of readers more quickly than ever before. Indeed, as Mathias's word *engine* suggests, with the expansion of modern publishing, it had begun to appear as though modern writing, too, had started to conform to the accelerated production rhythms of the Industrial Revolution. (The nervousness aroused by these developments, anticipations of the twentieth century's mass culture, is also registered in Wordsworth's Preface, which proposes as one cause of the "almost savage torpor" found among Wordsworth's countrymen and women, city-dwellers especially, the "rapid communication of intelligence" provided by the new popular press.) The spectacle of new sorts of people enlisting as authors and the multiplication of new venues for their writings generated gloomy warnings about overproduction and an accompanying debasement of artistic standards.

The genius poet was therefore shadowed throughout the Romantic period's literary discussion by a less admirable double, the Grub Street hack. *Poet* could in this era designate the visionary and universal benefactor profiled in Wordsworth's Preface and Shelley's *Defence of Poetry*, but it also evoked an impoverished and pretentious truant from a more honest trade, a misguided *romantic scribbler*. (That last phrase, often bandied about in this era, reminds us that even as the term *romantic* became synonymous with an admirable responsiveness to the promptings of imagination, it never completely shed its association with a deplorable and impractical deviation from common sense.) As Mary Robinson mischievously pointed out, it was a mistake to equate "the airy throne/ Of bold imagination, rapture fraught/ Above the herds of mortals" with a desolate mountaintop or isolated green dell, even though the period's poetic speakers tended to picture themselves in such sublime settings. The poet's haunt was in mundane reality likely to be a shabby, low-rent attic. Many motives drove the poets who in this era tried to make poetry new by reviving what was old and who thereby contrived to bypass the eighteenth-century poets whose heirs they were supposed to be: their medievalisms and primitivisms were, for a start, reactions against the neoclassical canons of good taste, as well as expressions of a new nationalism. But certainly ideas about the literary past's exemption from the commercial pressures of the present also helped make the outmoded old romances a radically new source of inspiration for this period, precisely because of rather than despite their historical distance. The energy invested at this moment in the scholarly investigation and poetic imitation of the ballads being sung or chanted by common people in the streets and fields suggests something similar. It registers the fascination that the participants in literate culture who listened in on these performances were inclined to ascribe to a cultural form whose origins predated the invention of the printing press and the advent of a print market. The ballad was transmitted by word of mouth and not by commercial exchange.

The double image of the poet—product of an era that both idealized poetry and fretted over its standing in modern, commercial society—is an important context for the questions centering Wordsworth's 1802 Preface, his retroactive statement of the principles guiding him in the poems he contributed to *Lyrical Ballads.* "What is meant by the word Poet? What is a Poet?" The questions were the more urgent because in a fractious period, there was increased pressure on the aesthetic sphere to act as a site in which human beings could rediscover the commonalities linking them as humans, as Wordsworth's definition of the poet as a figure of unification, "bind[ing] together . . . the vast empire of human society," suggests. One way to approach the period's new poetries and isolate some of the distinctive trends that were precipitated out of a welter of reforms and radical innovations is to start by tracing the shifting conceptions of poet and poetry that emerged then. If by taking this approach we take our cue from Wordsworth's Preface, we should also acknowledge that his manifesto for a new poetics can be deemed representative only to a limited extent. Wordsworth would have wished it otherwise, but

Contrasting views of the Romantic poet. On the left, Henry Fuseli, "The Poet's Vision," unused design for frontispiece to William Cowper's *Poems* (1807). On the right, Henry Heath, "Fine Arts, Pt. 1: Poetry," published August 8, 1826.

during this era of revolution definitions of good poetry, like definitions of the good society, were sure to create as much contention as consensus.

Concepts of the Poet and the Poem

Seeking a stable foundation on which social institutions might be constructed, eighteenth-century British philosophers had devoted much energy to demonstrating that human nature must be everywhere the same, because it everywhere derived from individuals' shared sensory experience of an external world that could be objectively represented. As the century went on, however, philosophers began emphasizing—and poets began developing a new language for—individual variations in perception and the capacity the receptive consciousness has to filter and to re-create reality. This was a shift Wordsworth registered when in his Preface he located the source of a poem not in outer nature but in the psychology of the individual poet. What distinguished the poems of *Lyrical Ballads* from the popular poetry of the day Wordsworth declared, vindicating his own departures from those norms, is that "[t]he feeling therein developed gives importance to the action and situation, and not the action and situation to the feeling." Wordsworth maintained, in continuation, that "[A]ll good poetry," was, at the moment of composition, "the spontaneous overflow of powerful feelings." Other contemporary discussions of poetry concurred with this account by referring likewise to the mind, emotions, and imagination of the poet for the origin, content, and defining attributes of a poem. "The poet, the man of strong feelings, gives us only an image of his mind, . . . marking the impression which nature had made on his own heart," Wollstonecraft wrote in an essay that appeared in the *Monthly Magazine* the year before the first edition of *Lyrical Ballads*. Though Romantic poetry is interchangeable for many modern readers with "nature poetry" (an equation that William Godwin, her widower, endorsed when he reprinted Wollstonecraft's essay under a new title, "On Poetry, and Our Relish for the Beauties of Nature"), this characterization of Romantic poetics risks downplaying the poets' emphatic attention to the operations of consciousness. Certainly, many poets participated enthusiastically in the touring of picturesque scenery that was a new leisure activity of their age. Wordsworth, Coleridge, and Southey, the Lake School, even set up their households in the midst of that scenery, announcing in their residential arrangements as well as their works their antipathy to "the increasing accumulation of men in cities" and faith in the restorative powers of a benevolent Nature. Even so, it is fair to say that when the great Romantic lyrics—Smith's *Beachy Head*, Wordsworth's "Tintern Abbey," Coleridge's "Frost at Midnight," Keats's "Nightingale"—remark on an aspect in the natural scene, this attention to the external world serves only as stimulus to the most characteristic human activity, that of thinking.

Infused with this emphasis, the lyric poem written in the first person, which for much of literary history was regarded as a minor kind, thus became for many among the Romantics a major form and was often described as the most essentially poetic of all the genres. And in most Romantic lyrics the "I" is no longer a conventionally typical lyric speaker, such as the Petrarchan lover or Cavalier gallant of Elizabethan and seventeenth-century love poems, but one who shares recognizable traits with the poet. The experiences and states of mind expressed by the lyric speaker often accord closely with the known facts of the poet's life.

This reinvention of the lyric complicated established understandings of the gender of authorship. It may not be an accident, some critics suggest, that Wordsworth in his Preface defines poetry as "the real language of men" and the Poet as a "man speaking to men": Wordsworth, who began to publish when women such as Robinson and Charlotte Smith occupied the vanguard of the new personal poetry, might have decided that to establish the distinctiveness of his project he needed to counterbalance his emphasis on his feelings with an emphasis on those feelings' "manly" dignity. This is not to say that women writers' relationship to the new ideas about poetry was straightforward either. In one of her prefaces Smith says that she anticipates being criticized for "bringing forward 'with querulous egotism,' the mention of myself." For many female poets the other challenge those ideas about poetry posed might have consisted in their potential to reinforce the old, prejudicial idea that their sex—traditionally seen as creatures of feeling rather than intellect—wrote about their own experiences because they were capable of nothing else. For male poets the risks of poetic self-revelation were different—and in some measure they were actively seized by those who, like Coleridge and Percy Shelley, intimated darkly that the introspective tendency and emotional sensitivity that made someone a poetic genius could also lead him to melancholy and madness.

It was not only the lyric that registered these new accounts of the poet. Byron confounded his contemporaries' expectations about which poetic genre was best suited to self-revelation by inviting his audience to equate the heroes of *Childe Harold, Manfred,* and *Don Juan* with their author, and to see these fictional protagonists' experiences as disclosing the deep truths of his secret self. Wordsworth's *Prelude* represents an extreme instance of this tendency to self-reference. Though the poem, half a century in the making, is of epic length and seriousness, its subject is not, as is customary in an epic, history on a world-changing scale but the growth of the poet's mind: "a thing unprecedented in Literary history that a man should talk so much about himself," Wordsworth admitted.

Spontaneity and the Impulses of Feeling

In traditional poetics, poetry had been regarded as supremely an art—an art that in modern times was practiced by poets who had assimilated classical precedents, were aware of the "rules" governing the kind of poem they are writing, and (except for the happy touches that, as Alexander Pope said, are "beyond the reach of art") deliberately employed tested means to achieve premeditated effects on an audience. But in her 1797 *Monthly Magazine* essay, Wollstonecraft foretold a shift in aesthetic doctrine when she wrote that "[t]he silken wings of fancy are shrivelled by rules," and that "a desire of attaining elegance of diction occasions an attention to words, incompatible with sublime, impassioned thoughts." In Wordsworth's account in the Preface, although the composition of a poem originates from "emotion recollected in tranquillity" and may be preceded and followed by reflection, the immediate act of composition must be spontaneous—impulsive, artless, and free from rules. Keats listed as an "axiom" a similar proposition—that "if poetry comes not as naturally as the leaves to a tree it had better not come at all."

On occasion in this period's discussions of poetics, this interest in a poetry that came naturally could act in concert with that nostalgia, already discussed, which abandoned the prosaic here-and-now for the more romantic possibilities housed in a remote, preliterate past. For instance, for many poets of the period, the ancient bard, a composite figure resembling at once the biblical prophets, Homer, Milton, and the harp-playing patriots whom eighteenth-century antiquarians had located in a legendary Dark Ages Britain, was a charismatic role model. Imagining the songs a bard might have sung in long-ago times made it easier to conceive an alternative to the mundane language of modernity—a natural, oral poetry, blissfully unconscious of modern decorums and artificial conventions and sublimely irreducible to rule or measure. (Though they chafed against this expectation, writers from the rural working class—Robert Burns and later John Clare—could be expected, by virtue of their perceived distance from the restraint and refinement of civilized discourse, to play a comparable role inside modern culture, that of peasant poet or natural genius.) When, after the end of the Napoleonic war, writers like Byron and Percy and Mary Shelley traveled to Italy, taking these bardic ideals with them, they became enthralled with the arts of the improvisatore and improvisatrice, men and women whose electrifying oral performances of poetry involved no texts but those of immediate inspiration.

The Bard. Frontispiece by Thomas Rowlandson for Edward Jones, *The Bardic Museum of Primitive British Literature* (1802), a collection of traditional Welsh melodies. Rowlandson pictures the bard as a figure unifying his community.

One writer who praised and emulated that rhapsodic spontaneity, Percy Shelley, thought it "an error to assert that the finest passages of poetry are produced by labour and study." He suggested instead that these were the products of an unconscious creativity: "A great statue or picture grows under the power of the artist as a child in the mother's womb."

The emphasis in this period on unlabored art and on the spontaneous activity of the imagination producing it, and the premium placed on the immediacy of the relationship between author and poem, are linked to a belief in the essential role of passion. According to this view (which connects the literary productions of the Romantic period to the poetry and fiction of sensibility written earlier in the eighteenth century), the intuitive feelings of "the heart" had to supplement the judgments of the purely logical faculty, "the head." "Deep thinking," Coleridge wrote, "is attainable only by a man of deep feeling"; hence, "a metaphysical solution that does not tell you something in the heart is grievously to be suspected as apocryphal."

Glorification of the Ordinary

In the lecture he gave "On the Living Poets" in 1818 Hazlitt declared the poetry of the Lake school, with Wordsworth at its head, to be the literary equivalent of the French Revolution, a translation of political change into poetical experiment. "Kings and queens were dethroned from their rank and station in legitimate tragedy or epic poetry, as they were decapitated elsewhere. . . . The paradox [these poets] set out with was that all things are by nature, equally fit subjects for poetry; or that if there is any preference to give, those that are the meanest [i.e., most humble] and most unpromising are the best." Furthermore, as Hazlitt pointed out, the Lake School had done more than take the subjects of serious poems from the lives of humble country folk; it overtly elicited a genteel audience's sympathies for the disgraced, outcast, and delinquent—"convicts, female vagrants, gypsies . . . idiot boys and mad mothers," in Hazlitt's list. To some extent Hazlitt's analogizing between poetic and political experiments suggests more about him than the living poets he discusses: an avid youthful reader of Jean-Jacques Rousseau, he sounds as though he took to heart the Swiss-French philosopher's advocacy of a simplicity of manners against aristocratic corruption. Still, Hazlitt would have found support for his characterization of the Lake School from Wordsworth's statement in the Preface that his aim in *Lyrical Ballads* was "to choose incidents and situations from common life." For Wordsworth's polemical purposes, it was in "humble and rustic life" that a natural language—"a language really spoken by men" and "incorporated with the beautiful and permanent forms of nature"—was to be found, and the speech of rustics was in the Preface promoted as a cure for the ailments of the overcivilized.

Hazlitt would have known as well that later-eighteenth-century writers had already experimented with the simple treatment of simple subjects. Burns had with great success represented "the rural scenes and rural pleasures of [his] natal Soil," and in a language aiming to be true to the rhythms of the Scots language. Women poets, too—Barbauld, Robinson—assimilated to their poems the subject matter of everyday life. Many later eighteenth-century writers had taken their cue from the stark simplicity of the popular ballad: the ballad's appeal for an up-market, metropolitan readership, capitalized on by eighteenth-century collections like Percy's *Reliques of Ancient*

English Poetry, was in a part a function of the contrast between primitive plainness and outright crudity of these song traditions and the tame, elaborate poetic diction defining poetry's modern milieu.

Once it had arrived on this scene Wordsworth's Preface of 1802 underwrote such poetic practice with a theory that inverted the traditional hierarchy of poetic genres, subjects, and styles. It elevated humble life and the plain style, which in earlier theory were appropriate only for the pastoral, the genre at the bottom of the traditional hierarchy, into the principal subject and medium for poetry in general. Byron reacted with scorn to this poetic program and facetiously summoned ghosts from the eighteenth century to help him protest against what *he* perceived as Wordsworth's bathos:

> "Peddlers," and "Boats," and "Wagons"! Oh! ye shades
> Of Pope and Dryden, are we come to this?

Yet Wordsworth's project was not simply to represent the world as it is but, as he explained in his Preface, to throw over "situations from common life . . . a certain coloring of imagination, whereby ordinary things should be presented to the mind in an unusual aspect." No one can read his poems without noticing the reverence with which he invests words that for earlier writers had been derogatory—words such as *common, ordinary, everyday, humble*. Wordsworth's aim was to shatter the lethargy of custom so as to refresh our sense of wonder in the everyday and the lowly.

In the eighteenth century Samuel Johnson had said that "wonder is a pause of reason"—"the effect of novelty upon ignorance." But for many Romantics, to arouse in the sophisticated mind that sense of wonder presumed to be felt by the ignorant and the innocent—to renew the universe, Percy Shelley wrote, "after it has been blunted by reiteration"—was a major function of poetry. Commenting on the imaginative quality of Wordsworth's early verse, Coleridge remarked in *Biographia Literaria*: "To combine the child's sense of wonder and novelty with the appearances, which every day for perhaps forty years had rendered familiar . . . this is the character and privilege of genius." Contributing to this poetry of the child's-eye view, Barbauld wrote a poem centered on an observer's effort to imagine the unknowable perspective of a being for whom thought and sensation are not yet begun—a "little invisible being who is expected soon to become visible" but is still in its mother's womb.

The Supernatural, the Romance, and Psychological Extremes

There was a counterpoint to this poetry devoted to reviving the wonder of the familiar—"characters and incidents such as will be found in every village and its vicinity"—and proposing the authenticity of that local knowledge that long familiarity brings: a poetry that instead was founded on frank violation of natural laws and the ordinary course of events and that thereby cultivated the romantic in the understanding of that term that was to the forefront during the Romantic period itself. Coleridge contrasts these two sorts of poem when in *Biographia Literaria* he describes the division of labor organizing his collaboration with Wordsworth on *Lyrical Ballads*: his responsibility was poetry in which "the incidents and agents were to be, in part at least, supernatural, or at least romantic." Stories of bewitchings, hauntings, and possession—shaped by antiquated treatises on demonology, folklore, and Gothic novels—supplied Coleridge in poems such as *Rime of the Ancient Mariner, Christabel*, and "Kubla Khan" with the means of impressing on readers a sense of occult powers and unknown modes of being.

Poems like these, as Coleridge's epithet "romantic" suggests, were often grouped together by contemporaries under the medievalizing rubric "romance." On the one hand romances were writings that turned, in their quest for settings conducive to supernatural happenings, to distant pasts, faraway, exotic places, or both—Keats's "perilous seas, in faery lands forlorn" or the China of "Kubla Khan." On the other hand romance also named a homegrown, native tradition of literature, made unfamiliar and alien by the passage of time. For many authors, starting with Horace Walpole, whose *Castle of Otranto* (1764) began the tradition of Gothic fiction, writing under the banner of romance meant reclaiming their national birthright: a literature of imagination—associated, above all, with Spenser and the Shakespeare of fairy magic and witchcraft—that had been forced underground by the Enlightenment's emphasis on reason. Byron negotiated between romance's two sets of associations in *Childe Harold*, having his hero travel in far-off Albania and become entranced by the inhabitants' savage songs, but also giving the poem the subtitle "A Romaunt" (an archaic spelling of romance) and writing it in Spenserian stanzas. This was the same stanzaic form, neglected for much of the eighteenth century, that Keats drew on for *The Eve of St. Agnes*, the poem in which he proved himself a master of that Romantic mode that establishes a medieval setting for events violating our sense of realistic probability. The Romantic period's "medieval revival" was also promoted by women: Robinson, for instance (author of "Old English," "Monkish," and "Gothic" Tales), as well as Letitia Landon, Felicia Hemans, and others, women who often matched the arch-medievalist Sir Walter Scott in the historical learning they brought to their compositions.

The "addition of strangeness to beauty" that Walter Pater near the end of the nineteenth century would identify as a key Romantic tendency is seen not only in this concern with the exotic and archaic landscapes of romance but also in an interest in the mysteries of mental life and determination to investigate psychological extremes. Coleridge and Thomas De Quincey shared an interest in dreams and nightmares and in the altered consciousness they experienced under their addiction to opium. In his odes, as in the quasi-medieval "ballad" "La Belle Dame sans Merci," Keats recorded strange mixtures of pleasure and pain with extraordinary sensitivity, pondering the destructive aspects of sexuality and the erotic quality of the longing for death. And Byron made repeated use of the fascination of the forbidden and the appeal of the terrifying yet seductive Satanic hero.

There were, of course, writers who resisted these poetic engagements with fantasized landscapes and strange passions. Significant dissent came from some women writers, who, given accounts of their sex as especially susceptible to the delusions or romantic love, had particular reason to continue the Enlightenment program and promote the rational regulation of emotion. Barbauld wrote a poem gently advising the young Coleridge not to prolong his stay in the "fairy bower" of romance but to engage actively with the world as it is. Often satirical when she assesses characters who imagine themselves the pitiable victims of their own powerful feelings, Jane Austen had her heroine in *Persuasion*, while conversing with a melancholy, Byron-reading young man, caution him against overindulgence in Byron's "impassioned descriptions of hopeless agony" and "prescribe" to him a "larger allowance of prose in his daily study." And yet this heroine, having "been forced into prudence in her youth," has "learned romance as she grew older." The reversal of the sequence that usually orders the story line of female socialization suggests a receptivity to romance's allure—the allure of the improbable—that links Austen to the spirit of the age.

Individualism and Alienation

Another feature of Byron's poetry that attracted notice and, in some quarters, censure was its insistence on his or his hero's self-sufficiency. Hazlitt, for instance, borrowed lines from Shakespeare's *Coriolanus* to object to Byron's habit of spurning human connection "[a]s if a man were author of himself, / And owned no other kin." The audacious individualism that Hazlitt questions in this passage from *The Spirit of the Age* was, however, central to the celebrations of creativity occupying many Romantic-period writers. Indeed, in the Preface, Wordsworth had already characterized his poetic experimentation in *Lyrical Ballads* as an exercise in artistic self-sufficiency. The Preface has been read as a document in which Wordsworth, proving himself a self-made man, arranges for his disinheritance—arranges to cut himself off, he says, "from a large portion of the phrases and figures of speech which from father to son have long been regarded as the common inheritance of Poets." The German philosophers who generated many of the characteristic ideas of European Romanticism had likewise developed an account of how individuals might author and create themselves. In the work of Immanuel Kant and others, the human mind was described as creating the universe it perceived and so creating its own experience. Mind is "not passive," Kant's admirer Coleridge wrote, but "made in God's image, and that too in the sublimest sense—the Image of the *Creator*." And Wordsworth declared in *The Prelude* that the individual mind "Even as an agent of the one great mind, / creates, creator and receiver both." The Romantic period, the epoch of free enterprise, imperial expansion, and boundless revolutionary hope, was also an epoch of individualism in which philosophers and poets alike put an extraordinarily high estimate on human potentialities.

In representing this expanded scope for individual initiative, much poetry of the period redefined heroism and made a ceaseless striving for the unattainable its crucial element. Viewed by moralists of previous ages as sin or lamentable error, longings that can never be satisfied—in Percy Shelley's phrase, "the desire of the moth for a star"—came to be revalued as the glory of human nature. "Less than everything," Blake announced, "cannot satisfy man." Discussions of the nature of art developed similarly. The German philosopher Friedrich Schlegel's proposal that poetry "should forever be becoming and never be perfected" supplied a way to understand the unfinished, "fragment" poems of the period ("Kubla Khan" most famously) not as failures but instead as confirmations that the most poetic poetry was defined as much by what was absent as by what was present: the poem, in this understanding, was a fragmentary trace of an original conception that was too grand ever to be fully realized. This defiant attitude toward limits also made many writers impatient with the conceptions of literary genre they inherited from the past. The result was that, creating new genres from old, they produced an astonishing variety of hybrid forms constructed on fresh principles of organization and style: "elegiac sonnets," "lyrical ballads," the poetic autobiography of *The Prelude*, Percy Shelley's "lyric drama" of cosmic reach, *Prometheus Unbound*, and (in the field of prose) the "historical novels" of Scott and the complex interweaving of letters, reported oral confessions, and interpolated tales that is Mary Shelley's *Frankenstein*.

In this context many writers' choice to portray poetry as a product of solitude and poets as loners might be understood as a means of reinforcing the individuality of their vision. (The sociability of the extroverted narrator of *Don Juan*, who is forever buttonholing "the gentle reader," is exceptional— Byron's way of harkening back to the satire of the eighteenth century.) And the appeal that nature poetry had for many writers of the period can be attributed to a determination to idealize the natural scene as a site where the individual could find freedom from social laws, an idealization that was easier to sustain when nature was, as often in the era, represented not as cultivated fields but as uninhabitable wild wastes, unplowed uplands, caves, and chasms. Rural *community*, threatened by the enclosures that were breaking up village life, was a tenuous presence in poetry as well.

Wordsworth's imagination is typically released, for instance, by the sudden apparition of a single figure, stark and solitary against a natural background; the terms *solitary, by one self, alone* sound through his poems. In the poetry of Coleridge, Shelley, and Byron (before *Don Juan* launched Byron's own satire on Byronism), the desolate landscapes are often the haunts of disillusioned visionaries and accursed outlaws, figures whose thwarted ambitions and torments connect them, variously, to Cain, the Wandering Jew, Satan, and even Napoleon. A variant of this figure is Prometheus, the hero of classical mythology, who is Satan-like in setting himself in opposition to God, but who, unlike Satan, is the champion rather than the enemy of the human race. Mary Shelley subjected this hero, central to her husband's mythmaking, to ironic rewriting in *Frankenstein*: Victor Frankenstein, a "Modern Prometheus," is far from championing humankind. For other women writers of the period, and for Shelley in her later novels, the equivalent to these half-charismatic, half-condemnable figures of alienation is the woman of "genius." In a world in which—as Wollstonecraft complained in the *Rights of Woman*—"all women are to be levelled by meekness and docility, into one character of . . . gentle compliance," the woman who in "unfeminine" fashion claimed a distinctive individuality did not gain authority but risked ostracism. As for the woman of genius, in writings by Robinson, Hemans, and Landon particularly, her story was often told as a modern variation on ancient legends of the Greek Sappho, the ill-fated female poet who had triumphed in poetry but died of love. Pressured by the emergent Victorianism of the 1820s and playing it safe, Hemans especially was careful to associate genius with self-inflicted sorrow and happiness with a woman's embrace of her domestic calling.

WRITING IN THE MARKETPLACE AND THE LAW COURTS

Even Romantics who wished to associate literature with isolated poets holding mute converse with their souls had to acknowledge that in real life the writer did not dwell in solitude but confronted, and was accountable to, a crowd. For many commentators the most revolutionary aspect of the age was the spread of literacy and the dramatic expansion of the potential audi-

Printing Press. George Cruikshank's image of a printing press in human form, superhero and harbinger of modern liberty, opens William Hone's satiric pamphlet *The Political Showman—At Home!* (1821).

ence for literature. This revolution, like the Revolution in France, occasioned a conservative reaction: the worry, frequently expressed as books ceased to be written exclusively for an elite, that this bigger audience (by 1830, about half of England's population of fourteen million) would be less qualified to judge or understand what it read. Beginning in the 1780s, more members of the working classes had learned to read as a result of lessons provided in Sunday schools (informal sites for the education of the poor that long antedated state-supported schools). At the same time reading matter became more plentiful and cheaper, thanks to innovations in retailing—the cut-rate sales of remaindered books and the spread of circulating libraries where volumes could be "rented"—and thanks to technological developments. By the end of the period, printing presses were driven by steam engines, and the manufacture of paper had been mechanized; publishers had mastered publicity, the art (as it was called) of "the puff." Surveying the consequences of these changes, Coleridge muttered darkly about that "misgrowth," "a Reading Public," making it sound like something freakish and pathological. Books had become a big business, one enrolling increasing numbers of individuals who found it possible to do without the assistance of wealthy patrons and who, accordingly, looked to this public for their hopes of survival. A few writers became celebrities, invested with a glamour that formerly had been reserved for royalty and that we nowadays save for movie stars. This was the case for the best-selling Byron, particularly, whose enthusiastic public could by the 1830s purchase dinner services imprinted with illustrations from his life and works.

How such popular acclaim was to be understood and how the new reading public that bestowed it (and took it away) could possibly be reformed or monitored when, as Coleridge's term *misgrowth* suggests, its limits and composition seemed unknowable: these were pressing questions for the age. Opponents of the French Revolution and political reform at home pondered a frightening possibility: if "events . . . [had] made us a world of readers" (as Coleridge put it, thinking of how newspapers had proliferated in response to the political upheavals), it might also be true that readers could *make* events in turn, that the new members of the audience for print would demand a part in the drama of national politics. Conservatives were well aware of arguments conjecturing that the Revolution had been the result of the invention of the printing press three centuries before. They certainly could not forget that Paine's *Rights of Man*—not the reading matter for the poor the Sunday-school movement had envisioned—had sold an astonishing two hundred thousand copies in a year.

However, the British state had lacked legal provisions for the prepublication censorship of books since 1695, which was when the last Licensing Act had lapsed. Throughout the Romantic period therefore the Crown tried out other methods for policing reading and criminalizing certain practices of authoring and publishing. Paine was in absentia found guilty of sedition, for instance, and in 1817 the radical publisher William Hone narrowly escaped conviction for blasphemy. Another government strategy was to use taxes to inflate the prices of printed matter and so keep political information out of the hands of the poor without exactly violating the freedom of the press. In the meantime worries about how the nation would fare now that "the people" read were matched by worries about how to regulate the reading done by women. In 1807 the bowdlerized edition was born, as the Reverend Thomas Bowdler and his sister Henrietta produced *The Family Shakespeare*, concocting a Bard who, his indelicacies expurgated, could be sanctioned family fare.

Commentators who condemned the publishing industry as a scene of criminality also cited the frequency with which, during this chaotic time, best-selling books ended up republished in unauthorized, "pirated" editions. Novels were the pirates' favorite targets. But the radical underground of London's printing industry also appropriated one of the most politically daring works of Percy Shelley, *Queen Mab*, and by keeping it in print, and accessible in cheap editions, thwarted attempts to posthumously sanitize the poet's reputation. And in 1817 Southey, by then a Tory and the King-dom's Poet Laureate, was embarrassed to find his insurrectionary drama of 1794, *Wat Tyler*, published without his permission. There was no chance, Southey learned, that the publishers who had filched his play and put this souvenir of his youthful radicalism into circulation would be punished. The court refused to grant an injunction, citing the precedent that there could be no protection for publications deemed injurious to the public.

OTHER LITERARY FORMS

Prose

Although we now know the Romantic period as an age of poetry, centered on works of imagination, nonfiction prose forms—essays, reviews, political pamphlets—flourished during the epoch, as writers seized the opportunity to speak to and for the era's new audiences. In eighteenth-century England, prose, particularly in the urbane, accessible style that writers such as Joseph Addison and David Hume cultivated in their essays, had been valued as the medium of sociable exchange that could integrate different points of view and unify the public space known as the "republic of letters." That ideal of civil discussion came under pressure in the Romantic period, however, since by then many intellectuals were uncertain whether a republic of letters could survive the arrival of those new readers, "the people," and whether in this age of class awareness such a thing as a unified public culture was even possible. Those uncertainties are never far from the surface in the master-pieces of Romantic prose—a category that ranges from the pamphleteering that drew Burke, Wollstonecraft, and Paine into the Revolution controversy of the 1790s, to the periodical essays, with suggestive titles like *The Watchman* and *The Friend*, in which Coleridge turned controversialist, to the magazine writing of Hazlitt, Charles Lamb, and De Quincey in the 1820s.

The issue of how the writer should relate to audience—as watchman or friend?—was especially tricky, because this period, when so many more people defined themselves as readers, saw the emergence of a new species of specialist reader. This was the critic, who, perhaps problematically, was empowered to tell all the others what to read. Following the establishment in 1802 of the *Edinburgh Review* and in 1809 of the *Quarterly Review*, a new professionalized breed of book reviewer claimed a degree of cultural authority to which eighteenth-century critics had never aspired. Whereas later-eighteenth-century periodicals such as the *Monthly Review* and *Critical Review* had aimed to notice almost everything in print, the *Edinburgh* and *Quarterly* limited themselves to about fifteen books per issue. The selectivity enabled them to make decisive statements about what would count as culture and what would fall beyond the pale. They also conceptu-alized criticism as a space of discipline, in which the reputations of the writers under review were as likely to be marred as they were to be made. The stern Latin motto of the *Edinburgh* (founded by lawyers) translates as "the judge is condemned when the guilty go free." The continuing tension in the relations between criticism and literature and doubt about whether critical prose can be literature—whether it can have artistic value as well as social utility—are legacies from the Romantic era. Hazlitt wondered self-consciously in an essay on criticism whether his was not in fact a critical rather than a poetical age and whether "no great works of genius appear, because so much is said and written about them."

Hazlitt participated importantly in another development. In 1820 the founding editor of the *London Magazine* gathered a group of writers, Hazlitt, Lamb, and De Quincey, who in the *London*'s pages collectively developed the Romantic form known as the familiar essay: intimate-feeling commen-taries, often presented as if prompted by incidents in the authors' private lives, on an eclectic range of topics, from pork to prizefighting. In some of his essays, Hazlitt modeled an account of the individual's response to works of art as most important not for how, for instance, it prepares that person for public citizenship, but for what it helps him discover about his personality. For their essays Lamb and De Quincey developed a style that harkened back to writers who flourished before the republic of letters and who had more idiosyncratic eccentricities than eighteenth-century decorum would have allowed. Though these essayists were very differently circumstanced from the Romantic poets who were their friends—paid by the page and writing to a deadline, for a start—their works thus parallel the poets' in also turning toward the subjective. One consequence of the essayists' cultivation of intimacy and preference for the impressionistic over the systematic is that, when we track the history of prose to the 1820s, we see it end up in a place very different from the one it occupies at the start of the Romantic period. Participants in the Revolution controversy of the 1790s had claimed to speak for all England. By the close of the period the achievement of the familiar essay was to have brought the medium of prose within the category of "the literary"—but by distancing it from public life.

Drama

Whether the plays composed during the Romantic period can qualify as literature has been, by contrast, more of a puzzle. England throughout this period had a vibrant theatrical culture. Theater criticism, practiced with flair by Hazlitt and Lamb, emerged as a new prose genre; actors like Sarah Siddons and Edmund Kean numbered the poets among their admirers and found their way into Romantic poetry; Mary Robinson was known as an actor before she was known as an author. But there were many restrictions limiting what could be staged in England and many calls for reform. As places where crowds gathered, theaters were always closely watched by suspicious government officials. The English had habitually extolled their theater as a site of social mixing—a mirror to the political order in that it supplied all the classes in the nation (those who, depending on how their tickets were priced, frequented the box, the pit, or the gallery) with another sort of representative assembly. But during this era *disorder* seemed the rule: riots broke out at Covent Garden in 1792 and 1809. The link between drama and disorder was one reason that new dramas had to meet the approval of a censor before they could be performed, a rule in place since 1737. Another restriction was that only the Theaters Royal (in London, Drury Lane, and Covent Garden) had the legal right to produce "legitimate" (spoken word) drama, leaving the other stages limited to entertainments—pantomimes and melodramas mainly—in which dialogue was by regulation always combined with music. An evening's entertainment focused on legitimate drama would not have been so different. The stages and auditoriums of the two theaters royal were huge spaces, which encouraged their managers to favor grandiose spectacles or, more precisely, multimedia experiences, involving musicians, dancers, and artists who designed scenery, besides players and playwrights.

This theatrical culture's demotion of *words* might explain why the poets of the era, however stage-struck, found drama uncongenial. Nonetheless, almost all tried their hands at the form, tempted by the knowledge that the plays of certain of their (now less esteemed) contemporaries—Hannah Cowley and Charles Maturin, for example—had met with immense acclaim. Some of the poets' plays were composed to be read rather than performed: "closet dramas," such as Byron's *Manfred*, Percy Shelley's *Prometheus Unbound*, and most of Joanna Baillie's *Plays on the Passions*, permitted experimentation with topic and form. Others were written expressly for the stage, but their authors were hampered by their inexperience and tendency, exacerbated by the censorship that encouraged them to seek safe subject matter in the past, to imitate the style of Elizabethan and Jacobean drama. There were exceptions to this discouraging record. Coleridge's tragedy *Remorse*, for instance, was a minor hit and ran for twenty nights in 1813. The most capable dramatist among the poets was, surprisingly, Percy Shelley. His powerful tragedy *The Cenci* (1820), the story of a monstrous father who rapes his daughter and is murdered by her in turn, was deemed unstageable on political rather than artistic or technical grounds. It had no chance of getting by the Examiner of Plays; indeed, by thematizing the unspeakable topic of incest, Shelley predicted his own censoring.

The Novel

Novels at the start of the Romantic period were immensely popular but— as far as critics and some of the form's half-ashamed practitioners were concerned—not quite respectable. Loose in structure, they seemed to require fewer skills than other literary genres. This genre lacked the classic pedigree claimed by poetry and drama. It attracted (or so detractors declared) an undue proportion of readers who were women, and who, by consuming its escapist stories of romantic love, risked developing false ideas of life. It likewise attracted (so some of these same critics complained) too many *writers* who were women. (By the 1780s women were publishing as many novels as men.) Because of its popularity, the form also focused commentators' anxieties about the expansion of the book market and commercialization of literature: hence late-eighteenth-century reviewers of new novels often sarcastically described them as mass-produced commodities, not authored exactly, but instead stamped out automatically in "novel-mills." Matters changed decisively, however, starting around 1814. Reviews of Scott's *Waverley* series of historical novels and then a review that Scott wrote of Austen's *Emma* declared a renaissance—"a new style of novel." By this time, too, the genre had its historians, who delineated the novel's origins and rise and in this manner established its particularity against the more reputable literary forms. It was having a canon created for it too; figures like Barbauld and Scott compiled and introduced collections of the best novels. So equipped, the novel began to endanger poetry's long-held monopoly on literary prestige.

There had in fact been earlier signs of these new ambitions for the genre, although reviewers did not then know what to make of them. The last decade of the eighteenth century saw bold experiments with novels' form and subject matter—in particular, new ways of linking fiction with philosophy and history. Rather than, as one reviewer put it, contentedly remaining in a "region of their own," some novels showed signs of having designs on the real world. The writers now known as the Jacobin novelists used the form to test political theories and represent the political upheavals of the age. Thus in *Caleb Williams, or, Things as They Are*, William Godwin (husband of Mary Wollstonecraft, father of Mary Shelley) set out, he said, to "write a tale, that shall constitute an epoch in the mind of the reader, that no one, after he had read it, shall ever be exactly the same": the result was a chilling novel of surveillance and entrapment in which a servant recounts the persecutions he suffers at the hands of the master whose secret past he has detected. (The disturbing cat-and-mouse game between the two gets rewritten two decades later as the conclusion to *Frankenstein*, a novel that, among many other things, represents Shelley's tribute to the philosophical fictions of her parents.) Loyalists attacked the Jacobins with their own weapons and, in making novels their ammunition, contributed in turn to enhancing the genre's cultural presence.

The Novel. Illustration from 1787 by James
Northcote of a scene in William Hayley's didactic
poem *The Triumphs of Temper* (1781): the heroine's
maiden aunt has just caught her in possession of a
novel and seized the book as "filthy trash"—while
secretly intending to keep it for herself.

Another innovation in novel writing took shape, strangely enough, as a
recovery of what was old. Writers whom we now describe as the Gothic
novelists revisited the romance, the genre identified as the primitive forerunner of the modern novel, looking to a medieval (i.e., "Gothic") Europe
that they pictured as a place of gloomy castles, devious Catholic monks,
and stealthy ghosts. These authors—first Walpole, followed by Clara Reeve,
Sophia Lee, Matthew Lewis, and the hugely popular Ann Radcliffe—
developed for the novel a repertory of settings and story lines meant to
purvey to readers the pleasurable terror of regression to a premodern, pre-
rational state. This Gothic turn was another instance of the period's
"romance revival," another variation on the effort to renew the literature of
the present by reworking the past. Gothic fiction was thus promoted in
terms running parallel to those in accounts of the powers of poetry: when
novels break with humdrum reality, Barbauld explained, "our imagination,
darting forth, explores with rapture the new world which is laid open to its
view, and rejoices in the expansion of its powers."

Possibly this "new world" was meant to supply Romantic-period readers
with an escape route from the present and from what Godwin called "things
as they are." Certainly, the pasts that Gothic novelists conjure up are conceived of in fanciful, freewheeling ways; it is comical just how often a Radcliffe heroine who is supposed to inhabit sixteenth-century France can act
like a proper English girl on the marriage market in the 1790s. But even that
example of anachronism might suggest that some Gothic novelists were inviting readers to assess their stories as engaging the questions of the day. Gothic
horrors gave many writers a language in which to examine the nature of
power—the elements of sadism and masochism in the relations between men

and women, for instance. And frequently the Gothic novelists probe the very ideas of historical accuracy and legitimacy that critics use against them, and meditate on who is authorized to tell the story of the past and who is not.

The ascendancy of the novel in the early nineteenth century is in many ways a function of fiction writers' new self-consciousness about their relation to works of history. By 1814 the novelist and historian encroached on each other's territory more than ever. This was not exactly because nineteenth-century novelists were renewing their commitment to probability and realism (although, defining themselves against the critically reviled Gothic novelists, many were) but rather because the nature of things historical was also being reinvented. In light of the Revolution, history's traditional emphasis on public affairs and great men had begun to give way to an emphasis on beliefs, customs, everyday habits—the approach we now identify with social history. Novelists pursued similar interests: in works like *Castle Rackrent*, Maria Edgeworth, for instance, provides an almost anthropological account of the way of life of a bygone Ireland. The only novelist before Scott whom the influential *Edinburgh Review* took seriously, Edgeworth builds into her "national tales" details about local practices that demonstrate how people's ways of seeing are rooted in the particularities of their native places. Scott learned from her, incorporating her regionalism into his new style of historical novels, in which, with deeply moving results, he also portrayed the past as a place of adventure, pageantry, and grandeur.

Scott and Edgeworth establish the master theme of the early-nineteenth-century novel: the question of how the individual consciousness intermeshes with larger social structures, of how far character is the product of history and how far it is not. Jane Austen's brilliance as a satirist of the English leisure class often prompts literary historians to compare her works to witty Restoration and eighteenth-century comedies. But she too helped bring this theme to the forefront of novel writing, devising new ways of articulating the relationship between the psychological history of the individual and the history of society and, with unsurpassed psychological insight, creating unforgettable heroines who live in time and change. As with other Romantics, Austen's topic is revolution—revolutions of the mind. The momentous event in her fictions, which resemble Wordsworth's poetry in finding out the extraordinary in the everyday, is the change of mind that creates the possibility of love. Contrasting his own "big bow-wow strain" with Austen's nuance, Scott wrote that Austen "had a talent for describing the involvements and feelings and characters of ordinary life, which is to me the most wonderful I ever met with." Nineteenth-century reviewers of his triumphant *Waverley* series were certain that Scott's example foretold the future of novel writing. He, however, recognized the extent to which Austen had also changed the genre in which she worked, by developing a new novelistic language for the workings of the mind in flux.

The Romantic Period

TEXTS	CONTEXTS
1773 Anna Letitia Aikin (later Barbauld), *Poems*	1773 East India Act brings large portions of the Indian subcontinent under British government control
1774 J. W. von Goethe, *The Sorrows of Young Werther*	
	1775 American War of Independence (1775–83)
1776 Adam Smith, *The Wealth of Nations*	
1778 Frances Burney, *Evelina*	
1779 Samuel Johnson, *Lives of the English Poets* (1779–81)	
	1780 Gordon Riots in London
1781 Immanuel Kant, *Critique of Pure Reason*. Jean-Jacques Rousseau, *Confessions*. J. C. Friedrich Schiller, *The Robbers*	
	1783 William Pitt becomes prime minister (serving until 1801 and again in 1804–6)
1784 Charlotte Smith, *Elegiac Sonnets*	1784 Death of Samuel Johnson. Warren Hastings and Sir William Jones found the Asiatic Society in Calcutta
1785 William Cowper, *The Task*	
1786 William Beckford, *Vathek*. Robert Burns, *Poems, Chiefly in the Scottish Dialect*	
	1787 W. A. Mozart, *Don Giovanni*. Society for the Abolition of the Slave Trade founded
1789 Jeremy Bentham, *Principles of Morals and Legislation*. William Blake, *Songs of Innocence*	1789 Fall of the Bastille (beginning of the French Revolution)
1790 Joanna Baillie, *Poems*. Blake, *The Marriage of Heaven and Hell*. Edmund Burke, *Reflections on the Revolution in France*	1790 J. M. W. Turner first exhibits at the Royal Academy
1791 William Gilpin, *Observations on the River Wye*. Thomas Paine, *Rights of Man*. Ann Radcliffe, *The Romance of the Forest*	1791 Revolution in Santo Domingo (modern Haiti)
1792 Mary Wollstonecraft, *A Vindication of the Rights of Woman*	1792 September Massacres in Paris. First gas lights in Britain
1793 William Godwin, *Political Justice*	1793 Execution of Louis XVI and Marie Antoinette. France declares war against Britain (and then Britain against France). The Reign of Terror
1794 Blake, *Songs of Experience*. Godwin, *Caleb Williams*. Radcliffe, *The Mysteries of Udolpho*	1794 The fall of Robespierre. Trials for high treason of members of the London Corresponding Society
	1795 Pitt's Gagging Acts suppress freedom of speech and assembly in Britain
1796 Matthew Gregory Lewis, *The Monk*	
	1797 Mary Wollstonecraft dies from complications of childbirth

TEXTS	CONTEXTS
1798 Baillie, *Plays on the Passions*, volume 1. Bentham, *Political Economy*. Thomas Malthus, *An Essay on the Principle of Population*. William Wordsworth and Samuel Taylor Coleridge, *Lyrical Ballads*	1798 Rebellion in Ireland
1800 Maria Edgeworth, *Castle Rackrent*. Mary Robinson, *Lyrical Tales*	
	1801 Parliamentary Union of Ireland and Great Britain
1802–3 Walter Scott, *Minstrelsy of the Scottish Border*	1802 Treaty of Amiens. *Edinburgh Review* founded. John Constable first exhibits at the Royal Academy
	1804 Napoleon crowned emperor. Founding of the republic of Haiti
1805 Scott, *The Lay of the Last Minstrel*	1805 The French fleet defeated by the British at Trafalgar
1807 Wordsworth, *Poems in Two Volumes* Charlotte Smith, *Beachy Head*	1807 Abolition of the slave trade
1808 Goethe, *Faust*, part I	1808 Ludwig van Beethoven, *Symphonies* 5 and 6
	1809 *Quarterly Review* founded
1811 Jane Austen, *Sense and Sensibility*	1811 The Prince of Wales becomes regent for George III, who is declared incurably insane
1812 Lord Byron, *Childe Harold's Pilgrimage*, cantos 1 and 2. Felicia Hemans, *The Domestic Affections*. Barbauld, *Eighteen Hundred and Eleven*	1812 War between Britain and the United States (1812–15)
1813 Austen, *Pride and Prejudice*. Byron, *The Giaour*	1813 Renewal of charter of East India Company, with "pious clause," authorizing missionary activity on the Indian subcontinent
1814 Scott, *Waverley*. Wordsworth, *The Excursion*	
	1815 Napoleon defeated at Waterloo. Corn Laws passed, protecting economic interests of the landed aristocracy
1816 Byron, *Childe Harold*, cantos 3 and 4. Coleridge, *Christabel*, "Kubla Khan." Percy Shelley, *Alastor*	
1817 Byron, *Manfred*. Coleridge, *Biographia Literaria* and *Sibylline Leaves*. John Keats, *Poems*	1817 *Blackwood's Edinburgh Magazine* founded. Death of Princess Charlotte. Death of Jane Austen
1818 Austen, *Persuasion* and *Northanger Abbey*. Keats, *Endymion*. Thomas Love Peacock, *Nightmare Abbey*. Mary Shelley, *Frankenstein*	
1819 Byron, *Don Juan*, cantos 1 and 2. Percy Shelley, *The Mask of Anarchy*	1819 "Peterloo Massacre" in Manchester
1820 John Clare, *Poems Descriptive of Rural Life*. Keats, *Lamia, Isabella, The Eve of St. Agnes, and Other Poems*. Percy Shelley, *Prometheus Unbound*	1820 Death of George III; accession of George IV. *London Magazine* founded

TEXTS	CONTEXTS
1821 Thomas De Quincey, *Confessions of an English Opium-Eater*. Percy Shelley, *Adonais*. Clare, *The Village Minstrel*	**1821** Deaths of Keats in Rome and Napoleon at St. Helena
	1822 Franz Schubert, *Unfinished Symphony*. Death of Percy Shelley in the Bay of Spezia, near Lerici, Italy
1823 Charles Lamb, *Essays of Elia*	
1824 Letitia Landon, *The Improvisatrice*	**1824** Death of Byron in Missolonghi
1825 William Hazlitt, *The Spirit of the Age*	
1826 Mary Shelley, *The Last Man*	
1827 Clare, *The Shepherd's Calendar*	
1828 Hemans, *Records of Woman*	**1828** Parliamentary repeal of the Test and Corporation Acts excluding Dissenters from state offices
	1829 Catholic Emancipation
1830 Charles Lyell, *Principles of Geology* (1830–33). Alfred Tennyson, *Poems, Chiefly Lyrical*	**1830** Death of George IV; accession of William IV. Revolution in France
	1832 First Reform Bill
1835 Clare, *The Rural Muse*	

Balladry and Ballad Revivals

Through the eighteenth century many commentators (Joseph Addison in his *Spectator* essays of 1711 most famously) proposed that polished modern poetry might not hold its own when compared to "darling songs of the common people" such as "The Children in the Wood" or "Chevy Chase." By the end of the century authors and scholars not only haunted the city streets where Addison had encountered itinerant ballad singers hawking the crudely printed broadsides that contained those songs, hunting for the "majestic simplicity" that Addison had celebrated, they also headed to remote, undeveloped parts of Britain and to the border regions between the Scottish Highlands and Lowlands and between Scotland and England especially. They made a systematic effort to write down and then put into print the words to the tunes and chants they heard there. These were the stages by which literary culture began to engage, sometimes squeamishly, with an oral culture associated with sensational stories (of infanticide, bloody feuds, supernatural events, illicit sex) and with illiterate and barely literate people, the unnamed shepherds and old servant women, for instance, who served as the sources for Sir Walter Scott's ballad collection *The Minstrelsy of the Scottish Border* (1802–3).

Through popular ballads, these collectors sought an alternative to the refinement and elegance that were supposed to regulate eighteenth-century literary culture. In the people who remembered and performed them, they hoped to encounter living relics of a lost past, closer to nature than modern times: a hope that made Romantic-period ballad scholarship a dry run for the discipline of folklore that would come onto the scene at the nineteenth century's end. It was "in the first ages of society," the professor of Rhetoric at Edinburgh University Hugh Blair declared in 1765, that poetry was "most glowing and animated." Ballad revivals seemed a way to recover the primal energies that poetry was thought to have lost as a consequence of Enlightenment, the standardization of the English language, and the triumph of good taste.

Ballads are tricky to locate historically. This is because these narrative poems have a complicated relationship to authorship. Those who sing or recite them invariably change, even recompose, them, and, accordingly, when one speaks of "Sir Patrick Spens," one is actually speaking of a number of poems telling the same story in different words. In different localities, different versions will prevail. Early editions of *The Norton Anthology of English Literature* presented ballads as belonging to medieval literature. This presentation registered the impact of theories, like the one that Thomas Percy elaborated as the compiler of *Reliques of Ancient English Poetry* (1765), that proposed that the songs sung by eighteenth-century balladeers actually represented the corrupted remnants of a romantic literature of the Middle Ages. Ballads, Percy and his followers insisted, were originally the works of court minstrels who enjoyed a social centrality denied to modern poets; balladry decisively predated the commercial networks established with the advent of print technology. Scholars nowadays place the origin of much of the ballad canon later, from the seventeenth century on, and they believe print has played a larger part in the transmission of oral culture across time than eighteenth- and nineteenth-century collectors were willing to accept.

Arranging for ballads to head up the Romantic period, as this edition does, is a way to acknowledge how generative balladry was for Romantic poetics. It fueled the interest that many Romantic poets took in the sound effects that might reconnect printed poetry to the living voice. It prompted the sort of experimentation with genres that Wordsworth and Coleridge signaled with their title *Lyrical Ballads*. It also fueled the primitivism of the period: authors' and readers' nostalgia for a lost world shaped by the immediate contact between singers and their auditors, and not by the mediation of an impersonal market in printed books.

Their basis in song lends ballads their distinctive features: their regular meter and use of refrain and repetition; their characteristic stanzaic form ("ballad stanzas" are quatrains of alternating four-beat and three-beat lines, with a rhyme scheme abcb). As Addison recognized, the stark simplicity of the ballads helps them take hold of their audience's imaginations. They haunt us—and continue to be performed by modern musicians—not just because of their tunes but also because these pared-down narratives enigmatically refuse to elaborate on the dramatic incidents at their centers.

Though the spelling has been modernized, the texts we give here as examples of ballads are based on those provided in books that Romantic authors would have read. Near the end of the nineteenth century, Francis James Child synthesized the work of previous ballad scholars in his comprehensive and still-standard collection *English and Scottish Popular Ballads* (1888–92); the numbers under which Child lists these ballads are provided in the notes.

Lord Randall[1]

"Oh where ha'e ye been, Lord Randall my son?
O where ha'e ye been, my handsome young man?"
  "I ha'e been to the wild wood: mother, make my bed soon,
  For I'm weary wi' hunting, and fain° wald° lie   *gladly / would*
    down."

5 "Where gat ye your dinner, Lord Randall my son?
Where gat ye your dinner, my handsome young man?"
  "I dined wi' my true love: mother, make my bed soon,
  For I'm weary wi' hunting, and fain wald lie down."

"What gat ye to your dinner, Lord Randall my son?
10 What gat ye to your dinner, my handsome young man?"
  "I gat eels boiled in broo:° mother, make my bed soon,   *broth*
  For I'm weary wi' hunting and fain wald lie down."

"What became of your bloodhounds, Lord Randall my son?
What became of your bloodhounds, my handsome young man?"
15 "O they swelled and they died: mother, make my bed soon,
  For I'm weary wi' hunting and fain wald lie down."

"O I fear ye are poisoned, Lord Randall my son!
O I fear ye are poisoned, my handsome young man!"
  "Oh yes, I am poisoned: mother, make my bed soon,
20 For I'm sick at the heart, and I fain wald lie down."

1. Child, no. 12D. From Scott's *Minstrelsy* (1803).

Bonny Barbara Allan[1]

It was in and about the Martinmas° time,   *November 11*
 When the green leaves were a-fallin';
That Sir John Graeme in the West Country
 Fell in love with Barbara Allan.

5 He sent his man down through the town
 To the place where she was dwellin':
"O haste and come to my master dear,
 Gin° ye be Barbara Allan."   *if*

O hooly,° hooly rase° she up,   *gently / rose*
10 To the place where he was lyin',
And when she drew the curtain by:
 "Young man, I think you're dyin'."

"O it's I'm sick, and very, very sick,
 And 'tis a' for Barbara Allan."
15 "O the better for me ye sal° never be,   *shall*
 Though your heart's blood were a-spillin'.

"O dinna ye mind,[2] young man," said she,
 "When ye the cups were fillin',
That ye made the healths gae° round and round, *go*
20 And slighted Barbara Allan?"

He turned his face unto the wall,
 And death with him was dealin':
"Adieu, adieu, my dear friends all,
 And be kind to Barbara Allan."

25 And slowly, slowly, rase she up,
 And slowly, slowly left him;
And sighing said she could not stay,
 Since death of life had reft° him.   *deprived*

She had not gane° a mile but twa,°   *gone / two*
30 When she heard the dead-bell knellin',
And every jow° that the dead-bell ga'ed°   *stroke / made*
 It cried, "Woe to Barbara Allan!"

"O mother, mother, make my bed,
 O make it soft and narrow:
35 Since my love died for me today,
 I'll die for him tomorrow."

---

1. Child, no. 84A. From Allan Ramsay's *The Tea-Table Miscellany; or . . . choice songs, Scots and English* (10th ed., 1740). In 1666 the diarist Samuel Pepys, whose collection of broadside ballads is preserved at Magdalene College, Cambridge University, reported the "perfect pleasure" with which he heard an actress sing "her little Scotch song of Barbary Allen."
2. Don't you remember.

The Wife of Usher's Well[1]

There lived a wife at Usher's Well,
    And a wealthy wife was she;
She had three stout and stalwart sons,
    And sent them o'er the sea.

5 They hadna' been a week from her,
    A week but barely ane,°   *one*
When word came to the carlin° wife   *old*
    That her three sons were gane.°   *gone*

They hadna' been a week from her,
10   A week but barely three,
When word came to the carlin wife
    That her sons she'd never see.

"I wish the wind may never cease
    Nor fashes° in the flood,   *disturbances*
15 Till my three sons come hame° to me,   *home*
    In earthly flesh and blood."

It fell about the Martinmas,°   *November 11*
    When nights are long and mirk,°   *dark*
The carlin wife's three sons came hame,
20   And their hats were o' the birk.[2]

It neither grew in sike° nor ditch,   *field*
    Nor yet in ony sheugh,°   *furrow*
But at the gates o' Paradise
    That birk grew fair eneugh.

25 "Blow up the fire, my maidens,
    Bring water from the well:
For a' my house shall feast this night,
    Since my three sons are well."

And she has made to them a bed,
30   She's made it large and wide,
And she's ta'en her mantle her about,
    Sat down at the bedside.

Up then crew the red, red cock,
    And up and crew the gray.
35 The eldest to the youngest said,
    "'Tis time we were away."[3]

---

1. Child, no. 79A. From Scott's *Minstrelsy* (1802), which bases its text "on the recitation of an old woman" living in West Lothian, a rural district to the west of Edinburgh.

2. Birch. Those returning from the dead were thought to wear vegetation on their heads.
3. The dead must return to their graves at cockcrow.

The cock he hadna' crawed but once,
  And clapped his wings at a',
When the youngest to the eldest said,
40   "Brother, we must awa'.°   *away*

"The cock doth craw, the day doth daw,°   *dawn*
  The channerin'° worm doth chide: *fretting*
Gin° we be missed out o' our place,   *if*
  A sair pain we maun bide.⁴

45 "Fare ye weel,° my mother dear,   *well*
  Fareweel to barn and byre.°   *cow house*
And fare ye weel, the bonny lass
  That kindles my mother's fire."

The Three Ravens[1]

There were three ravens sat on a tree,
  Down a down, hay down, hay down
There were three ravens sat on a tree,
  With a down
5 There were three ravens sat on a tree,
They were as black as they might be,
  With a down, derry, derry, derry, down, down.[2]

The one of them said to his mate,
"Where shall we our breakfast take?"

10 "Down in yonder green field
There lies a knight slain under his shield.

"His hounds they lie down at his feet,
So well they can their master keep.

"His hawks they fly so eagerly,°   *fiercely*
15 There's no fowl° dare him come nigh."   *bird*

Down there comes a fallow° doe,   *red-brown*
As great with young as she might go.°   *walk*

She lifted up his bloody head,
And kissed his wounds that were so red.

20 She got him up upon her back,
And carried him to earthen lake.°   *pit*

---

4. A sore pain we must abide.
1. Child, no. 26A. The text is that of the first version to appear in print, in Thomas Ravenscroft's songbook *Melismata* (1611), reprinted in Joseph Ritson's *Ancient Songs* (1790).
2. The following stanzas take the same pattern with the repetition of the first line and the refrains.

She buried him before the prime;[3]
She was dead herself ere evensong time.

God send every gentleman
25 Such hawks, such hounds, and such a lemman.°   *mistress*

Sir Patrick Spens[1]

The king sits in Dumferline town,
    Drinking the blude-reid° wine: *bloodred*
"O whar will I get a guid sailor
    To sail this ship of mine?"

5 Up and spak an eldern° knicht,   *ancient*
    Sat at the king's richt knee:
"Sir Patrick Spens is the best sailor
    That sails upon the sea."

The king has written a braid° letter   *broad*
10   And signed it wi' his hand,
And sent it to Sir Patrick Spens,
    Was walking on the sand.

The first line that Sir Patrick read,
    A loud lauch° lauched he;   *laugh*
15 The next line that Sir Patrick read,
    The tear blinded his ee.°   *eye*

"O wha° is this has done this deed,   *who*
    This ill deed done to me,
To send me out this time o' the year,
20   To sail upon the sea?

"Make haste, make haste, my mirry men all,
    Our guid ship sails the morn."
"O say na° sae,° my master dear,   *not / so*
    For I fear a deadly storm.

25 "Late late yestre'en I saw the new moon
    Wi' the auld° moon in her arm,   *old*
And I fear, I fear, my dear master,
    That we will come to harm."

O our Scots nobles were richt laith°   *loath*
30   To weet° their cork-heeled shoon,°   *wet / shoes*

3. The first hour of the morning.
1. Child, no. 58A. From Percy's *Reliques* (1765), where Percy declares himself sure that the ballad has a basis in history but fails to pinpoint just when "this fatal expedition happened that proved so destructive to the Scottish nobles." The version in Scott's *Minstrelsy* (1803) includes a stanza that describes Sir Patrick Spens's ship as bound for Norway, where Spens is to collect the daughter of the Norwegian king.

But lang owre° a' the play were played   *ere*
    Their hats they swam aboon.°   *above*

O lang, lang may their ladies sit,
    Wi' their fans into their hand,
35 Or e'er they see Sir Patrick Spens
    Come sailing to the land.

O lang, lang may the ladies stand,
    Wi' their gold kembs° in their hair,   *combs*
Waiting for their ain° dear lords,   *own*
40   For they'll see thame na mair.°   *more*

Half o'er,° half o'er to Aberdour   *halfway over*
    It's fifty fadom° deep,   *fathoms*
And there lies guid Sir Patrick Spens,
    Wi' the Scots lords at his feet.

The Dæmon-lover[1]

"O where have you been, my long, long love,
    This long seven years and mair?"
"O I'm come to seek my former vows,
    Ye granted me before."

5 "O hold your tongue of your former vows,
    For they will breed sad strife;
O hold your tongue of your former vows,
    For I am become a wife."

He turned him right and round about,
10   And the tear blinded his e'e;°   *eye*
"I wad never hae trodden on Irish ground,
    If it had not been for thee."

"I might hae had a king's daughter,
    Far, far beyond the sea;
15 I might have had a king's daughter,
    Had it not been for love o' thee."

"If ye might have had a king's daughter,
    Yer sel ye had to blame;
Ye might have taken the king's daughter,
20   For ye kend° that I was nane."   *knew*

1. Child, no. 243F. From Scott's *Minstrelsy* (5th ed., 1812), a ballad contributed by Scott's friend William Laidlaw, who took it down from the recitation of one Walter Grieve and also "improved" it with four stanzas (6, 12, 17, 18) of his own authoring: the authenticity that balladry promised was sometimes an object of fabrication. In the United States, this ballad has been handed down with the title "The House Carpenter," the trade of the husband whom the woman leaves behind.

"O faulse are the vows of womankind,
    But fair is their faulse bodie;
I never wad hae trodden on Irish ground,
    Had it not been for love o' thee."

25   "If I was to leave my husband dear,
    And my two babes also,
O what have you to take me to,
    If with you I should go?"

"I hae seven ships upon the sea,
30   The eighth brought me to land;
With four-and-twenty bold mariners,
    And music on every hand."

She has taken up her two little babes,
    Kissed them baith cheek and chin;
35   "O fair ye weel, my ain two babes,
    For I'll never see you again."

She set her foot upon the ship,
    No mariners could she behold;
But the sails were o' the taffetie,
40   And the masts o' the beaten gold.

She had not sailed a league, a league,
    A league but barely three,
When dismal grew his countenance,
    And drumlie° grew his e'e.   *troubled*

45   The masts, that were like the beaten gold,
    Bent not on the heaving seas;
But the sails, that were o' the taffetie,
    Fill'd not in the east land breeze.

They had not sail'd a league, a league,
50   A league but barely three,
Until she espied his cloven foot,
    And she wept right bitterlie.

"O hold your tongue of your weeping," says he,
    "Of your weeping now let me be;
55   I will shew you how the lilies grow
    On the banks of Italy."

"O what hills are yon, yon pleasant hills,
    That the sun shines sweetly on?"
"O yon are the hills of heaven," he said,
60   "Where you will never win."

"O whaten a mountain is yon," she said,
    "All so dreary wi' frost and snow?"
"O yon is the mountain of hell," he cried,
    "Where you and I will go."

65 And aye when she turn'd her round about,
    Aye taller he seem'd for to be;
Until that the tops o' that gallant ship
    Nae taller were than he.

The clouds grew dark, and the wind grew loud,
70 And the levin° fill'd her e'e;   *lightning*
And waesome wail'd the snaw-white sprites
    Upon the gurlie° sea.   *stormy*

He struck the tap-mast wi' his hand,
    The fore-mast wi' his knee;
75 And he brake that gallant ship in twain,
    And sank her in the sea.

ANNA LETITIA BARBAULD
1743–1825

Anna Barbauld, born Anna Letitia Aikin, received an unusual education from her father, who was a minister and a teacher at the Warrington Academy in Lancashire, the great educational center for the Nonconformist community, whose religion barred them from admission to the universities of Oxford and Cambridge. During the eighteenth century Dissenting academies such as Warrington had developed a modern curriculum in the natural sciences as well as in modern languages and English literature. This progressive educational program deviated significantly from the curriculum, scarcely altered since the sixteenth century, that was supplied by the old universities. The benefits Barbauld received from her exposure to an educational system that the Dissenters had designed with their sons in mind are suggested by the astounding versatility of her literary career.

She made her literary debut in 1773 with *Poems* and *Miscellaneous Pieces in Prose*, the latter co-written with her brother John. The books immediately established her as a leading author. Her marriage the next year to Rochemont Barbauld, a Dissenting minister like her father, and their decision to set up a boys' school together therefore struck the critic Samuel Johnson as squandering this woman's own unusual education: "Miss [Aikin] was an instance of early cultivation, but in what did it terminate?" Thereafter, until Rochemont Barbauld's increasing mental instability necessitated the closing of their school, Barbauld divided her time between writing and teaching the younger boys. Because of the popularity of Barbauld's *Lessons for Children* (1778–79) and *Hymns in Prose for Children* (1781), William Hazlitt was recording a common experience when he recalled that he read her books "before those of any other author . . . , when I was learning to spell words of one syllable." This writing for child audiences registered Barbauld's Enlightenment faith in human potential.

Her fame continued to grow in the 1790s, and in 1797 the up-and-coming poet Samuel Taylor Coleridge walked forty miles to meet her. During this decade Barbauld contributed poetry to her brother John's *Monthly Magazine*, published her "Epistle to William Wilberforce" attacking British involvement in the slave trade, and wrote pamphlets that opposed the war with France and campaigned for the repeal of the Test Acts that had barred participation in the public life of the nation to Nonconformists (those men who would not subscribe, as "tests" of their loyalty, to the thirty-nine Articles of the Established Church). She accompanied this writing with editing, producing editions of William Collins's poems (1797) and the novelist Samuel Richardson's letters (1804). Her fifty-volume compilation *The British Novelists* (1810) was the first attempt to establish a national canon in fiction and thereby do for the novel what Samuel Johnson's *Works of the English Poets* (1779–81) had done for poetry. Its introductory essay, "On the Origin and Progress of Novel-Writing," makes a pioneering argument for the educational and artistic value of the still disreputable genre.

Barbauld's last major work was *Eighteen Hundred and Eleven* (1812), a long poem that despairs over the war with France (then in its seventeenth year) and the corruption of English consumer society. (An excerpt may be found in "Romantic Literature and Wartime," on p. 754.) Critics were unnerved, even disgusted, by the poem's apocalyptic vision of a future in which England, its pride humbled, would lie in ruins—the more so because of its author's gender. The Tory critic John Wilson Croker thus warned Barbauld "to desist from satire": it was not up to a "lady-author" to sally forth from her knitting and say how "the empire might . . . be saved." Despite this abuse, Barbauld did not stop writing. She continued, as had long been her practice, to circulate work in manuscript and published a few poems in magazines. The posthumous collection of Barbauld's *Works* her niece Lucy Aikin brought out in 1825 contained several previously unpublished pieces.

The Mouse's Petition[1]

Found in the trap where he had been confined all night by Dr. Priestley,
for the sake of making experiments with different kinds of air

"Parcere subjectis, et debellare superbos."
—Virgil

Oh hear a pensive prisoner's prayer,
For liberty that sighs;
And never let thine heart be shut
Against the wretch's cries.

5   For here forlorn and sad I sit,
Within the wiry gate;
And tremble at th' approaching morn,
Which brings impending fate.

If e'er thy breast with freedom glow'd,
10   And spurn'd a tyrant's chain,
Let not thy strong oppressive force
A free-born mouse detain.

1. Addressed to the clergyman, political theorist, and scientist Joseph Priestley (1733–1804), who at this time was the most distinguished teacher at the Nonconformist Protestant Warrington Academy, where Barbauld's father was also a member of the faculty. The imagined speaker (the petitioning mouse) is destined to participate in just the sort of experiment that led Priestley, a few years later, to the discovery of "phlogiston"— what we now call oxygen. Tradition has it that when Barbauld showed him the lines, Priestley set the mouse free. According to Barbauld's modern editors, the poem was many times reprinted and was a favorite to assign students for memorizing. The Latin epigraph is from *The Aeneid* 6.853, "To spare the humbled, and to tame in war the proud."

Oh do not stain with guiltless blood
Thy hospitable hearth;
15 Nor triumph that thy wiles betray'd
A prize so little worth.

The scatter'd gleanings of a feast
My frugal meals supply;
But if thine unrelenting heart
20 That slender boon deny,

The cheerful light, the vital air,
Are blessings widely given;
Let nature's commoners enjoy
The common gifts of heaven.

25 The well-taught philosophic mind
To all compassion gives;
Casts round the world an equal eye,
And feels for all that lives.

If mind, as ancient sages taught,[2]
30 A never dying flame,
Still shifts through matter's varying forms,
In every form the same,

Beware, lest in the worm you crush
A brother's soul you find;
35 And tremble lest thy luckless hand
Dislodge a kindred mind.

Or, if this transient gleam of day
Be *all* of life we share,
Let pity plead within thy breast
40 That little *all* to spare.

So may thy hospitable board
With health and peace be crown'd;
And every charm of heartfelt ease
Beneath thy roof be found.

45 So, when destruction lurks unseen,
Which men, like mice, may share,
May some kind angel clear thy path,
And break the hidden snare.

ca. 1771   1773

2. Lines 29–36 play on the idea of transmigration of souls, a doctrine that Priestley believed until the
early 1770s.

An Inventory of the Furniture in Dr. Priestley's Study

A map of every country known,[1]
With not a foot of land his own.
A list of folks that kicked a dust
On this poor globe, from Ptol. the First;[2]
5   He hopes,—indeed it is but fair,—
Some day to get a corner there.
A group of all the British kings,
Fair emblem! on a packthread swings.
The Fathers, ranged in goodly row,[3]
10   A decent, venerable show,
Writ a great while ago, they tell us,
And many an inch o'ertop their fellows.
A Juvenal[4] to hunt for mottos;
And Ovid's tales of nymphs and grottos.[5]
15   The meek-robed lawyers, all in white;
Pure as the lamb,—at least, to sight.
A shelf of bottles, jar and phial,°   *vial*
By which the rogues he can defy all,—
All filled with lightning keen and genuine,
20   And many a little imp he'll pen you in;
Which, like Le Sage's sprite, let out,
Among the neighbours makes a rout;[6]
Brings down the lightning on their houses,
And kills their geese, and frights their spouses.
25   A rare thermometer, by which
He settles, to the nicest pitch,
The just degrees of heat, to raise
Sermons, or politics, or plays.
Papers and books, a strange mixed olio,
30   From shilling touch° to pompous folio;   *cheap pamphlet*
Answer, remark, reply, rejoinder,
Fresh from the mint, all stamped and coined here;
Like new-made glass, set by to cool,
Before it bears the workman's tool.
35   A blotted proof-sheet, wet from Bowling.[7]
—"How can a man his anger hold in?"—
Forgotten rimes, and college themes,
Worm-eaten plans, and embryo schemes;—
A mass of heterogeneous matter,
40   A chaos dark, nor land nor water;—
New books, like new-born infants, stand,
Waiting the printer's clothing hand;—
Others, a motley ragged brood,

1. The maps, historical charts, books, and scientific apparatus are all part of the "furniture" (furnishings) of Joseph Priestley's study (see p. 40, n. 1).
2. Ptolemy I (ca. 367–283 B.C.E.), founder of the Ptolemaic dynasty in Egypt.
3. The works of the Catholic Church Fathers.
4. Roman satirist.
5. Ovid's *Metamorphoses*.
6. In René LeSage's *Le Diable Boîteux* (1707), a laboratory-created spirit lifts the roofs from the neighbors' houses, exposing their private lives and creating havoc.
7. Presumably a local printer.

Their limbs unfashioned all, and rude,
45 Like Cadmus' half-formed men appear;[8]
One rears a helm, one lifts a spear,
And feet were lopped and fingers torn
Before their fellow limbs were born;
A leg began to kick and sprawl
50 Before the head was seen at all,
Which quiet as a mushroom lay
Till crumbling hillocks gave it way;
And all, like controversial writing,
Were born with teeth, and sprung up fighting.
55   "But what is this," I hear you cry,
"Which saucily provokes my eye?"—
A thing unknown, without a name,
Born of the air and doomed to flame.

ca. 1771   1825

A Summer Evening's Meditation[1]

'Tis past! The sultry tyrant of the south
Has spent his short-lived rage; more grateful° hours   *pleasing*
Move silent on; the skies no more repel
The dazzled sight, but with mild maiden beams
5 Of tempered lustre court the cherished eye
To wander o'er their sphere; where, hung aloft,
Dian's bright crescent, like a silver bow
New strung in heaven, lifts high its beamy horns
Impatient for the night, and seems to push
10 Her brother° down the sky. Fair Venus shines   *Apollo*
Even in the eye of day; with sweetest beam
Propitious shines, and shakes a trembling flood
Of softened radiance from her dewy locks.
The shadows spread apace; while meekened[2] Eve,
15 Her cheek yet warm with blushes, slow retires
Through the Hesperian gardens of the west,
And shuts the gates of day. 'Tis now the hour
When Contemplation from her sunless haunts,
The cool damp grotto, or the lonely depth
20 Of unpierced woods, where wrapt in solid shade
She mused away the gaudy hours of noon,
And fed on thoughts unripened by the sun,
Moves forward; and with radiant finger points

8. Armed men created when Cadmus sowed the earth with the teeth of a dragon he had killed (Ovid's *Metamorphoses* 3.95–114).
1. This poem looks backward to poems such as William Collins's "Ode to Evening" (1748), Anne Finch's "A Nocturnal Reverie" (1713), and even to Milton's description in book 2 of *Paradise Lost* of Satan's daring navigation of the realm of Chaos. At the same time Barbauld's excursion-and-return structure anticipates the high flights (and returns) of later lyrics by Coleridge, Percy Shelley, and Keats. But her account of the journey, with its references to Diana's crescent (line 7) and Venus's sweetest beams (10 and 11) is *differently* gendered: this soul that launches "into the trackless deeps" (82) is clearly female.
2. Softened, made meek.

To yon blue concave swelled by breath divine,
25 Where, one by one, the living eyes of heaven
Awake, quick kindling o'er the face of ether
One boundless blaze; ten thousand trembling fires,
And dancing lustres, where the unsteady eye,
Restless and dazzled, wanders unconfined
30 O'er all this field of glories; spacious field,
And worthy of the Master: he, whose hand
With hieroglyphics elder than the Nile
Inscribed the mystic tablet, hung on high
To public gaze, and said, "Adore, O man!
35 The finger of thy God." From what pure wells
Of milky light, what soft o'erflowing urn,
Are all these lamps so fill'd? these friendly lamps,
For ever streaming o'er the azure deep
To point our path, and light us to our home.
40 How soft they slide along their lucid spheres!
And silent as the foot of Time, fulfill
Their destined courses: Nature's self is hushed,
And, but° a scattered leaf, which rustles through   *except for*
The thick-wove foliage, not a sound is heard
45 To break the midnight air; though the raised ear,
Intensely listening, drinks in every breath.
How deep the silence, yet how loud the praise!
But are they silent all? or is there not
A tongue in every star, that talks with man,
50 And woos him to be wise? nor woos in vain:
This dead of midnight is the noon of thought,
And Wisdom mounts her zenith with the stars.
At this still hour the self-collected soul
Turns inward, and beholds a stranger there
55 Of high descent, and more than mortal rank;
An embryo God; a spark of fire divine,
Which must burn on for ages, when the sun,—
Fair transitory creature of a day!—
Has closed his golden eye, and wrapt in shades
60 Forgets his wonted journey through the east.

Ye citadels of light, and seats of Gods!
Perhaps my future home, from whence the soul,
Revolving° periods past, may oft look back   *meditating on*
With recollected tenderness on all
65 The various busy scenes she left below,
Its deep-laid projects and its strange events,
As on some fond and doting tale that soothed
Her infant hours—O be it lawful now
To tread the hallowed circle of your courts,
70 And with mute wonder and delighted awe
Approach your burning confines. Seized in thought,
On Fancy's wild and roving wing I sail,
From the green borders of the peopled Earth,
And the pale Moon, her duteous fair attendant;
75 From solitary Mars; from the vast orb
Of Jupiter, whose huge gigantic bulk

Dances in ether like the lightest leaf;
To the dim verge, the suburbs of the system,
Where cheerless Saturn[3] 'midst his watery moons
80 Girt with a lucid zone,° in gloomy pomp,   *belt*
Sits like an exiled monarch: fearless thence
I launch into the trackless deeps of space,
Where, burning round, ten thousand suns appear,
Of elder beam, which ask no leave to shine
85 Of our terrestrial star, nor borrow light
From the proud regent of our scanty day;
Sons of the morning, first-born of creation,
And only less than Him who marks their track,
And guides their fiery wheels. Here must I stop,
90 Or is there aught beyond? What hand unseen
Impels me onward through the glowing orbs
Of habitable nature, far remote,
To the dread confines of eternal night,
To solitudes of vast unpeopled space,
95 The deserts of creation, wide and wild;
Where embryo systems and unkindled suns
Sleep in the womb of chaos? fancy droops,
And thought astonished stops her bold career.
But O thou mighty mind! whose powerful word
100 Said, thus let all things be, and thus they were,[4]
Where shall I seek thy presence? how unblamed
Invoke thy dread perfection?
Have the broad eyelids of the morn beheld thee?
Or does the beamy shoulder of Orion
105 Support thy throne? O look with pity down
On erring, guilty man! not in thy names
Of terror clad; not with those thunders armed
That conscious Sinai felt, when fear appalled
The scattered tribes;[5]—thou hast a gentler voice,
110 That whispers comfort to the swelling heart,
Abashed, yet longing to behold her Maker.

But now my soul, unused to stretch her powers
In flight so daring, drops her weary wing,
And seeks again the known accustomed spot,
115 Drest up with sun, and shade, and lawns, and streams,
A mansion fair, and spacious for its guest,
And full replete with wonders. Let me here,
Content and grateful, wait the appointed time,
And ripen for the skies: the hour will come
120 When all these splendours bursting on my sight
Shall stand unveiled, and to my ravished sense
Unlock the glories of the world unknown.

1773

---

3. Saturn marked the outmost bounds of the solar system until the discovery of Uranus in 1781.
4. An echo of Genesis 1.3.
5. When God came down to deliver the Ten Commandments "there were thunders and lightnings . . . so that all the people . . . trembled" (Exodus 19.16).

Epistle to William Wilberforce, Esq., on the Rejection of the Bill for Abolishing the Slave Trade[1]

Cease, Wilberforce, to urge thy generous aim!
Thy Country knows the sin, and stands the shame!
The Preacher, Poet, Senator in vain
Has rattled in her sight the Negro's chain;
5 With his deep groans assail'd her startled ear,
And rent the veil that hid his constant tear;
Forc'd her averted eyes his stripes to scan,
Beneath the bloody scourge laid bare the man,
Claim'd Pity's tear, urg'd Conscience' strong control,
10 And flash'd conviction on her shrinking soul.
The Muse too, soon awak'd, with ready tongue
At Mercy's shrine applausive° paeans rung;   *approving*
And Freedom's eager sons, in vain foretold
A new Astrean reign,° an age of gold: *reign of justice*
15 She knows and she persists—Still Afric bleeds,
Uncheck'd, the human traffic still proceeds;
She stamps her infamy to future time,
And on her harden'd forehead seals the crime.
In vain, to thy white standard gathering round,
20 Wit, Worth, and Parts and Eloquence are found:
In vain, to push to birth thy great design,
Contending chiefs, and hostile virtues join;
All, from conflicting ranks, of power possest
To rouse, to melt, or to inform the breast.
25 Where seasoned tools of Avarice prevail,
A Nation's eloquence, combined, must fail:
Each flimsy sophistry by turns they try;
The plausive° argument, the daring lie,   *specious*
The artful gloss, that moral sense confounds,
30 Th' acknowledged thirst of gain that honour wounds:
Bane of ingenuous minds, th' unfeeling sneer,
Which, sudden, turns to stone the falling tear:
They search assiduous, with inverted skill,
For forms of wrong, and precedents of ill;
35 With impious mockery wrest the sacred page,
And glean up crimes from each remoter age:
Wrung Nature's tortures, shuddering, while you tell,
From scoffing fiends bursts forth the laugh of hell;
In Britain's senate, Misery's pangs give birth
40 To jests unseemly, and to horrid mirth—
Forbear!—thy virtues but provoke our doom,
And swell th' account of vengeance yet to come;
For, not unmark'd in Heaven's impartial plan,
Shall man, proud worm, contemn his fellow-man?

---

1. On April 18, 1791, the politician and humanitarian Wilberforce (1759–1833) presented a motion in the House of Commons to abolish the slave trade. The motion was rejected a day later by a vote of 163 to 88. Sixteen years passed before the trade was outlawed in the British West Indies (1807), and another twenty-six before slavery itself was abolished (1833).

45　And injur'd Afric, by herself redrest,
　　Darts her own serpents at her Tyrant's breast.
　　Each vice, to minds deprav'd by bondage known,
　　With sure contagion fastens on his own;
　　In sickly languors melts his nerveless frame,
50　And blows to rage impetuous Passion's flame:
　　Fermenting swift, the fiery venom gains
　　The milky innocence of infant veins;
　　There swells the stubborn will, damps learning's fire,
　　The whirlwind wakes of uncontrol'd desire,
55　Sears the young heart to images of woe,
　　And blasts the buds of Virtue as they blow.°　　　　　　　*bloom*
　　　　Lo! where reclin'd, pale Beauty courts the breeze,
　　Diffus'd on sofas of voluptuous ease;
　　With anxious awe, her menial train around,
60　Catch her faint whispers of half-utter'd sound;
　　See her, in monstrous fellowship, unite
　　At once the Scythian, and the Sybarite;[2]
　　Blending repugnant vices, misallied,
　　Which *frugal* nature purpos'd to divide;
65　See her, with indolence to fierceness join'd,
　　Of body delicate, infirm of mind,
　　With languid tones imperious mandates urge;
　　With arm recumbent wield the household scourge;
　　And with unruffled mien, and placid sounds,
70　Contriving torture, and inflicting wounds.
　　　　Nor, in their palmy walks and spicy groves,
　　The form benign of rural Pleasure roves;
　　No milk-maid's song, or hum of village talk,
　　Sooths the lone Poet in his evening walk:
75　No willing arm the flail unwearied plies,
　　Where the mix'd sounds of cheerful labour rise;
　　No blooming maids and frolic swains are seen
　　To pay gay homage to their harvest queen:
　　No heart-expanding scenes their eyes must prove
80　Of thriving industry, and faithful love:
　　But shrieks and yells disturb the balmy air,
　　Dumb sullen looks of woe announce despair,
　　And angry eyes through dusky features glare.
　　Far from the sounding lash the Muses fly,
85　And sensual riot drowns each finer joy.
　　　　Nor less from the gay East, on essenc'd wings,
　　Breathing unnam'd perfumes, Contagion springs;
　　The soft luxurious plague alike pervades
　　The marble palaces, and rural shades;
90　Hence, throng'd Augusta° builds her rosy bowers,　　　　*London*
　　And decks in summer wreaths her smoky towers;
　　And hence, in summer bow'rs, Art's costly hand
　　Pours courtly splendours o'er the dazzled land:
　　The manners melt—One undistinguish'd blaze
95　O'erwhelms the sober pomp of elder days;

2. I.e., the contraries of pastoral wildness and effeminate voluptuousness.

Corruption follows with gigantic stride,
And scarce vouchsafes his shameless front to hide:
The spreading leprosy taints ev'ry part,
Infects each limb, and sickens at the heart.
100 Simplicity! most dear of rural maids,
Weeping resigns her violated shades:
Stern Independance from his glebe° retires,　　　　　*cultivated land*
And anxious Freedom eyes her drooping fires;
By foreign wealth are British morals chang'd,
105 And Afric's sons, and India's, smile aveng'd.
　　For you, whose temper'd ardour long has borne
Untir'd the labour, and unmov'd the scorn;
In Virtue's fasti° be inscrib'd your fame,　　　　　*records*
And utter'd yours with Howard's honour'd name,[3]
110 Friends of the friendless—Hail, ye generous band!
Whose efforts yet arrest Heav'n's lifted hand,
Around whose steady brows, in union bright,
The civic wreath, and Christian's palm unite:
Your merit stands, no greater and no less,
115 Without, or with the varnish of success;
But seek no more to break a Nation's fall,
For ye have sav'd yourselves—and that is all.
Succeeding times your struggles, and their fate,
With mingled shame and triumph shall relate,
120 While faithful History, in her various page,
Marking the features of this motley age,
To shed a glory, and to fix a stain,
Tells how you strove, and that you strove in vain.

1791　　　　　　　　　　　　　　　　　　　　　　　　　1791

The Rights of Woman[1]

Yes, injured Woman! rise, assert thy right!
Woman! too long degraded, scorned, opprest;
O born to rule in partial° Law's despite,　　　　　*biased*
Resume thy native empire o'er the breast!

5　Go forth arrayed in panoply° divine;　　　　　*suit of armor*
That angel pureness which admits no stain;
Go, bid proud Man his boasted rule resign,
And kiss the golden sceptre of thy reign.

Go, gird thyself with grace; collect thy store
10　Of bright artillery glancing from afar;
Soft melting tones thy thundering cannon's roar,
Blushes and fears thy magazine° of war.　　　　　*storehouse of arms*

3. John Howard (1726–1790), philanthropist
and prison and public health reformer.
1. A response—seemingly favorable until the last
two stanzas—to Mary Wollstonecraft's *A Vindication of the Rights of Woman* (1792). In chapter 4
of *Vindication*, Wollstonecraft had singled out
Barbauld's poem "To a Lady with Some Painted
Flowers" as evidence that even women of sense
were capable of adopting the masculine-centered
gender code that identified the feminine with the
ornamental and the frivolous.

Thy rights are empire: urge no meaner claim,—
Felt, not defined, and if debated, lost;
15 Like sacred mysteries, which withheld from fame,
Shunning discussion, are revered the most.

Try all that wit and art suggest to bend
Of thy imperial foe the stubborn knee;
Make treacherous Man thy subject, not thy friend;
20 Thou mayst command, but never canst be free.

Awe the licentious, and restrain the rude;
Soften the sullen, clear the cloudy brow:
Be, more than princes' gifts, thy favours sued;—
She hazards all, who will the least allow.

25 But hope not, courted idol of mankind,
On this proud eminence secure to stay;
Subduing and subdued, thou soon shalt find
Thy coldness soften, and thy pride give way.

Then, then, abandon each ambitious thought,
30 Conquest or rule thy heart shall feebly move,
In Nature's school, by her soft maxims taught,
That separate rights are lost in mutual love.

ca. 1792–95   1825

To a Little Invisible Being
Who Is Expected Soon to Become Visible

Germ of new life, whose powers expanding slow
For many a moon their full perfection wait,—
Haste, precious pledge of happy love, to go
Auspicious borne through life's mysterious gate.

5 What powers lie folded in thy curious frame,—
Senses from objects locked, and mind from thought!
How little canst thou guess thy lofty claim
To grasp at all the worlds the Almighty wrought!

And see, the genial season's warmth to share,
10 Fresh younglings° shoot, and opening roses glow!   *young plants*
Swarms of new life exulting fill the air,—
Haste, infant bud of being, haste to blow!°   *bloom*

For thee the nurse prepares her lulling songs,
The eager matrons count the lingering day;
15 But far the most thy anxious parent longs
On thy soft cheek a mother's kiss to lay.

She only asks to lay her burden down,
That her glad arms that burden may resume;

And nature's sharpest pangs her wishes crown,
20 That free thee living from thy living tomb.

She longs to fold to her maternal breast
Part of herself, yet to herself unknown;
To see and to salute the stranger guest,
Fed with her life through many a tedious moon.

25 Come, reap thy rich inheritance of love!
Bask in the fondness of a Mother's eye!
Nor wit nor eloquence her heart shall move
Like the first accents of thy feeble cry.

Haste, little captive, burst thy prison doors!
30 Launch on the living world, and spring to light!
Nature for thee displays her various stores,
Opens her thousand inlets of delight.

If charmed verse or muttered prayers had power,
With favouring spells to speed thee on thy way,
35 Anxious I'd bid my beads° each passing hour,   *offer a prayer*
Till thy wished smile thy mother's pangs o'erpay.°   *more than compensate*

ca. 1795?   1825

Inscription for an Ice-House[1]

Stranger, approach! within this iron door
Thrice locked and bolted, this rude arch beneath
That vaults with ponderous stone the cell; confined
By man, the great magician, who controuls
5 Fire, earth and air, and genii of the storm,
And bends the most remote and opposite things
To do him service and perform his will,—
A giant sits; stern Winter; here he piles,
While summer glows around, and southern gales
10 Dissolve the fainting world, his treasured snows
Within the rugged cave.—Stranger, approach!
He will not cramp thy limbs with sudden age,
Nor wither with his touch the coyest flower
That decks thy scented hair. Indignant hero,
15 Like fettered Sampson when his might was spent
In puny feats to glad the festive halls
Of Gaza's wealthy sons;[2] or he who sat

1. Predating the modern refrigerator by centuries, buildings called icehouses were fashionable additions to the grounds of 18th-century manor houses. The ice they stored, usually obtained in winter from nearby ponds or rivers, would be used during the summer to preserve food, chill drinks, or make ice cream. Barbauld's inscription was composed for the icehouse built by a family friend, the reform-minded member of parliament William Smith.
2. In Judges 16 the Israelite hero Sampson is captured by the Philistines following his betrayal by his wife, Delilah, who has cut his hair and robbed him of his strength. As Sampson's hair begins to grow back, he regains his powers, and his captors foolhardily arrange for him to entertain them in their temple with his feats of strength.

Midst laughing girls submiss, and patient twirled
The slender spindle in his sinewy grasp;[3]
20 The rugged power, fair Pleasure's minister,
Exerts his art to deck the genial board;°   *dining table*
Congeals the melting peach, the nectarine smooth,
Burnished and glowing from the sunny wall;
Darts sudden frost into the crimson veins
25 Of the moist berry; moulds the sugared hail;[4]
Cools with his icy breath our flowing cups;
Or gives to the fresh dairy's nectared bowls
A quicker zest. Sullen he plies his task,
And on his shaking fingers counts the weeks
30 Of lingering Summer, mindful of his hour
To rush in whirlwinds forth, and rule the year.

1795   1825

Washing-Day

> . . . *and their voice,*
> *Turning again towards childish treble, pipes*
> *And whistles in its sound.*[1]

The Muses are turned gossips; they have lost
The buskined° step, and clear high-sounding phrase,   *tragic, elevated*
Language of gods. Come then, domestic Muse,
In slipshod measure loosely prattling on
5   Of farm or orchard, pleasant curds and cream,
Or drowning flies, or shoe lost in the mire
By little whimpering boy, with rueful face;
Come, Muse; and sing the dreaded Washing-Day.
Ye who beneath the yoke of wedlock bend,
10 With bowed soul, full well ye ken° the day   *know*
Which week, smooth sliding after week, brings on
Too soon;—for to that day nor peace belongs
Nor comfort;—ere the first gray streak of dawn,
The red-armed washers come and chase repose.
15 Nor pleasant smile, nor quaint device of mirth,
E'er visited that day: the very cat,
From the wet kitchen scared, and reeking hearth,
Visits the parlour,—an unwonted° guest.   *unaccustomed*
The silent breakfast-meal is soon dispatched;
20 Uninterrupted, save by anxious looks
Cast at the lowering sky, if sky should lower.
From that last evil, O preserve us, heavens!

---

3. Barbauld refers to the episode in the adventures of Hercules, in which the hero, in humiliating servitude under the queen of Lydia, puts down his weapons and takes to assisting Omphale and her waiting women with their spinning.
4. An echo of James Thomson's description in *The Seasons* (1743) of how the "grim tyrant," Winter, "arms his winds with all-subduing frost / Moulds his fierce hail, and treasures up his snows, / With which he now oppresses half the globe" (lines 898–901).
1. Loosely quoted from Shakespeare's *As You Like It* 2.7.160–62.

For should the skies pour down, adieu to all
Remains of quiet: then expect to hear
25 Of sad disasters,—dirt and gravel stains
Hard to efface, and loaded lines at once
Snapped short,—and linen-horse° by dog thrown down,   *drying rack*
And all the petty miseries of life.
Saints have been calm while stretched upon the rack,
30 And Guatimozin[2] smiled on burning coals;
But never yet did housewife notable
Greet with a smile a rainy washing-day.
—But grant the welkin° fair, require not thou   *sky*
Who call'st thyself perchance the master there,
35 Or study swept or nicely dusted coat,
Or usual 'tendance;—ask not, indiscreet,
Thy stockings mended, though the yawning rents
Gape wide as Erebus;° nor hope to find   *the underworld*
Some snug recess impervious: shouldst thou try
40 The 'customed garden walks, thine eye shall rue
The budding fragrance of thy tender shrubs,
Myrtle or rose, all crushed beneath the weight
Of coarse checked apron,—with impatient hand
Twitched off when showers impend: or crossing lines
45 Shall mar thy musings, as the wet cold sheet
Flaps in thy face abrupt. Woe to the friend
Whose evil stars have urged him forth to claim
On such a day the hospitable rites!
Looks, blank at best, and stinted courtesy,
50 Shall he receive. Vainly he feeds his hopes
With dinner of roast chicken, savoury pie,
Or tart or pudding:—pudding he nor tart
That day shall eat; nor, though the husband try,
Mending what can't be helped, to kindle mirth
55 From cheer deficient, shall his consort's brow
Clear up propitious:—the unlucky guest
In silence dines, and early slinks away.
I well remember, when a child, the awe
This day struck into me; for then the maids,
60 I scarce knew why, looked cross, and drove me from them;
Nor soft caress could I obtain, nor hope
Usual indulgencies; jelly or creams,
Relic of costly suppers, and set by
For me, their petted one; or buttered toast,
65 When butter was forbid; or thrilling tale
Of ghost or witch, or murder—so I went
And sheltered me beside the parlour fire:
There my dear grandmother, eldest of forms,
Tended the little ones, and watched from harm,
70 Anxiously fond, though oft her spectacles
With elfin cunning hid, and oft the pins
Drawn from her ravelled stocking, might have soured

2. The last Aztec emperor (Cuanhtémoc, d. 1525), who was tortured and executed by the Spanish conquistadors.

One less indulgent.—
At intervals my mother's voice was heard,
75 Urging dispatch: briskly the work went on,
All hands employed to wash, to rinse, to wring,
To fold, and starch, and clap,° and iron, and plait.   *flatten*
Then would I sit me down, and ponder much
Why washings were. Sometimes through hollow bowl
80 Of pipe amused we blew, and sent aloft
The floating bubbles; little dreaming then
To see, Montgolfier,[3] thy silken ball
Ride buoyant through the clouds—so near approach
The sports of children and the toils of men.
85 Earth, air, and sky, and ocean, hath its bubbles,[4]
And verse is one of them—this most of all.

1797

The Caterpillar

No, helpless thing, I cannot harm thee now;
Depart in peace, thy little life is safe,
For I have scanned thy form with curious eye,
Noted the silver line that streaks thy back,
5 The azure and the orange that divide
Thy velvet sides; thee, houseless wanderer,
My garment has enfolded, and my arm
Felt the light pressure of thy hairy feet;
Thou hast curled round my finger; from its tip,
10 Precipitous descent! with stretched out neck,
Bending thy head in airy vacancy,
This way and that, inquiring, thou hast seemed
To ask protection; now, I cannot kill thee.
Yet I have sworn perdition to thy race,
15 And recent from the slaughter am I come
Of tribes and embryo nations: I have sought
With sharpened eye and persecuting zeal,
Where, folded in their silken webs they lay
Thriving and happy; swept them from the tree
20 And crushed whole families beneath my foot;
Or, sudden, poured on their devoted° heads   *doomed*
The vials of destruction.°—This I've done,   *pesticide*
Nor felt the touch of pity: but when thou,—
A single wretch, escaped the general doom,
25 Making me feel and clearly recognise
Thine individual existence, life,
And fellowship of sense with all that breathes,—
Present'st thyself before me, I relent,
And cannot hurt thy weakness.—So the storm

---

3. Brothers Joseph-Michel and Jacques-Étienne Montgolfier successfully launched the first hot-air balloon, at Annonay, France, in 1783.

4. Cf. Shakespeare's *Macbeth* 1.3.77: "The earth hath bubbles, as the water has."

30 Of horrid war, o'erwhelming cities, fields,
And peaceful villages, rolls dreadful on:
The victor shouts triumphant; he enjoys
The roar of cannon and the clang of arms,
And urges, by no soft relentings stopped,
35 The work of death and carnage. Yet should one,
A single sufferer from the field escaped,
Panting and pale, and bleeding at his feet,
Lift his imploring eyes,—the hero weeps;
He is grown human, and capricious Pity,
40 Which would not stir for thousands, melts for one
With sympathy spontaneous:—'Tis not Virtue,
Yet 'tis the weakness of a virtuous mind.

ca. 1816?   1825

CHARLOTTE SMITH
1749–1806

The melancholy of Charlotte Smith's poems was no mere literary posture. After her father married for the second time, she herself was married off, at the age of fifteen, and bore a dozen children (three of whom died in infancy or childhood), before permanently separating from her husband, Benjamin Smith, because of his abusive temper, infidelities, and financial irresponsibility. She began writing to make money when her husband was imprisoned for debt in 1783. Her first book, *Elegiac Sonnets, and Other Essays by Charlotte Smith of Bignor Park, Sussex,* came out in 1784 and went through nine expanding editions in the following sixteen years.

Beginning with the 1788 publication of *Emmeline,* Smith also enjoyed considerable success as a novelist, rapidly producing nine more novels within the decade, including *Desmond* (1792), *The Old Manor House* (1793), *The Banished Man* (1794), and *The Young Philosopher* (1798). She also wrote books for children and, once, for the stage. The liberal political views espoused in her novels made the books key contributions to the Revolution Controversy in Britain. This was also the case with her eight-hundred-line blank verse poem *The Emigrants* (1793), which both evokes the suffering endured by political refugees from France and links their plight to that of the poet herself, who as a woman has discovered the emptiness of her native land's "boast / Of equal law." Such views earned Smith a place of dishonor, alongside Mary Wollstonecraft and Anna Letitia Barbauld, in Richard Polwhele's conservative satire *The Unsex'd Females* (1797), which scolds her for having suffered "her mind to be infected with the Gallic mania."

The sonnet as a form, after its great flourishing in the Renaissance in the hands of Sidney, Spenser, Shakespeare, Donne, and Milton, dropped out of fashion in the eighteenth century. It was, Samuel Johnson declared in his *Dictionary* (1755), "not very suitable to the English language." Its revival toward the end of that century—by Coleridge in the 1790s; Wordsworth (who wrote some five hundred sonnets beginning in 1802); and in the next generation, Shelley and Keats—was largely the result of Smith's influential refashioning of the sonnet as a medium of mournful feeling. In the introduction to his privately printed "sheet of sonnets" in

1796, Coleridge noted that "Charlotte Smith and [William Lisle] Bowles are they who first made the Sonnet popular among the present English," but in fact, in his *Fourteen Sonnets* of 1789 Bowles was simply following in Smith's footsteps.

In that commentary on the sonnet Coleridge made Smith his principal example when he remarked that "those Sonnets appear to me the most exquisite, in which moral Sentiments, Affections, or Feelings, are deduced from, and associated with, the scenery of Nature." Subsequently, of course, the connecting of feelings and nature became recognized as a central theme and strategy in Romantic literature, especially in the lyric poetry we associate with Coleridge and Wordsworth. But Smith's engagement with nature differs in illuminating ways from theirs. This is in part because of its quasi-scientific insistence on the faithful rendering of detail (one of Smith's sonnets is addressed to the "goddess of botany") and because of the other-

Frontispiece to the 1788 edition of *Elegiac Sonnets*, showing the "Queen of the Silver Bowl."

ness and multitudinousness in the natural world which that detail discloses. This carefully realized close-up view of nature is central to her masterpiece, the posthumously published *Beachy Head* (1807), where it gets combined, to startling effect, with a sense of the vast—immense vistas of geological time, for instance, or the distances covered by ships voyaging between Britain and her Asian colonies. Named for the headland forming the southernmost point in Sussex, the likely beachhead for the French invasion that early-nineteenth-century English people anticipated fearfully, *Beachy Head* brings together personal memories, natural history, and national history in a mix that is without parallel in the period.

From Elegiac Sonnets

Written at the Close of Spring

The garlands fade that Spring so lately wove,
    Each simple flower, which she had nursed in dew,
Anemonies,[1] that spangled every grove,
    The primrose wan, and hare-bell mildly blue.
5 No more shall violets linger in the dell,
    Or purple orchis variegate the plain,

---

1. Anemonies. *Anemony Nemeroso.* The wood Anemone [Smith's note].

Till Spring again shall call forth every bell,
   And dress with humid hands her wreaths again.—
Ah! poor humanity! so frail, so fair,
10   Are the fond visions of thy early day,
Till tyrant passion, and corrosive care,
   Bid all thy fairy colors fade away!
Another May new buds and flowers shall bring;
Ah! why has happiness—no second Spring?

1784

To Sleep

Come, balmy Sleep! tired nature's soft resort!
   On these sad temples all thy poppies shed;
And bid gay dreams, from Morpheus'[1] airy court,
   Float in light vision round my aching head!
5   Secure of all thy blessings, partial[2] Power!
   On his hard bed the peasant throws him down;
And the poor sea boy, in the rudest hour,
   Enjoys thee more than he who wears a crown.[3]
Clasp'd in her faithful shepherd's guardian arms,
10   Well may the village girl sweet slumbers prove
And they, O gentle Sleep! still taste thy charms,
   Who wake to labor, liberty, and love.
But still thy opiate aid dost thou deny
To calm the anxious breast; to close the streaming eye.

1784

To Night

I love thee, mournful, sober-suited Night!
   When the faint moon, yet lingering in her wane,
And veil'd in clouds, with pale uncertain light
   Hangs o'er the waters of the restless main.
5   In deep depression sunk, the enfeebled mind
   Will to the deaf cold elements complain,
   And tell the embosom'd grief, however vain,
To sullen surges and the viewless wind.
Though no repose on thy dark breast I find,
10   I still enjoy thee—cheerless as thou art;
   For in thy quiet gloom the exhausted heart
Is calm, though wretched; hopeless, yet resign'd.

---

1. Greek god of dreams.
2. Friendly, but also biased.
3. Wilt thou upon the high and giddy mast / seal up the ship boy's eyes, and rock his brains / In

cradle of the rude impetuous surge? Shakespeare's *Henry IV* [Smith's note]. It was "imperious surge" in the original.

While to the winds and waves its sorrows given,
May reach—though lost on earth—the ear of Heaven!

1788

Written in the Church-Yard at Middleton in Sussex[1]

Press'd by the Moon, mute arbitress of tides,
  While the loud equinox its power combines,
  The sea no more its swelling surge confines,
But o'er the shrinking land sublimely rides.
5 The wild blast, rising from the Western cave,
  Drives the huge billows from their heaving bed;
  Tears from their grassy tombs the village dead,
And breaks the silent sabbath of the grave!
With shells and sea-weed mingled, on the shore
10 Lo! their bones whiten in the frequent wave;
  But vain to them the winds and waters rave;
They hear the warring elements no more:
While I am doom'd—by life's long storm opprest,
To gaze with envy on their gloomy rest.

1789

To Fancy

Thee, Queen of Shadows!—shall I still invoke,
  Still love the scenes thy sportive pencil drew,
When on mine eyes the early radiance broke
  Which shew'd the beauteous, rather than the true!
5 Alas! long since, those glowing tints are dead,
  And now 'tis thine in darkest hues to dress[1]
The spot where pale Experience hangs her head
  O'er the sad grave of murder'd Happiness!
Thro' thy false medium then, no longer view'd,
10 May fancy'd pain and fancy'd pleasure fly,
  And I, as from me all thy dreams depart,
Be to my wayward destiny subdu'd;
  Nor seek perfection with a poet's eye,
  Nor suffer anguish with a poet's heart!

1789

1. Middleton is a village on the margin of the sea, in Sussex, containing only two or three houses. There were formerly several acres of ground between its small church and the sea, which now, by its continual encroachments, approaches within a few feet of this half ruined and humble edifice. The wall, which once surrounded the churchyard, is entirely swept away, many of the graves broken up, and the remains of bodies interred washed into the sea: whence human bones are found among the sand and shingles on the shore [Smith's note].
1. Make ready, prepare.

On Being Cautioned against Walking on an
Headland Overlooking the Sea, Because
It Was Frequented by a Lunatic

Is there a solitary wretch who hies
    To the tall cliff, with starting pace or slow,
And, measuring, views with wild and hollow eyes
    Its distance from the waves that chide below;
5 Who, as the sea-born gale with frequent sighs
    Chills his cold bed upon the mountain turf,
With hoarse, half-utter'd lamentation, lies
    Murmuring responses to the dashing surf?
In moody sadness, on the giddy brink,
10   I see him more with envy than with fear;
He has no *nice felicities* that shrink[1]
    From giant horrors; wildly wandering here,
He seems (uncursed with reason) not to know
The depth or the duration of his woe.

1797

To the Insect of the Gossamer[1]

Small, viewless Aeronaut,[2] that by the line
    Of Gossamer suspended, in mid air
    Float'st on a sun beam—Living Atom, where
Ends thy breeze-guided voyage;—with what design
5   In Aether[3] dost thou launch thy form minute,
Mocking the eye?—Alas! before the veil
Of denser clouds shall hide thee, the pursuit
Of the keen Swift[4] may end thy fairy sail!—
Thus on the golden thread that Fancy weaves
10   Buoyant, as Hope's illusive° flattery breathes,   *illusory*
The young and visionary Poet leaves
Life's dull realities, while sevenfold wreaths
Of rainbow-light around his head revolve.
Ah! soon at Sorrow's touch the radiant dreams dissolve!

1797

1. "'Tis delicate felicity that shrinks / when rocking winds are loud." Walpole [Smith's note]. Smith is citing Horace Walpole's 1768 tragedy *The Mysterious Mother* I.70.

1. A long endnote accompanied this sonnet in *Elegiac Sonnets and Other Poems*: "The almost imperceptible threads floating in the air, towards the end of Summer or Autumn, in a still evening, sometimes are so numerous as to be felt on the face and hands. It is on these that a minute species of spider convey themselves from place to place; sometimes rising with the wind to a great height in the air." Smith continues by quoting descriptions of this phenomenon from the *Encyclopedia Britannica* and the scientist-poet Erasmus Darwin's *The Economy of Vegetation* (1791). She then turns

to Shakespeare's *Romeo and Juliet*, where Mercutio imagines the fairy queen Mab guiding the tiny beings who draw her carriage with reins made from the "smallest spider's web" (1.4.61), and where Friar Laurence reacts to Juliet's arrival at his cell by observing that "A lover may bestride the Gossamer / That idles in the wanton Summer air, / And yet not fall" (2.6.18–20). (Smith's note mistakenly assigns this speech to Juliet herself.)

2. *Aeronaut* can designate both a human balloonist, who floats through the air, and the kind of spider that does the same.

3. Air. The term was still sometimes used to designate the regions of space above the clouds or the refined, pure atmosphere breathed in heaven.

4. An insect-eating bird.

The Sea View[1]

The upland shepherd, as reclined he lies
  On the soft turf that clothes the mountain brow,
Marks the bright sea-line mingling with the skies;
  Or from his course celestial, sinking slow,
5   The summer-sun in purple radiance low,
Blaze on the western waters; the wide scene
  Magnificent, and tranquil, seems to spread
Even o'er the rustic's breast a joy serene,
  When, like dark plague-spots by the Demons shed,
10 Charged deep with death, upon the waves, far seen,
  Move the war-freighted ships; and fierce and red,
  Flash their destructive fire.—The mangled dead
And dying victims then pollute the flood.
Ah! thus man spoils Heaven's glorious works with blood!

1797

The Swallow[1]

The gorse[2] is yellow on the heath,
  The banks with speed well[3] flowers are gay,
The oaks are budding; and beneath,
The hawthorn soon will bear the wreath,
5   The silver wreath of May.

The welcome guest of settled Spring,
  The Swallow too is come at last;
Just at sun-set, when thrushes sing,
I saw her dash with rapid wing,
10   And hail'd her as she pass'd.

Come, summer visitant, attach
  To my reed° roof your nest of clay,   *thatched*
And let my ear your music catch
Low twittering underneath the thatch
15   At the gray dawn of day.

As fables tell, an Indian Sage,[4]
  The Hindostani woods among,
Could in his desert hermitage,

1. Suggested by the recollection of having seen, some years since, on a beautiful evening of Summer, an engagement between two armed ships, from the high down called the Beacon Hill, near Brighthelmstone [Smith's note]. Smith is referring to a location near Brighton.
1. This poem appeared posthumously in 1807 both in the last of Smith's books for children, the ornithological handbook *The History of Birds*, and in her *Beachy Head, Fables, and Other*
Poems, the source of the text used here.
2. The Gorse-Furze.—Ulex Europæus. Called so in many counties of England [Smith's note].
3. Veronica chamœdrys.—This elegant flower, though not celebrated like the Primrose, Cowslip, and Daisy, is in all its varieties one of the most beautiful of our indigenous plants [Smith's note].
4. There are two or three fables that relate the knowledge acquired by some Indian recluse, of the language of birds [Smith's note].

As if 'twere mark'd in written page,
20   Translate the wild bird's song,

I wish I did his power possess,
    That I might learn, fleet bird, from thee,
What our vain systems only guess,
And know from what wide wilderness
25   You came across the sea.

I would a little while restrain
    Your rapid wing, that I might hear
Whether on clouds that bring the rain,
You sail'd above the western main,
30   The wind your charioteer.

In Afric, does the sultry gale
    Thro' spicy bower, and palmy grove,
Bear the repeated Cuckoo's tale?
Dwells *there* a time, the wandering Rail
35   Or the itinerant Dove?[5]

Were you in Asia? O relate,
    If there your fabled sister's woes
She seem'd in sorrow to narrate;
Or sings she but to celebrate
40   Her nuptials with the rose?[6]

I would enquire how journeying long,
    The vast and pathless ocean o'er,
You ply again those pinions strong,
And come to build anew among[7]
45   The scenes you left before;

But if, as colder breezes blow,
    Prophetic of the waning year,
You hide, tho' none know when or how,
In the cliff's excavated brow,[8]
50   And linger torpid here;

---

5. The Cuckoo, the Rail, and many species of Doves, are all emigrants [Smith's note].

6. Alluding to the Ovidian fable of the Metamorphosis of Procne and Philomela into the Swallow and the Nightingale; and to the oriental story of the Loves of the Nightingale and the Rose; which is told with much elegant extravagance in the Botanic Garden [Smith's note]. In *The Loves of the Plants,* Part 1 of his *Botanic Garden* of 1789, Erasmus Darwin set out in verse supplemented by "philosophical notes" the influential method for determining botanical genera and species that Carolus Linnaeus pioneered earlier in the century. Smith's reference to Darwin's poem, which made Linnaeus's Latin writings accessible to a broad audience, may be to a long footnote to canto 1, line 320, or to canto 4, lines 309–20. She couples Darwin's book with the fable of rape and female revenge found in book 6 of the classical Roman poet Ovid's *Metamorphoses.*

7. Accurate observers have remarked, that an equal number of these birds return every year to build in the places they frequented before; and that each pair set immediately about repairing a particular nest [Smith's note]. Although swallows' return to their nests is a well-known sign of spring, 18th- and early-19th-century scientists were mystified by where the birds might be during their absence. The matter was debated vigorously by figures such as Gilbert White, author in 1789 of *The Natural History and Antiquities of Selborne,* which Smith mentions in her note to line 58. Some debaters opted for migration, and others, hibernation, the "torpid state" Smith envisions.

8. Many persons have supported the idea, that the Hirundines linger concealed among rocks and hollows in a torpid state, and that all do not emigrate [Smith's note].

Thus lost to life, what favouring dream
 Bids you to happier hours awake;
And tells, that dancing in the beam,
The light gnat hovers o'er the stream,
55 The May-fly on the lake?

Or if, by instinct taught to know
 Approaching dearth of insect food;
To isles and willowy aits° you go,[9]   *small islands*
And crouding on the pliant bough,
60 Sink in the dimpling flood:

How learn ye, while the cold waves boom
 Your deep and ouzy couch above,
The time when flowers of promise bloom,
And call you from your transient tomb,
65 To light, and life, and love?

Alas! how little can be known,
 Her sacred veil where Nature draws;
Let baffled Science humbly own,
Her mysteries understood alone,
70 By *Him* who gives her laws.

1807

Beachy Head[1]

On thy stupendous summit, rock sublime!
That o'er the channel rear'd, half way at sea
The mariner at early morning hails,[2]
I would recline; while Fancy should go forth,
5 And represent the strange and awful hour
Of vast concussion;[3] when the Omnipotent
Stretch'd forth his arm, and rent the solid hills,
Bidding the impetuous main flood rush between
The rifted shores, and from the continent
10 Eternally divided this green isle.
Imperial lord of the high southern coast!
From thy projecting head-land I would mark
Far in the east the shades of night disperse,

9. Another opinion is, that the Swallows, at the time they disappear, assemble about rivers and ponds, and a number of them settling on the pliant boughs of willow and osier, sink by their weight into the water; at the bottom of which they remain torpid till the ensuing spring. For the foundation of these various theories, see "White's History of Selbourne" [Smith's note].
1. This is the longest of several works left in manuscript when Smith died in October 1806 and published in the posthumous volume *Beachy Head, Fables, and Other Poems* the following year. It is not known to what degree Smith considered the poem finished.
2. In crossing the Channel from the coast of France, Beachy-Head is the first land made [Smith's note].
3. Alluding to an idea that this Island was once joined to the continent of Europe, and torn from it by some convulsion in Nature. I confess I never could trace the resemblance between the two countries. Yet the cliffs about Dieppe, resemble the chalk cliffs on the Southern coast. But Normandy has no likeness whatever to the part of England opposite to it [Smith's note].

Melting and thinned, as from the dark blue wave
15   Emerging, brilliant rays of arrowy light°   *dawn*
Dart from the horizon; when the glorious sun
Just lifts above it his resplendent orb.
Advances now, with feathery silver touched,
The rippling tide of flood; glisten the sands,
20   While, inmates of the chalky clefts that scar
Thy sides precipitous, with shrill harsh cry,
Their white wings glancing in the level beam,
The terns, and gulls, and tarrocks, seek their food,[4]
And thy rough hollows echo to the voice
25   Of the gray choughs,[5] and ever restless daws,
With clamour, not unlike the chiding hounds,
While the lone shepherd, and his baying dog,
Drive to thy turfy crest his bleating flock.

The high meridian° of the day is past,   *noon*
30   And Ocean now, reflecting the calm Heaven,
Is of cerulean hue; and murmurs low
The tide of ebb, upon the level sands.
The sloop, her angular canvas shifting still,
Catches the light and variable airs
35   That but a little crisp the summer sea,
Dimpling its tranquil surface.

                    Afar off,
And just emerging from the arch immense
Where seem to part the elements, a fleet
Of fishing vessels stretch their lesser sails;
40   While more remote, and like a dubious spot
Just hanging in the horizon, laden deep,
The ship of commerce richly freighted, makes
Her slower progress, on her distant voyage,
Bound to the orient climates, where the sun
45   Matures the spice within its odorous shell,
And, rivalling the gray worm's filmy toil,[6]
Bursts from its pod the vegetable down;[7]
Which in long turban'd wreaths, from torrid heat
Defends the brows of Asia's countless castes.
50   There the Earth hides within her glowing breast
The beamy adamant,[8] and the round pearl
Enchased° in rugged covering; which the slave,   *enclosed*
With perilous and breathless toil, tears off
From the rough sea-rock, deep beneath the waves.
55   These are the toys of Nature; and her sport
Of little estimate in Reason's eye:
And they who reason, with abhorrence see

---

4. Terns. *Sterna hirundo,* or Sea Swallow. Gulls. *Larus canus.* Tarrocks. *Larus tridactylus* [Smith's note].
5. Gray choughs. *Corvus Graculus,* Cornish Choughs, or, as these birds are called by the Sussex people, Saddle-backed Crows, build in great numbers on this coast [Smith's note].

6. I.e., to produce silk.
7. Cotton. *Gossypium herbaceum* [Smith's note].
8. Diamonds, the hardest and most valuable of precious stones. For the extraordinary exertions of the Indians in diving for the pearl oysters, see the account of the Pearl fisheries in Percival's *View of Ceylon* [Smith's note].

Man, for such gaudes and baubles, violate
The sacred freedom of his fellow man—
60 Erroneous estimate! As Heaven's pure air,
Fresh as it blows on this aërial height,
Or sound of seas upon the stony strand,
Or inland, the gay harmony of birds,
And winds that wander in the leafy woods;
65 Are to the unadulterate taste more worth
Than the elaborate harmony, brought out
From fretted stop° or modulated airs   *stringed instrument*
Of vocal science.—So the brightest gems,
Glancing resplendent on the regal crown,
70 Or trembling in the high born beauty's ear,
Are poor and paltry, to the lovely light
Of the fair star,° that as the day declines   *Venus*
Attendent on her queen, the crescent moon,
Bathes her bright tresses in the eastern wave.
75 For now the sun is verging to the sea,
And as he westward sinks, the floating clouds
Suspended, move upon the evening gale,
And gathering round his orb, as if to shade
The insufferable brightness, they resign
80 Their gauzy whiteness; and more warm'd, assume
All hues of purple. There, transparent gold
Mingles with ruby tints, and sapphire gleams,
And colours, such as Nature through her works
Shews only in the ethereal canopy.
85 Thither aspiring Fancy fondly soars,
Wandering sublime thro' visionary vales,
Where bright pavilions rise, and trophies, fann'd
By airs celestial; and adorn'd with wreaths
Of flowers that bloom amid elysian bowers.
90 Now bright, and brighter still the colours glow,
Till half the lustrous orb within the flood
Seems to retire: the flood reflecting still
Its splendor, and in mimic glory drest;
Till the last ray shot upward, fires the clouds
95 With blazing crimson; then in paler light,
Long lines of tenderer radiance, lingering yield
To partial darkness; and on the opposing side
The early moon distinctly rising, throws
Her pearly brilliance on the trembling tide.

100 The fishermen, who at set seasons pass
Many a league off at sea their toiling night,
Now hail their comrades, from their daily task
Returning; and make ready for their own,
With the night tide commencing:—The night tide
105 Bears a dark vessel on, whose hull and sails
Mark her a coaster[9] from the north. Her keel
Now ploughs the sand; and sidelong now she leans,

9. Ship that sails along the coast.

While with loud clamours her athletic crew
Unload her; and resounds the busy hum
110 Along the wave-worn rocks. Yet more remote
Where the rough cliff hangs beetling° o'er its base,   *projecting*
All breathes repose; the water's rippling sound
Scarce heard; but now and then the sea-snipe's[1] cry
Just tells that something living is abroad;
115 And sometimes crossing on the moonbright line,
Glimmers the skiff, faintly discern'd awhile,
Then lost in shadow.

Contemplation here,
High on her throne of rock, aloof may sit,
And bid recording Memory unfold
120 Her scroll voluminous—bid her retrace
The period, when from Neustria's hostile shore°   *Normandy*
The Norman launch'd his galleys, and the bay
O'er which that mass of ruin[2] frowns even now
In vain and sullen menace, then received
125 The new invaders; a proud martial race,
Of Scandinavia[3] the undaunted sons,

1. In crossing the channel this bird is heard at night, uttering a short cry, and flitting along near the surface of the waves. The sailors call it the Sea Snipe; but I can find no species of sea bird of which this is the vulgar name. A bird so called inhabits the Lake of Geneva [Smith's note].
2. Pevensey Castle [Smith's note].
3. The Scandinavians (modern Norway, Sweden, Denmark, Lapland, &c.) and other inhabitants of the north, began towards the end of the 8th century, to leave their inhospitable climate in search of the produce of more fortunate countries.
    The North-men made inroads on the coasts of France; and carrying back immense booty, excited their compatriots to engage in the same piratical voyages: and they were afterwards joined by numbers of necessitous and daring adventurers from the coasts of Provence and Sicily.
    In 844, these wandering innovators had a great number of vessels at sea; and again visiting the coasts of France, Spain, and England, the following year they penetrated even to Paris: and the unfortunate Charles the Bald, king of France, purchased at a high price, the retreat of the banditti he had no other means of repelling.
    These successful expeditions continued for some time; till Rollo, otherwise Raoul, assembled a number of followers, and after a descent on England, crossed the channel, and made himself master of Rouen, which he fortified. Charles the Simple, unable to contend with Rollo, offered to resign to him some of the northern provinces, and to give him his daughter in marriage. Neustria, since called Normandy, was granted to him, and afterwards Brittany. He added the more solid virtues of the legislator to the fierce valour of the conqueror—converted to Christianity, he established justice, and repressed the excesses of his Danish subjects, till then accustomed to live only by plunder. His name became the signal for pursuing those who violated the laws; as well as the cry of Haro, still so usual in Normandy. The Danes and Francs produced a race of men celebrated for their valour; and it was a small party of these that in 983, having been on a pilgrimage to Jerusalem, arrived on their return at Salerno, and found the town surrounded by Mahometans, whom the Salernians were bribing to leave their coast. The Normans represented to them the baseness and cowardice of such submission; and notwithstanding the inequality of their numbers, they boldly attacked the Saracen camp, and drove the infidels to their ships. The prince of Salerno, astonished at their successful audacity, would have loaded them with the marks of his gratitude; but refusing every reward, they returned to their own country, from whence, however, other bodies of Normans passed into Sicily (anciently called Trinacria); and many of them entered into the service of the emperor of the East, others of the Pope, and the duke of Naples was happy to engage a small party of them in defence of his newly founded dutchy. Soon afterwards three brothers of Coutance, the sons of Tancred de Hauteville, Guillaume Fier-a-bras, Drogon, and Humfroi, joining the Normans established at Aversa, became masters of the fertile island of Sicily; and Robert Guiscard joining them, the Normans became sovereigns both of Sicily and Naples (Parthenope). How William, the natural son of Robert, duke of Normandy, possessed himself of England, is too well known to be repeated here. William sailing from St. Valori, landed in the bay of Pevensey; and at the place now called Battle, met the English forces under Harold: an esquire (ecuyer) called Taillefer, mounted on an armed horse, led on the Normans, singing in a thundering tone the war song of Rollo. He threw himself among the English, and was killed on the first onset. In a marsh not far from Hastings, the skeletons of an armed man and horse were found a few years since, which are believed to have belonged to the Normans, as a party of their horse, deceived in the nature of the ground, perished in the morass [Smith's note].

Whom Dogon, Fier-a-bras, and Humfroi led
To conquest: while Trinacria to their power
Yielded her wheaten garland; and when thou,
130 Parthenope! within thy fertile bay
Receiv'd the victors—

           In the mailed ranks
Of Normans landing on the British coast
Rode Taillefer; and with astounding voice
Thunder'd the war song daring Roland sang
135 First in the fierce contention: vainly brave,
One not inglorious struggle England made—
But failing, saw the Saxon heptarchy[4]
Finish for ever.——Then the holy pile,[5]
Yet seen upon the field of conquest, rose,
140 Where to appease heaven's wrath for so much blood,
The conqueror bade unceasing prayers ascend,
And requiems for the slayers and the slain.
But let not modern Gallia° form from hence   _France_
Presumptuous hopes, that ever thou again,
145 Queen of the isles! shalt crouch to foreign arms.
The enervate sons of Italy may yield;
And the Iberian, all his trophies torn
And wrapp'd in Superstition's monkish weed,
May shelter his abasement, and put on
150 Degrading fetters. Never, never thou!
Imperial mistress of the obedient sea;
But thou, in thy integrity secure,
Shalt now undaunted meet a world in arms.

England! 'twas where this promontory rears
155 Its rugged brow above the channel wave,
Parting the hostile nations, that thy fame,
Thy naval fame was tarnish'd, at what time
Thou, leagued with the Batavian,° gavest to France[6]   _Dutch_
One day of triumph—triumph the more loud,
160 Because even then so rare. Oh! well redeem'd,
Since, by a series of illustrious men,
Such as no other country ever rear'd,
To vindicate her cause. It is a list

4. The seven kingdoms of Saxon England.
5. Battle Abbey was raised by the Conqueror, and endowed with an ample revenue, that masses might be said night and day for the souls of those who perished in battle [Smith's note].
6. In 1690, King William being then in Ireland, Tourville, the French admiral, arrived on the coast of England. His fleet consisted of seventy-eight large ships, and twenty-two fire-ships. Lord Torrington, the English admiral, lay at St. Helens, with only forty English and a few Dutch ships; and conscious of the disadvantage under which he should give battle, he ran up between the enemy's fleet and the coast, to protect it. The queen's council, dictated to by Russel, persuaded her to order Torrington to venture a battle. The orders Torrington appears to have obeyed reluctantly: his fleet now consisted of twenty-two Dutch and thirty-four English ships. Evertson, the Dutch admiral, was eager to obtain glory; Torrington, more cautious, reflected on the importance of the stake. The consequence was, that the Dutch rashly sailing on were surrounded, and Torrington, solicitous to recover this false step, placed himself with difficulty between the Dutch and French;—but three Dutch ships were burnt, two of their admirals killed, and almost all their ships disabled. The English and Dutch declining a second engagement, retired towards the mouth of the Thames. The French, from ignorance of the coast, and misunderstanding among each other, failed to take all the advantage they might have done of this victory [Smith's note].

Which, as Fame echoes it, blanches the cheek
165 Of bold Ambition; while the despot feels
The extorted sceptre tremble in his grasp.

From even the proudest roll° by glory fill'd,   *historical record*
How gladly the reflecting mind returns
To simple scenes of peace and industry,
170 Where, bosom'd in some valley of the hills
Stands the lone farm; its gate with tawny ricks°   *hay stacks*
Surrounded, and with granaries and sheds,
Roof'd with green mosses, and by elms and ash
Partially shaded; and not far remov'd
175 The hut of sea-flints built; the humble home
Of one, who sometimes watches on the heights,[7]
When hid in the cold mist of passing clouds,
The flock, with dripping fleeces, are dispers'd
O'er the wide down; then from some ridged point
180 That overlooks the sea, his eager eye
Watches the bark that for his signal waits
To land its merchandize:—Quitting for this
Clandestine traffic his more honest toil,
The crook abandoning, he braves himself
185 The heaviest snow-storm of December's night,
When with conflicting winds the ocean raves,
And on the tossing boat, unfearing mounts
To meet the partners of the perilous trade,
And share their hazard. Well it were for him,
190 If no such commerce of destruction known,
He were content with what the earth affords
To human labour; even where she seems
Reluctant most. More happy is the hind,°   *peasant*
Who, with his own hands rears on some black moor,
195 Or turbary,° his independent hut   *peat bog*
Cover'd with heather, whence the slow white smoke
Of smouldering peat arises——A few sheep,
His best possession, with his children share
The rugged shed when wintry tempests blow;
200 But, when with Spring's return the green blades rise
Amid the russet heath, the household live
Joint tenants of the waste° throughout the day,   *uncultivated land*
And often, from her nest, among the swamps,
Where the gemm'd sun-dew grows, or fring'd buck-bean,[8]
205 They scare the plover,[9] that with plaintive cries
Flutters, as° sorely wounded, down the wind.   *pretending to be*
Rude, and but just remov'd from savage life
Is the rough dweller among scenes like these,
(Scenes all unlike the poet's fabling dreams

---

7. The shepherds and labourers of this tract of country, a hardy and athletic race of men, are almost universally engaged in the contraband trade, carried on for the coarsest and most destructive spirits, with the opposite coast. When no other vessel will venture to sea, these men hazard their lives to elude the watchfulness of the Revenue officers, and to secure their cargoes [Smith's note].
8. Sun-dew. *Drosera rotundifolia.* Buck-bean. *Menyanthes trifoliatum* [Smith's note].
9. Plover. *Tringa vanellus* [Smith's note].

210 Describing Arcady[1])—But he is free;
The dread that follows on illegal acts
He never feels; and his industrious mate
Shares in his labour. Where the brook is traced
By crowding osiers,° and the black coot[2] hides   *willows*
215 Among the plashy reeds, her diving brood,
The matron wades; gathering the long green rush[3]
That well prepar'd hereafter lends its light
To her poor cottage, dark and cheerless else
Thro' the drear hours of Winter. Otherwhile
220 She leads her infant group where charlock° grows   *wild mustard*
"Unprofitably gay,"[4] or to the fields,
Where congregate the linnet and the finch,
That on the thistles, so profusely spread,
Feast in the desert; the poor family
225 Early resort, extirpating with care
These, and the gaudier mischief of the ground;
Then flames the high rais'd heap; seen afar off
Like hostile war-fires flashing to the sky.[5]
Another task is theirs: On fields that shew
230 As° angry Heaven had rain'd sterility,   *as if*
Stony and cold, and hostile to the plough,
Where clamouring loud, the evening curlew[6] runs
And drops her spotted eggs among the flints;
The mother and the children pile the stones
235 In rugged pyramids;—and all this toil
They patiently encounter; well content
On their flock bed[7] to slumber undisturb'd
Beneath the smoky roof they call their own.
Oh! little knows the sturdy hind, who stands
240 Gazing, with looks where envy and contempt
Are often strangely mingled, on the car°   *carriage*
Where prosperous Fortune sits; what secret care
Or sick satiety is often hid,
Beneath the splendid outside: *He* knows not
245 How frequently the child of Luxury
Enjoying nothing, flies from place to place
In chase of pleasure that eludes his grasp;
And that content is e'en less found by him,
Than by the labourer, whose pick-axe smooths
250 The road before his chariot; and who doffs
What *was* an hat; and as the train pass on,
Thinks how one day's expenditure, like this,
Would cheer him for long months, when to his toil
The frozen earth closes her marble breast.
255 Ah! who *is* happy? Happiness! a word

1. Arcadia, an imagined land of peace and simplicity.
2. Coot. *Fulica aterrima* [Smith's note].
3. A reedy plant burned for light.
4. "With blossom'd furze, unprofitably gay." Goldsmith [Smith's note]. Smith is citing Oliver Goldsmith's *The Deserted Village*, line 194.
5. The Beacons formerly lighted up on the hills to give notice of the approach of an enemy. These signals would still be used in case of alarm, if the Telegraph [the signaling apparatus] now substituted could not be distinguished on account of fog or darkness [Smith's note].
6. Curlew. *Charadrius oedienemus* [Smith's note].
7. A bed stuffed with tufts of wool.

That like false fire,° from marsh effluvia born,   *will-o'-the-wisp*
Misleads the wanderer, destin'd to contend
In the world's wilderness, with want or woe—
Yet *they* are happy, who have never ask'd
260 What good or evil means. The boy
That on the river's margin gaily plays,
Has heard that Death is there.—He knows not Death,
And therefore fears it not; and venturing in
He gains a bullrush, or a minnow—then,
265 At certain peril, for a worthless prize,
A crow's, or raven's nest, he climbs the boll°   *bole, trunk*
Of some tall pine; and of his prowess proud,
Is for a moment happy. Are *your* cares,
Ye who despise him, never worse applied?
270 The village girl is happy, who sets forth
To distant fair, gay in her Sunday suit,
With cherry colour'd knots, and flourish'd shawl,
And bonnet newly purchas'd. So is he
Her little brother, who his mimic drum
275 Beats, till he drowns her rural lovers' oaths
Of constant faith, and still increasing love;
Ah! yet a while, and half those oaths believ'd,
Her happiness is vanish'd; and the boy
While yet a stripling, finds the sound he lov'd
280 Has led him on, till he has given up
His freedom, and his happiness together.
I once was happy, when while yet a child,
I learn'd to love these upland solitudes,
And, when elastic as the mountain air,
285 To my light spirit, care was yet unknown
And evil unforseen:—Early it came,
And childhood scarcely passed, I was condemned,
A guiltless exile, silently to sigh,
While Memory, with faithful pencil, drew
290 The contrast; and regretting, I compar'd
With the polluted smoky atmosphere
And dark and stifling streets, the southern hills
That to the setting Sun, their graceful heads
Rearing, o'erlook the frith,° where Vecta[8] breaks   *firth, inlet*
295 With her white rocks, the strong impetuous tide,
When western winds the vast Atlantic urge
To thunder on the coast.—Haunts of my youth!
Scenes of fond day dreams, I behold ye yet!
Where 'twas so pleasant by thy northern slopes
300 To climb the winding sheep-path, aided oft
By scatter'd thorns: whose spiny branches bore
Small woolly tufts, spoils of the vagrant lamb
There seeking shelter from the noon-day sun;
And pleasant, seated on the short soft turf,

---

8. Vecta. The Isle of Wight, which breaks the force of the waves when they are driven by southwest winds against this long and open coast. It is somewhere described as "Vecta shouldering the Western Waves" [Smith's note].

305   To look beneath upon the hollow way
      While heavily upward mov'd the labouring wain,°   *wagon*
      And stalking slowly by, the sturdy hind
      To ease his panting team, stopp'd with a stone
      The grating wheel.

                       Advancing higher still
310   The prospect widens, and the village church
      But little, o'er the lowly roofs around
      Rears its gray belfry, and its simple vane;
      Those lowly roofs of thatch are half conceal'd
      By the rude arms of trees, lovely in spring,[9]
315   When on each bough, the rosy-tinctur'd bloom
      Sits thick, and promises autumnal plenty.
      For even those orchards round the Norman Farms,
      Which, as their owners mark the promis'd fruit,
      Console them for the vineyards of the south,
      Surpass not these.

320   Where woods of ash, and beech,
      And partial copses, fringe the green hill foot,
      The upland shepherd rears his modest home,
      There wanders by, a little nameless stream
      That from the hill wells forth, bright now and clear,
325   Or after rain with chalky mixture gray,
      But still refreshing in its shallow course,
      The cottage garden; most for use design'd,
      Yet not of beauty destitute. The vine
      Mantles the little casement; yet the briar
330   Drops fragrant dew among the July flowers;
      And pansies rayed, and freak'd and mottled pinks
      Grow among balm, and rosemary and rue;
      There honeysuckles flaunt, and roses blow
      Almost uncultured:° Some with dark green leaves   *uncultivated*
335   Contrast their flowers of pure unsullied white;
      Others, like velvet robes of regal state
      Of richest crimson, while in thorny moss
      Enshrined and cradled, the most lovely, wear
      The hues of youthful beauty's glowing cheek.—
340   With fond regret I recollect e'en now
      In Spring and Summer, what delight I felt
      Among these cottage gardens, and how much
      Such artless nosegays, knotted with a rush
      By village housewife or her ruddy maid,
345   Were welcome to me; soon and simply pleas'd.

      An early worshipper at Nature's shrine,
      I loved her rudest scenes—warrens,° and heaths,   *land for breeding*

---

9. Every cottage in this country has its orchard; and I imagine that not even those of Herefordshire, or Worcestershire, exhibit a more beautiful prospect, when the trees are in bloom, and the "Primavera candida e vermiglia," is every where so enchanting [Smith's note]. Smith is quoting Petrarch's sonnet 310, "pure and ruddy spring."

And yellow commons, and birch-shaded hollows,
And hedge rows, bordering unfrequented lanes
350 Bowered with wild roses, and the clasping woodbine
Where purple tassels of the tangling vetch[1]
With bittersweet, and bryony inweave,[2]
And the dew fills the silver bindweed's[3] cups.—
I loved to trace the brooks whose humid banks
355 Nourish the harebell, and the freckled pagil;[4]
And stroll among o'ershadowing woods of beech,
Lending in Summer, from the heats of noon
A whispering shade; while haply there reclines
Some pensive lover of uncultur'd flowers,°   *wildflowers*
360 Who, from the tumps° with bright green mosses clad,   *hillocks, mounds*
Plucks the wood sorrel,[5] with its light thin leaves,
Heart-shaped, and triply folded; and its root
Creeping like beaded coral; or who there
Gathers, the copse's pride, anémones,[6]
365 With rays like golden studs on ivory laid
Most delicate: but touch'd with purple clouds,
Fit crown for April's fair but changeful brow.

Ah! hills so early loved! in fancy still
I breathe your pure keen air; and still behold
370 Those widely spreading views, mocking alike
The Poet and the Painter's utmost art.
And still, observing objects more minute,
Wondering remark the strange and foreign forms
Of sea-shells; with the pale calcareous° soil   *chalky*
375 Mingled, and seeming of resembling substance.[7]
Tho' surely the blue Ocean (from the heights
Where the downs westward trend, but dimly seen)
Here never roll'd its surge. Does Nature then
Mimic, in wanton mood, fantastic shapes
380 Of bivalves, and inwreathed volutes,[8] that cling
To the dark sea-rock of the wat'ry world?
Or did this range of chalky mountains, once[9]
Form a vast basin, where the Ocean waves

1. Vetch. *Vicia sylvatica* [Smith's note].
2. Bittersweet. *Solatium dulcamara.* Bryony. *Bryonia alba* [Smith's note].
3. Bindweed. *Convolvulus septum* [Smith's note].
4. Harebell. *Hyacinthus non scriptus.* Pagil. *Primula veris* [Smith's note].
5. Sorrel. *Oxalis acetosella* [Smith's note].
6. Anémones. *Anemóne nemorosa.* It appears to be settled on late and excellent authorities, that this word should not be accented on the second syllable, but on the penultima. I have however ventured the more known accentuation, as more generally used, and suiting better the nature of my verse [Smith's note].
7. Among the crumbling chalk I have often found shells, some quite in a fossil state and hardly distinguishable from chalk. Others appeared more recent; cockles, muscles, and periwinkles, I well remember, were among the number; and some whose names I do not know. A great number were like those of small land snails. It is now many years since I made these observations. The appearance of sea-shells so far from the sea excited my surprise, though I then knew nothing of natural history. I have never read any of the late theories of the earth, nor was I ever satisfied with the attempts to explain many of the phenomena which call forth conjecture in those books I happened to have had access to on this subject [Smith's note].
8. Spiral-shelled mollusks such as periwinkles. "Bivalves": hinge-shelled mollusks such as clams and oysters.
9. The theory here slightly hinted at, is taken from an idea started by Mr. White [Smith's note]. Smith is referring to Gilbert White, author of *The Natural History and Antiquities of Selborne,* 1789.

Swell'd fathomless? What time these fossil shells,
385 Buoy'd on their native element, were thrown
Among the imbedding calx:° when the huge hill   *lime*
Its giant bulk heaved, and in strange ferment
Grew up a guardian barrier, 'twixt the sea
And the green level of the sylvan weald.¹

390 Ah! very vain is Science' proudest boast,
And but a little light its flame yet lends
To its most ardent votaries; since from whence
These fossil forms are seen, is but conjecture,
Food for vague theories, or vain dispute,
395 While to his daily task the peasant goes,
Unheeding such inquiry; with no care
But that the kindly change of sun and shower,
Fit for his toil the earth he cultivates.
As little recks the herdsman of the hill,
400 Who on some turfy knoll, idly reclined,
Watches his wether° flock, that deep beneath   *male sheep*
Rest the remains of men, of whom is left²
No traces in the records of mankind,
Save what these half obliterated mounds
405 And half fill'd trenches doubtfully impart
To some lone antiquary; who on times remote,
Since which two thousand years have roll'd away,
Loves to contemplate. He perhaps may trace,
Or fancy he can trace, the oblong square
410 Where the mail'd legions, under Claudius,³ rear'd
The rampire,° or excavated fosse° delved;   *rampart / ditch*
What time the huge unwieldy Elephant⁴

1. The Sussex Weald, a wooded tract of land between the North and South Downs.
2. These Downs are not only marked with traces of encampments, which from their forms are called Roman or Danish; but there are numerous tumuli [burial mounds] among them. Some of which having been opened a few years ago, were supposed by a learned antiquary to contain the remains of the original natives of the country [Smith's note].
3. That the legions of Claudius [10 B.C.E.–54 C.E.] were in this part of Britain appears certain. Since this emperor received the submission of Cantii, Atrebates, Irenobates, and Regni, in which latter denomination were included the people of Sussex [Smith's note].
4. In the year 1740, some workmen digging in the park at Burton in Sussex, discovered, nine feet below the surface, the teeth and bones of an elephant; two of the former were seven feet eight inches in length. There were besides these, tusks, one of which broke in removing it, a grinder not at all decayed, and a part of the jaw-bone, with bones of the knee and thigh, and several others. Some of them remained very lately at Burton House, the seat of John Biddulph, Esq. Others were in possession of the Rev. Dr. Langrish, minister of Petworth at that period, who was present when some of these bones were taken up, and gave it as his opinion, that they had remained there since the universal deluge [the Flood]. The Romans under the Emperor Claudius probably brought elephants into Britain. Milton, in the Second Book of his History [of Britain], in speaking of the expedition, says that "He like a great eastern king, with armed elephants, marched through Gallia." This is given on the authority of Dion Cassius, in his Life of the Emperor Claudius. It has therefore been conjectured, that the bones found at Burton might have been those of one of these elephants, who perished there soon after its landing; or dying on the high downs, one of which, called Duncton Hill, rises immediately above Burton Park, the bones might have been washed down by the torrents of rain, and buried deep in the soil. They were not found together, but scattered at some distance from each other. The two tusks were twenty feet apart. I had often heard of the elephant's bones at Burton, but never saw them; and I have no books to refer to. I think I saw, in what is now called the National Museum at Paris, the very large bones of an elephant, which were found in North America: though it is certain that this enormous animal is never seen in its natural state, but in the countries under the torrid zone of the old world. I have, since making this note, been told that the bones of the rhinoceros and hippopotamus have been found in America [Smith's note].

Auxiliary reluctant, hither led,
From Afric's forest glooms and tawny sands,
415 First felt the Northern blast, and his vast frame
Sunk useless; whence in after ages found,
The wondering hinds, on those enormous bones
Gaz'd; and in giants[5] dwelling on the hills
Believed and marvell'd.—

     Hither, Ambition come!
420 Come and behold the nothingness of all
For which you carry thro' the oppressed Earth,
War, and its train of horrors—see where tread
The innumerous° hoofs of flocks above the works   *countless*
By which the warrior sought to register
425 His glory, and immortalize his name.—
The pirate Dane,[6] who from his circular camp
Bore in destructive robbery, fire and sword
Down thro' the vale, sleeps unremember'd here;
And here, beneath the green sward, rests alike
430 The savage native,[7] who his acorn meal
Shar'd with the herds, that ranged the pathless woods;
And the centurion, who on these wide hills
Encamping, planted the Imperial Eagle.°   *the Roman standard*
All, with the lapse of Time, have passed away,
435 Even as the clouds, with dark and dragon shapes,
Or like vast promontories crown'd with towers,
Cast their broad shadows on the downs: then sail
Far to the northward, and their transient gloom
Is soon forgotten.

    But from thoughts like these,
440 By human crimes suggested, let us turn
To where a more attractive study courts
The wanderer of the hills; while shepherd girls
Will from among the fescue[8] bring him flowers,
Of wonderous mockery; some resembling bees
445 In velvet vest, intent on their sweet toil,[9]
While others mimic flies,[1] that lightly sport
In the green shade, or float along the pool,
But here seen perch'd upon the slender stalk,
And gathering honey dew. While in the breeze

---

5. The peasants believe that the large bones sometimes found belonged to giants, who formerly lived on the hills. The devil also has a great deal to do with the remarkable forms of hill and vale: the Devil's Punch Bowl, the Devil's Leaps, and the Devil's Dyke, are names given to deep hollows, or high and abrupt ridges, in this and the neighbouring county [Smith's note].
6. The incursions of the Danes were for many ages the scourge of this island [Smith's note].
7. The Aborigines of this country lived in woods, unsheltered but by trees and caves; and were probably as truly savage as any of those who are now termed so [Smith's note].
8. The grass called Sheep's Fescue (*Festuca ovina*), clothes these Downs with the softest turf [Smith's note].
9. *Ophrys apifera*, Bee Ophrys, or Orchis found plentifully on the hills, as well as the next [Smith's note].
1. *Ophrys muscifera*. Fly Orchis. Linnæus, misled by the variations to which some of this tribe are really subject, has perhaps too rashly esteemed all those which resemble insects, as forming only one species, which he terms Ophrys insecti fera. See *English Botany* [Smith's note].

450   That wafts the thistle's plumed seed along,
      Blue bells wave tremulous. The mountain thyme[2]
      Purples the hassock° of the heaving mole,   *tuft of grass*
      And the short turf is gay with tormentil,[3]
      And bird's foot trefoil, and the lesser tribes
455   Of hawkweed;[4] spangling it with fringed stars.—
      Near where a richer tract of cultur'd land
      Slopes to the south; and burnished by the sun,
      Bend in the gale of August, floods of corn;
      The guardian of the flock, with watchful care,[5]
460   Repels by voice and dog the encroaching sheep—
      While his boy visits every wired trap[6]
      That scars the turf; and from the pit-falls takes
      The timid migrants,[7] who from distant wilds,
      Warrens, and stone quarries, are destined thus
465   To lose their short existence. But unsought
      By Luxury yet, the Shepherd still protects
      The social bird,[8] who from his native haunts
      Of willowy current, or the rushy pool,
      Follows the fleecy crowd, and flirts and skims,
      In fellowship among them.

470   Where the knoll
      More elevated takes the changeful winds,
      The windmill rears its vanes; and thitherward
      With his white load,° the master travelling,   *load of grain*
      Scares the rooks rising slow on whispering wings,
475   While o'er his head, before the summer sun
      Lights up the blue expanse, heard more than seen,
      The lark sings matins; and above the clouds
      Floating, embathes his spotted breast in dew.
      Beneath the shadow of a gnarled thorn,
480   Bent by the sea blast[9] from a seat of turf

2. Blue bells. *Campanula rotundifolia.* Mountain thyme. *Thymus serpyllum.* "It is a common notion, that the flesh of sheep which feeds upon aromatic plants, particularly wild thyme, is superior in flavour to other mutton. The truth is, that sheep do not crop these aromatic plants, unless now and then by accident, or when they are first turned on hungry to downs, heaths, or commons; but the soil and situations favourable to aromatic plants, produce a short sweet pasturage, best adapted to feeding sheep, whom nature designed for mountains, and not for turnip grounds and rich meadows. The attachment of bees to this, and other aromatic plants, is well known." Martyn's Miller [Smith's note]. Smith is citing Thomas Martyn's revision of Philip Miller's *The Gardener's and Botanist's Dictionary,* 1797–1807.
3. Tormentil. *Tormentilla reptans* [Smith's note].
4. Bird's foot trefoil. *Trifolium ornithopoides.* Hawkweed. *Hieracium,* many sorts [Smith's note].
5. The downs, especially to the south, where they are less abrupt, are in many places under the plough; and the attention of the shepherds is

there particularly required to keep the flocks from trespassing [Smith's note].
6. Square holes cut in the turf, into which a wire noose is fixed, to catch Wheatears. Mr. White [*Natural History of Selborne*] says, that these birds (*Motacilla oenanthe*) are never taken beyond the river Adur, and Beding Hill; but this is certainly a mistake [Smith's note].
7. These birds are extremely fearful, and on the slightest appearance of a cloud, run for shelter to the first rut, or heap of stone, that they see [Smith's note].
8. The Yellow Wagtail. *Motacilla flava.* It frequents the banks of rivulets in winter, making its nest in meadows and corn-fields. But after the breeding season is over, it haunts downs and sheepwalks, and is seen constantly among the flocks, probably for the sake of the insects it picks up. In France the shepherds call it *La Bergeronette,* and say it often gives them, by its cry, notice of approaching danger [Smith's note].
9. The strong winds from the south-west occasion almost all the trees, which on these hills are exposed to it, to grow the other way [Smith's note].

With fairy nosegays strewn, how wide the view![1]
Till in the distant north it melts away,
And mingles indiscriminate with clouds:
But if the eye could reach so far, the mart
485 Of England's capital, its domes and spires
Might be perceived.—Yet hence the distant range
Of Kentish hills,[2] appear in purple haze;
And nearer, undulate the wooded heights,
And airy summits,[3] that above the mole°   cliff
490 Rise in green beauty; and the beacon'd ridge
Of Black-down[4] shagg'd with heath, and swelling rude
Like a dark island from the vale; its brow
Catching the last rays of the evening sun
That gleam between the nearer park's old oaks,
495 Then lighten up the river, and make prominent
The portal, and the ruin'd battlements[5]
Of that dismantled fortress; rais'd what time
The Conqueror's successors fiercely fought,
Tearing with civil feuds the desolate land.
500 But now a tiller of the soil dwells there,
And of the turret's loop'd and rafter'd halls
Has made an humbler homestead—Where he sees,
Instead of armed foemen, herds that graze
Along his yellow meadows; or his flocks
505 At evening from the upland driv'n to fold.—

In such a castellated mansion once
A stranger chose his home; and where hard by
In rude disorder fallen, and hid with brushwood
Lay fragments gray of towers and buttresses,
510 Among the ruins, often he would muse.—
His rustic meal soon ended, he was wont
To wander forth, listening the evening sounds
Of rushing milldam,[6] or the distant team,
Or night-jar, chasing fern-flies:[7] the tir'd hind

1. So extensive are some of the views from these hills, that only the want of power in the human eye to travel so far, prevents London itself being discerned. Description falls so infinitely short of the reality, that only here and there, distinct features can be given [Smith's note].
2. A scar of chalk in a hill beyond Sevenoaks in Kent, is very distinctly seen of a clear day [Smith's note].
3. The hills about Dorking in Surry; over almost the whole extent of which county the prospect extends [Smith's note].
4. This is an high ridge, extending between Sussex and Surry. It is covered with heath, and has almost always a dark appearance. On it is a telegraph [Smith's note].
5. In this country there are several of the fortresses or castles built by Stephen of Blois [King of England, 1135–54], in his contention for the kingdom, with the daughter of Henry the First, the empress Matilda. Some of these are now converted into farm houses [Smith's note].
6. I.e., the water in the dammed millstream.
7. Dr. Aikin remarks, I believe, in his essay "On

the Application of Natural History to the Purposes of Poetry," how many of our best poets have noticed the same circumstance, the hum of the Dor Beetle (Scaraboeus stercorarius) among the sounds heard by the evening wanderer. I remember only one instance in which the more remarkable, though by no means uncommon noise, of the Fern Owl, or Goatsucker, is mentioned. It is called the Night Hawk, the Jar Bird, the Churn Owl, and the Fern Owl, from its feeding on the Scaraboeus solstitialis, or Fern Chafer, which it catches while on the wing with its claws, the middle toe of which is long and curiously serrated, on purpose to hold them. It was this bird that was intended to be described in the Forty-second sonnet. I was mistaken in supposing it as visible in November; it is a migrant, and leaves this country in August. I had often seen and heard it, but I did not then know its name or history. It is called Goatsucker (Caprimulgus), from a strange prejudice taken against it by the Italians, who assert that it sucks their goats; and the peasants of England still believe that a disease in the backs of their cattle, occasioned by a fly, which deposits its egg under the skin, and

515 Pass'd him at nightfall, wondering he should sit
On the hill top so late: they from the coast
Who sought by-paths with their clandestine load,°   *smuggled goods*
Saw with suspicious doubt, the lonely man
Cross on their way: but village maidens thought
520 His senses injur'd; and with pity say
That he, poor youth! must have been cross'd in love—
For often, stretch'd upon the mountain turf
With folded arms, and eyes intently fix'd
Where ancient elms and firs obscured a grange,°   *farm*
525 Some little space within the vale below,
They heard him, as complaining of his fate,
And to the murmuring wind, of cold neglect
And baffled hope he told.—The peasant girls
These plaintive sounds remember, and even now
530 Among them may be heard the stranger's songs.

     Were I a Shepherd on the hill
         And ever as the mists withdrew
     Could see the willows of the rill
     Shading the footway to the mill
535   Where once I walk'd with you—

     And as away Night's shadows sail,
         And sounds of birds and brooks arise,
     Believe, that from the woody vale
     I hear your voice upon the gale
540   In soothing melodies;

     And viewing from the Alpine height,
         The prospect dress'd in hues of air,
     Could say, while transient colours bright
     Touch'd the fair scene with dewy light,
545   'Tis, that *her* eyes are there!

     I think, I could endure my lot
         And linger on a few short years,
     And then, by all but you forgot,
     Sleep, where the turf that clothes the spot
550   May claim some pitying tears.

     For 'tis not easy to forget
         One, who thro' life has lov'd you still,
     And you, however late, might yet
     With sighs to Memory giv'n, regret°   *recall with regret*
555   The Shepherd of the Hill.

---

raises a boil, sometimes fatal to calves, is the work of this bird, which they call a Puckeridge. Nothing can convince them that their beasts are not injured by this bird, which they therefore hold in abhorrence [Smith's note]. Smith refers at the beginning to John Aikin's *An Essay on the Application of Natural History to Poetry*, 1777, and in the middle to sonnet 42 in her own *Elegiac Sonnets*.

Yet otherwhile it seem'd as if young Hope
Her flattering pencil gave to Fancy's hand,
And in his wanderings, rear'd to sooth his soul
Ideal bowers of pleasure.—Then, of Solitude
560 And of his hermit life, still more enamour'd,
His home was in the forest; and wild fruits
And bread sustain'd him. There in early spring
The Barkmen[8] found him, e'er the sun arose;
There at their daily toil, the Wedgecutters[9]
565 Beheld him thro' the distant thicket move.
The shaggy dog following the truffle hunter,[1]
Bark'd at the loiterer; and perchance at night
Belated villagers from fair or wake,
While the fresh night-wind let the moonbeams in
570 Between the swaying boughs, just saw him pass,
And then in silence, gliding like a ghost
He vanish'd! Lost among the deepening gloom.—
But near one ancient tree, whose wreathed roots
Form'd a rude couch, love-songs and scatter'd rhymes,
575 Unfinish'd sentences, or half erased,
And rhapsodies like this, were sometimes found—

Let us to woodland wilds repair
   While yet the glittering night-dews seem
To wait the freshly-breathing air,
580   Precursive of the morning beam,
That rising with advancing day,
Scatters the silver drops away.

An elm, uprooted by the storm,
   The trunk with mosses gray and green,
585 Shall make for us a rustic form,
   Where lighter grows the forest scene;
And far among the bowery shades,
Are ferny lawns and grassy glades.

Retiring May to lovely June
590   Her latest garland now resigns;
The banks with cuckoo-flowers[2] are strewn,
   The woodwalks blue with columbines,[3]
And with its reeds, the wandering stream
Reflects the flag-flower's[4] golden gleam.

595 There, feathering down the turf to meet,
   Their shadowy arms the beeches spread,
While high above our sylvan seat,

8. As soon as the sap begins to rise, the trees intended for felling are cut and barked. At which time the men who are employed in that business pass whole days in the woods [Smith's note].
9. The wedges used in ship-building are made of beech wood, and great numbers are cut every year in the woods near the Downs [Smith's note].
1. Truffles are found under the beech woods, by means of small dogs trained to hunt them by the scent [Smith's note].

2. Cuckoo-flowers. *Lychnis dioica.* Shakespeare describes the Cuckoo buds as being yellow [*Love's Labor's Lost* 5.2.871]. He probably meant the numerous Ranunculi, or March marigolds (*Caltha palustris*) which so gild the meadows in Spring; but poets have never been botanists. The Cuckoo flower is the *Lychnis floscuculi* [Smith's note].
3. Columbines. *Aquilegia vulgaris* [Smith's note].
4. Flag-flower. *Iris pseudacorus* [Smith's note].

Lifts the light ash its airy head;
And later leaved, the oaks between
600   Extend their boughs of vernal green.

The slender birch its paper rind
   Seems offering to divided love,
And shuddering even without a wind
   Aspens, their paler foliage move,
605   As If some spirit of the air
Breath'd a low sigh in passing there.

The Squirrel in his frolic mood,
   Will fearless bound among the boughs;
Yaffils[5] laugh loudly thro' the wood,
610   And murmuring ring-doves tell their vows;
While we, as sweetest woodscents rise,
Listen to woodland melodies.

And I'll contrive a sylvan room
   Against the time of summer heat,
615   Where leaves, inwoven in Nature's loom,
   Shall canopy our green retreat;
And gales that "close the eye of day"[6]
Shall linger, e'er they die away.

And when a sere and sallow hue
620   From early frost the bower receives,
I'll dress the sand rock cave for you,
   And strew the floor with heath and leaves,
That you, against the autumnal air
May find securer shelter there.

625   The Nightingale will then have ceas'd
   To sing her moonlight serenade;
But the gay bird with blushing breast,[7]
   And Woodlarks[8] still will haunt the shade,
And by the borders of the spring
630   Reed-wrens[9] will yet be carolling.

The forest hermit's lonely cave
   None but such soothing sounds shall reach,
Or hardly heard, the distant wave
   Slow breaking on the stony beach;
635   Or winds, that now sigh soft and low,
Now make wild music as they blow.

5. Yaffils. Woodpeckers (*Picus*); three or four species in Britain [Smith's note].
6. "And liquid notes that close the eye of day." Milton [Sonnet 1, "O Nightingale"]. The idea here meant to be conveyed is of the evening wind, so welcome after a hot day of Summer, and which appears to sooth and lull all nature into tranquillity [Smith's note].

7. The Robin (*Motacilla rubecula*), which is always heard after other songsters have ceased to sing [Smith's note].
8. The Woodlark (*Alauda nemorosa*), sings very late [Smith's note].
9. Reed-wrens (*Motacilla arundinacea*), sing all the summer and autumn, and are often heard during the night [Smith's note].

And then, before the chilling North
　　The tawny foliage falling light,
Seems, as it flits along the earth,
640　　The footfall of the busy Sprite,
Who wrapt in pale autumnal gloom,
Calls up the mist-born Mushroom.

Oh! could I hear your soft voice there,
　　And see you in the forest green
645 All beauteous as you are, more fair
　　You'd look, amid the sylvan scene,
And in a wood-girl's simple guise,
Be still more lovely in mine eyes.

Ye phantoms of unreal delight,
650　　Visions of fond delirium born!
Rise not on my deluded sight,
　　Then leave me drooping and forlorn
To know, such bliss can never be,
Unless Amanda loved like me.

655 The visionary, nursing dreams like these,
Is not indeed unhappy. Summer woods
Wave over him, and whisper as they wave,
Some future blessings he may yet enjoy.
And as above him sail the silver clouds,
660 He follows them in thought to distant climes,
Where, far from the cold policy of this,
Dividing him from her he fondly loves,
He, in some island of the southern sea,[1]
May haply build his cane-constructed bower
665 Beneath the bread-fruit, or aspiring palm,
With long green foliage rippling in the gale.
Oh! let him cherish his ideal bliss—
For what is life, when Hope has ceas'd to strew
Her fragile flowers along its thorny way?
670 And sad and gloomy are his days, who lives
Of Hope abandon'd!

　　　　　Just beneath the rock
Where Beachy overpeers the channel wave,
Within a cavern mined by wintry tides
Dwelt one,[2] who long disgusted with the world

1. An allusion to the visionary delights of the newly discovered islands [Polynesia], where it was at first believed men lived in a state of simplicity and happiness; but where, as later enquiries have ascertained, that exemption from toil, which the fertility of their country gives them, produces the grossest vices; and a degree of corruption that late navigators think will end in the extirpation of the whole people in a few years [Smith's note].
2. In a cavern almost immediately under the cliff called Beachy Head, there lived, as the people of the country believed, a man of the name of Darby, who for many years had no other abode than this cave, and subsisted almost entirely on shell-fish. He had often administered assistance to shipwrecked mariners; but venturing into the sea on this charitable mission during a violent equinoctial storm, he himself perished. As it is above thirty years since I heard this tradition of Parson Darby (for so I think he was called): it may now perhaps be forgotten [Smith's note].

675 And all its ways, appear'd to suffer life
Rather than live; the soul-reviving gale,
Fanning the bean-field, or the thymy° heath,   *abounding in thyme*
Had not for many summers breathed on him;
And nothing mark'd to him the season's change,
680 Save that more gently rose the placid sea,
And that the birds which winter on the coast
Gave place to other migrants; save that the fog,
Hovering no more above the beetling cliffs
Betray'd not then the little careless sheep[3]
685 On the brink grazing, while their headlong fall
Near the lone Hermit's flint-surrounded home,
Claim'd unavailing pity; for his heart
Was feelingly alive to all that breath'd;
And outraged as he was, in sanguine youth,
690 By human crimes, he still acutely felt
For human misery.

                Wandering on the beach,
He learn'd to augur from the clouds of heaven,
And from the changing colours of the sea,
And sullen murmurs of the hollow cliffs,
695 Or the dark porpoises,[4] that near the shore
Gambol'd and sported on the level brine
When tempests were approaching: then at night
He listen'd to the wind; and as it drove
The billows with o'erwhelming vehemence
700 He, starting from his rugged couch, went forth
And hazarding a life, too valueless,
He waded thro' the waves, with plank or pole
Towards where the mariner in conflict dread
Was buffeting for life the roaring surge;
705 And now just seen, now lost in foaming gulphs,
The dismal gleaming of the clouded moon
Shew'd the dire peril. Often he had snatch'd
From the wild billows, some unhappy man
Who liv'd to bless the hermit of the rocks.
710 But if his generous cares were all in vain,
And with slow swell the tide of morning bore
Some blue swol'n cor'se° to land; the pale recluse   *corpse*
Dug in the chalk a sepulchre—above
Where the dank sea-wrack° mark'd the utmost tide,   *refuse from the sea*
715 And with his prayers perform'd the obsequies
For the poor helpless stranger.

                One dark night
The equinoctial wind blew south by west,
Fierce on the shore;—the bellowing cliffs were shook
Even to their stony base, and fragments fell
720 Flashing and thundering on the angry flood.

3. Sometimes in thick weather the sheep feeding on the summit of the cliff, miss their footing,
and are killed by the fall [Smith's note].

4. Dark porpoises. *Delphinus phocœna* [Smith's
note].

At day-break, anxious for the lonely man,
His cave the mountain shepherds visited,
Tho' sand and banks of weeds had choak'd their way.—
He was not in it; but his drowned cor'se
725 By the waves wafted, near his former home
Receiv'd the rites of burial. Those who read
Chisel'd within the rock, these mournful lines,
Memorials of his sufferings, did not grieve,
That dying in the cause of charity
730 His spirit, from its earthly bondage freed,
Had to some better region fled for ever.

1806   1807

MARY ROBINSON
1757?–1800

Mary Robinson, whom the *Dictionary of National Biography*, at the beginning of a long entry, describes as "actress, author, and mistress of George, Prince of Wales," lived a more sensational life than any other poet of the period, Byron and Shelley included. Her father was a Bristol whaler, her mother a woman of "genteel background" who, after her husband deserted the family, ran a school for girls. At fifteen Mary was married to Thomas Robinson, an articled law clerk who seemed a good match but quickly proved a gambler and libertine; he was arrested for debt, and Mary and her infant daughter spent a year with him in debtors' prison, where, to pass the time, she began writing poetry. Her first pieces appeared in a two-volume *Poems* published under the patronage of the duchess of Devonshire in 1775.

In December 1776, accepting a long-standing invitation of David Garrick, the actor-manager of the Drury Lane theater, Robinson made her stage debut as Juliet, and for the next four years she was constantly before the public—in thirty or more principal roles, nine of them in plays by Shakespeare. A beauty and leader of fashion, she attracted many suitors and was painted by many of the leading portraitists of the day, including George Romney, Thomas Gainsborough, and Sir Joshua Reynolds, president of the Royal Academy. At a command performance of *The Winter's Tale* in December 1779, playing the role of Perdita, Robinson captivated the teenaged prince of Wales and, after negotiating financial compensation in the form of a £20,000 bond (because she would have to give up her acting career), became his mistress. As a royal mistress, she was even more exposed to the public eye than she had been on the stage; years after the prince abandoned her, ribald speculation about the erotic adventures of "Perdita" continued to engross gossip columnists and satiric cartoonists. Robinson's attempt, following the prince's desertion, to sue for the promised £20,000 failed, but through the efforts of the Whig parliamentarian Charles James Fox, another famous man who may have been her lover, she received an annuity from the prince of £500 per year. At twenty-five she formed an attachment with Banastre Tarleton, an army officer who had just returned from the war in America and was embarking on a career in Parliament. That attachment lasted ten years, until Tarleton married an heiress. Robinson was by this time in poor health and, as a consequence of either a miscarriage (in some accounts) or rheumatic fever (in others), was paralyzed from the waist down. Even in this condition she made a striking public figure, as four liveried servants, covering their arms with long white sleeves, bore her from the opera house to her waiting carriage. A savvy self-publicist, she appears to have been well aware of the part she played in the spectacle that was fashionable London, accepting and even embracing (in the words of her modern editor, Judith Pascoe) her role as "the most attractive object in a large urban display."

Literature became Robinson's principal activity and source of income when she was in her early thirties. In 1788 and 1789, writing under the pen name "Laura Maria" and sending her verse to the papers the *World* and the *Oracle*, she entered into a passionate poetical correspondence with "Della Crusca" (pseudonym of the poet Robert Merry, who had already participated in a similar public flirtation in the periodical press, in the series of love poems he exchanged with "Anna Matilda," the poet Hannah Cowley). When, in her *Poems* of 1791, Robinson reprinted some of these "effusions" of feeling, she attracted six hundred subscribers. In 1796 she contributed to the English revival of the sonnet with her Petrarchan series *Sappho and Phaon*. In the 1790s she also authored seven novels, beginning in 1792 with *Vacenza, or The Dangers of Credulity*. She succeeded Robert Southey in the influential office of poetry editor of the *Morning Post* in 1799. Other writings by Robinson include her political tracts *Impartial Reflections on the Present Situation of the Queen of France* (1793) and *Thoughts on the Condition of Women, and on the Injustice of Mental Subordination* (1799) and her posthumous *Memoirs* (1801), an autobiography whose description of a woman's poetic vocation makes it (like Robinson's critical discussion of the Greek poet of passion Sappho) exceptional in an era now better known for its models of masculine artistry.

Robinson is one of the accomplished writers of blank verse in the 1790s (as in "London's Summer Morning") as well as one of the most irrepressibly musical in many different forms of rhyme. Outspokenly liberal in its politics, good-humored, satirical, and sentimental by turns, her late verse in particular exemplifies what Stuart Curran calls "the new realism that will impel English poetry into the nineteenth century." *Lyrical Tales* (1800), the final volume of Robinson's poetry to be published in her lifetime, appeared the month before the second edition of Wordsworth and Coleridge's *Lyrical Ballads*—from the same publisher and printer and in exactly the same format and typography (Wordsworth, in reaction, tried to change his own title to *Poems by W. Wordsworth*). Robinson's "The Poor Singing Dame" is modeled on the most popular of Wordsworth's 1798 ballads, "Goody Blake and Harry Gill." Wordsworth in turn based one of his pieces ("The Seven Sisters; or, The Solitude of Binnorie") on the elaborate metrical scheme of Robinson's "The Haunted Beach," a poem that prompted Coleridge to exclaim to Southey, when he first saw it in the *Morning Post*, "the Metre—ay! that Woman has an Ear." Coleridge admired her "undoubted Genius," and Robinson returned the compliment in one of her last poems, "To the Poet Coleridge," a shrewd reading of "Kubla Khan" sixteen years before it first got into print.

January, 1795[1]

Pavement slipp'ry, people sneezing,
Lords in ermine, beggars freezing;
Titled gluttons dainties carving,
Genius in a garret starving.

1. First published in the *Morning Post* as the work of "Portia."

5   Lofty mansions, warm and spacious;
Courtiers cringing and voracious;
Misers scarce the wretched heeding;
Gallant soldiers fighting, bleeding.

Wives who laugh at passive spouses;
10   Theatres, and meeting-houses;
Balls, where simp'ring misses languish;
Hospitals, and groans of anguish.

Arts and sciences bewailing;
Commerce drooping, credit failing;
15   Placemen° mocking subjects loyal;   *political appointees*
Separations, weddings royal.

Authors who can't earn a dinner;
Many a subtle rogue a winner;
Fugitives for shelter seeking;
20   Misers hoarding, tradesmen breaking.°   *going bankrupt*

Taste and talents quite deserted;
All the laws of truth perverted;
Arrogance o'er merit soaring;
Merit silently deploring.

25   Ladies gambling night and morning;
Fools the works of genius scorning;
Ancient dames for girls mistaken,
Youthful damsels quite forsaken.

Some in luxury delighting;
30   More in talking than in fighting;
Lovers old, and beaux decrepid;
Lordlings empty and insipid.

Poets, painters, and musicians;
Lawyers, doctors, politicians:
35   Pamphlets, newspapers, and odes,
Seeking fame by diff'rent roads.

Gallant souls with empty purses;
Gen'rals only fit for nurses;
School-boys, smit with martial spirit,
40   Taking place of vet'ran merit.

Honest men who can't get places,
Knaves who shew unblushing faces;
Ruin hasten'd, peace retarded;
Candor spurn'd, and art rewarded.

1795   1806

London's Summer Morning

Who has not wak'd to list the busy sounds
Of summer's morning, in the sultry smoke
Of noisy London? On the pavement hot
The sooty chimney-boy, with dingy face
5 And tatter'd covering, shrilly bawls his trade,
Rousing the sleepy housemaid. At the door
The milk-pail rattles, and the tinkling bell
Proclaims the dustman's° office; while the street   trash collector's
Is lost in clouds impervious. Now begins
10 The din of hackney-coaches, waggons, carts;
While tinmen's shops, and noisy trunk-makers,
Knife-grinders, coopers, squeaking cork-cutters,
Fruit-barrows, and the hunger-giving cries
Of vegetable venders, fill the air.
15 Now ev'ry shop displays its varied trade,
And the fresh-sprinkled pavement cools the feet
Of early walkers. At the private door
The ruddy housemaid twirls the busy mop,[1]
Annoying the smart 'prentice, or neat girl,
20 Tripping with band-box[2] lightly. Now the sun
Darts burning splendor on the glitt'ring pane,
Save where the canvas awning throws a shade
On the gay merchandise. Now, spruce and trim,
In shops (where beauty smiles with industry)
25 Sits the smart damsel; while the passenger°   passerby
Peeps through the window, watching ev'ry charm.
Now pastry dainties catch the eye minute
Of humming insects, while the limy snare[3]
Waits to enthral them. Now the lamp-lighter
30 Mounts the tall ladder, nimbly venturous,
To trim the half-fill'd lamp; while at his feet
The pot-boy[4] yells discordant! All along
The sultry pavement, the old-clothes-man cries
In tone monotonous, and side-long views
35 The area for his traffic: now the bag
Is slily open'd, and the half-worn suit
(Sometimes the pilfer'd treasure of the base
Domestic spoiler), for one half its worth,
Sinks in the green abyss. The porter now
40 Bears his huge load along the burning way;
And the poor poet wakes from busy dreams,
To paint the summer morning.

1795–1800   1800

---

1. An echo of Jonathan Swift's urban pastoral "A Description of the Morning" (1709), in which Moll whirls "her mop with dex'trous airs" (line 7).
2. Box for hats, gloves, etc.
3. Sticky substance used to catch insects.
4. Servant from a nearby pub.

The Poor Singing Dame

Beneath an old wall, that went round an old castle,
    For many a year, with brown ivy o'erspread,
A neat little hovel, its lowly roof raising,
    Defied the wild winds that howl'd over its shed:
5 The turrets, that frown'd on the poor simple dwelling,
    Were rock'd to and fro, when the tempest would roar,
And the river, that down the rich valley was swelling,
    Flow'd swiftly beside the green step of its door.

The summer sun gilded the rushy roof slanting,
10   The bright dews bespangled its ivy-bound hedge,
And above, on the ramparts, the sweet birds were chanting,
    And wild buds thick dappled the clear river's edge.
When the castle's rich chambers were haunted and dreary,
    The poor little hovel was still and secure;
15 And no robber e'er enter'd, nor goblin nor fairy,
    For the splendors of pride had no charms to allure.

The Lord of the castle, a proud surly ruler,
    Oft heard the low dwelling with sweet music ring,
For the old Dame that liv'd in the little hut cheerly,
20   Would sit at her wheel, and would merrily sing:
When with revels the castle's great hall was resounding,
    The old Dame was sleeping, not dreaming of fear;
And when over the mountains the huntsmen were bounding
    She would open her lattice, their clamors to hear.

25 To the merry-ton'd horn she would dance on the threshold,
    And louder, and louder, repeat her old song:
And when winter its mantle of frost was displaying,
    She caroll'd, undaunted, the bare woods among:
She would gather dry fern, ever happy and singing,
30   With her cake of brown bread, and her jug of brown beer,
And would smile when she heard the great castle-bell ringing,
    Inviting the proud—to their prodigal cheer.

Thus she liv'd, ever patient and ever contented,
    Till envy the Lord of the castle possess'd,
35 For he hated that poverty should be so cheerful,
    While care could the fav'rites of fortune molest;
He sent his bold yeomen with threats to prevent her,
    And still would she carol her sweet roundelay;
At last, an old steward relentless he sent her—
40   Who bore her, all trembling, to prison away!

Three weeks did she languish, then died broken-hearted,
    Poor Dame! how the death-bell did mournfully sound!
And along the green path six young bachelors bore her,
    And laid her for ever beneath the cold ground!
45 And the primroses pale 'mid the long grass were growing,
    The bright dews of twilight bespangled her grave,

And morn heard the breezes of summer soft blowing
　　To bid the fresh flow'rets in sympathy wave.

The Lord of the castle, from that fatal moment
50　　When poor singing Mary was laid in her grave,
Each night was surrounded by screech-owls appalling,
　　Which o'er the black turrets their pinions would wave!
On the ramparts that frown'd on the river, swift flowing,
　　They hover'd, still hooting a terrible song,
55　When his windows would rattle, the winter blast blowing,
　　They would shriek like a ghost, the dark alleys among!

Wherever he wander'd they follow'd him crying,
　　At dawnlight, at eve, still they haunted his way!
When the moon shone across the wide common they hooted,
60　　Nor quitted his path till the blazing of day.
His bones began wasting, his flesh was decaying,
　　And he hung his proud head, and he perish'd with shame;
And the tomb of rich marble, no soft tear displaying,
　　O'ershadows the grave of the Poor Singing Dame!

1799–1800　　　　　　　　　　　　　　　　　　　　　　1800

The Haunted Beach

　　Upon a lonely desart Beach,
　　　　Where the white foam was scatter'd,
　　A little shed uprear'd its head,
　　　　Though lofty barks° were shatter'd.　　　　　*ships*
5　　The sea-weeds gath'ring near the door
　　　　A somber path display'd;
　　And, all around, the deaf'ning roar
　　Re-echo'd on the chalky shore,
　　　　By the green billows made.

10　Above a jutting cliff was seen
　　　　Where Sea Birds hover'd, craving;
　　And all around the craggs were bound
　　　　With weeds—for ever waving.
　　And here and there, a cavern wide
15　　　　Its shad'wy jaws display'd;
　　And near the sands, at ebb of tide,
　　A shiver'd mast was seen to ride
　　　　Where the green billows stray'd.

　　And often, while the moaning wind
20　　　　Stole o'er the Summer Ocean,
　　The moonlight scene was all serene,
　　　　The waters scarce in motion;
　　Then, while the smoothly slanting sand
　　　　The tall cliff wrapp'd in shade,
25　The Fisherman beheld a band

Of Spectres gliding hand in hand—
   Where the green billows play'd.

And pale their faces were as snow,
   And sullenly they wander'd;
30 And to the skies with hollow eyes
   They look'd as though they ponder'd.
And sometimes, from their hammock shroud,
   They dismal howlings made,
And while the blast blew strong and loud
35 The clear moon mark'd the ghastly crowd,
   Where the green billows play'd!

And then above the haunted hut
   The Curlews screaming hover'd;
And the low door, with furious roar,
40   The frothy breakers cover'd.
For in the Fisherman's lone shed
   A murder'd man was laid,
With ten wide gashes in his head,
And deep was made his sandy bed
45   Where the green billows play'd.

A shipwreck'd Mariner was he,
   Doom'd from his home to sever;
Who swore to be through wind and sea
   Firm and undaunted ever!
50 And when the wave resistless roll'd,
   About his arm he made
A packet rich of Spanish gold,
And, like a British sailor bold,
   Plung'd where the billows play'd!

55 The Spectre band, his messmates brave,
   Sunk in the yawning ocean,
While to the mast he lash'd him fast,
   And brav'd the storm's commotion.
The winter moon upon the sand
60   A silv'ry carpet made,
And mark'd the Sailor reach the land,
And mark'd his murd'rer wash his hand
   Where the green billows play'd.

And since that hour the Fisherman
65   Has toil'd and toil'd in vain;
For all the night the moony light
   Gleams on the specter'd main!
And when the skies are veil'd in gloom,
   The Murd'rer's liquid way
70 Bounds o'er the deeply yawning tomb,
And flashing fires the sands illume,
   Where the green billows play!

     Full thirty years his task has been
        Day after day more weary;
75   For Heav'n design'd his guilty mind
        Should dwell on prospects dreary.
     Bound by a strong and mystic chain,
        He has not pow'r to stray;
     But destin'd mis'ry to sustain,
80   He wastes, in Solitude and Pain,
        A loathsome life away.

1800

The Poet's Garret

     Come, sportive fancy! come with me, and trace
     The poet's attic home! the lofty seat
     Of the heav'n-tutor'd nine!° the airy throne   *the muses*
     Of bold imagination, rapture fraught
5   Above the herds of mortals. All around
     A solemn stillness seems to guard the scene,
     Nursing the brood of thought—a thriving brood
     In the rich mazes of the cultur'd brain.
     Upon thy altar, an old worm-eat board,
10 The pannel of a broken door, or lid
     Of a strong coffer, plac'd on three-legg'd stool,
     Stand quires of paper, white and beautiful!
     Paper, by destiny ordain'd to be
     Scrawl'd o'er and blotted; dash'd, and scratch'd, and torn;
15 Or mark'd with lines severe, or scatter'd wide
     In rage impetuous! Sonnet, song, and ode,
     Satire, and epigram, and smart charade;
     Neat paragraph, or legendary tale,
     Of short and simple metre, each by turns
20 Will there delight the reader.

                   On the bed
     Lies an old rusty° suit of "solemn black,"—   *shabby*
     Brush'd thread-bare, and, with brown, unglossy hue,
     Grown somewhat ancient. On the floor is seen
     A pair of silken hose, whose footing bad
25 Shews they are trav'llers, but who still bear
     Marks somewhat *holy.* At the scanty fire
     A chop turns round, by packthread strongly held;
     And on the blacken'd bar a vessel shines
     Of batter'd pewter, just half fill'd, and warm,
30 With Whitbread's bev'rage pure.[1] The kitten purs,
     Anticipating dinner; while the wind
     Whistles thro' broken panes, and drifted snow

---

1. Beer from Samuel Whitbread's brewery.

Carpets the parapet with spotless garb,
Of vestal coldness. Now the sullen hour
35 (The fifth hour after noon) with dusky hand
Closes the lids of day. The farthing light
Gleams thro' the cobwebb'd chamber, and the bard
Concludes his pen's hard labour. Now he eats
With appetite voracious! nothing sad
40 That he with costly plate, and napkins fine,
Nor china rich, nor fork of silver, greets
His eye or palate. On his lyric board
A sheet of paper serves for table-cloth;
An heap of salt is serv'd,—oh! heav'nly treat!
45 On ode Pindaric![2] while his tuneful puss
Scratches his slipper for her fragment sweet,
And sings her love-song soft, yet mournfully.
Mocking the pillar Doric, or the roof
Of architecture Gothic, all around
50 The well-known ballads flit, of Grub-street fame![3]
The casement, broke, gives breath celestial
To the long dying-speech; or gently fans
The love-inflaming sonnet. All around
Small scraps of paper lie, torn vestiges
55 Of an unquiet fancy. Here a page
Of flights poetic—there a dedication—
A list of dramatis personæ, bold,
Of heroes yet unborn, and lofty dames
Of perishable compound, light as fair,
60 But sentenc'd to oblivion![4]

On a shelf,
(Yclept[5] a mantle-piece) a phial stands,
Half fill'd with potent spirits!—spirits strong,
Which sometimes haunt the poet's restless brain,
And fill his mind with fancies whimsical.
65 Poor poet! happy art thou, thus remov'd
From pride and folly! for in thy domain
Thou can'st command thy subjects; fill thy lines;
Wield th' all-conqu'ring weapon heav'n bestows
On the grey goose's wing!° which, tow'ring high,   *goose-quill pen*
70 Bears thy sick fancy to immortal fame!

1800   1806

---

2. The tablecloth is an ode written in the manner of the Classical Greek poet Pindar (ca. 518–438 B.C.E.).

3. Originally the name for a London street (now Milton Street) that through the 18th century was often inhabited by third-rate authors churning out writing for money. The term came to designate literary hackwork generally.

4. Compare in Alexander Pope's *Dunciad* (1743) the description of this mock-epic's dunce in chief, glimpsed at a moment of writer's block: "Round him much Embryo, much Abortion lay, / Much future Ode, and abdicated Play" (1.121–22).

5. Called; the word was an archaism in Robinson's time, associated with antiquated poetry.

To the Poet Coleridge[1]

Rapt in the visionary theme!
   Spirit divine! with thee I'll wander,
Where the blue, wavy, lucid stream,
   'Mid forest glooms, shall slow meander!
5 With thee I'll trace the circling bounds
   Of thy new Paradise extended;
And listen to the varying sounds
   Of winds, and foamy torrents blended.

Now by the source which lab'ring heaves
10   The mystic fountain, bubbling, panting,
While gossamer° its net-work weaves,   *filmy cobweb*
   Adown the blue lawn slanting!
I'll mark thy *sunny dome*, and view
Thy *caves of ice*, thy fields of dew!
15 Thy ever-blooming mead, whose flow'r
Waves to the cold breath of the moonlight hour!
Or when the day-star, peering bright
On the grey wing of parting night;
While more than vegetating pow'r
20 Throbs grateful to the burning hour,
As summer's whisper'd sighs unfold
Her million, million buds of gold;
Then will I climb the breezy bounds,
   Of thy new Paradise extended,
25 And listen to the distant sounds
   Of winds, and foamy torrents blended!

Spirit divine! with thee I'll trace
Imagination's boundless space!
With thee, beneath thy *sunny dome*,
30   I'll listen to the minstrel's lay,
   Hymning the gradual close of day;
In *caves of ice* enchanted roam,
Where on the glitt'ring entrance plays
The moon's-beam with its silv'ry rays;
35   Or, when the glassy stream,
     That through the deep dell flows,
Flashes the noon's hot beam;
   The noon's hot beam, that midway shows
Thy flaming temple, studded o'er
40 With all Peruvia's° lustrous store!   *Peru's*
There will I trace the circling bounds
   Of thy new Paradise extended!
And listen to the awful sounds,
   Of winds, and foamy torrents blended!

---

1. This poem is a tribute to, and running commentary on, Coleridge's "Kubla Khan," which Robinson read in manuscript (Coleridge had drafted it in 1797 but did not publish it until 1816).

45   And now I'll pause to catch the moan
      Of distant breezes, cavern-pent;
   Now, ere the twilight tints are flown,
   Purpling the landscape, far and wide,
   On the dark promontory's side
50   I'll gather wild flow'rs, dew besprent,°   *sprinkled*
   And weave a crown for thee,
   Genius of Heav'n-taught poesy!
   While, op'ning to my wond'ring eyes,
   Thou bidst a new creation rise,
55   I'll raptur'd trace the circling bounds
      Of thy rich Paradise extended,
   And listen to the varying sounds
      Of winds, and foaming torrents blended.

   And now, with lofty tones inviting,
60   Thy nymph, her dulcimer swift smiting,
   Shall wake me in ecstatic measures!
   Far, far remov'd from mortal pleasures!
     In cadence rich, in cadence strong,
   Proving the wondrous witcheries of song!
65   I hear her voice! thy *sunny dome*,
   Thy *caves of ice*, aloud repeat,
   Vibrations, madd'ning sweet,
   Calling the visionary wand'rer home.
   She sings of thee, O favor'd child
70   Of *minstrelsy*, sublimely wild!
   Of thee, whose soul can feel the tone
   Which gives to airy dreams *a magic* all thy own!

Oct. 1800   1801

The Savage of Aveyron[1]

   'Twas in the mazes of a wood,
   The lonely wood of AVEYRON,
   I heard a melancholy tone:—
     It seem'd to freeze my blood!
5   A torrent near was flowing fast,

1. In remarks prefacing this poem on its first publication in the *Memoirs of the Late Mrs. Robinson*, Robinson's daughter and posthumous editor explained that her mother, then in her final illness, wrote it after reading "various accounts of a SAVAGE BOY, lately discovered in the *Forest of Aveyron* [in southern France] and said then to be existing in Paris. Frequent instances of this kind have occurred in the history of Man, and conjecture has almost uniformly been bewildered respecting the origin of such figures. In countries where BANDITTI have been known to reside, imagination may be allowed the exercise of its powers; and Reason may ruminate on the possibility, as well as the probability, of such an interesting history as that of THE SAVAGE OF AVEYRON."

In 1799 hunters at last captured this feral boy, who for several years had been spotted living alone in the woods, subsisting on acorns and roots. He appeared at that point to be about twelve years old. Efforts to educate Victor, as he came to be called, to teach him speech and attach him to social life, began soon after. Largely unsuccessful, these efforts were nevertheless watched closely, in the hope that they would resolve longstanding controversies about the boundaries and potential of human nature. The mystery of Victor's origins was never solved. He died, still an inmate of the Paris Institution for the Deaf and Mute, in 1828.

And hollow was the midnight blast
As o'er the leafless woods it past,
   While terror-fraught I stood!
O! mazy woods of AVEYRON!
10   O! wilds of dreary solitude!
   Amid thy thorny alleys rude
I thought myself alone!
    I thought no living thing could be
    So weary of the world as me,—
15 While on my winding path the pale moon shone.

    Sometimes the tone was loud and sad,
And sometimes dulcet, faint, and slow;
And then a tone of frantic woe:
    It almost made me mad.
20 The burthen was "Alone! alone!"
And then the heart did feebly groan;—
Then suddenly a cheerful tone
    Proclaim'd a spirit glad!
O! mazy woods of AVEYRON!
25   O! wilds of dreary solitude!
   Amid your thorny alleys rude
I wish'd myself—a traveller alone.

    "Alone!" I heard the wild boy say,—
And swift he climb'd a blasted oak:
30 And there, while morning's herald woke,
    He watch'd the opening day.
Yet dark and sunken was his eye,
Like a lorn° maniac's, wild and shy,   *forlorn*
And scowling like a winter sky,
35   Without one beaming ray!
Then, mazy woods of AVEYRON!
    Then, wilds of dreary solitude!
   Amid thy thorny alleys rude
I sigh'd to be—a traveller alone.

40   "Alone, alone!" I heard him shriek,
'Twas like the shriek of dying man!
And then to mutter he began,—
    But, O! *he could not speak!*
I saw him point to Heav'n, and sigh,
45 The big drop trembl'd in his eye;
And slowly from the yellow sky,
    I saw the pale morn break.
I saw the woods of AVEYRON.
    Their wilds of dreary solitude:
50   I mark'd their thorny alleys rude,
And wish'd to be—a traveller alone!

    His hair was long and black, and he
From infancy *alone* had been:
For since his fifth year he had seen,

55   None mark'd his destiny!
No mortal ear had heard his groan,
For him no beam of Hope had shone:
While sad he sigh'd—*"alone, alone!"*
   Beneath the blasted tree.
60 And then, O! woods of AVEYRON,
   O! wilds of dreary solitude,
   Amid your thorny alleys rude
I thought myself a traveller—alone.

   And now upon the blasted tree
65 He carv'd *three* notches, broad and long,
And all the while he sang a song—
   Of nature's melody!
And though of words he nothing knew,
And, though his dulcet tones were few,
70 Across the yielding bark he drew,
   Deep sighing, notches THREE.
O! mazy woods of AVEYRON,
   O! wilds of dreary solitude,
   Amid your thorny alleys rude
75 Upon this BLASTED OAK no sun beam shone!

   And now he pointed one, two, three;
Again he shriek'd with wild dismay;
And now he paced the thorny way,
   Quitting the blasted tree.
80 It was a dark December morn,
The dew was frozen on the thorn:
But to a wretch so sad, so lorn,
   All days alike would be!
Yet, mazy woods of AVEYRON,
85   Yet, wilds of dreary solitude,
   Amid your frosty alleys rude
I wish'd to be—a traveller alone.

   He follow'd me along the wood
To a small grot° his hands had made,   *cave, grotto*
90 Deep in a black rock's sullen shade,
   Beside a tumbling flood.
Upon the earth I saw him spread
Of wither'd leaves a narrow bed,
Yellow as gold, and streak'd with red,
95   They look'd like streaks of blood!
Pull'd from the woods of AVEYRON,
   And scatter'd o'er the solitude
   By midnight whirlwinds strong and rude,
To pillow the scorch'd brain that throbb'd alone.

100   Wild berries were his winter food,
With them his sallow lip was dy'd;
On chestnuts wild he fed beside,
   Steep'd in the foamy flood.

Chequer'd with scars his breast was seen,
105 Wounds streaming fresh with anguish keen,
And marks where other wounds had been
   Torn by the brambles rude.
Such was the boy of AVEYRON,
   The tenant of that solitude,
110   Where still, by misery unsubdued,
He wander'd *nine long winters*, all alone.

   Before the step of his rude throne,
The *squirrel* sported, tame and gay;
The *dormouse* slept its life away,
115   Nor heard his midnight groan.
About his form a garb he wore,
Ragged it was, and mark'd with gore,
And yet, where'er 'twas folded o'er,
   Full many a spangle shone!
120 Like little stars, O! AVEYRON,
   They gleam'd amid thy solitude;
   Or like, along thy alleys rude,
The summer dew-drops sparkling in the sun.

It once had been a lady's vest,°   *robe, gown*
125 White as the whitest mountain's snow,
Till ruffian hands had taught to flow
   The fountain of her breast!
Remembrance bade the WILD BOY trace
Her beauteous form, her angel face,
130 Her eye that beam'd with Heavenly grace.
   Her fainting voice that blest,—
When in the woods of AVEYRON,
   Deep in their deepest solitude,
   Three barb'rous ruffians shed her blood,
135 And mock'd, with cruel taunts, her dying groan.

   Remembrance trac'd the summer bright,
When all the trees were fresh and green,
When lost, the alleys long between,
   The lady past the night:
140 She past the night, bewilder'd wild,
She past it with her fearless child,
Who raised his little arms, and smil'd
   To see the morning light.
While in the woods of AVEYRON,
145   Beneath the broad oak's canopy.
   She mark'd aghast the RUFFIANS THREE,
Waiting to seize the traveller alone!

   Beneath the broad oak's canopy
The lovely lady's bones were laid;
150 But since that hour no breeze has play'd
   About the blasted tree!
The leaves all wither'd ere the sun

His next day's rapid course had run,
And ere the summer day was done
155   It winter seem'd to be:
And still: O! woods of AVEYRON,
  Amid thy dreary solitude
  The oak a sapless trunk has stood,
To mark the spot where MURDER foul was done!

160   From HER the WILD BOY learn'd "ALONE,"
She tried to say, *my babe will die!*
But angels caught her parting sigh,
  The BABE her *dying tone.*
And from that hour the BOY has been
165   Lord of the solitary scene,
Wand'ring the dreary shades between,
  Making his dismal moan!
Till, mazy woods of AVEYRON,
  Dark wilds of dreary solitude,
170   Amid your thorny alleys rude
I thought myself alone.
  And could a wretch more wretched be,
  More wild, or fancy-fraught than he,
Whose melancholy tale would pierce AN HEART OF STONE.

1801

The Slave Trade and the
Literature of Abolition

ate-eighteenth-century Britons prided themselves on how their constitution safe-guarded individual liberty. Yet their economy depended increasingly on wealth obtained through the enslavement of others. Members of Parliament and even the missionary arm of the Anglican Church numbered among the absentee owners of Caribbean plantations that exploited the labor of enslaved Africans. The maritime industries of Bristol and Liverpool were heavily involved in procuring this labor supply. Beginning in the seventeenth century, a "triangular trade" had been established, which saw ships sail to the west coast of Africa to buy or kidnap human cargo, voyage across the Atlantic to the New World where those slaves would be sold at a tremendous premium, and then, in the third leg of the triangle, return to Britain carrying the colonial goods that fed Europeans' growing appetites for tobacco, rum, and sugar. By the 1790s more than 40,000 Africans annually were being packed into British slave ships. The mortality rate for these people during the horrific Middle Passage has been estimated at one in six. One-third died within three years of disembarking in the West Indies, from tropical diseases or the mistreatment and sexual abuse meted out to them on the plantations.

Through the first three-quarters of the eighteenth century, those few British people who had considered these evils at all had for the most part rationalized them away. Slavery seemed simply the cost of doing business in the New World, and the West Indian planters' rights to secure possession of their property, even property in persons, appeared beyond challenge. The link between slave labor and the consumer pleasures that defined their daily lives escaped most people's notice. "How little think the giddy and the gay / While sipping o'er the sweets of charming tea, / . . . How oft their lux'ry robs the wretch of rest," lamented one Mary Birkett in her 1789 poem on the slave trade. Whereas across the Atlantic the white settlers of the southern United States and the white elites of the Sugar Islands were outnumbered and continually anxious, with reason, that the enslaved might revolt and avenge their wrongs, white Britons, by contrast, contrived to enjoy the fruits of slavery without meditating on its costs.

The movement for abolishing the slave trade that was launched in the 1780s challenged that willful ignorance. The abolitionists mobilized the power that the stories and poems they distributed had to break down the boundaries between "out there" and "in here"; they brought distant suffering and violence home. Almost every major poet working in the late eighteenth century wrote for their cause. (For proslavery writers, by contrast, prose was overwhelmingly the medium of choice.) In amassing, in an often lurid idiom, a dossier of national crime, this literature changed how the public thought about collective moral responsibility. It also evidenced the power that might accrue to those who harnessed the emergent force of mass literacy.

At its 1787 launch the Society for Effecting the Abolition of the Trade in Slaves comprised only a small circle: Thomas Clarkson, most famously, the lawyer Granville Sharp, the Quaker publisher James Phillips, and a few others. Nonetheless, abolitionism fast became a popular movement. That same year, two-thirds of the adult male population of Manchester signed petitions calling on Parliament to investigate the trade. Later 300,000 families pledged to abstain from purchasing Caribbean sugar. Though marginalized by later historians, members of Britain's black community, an impoverished group who at this time numbered ten to fifteen thousand, also found public voices in the struggle. There were black writers such as Olaudah Equiano and Ottobah Cuguano and, before them, figures such as James Somerset, the slave who

95

had the audacity to test white men's law and so force the judiciary to declare outright, in the Mansfield Judgement of 1772, that in fact there was no legal basis for slavery on English ground.

It was difficult for these activists to parlay altered public opinion into legislative action. William Wilberforce, the Society's chief representative in Parliament, was consistently outmaneuvered by proslavery politicians, who variously dismissed the witnesses he introduced, cited biblical precedents legitimizing modern slavery, or insisted that, thanks to their owners' benevolent care, West Indian slaves were better off than British laborers. His motions for abolition were repeatedly voted down or allowed to die in committee, defeats bitterly memorialized in Anna Letitia Barbauld's 1791 poem "Epistle to William Wilberforce" (on p. 46). The radical turn that revolutionary activity in France took in the 1790s proved another setback. Proslavery agitators seized the opportunity to portray abolition as dangerous to social stability. The petitioning among white British subjects that had occurred in the early stages of the abolitionist campaigning looked different in this altered context: a menacing attempt on the part of the governed to overawe their rightful governors. Then revolution in the French sugar colony of Saint Domingue (modern Haiti), led by former slaves Jean-Jacques Dessalines and Toussaint l'Ouverture, occasioned a new racist demonology: the carnage was decried as the inevitable consequence of recklessly introducing primitive minds to modern politics' "schemes of perfection."

Nonetheless, subsequent events made apparent the penalties Britain would pay for continued support of colonial slavery. The few British soldiers who survived their tours of duty in the West Indies during the Revolutionary and Napoleonic Wars returned with news of just how resolute an enemy slaves seeking their freedom could be. Napoleon's reintroduction of slavery into the French Empire in 1802 enabled supporters of abolition to parry the suggestion that the disruption of this lucrative British industry would aid Britain's commercial rivals: instead they could link support for their cause to the war effort. In 1807 Parliament at last voted for abolition.

Wishfully, Wilberforce, Clarkson, and their associates had proposed that with the ending of the trade, slavery itself would naturally and immediately cease to be. In fact, freedom was long in arriving in the empire. It took twenty-six years; another wave of political agitation in England spearheaded by a new antislavery society; bloody rebellions in Barbados (1816), Guyana (1823), and Jamaica (1831); and finally a reform of Parliament that reduced the number of votes controlled by the West Indian interests before the Emancipation Bill was enacted.

The strategies for depicting violence, suffering, and retaliation that anti- and proslavery writers developed over the course of this long debate altered the cultural landscape. The influence of their writings is discernible throughout Romantic literature, in Romantic authors' apocalyptic imaginings, explorations of themes of guilt and confession, interest in the workings of pity, and consciousness of how language can fail in the face of atrocity. The texts that follow, which in the main document the early phase of the abolitionist movement, suggest the variety of moves writers made to galvanize the attention of the reading public.

JOHN NEWTON

John Newton (1725–1807) is remembered today as the author of "Amazing Grace," a beautiful hymn interwoven in complex ways with the history of slavery. By 1852 the hymn was so important to the tradition of African American gospel music that the novelist Harriet Beecher Stowe arranged for her slave hero in *Uncle Tom's Cabin* to sing it at a moment of despondency. There is a second, conflicting way, though, in which "Amazing Grace" is linked to the history of slavery—through the biography of its author. When in 1779 Newton wrote "Faith's Review and Expectation" (as "Amazing Grace" was originally titled), he was already a celebrity minister in the Anglican Church, famous for the narrative of his spiritual awakening he had published in 1764. He was also a former captain of a slave ship, who during the 1750s had made three voyages down Africa's Windward coast, doing so *after* his conversion. Late in life, Newton looked back at his slaver past a second time as he stepped forth in print as a champion of abolition. To read "Amazing Grace" alongside this book *Thoughts upon the African Slave Trade* (1788), which Newton presented as his act of "public confession," is to see how Evangelical Christianity's themes of sin and redemption provided a framework for the abolitionists' political engagement. It suggests how the abolitionists' preoccupation with their own spiritual welfare would overshadow sometimes their consciousness of African suffering.

Faith's Review and Expectation
(Amazing Grace)

Amazing grace! (how sweet the sound)
    That sav'd a wretch like me!
I once was lost, but now am found,
    Was blind, but now I see.

5 'Twas grace that taught my heart to fear,
    And grace my fears reliev'd;
How precious did that grace appear,
    The hour I first believ'd!

Thro' many dangers, toils and snares,
10   I have already come;
'Tis grace has brought me safe thus far,
    And grace will lead me home.

The Lord has promis'd good to me,
    His word my hope secures;
15 He will my shield and portion be,
    As long as life endures.

Yes, when this flesh and heart shall fail,
    And mortal life shall cease;
I shall possess, within the vail,
20   A life of joy and peace.

> The earth shall soon dissolve like snow,
> The sun forbear to shine;
> But God who call'd me here below,
> Will be for ever mine.

1779

THOMAS CLARKSON

Thomas Clarkson (1760–1846) was merely seeking academic honors when he chanced to enter a Latin composition contest on the topic of slavery. However, the evidence the recent Cambridge graduate gathered to prepare his essay shocked him deeply. He won the prize and had an epiphany: "A thought came into my mind," he wrote, looking back in his riveting *History of the Rise, Progress and Accomplishment of the Abolition of the Slave-Trade* (1808), "that if the contents of the Essay were true, it was time some person should see these calamities to their end." Forgoing the church career that awaited him, Clarkson arranged to publish an English version of his essay and began traveling. This determined activist would cover 35,000 miles on horseback over the following seven years. He scoured England for witnesses who might testify to the suffering that slavery inflicted on its victims, a group that for Clarkson, as for Newton, included the working-class seamen who were often "impressed"—recruited by force—into its service. Sometimes at great risk to himself (the Liverpool merchants wanted him dead), he assembled the first comprehensive account of the slave trade. Whether by excavating ships' muster rolls stored in London's Custom House or inventorying the shackles, thumbscrews, and instruments for force feeding that he found for sale in Liverpool marine supply shops, Clarkson empowered abolitionism with hard facts. Clarkson's genius, however, also lay in his realization that antislavery writing would need to tap the resources of imaginative literature so as to bring those facts from faraway up close and prompt readers to reimagine themselves as witnesses to slavery's atrocities. Pivoting on what the author calls an "Imaginary scene in Africa" and an "Imaginary conversation with an African," the first text reprinted here, from the opening of part III of Clarkson's *Essay* (the revised 1788 edition), suggests his technique. In the second excerpt from his *Essay*, Clarkson first details the "accommodation" slaves experience during the Middle Passage and then tells the story of a particular voyage: that of the *Zong*, whose captain in September 1781 ordered more than a hundred slaves thrown overboard so that the ship's owners could collect on the insurance policy they had taken out on their cargo.

From Essay on the Slavery and Commerce of the Human Species

From *Part III, Chapter 1 ("Imaginary conversation with an African")*

* * *

I shall suppose myself on a particular part of the continent of Africa, and relate a scene, which, from its agreement with unquestionable facts, might not unreasonably be presumed to have been presented to my view, had I been actually there.

And first, I will turn my eyes to the cloud of dust that is before me. It seems to advance rapidly, and, accompanied with dismal shrieks and yellings, to make the very air, that is above it, tremble as it rolls along. What can possibly be the cause? I will inquire of that melancholy African, who is walking dejected upon the shore; whose eyes are stedfastly fixed on the approaching object, and whose heart, if I can judge from the appearance of his countenance, must be greatly agitated.

"Alas!" says the the unhappy African, "the cloud that you see approaching, rises from a train of wretched slaves. They are going to the ships behind you. They are destined for the English colonies, and, if you will stay here but for a little time, you will see them pass. They arrived here about two days ago from the inland country. I saw the fleet come in, which had gone to fetch them, and, upon looking into the different canoes, found them lying at the bottom, their hands and feet being tied together. As soon as they were landed, they were conveyed to the houses of the black traders, which you see at a little distance, where they were immediately oiled, and fed, and made up for sale." * * *

We then discovered that the inhabitants of the depopulated village had all of them passed us, and that the part of the train, to which we were now opposite, was a body of kidnapped people. Here we indulged our imagination. We thought we beheld in one of them a father, in another an husband, and in another a son, each of whom was forced from his various and tender connections, and without even the opportunity of bidding them adieu. While we were engaged in these and other melancholy reflections, the whole body of slaves had intirely passed us. We turned almost insensibly to look at them again, when we discovered an unhappy man at the end of the train, who could scarcely keep pace with the rest. His feet seemed to have suffered much, either from the fetters, which had confined them in the canoe, or from long and constant travelling, for he was limping painfully along.

"This man," resumes the African, "has travelled a considerable way. He lived at a great distance from hence, and had a large family, for whom he was daily to provide. As he went out one night to a neighbouring spring, to procure water for his thirsty children, he was kidnapped by two *slave-hunters*, who sold him in the morning to some country merchants for a *bar of iron*. These drove him with other slaves, procured almost in the same manner, to the nearest market, where some of the travelling traders purchased him for a *pistol*. These handed him down to the fair, from whence the canoes fetched him. His wife and children have been long waiting for his return. But he is gone for ever from their sight: and they must be now disconsolate, being certain by his delay, that he must have fallen into the hands of the *Christians*."

"And now, as I have mentioned the name of *Christians*, a name, by which the Europeans distinguish themselves from us, I could wish to be informed of the meaning which such an appellation may convey. They consider themselves as *men*, but us unfortunate Africans, whom they term *Heathens*, as the beasts that serve us. But ah! how different is the fact! What is *Christianity*, but a system of *murder* and *oppression*? The cries and yells of the unfortunate people, who are now soon to embark for the regions of servitude, have already pierced my heart. Have you not heard me sigh while we have been talking? Do you not see the tears that now trickle down my cheeks? and yet these hardened *Christians* are unable to be moved at all: nay, they will scourge them amidst their groans, and even smile, while they are torturing them to death. Happy, happy Heathenism! which can detest the vices of Christianity, and feel for the distresses of mankind."

"But" I reply, "You are totally mistaking: *Christianity* is the most perfect and lovely of moral systems. It blesses even the hand of persecution itself, and returns good for evil. But the people against whom you so justly declaim, are not *Christians*. They are *infidels*. They are *monsters*. They are out of the common course of nature. Their countrymen at home are generous and brave. They support the sick, the lame, and the blind. They fly to the succour of the distressed. They have noble and stately buildings for the sole purpose of benevolence. They are in short, of all nations, the most remarkable for humanity and justice."

"But why then," replies the honest African, "do they suffer this? Why is Africa a scene of blood and desolation? Why are her children wrested from her, to administer to the luxuries and greatness of those whom they never offended? And why are these dismal cries in vain?"

"Alas!" I reply again, "can the cries and groans, with which the air now trembles, be heard across this extensive continent? Can the southern winds convey them to the ear of Britain? If they could reach the generous Englishman at home, they would pierce his heart, as they have already pierced your own. He would sympathize with you in your distress. He would be enraged at the conduct of his countrymen, and resist their tyranny."—

But here a shriek unusually loud, accompanied with a dreadful rattling of chains, interrupted the discourse. * * *

From *Part III, Chapter 3* (*"The dimensions of a slave vessel" and the* Zong *Incident*)

* * *

As much has been said by the advocates for this trade, of the accommodation which slaves experience during the middle passage, I shall say a few words on that head.

The height of their apartments varies of course according to the size of the vessel, but may be stated to be from six feet to less than three; so that it is impossible for them to stand erect in most of the vessels that transport them, and in some scarcely to sit down in the same posture.

In cases of this kind it is better to be explicit, and to mention particular facts. I shall therefore give the reader the dimensions of two vessels that sailed about six months ago, from a British port to the Coast of Africa, for slaves. I do not mean as tenders[1] to other ships, but to collect them on their own account, and to carry them to the colonies.

One of them was a vessel of *twenty-five* tons. The length of the upper part of the hold, or roof of the rooms where the slaves were to be confined, was thirty-one feet. The greatest breadth of the bottom or floor, was ten feet four inches, and the least five. The depth or height, was rather less than four. This vessel was calculated, and sailed for *seventy* slaves.

1. Small supply boats.

It is clear that none of the unfortunate people, perhaps at this moment on board, can stand upright, but that they must sit down, and contract their limbs within the limits of little more than three square feet, during the whole of the middle passage. I cannot compare the scene on board this vessel, to any other than that of a pen of sheep; with this difference only, that the one have the advantages of a wholesome air, while that, which the others breathe, is putrid.

The other vessel measured *eleven* tons. The length of the apartment for the slaves was twenty-two feet. The greatest breadth of the floor eight, and the least four. The depth was two feet eight inches. This vessel was calculated and sailed for *thirty* slaves.

Any person of a moderate height, standing upon dry ground, by the side of this vessel, might overlook every thing upon the deck; as her height from the keel to the beam was but five feet eight inches, three of which were engrossed by ballast, cargo, and provisions, and the rest was left for—*slaves*.

The only idea, that will perhaps strike the reader, in examining these dimensions, will be, that the apartment must be in shape and size, as well as in heat, similar to an *oven*. I know of no other object of just comparison; and to shew how preposterously the advocates for slavery talk, when they declaim upon the accommodations for slaves; this very *boat* was built for the pleasure and convenience of about *six* free people upon the Severn.[2]

If it should be said that the larger vessels have better accommodations, I reply, that it can only be in the height of the room, the slaves being stowed equally close. I assert farther, that in some of these they have not had so much room upon the floor by one square foot, as in those, which have been just specified; for I have known the number of slaves, which many of them have carried, and have had their apartments measured.

Being stowed then in the manner thus described, they soon begin to experience the effects, which might naturally be presumed to arise from their situation. In consequence of the pestilential breath of so many confined in so small a space, they become sickly, and from the vicissitude of heat and cold, of heat when confined below, and of cold when suddenly brought up for air, a flux[3] is generated. Whenever this disorder attacks them, no pen can be adequate to the task of describing their situation.

Imagine only for a moment the gratings to be opened, but particularly after a rain, which has occasioned them to be covered for some time.

The first scene that presents itself, is a cluster of unhappy people, who, overcome by excessive heat and stench, have fainted away.

The next that occurs, is that of one of them endeavouring to press forward to the light, to catch a mouthful of wholesome air, but hindered by the partner of his chains, who is lying dead at his feet, and whom he has not sufficient strength to drag after him.

The third is conspicuous in the instance of those, who are just on the point of fainting, and who are wallowing in the blood and mucus of the intestines, with which the floor is covered.

Such are the scenes, that universally present themselves in the case supposed; and how agonizing and insufferable their situation must have been during this period of their confinement, none, I believe, can possibly conceive, unless they had been the partners of their chains.

2. River that flows into the Bristol Channel in the West of England.
3. Diarrhea or dysentery.

* * *

With respect to the conduct of the *receivers*, I shall mention an instance, which happened in September of the year 1781.

The captain of a ship, then on the middle passage, had lost a considerable number of his slaves by death. The mortality was still spreading, and so rapidly, that it was impossible to say either where, or when it would end. Thus circumstanced, and uneasy at the thought of the loss which was likely to accrue to his owners, he began to rack his ingenuity to repair it. He came at length to the diabolical resolution of selecting those that were the most sickly, and of throwing them into the sea: conceiving, that if he could plead a necessity for the deed, the loss would devolve from the owners to the underwriters of the vessel.

The plea, which he proposed to set up, was a want of water, though neither the seamen nor the slaves had been put upon short allowance.

Thus armed, as he imagined, with an invincible excuse, he began to execute his design. He selected accordingly *one hundred* and *thirty-two* of the most sickly of the slaves. *Fifty-four* of these were immediately thrown into the sea, and *forty-two* were made to be partakers of their fate on the succeeding day.

But here, as if Providence expressly disapproved of the design, and had determined to cut off his excuse for sacrificing the rest, and exhibit a proof against him, a shower of rain immediately succeeded the transaction, and lasted for three days.

Notwithstanding this, the *remaining twenty-six* were brought upon deck to complete the number of victims, which avarice had at first determined to sacrifice to her shrine. The first sixteen submitted to be thrown into the sea; but the rest, with a noble resolution, would not suffer the contaminated *receivers* to touch them, but leapt after their companions, and shared their fate.

Thus was perpetrated a deed, unparalleled in the memory of man, or in the history of former times, and of so black and complicated a nature, that were it to be perpetuated to future generations, and to rest on the testimony of an individual, it could not possibly be believed.

I have now afforded a specimen, though in a manner inadequate to convey a just idea, of the different tragical scenes, that happen during the middle passage, and before the arrival of the vessels at their destined ports. To mention others, would be only to increase a painful, and to perform an unnecessary task. I shall therefore close my description here, sorry that, though I have studied to be concise, I should have felt myself obliged to lay open to the feelings of the reader, such a source of uneasiness and pain.

1788

WILLIAM COWPER

T he life of William Cowper (1731–1800) was darkened by recurrent struggles with mental illness and, in later years, by his conviction of his certain damnation: his attempt at suicide in 1763 was, he believed, the one sin for which no divine forgiveness could be obtained. Cowper sought relief from this knowledge of his outcast condition in country seclusion. Fleeing London, where he had studied law, in 1768 he settled with his friends the Unwins in rural Olney. There Cowper became a neighbor of John Newton with whom he co-authored the *Olney Hymns* (1779). The poetry he published afterward, especially his long poem in meditative blank verse, *The Task* (1785), made him the most widely read poet of his generation, an inspiration for Charlotte Smith, Blake, Wordsworth, and Coleridge. Also contributing to Cowper's fame were the handful of short poems supporting abolition that he published in the late 1780s. "The Negro's Complaint"—one of the most powerful of these poems thanks to its unsettling use of ballad form and its self-asserting speaker prophesying divine retribution—was commissioned by the Society for Effecting the Abolition of the Trade in Slaves. They added the subtitle "A subject for conversation at the tea table" and arranged for thousands of copies to be printed and mailed across England.

The Negro's Complaint

To the tune of "Hosier's Ghost" or
As near Porto Bello lying.

Forced from Home and all its pleasures
  Afric's coast I left forlorn,
To encrease a stranger's treasures
  O'er the raging billows borne;
5 Men from England bought and sold me,
  Pay'd my price in paltry gold,
But though slave they have enroll'd me
  Minds are never to be sold.

Still in thought as free as ever
10 What are England's rights, I ask,
Me from my delights to sever,
  Me to torture, me to task?
Fleecy locks and black complexion
  Cannot forfeit Nature's claim;
15 Skins may differ, but Affection
  Dwells in White and Black the same.

Why did all-creating Nature
  Make the plant for which we toil?
Sighs must fan it, tears must water,
20 Sweat of ours must dress[1] the soil.
Think, ye Masters iron-hearted
  Lolling at your jovial boards,°   *dining tables*
Think how many backs have smarted
  For the sweets your Cane affords.

25 Is there, as ye sometimes tell us,
  Is there One who reigns on high?
Has he bid you buy and sell us
  Speaking from his throne the sky?
Ask him if your knotted scourges,

---

1. Fertilize. One thing that makes sugar cane production extraordinarily labor intensive is that sugar cane thrives only with heavy manuring.

30   Matches, blood-extorting screws°   *thumbscrews*
        Are the means that Duty urges
        Agents of his Will to use?

        Hark—He answers. Wild tornadoes
        Strewing yonder flood with wrecks,
35   Wasting Towns, Plantations, Meadows,
        Are the voice with which he speaks.
        He foreseeing what vexations
        Afric's sons should undergo,
        Fix'd their Tyrants' habitations
40   Where his whirlwinds answer—No.

        By our blood in Afric wasted
        'Ere our necks received the chain,
        By the mis'ries that we tasted
        Crossing in your barks° the main,°   *ships / ocean*
45   By our suff'rings since ye brought us
        To the man-degrading mart,
        All sustain'd with patience taught us
        Only by a broken heart—

        Deem our nation Brutes no longer
50   'Till some reason ye shall find
        Worthier of regard and stronger
        Than the Colour of our Kind.
        Slaves of Gold! Whose sordid dealings
        Tarnish all your boasted pow'rs
55   Prove that *You* have Human Feelings
        'Ere ye proudly question *Ours.*

1788   1789

OLAUDAH EQUIANO

"Written by Himself": the words concluding the title given to Equiano's 1789 memoir themselves make a statement about this African's literacy and membership in the community of rational argumentation. "The life of an African written by himself is certainly a curiosity," wrote Mary Wollstonecraft in her review, "as it has been a favourite philosophic whim to degrade the numerous nations, on whom the sun-beams more directly dart, . . . and hastily to conclude that nature . . . designed to stamp them with a mark of slavery." "Written by Himself" also encapsulates the challenge that his *Narrative* posed not only to British racism but also to the iconography of African passivity elaborated in many abolitionist writings. These tended to picture the slave trade's black victims as recipients either of white people's malice or their mercy: in this iconography suicide was blacks' only self-assertive act.

Recent archival discoveries indicate that Equiano (ca. 1745–1797) must at some moments in his life have told people that he had been born in South Carolina. However, many scholars continue to accept the account of his upbringing he gives within his memoir. There he identifies himself as an African by birth and explains how his idyllic childhood in what is now modern Nigeria was brought to a traumatic end when he was kidnapped by slave traders. He was shipped first to Barbados and then to North America, ending up the property of a British naval officer. He remained six years in the service of Michael Pascal, obtaining some informal education and undergoing Christian baptism. In 1763 Pascal abruptly sold him, despite previously encouraging the young man in the belief that his service had already won him his liberty. Eventually, in 1766, the Quaker who was Equiano's next purchaser permitted him to buy his freedom. The price was £40, money that Equiano earned through the skilful trading he did on the side while laboring on this master's ships. As a freeman Equiano exercised many trades before turning author: hairdresser, seaman aboard a polar expedition, even overseer on a Central American plantation founded

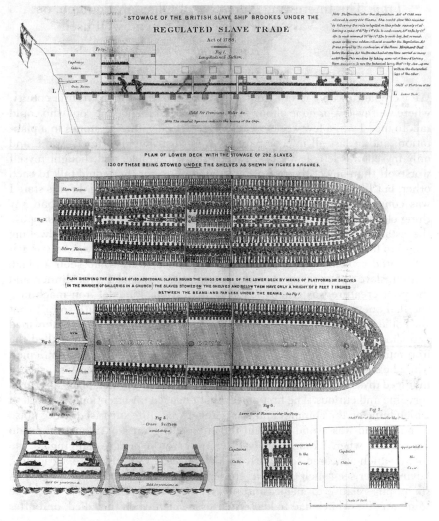

The Slave Ship *Brookes*. This engraving of the plan of a Liverpool-based slave ship, stowed with its human cargo, was published in 1789 by the Society for Effecting the Abolition of the Trade in Slaves and made, Thomas Clarkson recalled, "an instantaneous impression of horror upon all who saw it."

on slave labor. After his return to London in 1779 he both became involved in Clarkson's Committee and made allies among the working-class membership of the radical London Corresponding Society. He spent the final years of his life lecturing to promote abolition and his book, which went through multiple editions and brought Equiano the prosperity that enabled him to support in comfort his English wife and their two daughters.

Throughout the *Interesting Narrative*, which is simultaneously a travelogue, an intervention into the abolition debate, and a spiritual autobiography, Equiano construes the events of his life as a series of providential deliverances. It is part of the complex art of his narrative that, however extensive these debts to God, he comes across, as well, as one of the period's most resolute self-made men.

From The Interesting Narrative of Olaudah Equiano, or Gustavus Vassa, the African, Written by Himself

From *Chapter 3*

[FROM VIRGINIA TO ENGLAND]

We were landed up a river a good way from the sea, about Virginia county, where we saw few or none of our native Africans, and not one soul who could talk to me.[1] I was a few weeks weeding grass, and gathering stones in a plantation; and at last all my companions were distributed different ways, and only myself was left. I was now exceedingly miserable, and thought myself worse off than any of the rest of my companions; for they could talk to each other, but I had no person to speak to that I could understand. In this state I was constantly grieving and pining and wishing for death rather than any thing else. While I was in this plantation the gentleman, to whom I suppose the estate belonged, being unwell, I was one day sent for to his dwelling house to fan him; when I came into the room where he was I was very much affrighted at some things I saw, and the more so as I had seen a black woman slave as I came through the house, who was cooking the dinner, and the poor creature was cruelly loaded with various kinds of iron machines; she had one particularly on her head, which locked her mouth so fast that she could scarcely speak; and could not eat nor drink. I was much astonished and shocked at this contrivance, which I afterwards learned was called the iron muzzle. Soon after I had a fan put into my hand, to fan the gentleman while he slept; and so I did indeed with great fear. While he was fast asleep I indulged myself a great deal in looking about the room, which to me appeared very fine and curious. The first object that engaged my attention was a watch which hung on the chimney and was going. I was quite surprised at the noise it made, and was afraid it would tell the gentleman any thing I might do amiss: and when I immediately after observed a picture hanging in the room, which appeared constantly to look at me, I was still more affrighted, having never seen such things as these before. At one time I thought it was something relative to magic; and not seeing it move I thought it might be some way the whites had to keep their great men when they died, and offer

---

1. We pick up Equiano's story when, a young boy, having survived the voyage from Africa, he commences his life as a slave on a Virginia plantation. (For his account of the Middle Passage, see the excerpts from his *Narrative* in the NAEL Archive.)

them libation as we used to do to our friendly spirits. In this state of anxiety I remained till my master awoke, when I was dismissed out of the room, to my no small satisfaction and relief; for I thought that these people were all made up of wonders. In this place I was called Jacob; but on board the African snow[2] was called Michael. I had been some time in this miserable, forlorn, and much dejected state, without having any one to talk to, which made my life a burden, when the kind and unknown hand of the Creator (who in very deed leads the blind in a way they know not) now began to appear, to my comfort; for one day the captain of a merchant ship, called the Industrious Bee, came on some business to my master's house. This gentleman, whose name was Michael Henry Pascal, was a lieutenant in the royal navy, but now commanded this trading ship, which was somewhere in the confines of the county many miles off. While he was at my master's house it happened that he saw me, and liked me so well that he made a purchase of me. I think I have often heard him say he gave thirty or forty pounds sterling for me; but I do not now remember which. However, he meant me for a present to some of his friends in England: and I was sent accordingly from the house of my then master, one Mr. Campbell, to the place where the ship lay; I was conducted on horseback by an elderly black man (a mode of travelling which appeared very odd to me). When I arrived I was carried on board a fine large ship, loaded with tobacco, &c. and just ready to sail for England. I now thought my condition much mended; I had sails to lie on, and plenty of good victuals to eat; and every body on board used me very kindly, quite contrary to what I had seen of any white people before; I therefore began to think that they were not all of the same disposition. A few days after I was on board we sailed for England. I was still at a loss to conjecture my destiny. By this time, however, I could smatter a little imperfect English; and I wanted to know as well as I could where we were going. Some of the people of the ship used to tell me they were going to carry me back to my own country, and this made me very happy. I was quite rejoiced at the sound of going back; and thought if I should get home what wonders I should have to tell. But I was reserved for another fate, and was soon undeceived when we came within sight of the English coast. While I was on board this ship, my captain and master named me *Gustavus Vasa*.[3] I at that time began to understand him a little, and refused to be called so, and told him as well as I could that I would be called Jacob; but he said I should not, and still called me Gustavus; and when I refused to answer to my new name, which at first I did, it gained me many a cuff; so at length I submitted, and was obliged to bear the present name, by which I have been known ever since.

* * *

It was about the beginning of the spring 1757 when I arrived in England; and I was near twelve years of age at that time. I was very much struck with the buildings and the pavement of the streets in Falmouth:[4] and, indeed, any object I saw filled me with new surprise. One morning, when I got upon deck, I saw it covered all over with the snow that fell over-night: as I had

---

2. A two-masted vessel equipped with an additional half-mast.
3. After the Swedish nobleman (1496–1560) who led a successful revolt against Danish rule of his country and became Sweden's king.
4. Harbor town on England's southwest coast.

never seen any thing of the kind before, I thought it was salt; so I immediately ran down to the mate and desired him, as well as I could, to come and see how somebody in the night had thrown salt all over the deck. He, knowing what it was, desired me to bring some of it down to him: accordingly I took up a handful of it, which I found very cold indeed; and when I brought it to him he desired me to taste it. I did so, and I was surprised beyond measure. I then asked him what it was; he told me it was snow: but I could not in anywise understand him. He asked me if we had no such thing in my country; and I told him, No. I then asked him the use of it, and who made it; he told me a great man in the heavens, called God: but here again I was to all intents and purposes at a loss to understand him; and the more so, when a little after I saw the air filled with it, in a heavy shower, which fell down on the same day. After this I went to church; and having never been at such a place before, I was again amazed at seeing and hearing the service. I asked all I could about it; and they gave me to understand it was worshipping God, who made us and all things. I was still at a great loss, and soon got into an endless field of inquiries, as well as I was able to speak and ask about things. However, my little friend Dick[5] used to be my best interpreter; for I could make free with him, and he always instructed me with pleasure: and from what I could understand by him of this God, and in seeing these white people did not sell one another, as we did, I was much pleased; and in this I thought they were much happier than we Africans. I was astonished at the wisdom of the white people in all things I saw; but was amazed at their not sacrificing, or making any offerings, and eating with unwashed hands, and touching the dead. I likewise could not help remarking the particular slenderness of their women, which I did not at first like; and I thought they were not so modest and shamefaced as the African women.

I had often seen my master and Dick employed in reading; and I had a great curiosity to talk to the books, as I thought they did; and so to learn how all things had a beginning: for that purpose I have often taken up a book, and have talked to it, and then put my ears to it, when alone, in hopes it would answer me; and I have been very much concerned when I found it remained silent.

My master lodged at the house of a gentleman in Falmouth, who had a fine little daughter about six or seven years of age, and she grew prodigiously fond of me; insomuch that we used to eat together, and had servants to wait on us. I was so much caressed by this family that it often reminded me of the treatment I had received from my little noble African master.[6] After I had been here a few days, I was sent on board of the ship; but the child cried so much after me that nothing could pacify her till I was sent for again. It is ludicrous enough, that I began to fear I should be betrothed to this young lady; and when my master asked me if I would stay there with her behind him, as he was going away with the ship, which had taken in the tobacco again, I cried immediately, and said I would not leave her. At last, by stealth, one night I was sent on board the ship again; and in a little time we sailed for Guernsey, where she was in part owned by a merchant, one Nicholas Doberry. As I was

5. Richard Baker, the white American boy who befriended Equiano during the voyage from Virginia.
6. Before being traded to the Englishmen who would convey him across the Atlantic, Equiano had been a slave within an African household, where he became the playmate of the son.

now amongst a people who had not their faces scarred, like some of the African nations where I had been, I was very glad I did not let them ornament me in that manner when I was with them. When we arrived at Guernsey, my master placed me to board and lodge with one of his mates, who had a wife and family there; and some months afterwards he went to England, and left me in care of this mate, together with my friend Dick: This mate had a little daughter, aged about five or six years, with whom I used to be much delighted. I had often observed that when her mother washed her face it looked very rosy; but when she washed mine it did not look so: I therefore tried oftentimes myself if I could not by washing make my face of the same colour as my little play-mate (Mary), but it was all in vain; and I now began to be mortified at the difference in our complexions.

* * *

From *Chapter 4*

[SOLD AGAIN]

I thought now of nothing but being freed, and working for myself, and thereby getting money to enable me to get a good education; for I always had a great desire to be able at least to read and write; and while I was on shipboard I had endeavoured to improve myself in both. While I was in the Ætna[7] particularly, the captain's clerk taught me to write, and gave me a smattering of arithmetic as far as the rule of three. There was also one Daniel Queen, about forty years of age, a man very well educated, who messed with me[8] on board this ship, and he likewise dressed and attended the captain. Fortunately this man soon became very much attached to me, and took very great pains to instruct me in many things. He taught me to shave and dress hair a little, and also to read in the Bible, explaining many passages to me, which I did not comprehend. I was wonderfully surprised to see the laws and rules of my country written almost exactly here; a circumstance which I believe tended to impress our manners and customs more deeply on my memory. I used to tell him of this resemblance; and many a time we have sat up the whole night together at this employment. In short, he was like a father to me; and some even used to call me after his name; they also styled me the black Christian. Indeed I almost loved him with the affection of a son. Many things I have denied myself that he might have them; and when I used to play at marbles or any other game, and won a few halfpence, or got any little money, which I sometimes did, for shaving any one, I used to buy him a little sugar or tobacco, as far as my stock of money would go. He used to say, that he and I never should part; and that, when our ship was paid off, as I was as free as himself or any other man on board, he would instruct me in his business, by which I might gain a good livelihood. This gave me new life and spirits; and my heart burned within me, while I thought the time long till I obtained my freedom. For though my master had not promised it to me, yet, besides the assurances I had received that he had no right to detain me, he

7. Pascal was given command of this Royal Navy ship in 1759, at the height of the Seven Years' War with France.

8. Dined together, as a fellow member of the crew.

always treated me with the greatest kindness, and reposed in me an unbounded confidence; he even paid attention to my morals; and would never suffer me to deceive him, or tell lies, of which he used to tell me the consequences; and that if I did so God would not love me; so that, from all this tenderness, I had never once supposed, in all my dreams of freedom, that he would think of detaining me any longer than I wished.

In pursuance of our orders we sailed from Portsmouth for the Thames, and arrived at Deptford[9] the 10th of December, where we cast anchor just as it was high water. The ship was up about half an hour, when my master ordered the barge to be manned; and all in an instant, without having before given me the least reason to suspect any thing of the matter, he forced me into the barge; saying, I was going to leave him, but he would take care I should not. I was so struck with the unexpectedness of this proceeding, that for some time I did not make a reply, only I made an offer to go for my books and chest of clothes, but he swore I should not move out of his sight; and if I did he would cut my throat, at the same time taking his hanger.[1] I began, however, to collect myself; and, plucking up courage, I told him I was free, and he could not by law serve me so. But this only enraged him the more; and he continued to swear, and said he would soon let me know whether he would or not, and at that instant sprung himself into the barge from the ship, to the astonishment and sorrow of all on board. The tide, rather unluckily for me, had just turned downward, so that we quickly fell down the river along with it, till we came among some outward-bound West Indiamen; for he was resolved to put me on board the first vessel he could get to receive me. The boat's crew, who pulled against their will, became quite faint different times, and would have gone ashore; but he would not let them. Some of them strove then to cheer me, and told me he could not sell me, and that they would stand by me, which revived me a little; and I still entertained hopes; for as they pulled along he asked some vessels to receive me, but they could not. But, just as we had got a little below Gravesend, we came alongside of a ship which was going away the next tide for the West Indies; her name was the Charming Sally, Captain James Doran; and my master went on board and agreed with him for me; and in a little time I was sent for into the cabin. When I came there Captain Doran asked me if I knew him; I answered that I did not; "Then," said he "you are now my slave." I told him my master could not sell me to him, nor to any one else. "Why," said he, "did not your master buy you?" I confessed he did. "But I have served him," said I, "many years, and he has taken all my wages and prize-money,[2] for I only got one sixpence during the war; besides this I have been baptized;[3] and by the laws of the land no man has a right to sell me:" And I added, that I had heard a lawyer and others at different times tell my master so. They both then said that those people who told me so were not my friends; but I replied—it was very extraordinary that other people did not know the law as well as they. Upon this Captain Doran said I talked too much English; and if I did not behave

9. Site of the Royal Dockyards on the Thames River, east of London. Portsmouth is a port on England's south coast.
1. Short sword.
2. Ships captured in naval battles were sold, along with their cargoes, and the money was dis-

tributed among the victorious crew as prizes.
3. Though it had been formally repudiated in 1729 in a legal opinion issued by England's attorney general and solicitor general, the belief that their baptism as Christians should automatically release individuals from slavery persisted.

myself well, and be quiet, he had a method on board to make me. I was too well convinced of his power over me to doubt what he said; and my former sufferings in the slaveship presenting themselves to my mind, the recollection of them made me shudder.

* * *

From *Chapter 5*

[CRUELTY OF THE WEST INDIAN PLANTERS]

On the 13th of February 1763, from the mast-head, we descried our destined island Montserrat; and soon after I beheld those

"Regions of sorrow, doleful shades, where peace
And rest can rarely dwell. Hope never comes
That comes to all, but torture without end
Still urges."[4]

At the sight of this land of bondage, a fresh horror ran through all my frame, and chilled me to the heart. My former slavery now rose in dreadful review to my mind, and displayed nothing but misery, stripes, and chains; and, in the first paroxysm of my grief, I called upon God's thunder, and his avenging power, to direct the stroke of death to me, rather than permit me to become a slave, and be sold from lord to lord.

* * *

While I was in Montserrat I knew a negro man, named Emanuel Sankey, who endeavoured to escape from his miserable bondage, by concealing himself on board of a London ship: but fate did not favour the poor oppressed man; for, being discovered when the vessel was under sail, he was delivered up again to his master. This *Christian master* immediately pinned the wretch down to the ground at each wrist and ancle, and then took some sticks of sealing wax, and lighted them, and dropped it all over his back. There was another master who was noted for cruelty; and I believe he had not a slave but what had been cut, and had pieces fairly taken out of the flesh: and, after they had been punished thus, he used to make them get into a long wooden box or case he had for that purpose, in which he shut them up during pleasure. It was just about the height and breadth of a man; and the poor wretches had no room, when in the case, to move.

It was very common in several of the islands, particularly in St. Kitt's, for the slaves to be branded with the initial letters of their master's name; and a load of heavy iron hooks hung about their necks. Indeed on the most trifling occasions they were loaded with chains; and often instruments of torture were added. The iron muzzle, thumb screws, &c. are so well known, as not to need a description, and were sometimes applied for the slightest faults. I have seen a negro beaten till some of his bones were broken, for even letting a pot boil over. Is it surprising that usage like this should drive the poor creatures to despair, and make them seek a refuge in death from those evils which render their lives intolerable—while,

---

4. From Milton's description of hell: *Paradise Lost* 1.65–68, slightly misquoted (where Milton wrote "never," Equiano writes "rarely").

"With shuddering horror pale, and eyes aghast,
They view their lamentable lot, and find
No rest!"[5]

1789

5. Again citing Milton's description of hell: *Paradise Lost* 2.616–18.
  The merchant to whom, after their arrival in Montserrat, Captain Doran sells Equiano

eventually permits him to purchase his freedom. For Equiano's account of how he obtains that money and gains his liberty, see the concluding excerpt from his *Narrative* in the NAEL Archive.

HANNAH MORE AND EAGLESFIELD SMITH

The complicated publication history of "The Sorrows of Yamba" hints at how the abolitionist cause could yoke together people from divergent backgrounds and with conflicting political views. The poem was long identified as a work by Hannah More (1745–1833), an author who began her career as a playwright, but who in the 1780s, prompted by her growing Evangelicalism and the spiritual counsel of John Newton, turned her formidable energies instead to charity work and didactic and polemical writings. Some of these writings urged moral reformation on fashionable ladies. Others aimed to inculcate habits of piety, industry, and submissiveness in the newly literate poor and to steer them away from the ideas of equality filling books such as Thomas Paine's *Rights of Man*. "The Sorrows of Yamba" debuted in print as part of the "Cheap Repository," a series of tracts targeting this sector of the reading public that More and her sisters began publishing anonymously in 1795. Philanthropists bought up millions of these tracts, priced at a halfpence or penny each, so as to distribute their "entertaining" yet "useful" stories and ballads in Sunday schools, workhouses, and prisons; an Anglican bishop sent trunkfuls to the West Indies. Romanticist scholar Alan Richardson has discovered, however, that the Cheap Repository version of "The Sorrows" reworks a poem that Scottish author Eaglesfield Smith (ca. 1770–1838) appears to have sent to More in manuscript form and which he subsequently republished in the *Universal Magazine* in 1797, perhaps to reassert his authorship. Little is known about Smith, but another of his poems suggests a sympathy for the French Revolution that More would have deplored. More's far-reaching alterations of Smith's original poem converted a tragedy to a conversion narrative. The missionary who appears at line 81 in time to rescue Yamba from suicide and to redeem the reputation of white Englishmen is her invention.

From The Sorrows of Yamba; or, the Negro Woman's Lamentation

To the Tune of *Hosier's Ghost*

In St. Lucie's distant isle,[1]
  Still with Afric's love I burn;
Parted many a thousand mile,
  Never, never to return.

1. Saint Lucia, island in the eastern Caribbean Sea, claimed through the 18th century by both Britain and France.

5   Come, kind death! and give me rest;
       Yamba has no friend but thee;
    Thou canst ease my throbbing breast;
       Thou canst set the Prisoner free.

    Down my cheeks the tears are dripping,
10   Broken is my heart with grief;
    Mangled my poor flesh with whipping,
       Come, kind Death! and bring relief.

    Born on Afric's golden coast,
       Once I was as blest as you;
15   Parents tender I could boast,
       Husband dear, and children too.

    Whity man he came from far,
       Sailing o'er the briny flood;
    Who, with help of British Tar,°   *sailor*
20   Buys up human flesh and blood.

    With the baby, at my breast
       (Other two were sleeping by)
    In my hut I sat at rest,
       With no thought of danger nigh.

25   From the bush at even-tide,
       Rush'd the fierce man-stealing crew;
    Seiz'd the children by my side,
       Seiz'd the wretched Yamba too.

    Then for love of filthy gold,
30   Strait they bore me to the sea,
    Cramm'd me down a Slave-ship's hold,
       Where were hundreds stow'd like me.

    Naked on the platform lying,
       Now we cross the tumbling wave;
35   Shrieking, sickening, fainting, dying;
       Deed of shame for Britons brave!

    At the savage Captain's beck,
       Now, like brutes, they make us prance;
    Smack the cat[2] about the deck,
40   And in scorn they bid us dance.

    Nauseous horse-beans they bring nigh,
       Sick and sad we cannot eat;
    Cat must cure the sulks, they cry,
       Down their throats we'll force the meat.

45   I, in groaning pass'd the night,
       And did roll my aching head;

2. Whip called the "cat o' nine tails."

At the break of morning light,
  My poor child was cold and dead.

Happy, happy, there she lies;
50   Thou shalt feel the lash no more;
Thus full many a Negro dies,
  Ere we reach the destin'd shore.

Thee, sweet infant, none shall sell;
  Thou hast gain'd a wat'ry grave;
55 Clean escap'd the tyrants fell,
  While thy mother lives a slave.

          *   *   *

Mourning thus my wretched state
  (Ne'er may I forget the day)
75 Once in dusk of evening late,
  Far from home I dar'd to stray.

Dar'd, alas! with impious haste,
  Tow'rds the roaring sea to fly;
Death itself I long'd to taste,
80 Long'd to cast me in and die.

There I met upon the Strand,°   beach
  English Missionary good;
He had Bible book in hand,
  Which poor me no understood.

85 Led by pity from afar,
  He had left his native ground;
Thus, if some inflict a scar,
  Others fly to cure the wound.

Strait he pull'd me from the shore,
90 Bid me no self-murder do;
Talk'd of state when life is o'er,
  All from Bible good and true.

Then he led me to his cot,°   cottage
  Sooth'd and pitied all my woe;
95 Told me 'twas the Christian's lot,
  Much to suffer here below.

Told me then of God's dear Son,
  (Strange and wond'rous is the story)
What sad wrong to him was done,
100 Tho' he was the Lord of Glory

Told me, too, like one who knew him,
  (Can such love as this be true?)
How he died for them that slew him,
  Died for wretched Yamba too.

          *   *   *

125 Now I'll bless my cruel capture,
       (Hence I've known a Saviour's name)
    Till my grief is turn'd to rapture,
       And I half forget the blame.

    But tho' here a Convert rare,
130   Thanks her God for Grace divine;
    Let not man the glory share;
       Sinner, still the guilt is thine.

    Here an injured Slave forgives,
       There a host for vengeance cry;
135 Here a single Yamba lives,
       There a thousand droop and die.

                        *   *   *

                                        1795, 1797

SAMUEL TAYLOR COLERIDGE

When Coleridge and his friend Robert Southey were still planning the utopian community they hoped to establish in the Pennsylvanian wilderness,
they decided to raise funds by giving public lectures and charging admission. One of
Coleridge's lectures, given in Bristol in June 1795, was on the slave trade, an incen-
diary topic given the sources of Bristol's prosperity. Coleridge reworked his lecture
for the fourth number of his periodical *The Watchman* in March 1796. In its climax,
reproduced here, he proposes that for ethical reasons abolition should come about
not through legislation but as the consequence of British consumers' determination
to abstain from slave-grown sugar. The dining rooms in which families consume
their jams and sweetened tea are, in Coleridge's account, scenes of a deplorable failure of the moral imagination. Even women, he suggests, who are excessively ready to
empathize with the imaginary victims they encounter in their sentimental novels,
are blind to the cruelties that bring West Indian commodities to their tables.
Coleridge's lecture reveals how abolitionist rhetoric built on a long tradition of moral
strictures associating corruption and a modern taste for luxury goods.

From On the Slave Trade

                        *   *   *

The Abbé Raynal[1] computes that at the time of his writing, nine millions of
slaves had been consumed by the Europeans—add one million since, (for
it is near thirty years since his book was first published) and recollect, that
for one procured ten at least are slaughtered, that a fifth die in the pas-

---

1. Guillaume-Thomas-François Raynal, author of
the *Histoire des deux Indes* (History of the East
and West Indies), a history in French of the
wrongs of empire that became a global best seller
after its first appearance in 1770.

sage, and a third in the seasoning; and the calculation will amount to ONE HUNDRED and EIGHTY MILLION! Ye who have joined in this confederacy, ask of yourselves this fearful question—"if the God of Justice inflict on us that mass only of anguish which we have wantonly heaped on our brethren, what must a state of retribution be?" But who are they who have joined in this tartarean confederacy? Who are these kidnappers, and assassins? In all reasonings neglecting the intermediate links we attribute the final effect to the first cause. And what is the first and constantly acting cause of the Slave-trade? That cause, by which it exists and deprived of which it would immediately cease? Is it not self-evidently the consumption of its products? And does not then the guilt rest on the consumers? And is it not an allowed axiom in morality, that wickedness may be multiplied, but cannot be divided; and that the guilt of all, attaches to each one who is knowingly an accomplice? Think not of the slave-captains and slaveholders! these very men, their darkened minds, and brutalized hearts, will prove one part of the dreadful charge against you! They are more to be pitied than the slaves; because more depraved. I address myself to you who independently of all political distinctions, profess yourself Christians! As you hope to live with Christ hereafter, you are commanded to do unto others as ye would that others should do unto you. Would *you* choose, that a slave merchant should incite an intoxicated Chieftain to make war on your Country, and murder your Wife and Children before your face, or drag them with yourself to the Market? Would you choose to be sold? to have the hot iron hiss upon your breasts, after having been crammed into the hold of a Ship with so many fellow-victims, that the heat and stench, arising from your diseased bodies, should rot the very planks? Would *you*, that others should do this unto *you*? and if you shudder with selfish horror at the bare idea, do you yet dare be the occasion of it to others?—The application to the Legislature was altogether wrong. I am not convinced that on any occasion a Christian is justified in calling for the interference of secular power; but on the present occasion it was superfluous. If only one tenth part among you who profess yourselves Christians; if one half only of the Petitioners; instead of bustling about with ostentatious sensibility, were to leave off—not *all* the West-India commodities—but only Sugar and Rum, the one useless and the other pernicious—all this misery might be stopped. Gracious Heaven! At your meals you rise up, and pressing your hands to your bosoms, you lift up your eyes to God, and say, "O Lord! bless the food which thou hast given us!" A part of that food among most of you, is sweetened with Brother's Blood. "Lord! bless the food which thou hast given us?" O Blasphemy! Did God give food mingled with the blood of the Murdered? Will God bless the food which is polluted with the Blood of his own innocent children? Surely if the inspired Philanthropist of Galilee[2] were to revisit Earth, and be among the Feasters as at Cana, he would not now change water into wine, but convert the produce into the things producing, the occasion into the things occasioned. Then with our fleshly eye should we behold what even now Imagination ought to paint to us; instead of conserves, tears and blood, and for music, groanings and the loud peals of the lash!

---

2. I.e., Jesus Christ; the first miracle recounted in the Gospel of John occurs when he turns water into wine to supply the guests attending a wedding feast. See John 2.1–11.

There is observable among the Many a false and bastard sensibility that prompts them to remove those evils and those evils alone, which by hideous spectacle or clamorous outcry are present to their senses, and disturb their selfish enjoyments. Other miseries, though equally certain and far more horrible, they not only do not endeavour to remedy—they support, they fatten on them. Provided the dunghill be not before their parlour window, they are well content to know that it exists, and that it is the hot-bed of their pestilent luxuries.—To this grievous failing we must attribute the frequency of wars, and the continuance of the Slave-trade. The merchant finds no argument against it in his ledger: the citizen at the crouded feast is not nauseated by the stench and filth of the slave-vessel—the fine lady's nerves are not shattered by the shrieks! She sips a beverage sweetened with human blood, even while she is weeping over the refined sorrows of Werter or of Clementina.[3] Sensibility is not Benevolence. Nay, by making us tremblingly alive to trifling misfortunes, it frequently prevents it, and induces effeminate and cowardly selfishness. Our own sorrows, like the Princes of Hell in Milton's Pandemonium, sit enthroned "bulky and vast:" while the miseries of our fellow-creatures dwindle into pigmy forms, and are crouded, an innumerable multitude, into some dark corner of the heart.[4] There is one criterion by which we may always distinguish benevolence from mere sensibility—Benevolence impels to action, and is accompanied by self-denial.

1795   1796

3. A suffering heroine in Samuel Richardson's *Sir Charles Grandison* (1753–54). Werter is the hero of Goethe's novel *The Sorrows of Young Werther* (1774), For a similar satire—rather more playful—on how the culture of the fashionable novel encouraged a female readership to pride themselves on their sensibility, i.e., their emotional sensitivity, see Jane Austen, "Love and Friendship," on p. 553 in this volume.

4. Coleridge remembers how in book 1 of *Paradise Lost* the rank and file of Satan's followers must dwindle from "giant" to "pigmean" size so that they can all squeeze inside the palace of Pandemonium (lines 778, 780); meanwhile their leaders sit enthroned "in their own dimensions like themselves" (line 793).

WILLIAM COBBETT

The *Political Register*, a digest of news combined with commentary that appeared weekly from 1802 until 1835, made William Cobbett (1763–1835) the most influential journalist of the nineteenth century. The paper began as a loyalist organ, but, over time, as Cobbett came to support parliamentary reform, it morphed into the vehicle for an increasingly heated criticism of the government. When Cobbett launched a broadside version of the *Political Register* in 1816, priced at two pence to target working-class readers, his former allies condemned him for "poisoning the minds of the people." In this long, varied career, Cobbett's loathing for William Wilberforce was one of the few constants, with another being Cobbett's suspicion of the abolitionist cause embraced by Wilberforce and his fellow Evangelical do-gooders: mere sentimentalism, or even a plot, Cobbett sometimes implied, to direct attention away from the plight of English workers—"poor white slaves in this kingdom." A *Political Register* essay from 1823 called on Wilberforce to ponder the lives of factory workers paid starvation wages, "and then believe, if you can, . . . that we shall think you a man of humanity, making as you do such a bawling about [the blacks'] imaginary sufferings, and saying not a word about the sufferings of . . . your own country people." Olaudah Equiano's career illustrated how working-class radicalism and abolition could be fused (see p. 104), but Cobbett, convinced of Africans' racial inferiority, would not contemplate such solidarity. The editorial excerpted here appeared in the *Political Register* in the first year of its run, just as the parliamentary campaign for abolition was reviving. It takes the form of a letter that Cobbett claims to have sent six years earlier to the bishop of Rochester, warning this member of the House of Lords of dire consequences should the Abolition Bill pass.

From Slave Trade

* * *

That the sacred Scriptures of the Old and New Testament authorize a slave trade, your lordship dares not deny; nay, my lord, you must allow they do more. Under the law, the slave trade is in a manner commanded by God Almighty, and under the Gospel dispensation, the holding in slavery persons purchased as slaves, is not only mentioned by our blessed Saviour and his apostles, without censure or disapprobation, but rules are given by St. Paul and 1st Peter, how slaves ought to demean themselves to their masters.

* * *

If the purchasing slaves be now inhuman and unjust, it must always have been so; and the keeping persons in slavery, so unjustly acquired, must have been equally so: and your lordship must either allow the purchase and possession of slaves to be consistent with the law of God (unless you can shew when that law was abrogated) or acknowledge that the patriarchs, prophets, apostles, martyrs, saints, confessors, fathers, and bishops of the church of God, both under the law and the Gospel, who have purchased, sold, or possessed slaves (bond men and bond maids), have acted with cruelty, oppression, inhumanity, and injustice. Such an opinion would be directly contrary to those doctrines which your lordship teaches, and which you and Mr. Wilberforce profess to believe.

This notable discovery, of the inhumanity and injustice of the slave trade, has never been made until the present aera of anarchy and confusion, wherein impious men have presumed to set up their own ideas of humanity and justice (in contradiction to the laws of God) as the standard of perfection.

* * *

It may have hitherto escaped your lordship's attention, that the present attack on the property and reputation of the West-India planters, and the African merchants, originates from the same set of people who, one hundred and fifty years ago, voted peers and bishops to be useless. Do you think, my lord, these people to have so far changed their principles, as not to have as strong an inclination as formerly, "to bind kings in chains, and nobles in links of iron?"[1] Can you, my Lord, suppose these people less capable of injuring your lordships than they were, in the middle of the last century, because they have

---

1. A reference to the dismantling of the Anglican Church that occurred during Oliver Cromwell's Protectorate, at the height of Puritan power in England (1649–60). The quotation is from Psalms 149.8, often cited as a description of the Puritans' goals.

for their allies the philosophers, the illuminers, the atheists, and the jacobins of France? What these people have been capable of, they have already shewn you; they have availed themselves of the mistaken zeal of Mr. Wilberforce, the humane society in the Old Jewry,[2] and their missionary, the Rev. Mr. Clarkson, in preaching the doctrines of liberty and equality to the negroes.

Under pretence of abolishing slavery, and the slave trade, they have not only been the means of spreading ruin and desolation throughout the French West-India colonies, and in some of those belonging to Great-Britain (*St. Vincent's* and *Grenada*), inhabited by Frenchmen; but also of abolishing the Christian religion; imprisoning, banishing, or murdering nobles, bishops, and priests; and, as heretofore, of converting churches, and other buildings dedicated to religion, into arsenals, stables, and slaughter-houses; while the rents, revenues, and tythes of peers, bishops, and priests, have been the reward of the spoilers.

My Lord, the principal means whereby the anarchists of France have been enabled to effect their dreadful, rebellious, and anti-christian purposes, were by encouraging a disbelief of the sacred Scriptures, and revealed religion. Will the setting at naught and slighting the authority of the Scriptures (which are a strong support of our claim of right to buy slaves), strengthen that belief in them, which is the best and surest foundation on which the title of your lordships to the respect of the laity is built?

* * *

1796?   1802

2. Name of the street in the City of London where the Committee for Effecting the Abolition of the Trade in Slaves was headquartered.

MARY PRINCE

I n 1831 Mary Prince, born a slave in Bermuda sometime around 1788, then living as a freewoman in London, became the English tradition's first black female autobiographer. As the journalist Thomas Pringle explains in the preface that vouches for this often devastating memoir's authenticity, the "idea of writing Mary Prince's history was first suggested by herself." "She wished it to be done, she said"—Pringle, secretary of the Anti-Slavery Society, furthered her project by arranging for a white lady visitor to take down her words—so the "good people in England might hear from a slave what a slave had felt and suffered."

Prince's motives for recalling past sufferings were personal as well. In England, where Prince's last owner, the merchant John Wood, had brought her in 1828 to labor as a washerwoman and nanny to his children, emancipation had been the law of the land since the Mansfield Judgment. Prince was therefore quick to recognize that Wood had inadvertently presented her with an opportunity: "I knew that I was free in England," she explains. If, however, Prince returned to the West Indies, so as to rejoin the husband her master had forced her to leave behind, she would forfeit that freedom and revert to her slave status. *The History of Mary Prince* protests this dilemma. It demonstrated to the reading public of 1831, who bought up three editions of the pamphlet, that their complacency about the morality of empire was premature and that the freedom black subjects could claim under the empire's laws remained fatally qualified.

Soon after 1831 Prince disappears from the historical record. It is unknown whether publication of the *History* proved effective for Prince personally, but it doubtless helped speed passage of the Emancipation Bill in 1833.

From The History of Mary Prince, A West Indian Slave, Related by Herself

* * *

My new master was one of the owners or holders of the salt ponds,[1] and he received a certain sum for every slave that worked upon his premises, whether they were young or old. This sum was allowed him out of the profits arising from the salt works. I was immediately sent to work in the salt water with the rest of the slaves. This work was perfectly new to me. I was given a half barrel and a shovel, and had to stand up to my knees in the water, from four o'clock in the morning till nine, when we were given some Indian corn boiled in water, which we were obliged to swallow as fast as we could for fear the rain should come on and melt the salt. We were then called again to our tasks, and worked through the heat of the day; the sun flaming upon our heads like fire, and raising salt blisters in those parts which were not completely covered. Our feet and legs, from standing in the salt water for so many hours, soon became full of dreadful boils, which eat down in some cases to the very bone, afflicting the sufferers with great torment. We came home at twelve; ate our corn soup, called *blawly*, as fast as we could, and went back to our employment till dark at night. We then shovelled up the salt in large heaps, and went down to the sea, where we washed the pickle from our limbs, and cleaned the barrows and shovels from the salt. When we returned to the house, our master gave us each our allowance of raw Indian corn, which we pounded in a mortar and boiled in water for our suppers.

We slept in a long shed, divided into narrow slips, like the stalls used for cattle. Boards fixed upon stakes driven into the ground, without mat or covering, were our only beds. On Sundays, after we had washed the salt bags, and done other work required of us, we went into the bush and cut the long soft grass, of which we made trusses for our legs and feet to rest upon, for they were so full of the salt boils that we could get no rest lying upon the bare boards.

Though we worked from morning till night, there was no satisfying Mr. D——.[2] I hoped, when I left Capt. I——, that I should have been better off, but I found it was but going from one butcher to another. There was this

1. In this section Prince describes her decade of suffering as part of the labor force used in the Turks Islands to harvest salt from the *salinas*, local catchments for seawater.

2. In the Preface Pringle explains that he has suppressed the names of some of Prince's owners, Mr. D—— among them, for fear of disturbing their surviving relations. To what extent the *His-* *tory* is also marked by less visible acts of censorship—whether, as seems likely, some details in Prince's oral account, especially those involving her sexual exploitation by her masters, were omitted when it was set down in writing—is a question that scholars of slave narratives often debate.

difference between them: my former master used to beat me while raging and foaming with passion; Mr. D—— was usually quite calm. He would stand by and give orders for a slave to be cruelly whipped, and assist in the punishment, without moving a muscle of his face; walking about and taking snuff with the greatest composure. Nothing could touch his hard heart—neither sighs, nor tears, nor prayers, nor streaming blood; he was deaf to our cries, and careless of our sufferings.—Mr. D—— has often stripped me naked, hung me up by the wrists, and beat me with the cow-skin,[3] with his own hand, till my body was raw with gashes. Yet there was nothing very remarkable in this; for it might serve as a sample of the common usage of the slaves on that horrible island.

＊　＊　＊

I still live in the hope that God will find a way to give me my liberty, and give me back to my husband. I endeavour to keep down my fretting, and to leave all to Him, for he knows what is good for me better than I know myself. Yet, I must confess, I find it a hard and heavy task to do so.

I am often much vexed, and I feel great sorrow when I hear some people in this country say, that the slaves do not need better usage, and do not want to be free.[4] They believe the foreign people,[5] who deceive them, and say slaves are happy. I say, Not so. How can slaves be happy when they have the halter round their neck and the whip upon their back? and are disgraced and thought no more of than beasts?—and are separated from their mothers, and husbands, and children, and sisters, just as cattle are sold and separated? Is it happiness for a driver in the field to take down his wife or sister or child, and strip them, and whip them in such a disgraceful manner?—women that have had children exposed in the open field to shame! There is no modesty or decency shown by the owner to his slaves; men, women, and children are exposed alike. Since I have been here I have often wondered how English people can go out into the West Indies and act in such a beastly manner. But when they go to the West Indies, they forget God and all feeling of shame, I think, since they can see and do such things. They tie up slaves like hogs—moor[6] them up like cattle, and they lick them, so as hogs, or cattle, or horses never were flogged;—and yet they come home and say, and make some good people believe, that slaves don't want to get out of slavery. But they put a cloak about the truth. It is not so. All slaves want to be free—to be free is very sweet. I will say the truth to English people who may read this history that my good friend, Miss S——,[7] is now writing down for me. I have been a slave myself—I know what slaves feel—I can tell by myself what other slaves feel, and by what they have told me. The man that says slaves be quite happy in slavery—that they don't want to be free—that man is either ignorant or a lying person. I never heard a slave say so. I never heard a Buckra man[8] say so, till I heard tell of it in England. Such people ought to be ashamed of themselves. They can't do without slaves, they say. What's the reason they can't do without slaves as well as in England? No slaves here—no whips—no stocks—no punishment, except for wicked people. They hire servants in England; and if they don't like

3. A type of whip.
4. The whole of this paragraph especially, is given as nearly as was possible in Mary's precise words [Pringle's note].
5. She means West Indians [Pringle's note].
6. A West Indian phrase: to fasten or tie up [Pringle's note].

7. Susanna Strickland (1803–1885), better known by her married name, Susanna Moodie. In 1832, after her marriage to John Moodie, she emigrated to Ontario, where she earned fame as the author of several books documenting life in the Canadian colony.
8. White man.

them, they send them away: they can't lick them. Let them work ever so hard in England, they are far better off than slaves. If they get a bad master, they give warning and go hire to another. They have their liberty. That's just what *we* want. We don't mind hard work, if we had proper treatment, and proper wages like English servants, and proper time given in the week to keep us from breaking the Sabbath. But they won't give it; they will have work— work—work, night and day, sick or well, till we are quite done up; and we must not speak up nor look amiss, however much we be abused. And then when we are quite done up, who cares for us, more than for a lame horse? This is slavery. I tell it to let English people know the truth; and I hope they will never leave off to pray God, and call loud to the great King of England, till all the poor blacks be given free, and slavery done up for evermore.

1831

WILLIAM BLAKE
1757–1827

W hat William Blake called his "Spiritual Life" was as varied, free, and dramatic as his "Corporeal Life" was simple, limited, and unadventurous. His father was a London tradesman. His only formal education was in art: at the age of ten he entered a drawing school, and later he studied for a time at the school of the Royal Academy of Arts. At fourteen he entered an apprenticeship for seven years to a well-known engraver, James Basire, and began reading widely in his free time and trying his hand at poetry. At twenty-four he married Catherine Boucher, daughter of a market gardener. She was then illiterate, but Blake taught her to read and to help him in his engraving and printing. In the early and somewhat sentimentalized biographies, Catherine is represented as an ideal wife for an unorthodox and impecunious genius. Blake, however, must have been a trying domestic partner, and his vehement attacks on the torment caused by a possessive, jealous female will, which reached their height in 1793 and remained prominent in his writings for another decade, probably reflect a troubled period at home. The couple was childless.

The Blakes for a time enjoyed a moderate prosperity while Blake gave drawing lessons, illustrated books, and engraved designs made by other artists. When the demand for his work slackened, Blake in 1800 moved to a cottage at Felpham, on the Sussex seacoast, to take advantage of the patronage of the wealthy amateur of the arts and biographer William Hayley (also a supporter of Charlotte Smith), who with the best of narrow intentions tried to transform Blake into a conventional artist and breadwinner. But the caged eagle soon rebelled. Hayley, Blake wrote, "is the Enemy of my Spiritual Life while he pretends to be the Friend of my Corporeal."

At Felpham in 1803 occurred an event that left a permanent mark on Blake's mind and art—an altercation with one John Schofield, a private in the Royal Dragoons. Blake ordered the soldier out of his garden and, when Schofield replied with threats and curses against Blake and his wife, pushed him the fifty yards to the inn where he was quartered. Schofield brought charges that Blake had uttered seditious statements about king and country. Because England was at war with France, sedition was a hanging offense. Blake was acquitted—an event, according to a newspaper account, "which so gratified the auditory that the court was . . . thrown into an uproar by their

noisy exultations." Nevertheless Schofield, his fellow soldier Cock, and other participants in the trial haunted Blake's imagination and were enlarged to demonic characters who play a sinister role in *Jerusalem*. The event exacerbated Blake's sense that
ominous forces were at work in the contemporary world and led him to complicate
the symbolic and allusive style by which he veiled the radical religious, moral, and
political opinions that he expressed in his poems.

The dominant literary and artistic fashion of Blake's youth involved the notion
that the future of British culture would involve the recovery, through archaeology as
well as literary history, of an all but lost past. As an apprentice engraver who learned
to draw by sketching the medieval monuments of London churches, Blake began his
artistic career in the thick of that antiquarianism. It also informs his early lyric
poetry. *Poetical Sketches*, published when he was twenty-six, suggests Blake's affinities
with a group of later eighteenth-century writers that includes Thomas Warton, poet
and student of Middle English romance and Elizabethan verse; Thomas Gray, translator from Old Icelandic and Welsh and author, in 1757, of "The Bard," a poem about
the English conquest of Wales; Thomas Percy, the editor of the ballad collection
Reliques of Ancient English Poetry (1765); and James Macpherson, who came before
the public in the 1760s claiming to be the translator of the epic verse of a third-
century Gaelic bard named Ossian. Like these figures, Blake located the sources of
poetic inspiration in an archaic native tradition that, according to the prevailing
view of national history, had ended up eclipsed after the seventeenth century, when
French court culture, manners, and morals began their cultural ascendancy. Even in
their orientation to a visionary culture, the bards of Blake's later Prophetic Books
retain an association with this imagined version of a primitive past.

Poetical Sketches was the only book of Blake's to be set in type according to customary methods. In 1788 he began to experiment with relief etching, a method that
he called "illuminated printing" (a term associating his works with the illuminated
manuscripts of the Middle Ages) and used to produce most of his books of poems.
Working directly on a copper plate with pens, brushes, and an acid-resistant medium,
he wrote the text in reverse (so that it would print in the normal order) and also drew
the illustration; he then etched the plate in acid to eat away the untreated copper and
leave the design standing in relief. The pages printed from such plates were colored
by hand in watercolors, often by Catherine Blake, and stitched together to make up a
volume. This process was laborious and time-consuming, and Blake printed very few
copies of his books; for example, of *Songs of Innocence and of Experience* only twenty-
eight copies (some of them incomplete) are known to exist; of *The Book of Thel*, sixteen; of *The Marriage of Heaven and Hell*, nine; and of *Jerusalem*, five.

To read a Blake poem without the pictures is to miss something important: Blake
places words and images in a relationship that is sometimes mutually enlightening
and sometimes turbulent, and that relationship is an aspect of the poem's argument.
In this mode of relief etching, he published *Songs of Innocence* (1789), then added
supplementary poems and printed *Songs of Innocence and of Experience* (1794). The
two groups of poems represent the world as it is envisioned by what he calls "two
contrary states of the human soul."

Gradually Blake's thinking about human history and his experience of life and
suffering articulated themselves in the "Giant Forms" and their actions, which came
to constitute a complete mythology. As Blake's mythical character Los said, speaking
for all imaginative artists, "I must Create a System or be enslaved by another Man's."
This coherent but constantly altering and enlarging system composed the subject
matter first of Blake's "minor prophecies," completed by 1795, and then of the major
prophetic books on which he continued working until about 1820: *The Four Zoas*,
Milton, and *Jerusalem*.

In his sixties Blake gave up poetry to devote himself to pictorial art. In the course of
his life, he produced hundreds of paintings and engravings, many of them illustrations
for the work of other poets, including a representation of Chaucer's Canterbury pilgrims, a superb set of designs for the Book of Job, and a series of illustrations of Dante,
on which he was still hard at work when he died. At the time of his death, Blake was

little known as an artist and almost entirely unknown as a poet. In the mid-nineteenth century he acquired a group of admirers among the Pre-Raphaelites, who regarded him as a precursor. Since the mid-1920s Blake has finally come into his own, both in poetry and in painting, as one of the most dedicated, intellectually challenging, and astonishingly original artists. His marked influence ranges from William Butler Yeats, who edited Blake's writings and modeled his own system of mythology on Blake's, to Allen Ginsberg and other Beat writers, Philip Pullman's His Dark Materials trilogy, and the graphic novels of the present day.

The explication of Blake's cryptic prophetic books has been the preoccupation of many scholars. Blake wrote them in the persona, or "voice," of "the Bard! / Who Present, Past, & Future sees"—that is, as a British poet who follows Spenser, and especially Milton, in a lineage going back to the prophets of the Bible. "The Nature of my Work," he said, "is Visionary or Imaginative." What Blake meant by the key terms *vision* and *imagination,* however, is often misinterpreted by taking literally what he, speaking the traditional language of his great predecessors, intended in a figurative sense. "That which can be made Explicit to the Idiot," he declared, "is not worth my care." Blake was a born ironist who enjoyed mystifying his well-meaning but literal-minded friends and who took a defiant pleasure in shocking the dull and complacent "angels" of his day by being deliberately outrageous in representing his work and opinions.

Blake declared that "all he knew was in the Bible" and that "The Old & New Testaments are the Great Code of Art." This is an exaggeration of the truth that all his prophetic writings deal, in various formulations, with some aspects of the overall biblical plot of the creation and the Fall, the history of the generations of humanity in the fallen world, redemption, and the promise of a recovery of Eden and of a New Jerusalem. These events, however, Blake interprets in what he calls "the spiritual sense." For such a procedure he had considerable precedent, not in the neoplatonic and occult thinkers with whom some modern commentators align him, but in the "spiritual" interpreters of the Bible among the radical Protestant sects in seventeenth- and eighteenth-century England. In *The French Revolution, America: A Prophecy, Europe: A Prophecy,* and the trenchant prophetic satire *The Marriage of Heaven and Hell*—all of which Blake wrote in the early 1790s while he was an ardent supporter of the French Revolution—he, like Wordsworth, Coleridge, Southey, and a number of radical English theologians, represented the contemporary revolution as the purifying violence that, according to biblical prophecy, portended the imminent redemption of humanity and the world. (For discussion of these apocalyptic expectations, see "The French Revolution" in the NAEL Archive.) In Blake's later poems Orc, the fiery spirit of violent revolution, gives way as a central personage to Los, the type of the visionary imagination in the fallen world.

BLAKE'S MYTHMAKING

Blake's first attempt to articulate his full myth of humanity's present, past, and future was *The Four Zoas,* begun in 1796 or 1797. A passage from the opening statement of its theme exemplifies the long verse line (what Blake called "the march of long resounding strong heroic verse") in which he wrote his Prophetic Books and will serve also to outline the Books' vision:

> Four Mighty Ones are in every Man; a Perfect Unity
> Cannot Exist, but from the Universal Brotherhood of Eden,
> The Universal Man. To Whom be Glory Evermore, Amen. . . .
> Los was the fourth immortal starry one, & in the Earth
> Of a bright Universe Empery attended day & night
> Days & nights of revolving joy, Urthona was his name
> In Eden; in the Auricular Nerves of Human life
> Which is the Earth of Eden, he his Emanations propagated. . . .
>   Daughter of Beulah, Sing
> His fall into Division & his Resurrection to Unity.

Blake's mythical premise, or starting point, is not a transcendent God but the "Universal Man" who is God and who incorporates the cosmos as well. (Blake elsewhere describes this founding image as "the Human Form Divine" and names him "Albion.") The Fall, in this myth, is not the fall of humanity away from God but a falling apart of primal people, a "fall into Division." In this event the original sin is what Blake calls "Selfhood," the attempt of an isolated part to be self-sufficient. The breakup of the all-inclusive Universal Man in Eden into exiled parts, it is evident, serves to identify the Fall with the creation—the creation not only of man and of nature as we ordinarily know them but also of a separate sky god who is alien from humanity. Universal Man divides first into the "Four Mighty Ones" who are the Zoas, or chief powers and component aspects of humanity, and these in turn divide sexually into male Spectres and female Emanations. (Thus in the quoted passage the Zoa known in the unfallen state of Eden as Urthona, the imaginative power, separates into the form of Los in the fallen world.) In addition to Eden there are three successively lower "states" of being in the fallen world, which Blake calls Beulah (a pastoral condition of easy and relaxed innocence, without clash of "contraries"), Generation (the realm of common human experience, suffering, and conflicting contraries), and Ulro (Blake's hell, the lowest state, or limit, of bleak rationality, tyranny, static negation, and isolated Selfhood). The fallen world moves through the cycles of its history, successively approaching and falling away from redemption, until, by the agency of the Redeemer (who is equated with the human imagination and is most potently operative in the prophetic poet), it will culminate in an apocalypse. In terms of his controlling image of the Universal Man, Blake describes this apocalypse as a return to the original, undivided condition, "his Resurrection to Unity."

What is confusing to many readers is that Blake alternates this representation of the Fall (as a fragmentation of the one Primal Man into separate parts) with a different kind of representation, in terms of two sharply opposed ways of seeing the universe. In this latter mode the Fall is a catastrophic change from imaginative insight (which sees the cosmos as unified and humanized) to sight by the physical eye (which sees the cosmos as a multitude of isolated individuals in an inhuman and alien nature). In terms of this distinction, the apocalypse toward which Blake as imaginative artist strives unceasingly will enable men and women once again to envision all beings as participant in the individual life that he calls "the Universal Brotherhood of Eden"— that is, a humanized world in which all individuals, in familial union, can feel at home.

The text for Blake's writings is that of *The Complete Poetry and Prose of William Blake,* edited by David V. Erdman and Harold Bloom (rev. ed., Berkeley, 1982). Blake's erratic spelling and punctuation have been altered when the original form might mislead the reader. The editors are grateful for the expert advice of Joseph Viscomi, Robert Essick, and Alexander S. Gourlay in editing the selections from Blake.

All Religions Are One[1]

The Voice of one crying in the Wilderness[2]

The Argument. As the true method of knowledge is experiment the true faculty of knowing must be the faculty which experiences. This faculty I treat of.

1. This and the following two selections are early illuminated works, probably etched in 1788. They are directed both against 18th-century Deism, or "natural religion" (which bases its religious tenets not on scriptural revelation but on evidences of God in the natural or "organic" world), and against Christian orthodoxy, whose creed is based on a particular Scripture. In this selection Blake ironically accepts the Deistic view that all particular religions are variants of the one true religion but rejects the Deists' "Argument" that this religion is grounded on reasoning from sense experience. He attributes the one religion instead to the innate possession by all people of "Poetic Genius," i.e., of a capacity for imaginative vision.

2. Applied in the Gospels (e.g., Matthew 3.3) to John the Baptist, regarded as fulfilling the prophecy in Isaiah 39.3. Blake applies the phrase to himself, as a later prophetic voice in an alien time.

PRINCIPLE 1st. That the Poetic Genius is the true Man, and that the body or outward form of Man is derived from the Poetic Genius. Likewise that the forms of all things are derived from their Genius, which by the Ancients was call'd an Angel & Spirit & Demon.

PRINCIPLE 2d. As all men are alike in outward form, So (and with the same infinite variety) all are alike in the Poetic Genius.

PRINCIPLE 3d. No man can think write or speak from his heart, but he must intend truth. Thus all sects of Philosophy are from the Poetic Genius, adapted to the weaknesses of every individual.

PRINCIPLE 4. As none by travelling over known lands can find out the unknown, So from already acquired knowledge Man could not acquire more. Therefore an universal Poetic Genius exists.

PRINCIPLE 5. The Religions of all Nations are derived from each Nation's different reception of the Poetic Genius, which is everywhere call'd the Spirit of Prophecy.

PRINCIPLE 6. The Jewish & Christian Testaments are An original derivation from the Poetic Genius. This is necessary from the confined nature of bodily sensation.

PRINCIPLE 7th. As all men are alike (tho' infinitely various), So all Religions & as all similars have one source.

The true Man is the source, he being the Poetic Genius.

1788

There Is No Natural Religion[1]

[a]

The Argument. Man has no notion of moral fitness but from Education. Naturally he is only a natural organ subject to Sense.

I. Man cannot naturally Percieve but through his natural or bodily organs.

II. Man by his reasoning power can only compare & judge of what he has already perciev'd.

III. From a perception of only 3 senses or 3 elements none could deduce a fourth or fifth.

IV. None could have other than natural or organic thoughts if he had none but organic perceptions.

V. Man's desires are limited by his perceptions; none can desire what he has not perciev'd.

VI. The desires & perceptions of man, untaught by any thing but organs of sense, must be limited to objects of sense.

Conclusion. If it were not for the Poetic or Prophetic character the Philosophic & Experimental would soon be at the ratio of all things, & stand still unable to do other than repeat the same dull round over again.

1788

---

1. In this selection Blake presents his version of English empiricism, which derives all mental content (including the evidences from which, in "natural religion," reason is held to prove the existence of God) from perceptions by the physical senses.

There Is No Natural Religion[1]

[b]

I. Man's perceptions are not bounded by organs of perception; he percieves more than sense (tho' ever so acute) can discover.

II. Reason, or the ratio[2] of all we have already known, is not the same that it shall be when we know more.

[III lacking]

IV. The bounded is loathed by its possessor. The same dull round even of a universe would soon become a mill with complicated wheels.

V. If the many become the same as the few when possess'd, More! More! is the cry of a mistaken soul. Less than All cannot satisfy Man.

VI. If any could desire what he is incapable of possessing, despair must be his eternal lot.

VII. The desire of Man being Infinite, the possession is Infinite & himself Infinite.

Application. He who sees the Infinite in all things sees God. He who sees the Ratio only sees himself only.

Therefore God becomes as we are, that we may be as he is.

1788

From Songs of Innocence and of Experience[1]

SHEWING THE TWO CONTRARY STATES OF THE HUMAN SOUL

From Songs of Innocence

Introduction

Piping down the valleys wild
Piping songs of pleasant glee
On a cloud I saw a child,
And he laughing said to me,

---

1. In this third document Blake presents his assertions (in opposition to those in the preceding tract) that knowledge is not limited to the physical senses, but is as unbounded as the infinite desires of humankind and its godlike capacity for infinite vision.

2. In Latin *ratio* signifies both "reason" and "calculation." Blake applies the term derogatorily to the 18th-century concept of reason as a calculating faculty whose operations are limited to sense perceptions.

1. *Songs of Innocence* was etched in 1789, and in 1794 was combined with additional poems under the title *Songs of Innocence and of Experience*; this collection was reprinted at various later times with varying arrangements of the poems. In his songs of innocence Blake assumes the stance that he is writing "happy songs / Every child may joy to hear," but they do not all depict an innocent and happy world; many of them incorporate injustice,

evil, and suffering. These aspects of the fallen world, however, are represented as they appear to a "state" of the human soul that Blake calls "innocence" and that he expresses in a simple pastoral language, in the tradition both of Isaac Watts's widely read *Divine Songs for Children* (1715) and of the picture books for child readers pioneered by mid-18th-century booksellers such as John Newbery. The vision of the same world, as it appears to the "contrary" state of the soul that Blake calls "experience," is an ugly and terrifying one of poverty, disease, prostitution, war, and social, institutional, and sexual repression, epitomized in the ghastly representation of modern London. Though each stands as an independent poem, a number of the songs of innocence have a matched counterpart, or "contrary," in the songs of experience. Thus "Infant Joy" is paired with "Infant Sorrow," and the meek "Lamb" reveals its other aspect of divinity in the flaming, wrathful "Tyger."

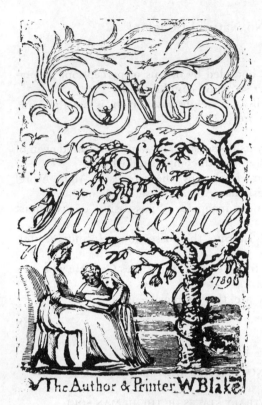

Separate title page for *Songs of Innocence* (1789), *Songs of Innocence and of Experience*, plate 3, copy C, ca. 1801.

5   Pipe a song about a Lamb;
    So I piped with merry chear;
    Piper pipe that song again—
    So I piped, he wept to hear.

    Drop thy pipe thy happy pipe
10   Sing thy songs of happy chear;
    So I sung the same again
    While he wept with joy to hear.

    Piper sit thee down and write
    In a book that all may read—
15   So he vanish'd from my sight.
    And I pluck'd a hollow reed,

    And I made a rural pen,
    And I stain'd the water clear,
    And I wrote my happy songs
20   Every child may joy to hear.

1789

The Ecchoing Green

The Sun does arise,
And make happy the skies.
The merry bells ring
To welcome the Spring.
5   The sky-lark and thrush,
The birds of the bush,
Sing louder around,
To the bells' chearful sound.
While our sports shall be seen
10   On the Ecchoing Green.

Old John with white hair
Does laugh away care,
Sitting under the oak,
Among the old folk.
15   They laugh at our play,
And soon they all say:
Such, such were the joys.
When we all, girls & boys,
In our youth-time were seen,
20   On the Ecchoing Green.

Till the little ones weary
No more can be merry
The sun does descend,
And our sports have an end:
25   Round the laps of their mothers,
Many sisters and brothers,
Like birds in their nest,
Are ready for rest;
And sport no more seen,
30   On the darkening Green.

1789

The Lamb[1]

Little Lamb, who made thee?
  Dost thou know who made thee?
Gave thee life & bid thee feed,
By the stream & o'er the mead;
5 Gave thee clothing of delight,
Softest clothing wooly bright;
Gave thee such a tender voice,
Making all the vales rejoice!
  Little Lamb who made thee?
10 Dost thou know who made thee?

---

1. The opening of this poem mimes the form of the catechistic questions and answers customarily used for children's religious instruction.

Little Lamb I'll tell thee,
Little Lamb I'll tell thee!
He is callèd by thy name,
For he calls himself a Lamb;
15   He is meek & he is mild,
He became a little child;
I a child & thou a lamb,
We are callèd by his name.
    Little Lamb God bless thee.
20   Little Lamb God bless thee.

1789

The Little Black Boy

My mother bore me in the southern wild,
And I am black, but O! my soul is white;
White as an angel is the English child,
But I am black as if bereav'd of light.

5   My mother taught me underneath a tree,
And sitting down before the heat of day,
She took me on her lap and kissèd me,
And pointing to the east, began to say:

Look on the rising sun: there God does live
10   And gives his light, and gives his heat away;
And flowers and trees and beasts and men receive
Comfort in morning, joy in the noon day.

And we are put on earth a little space,
That we may learn to bear the beams of love,
15   And these black bodies and this sun-burnt face
Is but a cloud, and like a shady grove.

For when our souls have learn'd the heat to bear,
The cloud will vanish; we shall hear his voice,
Saying: Come out from the grove, my love & care,
20   And round my golden tent like lambs rejoice.

Thus did my mother say, and kissèd me;
And thus I say to little English boy:
When I from black and he from white cloud free,
And round the tent of God like lambs we joy,

25   I'll shade him from the heat till he can bear
To lean in joy upon our father's knee.
And then I'll stand and stroke his silver hair,
And be like him, and he will then love me.

1789

The Chimney Sweeper

When my mother died I was very young,
And my father sold me while yet my tongue
Could scarcely cry 'weep! 'weep! 'weep! 'weep![1]
So your chimneys I sweep & in soot I sleep.

5   There's little Tom Dacre, who cried when his head
That curl'd like a lamb's back, was shav'd, so I said,
Hush, Tom! never mind it, for when your head's bare,
You know that the soot cannot spoil your white hair.

And so he was quiet, & that very night,
10   As Tom was a-sleeping he had such a sight!
That thousands of sweepers, Dick, Joe, Ned, & Jack,
Were all of them lock'd up in coffins of black;

And by came an Angel who had a bright key,
And he open'd the coffins & set them all free;
15   Then down a green plain, leaping, laughing they run,
And wash in a river and shine in the Sun.

Then naked & white, all their bags left behind,
They rise upon clouds, and sport in the wind.
And the Angel told Tom, if he'd be a good boy,
20   He'd have God for his father & never want joy.

And so Tom awoke; and we rose in the dark
And got with our bags & our brushes to work.
Tho' the morning was cold, Tom was happy & warm;
So if all do their duty, they need not fear harm.

1789

The Divine Image

To Mercy, Pity, Peace, and Love,
All pray in their distress,
And to these virtues of delight
Return their thankfulness.

5   For Mercy, Pity, Peace, and Love,
Is God, our father dear:
And Mercy, Pity, Peace, and Love,
Is Man, his child and care.

For Mercy has a human heart,
10   Pity, a human face,

---

1. The child's lisping attempt at the chimney sweeper's street cry, "Sweep! Sweep!"

And Love, the human form divine,
And Peace, the human dress.

Then every man of every clime,
That prays in his distress,
15 Prays to the human form divine,
Love, Mercy, Pity, Peace.

And all must love the human form,
In heathen, Turk, or Jew.
Where Mercy, Love, & Pity dwell,
20 There God is dwelling too.

1789

Holy Thursday[1]

'Twas on a Holy Thursday, their innocent faces clean,
The children walking two & two, in red & blue & green;
Grey headed beadles[2] walkd before with wands as white as snow,
Till into the high dome of Paul's they like Thames' waters flow.

5 O what a multitude they seemd, these flowers of London town!
Seated in companies they sit with radiance all their own.
The hum of multitudes was there, but multitudes of lambs,
Thousands of little boys & girls raising their innocent hands.

Now like a mighty wind they raise to heaven the voice of song,
10 Or like harmonious thunderings the seats of heaven among.
Beneath them sit the agèd men, wise guardians of the poor;
Then cherish pity, lest you drive an angel from your door.[3]

ca. 1784   1789

Nurse's Song

When the voices of children are heard on the green
And laughing is heard on the hill,
My heart is at rest within my breast
And everything else is still.

5 Then come home my children, the sun is gone down
And the dews of night arise;
Come, come, leave off play, and let us away
Till the morning appears in the skies.

1. A special day during the Easter season when the poor (frequently orphaned) children of the charity schools of London—sometimes as many as 6,000—marched in a procession to a service at St. Paul's Cathedral.

2. Lower church officers, one of whose duties is to keep order.
3. Cf. Hebrews 13.2: "Be not forgetful to entertain strangers: for thereby some have entertained angels unawares."

No, no, let us play, for it is yet day
10 And we cannot go to sleep;
Besides, in the sky, the little birds fly
And the hills are all coverd with sheep.

Well, well, go & play till the light fades away
And then go home to bed.
15 The little ones leaped & shouted & laugh'd
And all the hills ecchoèd.

ca. 1784   1789

Infant Joy

I have no name,
I am but two days old.
What shall I call thee?
I happy am,
5   Joy is my name.
Sweet joy befall thee!

Pretty joy!
Sweet joy but two days old,
Sweet joy I call thee;
10   Thou dost smile,
I sing the while—
Sweet joy befall thee.

1789

On Anothers Sorrow

Can I see anothers woe,
And not be in sorrow too.
Can I see anothers grief,
And not seek for kind relief.

5   Can I see a falling tear,
And not feel my sorrows share,
Can a father see his child,
Weep, nor be with sorrow fill'd.

Can a mother sit and hear,
10   An infant groan an infant fear—
No no never can it be.
Never never can it be.

And can he who smiles on all
Hear the wren with sorrows small,

15 Hear the small birds grief & care
Hear the woes that infants bear—

And not sit beside the nest
Pouring pity in their breast,
And not sit the cradle near
20 Weeping tear on infants tear.

And not sit both night & day,
Wiping all our tears away.
O! no never can it be.
Never never can it be.

25 He doth give his joy to all.
He becomes an infant small.
He becomes a man of woe
He doth feel the sorrow too.

Think not, thou canst sigh a sigh,
30 And thy maker is not by.
Think not, thou canst weep a tear,
And thy maker is not near.

O! he gives to us his joy,
That our grief he may destroy
35 Till our grief is fled & gone
He doth sit by us and moan

1789

FROM SONGS OF EXPERIENCE

Introduction

Hear the voice of the Bard!
Who Present, Past, & Future sees;
Whose ears have heard
The Holy Word
5 That walk'd among the ancient trees;[1]

Calling the lapsèd Soul[2]
And weeping in the evening dew,
That might controll[3]
The starry pole,
10 And fallen, fallen light renew!

O Earth, O Earth, return!
Arise from out the dewy grass;

---

1. Genesis 3.8: "And [Adam and Eve] heard the voice of the Lord God walking in the garden in the cool of the day." "The Bard," or poet-prophet, whose imagination is not bound by time, has heard the voice of the Lord in Eden.
2. The syntax leaves it ambiguous whether it is

"the Bard" or "the Holy Word" who calls to the fallen ("lapsèd") soul and to the fallen earth to stop the natural cycle of light and darkness.
3. The likely syntax is that "Soul" is the subject of "might controll."

Separate title page for *Songs of Experience* (1794), *Songs of Innocence and of Experience*, plate 29, copy Z, ca. 1801.

Night is worn,
And the morn
15 Rises from the slumberous mass.

Turn away no more;
Why wilt thou turn away?
The starry floor
The watry shore[4]
20 Is giv'n thee till the break of day.

1794

Earth's Answer[1]

Earth rais'd up her head,
From the darkness dread & drear.
Her light fled:
Stony dread!
5 And her locks cover'd with grey despair.

---

4. In Blake's recurrent symbolism the starry sky ("floor") signifies rigid rational order and the sea signifies chaos.

1. The Earth explains why she, the natural world, cannot by her unaided endeavors renew the fallen light.

Prison'd on watry shore
Starry Jealousy does keep my den,
Cold and hoar
Weeping o'er
10 I hear the Father of the ancient men.[2]

Selfish father of men,
Cruel, jealous, selfish fear!
Can delight
Chain'd in night
15 The virgins of youth and morning bear?

Does spring hide its joy
When buds and blossoms grow?
Does the sower
Sow by night,
20 Or the plowman in darkness plow?

Break this heavy chain
That does freeze my bones around;
Selfish! vain!
Eternal bane!
25 That free Love with bondage bound.

1794

The Clod & the Pebble

Love seeketh not Itself to please,
Nor for itself hath any care;
But for another gives its ease,
And builds a Heaven in Hell's despair.

5   So sang a little Clod of Clay,
       Trodden with the cattle's feet;
       But a Pebble of the brook,
       Warbled out these metres meet:

Love seeketh only Self to please,
10 To bind another to its delight;
Joys in another's loss of ease,
And builds a Hell in Heaven's despite.

1794

2. This is the character that Blake later named "Urizen" in his prophetic works. He is the tyrant who binds the mind to the natural world and also imposes a moral bondage on sexual desire and other modes of human energy.

Holy Thursday

Is this a holy thing to see,
In a rich and fruitful land,
Babes reduced to misery,
Fed with cold and usurous hand?

5   Is that trembling cry a song?
Can it be a song of joy?
And so many children poor?
It is a land of poverty!

And their sun does never shine,
10   And their fields are bleak & bare,
And their ways are fill'd with thorns;
It is eternal winter there.

For where-e'er the sun does shine,
And where-e'er the rain does fall,
15   Babe can never hunger there,
Nor poverty the mind appall.

1794

The Chimney Sweeper

A little black thing among the snow
Crying 'weep, 'weep, in notes of woe!
Where are thy father & mother? say?
They are both gone up to the church to pray.

5   Because I was happy upon the heath,
And smil'd among the winter's snow;
They clothed me in the clothes of death,
And taught me to sing the notes of woe.

And because I am happy, & dance & sing,
10   They think they have done me no injury,
And are gone to praise God & his Priest & King,
Who make up a heaven of our misery.

1790–92   1794

Nurse's Song

When the voices of children are heard on the green
And whisperings are in the dale,
The days of my youth rise fresh in my mind,
My face turns green and pale.

5 Then come home my children, the sun is gone down
And the dews of night arise;
Your spring & your day are wasted in play,
And your winter and night in disguise.

1794

The Sick Rose

O Rose, thou art sick.
The invisible worm
That flies in the night
In the howling storm

5 Has found out thy bed
Of crimson joy,
And his dark secret love
Does thy life destroy.

1794

The Fly

Little Fly
Thy summer's play
My thoughtless hand
Has brush'd away

5 Am not I
A fly like thee?
Or art not thou
A man like me?

For I dance
10 And drink & sing,
Till some blind hand
Shall brush my wing.

If thought is life
And strength & breath,
15 And the want
Of thought is death;

Then am I
A happy fly,
If I live,
20 Or if I die.

1794

"The Tyger," *Songs of Innocence and of Experience*, plate 52, copy C, ca. 1801.

The Tyger[1]

Tyger! Tyger! burning bright
In the forests of the night,
What immortal hand or eye
Could frame thy fearful symmetry?

5 In what distant deeps or skies
Burnt the fire of thine eyes?
On what wings dare he aspire?
What the hand dare seize the fire?

And what shoulder, & what art,
10 Could twist the sinews of thy heart?
And when thy heart began to beat,
What dread hand? & what dread feet?

---

1. For the author's revisions while composing "The Tyger," see "Poems in Process," in the NAEL Archive.

What the hammer? what the chain?
In what furnace was thy brain?
15 What the anvil? what dread grasp
Dare its deadly terrors clasp?

When the stars threw down their spears[2]
And water'd heaven with their tears,
Did he smile his work to see?
20 Did he who made the Lamb make thee?

Tyger! Tyger! burning bright
In the forests of the night,
What immortal hand or eye
Dare frame thy fearful symmetry?

1790–92   1794

My Pretty Rose Tree

A flower was offerd to me;
Such a flower as May never bore,
But I said, I've a Pretty Rose-tree,
And I passed the sweet flower o'er.

5 Then I went to my Pretty Rose-tree,
To tend her by day and by night.
But my Rose turnd away with jealousy,
And her thorns were my only delight.

1794

Ah! Sun-flower

Ah Sun-flower! weary of time,
Who countest the steps of the Sun,
Seeking after that sweet golden clime
Where the traveller's journey is done;

5 Where the Youth pined away with desire,
And the pale Virgin shrouded in snow,
Arise from their graves and aspire,
Where my Sun-flower wishes to go.

1794

---

2. "Threw down" is ambiguous and may signify that the stars either "surrendered" or "hurled down" their spears.

The Garden of Love

I went to the Garden of Love,
And saw what I never had seen:
A Chapel was built in the midst,
Where I used to play on the green.

5 And the gates of this Chapel were shut,
And Thou shalt not writ over the door;
So I turn'd to the Garden of Love,
That so many sweet flowers bore,

And I saw it was filled with graves,
10 And tomb-stones where flowers should be;
And Priests in black gowns were walking their rounds,
And binding with briars my joys & desires.

1794

London

I wander thro' each charter'd[1] street,
Near where the charter'd Thames does flow,
And mark in every face I meet
Marks of weakness, marks of woe.

5 In every cry of every Man,
In every Infant's cry of fear,
In every voice, in every ban,[2]
The mind-forg'd manacles I hear:

How the Chimney-sweeper's cry
10 Every blackning Church appalls,
And the hapless Soldier's sigh
Runs in blood down Palace walls.

But most thro' midnight streets I hear
How the youthful Harlot's curse
15 Blasts the new-born Infant's tear,[3]
And blights with plagues the Marriage hearse.[4]

1794

1. "Given liberty," but also, ironically, "preempted as private property, and rented out."
2. The various meanings of *ban* are relevant (political and legal prohibition, curse, public condemnation) as well as "banns" (marriage proclamation).
3. Most critics read this line as implying prenatal blindness, resulting from a parent's venereal disease (the "plagues" of line 16) by earlier infection from the harlot.
4. In the older sense: "converts the marriage bed into a bier." Or possibly, because the current sense of the word had also come into use in Blake's day, "converts the marriage coach into a funeral hearse."

"London," *Songs of Innocence and of Experience*, plate 51, copy C, ca. 1801.

The Human Abstract[1]

Pity would be no more,
If we did not make somebody Poor;
And Mercy no more could be,
If all were as happy as we;

5 And mutual fear brings peace,
Till the selfish loves increase;
Then Cruelty knits a snare,
And spreads his baits with care.

He sits down with holy fears,
10 And waters the ground with tears;
Then Humility takes its root
Underneath his foot.

Soon spreads the dismal shade
Of Mystery over his head;
15 And the Catterpiller and Fly
Feed on the Mystery.

1. The matched contrary to "The Divine Image" in *Songs of Innocence.* The virtues of the earlier poem, "Mercy, Pity, Peace, and Love," are now represented as possible marks for exploitation, cruelty, conflict, and hypocritical humility.

"The Human Abstract," *Songs of Innocence and Experience*, plate 47, copy Y, 1825.

And it bears the fruit of Deceit,
Ruddy and sweet to eat;
And the Raven his nest has made
20 In its thickest shade.

The Gods of the earth and sea,
Sought thro' Nature to find this Tree,
But their search was all in vain:
There grows one in the Human Brain.

1790–92   1794

Infant Sorrow

My mother groand! my father wept.
Into the dangerous world I leapt,
Helpless, naked, piping loud;
Like a fiend hid in a cloud.

5 Struggling in my father's hands,
Striving against my swadling bands;
Bound and weary I thought best
To sulk upon my mother's breast.

1794

A Poison Tree

I was angry with my friend:
I told my wrath, my wrath did end.
I was angry with my foe:
I told it not, my wrath did grow.

5   And I waterd it in fears,
Night & morning with my tears;
And I sunnèd it with smiles,
And with soft deceitful wiles.

And it grew both day and night,
10 Till it bore an apple bright.
And my foe beheld it shine,
And he knew that it was mine,

And into my garden stole,
When the night had veild the pole;
15 In the morning glad I see
My foe outstretchd beneath the tree.

1794

To Tirzah[1]

Whate'er is Born of Mortal Birth
Must be consumèd with the Earth
To rise from Generation free;
Then what have I to do with thee?[2]

5 The Sexes sprung from Shame & Pride,
Blow'd° in the morn, in evening died;   *blossomed*
But Mercy changd Death into Sleep;
The Sexes rose to work & weep.

Thou, Mother of my Mortal part,
10 With cruelty didst mould my Heart,
And with false self-deceiving tears
Didst bind my Nostrils, Eyes, & Ears.

Didst close my Tongue in senseless clay
And me to Mortal Life betray.

1. Tirzah was the capital of the northern kingdom of Israel and is conceived by Blake in opposition to Jerusalem, capital of the southern kingdom of Judah, whose tribes had been redeemed from captivity. In this poem, which was added to late versions of *Songs of Experience*, Tirzah is represented as the mother—in the realm of material nature and "Generation"—of the mortal body, with its restrictive senses.
2. Echoing the words of Christ to his mother at the marriage in Cana, John 2.4: "Woman, what have I to do with thee? mine hour is not yet come."

15   The Death of Jesus set me free;
      Then what have I to do with thee?

ca. 1805

A Divine Image[1]

Cruelty has a Human Heart
And Jealousy a Human Face,
Terror, the Human Form Divine,
And Secrecy, the Human Dress.

5   The Human Dress is forgèd Iron,
     The Human Form, a fiery Forge,
     The Human Face, a Furnace seal'd,
     The Human Heart, its hungry Gorge.°   *mouth, stomach*

1790–91

The Book of Thel   Although Blake dated the etched poem 1789, its composition probably extended to 1791, so that he was working on it at the time he was writing the *Songs of Innocence* and some of the *Songs of Experience*. *The Book of Thel* treats the same two "states"; now, however, Blake employs the narrative instead of the lyrical mode and embodies aspects of the developing myth that was fully enacted in his later prophetic books. And like the major prophecies, this poem is written in the fourteener, a long line of seven stresses.

Thel is represented as a virgin dwelling in the Vales of Har, which seems equivalent to the sheltered state of pastoral peace and innocence in Blake's *Songs of Innocence*. Here, however, Thel feels useless and unfulfilled and appeals for comfort, unavailingly, to various beings who are contented with their roles in Har. Finally, the Clay invites Thel to try the experiment of assuming embodied life. Part 4 (plate 6) expresses the brutal shock of the revelation to Thel of the experience of sexual desire—a revelation from which she flees in terror back to her sheltered, if unsatisfying, existence in Har.

Some commentators propose that Thel is an unborn soul who rejects the ordeal of an embodied life in the material world. Others propose that Thel is a human virgin who shrinks from experiencing a life of adult sexuality. It is possible, however, to read Blake's little myth as comprehending both these areas of significance. The reader does not need to know Blake's mythology inside and out to recognize the broad symbolic reach of this poem in ordinary human experience—the elemental failure of nerve to meet the challenge of life as it is, the timid incapacity to risk the conflict, physicality, pain, and loss without which there is no possibility either of growth or of creativity.

---

1. Blake omitted this poem from all but one copy of *Songs of Experience*, probably because "The Human Abstract" served as a more comprehensive and subtle contrary to "The Divine Image" in *Songs of Innocence*.

The Book of Thel

PLATE i[1]

Thel's Motto

Does the Eagle know what is in the pit?
Or wilt thou go ask the Mole?
Can Wisdom be put in a silver rod?
Or Love in a golden bowl?[2]

PLATE 1

1

The daughters of Mne[3] Seraphim led round their sunny flocks,
All but the youngest; she in paleness sought the secret air,
To fade away like morning beauty from her mortal day;
Down by the river of Adona her soft voice is heard,
5 And thus her gentle lamentation falls like morning dew:

"O life of this our spring! why fades the lotus of the water?
Why fade these children of the spring? born but to smile & fall.
Ah! Thel is like a watry bow, and like a parting cloud,
Like a reflection in a glass, like shadows in the water,
10 Like dreams of infants, like a smile upon an infant's face,
Like the dove's voice, like transient day, like music in the air.
Ah! gentle may I lay me down, and gentle rest my head,
And gentle sleep the sleep of death, and gentle hear the voice
Of him that walketh in the garden in the evening time."[4]

———————

15 The Lilly of the valley breathing in the humble grass
Answer'd the lovely maid and said: "I am a watry weed,
And I am very small, and love to dwell in lowly vales;
So weak, the gilded butterfly scarce perches on my head;
Yet I am visited from heaven, and he that smiles on all
20 Walks in the valley and each morn over me spreads his hand,
Saying: 'Rejoice, thou humble grass, thou new-born lilly flower,
Thou gentle maid of silent valleys and of modest brooks;
For thou shalt be clothed in light, and fed with morning manna,
Till summer's heat melts thee beside the fountains and the springs
25 To flourish in eternal vales.' Then why should Thel complain?

1. The plate numbers identify the page, each with its own pictorial design, as originally printed by Blake. These numbers are reproduced here because they are frequently used in references to Blake's writings.
2. Ecclesiastes 12.5–6 describes a time when "fears shall be in the way . . . and desire shall fail: because man goeth to his long home, and the mourners go about the streets: Or ever the silver cord be loosed, or the golden bowl be broken."

Perhaps Blake changed the silver cord to a rod to make it, with the golden bowl, a sexual symbol.
3. There has been much speculation about this curious term. It may be an abbreviation for the name "Mnetha," the goddess of the Vales of Har in Blake's earlier poem *Tiriel*.
4. Genesis 3.8: "And they heard the voice of the Lord God walking in the garden in the cool of the day."

Title page of *The Book of Thel*
(1789), plate ii, copy N, ca. 1815

PLATE 2

Why should the mistress of the vales of Har utter a sigh?"

She ceasd & smild in tears, then sat down in her silver shrine.

Thel answerd: "O thou little virgin of the peaceful valley,
Giving to those that cannot crave, the voiceless, the o'ertired;[5]
5   Thy breath doth nourish the innocent lamb, he smells thy milky
        garments,
He crops thy flowers, while thou sittest smiling in his face,
Wiping his mild and meekin° mouth from all contagious taints.   *humble*
Thy wine doth purify the golden honey; thy perfume,
Which thou dost scatter on every little blade of grass that springs,
10   Revives the milkèd cow, & tames the fire-breathing steed.
But Thel is like a faint cloud kindled at the rising sun:
I vanish from my pearly throne, and who shall find my place?"

"Queen of the vales," the Lilly answered, "ask the tender cloud,
And it shall tell thee why it glitters in the morning sky,
15   And why it scatters its bright beauty thro' the humid air.

---

5. Some scholars, looking to the taming of "the fire-breathing steed" in line 10, construe this word as
"o'erfired."

Descend, O little cloud, & hover before the eyes of Thel."
The Cloud descended, and the Lilly bowd her modest head,
And went to mind her numerous charge among the verdant grass.

PLATE 3

2

"O little Cloud," the virgin said, "I charge thee tell to me,
Why thou complainest not when in one hour thou fade away:
Then we shall seek thee but not find; ah, Thel is like to Thee.
I pass away, yet I complain, and no one hears my voice."

5   The Cloud then shew'd his golden head & his bright form emerg'd,
Hovering and glittering on the air before the face of Thel.

"O virgin, know'st thou not our steeds drink of the golden springs
Where Luvah[6] doth renew his horses? Look'st thou on my youth,
And fearest thou because I vanish and am seen no more,
10   Nothing remains? O maid, I tell thee, when I pass away,
It is to tenfold life, to love, to peace, and raptures holy:
Unseen descending, weigh my light wings upon balmy flowers,
And court the fair eyed dew, to take me to her shining tent;
The weeping virgin trembling kneels before the risen sun,
15   Till we arise link'd in a golden band, and never part,
But walk united, bearing food to all our tender flowers."

"Dost thou O little Cloud? I fear that I am not like thee;
For I walk through the vales of Har and smell the sweetest flowers,
But I feed not the little flowers; I hear the warbling birds,
20   But I feed not the warbling birds; they fly and seek their food;
But Thel delights in these no more, because I fade away,
And all shall say, 'Without a use this shining woman liv'd,
Or did she only live to be at death the food of worms?'"

The Cloud reclind upon his airy throne and answer'd thus:

25   "Then if thou art the food of worms, O virgin of the skies,
How great thy use, how great thy blessing! Every thing that lives
Lives not alone, nor for itself; fear not, and I will call
The weak worm from its lowly bed, and thou shalt hear its voice.
Come forth, worm of the silent valley, to thy pensive queen."

————————————

30   The helpless worm arose, and sat upon the Lilly's leaf,
And the bright Cloud saild on, to find his partner in the vale.

6. The earliest mention in Blake's work of one of his "Giant Forms," the Zoas. Luvah is the mythical embodiment of the passional and sexual aspect of humankind. He is represented here, like the Greek Phoebus Apollo, as the driver of the chariot of the sun; he repairs to the Vales of Har simply to rest and water his horses. The cloud in this passage describes the cycle of water, from cloud to rain and (by the vaporizing action of the sun on water) back to the cloud.

PLATE 4

3

Then Thel astonish'd view'd the Worm upon its dewy bed.

"Art thou a Worm? Image of weakness, art thou but a Worm?
I see thee like an infant wrapped in the Lilly's leaf;
Ah, weep not, little voice, thou can'st not speak, but thou can'st weep.
5   Is this a Worm? I see thee lay helpless & naked, weeping,
And none to answer, none to cherish thee with mother's smiles."

The Clod of Clay heard the Worm's voice, & raisd her pitying head;
She bow'd over the weeping infant, and her life exhal'd
In milky fondness; then on Thel she fix'd her humble eyes.

10   "O beauty of the vales of Har! we live not for ourselves;
Thou seest me the meanest thing, and so I am indeed;
My bosom of itself is cold, and of itself is dark,

PLATE 5

But he that loves the lowly, pours his oil upon my head,
And kisses me, and binds his nuptial bands around my breast,
And says: 'Thou mother of my children, I have lovèd thee,
And I have given thee a crown that none can take away.'
5   But how this is, sweet maid, I know not, and I cannot know;
I ponder, and I cannot ponder; yet I live and love."

The daughter of beauty wip'd her pitying tears with her white veil,
And said: "Alas! I knew not this, and therefore did I weep.
That God would love a Worm, I knew, and punish the evil foot
10   That, wilful, bruis'd its helpless form; but that he cherish'd it
With milk and oil I never knew; and therefore did I weep,
And I complaind in the mild air, because I fade away,
And lay me down in thy cold bed, and leave my shining lot."

"Queen of the vales," the matron Clay answered, "I heard thy sighs,
15   And all thy moans flew o'er my roof, but I have call'd them down.
Wilt thou, O Queen, enter my house? 'tis given thee to enter
And to return; fear nothing, enter with thy virgin feet."

PLATE 6

4

The eternal gates' terrific porter lifted the northern bar:[7]
Thel enter'd in & saw the secrets of the land unknown.
She saw the couches of the dead, & where the fibrous roots
Of every heart on earth infixes deep its restless twists:
5   A land of sorrows & of tears where never smile was seen.

---

7. Homer, in *Odyssey* 13, described the Cave of the Naiades, of which the northern gate is for mortals and the southern gate for gods. The Neo-platonist Porphyry had allegorized it as an account of the descent of the soul into matter and then its return.

She wanderd in the land of clouds thro' valleys dark, listning
Dolours & lamentations; waiting oft beside a dewy grave,
She stood in silence, listning to the voices of the ground,
Till to her own grave plot she came, & there she sat down,
10   And heard this voice of sorrow breathed from the hollow pit:

"Why cannot the Ear be closed to its own destruction?
Or the glistning Eye to the poison of a smile?
Why are Eyelids stord with arrows ready drawn,
Where a thousand fighting men in ambush lie?
15   Or an Eye of gifts & graces, show'ring fruits & coinèd gold?
Why a Tongue impress'd with honey from every wind?
Why an Ear, a whirlpool fierce to draw creations in?
Why a Nostril wide inhaling terror, trembling, & affright?
Why a tender curb upon the youthful burning boy?
20   Why a little curtain of flesh on the bed of our desire?"

The Virgin started from her seat, & with a shriek
Fled back unhinderd till she came into the vales of Har.

1789–91

Visions of the Daughters of Albion   This work, dated 1793 on the
title page, is one of Blake's early illuminated books, and like his later and longer
works is written in what Blake called "the long resounding strong heroic verse" of
seven-foot lines. Unlike the timid heroine of *The Book of Thel*, the virgin Oothoon
dares to break through into adult sexuality (symbolized by her plucking a marigold
and placing it between her breasts) and sets out joyously to join her lover, Theotormon, whose realm is the Atlantic Ocean. She is stopped and raped by Bromion, who
appears as a thunderstorm (1.16–17). The jealous Theotormon, condemning the
victim as well as the rapist, binds the two "back to back" in a cave and sits weeping
on the threshold. The rest of the work consists of monologues by the three characters, who remain fixed in these postures. Throughout this stage tableau the Daughters of Albion serve as the chorus who, in a recurrent refrain, echo the "woes" and
"sighs" of Oothoon, but not her call to rebellion.
    This simple drama is densely significant, for as Blake's compressed allusions
indicate, the characters, events, and monologues have diverse areas of application.
Blake's abrupt opening word, which he etched in very large letters, is *Enslav'd*, and
the work as a whole embodies his view that contemporary men, and even more
women, in a spiritual parallel to shackled African slaves, are in bondage to oppressive concepts and codes in all aspects of perception, thought, social institutions,
and actions. As indicated by the refrain of the Daughters of Albion (that is, contemporary Englishwomen), Oothoon in one aspect represents the sexual disabilities and slavelike status of all women in a male-dominated society. But as "the
soft soul of America" (1.3) she is also the revolutionary nation that had recently
won political emancipation, yet continued to tolerate an agricultural system that
involved black slavery and to acquiesce in the crass economic exploitation of her
"soft American plains." At the same time Oothoon is represented in the situation
of a black female slave who has been branded, whipped, raped, and impregnated
by her master.
    Correlatively, the speeches of the boastful Bromion show him to be not only a
sexual exploiter of women and a cruel and acquisitive slave owner but also a general

proponent of the use of force to achieve mastery in wars, in an oppressive legal system, and in a religious morality based on the fear of hell (4.19–24). Theotormon is represented as even more contemptible. Broken and paralyzed by the prohibitions of a puritanical religion, he denies any possibility of achieving "joys" in this life, despairs of the power of intellect and imagination to improve the human condition and, rationalizing his own incapacity, bewails Oothoon's daring to think and act other than he does.

Oothoon's long and passionate oration that concludes the poem (plates 5–8) celebrates a free sexual life for both women and men. Blake, however, uses this open and unpossessive sexuality to typify the realization of all human potentialities and to represent an outgoing altruism, as opposed to an enclosed self-centeredness, "the self-love that envies all." To such a suspicious egotism, as her allusions indicate, Oothoon attributes the tyranny of uniform moral laws imposed on variable individuals, a rigidly institutional religion, the acquisitiveness that drives the system of commerce, and the property rights in another person that are established by the marriage contract.

Blake's poem reflects some prominent happenings of the years of its composition, 1791–93. This was not only the time when the revolutionary spirit had moved from America to France with tremendous consequences in England, but also the time of rebellions by African slaves in the Western Hemisphere and of widespread debate in England about the abolition of the slave trade. Blake, while composing the *Visions*, had illustrated the sadistic punishments inflicted on rebellious slaves in his engravings for J. G. Stedman's *A Narrative, of a Five Years' Expedition, against the Revolted Negroes of Surinam* (see David Erdman, *Blake: Prophet against Empire*, chapter 10). Blake's championing of women's liberation parallels some of the views expressed in the *Vindication of the Rights of Woman* published in 1792 by Mary Wollstonecraft, whom Blake knew and admired, and for whom he had illustrated a book the year before.

Visions of the Daughters of Albion

The Eye sees more than the Heart knows.

PLATE iii

The Argument

I loved Theotormon
And I was not ashamed
I trembled in my virgin fears
And I hid in Leutha's[1] vale!

5   I plucked Leutha's flower,
And I rose up from the vale;
But the terrible thunders tore
My virgin mantle in twain.

---

1. In some poems by Blake, Leutha is represented as a female figure who is beautiful and seductive but treacherous.

Frontispiece, *Visions of the Daughters of Albion* (1793), plate 1, copy P, ca. 1815

PLATE 1

Visions

ENSLAV'D, the Daughters of Albion weep: a trembling lamentation
Upon their mountains; in their valleys, sighs toward America.

For the soft soul of America, Oothoon[2] wandered in woe,
Along the vales of Leutha seeking flowers to comfort her;
5   And thus she spoke to the bright Marygold of Leutha's vale:

"Art thou a flower! art thou a nymph! I see thee now a flower,
Now a nymph! I dare not pluck thee from thy dewy bed!"

The Golden nymph replied: "Pluck thou my flower Oothoon the mild.
Another flower shall spring, because the soul of sweet delight
10   Can never pass away." She ceas'd & closd her golden shrine.

Then Oothoon pluck'd the flower saying, "I pluck thee from thy bed,
Sweet flower, and put thee here to glow between my breasts,
And thus I turn my face to where my whole soul seeks."

Over the waves she went in wing'd exulting swift delight;
15   And over Theotormon's reign took her impetuous course.

Bromion rent her with his thunders. On his stormy bed
Lay the faint maid, and soon her woes appalld his thunders hoarse.

———————————

2. The name is adapted by Blake from a character in James Macpherson's pretended translations, in the 1760s, from the ancient British bard Ossian. After her husband goes off to war, Macpherson's Oithona is abducted, raped, and imprisoned by a rejected suitor.

Bromion spoke: "Behold this harlot here on Bromion's bed,
And let the jealous dolphins sport around the lovely maid;
20 Thy soft American plains are mine, and mine thy north & south:
Stampt with my signet[3] are the swarthy children of the sun:
They are obedient, they resist not, they obey the scourge:
Their daughters worship terrors and obey the violent.

PLATE 2

Now thou maist marry Bromion's harlot, and protect the child
Of Bromion's rage, that Oothoon shall put forth in nine moons' time."[4]
Then storms rent Theotormon's limbs; he rolld his waves around,
And folded his black jealous waters round the adulterate pair;
5 Bound back to back in Bromion's caves terror & meekness dwell.

At entrance Theotormon sits wearing the threshold hard
With secret tears; beneath him sound like waves on a desart shore
The voice of slaves beneath the sun, and children bought with money,
That shiver in religious caves beneath the burning fires
10 Of lust, that belch incessant from the summits of the earth.

Oothoon weeps not: she cannot weep! her tears are locked up;
But she can howl incessant, writhing her soft snowy limbs,
And calling Theotormon's Eagles to prey upon her flesh.[5]

"I call with holy voice! kings of the sounding air,
15 Rend away this defiled bosom that I may reflect
The image of Theotormon on my pure transparent breast."

The Eagles at her call descend & rend their bleeding prey;
Theotormon severely smiles; her soul reflects the smile,
As the clear spring mudded with feet of beasts grows pure & smiles.

20 The Daughters of Albion hear her woes, & eccho back her sighs.

"Why does my Theotormon sit weeping upon the threshold,
And Oothoon hovers by his side, perswading him in vain?
I cry, 'Arise O Theotormon, for the village dog
Barks at the breaking day, the nightingale has done lamenting,
25 The lark does rustle in the ripe corn, and the Eagle returns
From nightly prey, and lifts his golden beak to the pure east,
Shaking the dust from his immortal pinions to awake
The sun that sleeps too long. Arise my Theotormon, I am pure;
Because the night is gone that clos'd me in its deadly black.'
30 They told me that the night & day were all that I could see;
They told me that I had five senses to inclose me up,
And they inclos'd my infinite brain into a narrow circle,
And sunk my heart into the Abyss, a red round globe hot burning,

---

3. A small seal or stamp. The allusion is to the branding of slaves by their owners.
4. Pregnancy enhanced the market value of a female slave in America.

5. The implied parallel is to Zeus's punishment of Prometheus for befriending the human race, by setting an eagle to devour his liver.

Till all from life I was obliterated and erased.
35 Instead of morn arises a bright shadow, like an eye
In the eastern cloud,[6] instead of night a sickly charnel house,
That Theotormon hears me not! to him the night and morn
Are both alike: a night of sighs, a morning of fresh tears;

PLATE 3

And none but Bromion can hear my lamentations.

"With what sense is it that the chicken shuns the ravenous hawk?
With what sense does the tame pigeon measure out the expanse?
With what sense does the bee form cells? have not the mouse & frog
5   Eyes and ears and sense of touch? yet are their habitations
And their pursuits as different as their forms and as their joys.
Ask the wild ass why he refuses burdens, and the meek camel
Why he loves man; is it because of eye, ear, mouth, or skin,
Or breathing nostrils? No, for these the wolf and tyger have.
10 Ask the blind worm the secrets of the grave, and why her spires
Love to curl round the bones of death; and ask the rav'nous snake
Where she gets poison, & the wing'd eagle why he loves the sun,
And then tell me the thoughts of man, that have been hid of old.[7]

"Silent I hover all the night, and all day could be silent,
15 If Theotormon once would turn his loved eyes upon me.
How can I be defild when I reflect thy image pure?
Sweetest the fruit that the worm feeds on, & the soul prey'd on by woe,
The new wash'd lamb ting'd with the village smoke, & the bright swan
By the red earth of our immortal river:[8] I bathe my wings,
20 And I am white and pure to hover round Theotormon's breast."

Then Theotormon broke his silence, and he answered:

"Tell me what is the night or day to one o'erflowd with woe?
Tell me what is a thought? & of what substance is it made?
Tell me what is a joy? & in what gardens do joys grow?
25 And in what rivers swim the sorrows? and upon what mountains

PLATE 4

Wave shadows of discontent? and in what houses dwell the wretched
Drunken with woe, forgotten, and shut up from cold despair?

"Tell me where dwell the thoughts, forgotten till thou call them forth?
Tell me where dwell the joys of old! & where the ancient loves?
5   And when will they renew again & the night of oblivion past?

6. The contrast is between the physical sun perceived by the constricted ("inclos'd," line 32) sensible eye and "the breaking day" (line 24) of a new era perceived by Oothoon's liberated vision.
7. Oothoon implies that "thoughts" (powers of conceiving a liberated life in a better world) are as innate to human beings as instinctual patterns of behavior are to other species of living things.
8. "Red earth": the etymological meaning of the Hebrew name *Adam* (cf. *The Marriage of Heaven and Hell* 2.13, p. 159). "Immortal river": may refer to the "river" that "went out of Eden" (Genesis 2.10).

That I might traverse times & spaces far remote and bring
Comforts into a present sorrow and a night of pain.
Where goest thou, O thought? to what remote land is thy flight?
If thou returnest to the present moment of affliction
10   Wilt thou bring comforts on thy wings and dews and honey and balm,
Or poison from the desart wilds, from the eyes of the envier?"

Then Bromion said, and shook the cavern with his lamentation:

"Thou knowest that the ancient trees seen by thine eyes have fruit;
But knowest thou that trees and fruits flourish upon the earth
15   To gratify senses unknown? trees beasts and birds unknown:
Unknown, not unpercievd, spread in the infinite microscope,
In places yet unvisited by the voyager, and in worlds
Over another kind of seas, and in atmospheres unknown?
Ah! are there other wars, beside the wars of sword and fire?
20   And are there other sorrows, beside the sorrows of poverty?
And are there other joys, beside the joys of riches and ease?
And is there not one law for both the lion and the ox?[9]
And is there not eternal fire, and eternal chains?
To bind the phantoms of existence from eternal life?"

25   Then Oothoon waited silent all the day and all the night,

PLATE 5

But when the morn arose, her lamentation renewd.
The Daughters of Albion hear her woes, & eccho back her sighs.

"O Urizen![1] Creator of men! mistaken Demon of heaven:
Thy joys are tears! thy labour vain, to form men to thine image.
5   How can one joy absorb another? are not different joys
Holy, eternal, infinite! and each joy is a Love.

"Does not the great mouth laugh at a gift? & the narrow eyelids mock
At the labour that is above payment? and wilt thou take the ape
For thy councellor? or the dog for a schoolmaster to thy children?
10   Does he who contemns poverty, and he who turns with abhorrence
From usury, feel the same passion, or are they movcd alike?
How can the giver of gifts experience the delights of the merchant?
How the industrious citizen the pains of the husbandman?
How different far the fat fed hireling with hollow drum,
15   Who buys whole corn fields into wastes,[2] and sings upon the heath:
How different their eye and ear! how different the world to them!
With what sense does the parson claim the labour of the farmer?
What are his nets & gins° & traps? & how does he surround him   *snares*

---

9. The last line of *The Marriage of Heaven and Hell* proclaims: "One Law for the Lion & Ox is Oppression."
1. This is the first occurrence of the name "Urizen" in Blake (the name can be pronounced either as "your reason" or as an echo of "horizon"). Oothoon's liberated vision recognizes the error in the way God is conceived in conventional religion.
2. Probably a compressed allusion both to the wealthy landowner who converts fertile fields into a game preserve and to the army recruiting officer ("with hollow drum") who strips the land of its agricultural laborers.

With cold floods of abstraction, and with forests of solitude,
20　To build him castles and high spires, where kings & priests may dwell?
Till she who burns with youth, and knows no fixed lot, is bound
In spells of law to one she loaths; and must she drag the chain
Of life, in weary lust? must chilling murderous thoughts obscure
The clear heaven of her eternal spring? to bear the wintry rage
25　Of a harsh terror, driv'n to madness, bound to hold a rod
Over her shrinking shoulders all the day, & all the night
To turn the wheel of false desire, and longings that wake her womb
To the abhorred birth of cherubs in the human form
That live a pestilence & die a meteor & are no more;
30　Till the child dwell with one he hates, and do the deed he loaths,
And the impure scourge force his seed into its unripe birth
E'er yet his eyelids can behold the arrows of the day?[3]

"Does the whale worship at thy footsteps as the hungry dog?
Or does he scent the mountain prey, because his nostrils wide
35　Draw in the ocean? does his eye discern the flying cloud
As the raven's eye? or does he measure the expanse like the vulture?
Does the still spider view the cliffs where eagles hide their young?
Or does the fly rejoice because the harvest is brought in?
Does not the eagle scorn the earth & despise the treasures beneath?
40　But the mole knoweth what is there, & the worm shall tell it thee.
Does not the worm erect a pillar in the mouldering church yard,

PLATE 6

And a palace of eternity in the jaws of the hungry grave?
Over his porch these words are written: 'Take thy bliss O Man!
And sweet shall be thy taste & sweet thy infant joys renew!'

"Infancy, fearless, lustful, happy! nestling for delight
5　In laps of pleasure; Innocence! honest, open, seeking
The vigorous joys of morning light, open to virgin bliss,
Who taught thee modesty, subtil modesty? Child of night & sleep,
When thou awakest wilt thou dissemble all thy secret joys,
Or wert thou not awake when all this mystery was disclos'd?
10　Then com'st thou forth a modest virgin, knowing to dissemble,
With nets found under thy night pillow to catch virgin joy,
And brand it with the name of whore, & sell it in the night,
In silence, ev'n without a whisper, and in seeming sleep.[4]
Religious dreams and holy vespers light thy smoky fires;
15　Once were thy fires lighted by the eyes of honest morn.
And does my Theotormon seek this hypocrite modesty,
This knowing, artful, secret, fearful, cautious, trembling hypocrite?
Then is Oothoon a whore indeed! and all the virgin joys
Of life are harlots, and Theotormon is a sick man's dream,
20　And Oothoon is the crafty slave of selfish holiness.

3. The reference is to the begetting of children, both in actual slavery and in the metaphoric slavery of a loveless marriage, from generation to generation.
4. Oothoon contrasts the natural, innocent sensuality of an infant to the sort of modesty characterizing the adult virgin, a false modesty that, Mary Wollstonecraft had observed in her *Vindication of the Rights of Woman*, is "merely a respect for the opinion of the world."

"But Oothoon is not so; a virgin fill'd with virgin fancies
Open to joy and to delight where ever beauty appears.
If in the morning sun I find it, there my eyes are fix'd

PLATE 7

In happy copulation; if in evening mild, wearied with work,
Sit on a bank and draw the pleasures of this free born joy.

"The moment of desire! the moment of desire! The virgin
That pines for man shall awaken her womb to enormous joys
5   In the secret shadows of her chamber; the youth shut up from
The lustful joy shall forget to generate & create an amorous image
In the shadows of his curtains and in the folds of his silent pillow.[5]
Are not these the places of religion? the rewards of continence?
The self enjoyings of self denial? Why dost seek religion?
10 Is it because acts are not lovely, that thou seekest solitude,
Where the horrible darkness is impressed with reflections of desire?

"Father of Jealousy,[6] be thou accursed from the earth!
Why hast thou taught my Theotormon this accursed thing?
Till beauty fades from off my shoulders, darken'd and cast out,
15 A solitary shadow wailing on the margin of non-entity.

"I cry, Love! Love! Love! happy happy Love! free as the mountain wind!
Can that be Love, that drinks another as a sponge drinks water?
That clouds with jealousy his nights, with weepings all the day,
To spin a web of age around him, grey and hoary! dark!
20 Till his eyes sicken at the fruit that hangs before his sight.
Such is self-love that envies all! a creeping skeleton
With lamplike eyes watching around the frozen marriage bed.

"But silken nets and traps of adamant[7] will Oothoon spread,
And catch for thee girls of mild silver, or of furious gold;
25 I'll lie beside thee on a bank & view their wanton play
In lovely copulation bliss on bliss with Theotormon:
Red as the rosy morning, lustful as the first born beam,
Oothoon shall view his dear delight, nor e'er with jealous cloud
Come in the heaven of generous love; nor selfish blightings bring.

30 "Does the sun walk in glorious raiment on the secret floor

PLATE 8

Where the cold miser spreads his gold? or does the bright cloud drop
On his stone threshold? does his eye behold the beam that brings
Expansion to the eye of pity? or will he bind himself
Beside the ox to thy hard furrow? does not that mild beam blot
5   The bat, the owl, the glowing tyger, and the king of night?

---

5. Blake is describing masturbation.
6. I.e., Urizen (5.3), the God who prohibits the
satisfaction of human desires.

7. A legendary stone believed to be unbreakable.
(The name is derived from the Greek word for
diamond.)

The sea fowl takes the wintry blast for a cov'ring to her limbs,
And the wild snake the pestilence to adorn him with gems & gold.
And trees & birds & beasts & men behold their eternal joy.
Arise you little glancing wings, and sing your infant joy!
10   Arise and drink your bliss, for every thing that lives is holy!"[8]

Thus every morning wails Oothoon, but Theotormon sits
Upon the margind ocean conversing with shadows dire.

The Daughters of Albion hear her woes, & eccho back her sighs.

1791–93   1793

The Marriage of Heaven and Hell

This, the most immediately accessible of Blake's longer works, is a vigorous, deliberately outrageous, and at times comic onslaught against timidly conventional and self-righteous members of society as well as against stock opinions of orthodox Christian piety and morality. The seeming simplicity of Blake's satiric attitude, however, is deceptive.

Initially, Blake accepts the terminology of standard Christian morality ("what the religious call Good & Evil") but reverses its values. In this conventional use Evil, which is manifested by the class of beings called Devils and which consigns wrongdoers to the orthodox Hell, is everything associated with the body and its desires and consists essentially of energy, abundance, actions, and freedom. Conventional Good, which is manifested by Angels and guarantees its adherents a place in the orthodox Heaven, is associated with the Soul (regarded as entirely separate from the body) and consists of the contrary qualities of reason, restraint, passivity, and prohibition. Blandly adopting these conventional oppositions, Blake elects to assume the diabolic persona—what he calls "the voice of the Devil"—and to utter "Proverbs of Hell."

But this stance is only a first stage in Blake's complex irony, designed to startle the reader into recognizing the inadequacy of conventional moral categories. As he also says in the opening summary, "Without Contraries is no progression," and "Reason and Energy" are both "necessary to Human existence." It turns out that Blake subordinates his reversal of conventional values under a more inclusive point of view, according to which the real Good, as distinguished from the merely ironic Good, is not abandonment of all restraints but a "marriage," or union of the contraries, of desire and restraint, energy and reason, the promptings of Hell and the denials of Heaven—or as Blake calls these contraries in plate 16, "the Prolific" and "the Devouring." These two classes, he adds, "should be enemies," and "whoever tries to reconcile them seeks to destroy existence." Implicit in Blake's satire is the view that the good and abundant life consists in the sustained tension, without victory or suppression, of co-present oppositions.

When Blake composed this unique work in the early 1790s, his city of London was teeming with religious mystics, astrologers, and sometimes bawdy freethinkers who were determined to challenge the Established Church's monopoly on spirituality and who were reviving the link, created in the seventeenth century, between enthusiasm in religion and political revolution. The work is also a response to the writings of the visionary Swedish theologian Emanuel Swedenborg, whom Blake had at first admired but then had come to recognize as a conventional Angel in the disguise of a radical Devil. In plate 3 the writings of

---

8. This last phrase is also the concluding line of "A Song of Liberty," appended to *The Marriage of Heaven and Hell*.

Swedenborg are described as the winding clothes Blake discards as he is resurrected from the tomb of his past self, as a poet-prophet who heralds the apocalyptic promise of his age. Blake shared the expectations of a number of radical English writers, including the young poets Wordsworth, Coleridge, and Southey, that the French Revolution was the violent stage that, as the biblical prophets foresaw, immediately preceded the millennium. The double role of *The Marriage* as both satire and revolutionary prophecy is made explicit in *A Song of Liberty*, which Blake etched in 1792 and added as a coda.

The Marriage of Heaven and Hell

PLATE 2

The Argument

Rintrah[1] roars & shakes his fires in the burdend air;
Hungry clouds swag on the deep.

Once meek, and in a perilous path,
The just man kept his course along
5   The vale of death.
Roses are planted where thorns grow,
And on the barren heath
Sing the honey bees.

Then the perilous path was planted,
10   And a river, and a spring,
On every cliff and tomb;
And on the bleached bones
Red clay[2] brought forth;

Till the villain left the paths of ease,
15   To walk in perilous paths, and drive
The just man into barren climes.

Now the sneaking serpent walks
In mild humility,
And the just man rages in the wilds
20   Where lions roam.

Rintrah roars & shakes his fires in the burdend air;
Hungry clouds swag on the deep.

---

1. Rintrah plays the role of the angry Old Testament prophet Elijah as well as of John the Baptist, the voice "crying in the wilderness" (Matthew 3), preparing the way for Christ the Messiah. It has been plausibly suggested that stanzas 2–5 summarize the course of biblical history to the present time. "Once" (line 3) refers to Old Testament history after the Fall; "Then" (line 9) is the time of the birth of Christ. "Till" (line 14) identifies the era when Christianity was perverted into an institutional reli-

gion. "Now" (line 17) is the time of the wrathful portent of the French Revolution. In this final era the hypocritical serpent represents the priest of the "angels" in the poem, while "the just man" is embodied in Blake, a raging poet and prophet in the guise of a devil. "Swag" (line 2): sag, hang down.
2. In Hebrew the literal meaning of *Adam*, or created man. The probable reference is to the birth of the Redeemer, the new Adam.

PLATE 3

As a new heaven is begun, and it is now thirty-three years since its advent, the Eternal Hell revives. And lo! Swedenborg[3] is the Angel sitting at the tomb; his writings are the linen clothes folded up. Now is the dominion of Edom, & the return of Adam into Paradise; see Isaiah xxxiv & XXXV Chap.[4]

Without Contraries is no progression. Attraction and Repulsion, Reason and Energy, Love and Hate, are necessary to Human existence.

From these contraries spring what the religious call Good & Evil. Good is the passive that obeys Reason. Evil is the active springing from Energy.

Good is Heaven. Evil is Hell.

PLATE 4

The Voice of the Devil

All Bibles or sacred codes have been the causes of the following Errors:

1. That Man has two real existing principles; Viz: a Body & a Soul.

2. That Energy, calld Evil, is alone from the Body, & that Reason, calld Good, is alone from the Soul.

3. That God will torment Man in Eternity for following his Energies.

But the following Contraries to these are True:

1. Man has no Body distinct from his Soul; for that calld Body is a portion of Soul discernd by the five Senses, the chief inlets of Soul in this age.

2. Energy is the only life, and is from the Body; and Reason is the bound or outward circumference of Energy.

3. Energy is Eternal Delight.

PLATE 5

Those who restrain desire, do so because theirs is weak enough to be restrained; and the restrainer or reason usurps its place & governs the unwilling.

And being restraind, it by degrees becomes passive, till it is only the shadow of desire.

The history of this is written in *Paradise Lost*,[5] & the Governor or Reason is call'd Messiah.

---

3. Emanuel Swedenborg (1688–1772), Swedish scientist and religious philosopher, had predicted, on the basis of his visions, that the Last Judgment and the coming of the Kingdom of Heaven would occur in 1757. This was precisely the year of Blake's birth. Now, in 1790, Blake is thirty-three, the age at which Christ had been resurrected from the tomb; correspondingly, Blake rises from the tomb of his past life in his new role as imaginative artist who will redeem his age. But, Blake ironically comments, the works he will engrave in his resurrection will constitute the Eternal Hell, the contrary brought into simultaneous being by Swedenborg's limited New Heaven.

4. Isaiah 34 prophesies "the day of the Lord's vengeance," a time of violent destruction and bloodshed; Isaiah 35 prophesies the redemption to follow, in which "the desert shall . . . blossom as the rose," "in the wilderness shall waters break out, and streams in the desert," and "no lion shall be there," but "an highway shall be there . . . and it shall be called The way of holiness" (cf. "The Argument," lines 3–11, 20). Blake combines with these chapters Isaiah 63, in which "Edom" is the place from which comes the man whose garments are red with the blood he has spilled; for as he says, "the day of vengeance is in mine heart, and the year of my redeemed is come." Blake interprets this last phrase as predicting the time when Adam would regain his lost Paradise. Also relevant is Genesis 36.1, where the Edomites are identified as the descendants of the disinherited Esau, cheated out of his father's blessing by Jacob.

5. What follows, to the end of this section, is Blake's "diabolical" reading of Milton's *Paradise Lost*. For other Romantic comments on the magnificence of Milton's Satan see "The Satanic and Byronic Hero" in the NAEL Archive.

And the original Archangel, or possessor of the command of the heavenly host, is call'd the Devil or Satan, and his children are call'd Sin & Death.[6]

But in the Book of Job, Milton's Messiah is call'd Satan.[7]

For this history has been adopted by both parties.

It indeed appear'd to Reason as if Desire was cast out; but the Devil's account is, that the Messi[PLATE 6]ah fell, & formed a heaven of what he stole from the Abyss.

This is shewn in the Gospel, where he prays to the Father to send the comforter or Desire that Reason may have Ideas to build on,[8] the Jehovah of the Bible being no other than he who dwells in flaming fire. Know that after Christ's death, he became Jehovah.

But in Milton, the Father is Destiny, the Son, a Ratio[9] of the five senses, & the Holy-ghost, Vacuum!

Note. The reason Milton wrote in fetters when he wrote of Angels & God, and at liberty when of Devils & Hell, is because he was a true Poet and of the Devil's party without knowing it.

A Memorable Fancy[1]

As I was walking among the fires of hell, delighted with the enjoyments of Genius, which to Angels look like torment and insanity, I collected some of their Proverbs; thinking that as the sayings used in a nation mark its character, so the Proverbs of Hell shew the nature of Infernal wisdom better than any description of buildings or garments.

When I came home, on the abyss of the five senses, where a flat sided steep frowns over the present world, I saw a mighty Devil[2] folded in black clouds, hovering on the sides of the rock; with cor[PLATE 7]roding fires he wrote the following sentence now perceived by the minds of men, & read by them on earth:

> How do you know but ev'ry Bird that cuts the airy way,
> Is an immense world of delight, clos'd by your senses five?

Proverbs of Hell[3]

In seed time learn, in harvest teach, in winter enjoy.
Drive your cart and your plow over the bones of the dead.
The road of excess leads to the palace of wisdom.
Prudence is a rich ugly old maid courted by Incapacity.
5   He who desires but acts not, breeds pestilence.

6. Satan's giving birth to Sin and then incestuously begetting Death upon her is described in *Paradise Lost* 2.745ff.; the war in heaven, referred to three lines below, in which the Messiah defeated Satan and drove him out of heaven, is described in 6.824ff.

7. In the Book of Job, Satan plays the role of Job's moral accuser and physical tormentor.

8. Possibly John 14.16–17, where Christ says he "will pray the Father, and he shall give you another Comforter . . . Even the Spirit of truth."

9. The Latin *ratio* means both "reason" and "sum." Blake applies the term to the 18th-century view, following the empiricist philosophy of John Locke, that the content of the mind, on which the

faculty of reason operates, is limited to the sum of the experience acquired by the five senses.

1. Blake parodies Swedenborg's accounts, in his *Memorable Relations*, of his conversations with the inhabitants during his spiritual trips to heaven.

2. The "mighty Devil" is Blake, as he sees himself reflected in the shiny plate on which he is etching this very passage with "corroding fires," i.e., the acid used in the etching process. See also the third from last sentence in plate 14.

3. A "diabolic" version of the Book of Proverbs in the Old Testament, which also incorporates sly allusions to 18th-century books of piety such as Isaac Watts's *Divine Songs*.

The cut worm forgives the plow.
Dip him in the river who loves water.
A fool sees not the same tree that a wise man sees.
He whose face gives no light, shall never become a star.
10 Eternity is in love with the productions of time.
The busy bee has no time for sorrow.
The hours of folly are measur'd by the clock; but of wisdom, no clock can
    measure.
All wholsom food is caught without a net or a trap.
Bring out number, weight, & measure in a year of dearth.
15 No bird soars too high, if he soars with his own wings.
A dead body revenges not injuries.
The most sublime act is to set another before you.
If the fool would persist in his folly he would become wise.
Folly is the cloke of knavery.
20 Shame is Pride's cloke.

PLATE 8

Prisons are built with stones of Law, Brothels with bricks of Religion.
The pride of the peacock is the glory of God.
The lust of the goat is the bounty of God.
The wrath of the lion is the wisdom of God.
5 The nakedness of woman is the work of God.
Excess of sorrow laughs. Excess of joy weeps.
The roaring of lions, the howling of wolves, the raging of the stormy sea,
    and the destructive sword, are portions of eternity too great for the
    eye of man.
The fox condemns the trap, not himself.
Joys impregnate. Sorrows bring forth.
10 Let man wear the fell of the lion, woman the fleece of the sheep.
The bird a nest, the spider a web, man friendship.
The selfish smiling fool & the sullen frowning fool shall be both thought
    wise, that they may be a rod.
What is now proved was once only imagin'd.
The rat, the mouse, the fox, the rabbit watch the roots; the lion, the tyger,
    the horse, the elephant, watch the fruits,
15 The cistern contains; the fountain overflows.
One thought fills immensity.
Always be ready to speak your mind, and a base man will avoid you.
Every thing possible to be believ'd is an image of truth.
The eagle never lost so much time as when he submitted to learn of the crow.

PLATE 9

The fox provides for himself, but God provides for the lion.
Think in the morning, Act in the noon, Eat in the evening, Sleep in the
    night.
He who has sufferd you to impose on him knows you.
As the plow follows words, so God rewards prayers.
5 The tygers of wrath are wiser than the horses of instruction.
Expect poison from the standing water.
You never know what is enough unless you know what is more than enough.

Listen to the fool's reproach! it is a kingly title!
The eyes of fire, the nostrils of air, the mouth of water, the beard of earth.
10 The weak in courage is strong in cunning.
The apple tree never asks the beech how he shall grow, nor the lion the
     horse, how he shall take his prey.
The thankful reciever bears a plentiful harvest.
If others had not been foolish, we should be so.
The soul of sweet delight can never be defil'd.
15 When thou seest an Eagle, thou seest a portion of Genius; lift up thy head!
As the catterpiller chooses the fairest leaves to lay her eggs on, so the priest
     lays his curse on the fairest joys.
To create a little flower is the labour of ages.
Damn braces; Bless relaxes.
The best wine is the oldest, the best water the newest.
20 Prayers plow not! Praises reap not!
Joys laugh not! Sorrows weep not!

PLATE 10

The head Sublime, the heart Pathos, the genitals Beauty, the hands & feet
    Proportion.
As the air to a bird or the sea to a fish, so is contempt to the contemptible.
The crow wish'd every thing was black, the owl that every thing was white.
Exuberance is Beauty.
5 If the lion was advised by the fox, he would be cunning.
Improvement makes strait roads, but the crooked roads without
     Improvement are roads of Genius.
Sooner murder an infant in its cradle than nurse unacted desires.
Where man is not, nature is barren.
Truth can never be told so as to be understood, and not be believ'd.
10   Enough! or Too much.

PLATE 11

    The ancient Poets animated all sensible objects with Gods or Geniuses,
calling them by the names and adorning them with the properties of woods,
rivers, mountains, lakes, cities, nations, and whatever their enlarged & numerous senses could perceive.

    And particularly they studied the genius of each city & country, placing it
under its mental deity.

    Till a system was formed, which some took advantage of & enslav'd the
vulgar by attempting to realize or abstract the mental deities from their
objects; thus began Priesthood,

    Choosing forms of worship from poetic tales.

    And at length they pronounced that the Gods had ordered such things.

    Thus men forgot that All deities reside in the human breast.

PLATE 12

A Memorable Fancy

    The Prophets Isaiah and Ezekiel dined with me, and I asked them how
they dared so roundly to assert that God spake to them; and whether they

did not think at the time that they would be misunderstood, & so be the cause of imposition.

Isaiah answer'd: "I saw no God, nor heard any, in a finite organical perception; but my senses discover'd the infinite in every thing, and as I was then perswaded, & remain confirm'd, that the voice of honest indignation is the voice of God, I cared not for consequences, but wrote."

Then I asked: "Does a firm perswasion that a thing is so, make it so?"

He replied: "All poets believe that it does, & in ages of imagination this firm perswasion removed mountains; but many are not capable of a firm perswasion of any thing."

Then Ezekiel said: "The philosophy of the East taught the first principles of human perception. Some nations held one principle for the origin & some another; we of Israel taught that the Poetic Genius (as you now call it) was the first principle and all the others merely derivative, which was the cause of our despising the Priests & Philosophers of other countries, and prophecying that all Gods [PLATE 13] would at last be proved to originate in ours & to be the tributaries of the Poetic Genius; it was this that our great poet, King David, desired so fervently & invokes so pathetically, saying by this he conquers enemies & governs kingdoms; and we so loved our God, that we cursed in his name all the deities of surrounding nations, and asserted that they had rebelled; from these opinions the vulgar came to think that all nations would at last be subject to the Jews."

"This," said he, "like all firm perswasions, is come to pass, for all nations believe the Jews' code and worship the Jews' god, and what greater subjection can be?"

I heard this with some wonder, & must confess my own conviction. After dinner I ask'd Isaiah to favour the world with his lost works; he said none of equal value was lost. Ezekiel said the same of his.

I also asked Isaiah what made him go naked and barefoot three years? He answered, "the same that made our friend Diogenes,[4] the Grecian."

I then asked Ezekiel why he eat dung, & lay so long on his right & left side?[5] He answered, "the desire of raising other men into a perception of the infinite; this the North American tribes practise, & is he honest who resists his genius or conscience only for the sake of present ease or gratification?"

PLATE 14

The ancient tradition that the world will be consumed in fire at the end of six thousand years is true, as I have heard from Hell.

For the cherub with his flaming sword is hereby commanded to leave his guard at the tree of life;[6] and when he does, the whole creation will be consumed, and appear infinite and holy, whereas it now appears finite & corrupt.

This will come to pass by an improvement of sensual enjoyment.

But first the notion that man has a body distinct from his soul is to be expunged; this I shall do, by printing in the infernal method, by corrosives,

4. Greek Cynic (4th century), whose extreme repudiation of civilized customs gave rise to anecdotes that he had renounced clothing. In Isaiah 20.2–3 the prophet, at the Lord's command, walked "naked and barefoot" for three years.
5. The Lord gave these instructions to the prophet Ezekiel (4.4–6).
6. In Genesis 3.24, when the Lord drove Adam and Eve from the Garden of Eden, he had placed Cherubim and a flaming sword at the eastern end "to keep the way of the tree of life."

which in Hell are salutary and medicinal, melting apparent surfaces away, and displaying the infinite which was hid.[7]

If the doors of perception were cleansed every thing would appear to man as it is, infinite.

For man has closed himself up, till he sees all things thro' narrow chinks of his cavern.

PLATE 15

A Memorable Fancy

I was in a Printing house[8] in Hell & saw the method in which knowledge is transmitted from generation to generation.

In the first chamber was a Dragon-Man, clearing away the rubbish from a cave's mouth; within, a number of Dragons were hollowing the cave.

In the second chamber was a Viper folding round the rock & the cave, and others adorning it with gold, silver, and precious stones.

In the third chamber was an Eagle with wings and feathers of air; he caused the inside of the cave to be infinite; around were numbers of Eagle-like men, who built palaces in the immense cliffs.

In the fourth chamber were Lions of flaming fire, raging around & melting the metals into living fluids.

In the fifth chamber were Unnam'd forms, which cast the metals into the expanse.

There they were receiv'd by Men who occupied the sixth chamber, and took the forms of books & were arranged in libraries.[9]

PLATE 16

The Giants[1] who formed this world into its sensual existence, and now seem to live in it in chains, are in truth the causes of its life & the sources of all activity; but the chains are the cunning of weak and tame minds which have power to resist energy; according to the proverb, the weak in courage is strong in cunning.

Thus one portion of being is the Prolific, the other, the Devouring; to the Devourer it seems as if the producer was in his chains, but it is not so; he only takes portions of existence and fancies that the whole.

But the Prolific would cease to be Prolific unless the Devourer as a sea received the excess of his delights.

Some will say, "Is not God alone the Prolific?" I answer, "God only Acts & Is, in existing beings or Men."

These two classes of men are always upon earth, & they should be enemies; whoever tries [PLATE 17] to reconcile them seeks to destroy existence.

Religion is an endeavour to reconcile the two.

Note. Jesus Christ did not wish to unite but to separate them, as in the Parable of sheep and goats! & he says, "I came not to send Peace but a Sword."[2]

---

7. See p. 161, n. 2.
8. A covert pun runs through this section: workers, ink-blackened, who did the dirty work in the printing houses of the period were humorously known as "printer's devils."
9. In this "Memorable Fancy" Blake allegorizes his procedure in designing, etching, printing,

and binding his works of imaginative genius.
1. In this section human creative energies, called "the Prolific," in their relation to their indispensable contrary, "the Devourer."
2. Matthew 10.34. The parable of the sheep and the goats is in Matthew 25.32–33.

Messiah or Satan or Tempter was formerly thought to be one of the Ante-diluvians[3] who are our Energies.

A Memorable Fancy

An Angel came to me and said: "O pitiable foolish young man! O horrible! O dreadful state! consider the hot burning dungeon thou art preparing for thyself to all eternity, to which thou art going in such career."

I said: "Perhaps you will be willing to shew me my eternal lot, & we will contemplate together upon it and see whether your lot or mine is most desirable."

So he took me thro' a stable & thro' a church & down into the church vault at the end of which was a mill; thro' the mill we went, and came to a cave; down the winding cavern we groped our tedious way till a void boundless as a nether sky appeared beneath us, & we held by the roots of trees and hung over this immensity, but I said: "If you please, we will commit ourselves to this void, and see whether Providence is here also, if you will not I will." But he answered: "Do not presume, O young man, but as we here remain, behold thy lot which will soon appear when the darkness passes away."[4]

So I remain with him sitting in the twisted [PLATE 18] root of an oak; he was suspended in a fungus which hung with the head downward into the deep.

By degrees we beheld the infinite Abyss, fiery as the smoke of a burning city; beneath us at an immense distance was the sun, black but shining; round it were fiery tracks on which revolv'd vast spiders, crawling after their prey, which flew, or rather swum in the infinite deep, in the most terrific shapes of animals sprung from corruption; & the air was full of them, & seemed composed of them; these are Devils, and are called Powers of the air. I now asked my companion which was my eternal lot? He said, "Between the black & white spiders."

But now, from between the black & white spiders a cloud and fire burst and rolled thro the deep, blackning all beneath, so that the nether deep grew black as a sea & rolled with a terrible noise. Beneath us was nothing now to be seen but a black tempest, till looking east between the clouds & the waves, we saw a cataract of blood mixed with fire, and not many stones' throw from us appeared and sunk again the scaly fold of a monstrous serpent. At last to the east, distant about three degrees, appeared a fiery crest above the waves. Slowly it reared like a ridge of golden rocks till we discovered two globes of crimson fire, from which the sea fled away in clouds of smoke. And now we saw it was the head of Leviathan;[5] his forehead was divided into streaks of green & purple like those on a tyger's forehead; soon we saw his mouth & red gills hang just above the raging foam, tinging the black deep with beams of blood, advancing toward [PLATE 19] us with all the fury of a spiritual existence.

---

3. Those who lived before Noah's Flood.
4. The "stable" is where Jesus was born, which, allegorically, leads to the "church" founded in his name and to the "vault" where this institution effectually buried him. The "mill" in Blake is a symbol of mechanical and analytic philosophy; through this the pilgrims pass into the twisting cave of rationalistic theology and descend to an underworld that is an empty abyss. The point of this Blakean equivalent of a carnival funhouse is that only after you have thoroughly confused yourself by this tortuous approach, and only if you then (as in the next two paragraphs) stare at this topsy-turvy emptiness long enough, will the void gradually assume the semblance of the comic horrors of the fantasized Hell of religious orthodoxy.
5. The biblical sea monster.

My friend the Angel climb'd up from his station into the mill. I remain'd alone, & then this appearance was no more, but I found myself sitting on a pleasant bank beside a river by moon light, hearing a harper who sung to the harp, & his theme was: "The man who never alters his opinion is like standing water, & breeds reptiles of the mind."

But I arose, and sought for the mill, & there I found my Angel, who surprised asked me how I escaped?

I answered: "All that we saw was owing to your metaphysics: for when you ran away, I found myself on a bank by moonlight hearing a harper. But now we have seen my eternal lot, shall I shew you yours? He laughd at my proposal; but I by force suddenly caught him in my arms, & flew westerly thro' the night, til we were elevated above the earth's shadow; then I flung myself with him directly into the body of the sun. Here I clothed myself in white, & taking in my hand Swedenborg's volumes, sunk from the glorious clime, and passed all the planets till we came to Saturn. Here I staid to rest & then leap'd into the void between Saturn & the fixed stars.[6]

"Here," said I, "is your lot, in this space, if space it may be calld." Soon we saw the stable and the church, & I took him to the altar and open'd the Bible, and lo! it was a deep pit, into which I descended, driving the Angel before me. Soon we saw seven houses of brick;[7] one we enterd; in it were a [PLATE 20] number of monkeys, baboons, & all of that species, chaind by the middle, grinning and snatching at one another, but withheld by the shortness of their chains. However, I saw that they sometimes grew numerous, and then the weak were caught by the strong, and with a grinning aspect, first coupled with & then devourd, by plucking off first one limb and then another till the body was left a helpless trunk. This, after grinning & kissing it with seeming fondness, they devour'd too; and here & there I saw one savourily picking the flesh off of his own tail. As the stench terribly annoyd us both, we went into the mill, & I in my hand brought the skeleton of a body, which in the mill was Aristotle's Analytics.[8]

So the Angel said: "Thy phantasy has imposed upon me, & thou oughtest to be ashamed."

I answered: "We impose on one another, & it is but lost time to converse with you whose works are only Analytics."

Opposition is true Friendship.

PLATE 21

I have always found that Angels have the vanity to speak of themselves as the only wise; this they do with a confident insolence sprouting from systematic reasoning.

Thus Swedenborg boasts that what he writes is new; tho' it is only the Contents or Index of already publish'd books.

A man carried a monkey about for a shew, & because he was a little wiser than the monkey, grew vain, and conceiv'd himself as much wiser than seven

---

6. In the Ptolemaic world picture, Saturn was in the outermost planetary sphere; beyond it was the sphere of the fixed stars.
7. The "seven churches which are in Asia," to which John addresses the Book of Revelation 1.4.

Blake now forces on the angel his own diabolic view of angelic biblical exegesis, theological speculation and disputation, and Hell.
8. Aristotle's treatises on logic.

men. It is so with Swedenborg; he shews the folly of churches & exposes hypocrites, till he imagines that all are religious, & himself the single [PLATE 22] one on earth that ever broke a net.

Now hear a plain fact: Swedenborg has not written one new truth. Now hear another: he has written all the old falshoods.

And now hear the reason: He conversed with Angels who are all religious, & conversed not with Devils, who all hate religion, for he was incapable thro' his conceited notions.

Thus Swedenborg's writings are a recapitulation of all superficial opinions, and an analysis of the more sublime, but no further.

Have now another plain fact: Any man of mechanical talents may from the writings of Paracelsus or Jacob Behmen[9] produce ten thousand volumes of equal value with Swedenborg's, and from those of Dante or Shakespear, an infinite number.

But when he has done this, let him not say that he knows better than his master, for he only holds a candle in sunshine.

A Memorable Fancy

Once I saw a Devil in a flame of fire, who arose before an Angel that sat on a cloud, and the Devil utterd these words:

"The worship of God is, Honouring his gifts in other men, each according to his genius, and loving the [PLATE 23] greatest men best. Those who envy or calumniate great men hate God, for there is no other God."

The Angel hearing this became almost blue; but mastering himself, he grew yellow, & at last white, pink, & smiling, and then replied:

"Thou Idolater, is not God One? & is not he visible in Jesus Christ? and has not Jesus Christ given his sanction to the law of ten commandments, and are not all other men fools, sinners, & nothings?"

The Devil answer'd; "Bray a fool in a mortar with wheat, yet shall not his folly be beaten out of him.[1] If Jesus Christ is the greatest man, you ought to love him in the greatest degree. Now hear how he has given his sanction to the law of ten commandments: did he not mock at the sabbath, and so mock the sabbath's God?[2] murder those who were murderd because of him? turn away the law from the woman taken in adultery?[3] steal the labor of others to support him? bear false witness when he omitted making a defence before Pilate?[4] covet when he pray'd for his disciples, and when he bid them shake off the dust of their feet against such as refused to lodge them?[5] I tell you, no virtue can exist without breaking these ten commandments. Jesus was all virtue, and acted from im[PLATE 24]pulse, not from rules."

When he had so spoken, I beheld the Angel, who stretched out his arms embracing the flame of fire, & he was consumed and arose as Elijah.[6]

9. Jakob Boehme (1575–1624), a German shoemaker who developed a theosophical system that has had persisting influence on both theological and metaphysical speculation. Paracelsus (1493–1541), a Swiss physician and a pioneer in empirical medicine, was also a prominent theorist of the occult.
1. Proverbs 27.22: "Though thou shouldst bray a fool in a mortar among wheat with a pestle, yet will not his foolishness depart from him." "Bray":

pound into small pieces.
2. Mark 2.27: "The sabbath was made for man."
3. Cf. John 8.2–11.
4. Cf. Matthew 27.13–14.
5. Matthew 10.14: "Whosoever shall not receive you . . . when ye depart . . . shake off the dust of your feet."
6. In 2 Kings 2.11 the prophet Elijah "went up by a whirlwind into heaven," borne by "a chariot of fire."

Note. This Angel, who is now become a Devil, is my particular friend; we often read the Bible together in its infernal or diabolical sense, which the world shall have if they behave well.

I have also The Bible of Hell,[7] which the world shall have whether they will or no.

One Law for the Lion & Ox is Oppression.

1790–93   1790–93

PLATE 25

A Song of Liberty[1]

1. The Eternal Female groand! it was heard over all the Earth.

2. Albion's[2] coast is sick, silent; the American meadows faint!

3. Shadows of Prophecy shiver along by the lakes and the rivers and mutter across the ocean. France, rend down thy dungeon![3]

4. Golden Spain, burst the barriers of old Rome!

5. Cast thy keys, O Rome,[4] into the deep down falling, even to eternity down falling,

6. And weep.[5]

7. In her trembling hands she took the new born terror, howling.

8. On those infinite mountains of light now barr'd out by the Atlantic sea,[6] the new born fire stood before the starry king![7]

9. Flag'd with grey brow'd snows and thunderous visages, the jealous wings wav'd over the deep.

10. The speary hand burned aloft, unbuckled was the shield, forth went the hand of jealousy among the flaming hair, and [PLATE 26] hurl'd the new born wonder thro' the starry night.

11. The fire, the fire, is falling!

12. Look up! look up! O citizen of London, enlarge thy countenance! O Jew, leave counting gold! return to thy oil and wine. O African! black African! (Go, wingèd thought, widen his forehead.)

13. The fiery limbs, the flaming hair, shot like the sinking sun into the western sea.

14. Wak'd from his eternal sleep, the hoary element[8] roaring fled away:

7. I.e., the poems and designs that Blake is working on.
1. Blake etched this poem in 1792 and sometimes bound it as an appendix to *The Marriage of Heaven and Hell*. It recounts the birth, manifested in the contemporary events in France, of the flaming Spirit of Revolution (whom Blake later called Orc), and describes his conflict with the tyrannical sky god (whom Blake later called Urizen). The poem ends with the portent of the Spirit of Revolution shattering the ten commandments, or prohibitions against political, religious, and moral liberty, and bringing in a free and joyous new world.
2. England's.
3. The political prison, the Bastille, was destroyed by the French revolutionaries in 1789.
4. The keys of Rome, a symbol of Papal power.
5. Echoing, among others, John 11.35 ("Jesus wept") and Revelation 18.11 (which states that at the fall of Babylon, "the merchants of the earth shall weep and mourn for her").
6. The legendary continent of Atlantis, sunk beneath the sea, which Blake uses to represent the condition before the Fall.
7. Blake often uses the stars, in their fixed courses, as a symbol of the law-governed Newtonian universe.
8. The sea, which to Blake represents a devouring chaos.

15. Down rushd, beating his wings in vain, the jealous king; his grey brow'd councellors, thunderous warriors, curl'd veterans, among helms, and shields, and chariots, horses, elephants; banners, castles, slings and rocks,
16. Falling, rushing, ruining! buried in the ruins, on Urthona's dens;
17. All night beneath the ruins; then, their sullen flames faded, emerge round the gloomy king,
18. With thunder and fire, leading his starry hosts thro' the waste wilderness [PLATE 27] he promulgates his ten commands, glancing his beamy eyelids over the deep in dark dismay,
19. Where the son of fire in his eastern cloud, while the morning plumes her golden breast,
20. Spurning the clouds written with curses, stamps the stony law[9] to dust, loosing the eternal horses from the dens of night, crying:

"Empire is no more! and now the lion & wolf shall cease."[1]

Chorus

Let the Priests of the Raven of dawn, no longer in deadly black, with hoarse note curse the sons of joy. Nor his accepted brethren, whom, tyrant, he calls free, lay the bound or build the roof. Nor pale religious letchery call that virginity, that wishes but acts not!

For every thing that lives is Holy.

1792   1792

FROM BLAKE'S NOTEBOOK[1]

Mock on, Mock on, Voltaire, Rousseau

Mock on, Mock on, Voltaire, Rousseau;[2]
Mock on, Mock on, 'tis all in vain.
You throw the sand against the wind,
And the wind blows it back again;

5   And every sand becomes a Gem
Reflected in the beams divine;

9. I.e., the Ten Commandments (verse 18), which the "finger of God" had written on "tables [tablets] of stone" (Exodus 31.18).
1. Cf. Isaiah's prophecy, 65.17–25, of "new heavens and a new earth," when "The wolf and the lamb shall feed together, and the lion shall eat straw like the bullock."
1. A commonplace book in which Blake drew sketches and jotted down verses and memoranda between the late 1780s and 1810. It is known as the Rossetti manuscript because it later came into the possession of the poet and painter Dante Gabriel Rossetti. These poems were first published in imperfect form in 1863, then transcribed from the manuscript by Geoffrey Keynes in 1935.
2. Blake regards both Voltaire and Rousseau, French writers often hailed as the authors of the Revolution, as representing rationalism and Deism.

Blown back, they blind the mocking Eye,
But still in Israel's paths they shine.

The Atoms of Democritus[3]
10 And Newton's Particles of light[4]
Are sands upon the Red sea shore,
Where Israel's tents do shine so bright.

Never pain to tell thy love

Never pain to tell thy love
Love that never told can be,
For the gentle wind does move
Silently, invisibly.

5 I told my love, I told my love,
I told her all my heart,
Trembling, cold, in ghastly fears—
Ah, she doth depart.

Soon as she was gone from me
10 A traveller came by
Silently, invisibly—
O, was no deny.

I askèd a thief

I askèd a thief to steal me a peach,
He turned up his eyes;
I ask'd a lithe lady to lie her down,
Holy & meek she cries.

5 As soon as I went
An angel came.
He wink'd at the thief
And smild at the dame—

And without one word said
10 Had a peach from the tree
And still as a maid
Enjoy'd the lady.

1796

---

3. Democritus (460–362 B.C.E.) proposed that atoms were the ultimate components of the universe.

4. Newton in his *Opticks* hypothesized that light consisted of minute material particles.

And did those feet[1]

And did those feet in ancient time
Walk upon England's mountains green?
And was the holy Lamb of God
On England's pleasant pastures seen?

5 And did the Countenance Divine
Shine forth upon our clouded hills?
And was Jerusalem builded here,
Among those dark Satanic Mills?[2]

Bring me my Bow of burning gold,
10 Bring me my Arrows of desire,
Bring me my Spear; O clouds unfold!
Bring me my Chariot of fire!

I will not cease from Mental Fight,
Nor shall my Sword sleep in my hand,
15 Till we have built Jerusalem
In England's green & pleasant Land.

ca. 1804–10   ca. 1804–10

Two Letters on Sight and Vision[1]

To Dr. John Trusler (Aug. 23, 1799)

Revd Sir

I really am sorry that you are falln out with the Spiritual World, Especially if I should have to answer for it. I feel very sorry that your Ideas & Mine on Moral Painting differ so much as to have made you angry with my method of Study. If I am wrong, I am wrong in good company. I had hoped your plan comprehended All Species of this Art, & Especially that you would not regret that Species which gives Existence to Every other, namely Visions of Eternity. You say that I want somebody to Elucidate my Ideas. But you ought to know that What is Grand is necessarily obscure to Weak men. That which can be made Explicit to the Idiot is not worth my care. The wisest of the Ancients

---

1. These quatrains occur in the preface to Blake's prophetic poem *Milton*. There is an ancient belief that Jesus came to England with Joseph of Arimathea, the merchant who is identified in the Gospels as making the arrangements for Christ's burial following the crucifixion. Blake adapts the legend to his own conception of a spiritual Israel, in which the significance of biblical events is as relevant to England as to Palestine. By a particularly Blakean irony, this poem of mental war in the service of apocalyptic desire is widely used as a hymn, national anthem, or school song by just those establishment figures whom Blake would call "angels."
2. There may be an allusion here to industrial

England, but the mill is also Blake's symbol for a mechanistic and utilitarian worldview, according to which, as he said elsewhere, "the same dull round, even of a universe" becomes "a mill with complicated wheels."
1. Blake wrote these pronouncements about the difference between "corporeal" sight and imaginative vision at times when a friend, a patron, or the need for money was putting pressure on him to turn from his visionary art to more fashionable modes of representation. The first letter is a passionate response to John Trusler (1735–1820), clergyman and author, who had objected to some of Blake's visionary art.

considerd what is not too Explicit as the fittest for Instruction, because it rouzes the faculties to act. I name Moses, Solomon, Esop, Homer, Plato.

But as you have favored me with your remarks on my Design, permit me in return to defend it against a mistaken one, which is, That I have supposed Malevolence without a Cause.[2]—Is not Merit in one a Cause of Envy in another, & Serenity & Happiness & Beauty a Cause of Malevolence? But Want of Money & the Distress of A Thief can never be alleged as the Cause of his Thievery, for many honest people endure greater hardships with Fortitude. We must therefore seek the Cause elsewhere than in want of Money, for that is the Miser's passion, not the Thief's.

I have therefore proved your Reasonings Ill proportioned, which you can never prove my figures to be. They are those of Michael Angelo, Rafael, & the Antique, & of the best living Models. I perceive that your Eye is perverted by Caricature Prints,[3] which ought not to abound so much as they do. Fun I love, but too much Fun is of all things the most loathsom. Mirth is better than Fun, & Happiness is better than Mirth—I feel that a Man may be happy in This World. And I know that This World Is a World of Imagination & Vision. I see Every thing I paint In This World, but Every body does not see alike. To the Eyes of a Miser a Guinea is more beautiful than the Sun, & a bag worn with the use of Money has more beautiful proportions than a Vine filled with Grapes. The tree which moves some to tears of joy is in the Eyes of others only a Green thing that stands in the way. Some See Nature all Ridicule & Deformity, & by these I shall not regulate my proportions; & Some Scarce see Nature at all. But to the Eyes of the Man of Imagination Nature is Imagination itself. As a man is, So he Sees. As the Eye is formed, such are its Powers. You certainly Mistake when you say that the Visions of Fancy are not to be found in This World. To Me This World is all One continued Vision of Fancy or Imagination, & I feel Flatterd when I am told So. What is it sets Homer, Virgil, & Milton in so high a rank of Art? Why is the Bible more Entertaining & Instructive than any other book? Is it not because they are addressed to the Imagination, which is Spiritual Sensation, & but mediately to the Understanding or Reason? Such is True Painting, and such was alone valued by the Greeks & the best modern Artists. Consider what Lord Bacon says, "Sense sends over to Imagination before Reason have judged, & Reason sends over to Imagination before the Decree can be acted." See Advancem' of Learning, Part 2, P. 47 of first Edition.

But I am happy to find a Great Majority of Fellow Mortals who can Elucidate My Visions, & Particularly they have been Elucidated by Children, who have taken a greater delight in contemplating my Pictures than I even hoped. Neither Youth nor Childhood is Folly or Incapacity. Some Children are Fools, & so are some Old Men. But There is a vast Majority on the side of Imagination or Spiritual Sensation.

To Engrave after another Painter is infinitely more laborious than to Engrave one's own Inventions. And of the Size you require my price has been Thirty Guineas, & I cannot afford to do it for less. I had Twelve for the Head I sent you as a Specimen; but after my own designs, I could do at least

2. Blake had made a watercolor drawing (which has survived) illustrating Malevolence. He described this design in an earlier letter: "A Father, taking leave of his Wife & Child, Is watch'd by two Fiends incarnate, with intention that when his back is turned they will murder the mother & her infant."
3. Pictures of people with ludicrously exaggerated features, like, for instance, James Gillray's.

Six times the quantity of labour in the same time, which will account for the difference of price, as also that Chalk Engraving is at least six times as laborious as Aqua tinta. I have no objection to Engraving after another Artist. Engraving is the profession I was apprenticed to, & should never have attempted to live by any thing else, If orders had not come in for my Designs & Paintings, which I have the pleasure to tell you are Increasing Every Day. Thus If I am a Painter, it is not to be attributed to Seeking after. But I am contented whether I live by Painting or Engraving.

I am Revd Sir Your very obedient servant,

William Blake

To George Cumberland[4] (Apr. 12, 1827)

Dear Cumberland

I have been very near the Gates of Death & have returned very weak & an Old Man feeble & tottering, but not in Spirit & Life not in The Real Man The Imagination which Liveth for Ever. In that I am stronger & stronger as this Foolish Body decays. I thank you for the Pains you have taken with Poor Job.[5] I know too well that a great majority of Englishmen are fond of The Indefinite, which they Measure by Newton's Doctrine of the Fluxions of an Atom,[6] a Thing that does not Exist. These are Politicians & think that Republican Art[7] is Inimical to their Atom. For a Line or Lineament is not formed by Chance; a Line is a Line in its Minutest Subdivision[s]; Strait or Crooked, It is Itself, & Not Intermeasurable with or by any Thing Else. Such is Job, but since the French Revolution Englishmen are all Intermeasurable One by Another; Certainly a happy state of Agreement, to which I for One do not Agree. God keep me from the Divinity of Yes & No too, The Yea Nay Creeping Jesus, from supposing Up & Down to be the same Thing, as all Experimentalists must suppose.

You are desirous, I know, to dispose of some of my Works & to make [them] Pleasing. I am obliged to you & to all who do so. But having none remaining of all that I had Printed, I cannot Print more Except at a great loss, for at the time I printed those things I had a whole House to range in; now I am shut up in a Corner, therefore am forced to ask a Price for them that I scarce expect to get from a Stranger. I am now Printing a Set of the Songs of Innocence & Experience for a Friend at Ten Guineas, which I cannot do under Six Months consistent with my other Work, so that I have little hope of doing any more of such things. The Last Work I produced is a Poem Entitled "Jerusalem the Emanation of the Giant Albion," but find that to Print it will Cost my Time the amount of Twenty Guineas. One I have Finishd; it contains 100 Plates but it is not likely that I shall get a Customer for it.

As you wish me to send you a list with the Prices of these things they are as follows:

---

4. A businessman who was an old and loyal friend of Blake and a buyer of his illuminated books. Blake wrote this letter only four months before he died on Aug. 4, 1827.
5. Cumberland was trying to interest his friends in buying a set of Blake's engravings, *Illustrations of the Book of Job.*

6. Isaac Newton's *Method of Fluxions* (1704) announced his discovery of the infinitesimal calculus. To Blake, Newton was the archrepresentative of materialist philosophy.
7. I.e., a free art, not subject to authoritarian control, and suited to the free citizens of a republic (rather than the subjects of a monarch).

	£	s	d
America	6.	6.	0
Europe	6.	6.	0
Visions &^{c}	5.	5.	0
Thel	3.	3.	0
Songs of Inn. & Exp.	10.	10.	0
Urizen	6.	6.	0

The Little Card[8] I will do as soon as Possible, but when you Consider that I have been reduced to a Skeleton, from which I am slowly recovering, you will I hope have Patience with me.

Flaxman[9] is Gone & we must All soon follow, every one to his Own Eternal House, Leaving the Delusive Goddess Nature & her Laws to get into Freedom from all Law of the Members into The Mind, in which every one is King & Priest in his own House. God Send it so on Earth as it is in Heaven.

I am, Dear Sir, Yours Affectionately

WILLIAM BLAKE

8. A small illustrated name card that Blake executed for Cumberland; it was his last engraving.
9. John Flaxman, a well-known sculptor of the time and illustrator of Homer and Dante, had died the preceding December.

ROBERT BURNS
1759–1796

When Robert Burns published *Poems, Chiefly in the Scottish Dialect* in 1786, he was immediately hailed by the Edinburgh establishment as an instance of the natural genius, a "Heaven-taught ploughman" whose poems owed nothing to literary study, but instead represented the spontaneous overflow of his native feelings. Burns took care to call attention to those qualities in his verse—the undisciplined energy and rustic simplicity—that suited the temper of an age worried that modern refinement and propriety had undermined the vigor of poetry. But even though he cast himself (in the half-modest, half-defiant words of his Preface to *Poems*) as someone "unacquainted with the necessary requisites for commencing Poet by rule," Burns was in fact a widely read (although largely self-educated) man and a careful craftsman who turned to two earlier traditions for his poetic models. One of these was an oral tradition of folklore and popular balladry. The other was the highly developed literary tradition of poetry written in Scots or Lallans—the distinct English of Lowland Scotland.

His father—William Burnes, as he spelled his name—was a God-fearing and hard-working farmer of Ayrshire, a county in southwestern Scotland, who, unable to make a go of it in a period of hard times and high rents, died in 1784 broken in body and spirit. Robert, with his brother Gilbert, was forced to do the heavy work of a man while still a boy and began to show signs of the heart trouble of which he was to die when only thirty-seven. Although his father had the Scottish esteem for education and saw to it that his sons attended school whenever they could, Burns's education in literature, theology, politics, and philosophy came mainly from his own reading. At the age of fifteen, he fell in love and was inspired by that event to write his first song. "Thus," he said, "with me began Love and Poesy." After he reached maturity, he practiced at both. He began a series of love affairs, fathering in 1785 the first of a number of illegitimate children. He also extended greatly the range and quantity of his attempts at poetry. So rapid was his development that by the time he published the Kilmarnock edition, at the age of twenty-seven, he had written all but a few of his greatest long poems.

The Kilmarnock volume (so named from the town in which it was published) is one of the most remarkable first volumes by any British poet, and it had a great and immediate success. Burns was acclaimed "Caledonia's Bard" and championed by intellectuals and gentlefolk when he visited the city of Edinburgh soon after his book came out. The peasant-poet demonstrated that he could more than hold his own as an urbane conversationalist and debater. But he was also wise enough to realize that once the novelty wore off, his eminence in this society would not endure. He had a fierce pride that was quick to resent any hint of contempt or condescension toward himself as a man of low degree. His sympathies were democratic, and even in 1793 and 1794, when partisans of parliamentary reform were being prosecuted for sedition in Edinburgh and Glasgow, he remained (like William Blake in London) an outspoken admirer of the republican revolutions in America and France. In religion too he was a radical. Against the strict Calvinism of the Presbyterian kirk (church) in which he had been raised, Burns was known to profess "the Religion of Sentiment and Reason." A letter of December 1789, in which he seizes the chance to play a free-thinking Son "of Satan," merrily proclaims his intention to take up a theme that will, he says, be "pregnant with all the stores of Learning, from Moses & Confucius to [Benjamin] Franklin & [Joseph] Priestl[e]y—in short . . . I intend to write Baudy." Burns's satires on the kirk and taste for bawdy vulgarity could offend. Furthermore, his promiscuity gained him considerable notoriety, less because womanizing was out of the common order for the time than because he flaunted it. Many of the friendships that he made in high society fell apart, and Burns's later visits to Edinburgh were less successful than the first.

In 1788 Burns was given a commission as excise officer, or tax inspector, and he settled down with Jean Armour, a former lover, now his wife, at Ellisland, near Dumfries, combining his official duties with farming. This was the fourth farm on which Burns had worked; and when it, like the others, failed, he moved his family to the lively country town of Dumfries. Here he was fairly happy, despite recurrent illness and a chronic shortage of money. He performed his official duties efficiently and was respected by his fellow townspeople and esteemed by his superiors; he was a devoted family man and father; and he accumulated a circle of intimates to whom he could repair for conversation and conviviality. In 1787 James Johnson, an engraver, had enlisted Burns's aid in collecting Scottish ballads for an anthology called *The Scots Musical Museum*. Burns soon became the real editor for several volumes of this work, devoting all of his free time to collecting, editing, restoring, and imitating traditional songs, and to writing verses of his own to traditional dance tunes. Almost all of his creative work during the last twelve years of his life went into the writing of songs for the *Musical Museum* and for George Thomson's *Select Collection of Original Scottish Airs*. This was for Burns a devoted labor of love and patriotism, done anonymously, for which he refused to accept any pay, although badly in need of money; and he continued the work when he was literally on his deathbed.

Because of its use of Scots, the language spoken by most eighteenth-century Scottish people (lower and upper class alike), and because, in addition, of its lyricism and engagement with folk culture, Burns's verse is often said to anticipate William Wordsworth's idea of a poetry founded on "a selection of language really used by men." This account is based primarily on his songs. By far the major portion of the poems that he published under his own name are concerned with men and manners and are written in the literary forms that had been favored by earlier eighteenth-century poets. They include brilliant satire in a variety of modes, a number of fine verse epistles to friends and fellow poets, and one masterpiece of mock-heroic (or at any rate seriocomic) narrative, "Tam o' Shanter." It can be argued that, next to Pope, Burns is the greatest eighteenth-century master of these literary types. (Byron would later claim those forms for his own generation.) Yet Burns's writings in satire, epistle, and mock-heroic are remote from Pope's in their heartiness and verve, no less than in their dialect and intricate stanza forms. The reason for the difference is that Burns turned for his models not to Horace and the English neoclassic tradition but to the native tradition that had been established in the golden age of Scots poetry by Robert Henryson, William Dunbar, Gavin Douglas, and other Scottish Chaucerians of the fifteenth and sixteenth centuries. He knew this literature through his eighteenth-century Scottish predecessors, especially Allan Ramsay and Robert Fergusson, who had collected some of the old poems and written new ones based on the old models. Burns improved greatly on these predecessors, but he derived from them much that is characteristic in his literary forms, subjects, diction, and stanzas.

Burns's songs, which number more than three hundred, have, however, in themselves been enough to sustain his poetic reputation. They made him, for a start, a central figure for his contemporaries' discussions of how music, valued by them for awakening sympathies that reason could not rouse, might serve as the foundation of a national identity. (William Wordsworth would explore this new notion of "national music"—of ethnically marked melody—in his 1805 poem "The Solitary Reaper.") But beyond being the bard of Scots nationalism, Burns is a songwriter for all English-speaking people. Evidence of that standing is supplied each New Year's Eve, when, moved once again to acknowledge their common bondage to time, men and women join hands and sing "Auld Lang Syne," to an old tune that Burns refitted with his new words.

To a Mouse

On turning her up in her Nest, with the Plough, November 1785[1]

Wee, sleekit,° cowrin,° tim'rous beastie,   *sleek / cowering*
    O, what a pannic's in thy breastie!
Thou need na start awa sae hasty,
        Wi' bickering brattle![2]
5 I wad be laith° to rin° an' chase thee,   *loath / run*
      Wi' murd'ring *pattle!*°   *plowstaff*

    I'm truly sorry Man's dominion
Has broken Nature's social union,
An' justifies that ill opinion,
10   Which makes thee startle
At me, thy poor, earth-born companion,
        An' *fellow-mortal!*

    I doubt na, whyles,° but thou may thieve;   *sometimes*
What then? Poor beastie, thou maun° live!   *must*
15 A *daimen-icker* in a *thrave*[3]
        'S a sma' request;
I'll get a blessin wi' the lave,°   *remainder*
        An' never miss't!

1. Burns's brother claimed this poem was composed while the poet was actually holding the plow.
2. With headlong scamper.
3. An occasional ear in twenty-four sheaves.

Thy wee bit *housie*, too, in ruin!
20 Its silly wa's° the win's are strewin!   *frail walls*
An' naething, now, to big° a new ane   *build*
   O' foggage° green!   *coarse grass*
An' bleak December's winds ensuin,
   Baith snell° an' keen!   *bitter*

25 Thou saw the fields laid bare an' waste,
An' weary Winter comin fast,
An' cozie here, beneath the blast,
   Thou thought to dwell,
Till crash! the cruel *coulter*° past   *cutter blade*
30   Out thro' thy cell.

That wee-bit heap o' leaves an' stibble,°   *stubble*
Has cost thee monie a weary nibble!
Now thou's turn'd out, for a' thy trouble,
   But° house or hald,[4]   *without*
35 To thole° the Winter's sleety dribble,   *endure*
   An' cranreuch° cauld!   *hoarfrost*

But, Mousie, thou art no thy lane,°   *not alone*
In proving *foresight* may be vain:
The best-laid schemes o' *Mice* an' *Men*
40   Gang aft a-gley,[5]
An' lea'e us nought but grief an' pain,
   For promis'd joy!

Still thou art blest, compar'd wi' *me!*
The present only toucheth thee:
45 But, Och! I backward cast my e'e°   *eye*
   On prospects drear!
An' forward, tho' I canna *see*,
   I *guess* an' *fear!*

1785   1786

To a Louse

On seeing one on a Lady's Bonnet at Church

Ha! whare ye gaun, ye crowlin° ferlie!°   *crawling / wonder*
Your impudence protects you sairlie:°   *sorely*
I canna say but ye strunt° rarely,   *strut*
   Owre gauze and lace;
5 Tho' faith, I fear, ye dine but sparely
   On sic a place.

4. Hold, holding (i.e., land).
5. Go often awry.

Ye ugly, creepin, blastit wonner,°   *wonder*
Detested, shunn'd, by saunt° an' sinner,   *saint*
How daur ye set your fit° upon her,   *foot*
10   Sae fine a Lady!
Gae somewhere else and seek your dinner,
     On some poor body.

Swith,° in some beggar's haffet° squattle;° *swift / hair / sprawl*
There ye may creep, and sprawl, and sprattle°   *struggle*
15 Wi' ither kindred, jumping cattle,
     In shoals and nations;
Whare *horn* nor *bane*[1] ne'er dare unsettle
     Your thick plantations.

Now haud° you there, ye're out o' sight,   *hold*
20 Below the fatt'rels,° snug and tight;   *ribbon ends*
Na faith ye yet![2] ye'll no be right
     'Till ye've got on it,
The vera tapmost, tow'ring height
     O' *Miss's bonnet*.

25 My sooth! right bauld ye set your nose out,
As plump an' gray as onie grozet:°   *gooseberry*
O for some rank, mercurial rozet,°   *rosin*
    Or fell,° red smeddum,°   *sharp / powder*
I'd gie you sic a hearty dose o't,
30   Wad dress your droddum!°   *buttocks*

I wad na been surpris'd to spy.
You on an auld wife's flainen toy;°   *flannel cap*
Or aiblins° some bit duddie° boy,   *perhaps / ragged*
    On's wyliecoat;°   *undershirt*
35 But Miss's fine *Lunardi!*[3] fie!
     How daur ye do't?

O, *Jenny*, dinna toss your head,
An' set your beauties a' abread!°   *abroad*
Ye little ken° what cursed speed   *know*
40   The blastie's° makin!   *creature's*
Thae° *winks* and *finger-ends*, I dread,   *those*
     Are notice takin!

O wad some Pow'r the giftie gie us
To see oursels as others see us!
45 It wad frae monie a blunder free us
     An' foolish notion:
What airs in dress an' gait wad lea'e us,
     And ev'n Devotion![4]

1785   1786

---

1. I.e., fine-tooth comb made of bone ("bane").
2. Confound you!
3. A balloon-shaped bonnet, named after Vin-cenzo Lunardi, who made a number of balloon flights in the 1780s.
4. I.e., affected piety.

Green Grow the Rashes

A FRAGMENT.

CHORUS.

Green grow the rashes,° O;   rushes
Green grow the rashes, O;
The sweetest hours that e'er I spend,
Are spent among the lasses, O.

I

5   There's nought but care on ev'ry han',
      In ev'ry hour that passes, O:
What signifies the life o' man,
      An' 'twere na for the lasses, O.
               Green grow, etc.

II

The warly° race may riches chase,   worldly
10   An' riches still may fly them, O;
An' tho' at last they catch them fast,
      Their hearts can ne'er enjoy them, O.
               Green grow, etc.

III

But gie me a canny° hour at e'en,°   quiet / evening
      My arms about my Dearie, O;
15   An' warly cares, an' warly men,
      May a' gae tapsalteerie,° O!   topsy-turvy
               Green grow, etc.

IV

For you sae douse,° ye sneer at this,   prudent
      Ye're nought but senseless asses, O:
The wisest Man[1] the warl' e'er saw,
20   He dearly lov'd the lasses, O.
               Green grow, etc.

V

Auld Nature swears, the lovely Dears
      Her noblest work she classes, O:
Her prentice° han' she try'd on man,   apprentice
      An' then she made the lasses, O.
               Green grow, etc.

1784   1787

1. Solomon, the Old Testament king who "loved many strange women" (1 Kings 11.1).

Holy Willie's Prayer[1]

O thou, wha° in the heavens dost dwell,   *who*
Wha, as it pleases best thysel',
Sends ane° to heaven and ten to hell,   *one*
    A' for thy glory,
5 And no for any guid or ill
    They've done afore thee!

I bless and praise thy matchless might,
Whan thousands thou hast left in night,
That I am here afore thy sight,
10   For gifts an' grace
A burnin' an' a shinin' light,
    To a' this place.

What was I, or my generation,°   *ancestry*
That I should get such exaltation,
15 I wha deserve sic just damnation,
    For broken laws,
Five thousand years 'fore my creation,
    Thro' Adam's cause.

When frae my mither's womb I fell,
20 Thou might hae plunged me in hell,
To gnash my gums, to weep and wail,[2]
    In burnin' lake,
Whar damned devils roar and yell,
    Chain'd to a stake.

25 Yet I am here a chosen sample,
To show thy grace is great an' ample;
I'm here a pillar in thy temple,
    Strong as a rock,

1. This satire, which takes the form of a dramatic monologue, was inspired by William Fisher, a self-righteous church elder in the same Ayrshire parish that in 1785 had forced Burns and Betty Paton to do public penance for "fornication." The poem is directed against a basic Calvinist tenet of the old Scottish kirk: Holy Willie assumes that as one of a small minority, God's "elect," he has been predestined for grace, no matter what deeds he does in this world.

Aiming to avoid giving offense, Burns prudently excluded "Holy Willie's Prayer" from collections he published during his lifetime, though he did circulate the poem in manuscript. One of those manuscripts must have been the source used by the publishers who, likely without the poet's permission, printed the poem in 1789, in an anonymous eight-page pamphlet titled *The Prayer of Holy Willie, A Canting, Hypocritical Kirk Elder.*

Another manuscript version of "Holy Willie's Prayer," in what is known as the Glenriddell Manuscript, includes a prologue that outlines Burns's "Argument" as follows: "Holy Willie was a rather oldish bachelor Elder in the parish of Mauchline, & much & justly famed for that polemical chattering which ends in tippling Orthodoxy, & for that Spiritualized Bawdry which refines to Liquorish Devotion.—In a Sessional process [a trial carried on under the auspices of the Kirk government] with a gentleman in Mauchline, a Mr. Gavin Hamilton, Holy Willie, and his priest, father Auld, after full hearing of the Presbytery of Ayr, came off but second best; owing partly to the oratorical powers of Mr. Robert Aiken, Mr. Hamilton's Counsel; but chiefly to Mr. Hamilton's being one of the most irreproachable & truly respectable characters in the country.—On losing his Process, the Muse overheard him [Holy Willie] at his devotions as follows—." The Glenriddell manuscript also gives the poem an epigraph from Alexander Pope's *The Rape of the Lock.* "And send the Godly in a pet to pray—."

2. An echo of Matthew 8.12; "the children of the kingdom shall be cast out into outer darkness: there shall be weeping and gnashing of teeth."

A guide, a buckler° an' example   shield
30   To a' thy flock.

But yet, O L—d! confess I must,
At times I'm fash'd° wi' fleshly lust;   troubled
An' sometimes too, wi' warldly trust°   duty
          Vile self gets in;
35   But thou remembers we are dust,
          Defil'd in sin.

O L—d! yestreen,° thou kens, wi' Meg,   yesterday night
Thy pardon I sincerely beg,
O! may it ne'er be a livin' plague
40   To my dishonour,
An' I'll ne'er lift a lawless l—g°   leg
          Again upon her.

Besides, I farther maun° allow,   must
Wi Lizie's lass, three times I trow;°   believe
45   But, L—d, that Friday I was fow,°   drunk
          When I came near her,
Or else, thou kens, thy *servant true*,
          Wad ne'er hae steer'd° her.   molested

Maybe thou lets this *fleshly thorn*
50   Beset thy servant e'en and morn,[3]
Lest he owre high and proud shou'd turn,
          'Cause he's sae *gifted*;
If sae, thy han' maun e'en be born,
          Until thou lift it.

55   L—d bless thy Chosen in this place,
For *here* thou hast a *chosen race*;
But G—d confound their stubborn face,
          And blast their name,
Wha bring thy elders to disgrace
60   An' public shame.

L—d mind G—n H—n's[4] deserts,
He drinks, an' swears, an' plays at carts,°   cards
Yet has sae mony takin' arts,
          Wi' grit an' sma',°   great and small
65   Frae G—d's an priest the people's hearts
          He steals awa'.

An' whan we chasten'd him therefore,
Thou kens how he bred sic a splore,°   disturbance
As set the warld in a roar

---

3. An echo of 2 Corinthians 12.7: "there was given to me a thorn in the flesh, the messenger of Satan to buffet me, lest I should be exalted above measure."
4. Burns's friend Gavin Hamilton, whom Holy Willie had brought up on moral charges before the kirk session of the Presbytery of Ayr. As Burns explained in the manuscript Argument, Hamilton was defended by his counsel, Robert Aiken (referred to in line 79).

70   O' laughin' at us;
Curse thou his basket and his store,
         Kail° an' potatoes.   *broth*

L—d hear my earnest cry an' pray'r,
Against that presbyt'ry o' Ayr;
75 Thy strong right hand, L—d make it bare,
         Upo' their heads,
L—d weigh it down, and dinna spare,
         For their misdeeds.

O L—d my G—d, that glib-tongu'd A—n,°   *Aiken*
80 My very heart an' saul° are quakin',   *soul*
To think how we stood sweatin' shakin',
         An' p—d wi' dread,
While he wi' hingin'° lips and snakin'[5]   *hanging*
         Held up his head.

85 L—d in the day of vengeance try him,
L—d visit them wha did employ him,
An' pass not in thy mercy by 'em,
         Nor hear their pray'r;
But for thy people's sake destroy 'em,
90   And dinna spare.

But, L—d remember me and mine
Wi' mercies temp'ral and divine,
That I for gear° and grace may shine,   *riches*
         Extoll'd by name,
95 An' a' the glory shall be thine,
         Amen, Amen!

1785   1789, 1799

Tam o' Shanter: A Tale[1]

Of Brownyis and of Bogillis full is this buke.
        GAWIN DOUGLAS

When chapmen billies° leave the street,   *peddler fellows*
And drouthy° neebors, neebors meet,   *thirsty*
As market-days are wearing late,

5. Burns's modern editor, Robert Irvine, suggests that in "snaking," Aiken may be sniffing contemptuously.

1. This mock-heroic poem, written to order for a 1791 book on Scottish antiquities, is based on a witch story told about Alloway Kirk, the ruins of a 16th-century church near Burns's house in Ayr. Burns recognized that "Tam o' Shanter" was his masterpiece: true, he admitted in a letter, it exhibited "a spice of roguish waggery that might be spared," but it also showed "a force of genius, and a finishing polish, that I despair of ever excelling." The epigraph, added when "Tam o' Shanter" was republished in the 1793 edition of *Poems, chiefly in the Scottish Dialect,* is from the prologue to book 6 of Gavin Douglas's 16th-century Scots translation of Virgil's *Aeneid.* In this book the epic hero Aeneas, soon to be the founder of Rome, descends into the world of the dead. See the NAEL Archive for a recording of "Tam o' Shanter."

An' folk begin to tak the gate;°   *road*
5 While we sit bousing at the nappy,°   *strong ale*
And getting fou° and unco° happy,   *drunk / very*
We think na on the lang Scots miles,[2]
The mosses, waters, slaps,° and styles,   *gaps in fences*
That lie between us and our hame,
10 Whare sits our sulky sullen dame,
Gathering her brows like gathering storm,
Nursing her wrath to keep it warm.

    This truth fand° honest *Tam o' Shanter*,   *found*
As he frae Ayr ae night did canter,
15 (Auld Ayr, wham ne'er a town surpasses,
For honest men and bonny lasses).

    O *Tam!* hadst thou but been sae wise,
As ta'en thy ain wife *Kate's* advice!
She tauld thee weel thou was a skellum,°   *rascal*
20 A blethering,° blustering, drunken blellum;° *chattering / babbler*
That frae November till October,
Ae° market-day thou was nae sober;   *one*
That ilka° melder,[3] wi' the miller,   *every*
Thou sat as lang as thou had siller;°   *silver, money*
25 That every naig° was ca'd° a shoe on,   *nag / driven*
The smith and thee gat roaring fou on;
That at the L—d's house, even on Sunday,
Thou drank wi' Kirkton Jean till Monday.
She prophesied that late or soon,
30 Thou would be found deep drown'd in Doon;
Or catch'd wi' warlocks in the mirk,°   *night*
By *Aloway's* auld haunted kirk.

    Ah, gentle dames! it gars° me greet,°   *makes / weep*
To think how mony counsels sweet,
35 How mony lengthen'd sage advices,
The husband frae the wife despises!

    But to our tale: Ae market-night,
Tam had got planted unco right;
Fast by an ingle,° bleezing° finely,   *fireplace / blazing*
40 Wi' reaming swats,° that drank divinely; *foaming new ale*
And at his elbow, Souter° *Johnny*,   *shoemaker*
His ancient, trusty, drouthy crony;
Tam lo'ed him like a vera brither;
They had been fou for weeks thegither.
45 The night drave on wi' sangs and clatter;
And ay the ale was growing better:
The landlady and *Tam* grew gracious,
Wi' favours, secret, sweet, and precious:
The Souter tauld his queerest stories;

---

2. Scots miles measured just over two hundred feet longer than English miles.
3. The amount of grain processed at a single grinding.

50   The landlord's laugh was ready chorus:
The storm without might rair° and rustle,   *roar*
Tam did na mind the storm a whistle.

    Care, mad to see a man sae happy,
E'en drown'd himself amang the nappy:
55   As bees flee hame wi' lades o' treasure,
The minutes wing'd their way wi' pleasure:
Kings may be blest, but *Tam* was glorious,
O'er a' the ills o' life victorious!

    But pleasures are like poppies spread,
60   You seize the flower, its bloom is shed;
Or like the snow falls in the river,
A moment white—then melts for ever;
Or like the borealis race,
That flit ere you can point their place;
65   Or like the rainbow's lovely form
Evanishing amid the storm.—
Nae man can tether time or tide;
The hour approaches Tam maun° ride;   *must*
That hour, o' night's black arch the key-stane,
70   That dreary hour he mounts his beast in;
And sic a night he taks the road in,
As ne'er poor sinner was abroad in.

    The wind blew as 'twad blawn its last;
The rattling showers rose on the blast;
75   The speedy gleams the darkness swallow'd;
Loud, deep, and lang, the thunder bellow'd:
That night, a child might understand,
The Deil° had business on his hand.   *Devil*

    Weel mounted on his gray mare, *Meg*,[4]
80   A better never lifted leg,[5]
Tam skelpit° on thro' dub° and mire,   *slapped / puddle*
Despising wind, and rain, and fire;
Whiles holding fast his gude blue bonnet;
Whiles crooning o'er some auld Scots sonnet;
85   Whiles glowring° round wi' prudent cares,   *staring*
Lest bogles° catch him unawares: *bogeymen*
Kirk-Alloway was drawing nigh,
Whare ghaists° and houlets° nightly cry.—   *ghosts / owls*

    By this time he was cross the ford,
90   Whare, in the snaw, the chapman smoor'd;[6]
And past the birks° and meikle stane,°   *birches / big stone*
Whare drunken *Charlie* brak's neck-bane;

4. Tam's horse, Meg (also called Maggie), occasions the poem's bawdiest wordplay.
5. Cf. this "lifted leg" to Willie's use of the term
about himself in line 41 of "Holy Willie's Prayer" (p. 182).
6. The peddler smothered.

And thro' the whins, and by the cairn,[7]
Whare hunters fand the murder'd bairn;°   *child*
95   And near the thorn, aboon the well,
Whare *Mungo's* mither hang'd hersel.—
Before him *Doon* pours all his floods;
The doubling storm roars thro' the woods;
The lightnings flash from pole to pole;
100   Near and more near the thunders roll:
When, glimmering thro' the groaning trees,
Kirk-Alloway seem'd in a bleeze;°   *blaze*
Thro' ilka bore° the beams were glancing;   *hole*
And loud resounded mirth and dancing.—

105   Inspiring bold *John Barleycorn!*
What dangers thou canst make us scorn!
Wi' tippeny,[8] we fear nae evil;
Wi' usquabae,° we'll face the devil!—   *whiskey*
The swats sae ream'd in *Tammie's* noddle,
110   Fair play, he car'd na deils a boddle.[9]
But *Maggie* stood right sair astonish'd,
Till, by the heel and hand admonish'd,
She ventured forward on the light;
And, wow! *Tam* saw an unco° sight!   *strange*

115   Warlocks and witches in a dance;
Nae cotillion brent new° frae *France*,   *brand new*
But hornpipes, jigs, strathspeys,[1] and reels,
Put life and mettle in their heels.
A winnock-bunker° in the east,   *window seat*
120   There sat auld Nick, in shape o' beast;
A towzie tyke,° black, grim, and large,   *shaggy dog*
To gie them music was his charge:
He screw'd the pipes and gart° them skirl,°   *made / screech*
Till roof and rafters a' did dirl.°   *rattle*
125   Coffins stood round, like open presses,
That shaw'd the dead in their last dresses:
And by some devilish cantraip° slight   *charm, spell*
Each in its cauld hand held a light.—
By which heroic *Tam* was able
130   To note upon the haly° table,   *holy*
A murderer's banes in gibbet airns;°   *irons*
Twa span-lang,[2] wee, unchristen'd bairns;
A thief, new-cutted frae a rape,°   *rope*
Wi' his last gasp his gab° did gape;   *mouth*
135   Five tomahawks, wi' blude red-rusted;
Five scymitars, wi' murder crusted;
A garter, which a babe had strangled;
A knife, a father's throat had mangled,
Whom his ain son o' life bereft,

---

7. Stones heaped up as a memorial. "Whins": furze, an evergreen shrub.
8. Two penny (usually of weak beer).
9. A very small copper coin. I.e., the weak beer frothed up so much in Tam's brain ("noddle") that he didn't care a farthing about devils ("deils").
1. A slow Highland dance.
2. Two spans long (a span is the distance from outstretched thumb to little finger).

140   The grey hairs yet stack° to the heft;   *stuck*
        Wi' mair o' horrible and awefu',
        Which even to name wad be unlawfu'.

        As *Tammie* glowr'd, amaz'd, and curious,
        The mirth and fun grew fast and furious:
145   The piper loud and louder blew;
        The dancers quick and quicker flew;
        They reel'd, they set, they cross'd, they cleekit,°   *joined hands*
        Till ilka carlin swat and reekit,[3]
        And coost her duddies to the wark,[4]
150   And linket° at it in her sark![5]   *tripped lightly*

        Now, *Tam, O Tam!* had thae been queans,°   *girls*
        A' plump and strapping in their teens,
        Their sarks, instead o' creeshie flannen,°   *greasy flannel*
        Been snaw-white seventeen hunder linnen![6]
155   Thir° breeks o' mine, my only pair,   *these*
        That ance were plush, o' gude blue hair,
        I wad hae gi'en them off my hurdies,°   *buttocks*
        For ae blink o' the bonie burdies!°   *bonny (pretty) girls*

        But wither'd beldams,° auld and droll,   *hags*
160   Rigwoodie° hags wad spean° a foal,   *ugly / wean*
        Lowping° and flinging on a crummock,°   *leaping / staff*
        I wonder didna turn thy stomach.

        But *Tam* kend what was what fu' brawlie,°   *finely*
        There was ae winsome wench and wawlie,°   *strapping*
165   That night enlisted in the core,°   *corps*
        (Lang after kend on *Carrick* shore;
        For mony a beast to dead she shot,
        And perish'd mony a bony boat,
        And shook baith meikle corn and bear,°   *barley*
170   And kept the country-side in fear)
        Her cutty° sark, o' Paisley[7] harn°,   *short / yarn*
        That while a lassie she had worn,
        In longitude tho' sorely scanty,
        It was her best, and she was vauntie.°—   *proud*
175   Ah! little kend thy reverend grannie,
        That sark she coft° for her wee Nannie,   *bought*
        Wi' twa pund Scots ('twas a' her riches),
        Wad ever grac'd a dance of witches!

        But here my Muse her wing maun cour;°   *lower*
180   Sic flights are far beyond her pow'r;
        To sing how Nannie lap and flang,
        (A souple jade° she was, and strang),   *hussie*
        And how *Tam* stood, like ane bewitch'd,
        And thought his very een° enrich'd;   *eyes*

3. Until every old woman did sweat and smoke.   6. Very fine linen.
4. Cast off her clothes for the work.   7. A major center of textile production.
5. Shirt (underclothes).

185   Even Satan glowr'd, and fidg'd fu' fain,[8]
     And hotch'd° and blew wi' might and main: *jerked*
     Till first ae caper, syne° anither,   *then*
     Tam tint° his reason a' thegither,   *lost*
     And roars out, "Weel done, Cutty-sark!"
190   And in an instant all was dark:
     And scarcely had he Maggie rallied,
     When out the hellish legion sallied.

     As bees bizz out wi' angry fyke,°   *fuss*
     When plundering herds° assail their byke;°   *herdsmen / hive*
195   As open° pussie's mortal foes,   *begin to bark*
     When, pop! she starts before their nose;
     As eager runs the market-crowd,
     When "Catch the thief!" resounds aloud;
     So Maggie runs, the witches follow,
200   Wi' mony an eldritch° skreech and hollow.   *unearthly*

     Ah, *Tam!* Ah, *Tam!* thou'll get thy fairin'![9]
     In hell they'll roast thee like a herrin!
     In vain thy *Kate* awaits thy comin!
     Kate soon will be a woefu' woman!
205   Now, do thy speedy utmost, Meg,
     And win the key-stane[1] of the brig;°   *bridge*
     There at them thou thy tail may toss,
     A running stream they dare na cross.
     But ere the key-stane she could make,
210   The fient° a tail she had to shake!   *devil*
     For Nannie, far before the rest,
     Hard upon noble Maggie prest,
     And flew at Tam wi' furious ettle;°   *intent*
     But little wist° she Maggie's mettle—   *knew*
215   Ae spring brought off her master hale,°   *whole*
     But left behind her ain grey tail:
     The carlin claught° her by the rump,   *clutched*
     And left poor Maggie scarce a stump.[2]

     Now, wha this tale o' truth shall read,
220   Ilk man and mother's son, take heed:
     Whene'er to drink you are inclin'd,
     Or cutty-sarks run in your mind,
     Think, ye may buy the joys o'er dear,
     Remember Tam o' Shanter's mare.

1790   1791, 1793

---

8. Fidgeted with pleasure.
9. Literally, a present brought home from a fair. I.e., Tam will get his just deserts.
1. It is a well known fact that witches, or any evil spirits, have no power to follow a poor wight any farther than the middle of the next running stream. It may be proper likewise to mention to the benighted traveller, that when he falls in with *bogles*, whatever danger may be in his going forward, there is much more hazard in turning back [Burns's note].
2. I.e., she had no tail left at all.

Such a Parcel of Rogues in a Nation

Fareweel to a' our Scottish fame,
   Fareweel our ancient glory!
Fareweel ev'n to the Scottish name,
   Sae famed in martial story!
5 Now Sark rins over Solway sands,
   An' Tweed rins to the ocean,
To mark where England's province stands—
   Such a parcel of rogues in a nation!

What force or guile could not subdue
10   Thro' many warlike ages
Is wrought now by a coward few
   For hireling traitors' wages.
The English steel we could disdain,
   Secure in valour's station;
15 But English gold has been our bane—
   Such a parcel of rogues in a nation!

O, would, or I had seen the day
   That Treason thus could sell us,
My auld grey head had lien in clay
20   Wi' Bruce and loyal Wallace![1]
But pith and power,° till my last hour   *with all my strength*
   I'll mak this declaration:—
'We're bought and sold for English gold'—
   Such a parcel of rogues in a nation!

1792

Robert Bruce's March to Bannockburn[1]

[Scots, Wha Hae]

Scots, wha hae wi' Wallace[2] bled,
Scots, wham Bruce has aften led,
Welcome to your gory bed
    Or to victorie!

5 Now's the day, and now's the hour;
See the front o' battle lour,
See approach proud Edward's power—
    Chains and slaverie!

1. For Bruce and Wallace, see "Robert Bruce's March to Bannockburn," below, nn. 1 and 2.
1. Burns's words are set to the old tune to which, it was said, Robert Bruce's Scottish army had marched when it went to battle against the English invaders in 1314. This marching song is at once a historical reconstruction and an anthem for the revolutionary 1790s. Burns's turn to song writing in the last few years of his life might, the critic Marilyn Butler suggested, have had to do with the fact that songs like these, transmitted aurally, were more likely than compositions in other modes to slip past the scrutiny of a censorious government.
2. William Wallace (1272–1305), the great Scottish warrior in the wars against the English.

Wha will be a traitor knave?
10 Wha can fill a coward's grave?
Wha sae base as be a slave?—
      Let him turn, and flee!

Wha for Scotland's King and Law
Freedom's sword will strongly draw,
15 Freeman stand or freeman fa',
      Let him follow me!

By Oppression's woes and pains,
By your sons in servile chains,
We will drain our dearest veins
20   But they shall be free!

Lay the proud usurpers low!
Tyrants fall in every foe!
Liberty's in every blow!
      Let us do, or die!

1793   1794, 1815

Song: For a' that and a' that[1]

Is there for honest Poverty
  That hings,° his head, an' a' that?   *hangs*
The coward slave, we pass him by—
  We dare be poor for a' that!
5 For a' that, an' a' that,
  Our toils obscure, an' a' that,
The rank is but the guinea's stamp,°   *inscription on a coin*
  The Man's the gowd° for a' that.   *gold*

What though on hamely fare we dine,
10   Wear hoddin grey,[2] an' a' that?
Gie° fools their silks, and knaves their wine—   *give*
  A Man's a Man for a' that.
For a' that, an a' that,
  Their tinsel show, an' a' that,
15 The honest man, tho' e'er sae poor,
  Is king o' men for a' that.

Ye see yon birkie° ca'd 'a lord,'   *fellow*
  Wha struts, an' stares, an' a' that?
Tho' hundreds worship at his word,
20   He's but a cuif° for a' that.   *dolt*
For a' that, an' a' that,
  His ribband, star, an' a' that,

---

1. This song was set to a dance tune, known as
"Lady Macintosh's Reel," that Burns had drawn
on for previous songs.
2. A coarse cloth of undyed wool.

    The man o' independent mind,
      He looks an' laughs at a' that.

25 A prince can mak a belted knight,
      A marquis, duke, an' a' that!
    But an honest man's aboon° his might—   *above*
      Guid faith, he mauna fa' that![3]
    For a' that, an' a' that,
30   Their dignities, an' a' that,
    The pith o' sense an' pride o' worth
      Are higher rank than a' that.

    Then let us pray that come it may
      (As come it will for a' that)
35 That Sense and Worth o'er a' the earth
      Shall bear the gree° an' a' that!   *win the prize*
    For a' that, an' a' that,
      It's comin yet for a' that,
    That Man to Man the world o'er
      Shall brithers be for a' that.

1795   1795

A Red, Red Rose[1]

    O, my Luve is like a red, red rose,
      That's newly sprung in June.
    O, my luve is like the melodie,
      That's sweetly play'd in tune.

5   As fair art thou, my bonie lass,
      So deep in luve am I,
    And I will luve thee still, my Dear,
      Till a' the seas gang° dry.   *go*

    Till a' the seas gang dry, my Dear,
10   And the rocks melt wi' the sun!
    O I will luve thee still, my dear,
      While the sands o' life shall run.

    And fare thee weel, my only Luve,
      And fare thee weel, a while!
15 And I will come again, my luve,
      Tho' it were ten thousand mile!

1794   1796

---

3. Must not claim that.
1. Like many of Burns's lyrics, this one incorporates elements from several contemporary ballads.

Auld Lang Syne[1]

CHORUS.

For auld lang syne, my jo,°   *sweetheart*
   For auld lang syne,
We'll tak a cup o' kindness yet
   For auld lang syne!

5 Should auld acquaintance be forgot,
   And never brought to mind?
Should auld acquaintance be forgot,
   And auld lang syne!

And surely ye'll be° your pint-stowp,°   *pay for / pint cup*
10   And surely I'll be mine,
And we'll tak a cup o' kindness yet
   For auld lang syne!

We twa° hae run about the braes,°   *two / slopes*
   And pou'd° the gowans° fine,   *pulled / daisies*
15 But we've wander'd monie a weary fit
   Sin' auld lang syne.

We twa hae paidl'd in the burn°   *stream*
   Frae morning sun till dine,°   *dinner, noon*
But seas between us braid° hae roar'd   *broad*
20   Sin' auld lang syne.

And there's a hand, my trusty fiere,°   *friend*
   And gie's a hand o' thine,
And we'll tak a right guid-willie waught°   *hearty swig*
   For auld lang syne!

1796

1. Long ago.

The Revolution Controversy and the "Spirit of the Age"

In a letter to Byron in 1816 Percy Shelley called the French Revolution "the master theme of the epoch in which we live." The closing sentences of his "Defence of Poetry" assert, similarly, that, because of the repercussions of the Revolution, English literature "has arisen as it were from a new birth." The "electric life that burns" within the great poets of the time, Shelley continues, expresses "less their spirit than the spirit of the age." Such judgments were widely shared: the literature of Romanticism, early and late, cannot be understood historically without acknowledgment of how these works' distinctive modes of imagining and feeling were shaped first by the promise, then by the tragedy, of the great events in France. In the generation preceding Shelley's several authors had expressed an enthusiasm for those political transformations that in its intensity resembled a religious awakening. Many tried to make sense of events in terms borrowed from the Bible, interpreting the Revolution as fulfilling the promise, guaranteed by an infallible text, that a short period of violence would ultimately usher in an era of universal peace in which the world will begin anew. (See "The French Revolution: Apocalyptic Expectations" in the NAEL Archive.) And even after what they considered the failure of the revolutionary promise—signaled by the executions of the king and queen, the massacres during the Reign of Terror under Robespierre, the wars of imperial conquest under Napoleon—many authors held fast, despite a pervasive disenchantment, to their dreams of radical transformation. Twenty years on, when Shelley wrote, it must have seemed, following the defeat of Napoleon's armies and restoration of the European monarchies, as though the clock had been turned back and the old political order had been reestablished on even firmer foundations than before. Shelley and many other Romantic authors, however, continued in the belief that the hopes aroused by the Revolution remained relevant, even essential, for their moment.

That Revolution began with the storming of the Bastille and freeing of a handful of political prisoners by an angry mob of Parisians on July 14, 1789. A month later, the new National Assembly passed the Declaration of the Rights of Man. Six weeks after, in early October, citizens marched to the royal palace of Versailles and arrested King Louis XVI and his queen, Marie Antoinette, confining them to the Tuileries palace in Paris. These happenings were almost immediately reported in the London newspapers, quick to recognize a commercial opportunity. British liberals applauded the revolutionists' proclamation of natural rights and equality. The radicals were ecstatic, believing the moment was ripe for Britain to embrace political change as well. Conservatives, who referred to themselves "loyalists," thus casting others' reformist principles as treason, were first wary and then horrified. Most alarming to them, perhaps, was the emergent view that politics was the legitimate business of the common people and should not be monopolized by an aristocratic elite.

It did not escape the notice of British onlookers that during the revolutionists' festivities, printing presses were carried along in the parades—the French republic's way of honoring the technology that made it possible to spread new political ideas and to include the masses in their discussion. This section documents how, through the early 1790s, a frenzied pamphlet war over the meanings of the French Revolution kept the printing presses of England busy in their turn. Sales in London's printmaking businesses were likewise boosted by the excitement, which provided visual artists, satirists especially, with unprecedented opportunities.

This English debate about the Revolution was initiated by Richard Price's sermon, *A Discourse on the Love of Our Country*, which he delivered a month after the imprisonment of the French king and queen. When a year later Edmund Burke published a rebuttal to Price, his *Reflections on the Revolution in France*, the controversy heated up. *Reflections* drew more than fifty further responses, from Mary Wollstonecraft, in her *Vindication of the Rights of Men* (1790), and Thomas Paine, in his *Rights Of Man* (1791), most famously. The extracts we have chosen convey the wildly divergent tones those four writers brought to their debating: euphoric in Price; declamatory and sometimes blatantly sensationalist in Burke; forthrightly contemptuous in Wollstonecraft, who mocks her opponent's rhapsodic style; pointed and plain in Paine, who purposefully develops an accessible style meant to appeal to the newly literate. The loyalists soon found that, despite their belief that the common people were better suited intellectually to deference than to discussion, they too needed to mobilize popular support and address Paine's broad audience. The British government therefore launched a full-throttled propaganda campaign of its own—an attempt to communicate conservative ideas across the barriers of social class that itself represented a radical break with tradition. This section ends by sampling the pivotal contributions to that campaign that the brilliant artist James Gillray made in the dozens of political prints that he etched during the 1790s—works that seem to have begun as pictorial synopses of loyalist pamphlets, but whose shock tactics took them far beyond that assigned function. Gillray's exaggerated depictions of English radicals and members of the Parisian mob made revolutionary ideas look depraved and a tad ludicrous and convinced many that total anarchy was the inevitable consequence of any mass movement for political reform.

RICHARD PRICE

Richard Price (1723–1791) was a Unitarian minister in London and a writer on moral philosophy, population, and the national debt, among other topics. The full title of his sermon, which prompted Burke's *Reflections* and in turn the scores of responses to Burke, is *A Discourse on the Love of Our Country, Delivered on Nov. 4, 1789, at the Meeting-House in the Old Jewry, to the Society for Commemorating the Revolution in Great Britain.* The London Revolution Society had been founded a year earlier to mark the hundredth anniversary of the "bloodless" Glorious Revolution of 1688, which ended the short reign of King James II and produced the Declaration of Right, establishing a limited monarchy and guaranteeing the civil rights of privileged classes. The first two-thirds of the extracts given here commemorate that Revolution; in the final third, beginning "What an eventful period is this!" Price greets with religious fervor "two other Revolutions, both glorious," the American and the French. The *Discourse* went through six editions in its first year of publication.

From A Discourse on the Love of Our Country

We are met to thank God for that event in this country to which the name of THE REVOLUTION has been given; and which, for more than a century, it has been usual for the friends of freedom, and more especially Protestant Dissenters, under the title of the REVOLUTION SOCIETY, to celebrate with expressions of joy and exultation. * * * By a bloodless victory, the fetters which despotism had been long preparing for us were broken; the rights of the people were asserted, a tyrant expelled, and a Sovereign of our own choice appointed in his room. Security was given to our property, and our consciences were emancipated. The bounds of free enquiry were enlarged; the volume in which are the words of eternal life, was laid more open to our examination; and that *aera* of light and liberty was introduced among us, by which we have been made an example to other kingdoms, and became the instructors of the world. Had it not been for this deliverance, the probability is, that, instead of being thus distinguished, we should now have been a base people, groaning under the infamy and misery of popery and slavery. Let us, therefore, offer thanksgivings to God, the author of all our blessings. * * *

It is well known that King James was not far from gaining his purpose; and that probably he would have succeeded, had he been less in a hurry. But he was a fool as well as a bigot. He wanted courage as well as prudence; and, therefore, fled, and left us to settle quietly for ourselves that constitution of government which is now our boast. We have particular reason, as Protestant Dissenters, to rejoice on this occasion. It was at this time we were rescued from persecution, and obtained the liberty of worshipping God in the manner we think most acceptable to him. It was then our meeting houses were opened, our worship was taken under the protection of the law, and the principles of toleration gained a triumph. We have, therefore, on this occasion, peculiar reasons for thanksgiving.—But let us remember that we ought not to satisfy ourselves with thanksgivings. Our gratitude, if genuine, will be accompanied with endeavours to give stability to the deliverance our country has obtained, and to extend and improve the happiness with which the Revolution has blest us.—Let us, in particular, take care not to forget the principles of the Revolution. This Society has, very properly, in its Reports, held out these principles, as an instruction to the public. I will only take notice of the three following:

First: The right to liberty of conscience in religious matters.

Secondly: The right to resist power when abused. And,

Thirdly: The right to chuse our own governors; to cashier them for misconduct; and to frame a government for ourselves.

* * *

I would farther direct you to remember, that though the Revolution was a great work, it was by no means a perfect work; and that all was not then gained which was necessary to put the kingdom in the secure and complete possession of the blessings of liberty.—In particular, you should recollect, that the toleration then obtained was imperfect. It included only those who could declare their faith in the doctrinal articles of the church of England. It has, indeed, been since extended, but not sufficiently; for there still exist penal laws on account of religious opinions, which (were they carried into execution) would shut up many of our places of worship, and silence and imprison some of our ablest and best men.—The TEST LAWS are also still in force; and deprive of eligibility to civil and military offices, all who cannot conform to the established worship. It is with great pleasure I find that the body of Protestant Dissenters, though defeated in two late attempts to deliver their country from this disgrace to it, have determined to persevere. Should they at last succeed, they will have the satisfaction, not only of removing from themselves a proscription they do not deserve, but of contributing to lessen the number of public iniquities. For I cannot call by a gentler name, laws which convert an ordinance appointed by our Saviour to commemorate his death, into an instrument of oppressive policy, and a qualification of rakes and atheists for civil posts.—I have said, *should* they succeed—but perhaps I ought not to suggest a doubt about their success. And, indeed, when I consider that in Scotland the established church is defended by no such test— that in Ireland it has been abolished—that in a great neighbouring country it has been declared to be an indefeasible right of all citizens to be equally eligible to public offices—that in the same kingdom a professed Dissenter from the established church holds the first office in the state—that in the Emperor's dominions *Jews* have been lately admitted to the enjoyment of equal privileges with other citizens—and that in this very country, a Dissenter, though excluded from the power of *executing* the laws, yet is allowed to be employed in *making* them.—When, I say, I consider such facts as these, I am disposed to think it impossible that the enemies of the repeal of the Test Laws should not soon become ashamed, and give up their opposition.

But the most important instance of the imperfect state in which the Revolution left our constitution, is the *inequality of our representation.* I think, indeed, this defect in our constitution so gross and so palpable, as to make it excellent chiefly in form and theory. You should remember that a representation in the legislature of a kingdom is the *basis* of constitutional liberty in it, and of all legitimate government; and that without it a government is nothing but an usurpation. When the representation is fair and equal, and at the same time vested with such powers as our House of Commons possesses, a kingdom may be said to govern itself, and consequently to possess true liberty. When the representation is partial, a kingdom possesses liberty only partially; and if extremely partial, it only gives a *semblance* of liberty; but if not only extremely partial, but corruptly chosen, and under corrupt influence after being chosen, it becomes a *nuisance*, and produces the worst of all forms of government—a government by corruption, a government carried on and supported by spreading venality and profligacy through a kingdom. May heaven preserve this kingdom from a calamity so dreadful! It is the point of depravity to which abuses under such a government as ours naturally tend, and the last stage of national unhappiness. We are, at present, I hope, at a great distance from it. But it cannot be pretended that there are no advances towards it, or that there is no reason for apprehension and alarm.

* * *

What an eventful period is this! I am thankful that I have lived to it; and I could almost say, *Lord, now lettest thou thy servant depart in peace, for mine eyes have seen thy salvation* [Luke 2.29–30]. I have lived to see a diffusion of knowledge, which has undermined superstition and error—I have lived to see the rights of men better understood than ever; and nations panting for liberty, which seemed to have lost the idea of it.—I have lived to see THIRTY MILLIONS of people, indignant and resolute, spurning at slavery, and demanding liberty with an irresistible voice; their king led in triumph, and an arbitrary monarch surrendering himself to his subjects.—After sharing in the benefits of one Revolution, I have been spared to be a witness to two other Revolutions, both glorious.—And now, methinks, I see the ardour for liberty catching and spreading; a general amendment beginning in human affairs; the dominion of kings changed for the dominion of laws, and the dominion of priests giving way to the dominion of reason and conscience.

Be encouraged, all ye friends of freedom, and writers in its defence! The times are auspicious. Your labours have not been in vain. Behold kingdoms, admonished by you, starting from sleep, breaking their fetters, and claiming justice from their oppressors! Behold, the light you have struck out, after setting *America* free, reflected to *France*, and there kindled into a blaze that lays despotism in ashes, and warms and illuminates *Europe*!

Tremble all ye oppressors of the world! Take warning all ye supporters of slavish governments, and slavish hierarchies! Call no more (absurdly and wickedly) REFORMATION, innovation. You cannot now hold the world in darkness. Struggle no longer against increasing light and liberality. Restore to mankind their rights; and consent to the correction of abuses, before they and you are destroyed together.

1789

EDMUND BURKE

The great statesman and political theorist Edmund Burke (1729–1797) read Price's *Discourse* in January 1790 and immediately began drafting his *Reflections on the Revolution in France* as a reply in the form of a letter (as the lengthy subtitle describes it) "Intended to Have Been Sent to a Gentleman in Paris" (a Frenchman who had written to Burke soliciting the British parliamentarian's opinion of events in his country). The work was published at the beginning of November and was an instant bestseller: thirteen thousand copies were purchased in the first five weeks, and by the following September it had gone through eleven editions. Clearly, part of its appeal to contemporary readers lay in the highly wrought accounts of the mob's violent treatment of the French king and queen (who at the time Burke was writing were imprisoned in Paris and would be executed three years later, in January and October 1793). *Reflections* has become the classic, most eloquent statement of British conservatism favoring monarchy, aristocracy, property, hereditary succession, and the wisdom of the ages. Earlier in his career Burke had championed many liberal causes and sided with the Americans in their war for independence; opponents and allies alike were surprised at the strength of his conviction that the French Revolution was a disaster and the revolutionists "a swinish multitude."

From Reflections on the Revolution in France

* * * All circumstances taken together, the French revolution is the most astonishing that has hitherto happened in the world. The most wonderful things are brought about in many instances by means the most absurd and ridiculous; in the most ridiculous modes; and apparently, by the most contemptible instruments. Every thing seems out of nature in this strange chaos of levity and ferocity, and of all sorts of crimes jumbled together with all sorts of follies. In viewing this monstrous tragi-comic scene, the most opposite

passions necessarily succeed, and sometimes mix with each other in the mind; alternate contempt and indignation; alternate laughter and tears; alternate scorn and horror.

* * *

You will observe, that from Magna Charta to the Declaration of Right,[1] it has been the uniform policy of our constitution to claim and assert our liberties, as an *entailed inheritance*[2] derived to us from our forefathers, and to be transmitted to our posterity; as an estate specially belonging to the people of this kingdom without any reference whatever to any other more general or prior right. By this means our constitution preserves an unity in so great a diversity of its parts. We have an inheritable crown; an inheritable peerage; and an house of commons and a people inheriting privileges, franchises, and liberties, from a long line of ancestors.

This policy appears to me to be the result of profound reflection; or rather the happy effect of following nature, which is wisdom without reflection, and above it. A spirit of innovation is generally the result of a selfish temper and confined views. People will not look forward to posterity, who never look backward to their ancestors. Besides, the people of England well know, that the idea of inheritance furnishes a sure principle of conservation, and a sure principle of transmission; without at all excluding a principle of improvement. It leaves acquisition free; but it secures what it acquires. Whatever advantages are obtained by a state proceeding on these maxims, are locked fast as in a sort of family settlement; grasped as in a kind of mortmain[3] for ever. By a constitutional policy, working after the pattern of nature, we receive, we hold, we transmit our government and our privileges, in the same manner in which we enjoy and transmit our property and our lives. The institutions of policy, the goods of fortune, the gifts of Providence, are handed down, to us and from us, in the same course and order. Our political system is placed in a just correspondence and symmetry with the order of the world, and with the mode of existence decreed to a permanent body composed of transitory parts; wherein, by the disposition of a stupendous wisdom, moulding together the great mysterious incorporation of the human race, the whole, at one time, is never old, or middle-aged, or young, but in a condition of unchangeable constancy, moves on through the varied tenour of perpetual decay, fall, renovation, and progression. Thus, by preserving the method of nature in the conduct of the state, in what we improve we are never wholly new; in what we retain we are never wholly obsolete. By adhering in this manner and on those principles to our forefathers, we are guided not by the superstition of antiquarians, but by the spirit of philosophic analogy. In this choice of inheritance we have given to our frame of polity the image of a relation in blood; binding up the constitution of our country with our dearest domestic ties; adopting our fundamental laws into the bosom of our family affections; keeping inseparable, and cherishing with the warmth

1. The Magna Carta, the "great charter" of English personal and political liberty, dates from 1215. The Declaration of Right, another cornerstone of the English constitution, was a product of the Glorious Revolution of 1688.
2. An entail is a legal device that prescribes the line of succession along which a piece of family property must pass and that thereby prevents future generations of heirs from making their own decisions about that property.
3. A legal term (literally, "dead hand") for the perpetual holding of lands by an ecclesiastical or other corporation.

of all their combined and mutually reflected charities, our state, our hearths, our sepulchres, and our altars.

Through the same plan of a conformity to nature in our artificial institutions, and by calling in the aid of her unerring and powerful instincts, to fortify the fallible and feeble contrivances of our reason, we have derived several other, and those no small benefits, from considering our liberties in the light of an inheritance. Always acting as if in the presence of canonized forefathers, the spirit of freedom, leading in itself to misrule and excess, is tempered with an awful gravity. This idea of a liberal descent inspires us with a sense of habitual native dignity, which prevents that upstart insolence almost inevitably adhering to and disgracing those who are the first acquirers of any distinction. By this means our liberty becomes a noble freedom. It carries an imposing and majestic aspect. It has a pedigree and illustrating ancestors. It has its bearings and its ensigns armorial. It has its gallery of portraits; its monumental inscriptions; its records, evidences, and titles. We procure reverence to our civil institutions on the principle upon which nature teaches us to revere individual men; on account of their age; and on account of those from whom they are descended. All your sophisters[4] cannot produce any thing better adapted to preserve a rational and manly freedom than the course that we have pursued, who have chosen our nature rather than our speculations, our breasts rather than our inventions, for the great conservatories and magazines[5] of our rights and privileges.

*　*　*

Far am I from denying in theory; full as far is my heart from withholding in practice (if I were of power to give or to withhold) the *real* rights of men. In denying their false claims of right, I do not mean to injure those which are real, and are such as their pretended rights would totally destroy. If civil society be made for the advantage of man, all the advantages for which it is made become his right. It is an institution of beneficence; and law itself is only beneficence acting by a rule. Men have a right to live by that rule; they have a right to justice; as between their fellows, whether their fellows are in politic function or in ordinary occupation. They have a right to the fruits of their industry; and to the means of making their industry fruitful. They have a right to the acquisitions of their parents; to the nourishment and improvement of their offspring; to instruction in life, and to consolation in death. Whatever each man can separately do, without trespassing upon others, he has a right to do for himself; and he has a right to a fair portion of all which society, with all its combinations of skill and force, can do in his favor. In this partnership all men have equal rights; but not to equal things. He that has but five shillings in the partnership, has as good a right to it, as he that has five hundred pound has to his larger proportion. But he has not a right to an equal dividend in the product of the joint stock; and as to the share of power, authority, and direction which each individual ought to have in the management of the state, that I must deny to be amongst the direct original rights of man in civil society; for I have in my contemplation the civil social man, and no other. It is a thing to be settled by convention.

4. Persons reasoning with clever and fallacious arguments (from the name given to a sect of paid teachers of rhetoric and philosophy in ancient Athens).
5. Storehouses.

* * *

History, who keeps a durable record of all our acts, and exercises her awful censure over the proceedings of all sorts of sovereigns, will not forget, either those events, or the era of this liberal refinement in the intercourse of mankind. History will record, that on the morning of the 6th of October 1789, the king and queen of France, after a day of confusion, alarm, dismay, and slaughter, lay down, under the pledged security of public faith, to indulge nature in a few hours of respite, and troubled melancholy repose. From this sleep the queen was first startled by the voice of the centinel at her door, who cried out to her, to save herself by flight—that this was the last proof of fidelity he could give—that they were upon him, and he was dead. Instantly he was cut down. A band of cruel ruffians and assassins, reeking with his blood, rushed into the chamber of the queen, and pierced with an hundred strokes of bayonets and poniards the bed, from whence this persecuted woman had but just time to fly almost naked, and through ways unknown to the murderers had escaped to seek refuge at the feet of a king and husband, not secure of his own life for a moment.

This king, to say no more of him, and this queen, and their infant children (who once would have been the pride and hope of a great and generous people) were then forced to abandon the sanctuary of the most splendid palace in the world, which they left swimming in blood, polluted by massacre, and strewed with scattered limbs and mutilated carcases. Thence they were conducted into the capital of their kingdom. Two had been selected from the unprovoked, unresisted, promiscuous slaughter, which was made of the gentlemen of birth and family who composed the king's body guard. These two gentlemen, with all the parade of an execution of justice, were cruelly and publickly dragged to the block, and beheaded in the great court of the palace. Their heads were stuck upon spears, and led the procession; whilst the royal captives who followed in the train were slowly moved along, amidst the horrid yells, and shrilling screams, and frantic dances, and infamous contumelies, and all the unutterable abominations of the furies of hell, in the abused shape of the vilest of women. After they had been made to taste, drop by drop, more than the bitterness of death, in the slow torture of a journey of twelve miles, protracted to six hours, they were, under a guard, composed of those very soldiers who had thus conducted them through this famous triumph, lodged in one of the old palaces of Paris, now converted into a Bastile[6] for kings.

* * *

I hear that the august person,[7] who was the principal object of our preacher's triumph,[8] though he supported himself, felt much on that shameful occasion. As a man, it became him to feel for his wife and his children, and the faithful guards of his person, that were massacred in cold blood about him; as a prince, it became him to feel for the strange and frightful transformation of his civilized subjects, and to be more grieved for them, than solicitous for himself. It derogates little from his fortitude, while it adds infinitely to the

---

6. The Bastille was France's political prison.
7. King Louis XVI.
8. A reference to Price's exclamation, in the final selection printed on p. 196 from *A Dis-* *course on the Love of Our Country*, that he has lived to see the French "king led in triumph . . . an arbitrary monarch surrendering himself to his subjects."

honor of his humanity. I am very sorry to say it, very sorry indeed, that such personages are in a situation in which it is not unbecoming in us to praise the virtues of the great.

I hear, and I rejoice to hear, that the great lady, the other object of the triumph, has borne that day (one is interested that beings made for suffering should suffer well) and that she bears all the succeeding days, that she bears the imprisonment of her husband, and her own captivity, and the exile of her friends, and the insulting adulation of addresses, and the whole weight of her accumulated wrongs, with a serene patience, in a manner suited to her rank and race, and becoming the offspring of a sovereign distinguished for her piety and her courage;[9] that like her she has lofty sentiments; that she feels with the dignity of a Roman matron; that in the last extremity she will save herself from the last disgrace,[1] and that if she must fall, she will fall by no ignoble hand.

It is now sixteen or seventeen years since I saw the queen of France, then the dauphiness,[2] at Versailles; and surely never lighted on this orb, which she hardly seemed to touch, a more delightful vision. I saw her just above the horizon, decorating and cheering the elevated sphere she just began to move in,—glittering like the morning-star, full of life, and splendor, and joy. Oh! what a revolution! and what an heart must I have, to contemplate without emotion that elevation and that fall! Little did I dream when she added titles of veneration to those of enthusiastic, distant, respectful love, that she should ever be obliged to carry the sharp antidote against disgrace concealed in that bosom; little did I dream that I should have lived to see such disasters fallen upon her in a nation of gallant men, in a nation of men of honor and of cava-liers. I thought ten thousand swords must have leaped from their scabbards to avenge even a look that threatened her with insult.—But the age of chiv-alry is gone.—That of sophisters, oeconomists, and calculators, has suc-ceeded; and the glory of Europe is extinguished for ever. Never, never more, shall we behold that generous loyalty to rank and sex, that proud submis-sion, that dignified obedience, that subordination of the heart, which kept alive, even in servitude itself, the spirit of an exalted freedom. The unbought grace of life, the cheap defence of nations, the nurse of manly sentiment and heroic enterprize is gone! It is gone, that sensibility of principle, that chas-tity of honor, which felt a stain like a wound, which inspired courage whilst it mitigated ferocity, which ennobled whatever it touched, and under which vice itself lost half its evil, by losing all its grossness.

This mixed system of opinion and sentiment had its origin in the antient chivalry; and the principle, though varied in its appearance by the varying state of human affairs, subsisted and influenced through a long succession of generations, even to the time we live in. If it should ever be totally extin-guished, the loss I fear will be great. It is this which has given its character to modern Europe. It is this which has distinguished it under all its forms of government, and distinguished it to its advantage, from the states of Asia, and possibly from those states which flourished in the most brilliant periods of the antique world. It was this, which, without confounding ranks, had produced a noble equality, and handed it down through all the gradations of

9. Marie Antoinette was the daughter of Maria Theresa, empress of Austria.
1. Like the women of classical Rome when they endured defeat, Marie Antoinette, Burke sug-gests, will kill herself to preserve her chastity rather than suffer the disgrace of rape.
2. I.e., wife of the dauphin, who was heir to the throne of France.

social life. It was this opinion which mitigated kings into companions, and raised private men to be fellows with kings. Without force, or opposition, it subdued the fierceness of pride and power; it obliged sovereigns to submit to the soft collar of social esteem, compelled stern authority to submit to elegance, and gave a domination vanquisher of laws, to be subdued by manners.

But now all is to be changed. All the pleasing illusions, which made power gentle, and obedience liberal, which harmonized the different shades of life, and which, by a bland assimilation, incorporated into politics the sentiments which beautify and soften private society, are to be dissolved by this new conquering empire of light and reason. All the decent drapery of life is to be rudely torn off. All the superadded ideas, furnished from the wardrobe of a moral imagination, which the heart owns, and the understanding ratifies, as necessary to cover the defects of our naked shivering nature, and to raise it to dignity in our own estimation, are to be exploded as a ridiculous, absurd, and antiquated fashion.

On this scheme of things, a king is but a man; a queen is but a woman; a woman is but an animal; and an animal not of the highest order. All homage paid to the sex[3] in general as such, and without distinct views, is to be regarded as romance and folly. Regicide, and parricide, and sacrilege, are but fictions of superstition, corrupting jurisprudence by destroying its simplicity. The murder of a king, or a queen, or a bishop, or a father, are only common homicide; and if the people are by any chance, or in any way gainers by it, a sort of homicide much the most pardonable, and into which we ought not to make too severe a scrutiny.

On the scheme of this barbarous philosophy, which is the offspring of cold hearts and muddy understandings, and which is as void of solid wisdom, as it is destitute of all taste and elegance, laws are to be supported only by their own terrors, and by the concern, which each individual may find in them, from his own private speculations, or can spare to them from his own private interests. In the groves of *their* academy, at the end of every visto, you see nothing but the gallows. Nothing is left which engages the affections on the part of the commonwealth. On the principles of this mechanic philosophy, our institutions can never be embodied, if I may use the expression, in persons; so as to create in us love, veneration, admiration, or attachment. But that sort of reason which banishes the affections is incapable of filling their place. These public affections, combined with manners, are required sometimes as supplements, sometimes as correctives, always as aids to law. The precept given by a wise man, as well as a great critic, for the construction of poems, is equally true as to states. *Non satis est pulchra esse poemata, dulcia sunto.*[4] There ought to be a system of manners in every nation which a well-formed mind would be disposed to relish. To make us love our country, our country ought to be lovely.

But power, of some kind or other, will survive the shock in which manners and opinions perish; and it will find other and worse means for its support. The usurpation which, in order to subvert antient institutions, has destroyed antient principles, will hold power by arts similar to those by which it has acquired it. When the old feudal and chivalrous spirit of *Fealty*,[5] which,

---

3. Homage paid to women.
4. "It is not enough for poems to have beauty; they must be sweet, tender, affecting" (Latin;

Horace's *Ars Poetica* 99).
5. Fidelity of a vassal or feudal tenant to his lord.

by freeing kings from fear, freed both kings and subjects from the precautions of tyranny, shall be extinct in the minds of men, plots and assassinations will be anticipated by preventive murder and preventive confiscation, and that long roll of grim and bloody maxims, which form the political code of all power, not standing on its own honor, and the honor of those who are to obey it. Kings will be tyrants from policy when subjects are rebels from principle.

important idea France Burke believes

When antient opinions and rules of life are taken away, the loss cannot possibly be estimated. From that moment we have no compass to govern us, nor can we know distinctly to what port we steer. Europe undoubtedly, taken in a mass, was in a flourishing condition the day on which your Revolution was compleated. How much of that prosperous state was owing to the spirit of our old manners and opinions is not easy to say; but as such causes cannot be indifferent in their operation, we must presume, that, on the whole, their operation was beneficial.

if not following rules, great loss

We are but too apt to consider things in the state in which we find them, without sufficiently adverting to the causes by which they have been produced, and possibly may be upheld. Nothing is more certain, than that our manners, our civilization, and all the good things which are connected with manners, and with civilization, have, in this European world of ours, depended for ages upon two principles; and were indeed the result of both combined; I mean the spirit of a gentleman, and the spirit of religion. The nobility and the clergy, the one by profession, the other by patronage, kept learning in existence, even in the midst of arms and confusions, and whilst governments were rather in their causes than formed. Learning paid back what it received to nobility and to priesthood; and paid it with usury,[6] by enlarging their ideas, and by furnishing their minds. Happy if they had all continued to know their indissoluble union, and their proper place! Happy if learning, not debauched by ambition, had been satisfied to continue the instructor, and not aspired to be the master! Along with its natural protectors and guardians, learning will be cast into the mire, and trodden down under the hoofs of a swinish multitude.

If, as I suspect, modern letters owe more than they are always willing to own to antient manners, so do other interests which we value full as much as they are worth. Even commerce, and trade, and manufacture, the gods of our oeconomical politicians, are themselves perhaps but creatures; are themselves but effects, which, as first causes, we choose to worship. They certainly grew under the same shade in which learning flourished. They too may decay with their natural protecting principles. With you, for the present at least, they all threaten to disappear together. Where trade and manufactures are wanting to a people, and the spirit of nobility and religion remains, sentiment supplies, and not always ill supplies their place; but if commerce and the arts should be lost in an experiment to try how well a state may stand without these old fundamental principles, what sort of a thing must be a nation of gross, stupid, ferocious, and at the same time, poor and sordid barbarians, destitute of religion, honor, or manly pride, possessing nothing at present, and hoping for nothing hereafter?

I wish you may not be going fast, and by the shortest cut, to that horrible and disgustful situation. Already there appears a poverty of conception, a

6. Interest.

coarseness and vulgarity in all the proceedings of the assembly and of all their instructors. Their liberty is not liberal. Their science is presumptuous ignorance. Their humanity is savage and brutal.

* * *

1790

MARY WOLLSTONECRAFT

The first of the many published replies to Burke's *Reflections* was by Wollstonecraft, who appears elsewhere in this anthology as author of A *Vindication of the Rights of Woman* (1792), the landmark work in the history of feminism, and *Letters Written during a Short Residence in Sweden, Norway, and Denmark* (1796). Toward the end of 1790, when Burke's *Reflections* came out, she was working in London as a writer and translator for the radical publisher Joseph Johnson. Reading Burke, she was outraged at the weakness of his arguments and the exaggerated rhetoric with which he depicted the revolutionists as violators of royalty and womanhood. Always a rapid writer, she composed her reply, A *Vindication of the Rights of Men*, in a matter of days, and Johnson's printer set it in type as fast as the sheets of manuscript were turned in. It was published anonymously in November, less than a month after Burke's *Reflections* first appeared, and a second edition (this time with her name on the title page) was called for almost immediately.

From A Vindication of the Rights of Men

Advertisement

Mr. Burke's Reflections on the French Revolution first engaged my attention as the transient topic of the day; and reading it more for amusement than information, my indignation was roused by the sophistical arguments, that every moment crossed me, in the questionable shape of natural feelings and common sense.

Many pages of the following letter were the effusions of the moment; but, swelling imperceptibly to a considerable size, the idea was suggested of publishing a short vindication of *the Rights of Men.*

Not having leisure or patience to follow this desultory writer through all the devious tracks in which his fancy has started fresh game, I have confined my strictures, in a great measure, to the grand principles at which he has levelled many ingenious arguments in a very specious garb.

A *Letter to the Right Honorable Edmund Burke*

Sir,

It is not necessary, with courtly insincerity, to apologize to you for thus intruding on your precious time, nor to profess that I think it an honor to discuss an important subject with a man whose literary abilities have raised him to notice in the state. I have not yet learned to twist my periods,[1] nor, in the equivocal idiom of politeness, to disguise my sentiments, and imply what I should be afraid to utter: if, therefore, in the course of this epistle, I chance to express contempt, and even indignation, with some emphasis, I beseech you to believe that it is not a flight of fancy; for truth, in morals, has ever appeared to me the essence of the sublime; and, in taste, simplicity the only criterion of the beautiful. But I war not with an individual when I contend for the *rights of men* and the liberty of reason. You see I do not condescend to cull my words to avoid the invidious phrase, nor shall I be prevented from giving a manly definition of it, by the flimsy ridicule which a lively fancy has interwoven with the present acceptation of the term. Reverencing the rights of humanity, I shall dare to assert them; not intimidated by the horse laugh that you have raised, or waiting till time has wiped away the compassionate tears which you have elaborately labored to excite.

From the many just sentiments interspersed through the letter before me, and from the whole tendency of it, I should believe you to be a good, though a vain man, if some circumstances in your conduct did not render the inflexibility of your integrity doubtful; and for this vanity a knowledge of human nature enables me to discover such extenuating circumstances, in the very texture of your mind, that I am ready to call it amiable, and separate the public from the private character.

☆　☆　☆

Quitting now the flowers of rhetoric, let us, Sir, reason together; and, believe me, I should not have meddled with these troubled waters, in order to point out your inconsistencies, if your wit had not burnished up some rusty, baneful opinions, and swelled the shallow current of ridicule till it resembled the flow of reason, and presumed to be the test of truth.

I shall not attempt to follow you through "horse-way and foot-path;"[2] but, attacking the foundation of your opinions, I shall leave the superstructure to find a center of gravity on which it may lean till some strong blast puffs it into the air; or your teeming fancy, which the ripening judgment of sixty years has not tamed, produces another Chinese erection,[3] to stare, at every turn, the plain country people in the face, who bluntly call such an airy edifice—a folly.

The birthright of man, to give you, Sir, a short definition of this disputed right, is such a degree of liberty, civil and religious, as is compatible with the liberty of every other individual with whom he is united in a social compact, and the continued existence of that compact.

Liberty, in this simple, unsophisticated sense, I acknowledge, is a fair idea that has never yet received a form in the various governments that have been established on our beauteous globe; the demon of property has ever been at hand to encroach on the sacred rights of men, and to fence round with awful pomp laws that war with justice. But that it results from the eternal foundation of right—from immutable truth—who will presume to deny, that

1. Conceal the truth with elaborate sentence structures.
2. Shakespeare's *King Lear* 4.1.57.
3. Chinese pagodas were popular ornaments in late-18th-century British landscaping.

pretends to rationality—if reason has led them to build their morality[4] and religion on an everlasting foundation—the attributes of God?

I glow with indignation when I attempt, methodically, to unravel your slavish paradoxes, in which I can find no fixed first principle to refute; I shall not, therefore, condescend to shew where you affirm in one page what you deny in another; and how frequently you draw conclusions without any previous premises:—it would be something like cowardice to fight with a man who had never exercised the weapons with which his opponent chose to combat, and irksome to refute sentence after sentence in which the latent spirit of tyranny appeared. _[asserts that Burke's writing was tyrannical]_

I perceive, from the whole tenor of your Reflections, that you have a mortal antipathy to reason; but, if there is any thing like argument, or first principles, in your wild declamation, behold the result:—that we are to reverence the rust of antiquity, and term the unnatural customs, which ignorance and mistaken self-interest have consolidated, the sage fruit of experience: nay, that, if we do discover some errors, our _feelings_ should lead us to excuse, with blind love, or unprincipled filial affection, the venerable vestiges of ancient days. These are gothic[5] notions of beauty—the ivy is beautiful, but, when it insidiously destroys the trunk from which it receives support, who would not grub it up?

Further, that we ought cautiously to remain for ever in frozen inactivity, because a thaw, whilst it nourishes the soil, spreads a temporary inundation; and the fear of risking any personal present convenience should prevent a struggle for the most estimable advantages. This is sound reasoning, I grant, in the mouth of the rich and short-sighted.

Yes, Sir, the strong gained riches, the few have sacrificed the many to their vices; and, to be able to pamper their appetites, and supinely exist without exercising mind or body, they have ceased to be men.—Lost to the relish of true pleasure, such beings would, indeed, deserve compassion, if injustice was not softened by the tyrant's plea—necessity; if prescription was not raised as an immortal boundary against innovation. Their minds, in fact, instead of being cultivated, have been so warped by education, that it may require some ages to bring them back to nature, and enable them to see their true interest, with that degree of conviction which is necessary to influence their conduct.

The civilization which has taken place in Europe has been very partial, and, like every custom that an arbitrary point of honour has established, refines the manners at the expence of morals, by making sentiments and opinions current in conversation that have no root in the heart, or weight in the cooler resolves of the mind.—And what has stopped its progress?— hereditary property—hereditary honors. The man has been changed into an artificial monster by the station in which he was born, and the consequent homage that benumbed his faculties like the torpedo's[6] touch;—or a being, with a capacity of reasoning, would not have failed to discover, as his faculties unfolded, that true happiness arose from the friendship and intimacy which can only be enjoyed by equals; and that charity is not a condescending

---

4. As religion is included in my idea of morality, I should not have mentioned the term without specifying all the simple ideas which that comprehensive word generalizes; but as the charge of atheism has been very freely banded about in the letter I am considering, I wish to guard against misrepresentation [Wollstonecraft's note].
5. Barbarous.
6. Electric ray, a fish with a whiplike tail that gives an electric shock to those it touches.

distribution of alms, but an intercourse of good offices and mutual benefits, founded on respect for justice and humanity.

It is necessary emphatically to repeat, that there are rights which men inherit at their birth, as rational creatures, who were raised above the brute creation by their improvable faculties; and that, in receiving these, not from their forefathers but, from God, prescription can never undermine natural rights.

natural rights not given from forefathers

A father may dissipate his property without his child having any right to complain;—but should he attempt to sell him for a slave, or fetter him with laws contrary to reason; nature, in enabling him to discern good from evil, teaches him to break the ignoble chain, and not to believe that bread becomes flesh, and wine blood, because his parents swallowed the Eucharist with this blind persuasion.

There is no end to this implicit submission to authority—some where it must stop, or we return to barbarism; and the capacity of improvement, which gives us a natural sceptre on earth, is a cheat, an ignis-fatuus,[7] that leads us from inviting meadows into bogs and dung-hills. And if it be allowed that many of the precautions, with which any alteration was made, in our government, were prudent, it rather proves its weakness than substantiates an opinion of the soundness of the stamina, or the excellence of the constitution.

But on what principle Mr. Burke could defend American independence, I cannot conceive; for the whole tenor of his plausible arguments settles slavery on an everlasting foundation. Allowing his servile reverence for antiquity, and prudent attention to self-interest, to have the force which he insists on, the slave trade ought never to be abolished; and, because our ignorant forefathers, not understanding the native dignity of man, sanctioned a traffic that outrages every suggestion of reason and religion, we are to submit to the inhuman custom, and term an atrocious insult to humanity the love of our country, and a proper submission to the laws by which our property is secured.—Security of property! Behold, in a few words, the definition of English liberty. And to this selfish principle every nobler one is sacrificed.— The Briton takes place of the man, and the image of God is lost in the citizen! But it is not that enthusiastic flame which in Greece and Rome consumed every sordid passion: no, self is the focus; and the disparting rays rise not above our foggy atmosphere. But softly—it is only the property of the rich that is secure; the man who lives by the sweat of his brow has no asylum from oppression; the strong man may enter—when was the castle of the poor sacred? and the base informer steal him from the family that depend on his industry for subsistence.

* * *

But, among all your plausible arguments, and witty illustrations, your contempt for the poor always appears conspicuous, and rouses my indignation. The following paragraph in particular struck me, as breathing the most tyrannic spirit, and displaying the most factitious feelings. "Good order is the foundation of all good things. To be enabled to acquire, the people, without being servile, must be tractable and obedient. The magistrate must have his

---

7. The phosphorescent light (also known as will o' the wisp) that is said to appear in marshy landscapes and lead travelers off the path of safety.

reverence, the laws their authority. The body of the people must not find the principles of natural subordination by art rooted out of their minds. They *must* respect that property of which they *cannot* partake. *They must labor to obtain what by labor can be obtained; and when they find, as they commonly do, the success disproportioned to the endeavor, they must be taught their consolation in the final proportions of eternal justice.* Of this consolation, whoever deprives them, deadens their industry, and strikes at the root of all acquisition as of all conservation. He that does this, is the cruel oppressor, the merciless enemy, of the poor and wretched; at the same time that, by his wicked speculations, he exposes the fruits of successful industry, and the accumulations of fortune, (ah! there's the rub)[8] to the plunder of the negligent, the disappointed, and the unprosperous."

This is contemptible hard-hearted sophistry, in the specious form of humility, and submission to the will of Heaven.—It is, Sir, *possible* to render the poor happier in this world, without depriving them of the consolation which you gratuitously grant them in the next. They have a right to more comfort than they at present enjoy; and more comfort might be afforded them, without encroaching on the pleasures of the rich: not now waiting to enquire whether the rich have any right to exclusive pleasures. What do I say?—encroaching! No; if an intercourse were established between them, it would impart the only true pleasure that can be snatched in this land of shadows, this hard school of moral discipline.

I know, indeed, that there is often something disgusting in the distresses of poverty, at which the imagination revolts, and starts back to exercise itself in the more attractive Arcadia of fiction. The rich man builds a house, art and taste give it the highest finish. His gardens are planted, and the trees grow to recreate the fancy of the planter, though the temperature of the climate may rather force him to avoid the dangerous damps they exhale, than seek the umbrageous retreat. Every thing on the estate is cherished but man;—yet, to contribute to the happiness of man, is the most sublime of all enjoyments. But if, instead of sweeping pleasure-grounds, obelisks, temples, and elegant cottages,[9] as *objects* for the eye, the heart was allowed to beat true to nature, decent farms would be scattered over the estate, and plenty smile around. Instead of the poor being subject to the griping hand of an avaricious steward, they would be watched over with fatherly solicitude, by the man whose duty and pleasure it was to guard their happiness, and shield from rapacity the beings who, by the sweat of their brow, exalted him above his fellows.

I could almost imagine I see a man thus gathering blessings as he mounted the hill of life; or consolation, in those days when the spirits lag, and the tired heart finds no pleasure in them. It is not by squandering alms that the poor can be relieved, or improved—it is the fostering sun of kindness, the wisdom that finds them employments calculated to give them habits of virtue, that meliorates their condition. Love is only the fruit of love; condescension and authority may produce the obedience you applaud; but he has lost his heart of flesh who can see a fellow-creature humbled before him, and trembling at the frown of a being, whose heart is supplied

---

8. Cf. Shakespeare's *Hamlet* 3.1.67. The "rub" is the flaw in the reasoning.
9. A reference to the vogue for picturesque landscaping on aristocratic estates.

by the same vital current, and whose pride ought to be checked by a consciousness of having the same infirmities.

* * *

1790

THOMAS PAINE

Although he was born and lived his first thirty-seven years in England, Thomas Paine (1737–1809) enters the debate as a visitor from America, where by writing *Common Sense* (1776) and the sixteen *Crisis* pamphlets, beginning "These are the times that try men's souls" (1776–83), he had served as the most effective propagandist for American independence. His *Rights of Man: Being an Answer to Mr. Burke's Attack on the French Revolution*, published in March 1791 with a dedication "To George Washington, President of the United States of America," has the full weight of the American revolutionary experience behind it and is the strongest statement against hereditary monarchy of any of the works replying to Burke in this "war of pamphlets." Paine published a second part of *Rights of Man* the following year and, when charged with treason by the British, fled to France, where he was made a citizen and a member of the Convention. With the fall of the more moderate Girondists, he was imprisoned by the Jacobins for a year in 1793–94, during which he wrote his last famous work, *The Age of Reason* (1794).

From Rights of Man

Among the incivilities by which nations or individuals provoke and irritate each other, Mr. Burke's pamphlet on the French Revolution is an extraordinary instance. Neither the people of France, nor the National Assembly, were troubling themselves about the affairs of England, or the English Parliament; and why Mr. Burke should commence an unprovoked attack upon them, both in parliament and in public, is a conduct that cannot be pardoned on the score of manners, nor justified on that of policy.

There is scarcely an epithet of abuse to be found in the English language with which Mr. Burke has not loaded the French nation and the National Assembly. Every thing which rancor, prejudice, ignorance or knowledge could suggest, are poured forth in the copious fury of near four hundred pages. In the strain and on the plan Mr. Burke was writing, he might have written on to as many thousands. When the tongue or the pen is let loose in a frenzy of passion, it is the man, and not the subject, that becomes exhausted.

Hitherto Mr. Burke has been mistaken and disappointed in the opinions he had formed of the affairs of France; but such is the ingenuity of his hope, or the malignancy of his despair, that it furnishes him with new pretences to go on. There was a time when it was impossible to make Mr. Burke believe there would be any revolution in France. His opinion then was, that the

French had neither spirit to undertake it, nor fortitude to support it; and now that there is one, he seeks an escape by condemning it.

* * *

There never did, there never will, and there never can exist a parliament, or any description of men, or any generation of men, in any country, possessed of the right or the power of binding and controuling posterity to the *"end of time,"* or of commanding for ever how the world shall be governed, or who shall govern it; and therefore, all such clauses, acts or declarations, by which the makers of them attempt to do what they have neither the right nor the power to do, nor the power to execute, are in themselves null and void.—Every age and generation must be as free to act for itself, *in all cases,* as the ages and generations which preceded it. The vanity and presumption of governing beyond the grave, is the most ridiculous and insolent of all tyrannies. Man has no property in man; neither has any generation a property in the generations which are to follow. The parliament or the people of 1688, or of any other period, had no more right to dispose of the people of the present day, or to bind or to controul them *in any shape whatever,* than the parliament or the people of the present day have to dispose of, bind or controul those who are to live a hundred or a thousand years hence. Every generation is, and must be, competent to all the purposes which its occasions require. It is the living, and not the dead, that are to be accommodated. When man ceases to be, his power and his wants cease with him; and having no longer any participation in the concerns of this world, he has no longer any authority in directing who shall be its governors, or how its government shall be organized, or how administered.

I am not contending for nor against any form of government, nor for nor against any party here or elsewhere. That which a whole nation chooses to do, it has a right to do. Mr. Burke says, No. Where then *does* the right exist? I am contending for the rights of the *living,* and against their being willed away, and controuled and contracted for, by the manuscript assumed authority of the dead; and Mr. Burke is contending for the authority of the dead over the rights and freedom of the living.

* * *

"We have seen," says Mr. Burke, "the French rebel against a mild and lawful Monarch, with more fury, outrage, and insult, than any people has been known to rise against the most illegal usurper, or the most sanguinary tyrant."—This is one among a thousand other instances, in which Mr. Burke shews that he is ignorant of the springs and principles of the French revolution.

It was not against Louis the XVIth, but against the despotic principles of the government, that the nation revolted. These principles had not their origin in him, but in the original establishment, many centuries back; and they were become too deeply rooted to be removed, and the augean stable[1] of parasites and plunderers too abominably filthy to be cleansed, by any thing short of a complete and universal revolution. When it becomes necessary to do a thing, the whole heart and soul should go into the measure, or not

---

1. King Augeas's stable, housing three thousand oxen and neglected for decades, was a classical symbol of filth and corruption. Hercules cleaned it by changing the course of a river.

attempt it. That crisis was then arrived, and there remained no choice but to act with determined vigor, or not to act at all. The King was known to be the friend of the nation, and this circumstance was favorable to the enterprise. Perhaps no man bred up in the style of an absolute King, ever possessed a heart so little disposed to the exercise of that species of power as the present King of France. But the principles of the government itself still remained the same. The Monarch and the monarchy were distinct and separate things; and it was against the established despotism of the latter, and not against the person or principles of the former, that the revolt commenced, and the revolution has been carried.

Mr. Burke does not attend to the distinction between *men* and *principles*; and therefore, he does not see that a revolt may take place against the despotism of the latter, while there lies no charge of despotism against the former.

The natural moderation of Louis the XVIth contributed nothing to alter the hereditary despotism of the monarchy. All the tyrannies of former reigns, acted under that hereditary despotism, were still liable to be revived in the hands of a successor. It was not the respite of a reign that would satisfy France, enlightened as she was then become. A casual discontinuance of the *practice* of despotism, is not a discontinuance of its *principles*; the former depends on the virtue of the individual who is in immediate possession of power; the latter, on the virtue and fortitude of the nation. In the case of Charles I and James II of England,[2] the revolt was against the personal despotism of the men; whereas in France, it was against the hereditary despotism of the established government. But men who can consign over the rights of posterity for ever on the authority of a moldy parchment, like Mr. Burke, are not qualified to judge of this revolution. It takes in a field too vast for their views to explore, and proceeds with a mightiness of reason they cannot keep pace with.

But there are many points of view in which this revolution may be considered. When despotism has established itself for ages in a country, as in France, it is not in the person of the King only that it resides. It has the appearance of being so in show, and in nominal authority; but it is not so in practice, and in fact. It has its standard every where. Every office and department has its despotism founded upon custom and usage. Every place has its Bastille,[3] and every Bastille its despot. The original hereditary despotism resident in the person of the King, divides and subdivides itself into a thousand shapes and forms, till at last the whole of it is acted by deputation. This was the case in France; and against this species of despotism, proceeding on through an endless labyrinth of office till the source of it is scarcely perceptible, there is no mode of redress. It strengthens itself by assuming the appearance of duty, and tyrannises under the pretence of obeying.

When a man reflects on the condition which France was in from the nature of her government, he will see other causes for revolt than those which immediately connect themselves with the person or character of Louis XVI. There were, if I may so express it, a thousand despotisms to be

---

2. Charles I was overthrown by the Civil War and executed in 1649. His son, James II, was dethroned in the Glorious Revolution of 1688.

3. France's political prison (where the French Revolution began on July 14, 1789).

reformed in France, which had grown up under the hereditary despotism of the monarchy, and became so rooted as to be in a great measure independent of it. Between the monarchy, the parliament, and the church, there was a *rivalship* of despotism; besides the feudal despotism operating locally, and the ministerial despotism operating every where. But Mr. Burke, by considering the King as the only possible object of a revolt, speaks as if France was a village, in which every thing that passed must be known to its commanding officer, and no oppression could be acted but what he could immediately control. Mr. Burke might have been in the Bastille his whole life, as well under Louis XVI as Louis XIV and neither the one nor the other have known that such a man as Mr. Burke existed. The despotic principles of the government were the same in both reigns, though the dispositions of the men were as remote as tyranny and benevolence.

What Mr. Burke considers as a reproach to the French Revolution (that of bringing it forward under a reign more mild than the preceding ones), is one of its highest honors. The revolutions that have taken place in other European countries, have been excited by personal hatred. The rage was against the man, and he became the victim. But, in the instance of France, we see a revolution generated in the rational contemplation of the rights of man, and distinguishing from the beginning between persons and principles.

But Mr. Burke appears to have no idea of principles, when he is contemplating governments. "Ten years ago," says he, "I could have felicitated France on her having a government, without enquiring what the nature of that government was, or how it was administered." Is this the language of a rational man? Is it the language of a heart feeling as it ought to feel for the rights and happiness of the human race? On this ground, Mr. Burke must compliment every government in the world, while the victims who suffer under them, whether sold into slavery, or tortured out of existence, are wholly forgotten. It is power, and not principles, that Mr. Burke venerates; and under this abominable depravity, he is disqualified to judge between them.—Thus much for his opinion as to the occasions of the French Revolution.

* * *

As to the tragic paintings by which Mr. Burke has outraged his own imagination, and seeks to work upon that of his readers, they are very well calculated for theatrical representation, where facts are manufactured for the sake of show, and accommodated to produce, through the weakness of sympathy, a weeping effect. But Mr. Burke should recollect that he is writing History, and not *Plays*; and that his readers will expect truth, and not the spouting rant of high-toned exclamation.

When we see a man dramatically lamenting in a publication intended to be believed, that, "*The age of chivalry is gone!* that *The glory of Europe is extinguished for ever!* that *The unbought grace of life* (if any one knows what it is), *the cheap defence of nations, the nurse of manly sentiment and heroic enterprize, is gone!*" and all this because the Quixote[4] age of chivalric nonsense is gone, What opinion can we form of his judgment, or what regard can we pay to his facts? In the rhapsody of his imagination, he has discov-

4. Insanely idealistic; from the hero of Cervantes' romance, who famously mistakes windmills for his foes the giants.

ered a world of windmills, and his sorrows are, that there are no Quixotes
to attack them. But if the age of aristocracy, like that of chivalry, should
fall, and they had originally some connection, Mr. Burke, the trumpeter of
the Order, may continue his parody to the end, and finish with exclaiming,
"*Othello's occupation's gone!*"[5]

Notwithstanding Mr. Burke's horrid paintings, when the French Revolution is compared with that of other countries, the astonishment will be,
that it is marked with so few sacrifices; but this astonishment will cease
when we reflect that *principles*, and not *persons*, were the meditated objects
of destruction. The mind of the nation was acted upon by a higher stimulus
than what the consideration of persons could inspire, and sought a higher
conquest than could be produced by the downfall of an enemy. * * *

1791

5. Shakespeare's *Othello* 3.3.362; Othello's feeling, when he thinks Desdemona has been unfaithful,
that his life is over.

JAMES GILLRAY

I n the mid-eighteenth century, the artist William Hogarth's success with the
prints he called his "modern moral subjects" had demonstrated that people who
trained as engravers could be something more than practitioners of a mechanical
art, replicating in reproducible form the paintings of others. They could also claim
considerable moral authority as witty social critics. Satiric prints in the tradition
Hogarth helped establish were a thriving commercial concern by the time the
twenty-one-year old James Gillray (1757–1815) enrolled (along with William Blake)
as a student of engraving at the Royal Academy of Art. Especially popular at this
time were political caricatures, the form of portraiture, deftly balanced between a
realistic visual idiom and a grotesque one, that continues to be used to pillory public figures and their pretensions. Straitlaced foreign visitors frequently marveled
over the laughing crowds that would gather around the windows of the London
print shops where these were displayed. By the end of the 1780s, Gillray, originally
from a working-class family, had become a celebrity thanks to the verve with
which he captured the likenesses of politicians—even the Royal Family—in etched
portraits that comically heightened the physical particularities that made them
their distinct selves. With the outbreak of the French Revolution, these images
also proved well suited to registering the yawning gap between the high-minded
idealism of the revolutionaries and the sordid realities of their Revolution. The
imaginative power that infused Gillray's depictions of French revolutionists and
their English sympathizers struck many as the equivalent in visual art to the verbal
art that Thomas Paine had complained about in his encounter with "Mr. Burke's
horrid paintings." It is not surprising therefore to learn that after 1797 Gillray was
secretly on the government payroll, for assisting in the campaign to discredit the
radical opposition. Still, with their characteristic mix of fury and glee, his prints
make it difficult for attentive viewers to pin down his political allegiances.
Straightforward propaganda they are not. Unbalanced, blending in a combustible
compound the high-minded history paintings Gillray studied at the Royal Academy and the crude energies of popular culture, these images can throw us off balance in our turn.

Smelling out a Rat;—or The Atheistical Revolutionist disturbed in his Midnight Calculations. Published December 3, 1790. This print commemorating the attack on Richard Price that Burke made in his *Reflections on the Revolution in France* was etched only six months after Gillray engraved James Northcote's heroic painting of the liberation of the Bastille prisoners (see color insert). That Gillray had since then changed sides in the revolution controversy, falling in line with Burke's equation of the revolution with destruction not salvation, is suggested by the print's title and many details. The painting on the wall behind Price's desk depicts the beheading of England's King Charles I in the Civil War of the 1640s. On the study floor Price's offending sermon lies beside a book with the seditious title *Treatise . . . on the Absurdity of Serving God and Honoring the King*. But how sincere was Gillray's newfound allegiance to Burke, given that an outsize nose and spectacles here make Burke appear a fanatical monster? Price, only lightly caricatured, may be the rat of the title but he has been permitted to retain his humanity.

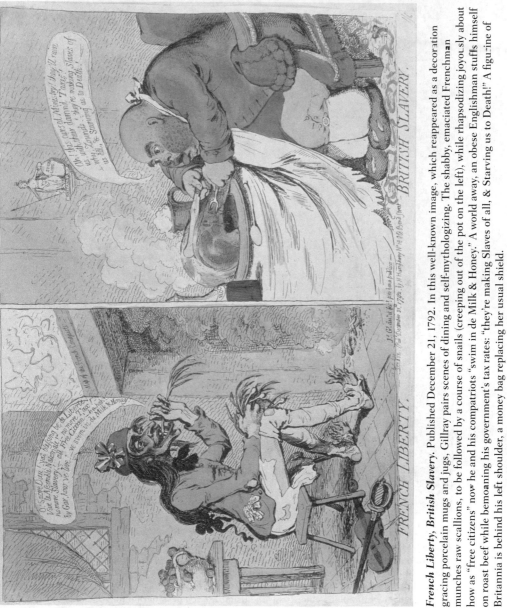

French Liberty, British Slavery. Published December 21, 1792. In this well-known image, which reappeared as a decoration gracing porcelain mugs and jugs, Gillray pairs scenes of dining and self-mythologizing. The shabby, emaciated Frenchman munches raw scallions, to be followed by a course of snails (creeping out of the pot on the left), while rhapsodizing joyously about how as "free citizens" now he and his compatriots "swim in de Milk & Honey." A world away, an obese Englishman stuffs himself on roast beef while bemoaning his government's tax rates: "they're making Slaves of all, & Starving us to Death!" A figurine of Britannia is behind his left shoulder, a money bag replacing her usual shield.

The Zenith of French Glory; _ The Pinnacle of Liberty.
Religion, Justice, Loyalty, & all the Bugbears of Unenlightened Minds, Farewell!

The Zenith of French Glory;—The Pinnacle of Liberty. Published February 12, 1793.
The news that reached London on January 24, 1793, of the French National Convention's
execution of King Louis XVI three days earlier occasioned this ferocious print. It shows
one of Gillray's specimen sans-culottes enjoying a good view of the guillotine and its royal
victim, his right foot set jauntily atop the neck of one of the clergymen who have been
strung up below him. (Sans-culotte was the usual French designation for a member of the
lower classes, because working men wore long trousers instead of the knee-breeches
favored by male aristocrats and bourgeois. Gillray delighted in translating the term
literally and scurrilously, and the posteriors of his Frenchmen are often visible, as here,
through their rags.) In the colored version of the print, the execution platform appears to
be located in a lake of blood, the effect of the red caps worn by the mob of sans-culottes
who surround it. The cathedral that is in flames and the paper reading "Bon soir
Monsieur" ("Good night sir") that has been nailed atop the crucifix on the picture's right
add apocalyptic notes to the horror of the scene.

The British Butcher, Supplying John Bull with a Substitute for Bread. Published July 6, 1795. John Bull, the embodiment of ordinary Englishness, is a stock character in Gillray's prints. Bull is the closest we approach to innocence in Gillray's villainous world and yet he cuts a shambling figure: Gillray portrays him as hopelessly susceptible to politicians' manipulations. This print was published at the height of a food shortage brought on by a bad harvest and exacerbated by the demands of the war against France. Prime Minister Pitt is pictured as a butcher, arrogantly explaining to his customer John Bull that because he cannot afford bread, he must accept meat: "A Crown, take it or leave it." The posters that are pasted on the side of Pitt's butcher's block and that juxtapose the prices for provisions with the monthly wages for working men suggest Bull's problem: either he can starve or he can obtain higher wages by enlisting as a soldier for the Crown and so risk being butchered himself. In a similar scene involving this duo, from November 1796, Gillray pictures the prime minister holding a money-bag and saying, "More Money John! to defend you from the Bloody, the Cannibal French . . . They're a coming!" The caption tells us that Bull, imaged with his trousers in his hand, is "giving his Breeches to save his Bacon": a hint that Bull may turn sans-culotte himself.

MARY WOLLSTONECRAFT
1759–1797

Mary Wollstonecraft's father inherited a substantial fortune and set himself up as a gentleman farmer. He was, however, both extravagant and incompetent, and as one farm after another failed, he became moody and violent and sought solace in heavy bouts of drinking and in tyrannizing his submissive wife. Mary was the second of five children and the oldest daughter. She later told her husband, William Godwin, that she used to throw herself in front of her mother to protect her from her father's blows, and that she sometimes slept outside the door of her parents' bedroom to intervene if her father should break out in a drunken rage. The solace of Mary's early life was her fervent attachment to Fanny Blood, an accomplished girl two years her senior; their friendship, which began when Mary was sixteen, endured and deepened until Fanny's death.

At the age of nineteen, Mary Wollstonecraft left home to take a position as companion to a well-to-do widow living in Bath, where for the first time she had the opportunity to observe—and scorn—the social life of the upper classes at the most fashionable of English resort cities. Having left her job in 1780 to nurse her dying mother through a long and harrowing illness, Wollstonecraft next went to live with the Bloods, where her work helped sustain the struggling family. Her sister Eliza meanwhile had married and, in 1784, after the birth of a daughter, suffered a nervous breakdown. Convinced that her sister's collapse was the result of her husband's cruelty and abuse, Wollstonecraft persuaded her to abandon husband and child and flee to London. Because a divorce at that time was not commonly available, and a fugitive wife could be forced to return to her husband, the two women hid in secret quarters while awaiting the grant of a legal separation. The infant, automatically given into the father's custody, died before she was a year old.

The penniless women, together with Fanny Blood and Wollstonecraft's other sister, Everina, established a girls' school at Newington Green, near London. The project flourished at first, and at Newington, Wollstonecraft was befriended by the Reverend Richard Price, the radical author who was soon to play a leading role in the British debates about the Revolution in France, and whose kindly guidance helped shape her social and political opinions. Blood, although already ill with tuberculosis, went to Lisbon to marry her longtime suitor, Hugh Skeys, and quickly became pregnant. Wollstonecraft rushed to Lisbon to attend her friend's childbirth, only to have Fanny die in her arms; the infant died soon afterward. The loss threw Wollstonecraft (already subject to bouts of depression) into black despair, which was heightened when she found that the school at Newington was in bad financial straits and had to be closed. Tormented by creditors, she rallied her energies to write her first book, *Thoughts on the Education of Daughters* (1786), a conventional and pious series of essays, and took up a position as governess for several daughters in the Anglo-Irish family of Viscount Kingsborough, a man of great wealth whose seat was in County Cork, Ireland.

The Kingsboroughs were well intentioned and did their best to introduce Wollstonecraft into the busy trivialities of their social life. But the ambiguity of her position as governess, halfway between a servant and a member of the family, was galling. An antagonism developed between Wollstonecraft and Lady Kingsborough, in part because the children feared their mother and adored their governess. Wollstonecraft was dismissed. She returned to London, where Joseph Johnson in 1788 published *Mary, a Fiction*, a novel, as Wollstonecraft described it, about "the mind of a woman who has thinking powers." Johnson also published her book for children, *Original Stories from Real Life*, a considerable success that was translated into German and quickly achieved a second English edition illustrated with engravings by William Blake. Wollstonecraft was befriended and subsidized by Johnson, the major publisher in England of radical and reformist books, and she took a prominent place among the writers (including notables such as Barbauld and Coleridge) whom he regularly entertained at his rooms in St. Paul's Churchyard. She published translations from French and German (she had taught herself both languages) and began reviewing books for Johnson's newly founded journal, the *Analytical Review*. Though still in straitened circumstances, she helped support her two sisters and her improvident and importunate father and was also generous with funds—and with advice—to one of her brothers and to the indigent family of Fanny Blood.

In 1790 Edmund Burke's *Reflections on the Revolution in France*—an eloquent and powerful attack on the French Revolution and its English sympathizers—quickly evoked Wollstonecraft's response, *A Vindication of the Rights of Men*. This was a formidable piece of argumentation; its most potent passages represent the disabilities and sufferings of the English lower classes and impugn the motives and sentiments of Burke. This work, the first book-length reply to Burke, scored an immediate success, although it was soon submerged in the flood of other replies, most notably Thomas Paine's classic *Rights of Man* (1791–92). In 1792 Wollstonecraft focused her defense of the underprivileged on her own sex and wrote, in six weeks of intense effort, *A Vindication of the Rights of Woman*.

Earlier writers in both France and England had proposed that, given equivalent educations, women would equal men in achievement. Wollstonecraft was particularly indebted to the historian Catharine Macaulay, whose *Letters on Education* (1790) she had reviewed enthusiastically. At the same time Wollstonecraft was contributing to a long-running discussion of human rights that in Britain dated back to John Locke's publication of the *Second Treatise of Civil Government* (1690). Prefaced with a letter addressed to the French politician Bishop Talleyrand, the *Vindication* was in part her rejoinder to the inconsistent actions of France's National Assembly, which in 1791 had formally denied to all Frenchwomen the rights of citizens, even as, ironically enough, it set about celebrating the "universal rights of man."

Her book was also unprecedented in its firsthand observations of the disabilities and indignities suffered by women and in the articulateness and passion with which it exposed and decried this injustice. Wollstonecraft's views were conspicuously radical at a time when women had no political rights; were limited to a few lowly vocations as servants, nurses, governesses, and petty shopkeepers; and were legally nonpersons who lost their property to their husbands at marriage and were incapable of instituting an action in the courts of law. An impressive feature of her book, for all its vehemence, is the clear-sightedness and balance of her analysis of the social conditions of the time, as they affect men as well as women. She perceives that women constitute an oppressed class that cuts across the standard hierarchy of social classes; she shows that women, because they are denied their rights as human beings, have been forced to seek their ends by means of coquetry and cunning, the weapons of the weak; and having demonstrated that it is contrary to reason to expect virtue from those who are not free, she also recognizes that men, no less than women, inherit their roles, and that the wielding of irresponsible power corrupts the oppressor no less than it distorts the oppressed. Hence her surprising and telling comparisons between women on the one hand and men of the nobility and military on the other as classes whose values and behavior have been distorted because their social roles prevent them from becoming fully human. In writing this pioneering work, Wollstonecraft found the cause that she was to pursue the rest of her life.

In December 1792 Wollstonecraft went to Paris to observe the Revolution firsthand. During the years that she lived in France, 1793–94, the early period of moderation was succeeded by extremism and violence. In Paris she joined a group of English, American, and European expatriates sympathetic to the Revolution and fell in love with Gilbert Imlay, a personable American who had briefly been an officer in the American Revolutionary Army and was the author of a widely read book on the Kentucky backwoods, where he had been an explorer. He played the role in Paris of an American frontiersman and child of nature, but was in fact an adventurer who had left America to avoid prosecution for debt and for freewheeling speculations in Kentucky land. He was also unscrupulous in his relations with women. The two became lovers, and their daughter, Fanny Imlay, was born in May 1794. Imlay, who was often absent on mysterious business deals, left mother and daughter for a visit to London that he kept protracting. After the publication of her book *An Historical and Moral View of the Origin and Progress of the French Revolution* (1794), Wollstonecraft followed Imlay to London, where, convinced that he no longer loved her, she tried to commit suicide. The attempt, however, was discovered and prevented by Imlay. To get her out of the way, he persuaded her to take a trip as his business envoy to the Scandinavian countries. Although this was then a region of poor or impassible roads and primitive accommodations, the intrepid Wollstonecraft traveled there for four months, sometimes in the wilds, accompanied by the year-old Fanny and a French nursemaid.

Back in London, Wollstonecraft discovered that Imlay was living with a new mistress, an actress. Finally convinced he was lost to her, she hurled herself from a bridge into the Thames but was rescued by a passerby. Imlay departed with his actress to Paris. Wollstonecraft, resourceful as always, used the letters she had written to Imlay to compose a book, *Letters Written during a Short Residence in Sweden, Norway, and Denmark* (1796), full of sharp observations of politics, the lives of Scandinavian women, and the austere northern landscape.

In the same year Wollstonecraft renewed an earlier acquaintance with the philosopher William Godwin. His *Inquiry Concerning Political Justice* (1793), the most drastic proposal for restructuring the political and social order yet published in England, together with his novel of terror, *Caleb Williams* (1794), which embodies his social views, had made him the most famed radical writer of his time. The austerely rationalistic philosopher, then forty years of age, had an unexpected capacity for deep feeling, and what began as a flirtation soon ripened into affection and (as their letters show) passionate physical love. She wrote Godwin, with what was for the time remarkable outspokenness on the part of a woman: "Now by these presents [i.e., this document] let me assure you that you are not only in my heart, but my veins, this morning. I turn from you half abashed—yet you haunt me, and some look, word or touch thrills through my whole frame. . . . When the heart and reason accord there is no flying from voluptuous sensations, do what a woman can." Wollstonecraft was soon pregnant once more, and Godwin (who had in his *Inquiry* attacked the institution of marriage as a base form of property rights in human beings) braved the ridicule of his radical friends and conservative enemies by marrying her.

They set up a household together, but Godwin also kept separate quarters in which to do his writing, and they further salvaged their principles by agreeing to live separate social lives. Wollstonecraft was able to enjoy this arrangement for only six months. She began writing *The Wrongs of Woman*, a novel about marriage and motherhood that uses its Gothic setting inside a dilapidated madhouse to explore how women are confined both by unjust marriage laws and by their own romantic illusions. On August 30, 1797, she gave birth to a daughter, Mary Wollstonecraft Godwin, later the author of *Frankenstein* and wife of Percy Shelley. The delivery was not difficult, but resulted in massive blood poisoning. After ten days of agony, she lapsed into a coma and died. Her last whispered words were about her husband: "He is the kindest, best man in the world." Godwin wrote to a friend, announcing her death: "I firmly believe that there does not exist her equal in the world. I know from experience we were formed to make each other happy."

To distract himself in his grief, Godwin published in 1798 *Memoirs of the Author of "A Vindication of the Rights of Woman,"* in which he told, with the total candor on which he prided himself, of her affairs with Imlay and himself, her attempts at suicide, and her freethinking in matters of religion and sexual relationships. In four companion volumes of her *Posthumous Works,* he indiscreetly included her love letters to Imlay along with the unfinished *Wrongs of Woman.* The reaction to these revelations was immediate and ugly. The conservative satirist the Reverend Richard Polwhele, for instance, remarked gloatingly on how it appeared to him providential that as a proponent of sexual equality Wollstonecraft should have died in childbirth—"a death that strongly marked the distinction of the sexes, by pointing out the destiny of women, and the diseases to which they are liable." The unintended consequence of Godwin's candor was that Wollstonecraft came to be saddled with a scandalous reputation so enduring that through the Victorian era advocates of the equality of women circumspectly avoided explicit reference to her *Vindication.* Even John Stuart Mill, in his *Subjection of Women* (1869), neglected to mention the work. It was only in the twentieth century, and especially in the later decades, that Wollstonecraft's *Vindication* gained recognition as a classic in the literature not only of women's rights but of social analysis as well.

From A Vindication of the Rights of Woman

From *The Dedication to M. Talleyrand-Périgord*[1]

* * *

Contending for the rights of woman, my main argument is built on this simple principle, that if she be not prepared by education to become the companion of man, she will stop the progress of knowledge and virtue; for truth must be common to all, or it will be inefficacious with respect to its influence on general practice. And how can woman be expected to co-operate unless she know why she ought to be virtuous? unless freedom strengthen her reason till she comprehend her duty, and see in what manner it is connected with her real good? If children are to be educated to understand the true principle of patriotism, their mother must be a patriot; and the love of mankind, from which an orderly train of virtues spring, can only be produced by considering the moral and civil interest of mankind; but the education and situation of woman, at present, shuts her out from such investigations.

In this work I have produced many arguments, which to me were conclusive, to prove that the prevailing notion respecting a sexual[2] character was subversive of morality, and I have contended, that to render the human body and mind more perfect, chastity must more universally prevail, and that chastity will never be respected in the male world till the person of a woman is not, as it were, idolized, when little virtue or sense embellish it with the grand traces of mental beauty, or the interesting simplicity of affection.

Consider, Sir, dispassionately, these observations—for a glimpse of this truth seemed to open before you when you observed, 'that to see one half of the human race excluded by the other from all participation of government, was a political phænomenon that, according to abstract principles, it was impossible to explain.' If so, on what does your constitution rest?[3] If the

1. In 1791 Charles Maurice de Talleyrand-Périgord submitted a report on public education to France's new Constituent Assembly.
2. Here as elsewhere in the *Vindication,* the word *sexual* is equivalent to the modern term *gender-specific.*
3. In France's Constitution of 1791 only males over twenty-five were citizens. Women were not to get the vote until 1944.

abstract rights of man will bear discussion and explanation, those of woman, by a parity of reasoning, will not shrink from the same test: though a different opinion prevails in this country, built on the very arguments which you use to justify the oppression of woman—prescription.[4]

Consider, I address you as a legislator, whether, when men contend for their freedom, and to be allowed to judge for themselves respecting their own happiness, it be not inconsistent and unjust to subjugate women, even though you firmly believe that you are acting in the manner best calculated to promote their happiness? Who made man the exclusive judge, if woman partake with him the gift of reason?

In this style, argue tyrants of every denomination, from the weak king to the weak father of a family; they are all eager to crush reason; yet always assert that they usurp its throne only to be useful. Do you not act a similar part, when you *force* all women, by denying them civil and political rights, to remain immured in their families groping in the dark? for surely, Sir, you will not assert, that a duty can be binding which is not founded on reason? If indeed this be their destination, arguments may be drawn from reason: and thus augustly supported, the more understanding women acquire, the more they will be attached to their duty—comprehending it—for unless they comprehend it, unless their morals be fixed on the same immutable principle as those of man, no authority can make them discharge it in a virtuous manner. They may be convenient slaves, but slavery will have its constant effect, degrading the master and the abject dependent.

But, if women are to be excluded, without having a voice, from a participation of the natural rights of mankind, prove first, to ward off the charge of injustice and inconsistency, that they want reason—else this flaw in your NEW CONSTITUTION will ever shew that man must, in some shape, act like a tyrant, and tyranny, in whatever part of society it rears its brazen front, will ever undermine morality.

I have repeatedly asserted, and produced what appeared to me irrefragable arguments drawn from matters of fact, to prove my assertion, that women cannot, by force, be confined to domestic concerns; for they will, however ignorant, intermeddle with more weighty affairs, neglecting private duties only to disturb, by cunning tricks, the orderly plans of reason which rise above their comprehension.

Besides, whilst they are only made to acquire personal accomplishments, men will seek for pleasure in variety, and faithless husbands will make faithless wives; such ignorant beings, indeed, will be very excusable when, not taught to respect public good, nor allowed any civil rights, they attempt to do themselves justice by retaliation.

The box of mischief thus opened in society,[5] what is to preserve private virtue, the only security of public freedom and universal happiness?

---

4. Samuel Johnson's *Dictionary of the English Language* of 1755 (the later 18th century's authoritative guide to usage) defines *prescription* as "rules produced and authorised by long custom: custom continued till it has the force of law." In her first *Vindication* Wollstonecraft noted how the doctrine of prescription motivated Edmund Burke's antagonism toward the dismantling of inherited privileges in revolutionary France and, accordingly, identified his *Reflections on the Revolution* as championing the rich, who invoke "prescription," she asserted, as "an immortal boundary against innovation."

5. Refers to the story of Pandora, who in Greek mythology was the first woman, and to her opening of the box that Zeus, king of the gods, had sent down to earth with her. That action released evil into the world.

Let there be then no coercion *established* in society, and the common law of gravity prevailing, the sexes will fall into their proper places. And, now that more equitable laws are forming your citizens, marriage may become more sacred: your young men may choose wives from motives of affection, and your maidens allow love to root out vanity.

The father of a family will not then weaken his constitution and debase his sentiments, by visiting the harlot, nor forget, in obeying the call of appetite, the purpose for which it was implanted. And, the mother will not neglect her children to practise the arts of coquetry, when sense and modesty secure her the friendship of her husband.

But, till men become attentive to the duty of a father, it is vain to expect women to spend that time in their nursery which they, 'wise in their generation,'[6] choose to spend at their glass; for this exertion of cunning is only an instinct of nature to enable them to obtain indirectly a little of that power of which they are unjustly denied a share: for, if women are not permitted to enjoy legitimate rights, they will render both men and themselves vicious, to obtain illicit privileges.

I wish, Sir, to set some investigations of this kind afloat in France; and should they lead to a confirmation of my principles, when your constitution is revised the Rights of Woman may be respected, if it be fully proved that reason calls for this respect, and loudly demands Justice for one half of the human race.

I am, Sir,
Your's respectfully,
M. W.

* * *

Introduction

After considering the historic page, and viewing the living world with anxious solicitude, the most melancholy emotions of sorrowful indignation have depressed my spirits, and I have sighed when obliged to confess, that either nature has made a great difference between man and man, or that the civilization which has hitherto taken place in the world has been very partial. I have turned over various books written on the subject of education, and patiently observed the conduct of parents and the management of schools; but what has been the result?—a profound conviction that the neglected education of my fellow-creatures is the grand source of the misery I deplore; and that women, in particular, are rendered weak and wretched by a variety of concurring causes, originating from one hasty conclusion. The conduct and manners of women, in fact, evidently prove that their minds are not in a healthy state; for, like the flowers which are planted in too rich a soil, strength and usefulness are sacrificed to beauty; and the flaunting leaves, after having pleased a fastidious eye, fade, disregarded on the stalk, long before the season when they ought to have arrived at maturity.—One cause of this barren blooming[7] I attribute to a false system of education, gathered

6. Luke 16.8: "For the children of this world are in their generation wiser than the children of light."
7. Wollstonecraft compares women to "luxuri-ants," botanical science's technical term for those plants that late-18th-century gardeners, drawing on the latest techniques, cultivated for their showy blooms and at the expense of their seeds.

from the books written on this subject by men who, considering females rather as women than human creatures, have been more anxious to make them alluring mistresses than affectionate wives and rational mothers; and the understanding of the sex has been so bubbled[8] by this specious homage, that the civilized women of the present century, with a few exceptions, are only anxious to inspire love, when they ought to cherish a nobler ambition, and by their abilities and virtues exact respect.

In a treatise, therefore, on female rights and manners, the works which have been particularly written for their improvement must not be overlooked; especially when it is asserted, in direct terms, that the minds of women are enfeebled by false refinement; that the books of instruction, written by men of genius, have had the same tendency as more frivolous productions; and that, in the true style of Mahometanism, they are treated as a kind of subordinate beings,[9] and not as a part of the human species, when improveable reason is allowed to be the dignified distinction which raises men above the brute creation, and puts a natural sceptre in a feeble hand.

Yet, because I am a woman, I would not lead my readers to suppose that I mean violently to agitate the contested question respecting the equality or inferiority of the sex; but as the subject lies in my way, and I cannot pass it over without subjecting the main tendency of my reasoning to misconstruction, I shall stop a moment to deliver, in a few words, my opinion.—In the government of the physical world it is observable that the female in point of strength is, in general, inferior to the male. This is the law of nature; and it does not appear to be suspended or abrogated in favour of woman. A degree of physical superiority cannot, therefore, be denied—and it is a noble prerogative! But not content with this natural pre-eminence, men endeavour to sink us still lower, merely to render us alluring objects for a moment; and women, intoxicated by the adoration which men, under the influence of their senses, pay them, do not seek to obtain a durable interest in their hearts, or to become the friends of the fellow creatures who find amusement in their society.

I am aware of an obvious inference:—from every quarter have I heard exclamations against masculine women; but where are they to be found? If by this appellation men mean to inveigh against their ardour in hunting, shooting, and gaming, I shall most cordially join in the cry; but if it be against the imitation of manly virtues, or, more properly speaking, the attainment of those talents and virtues, the exercise of which ennobles the human character, and which raise females in the scale of animal being, when they are comprehensively termed mankind;—all those who view them with a philosophic eye must, I should think, wish with me, that they may every day grow more and more masculine.

This discussion naturally divides the subject. I shall first consider women in the grand light of human creatures, who, in common with men, are placed on this earth to unfold their faculties; and afterwards I shall more particularly point out their peculiar designation.

I wish also to steer clear of an error which many respectable writers have fallen into; for the instruction which has hitherto been addressed to women,

8. Deluded, cheated (archaic).
9. It was a common but mistaken opinion among Europeans that in the Koran, the sacred text of Islam, the Prophet Mohammed taught that women have no souls and would not be permitted an afterlife.

has rather been applicable to *ladies*, if the little indirect advice, that is scattered through Sandford and Merton,[1] be excepted; but, addressing my sex in a firmer tone, I pay particular attention to those in the middle class, because they appear to be in the most natural state.[2] Perhaps the seeds of false-refinement, immorality, and vanity, have ever been shed by the great. Weak, artificial beings, raised above the common wants and affections of their race, in a premature unnatural manner, undermine the very foundation of virtue, and spread corruption through the whole mass of society! As a class of mankind they have the strongest claim to pity; the education of the rich tends to render them vain and helpless, and the unfolding mind is not strengthened by the practice of those duties which dignify the human character.—They only live to amuse themselves, and by the same law which in nature invariably produces certain effects, they soon only afford barren amusement.

But as I purpose taking a separate view of the different ranks of society, and of the moral character of women, in each, this hint is, for the present, sufficient; and I have only alluded to the subject, because it appears to me to be the very essence of an introduction to give a cursory account of the contents of the work it introduces.

My own sex, I hope, will excuse me, if I treat them like rational creatures, instead of flattering their *fascinating* graces, and viewing them as if they were in a state of perpetual childhood, unable to stand alone. I earnestly wish to point out in what true dignity and human happiness consists—I wish to persuade women to endeavour to acquire strength, both of mind and body, and to convince them that the soft phrases, susceptibility of heart, delicacy of sentiment, and refinement of taste, are almost synonymous with epithets of weakness, and that those beings who are only the objects of pity and that kind of love, which has been termed its sister, will soon become objects of contempt.

Dismissing then those pretty feminine phrases, which the men condescendingly use to soften our slavish dependence, and despising that weak elegancy of mind, exquisite sensibility, and sweet docility of manners, supposed to be the sexual characteristics of the weaker vessel, I wish to shew that elegance is inferior to virtue, that the first object of laudable ambition is to obtain a character as a human being, regardless of the distinction of sex; and that secondary views should be brought to this simple touchstone.

This is a rough sketch of my plan; and should I express my conviction with the energetic emotions that I feel whenever I think of the subject, the dictates of experience and reflection will be felt by some of my readers. Animated by this important object, I shall disdain to cull my phrases or polish my style;—I aim at being useful, and sincerity will render me unaffected; for, wishing rather to persuade by the force of my arguments, than dazzle by the elegance of my language, I shall not waste my time in rounding periods,[3] or in fabricating the turgid bombast of artificial feelings, which, coming from the head, never reach the heart.—I shall be employed about things, not words!—and, anxious to render my sex more respectable members of society,

---

1. *Sandford and Merton*, a children's book by Thomas Day (1786–89), is the story of Tommy Merton, a spoiled wealthy child who is befriended by Harry Sandford, a poor but principled lad.
2. Wollstonecraft considers the middle classes to be more "natural" and also more educable than the aristocracy—"the great"—because they are as yet uncorrupted by the artificiality of leisure-class life.
3. Formulating balanced sentences.

I shall try to avoid that flowery diction which has slided from essays into novels, and from novels into familiar letters and conversation.

These pretty superlatives, dropping glibly from the tongue, vitiate the taste, and create a kind of sickly delicacy that turns away from simple unadorned truth; and a deluge of false sentiments and overstretched feelings, stifling the natural emotions of the heart, render the domestic pleasures insipid, that ought to sweeten the exercise of those severe duties, which educate a rational and immortal being for a nobler field of action.

The education of women has, of late, been more attended to than formerly; yet they are still reckoned a frivolous sex, and ridiculed or pitied by the writers who endeavour by satire or instruction to improve them. It is acknowledged that they spend many of the first years of their lives in acquiring a smattering of accomplishments;[4] meanwhile strength of body and mind are sacrificed to libertine notions of beauty, to the desire of establishing themselves,—the only way women can rise in the world,—by marriage. And this desire making mere animals of them, when they marry they act as such children may be expected to act:—they dress; they paint, and nickname God's creatures.[5] Surely these weak beings are only fit for a seraglio![6]— Can they be expected to govern a family with judgment, or take care of the poor babes whom they bring into the world?

If then it can be fairly deduced from the present conduct of the sex, from the prevalent fondness for pleasure which takes place of ambition and those nobler passions that open and enlarge the soul; that the instruction which women have hitherto received has only tended, with the constitution of civil society, to render them insignificant objects of desire—mere propagators of fools!—if it can be proved that in aiming to accomplish them, without cultivating their understandings, they are taken out of their sphere of duties, and made ridiculous and useless when the short-lived bloom of beauty is over,[7] I presume that *rational* men will excuse me for endeavouring to persuade them to become more masculine and respectable.

Indeed the word masculine is only a bugbear: there is little reason to fear that women will acquire too much courage or fortitude; for their apparent inferiority with respect to bodily strength, must render them, in some degree, dependent on men in the various relations of life; but why should it be increased by prejudices that give a sex to virtue, and confound simple truths with sensual reveries?

Women are, in fact, so much degraded by mistaken notions of female excellence, that I do not mean to add a paradox when I assert, that this artificial weakness produces a propensity to tyrannize, and gives birth to cunning, the natural opponent of strength, which leads them to play off those contemptible infantine airs that undermine esteem even whilst they excite desire. Let men become more chaste and modest, and if women do not grow wiser in the

---

4. I.e., the lessons in music, dancing, art, and needlework that were central elements in the education provided for genteel young women and that were supposed to enhance their value on the marriage market.
5. Shakespeare's Hamlet, charging Ophelia with the faults characteristic of women, says, "you jig, you amble, and you lisp and nickname God's creatures" (*Hamlet* 3.1.143–44).
6. Harem, the women's quarters in a Muslim

household.
7. A lively writer, I cannot recollect his name, asks what business women turned of forty have to do in the world? [Wollstonecraft's note]. Perhaps Wollstonecraft is referring to a passage in Frances Burney's popular novel *Evelina* spoken by the licentious Lord Merton: "I don't know what the devil a woman lives for after thirty: she is only in other folks' way."

same ratio, it will be clear that they have weaker understandings. It seems scarcely necessary to say, that I now speak of the sex in general. Many individuals have more sense than their male relatives; and, as nothing preponderates where there is a constant struggle for an equilibrium, without it has naturally more gravity, some women govern their husbands without degrading themselves, because intellect will always govern.

* * *

Chapter 2. The Prevailing Opinion of a Sexual Character Discussed

To account for, and excuse the tyranny of man, many ingenious arguments have been brought forward to prove, that the two sexes, in the acquirement of virtue, ought to aim at attaining a very different character: or, to speak explicitly, women are not allowed to have sufficient strength of mind to acquire what really deserves the name of virtue. Yet it should seem, allowing them to have souls, that there is but one way appointed by Providence to lead *mankind* to either virtue or happiness.

If then women are not a swarm of ephemeron triflers, why should they be kept in ignorance under the specious name of innocence? Men complain, and with reason, of the follies and caprices of our sex, when they do not keenly satirize our headstrong passions and groveling vices.—Behold, I should answer, the natural effect of ignorance! The mind will ever be unstable that has only prejudices to rest on, and the current will run with destructive fury when there are no barriers to break its force. Women are told from their infancy, and taught by the example of their mothers, that a little knowledge of human weakness, justly termed cunning, softness of temper, *outward* obedience, and a scrupulous attention to a puerile kind of propriety, will obtain for them the protection of man; and should they be beautiful, every thing else is needless, for, at least, twenty years of their lives.

Thus Milton describes our first frail mother; though when he tells us that women are formed for softness and sweet attractive grace,[8] I cannot comprehend his meaning, unless, in the true Mahometan strain, he meant to deprive us of souls, and insinuate that we were beings only designed by sweet attractive grace, and docile blind obedience, to gratify the senses of man when he can no longer soar on the wing of contemplation.

How grossly do they insult us who thus advise us only to render ourselves gentle, domestic brutes! For instance, the winning softness so warmly, and frequently, recommended, that governs by obeying. What childish expressions, and how insignificant is the being—can it be an immortal one? who will condescend to govern by such sinister methods! 'Certainly,' says Lord Bacon, 'man is of kin to the beasts by his body; and if he be not of kin to God by his spirit, he is a base and ignoble creature!'[9] Men, indeed, appear to me to act in a very unphilosophical manner when they try to secure the good conduct of women by attempting to keep them always in a state of childhood. Rousseau[1] was more consistent when he wished to stop the progress

---

8. Milton asserts the authority of man over woman on the grounds that "For contemplation he and valor formed, / For softness she and sweet attractive grace; / He for God only, she for God in him" (*Paradise Lost* 4.298ff).

9. Francis Bacon, Essay XVI, "Of Atheism."

1. Throughout his writings Jean-Jacques Rousseau (1712–1778) argued against the notion that civilization and rationality brought moral perfection, proposing that virtuous societies were instead the primitive ones that remained closest to nature.

of reason in both sexes, for if men eat of the tree of knowledge, women will come in for a taste; but, from the imperfect cultivation which their understandings now receive, they only attain a knowledge of evil.[2]

Children, I grant, should be innocent; but when the epithet is applied to men, or women, it is but a civil term for weakness. For if it be allowed that women were destined by Providence to acquire human virtues, and by the exercise of their understandings, that stability of character which is the firmest ground to rest our future hopes upon, they must be permitted to turn to the fountain of light, and not forced to shape their course by the twinkling of a mere satellite. Milton, I grant, was of a very different opinion; for he only bends to the indefeasible right of beauty, though it would be difficult to render two passages which I now mean to contrast, consistent. But into similar inconsistencies are great men often led by their senses.

> To whom thus Eve with *perfect beauty* adorn'd.
> My Author and Disposer, what thou bidst
> *Unargued* I obey; So God ordains;
> God is *thy law, thou mine:* to know no more
> Is Woman's *happiest* knowledge and her *praise.*[3]

These are exactly the arguments that I have used to children; but I have added, your reason is now gaining strength, and, till it arrives at some degree of maturity, you must look up to me for advice—then you ought to *think*, and only rely on God.

Yet in the following lines Milton seems to coincide with me; when he makes Adam thus expostulate with his Maker.

> Hast thou not made me here thy substitute,
> And these inferior far beneath me set?
> Among *unequals* what society
> Can sort, what harmony or true delight?
> Which must be mutual, in proportion due
> Giv'n and receiv'd; but in *disparity*
> The one intense, the other still remiss
> Cannot well suit with either, but soon prove
> Tedious alike: of *fellowship* I speak
> Such as I seek, fit to participate
> All rational delight—[4]

In treating, therefore, of the manners of women, let us, disregarding sensual arguments, trace what we should endeavour to make them in order to co-operate, if the expression be not too bold, with the supreme Being.

By individual education, I mean, for the sense of the word is not precisely defined, such an attention to a child as will slowly sharpen the senses, form the temper,[5] regulate the passions as they begin to ferment, and set the understanding to work before the body arrives at maturity; so that the man may only have to proceed, not to begin, the important task of learning to think and reason.

---

2. Both Adam and Eve ate the fruit from the tree of knowledge of good and evil in the garden of Eden. In the fallen state both men and women need to work at virtue, but according to Wollstonecraft, women have been denied the education, and thus the means, to attain it.

3. *Paradise Lost* IV.634–38. The italics are Wollstonecraft's.
4. *Paradise Lost* VIII.381–92. The italics are Wollstonecraft's.
5. Temperament, character.

To prevent any misconstruction, I must add, that I do not believe that a private education[6] can work the wonders which some sanguine writers have attributed to it. Men and women must be educated, in a great degree, by the opinions and manners of the society they live in. In every age there has been a stream of popular opinion that has carried all before it, and given a family character, as it were, to the century. It may then fairly be inferred, that, till society be differently constituted, much cannot be expected from education. It is, however, sufficient for my present purpose to assert, that, whatever effect circumstances have on the abilities, every being may become virtuous by the exercise of its own reason; for if but one being was created with vicious inclinations, that is positively bad, what can save us from atheism? or if we worship a God, is not that God a devil?

Consequently, the most perfect education, in my opinion, is such an exercise of the understanding as is best calculated to strengthen the body and form the heart. Or, in other words, to enable the individual to attain such habits of virtue as will render it independent. In fact, it is a farce to call any being virtuous whose virtues do not result from the exercise of its own reason. This was Rousseau's opinion respecting men: I extend it to women, and confidently assert that they have been drawn out of their sphere by false refinement, and not by an endeavour to acquire masculine qualities. Still the regal homage which they receive is so intoxicating, that till the manners of the times are changed, and formed on more reasonable principles, it may be impossible to convince them that the illegitimate power, which they obtain, by degrading themselves, is a curse, and that they must return to nature and equality if they wish to secure the placid satisfaction that unsophisticated affections impart. But for this epoch we must wait—wait, perhaps, till kings and nobles, enlightened by reason, and, preferring the real dignity of man to childish state, throw off their gaudy hereditary trappings: and if then women do not resign the arbitrary power of beauty—they will prove that they have *less* mind than man.

I may be accused of arrogance; still I must declare what I firmly believe, that all the writers who have written on the subject of female education and manners from Rousseau to Dr. Gregory,[7] have contributed to render women more artificial, weak characters, than they would otherwise have been; and, consequently, more useless members of society. I might have expressed this conviction in a lower key; but I am afraid it would have been the whine of affectation, and not the faithful expression of my feelings, of the clear result, which experience and reflection have led me to draw. When I come to that division of the subject, I shall advert to the passages that I more particularly disapprove of, in the works of the authors I have just alluded to; but it is first necessary to observe, that my objection extends to the whole purport of those books, which tend, in my opinion, to degrade one half of the human species, and render women pleasing at the expense of every solid virtue.

Though, to reason on Rousseau's ground, if man did attain a degree of perfection of mind when his body arrived at maturity, it might be proper, in order to make a man and his wife *one*, that she should rely entirely on his under-

6. Education at home.
7. John Gregory (1724–1773), Scottish physician, philosopher, and professor at the University of Edinburgh. In her edited anthology *The Female Reader* (1789) Wollstonecraft had quoted extensively from Gregory's widely read advice book, *A Father's Legacy to His Daughters* (1774). Here she returns to that work in a more critical spirit.

standing; and the graceful ivy, clasping the oak that supported it, would form a whole in which strength and beauty would be equally conspicuous. But, alas! husbands, as well as their helpmates, are often only overgrown children; nay, thanks to early debauchery, scarcely men in their outward form—and if the blind lead the blind, one need not come from heaven to tell us the consequence.[8]

Many are the causes that, in the present corrupt state of society, contribute to enslave women by cramping their understandings and sharpening their senses. One, perhaps, that silently does more mischief than all the rest, is their disregard of order.

To do every thing in an orderly manner, is a most important precept, which women, who, generally speaking, receive only a disorderly kind of education, seldom attend to with that degree of exactness that men, who from their infancy are broken into method, observe. This negligent kind of guess-work, for what other epithet can be used to point out the random exertions of a sort of instinctive common sense, never brought to the test of reason? prevents their generalizing matters of fact—so they do to-day, what they did yesterday, merely because they did it yesterday.

This contempt of the understanding in early life has more baneful consequences than is commonly supposed; for the little knowledge which women of strong minds attain, is, from various circumstances, of a more desultory kind than the knowledge of men, and it is acquired more by sheer observations on real life, than from comparing what has been individually observed with the results of experience generalized by speculation. Led by their dependent situation and domestic employments more into society, what they learn is rather by snatches; and as learning is with them, in general, only a secondary thing, they do not pursue any one branch with that persevering ardour necessary to give vigour to the faculties, and clearness to the judgment. In the present state of society, a little learning is required to support the character of a gentleman; and boys are obliged to submit to a few years of discipline. But in the education of women, the cultivation of the understanding is always subordinate to the acquirement of some corporeal accomplishment; even while enervated by confinement and false notions of modesty, the body is prevented from attaining that grace and beauty which relaxed half-formed limbs never exhibit. Besides, in youth their faculties are not brought forward by emulation; and having no serious scientific study, if they have natural sagacity it is turned too soon on life and manners. They dwell on effects, and modifications, without tracing them back to causes; and complicated rules to adjust behaviour are a weak substitute for simple principles.

As a proof that education gives this appearance of weakness to females, we may instance the example of military men, who are, like them, sent into the world before their minds have been stored with knowledge or fortified by principles. The consequences are similar; soldiers acquire a little superficial knowledge, snatched from the muddy current of conversation, and, from continually mixing with society, they gain, what is termed a knowledge of the world; and this acquaintance with manners and customs has frequently been confounded with a knowledge of the human heart. But can the crude fruit of casual observation, never brought to the test of judgment, formed by compar-

---

8. Matthew 15.14: "And if the blind lead the blind, both shall fall into the ditch." "One . . . from heaven": Jesus.

ing speculation and experience, deserve such a distinction? Soldiers, as well as women, practice the minor virtues with punctilious politeness. Where is then the sexual difference, when the education has been the same? All the difference that I can discern, arises from the superior advantage of liberty, which enables the former to see more of life.

It is wandering from my present subject, perhaps, to make a political remark; but, as it was produced naturally by the train of my reflections, I shall not pass it silently over.

Standing armies can never consist of resolute, robust men, they may be well disciplined machines, but they will seldom contain men under the influence of strong passions, or with very vigorous faculties. And as for any depth of understanding, I will venture to affirm, that it is as rarely to be found in the army as amongst women; and the cause, I maintain, is the same. It may be further observed, that officers are also particularly attentive to their persons, fond of dancing, crowded rooms, adventures, and ridicule.[9] Like the *fair* sex,[1] the business of their lives is gallantry.—They were taught to please, and they only live to please. Yet they do not lose their rank in the distinction of sexes, for they are still reckoned superior to women, though in what their superiority consists, beyond what I have just mentioned, it is difficult to discover.

The great misfortune is this, that they both acquire manners before morals, and a knowledge of life before they have, from reflection, any acquaintance with the grand ideal outline of human nature. The consequence is natural; satisfied with common nature, they become a prey to prejudices, and taking all their opinions on credit, they blindly submit to authority. So that, if they have any sense, it is a kind of instinctive glance, that catches proportions, and decides with respect to manners; but fails when arguments are to be pursued below the surface, or opinions analyzed.

May not the same remark be applied to women? Nay, the argument may be carried still further, for they are both thrown out of a useful station by the unnatural distinctions established in civilized life. Riches and hereditary honours have made cyphers of women to give consequence to the numerical figure;[2] and idleness has produced a mixture of gallantry and despotism into society, which leads the very men who are the slaves of their mistresses to tyrannize over their sisters, wives, and daughters. This is only keeping them in rank and file, it is true. Strengthen the female mind by enlarging it, and there will be an end to blind obedience; but, as blind obedience is ever sought for by power, tyrants and sensualists are in the right when they endeavour to keep women in the dark, because the former only want slaves, and the latter a play-thing. The sensualist, indeed, has been the most dangerous of tyrants, and women have been duped by their lovers, as princes by their ministers, whilst dreaming that they reigned over them.

I now principally allude to Rousseau, for his character of Sophia[3] is, undoubtedly, a captivating one, though it appears to me grossly unnatural;

9. Why should women be censured with petulant acrimony, because they seem to have a passion for a scarlet coat? Has not education placed them more on a level with soldiers than any other class of men? [Wollstonecraft's note].
1. Women.
2. As a zero added to a number multiplies its value by a factor of ten, in a hierarchical society women magnify the status of the men with whom they are allied.
3. "*Sophie ou la Femme*" is the title of book V of *Émile*, Rousseau's blend of educational treatise and novel. Having tracked the development of Émile, his imaginary pupil, up to age twenty, Rousseau invents the character of Sophie (Sophia in the 1762 English translation) to supply his hero with a wife and to address, belatedly, the topic of female education.

however it is not the superstructure, but the foundation of her character, the principles on which her education was built, that I mean to attack; nay, warmly as I admire the genius of that able writer, whose opinions I shall often have occasion to cite, indignation always takes place of admiration, and the rigid frown of insulted virtue effaces the smile of complacency, which his eloquent periods are wont to raise, when I read his voluptuous reveries. Is this the man, who, in his ardour for virtue, would banish all the soft arts of peace, and almost carry us back to Spartan discipline? Is this the man who delights to paint the useful struggles of passion, the triumphs of good dispositions, and the heroic flights which carry the glowing soul out of itself?—How are these mighty sentiments lowered when he describes the pretty foot and enticing airs of his little favourite! But, for the present, I wave[4] the subject, and, instead of severely reprehending the transient effusions of overweening sensibility, I shall only observe, that whoever has cast a benevolent eye on society, must often have been gratified by the sight of a humble mutual love, not dignified by sentiment, or strengthened by a union in intellectual pursuits. The domestic trifles of the day have afforded matters for cheerful converse, and innocent caresses have softened toils which did not require great exercise of mind or stretch of thought: yet, has not the sight of this moderate felicity excited more tenderness than respect? An emotion similar to what we feel when children are playing, or animals sporting,[5] whilst the contemplation of the noble struggles of suffering merit has raised admiration, and carried our thoughts to that world where sensation will give place to reason.

Women are, therefore, to be considered either as moral beings, or so weak that they must be entirely subjected to the superior faculties of men.

Let us examine this question. Rousseau declares that a woman should never, for a moment, feel herself independent, that she should be governed by fear to exercise her natural cunning, and made a coquetish slave in order to render her a more alluring object of desire, a *sweeter* companion to man, whenever he chooses to relax himself. He carries the arguments, which he pretends to draw from the indications of nature, still further, and insinuates that truth and fortitude, the corner stones of all human virtue, should be cultivated with certain restrictions, because, with respect to the female character, obedience is the grand lesson which ought to be impressed with unrelenting rigour.[6]

What nonsense! when will a great man arise with sufficient strength of mind to puff away the fumes which pride and sensuality have thus spread over the subject! If women are by nature inferior to men, their virtues must be the same in quality, if not in degree, or virtue is a relative idea; conse-

---

4. A common spelling for "waive" in the eighteenth century.
5. Similar feelings has Milton's pleasing picture of paradisiacal happiness ever raised in my mind; yet, instead of envying the lovely pair, I have, with conscious dignity, or Satanic pride, turned to hell for sublimer objects. In the same style, when viewing some noble monument of human art, I have traced the emanation of the Deity in the order I admired, till, descending from that giddy height, I have caught myself contemplating the grandest of all human sights;—for fancy quickly placed, in some solitary recess, an outcast of fortune, rising superior to passion and discontent

[Wollstonecraft's note]. Wollstonecraft is referring to the portrait of Adam and Eve in book IV of Milton's *Paradise Lost* and stating what has since become a critical commonplace, that Milton's Eden, for all its bliss, is not as compelling as his suffering Satan.
6. *Émile*: "The first and most important qualification in a woman is good nature or sweetness of temper: formed to obey a being so imperfect as man, often full of vices, and always full of faults, she ought to learn betimes even to suffer injustice, and to bear the insults of a husband without complaint: it is not for his sake, but her own, that she should be of a mild disposition."

quently, their conduct should be founded on the same principles, and have the same aim.

Connected with man as daughters, wives, and mothers, their moral character may be estimated by their manner of fulfilling those simple duties; but the end, the grand end of their exertions should be to unfold their own faculties and acquire the dignity of conscious virtue. They may try to render their road pleasant; but ought never to forget, in common with man, that life yields not the felicity which can satisfy an immortal soul. I do not mean to insinuate, that either sex should be so lost in abstract reflections or distant views, as to forget the affections and duties that lie before them, and are, in truth, the means appointed to produce the fruit of life; on the contrary, I would warmly recommend them, even while I assert, that they afford most satisfaction when they are considered in their true, sober light.

Probably the prevailing opinion, that woman was created for man, may have taken its rise from Moses's poetical story;[7] yet, as very few, it is presumed, who have bestowed any serious thought on the subject, ever supposed that Eve was, literally speaking, one of Adam's ribs, the deduction must be allowed to fall to the ground; or, only be so far admitted as it proves that man, from the remotest antiquity, found it convenient to exert his strength to subjugate his companion, and his invention to shew that she ought to have her neck bent under the yoke, because the whole creation was only created for his convenience or pleasure.

Let it not be concluded that I wish to invert the order of things; I have already granted, that, from the constitution of their bodies, men seem to be designed by Providence to attain a greater degree of virtue. I speak collectively of the whole sex; but I see not the shadow of a reason to conclude that their virtues should differ in respect to their nature. In fact, how can they, if virtue has only one eternal standard? I must therefore, if I reason consequentially, as strenuously maintain that they have the same simple direction, as that there is a God.

It follows then that cunning should not be opposed to wisdom, little cares to great exertions, or insipid softness, varnished over with the name of gentleness, to that fortitude which grand views alone can inspire.

I shall be told that woman would then lose many of her peculiar graces, and the opinion of a well known poet might be quoted to refute my unqualified assertion. For Pope has said, in the name of the whole male sex,

> Yet ne'er so sure our passion to create,
> As when she touch'd the brink of all we hate.[8]

In what light this sally places men and women, I shall leave to the judicious to determine; meanwhile I shall content myself with observing, that I cannot discover why, unless they are mortal, females should always be degraded by being made subservient to love or lust.

To speak disrespectfully of love is, I know, high treason against sentiment and fine feelings; but I wish to speak the simple language of truth, and rather to address the head than the heart. To endeavour to reason love

7. See Genesis 2.21–23 for one account of the creation of woman. Moses was thought to be the author of the first five books of the Old Testament (the Pentateuch).

8. Alexander Pope, "Of the Characters of Women," Epistle 2, lines 51–52, of his *Moral Essays* (1735).

out of the world, would be to out Quixote Cervantes,[9] and equally offend against common sense; but an endeavour to restrain this tumultuous passion, and to prove that it should not be allowed to dethrone superior powers, or to usurp the sceptre which the understanding should ever coolly wield, appears less wild.

Youth is the season for love in both sexes; but in those days of thoughtless enjoyment provision should be made for the more important years of life, when reflection takes place of sensation. But Rousseau, and most of the male writers who have followed his steps, have warmly inculcated that the whole tendency of female education ought to be directed to one point:—to render them pleasing.

Let me reason with the supporters of this opinion who have any knowledge of human nature, do they imagine that marriage can eradicate the habitude of life? The woman who has only been taught to please will soon find that her charms are oblique sunbeams, and that they cannot have much effect on her husband's heart when they are seen every day, when the summer is passed and gone. Will she then have sufficient native energy to look into herself for comfort, and cultivate her dormant faculties? or, is it not more rational to expect that she will try to please other men; and, in the emotions raised by the expectation of new conquests, endeavour to forget the mortification her love or pride has received? When the husband ceases to be a lover—and the time will inevitably come, her desire of pleasing will then grow languid, or become a spring of bitterness; and love, perhaps, the most evanescent of all passions, gives place to jealousy or vanity.

I now speak of women who are restrained by principle or prejudice; such women, though they would shrink from an intrigue with real abhorrence, yet, nevertheless, wish to be convinced by the homage of gallantry that they are cruelly neglected by their husbands; or, days and weeks are spent in dreaming of the happiness enjoyed by congenial souls till their health is undermined and their spirits broken by discontent. How then can the great art of pleasing be such a necessary study? it is only useful to a mistress; the chaste wife, and serious mother, should only consider her power to please as the polish of her virtues, and the affection of her husband as one of the comforts that render her task less difficult and her life happier.—But, whether she be loved or neglected, her first wish should be to make herself respectable, and not to rely for all her happiness on a being subject to like infirmities with herself.

The worthy Dr. Gregory fell into a similar error. I respect his heart; but entirely disapprove of his celebrated Legacy to his Daughters.

He advises them to cultivate a fondness for dress, because a fondness for dress, he asserts, is natural to them.[1] I am unable to comprehend what either he or Rousseau mean, when they frequently use this indefinite term.[2] If they told us that in a pre-existent state the soul was fond of dress, and brought this inclination with it into a new body, I should listen to them with a half smile, as I often do when I hear a rant about innate elegance.—But if he only meant to say that the exercise of the faculties will produce this fondness—I

9. I.e., to outdo the idealistic but ineffectual hero of Miguel de Cervantes' Don Quixote (1605) in trying to accomplish the impossible.
1. "The love of dress is natural to you, and there-
fore it is proper and reasonable." John Gregory, A Father's Legacy to His Daughters, 2nd ed. (London, 1775).
2. I.e., "natural."

deny it.—It is not natural; but arises, like false ambition in men, from a love of power.

Dr. Gregory goes much further; he actually recommends dissimulation, and advises an innocent girl to give the lie to her feelings, and not dance with spirit, when gaiety of heart would make her feel eloquent without making her gestures immodest. In the name of truth and common sense, why should not one woman acknowledge that she can take more exercise than another? or, in other words, that she has a sound constitution; and why, to damp innocent vivacity, is she darkly to be told that men will draw conclusions which she little thinks of?[3]—Let the libertine draw what inference he pleases; but, I hope, that no sensible mother will restrain the natural frankness of youth by instilling such indecent cautions. Out of the abundance of the heart the mouth speaketh;[4] and a wiser than Solomon[5] hath said, that the heart should be made clean, and not trivial ceremonies observed,[6] which it is not very difficult to fulfill with scrupulous exactness when vice reigns in the heart.

Women ought to endeavour to purify their heart; but can they do so when their uncultivated understandings make them entirely dependent on their senses for employment and amusement, when no noble pursuit sets them above the little vanities of the day, or enables them to curb the wild emotions that agitate a reed over which every passing breeze has power? To gain the affections of a virtuous man is affectation necessary? Nature has given woman a weaker frame than man; but, to ensure her husband's affections, must a wife, who by the exercise of her mind and body whilst she was discharging the duties of a daughter, wife, and mother, has allowed her constitution to retain its natural strength, and her nerves a healthy tone, is she, I say, to condescend to use art and feign a sickly delicacy in order to secure her husband's affection? Weakness may excite tenderness, and gratify the arrogant pride of man; but the lordly caresses of a protector will not gratify a noble mind that pants for, and deserves to be respected. Fondness is a poor substitute for friendship!

In a seraglio, I grant, that all these arts are necessary; the epicure must have his palate tickled, or he will sink into apathy; but have women so little ambition as to be satisfied with such a condition? Can they supinely dream life away in the lap of pleasure, or the languor of weariness, rather than assert their claim to pursue reasonable pleasures and render themselves conspicuous by practising the virtues which dignify mankind? Surely she has not an immortal soul who can loiter life away merely employed to adorn her person, that she may amuse the languid hours, and soften the cares of a fellow-creature who is willing to be enlivened by her smiles and tricks, when the serious business of life is over.

Besides, the woman who strengthens her body and exercises her mind will, by managing her family and practising various virtues, become the friend, and not the humble dependent of her husband; and if she, by possessing such substantial qualities, merit his regard, she will not find it necessary

---

3. For this and the previous sentence see Gregory: "I would have you to dance with spirit; but never allow yourselves to be so far transported with mirth, as to forget the delicacy of your sex.— Many a girl dancing in the gaiety and innocence of her heart, is thought to discover a spirit she little dreams of."

4. Matthew 12.34.
5. I.e., Jesus, who describes himself in comparable terms in Luke 11.31.
6. In Luke 11.39–44 and Matthew 23.25–28, Jesus speaks of purifying the inner self and denounces the Pharisees' self-righteous observance of the letter of the law.

to conceal her affection, nor to pretend to an unnatural coldness of constitution to excite her husband's passions. In fact, if we revert to history, we shall find that the women who have distinguished themselves have neither been the most beautiful nor the most gentle of their sex.

Nature, or, to speak with strict propriety, God, has made all things right; but man has sought him out many inventions to mar the work. I now allude to that part of Dr. Gregory's treatise, where he advises a wife never to let her husband know the extent of her sensibility or affection.[7] Voluptuous precaution, and as ineffectual as absurd.—Love, from its very nature, must be transitory. To seek for a secret that would render it constant, would be as wild a search as for the philosopher's stone, or the grand panacea:[8] and the discovery would be equally useless, or rather pernicious to mankind. The most holy band of society is friendship. It has been well said, by a shrewd satirist, "that rare as true love is, true friendship is still rarer."[9]

This is an obvious truth, and the cause not lying deep, will not elude a slight glance of inquiry.

Love, the common passion, in which chance and sensation take place of choice and reason, is, in some degree, felt by the mass of mankind; for it is not necessary to speak, at present, of the emotions that rise above or sink below love. This passion, naturally increased by suspense and difficulties, draws the mind out of its accustomed state, and exalts the affections; but the security of marriage, allowing the fever of love to subside, a healthy temperature is thought insipid, only by those who have not sufficient intellect to substitute the calm tenderness of friendship, the confidence of respect, instead of blind admiration, and the sensual emotions of fondness.

This is, must be, the course of nature.—Friendship or indifference inevitably succeeds love.—And this constitution seems perfectly to harmonize with the system of government which prevails in the moral world. Passions are spurs to action, and open the mind; but they sink into mere appetites, become a personal and momentary gratification, when the object is gained, and the satisfied mind rests in enjoyment. The man who had some virtue whilst he was struggling for a crown, often becomes a voluptuous tyrant when it graces his brow; and, when the lover is not lost in the husband, the dotard, a prey to childish caprices, and fond jealousies, neglects the serious duties of life, and the caresses which should excite confidence in his children are lavished on the overgrown child, his wife.

In order to fulfil the duties of life, and to be able to pursue with vigour the various employments which form the moral character, a master and mistress of a family ought not to continue to love each other with passion. I mean to say, that they ought not to indulge those emotions which disturb the order of society, and engross the thoughts that should be otherwise employed. The mind that has never been engrossed by one object wants vigour—if it can long be so, it is weak.

A mistaken education, a narrow, uncultivated mind, and many sexual prejudices, tend to make women more constant than men; but, for the present, I shall not touch on this branch of the subject. I will go still further, and

7. Gregory: "If you love him, let me advise you never to discover to him the full extent of your love, no, not although you marry him."
8. A medicine reputed to cure all diseases. "Philosopher's stone": sought by alchemists because it was supposed to have the power to transmute base metals into gold.
9. La Rochefoucauld (1613–1680, French noble), *Les Maximes*, No. 473.

advance, without dreaming of a paradox, that an unhappy marriage is often very advantageous to a family, and that the neglected wife is, in general, the best mother.[1] And this would almost always be the consequence if the female mind were more enlarged: for, it seems to be the common dispensation of Providence, that what we gain in present enjoyment should be deducted from the treasure of life, experience; and that when we are gathering the flowers of the day and revelling in pleasure, the solid fruit of toil and wisdom should not be caught at the same time. The way lies before us, we must turn to the right or left; and he who will pass life away in bounding from one pleasure to another, must not complain if he acquire neither wisdom nor respectability of character.

Supposing, for a moment, that the soul is not immortal, and that man was only created for the present scene,—I think we should have reason to complain that love, infantine fondness, ever grew insipid and palled upon the sense. Let us eat, drink, and love, for tomorrow we die, would be, in fact, the language of reason, the morality of life; and who but a fool would part with a reality for a fleeting shadow? But, if awed by observing the improbable[2] powers of the mind, we disdain to confine our wishes or thoughts to such a comparatively mean field of action, that only appears grand and important, as it is connected with a boundless prospect and sublime hopes, what necessity is there for falsehood in conduct, and why must the sacred majesty of truth be violated to detain a deceitful good that saps the very foundation of virtue? Why must the female mind be tainted by coquetish arts to gratify the sensualist, and prevent love from subsiding into friendship, or compassionate tenderness, when there are not qualities on which friendship can be built? Let the honest heart shew itself, and *reason* teach passion to submit to necessity; or, let the dignified pursuit of virtue and knowledge raise the mind above those emotions which rather imbitter than sweeten the cup of life, when they are not restrained within due bounds.

I do not mean to allude to the romantic passion, which is the concomitant of genius.—Who can clip its wing? But that grand passion not proportioned to the puny enjoyments of life, is only true to the sentiment, and feeds on itself. The passions which have been celebrated for their durability have always been unfortunate. They have acquired strength by absence and constitutional melancholy.—The fancy[3] has hovered round a form of beauty dimly seen—but familiarity might have turned admiration into disgust; or, at least, into indifference, and allowed the imagination leisure to start fresh game. With perfect propriety, according to this view of things, does Rousseau make the mistress of his soul, Eloisa, love St. Preux, when life was fading before her;[4] but this is no proof of the immortality of the passion.

Of the same complexion is Dr. Gregory's advice respecting delicacy of sentiment, which he advises a woman not to acquire, if she have determined to marry.[5] This determination, however, perfectly consistent with his former

1. Wollstonecraft's point is that a woman who is not preoccupied with her husband (and his attentions to her) has more time and energy for her children.
2. The first edition reads "improvable" here, which makes more sense in context.
3. Imagination.
4. In Rousseau's *Julie; ou la Nouvelle Héloïse* (1761), the heroine, Julie, reveals her long-held passionate love for St. Preux as she is dying, even though she has been a faithful wife to Wolmar since her marriage.
5. Gregory: "But if you find that marriage is absolutely essential to your happiness . . . shun . . . reading and conversation that warms the imagination, which engages and softens the heart, and raises the taste above the level of common life . . . [otherwise] you may be tired with insipidity and dullness; shocked with indelicacy, or mortified by indifference."

advice, he calls *indelicate*, and earnestly persuades his daughters to conceal it, though it may govern their conduct;—as if it were indelicate to have the common appetites of human nature.

Noble morality! and consistent with the cautious prudence of a little soul that cannot extend its views beyond the present minute division of existence. If all the faculties of woman's mind are only to be cultivated as they respect her dependence on man; if, when a husband be obtained, she have arrived at her goal, and meanly proud rests satisfied with such a paltry crown, let her grovel contentedly, scarcely raised by her employments above the animal kingdom; but, if, struggling for the prize of her high calling,[6] she look beyond the present scene, let her cultivate her understanding without stopping to consider what character the husband may have whom she is destined to marry. Let her only determine, without being too anxious about present happiness, to acquire the qualities that ennoble a rational being, and a rough inelegant husband may shock her taste without destroying her peace of mind. She will not model her soul to suit the frailties of her companion, but to bear with them: his character may be a trial, but not an impediment to virtue.

If Dr. Gregory confined his remark to romantic expectations of constant love and congenial feelings, he should have recollected that experience will banish what advice can never make us cease to wish for, when the imagination is kept alive at the expence of reason.

I own it frequently happens that women who have fostered a romantic unnatural delicacy of feeling, waste their[7] lives in *imagining* how happy they should have been with a husband who could love them with a fervid increasing affection every day, and all day. But they might as well pine married as single—and would not be a jot more unhappy with a bad husband than longing for a good one. That a proper education; or, to speak with more precision, a well stored mind, would enable a woman to support a single life with dignity, I grant; but that she should avoid cultivating her taste, lest her husband should occasionally shock it, is quitting a substance for a shadow. To say the truth, I do not know of what use is an improved taste, if the individual be not rendered more independent of the casualties of life; if new sources of enjoyment, only dependent on the solitary operations of the mind, are not opened. People of taste, married or single, without distinction, will ever be disgusted by various things that touch not less observing minds. On this conclusion the argument must not be allowed to hinge; but in the whole sum of enjoyment is taste to be denominated a blessing?

The question is, whether it procures most pain or pleasure? The answer will decide the propriety of Dr. Gregory's advice, and shew how absurd and tyrannic it is thus to lay down a system of slavery; or to attempt to educate moral beings by any other rules than those deduced from pure reason, which apply to the whole species.

Gentleness of manners, forbearance and long-suffering, are such amiable Godlike qualities, that in sublime poetic strains the Deity has been invested with them; and, perhaps, no representation of his goodness so strongly fastens on the human affections as those that represent him abundant in mercy and willing to pardon.[8] Gentleness, considered in this point of view, bears on

6. An echo of Philippians 3.14, where Saint Paul writes, "I press toward the mark for the prize of the high calling of God in Christ Jesus."
7. For example, the herd of Novelists [Wollstonecraft's note].
8. Isaiah 55.7: "And he will have mercy upon him; and to our God, for he will abundantly pardon."

its front all the characteristics of grandeur, combined with the winning graces of condescension; but what a different aspect it assumes when it is the submissive demeanour of dependence, the support of weakness that loves, because it wants protection; and is forbearing, because it must silently endure injuries; smiling under the lash at which it dare not snarl. Abject as this picture appears, it is the portrait of an accomplished woman, according to the received opinion of female excellence separated by specious reasoners from human excellence. Or, they[9] kindly restore the rib, and make one moral being of a man and woman; not forgetting to give her all the 'submissive charms,'[1]

How women are to exist in that state where there is to be neither marrying nor giving in marriage, we are not told.[2] For though moralists have agreed that the tenor of life seems to prove that *man* is prepared by various circumstances for a future state, they constantly concur in advising *woman* only to provide for the present. Gentleness, docility, and a spaniel-like affection are, on this ground, consistently recommended as the cardinal virtues of the sex; and, disregarding the arbitrary economy of nature, one writer has declared that it is masculine for a woman to be melancholy.[3] She was created to be the toy of man, his rattle, and it must jingle in his ears whenever, dismissing reason, he chooses to be amused.

To recommend gentleness, indeed, on a broad basis is strictly philosophical. A frail being should labour to be gentle. But when forbearance confounds right and wrong, it ceases to be a virtue; and, however convenient it may be found in a companion—that companion will ever be considered as an inferior, and only inspire a vapid tenderness, which easily degenerates into contempt. Still, if advice could really make a being gentle, whose natural disposition admitted not of such a fine polish, something towards the advancement of order would be attained; but if, as might quickly be demonstrated, only affectation be produced by this indiscriminate counsel, which throws a stumbling-block in the way of gradual improvement, and true melioration of temper, the sex is not much benefited by sacrificing solid virtues to the attainment of superficial graces, though for a few years they may procure the individuals regal sway.

As a philosopher, I read with indignation the plausible epithets which men use to soften their insults; and, as a moralist, I ask what is meant by such heterogeneous associations, as fair defects, amiable weaknesses, &c.?[4] If there be but one criterion of morals, but one archetype for man, women appear to be suspended by destiny, according to the vulgar tale of Mahomet's coffin;[5] they have neither the unerring instinct of brutes, nor are allowed to fix the eye of reason on a perfect model. They were made to be loved, and must not aim at respect, lest they should be hunted out of society as masculine.

9. Vide Rousseau, and Swedenborg [Wollstonecraft's note]. The Swedish mystic Emanuel Swedenborg (1688–1772) believed that in the afterlife each married couple would form a single angel, with the wife contributing her capacity for love and the husband his wisdom.

1. *Paradise Lost* IV.497–99: "he in delight / Both of her Beauty and submissive charms / Smil'd with superior love."

2. An echo of Jesus's account of the resurrection in Matthew 22.30.

3. Perhaps a recollection of Edmund Burke's *Philosophical Enquiry into the Origins of Our Ideas of the Sublime and the Beautiful* (1757). In attempting to distinguish the aesthetic category of "the beautiful" from the aesthetic category of "the sublime," Burke resorts frequently to analogy and so devotes many pages to outlining his notions of the distinctions that separate femininity from masculinity.

4. *Paradise Lost* X.891–92: "This fair defect / Of nature"; and Pope, "Of the Characters of Women," line 44: "Fine by defect, and delicately weak."

5. Wollstonecraft refers to a discredited European legend maintaining that at Mohammed's tomb in Medina giant magnets were used to suspend his coffin in midair.

But to view the subject in another point of view. Do passive indolent women make the best wives? Confining our discussion to the present moment of existence, let us see how such weak creatures perform their part? Do the women who, by the attainment of a few superficial accomplishments, have strengthened the prevailing prejudice, merely contribute to the happiness of their husbands? Do they display their charms merely to amuse them? And have women, who have early imbibed notions of passive obedience, sufficient character to manage a family or educate children? So far from it, that, after surveying the history of woman, I cannot help, agreeing with the severest satirist, considering the sex as the weakest as well as the most oppressed half of the species. What does history disclose but marks of inferiority, and how few women have emancipated themselves from the galling yoke of sovereign man?—So few, that the exceptions remind me of an ingenious conjecture respecting Newton: that he was probably a being of a superior order, accidentally caged in a human body.[6] Following the same train of thinking, I have been led to imagine that the few extraordinary women who have rushed in eccentrical directions out of the orbit prescribed to their sex, were *male* spirits, confined by mistake in female frames. But if it be not philosophical to think of sex when the soul is mentioned, the inferiority must depend on the organs; or the heavenly fire, which is to ferment the clay, is not given in equal portions.

But avoiding, as I have hitherto done, any direct comparison of the two sexes collectively, or frankly acknowledging the inferiority of woman, according to the present appearance of things, I shall only insist that men have increased that inferiority till women are almost sunk below the standard of rational creatures. Let their faculties have room to unfold, and their virtues to gain strength, and then determine where the whole sex must stand in the intellectual scale. Yet let it be remembered, that for a small number of distinguished women I do not ask a place.

It is difficult for us purblind mortals to say to what height human discoveries and improvements may arrive when the gloom of despotism subsides, which makes us stumble at every step; but, when morality shall be settled on a more solid basis, then, without being gifted with a prophetic spirit, I will venture to predict that woman will be either the friend or slave of man. We shall not, as at present, doubt whether she is a moral agent, or the link which unites man with brutes. But, should it then appear, that like the brutes they were principally created for the use of man, he will let them patiently bite the bridle, and not mock them with empty praise; or, should their rationality be proved, he will not impede their improvement merely to gratify his sensual appetites. He will not, with all the graces of rhetoric, advise them to submit implicitly their understanding to the guidance of man. He will not, when he treats of the education of women, assert that they ought never to have the free use of reason, nor would he recommend cunning and dissimulation to beings who are acquiring, in like manner as himself, the virtues of humanity.

Surely there can be but one rule of right, if morality has an eternal foundation, and whoever sacrifices virtue, strictly so called, to present conve-

6. Possibly a reference to Pope's 1733–34 *Essay on Man*, Epistle II, lines 31–34: "Superior beings, when of late they saw / A mortal Man unfold all Nature's law, / Admir'd such wisdom in an earthly shape, / And shew'd a NEWTON as we shew an Ape." Isaac Newton (1643–1727) was revered across Europe for his foundational work of physics, the *Principia* (1687), in which he formulated the laws of gravitation and motion.

nience, or whose *duty* it is to act in such a manner, lives only for the passing day, and cannot be an accountable creature.

The poet then should have dropped his sneer when he says,

> If weak women go astray,
> The stars are more in fault than they.[7]

For that they are bound by the adamantine chain of destiny is most certain, if it be proved that they are never to exercise their own reason, never to be independent, never to rise above opinion, or to feel the dignity of a rational will that only bows to God, and often forgets that the universe contains any being but itself and the model of perfection to which its ardent gaze is turned, to adore attributes that, softened into virtues, may be imitated in kind, though the degree overwhelms the enraptured mind.

If I say, for I would not impress by declamation when Reason offers her sober light, if they be really capable of acting like rational creatures, let them not be treated like slaves; or, like the brutes who are dependent on the reason of man, when they associate with him; but cultivate their minds, give them the salutary, sublime curb of principle, and let them attain conscious dignity by feeling themselves only dependent on God. Teach them, in common with man, to submit to necessity, instead of giving, to render them more pleasing, a sex to morals.

Further, should experience prove that they cannot attain the same degree of strength of mind, perseverance, and fortitude, let their virtues be the same in kind, though they may vainly struggle for the same degree; and the superiority of man will be equally clear, if not clearer; and truth, as it is a simple principle, which admits of no modification, would be common to both. Nay, the order of society as it is at present regulated would not be inverted, for woman would then only have the rank that reason assigned her, and arts could not be practised to bring the balance even, much less to turn it.

These may be termed Utopian dreams.—Thanks to that Being who impressed them on my soul, and gave me sufficient strength of mind to dare to exert my own reason, till, becoming dependent only on him for the support of my virtue, I view, with indignation, the mistaken notions that enslave my sex.

I love man as my fellow; but his scepter, real, or usurped, extends not to me, unless the reason of an individual demands my homage; and even then the submission is to reason, and not to man. In fact, the conduct of an accountable being must be regulated by the operations of its own reason; or on what foundation rests the throne of God?

It appears to me necessary to dwell on these obvious truths, because females have been insulated, as it were; and, while they have been stripped of the virtues that should clothe humanity, they have been decked with artificial graces that enable them to exercise a short-lived tyranny. Love, in their bosoms, taking place of every nobler passion, their sole ambition is to be fair, to raise emotion instead of inspiring respect; and this ignoble desire, like the servility in absolute monarchies, destroys all strength of character. Liberty is the mother of virtue, and if women be, by their very constitution,

---

7. Matthew Prior, "Hans Carvel" (1700), lines 11–12.

slaves, and not allowed to breathe the sharp invigorating air of freedom, they must ever languish like exotics,[8] and be reckoned beautiful flaws in nature.

As to the argument respecting the subjection in which the sex has ever been held, it retorts on man. The many have always been enthralled by the few; and monsters, who scarcely have shewn any discernment of human excellence, have tyrannized over thousands of their fellow-creatures. Why have men of superiour endowments submitted to such degradation? For, is it not universally acknowledged that kings, viewed collectively, have ever been inferior, in abilities and virtue, to the same number of men taken from the common mass of mankind—yet, have they not, and are they not still treated with a degree of reverence that is an insult to reason? China is not the only country where a living man has been made a God.[9] *Men* have submitted to superior strength to enjoy with impunity the pleasure of the moment— *women* have only done the same, and therefore till it is proved that the courtier, who servilely resigns the birthright of a man, is not a moral agent, it cannot be demonstrated that woman is essentially inferior to man because she has always been subjugated.

Brutal force has hitherto governed the world, and that the science of politics is in its infancy, is evident from philosophers scrupling to give the knowledge most useful to man that determinate distinction.

I shall not pursue this argument any further than to establish an obvious inference, that as sound politics diffuse liberty, mankind, including woman, will become more wise and virtuous.

From *Chapter 4. Observations on the State of Degradation to Which Woman Is Reduced by Various Causes.*

* * *

In the middle rank of life, to continue the comparison,[1] men, in their youth, are prepared for professions, and marriage is not considered as the grand feature in their lives; whilst women, on the contrary, have no other scheme to sharpen their faculties. It is not business, extensive plans, or any of the excursive flights of ambition, that engross their attention; no, their thoughts are not employed in rearing such noble structures. To rise in the world, and have the liberty of running from pleasure to pleasure, they must marry advantageously, and to this object their time is sacrificed, and their persons often legally prostituted. A man when he enters any profession has his eye steadily fixed on some future advantage (and the mind gains great strength by having all its efforts directed to one point), and, full of his business, pleasure is considered as mere relaxation; whilst women seek for pleasure as the main purpose of existence. In fact, from the education, which they receive from society, the love of pleasure may be said to govern them all; but does this prove that there is a sex in souls? It would be just as rational to declare

---

8. Hothouse plants, which do not thrive in the English climate. Wollstonecraft also echoes here the language of the *Mansfield Judgment* of 1772, the legal decision that prohibited slavery within England by declaring "the air of England . . . too pure for slaves to breathe in."

9. The emperors of China were known as the "sons of heaven."
1. I.e., her comparison between the social expectations that shape men and those that shape women and lead them to "degradation."

that the courtiers in France, when a destructive system of despotism had formed their character, were not men, because liberty, virtue, and humanity, were sacrificed to pleasure and vanity.—Fatal passions, which have ever domineered over the *whole* race!

The same love of pleasure, fostered by the whole tendency of their education, gives a trifling turn to the conduct of women in most circumstances: for instance, they are ever anxious about secondary things; and on the watch for adventures, instead of being occupied by duties.

A man, when he undertakes a journey, has, in general, the end in view; a woman thinks more of the incidental occurrences, the strange things that may possibly occur on the road; the impression that she may make on her fellow-travellers; and, above all, she is anxiously intent on the care of the finery that she carries with her, which is more than ever a part of herself, when going to figure on a new scene; when, to use an apt French turn of expression, she is going to produce a sensation.—Can dignity of mind exist with such trivial cares?

In short, women, in general, as well as the rich of both sexes, have acquired all the follies and vices of civilization, and missed the useful fruit. It is not necessary for me always to premise, that I speak of the condition of the whole sex, leaving exceptions out of the question. Their senses are inflamed, and their understandings neglected, consequently they become the prey of their senses, delicately termed sensibility, and are blown about by every momentary gust of feeling. Civilized women are, therefore, so weakened by false refinement, that, respecting morals, their condition is much below what it would be were they left in a state nearer to nature. Ever restless and anxious, their over exercised sensibility not only renders them uncomfortable themselves, but troublesome, to use a soft phrase, to others. All their thoughts turn on things calculated to excite emotion; and feeling, when they should reason, their conduct is unstable, and their opinions are wavering—not the wavering produced by deliberation or progressive views, but by contradictory emotions. By fits and starts they are warm in many pursuits; yet this warmth, never concentrated into perseverance, soon exhausts itself; exhaled by its own heat, or meeting with some other fleeting passion, to which reason has never given any specific gravity, neutrality ensues. Miserable, indeed, must be that being whose cultivation of mind has only tended to inflame its passions! A distinction should be made between inflaming and strengthening them. The passions thus pampered, whilst the judgment is left unformed, what can be expected to ensue?—Undoubtedly, a mixture of madness and folly!

This observation should not be confined to the *fair* sex; however, at present, I only mean to apply it to them.

Novels, music, poetry, and gallantry, all tend to make women the creatures of sensation, and their character is thus formed in the mould of folly during the time they are acquiring accomplishments, the only improvement they are excited, by their station in society, to acquire. This overstretched sensibility naturally relaxes the other powers of the mind, and prevents intellect from attaining that sovereignty which it ought to attain to render a rational creature useful to others, and content with its own station: for the exercise of the understanding, as life advances, is the only method pointed out by nature to calm the passions.

Satiety has a very different effect, and I have often been forcibly struck by an emphatical description of damnation:—when the spirit is represented as continually hovering with abortive eagerness round the defied body, unable to enjoy any thing without the organs of sense. Yet, to their senses, are women made slaves, because it is by their sensibility that they obtain present power.

And will moralists pretend to assert, that this is the condition in which one half of the human race should be encouraged to remain with listless inactivity and stupid acquiescence? Kind instructors! what were we created for? To remain, it may be said, innocent; they mean in a state of childhood.—We might as well never have been born, unless it were necessary that we should be created to enable man to acquire the noble privilege of reason, the power of discerning good from evil, whilst we lie down in the dust from whence we were taken, never to rise again.—

It would be an endless task to trace the variety of meannesses, cares, and sorrows, into which women are plunged by the prevailing opinion, that they were created rather to feel than reason, and that all the power they obtain, must be obtained by their charms and weakness:

Fine by defect, and amiably weak![2]

And, made by this amiable weakness entirely dependent, excepting what they gain by illicit sway, on man, not only for protection, but advice, is it surprising that, neglecting the duties that reason alone points out, and shrinking from trials calculated to strengthen their minds, they only exert themselves to give their defects a graceful covering, which may serve to heighten their charms in the eye of the voluptuary, though it sink them below the scale of moral excellence?

Fragile in every sense of the word, they are obliged to look up to man for every comfort. In the most trifling dangers they cling to their support, with parasitical tenacity, piteously demanding succour; and their *natural* protector extends his arm, or lifts up his voice, to guard the lovely trembler—from what? Perhaps the frown of an old cow, or the jump of a mouse; a rat, would be a serious danger. In the name of reason, and even common sense, what can save such beings from contempt; even though they be soft and fair?

These fears, when not affected, may produce some pretty attitudes; but they shew a degree of imbecility which degrades a rational creature in a way women are not aware of—for love and esteem are very distinct things.

I am fully persuaded that we should hear of none of these infantine airs, if girls were allowed to take sufficient exercise, and not confined in close rooms till their muscles are relaxed, and their powers of digestion destroyed. To carry the remark still further, if fear in girls, instead of being cherished, perhaps, created, were treated in the same manner as cowardice in boys, we should quickly see women with more dignified aspects. It is true, they could not then with equal propriety be termed the sweet flowers that smile in the walk of man; but they would be more respectable members of society, and discharge the important duties of life by the light of their own reason. 'Educate women like men,' says Rousseau, 'and the more they resemble our sex the less power will they have over us.'[3] This is the very point I aim at. I do not wish them to have power over men; but over themselves.

---

2. A misquotation of Pope, "Of the Characters of Women," line 44: "Fine by defect, and delicately weak."

3. The passage continues: "and when once they become like ourselves, we shall then be truly their masters" (*Émile*).

In the same strain have I heard men argue against instructing the poor; for many are the forms that aristocracy assumes. 'Teach them to read and write,' say they, 'and you take them out of the station assigned them by nature.' An eloquent Frenchman has answered them, I will borrow his sentiments. But they know not, when they make man a brute, that they may expect every instant to see him transformed into a ferocious beast.[4] Without knowledge there can be no morality!

Ignorance is a frail base for virtue! Yet, that it is the condition for which woman was organized, has been insisted upon by the writers who have most vehemently argued in, favour of the superiority of man; a superiority not in degree, but essence; though, to soften the argument, they have laboured to prove, with chivalrous generosity, that the sexes ought not to be compared; man was made to reason, woman to feel: and that together, flesh and spirit, they make the most perfect whole, by blending happily reason and sensibility into one character.

And what is sensibility? 'Quickness of sensation; quickness of perception; delicacy.' Thus is it defined by Dr. Johnson;[5] and the definition gives me no other idea than of the most exquisitely polished instinct. I discern not a trace of the image of God in either sensation or matter. Refined seventy times seven,[6] they are still material; intellect dwells not there; nor will fire ever make lead gold!

I come round to my old argument; if woman be allowed to have an immortal soul, she must have, as the employment of life, an understanding to improve. And when, to render the present state more complete, though every thing proves it to be but a fraction of a mighty sum, she is incited by present gratification to forget her grand destination, nature is counteracted, or she was born only to procreate and rot. Or, granting brutes, of every description, a soul, though not a reasonable one, the exercise of instinct and sensibility may be the step, which they are to take, in this life, towards the attainment of reason in the next; so that through all eternity they will lag behind man, who, why we cannot tell, had the power given him of attaining reason in his first mode of existence.

When I treat of the peculiar duties of women, as I should treat of the peculiar duties of a citizen or father, it will be found that I do not mean to insinuate that they should be taken out of their families, speaking of the majority. 'He that hath wife and children,' says Lord Bacon, 'hath given hostages to fortune; for they are impediments to great enterprises, either of virtue or mischief. Certainly the best works, and of greatest merit for the public, have proceeded from the unmarried or childless men.'[7] I say the same of women. But, the welfare of society is not built on extraordinary exertions; and were it more reasonably organized, there would be still less need of great abilities, or heroic virtues.

In the regulation of a family, in the education of children, understanding, in an unsophisticated sense, is particularly required: strength both of body

4. Wollstonecraft might be remembering a remark made in 1790 by the statesman Mirabeau, responding to the aggressive tone of the debates in revolutionary France's new Constituent Assembly and reflecting, more generally, on the power the common people had come to exercise in the nation's political arguments: "you have loosed the bull: do you expect he will not use his horns?"

5. Wollstonecraft cites the emended definition Johnson included in the fourth (1773) edition of his *Dictionary*.
6. Matthew 18.22: "Jesus saith unto him, I say not unto thee, Until seven times: but, Until seventy times seven."
7. Francis Bacon, Essay VIII, "Of Marriage and the Single Life."

and mind; yet the men who, by their writings, have most earnestly laboured to domesticate women, have endeavoured, by arguments dictated by a gross appetite, which satiety had rendered fastidious, to weaken their bodies and cramp their minds. But, if even by these sinister methods they really *persuaded* women, by working on their feelings, to stay at home, and fulfil the duties of a mother and mistress of a family, I should cautiously oppose opinions that led women to right conduct, by prevailing on them to make the discharge of such important duties the main business of life, though reason were insulted. Yet, and I appeal to experience, if by neglecting the understanding they be as much, nay, more detached from these domestic employments, than they could be by the most serious intellectual pursuit, though it may be observed, that the mass of mankind will never vigorously pursue an intellectual object,[8] I may be allowed to infer that reason is absolutely necessary to enable a woman to perform any duty properly, and I must again repeat, that sensibility is not reason.

The comparison with the rich still occurs to me; for, when men neglect the duties of humanity, women will follow their example; a common stream hurries them both along with thoughtless celerity. Riches and honours prevent a man from enlarging his understanding, and enervate all his powers by reversing the order of nature, which has ever made true pleasure the reward of labour. Pleasure—enervating pleasure is, likewise, within women's reach without earning it. But, till hereditary possessions are spread abroad, how can we expect men to be proud of virtue? And, till they are, women will govern them by the most direct means, neglecting their dull domestic duties to catch the pleasure that sits lightly on the wing of time.

'The power of the woman,' says some author, 'is her sensibility';[9] and men, not aware of the consequence, do all they can to make this power swallow up every other. Those who constantly employ their sensibility will have most: for example; poets, painters, and composers.[1] Yet, when the sensibility is thus increased at the expence of reason, and even the imagination, why do philosophical men complain of their fickleness? The sexual attention of man particularly acts on female sensibility, and this sympathy has been exercised from their youth up. A husband cannot long pay those attentions with the passion necessary to excite lively emotions, and the heart, accustomed to lively emotions, turns to a new lover, or pines in secret, the prey of virtue or prudence. I mean when the heart has really been rendered susceptible, and the taste formed; for I am apt to conclude, from what I have seen in fashionable life, that vanity is oftener fostered than sensibility by the mode of education, and the intercourse between the sexes, which I have reprobated; and that coquetry more frequently proceeds from vanity than from that inconstancy, which overstrained sensibility naturally produces.

Another argument that has had great weight with me, must, I think, have some force with every considerate benevolent heart. Girls who have been thus weakly educated, are often cruelly left by their parents without any

---

8. The mass of mankind are rather the slaves of their appetites than of their passions [Wollstonecraft's note].

9. Possibly a recollection of *A Father's Legacy to His Daughters*, in which Gregory, discussing women's blushing, asserts "That extreme sensibility which it indicates, may be a weakness and incumbrance in our sex . . . but in yours it is peculiarly engaging."

1. Men of these descriptions pour it into their compositions, to amalgamate the gross materials; and, moulding them with passion, give to the inert body a soul; but, in woman's imagination, love alone concentrates these ethereal beams [Wollstonecraft's note].

provision; and, of course, are dependent on, not only the reason, but the bounty of their brothers. These brothers are, to view the fairest side of the question, good sort of men, and give as a favour, what children of the same parents had an equal right to. In this equivocal humiliating situation, a docile female may remain some time, with a tolerable degree of comfort. But, when the brother marries, a probable circumstance, from being considered as the mistress of the family, she is viewed with averted looks as an intruder, an unnecessary burden on the benevolence of the master of the house, and his new partner.

Who can recount the misery, which many unfortunate beings, whose minds and bodies are equally weak, suffer in such situations—unable to work, and ashamed to beg? The wife, a cold-hearted, narrow-minded, woman, and this is not an unfair supposition; for the present mode of education does not tend to enlarge the heart any more than the understanding, is jealous of the little kindness which her husband shews to his relations; and her sensibility not rising to humanity, she is displeased at seeing the property of *her* children lavished on an helpless sister.

These are matters of fact, which have come under my eye again and again. The consequence is obvious, the wife has recourse to cunning to undermine the habitual affection, which she is afraid openly to oppose; and neither tears nor caresses are spared till the spy is worked out of her home, and thrown on the world, unprepared for its difficulties; or sent, as a great effort of generosity, or from some regard to propriety, with a small stipend, and an uncultivated mind, into joyless solitude.

These two women may be much upon a par, with respect to reason and humanity; and changing situations, might have acted just the same selfish part; but had they been differently educated, the case would also have been very different. The wife would not have had that sensibility, of which self is the centre, and reason might have taught her not to expect, and not even to be flattered by, the affection of her husband, if it led him to violate prior duties. She would wish not to love him merely because he loved her, but on account of his virtues; and the sister might have been able to struggle for herself instead of eating the bitter bread of dependence.

I am, indeed, persuaded that the heart, as well as the understanding, is opened by cultivation; and by, which may not appear so clear, strengthening the organs; I am not now talking of momentary flashes of sensibility, but of affections. And, perhaps, in the education of both sexes, the most difficult task is so to adjust instruction as not to narrow the understanding, whilst the heart is warmed by the generous juices of spring, just raised by the electric fermentation of the season; nor to dry up the feelings by employing the mind in investigations remote from life.

With respect to women, when they receive a careful education, they are either made fine ladies, brimful of sensibility, and teeming with capricious fancies; or mere notable women.[2] The latter are often friendly, honest creatures, and have a shrewd kind of good sense joined with worldly prudence, that often render them more useful members of society than the fine sentimental lady, though they possess neither greatness of mind nor taste. The intellectual world is shut against them; take them out of their family or neigh-

2. I.e., industrious and energetic housewives.

bourhood, and they stand still; the mind finding no employment, for literature affords a fund of amusement which they have never sought to relish, but
frequently to despise. The sentiments and taste of more cultivated minds
appear ridiculous, even in those whom chance and family connections have
led them to love; but in mere acquaintance they think it all affectation.

A man of sense can only love such a woman on account of her sex, and
respect her, because she is a trusty servant. He lets her, to preserve his own
peace, scold the servants, and go to church in clothes made of the very best
materials. A man of her own size of understanding would, probably, not
agree so well with her; for he might wish to encroach on her prerogative, and
manage some domestic concerns himself. Yet women, whose minds are not
enlarged by cultivation, or the natural selfishness of sensibility expanded by
reflection, are very unfit to manage a family; for, by an undue stretch of
power, they are always tyrannizing to support a superiority that only rests on
the arbitrary distinction of fortune. The evil is sometimes more serious,
and domestics are deprived of innocent indulgences, and made to work
beyond their strength, in order to enable the notable woman to keep a better
table, and outshine her neighbours in finery and parade. If she attend to her
children, it is, in general, to dress them in a costly manner—and, whether this
attention arise from vanity or fondness, it is equally pernicious.

Besides, how many women of this description pass their days; or, at least,
their evenings, discontentedly. Their husbands acknowledge that they are
good managers, and chaste wives; but leave home to seek for more agreeable,
may I be allowed to use a significant French word, *piquant*[3] society; and the
patient drudge, who fulfils her task, like a blind horse in a mill, is defrauded
of her just reward; for the wages due to her are the caresses of her husband;
and women who have so few resources in themselves, do not very patiently
bear this privation of a natural right.

A fine lady, on the contrary, has been taught to look down with contempt
on the vulgar employments of life; though she has only been incited to
acquire accomplishments that rise a degree above sense; for even corporeal
accomplishments cannot be acquired with any degree of precision unless the
understanding has been strengthened by exercise. Without a foundation of
principles taste is superficial, grace must arise from something deeper than
imitation. The imagination, however, is heated, and the feelings rendered
fastidious, if not sophisticated; or, a counterpoise of judgment is not acquired,
when the heart still remains artless, though it becomes too tender.

These women are often amiable; and their hearts are really more sensible
to general benevolence, more alive to the sentiments that civilize life, than
the square-elbowed family drudge; but, wanting a due proportion of reflection
and self-government, they only inspire love; and are the mistresses of their
husbands, whilst they have any hold on their affections; and the platonic
friends of his male acquaintance. These are the fair defects in nature; the
women who appear to be created not to enjoy the fellowship of man, but to
save him from sinking into absolute brutality, by rubbing off the rough
angles of his character; and by playful dalliance to give some dignity to the
appetite that draws him to them.—Gracious Creator of the whole human
race! hast thou created such a being as woman, who can trace thy wisdom in

3. Stimulating.

thy works, and feel that thou alone art by thy nature exalted above her,—for no better purpose?—Can she believe that she was only made to submit to man, her equal, a being, who, like her, was sent into the world to acquire virtue?—Can she consent to be occupied merely to please him; merely to adorn the earth, when her soul is capable of rising to thee?—And can she rest supinely dependent on man for reason, when she ought to mount with him the arduous steeps of knowledge?—

Yet, if love be the supreme good, let women be only educated to inspire it, and let every charm be polished to intoxicate the senses; but, if they be moral beings, let them have a chance to become intelligent; and let love to man be only a part of that glowing flame of universal love, which, after encircling humanity, mounts in grateful incense to God.

* * *

1792

Letters Written during a Short Residence in Sweden, Norway, and Denmark

Writing to a friend in March 1797, the poet Robert Southey declared himself haunted by a book of travels that the firm of Joseph Johnson had published at the start of the preceding year: Mary Wollstonecraft, Southey enthused, "has made me in love with a cold climate, and frost and snow, with a northern moonlight." Wollstonecraft had set out on her arduous and sometimes dangerous five-month journey through the Scandinavian countries in June 1795, taking with her Fanny, her year-old infant, and Marguerite, a French maid who had earlier accompanied her from Paris to London. Fanny's father, Gilbert Imlay—author, inaugurator of sometimes shady commercial deals, and inveterate philanderer—had devised this scheme of sending Wollstonecraft as his business agent to the northern countries, thus leaving himself free to pursue an affair with another woman. Upon returning to London in September 1795, Wollstonecraft prepared for publication the letters that she had written to Imlay during the trip. Contemporary readers were left to speculate about the identity of the *you* to whom the letters were addressed and to ponder the suggestion that the letters' unhappy author had once been romantically involved with this unnamed correspondent. For many this tantalizingly sketchy love story gave the *Letters* their fascination. Writing in his *Memoirs* of Wollstonecraft, William Godwin declared, "If ever there was a book calculated to make a man in love with its author, this appears to me the book."

By the late eighteenth century, travel writing had begun to develop into a philosophical genre—a forum for comparative inquiries into the effects various sorts of political institutions and legal systems had on people's everyday lives and a forum in which commentators assessed the costs, as well as the benefits, of social and economic progress. Wollstonecraft had reviewed travelogues for Johnson's *Analytical Review*, and she contributed to this development in her turn with these discussions of Europe's northern fringe, a remote, unmodernized region that until then had rarely figured on travelers' itineraries. In the letters she thus remarks insightfully on the relations between rich and poor in the communities she visits, on the people's responses to the political tumults of the era, and, especially, on the situation of women and the petty despotisms of family life. Yet she also responds ardently to the sublime natural scenery of Scandinavia, and moves easily from those aesthetic contemplations to meditations on death and the possibility of an afterlife—reveries she intersperses with her sharply realistic observations of the world around her.

From Letters Written during a Short Residence in Sweden, Norway, and Denmark

Advertisement

The writing travels, or memoirs, has ever been a pleasant employment; for vanity or sensibility always renders it interesting. In writing these desultory letters, I found I could not avoid being continually the first person—"the little hero of each tale."[1] I tried to correct this fault, if it be one, for they were designed for publication; but in proportion as I arranged my thoughts, my letter, I found, became stiff and affected: I, therefore, determined to let my remarks and reflections flow unrestrained, as I perceived that I could not give a just description of what I saw, but by relating the effect different objects had produced on my mind and feelings, whilst the impression was still fresh.

A person has a right, I have sometimes thought, when amused by a witty or interesting egotist, to talk of himself when he can win on our attention by acquiring our affection. Whether I deserve to rank amongst this privileged number, my readers alone can judge—and I give them leave to shut the book, if they do not wish to become better acquainted with me.

My plan was simply to endeavor to give a just view of the present state of the countries I have passed through, as far as I could obtain information during so short a residence; avoiding those details which, without being very useful to travelers who follow the same route, appear very insipid to those who only accompany you in their chair.

Letter 1

Eleven days of weariness on board a vessel not intended for the accommodation of passengers have so exhausted my spirits, to say nothing of the other causes, with which you are already sufficiently acquainted, that it is with some difficulty I adhere to my determination of giving you my observations, as I travel through new scenes, whilst warmed with the impression they have made on me.

The captain, as I mentioned to you, promised to put me on shore at Arendall, or Gothenburg, in his way to Elsineur;[2] but contrary winds obliged us to pass both places during the night. In the morning, however, after we had lost sight of the entrance of the latter bay, the vessel was becalmed; and the captain, to oblige me, hanging out a signal for a pilot, bore down towards the shore.

My attention was particularly directed to the lighthouse; and you can scarcely imagine with what anxiety I watched two long hours for a boat to emancipate me—still no one appeared. Every cloud that flitted on the horizon was hailed as a liberator, till approaching nearer, like most of the prospects sketched by hope, it dissolved under the eye into disappointment.

Weary of expectation, I then began to converse with the captain on the subject; and, from the tenor of the information my questions drew forth, I soon concluded, that, if I waited for a boat, I had little chance of getting on shore at this place. Despotism, as is usually the case, I found had here

---

1. Edward Young, *Love of Fame, the Universal Passion* (1725), line 116.
2. Helsingør, Denmark. "Arendall": in Norway

[Wollstonecraft's note]. "Gothenburg": i.e., Göteborg, Sweden. Gilbert Imlay's business partner was based in this town.

cramped the industry of man. The pilots being paid by the king, and scant-ily, they will not run into any danger, or even quit their hovels, if they can possibly avoid it, only to fulfil what is termed their duty. How different is it on the English coast, where, in the most stormy weather, boats immediately hail you, brought out by the expectation of extraordinary profit.

Disliking to sail for Elsineur, and still more to lie at anchor, or cruise about the coast for several days, I exerted all my rhetoric to prevail on the captain to let me have the ship's boat; and though I added the most forcible of arguments, I for a long time addressed him in vain.

It is a kind of rule at sea, not to send out a boat. The captain was a good-natured man; but men with common minds seldom break through general rules. Prudence is ever the resort of weakness; and they rarely go as far as they may in any undertaking, who are determined not to go beyond it on any account. If, however, I had some trouble with the captain, I did not lose much time with the sailors; for they, all alacrity, hoisted out the boat, the moment I obtained permission, and promised to row me to the lighthouse.

I did not once allow myself to doubt of obtaining a conveyance from thence round the rocks—and then away for Gothenburg—confinement is so unpleasant.

The day was fine; and I enjoyed the water till, approaching the little island, poor Marguerite, whose timidity always acts as a feeler before her adventur-ing spirit, began to wonder at our not seeing any inhabitants. I did not listen to her. But when, on landing, the same silence prevailed, I caught the alarm, which was not lessened by the sight of two old men, whom we forced out of their wretched hut. Scarcely human in their appearance, we with difficulty obtained an intelligible reply to our questions—the result of which was, that they had no boat, and were not allowed to quit their post, on any pretense. But, they informed us, that there was at the other side, eight or ten miles over, a pilot's dwelling; two guineas[3] tempted the sailors to risk the captain's displeasure, and once more embark to row me over.

The weather was pleasant, and the appearance of the shore so grand, that I should have enjoyed the two hours it took to reach it, but for the fatigue which was too visible in the countenances of the sailors who, instead of uttering a complaint, were, with the thoughtless hilarity peculiar to them, joking about the possibility of the captain's taking advantage of a slight west-erly breeze, which was springing up, to sail without them. Yet, in spite of their good humor, I could not help growing uneasy when the shore, reced-ing, as it were, as we advanced, seemed to promise no end to their toil. This anxiety increased when, turning into the most picturesque bay I ever saw, my eyes sought in vain for the vestige of a human habitation. Before I could determine what step to take in such a dilemma, for I could not bear to think of returning to the ship, the sight of a barge relieved me, and we hastened towards it for information. We were immediately directed to pass some jut-ting rocks when we should see a pilot's hut.

There was a solemn silence in this scene, which made itself be felt. The sunbeams that played on the ocean, scarcely ruffled by the lightest breeze, contrasted with the huge, dark rocks, that looked like the rude materials of creation forming the barrier of unwrought space, forcibly struck me; but I

---

3. A British gold coin worth one pound and a shilling.

should not have been sorry if the cottage had not appeared equally tranquil. Approaching a retreat where strangers, especially women, so seldom appeared, I wondered that curiosity did not bring the beings who inhabited it to the windows or door. I did not immediately recollect that men who remain so near the brute creation, as only to exert themselves to find the food necessary to sustain life, have little or no imagination to call forth the curiosity necessary to fructify the faint glimmerings of mind which entitles them to rank as lords of the creation.—Had they either, they could not contentedly remain rooted in the clods they so indolently cultivate.

Whilst the sailors went to seek for the sluggish inhabitants, these conclusions occurred to me; and, recollecting the extreme fondness which the Parisians ever testify for novelty, their very curiosity appeared to me a proof of the progress they had made in refinement. Yes; in the art of living—in the art of escaping from the cares which embarrass the first steps towards the attainment of the pleasures of social life.

The pilots informed the sailors that they were under the direction of a lieutenant retired from the service, who spoke English; adding, that they could do nothing without his orders; and even the offer of money could hardly conquer their laziness, and prevail on them to accompany us to his dwelling. They would not go with me alone which I wanted them to have done, because I wished to dismiss the sailors as soon as possible. Once more we rowed off, they following tardily, till, turning round another bold protuberance of the rocks, we saw a boat making towards us, and soon learnt that it was the lieutenant himself, coming with some earnestness to see who we were.

To save the sailors any further toil, I had my baggage instantly removed into his boat; for, as he could speak English, a previous parley was not necessary; though Marguerite's respect for me could hardly keep her from expressing the fear, strongly marked on her countenance, which my putting ourselves into the power of a strange man excited. He pointed out his cottage; and, drawing near to it, I was not sorry to see a female figure, though I had not, like Marguerite, been thinking of robberies, murders, or the other evil[4] which instantly, as the sailors would have said, runs foul of a woman's imagination.

On entering, I was still better pleased to find a clean house, with some degree of rural elegance. The beds were of muslin, coarse it is true, but dazzlingly white; and the floor was strewed over with little sprigs of juniper (the custom, as I afterwards found, of the country), which formed a contrast with the curtains and produced an agreeable sensation of freshness, to soften the ardor of noon. Still nothing was so pleasing as the alacrity of hospitality—all that the house afforded was quickly spread on the whitest linen.—Remember I had just left the vessel, where, without being fastidious, I had continually been disgusted. Fish, milk, butter, and cheese, and I am sorry to add, brandy, the bane of this country, were spread on the board. After we had dined, hospitality made them, with some degree of mystery, bring us some excellent coffee. I did not then know that it was prohibited.[5]

The good man of the house apologized for coming in continually, but declared that he was so glad to speak English, he could not stay out. He need

4. Rape.
5. The law then prohibited the import or consumption of coffee.

not have apologized; I was equally glad of his company. With the wife I could only exchange smiles; and she was employed observing the make of our clothes. My hands, I found, had first led her to discover that I was the lady. I had, of course, my quantum of reverences; for the politeness of the north seems to partake of the coldness of the climate, and the rigidity of its iron sinewed rocks. Amongst the peasantry, there is, however, so much of the simplicity of the golden age in this land of flint—so much overflowing of heart, and fellow-feeling, that only benevolence, and the honest sympathy of nature, diffused smiles over my countenance when they kept me standing, regardless of my fatigue, whilst they dropt courtesy after courtesy.

The situation of this house was beautiful, though chosen for convenience. The master being the officer who commanded all the pilots on the coast, and the person appointed to guard wrecks, it was necessary for him to fix on a spot that would overlook the whole bay. As he had seen some service, he wore, not without a pride I thought becoming, a badge to prove that he had merited well of his country. It was happy, I thought, that he had been paid in honor; for the stipend he received was little more than twelve pounds a year.—I do not trouble myself or you with the calculation of Swedish ducats. Thus, my friend, you perceive the necessity of *perquisites*.[6] This same narrow policy runs through every thing. I shall have occasion further to animadvert on it.

Though my host amused me with an account of himself, which gave me an idea of the manners of the people I was about to visit, I was eager to climb the rocks to view the country, and see whether the honest tars had regained their ship. With the help of the lieutenant's telescope I saw the vessel underway with a fair though gentle gale. The sea was calm, playful even as the most shallow stream, and on the vast bason[7] I did not see a dark speck to indicate the boat. My conductors were consequently arrived.

Straying further my eye was attracted by the sight of some heart's-ease[8] that peeped through the rocks. I caught at it as a good omen, and going to preserve it in a letter that had not conveyed balm to my heart, a cruel remembrance suffused my eyes; but it passed away like an April shower. If you are deep read in Shakspeare, you will recollect that this was the little western flower tinged by love's dart, which "maidens call love in idleness."[9] The gaiety of my babe was unmixed; regardless of omens or sentiments, she found a few wild strawberries more grateful[1] than flowers or fancies.

The lieutenant informed me that this was a commodious bay. Of that I could not judge, though I felt its picturesque beauty. Rocks were piled on rocks, forming a suitable bulwark to the ocean. Come no further, they emphatically said, turning their dark sides to the waves to augment the idle roar. The view was sterile: still little patches of earth, of the most exquisite verdure, enameled with the sweetest wild flowers, seemed to promise the goats and a few straggling cows luxurious herbage. How silent and peaceful was the scene. I gazed around with rapture, and felt more of that spontaneous pleasure which gives credibility to our expectation of happiness, than

---

6. Payments in addition to salary. The suggestion is of income derived from bribes or smuggling.
7. I.e., basin.
8. A small wildflower, variously colored. Wollstonecraft goes on to make the first of many veiled allusions to her faithless lover Imlay, to whom

these letters are addressed.
9. Popular name for the pansy, whose juice Oberon put on the sleeping Titania's eyes to make her dote on the next person she saw (Shakespeare's *A Midsummer Night's Dream* 2.1.165–72).
1. Pleasing.

I had for a long, long time before. I forgot the horrors I had witnessed in France,[2] which had cast a gloom over all nature, and suffering the enthusiasm of my character, too often, gracious God! damped by the tears of disappointed affection, to be lighted up afresh, care took wing while simple fellow feeling expanded my heart.

To prolong this enjoyment, I readily assented to the proposal of our host to pay a visit to a family, the master of which spoke English, who was the drollest dog in the country, he added, repeating some of his stories, with a hearty laugh.

I walked on, still delighted with the rude beauties of the scene; for the sublime often gave place imperceptibly to the beautiful, dilating the emotions which were painfully concentrated.

When we entered this abode, the largest I had yet seen, I was introduced to a numerous family; but the father, from whom I was led to expect so much entertainment, was absent. The lieutenant consequently was obliged to be the interpreter of our reciprocal compliments. The phrases were awkwardly transmitted, it is true; but looks and gestures were sufficient to make them intelligible and interesting. The girls were all vivacity, and respect for me could scarcely keep them from romping with my host, who, asking for a pinch of snuff, was presented with a box, out of which an artificial mouse, fastened to the bottom, sprung. Though this trick had doubtless been played time out of mind, yet the laughter it excited was not less genuine.

They were overflowing with civility; but to prevent their almost killing my babe with kindness, I was obliged to shorten my visit; and two or three of the girls accompanied us, bringing with them a part of whatever the house afforded to contribute towards rendering my supper more plentiful; and plentiful in fact it was, though I with difficulty did honor to some of the dishes, not relishing the quantity of sugar and spices put into every thing. At supper my host told me bluntly that I was a woman of observation, for I asked him *men's questions*.

The arrangements for my journey were quickly made; I could only have a car with post-horses, as I did not choose to wait till a carriage could be sent for to Gothenburg. The expense of my journey, about one or two and twenty English miles, I found would not amount to more than eleven or twelve shillings, paying, he assured me, generously. I gave him a guinea and a half. But it was with the greatest difficulty that I could make him take so much, indeed any thing for my lodging and fare. He declared that it was next to robbing me, explaining how much I ought to pay on the road. However, as I was positive, he took the guinea for himself; but, as a condition, insisted on accompanying me, to prevent my meeting with any trouble or imposition on the way.

I then retired to my apartment with regret. The night was so fine, that I would gladly have rambled about much longer; yet recollecting that I must rise very early, I reluctantly went to bed: but my senses had been so awake, and my imagination still continued so busy, that I sought for rest in vain. Rising before six, I scented the sweet morning air; I had long before heard the birds twittering to hail the dawning day, though it could scarcely have been allowed to have departed.

Nothing, in fact, can equal the beauty of the northern summer's evening and night; if night it may be called that only wants the glare of day, the full

2. Wollstonecraft had lived in France at the time of the Reign of Terror under Robespierre (1793–94).

light, which frequently seems so impertinent; for I could write at midnight very well without a candle. I contemplated all nature at rest; the rocks, even grown darker in their appearance, looked as if they partook of the general repose, and reclined more heavily on their foundation.—What, I exclaimed, is this active principle which keeps me still awake?—Why fly my thoughts abroad when every thing around me appears at home? My child was sleeping with equal calmness—innocent and sweet as the closing flowers.—Some recollections, attached to the idea of home, mingled with reflections respecting the state of society I had been contemplating that evening, made a tear drop on the rosy cheek I had just kissed; and emotions that trembled on the brink of ectasy and agony gave a poignancy to my sensations, which made me feel more alive than usual.

What are these imperious sympathies? How frequently has melancholy and even misanthropy taken possession of me, when the world has disgusted me, and friends have proved unkind. I have then considered myself as a particle broken off from the grand mass of mankind;—I was alone, till some involuntary sympathetic emotion, like the attraction of adhesion,[3] made me feel that I was still a part of a mighty whole, from which I could not sever myself—not, perhaps, for the reflection has been carried very far, by snapping the thread of an existence which loses its charms in proportion as the cruel experience of life stops or poisons the current of the heart. Futurity, what hast thou not to give to those who know that there is such a thing as happiness! I speak not of philosophical contentment, though pain has afforded them the strongest conviction of it.

After our coffee and milk, for the mistress of the house had been roused long before us by her hospitality, my baggage was taken forward in a boat by my host, because the car could not safely have been brought to the house.

The road at first was very rocky and troublesome; but our driver was careful, and the horses accustomed to the frequent and sudden acclivities and descents; so that not apprehending any danger, I played with my girl, whom I would not leave to Marguerite's care, on account of her timidity.

Stopping at a little inn to bait[4] the horses, I saw the first countenance in Sweden that displeased me, though the man was better dressed than any one who had as yet fallen in my way. An altercation took place between him and my host, the purport of which I could not guess, excepting that I was the occasion of it, be it what it would. The sequel was his leaving the house angrily; and I was immediately informed that he was the custom-house officer. The professional had indeed effaced the national character, for living as he did with these frank hospitable people, still only the exciseman appeared,—the counterpart of some I had met with in England and France. I was unprovided with a passport, not having entered any great town. At Gothenburg I knew I could immediately obtain one, and only the trouble made me object to the searching my trunks. He blustered for money; but the lieutenant was determined to guard me, according to promise, from imposition.

To avoid being interrogated at the town-gate, and obliged to go in the rain to give an account of myself, merely a form, before we could get the refreshment we stood in need of, he requested us to descend, I might have said step, from our car, and walk into town.

3. The physical attraction between two different substances.
4. Feed.

I expected to have found a tolerable inn, but was ushered into a most comfortless one; and, because it was about five o'clock, three or four hours after their dining hour, I could not prevail on them to give me any thing warm to eat.

The appearance of the accommodations obliged me to deliver one of my recommendatory letters, and the gentleman, to whom it was addressed, sent to look out for a lodging for me whilst I partook of his supper. As nothing passed at this supper to characterize the country, I shall here close my letter.

Your's truly.

From *Letter* 5

Had I determined to travel in Sweden merely for pleasure, I should probably have chosen the road to Stockholm, though convinced, by repeated observation, that the manners of a people are best discriminated in the country. The inhabitants of the capital are all of the same genus; for the varieties in the species we must, therefore, search where the habitations of men are so separated as to allow the difference of climate to have its natural effect. And with this difference we are, perhaps, most forcibly struck at the first view, just as we form an estimate of the leading traits of a character at the first glance, of which intimacy afterwards makes us almost lose sight.

As my affairs called me to Stromstad (the frontier town of Sweden) in my way to Norway, I was to pass over, I heard, the most uncultivated part of the country.[5] Still I believe that the grand features of Sweden are the same every where, and it is only the grand features that admit of description. There is an individuality in every prospect, which remains in the memory as forcibly depicted as the particular features that have arrested our attention; yet we cannot find words to discriminate that individuality so as to enable a stranger to say, this is the face, that the view. We may amuse by setting the imagination to work; but we cannot store the memory with a fact.

As I wish to give you a general idea of this country, I shall continue in my desultory manner to make such observations and reflections as the circumstances draw forth, without losing time, by endeavouring to arrange them.

* * *

We arrived early the second evening at a little village called Quistram,[6] where we had determined to pass the night; having been informed that we should not afterwards find a tolerable inn until we reached Stromstad.

Advancing towards Quistram, as the sun was beginning to decline, I was particularly impressed by the beauty of the situation. The road was on the declivity of a rocky mountain, slightly covered with a mossy herbage and vagrant firs. At the bottom, a river, straggling amongst the recesses of stone, was hastening forward to the ocean and its grey rocks, of which we had a prospect on the left, whilst on the right it stole peacefully forward into the meadows, losing itself in a thickly wooded rising ground. As we drew near, the loveliest banks of wild flowers variegated the prospect, and promised to

5. Wollstonecraft has temporarily left behind in Gothenburg (modern-day Göteborg) her baby and the maid, Marguerite, and is now traveling north up Sweden's southwest coast to the border with Norway.

6. Located at about the halfway mark of the journey between Göteborg and the border.

exhale odours to add to the sweetness of the air, the purity of which you could almost see, alas! not smell, for the putrifying herrings, which they use as manure, after the oil has been extracted, spread over the patches of earth, claimed by cultivation, destroyed every other.

It was intolerable, and entered with us into the inn, which was in other respects a charming retreat.

Whilst supper was preparing I crossed the bridge, and strolled by the river, listening to its murmurs. Approaching the bank, the beauty of which had attracted my attention in the carriage, I recognized many of my old acquaintance growing with great luxuriancy.

Seated on it, I could not avoid noting an obvious remark. Sweden appeared to me the country in the world most proper to form the botanist and natural historian: every object seemed to remind me of the creation of things, of the first efforts of sportive nature. When a country arrives at a certain state of perfection, it looks as if it were made so; and curiosity is not excited. Besides, in social life too many objects occur for any to be distinctly observed by the generality of mankind; yet a contemplative man, or poet, in the country, I do not mean the country adjacent to cities, feels and sees what would escape vulgar eyes, and draws suitable inferences. This train of reflections might have led me further, in every sense of the word; but I could not escape from the detestable evaporation of the herrings, which poisoned all my pleasure.

After making a tolerable supper, for it is not easy to get fresh provisions on the road, I retired, to be lulled to sleep by the murmuring of a stream, of which I with great difficulty obtained sufficient to perform my daily ablutions.

The last battle between the Danes and Swedes, which gave new life to their ancient enmity, was fought at this place 1788;[7] only seventeen or eighteen were killed; for the great superiority of the Danes and Norwegians obliged the Swedes to submit; but sickness, and a scarcity of provisions, proved very fatal to their opponents, on their return.

It would be very easy to search for the particulars of this engagement in the publications of the day; but as this manner of filling my pages does not come within my plan, I probably should not have remarked that the battle was fought here, were it not to relate an anecdote which I had from good authority.

I noticed, when I first mentioned this place to you, that we descended a steep before we came to the inn; an immense ridge of rocks stretching out on one side. The inn was sheltered under them; and about a hundred yards from it was a bridge that crossed the river, whose murmurs I have celebrated; it was not fordable. The Swedish general received orders to stop at the bridge, and dispute the passage; a most advantageous post for an army so much inferior in force: but the influence of beauty is not confined to courts. The mistress of the inn was handsome: when I saw her there were still some remains of beauty; and, to preserve her house, the general gave up the only tenable station. He was afterwards broke[8] for contempt of orders.

Approaching the frontiers, consequently the sea, nature resumed an aspect ruder and ruder, or rather seemed the bones of the world waiting to

7. A reference to the Russo-Swedish war of 1788– 90, in which Sweden's foes Denmark and Norway became involved because of treaty obligations.
8. I.e., stripped of his rank.

be clothed with every thing necessary to give life and beauty. Still it was sublime.

The clouds caught their hue of the rocks that menaced them. The sun appeared afraid to shine, the birds ceased to sing, and the flowers to bloom; but the eagle fixed his nest high amongst the rocks, and the vulture hovered over this abode of desolation. The farm houses, in which only poverty resided, were formed of logs scarcely keeping off the cold and drifting snow; out of them the inhabitants seldom peeped, and the sports or prattling of children was neither seen nor heard. The current of life seemed congealed at the source: all were not frozen; for it was summer, you remember; but everything appeared so dull, that I waited to see ice, in order to reconcile me to the absence of gaiety.

The day before, my attention had frequently been attracted by the wild beauties of the country we passed through.

The rocks which tossed their fantastic heads so high were often covered with pines and firs, varied in the most picturesque manner. Little woods filled up the recesses, when forests did not darken the scene; and vallies and glens, cleared of the trees, displayed a dazzling verdure which contrasted with the gloom of the shading pines. The eye stole into many a covert where tranquillity seemed to have taken up her abode, and the number of little lakes that continually presented themselves added to the peaceful composure of the scenery. The little cultivation which appeared did not break the enchantment, nor did castles rear their turrets aloft to crush the cottages, and prove that man is more savage than the natives of the woods. I heard of the bears, but never saw them stalk forth, which I was sorry for; I wished to have seen one in its wild state. In the winter, I am told, they sometimes catch a stray cow, which is a heavy loss to the owner.

The farms are small. Indeed most of the houses we saw on the road indicated poverty, or rather that the people could just live. Towards the frontiers they grew worse and worse in their appearance, as if not willing to put sterility itself out of countenance. No gardens smiled round the habitations, not a potato or cabbage to eat with the fish drying on a stick near the door. A little grain here and there appeared, the long stalks of which you might almost reckon. The day was gloomy when we passed over this rejected spot, the wind bleak, and winter seemed to be contending with nature, faintly struggling to change the season. Surely, thought I, if the sun ever shines here, it cannot warm these stones; moss only cleaves to them, partaking of their hardness; and nothing like vegetable life appears to chear with hope the heart.

So far from thinking that the primitive inhabitants of the world lived in a southern climate, where Paradise spontaneously arose, I am led to infer, from various circumstances, that the first dwelling of man happened to be a spot like this which led him to adore a sun so seldom seen; for this worship, which probably preceded that of demons or demi-gods, certainly never began in a southern climate, where the continual presence of the sun prevented its being considered as a good; or rather the want of it never being felt, this glorious luminary would carelessly have diffused its blessings without being hailed as a benefactor. Man must therefore have been placed in the north, to tempt him to run after the sun, in order that the different parts of the earth might be peopled. Nor do I wonder that hordes of barbarians always poured out of these regions to seek for milder climes, when nothing like cultivation attached them to the soil; especially when we take into the view that the adventuring spirit, common to man, is naturally stronger and more general during the infancy of society. The conduct of the followers of Mahomet,[9] and the crusaders, will sufficiently corroborate my assertion.

Approaching nearer to Stromstad, the appearance of the town proved to be quite in character with the country we had just passed through. I hesitated to use the word country, yet could not find another; still it would sound absurd to talk of fields of rocks.

The town was built on, and under them. Three or four weather-beaten trees were shrinking from the wind; and the grass grew so sparingly, that I could not avoid thinking Dr. Johnson's hyperbolical assertion "that the man merited well of his country who made a few blades of grass grow where they never grew before," might here have been uttered with strict propriety.[1] The steeple likewise towered aloft; for what is a church, even amongst the Lutherans, without a steeple? But to prevent mischief in such an exposed situation, it is wisely placed on a rock at some distance, not to endanger the roof of the church.

Rambling about, I saw the door open, and entered, when to my great surprise I found the clergyman reading prayers, with only the clerk attending. I instantly thought of Swift's "Dearly beloved Roger;"[2] but on enquiry I learnt that some one had died that morning, and in Sweden it is customary to pray for the dead.

The sun, who I suspected never dared to shine, began now to convince me that he came forth only to torment; for though the wind was still cutting, the rocks became intolerably warm under my feet; whilst the herring effluvia, which I before found so very offensive, once more assailed me. I hastened back to the house of a merchant, the little sovereign of the place, because he was by far the richest, though not the mayor.

Here we were most hospitably received, and introduced to a very fine and numerous family. I have before mentioned to you the lillies of the north, I might have added, water lillies, for the complexion of many, even of the young women seem to be bleached on the bosom of snow. But in this youthful circle the roses bloomed with all their wonted freshness, and I wondered from whence the fire was stolen which sparkled in their fine blue eyes.

Here we slept; and I rose early in the morning to prepare for my little voyage to Norway. I had determined to go by water, and was to leave my companions behind; but not getting a boat immediately, and the wind being high and unfavourable, I was told that it was not safe to go to sea during such boisterous weather; I was therefore obliged to wait for the morrow, and had the present day on my hands; which I feared would be irksome, because the family, who possessed about a dozen French words amongst them, and not an English phrase, were anxious to amuse me, and would not let me remain alone in my room. The town we had already walked round and round; and if

9. I.e., Mohammed.
1. Probably thinking of his travelogue *A Journey to the Western Islands of Scotland* (1775), which frequently deplores the barrenness of the Highlands, Wollstonecraft mistakenly ascribes to Samuel Johnson an assertion in fact uttered by the King of Brobdingnag in Jonathan Swift's *Gulliver's Travels* (1726). Gulliver reports that King's opinion that whoever could make "two blades of grass to grow upon a spot of ground where only one grew

before" served his nation more "than the whole race of politicians put together."
2. The prayer services that during 1700 Swift conducted as vicar of Laracor (in County Meath, Ireland) were thinly attended. The legend goes that he arrived in church one day to find nobody present except his clerk Roger Cox, which necessitated some rewording of the customary address to the congregation. Swift began the service with the words, "Dearly beloved Roger."

we advanced farther on the coast, it was still to view the same unvaried immensity of water, surrounded by barrenness.

The gentlemen wishing to peep into Norway, proposed going to Frederics-hall, the first town, the distance was only three Swedish miles.[3] There, and back again, was but a day's journey, and would not, I thought, interfere with my voyage. I agreed, and invited the eldest and prettiest of the girls to accompany us. I invited her, because I liked to see a beautiful face animated by pleasure, and to have an opportunity of regarding the country, whilst the gentlemen were amusing themselves with her.

I did not know, for I had not thought of it, that we were to scale some of the most mountainous cliffs of Sweden, in our way to the ferry which separates the two countries.

Entering amongst the cliffs, we were sheltered from the wind; warm sunbeams began to play, streams to flow, and groves of pines diversified the rocks. Sometimes they became suddenly bare and sublime. Once, in particular, after mounting the most terrific precipice, we had to pass through a tremendous defile, where the closing chasm seemed to threaten us with instant destruction, when turning quickly, verdant meadows and a beautiful lake relieved and charmed my eyes.

I have never travelled through Switzerland; but one of my companions assured me, that I should not there find any thing superior, if equal to the wild grandeur of these views.

As we had not taken this excursion into our plan, the horses had not been previously ordered, which obliged us to wait two hours at the first post. The day was wearing away. The road was so bad, that walking up the precipices consumed the time insensibly. But as we desired horses at each post ready at a certain hour, we reckoned on returning more speedily.

We stopt to dine at a tolerable farm. They brought us out ham, butter, cheese, and milk; and the charge was so moderate, that I scattered a little money amongst the children who were peeping at us, in order to pay them for their trouble.

Arrived at the ferry, we were still detained; for the people who attend at the ferries have a stupid kind of sluggishness in their manner, which is very provoking when you are in haste. At present I did not feel it; for scrambling up the cliffs, my eye followed the river as it rolled between the grand rocky banks; and to complete the scenery, they were covered with firs and pines, through which the wind rustled, as if it were lulling itself to sleep with the declining sun.

Behold us now in Norway; and I could not avoid feeling surprise at observing the difference in the manners of the inhabitants of the two sides of the river; for everything shews that the Norwegians are more industrious and more opulent. The Swedes, for neighbours are seldom the best friends, accuse the Norwegians of knavery, and they retaliate by bringing a charge of hypocrisy against the Swedes. Local circumstances probably render both unjust, speaking from their feelings, rather than reason: and is this astonishing when we consider that most writers of travels have done the same, whose works have served as materials for the compilers of universal histories. All are eager to give a national character; which is rarely just, because they do

---

3. In an earlier note Wollstonecraft explains that a Swedish mile is nearly six English miles.

not discriminate the natural from the acquired difference. The natural, I believe, on due consideration, will be found to consist merely in the degree of vivacity or thoughtfulness, pleasure, or pain, inspired by the climate, whilst the varieties which the forms of government, including religion, produce, are much more numerous and unstable.

A people have been characterized as stupid by nature; what a paradox! because they did not consider that slaves, having no object to stimulate industry, have not their faculties sharpened by the only thing that can exercise them, self-interest. Others have been brought forward as brutes, having no aptitude for the arts and sciences, only because the progress of improvement had not reached that stage which produces them.

Those writers who have considered the history of man, or of the human mind, on a more enlarged scale, have fallen into similar errors, not reflecting that the passions are weak where the necessaries of life are too hardly or too easily obtained.

Travellers who require that every nation should resemble their native country, had better stay at home. It is, for example, absurd to blame a people for not having that degree of personal cleanliness and elegance of manners which only refinement of taste produces, and will produce every where in proportion as society attains a general polish. The most essential service, I presume, that authors could render to society, would be to promote inquiry and discussion, instead of making those dogmatical assertions which only appear calculated to gird the human mind round with imaginary circles, like the paper globe which represents the one he inhabits.

This spirit of inquiry is the characteristic of the present century, from which the succeeding will, I am persuaded, receive a great accumulation of knowledge; and doubtless its diffusion will in a great measure destroy the factitious national characters which have been supposed permanent, though only rendered so by the permanency of ignorance.

Arriving at Fredericshall, at the siege of which Charles XII lost his life,[4] we had only time to take a transient view of it, whilst they were preparing us some refreshment.

Poor Charles! I thought of him with respect. I have always felt the same for Alexander;[5] with whom he has been classed as a madman, by several writers, who have reasoned superficially, confounding the morals of the day with the few grand principles on which unchangeable morality rests. Making no allowance for the ignorance and prejudices of the period, they do not perceive how much they themselves are indebted to general improvement for the acquirements, and even the virtues, which they would not have had the force of mind to attain, by their individual exertions in a less advanced state of society.

The evening was fine, as is usual at this season; and the refreshing odour of the pine woods became more perceptible; for it was nine o'clock when we left Fredericshall. At the ferry we were detained by a dispute relative to our

4. Charles XII was the celebrated warrior king, known as "the Lion of the North," who ruled Sweden from 1697 to 1718. He was shot while inspecting the trenches, as his army besieged a Norwegian fortress in what is now the modern town of Halden.
5. There was debate through the 18th century as to whether the military conquests of Alexander the Great (356–323 B.C.E.) should be seen as glorious or criminal, heroic or insane. The linkage of Alexander and Charles XII was conventional: in a *Champion* essay of 1740 the novelist Henry Fielding had, for instance, depicted them both as brutal madmen.

Swedish passport, which we did not think of getting countersigned in Norway. Midnight was coming on; yet it might with such propriety have been termed the noon of night, that had Young ever travelled towards the north, I should not have wondered at his becoming enamoured of the moon.[6] But it is not the queen of night alone who reigns here in all her splendor, though the sun, loitering just below the horizon, decks her with a golden tinge from his car, illuminating the cliffs that hide him; the heavens also, of a clear softened blue, throw her forward, and the evening star appears a lesser moon to the naked eye. The huge shadows of the rocks, fringed with firs, concentrating the views, without darkening them, excited that tender melancholy which, sublimating the imagination, exalts, rather than depresses the mind.

My companions fell asleep:—fortunately they did not snore; and I contemplated, fearless of idle questions, a night such as I had never before seen or felt to charm the senses, and calm the heart. The very air was balmy, as it freshened into morn, producing the most voluptuous sensations. A vague pleasurable sentiment absorbed me, as I opened my bosom to the embraces of nature; and my soul rose to its author, with the chirping of the solitary birds, which began to feel, rather than see, advancing day. I had leisure to mark its progress. The grey morn, streaked with silvery rays, ushered in the orient beams,—how beautifully varying into purple!—yet, I was sorry to lose the soft watry clouds which preceded them, exciting a kind of expectation that made me almost afraid to breathe, lest I should break the charm. I saw the sun—and sighed.

One of my companions, now awake, perceiving that the postillion had mistaken the road, began to swear at him, and roused the other two, who reluctantly shook off sleep.

We had immediately to measure back our steps, and did not reach Stromstad before five in the morning.

The wind had changed in the night, and my boat was ready.

A dish of coffee, and fresh linen, recruited my spirits; and I directly set out again for Norway; purposing to land much higher up the cost.

Wrapping my great coat round me, I lay down on some sails at the bottom of the boat, its motion rocking me to rest, till a discourteous wave interrupted my slumbers, and obliged me to rise and feel a solitariness which was not so soothing as that of the past night.

Adieu!

1795   1796

---

6. The third book of Edward Young's popular long poem *Night Thoughts on Life, Death, and Immortality* (1742–45) begins by invoking the moon as Young's muse.

MARIA EDGEWORTH
1768–1849

Maria Edgeworth's publishing career earned her more than £11,000—an enormous sum. It also made the novel, regularly reviled by critics in the late eighteenth century, a respectable form. After 1804, the editor Francis Jeffrey attended respectfully in the pages of his *Edinburgh Review* to each of Edgeworth's publications, remarking on how in her hands fiction had become an edifying medium for serious ideas.

Edgeworth was born in Oxfordshire on New Year's Day, 1768, the second child of Richard Lovell Edgeworth and Anna Maria Elers, who died when her daughter was five. (Richard Lovell Edgeworth married three more times, each new wife younger than her predecessor, and eventually fathered twenty-two children.) Maria Edgeworth spent most of her childhood in fashionable boarding schools in England, until her father, in a spirit of patriotism and optimism about social progress, decided to dedicate himself to the family estate in Ireland that had been his birthplace. In 1782 he sent for Maria to join him, his third wife, and Maria's half-brothers and half-sisters at Edgeworthstown, source of the Protestant Edgeworths' wealth since the early seventeenth century, when the property had been confiscated from a Catholic family. For the rest of her life, that manor house in rural County Longford would remain home for Edgeworth, who in 1802 rejected a marriage proposal from a Swedish diplomat.

Brimming over with children, with books, and (it was reported) with "ingenious mechanical devices" (some of them Richard Lovell Edgeworth's inventions), this home doubled as a laboratory for her father's experiments in education, up-to-the-minute agricultural techniques, and enlightened landlord-tenant relations. From the age of fourteen, Edgeworth assumed a central role in those experiments. She took up the business of estate management. She taught the younger children. At her father's prompting, she began a course of reading in political and economic theory, starting with Adam Smith's *The Wealth of Nations*.

Eventually Maria Edgeworth also began to write. *Letters for Literary Ladies* (1795), a novelistic defense of women's education, was followed by *The Parent's Assistant* (1796) and *Practical Education* (1798), treatises on pedagogy she co-authored with her father, and by the first of her influential collections of stories for children (*Early Lessons*, 1801). In 1800 she published *Castle Rackrent*, her masterpiece. *Rackrent* inaugurated Edgeworth's series of narratives memorializing the vanishing ways of life of rural Ireland, a project continued by *Ennui* (1809), *The Absentee* (1812), and *Ormond* (1819). Edgeworth's study of the Enlightenment social sciences is easy to trace in these regional fictions, and these concerns were a factor that helped secure their reputation among the reviewers. Not only had Edgeworth managed to associate the novel with a more intellectually prestigious discourse but, by packaging her representations of Ireland's picturesque folk culture in this way, she was also able to tap the authority of a system of economic and political analysis that, in its claims to be scientifically impartial, seemed to many to offer a counterweight to the ugly prejudices that were the legacies of that nation's history of colonial conquest.

The year Richard Lovell Edgeworth settled in Ireland, 1782, seemed an auspicious moment for a reformer like him. The Parliament in Dublin had just won legislative independence, and it appeared as though penal laws targeting Catholics would soon be relaxed. But this confidence that a new era of civil harmony was dawning was quickly shattered. In 1798 armed insurrection, involving both Catholic peasants and middle-class Protestants from the North, engulfed Ireland. The rising was soon repressed, with extreme brutality. Introduced in 1800 as a security measure by a British state horrified at the news that French expeditionary forces had planned to aid the rebels, an Act of Union abolished the Dublin Parliament and incorporated Ireland into the United Kingdom. However, as Byron observed in an address to the House of Lords, to call the ensuing political situation a Union was to abuse the term: "If it must be called an Union, it is the union of the shark with his prey." The native Catholic population would long remain without civil rights. Indeed, when Edgeworth died in 1849 at the age of eighty-three, Ireland was once again a scene of violent insurrection as well as of horrendous famine.

An anecdote in Edgeworth's 1820 memoir of her father conveys a sense of the ambiguous position that the Protestant Anglo-Irish—neither English exactly, nor Irish, neither outsiders nor natives—occupied in this tense political context. Edgeworth recounts how, after their family escaped from the Catholic rebels who in 1798 occupied the countryside around Edgeworthstown, Richard Lovell Edgeworth was nearly lynched by a mob from the Protestant county town where the Edgeworths had taken refuge, who were certain (such were the suspicions aroused by his nonsectarian politics) that he was a rebel sympathizer and a French spy.

The 1802 tale that we have selected as an example of Maria Edgeworth's fiction, "The Irish Incognito"—part trickster tale from the folk tradition, part philosophical meditation on the precariousness of personal identity—also captures something of this experience of living between cultures. Starting with the first disorienting sentence, which introduces a hero who sports the ultra-English name of John Bull but who is also a native son of Cork, this treatment of cultural difference is distinguished by some slippery ironies. (A town on Ireland's south coast, Cork, of course, is home to the legendary Blarney Stone, which grants Irish people their gift of gab.) The tale might well have promoted tolerance for British diversity among its original readers: unlike many of his namesakes of the era, this "John Bull" is eminently likeable. But (as with the more biting satires that Jonathan Swift had penned in Dublin eighty years before) it would also have perplexed these readers' preconceived notions about *who* exactly was *who* within that hybrid political entity called "the United Kingdom of Great Britain and Ireland."

The Irish Incognito[1]

Sir John Bull was a native of Ireland, *bred* and *born* in the city of Cork. His real name was Phelim O'Mooney, and he was by profession a *stocah*, or walking gentleman; that is, a person who is too proud to earn his bread, and too poor to have bread without earning it. He had always been told that none of his ancestors had ever been in trade or business of any kind, and he resolved, when a boy, never to *demean* himself and family, as his elder brother had done, by becoming a rich merchant. When he grew up to be a young man, he kept this spirited resolution as long as he had a relation or

1. Although written solely by Maria Edgeworth, "The Irish Incognito" forms the culminating chapter of a book that was published under both her name and her father's (her *Memoir* of her father states that he contributed passages to a few of the other chapters). This book was the *Essay on Irish Bulls*, which went through three revised editions between 1802 and 1808, before being included, in its 1808 version, in Maria Edgeworth's eighteen-volume collected *Tales and*

Novels of 1832. That edition provides the basis for the text we give here. A "bull" is a verbal blunder, an expression containing a contradiction that goes unperceived by the speaker. To collect "Irish bulls" as the *Essay* does is, on the face of it, to contribute to a longstanding English tradition of jokes about the dim-witted Irish, but the Edgeworths' relationship to that tradition turned out to be quite complicated.

friend in the world who would let him hang upon them; but when he was shaken off by all, what could he do but go into business? He chose the most genteel, however; he became a wine merchant. I'm *only* a wine merchant, said he to himself, and that is next door to being nothing at all. His brother furnished his cellars; and Mr. Phelim O'Mooney, upon the strength of the wine that he had in his cellars, and of the money he expected to make of it, immediately married a wife, set up a gig, and gave excellent dinners to men who were ten times richer than he even ever *expected* to be. In return for these excellent dinners, his new friends bought all their wine from Mr. O'Mooney, and never paid for it; he lived upon credit himself, and gave all his friends credit, till he became a bankrupt. Then nobody came to dine with him, and every body found out that he had been very imprudent; and he was obliged to sell his gig, but not before it had broken his wife's neck; so that when accounts came to be finally settled, he was not much worse than when he began the world, the loss falling upon his creditors, and he being, as he observed, free to begin life again, with the advantage of being once more a bachelor. He was such a good-natured, freehearted fellow, that every body liked him, even his creditors. His wife's relations made up the sum of five hundred pounds for him, and his brother offered to take him into his firm as partner; but O'Mooney preferred, he said, going to try, or rather to make, his fortune in England, as he did not doubt but he should by marriage, being, as he did not scruple to acknowledge, a personable, clever-looking man, and a great favourite with the sex.[2]

"My last wife I married for love, my next I expect will do the same by me, and of course the money must come on her side this time," said our hero, half jesting, half in earnest. His elder and wiser brother, the merchant, whom he still held in more than sufficient contempt, ventured to hint some slight objections to this scheme of Phelim's seeking fortune in England. He observed that so many had gone upon this plan already, that there was rather a prejudice in England against Irish adventurers.

This could not affect *him* any ways, Phelim replied, because he did not mean to appear in England as an Irishman at all.

"How then?"

"As an Englishman, since that is most agreeable."

"How can that be?"

"Who should hinder it?"

His brother, hesitatingly, said "Yourself."

"Myself!—What part of myself? Is it my tongue?—You'll acknowledge, brother, that I do not speak with the brogue."

It was true that Phelim did not speak with any Irish brogue: his mother was an English woman, and he had lived much with English officers in Cork, and he had studied and imitated their manner of speaking so successfully, that no one, merely by his accent, could have guessed that he was an Irishman.

"Hey! brother, I say!" continued Phelim, in a triumphant English tone; "I never was taken for an Irishman in my life. Colonel Broadman told me the other day, I spoke English better than the English themselves; that he should take me for an Englishman, in any part of the known world, the moment I

2. Women.

opened my lips. You must allow that not the smallest particle of brogue is discernible on my tongue."

His brother allowed that not the smallest particle of brogue was to be discerned upon Phelim's tongue, but feared that some Irish idiom might be perceived in his conversation. And then the name of O'Mooney!

"Oh, as to that, I need not trouble an act of parliament, or even a king's letter, just to change my name for a season; at the worst, I can travel and appear incognito."

"Always?"

"No: only just till I'm upon good terms with the lady—Mrs. Phelim O'Mooney, that is to be, God willing. Never fear, nor shake your head, brother; *you* men of business are out of this line, and not proper judges: I beg your pardon for saying so, but as you are my own brother, and nobody by, you'll excuse me."

His brother did excuse him, but continued silent for some minutes; he was pondering upon the means of persuading Phelim to give up this scheme.

"I would lay you any wager, my dear Phelim," said he, "that you could not continue four days in England incognito."

"Done!" cried Phelim. "Done for a hundred pounds; done for a thousand pounds, and welcome."

"But if you lose, how will you pay?"

"Faith! that's the last thing I thought of, being sure of winning."

"Then you will not object to any mode of payment I shall propose."

"None: only remembering always, that I was bankrupt last week, and shall be little better till I'm married; but then I'll pay you honestly if I lose."

"No, if you lose I must be paid before that time, my good sir," said his brother, laughing. "My bet is this:—I will lay you one hundred guineas that you do not remain four days in England incognito; be upon honour with me, and promise, that if you lose, you will, instead of laying down a hundred guineas, come back immediately, and settle quietly again to business."

The word *business* was always odious to our hero's proud ears; but he thought himself so secure of winning his wager, that he willingly bound himself in a penalty which he believed would never become due; and his generous brother, at parting, made the bet still more favourable, by allowing that Phelim should not be deemed the loser unless he was, in the course of the first four days after he touched English ground, detected eight times in being an Irishman.

"Eight times!" cried Phelim. "Good bye to a hundred guineas, brother, you may say."

"You may say," echoed his brother, and so they parted.

Mr. Phelim O'Mooney the next morning sailed from Cork harbour with a prosperous gale, and with a confidence in his own success which supplied the place of auspicious omens. He embarked at Cork, to go by long sea to London, and was driven into Deal, where Julius Caesar once landed before him, and with the same resolution to see and conquer.[3] It was early in the morning; having been very sea-sick, he was impatient, as soon as he got into the inn, for his breakfast: he was shown into a room where three ladies were

---

3. The Roman expeditionary force that invaded Britain in 55 B.C.E. landed in the southeast in the vicinity of the modern-day port of Deal. A later victory in Asia Minor occasioned Caesar's boast about how he "came, saw, and conquered."

waiting to go by the stage; his air of easy confidence was the best possible introduction.

"Would any of the company choose eggs?" said the waiter.

"I never touch an egg for my share," said O'Mooney, carelessly; he knew that it was supposed to be an Irish custom to eat eggs at breakfast; and when the malicious waiter afterwards set a plate full of eggs in salt upon the table, our hero magnanimously abstained from them; he even laughed heartily at a story told by one of the ladies of an Hibernian at Buxton, who declared that "no English hen ever laid a fresh egg."

O'Mooney got through breakfast much to his own satisfaction, and to that of the ladies, whom he had taken a proper occasion to call the *three graces*,[4] and whom he had informed that he was an *old* baronet of an English family, and that his name was Sir John Bull. The youngest of the graces civilly observed, "that whatever else he might he, she should never have taken him for an *old* baronet." The lady who made this speech was pretty, but O'Mooney had penetration enough to discover, in the course of the conversation, that she and her companions were far from being divinities; his three graces were a greengrocer's wife, a tallow chandler's widow, and a milliner. When he found that these ladies were likely to be his companions if he were to travel in the coach, he changed his plan, and ordered a post-chaise and four.

O'Mooney was not in danger of making any vulgar Irish blunders in paying his bill at an inn. No landlord or waiter could have suspected him, especially as he always left them to settle the matter first, and then looked over the bill and money with a careless gentility, saying, "Very right," or, "Very well, sir"; wisely calculating, that it was better to lose a few shillings on the road, than to lose a hundred pounds by the risk of Hibernian miscalculation.

Whilst the chaise was getting ready he went to the custom-house to look after his baggage. He found a red-hot countryman of his own there, roaring about four and fourpence, and fighting the battle of his trunks, in which he was ready to make affidavit there was not, nor never had been, any thing contraband; and when the custom-house officer replied by pulling out of one of them a piece of Irish poplin, the Hibernian fell immediately upon the Union, which he swore was Disunion, as the custom-house officers managed it. Sir John Bull appeared to much advantage all this time, maintaining a dignified silence; from his quiet appearance and deportment, the custom-house officers took it for granted that he was an Englishman. He was in no hurry; he begged *that* gentleman's business might be settled first; he would wait the officer's leisure, and as he spoke he played so dexterously with half-a-guinea between his fingers, as to make it visible only where he wished. The custom-house officer was his humble servant immediately; but the Hibernian would have been his enemy, if he had not conciliated him by observing, "that even Englishmen must allow there was something very like a bull in professing to make a complete identification of the two kingdoms, whilst, at the same time, certain regulations continued in full force to divide the countries by art, even more than the British channel does by nature."

Sir John talked so plausibly, and, above all, so candidly and coolly on Irish and English politics, that the custom-house officer conversed with him for a quarter of an hour without guessing of what country he was, till in an unlucky

4. A flowery compliment: in classical mythology the three graces are sister goddesses who bestow beauty and charm.

moment Phelim's heart got the better of his head. Joining in the praises bestowed by all parties on the conduct of a distinguished patriot of his country, he, in the height of his enthusiasm, inadvertently called him *the Speaker*.

"The *Speaker!*" said the officer.

"Yes, the Speaker—*our* Speaker" cried Phelim, with exultation.[5] He was not aware how he had betrayed himself, till the officer smiled and said—

"Sir, I really never should have found out that you were an Irishman but from the manner in which you named your countryman, who is as highly thought of by all parties in this country as in yours: your enthusiasm does honour to your heart."

"And to my head, I'm sure," said our hero, laughing with the best grace imaginable. "Well, I am glad you have found me out in this manner, though I lose the eighth part of a bet of a hundred guineas by it."

He explained the wager, and begged the custom-house officer to keep his secret, which he promised to do faithfully, and assured him, "that he should be happy to do any thing in his power to serve him." Whilst he was uttering these last words, there came in a snug, but soft-looking Englishman, who opining from the words "happy to do any thing in my power to serve you," that O'Mooney was a friend of the custom-house officer's, and encouraged by something affable and good-natured in our hero's countenance, crept up to him, and whispered a request—"Could you tell a body, sir, how to get out of the custom-house a very valuable box of Sèvre china that has been *laying* in the custom-house three weeks, and which I was commissioned to get out if I could, and bring up to town for a lady."

As a lady was in the case, O'Mooney's gallantry instantly made his good-nature effective. The box of Sèvre china was produced, and opened only as a matter of form, and only as a matter of curiosity its contents were examined—a beautiful set of Sèvre china and a pendule, said to have belonged to M. Egalité![6] "These things must be intended," said Phelim, "for some lady of superior taste or fortune."

As Phelim was a proficient in the Socratic art of putting judicious interrogatories, he was soon happily master of the principal points it concerned him to know: he learnt that the lady was rich—a spinster—of full age—at her own disposal—living with a single female companion at Blackheath[7]—furnishing a house there in a superior style—had two carriages—her Christian name Mary—her surname Sharperson.

O'Mooney, by the blessing of God, it shall soon be, thought Phelim. He politely offered the Englishman a place in his chaise for himself and Sèvre china, as it was for a lady, and would run great hazard in the stage, which besides was full. Mr. Queasy, for that was our soft Englishman's name, was astonished by our hero's condescension and affability, especially as he heard him called Sir John: he bowed sundry times as low as the fear of losing his wig would permit, and accepted the polite offer with many thanks for himself and the lady concerned.

5. John Foster, Baron Oriel, the last man to serve as speaker in the Irish House of Commons, before its abolition by the Act of Union in 1801.
6. Cousin to King Louis XVI and himself in line for the throne of France, Philippe, Duke of Orleans (1747–1793) assumed the surname Egalité ("Equality") as testimony of his support for the Revolution. The name change did not save him from the guillotine. The duke's Sèvre—expensive porcelain manufactured near Paris—and pendule (a pendulum clock) appear to have come on the market following his execution.
7. District of London.

Sir John Bull's chaise and four was soon ready and Queasy seated in the corner of it, and the Sèvre china safely stowed between his knees. Captain Murray, a Scotch officer, was standing at the inn door, with his eyes intently fixed on the letters that were worked in nails on the top of Sir John's trunk; the letters were P. O'M. Our hero, whose eyes were at least as quick as the Scotchman's, was alarmed lest this should lead to a second detection. He called instantly, with his usual presence of mind, to the ostler, and desired him to uncord *that* trunk, as it was not to go with him; raising his voice loud enough for all *the yard* to hear, he added—"It is not mine at all; it belongs to my friend, Mr. O'Mooney: let it be sent after me, at leisure, by the waggon, as directed, to the care of Sir John Bull."

Our hero was now giving his invention a prodigious quantity of superfluous trouble; and upon this occasion, as upon most others, he was more in danger from excess than deficiency of ingenuity: he was like the man in the fairy tale, who was obliged to tie his legs lest he should outrun the object of which he was in pursuit. The Scotch officer, though his eyes were fixed on the letters P. O'M., had none of the suspicions which Phelim was counteracting; he was only considering how he could ask for the third place in Sir John's chaise during the next stage, as he was in great haste to get to town upon particular business, and there were no other horses at the inn. When he heard that the heavy baggage was to go by the waggon, he took courage, and made his request. It was instantly granted by the good-natured Hibernian, who showed as much hospitality about his chaise as if it had been his house. Away they drove as fast as they could. Fresh dangers awaited him at the next inn. He left his hat upon the table in the hall whilst he went into the parlour, and when he returned, he heard some person inquiring what Irish gentleman was there. Our hero was terribly alarmed, for he saw that his hat was in the inquirer's hand, and he recollected that the name of Phelim O'Mooney was written in it. This the inquisitive gentleman did not see, for it was written in no very legible characters on the leather withinside of the front; but "F. Guest, hatter, Dame-street, Dublin," was a printed advertisement that could not be mistaken, and *that* was pasted within the crown. O'Mooney's presence of mind did not forsake him upon this emergency.

"My good sir," said he, turning to Queasy, who, without hearing one word of what was passing, was coming out of the parlour, with his own hat and gloves in his hand; "My good sir," continued he, loading him with parcels, "will you have the goodness to see these put into my carriage? I'll take care of your hat and gloves," added O'Mooney in a low voice. Queasy surrendered his hat and gloves instantly, unknowing wherefore; then squeezed forward with his load through the crowd, crying—"Waiter! hostler! pray, somebody put these into Sir John Bull's chaise."

Sir John Bull, equipped with Queasy's hat, marched deliberately through the defile, bowing with the air of at least an English county member[8] to this side and to that, as way was made for him to his carriage. No one suspected that the hat did not belong to him; no one, indeed, thought of the hat, for all eyes were fixed upon the man. Seated in the carriage, he threw money to the waiter, hostler, and boots, and drew up the glass, bidding the postilions

8. One of the members of Parliament who represented the counties of England.

drive on. By this cool self-possession our hero effected his retreat with successful generalship, leaving his new Dublin beaver behind him, without regret, as bona waviata.[9] Queasy, before whose eyes things passed continually without his seeing them, thanked Sir John for the care he had taken of his hat, drew on his gloves, and calculated aloud how long they should be going to the next stage. At the first town they passed through, O'Mooney bought a new hat, and Queasy deplored the unaccountable mistake by which Sir John's hat had been forgotten. No further *mistakes* happened upon the journey. The travellers rattled on, and neither 'stinted nor stayed'[1] till they arrived at Blackheath, at Miss Sharperson's. Sir John sat Queasy down without having given him the least hint of his designs upon the lady; but as he helped him out with the Sèvre china, he looked through the large opening double doors of the hall, and slightly said—"Upon my word, this seems to be a handsome house: it would be worth looking at, if the family were not at home."

"I am morally sure, Sir John," said the soft Queasy, "that Miss Sharperson would be happy to let you see the house to-night, and this minute, if she knew you were at the door, and who you were, and all your civility about me and the china.—Do, pray, walk in."

"Not for the world: a gentleman could not do such a thing without an invitation from the lady of the house herself."

"Oh, if that's all, I'll step up myself to the young lady; I'm certain she'll be proud—"

"Mr. Queasy, by no means; I would not have the lady disturbed for the world at this unseasonable hour.—It is too late—quite too late."

"Not at all, begging pardon, Sir John," said Queasy, taking out his watch: "only just tea-time by me.—Not at all unseasonable for any body; besides, the message is of my own head:—all, you know, if not well taken—"

Up the great staircase he made bold to go on his mission, as he thought, in defiance of Sir John's better judgment. He returned in a few minutes with a face of self-complacent exultation, *and* Miss Sharperson's compliments, and begs Sir John Bull will walk up and rest himself with a dish of tea, and has her thanks to him for the china.

Now Queasy, who had the highest possible opinion of Sir John Bull and of Miss Sharperson, whom he thought the two people of the greatest consequence and affability, had formed the notion that they were made for each other, and that it must be a match if they could but meet. The meeting he had now happily contrived and effected; and he had done his part for his friend Sir John, with Miss Sharperson, by as many exaggerations as he could utter in five minutes, concerning his perdigious politeness and courage, his fine person and carriage, his ancient family, and vast connections and importance wherever he appeared on the road, at inns, and over all England. He had previously, during the journey, done his part for his friend Miss Sharperson with Sir John, by stating that "she had a large fortune left her by her mother, and was to have twice as much from her grandmother; that she had thousands upon thousands in the funds, and an estate of two

9. *Bona waviata* is a Latin term applied in law to stolen goods that have been thrown away by their thief, who would rather lose them than be caught red-handed. It is applied here to the hero's "beaver," a type of hat made from beaver's fur.
1. I.e., by not stinting on money or food for the horses, they avoided any delay (stay).

thousand a year, called Rascàlly, in Scotland, besides plate and jewels without end."

Thus prepared, how could this lady and gentleman meet without falling desperately in love with each other!

Though a servant in handsome livery appeared ready to show Sir John up the great staircase, Mr. Queasy acted as a gentleman usher, or rather as showman. He nodded to Sir John as they passed across a long gallery and through an ante-chamber, threw open the doors of various apartments as he went along, crying—"Peep in! peep in! peep in here! peep in there!—Is not this spacious? Is not this elegant? Is not that grand? Did I say too much?" continued he, rubbing his hands with delight. "Did you ever see so magnificent and such highly-polished steel grates out of Lon'on?"

Sir John, conscious that the servant's eyes were upon him, smiled at this question, "looked superior down;" and though with reluctant complaisance he leaned his body to this side or to that, as Queasy pulled or swayed, yet he appeared totally regardless of the man's vulgar reflections. He had seen every thing as he passed, and was surprised at all he saw; but he evinced not the slightest symptom of astonishment. He was now ushered into a spacious, well lighted apartment: he entered with the easy, unembarrassed air of a man who was perfectly accustomed to such a home. His quick coup-d'oeil took in the whole at a single glance. Two magnificent candelabras stood on Egyptian tables[2] at the farther end of the room, and the lights were reflected on all sides from mirrors of no common size. Nothing seemed worthy to attract our hero's attention but the lady of the house, whom he approached with an air of distinguished respect. She was reclining on a Turkish sofa, her companion seated beside her, tuning a harp. Miss Sharperson half rose to receive Sir John: he paid his compliments with an easy, yet respectful air. He was thanked for his civilities to *the person* who had been commissioned to bring the box of Sèvre china from Deal.

"Vastly sorry it should have been so troublesome," Miss Sharperson said, in a voice fashionably unintelligible, and with a most becoming yet intimidating nonchalance of manner. Intimidating it might have been to any man but our hero; he, who had the happy talent of catching, wherever he went, the reigning manner of the place, replied to the lady in equal strains; and she, in her turn, seemed to look upon him more as her equal. Tea and coffee were served. *Nothings* were talked of quite easily by Sir John. He practised the art "not to admire," so as to give a justly high opinion of his taste, consequence, and knowledge of the world. Miss Sharperson, though her nonchalance was much diminished, continued to maintain a certain dignified reserve; whilst her companion, Miss Felicia Flat, condescended to ask Sir John, who had doubtless seen every fine house in England and on the continent, his opinion with respect to the furniture and finishing of the room, the placing of the Egyptian tables and the candelabras.

No mortal could have guessed by Sir John Bull's air, when he heard this question, that he had never seen a candelabra before in his life. He was so much, and yet seemingly so little upon his guard, he dealt so dexterously in generals, and evaded particulars so delicately, that he went through this dangerous conversation triumphantly. Careful not to protract his visit beyond the

2. Following the victory of the British Fleet against the French at the Battle of the Nile (1798), furnishings in an Egyptian style were the height of fashion.

bounds of propriety, he soon rose to take leave, and he mingled "intrusion, regret, late hour, happiness, and honour," so charmingly in his parting compliment, as to leave the most favourable impression on the minds of both the ladies, and to procure for himself an invitation to see the house next morning.

The first day was now ended, and our hero had been detected but once. He went to rest this night well satisfied with himself, but much more occupied with the hopes of marrying the heiress of Rascàlly than of winning a paltry bet.

The next day he waited upon the ladies in high spirits. Neither of them was *visible*, but Mr. Queasy had orders to show him the house, which he did with much exultation, dwelling particularly in his praises on the beautiful high polish of the steel grates. Queasy boasted that it was he who had recommended the ironmonger who furnished the house in that line; and that his bill, as he was proud to state, amounted to *many, many* hundreds. Sir John, who did not attend to one word Queasy said, went to examine the map of the Rascàlly estate, which was unrolled, and he had leisure to count the number of lords' and ladies' visiting tickets[3] which lay upon the chimney-piece. He saw names of the people of first quality and respectability: it was plain that Miss Sharperson must be a lady of high family as well as large fortune, else she would not be visited by persons of such distinction. Our hero's passion for her increased every moment. Her companion, Miss Flat, now appeared, and entered very freely into conversation with Sir John; and as he perceived that she was commissioned to sit in judgment upon him, he evaded all her leading questions with the skill of an Irish witness, but without giving any Hibernian answers. She was fairly at a fault. Miss Sharperson at length appeared, elegantly dressed; her person was genteel, and her face rather pretty. Sir John, at this instant, thought her beautiful, or seemed to think so. The ladies interchanged looks, and afterwards Sir John found a softness in his fair one's manner, a languishing tenderness in her eyes, in the tone of her voice, and at the same time a modest perplexity and reserve about her, which altogether persuaded him that he was quite right, and his brother quite wrong *en fait d'amour*.[4] Miss Flat appeared now to have the most self-possession of the three, and Miss Sharperson looked at her, from time to time, as if she asked leave to be in love. Sir John's visit lasted a full half hour before he was sensible of having been five minutes engaged in this delightful conversation.

Miss Sharperson's coach now came to the door: he handed her into it, and she gave him a parting look, which satisfied him all was yet safe in her heart. Miss Flat, as he handed her into the carriage, said, "Perhaps they should meet Sir John at Tunbridge,[5] where they were going in a few days." She added some words as she seated herself, which he scarcely noticed at the time, but they recurred afterwards disagreeably to his memory. The words were, "I'm so glad we've a roomy coach, for of all things it annoys me to be *squeedged* in a carriage."

This word *squeedged*, as he had not been used to it in Ireland, sounded to him extremely vulgar, and gave him suspicions of the most painful nature. He had the precaution, before he left Blackheath, to go into several shops,

3. The cards left by the people paying social calls on Miss Sharperson.
4. In matters concerning love (French).

5. Tunbridge Wells, a fashionable spa town in southeast England.

and to inquire something more concerning his fair ladies. All he heard was much to their advantage; that is, much to the advantage of Miss Sharperson's fortune. All agreed that she was a rich Scotch heiress. A rich Scotch heiress, Sir John wisely considered, might have an humble companion who spoke bad English. He concluded that *squeedged* was Scotch, blamed himself for his suspicions, and was more in love with his mistress and with himself than ever. As he returned to town, he framed the outline of a triumphant letter to his brother on his approaching marriage. The bet was a matter, at present, totally beneath his consideration. However, we must do him the justice to say, that like a man of honour he resolved that, as soon as he had won the lady's heart, he would *candidly* tell her his circumstances, and then leave her the choice either to marry him or break her heart, as she pleased. Just as he had formed this generous resolution, at a sudden turn of the road he overtook Miss Sharperson's coach: he bowed and looked in as he passed, when, to his astonishment, he saw, *squeedged* up in the corner by Miss Felicia, Mr. Queasy. He thought that this was a blunder in etiquette that would never have been made in Ireland. Perhaps his mistress was of the same opinion, for she hastily pulled down the blind as Sir John passed. A cold qualm came over the lover's heart. He lost no time in idle doubts and suspicions, but galloped on to town as fast as he could, and went immediately to call upon the Scotch officer with whom he had travelled, and whom he knew to be keen and prudent. He recollected the map of the Rascàlly estate, which he saw in Miss Sharperson's breakfast-room, and he remembered that the lands were said to lie in that part of Scotland from which Captain Murray came; from him he resolved to inquire into the state of the premises, before he should offer himself as tenant for life. Captain Murray assured him that there was no such place as Rascàlly in that part of Scotland; that he had never heard of any such person as Miss Sharperson, though he was acquainted with every family and every estate in the neighbourhood where she fabled hers to be. O'Mooney drew, from memory, the map of the Rascàlly estate. Captain Murray examined the boundaries, and assured him that his cousin the general's lands joined his own at the very spot which he described, and that unless two straight lines could enclose a space, the Rascàlly estate could not be found.

Sir John, naturally of a warm temper, proceeded, however, with prudence. The Scotch officer admired his sagacity in detecting this adventurer. Sir John waited at his hotel for Queasy, who had promised to call to let him know when the ladies would go to Tunbridge. Queasy came. Nothing could equal his astonishment and dismay when he was told the news.

"No such place as the Rascàlly estate! Then I'm an undone man! an undone man!" cried poor Queasy, bursting into tears: "but I'm certain it's impossible; and you'll find, Sir John, you've been misinformed. I would stake my life upon it, Miss Sharperson's a rich heiress, and has a rich grandmother. Why, she's five hundred pounds in my debt, and I know of her being thousands and thousands in the books of as good men as myself, to whom I've recommended her, which I wouldn't have done for my life if I had not known her to be solid. You'll find she'll prove a rich heiress, Sir John."

Sir John hoped so, but the proofs were not yet satisfactory. Queasy determined to inquire about her payments to certain creditors at Blackheath, and promised to give a decisive answer in the morning. O'Mooney saw that this man was too great a fool to be a knave; his perturbation was evidently the perturbation of a dupe, not of an accomplice: Queasy was made to "be an anvil, not a hammer."[6] In the midst of his own disappointment, our good-natured Hibernian really pitied this poor currier.[7]

The next morning Sir John went early to Blackheath. All was confusion at Miss Sharperson's house; the steps covered with grates and furniture of all sorts; porters carrying out looking-glasses, Egyptian tables, and candelabras; the noise of workmen was heard in every apartment; and louder than all the rest, O'Mooney heard the curses that were denounced against his rich heiress—curses such as are bestowed on a swindler in the moment of detection by the tradesmen whom she has ruined.

Our hero, who was of a most happy temper, congratulated himself upon having, by his own wit and prudence, escaped making the practical bull of marrying a female swindler.

Now that Phelim's immediate hopes of marrying a rich heiress were over, his bet with his brother appeared to him of more consequence, and he rejoiced in the reflection that this was the third day he had spent in England, and that he had but once been detected.—The ides of March[8] were come, but not passed!

"My lads," said he to the workmen, who were busy in carrying out the furniture from Miss Sharperson's house, "all hands are at work, I see, in saving what they can from the wreck of *the Sharperson*. She was as well-fitted out a vessel, and in as gallant trim, as any ship upon the face of the earth."

"Ship upon the face of the *yearth*!" repeated an English porter with a sneer; "ship upon the face of the water, you should say, master; but I take it you be's an Irishman."

O'Mooney had reason to be particularly vexed at being detected by this man, who spoke a miserable jargon, and who seemed not to have a very extensive range of ideas. He was one of those half-witted geniuses who catch at the shadow of an Irish bull. In fact, Phelim had merely made a lapsus linguae and had used an expression justifiable by the authority of the elegant and witty lord Chesterfield,[9] who said—no, who *wrote*—that the English navy is the finest navy *upon the face of the earth*! But it was in vain for our hero to argue the point; he was detected—no matter how or by whom. But this was only his second detection, and three of his four days of probation were past.

He dined this day at Captain Murray's. In the room in which they dined there was a picture of the captain, painted by Romney. Sir John, who happened to be seated opposite to it, observed that it was a very fine picture; the more he looked at it, the more he liked it. His admiration was at last unluckily expressed: he said, "That's an incomparable, an inimitable picture; it is absolutely *more like than the original*."[1]

A keen Scotch lady in company smiled, and repeated, "*More like than the original!* Sir John, if I had not been told by my relative here that you were an Englishman, I should have set you *doon*, from that speech, for an Irishman."

This unexpected detection brought the colour, for a moment, into Sir John's face; but immediately recovering his presence of mind, he said, "That

---

6. I.e., Queasy has not acted but been acted upon.
7. Someone who curries favor.
8. March 15. In Shakespeare's *Julius Caesar* 1.2, a soothsayer prophesies that Caesar will meet with danger on this date.
9. The hero's *lapsus linguae* (Latin for slip of the tongue) has a precedent in the writings of Philip

Dormer Stanhope, the fourth earl of Chesterfield (1694–1773), whose posthumously published letters to his illegitimate son secured him a reputation as a wit and a schemer.
1. This bull was really made [Edgeworth's note]. George Romney (1734–1802) painted society portraits and rural scenes.

was, I acknowledge, an excellent Irish bull; but in the course of my travels I have heard as good English bulls as Irish."

To this Captain Murray politely acceded, and he produced some laughable instances in support of the assertion, which gave the conversation a new turn.

O'Mooney felt extremely obliged to the captain for this, especially as he saw, by his countenance, that he also had suspicions of the truth. The first moment he found himself alone with Murray, our hero said to him, "Murray, you are too good a fellow to impose upon, even in jest. Your keen country-woman guessed the truth—I am an Irishman, but not a swindler. You shall hear why I conceal my country and name; only keep my secret till to-morrow night, or I shall lose a hundred guineas by my frankness."

O'Mooney then explained to him the nature of his bet. "This is only my third detection, and half of it voluntary, I might say, if I chose to higgle, which I scorn to do."

Captain Murray was so much pleased by this openness, that as he shook hands with O'Mooney, he said, "Give me leave to tell you, Sir, that even if you should lose your bet by this frank behaviour, you will have gained a better thing—a friend."

In the evening our hero went with his friend and a party of gentlemen to Maidenhead, near which place a battle was to be fought next day, between two famous pugilists, Bourke and Belcher.[2] At the appointed time the combatants appeared upon the stage; the whole boxing corps and the gentlemen *amateurs* crowded to behold the spectacle. Phelim O'Mooney's heart beat for the Irish champion Bourke; but he kept a guard upon his tongue, and had even the forbearance not to bet upon his countryman's head. How many rounds were fought, and how many minutes the fight lasted, how many blows were *put in* on each side, or which was the *game man* of the two, we forbear to decide or relate, as all this has been settled in the newspapers of the day; where also it was remarked, that Bourke, who lost the battle, "was put into a post-chaise, and left *standing* half an hour, while another fight took place. This was very scandalous on the part of his friends," says the humane newspaper historian, "as the poor man might possibly be dying."

Our hero O'Mooney's heart again got the better of his head. Forgetful of his bet, forgetful of every thing but humanity, he made his way up to the chaise, where Bourke was left. "How are you, my gay fellow?" said he. "Can you *see at all with the eye that's knocked out?*"

The brutal populace, who overheard this question, set up a roar of laughter: "A bull! a bull! an Irish bull! Did you hear the question this Irish gentleman asked his countryman?"

O'Mooney was detected a fourth time, and this time he was not ashamed. There was one man in the crowd who did not join in the laugh: a poor Irishman, of the name of Terence McDermod. He had in former times gone out a grousing, near Cork, with our hero; and the moment he heard his voice, he sprang forward, and with uncouth but honest demonstrations of joy, exclaimed, "Ah, my dear master! my dear young master! Phelim O'Mooney, Esq.[3] And I have found your honour alive again? By the blessing of God above, I'll never part you now till I die; and I'll go to the world's end to sarve *yees*."

2. The reference is to actual historical figures of the early 19th century—the bare-knuckle boxers Jem Belcher and Joe Bourke.

3. "Esquire"; designation given to men regarded as gentlemen.

O'Mooney wished him at the world's end this instant, yet could not prevail upon himself to check this affectionate follower of the O'Mooneys. He,
however, put half a crown into his hand, and hinted that if he wished really
to serve him, it must be at some other time. The poor fellow threw down the
money, saying, he would never leave him. "Bid me do any thing, barring that.
No, you shall never part me. Do what you plase with me, still I'll be close to
your heart, like your own shadow: knock me down if you will, and wilcome,
ten times a day, and I'll be up again like a ninepin: only let me sarve your
honour; I'll ask no wages nor take none."

There was no withstanding all this; and whether our hero's good-nature
deceived him we shall not determine, but he thought it most prudent, as he
could not get rid of Terence, to take him into his service, to let him into his
secret, to make him swear that he would never utter the name of Phelim
O'Mooney during the remainder of this day. Terence heard the secret of the
bet with joy, entered into the jest with all the readiness of an Irishman, and
with equal joy and readiness swore by the hind leg of the holy lamb that he
would never mention, even to his own dog, the name of Phelim O'Mooney,
Esq., good or bad, till past twelve o'clock; and further, that he would, till
the clock should strike that hour, call his master Sir John Bull, and nothing
else, to all men, women, and children, upon the floor of God's creation.

Satisfied with the fulness of this oath, O'Mooney resolved to return to
town with his man Terence McDermod. He, however, contrived, before he
got there, to make a practical bull, by which he was detected a fifth time.
He got into the coach which was driving *from* London instead of that which
was driving *to* London, and he would have been carried rapidly to Oxford,
had not his man Terence, after they had proceeded a mile and a half on the
wrong road, put his head down from the top of the coach, crying, as he
looked in at the window, "Master, Sir John Bull, are you there? Do you know
we're in the wrong box, going to Oxford?"

"Your master's an Irishman, dare to say, as well as yourself," said the
coachman, as he let Sir John out. He walked back to Maidenhead, and took
a chaise to town.

It was six o'clock when he got to London, and he went into a coffee-house
to dine. He sat down beside a gentleman who was reading the newspaper.
"Any news to-day, sir?"

The gentleman told him the news of the day, and then began to read aloud
some paragraphs in a strong Hibernian accent. Our hero was sorry that he
had met with another countryman; but he resolved to set a guard upon his
lips, and he knew that his own accent could not betray him. The stranger
read on till he came to a trial about a legacy which an old woman had left to
her cats. O'Mooney exclaimed, "I hate cats almost as much as old women;
and if I had been the English minister, I would have laid the *dog-tax* upon
cats."[4]

"If you had been the *Irish* minister, you mean," said the stranger, smiling;
"for I perceive now you are a countryman of my own."

"How can you think so, sir?" said O'Mooney: "You have no reason to suppose so from my accent, I believe."

"None in life—quite the contrary; for you speak remarkably pure English—
not the least note or half note of the brogue; but there's another sort of free-
mason sign by which we Hibernians know one another and are known all over

---

4. One of several new taxes introduced by Prime Minister Pitt to finance Britain's war against France.

the globe. Whether to call it a confusion of expressions or of ideas, I can't tell. Now an Englishman, if he had been saying what you did, sir, just now, would have taken time to separate the dog and the tax, and he would have put the tax upon cats, and let the dogs go about their business." Our hero, with his usual good-humour, acknowledged himself to be fairly detected.

"Well, sir," said the stranger, "if I had not found you out before by the blunder, I should be sure now you were my countryman by your good-humour. An Irishman can take what's said to him, provided no affront's meant, with more good-humour than any man on earth."

"Ay, that he can," cried O' Mooney: "he lends himself, like the whale, to be tickled even by the fellow with the harpoon, till he finds what he is about, and then he pays away, and pitches the fellow, boat and all, to the devil. Ah, countryman! you would give me credit indeed for my good humour if you knew what danger you have put me in by detecting me for an Irishman. I have been found out six times, and if I blunder twice more before twelve o'clock this night, I shall lose a hundred guineas by it: but I will make sure of my bet; for I will go home straight this minute, lock myself up in my room, and not say a word to any mortal till the watchman cries 'past twelve o'clock,'—then the fast and long Lent of my tongue will be fairly over; and if you'll meet me, my dear friend, at the King's Arms, we will have a good supper and keep Easter for ever."

Phelim, pursuant to his resolution, returned to his hotel, and shut himself up in his room, where he remained in perfect silence and consequent safety till about nine o'clock. Suddenly he heard a great huzzaing in the street; he looked out of the window, and saw that all the houses in the street were illuminated. His landlady came bustling into his apartment, followed by waiters with candles. His spirits instantly rose, though he did not clearly know the cause of the rejoicings. "I give you joy, ma'am. What are you all illuminating[5] for?" said he to his landlady.

"Thank you, sir, with all my heart. I am not sure. It is either for a great victory or the peace. Bob—waiter—step out and inquire for the gentleman."

The gentleman preferred stepping out to inquire for himself. The illuminations were in honour of the peace.[6] He totally forgot his bet, his silence, and his prudence, in his sympathy with the general joy. He walked rapidly from street to street, admiring the various elegant devices. A crowd was standing before the windows of a house that was illuminated with extraordinary splendour. He inquired whose it was, and was informed that it belonged to a contractor, who had made an immense fortune by the war.

"Then I'm sure these illuminations of his for the peace are none of the most sincere," said O'Mooney. The mob were of his opinion; and Phelim, who was now, alas! worked up to the proper pitch for blundering, added, by way of pleasing his audience still more—"If this contractor had *illuminated* in character, it should have been with *dark lanterns*."[7]

"Should it? by Jasus! that would be an Irish illumination," cried some one. "Arrah, honey! you're an Irishman, whoever you are, and have spoke your mind in character."

Sir John Bull was vexed that the piece of wit which he had aimed at the contractor had recoiled upon himself. "It is always, as my countryman observed, by having too much wit that I blunder. The deuce take me if I sport

5. Decorating with lights as a sign of celebration.
6. Probably the truce signed between Britain and France in October 1801, temporarily suspending hostilities after eight years of war.
7. Lanterns equipped with slides that allow their light to be hidden.

a single bon mot more this night. This is only my seventh detection, I have an eighth blunder still *to the good*; and if I can but keep my wit to myself till I am out of purgatory, then I shall be in heaven, and may sing Io triumphe[8] in spite of my brother."

Fortunately, Phelim had not made it any part of his bet that he should not speak to himself an Irish idiom, or that he should not think a bull. Resolved to be as obstinately silent as a monk of La Trappe,[9] he once more shut himself up in his cell, and fell fast asleep—dreamed that fat bulls of Basan[1] encompassed him round about—that he ran down a steep hill to escape them—that his foot slipped—he rolled to the bottom—felt the bull's horns in his side—heard the bull bellowing in his ears—wakened—and found Terence McDermod bellowing at his room door.

"Sir John Bull! Sir John Bull! murder! murder! my dear master, Sir John Bull! murder, robbery, and reward! let me in! for the love of the Holy Virgin! they are all after you!"

"Who? are you drunk, Terence?" said Sir John, opening the door.

"No, but they are mad—all mad."

"Who?"

"The constable. They are all mad entirely, and the lord mayor, all along with your honour's making me swear I would not tell your name. Sure they are all coming armed in a body to put you in jail for a forgery, unless I run back and tell them the truth—will I?"

"First tell me the truth, blunderer!"

"I'll make my affidavit I never blundered, plase your honour, but just went to the merchant's, as you ordered, with the draught, signed with the name I swore not to utter till past twelve. I presents the draught, and waits to be paid. 'Are you Mr. O'Mooney's servant?' says one of the clerks after a while. No, sir, not at all, sir,' said I; 'I'm Sir John Bull's, at your *sarvice*.' He puzzles and puzzles, and asks me did I bring the draught, and was that your writing at the bottom of it? I still said it was my master's writing, *Sir John Bull's*, and no other. They whispered from one up to t'other, and then said it was a forgery, as I overheard, and I must go before the mayor. With that, while the master, who was called down to be examined as to his opinion, was putting on his glasses to spell it out, I gives them, one and all, the slip, and whips out of the street door and home to give your honour notice, and have been breaking my heart at the door this half hour to make you hear—and now you have it all."

"I am in a worse dilemma now than when between the horns of the bull," thought Sir John: "I must now either tell my real name, avow myself an Irishman, and so lose my bet, or else go to gaol."

He preferred going to gaol. He resolved to pretend to be dumb, and he charged Terence not to betray him. The officers of justice came to take him up: Sir John resigned himself to them, making signs that he could not speak. He was carried before a magistrate. The merchant had never seen Mr. Phelim O'Mooney, but could swear to his handwriting and signature, having many of his letters and draughts. The draught in question was produced. Sir John Bull would neither acknowledge nor deny the signature, but in dumb

8. Greek cry of triumph.
9. Alluding to the vows of silence taken by the monks of the French Abbey of La Trappe.

1. A recollection of Psalms 22.12, where the Psalmist describes his anguish at being forsaken: "strong bulls of Bashan have beset me round."

show made signs of innocence. No art or persuasion could make him speak; he kept his fingers on his lips. One of the bailiffs offered to open Sir John's mouth. Sir John clenched his hand, in token that if they used violence he knew his remedy. To the magistrate he was all bows and respect: but the law, in spite of civility, must take its course.

Terence McDermod beat his breast, and called upon all the saints in the Irish calender when he saw the committal actually made out, and his dear master given over to the constables. Nothing but his own oath and his master's commanding eye, which was fixed upon him at this instant, could have made him forbear to utter, what he had never in his life been before so strongly tempted to tell—the truth.

Determined to win his wager, our hero suffered himself to be carried to a lock-up house, and persisted in keeping silence till the clock struck twelve! Then the charm was broken, and he spoke. He began talking to himself, and singing as loud as he possibly could. The next morning Terence, who was no longer bound by his oath to conceal Phelim's name, hastened to his master's correspondent in town, told the whole story, and O'Mooney was liberated. Having won his bet by his wit and steadiness, he had now the prudence to give up these adventuring schemes, to which he had so nearly become a dupe; he returned immediately to Ireland to his brother, and determined to settle quietly to business. His good brother paid him the hundred guineas most joyfully, declaring that he had never spent a hundred guineas better in his life than in recovering a brother. Phelim had now conquered his foolish dislike to trade: his brother took him into partnership, and Phelim O'Mooney never relapsed into Sir John Bull.

1802

WILLIAM WORDSWORTH

1770–1850

William Wordsworth was born in Cockermouth in West Cumberland, just on the northern fringe of the English Lake District. When his mother died, the eight-year-old boy was sent to school at Hawkshead, near Esthwaite Lake, in the heart of that sparsely populated region that he and Coleridge were to transform into one of the poetic centers of England. William and his three brothers boarded in the cottage of Ann Tyson, who gave the boys simple comfort, ample affection, and freedom to roam the countryside at will. A vigorous, unruly, and sometimes moody boy, William spent his free days and occasionally "half the night" in the sports and rambles described in the first two books of *The Prelude*, "drinking in" (to use one of his favorite metaphors) the natural sights and sounds, and getting to know the cottagers, shepherds, and solitary wanderers who moved through his imagination into his later poetry. He also found time to read voraciously in the books owned by his young headmaster, William Taylor, who encouraged him in his inclination to poetry.

John Wordsworth, the poet's father, died suddenly when William was thirteen, leaving to his five children mainly the substantial sum owed him by Lord Lonsdale, whom he had served as attorney and as steward of the huge Lonsdale estate. This harsh nobleman had yet to pay the debt when he died in 1802. Wordsworth was nevertheless able in 1787 to enter St. John's College, Cambridge University, where four years later he took his degree without distinction.

During the summer vacation of his third year at Cambridge (1790), Wordsworth and his closest college friend, the Welshman Robert Jones, journeyed on foot through France and the Alps (described in *The Prelude* 6) at the time when the French were joyously celebrating the first anniversary of the fall of the Bastille. Upon completing his course at Cambridge, Wordsworth spent four months in London, set off on another walking tour with Robert Jones through Wales (the time of the memorable ascent of Mount Snowdon in *The Prelude* 13), and then went back alone to France to master the language and qualify as a traveling tutor.

During his year in France (November 1791 to December 1792), Wordsworth became a fervent supporter of the French Revolution—which seemed to him and many others to promise a "glorious renovation" of society—and he fell in love with Annette Vallon, the daughter of a French surgeon at Blois. The two planned to marry, despite their differences in religion and political inclinations (Annette belonged to an old Catholic family whose sympathies were Royalist). But almost immediately after their daughter, Caroline, was born, lack of money forced Wordsworth to return to England. The outbreak of war made it impossible for him to rejoin Annette and Caroline. Wordsworth's guilt over this abandonment, his divided loyalties between England and France, and his gradual disillusion with the course of the Revolution brought him—according to his account in *The Prelude* 10 and 11—to the verge of an emotional breakdown, when "sick, wearied out with contrarieties," he "yielded up moral questions in despair." His suffering, his near-collapse, and the successful effort, after his break with his past, to reestablish "a saving intercourse with my true self," are the experiences that underlie many of his greatest poems.

At this critical point, a friend died and left Wordsworth a sum of money just sufficient to enable him to live by his poetry. In 1795 he settled in a rent-free house at Racedown, Dorsetshire, with his beloved sister, Dorothy, who now began her long career as confidante, inspirer, and secretary. At that same time Wordsworth met Samuel Taylor Coleridge. Two years later he moved to Alfoxden House, Somersetshire, to be near Coleridge, who lived four miles away at Nether Stowey. Here he entered at the age of twenty-seven on the delayed springtime of his poetic career.

Even while he had been an undergraduate at Cambridge, Coleridge claimed that he had detected signs of genius in Wordsworth's rather conventional poem about his tour in the Alps, *Descriptive Sketches*, published in 1793. Now he hailed Wordsworth unreservedly as "the best poet of the age." The two men met almost daily, talked for hours about poetry, and wrote prolifically. So close was their association that we find the same phrases occurring in poems by Wordsworth and Coleridge, as well as in the remarkable journals that Dorothy kept at the time; the two poets collaborated in some writings and freely traded thoughts and passages for others; and Coleridge even undertook to complete a few poems that Wordsworth had left unfinished. This close partnership, along with the hospitality the two households offered to another young radical writer, John Thelwall, aroused the paranoia of people in the neighborhood. Already fearful of a military invasion by France, they became convinced that Wordsworth and Coleridge were political plotters, not poets. The government sent spies to investigate, and the Wordsworths lost their lease.

Although brought to this abrupt end, that short period of collaboration resulted in one of the most important books of the era, *Lyrical Ballads, with a Few Other Poems*, published anonymously in 1798. This short volume opened with Coleridge's *Ancient Mariner* and included three other poems by Coleridge, some lyrics in which Wordsworth celebrated the experience of nature, and a number of verse anecdotes drawn from the lives of the rural poor. (The verse forms and the subject matter of this last set of poems—which includes "Simon Lee," "We Are Seven," and "The Thorn"—make evident the debt, announced in the very title of *Lyrical Ballads*, that Wordsworth's and Coleridge's book owed to the folk ballads that were being transcribed and anthologized in the later eighteenth century by collectors such as Thomas Percy and Robert Burns.) The book closed with Wordsworth's great descriptive and meditative poem in blank verse, "Tintern Abbey." This poem inaugurated what modern critics call Wordsworth's "myth of nature": his presentation of the "growth" of his mind to maturity, a process unfolding through the interaction between the inner world of the mind and the shaping force of external Nature.

William Hazlitt said that when he heard Coleridge read some of the newly written poems of *Lyrical Ballads* aloud, "the sense of a new style and a new spirit in poetry came over me," with something of the effect "that arises from the turning up of the fresh soil, or of the first welcome breath of spring." The reviewers were less enthusiastic, warning that, because of their simple language and subject matter, poems such as "Simon Lee" risked "vulgarity" or silliness. (For a sampling of these reactions, see "'Self-constituted judge of poesy': Reviewer vs. Poet in the Romantic Period" in the NAEL Archive.) Nevertheless *Lyrical Ballads* sold out in two years, and Wordsworth published under his own name a new edition, dated 1800, to which he added a second volume of poems. In his famous Preface to this edition, planned in close consultation with Coleridge, Wordsworth outlined a critical program that provided a retroactive rationale for the "experiments" the poems represented.

Late in 1799 William and Dorothy moved back permanently to their native lakes, settling at Grasmere in the little house later named Dove Cottage. Coleridge, following them, rented at Keswick, thirteen miles away. In 1802 Wordsworth finally came into his father's inheritance and, after an amicable settlement with Annette Vallon, married Mary Hutchinson, whom he had known since childhood. His life after that time had many sorrows: the drowning in 1805 of his favorite brother, John, a sea captain; the death in 1812 of two of his and Mary's five children; a growing rift with Coleridge, culminating in a bitter quarrel (1810) from which they were not completely reconciled for almost two decades; and, from the 1830s on, Dorothy's physical and mental illness. Over these years Wordsworth became, nonetheless, increasingly prosperous and famous. He also displayed a political and religious conservatism that disappointed readers who, like Hazlitt, had interpreted his early work as the expression of a "levelling Muse" that promoted democratic change. In 1813 a government sinecure, the position of stamp distributor (that is, revenue collector) for Westmorland, was bestowed on him—concrete evidence of his recognition as a national poet and of the alteration in the government's perception of his politics. Gradually, Wordsworth's residences, as he moved into more and more comfortable quarters, became standard stops for sightseers touring the Lakes. By 1843 he was poet laureate of Great Britain. He died in 1850 at the age of eighty. Only then did his executors publish his masterpiece, *The Prelude,* or *Growth of a Poet's Mind*, the autobiographical poem that he had written in two parts in 1799, expanded to its full length in 1805, and then continued to revise almost to the last decade of his long life.

Most of Wordsworth's greatest poetry had been written by 1807, when he published *Poems, in Two Volumes*. After *The Excursion* (1814) and the first collected edition of his poems (1815), although he continued to write prolifically and to work on the revisions for additional collected editions, his powers appeared to decline. The causes of that decline have been much debated. One seems to be inherent in the very nature of his writing. Wordsworth is above all the poet of the remembrance— also the reinterpretation—of things past. He frequently presents his poetry as the outgrowth of occasions on which objects or events in the present trigger a sudden renewal of feelings that he has experienced in youth, often without then realizing their import. In his prose portrait of Wordsworth for *The Spirit of the Age* William Hazlitt noticed this: for Wordsworth, he observed, there "is no image so insignificant that it has not in some mood or other found the way into his heart: no sound that does not awaken the memory of other years." But the memory of one's early emotional experience is not an inexhaustible resource for poetry, as Wordsworth recognized almost from the start of his career. In book 11 of *The 1805 Prelude* he already seems to be entertaining a premonition of future loss, in the lines that describe the recurrence of "spots of time" from his memories of childhood:

> The days gone by
> Come back upon me from the dawn almost
> Of life: the hiding-places of my power
> Seem open; I approach and then they close;
> I see by glimpses now, when age comes on
> May scarcely see at all.

The simple (maybe even prosy) lines, on the perplexities of memory, on the mystery that the self poses for the self, and on the sorrows and losses brought by time, announce an imminent imaginative failure. At the same time, contrariwise, they also suggest the reason Hazlitt in the same essay would declare Wordsworth's poetry preeminent among that of the living poets: "he has communicated interest and dignity to the primal movements of the heart of man."

From Lyrical Ballads

Goody Blake and Harry Gill

A True Story

Oh! what's the matter? what's the matter?
What is't that ails young Harry Gill?
That evermore his teeth they chatter,
Chatter, chatter, chatter still.
5 Of waistcoats Harry has no lack,

Good duffle grey, and flannel fine;
He has a blanket on his back,
And coats enough to smother nine.

In March, December, and in July,
10　'Tis all the same with Harry Gill;
The neighbours tell, and tell you truly,
His teeth they chatter, chatter still.
At night, at morning, and at noon,
'Tis all the same with Harry Gill;
15　Beneath the sun, beneath the moon,
His teeth they chatter, chatter still.

Young Harry was a lusty drover, *one who drives cattle or sheep*
And who so stout of limb as he?
His cheeks were red as ruddy clover,
20　His voice was like the voice of three.
Auld Goody[1] Blake was old and poor,
Ill fed she was, and thinly clad;
And any man who pass'd her door,
Might see how poor a hut she had,

25　All day she spun in her poor dwelling,
And then her three hours' work at night!
Alas! 'twas hardly worth the telling,
It would not pay for candle-light.
—This woman dwelt in Dorsetshire,
30　Her hut was on a cold hill-side,
And in that country coals are dear,
For they come far by wind and tide.

By the same fire to boil their pottage,
Two poor old dames, as I have known,
35　Will often live in one small cottage,
But she, poor woman, dwelt alone.
'Twas well enough when summer came,
The long, warm, lightsome summer-day,
Then at her door the *canty*° dame　　　　　　　　*lively*
40　Would sit, as any linnet gay.

But when the ice our streams did fetter,
Oh! then how her old bones would shake!
You would have said, if you had met her,
'Twas a hard time for Goody Blake.
45　Her evenings then were dull and dead;
Sad case it was, as you may think,
For very cold to go to bed,
And then for cold not sleep a wink.

Oh joy for her! when e'er in winter
50　The winds at night had made a rout,

---

1. Term of civility applied to a woman in humble life. "Auld": old.

And scatter'd many a lusty splinter,
And many a rotten bough about.
Yet never had she, well or sick,
As every man who knew her says,
55   A pile before-hand, wood or stick,
Enough to warm her for three days.

Now, when the frost was past enduring,
And made her poor old bones to ache,
Could any thing be more alluring,
60   Than an old hedge to Goody Blake?
And now and then, it must be said,
When her old bones were cold and chill,
She left her fire, or left her bed,
To seek the hedge of Harry Gill.

65   Now Harry he had long suspected
This trespass of old Goody Blake,
And vow'd that she should be detected,
And he on her would vengeance take.
And oft from his warm fire he'd go,
70   And to the fields his road would take,
And there, at night, in frost and snow,
He watch'd to seize old Goody Blake.

And once, behind a rick of barley,
Thus looking out did Harry stand;
75   The moon was full and shining clearly,
And crisp with frost the stubble-land.
—He hears a noise—he's all awake—
Again?—on tip-toe down the hill
He softly creeps—'Tis Goody Blake,
80   She's at the hedge of Harry Gill.

Right glad was he when he beheld her:
Stick after stick did Goody pull,
He stood behind a bush of elder,
Till she had filled her apron full.
85   When with her load she turned about,
The bye-road back again to take,
He started forward with a shout,
And sprang upon poor Goody Blake.

And fiercely by the arm he took her,
90   And by the arm he held her fast,
And fiercely by the arm he shook her,
And cried, "I've caught you then at last!"
Then Goody, who had nothing said,
Her bundle from her lap let fall;
95   And kneeling on the sticks, she pray'd
To God that is the judge of all.

She pray'd, her wither'd hand uprearing,
While Harry held her by the arm—
"God! who art never out of hearing,

100 O may he never more be warm!"
The cold, cold moon above her head,
Thus on her knees did Goody pray,
Young Harry heard what she had said,
And icy-cold he turned away.

105 He went complaining all the morrow
That he was cold and very chill:
His face was gloom, his heart was sorrow,
Alas! that day for Harry Gill!
That day he wore a riding-coat,
110 But not a whit the warmer he:
Another was on Thursday brought,
And ere the Sabbath he had three.

'Twas all in vain, a useless matter,
And blankets were about him pinn'd;
115 Yet still his jaws and teeth they clatter,
Like a loose casement in the wind.
And Harry's flesh it fell away;
And all who see him say 'tis plain,
That, live as long as live he may,
120 He never will be warm again.

evocative of the English countryside, where Wordsworth lived

No word to any man he utters,
A-bed or up, to young or old;
But ever to himself he mutters,
"Poor Harry Gill is very cold."
125 A-bed or up, by night or day;
His teeth they chatter, chatter still.
Now think, ye farmers all, I pray,
Of Goody Blake and Harry Gill.[2]

story that ends w/a strong moral

Mar. 1798   1798

Simon Lee[1]

The Old Huntsman

WITH AN INCIDENT IN WHICH HE WAS CONCERNED

In the sweet shire of Cardigan,[2]
Not far from pleasant Ivor-hall,

2. In the version of a Preface Wordsworth wrote for *Lyrical Ballads* in 1800 he remarked that through this tale he aimed "to draw attention to the truth that the power of the human imagination is sufficient to produce such changes even in our physical nature as might almost appear miraculous. The truth is an important one; the fact (for it is a *fact*) is a valuable illustration of it." Wordsworth found this fact when reading the latest speculations in psychological science. The poem reworks a case study in Erasmus Darwin's *Zoonomia; or, The Laws of Organic Life* (1796).

1. This old man had been huntsman to the Squires of Alfoxden. . . . I have, after an interval of 45 years, the image of the old man as fresh before my eyes as if I had seen him yesterday. The expression when the hounds were out, "I dearly love their voices," was word for word from his own lips [Wordsworth's note, 1843]. Wordsworth and Dorothy had lived at Alfoxden House, Somersetshire, in 1797–98.
2. Wordsworth relocates the incident from Somersetshire to Cardiganshire in Wales.

An old man dwells, a little man,—
'Tis said he once was tall.
5   Full five-and-thirty years he lived
A running huntsman[3] merry;
And still the centre of his cheek
Is red as a ripe cherry.

No man like him the horn could sound,
10   And hill and valley rang with glee
When Echo bandied, round and round,
The halloo of Simon Lee.
In those proud days, he little cared
For husbandry or tillage;
15   To blither tasks did Simon rouse
The sleepers of the village.

He all the country could outrun,
Could leave both man and horse behind;
And often, ere the chase was done,
20   He reeled, and was stone-blind.°   *totally blind*
And still there's something in the world
At which his heart rejoices;
For when the chiming hounds are out,
He dearly loves their voices!

25   But, oh the heavy change![4]—bereft
Of health, strength, friends, and kindred, see!
Old Simon to the world is left
In liveried[5] poverty.
His Master's dead,—and no one now
30   Dwells in the Hall of Ivor;
Men, dogs, and horses, all are dead;
He is the sole survivor.

And he is lean and he is sick;
His body, dwindled and awry,
35   Rests upon ankles swoln and thick;
His legs are thin and dry.
One prop he has, and only one,
His wife, an aged woman,
Lives with him, near the waterfall,
40   Upon the village Common.

Beside their moss-grown hut of clay,
Not twenty paces from the door,
A scrap of land they have, but they
Are poorest of the poor.
45   This scrap of land he from the heath
Enclosed when he was stronger;
But what to them avails the land
Which he can till no longer?

---

3. Manager of the hunt and the person in charge
of the hounds.
4. Cf. Milton's "Lycidas," line 37: "But O the

heavy change, now thou art gone."
5. Livery was the uniform worn by the male servants of a household.

Oft, working by her Husband's side,
50 Ruth does what Simon cannot do;
For she, with scanty cause for pride,
Is stouter° of the two.   *stronger, sturdier*
And, though you with your utmost skill
From labour could not wean them,
55 'Tis very, very little—all
That they can do between them.

Few months of life has he in store
As he to you will tell,
For still, the more he works, the more
60 Do his weak ankles swell.
My gentle Reader, I perceive
How patiently you've waited,
And now I fear that you expect
Some tale will be related.

65 O Reader! had you in your mind
Such stores as silent thought can bring,
O gentle Reader! you would find
A tale in every thing.
What more I have to say is short,
70 And you must kindly take it:
It is no tale; but, should you think,
Perhaps a tale you'll make it.

One summer-day I chanced to see
This old Man doing all he could
75 To unearth the root of an old tree,
A stump of rotten wood.
The mattock tottered in his hand;
So vain was his endeavour,
That at the root of the old tree
80 He might have worked for ever.

"You're overtasked, good Simon Lee,
Give me your tool," to him I said;
And at the word right gladly he
Received my proffered aid.
85 I struck, and with a single blow
The tangled root I severed,
At which the poor old Man so long
And vainly had endeavoured.

a simple act might mean more to someone diff.

The tears into his eyes were brought,
90 And thanks and praises seemed to run
So fast out of his heart, I thought
They never would have done.
—I've heard of hearts unkind, kind deeds
With coldness still returning;
95 Alas! the gratitude of men
Hath oftener left me mourning.

most men aren't often grateful when ppl helped them

1798   1798, 1845

We Are Seven[1]

————A simple Child,
That lightly draws its breath,
And feels its life in every limb,
What should it know of death?

5   I met a little cottage Girl:
She was eight years old, she said;
Her hair was thick with many a curl
That clustered round her head.

She had a rustic, woodland air,
10   And she was wildly clad:
Her eyes were fair, and very fair;
—Her beauty made me glad.

"Sisters and brothers, little Maid,
How many may you be?"
15   "How many? Seven in all," she said,
And wondering looked at me.

"And where are they? I pray you tell."
She answered, "Seven are we;
And two of us at Conway[2] dwell,
20   And two are gone to sea.

"Two of us in the church-yard lie,
My sister and my brother;
And, in the church-yard cottage, I
Dwell near them with my mother."

25   "You say that two at Conway dwell,
And two are gone to sea,
Yet ye are seven! I pray you tell,
Sweet Maid, how this may be."

Then did the little Maid reply,
30   "Seven boys and girls are we;
Two of us in the church-yard lie,
Beneath the church-yard tree."

"You run about, my little Maid,
Your limbs they are alive;
35   If two are in the church-yard laid,
Then ye are only five."

"Their graves are green, they may be seen,"
The little Maid replied,

---

1. Written at Alfoxden in the spring of 1798. . . .
The little girl who is the heroine I met within the
area of Goodrich Castle [in the Wye Valley north
of Tintern Abbey] in the year 1793 [Wordsworth's
note, 1843]. Wordsworth also tells us that, "while
walking to and fro," he composed the last stanza
first, beginning with the last line, and that
Coleridge contributed the first stanza.
2. A seaport town in north Wales.

"Twelve steps or more from my mother's door,
40 And they are side by side.

"My stockings there I often knit,
My kerchief there I hem;
And there upon the ground I sit,
And sing a song to them.

45 "And often after sun-set, Sir,
When it is light and fair,
I take my little porringer,[3]
And eat my supper there.

"The first that died was sister Jane;
50 In bed she moaning lay,
Till God released her of her pain;
And then she went away.

"So in the church-yard she was laid;
And, when the grass was dry,
55 Together round her grave we played,
My brother John and I.

"And when the ground was white with snow,
And I could run and slide,
My brother John was forced to go,
60 And he lies by her side."

"How many are you, then," said I,
"If they two are in heaven?"
Quick was the little Maid's reply,
"O Master! we are seven."

65 "But they are dead; those two are dead!
Their spirits are in heaven!"
'Twas throwing words away; for still
The little Maid would have her will,
And said, "Nay, we are seven!"

1798   1798, 1815

Lines Written in Early Spring

I heard a thousand blended notes,
While in a grove I sate reclined,
In that sweet mood when pleasant thoughts
Bring sad thoughts to the mind.

5 To her fair works did Nature link
The human soul that through me ran;

_____
3. Bowl for porridge.

And much it grieved my heart to think
What man has made of man.

Through primrose tufts, in that green bower,
10   The periwinkle[1] trailed its wreaths,
And 'tis my faith that every flower
Enjoys the air it breathes.

The birds around me hopped and played,
Their thoughts I cannot measure:—
15   But the least motion which they made,
It seemed a thrill of pleasure.

The budding twigs spread out their fan,
To catch the breezy air;
And I must think, do all I can,
20   That there was pleasure there.

If this belief from heaven be sent,
If such be Nature's holy plan,[2]
Have I not reason to lament
What man has made of man?

the word is so beautiful, yet humans distort that, do evil things, etc.

1798

1798, 1837

The Thorn[1]

I

"There is a Thorn[2]—it looks so old,
In truth, you'd find it hard to say
How it could ever have been young,

1. A trailing evergreen plant with small blue flowers (U.S. myrtle).
2. The version of these two lines in the *Lyrical Ballads* of 1798 reads: "If I these thoughts may not prevent, / If such be of my creed the plan."
1. Arose out of my observing, on the ridge of Quantock Hill [in Somersetshire], on a stormy day, a thorn which I had often past, in calm and bright weather, without noticing it. I said to myself, "Cannot I by some invention do as much to make this Thorn permanently an impressive object as the storm has made it to my eyes at this moment?" I began the poem accordingly, and composed it with great rapidity [Wordsworth's note, 1843]. In the prefatory Advertisement to the 1798 *Lyrical Ballads* Wordsworth wrote, "The poem of the Thorn . . . is not supposed to be spoken in the author's own person: the character of the loquacious narrator will sufficiently shew itself in the course of the story." In the editions of 1800–05 he elaborated in a separate note that reads, in part: "The character which I have here introduced speaking is sufficiently common. The Reader will perhaps have a general notion of it, if he has ever known a man, a Captain of a small trading vessel, for example, who, being past the middle age of life, had retired upon an annuity or small independent income to some village or country town of which he was not a native. . . . Such men, having little to do, become credulous and talkative from indolence; and from the same cause . . . they are prone to superstition. On which account it appeared to me proper to select a character like this to exhibit some of the general laws by which superstition acts upon the mind. Superstitious men are almost always men of slow faculties and deep feelings: their minds are not loose but adhesive; they have a reasonable share of imagination, by which word I mean the faculty which produces impressive effects out of simple elements. . . . It was my wish in this poem to show the manner in which such men cleave to the same ideas; and to follow the turns of passion . . . by which their conversation is swayed. . . . There is a numerous class of readers who imagine that the same words cannot be repeated without tautology: this is a great error. . . . Words, a Poet's words more particularly, ought to be weighed in the balance of feeling and not measured by the space they occupy upon paper."
2. Hawthorn, a thorny shrub or small tree.

It looks so old and grey.
5 Not higher than a two years' child
It stands erect, this aged Thorn;
No leaves it has, no prickly points;
It is a mass of knotted joints,
A wretched thing forlorn.
10 It stands erect, and like a stone
With lichens is it overgrown.

2

"Like rock or stone, it is o'ergrown,
With lichens to the very top,
And hung with heavy tufts of moss,
15 A melancholy crop:
Up from the earth these mosses creep,
And this poor Thorn they clasp it round
So close, you'd say that they are bent
With plain and manifest intent
20 To drag it to the ground;
And all have joined in one endeavour
To bury this poor Thorn for ever.

3

"High on a mountain's highest ridge,
Where oft the stormy winter gale
25 Cuts like a scythe, while through the clouds
It sweeps from vale to vale;
Not five yards from the mountain path,
This Thorn you on your left espy;
And to the left, three yards beyond,
30 You see a little muddy pond
Of water—never dry
Though but of compass small, and bare
To thirsty suns and parching air.

4

"And, close beside this aged Thorn,
35 There is a fresh and lovely sight,
A beauteous heap, a hill of moss,
Just half a foot in height.
All lovely colours there you see,
All colours that were ever seen;
40 And mossy network too is there,
As if by hand of lady fair
The work had woven been;
And cups,° the darlings of the eye,   *blossoms*
So deep is their vermilion dye.

5

45 "Ah me! what lovely tints are there
Of olive green and scarlet bright,

In spikes, in branches, and in stars,
Green, red, and pearly white!
This heap of earth o'ergrown with moss,
50   Which close beside the Thorn you see,
So fresh in all its beauteous dyes,
Is like an infant's grave in size,
As like as like can be:
But never, never any where,
55   An infant's grave was half so fair.

6

"Now would you see this aged Thorn,
This pond, and beauteous hill of moss,
You must take care and choose your time
The mountain when to cross.
60   For oft there sits between the heap
So like an infant's grave in size,
And that same pond of which I spoke,
A Woman in a scarlet cloak,
And to herself she cries,
65   'Oh misery! oh misery!
Oh woe is me! oh misery!'

7

"At all times of the day and night
This wretched Woman thither goes;
And she is known to every star,
70   And every wind that blows;
And there, beside the Thorn, she sits
When the blue daylight's in the skies,
And when the whirlwind's on the hill,
Or frosty air is keen and still,
75   And to herself she cries,
'Oh misery! oh misery!
Oh woe is me! oh misery!'"

8

"Now wherefore, thus, by day and night,
In rain, in tempest, and in snow,
80   Thus to the dreary mountain-top
Does this poor Woman go?
And why sits she beside the Thorn
When the blue daylight's in the sky
Or when the whirlwind's on the hill,
85   Or frosty air is keen and still,
And wherefore does she cry?—
O wherefore? wherefore? tell me why
Does she repeat that doleful cry?"

9

"I cannot tell; I wish I could;
90   For the true reason no one knows:

But would you gladly view the spot,
The spot to which she goes;
The hillock like an infant's grave,
The pond—and Thorn, so old and grey;
95 Pass by her door—'tis seldom shut—
And, if you see her in her hut—
Then to the spot away!
I never heard of such as dare
Approach the spot when she is there."

10

100 "But wherefore to the mountain-top
Can this unhappy Woman go,
Whatever star is in the skies,
Whatever wind may blow?"
"Full twenty years are past and gone
105 Since she (her name is Martha Ray)[3]
Gave with a maiden's true good-will
Her company to Stephen Hill;
And she was blithe and gay,
While friends and kindred all approved
110 Of him whom tenderly she loved.

11

"And they had fixed the wedding day,
The morning that must wed them both;
But Stephen to another Maid
Had sworn another oath;
115 And, with this other Maid, to church
Unthinking Stephen went—
Poor Martha! on that woeful day
A pang of pitiless dismay
Into her soul was sent;
120 A fire was kindled in her breast,
Which might not burn itself to rest.

12

"They say, full six months after this,
While yet the summer leaves were green,
She to the mountain-top would go,
125 And there was often seen.
What could she seek?—or wish to hide?
Her state to any eye was plain;
She was with child,° and she was mad;   *pregnant*
Yet often was she sober sad
130 From her exceeding pain.

---

3. Wordsworth gives the woman the name of the victim at the center of one of the 18th century's most famous murder trials. Martha Ray, mistress to a nobleman, was murdered in 1779 by a rejected suitor, a clergyman who claimed he had been driven to the deed by "love's madness." One of the illegitimate children whom this Martha Ray bore to the earl of Sandwich was Wordsworth's and Coleridge's friend Basil Montagu.

O guilty Father—would that death
Had saved him from that breach of faith!

13

"Sad case for such a brain to hold
Communion with a stirring child!
135   Sad case, as you may think, for one
Who had a brain so wild!
Last Christmas-eve we talked of this,
And grey-haired Wilfred of the glen
Held that the unborn infant wrought
140   About its mother's heart, and brought
Her senses back again:
And, when at last her time drew near,
Her looks were calm, her senses clear.

14

"More know I not, I wish I did,
145   And it should all be told to you;
For what became of this poor child
No mortal ever knew;
Nay—if a child to her was born
No earthly tongue could ever tell;
150   And if 'twas born alive or dead,
Far less could this with proof be said;
But some remember well,
That Martha Ray about this time
Would up the mountain often climb.

15

155   "And all that winter, when at night
The wind blew from the mountain-peak,
'Twas worth your while, though in the dark,
The churchyard path to seek:
For many a time and oft were heard
160   Cries coming from the mountain head:
Some plainly living voices were;
And others, I've heard many swear,
Were voices of the dead:
I cannot think, whate'er they say,
165   They had to do with Martha Ray.

16

"But that she goes to this old Thorn,
The Thorn which I described to you,
And there sits in a scarlet cloak,
I will be sworn is true.
170   For one day with my telescope,
To view the ocean wide and bright,
When to this country first I came,
Ere I had heard of Martha's name,

I climbed the mountain's height:—
175   A storm came on, and I could see
No object higher than my knee.

17

" 'Twas mist and rain, and storm and rain:
No screen, no fence could I discover;
And then the wind! in sooth, it was
180   A wind full ten times over.
I looked around, I thought I saw
A jutting crag,—and off I ran,
Head-foremost, through the driving rain,
The shelter of the crag to gain;
185   And, as I am a man,
Instead of jutting crag, I found
A Woman seated on the ground.

18

"I did not speak—I saw her face;
Her face!—it was enough for me;
190   I turned about and heard her cry,
'Oh misery! oh misery!'
And there she sits, until the moon
Through half the clear blue sky will go;
And, when the little breezes make
195   The waters of the pond to shake,
As all the country know,
She shudders, and you hear her cry,
'Oh misery! oh misery!' "

19

"But what's the Thorn? and what the pond?
200   And what the hill of moss to her?
And what the creeping breeze that comes
The little pond to stir?"
"I cannot tell; but some will say
She hanged her baby on the tree;
205   Some say she drowned it in the pond,
Which is a little step beyond:
But all and each agree,
The little Babe was buried there,
Beneath that hill of moss so fair.

20

210   "I've heard, the moss is spotted red
With drops of that poor infant's blood;
But kill a new-born infant thus,
I do not think she could!
Some say, if to the pond you go,
215   And fix on it a steady view,

The shadow of a babe you trace,
A baby and a baby's face,
And that it looks at you;
Whene'er you look on it, 'tis plain
220 The baby looks at you again.

21

"And some had sworn an oath that she
Should be to public justice brought;
And for the little infant's bones
With spades they would have sought.
225 But instantly the hill of moss
Before their eyes began to stir!
And, for full fifty yards around,
The grass—it shook upon the ground!
Yet all do still aver
230 The little Babe lies buried there,
Beneath that hill of moss so fair.

22

"I cannot tell how this may be,
But plain it is the Thorn is bound
With heavy tufts of moss that strive
235 To drag it to the ground;
And this I know, full many a time,
When she was on the mountain high,
By day, and in the silent night,
When all the stars shone clear and bright,
240 That I have heard her cry,
'Oh misery! oh misery!
Oh woe is me! oh misery!'"

Ma.–Apr. 1798   1798, 1845

Expostulation and Reply[1]

"Why, William, on that old grey stone,
Thus for the length of half a day,
Why, William, sit you thus alone,
And dream your time away?

5 "Where are your books?—that light bequeathed
To Beings else forlorn and blind!

---

1. This and the companion poem, "The Tables Turned," have often been attacked—and defended—as Wordsworth's own statement about the comparative merits of nature and of books. But they are a dialogue between two friends who rally one another by the usual device of overstating parts of a whole truth. In the 1798 Advertisement to Lyrical Ballads, Wordsworth said that the pieces originated in a conversation "with a friend who was somewhat unreasonably attached to modern books of moral philosophy." In 1843 he noted that the idea of learning when the mind is in a state of "wise passiveness" made this poem a favorite of the Quakers, who rejected religious ritual for informal and spontaneous worship.

Up! up! and drink the spirit breathed
From dead men to their kind.

"You look round on your Mother Earth,
10   As if she for no purpose bore you;
As if you were her first-born birth,
And none had lived before you!"

One morning thus, by Esthwaite lake,
When life was sweet, I knew not why,
15   To me my good friend Matthew spake,
And thus I made reply.

"The eye—it cannot choose but see;
We cannot bid the ear be still;
Our bodies feel, where'er they be,
20   Against or with our will.

"Nor less I deem that there are Powers
Which of themselves our minds impress;
That we can feed this mind of ours
In a wise passiveness.

25   "Think you, 'mid all this mighty sum
Of things for ever speaking,
That nothing of itself will come,
But we must still be seeking?

"—Then ask not wherefore, here, alone,
30   Conversing² as I may,
I sit upon this old grey stone,
And dream my time away."

Spring 1798   1798

author justifying his actions

The Tables Turned

An Evening Scene on the Same Subject

Up! up! my Friend, and quit your books;
Or surely you'll grow double:°   *double over*
Up! up! my Friend, and clear your looks;
Why all this toil and trouble?

5   The sun, above the mountain's head,
A freshening lustre mellow
Through all the long green fields has spread,
His first sweet evening yellow.

2. In the old sense of "communing" (with the "things for ever speaking").

Books! 'tis a dull and endless strife:
10 Come, hear the woodland linnet,°   *small finch*
How sweet his music! on my life,
There's more of wisdom in it.

And hark! how blithe the throstle° sings!   *song thrush*
He, too, is no mean preacher:
15 Come forth into the light of things,
Let Nature be your Teacher.

She has a world of ready wealth,
Our minds and hearts to bless—
Spontaneous wisdom breathed by health,
20 Truth breathed by cheerfulness.

One impulse from a vernal wood
May teach you more of man,
Of moral evil and of good,
Than all the sages can.

25 Sweet is the lore which Nature brings;
Our meddling intellect
Mis-shapes the beauteous forms of things:—
We murder to dissect.

Enough of Science and of Art;
30 Close up those barren leaves;°   *pages*
Come forth, and bring with you a heart
That watches and receives.

1798   1798, 1832

Old Man Travelling;

Animal Tranquillity and Decay, *a Sketch*

            The little hedge-row birds,
That peck along the road, regard him not.
He travels on, and in his face, his step,
His gait, is one expression; every limb,
5 His look and bending figure, all bespeak
A man who does not move with pain, but moves
With thought—He is insensibly subdued
To settled quiet: he is one by whom
All effort seems forgotten, one to whom
10 Long patience has such mild composure given,
That patience now doth seem a thing, of which
He hath no need. He is by nature led
To peace so perfect, that the young behold
With envy, what the old man hardly feels.
15 —I asked him whither he was bound, and what

The object of his journey; he replied
"Sir! I am going many miles to take
A last leave of my son, a mariner,
Who from a sea-fight has been brought to Falmouth,[1]

20   And there is dying in an hospital."[2]

1796–97

[handwritten note: old man feels little regarding the imminent death of his son?]

1798

Lines[1]

Composed a Few Miles above Tintern Abbey, on Revisiting the Banks of the Wye during a Tour, July 13, 1798

Five years have past; five summers, with the length
Of five long winters! and again I hear
These waters, rolling from their mountain-springs
With a soft inland murmur.[2]—Once again

5   Do I behold these steep and lofty cliffs,
That on a wild secluded scene impress
Thoughts of more deep seclusion; and connect
The landscape with the quiet of the sky.
The day is come when I again repose

10   Here, under this dark sycamore, and view
These plots of cottage-ground, these orchard-tufts,
Which at this season, with their unripe fruits,
Are clad in one green hue, and lose themselves
'Mid groves and copses. Once again I see

15   These hedge-rows, hardly hedge-rows, little lines
Of sportive wood run wild: these pastoral farms,
Green to the very door; and wreaths of smoke
Sent up, in silence, from among the trees!
With some uncertain notice, as might seem

20   Of vagrant dwellers in the houseless woods,
Or of some Hermit's cave, where by his fire
The Hermit sits alone.

[handwritten note: return to nature]

1. Port town in southwest England.
2. In his 1799 review of *Lyrical Ballads* Charles Burney objected to the antiwar sentiment he detected in this conclusion; see "'Self-constituted Judge of Poesy': Reviewer versus Poet in the Romantic Period" in the NAEL Archive. In the 1800 *Lyrical Ballads* Wordsworth cast lines 17–20 as reported rather than direct speech. Starting in 1815, reprints of the poem omitted the final five lines altogether.
1. No poem of mine was composed under circumstances more pleasant for me to remember than this. I began it upon leaving Tintern, after crossing the Wye, and concluded it just as I was entering Bristol in the evening, after a ramble of 4 or 5 days, with my sister. Not a line of it was altered, and not any part of it written down till I reached Bristol [Wordsworth's note, 1843]. The poem was printed as the last item in *Lyrical Ballads*.

Wordsworth had first visited the Wye valley and the ruins of Tintern Abbey, in Monmouthshire, while on a solitary walking tour in August 1793, when he was twenty-three years old. (See "Tintern Abbey, Tourism, and Romantic Landscape" in the NAEL Archive.) The puzzling difference between the present landscape and the remembered "picture of the mind" (line 61) gives rise to an intricately organized meditation, in which the poet reviews his past, evaluates the present, and (through his sister as intermediary) anticipates the future; he ends by rounding back quietly on the scene that had been his point of departure.
2. The river is not affected by the tides a few miles above Tintern [Wordsworth's note, 1798ff.]. Until 1845 the text had "sweet" for "soft," meaning fresh, not salty.

These beauteous forms,
Through a long absence, have not been to me
As is a landscape to a blind man's eye:
25　But oft, in lonely rooms, and 'mid the din
Of towns and cities, I have owed to them
In hours of weariness, sensations sweet,
Felt in the blood, and felt along the heart;
And passing even into my purer mind,
30　With tranquil restoration:—feelings too
Of unremembered pleasure: such, perhaps,
As have no slight or trivial influence
On that best portion of a good man's life,
His little, nameless, unremembered, acts
35　Of kindness and of love. Nor less, I trust,
To them I may have owed another gift,
Of aspect more sublime; that blessed mood,
In which the burthen° of the mystery,　　　　　　　　　　*burden*
In which the heavy and the weary weight
40　Of all this unintelligible world,
Is lightened:—that serene and blessed mood,
In which the affections gently lead us on,—
Until, the breath of this corporeal frame
And even the motion of our human blood
45　Almost suspended, we are laid asleep
In body, and become a living soul:
While with an eye made quiet by the power
Of harmony, and the deep power of joy,
We see into the life of things.

　　　　　　　　If this
50　Be but a vain belief, yet, oh! how oft—
In darkness and amid the many shapes
Of joyless daylight; when the fretful stir
Unprofitable, and the fever of the world,
Have hung upon the beatings of my heart—
55　How oft, in spirit, have I turned to thee,
O sylvan Wye! thou wanderer thro' the woods,
How often has my spirit turned to thee!

　　　And now, with gleams of half-extinguished thought,
With many recognitions dim and faint,
60　And somewhat of a sad perplexity,
The picture of the mind revives again:
While here I stand, not only with the sense
Of present pleasure, but with pleasing thoughts
That in this moment there is life and food
65　For future years. And so I dare to hope,
Though changed, no doubt, from what I was when first
I came among these hills; when like a roe°　　　　　　　*deer*
I bounded o'er the mountains, by the sides
Of the deep rivers, and the lonely streams,
70　Wherever nature led: more like a man
Flying from something that he dreads, than one

Who sought the thing he loved. For nature then
(The coarser pleasures of my boyish days,
And their glad animal movements all gone by)
75   To me was all in all.—I cannot paint
What then I was. The sounding cataract
Haunted me like a passion: the tall rock,
The mountain, and the deep and gloomy wood,
Their colours and their forms, were then to me
80   An appetite; a feeling and a love,
That had no need of a remoter charm,
By thought supplied, nor any interest
Unborrowed from the eye.—That time is past,
And all its aching joys are now no more,
85   And all its dizzy raptures.[3] Not for this
Faint° I, nor mourn nor murmur; other gifts   *lose heart*
Have followed; for such loss, I would believe,
Abundant recompense. For I have learned
To look on nature, not as in the hour
90   Of thoughtless youth; but hearing oftentimes
The still, sad music of humanity,
Nor harsh nor grating, though of ample power
To chasten and subdue. And I have felt
A presence that disturbs me with the joy
95   Of elevated thoughts; a sense sublime
Of something far more deeply interfused,
Whose dwelling is the light of setting suns,
And the round ocean and the living air,
And the blue sky, and in the mind of man:
100   A motion and a spirit, that impels
All thinking things, all objects of all thought,
And rolls through all things. Therefore am I still
A lover of the meadows and the woods,
And mountains; and of all that we behold
105   From this green earth; of all the mighty world
Of eye, and ear,—both what they half create,[4]
And what perceive; well pleased to recognise
In nature and the language of the sense,
The anchor of my purest thoughts, the nurse,
110   The guide, the guardian of my heart, and soul
Of all my moral being.

                    Nor perchance,
If I were not thus taught, should I the more
Suffer my genial spirits[5] to decay:
For thou art with me here upon the banks

---

3. Lines 66ff. contain Wordsworth's famed description of the three stages of his growing up, defined in terms of his evolving relations to the natural scene: the young boy's purely physical responsiveness (lines 73–74); the postadolescent's aching, dizzy, and equivocal passions—a love that is more like dread (lines 67–72, 75–85: this was his state of mind on the occasion of his first visit); his present state (lines 85ff.), in which for the first time he adds thought to sense.
4. This line has a close resemblance to an admirable line of Young, the exact expression of which I cannot recollect [Wordsworth's note, 1798ff.]. Edward Young in *Night Thoughts* (1744) says that the human senses "half create the wondrous world they see."
5. Creative powers. ("Genial" is here the adjectival form of the noun *genius*.)

115 Of this fair river; thou my dearest Friend,[6]
     My dear, dear Friend; and in thy voice I catch
     The language of my former heart, and read
     My former pleasures in the shooting lights
     Of thy wild eyes. Oh! yet a little while
120 May I behold in thee what I was once,
     My dear, dear Sister! and this prayer I make,
     Knowing that Nature never did betray
     The heart that loved her; 'tis her privilege,
     Through all the years of this our life, to lead
125 From joy to joy: for she can so inform
     The mind that is within us, so impress
     With quietness and beauty, and so feed
     With lofty thoughts, that neither evil tongues,[7]
     Rash judgments, nor the sneers of selfish men,
130 Nor greetings where no kindness is, nor all
     The dreary intercourse of daily life,
     Shall e'er prevail against us, or disturb
     Our cheerful faith, that all which we behold
     Is full of blessings. Therefore let the moon
135 Shine on thee in thy solitary walk;
     And let the misty mountain-winds be free
     To blow against thee: and, in after years,
     When these wild ecstasies shall be matured
     Into a sober pleasure; when thy mind
140 Shall be a mansion for all lovely forms,
     Thy memory be as a dwelling-place
     For all sweet sounds and harmonies; oh! then,
     If solitude, or fear, or pain, or grief,
     Should be thy portion,° with what healing thoughts   *inheritance, dowry*
145 Of tender joy wilt thou remember me,
     And these my exhortations! Nor, perchance—
     If I should be where I no more can hear
     Thy voice, nor catch from thy wild eyes these gleams
     Of past existence[8]—wilt thou then forget
150 That on the banks of this delightful stream
     We stood together; and that I, so long
     A worshipper of Nature, hither came
     Unwearied in that service; rather say
     With warmer love—oh! with far deeper zeal
155 Of holier love. Nor wilt thou then forget,
     That after many wanderings, many years
     Of absence, these steep woods and lofty cliffs,
     And this green pastoral landscape, were to me
     More dear, both for themselves and for thy sake!

July 1798   1798, 1815

---

6. His sister, Dorothy.
7. In the opening of *Paradise Lost* 7, Milton describes himself as fallen on "evil days" and "evil tongues" and with "dangers compassed round" (lines 26–27).
8. I.e., reminders of his own "past existence" five years earlier (see lines 116–19).

Preface to *Lyrical Ballads* (1802)   To the first edition of *Lyrical Ballads*, published jointly with Coleridge in 1798, Wordsworth prefixed an "Advertisement" asserting that the majority of the poems were "to be considered as experiments" to determine "how far the language of conversation in the middle and lower classes of society is adapted to the purposes of poetic pleasure." In the second, two-volume edition of 1800, Wordsworth, aided by frequent conversations with Coleridge, expanded the Advertisement into a preface that justified the poems not as experiments, but as exemplifying the principles of all good poetry. The Preface was enlarged for the third edition of *Lyrical Ballads*, published two years later. This last version of 1802 is reprinted here.

Although some of its ideas had antecedents in the later eighteenth century, the Preface as a whole deserves its reputation as a revolutionary manifesto about the nature of poetry. Like many radical statements, however, it claims to go back to the implicit principles that governed the great poetry of the past but have been perverted in recent practice. Most discussions of the Preface, following the lead of Coleridge in chapters 14 and 17 of his *Biographia Literaria*, have focused on Wordsworth's assertions about the valid language of poetry, on which he bases his attack on the "poetic diction" of eighteenth-century poets. As Coleridge pointed out, Wordsworth's argument about this issue is far from clear. However, Wordsworth's questioning of the underlying premises of neoclassical poetry went even further. His Preface implicitly denies the traditional assumption that the poetic genres constitute a hierarchy, from epic and tragedy at the top down through comedy, satire, pastoral, to the short lyric at the lowest reaches of the poetic scale; he also rejects the traditional principle of "decorum," which required the poet to arrange matters so that the poem's subject (especially the social class of its protagonists) and its level of diction conformed to the status of the literary kind on the poetic scale.

When Wordsworth asserted in the Preface that he deliberately chose to represent "incidents and situations from common life," he translated his democratic sympathies into critical terms, justifying his use of peasants, children, outcasts, criminals, and madwomen as serious subjects of poetic and even tragic concern. He also undertook to write in "a selection of language really used by men," on the grounds that there can be no "essential difference between the language of prose and metrical composition." In making this claim Wordsworth attacked the neoclassical principle that required the language, in many kinds of poems, to be elevated over everyday speech by a special, more refined and dignified diction and by artful figures of speech. Wordsworth's views about the valid language of poetry are based on the new premise that "all good poetry is the spontaneous overflow of powerful feelings"— spontaneous, that is, at the moment of composition, even though the process is influenced by prior thought and acquired poetic skill.

Wordsworth's assertions about the materials and diction of poetry have been greatly influential in expanding the range of serious literature to include the common people and ordinary things and events, as well as in justifying a poetry of sincerity rather than of artifice, expressed in the ordinary language of its time. But in the long view other aspects of his Preface have been no less significant in establishing its importance, not only as a turning point in English criticism but also as a central document in modern culture. Wordsworth feared that a new urban, industrial society's mass media and mass culture (glimpsed in the Preface when he refers derisively to contemporary Gothic novels and German melodramas) were threatening to blunt the human mind's "discriminatory powers" and to "reduce it to a state of almost savage torpor." He attributed to imaginative literature the primary role in keeping the human beings who live in such societies emotionally alive and morally sensitive. Literature, that is, could keep humans essentially human.

From Preface to *Lyrical Ballads, with Pastoral and Other Poems* (1802)

[THE SUBJECT AND LANGUAGE OF POETRY]

The first volume of these poems has already been submitted to general perusal. It was published, as an experiment, which, I hoped, might be of some use to ascertain, how far, by fitting to metrical arrangement a selection of the real language of men in a state of vivid sensation, that sort of pleasure and that quantity of pleasure may be imparted, which a poet may rationally endeavour to impart.

I had formed no very inaccurate estimate of the probable effect of those poems: I flattered myself that they who should be pleased with them would read them with more than common pleasure: and, on the other hand, I was well aware, that by those who should dislike them they would be read with more than common dislike. The result has differed from my expectation in this only, that I have pleased a greater number than I ventured to hope I should please.

For the sake of variety, and from a consciousness of my own weakness, I was induced to request the assistance of a friend, who furnished me with the poems of the *Ancient Mariner*, the *Foster-Mother's Tale*, the *Nightingale*, and the poem entitled *Love*. I should not, however, have requested this assistance, had I not believed that the poems of my friend[1] would in a great measure have the same tendency as my own, and that, though there would be found a difference, there would be found no discordance in the colours of our style; as our opinions on the subject of poetry do almost entirely coincide.

Several of my friends are anxious for the success of these poems from a belief, that, if the views with which they were composed were indeed realized, a class of poetry would be produced, well adapted to interest mankind permanently, and not unimportant in the multiplicity, and in the quality of its moral relations: and on this account they have advised me to prefix a systematic defence of the theory upon which the poems were written. But I was unwilling to undertake the task, because I knew that on this occasion the reader would look coldly upon my arguments, since I might be suspected of having been principally influenced by the selfish and foolish hope of *reasoning* him into an approbation of these particular poems: and I was still more unwilling to undertake the task, because, adequately to display my opinions, and fully to enforce my arguments, would require a space wholly disproportionate to the nature of a preface. For to treat the subject with the clearness and coherence of which I believe it susceptible, it would be necessary to give a full account of the present state of the public taste in this country, and to determine how far this taste is healthy or depraved; which, again, could not be determined, without pointing out, in what manner language and the human mind act and re-act on each other, and without retracing the revolutions, not of literature alone, but likewise of society itself. I have therefore altogether declined to enter regularly upon this defence; yet I am sensible, that there would be some impropriety in abruptly obtruding upon the public, without a few words of introduc-

---

1. The "friend" of course is Coleridge.

tion, poems so materially different from those upon which general approbation is at present bestowed.

It is supposed, that by the act of writing in verse an author makes a formal engagement that he will gratify certain known habits of association; that he not only thus apprizes the reader that certain classes of ideas and expressions will be found in his book, but that others will be carefully excluded. This exponent or symbol held forth by metrical language must in different eras of literature have excited very different expectations: for example, in the age of Catullus, Terence, and Lucretius and that of Statius or Claudian,[2] and in our own country, in the age of Shakespeare and Beaumont and Fletcher, and that of Donne and Cowley, or Dryden, or Pope. I will not take upon me to determine the exact import of the promise which by the act of writing in verse an author, in the present day, makes to his reader; but I am certain, it will appear to many persons that I have not fulfilled the terms of an engagement thus voluntarily contracted. They who have been accustomed to the gaudiness and inane phraseology of many modern writers, if they persist in reading this book to its conclusion, will, no doubt, frequently have to struggle with feelings of strangeness and awkwardness: they will look round for poetry, and will be induced to inquire by what species of courtesy these attempts can be permitted to assume that title. I hope therefore the reader will not censure me, if I attempt to state what I have proposed to myself to perform; and also (as far as the limits of a preface will permit) to explain some of the chief reasons which have determined me in the choice of my purpose: that at least he may be spared any unpleasant feeling of disappointment, and that I myself may be protected from the most dishonorable accusation which can be brought against an author, namely, that of an indolence which prevents him from endeavouring to ascertain what is his duty, or, when this duty is ascertained, prevents him from performing it.

The principal object, then, which I proposed to myself in these poems was to choose incidents and situations from common life, and to relate or describe them, throughout, as far as was possible, in a selection of language really used by men; and, at the same time, to throw over them a certain colouring of imagination, whereby ordinary things should be presented to the mind in an unusual way; and, further, and above all, to make these incidents and situations interesting by tracing in them, truly though not ostentatiously, the primary laws of our nature: chiefly, as far as regards the manner in which we associate ideas in a state of excitement. Low and rustic life was generally chosen, because in that condition, the essential passions of the heart find a better soil in which they can attain their maturity, are less under restraint, and speak a plainer and more emphatic language; because in that condition of life our elementary feelings co-exist in a state of greater simplicity, and, consequently, may be more accurately contemplated, and more forcibly communicated; because the manners of rural life germinate from those elementary feelings; and, from the necessary character of rural occupations, are more easily comprehended; and are more durable; and lastly, because in that condition the passions of men are incorporated with the beautiful and permanent forms of nature. The language, too, of these men

---

2. Wordsworth's implied contrast is between the naturalness and simplicity of the first three Roman poets (who wrote in the last two centuries B.C.E.) and the elaborate artifice of the last two Roman poets (Statius wrote in the 1st and Claudian in the 4th century C.E.).

is adopted (purified indeed from what appear to be its real defects, from all lasting and rational causes of dislike or disgust) because such men hourly communicate with the best objects from which the best part of language is originally derived; and because, from their rank in society and the sameness and narrow circle of their intercourse, being less under the influence of social vanity they convey their feelings and notions in simple and unelaborated expressions. Accordingly, such a language, arising out of repeated experience and regular feelings, is a more permanent, and a far more philosophical language, than that which is frequently substituted for it by poets, who think that they are conferring honour upon themselves and their art, in proportion as they separate themselves from the sympathies of men, and indulge in arbitrary and capricious habits of expression, in order to furnish food for fickle tastes, and fickle appetites, of their own creation.[3]

I cannot, however, be insensible of the present outcry against the triviality and meanness both of thought and language, which some of my contemporaries have occasionally introduced into their metrical compositions; and I acknowledge, that this defect, where it exists, is more dishonorable to the writer's own character than false refinement or arbitrary innovation, though I should contend at the same time that it is far less pernicious in the sum of its consequences. From such verses the poems in these volumes will be found distinguished at least by one mark of difference, that each of them has a worthy *purpose*. Not that I mean to say, that I always began to write with a distinct purpose formally conceived; but I believe that my habits of meditation have so formed my feelings, as that my descriptions of such objects as strongly excite those feelings, will be found to carry along with them a *purpose*. If in this opinion I am mistaken, I can have little right to the name of a poet. For all good poetry is the spontaneous overflow of powerful feelings: but though this be true, poems to which any value can be attached, were never produced on any variety of subjects but by a man who, being possessed of more than usual organic sensibility, had also thought long and deeply. For our continued influxes of feeling are modified and directed by our thoughts, which are indeed the representatives of all our past feelings; and, as by contemplating the relation of these general representatives to each other we discover what is really important to men, so, by the repetition and continuance of this act, our feelings will be connected with important subjects, till at length, if we be originally possessed of much sensibility, such habits of mind will be produced, that, by obeying blindly and mechanically the impulses of those habits, we shall describe objects, and utter sentiments, of such a nature and in such connection with each other, that the understanding of the being to whom we address ourselves, if he be in a healthful state of association, must necessarily be in some degree enlightened, and his affections ameliorated.

I have said that each of these poems has a purpose. I have also informed my reader what this purpose will be found principally to be: namely, to illustrate the manner in which our feelings and ideas are associated in a state of excitement. But, speaking in language somewhat more appropriate, it is to follow the fluxes and refluxes of the mind when agitated by the great and simple affections of our nature. This object I have endeavored in these short

---

3. It is worthwhile here to observe that the affecting parts of Chaucer are almost always expressed in language pure and universally intelligible even to this day [Wordsworth's note].

essays to attain by various means; by tracing the maternal passion through many of its more subtile[4] windings, as in the poems of the *Idiot Boy* and the *Mad Mother*; by accompanying the last struggles of a human being, at the approach of death, cleaving in solitude to life and society, as in the poem of the *Forsaken Indian*; by shewing, as in the stanzas entitled *We Are Seven*, the perplexity and obscurity which in childhood attend our notion of death, or rather our utter inability to admit that notion; or by displaying the strength of fraternal, or to speak more philosophically, of moral attachment when early associated with the great and beautiful objects of nature, as in *The Brothers*; or, as in the Incident of *Simon Lee*, by placing my reader in the way of receiving from ordinary moral sensations another and more salutary impression than we are accustomed to receive from them. It has also been part of my general purpose to attempt to sketch characters under the influence of less impassioned feelings, as in the *Two April Mornings, The Fountain, The Old Man Travelling, The Two Thieves*, &c., characters of which the elements are simple, belonging rather to nature than to manners,[5] such as exist now, and will probably always exist, and which from their constitution may be distinctly and profitably contemplated. I will not abuse the indulgence of my reader by dwelling longer upon this subject; but it is proper that I should mention one other circumstance which distinguishes these poems from the popular poetry of the day; it is this, that the feeling therein developed gives importance to the action and situation, and not the action and situation to the feeling. My meaning will be rendered perfectly intelligible by referring my reader to the poems entitled *Poor Susan* and the *Childless Father*, particularly to the last stanza of the latter poem.

I will not suffer a sense of false modesty to prevent me from asserting, that I point my reader's attention to this mark of distinction, far less for the sake of these particular poems than from the general importance of the subject. The subject is indeed important! For the human mind is capable of being excited without the application of gross[6] and violent stimulants; and he must have a very faint perception of its beauty and dignity who does not know this, and who does not further know, that one being is elevated above another, in proportion as he possesses this capability. It has therefore appeared to me, that to endeavour to produce or enlarge this capability is one of the best services in which, at any period, a writer can be engaged; but this service, excellent at all times, is especially so at the present day. For a multitude of causes, unknown to former times, are now acting with a combined force to blunt the discriminating powers of the mind, and, unfitting it for all voluntary exertion, to reduce it to a state of almost savage torpor. The most effective of these causes are the great national events which are daily taking place, and the increasing accumulation of men in cities, where the uniformity of their occupations produces a craving for extraordinary incident, which the rapid communication of intelligence hourly gratifies.[7] To this tendency of life and manners the literature and theatrical exhibitions of the country have conformed themselves. The invaluable works of our elder writers, I had almost said the works of Shakespeare and Milton, are driven into neglect by frantic novels, sickly and stu-

---

4. Subtle.
5. Social custom.
6. Coarse.

7. This was the period of the wars against France, of industrial urbanization, and of the rapid proliferation in England of daily newspapers.

pid German tragedies,[8] and deluges of idle and extravagant stories in verse.—When I think upon this degrading thirst after outrageous stimulation, I am almost ashamed to have spoken of the feeble effort with which I have endeavoured to counteract it; and, reflecting upon the magnitude of the general evil, I should be oppressed with no dishonorable melancholy, had I not a deep impression of certain inherent and indestructible qualities of the human mind, and likewise of certain powers in the great and permanent objects that act upon it which are equally inherent and indestructible; and did I not further add to this impression a belief, that the time is approaching when the evil will be systematically opposed, by men of greater powers, and with far more distinguished success.

Having dwelt thus long on the subjects and aim of these poems, I shall request the reader's permission to apprize him of a few circumstances relating to their *style*, in order, among other reasons, that I may not be censured for not having performed what I never attempted. The reader will find that personifications of abstract ideas[9] rarely occur in these volumes; and, I hope, are utterly rejected as an ordinary device to elevate the style, and raise it above prose. I have proposed to myself to imitate, and, as far as is possible, to adopt the very language of men; and assuredly such personifications do not make any natural or regular part of that language. They are, indeed, a figure of speech occasionally prompted by passion, and I have made use of them as such; but I have endeavoured utterly to reject them as a mechanical device of style, or as a family language which writers in metre seem to lay claim to by prescription. I have wished to keep my reader in the company of flesh and blood, persuaded that by so doing I shall interest him. I am, however, well aware that others who pursue a different track may interest him likewise; I do not interfere with their claim, I only wish to prefer a different claim of my own. There will also be found in these volumes little of what is usually called poetic diction;[1] I have taken as much pains to avoid it as others ordinarily take to produce it; this I have done for the reason already alleged, to bring my language near to the language of men, and further, because the pleasure which I have proposed to myself to impart is of a kind very different from that which is supposed by many persons to be the proper object of poetry. I do not know how, without being culpably particular, I can give my reader a more exact notion of the style in which I wished these poems to be written than by informing him that I have at all times endeavoured to look steadily at my subject, consequently, I hope that there is in these poems little falsehood of description, and that my ideas are expressed in language fitted to their respective importance. Something I must have gained by this practice, as it is friendly to one property of all good poetry, namely, good sense; but it has necessarily cut me off from a large portion of phrases and figures of speech which from father to son have long been regarded as the common inheritance of poets. I have also thought it expedient to restrict myself still further, having abstained from the use of many expressions, in

8. Wordsworth had in mind the "Gothic" terror novels by writers such as Ann Radcliffe and Matthew Gregory Lewis and the sentimental melodrama, then immensely popular in England, of August von Kotzebue and his German contemporaries.

9. This practice was common in 18th-century poetry. Samuel Johnson, for instance, in The

Vanity of Human Wishes (1749), has "Observation . . . survey[ing] mankind" and "Vengeance listen[ing] to the fool's request" (lines 1–2, 14).

1. In the sense of words, phrases, and figures of speech not commonly used in conversation or prose that are regarded as especially appropriate to poetry.

themselves proper and beautiful, but which have been foolishly repeated by bad poets, till such feelings of disgust are connected with them as it is scarcely possible by any art of association to overpower.

If in a poem there should be found a series of lines, or even a single line, in which the language, though naturally arranged and according to the strict laws of metre, does not differ from that of prose, there is a numerous class of critics, who, when they stumble upon these prosaisms as they call them, imagine that they have made a notable discovery, and exult over the poet as over a man ignorant of his own profession. Now these men would establish a canon of criticism which the reader will conclude he must utterly reject, if he wishes to be pleased with these volumes. And it would be a most easy task to prove to him, that not only the language of a large portion of every good poem, even of the most elevated character, must necessarily, except with reference to the metre, in no respect differ from that of good prose, but likewise that some of the most interesting parts of the best poems will be found to be strictly the language of prose, when prose is well written. The truth of this assertion might be demonstrated by innumerable passages from almost all the poetical writings, even of Milton himself. I have not space for much quotation; but, to illustrate the subject in a general manner, I will here adduce a short composition of Gray, who was at the head of those who by their reasonings have attempted to widen the space of separation betwixt prose and metrical composition, and was more than any other man curiously elaborate in the structure of his own poetic diction.[2]

> In vain to me the smiling mornings shine,
> And reddening Phoebus lifts his golden fire:
> The birds in vain their amorous descant join,
> Or cheerful fields resume their green attire:
> These ears, alas! for other notes repine;
> *A different object do these eyes require;*
> *My lonely anguish melts no heart but mine;*
> *And in my breast the imperfect joys expire;*
> Yet Morning smiles the busy race to cheer,
> And new-born pleasure brings to happier men;
> The fields to all their wonted tribute bear;
> To warm their little loves the birds complain.
> *I fruitless mourn to him that cannot hear*
> *And weep the more because I weep in vain.*

It will easily be perceived that the only part of this sonnet which is of any value is the lines printed in italics: it is equally obvious, that, except in the rhyme, and in the use of the single word "fruitless" for fruitlessly, which is so far a defect, the language of these lines does in no respect differ from that of prose.

By the foregoing quotation I have shewn that the language of prose may yet be well adapted to poetry; and I have previously asserted that a large portion of the language of every good poem can in no respect differ from that of good prose. I will go further. I do not doubt that it may be safely affirmed, that there neither is, nor can be, any essential difference between the language of

2. Thomas Gray (author in 1751 of the "Elegy Written in a Country Churchyard") had written, in a letter to Richard West, that "the language of the age is never the language of poetry." The poem that follows is Gray's "Sonnet on the Death of Richard West."

prose and metrical composition. We are fond of tracing the resemblance between poetry and painting, and, accordingly, we call them sisters: but where shall we find bonds of connection sufficiently strict to typify the affinity betwixt metrical and prose composition? They both speak by and to the same organs; the bodies in which both of them are clothed may be said to be of the same substance, their affections are kindred and almost identical, not necessarily differing even in degree; poetry[3] sheds no tears "such as Angels weep,"[4] but natural and human tears; she can boast of no celestial ichor[5] that distinguishes her vital juices from those of prose; the same human blood circulates through the veins of them both.

* * *

["WHAT IS A POET?"]

Taking up the subject, then, upon general grounds, I ask what is meant by the word "poet"? What is a poet? To whom does he address himself? And what language is to be expected from him? He is a man speaking to men: a man, it is true, endued with more lively sensibility, more enthusiasm and tenderness, who has a greater knowledge of human nature, and a more comprehensive soul, than are supposed to be common among mankind; a man pleased with his own passions and volitions, and who rejoices more than other men in the spirit of life that is in him; delighting to contemplate similar volitions and passions as manifested in the goings-on of the universe, and habitually impelled to create them where he does not find them. To these qualities he has added a disposition to be affected more than other men by absent things as if they were present; an ability of conjuring up in himself passions, which are indeed far from being the same as those produced by real events, yet (especially in those parts of the general sympathy which are pleasing and delightful) do more nearly resemble the passions produced by real events, than any thing which, from the motions of their own minds merely, other men are accustomed to feel in themselves; whence, and from practice, he has acquired a greater readiness and power in expressing what he thinks and feels, and especially those thoughts and feelings which, by his own choice, or from the structure of his own mind, arise in him without immediate external excitement.

But, whatever portion of this faculty we may suppose even the greatest poet to possess, there cannot be a doubt but that the language which it will suggest to him, must, in liveliness and truth, fall far short of that which is uttered by men in real life, under the actual pressure of those passions, certain shadows of which the poet thus produces, or feels to be produced, in himself. However exalted a notion we would wish to cherish of the character of a poet, it is obvious, that, while he describes and imitates passions, his situation is altogether slavish and mechanical, compared with the freedom and power of real and substantial action and suffering. So that it will

---

3. I here use the word "poetry" (though against my own judgment) as opposed to the word "prose," and synonymous with metrical composition. But much confusion has been introduced into criticism by this contradistinction of poetry and prose, instead of the more philosophical one of poetry and matter of fact, or science. The only strict antithesis to prose is metre; nor is this, in truth, a *strict* antithesis; because lines and passages of metre so naturally occur in writing prose, that it would be scarcely possible to avoid them, even were it desirable [Wordsworth's note].

4. Milton's *Paradise Lost* 1.620.

5. In Greek mythology the fluid in the veins of the gods.

be the wish of the poet to bring his feelings near to those of the persons whose feelings he describes, nay, for short spaces of time perhaps, to let himself slip into an entire delusion, and even confound and identify his own feelings with theirs; modifying only the language which is thus suggested to him, by a consideration that he describes for a particular purpose, that of giving pleasure. Here, then, he will apply the principle on which I have so much insisted, namely, that of selection; on this he will depend for removing what would otherwise be painful or disgusting in the passion; he will feel that there is no necessity to trick out[6] or to elevate nature: and, the more industriously he applies this principle, the deeper will be his faith that no words, which his fancy or imagination can suggest, will be to be compared with those which are the emanations of reality and truth.

But it may be said by those who do not object to the general spirit of these remarks, that, as it is impossible for the poet to produce upon all occasions language as exquisitely fitted for the passion as that which the real passion itself suggests, it is proper that he should consider himself as in the situation of a translator, who deems himself justified when he substitutes excellences of another kind for those which are unattainable by him; and endeavours occasionally to surpass his original, in order to make some amends for the general inferiority to which he feels that he must submit. But this would be to encourage idleness and unmanly despair. Further, it is the language of men who speak of what they do not understand; who talk of poetry as a matter of amusement and idle pleasure; who will converse with us as gravely about a *taste* for poetry, as they express it, as if it were a thing as indifferent as a taste for rope-dancing, or Frontiniac[7] or sherry. Aristotle, I have been told, hath said, that poetry is the most philosophic of all writing;[8] it is so: its object is truth, not individual and local, but general, and operative; not standing upon external testimony, but carried alive into the heart by passion; truth which is its own testimony, which gives strength and divinity to the tribunal to which it appeals, and receives them from the same tribunal. Poetry is the image of man and nature. The obstacles which stand in the way of the fidelity of the biographer and historian, and of their consequent utility, are incalculably greater than those which are to be encountered by the poet who has an adequate notion of the dignity of his art. The poet writes under one restriction only, namely, that of the necessity of giving immediate pleasure to a human being possessed of that information which may be expected from him, not as a lawyer, a physician, a mariner, an astronomer or a natural philosopher, but as a man. Except this one restriction, there is no object standing between the poet and the image of things; between this, and the biographer and historian there are a thousand.

Nor let this necessity of producing immediate pleasure be considered as a degradation of the poet's art. It is far otherwise. It is an acknowledgment of the beauty of the universe, an acknowledgment the more sincere because it is not formal, but indirect; it is a task light and easy to him who looks at the world in the spirit of love: further, it is a homage paid to the native and naked dignity of man, to the grand elementary principle of pleasure, by which he knows, and feels, and lives, and moves.[9] We have no sympathy but what is

---

6. Dress up.
7. A sweet wine made from muscat grapes. "Rope-dancing": tightrope walking.
8. Aristotle in fact said that "poetry is more philosophic than history, since its statements are of the nature of universals, whereas those of history are singulars" (*Poetics* 1451b).
9. A bold echo of the words of St. Paul, that in God "we live, and move, and have our being" (Acts 17.28).

propagated by pleasure: I would not be misunderstood; but wherever we sympathize with pain it will be found that the sympathy is produced and carried on by subtle combinations with pleasure. We have no knowledge, that is, no general principles drawn from the contemplation of particular facts, but what has been built up by pleasure, and exists in us by pleasure alone. The man of science, the chemist and mathematician, whatever difficulties and disgusts they may have had to struggle with, know and feel this. However painful may be the objects with which the anatomist's knowledge is connected, he feels that his knowledge is pleasure; and where he has no pleasure he has no knowledge. What then does the poet? He considers man and the objects that surround him as acting and re-acting upon each other, so as to produce an infinite complexity of pain and pleasure; he considers man in his own nature and in his ordinary life as contemplating this with a certain quantity of immediate knowledge, with certain convictions, intuitions, and deductions which by habit become of the nature of intuitions; he considers him as looking upon this complex scene of ideas and sensations, and finding every where objects that immediately excite in him sympathies which, from the necessities of his nature, are accompanied by an overbalance of enjoyment.

To this knowledge which all men carry about with them, and to these sympathies in which without any other discipline than that of our daily life we are fitted to take delight, the poet principally directs his attention. He considers man and nature as essentially adapted to each other, and the mind of man as naturally the mirror of the fairest and most interesting qualities of nature. And thus the poet, prompted by this feeling of pleasure which accompanies him through the whole course of his studies, converses with general nature with affections akin to those, which, through labour and length of time, the man of science has raised up in himself, by conversing with those particular parts of nature which are the objects of his studies. The knowledge both of the poet and the man of science is pleasure; but the knowledge of the one cleaves to us as a necessary part of our existence, our natural and unalienable inheritance; the other is a personal and individual acquisition, slow to come to us, and by no habitual and direct sympathy connecting us with our fellow-beings. The man of science seeks truth as a remote and unknown benefactor; he cherishes and loves it in his solitude: the poet, singing a song in which all human beings join with him, rejoices in the presence of truth as our visible friend and hourly companion. Poetry is the breath and finer spirit of all knowledge; it is the impassioned expression which is in the countenance of all science. Emphatically may it be said of the poet, as Shakespeare hath said of man, "that he looks before and after."[1] He is the rock of defence of human nature; an upholder and preserver, carrying everywhere with him relationship and love. In spite of difference of soil and climate, of language and manners, of laws and customs, in spite of things silently gone out of mind and things violently destroyed, the poet binds together by passion and knowledge the vast empire of human society, as it is spread over the whole earth, and over all time. The objects of the poet's thoughts are every where; though the eyes and senses of man are, it is true, his favorite guides, yet he will follow wheresoever he can find an atmosphere of sensation in which to move his wings. Poetry is the first

1. Cf. Shakespeare's *Hamlet* 4.4.9.27.

and last of all knowledge—it is as immortal as the heart of man. If the labours of men of science should ever create any material revolution, direct or indirect, in our condition, and in the impressions which we habitually receive, the poet will sleep then no more than at present, but he will be ready to follow the steps of the man of science, not only in those general indirect effects, but he will be at his side, carrying sensation into the midst of the objects of the science itself. The remotest discoveries of the chemist, the botanist, or mineralogist, will be as proper objects of the poet's art as any upon which it can be employed, if the time should ever come when these things shall be familiar to us, and the relations under which they are contemplated by the followers of these respective sciences shall be manifestly and palpably material to us as enjoying and suffering beings.[2] If the time should ever come when what is now called science, thus familiarized to men, shall be ready to put on, as it were, a form of flesh and blood, the poet will lend his divine spirit to aid the transfiguration, and will welcome the being thus produced, as a dear and genuine inmate of the household of man.—It is not, then, to be supposed that any one, who holds that sublime notion of poetry which I have attempted to convey, will break in upon the sanctity and truth of his pictures by transitory and accidental ornaments, and endeavour to excite admiration of himself by arts, the necessity of which must manifestly depend upon the assumed meanness of his subject.

What I have thus far said applies to poetry in general; but especially to those parts of composition where the poet speaks through the mouth of his characters; and upon this point it appears to have such weight that I will conclude, there are few persons, of good sense, who would not allow that the dramatic parts of composition are defective, in proportion as they deviate from the real language of nature, and are coloured by a diction of the poet's own, either peculiar to him as an individual poet, or belonging simply to poets in general, to a body of men who, from the circumstance of their compositions being in metre, it is expected will employ a particular language.

It is not, then, in the dramatic parts of composition that we look for this distinction of language; but still it may be proper and necessary where the poet speaks to us in his own person and character. To this I answer by referring my reader to the description which I have before given of a poet. Among the qualities which I have enumerated as principally conducing to form a poet, is implied nothing differing in kind from other men, but only in degree. The sum of what I have there said is, that the poet is chiefly distinguished from other men by a greater promptness to think and feel without immediate external excitement, and a greater power in expressing such thoughts and feelings as are produced in him in that manner. But these passions and thoughts and feelings are the general passions and thoughts and feelings of men. And with what are they connected? Undoubtedly with our moral sentiments and animal sensations, and with the causes which excite these; with the operations of the elements and the appearances of the visible universe; with storm and sunshine, with the revolutions[3] of the seasons, with cold and heat, with loss of friends and kindred, with injuries and resentments, gratitude and hope, with fear and sorrow. These, and the like, are the sensations

2. Wordsworth is at least right in anticipating the poetry of the machine. His sonnet "Steamboats, Viaducts, and Railways" is an early instance.
3. Recurrence.

and objects which the poet describes, as they are the sensations of other men, and the objects which interest them. The poet thinks and feels in the spirit of the passions of men. How, then, can his language differ in any material degree from that of all other men who feel vividly and see clearly? It might be *proved* that it is impossible. But supposing that this were not the case, the poet might then be allowed to use a peculiar language, when expressing his feelings for his own gratification, or that of men like himself. But poets do not write for poets alone, but for men. Unless therefore we are advocates for that admiration which depends upon ignorance, and that pleasure which arises from hearing what we do not understand, the poet must descend from this supposed height, and, in order to excite rational sympathy, he must express himself as other men express themselves. * * *

["EMOTION RECOLLECTED IN TRANQUILLITY"]

I have said that poetry is the spontaneous overflow of powerful feelings: it takes its origin from emotion recollected in tranquillity: the emotion is contemplated till by a species of reaction the tranquillity gradually disappears, and an emotion, kindred to that which was before the subject of contemplation, is gradually produced, and does itself actually exist in the mind. In this mood successful composition generally begins, and in a mood similar to this it is carried on; but the emotion, of whatever kind and in whatever degree, from various causes is qualified by various pleasures, so that in describing any passions whatsoever, which are voluntarily described, the mind will upon the whole be in a state of enjoyment. Now, if nature be thus cautious in preserving in a state of enjoyment a being thus employed, the poet ought to profit by the lesson thus held forth to him, and ought especially to take care, that whatever passions he communicates to his reader, those passions, if his reader's mind be sound and vigorous, should always be accompanied with an overbalance of pleasure. Now the music of harmonious metrical language, the sense of difficulty overcome, and the blind association of pleasure which has been previously received from works of rhyme or metre of the same or similar construction, an indistinct perception perpetually renewed of language closely resembling that of real life, and yet, in the circumstance of metre, differing from it so widely, all these imperceptibly make up a complex feeling of delight, which is of the most important use in tempering the painful feeling which will always be found intermingled with powerful descriptions of the deeper passions. This effect is always produced in pathetic and impassioned poetry; while, in lighter compositions, the ease and gracefulness with which the poet manages his numbers are themselves confessedly a principal source of the gratification of the reader. I might perhaps include all which it is *necessary* to say upon this subject by affirming, what few persons will deny, that, of two descriptions, either of passions, manners, or characters, each of them equally well executed, the one in prose and the other in verse, the verse will be read a hundred times where the prose is read once. * * *

I know that nothing would have so effectually contributed to further the end which I have in view, as to have shewn of what kind the pleasure is, and how the pleasure is produced, which is confessedly produced by metrical composition essentially different from that which I have here endeavoured to recommend: for the reader will say that he has been pleased by such composition; and what can I do more for him? The power of any art is limited; and he will suspect, that, if I propose to furnish him with new friends, it is only upon condition of his abandoning his old friends. Besides, as I have said, the reader is himself conscious of the pleasure which he has received from such composition, composition to which he has peculiarly attached the endearing name of poetry; and all men feel an habitual gratitude, and something of an honorable bigotry for the objects which have long continued to please them: we not only wish to be pleased, but to be pleased in that particular way in which we have been accustomed to be pleased. There is a host of arguments in these feelings; and I should be the less able to combat them successfully, as I am willing to allow, that, in order entirely to enjoy the poetry which I am recommending, it would be necessary to give up much of what is ordinarily enjoyed. But, would my limits have permitted me to point out how this pleasure is produced, I might have removed many obstacles, and assisted my reader in perceiving that the powers of language are not so limited as he may suppose; and that it is possible that poetry may give other enjoyments, of a purer, more lasting, and more exquisite nature. This part of my subject I have not altogether neglected; but it has been less my present aim to prove, that the interest excited by some other kinds of poetry is less vivid, and less worthy of the nobler powers of the mind, than to offer reasons for presuming, that, if the object which I have proposed to myself were adequately attained, a species of poetry would be produced, which is genuine poetry; in its nature well adapted to interest mankind permanently, and likewise important in the multiplicity and quality of its moral relations.

From what has been said, and from a perusal of the poems, the reader will be able clearly to perceive the object which I have proposed to myself: he will determine how far I have attained this object; and, what is a much more important question, whether it be worth attaining; and upon the decision of these two questions will rest my claim to the approbation of the public.

1800, 1802

Strange fits of passion have I known[1]

Strange fits of passion have I known:
And I will dare to tell,
But in the Lover's ear alone,
What once to me befel.

5 When she I loved looked every day
Fresh as a rose in June,
I to her cottage bent my way,
Beneath an evening moon.

---

1. This and the four following pieces are often grouped by editors as the "Lucy poems," even though "A slumber did my spirit seal" does not identify the "she" who is the subject of that poem. All but the last were written in 1799, while Wordsworth and his sister were in Germany and homesick. There has been diligent speculation about the identity of Lucy, but it remains speculation.

Upon the moon I fixed my eye,
10   All over the wide lea;
With quickening pace my horse drew nigh
Those paths so dear to me.

And now we reached the orchard-plot;
And, as we climbed the hill,
15   The sinking moon to Lucy's cot
Came near, and nearer still.

In one of those sweet dreams I slept,
Kind Nature's gentlest boon!
And all the while my eyes I kept
20   On the descending moon.

My horse moved on; hoof after hoof
He raised, and never stopped:
When down behind the cottage roof,
At once, the bright moon dropped.

25   What fond and wayward thoughts will slide
Into a Lover's head!
"O mercy!" to myself I cried,
"If Lucy should be dead!"[2]

1799   1800, 1836

She dwelt among the untrodden ways[1]

She dwelt among the untrodden ways
    Beside the springs of Dove,[2]
A Maid whom there were none to praise
    And very few to love:

5   A violet by a mossy stone
    Half hidden from the eye!
—Fair as a star, when only one
    Is shining in the sky.

She lived unknown, and few could know
10   When Lucy ceased to be;
But she is in her grave, and, oh,
    The difference to me!

1799   1800

---

2. An additional stanza in an earlier manuscript version demonstrates how a poem can be improved by omission of a passage that is, in itself, excellent poetry: "I told her this: her laughter light / Is ringing in my ears; / And when I think upon that night / My eyes are dim with tears."

1. For the author's revisions while composing this poem, see "Poems in Process," in the NAEL Archive.
2. There are several rivers by this name in England, including one in the Lake District.

Three years she grew

Three years she grew in sun and shower,
Then Nature said, "A lovelier flower
On earth was never sown;
This Child I to myself will take;
5   She shall be mine, and I will make
A Lady of my own.[1]

"Myself will to my darling be
Both law and impulse: and with me
The Girl, in rock and plain,
10   In earth and heaven, in glade and bower,
Shall feel an overseeing power
To kindle or restrain.

"She shall be sportive as the fawn
That wild with glee across the lawn
15   Or up the mountain springs;
And hers shall be the breathing balm,
And hers the silence and the calm
Of mute insensate things.

"The floating clouds their state shall lend
20   To her; for her the willow bend;
Nor shall she fail to see
Even in the motions of the Storm
Grace that shall mould the Maiden's form
By silent sympathy.

25   "The stars of midnight shall be dear
To her; and she shall lean her ear
In many a secret place
Where rivulets dance their wayward round,
And beauty born of murmuring sound
30   Shall pass into her face.

"And vital feelings of delight
Shall rear her form to stately height,
Her virgin bosom swell;
Such thoughts to Lucy I will give
35   While she and I together live
Here in this happy dell."

Thus Nature spake—the work was done—
How soon my Lucy's race was run!
She died, and left to me

---

1. I.e., Lucy was three years old when Nature made this promise; line 37 makes clear that Lucy had reached the maturity foretold in the sixth stanza when she died.

40 This heath, this calm, and quiet scene;
The memory of what has been,
And never more will be.

1799   1800, 1805

A slumber did my spirit seal

A slumber did my spirit seal;   *Sealed off from reality*
    I had no human fears:
She seemed a thing that could not feel
    The touch of earthly years.

5 No motion has she now, no force;   *dies between two stanzas*
    She neither hears nor sees;   *analepsis, lapses over*
Rolled round in earth's diurnal° course,   *and returns to event*   daily
    With rocks, and stones, and trees.

1799   1800

I travelled among unknown men

I travelled among unknown men,
    In lands beyond the sea;
Nor, England! did I know till then
    What love I bore to thee.

5 'Tis past, that melancholy dream!
    Nor will I quit thy shore
A second time; for still I seem
    To love thee more and more.

Among thy mountains did I feel
10   The joy of my desire;
And she I cherished turned her wheel
    Beside an English fire.

Thy mornings showed, thy nights concealed
    The bowers where Lucy played;
15 And thine too is the last green field
    That Lucy's eyes surveyed.

ca. 1801   1807, 1836

Nutting[1]

————————It seems a day
(I speak of one from many singled out)
One of those heavenly days that cannot die;
When, in the eagerness of boyish hope,
5 I left our cottage-threshold, sallying forth
With a huge wallet° o'er my shoulder slung,   *bag, knapsack*
A nutting-crook[2] in hand; and turned my steps
Tow'rd some far-distant wood, a Figure quaint,
Tricked out in proud disguise of cast-off weeds°   *clothes*
10 Which for that service had been husbanded,
By exhortation of my frugal Dame[3]—
Motley accoutrement, of power to smile
At thorns, and brakes,° and brambles,—and, in truth,   *thickets of ferns*
More ragged than need was! O'er pathless rocks,
15 Through beds of matted fern, and tangled thickets,
Forcing my way, I came to one dear nook
Unvisited, where not a broken bough
Drooped with its withered leaves, ungracious sign
Of devastation; but the hazels rose
20 Tall and erect, with tempting clusters hung,
A virgin scene!—A little while I stood,
Breathing with such suppression of the heart
As joy delights in; and, with wise restraint
Voluptuous, fearless of a rival, eyed
25 The banquet;—or beneath the trees I sate
Among the flowers, and with the flowers I played;
A temper known to those, who, after long
And weary expectation, have been blest
With sudden happiness beyond all hope.
30 Perhaps it was a bower beneath whose leaves
The violets of five seasons re-appear
And fade, unseen by any human eye;
Where fairy water-breaks[4] do murmur on
For ever; and I saw the sparkling foam,
35 And—with my cheek on one of those green stones
That, fleeced with moss, under the shady trees,
Lay round me, scattered like a flock of sheep—
I heard the murmur and the murmuring sound,
In that sweet mood when pleasure loves to pay
40 Tribute to ease; and, of its joy secure,
The heart luxuriates with indifferent things,
Wasting its kindliness on stocks[5] and stones,
And on the vacant air. Then up I rose,
And dragged to earth both branch and bough, with crash

---

1. Wordsworth said in 1843 that these lines, written in Germany in 1798, were "intended as part of a poem on my own life [*The Prelude*], but struck out as not being wanted there." He published them in the second edition of *Lyrical Ballads*, 1800.
2. Hooked stick used to shake tree branches and make nuts fall.
3. Ann Tyson, with whom Wordsworth lodged while at Hawkshead grammar school.
4. Places where the flow of a stream is broken by rocks.
5. Tree stumps. ("Stocks and stones" is a conventional expression for "inanimate things.")

45 And merciless ravage: and the shady nook
    Of hazels, and the green and mossy bower,
    Deformed and sullied, patiently gave up
    Their quiet being: and, unless I now
    Confound my present feelings with the past,
50 Ere from the mutilated bower I turned
    Exulting, rich beyond the wealth of kings,
    I felt a sense of pain when I beheld
    The silent trees, and saw the intruding sky.—
    Then, dearest Maiden,[6] move along these shades
55 In gentleness of heart; with gentle hand
    Touch—for there is a spirit in the woods.

1798   1800

The Ruined Cottage[1]

First Part

    'Twas summer and the sun was mounted high.
    Along the south the uplands feebly glared
    Through a pale steam, and all the northern downs
    In clearer air ascending shewed far off
5   Their surfaces with shadows dappled o'er
    Of deep embattled clouds: far as the sight
    Could reach those many shadows lay in spots
    Determined and unmoved, with steady beams
    Of clear and pleasant sunshine interposed;
10 Pleasant to him who on the soft cool moss
    Extends his careless limbs beside the root
    Of some huge oak whose aged branches make
    A twilight of their own, a dewy shade
    Where the wren warbles while the dreaming man,
15 Half-conscious of that soothing melody,
    With side-long eye looks out upon the scene,
    By those impending branches made more soft,
    More soft and distant. Other lot was mine.
    Across a bare wide Common I had toiled
20 With languid feet which by the slipp'ry ground
    Were baffled still, and when I stretched myself
    On the brown earth my limbs from very heat
    Could find no rest nor my weak arm disperse

---

6. In a manuscript passage originally intended to lead up to "Nutting," the maiden is called Lucy.
1. Wordsworth wrote *The Ruined Cottage* in 1797–98, then revised it several times before he finally published an expanded version of the story as book 1 of *The Excursion*, in 1814. *The Ruined Cottage* was not published as an independent poem until 1949, when it appeared in the fifth volume of *The Poetical Works of William Wordsworth*, edited by Ernest de Selincourt and Helen Darbishire, who printed a version known as "MS. B." The text reprinted here is from "MS. D," dated 1799, as transcribed by James

Butler in the Cornell Wordsworth volume, *"The Ruined Cottage" and "The Pedlar"* (1979).
    Concerning the principal narrator, introduced in line 33, Wordsworth said in 1843, "had I been born in a class which would have deprived me of what is called a liberal education, it is not unlikely that being strong in body; I should have taken to a way of life such as that in which my Pedlar passed the greater part of his days. . . . [T]he character I have represented in his person is chiefly an idea of what I fancied my own character might have become in his circumstances."

The insect host which gathered round my face
25 And joined their murmurs to the tedious noise
Of seeds of bursting gorse that crackled round.
I rose and turned towards a group of trees
Which midway in that level stood alone,
And thither come at length, beneath a shade
30 Of clustering elms that sprang from the same root
I found a ruined house, four naked walls
That stared upon each other. I looked round
And near the door I saw an aged Man,
Alone, and stretched upon the cottage bench;
35 An iron-pointed staff lay at his side.
With instantaneous joy I recognized
That pride of nature and of lowly life,
The venerable Armytage, a friend
As dear to me as is the setting sun.
40   Two days before
We had been fellow-travellers. I knew
That he was in this neighbourhood and now
Delighted found him here in the cool shade.
He lay, his pack of rustic merchandize
45 Pillowing his head—I guess he had no thought
Of his way-wandering life. His eyes were shut;
The shadows of the breezy elms above
Dappled his face. With thirsty heat oppress'd
At length I hailed him, glad to see his hat
50 Bedewed with water-drops, as if the brim
Had newly scoop'd a running stream. He rose
And pointing to a sun-flower bade me climb
The [   ]² wall where that same gaudy flower
Looked out upon the road. It was a plot
55 Of garden-ground, now wild, its matted weeds
Marked with the steps of those whom as they pass'd,
The goose-berry trees that shot in long lank slips,
Or currants hanging from their leafless stems
In scanty strings, had tempted to o'erleap
60 The broken wall. Within that cheerless spot,
Where two tall hedgerows of thick willow boughs
Joined in a damp cold nook, I found a well
Half-choked [with willow flowers and weeds.]³
I slaked my thirst and to the shady bench
65 Returned, and while I stood unbonneted
To catch the motion of the cooler air
The old Man said, "I see around me here
Things which you cannot see: we die, my Friend,
Nor we alone, but that which each man loved
70 And prized in his peculiar nook of earth
Dies with him or is changed, and very soon
Even of the good is no memorial left.
The Poets in their elegies and songs

2. The brackets here and in later lines mark blank spaces left unfilled in the manuscript.
3. Wordsworth penciled the bracketed phrase into a gap left in the manuscript.

Lamenting the departed call the groves,
75 They call upon the hills and streams to mourn,
And senseless[4] rocks, nor idly; for they speak
In these their invocations with a voice
Obedient to the strong creative power
Of human passion. Sympathies there are
80 More tranquil, yet perhaps of kindred birth,
That steal upon the meditative mind
And grow with thought. Beside yon spring I stood
And eyed its waters till we seemed to feel
One sadness, they and I. For them a bond
85 Of brotherhood is broken: time has been
When every day the touch of human hand
Disturbed their stillness, and they ministered
To human comfort. When I stooped to drink,
A spider's web hung to the water's edge,
90 And on the wet and slimy foot-stone lay
The useless fragment of a wooden bowl;
It moved my very heart. The day has been
When I could never pass this road but she
Who lived within these walls, when I appeared,
95 A daughter's welcome gave me, and I loved her
As my own child. O Sir! the good die first,
And they whose hearts are dry as summer dust
Burn to the socket. Many a passenger°   *passerby, traveler*
Has blessed poor Margaret for her gentle looks
100 When she upheld the cool refreshment drawn
From that forsaken spring, and no one came
But he was welcome, no one went away
But that it seemed she loved him. She is dead,
The worm is on her cheek, and this poor hut,
105 Stripp'd of its outward garb of household flowers,
Of rose and sweet-briar, offers to the wind
A cold bare wall whose earthy top is tricked
With weeds and the rank spear-grass. She is dead,
And nettles rot and adders sun themselves
110 Where we have sate together while she nurs'd
Her infant at her breast. The unshod Colt,
The wandring heifer and the Potter's ass,
Find shelter now within the chimney-wall
Where I have seen her evening hearth-stone blaze
115 And through the window spread upon the road
Its chearful light.—You will forgive me, Sir,
But often on this cottage do I muse
As on a picture, till my wiser mind
Sinks, yielding to the foolishness of grief.
120   She had a husband, an industrious man,
Sober and steady; I have heard her say
That he was up and busy at his loom
In summer ere the mower's scythe had swept
The dewy grass, and in the early spring

4. Incapable of sensation or perception.

125   Ere the last star had vanished. They who pass'd
      At evening, from behind the garden-fence
      Might hear his busy spade, which he would ply
      After his daily work till the day-light
      Was gone and every leaf and flower were lost
130   In the dark hedges. So they pass'd their days
      In peace and comfort, and two pretty babes
      Were their best hope next to the God in Heaven.
      —You may remember, now some ten years gone,
      Two blighting seasons when the fields were left
135   With half a harvest.[5] It pleased heaven to add
      A worse affliction in the plague of war:
      A happy land was stricken to the heart;
      'Twas a sad time of sorrow and distress:
      A wanderer among the cottages,
140   I with my pack of winter raiment saw
      The hardships of that season: many rich
      Sunk down as in a dream among the poor,
      And of the poor did many cease to be,
      And their place knew them not. Meanwhile, abridg'd°   *deprived*
145   Of daily comforts, gladly reconciled
      To numerous self-denials, Margaret
      Went struggling on through those calamitous years
      With chearful hope: but ere the second autumn
      A fever seized her husband. In disease
150   He lingered long, and when his strength returned
      He found the little he had stored to meet
      The hour of accident or crippling age
      Was all consumed. As I have said, 'twas now
      A time of trouble; shoals of artisans
155   Were from their daily labour turned away
      To hang for bread on parish charity,[6]
      They and their wives and children—happier far
      Could they have lived as do the little birds
      That peck along the hedges or the kite
160   That makes her dwelling in the mountain rocks.
      Ill fared it now with Robert, he who dwelt
      In this poor cottage; at his door he stood
      And whistled many a snatch of merry tunes
      That had no mirth in them, or with his knife
165   Carved uncouth figures on the heads of sticks,
      Then idly sought about through every nook
      Of house or garden any casual task
      Of use or ornament, and with a strange,
      Amusing but uneasy novelty
170   He blended where he might the various tasks
      Of summer, autumn, winter, and of spring.

5. As James Butler points out in his introduction, Wordsworth is purposely distancing his story in time. The "two blighting seasons" in fact occurred in 1794–95, only a few years before Wordsworth wrote *The Ruined Cottage*, when a bad harvest was followed by one of the worst winters on record. Much of the seed grain was destroyed in the ground, and the price of wheat nearly doubled.

6. The so-called able-bodied poor were entitled to receive from the parish in which they were settled the food, the clothing, and sometimes the cash that would help them over a crisis.

But this endured not; his good-humour soon
Became a weight in which no pleasure was,
And poverty brought on a petted° mood   *ill-tempered*
175   And a sore temper: day by day he drooped,
And he would leave his home, and to the town
Without an errand would he turn his steps
Or wander here and there among the fields.
One while he would speak lightly of his babes
180   And with a cruel tongue: at other times
He played with them wild freaks of merriment:
And 'twas a piteous thing to see the looks
Of the poor innocent children. 'Every smile,'
Said Margaret to me here beneath these trees,
185   'Made my heart bleed.'" At this the old Man paus'd
And looking up to those enormous elms
He said, "'Tis now the hour of deepest noon,
At this still season of repose and peace,
This hour when all things which are not at rest
190   Are chearful, while this multitude of flies
Fills all the air with happy melody,
Why should a tear be in an old man's eye?
Why should we thus with an untoward mind
And in the weakness of humanity
195   From natural wisdom turn our hearts away,
To natural comfort shut our eyes and ears,
And feeding on disquiet thus disturb
The calm of Nature with our restless thoughts?"

END OF THE FIRST PART

Second Part

He spake with somewhat of a solemn tone:
200   But when he ended there was in his face
Such easy chearfulness, a look so mild
That for a little time it stole away
All recollection, and that simple tale
Passed from my mind like a forgotten sound.
205   A while on trivial things we held discourse,
To me soon tasteless. In my own despite
I thought of that poor woman as of one
Whom I had known and loved. He had rehearsed
Her homely tale with such familiar power,
210   With such a[n active][7] countenance, an eye
So busy, that the things of which he spake
Seemed present, and, attention now relaxed,
There was a heartfelt chillness in my veins.
I rose, and turning from that breezy shade
215   Went out into the open air and stood
To drink the comfort of the warmer sun.
Long time I had not stayed ere, looking round
Upon that tranquil ruin, I returned

---

7. Wordsworth penciled the bracketed phrase into a gap left in the manuscript.

And begged of the old man that for my sake
220 He would resume his story. He replied,
"It were a wantonness° and would demand   *reckless ill-doing*
Severe reproof, if we were men whose hearts
Could hold vain dalliance with the misery
Even of the dead, contented thence to draw
225 A momentary pleasure never marked
By reason, barren of all future good.
But we have known that there is often found
In mournful thoughts, and always might be found,
A power to virtue friendly; were't not so,
230 I am a dreamer among men, indeed
An idle dreamer. 'Tis a common tale,
By moving accidents[8] uncharactered,
A tale of silent suffering, hardly clothed
In bodily form, and to the grosser sense
235 But ill adapted, scarcely palpable
To him who does not think. But at your bidding
I will proceed.
              While thus it fared with them
To whom this cottage till that hapless year
Had been a blessed home, it was my chance
240 To travel in a country far remote,
And glad I was when, halting by yon gate
That leads from the green lane, again I saw
These lofty elm-trees. Long I did not rest:
With many pleasant thoughts I cheer'd my way
245 O'er the flat common. At the door arrived,
I knocked, and when I entered with the hope
Of usual greeting, Margaret looked at me
A little while, then turned her head away
Speechless, and sitting down upon a chair
250 Wept bitterly. I wist not what to do
Or how to speak to her. Poor wretch! at last
She rose from off her seat—and then, oh Sir!
I cannot tell how she pronounced my name:
With fervent love, and with a face of grief
255 Unutterably helpless, and a look
That seem'd to cling upon me, she enquir'd
If I had seen her husband. As she spake
A strange surprize and fear came to my heart,
Nor had I power to answer ere she told
260 That he had disappeared—just two months gone.
He left his house; two wretched days had passed,
And on the third by the first break of light,
Within her casement full in view she saw
A purse of gold.[9] 'I trembled at the sight,'

---

8. Othello speaks "of most disastrous chances, / Of moving accidents by flood and field, / Of hair-breadth 'scapes" (Shakespeare, *Othello* 1.3.133–35).
9. The "bounty" that her husband had been paid for enlisting in the militia. The shortage of vol-

unteers and England's sharply rising military needs had in some counties forced the bounty up from about £1 in 1757 to more than £16 in 1796 (J. R. Western, *English Militia in the Eighteenth Century*, 1965).

265 Said Margaret, 'for I knew it was his hand
That placed it there, and on that very day
By one, a stranger, from my husband sent,
The tidings came that he had joined a troop
Of soldiers going to a distant land.
270 He left me thus—Poor Man! he had not heart
To take a farewell of me, and he feared
That I should follow with my babes, and sink
Beneath the misery of a soldier's life.'
This tale did Margaret tell with many tears:
275 And when she ended I had little power
To give her comfort, and was glad to take
Such words of hope from her own mouth as serv'd
To cheer us both: but long we had not talked
Ere we built up a pile of better thoughts,
280 And with a brighter eye she looked around
As if she had been shedding tears of joy.
We parted. It was then the early spring;
I left her busy with her garden tools;
And well remember, o'er that fence she looked,
285 And while I paced along the foot-way path
Called out, and sent a blessing after me
With tender chearfulness and with a voice
That seemed the very sound of happy thoughts.
    I roved o'er many a hill and many a dale
290 With this my weary load, in heat and cold,
Through many a wood, and many an open ground,
In sunshine or in shade, in wet or fair,
Now blithe, now drooping, as it might befal,
My best companions now the driving winds
295 And now the 'trotting brooks'[1] and whispering trees
And now the music of my own sad steps,
With many a short-lived thought that pass'd between
And disappeared. I came this way again
Towards the wane of summer, when the wheat
300 Was yellow, and the soft and bladed grass
Sprang up afresh and o'er the hay-field spread
Its tender green. When I had reached the door
I found that she was absent. In the shade
Where now we sit I waited her return.
305 Her cottage in its outward look appeared
As chearful as before; in any shew
Of neatness little changed, but that I thought
The honeysuckle crowded round the door
And from the wall hung down in heavier wreathes,
310 And knots of worthless stone-crop[2] started out
Along the window's edge, and grew like weeds
Against the lower panes. I turned aside
And stroll'd into her garden.—It was chang'd:
The unprofitable bindweed spread his bells

1. From Robert Burns ("To William Simpson," line 87).
2. A plant with yellow flowers that grows on walls and rocks.

315 From side to side and with unwieldy wreaths
 Had dragg'd the rose from its sustaining wall
 And bent it down to earth; the border-tufts—
 Daisy and thrift and lowly camomile
 And thyme—had straggled out into the paths
320 Which they were used° to deck. Ere this an hour   *accustomed*
 Was wasted. Back I turned my restless steps,
 And as I walked before the door it chanced
 A stranger passed, and guessing whom I sought
 He said that she was used to ramble far.
325 The sun was sinking in the west, and now
 I sate with sad impatience. From within
 Her solitary infant cried aloud.
 The spot though fair seemed very desolate,
 The longer I remained more desolate.
330 And, looking round, I saw the corner-stones,
 Till then unmark'd, on either side the door
 With dull red stains discoloured and stuck o'er
 With tufts and hairs of wool, as if the sheep
 That feed upon the commons³ thither came
335 Familiarly and found a couching-place
 Even at her threshold.—The house-clock struck eight;
 I turned and saw her distant a few steps.
 Her face was pale and thin, her figure too
 Was chang'd. As she unlocked the door she said,
340 'It grieves me you have waited here so long,
 But in good truth I've wandered much of late
 And sometimes, to my shame I speak, have need
 Of my best prayers to bring me back again.'
 While on the board she spread our evening meal
345 She told me she had lost her elder child,
 That he for months had been a serving-boy
 Apprenticed by the parish. 'I perceive
 You look at me, and you have cause. Today
 I have been travelling far, and many days
350 About the fields I wander, knowing this
 Only, that what I seek I cannot find.
 And so I waste my time: for I am changed;
 And to myself,' said she, 'have done much wrong,
 And to this helpless infant. I have slept
355 Weeping, and weeping I have waked; my tears
 Have flow'd as if my body were not such
 As others are, and I could never die.
 But I am now in mind and in my heart
 More easy, and I hope,' said she, 'that heaven
360 Will give me patience to endure the things
 Which I behold at home.' It would have grieved
 Your very heart to see her. Sir, I feel
 The story linger in my heart. I fear
 'Tis long and tedious, but my spirit clings
365 To that poor woman: so familiarly

---

3. Land belonging to the local community as a whole.

Do I perceive her manner, and her look
And presence, and so deeply do I feel
Her goodness, that not seldom in my walks
A momentary trance comes over me;
370   And to myself I seem to muse on one
By sorrow laid asleep or borne away,
A human being destined to awake
To human life, or something very near
To human life, when he shall come again
375   For whom she suffered. Sir, it would have griev'd
Your very soul to see her: evermore
Her eye-lids droop'd, her eyes were downward cast;
And when she at her table gave me food
She did not look at me. Her voice was low,
380   Her body was subdued. In every act
Pertaining to her house-affairs appeared
The careless stillness which a thinking mind
Gives to an idle matter—still she sighed,
But yet no motion of the breast was seen,
385   No heaving of the heart. While by the fire
We sate together, sighs came on my ear;
I knew not how, and hardly whence they came.
I took my staff, and when I kissed her babe
The tears stood in her eyes. I left her then
390   With the best hope and comfort I could give;
She thanked me for my will, but for my hope
It seemed she did not thank me.
                             I returned
And took my rounds along this road again
Ere on its sunny bank the primrose flower
395   Had chronicled the earliest day of spring.
I found her sad and drooping; she had learn'd
No tidings of her husband: if he lived
She knew not that he lived; if he were dead
She knew not he was dead. She seemed the same
400   In person [or]⁴ appearance, but her house
Bespoke a sleepy hand of negligence;
The floor was neither dry nor neat, the hearth
Was comfortless [   ],
The windows too were dim, and her few books,
405   Which, one upon the other, heretofore
Had been piled up against the corner-panes
In seemly order, now with straggling leaves
Lay scattered here and there, open or shut
As they had chanced to fall. Her infant babe
410   Had from its mother caught the trick of grief
And sighed among its playthings. Once again
I turned towards the garden-gate and saw
More plainly still that poverty and grief
Were now come nearer to her: the earth was hard,
415   With weeds defaced and knots of withered grass;

4. The word *or* was erased here; later manuscripts read "and."

No ridges there appeared of clear black mould,
No winter greenness; of her herbs and flowers
It seemed the better part were gnawed away
Or trampled on the earth; a chain of straw
420 Which had been twisted round the tender stem
Of a young apple-tree lay at its root;
The bark was nibbled round by truant sheep.
Margaret stood near, her infant in her arms,
And seeing that my eye was on the tree
425 She said, 'I fear it will be dead and gone
Ere Robert come again.' Towards the house
Together we returned, and she inquired
If I had any hope. But for her Babe
And for her little friendless Boy, she said,
430 She had no wish to live, that she must die
Of sorrow. Yet I saw the idle loom
Still in its place. His Sunday garments hung
Upon the self-same nail, his very staff
Stood undisturbed behind the door. And when
435 I passed this way beaten by Autumn winds
She told me that her little babe was dead
And she was left alone. That very time,
I yet remember, through the miry lane
She walked with me a mile, when the bare trees
440 Trickled with foggy damps, and in such sort
That any heart had ached to hear her begg'd
That wheresoe'er I went I still would ask
For him whom she had lost. We parted then,
Our final parting, for from that time forth
445 Did many seasons pass ere I returned
Into this tract again.
                              Five tedious years
She lingered in unquiet widowhood,
A wife and widow. Needs must it have been
A sore heart-wasting. I have heard, my friend,
450 That in that broken arbour she would sit
The idle length of half a sabbath day—
There, where you see the toadstool's lazy head—
And when a dog passed by she still would quit
The shade and look abroad. On this old Bench
455 For hours she sate, and evermore her eye
Was busy in the distance, shaping things
Which made her heart beat quick. Seest thou that path?
(The green-sward now has broken its grey line)
There to and fro she paced through many a day
460 Of the warm summer, from a belt of flax
That girt her waist spinning the long-drawn thread
With backward steps.—Yet ever as there passed
A man whose garments shewed the Soldier's red,
Or crippled Mendicant in Sailor's garb,
465 The little child who sate to turn the wheel
Ceased from his toil, and she with faltering voice,
Expecting still to learn her husband's fate,

Made many a fond inquiry; and when they
Whose presence gave no comfort were gone by,
470 Her heart was still more sad. And by yon gate
Which bars the traveller's road she often stood
And when a stranger horseman came, the latch
Would lift, and in his face look wistfully,
Most happy if from aught discovered there
475 Of tender feeling she might dare repeat
The same sad question. Meanwhile her poor hut
Sunk to decay, for he was gone whose hand
At the first nippings of October frost
Closed up each chink and with fresh bands of straw
480 Chequered the green-grown thatch. And so she lived
Through the long winter, reckless and alone,
Till this reft house by frost, and thaw, and rain
Was sapped; and when she slept the nightly damps
Did chill her breast, and in the stormy day
485 Her tattered clothes were ruffled by the wind
Even at the side of her own fire. Yet still
She loved this wretched spot, nor would for worlds
Have parted hence; and still that length of road
And this rude bench one torturing hope endeared,
490 Fast rooted at her heart, and here, my friend,
In sickness she remained, and here she died,
Last human tenant of these ruined walls."
   The old Man ceased: he saw that I was mov'd;
From that low Bench, rising instinctively,
495 I turned aside in weakness, nor had power
To thank him for the tale which he had told.
I stood, and leaning o'er the garden-gate
Reviewed that Woman's suff'rings, and it seemed
To comfort me while with a brother's love
500 I blessed her in the impotence of grief.
At length [towards] the [Cottage I returned]⁵
Fondly, and traced with milder interest
That secret spirit of humanity
Which, 'mid the calm oblivious tendencies
505 Of nature, 'mid her plants, her weeds, and flowers,
And silent overgrowings, still survived.
The old man, seeing this, resumed and said,
"My Friend, enough to sorrow have you given,
The purposes of wisdom ask no more;
510 Be wise and chearful, and no longer read
The forms of things with an unworthy eye.
She sleeps in the calm earth, and peace is here.
I well remember that those very plumes,
Those weeds, and the high spear-grass on that wall,
515 By mist and silent rain-drops silver'd o'er,
As once I passed did to my heart convey
So still an image of tranquillity,
So calm and still, and looked so beautiful

---

5. The words inside the brackets were added in MS. E.

Amid the uneasy thoughts which filled my mind,
520 That what we feel of sorrow and despair
From ruin and from change, and all the grief
The passing shews of being leave behind,
Appeared an idle dream that could not live
Where meditation was. I turned away
525 And walked along my road in happiness."
        He ceased. By this the sun declining shot
A slant and mellow radiance which began
To fall upon us where beneath the trees
We sate on that low bench, and now we felt,
530 Admonished thus, the sweet hour coming on.
A linnet warbled from those lofty elms,
A thrush sang loud, and other melodies,
At distance heard, peopled the milder air.
The old man rose and hoisted up his load.
535 Together casting then a farewell look
Upon those silent walls, we left the shade
And ere the stars were visible attained
A rustic inn, our evening resting-place.

THE END

1797–ca.1799   1949

Michael[1]

A Pastoral Poem

If from the public way you turn your steps
Up the tumultuous brook of Green-head Ghyll,[2]
You will suppose that with an upright path
Your feet must struggle; in such bold ascent
5 The pastoral mountains front you, face to face.
But, courage! for around that boisterous brook
The mountains have all opened out themselves,
And made a hidden valley of their own.
No habitation can be seen; but they
10 Who journey thither find themselves alone
With a few sheep, with rocks and stones, and kites°   hawks
That overhead are sailing in the sky.
It is in truth an utter solitude;

1. This poem is founded on the actual misfortunes of a family at Grasmere. For the account of the sheepfold, see Dorothy Wordsworth's *Grasmere Journals*, October 11, 1800 (pp. 411–12). Wordsworth wrote to Thomas Poole, on April 9, 1801, that he had attempted to picture a man "agitated by two of the most powerful affections of the human heart; the parental affection, and the love of property, *landed* property, including the feelings of inheritance, home, and personal and family independence." In another letter, sent, along with a copy of the 1800 *Lyrical Ballads*, January 14, 1801, to Charles James Fox, the leader of the opposition in Parliament, Wordsworth commented in a similar vein on how a "little tract of land" could serve, for the class of men whom he had represented in "Michael," as "a kind of permanent rallying point for their domestic feelings"; he also remarked, with regret, that this class, "small independent *proprietors* of land," was "rapidly disappearing." The subtitle shows Wordsworth's shift of the term "pastoral" from aristocratic make-believe to the tragic suffering of people in what he called "humble and rustic life."
2. A ravine forming the bed of a stream. Green-head Ghyll is not far from Wordsworth's cottage at Grasmere. The other places named in the poem are also in that vicinity.

Nor should I have made mention of this Dell
15 But for one object which you might pass by,
Might see and notice not. Beside the brook
Appears a straggling heap of unhewn stones!
And to that simple object appertains
A story—unenriched with strange events,
20 Yet not unfit, I deem, for the fireside,
Or for the summer shade. It was the first
Of those domestic tales that spake to me
Of Shepherds, dwellers in the valleys, men
Whom I already loved;—not verily
25 For their own sakes, but for the fields and hills
Where was their occupation and abode.
And hence this Tale, while I was yet a Boy
Careless of books, yet having felt the power
Of Nature, by the gentle agency
30 Of natural objects, led me on to feel
For passions that were not my own, and think
(At random and imperfectly indeed)
On man, the heart of man, and human life.
Therefore, although it be a history
35 Homely and rude, I will relate the same
For the delight of a few natural hearts;
And, with yet fonder feeling, for the sake
Of youthful Poets, who among these hills
Will be my second self when I am gone.

40   Upon the forest-side in Grasmere Vale
There dwelt a Shepherd, Michael was his name;
An old man, stout of heart, and strong of limb.
His bodily frame had been from youth to age
Of an unusual strength: his mind was keen,
45 Intense, and frugal, apt for all affairs,
And in his shepherd's calling he was prompt
And watchful more than ordinary men.
Hence had he learned the meaning of all winds,
Of blasts of every tone; and, oftentimes,
50 When others heeded not, he heard the South°   south wind
Make subterraneous music, like the noise
Of bagpipers on distant Highland hills.
The Shepherd, at such warning, of his flock
Bethought him, and he to himself would say,
55 "The winds are now devising work for me!"
And, truly, at all times, the storm, that drives
The traveller to a shelter, summoned him
Up to the mountains: he had been alone
Amid the heart of many thousand mists,
60 That came to him, and left him, on the heights.
So lived he till his eightieth year was past.
And grossly that man errs, who should suppose
That the green valleys, and the streams and rocks,
Were things indifferent to the Shepherd's thoughts.
65 Fields, where with cheerful spirits he had breathed

The common air; hills, which with vigorous step
He had so often climbed; which had impressed
So many incidents upon his mind
Of hardship, skill or courage, joy or fear;
70 Which, like a book, preserved the memory
Of the dumb animals, whom he had saved,
Had fed or sheltered, linking to such acts
The certainty of honourable gain;
Those fields, those hills—what could they less? had laid
75 Strong hold on his affections, were to him
A pleasurable feeling of blind love,
The pleasure which there is in life itself.

    His days had not been passed in singleness.
His Helpmate was a comely matron, old—
80 Though younger than himself full twenty years.
She was a woman of a stirring life,
Whose heart was in her house: two wheels she had
Of antique form; this large, for spinning wool;
That small, for flax; and if one wheel had rest,
85 It was because the other was at work.
The Pair had but one inmate in their house,
An only Child, who had been born to them
When Michael, telling° o'er his years, began   *counting*
To deem that he was old,—in shepherd's phrase,
90 With one foot in the grave. This only Son,
With two brave sheep-dogs tried° in many a storm,   *tested*
The one of an inestimable worth,
Made all their household. I may truly say,
That they were as a proverb in the vale
95 For endless industry. When day was gone,
And from their occupations out of doors
The Son and Father were come home, even then,
Their labour did not cease; unless when all
Turned to the cleanly supper-board, and there,
100 Each with a mess of pottage and skimmed milk,
Sat round the basket piled with oaten cakes,
And their plain home-made cheese. Yet when the meal
Was ended, Luke (for so the Son was named)
And his old Father both betook themselves
105 To such convenient work as might employ
Their hands by the fire-side; perhaps to card
Wool for the Housewife's spindle, or repair
Some injury done to sickle, flail, or scythe,
Or other implement of house or field.

110   Down from the ceiling, by the chimney's edge,
That in our ancient uncouth country style
With huge and black projection overbrowed
Large space beneath, as duly as the light
Of day grew dim the Housewife hung a lamp;
115 An aged utensil, which had performed
Service beyond all others of its kind.

Early at evening did it burn—and late,
Surviving comrade of uncounted hours,
Which, going by from year to year, had found,
120   And left the couple neither gay perhaps
Nor cheerful, yet with objects and with hopes,
Living a life of eager industry.
And now, when Luke had reached his eighteenth year,
There by the light of his old lamp they sate,
125   Father and Son, while far into the night
The Housewife plied her own peculiar work,
Making the cottage through the silent hours
Murmur as with the sound of summer flies.
This light was famous in its neighbourhood,
130   And was a public symbol of the life
That thrifty Pair had lived. For, as it chanced,
Their cottage on a plot of rising ground
Stood single, with large prospect, north and south,
High into Easedale, up to Dunmail-Raise,
135   And westward to the village near the lake;
And from this constant light, so regular
And so far seen, the House itself, by all
Who dwelt within the limits of the vale,
Both old and young, was named THE EVENING STAR.

140   Thus living on through such a length of years,
The Shepherd, if he loved himself, must needs
Have loved his Helpmate; but to Michael's heart
This son of his old age was yet more dear—
Less from instinctive tenderness, the same
145   Fond spirit that blindly works in the blood of all—
Than that a child, more than all other gifts
That earth can offer to declining man,
Brings hope with it, and forward-looking thoughts,
And stirrings of inquietude, when they
150   By tendency of nature needs must fail.
Exceeding was the love he bare to him,
His heart and his heart's joy! For oftentimes
Old Michael, while he was a babe in arms,
Had done him female service, not alone
155   For pastime and delight, as is the use
Of fathers, but with patient mind enforced
To acts of tenderness; and he had rocked
His cradle, as with a woman's gentle hand.

      And, in a later time, ere yet the Boy
160   Had put on boy's attire, did Michael love,
Albeit of a stern unbending mind,
To have the Young-one in his sight, when he
Wrought in the field, or on his shepherd's stool
Sate with a fettered sheep before him stretched
165   Under the large old oak, that near his door
Stood single, and, from matchless depth of shade,
Chosen for the Shearer's covert from the sun,

Thence in our rustic dialect was called
The CLIPPING TREE, a name which yet it bears.
170 There, while they two were sitting in the shade,
With others round them, earnest all and blithe,
Would Michael exercise his heart with looks
Of fond correction and reproof bestowed
Upon the Child, if he disturbed the sheep
175 By catching at their legs, or with his shouts
Scared them, while they lay still beneath the shears.

And when by Heaven's good grace the boy grew up
A healthy Lad, and carried in his cheek
Two steady roses that were five years old;
180 Then Michael from a winter coppice[3] cut
With his own hand a sapling, which he hooped
With iron, making it throughout in all
Due requisites a perfect shepherd's staff,
And gave it to the Boy; wherewith equipt
185 He as a watchman oftentimes was placed
At gate or gap, to stem or turn the flock;
And, to his office prematurely called,
There stood the urchin, as you will divine,
Something between a hindrance and a help;
190 And for this cause not always, I believe,
Receiving from his Father hire° of praise;   *wages*
Though nought was left undone which staff, or voice,
Or looks, or threatening gestures, could perform.

But soon as Luke, full ten years old, could stand
195 Against the mountain blasts; and to the heights,
Not fearing toil, nor length of weary ways,
He with his Father daily went, and they
Were as companions, why should I relate
That objects which the Shepherd loved before
200 Were dearer now? that from the Boy there came
Feelings and emanations—things which were
Light to the sun and music to the wind;
And that the old Man's heart seemed born again?

Thus in his father's sight the Boy grew up:
205 And now, when he had reached his eighteenth year,
He was his comfort and his daily hope.

While in this sort the simple household lived
From day to day, to Michael's ear there came
Distressful tidings. Long before the time
210 Of which I speak, the Shepherd had been bound
In surety for his brother's son, a man
Of an industrious life, and ample means;
But unforeseen misfortunes suddenly
Had prest upon him; and old Michael now

3. Grove of small trees.

215 Was summoned to discharge the forfeiture,
A grievous penalty, but little less
Than half his substance.[4] This unlooked-for claim,
At the first hearing, for a moment took
More hope out of his life than he supposed
220 That any old man ever could have lost.
As soon as he had armed himself with strength
To look his trouble in the face, it seemed
The Shepherd's sole resource to sell at once
A portion of his patrimonial fields.
225 Such was his first resolve; he thought again,
And his heart failed him. "Isabel," said he,
Two evenings after he had heard the news,
"I have been toiling more than seventy years,
And in the open sunshine of God's love
230 Have we all lived; yet if these fields of ours
Should pass into a stranger's hand, I think
That I could not lie quiet in my grave.
Our lot is a hard lot; the sun himself
Has scarcely been more diligent than I;
235 And I have lived to be a fool at last
To my own family. An evil man
That was, and made an evil choice, if he
Were false to us; and if he were not false,
There are ten thousand to whom loss like this
240 Had been no sorrow. I forgive him;—but
'Twere better to be dumb than to talk thus.

"When I began, my purpose was to speak
Of remedies and of a cheerful hope.
Our Luke shall leave us, Isabel; the land
245 Shall not go from us, and it shall be free;°   *unmortgaged*
He shall possess it, free as is the wind
That passes over it. We have, thou know'st,
Another kinsman—he will be our friend
In this distress. He is a prosperous man,
250 Thriving in trade—and Luke to him shall go,
And with his kinsman's help and his own thrift
He quickly will repair this loss, and then
He may return to us. If here he stay,
What can be done? Where every one is poor,
What can be gained?"
255   At this the old Man paused,
And Isabel sat silent, for her mind
Was busy, looking back into past times.
There's Richard Bateman,[5] thought she to herself,
He was a parish-boy[6]—at the church-door
260 They made a gathering for him, shillings, pence

4. Michael has guaranteed a loan for his nephew and now has lost the collateral, which amounts to half his financial worth.
5. The story alluded to here is well known in the country. The chapel is called Ings Chapel and is on the road leading from Kendal to Ambleside [Wordsworth's note, 1802–05].
6. A poor boy supported financially by the poor rates (taxes) paid out by the wealthier members of his parish.

And halfpennies, wherewith the neighbours bought
A basket, which they filled with pedlar's wares;
And, with this basket on his arm, the lad
Went up to London, found a master° there,   *employer*
265 Who, out of many, chose the trusty boy
To go and overlook his merchandise
Beyond the seas; where he grew wondrous rich,
And left estates and monies to the poor,
And, at his birth-place, built a chapel floored
270 With marble, which he sent from foreign lands.
These thoughts, and many others of like sort,
Passed quickly through the mind of Isabel,
And her face brightened. The old Man was glad,
And thus resumed:—"Well, Isabel! this scheme
275 These two days, has been meat and drink to me.
Far more than we have lost is left us yet.
—We have enough—I wish indeed that I
Were younger;—but this hope is a good hope.
Make ready Luke's best garments, of the best
280 Buy for him more, and let us send him forth
To-morrow, or the next day, or to-night:
—If he *could* go, the Boy should go to-night."

Here Michael ceased, and to the fields went forth
With a light heart. The Housewife for five days
285 Was restless morn and night, and all day long
Wrought on with her best fingers to prepare
Things needful for the journey of her son.
But Isabel was glad when Sunday came
To stop her in her work: for, when she lay
290 By Michael's side, she through the last two nights
Heard him, how he was troubled in his sleep:
And when they rose at morning she could see
That all his hopes were gone. That day at noon
She said to Luke, while they two by themselves
295 Were sitting at the door, "Thou must not go:
We have no other Child but thee to lose,
None to remember—do not go away,
For if thou leave thy Father he will die."
The Youth made answer with a jocund voice;
300 And Isabel, when she had told her fears,
Recovered heart. That evening her best fare
Did she bring forth, and all together sat
Like happy people round a Christmas fire.

With daylight Isabel resumed her work;
305 And all the ensuing week the house appeared
As cheerful as a grove in Spring: at length
The expected letter from their kinsman came,
With kind assurances that he would do
His utmost for the welfare of the Boy;
310 To which, requests were added, that forthwith
He might be sent to him. Ten times or more

The letter was read over; Isabel
Went forth to show it to the neighbours round;
Nor was there at that time on English land
315 A prouder heart than Luke's. When Isabel
Had to her house returned, the old Man said,
"He shall depart to-morrow." To this word
The Housewife answered, talking much of things
Which, if at such short notice he should go,
320 Would surely be forgotten. But at length
She gave consent, and Michael was at ease.

  Near the tumultuous brook of Green-head Ghyll,
In that deep valley, Michael had designed
To build a Sheep-fold;[7] and, before he heard
325 The tidings of his melancholy loss,
For this same purpose he had gathered up
A heap of stones, which by the streamlet's edge
Lay thrown together, ready for the work.
With Luke that evening thitherward he walked:
330 And soon as they had reached the place he stopped,
And thus the old Man spake to him:—"My Son,
To-morrow thou wilt leave me: with full heart
I look upon thee, for thou art the same
That wert a promise to me ere thy birth,
335 And all thy life hast been my daily joy.
I will relate to thee some little part
Of our two histories; 'twill do thee good
When thou art from me, even if I should touch
On things thou canst not know of.——After thou
340 First cam'st into the world—as oft befals
To new-born infants—thou didst sleep away
Two days, and blessings from thy Father's tongue
Then fell upon thee. Day by day passed on,
And still I loved thee with increasing love.
345 Never to living ear came sweeter sounds
Than when I heard thee by our own fire-side
First uttering, without words, a natural tune;
While thou, a feeding babe, didst in thy joy
Sing at thy Mother's breast. Month followed month,
350 And in the open fields my life was passed
And on the mountains; else I think that thou
Hadst been brought up upon thy Father's knees.
But we were playmates, Luke: among these hills,
As well thou knowest, in us the old and young
355 Have played together, nor with me didst thou
Lack any pleasure which a boy can know."
Luke had a manly heart; but at these words
He sobbed aloud. The old Man grasped his hand,
And said, "Nay, do not take it so—I see
360 That these are things of which I need not speak.

___

7. A sheepfold [pen for sheep] in these mountains is an unroofed building of stone walls, with different divisions [Wordsworth's note, 1802–05].

—Even to the utmost I have been to thee
A kind and a good Father: and herein
I but repay a gift which I myself
Received at others' hands; for, though now old
365 Beyond the common life of man, I still
Remember them who loved me in my youth.
Both of them sleep together: here they lived,
As all their Forefathers had done; and when
At length their time was come, they were not loth
370 To give their bodies to the family mould.°   *grave plot*
I wished that thou should'st live the life they lived:
But, 'tis a long time to look back, my Son,
And see so little gain from threescore years.
These fields were burthened° when they came to me;   *mortgaged*
375 Till I was forty years of age, not more
Than half of my inheritance was mine.
I toiled and toiled; God blessed me in my work,
And till these three weeks past the land was free.
—It looks as if it never could endure
380 Another Master. Heaven forgive me, Luke,
If I judge ill for thee, but it seems good
That thou should'st go."
                      At this the old Man paused;
Then, pointing to the stones near which they stood,
Thus, after a short silence, he resumed:
385 "This was a work for us; and now, my Son,
It is a work for me. But, lay one stone—
Here, lay it for me, Luke, with thine own hands.
Nay, Boy, be of good hope;—we both may live
To see a better day. At eighty-four
390 I still am strong and hale;—do thou thy part;
I will do mine.—I will begin again
With many tasks that were resigned to thee:
Up to the heights, and in among the storms,
Will I without thee go again, and do
395 All works which I was wont to do alone,
Before I knew thy face.—Heaven bless thee, Boy!
Thy heart these two weeks has been beating fast
With many hopes; it should be so—yes—yes—
I knew that thou could'st never have a wish
400 To leave me, Luke: thou hast been bound to me
Only by links of love: when thou art gone,
What will be left to us!—But, I forget
My purposes. Lay now the corner-stone,
As I requested; and hereafter, Luke,
405 When thou art gone away, should evil men
Be thy companions, think of me, my Son,
And of this moment; hither turn thy thoughts,
And God will strengthen thee: amid all fear
And all temptation, Luke, I pray that thou
410 May'st bear in mind the life thy Fathers lived,
Who, being innocent, did for that cause
Bestir them in good deeds. Now, fare thee well—

When thou return'st, thou in this place wilt see
A work which is not here: a covenant
415 'Twill be between us; but, whatever fate
Befal thee, I shall love thee to the last,
And bear thy memory with me to the grave."

The Shepherd ended here; and Luke stooped down,
And, as his Father had requested, laid
420 The first stone of the Sheep-fold. At the sight
The old Man's grief broke from him; to his heart
He pressed his Son, he kissèd him and wept;
And to the house together they returned.
—Hushed was that House in peace, or seeming peace,
425 Ere the night fell:—with morrow's dawn the Boy
Began his journey, and when he had reached
The public way, he put on a bold face;
And all the neighbours, as he passed their doors,
Came forth with wishes and with farewell prayers,
430 That followed him till he was out of sight.

A good report did from their Kinsman come,
Of Luke and his well-doing: and the Boy
Wrote loving letters, full of wondrous news,
Which, as the Housewife phrased it, were throughout
435 "The prettiest letters that were ever seen."
Both parents read them with rejoicing hearts.
So, many months passed on: and once again
The Shepherd went about his daily work
With confident and cheerful thoughts; and now
440 Sometimes when he could find a leisure hour
He to that valley took his way, and there
Wrought at the Sheep-fold. Meantime Luke began
To slacken in his duty; and, at length,
He in the dissolute city gave himself
445 To evil courses: ignominy and shame
Fell on him, so that he was driven at last
To seek a hiding-place beyond the seas.

There is a comfort in the strength of love;
'Twill make a thing endurable, which else
450 Would overset the brain, or break the heart:
I have conversed with more than one who well
Remember the old Man, and what he was
Years after he had heard this heavy news.
His bodily frame had been from youth to age
455 Of an unusual strength. Among the rocks
He went, and still looked up to sun and cloud,
And listened to the wind; and, as before
Performed all kinds of labour for his sheep,
And for the land, his small inheritance.
460 And to that hollow dell from time to time
Did he repair, to build the Fold of which
His flock had need. 'Tis not forgotten yet

The pity which was then in every heart
For the old Man—and 'tis believed by all
465 That many and many a day he thither went,
And never lifted up a single stone.

There, by the Sheep-fold, sometimes was he seen
Sitting alone, or with his faithful Dog,
Then old, beside him, lying at his feet.
470 The length of full seven years, from time to time,
He at the building of this Sheep-fold wrought,
And left the work unfinished when he died.
Three years, or little more, did Isabel
Survive her Husband: at her death the estate
475 Was sold, and went into a stranger's hand.
The Cottage which was named THE EVENING STAR
Is gone—the ploughshare has been through the ground
On which it stood;[8] great changes have been wrought
In all the neighbourhood:—yet the oak is left
480 That grew beside their door; and the remains
Of the unfinished Sheep-fold may be seen
Beside the boisterous brook of Green-head Ghyll.

Oct. 11–Dec. 9, 1800   1800, 1836

Resolution and Independence[1]

1

There was a roaring in the wind all night;
The rain came heavily and fell in floods;
But now the sun is rising calm and bright;
The birds are singing in the distant woods;
5 Over his own sweet voice the Stock-dove broods;
The Jay makes answer as the Magpie chatters;
And all the air is filled with pleasant noise of waters.

2

All things that love the sun are out of doors;
The sky rejoices in the morning's birth;
10 The grass is bright with rain-drops;—on the moors
The hare is running races in her mirth;
And with her feet she from the plashy earth
Raises a mist; that, glittering in the sun,
Runs with her all the way, wherever she doth run.

---

8. The land on which Michael's sheep had grazed
has been turned over to cultivation.
1. "This old man I met a few hundred yards from
my cottage," Wordsworth told Isabella Fenwick in
1843, and "the account of him is taken from his
own mouth." He wrote the poem eighteen months

after the meeting. For the account of the meeting
and the writing of the poem, which had the working title "The Leech Gatherer," see Dorothy Wordsworth's *Grasmere Journals*, October 3, 1800,
p. 411, and May 4 and 7, 1802, pp. 416 and 417.

3

15 I was a Traveller then upon the moor;
I saw the hare that raced about with joy;
I heard the woods and distant waters roar;
Or heard them not, as happy as a boy:
The pleasant season did my heart employ:
20 My old remembrances went from me wholly;
And all the ways of men, so vain and melancholy.

4

But, as it sometimes chanceth, from the might
Of joy in minds that can no further go,
As high as we have mounted in delight
25 In our dejection do we sink as low;
To me that morning did it happen so;
And fears and fancies thick upon me came;
Dim sadness—and blind thoughts, I knew not, nor could name.

5

I heard the sky-lark warbling in the sky;
30 And I bethought me of the playful hare:
Even such a happy Child of earth am I;
Even as these blissful creatures do I fare;
Far from the world I walk, and from all care;
But there may come another day to me—
35 Solitude, pain of heart, distress, and poverty.

6

My whole life I have lived in pleasant thought,
As if life's business were a summer mood;
As if all needful things would come unsought
To genial° faith, still rich in genial good;   *creative*
40 But how can He expect that others should
Build for him, sow for him, and at his call
Love him, who for himself will take no heed at all?

7

I thought of Chatterton,[2] the marvellous Boy,
The sleepless Soul that perished in his pride;
45 Of Him[3] who walked in glory and in joy

2. After his early death through drug overdose, a death believed by many to have been a suicide, the poet Thomas Chatterton (1752–1770) became a prime symbol of neglected boy genius for the Romantics. He came to public attention in his hometown of Bristol in the West of England as the discoverer of the long-lost manuscripts of a local 15th-century monk named "Thomas Rowley." Rowley's works—in fact Chatterton's own inventions—included many poems. His pseudo-Chaucerian "An Excelente Balade of Charitie" used the rhyme royal stanza form that Wordsworth employs here. Reports of the frustrations that Chatterton experienced in his attempts to interest the London literary establishment in such "discoveries" provided the seed for that Romantic mythmaking in which Wordsworth, Coleridge, and Keats participated.
3. Robert Burns, here considered, as Chatterton is, a natural poet who died young and poor, without adequate recognition, and who seemed to have hastened his death through dissipation.

Following his plough, along the mountain-side:
By our own spirits are we deified:
We Poets in our youth begin in gladness;
But thereof come in the end despondency and madness.

8

50   Now, whether it were by peculiar grace,
     A leading from above, a something given,
     Yet it befel, that, in this lonely place,
     When I with these untoward thoughts had striven,
     Beside a pool bare to the eye of heaven
55   I saw a Man before me unawares:
     The oldest man he seemed that ever wore grey hairs.

9

     As a huge stone is sometimes seen to lie
     Couched on the bald top of an eminence;
     Wonder to all who do the same espy,
60   By what means it could thither come, and whence;
     So that it seems a thing endued with sense:
     Like a sea-beast crawled forth, that on a shelf
     Of rock or sand reposeth, there to sun itself;

10

     Such seemed this Man,[4] not all alive nor dead,
65   Nor all asleep—in his extreme old age:
     His body was bent double, feet and head
     Coming together in life's pilgrimage;
     As if some dire constraint of pain, or rage
     Of sickness felt by him in times long past,
70   A more than human weight upon his frame had cast.

11

     Himself he propped, limbs, body, and pale face,
     Upon a long grey staff of shaven wood:
     And, still as I drew near with gentle pace,
     Upon the margin of that moorish flood
75   Motionless as a cloud the old Man stood,
     That heareth not the loud winds when they call;
     And moveth all together, if it move at all.

12

     At length, himself unsettling, he the pond
     Stirred with his staff, and fixedly did look

4. To outline his theory of the imagination, Wordsworth himself commented on lines 57–65 and
75–77, pointing out how the stone "is endowed
with something of the power of life to approximate
it to the sea-beast," the sea-beast is "stripped of
some of its vital qualities to assimilate it to the
stone," and the old man is divested of enough life
and motion to make "the two objects unite and
coalesce in just comparison." In this manner, he
stated, "the conferring, the abstracting, and the
modifying powers of the Imagination" were "all
brought into conjunction" (Preface to the *Poems* of
1815). Cf. Coleridge's definition of the imagination in *Biographia Literaria*, chap. 13 (p. 496).

80 Upon the muddy water, which he conned,°   *studied*
    As if he had been reading in a book:
    And now a stranger's privilege I took;
    And, drawing to his side, to him did say,
    "This morning gives us promise of a glorious day."

13

85 A gentle answer did the old Man make,
    In courteous speech which forth he slowly drew:
    And him with further words I thus bespake,
    "What occupation do you there pursue?
    This is a lonesome place for one like you."
90 Ere he replied, a flash of mild surprise
    Broke from the sable orbs of his yet-vivid eyes.

14

His words came feebly, from a feeble chest,
    But each in solemn order followed each,
    With something of a lofty utterance drest—
95 Choice word and measured phrase, above the reach
    Of ordinary men; a stately speech;
    Such as grave Livers[5] do in Scotland use,
    Religious men, who give to God and man their dues.

15

He told, that to these waters he had come
100 To gather leeches,[6] being old and poor:
    Employment hazardous and wearisome!
    And he had many hardships to endure:
    From pond to pond he roamed, from moor to moor;
    Housing, with God's good help, by choice or chance;
105 And in this way he gained an honest maintenance.

16

The old Man still stood talking by my side;
    But now his voice to me was like a stream
    Scarce heard; nor word from word could I divide;
    And the whole body of the Man did seem
110 Like one whom I had met with in a dream;
    Or like a man from some far region sent,
    To give me human strength, by apt admonishment.

17

My former thoughts returned: the fear that kills;
    And hope that is unwilling to be fed;
115 Cold, pain, and labour, and all fleshly ills;

5. Those who live gravely (as opposed to "loose livers," those who live for a life of pleasure).
6. Used by medical attendants to draw their patients' blood for curative purposes. A leech gatherer, bare legged in shallow water, stirred the water to attract them and, when they fastened themselves to his legs, picked them off.

And mighty Poets in their misery dead.
—Perplexed, and longing to be comforted,
My question eagerly did I renew,
"How is it that you live, and what is it you do?"

18

120 He with a smile did then his words repeat;
And said, that, gathering leeches, far and wide
He travelled; stirring thus about his feet
The waters of the pools where they abide.
"Once I could meet with them on every side;
125 But they have dwindled long by slow decay;
Yet still I persevere, and find them where I may."

19

While he was talking thus, the lonely place,
The old Man's shape, and speech—all troubled me:
In my mind's eye I seemed to see him pace
130 About the weary moors continually,
Wandering about alone and silently.
While I these thoughts within myself pursued,
He, having made a pause, the same discourse renewed.

20

And soon with this he other matter blended,
135 Cheerfully uttered, with demeanour kind,
But stately in the main; and when he ended,
I could have laughed myself to scorn to find
In that decrepit Man so firm a mind.
"God," said I, "be my help and stay[7] secure;
140 I'll think of the Leech-gatherer on the lonely moor!"

May 3–July 4, 1802   1807

I wandered lonely as a cloud[1]

I wandered lonely as a cloud
That floats on high o'er vales and hills,
When all at once I saw a crowd,
A host, of golden daffodils;
5   Beside the lake, beneath the trees,
Fluttering and dancing in the breeze.

Continuous as the stars that shine
And twinkle on the milky way,
They stretched in never-ending line
10   Along the margin of a bay:

7. Support (a noun).
1. For the original experience, two years earlier,

see Dorothy Wordsworth's *Grasmere Journals,*
April 15, 1802 (p. 414).

Ten thousand saw I at a glance,
Tossing their heads in sprightly dance.

The waves beside them danced; but they
Out-did the sparkling waves in glee:
15 A poet could not but be gay,
In such a jocund company:
I gazed—and gazed—but little thought
What wealth the show to me had brought:

For oft, when on my couch I lie
20 In vacant or in pensive mood,
They flash upon that inward eye
Which is the bliss of solitude;
And then my heart with pleasure fills,
And dances with the daffodils.

1804   1807, 1815

My heart leaps up

My heart leaps up when I behold
    A rainbow in the sky:
So was it when my life began;
So is it now I am a man;
5 So be it when I shall grow old,
    Or let me die!
The Child is father of the Man;
And I could wish my days to be
Bound each to each by natural piety.[1]

Mar. 26, 1802   1807

Ode: Intimations of Immortality   In 1843 Wordsworth said about this
ode to Isabella Fenwick:

> This was composed during my residence at Town End, Grasmere; two years at
> least passed between the writing of the four first stanzas and the remaining part.
> To the attentive and competent reader the whole sufficiently explains itself; but
> there may be no harm in adverting here to particular feelings or *experiences* of my
> own mind on which the structure of the poem partly rests. Nothing was more dif-
> ficult for me in childhood than to admit the notion of death as a state applicable to
> my own being. I have said elsewhere [in the opening stanza of "We Are Seven"]:
>
> > ——A simple Child,
> > That lightly draws its breath,
> > And feels its life in every limb,
> > What should it know of death!

---

1. Perhaps as distinguished from piety based on the Bible, in which the rainbow is the token of God's
promise to Noah and his descendants never again to send a flood to destroy the earth.

But it was not so much from [feelings] of animal vivacity that *my* difficulty came as from a sense of the indomitableness of the spirit within me. I used to brood over the stories of Enoch and Elijah [Genesis 5.22–24; 2 Kings 2.11], and almost to persuade myself that, whatever might become of others, I should be translated, in something of the same way, to heaven. With a feeling congenial to this, I was often unable to think of external things as having external existence, and I communed with all that I saw as something not apart from, but inherent in, my own immaterial nature. Many times while going to school have I grasped at a wall or tree to recall myself from this abyss of idealism to the reality. At that time I was afraid of such processes. In later periods of life I have deplored, as we have all reason to do, a subjugation of an opposite character, and have rejoiced over the remembrances, as is expressed in the lines—

> Obstinate questionings
> Of sense and outward things,
> Fallings from us, vanishings; etc.

To that dreamlike vividness and splendor which invest objects of sight in childhood, everyone, I believe, if he would look back, could bear testimony, and I need not dwell upon it here: but having in the Poem regarded it as presumptive evidence of a prior state of existence, I think it right to protest against a conclusion, which has given pain to some good and pious persons, that I meant to inculcate such a belief. It is far too shadowy a notion to be recommended to faith, as more than an element in our instincts of immortality. * * * [W]hen I was impelled to write this Poem on the 'Immortality of the Soul,' I took hold of the notion of pre-existence as having sufficient foundation in humanity for authorizing me to make for my purpose the best use of it I could as a Poet.

When he dictated this long note to Isabella Fenwick, at the age of seventy-two or seventy-three, Wordsworth was troubled by objections that his apparent claim for the preexistence of the soul violated the Christian belief that the soul, although it survives after death, does not exist before the birth of an individual. His claim in the note is that he refers to the preexistence of the soul not in order to set out a religious doctrine but only so as to deal "as a Poet" with a common human experience: that the passing of youth involves the loss of a freshness and radiance investing everything one sees. Coleridge's "Dejection: An Ode," which he wrote (in its earliest version) after he had heard the first four stanzas of Wordsworth's poem, employs a similar figurative technique for a comparable, though more devastating, experience of loss.

The original published text of this poem (in 1807) had as its title only "Ode," and then as epigraph *"Paulo maiora canamus"* (Latin for "Let us sing of somewhat higher things") from Virgil's *Eclogue 4.*

Ode

Intimations of Immortality from Recollections of Early Childhood

> The Child is Father of the Man;
> And I could wish my days to be
> Bound each to each by natural piety.[1]

---

1. The concluding lines of Wordsworth's "My heart leaps up" (p. 346).

1

There was a time when meadow, grove, and stream,
The earth, and every common sight,
    To me did seem
    Apparelled in celestial light,
5 The glory and the freshness of a dream.
It is not now as it hath been of yore;—
    Turn wheresoe'er I may,
    By night or day,
The things which I have seen I now can see no more.

2

10   The Rainbow comes and goes,
      And lovely is the Rose,
      The Moon doth with delight
Look round her when the heavens are bare,
      Waters on a starry night
15   Are beautiful and fair;
      The sunshine is a glorious birth;
      But yet I know, where'er I go,
That there hath past away a glory from the earth.

3

Now, while the birds thus sing a joyous song,
20   And while the young lambs bound
      As to the tabor's[2] sound,
To me alone there came a thought of grief:
A timely utterance[3] gave that thought relief,
And I again am strong:
25 The cataracts blow their trumpets from the steep;
No more shall grief of mine the season wrong;
I hear the Echoes through the mountains throng,
The Winds come to me from the fields of sleep,[4]
      And all the earth is gay;
30   Land and sea
    Give themselves up to jollity,
      And with the heart of May
    Doth every Beast keep holiday;—
      Thou Child of Joy,
35 Shout round me, let me hear thy shouts, thou happy
    Shepherd-boy!

4

Ye blessed Creatures, I have heard the call
Ye to each other make; I see

---

2. A small drum often used to beat time for dancing.
3. Perhaps "My heart leaps up," perhaps "Resolution and Independence," perhaps not a poem at
all.
4. Of the many suggested interpretations, the

simplest is "from the fields where they were sleeping." Wordsworth often associated a rising wind
with the revival of spirit and of poetic inspiration
(see, e.g., the opening passage of *The Prelude*, p.
362).

The heavens laugh with you in your jubilee;
　　　My heart is at your festival,
40　　　　My head hath its coronal,[5]
The fulness of your bliss, I feel—I feel it all.
　　　Oh evil day! if I were sullen
　　　While Earth herself is adorning,
　　　This sweet May-morning,
45　　　And the Children are culling
　　　　On every side,
　　　In a thousand valleys far and wide,
　　　Fresh flowers; while the sun shines warm,
And the Babe leaps up on his Mother's arm:—
50　　　I hear, I hear, with joy I hear!
　　　—But there's a Tree, of many, one,
A single Field which I have looked upon,
Both of them speak of something that is gone:
　　　The Pansy at my feet
55　　　Doth the same tale repeat:
Whither is fled the visionary gleam?
Where is it now, the glory and the dream?

5

Our birth is but a sleep and a forgetting:
The Soul that rises with us, our life's Star,[6]
60　　　Hath had elsewhere its setting,
　　　　And cometh from afar:
　　　Not in entire forgetfulness,
　　　And not in utter nakedness,
But trailing clouds of glory do we come
65　　　From God, who is our home:
Heaven lies about us in our infancy!
Shades of the prison-house begin to close
　　　Upon the growing Boy,
But He beholds the light, and whence it flows,
70　　　He sees it in his joy;
The Youth, who daily farther from the east
　　　Must travel, still is Nature's Priest,
　　　And by the vision splendid
　　　Is on his way attended;
75　At length the Man perceives it die away,
And fade into the light of common day.

6

Earth fills her lap with pleasures of her own;
Yearnings she hath in her own natural kind,
And, even with something of a Mother's mind,
80　　　And no unworthy aim,
　　　The homely[7] Nurse doth all she can

---

5. Circlet of wildflowers, with which the shepherd boys trimmed their hats in May.

6. The sun, as metaphor for the soul.
7. In the old sense: simple and friendly.

To make her Foster-child, her Inmate Man,
    Forget the glories he hath known,
And that imperial palace whence he came.

7

85   Behold the Child among his new-born blisses,
    A six years' Darling of a pigmy size!
    See, where 'mid work of his own hand he lies,
    Fretted[8] by sallies of his mother's kisses,
    With light upon him from his father's eyes!
90   See, at his feet, some little plan or chart,
    Some fragment from his dream of human life,
    Shaped by himself with newly-learnèd art;
        A wedding or a festival,
        A mourning or a funeral;
95   And this hath now his heart,
        And unto this he frames his song:
        Then will he fit his tongue
    To dialogues of business, love, or strife;
        But it will not be long
100   Ere this be thrown aside,
        And with new joy and pride
    The little Actor cons° another part;   *studies*
    Filling from time to time his "humorous stage"[9]
    With all the Persons, down to palsied Age,
105 That Life brings with her in her equipage;
        As if his whole vocation
        Were endless imitation.

8

Thou, whose exterior semblance doth belie
        Thy Soul's immensity;
110 Thou best Philosopher, who yet dost keep
    Thy heritage, thou Eye among the blind,
    That, deaf and silent, read'st the eternal deep,
    Haunted for ever by the eternal mind,—
        Mighty Prophet! Seer blest!
115   On whom those truths do rest,
    Which we are toiling all our lives to find,
    In darkness lost, the darkness of the grave;
    Thou, over whom thy Immortality
    Broods like the Day, a Master o'er a Slave,
120 A Presence which is not to be put by;
    Thou little Child, yet glorious in the might
    Of heaven-born freedom on thy being's height,
    Why with such earnest pains dost thou provoke
    The years to bring the inevitable yoke,
125 Thus blindly with thy blessedness at strife?

---

8. Irritated; or possibly in the old sense: check-
ered over.
9. From a sonnet by the Elizabethan poet Samuel
Daniel. In Daniel's era *humorous* meant "capricious" and also referred to the various characters
and temperaments ("humors") represented in
drama.

Full soon thy Soul shall have her earthly freight,
And custom lie upon thee with a weight,
Heavy as frost, and deep almost as life!

9

O joy! that in our embers
130   Is something that doth live,
That nature yet remembers
What was so fugitive!°   *fleeting*
The thought of our past years in me doth breed
Perpetual benediction: not indeed
135 For that which is most worthy to be blest;
Delight and liberty, the simple creed
Of Childhood, whether busy or at rest,
With new-fledged hope still fluttering in his breast:—
    Not for these I raise
140   The song of thanks and praise;
    But for those obstinate questionings
    Of sense and outward things,
    Fallings from us, vanishings;
    Blank misgivings of a Creature
145 Moving about in worlds not realised,[1]
High instincts before which our mortal Nature
Did tremble like a guilty Thing surprised:
    But for those first affections,
    Those shadowy recollections,
150   Which, be they what they may,
Are yet the fountain light of all our day,
Are yet a master light of all our seeing;
    Uphold us, cherish, and have power to make
Our noisy years seem moments in the being
155 Of the eternal Silence: truths that wake,
    To perish never;
Which neither listlessness, nor mad endeavour,
    Nor Man nor Boy,
Nor all that is at enmity with joy,
160 Can utterly abolish or destroy!
    Hence in a season of calm weather
    Though inland far we be,
Our Souls have sight of that immortal sea
    Which brought us hither,
165   Can in a moment travel thither,
And see the Children sport upon the shore,
And hear the mighty waters rolling evermore.

10

Then sing, ye Birds, sing, sing a joyous song!
    And let the young Lambs bound
170   As to the tabor's sound!
We in thought will join your throng,

---

1. Not seeming real (see Wordsworth's comment about "this abyss of idealism" in the headnote on
p. 347).

Ye that pipe and ye that play,
Ye that through your hearts to-day
Feel the gladness of the May!
175 What though the radiance which was once so bright
Be now for ever taken from my sight,
Though nothing can bring back the hour
Of splendour in the grass, of glory in the flower;
We will grieve not, rather find
180 Strength in what remains behind;
In the primal sympathy
Which having been must ever be;
In the soothing thoughts that spring
Out of human suffering;
185 In the faith that looks through death,
In years that bring the philosophic mind.

II

And O, ye Fountains, Meadows, Hills, and Groves,
Forebode° not any severing of our loves!   *predict, portend*
Yet in my heart of hearts I feel your might;
190 I only have relinquished one delight
To live beneath your more habitual sway.
I love the Brooks which down their channels fret,
Even more than when I tripped lightly as they;
The innocent brightness of a new-born Day
195   Is lovely yet;
The Clouds that gather round the setting sun
Do take a sober colouring from an eye
That hath kept watch o'er man's mortality;
Another race hath been, and other palms are won.[2]
200 Thanks to the human heart by which we live,
Thanks to its tenderness, its joys, and fears,
To me the meanest° flower that blows° can give   *lowliest / blooms*
Thoughts that do often lie too deep for tears.

1802–04   1807

The Solitary Reaper[1]

Behold her, single in the field,
Yon solitary Highland Lass!
Reaping and singing by herself;

---

2. In Greece foot races were often run for the prize of a branch or wreath of palm. Wordsworth's line echoes Paul, 1 Corinthians 9.24, who uses such races as a metaphor for life: "Know ye not that they which run in a race run all, but one receiveth the prize?"
1. One of the rare poems not based on Wordsworth's own experience. In a note published with the poem in 1807, Wordsworth says that it was suggested by a passage in Thomas Wilkinson's *Tours to the British Mountains* (1824), which he had seen in manuscript: "Passed a female who was reaping alone: she sung in Erse [the Gaelic language of Scotland] as she bended over her sickle; the sweetest human voice I ever heard: her strains were tenderly melancholy, and felt delicious, long after they were heard no more." In 1803 William and Mary Wordsworth, Dorothy Wordsworth, and Coleridge toured Scotland, making a pilgrimage to Robert Burns's grave and visiting places mentioned in Walter Scott's historical notes to his *Minstrelsy of the Scottish Border*.

Stop here, or gently pass!
5 Alone she cuts and binds the grain,
And sings a melancholy strain;
O listen! for the Vale profound
Is overflowing with the sound.

No Nightingale did ever chaunt
10 More welcome notes to weary bands
Of travellers in some shady haunt,
Among Arabian sands:
A voice so thrilling ne'er was heard
In spring-time from the Cuckoo-bird,
15 Breaking the silence of the seas
Among the farthest Hebrides.[2]

Will no one tell me what she sings?[3]
Perhaps the plaintive numbers° flow   *verses*
For old, unhappy, far-off things,
20 And battles long ago:
Or is it some more humble lay,
Familiar matter of to-day?
Some natural sorrow, loss, or pain,
That has been, and may be again?

25 Whate'er the theme, the Maiden sang
As if her song could have no ending;
I saw her singing at her work,
And o'er the sickle bending;—
I listened, motionless and still;
30 And, as I mounted up the hill,
The music in my heart I bore,
Long after it was heard no more.

Nov. 5, 1805   1807

Elegiac Stanzas

*Suggested by a Picture of Peele Castle, in a Storm,
Painted by Sir George Beaumont*[1]

I was thy neighbour once, thou rugged Pile!°   *building*
Four summer weeks I dwelt in sight of thee:
I saw thee every day; and all the while
Thy Form was sleeping on a glassy sea.

5 So pure the sky, so quiet was the air!
So like, so very like, was day to day!
Whene'er I looked, thy Image still was there;
It trembled, but it never passed away.

2. Islands off the west coast of Scotland.
3. The poet does not understand Erse, the language in which she sings.
1. A wealthy landscape painter who was Words-worth's patron and close friend. Peele Castle is on an island opposite Rampside, Lancashire, where Wordsworth had spent a month in 1794, twelve years before he saw Beaumont's painting.

How perfect was the calm! it seemed no sleep;
10 No mood, which season takes away, or brings:
I could have fancied that the mighty Deep
Was even the gentlest of all gentle Things.

Ah! THEN, if mine had been the Painter's hand,
To express what then I saw; and add the gleam,
15 The light that never was, on sea or land,
The consecration, and the Poet's dream;

I would have planted thee, thou hoary Pile
Amid a world how different from this!
Beside a sea that could not cease to smile;
20 On tranquil land, beneath a sky of bliss.

Thou shouldst have seemed a treasure-house divine
Of peaceful years; a chronicle of heaven;
—Of all the sunbeams that did ever shine
The very sweetest had to thee been given.

25 A Picture had it been of lasting ease,
Elysian[2] quiet, without toil or strife;
No motion but the moving tide, a breeze,
Or merely silent Nature's breathing life.

Such, in the fond illusion of my heart,
30 Such Picture would I at that time have made:
And seen the soul of truth in every part,
A stedfast peace that might not be betrayed.

So once it would have been,—'tis so no more;
I have submitted to a new control:
35 A power is gone, which nothing can restore;
A deep distress hath humanised my Soul.[3]

Not for a moment could I now behold
A smiling sea, and be what I have been:
The feeling of my loss will ne'er be old;
40 This, which I know, I speak with mind serene.

Then, Beaumont, Friend! who would have been the Friend,
If he had lived, of Him whom I deplore,°   *mourn*
This work of thine I blame not, but commend;
This sea in anger, and that dismal shore.

45 O 'tis a passionate Work!—yet wise and well,
Well chosen is the spirit that is here;
That Hulk° which labours in the deadly swell,   *ship*
This rueful sky, this pageantry of fear!

---

2. Referring to Elysium, in classical mythology the peaceful place where those favored by the gods dwelled after death.

3. Captain John Wordsworth, William's brother, had been drowned in a shipwreck on February 5, 1805. He is referred to in lines 41–42.

And this huge Castle, standing here sublime,
50 I love to see the look with which it braves,
Cased in the unfeeling armour of old time,
The lightning, the fierce wind, and trampling waves.

Farewell, farewell the heart that lives alone,
Housed in a dream, at distance from the Kind!°   humankind
55 Such happiness, wherever it be known,
Is to be pitied; for 'tis surely blind.

But welcome fortitude, and patient cheer,
And frequent sights of what is to be borne!
Such sights, or worse, as are before me here.—
60 Not without hope we suffer and we mourn.

Summer 1806   1807

SONNETS

Prefatory Sonnet [Nuns fret not][1]

Nuns fret not at their Convent's narrow room;
And Hermits are contented with their Cells;
And Students with their pensive Citadels:
Maids at the Wheel,° the Weaver at his Loom,   spinning wheel
5 Sit blithe and happy; Bees that soar for bloom,
High as the highest Peak of Furness Fells,[2]
Will murmur by the hour in Foxglove bells:
In truth, the prison, unto which we doom
Ourselves, no prison is: and hence to me,
10 In sundry moods, 'twas pastime to be bound
Within the Sonnet's scanty plot of ground:
Pleas'd if some Souls (for such there needs must be)
Who have felt the weight of too much liberty,
Should find short solace there, as I have found.

1802   1815

Composed upon Westminster Bridge,
September 3, 1802[1]

Earth has not any thing to show more fair:
Dull would he be of soul who could pass by

---

1. In *Poems in Two Volumes* (1807), this celebration of the restrictions of the sonnet form headed up the book's selection of sonnets. In old age Wordsworth remembered that his interest in the form was first revived when Dorothy read John Milton's sonnets aloud to him in 1802.
2. Hills forming the southwestern part of the Lake District.
1. The date of this experience was not September 3, but July 31, 1802. Its occasion was a trip to France, made possible by a brief truce in the war (see Dorothy Wordsworth's *Grasmere Journals,* July 1802, p. 417). Wordsworth's conflicted feelings about this return to France, where he had once supported the Revolution and loved Annette Vallon, inform a number of personal and political sonnets that he wrote in 1802, among them the four that follow.

A sight so touching in its majesty:
This City now doth, like a garment, wear
5 The beauty of the morning; silent, bare,
Ships, towers, domes, theatres, and temples lie
Open unto the fields, and to the sky;
All bright and glittering in the smokeless air.
Never did sun more beautifully steep
10 In his first splendour, valley, rock, or hill;
Ne'er saw I, never felt, a calm so deep!
The river glideth at his own sweet will:
Dear God! the very houses seem asleep;
And all that mighty heart is lying still!

1802   1807

It is a beauteous evening

It is a beauteous evening, calm and free,
The holy time is quiet as a Nun
Breathless with adoration; the broad sun
Is sinking down in its tranquillity;
5 The gentleness of heaven broods o'er the Sea:
Listen! the mighty Being is awake,
And doth with his eternal motion make
A sound like thunder—everlastingly.
Dear Child! dear Girl! that walkest with me here,[1]
10 If thou appear untouched by solemn thought,
Thy nature is not therefore less divine:
Thou liest in Abraham's bosom[2] all the year;
And worshipp'st at the Temple's inner shrine,
God being with thee when we know it not.

Aug. 1802   1807

To Toussaint l'Ouverture[1]

Toussaint, the most unhappy Man of Men!
Whether the rural Milk-maid by her Cow
Sing in thy hearing, or thou liest now
Alone in some deep dungeon's earless den,
5 O miserable Chieftain! where and when

1. The girl walking with Wordsworth is Caroline, his daughter by Annette Vallon. For the event described see Dorothy Wordsworth's *Grasmere Journals*, July 1802 (p. 417).
2. Where the souls destined for heaven rest after death. Luke 16.22: "And it came to pass, that the beggar died, and was carried by the angels into Abraham's bosom."
1. First published in the *Morning Post*, Feb. 2,

1803. François Dominique Toussaint, later called L'Ouverture (ca. 1743–1803), was a self-educated slave who became leader of the slave rebellion in Haiti and governor of Santo Domingo. For opposing Napoleon's edict reestablishing slavery (abolished in France and its colonial possessions in the early stages of the Revolution), Toussaint was arrested and taken to Paris in June 1802. He died in prison in April 1803.

Wilt thou find patience? Yet die not; do thou
Wear rather in thy bonds a cheerful brow:
Though fallen Thyself, never to rise again,
Live, and take comfort. Thou hast left behind
10   Powers that will work for thee; air, earth, and skies;
There's not a breathing of the common wind
That will forget thee; thou hast great allies;
Thy friends are exultations, agonies,
And love, and Man's unconquerable mind.

1802   1803

September 1st, 1802[1]

We had a fellow-Passenger who came
From Calais with us, gaudy in array,
A Negro Woman like a Lady gay,
Yet silent as a woman fearing blame;
5   Dejected, meek, yea pitiably tame,
She sat, from notice turning not away,
But on our proffered kindness still did lay
A weight of languid speech, or at the same
Was silent, motionless in eyes and face.
10   She was a Negro Woman driv'n from France,
Rejected like all others of that race,
Not one of whom may now find footing there;
This the poor Out-cast did to us declare,
Nor murmured at the unfeeling Ordinance.

1802   1803

London, 1802[1]

Milton! thou should'st be living at this hour:
England hath need of thee: she is a fen
Of stagnant waters: altar, sword, and pen,
Fireside, the heroic wealth of hall and bower,
5   Have forfeited their ancient English dower°   *endowment, gift*
Of inward happiness. We are selfish men;
Oh! raise us up, return to us again;
And give us manners, virtue, freedom, power.
Thy soul was like a Star, and dwelt apart:

1. First published, with the title "The Banished Negroes," in the *Morning Post*, Feb. 11, 1803. In 1827 Wordsworth added an explanatory headnote beneath the title: "Among the capricious acts of tyranny that disgraced those times, was the chasing of all Negroes from France by decree of the government: we had a Fellow-passenger who was one of the expelled."
1. One of a series "written immediately after my return from France to London, when I could not but be struck, as here described, with the vanity and parade of our own country . . . as contrasted with the quiet, and I may say the desolation, that the revolution had produced in France. This must be borne in mind, or else the reader may think that in this and the succeeding sonnets I have exaggerated the mischief engendered and fostered among us by undisturbed wealth" [Wordsworth's note, 1843].

10   Thou hadst a voice whose sound was like the sea:
     Pure as the naked heavens, majestic, free,
     So didst thou travel on life's common way,
     In cheerful godliness; and yet thy heart
     The lowliest duties on herself did lay.

Sept. 1802   1807

The world is too much with us

     The world is too much with us; late and soon,
     Getting and spending, we lay waste our powers:
     Little we see in Nature that is ours;
     We have given our hearts away, a sordid boon![1]
5   This Sea that bares her bosom to the moon;
     The winds that will be howling at all hours,
     And are up-gathered now like sleeping flowers;
     For this, for every thing, we are out of tune;
     It moves us not.—Great God! I'd rather be
10   A Pagan suckled in a creed outworn;
     So might I, standing on this pleasant lea,
     Have glimpses that would make me less forlorn;
     Have sight of Proteus rising from the sea;
     Or hear old Triton[2] blow his wreathèd horn.

1802–04   1807

Surprised by joy[1]

     Surprised by joy—impatient as the Wind
     I turned to share the transport—Oh! with whom
     But Thee, deep buried in the silent tomb,
     That spot which no vicissitude can find?
5   Love, faithful love, recalled thee to my mind—
     But how could I forget thee? Through what power,
     Even for the least division of an hour,
     Have I been so beguiled as to be blind
     To my most grievous loss!—That thought's return
10   Was the worst pang that sorrow ever bore,
     Save one, one only, when I stood forlorn,
     Knowing my heart's best treasure was no more;
     That neither present time, nor years unborn
     Could to my sight that heavenly face restore.

1813–14   1815

---

1. Gift. It is the act of giving the heart away that is sordid.
2. A sea deity, usually represented as blowing on a conch shell. Proteus was an old man of the sea who (in the *Odyssey*) could assume a variety of shapes. The description of Proteus echoes *Paradise Lost* 3.603–04, and that of Triton echoes Edmund Spenser's *Colin Clouts Come Home Againe*, lines 244–45.

1. This was in fact suggested by my daughter Catherine, long after her death [Wordsworth's note]. Catherine Wordsworth died June 4, 1812, at the age of four.

Mutability[1]

From low to high doth dissolution climb,
And sink from high to low, along a scale
Of awful° notes, whose concord shall not fail;   awe-inspiring
A musical but melancholy chime,
5   Which they can hear who meddle not with crime,
Nor avarice, nor over anxious care
Truth fails not; but her outward forms that bear
The longest date do melt like frosty rime,
That in the morning whitened hill and plain
10 And is no more; drop like the tower sublime
Of yesterday, which royally did wear
His crown of weeds, but could not even sustain
Some casual shout that broke the silent air,
Or the unimaginable touch of Time.

1821   1822

Steamboats, Viaducts, and Railways[1]

Motions and Means, on land and sea at war
With old poetic feeling, not for this,
Shall ye, by Poets even, be judged amiss!
Nor shall your presence, howsoe'er it mar
5   The loveliness of Nature, prove a bar
To the Mind's gaining that prophetic sense
Of future change, that point of vision, whence
May be discovered what in soul ye are.
In spite of all that beauty may disown
10 In your harsh features, Nature doth embrace
Her lawful offspring in Man's art; and Time,
Pleased with your triumphs o'er his brother Space,
Accepts from your bold hands the proffered crown
Of hope, and smiles on you with cheer sublime.

1833   1835

---

1. This late sonnet was included in an otherwise rather uninspired sequence, *Ecclesiastical Sonnets*, dealing with the history and ceremonies of the Church of England.
1. In late middle age Wordsworth demonstrates, as he had predicted in the Preface to *Lyrical Ballads*, that the poet will assimilate to his subject matter the "material revolution" produced by science.

The 1805 Prelude   We cannot be sure what William Wordsworth would have thought of the title by which readers now know his major work, *The Prelude, or Growth of a Poet's Mind*. The poet's widow gave the poem that title when her husband's literary executors published it in July 1850, three months after his death. Wordsworth himself had referred to it, variously, as "the poem to Coleridge" or "the poem on the growth of my own mind." Wordsworth's readership had known of the existence of this autobiographical poem since his 1814 publication of *The Excursion*, which had the subtitle "Being a portion of *The Recluse*." In the preface to that poem, which explained that *The Excursion* was part of a philosophical poem, still in preparation, titled *The Recluse*, Wordsworth revealed further that *The Recluse* would appear with a supplement: a poem, "long finished," he stated, that traced how Nature and Education had prepared the poet for executing the "arduous labour" which that philosophical poem would entail. This other poem—which is the one we now know as *The Prelude*—scrutinized his qualifications for that task. The "two Works have the same kind of relation to each other," he explained, as an ante-chapel has to a nave or "body of a gothic church."

Where *The Recluse* was never really begun, despite what that 1814 subtitle and preface indicated, *The Prelude*, by contrast, appears to have been a poem that Wordsworth could never really declare finished. He completed it, and then, rather than declaring it ready for the press, he completed it again. Revision occupied him for a half-century, claiming the time he had aimed to devote to *The Recluse*. Because he held it back from publication, this poem of self-scrutiny became a kind of lifetime companion to the poet, its account of his past altered to keep pace with the changes that age brought to its creator. The resulting gap between its dates of composition and date of publication is obliquely acknowledged in the title Mary Wordsworth devised. *The Prelude* was a good title, one of Wordsworth's executors observed, precisely because it would discourage readers from supposing that "it was his final production, instead of being, as it really is, one of his *earlier* works." Wordsworth had so arranged things, however, that when at last in 1850 it appeared as a book, this "earlier" work did double duty (in the words of Wordsworth scholar Mary Jacobus) as "a self-authored epitaph."

In 1926 Ernest de Selincourt, working from manuscripts, printed the version of the poem that Wordsworth completed in 1805, and which for many readers since then has become the preferred version. Other scholars later established the existence of a still earlier and shorter version that Wordsworth composed in 1798–99. The process that produced these three principal versions of *The Prelude*—1798–99; 1805; 1850—seems to have unfolded as follows.

1. While living in Germany during the autumn and winter of 1798–99 Wordsworth composed a number of blank verse passages about his formative experiences with nature, meaning thus to begin the philosophical poem Coleridge had urged him to write. Then, after settling with his sister, Dorothy, at Grasmere, what had first been intended as part of *The Recluse* evolved further, becoming a poem of almost a thousand lines, in two parts, that described his life up to the end of his school days. This poem corresponds to books 1 and 2 of later versions of *The Prelude*.

2. In 1801 Wordsworth began to expand this poem, adding the material that would ultimately form the beginning of book 3. He renewed this work in earnest at the start of 1804, with a new plan for a poem in five books. Scholars disagree as to whether this version, whose concluding book would have begun with the poet's vision on Mount Snowdon (later transposed to the poem's conclusion) and moved to the discussion of "spots of time" (later transposed to book 11), ever materialized. However, it is clear that by March 1804, Wordsworth had determined that the poem would require further enlarging. It would have to represent some of his experiences in France

during the 1790s and the failure of his hopes for the French Revolution, dramatizing the interaction of the imagination and historical forces, as well as the interaction of the imagination and nature. Adding books 6, then 9, and 10, and 8, he completed this new version in thirteen books in May 1805 and had Dorothy and his wife copy it out. This is the version printed in this volume, which reproduces the edition of the 1805 text that Jonathan Wordsworth, Stephen Gill, and M. H. Abrams prepared in 1979 for the Norton Critical Edition of *The Prelude*.

3. For the next thirty-five years, without altering in any essential way the *Prelude*'s subject matter or design, Wordsworth revised. This period also saw some parts of the poem published separately. "There was a boy" (from book 5) and "Simplon Pass" (from book 6), for example, appeared in Wordsworth's *Poems* of 1815. Coleridge (the first outside Wordsworth's family to encounter the 1805 text) had earlier published sections from books 1 and 6 in *The Friend*. The version of the whole poem his executors ushered into print in 1850 was in fourteen books, Wordsworth having split book 10 into two parts in 1832. The printer's copy was the transcript the poet's daughter and a friend had prepared in 1838 of the 1832 text, and into which Wordsworth and his clerk had later inserted corrections.

As this summary of the *Prelude*'s multiple recastings suggests, Wordsworth's vision of his poem—his view of himself, too—altered substantially over the years, at the start of the process especially. When he decided to enlarge the two-part *Prelude* of 1799, he committed himself to expanding lyric introspection to epic dimensions. It was "a thing unprecedented in Literary history," he observed in an 1805 letter that hints at this experiment with genre, "that a man should talk so much about himself." Between 1801 and 1805 he heightened his poem's style and incorporated allusions to earlier epics, self-consciously measuring his achievement as a poet-prophet against Milton's in *Paradise Lost*. Another prototype for his poem can be found in the tradition of spiritual autobiography that Saint Augustine had founded with his *Confessions* in the fourth century and that the scandalous Frenchman Jean-Jacques Rousseau had revived in the 1780s. Rousseau's *Confessions* made big, bold claims for the fascination of the author's subjectivity in all its unique intricacies, and Wordsworth's *Prelude* in some measure follows suit, as it personalizes epic and makes a literary form devoted to the public life of great collectivities (the fall of Troy or of Man) absorb representations of childhood anxieties and guilt that we might nowadays think of as belonging to a psychological case history. But as narrator, rather than narrated subject, Wordsworth insists on the wider import of this singular story. *The Prelude* thus asks to be read as the representative testimony of someone who (along with Coleridge, to whom the poem is addressed as a kind of letter, and along with an entire generation, in fact) has grappled with the traumatic experience of revolutionary optimism followed by defeat.

The poet has made it his urgent task to recover that lost faith: "I would enshrine the spirit of the past / For future restoration" (11.341–42). The persistent metaphor of *The Prelude*, shared with many autobiographies, is that of life as a circular journey. This poem of many wanderers and journeys concludes by installing the wandering poet back in his starting place. The prodigal son has completed the long journey home, after being lured into a crisis of identity by youthful radicalism and a residence in France. The poet declares the poem itself to be proof that he has realized the vocation he had queried at his setting-out. For many modern readers, however, much of the brilliance of *The Prelude* inheres in the passages in which the poet confesses to his failure to close the circle. What these readers value are Wordsworth's recurring expressions of doubt as to whether memory could ever bind the disparate materials of the individual's life into a coherent whole. A sense of the disjuncture between the man and the boy, the self who remembers and the self who is remembered, haunts this poem. This autobiographical enterprise demonstrates that sometimes self-estrangement—"I seem / Two consciousnesses—conscious of myself, / And of some other being" (2.31–33)—and self-knowledge proceed hand in hand.

Book First.

Introduction: Childhood and School-time

Oh there is blessing in this gentle breeze,
That blows from the green fields and from the clouds
And from the sky; it beats against my cheek,
And seems half conscious of the joy it gives.
5 O welcome messenger! O welcome friend!
A captive greets thee, coming from a house
Of bondage, from yon city's° walls set free,   *London's*
A prison where he hath been long immured.
Now I am free, enfranchised and at large,
10 May fix my habitation where I will.
What dwelling shall receive me, in what vale
Shall be my harbour, underneath what grove
Shall I take up my home, and what sweet stream
Shall with its murmurs lull me to my rest?
15 The earth is all before me¹—with a heart
Joyous, nor scared at its own liberty,
I look about, and should the guide I chuse
Be nothing better than a wandering cloud
I cannot miss my way. I breathe again—
20 Trances of thought and mountings of the mind
Come fast upon me. It is shaken off,
As by miraculous gift 'tis shaken off,
That burthen of my own unnatural self,
The heavy weight of many a weary day
25 Not mine, and such as were not made for me.
Long months of peace—if such bold word accord
With any promises of human life—
Long months of ease and undisturbed delight
Are mine in prospect.° Whither shall I turn,   *anticipation*
30 By road or pathway, or through open field,
Or shall a twig or any floating thing
Upon the river point me out my course?

Enough that I am free, for months to come
May dedicate myself to chosen tasks,
35 May quit the tiresome sea and dwell on shore—
If not a settler on the soil, at least
To drink wild water, and to pluck green herbs,
And gather fruits fresh from their native bough.
Nay more, if I may trust myself, this hour
40 Hath brought a gift that consecrates my joy;
For I, methought, while the sweet breath of heaven
Was blowing on my body, felt within
A corresponding mild creative breeze,
A vital breeze which travelled gently on
45 O'er things which it had made, and is become

---

1. One of many echoes from *Paradise Lost*, where the line is applied to Adam and Eve as they begin their new life after the fall and their expulsion from Eden: "The world was all before them" (12.646).

A tempest, a redundant° energy,   *abundant*
Vexing its own creation. 'Tis a power
That does not come unrecognised, a storm
Which, breaking up a long-continued frost,
50 Brings with it vernal° promises, the hope   *springtime*
Of active days, of dignity and thought,
Of prowess in an honorable field,
Pure passions, virtue, knowledge, and delight,
The holy life of music and of verse.[2]

55   Thus far, O friend,[3] did I, not used to make
A present joy the matter of my song,[4]
Pour out that day my soul in measured strains,
Even in the very words which I have here
Recorded. To the open fields I told
60 A prophesy; poetic numbers° came   *verses*
Spontaneously, and clothed in priestly robe
My spirit, thus singled out, as it might seem,
For holy services. Great hopes were mine:
My own voice cheared me, and, far more, the mind's
65 Internal echo of the imperfect sound—
To both I listened, drawing from them both
A chearful confidence in things to come.

        Whereat, being not unwilling now to give
A respite to this passion,[5] I paced on
70 Gently, with careless steps, and came erelong
To a green shady place where down I sate
Beneath a tree, slackening my thoughts by choice
And settling into gentler happiness.
'Twas autumn, and a calm and placid day
75 With warmth as much as needed from a sun
Two hours declined towards the west, a day
With silver clouds and sunshine on the grass,
And, in the sheltered grove where I was couched,
A perfect stillness. On the ground I lay
80 Passing through many thoughts, yet mainly such
As to myself pertained. I made a choice
Of one sweet vale[6] whither my steps should turn,
And saw, methought, the very house and fields
Present before my eyes; nor did I fail
85 To add meanwhile assurance of some work
Of glory there forthwith to be begun—

2. This opening passage (lines 1–54), which Wordsworth wrote in 1799, and which in book 7, line 4, he will call his "glad preamble," replaces a traditional epic's opening prayer to the Muse for inspiration. To be "inspired" is literally to be breathed or blown into by a divinity (in Latin *spirare* means both "to breathe" and "to blow"). The "breath of heaven" that blows on the poet's body in lines 41–42, answered by a breeze within (lines 42–43), fills that role here.
3. Samuel Taylor Coleridge, to whom Wordsworth

addresses the whole of the *Prelude*. For Coleridge's response, see "To William Wordsworth" (p. 489).
4. In the Preface to *Lyrical Ballads*, Wordsworth says that his poetry usually originates in "emotion recollected in tranquillity"; hence not, as in the preamble of lines 1–54, during the experience that it records.
5. I.e., willing to prolong the passion.
6. Grasmere, where Wordsworth settled with his sister, Dorothy, in December 1799.

Perhaps too there performed.[7] Thus long I lay
Cheared by the genial pillow of the earth
Beneath my head, soothed by a sense of touch
90   From the warm ground, that balanced me, else lost
Entirely, seeing nought, nought hearing, save
When here and there about the grove of oaks
Where was my bed, an acorn from the trees
Fell audibly, and with a startling sound.

95   Thus occupied in mind I lingered here
Contented, nor rose up until the sun
Had almost touched the horizon; bidding then
A farewell to the city left behind,
Even with the chance equipment of that hour
100   I journeyed towards the vale which I had chosen.
It was a splendid evening, and my soul
Did once again make trial of the strength
Restored to her afresh; nor did she want
Eolian visitations[8]—but the harp
105   Was soon defrauded, and the banded host
Of harmony dispersed in straggling sounds,
And lastly utter silence. 'Be it so,
It is an injury', said I, 'to this day
To think of any thing but present joy.'
110   So, like a peasant, I pursued my road
Beneath the evening sun, nor had one wish
Again to bend the sabbath of that time[9]
To a servile yoke. What need of many words?—
A pleasant loitering journey, through two days
115   Continued, brought me to my hermitage.°   *secluded dwelling*

        I spare to speak, my friend, of what ensued—
The admiration and the love, the life
In common things, the endless store of things
Rare, or at least so seeming, every day
120   Found all about me in one neighbourhood,
The self-congratulation,° the complete   *rejoicing*
Composure, and the happiness entire.
But speedily a longing in me rose
To brace myself to some determined aim,
125   Reading or thinking, either to lay up
New stores, or rescue from decay the old
By timely interference. I had hopes
Still higher, that with a frame of outward life
I might endue,° might fix in a visible home,   *invest*
130   Some portion of those phantoms of conceit,°   *mental images*
That had been floating loose about so long,
And to such beings temperately deal forth

---

7. The work is *The Recluse*, which Wordsworth
planned as his major poetic work but never finished.
8. Influences to which his soul responded as an
Eolian harp, placed in an open window, responds

with music to gusts of a breeze. For a description
of this instrument, named for Aeolus, the classical god of the winds, see Coleridge's *The Eolian
Harp*, p. 444, n. 1.
9. That time of rest.

The many feelings that oppressed my heart.
But I have been discouraged: gleams of light
135 Flash often from the east, then disappear,
And mock me with a sky that ripens not
Into a steady morning. If my mind,
Remembering the sweet promise of the past,
Would gladly grapple with some noble theme,
140 Vain is her wish—where'er she turns she finds
Impediments from day to day renewed.

    And now it would content me to yield up
Those lofty hopes awhile for present gifts
Of humbler industry. But, O dear friend,
145 The poet, gentle creature as he is,
Hath like the lover his unruly times—
His fits when he is neither sick nor well,
Though no distress be near him but his own
Unmanageable thoughts. The mind itself,
150 The meditative mind, best pleased perhaps
While she as duteous as the mother dove
Sits brooding,[1] lives not always to that end,
But hath less quiet instincts—goadings on
That drive her as in trouble through the groves.
155 With me is now such passion, which I blame
No otherwise than as it lasts too long.

    When, as becomes a man who would prepare
For such a glorious work, I through myself
Make rigorous inquisition, the report
160 Is often chearing; for I neither seem
To lack that first great gift, the vital soul,
Nor general truths which are themselves a sort
Of elements and agents, under-powers,
Subordinate helpers of the living mind.
165 Nor am I naked in external things,
Forms, images, nor numerous other aids
Of less regard, though won perhaps with toil,
And needful to build up a poet's praise.
Time, place, and manners,° these I seek, and these   *customs*
170 I find in plenteous store, but nowhere such
As may be singled out with steady choice—
No little band of yet remembered names
Whom I, in perfect confidence, might hope
To summon back from lonesome banishment
175 And make them inmates in the hearts of men
Now living, or to live in times to come.
Sometimes, mistaking vainly, as I fear,
Proud spring-tide swellings for a regular sea,
I settle on some British theme, some old

---

1. An echo of Milton's description in *Paradise Lost* of the original act of creation: the Holy Spirit, whom Milton calls on for inspiration, "Dovelike satst brooding on the vast Abyss / and mad'st it pregnant" (1.21–22).

180 Romantic tale by Milton left unsung;[2]
   More often resting at some gentle place
   Within the groves of chivalry I pipe
   Among the shepherds, with reposing knights
   Sit by a fountain-side and hear their tales.
185 Sometimes, more sternly moved, I would relate
   How vanquished Mithridates northward passed
   And, hidden in the cloud of years, became
   That Odin, father of a race by whom
   Perished the Roman Empire;[3] how the friends
190 And followers of Sertorius, out of Spain
   Flying, found shelter in the Fortunate Isles,
   And left their usages, their arts and laws,
   To disappear by a slow gradual death,
   To dwindle and to perish one by one,
195 Starved in those narrow bounds—but not the soul
   Of liberty, which fifteen hundred years
   Survived, and, when the European came
   With skill and power that could not be withstood,
   Did like a pestilence maintain its hold,
200 And wasted down by glorious death that race
   Of natural heroes.[4] Or I would record
   How in tyrannic times, some unknown man,
   Unheard of in the chronicles of kings,
   Suffered in silence for the love of truth;
205 How that one Frenchman, through continued force
   Of meditation on the inhuman deeds
   Of the first conquerors of the Indian Isles,
   Went single in his ministry across
   The ocean, not to comfort the oppressed,
210 But like a thirsty wind to roam about
   Withering the oppressor;[5] how Gustavus found
   Help at his need in Dalecarlia's mines;[6]
   How Wallace fought for Scotland, left the name
   Of Wallace[7] to be found like a wild flower
215 All over his dear country, left the deeds
   Of Wallace like a family of ghosts

2. In *Paradise Lost* 9.24–41 Milton relates that, in seeking a subject for his epic poem, he considered then rejected the "fabled Knights" of medieval romance.

3. Mithridates VI, king of Pontus in Asia Minor, was defeated by the Roman general Pompey in 66 B.C.E. Wordsworth finds epic potential in the legend that, following this defeat, he (in some versions, one of his chieftains) led his people in migration from Asia, north to Scandinavia; there he so impressed the inhabitants with his power that he was able to make them take him for a god, becoming the real-life prototype for the Norse god of war, Odin. In 1796 Coleridge and Robert Southey co-wrote an essay for Coleridge's journal *The Watchman* that retold this story, emphasizing Odin's choice of a dangerous freedom over Roman subjugation. This account of Odin links him to other figures whom Wordsworth here considers as potential subjects for his poem, all of them victims of and fighters against tyranny.

4. Sertorius, a Roman general temporarily allied with Mithridates, sought to establish an independent Roman republic in Spain. Following his assassination in 72 B.C.E. the republic was crushed, but there is a legend that his followers fled to the Canary Islands (known then as the "Fortunate Islands," line 191), where their descendants flourished until the arrival of Spanish conquistadors late in the 15th century.

5. Dominique de Gourges, a French gentleman who went in 1568 to Florida to avenge the massacre of the French by the Spaniards there [Wordsworth's note in the 1850 *Prelude*].

6. Gustavus Vassa (1496–1530) worked to advance Sweden's liberation from Danish rule while concealing himself in his country's Dalecarlia mines.

7. William Wallace, Scottish patriot, fought against the English until captured and executed in 1304. See Robert Burns's "Robert Bruce's March to Bannockburn," p. 189.

To people the steep rocks and river-banks,
Her natural sanctuaries, with a local soul
Of independence and stern liberty.
220 Sometimes it suits me better to shape out
Some tale from my own heart, more near akin
To my own passions and habitual thoughts,
Some variegated story, in the main
Lofty, with interchange of gentler things.
225 But deadening admonitions will succeed,
And the whole beauteous fabric seems to lack
Foundation, and withal appears throughout
Shadowy and unsubstantial.

                Then, last wish—
My last and favorite aspiration—then
230 I yearn towards some philosophic song
Of truth[8] that cherishes° our daily life,   *fosters tenderly*
With meditations passionate from deep
Recesses in man's heart, immortal verse
Thoughtfully fitted to the Orphean lyre;[9]
235 But from this awful° burthen I full soon   *solemn*
Take refuge, and beguile myself with trust
That mellower years will bring a riper mind
And clearer insight. Thus from day to day
I live a mockery of the brotherhood
240 Of vice and virtue, with no skill to part°   *distinguish*
Vague longing that is bred by want° of power,   *lack*
From paramount impulse not to be withstood;
A timorous capacity, from prudence;
From circumspection,° infinite delay.   *carefulness*
245 Humility and modest awe themselves
Betray me, serving often for a cloak
To a more subtle selfishness, that now
Doth lock my functions up in blank reserve,°   *total inaction*
Now dupes me by an over-anxious eye
250 That with a false activity beats off
Simplicity and self-presented truth.
Ah, better far than this to stray about
Voluptuously° through fields and rural walks   *luxuriously*
And ask no record of the hours given up
225 To vacant musing, unreproved neglect
Of all things, and deliberate holiday.
Far better never to have heard the name
Of zeal and just ambition than to live
Thus baffled by a mind that every hour
260 Turns recreant° to her task, takes heart again,   *unfaithful*
Then feels immediately some hollow thought
Hang like an interdict° upon her hopes.   *prohibition*
This is my lot; for either still I find

8. I.e., *The Recluse.*
9. The lyre of Orpheus. In Greek myth the singing and playing of Orpheus, a traditional figure
for the powers of poetry, enchanted both humans
and the natural world.

Some imperfection in the chosen theme,
265 Or see of absolute accomplishment
Much wanting—so much wanting—in myself
That I recoil and droop, and seek repose
In indolence from vain perplexity,
Unprofitably travelling towards the grave,
270 Like a false steward who hath much received
And renders nothing back.[1]

               Was it for this[2]
That one, the fairest of all rivers, loved
To blend his murmurs with my nurse's song,
And from his alder shades and rocky falls,
270 And from his fords and shallows, sent a voice
That flowed along my dreams? For this didst thou,
O Derwent, travelling over the green plains
Near my 'sweet birthplace',[3] didst thou, beauteous stream,
Make ceaseless music through the night and day,
280 Which with its steady cadence tempering
Our human waywardness, composed my thoughts
To more than infant softness, giving me
Among the fretful dwellings of mankind,
A knowledge, a dim earnest,° of the calm   *foretaste*
285 Which Nature breathes among the hills and groves?
When, having left his mountains, to the towers
Of Cockermouth that beauteous river came,
Behind my father's house he passed, close by,
Along the margin of our terrace walk.[4]
290 He was a playmate whom we dearly loved:
Oh, many a time have I, a five years' child,
A naked boy, in one delightful rill,
A little mill-race[5] severed from his stream,
Made one long bathing of a summer's day,
295 Basked in the sun, and plunged, and basked again,
Alternate, all a summer's day, or coursed
Over the sandy fields, leaping through groves
Of yellow grunsel;[6] or, when crag and hill,
The woods, and distant Skiddaw's[7] lofty height,
300 Were bronzed with a deep radiance, stood alone
Beneath the sky, as if I had been born
On Indian plains,[8] and from my mother's hut
Had run abroad in wantonness to sport,
A naked savage, in the thunder-shower.

---

1. The reference is to Christ's parable of the steward who fails to use his talents (literally, the coins his master has entrusted to him and, figuratively, his God-given abilities) in Matthew 25.14–30.
2. The two-part *Prelude* that Wordsworth wrote in 1798–99 begins with this abrupt question.
3. Quoting Coleridge's "Frost at Midnight," line 28.
4. The Derwent River flows by Cockermouth Castle and then past the garden terrace behind Wordsworth's childhood residence in Cockermouth, Cumbria.
5. The current that drives a mill wheel.
6. Or groundsel, a common European weed.
7. Skiddaw: one of the highest peaks in the Lake District, nine miles east of Cockermouth.
8. I.e., in America.

305   Fair seed-time had my soul, and I grew up
     Fostered alike by beauty and by fear,
     Much favored in my birthplace, and no less
     In that beloved vale[9] to which erelong
     I was transplanted. Well I call to mind—
     'Twas at an early age, ere I had seen
310   Nine summers—when upon the mountain slope
     The frost and breath of frosty wind had snapped
     The last autumnal crocus, 'twas my joy
     To wander half the night among the cliffs
     And the smooth hollows where the woodcocks ran
315   Along the open turf. In thought and wish
     That time, my shoulder all with springes° hung,   *bird snares*
     I was a fell destroyer. On the heights
     Scudding away from snare to snare, I plied
320   My anxious visitation, hurrying on,
     Still hurrying, hurrying onward. Moon and stars
     Were shining o'er my head; I was alone,
     And seemed to be a trouble to the peace
     That was among them. Sometimes it befel
325   In these night-wanderings, that a strong desire
     O'erpowered my better reason, and the bird
     Which was the captive of another's toils[1]
     Became my prey; and when the deed was done
     I heard among the solitary hills
330   Low breathings coming after me, and sounds
     Of undistinguishable motion, steps
     Almost as silent as the turf they trod.

     Nor less in springtime, when on southern banks
     The shining sun had from her knot of leaves
335   Decoyed the primrose flower, and when the vales
     And woods were warm, was I a plunderer then
     In the high places, on the lonesome peaks,
     Where'er among the mountains and the winds
     The mother-bird had built her lodge. Though mean°   *petty*
340   My object and inglorious, yet the end°   *result*
     Was not ignoble. Oh, when I have hung
     Above the raven's nest, by knots of grass
     And half-inch fissures in the slippery rock
     But ill sustained, and almost, as it seemed,
345   Suspended by the blast which blew amain,
     Shouldering the naked crag, oh, at that time
     While on the perilous ridge I hung alone,
     With what strange utterance did the loud dry wind
     Blow through my ears; the sky seemed not a sky
350   Of earth, and with what motion moved the clouds!

     The mind of man is framed even like the breath
     And harmony of music. There is a dark
     Invisible workmanship that reconciles

9. The valley of Esthwaite, thirty-five miles from   school after 1779.
Cockermouth, where Wordsworth attended   1. Snares or labors.

Discordant elements, and makes them move
355 In one society. Ah me, that all
The terrors, all the early miseries,
Regrets, vexations, lassitudes, that all
The thoughts and feelings which have been infused
Into my mind, should ever have made up
360 The calm existence that is mine when I
Am worthy of myself. Praise to the end,
Thanks likewise for the means! But I believe
That Nature, oftentimes, when she would frame
A favored being, from his earliest dawn
365 Of infancy doth open out the clouds
As at the touch of lightning, seeking him
With gentlest visitation; not the less,
Though haply° aiming at the self-same end,   *perhaps*
Does it delight her sometimes to employ
370 Severer interventions, ministry
More palpable—and so she dealt with me.

One evening—surely I was led by her—
I went alone into a shepherd's boat,
A skiff that to a willow-tree was tied
375 Within a rocky cove, its usual home.
'Twas by the shores of Patterdale, a vale
Wherein I was a stranger, thither come
A schoolboy traveller at the holidays.
Forth rambled from the village inn alone,
380 No sooner had I sight of this small skiff,
Discovered thus by unexpected chance,
Than I unloosed her tether and embarked.
The moon was up, the lake was shining clear
Among the hoary mountains; from the shore
385 I pushed, and struck the oars, and struck again
In cadence, and my little boat moved on
Even like a man who moves with stately step
Though bent on speed. It was an act of stealth
And troubled pleasure. Nor without the voice
390 Of mountain-echoes did my boat move on,
Leaving behind her still on either side
Small circles glittering idly in the moon,
Until they melted all into one track
Of sparkling light. A rocky steep uprose
395 Above the cavern of the willow-tree,
And now, as suited one who proudly rowed
With his best skill, I fixed a steady view
Upon the top of that same craggy ridge,
The bound of the horizon—for behind
400 Was nothing but the stars and the grey sky.[2]
She was an elfin pinnace;° lustily   *small boat*
I dipped my oars into the silent lake,
And as I rose upon the stroke my boat

---

2. To direct his boat in a straight line, the rower (sitting facing the stern of the boat) has fixed his eye on
a point on the ridge above the nearby shore, which blocks out the landscape behind.

Went heaving through the water like a swan—
405 When from behind that craggy steep, till then
The bound of the horizon, a huge cliff,
As if with voluntary power instinct,°   *endowed*
Upreared its head. I struck, and struck again,
And, growing still in stature, the huge cliff
410 Rose up between me and the stars, and still
With measured motion, like a living thing
Strode after me. With trembling hands I turned
And through the silent water stole my way
Back to the cavern of the willow-tree.
415 There, in her mooring-place, I left my bark
And through the meadows homeward went with grave
And serious thoughts; and after I had seen
That spectacle, for many days my brain
Worked with a dim and undetermined sense
420 Of unknown modes of being. In my thoughts
There was a darkness—call it solitude
Or blank desertion—no familiar shapes
Of hourly objects, images of trees,
Of sea or sky, no colours of green fields,
But huge and mighty forms that do not live
425 Like living men moved slowly through my mind
By day, and were the trouble of my dreams.

    Wisdom and spirit of the universe,
Thou soul that art the eternity of thought,
430 That giv'st to forms and images a breath
And everlasting motion—not in vain,
By day or star-light, thus from my first dawn
Of childhood didst thou intertwine for me
The passions that build up our human soul,
435 Not with the mean and vulgar° works of man,   *lowly, commonplace*
But with high objects, with enduring things,
With life and Nature, purifying thus
The elements of feeling and of thought,
And sanctifying by such discipline
440 Both pain and fear, until we recognise
A grandeur in the beatings of the heart.
Nor was this fellowship vouchsafed to me
With stinted kindness. In November days,
When vapours rolling down the valleys made
445 A lonely scene more lonesome, among woods
At noon, and 'mid the calm of summer nights
When by the margin of the trembling lake
Beneath the gloomy hills I homeward went
In solitude, such intercourse was mine—
450 'Twas mine among the fields both day and night,
And by the waters all the summer long.

    And in the frosty season, when the sun
Was set, and visible for many a mile
The cottage windows through the twilight blazed,
455 I heeded not the summons; happy time

It was indeed for all of us, to me
It was a time of rapture. Clear and loud
The village clock tolled six; I wheeled about
Proud and exulting, like an untired horse
460　That cares not for its home. All shod with steel°　　　*i.e., on skates*
We hissed along the polished ice in games
Confederate, imitative of the chace
And woodland pleasures, the resounding horn,
The pack loud bellowing, and the hunted hare.
465　So through the darkness and the cold we flew,
And not a voice was idle. With the din,
Meanwhile, the precipices rang aloud;
The leafless trees and every icy crag
Tinkled like iron; while the distant hills
470　Into the tumult sent an alien sound
Of melancholy, not unnoticed; while the stars,
Eastward, were sparkling clear, and in the west
The orange sky of evening died away.

　　Not seldom from the uproar I retired
475　Into a silent bay, or sportively
Glanced sideway,[3] leaving the tumultuous throng,
To cut across the image of a star
That gleamed upon the ice. And oftentimes
When we had given our bodies to the wind,
480　And all the shadowy banks on either side
Came sweeping through the darkness, spinning still
The rapid line of motion, then at once
Have I, reclining back upon my heels,
Stopped short—yet still the solitary cliffs
485　Wheeled by me, even as if the earth had rolled
With visible motion her diurnal° round.　　　*daily*
Behind me did they stretch in solemn train,°　　　*succession*
Feebler and feebler, and I stood and watched
Till all was tranquil as a dreamless sleep.

490　　Ye presences of Nature, in the sky
Or on the earth, ye visions of the hills
And souls of lonely places, can I think
A vulgar hope was yours when ye employed
Such ministry—when ye through many a year
495　Haunting me thus among my boyish sports,
On caves and trees, upon the woods and hills,
Impressed upon all forms the characters°　　　*signs*
Of danger or desire, and thus did make
The surface of the universal earth
500　With triumph, and delight, and hope, and fear,
Work° like a sea?　　　*seethe*

　　　　Not uselessly employed,
I might pursue this theme through every change
Of exercise and play to which the year

3. Moved off obliquely.

Did summon us in its delightful round.
505 We were a noisy crew; the sun in heaven
Beheld not vales more beautiful than ours,
Nor saw a race in happiness and joy
More worthy of the fields where they were sown.
I would record with no reluctant voice
510 The woods of autumn, and their hazel bowers
With milk-white clusters hung, the rod and line—
True symbol of the foolishness of hope—
Which with its strong enchantment led us on
By rocks and pools, shut out from every star
515 All the green summer, to forlorn cascades
Among the windings of the mountain brooks.
Unfading recollections—at this hour
The heart is almost mine with which I felt
From some hill-top on sunny afternoons
520 The kite, high up among the fleecy clouds,
Pull at its rein like an impatient courser,°   *racehorse*
Or, from the meadows sent on gusty days,
Beheld her breast the wind, then suddenly
Dashed headlong and rejected by the storm.

525   Ye lowly cottages in which we dwelt,
A ministration of your own was yours,
A sanctity, a safeguard, and a love.
Can I forget you, being as ye were
So beautiful among the pleasant fields
530 In which ye stood? Or can I here forget
The plain and seemly countenance with which
Ye dealt out your plain comforts? Yet had ye
Delights and exultations of your own:
Eager and never weary we pursued
535 Our home amusements by the warm peat fire
At evening, when with pencil and with slate,
In square divisions parcelled out, and all
With crosses and with cyphers scribbled o'er,°   *tic-tac-toe*
We schemed and puzzled, head opposed to head,
540 In strife too humble to be named in verse;
Or round the naked table, snow-white deal,°   *pine or fir*
Cherry, or maple, sate in close array,
And to the combat—lu or whist—led on
A thick-ribbed army, not as in the world
545 Neglected and ungratefully thrown by
Even for the very service they had wrought,
But husbanded through many a long campaign.
Uncouth assemblage was it, where no few
Had changed their functions—some, plebean cards
550 Which fate beyond the promise of their birth
Had glorified, and called to represent
The persons of departed potentates.[4]

4. The cards for these games of loo and whist
have changed their functions in ways that remind
us that *The Prelude* was begun soon after the
downfall of the French monarchy during the Revolution. The "potentate" cards—the kings, queens,
and jacks—have over time been lost from the

Oh, with what echoes on the board they fell!
Ironic diamonds—clubs, hearts, diamonds, spades,
555 A congregation piteously akin.
Cheap matter did they give to boyish wit,
Those sooty knaves, precipitated down
With scoffs and taunts like Vulcan out of heaven;[5]
The paramount ace, a moon in her eclipse;
560 Queens, gleaming through their splendour's last decay;
And monarchs, surly at the wrongs sustained
By royal visages. Meanwhile abroad
The heavy rain was falling, or the frost
Raged bitterly with keen and silent tooth;
565 And, interrupting the impassioned game,
From Esthwaite's neighbouring lake the splitting ice,
While it sank down towards the water, sent
Among the meadows and the hills its long
And dismal yellings, like the noise of wolves
570 When they are howling round the Bothnic main.°   *Baltic Sea*

   Nor, sedulous° as I have been to trace   *diligent*
How Nature by extrinsic passion first
Peopled my mind with beauteous forms or grand
And made me love them, may I well forget
575 How other pleasures have been mine, and joys
Of subtler origin—how I have felt,
Not seldom, even in that tempestuous time,
Those hallowed and pure motions of the sense
Which seem in their simplicity to own
580 An intellectual° charm, that calm delight   *spiritual*
Which, if I err not, surely must belong
To those first-born° affinities that fit   *innate*
Our new existence to existing things,
And, in our dawn of being, constitute
585 The bond of union betwixt life and joy.

   Yes, I remember when the changeful earth
And twice five seasons on my mind had stamped
The faces of the moving year, even then,
A child, I held unconscious intercourse
590 With the eternal beauty, drinking in
A pure organic pleasure from the lines
Of curling mist, or from the level plain
Of waters coloured by the steady clouds.
The sands of Westmoreland, the creeks and bays
595 Of Cumbria's° rocky limits, they can tell   *Cumberland's*
How when the sea threw off his evening shade
And to the shepherd's huts beneath the crags
Did send sweet notice of the rising moon,
How I have stood, to fancies such as these,

---

pack and so selected "plebean," or commoner,
cards have come to be used in their place.
5. Roman god of fire and the forge. His mother,

Juno, when he was born lame, threw him down
from Olympus, home of the gods.

600 Engrafted in the tenderness of thought,
   A stranger, linking with the spectacle
   No conscious memory of a kindred sight,
   And bringing with me no peculiar sense
   Of quietness or peace—yet I have stood
605 Even while mine eye has moved o'er three long leagues° *about 9 miles*
   Of shining water, gathering, as it seemed,
   Through every hair-breadth of that field of light
   New pleasure, like a bee among the flowers.

   Thus often in those fits of vulgar° joy *ordinary*
610 Which through all seasons on a child's pursuits
   Are prompt attendants, 'mid that giddy bliss
   Which like a tempest works along the blood
   And is forgotten, even then I felt
   Gleams like the flashing of a shield. The earth
615 And common face of Nature spake to me
   Rememberable things; sometimes, 'tis true,
   By chance collisions and quaint accidents—
   Like those ill-sorted unions, work supposed
   Of evil-minded fairies—yet not vain
620 Nor profitless, if haply they impressed
   Collateral° objects and appearances, *secondary*
   Albeit lifeless then, and doomed to sleep
   Until maturer seasons called them forth
   To impregnate and to elevate the mind.
625 And if the vulgar joy by its own weight
   Wearied itself out of the memory,
   The scenes which were a witness of that joy
   Remained, in their substantial lineaments
   Depicted on the brain, and to the eye
630 Were visible, a daily sight. And thus
   By the impressive discipline of fear,
   By pleasure and repeated happiness—
   So frequently repeated—and by force
   Of obscure feelings representative
635 Of joys that were forgotten, these same scenes,
   So beauteous and majestic in themselves,
   Though yet the day was distant, did at length
   Become habitually dear, and all
   Their hues and forms were by invisible links
640 Allied to the affections.

                    I began
   My story early, feeling, as I fear,
   The weakness of a human love for days
   Disowned by memory—ere the birth of spring
   Planting my snowdrops among winter snows.[6]
645 Nor will it seem to thee, my friend, so prompt
   In sympathy, that I have lengthened out

---

6. I.e., he fears that he may have mistakenly attributed his later thoughts to a time of life he can no longer remember.

With fond and feeble tongue a tedious tale.
Meanwhile my hope has been that I might fetch
Invigorating thoughts from former years,
650   Might fix the wavering balance of my mind,
And haply meet reproaches too, whose power
May spur me on, in manhood now mature,
To honorable toil. Yet should these hopes
Be vain, and thus should neither I be taught
655   To understand myself, nor thou to know
With better knowledge how the heart was framed
Of him thou lovest, need I dread from thee
Harsh judgments if I am so loth to quit
Those recollected hours that have the charm
660   Of visionary things,[7] and lovely forms
And sweet sensations, that throw back our life
And almost make our infancy itself
A visible scene on which the sun is shining?

One end hereby at least hath been attained—
665   My mind hath been revived—and if this mood
Desert me not, I will forthwith bring down
Through later years the story of my life.
The road lies plain before me. 'Tis a theme
Single and of determined bounds, and hence
670   I chuse it rather at this time than work
Of ampler or more varied argument,
Where I might be discomfited and lost,
And certain hopes are with me that to thee
This labour will be welcome, honoured friend.

From Book Second.

School-time (Continued)

[BOYHOOD ADVENTURES; "BLESSED THE INFANT BABE"]

Thus far, O friend, have we, though leaving much
Unvisited, endeavoured to retrace
My life through its first years, and measured back
The way I travelled when I first began
5   To love the woods and fields. The passion yet
Was in its birth, sustained, as might befal,
By nourishment that came unsought—for still
From week to week, from month to month, we lived
A round of tumult. Duly° were our games   *appropriately*
10   Prolonged in summer till the daylight failed:
No chair remained before the doors, the bench
And threshold steps were empty, fast asleep
The labourer and the old man who had sate

---

7. Things seen in a vision.

A later lingerer, yet the revelry
15 Continued and the loud uproar. At last,
When all the ground was dark and the huge clouds
Were edged with twinkling stars, to bed we went
With weary joints and with a beating mind.
Ah, is there one who ever has been young
20 And needs a monitory voice to tame
The pride of virtue and of intellect?
And is there one, the wisest and the best
Of all mankind, who does not sometimes wish
For things which cannot be, who would not give,
25 If so he might, to duty and to truth
The eagerness of infantine desire?
A tranquillizing spirit presses now
On my corporeal frame, so wide appears
The vacancy between me and those days,
30 Which yet have such self-presence in my mind
That sometimes when I think of them I seem
Two consciousnesses—conscious of myself,
And of some other being. A grey stone
Of native rock, left midway in the square
35 Of our small market-village, was the home
And centre of these joys; and when, returned
After long absence, thither I repaired,
I found that it was split and gone to build
A smart assembly-room that perked and flared
40 With wash and rough-cast, elbowing the ground
Which had been ours.[1] But let the fiddle scream,
And be ye happy! Yet, my friends,[2] I know
That more than one of you will think with me
Of those soft starry nights, and that old dame
45 From whom the stone was named, who there had sate
And watched her table with its huxter's wares,°   *peddlar's goods*
Assiduous through the length of sixty years.

    We ran a boisterous race, the year span round
With giddy motion; but the time approached
50 That brought with it a regular desire
For calmer pleasures—when the beauteous forms
Of Nature were collaterally attached[3]
To every scheme of holiday delight,
And every boyish sport, less grateful° else   *pleasing*
55 And languidly pursued. When summer came
It was the pastime of our afternoons
To beat along the plain of Windermere
With rival oars; and the selected bourne°   *destination*
Was now an island musical with birds
60 That sang for ever, now a sister isle
Beneath the oak's umbrageous° covert, sown   *shady*

1. The Hawkshead Town Hall, built in 1790.
2. Coleridge and John Wordsworth (William's brother), who had visited Hawkshead together
with William in November 1799.
3. Associated as an accompaniment.

With lilies-of-the-valley like a field,
And now a third small island where remained
An old stone table and a mouldered cave—
65 A hermit's history.[4] In such a race,
So ended, disappointment could be none,
Uneasiness, or pain, or jealousy;
We rested in the shade, all pleased alike,
Conquered and conqueror. Thus the pride of strength
70 And the vainglory of superior skill
Were interfused with objects which subdued
And tempered them, and gradually produced
A quiet independence of the heart.
And to my friend who knows me I may add,
75 Unapprehensive of reproof, that hence
Ensued a diffidence and modesty,
And I was taught to feel—perhaps too much—
The self-sufficing power of solitude.

No delicate viands sapped our bodily strength:
80 More than we wished we knew the blessing then
Of vigorous hunger, for our daily meals
Were frugal, Sabine fare[5]—and then, exclude
A little weekly stipend,[6] and we lived
Through three divisions of the quartered year
85 In pennyless poverty. But now, to school
Returned from the half-yearly holidays,
We came with purses more profusely filled,
Allowance which abundantly sufficed
To gratify the palate with repasts
90 More costly than the dame of whom I spake,
That ancient woman, and her board, supplied.
Hence inroads into distant vales, and long
Excursions far away among the hills,
Hence rustic dinners on the cool green ground—
95 Or in the woods, or near a river-side,
Or by some shady fountain°—while soft airs   spring or stream
Among the leaves were stirring, and the sun,
Unfelt, shone sweetly round us in our joy.

Nor is my aim neglected if I tell
100 How twice in the long length of those half-years
We from our funds perhaps with bolder hand
Drew largely, anxious for one day at least
To feel the motion of the galloping steed.
And with the good old innkeeper, in truth,
105 On such occasion sometimes we employed
Sly subterfuge, for the intended bound°   limit
Of the day's journey was too distant far

---

4. The 1850 *Prelude* clarifies that this is the island of Lady Holm, former site of a chapel dedicated to the Virgin Mary, by then a ruin.
5. Like the meals of the Roman poet Horace on his Sabine farm.

6. In his last year at school, Wordsworth had an allowance of sixpence a week; his younger brother Christopher, threepence. After the Midsummer and Christmas holidays (line 86), the boys received larger sums.

For any cautious man: a structure famed
Beyond its neighbourhood, the antique walls
110 Of that large abbey which within the Vale
Of Nightshade, to St Mary's honour built,
Stands yet, a mouldering pile[7] with fractured arch,
Belfry, and images, and living trees—
A holy scene. Along the smooth green turf
115 Our horses grazed. To more than inland peace
Left by the sea-wind passing overhead
(Though wind of roughest temper) trees and towers
May in that valley oftentimes be seen
Both silent and both motionless alike,
120 Such is the shelter that is there, and such
The safeguard for repose and quietness.

    Our steeds remounted, and the summons given,
With whip and spur we by the chauntry[8] flew
In uncouth race, and left the cross-legged knight,
125 And the stone abbot, and that single wren
Which one day sang so sweetly in the nave
Of the old church that, though from recent showers
The earth was comfortless, and, touched by faint
Internal breezes—sobbings of the place
130 And respirations—from the roofless walls
The shuddering ivy dripped large drops, yet still
So sweetly 'mid the gloom the invisible bird
Sang to itself that there I could have made
My dwelling-place, and lived for ever there
135 To hear such music. Through the walls we flew
And down the valley, and, a circuit made
In wantonness° of heart, through rough and smooth   *playfulness*
We scampered homeward. Oh, ye rocks and streams,
And that still spirit of the evening air,
140 Even in this joyous time I sometimes felt
Your presence, when, with slackened step, we breathed[9]
Along the sides of the steep hills, or when,
Lighted by gleams of moonlight from the sea,
We beat with thundering hoofs the level sand.

145   Upon the eastern shore of Windermere
Above the crescent of a pleasant bay
There was an inn,[1] no homely-featured shed,
Brother of the surrounding cottages,
But 'twas a splendid place, the door beset
150 With chaises, grooms, and liveries, and within
Decanters, glasses, and the blood-red wine.
In ancient times, or ere the hall was built
On the large island,[2] had this dwelling been
More worthy of a poet's love, a hut

---

7. The ruins of Furness Abbey, roughly twenty miles south of Hawkshead.
8. A chapel endowed for masses to be sung for the dead.
9. Slowed to let the horses catch their breath.
1. The White Lion inn at Bowness.
2. The Hall on Belle Isle in Lake Windermere had been built in the early 1780s.

155   Proud of its one bright fire and sycamore shade;
But though the rhymes were gone which once inscribed
The threshold, and large golden characters°   *letters*
On the blue-frosted signboard had usurped
The place of the old lion, in contempt
160   And mockery of the rustic painter's hand,
Yet to this hour the spot to me is dear
With all its foolish pomp. The garden lay
Upon a slope surmounted by the plain
Of a small bowling-green; beneath us stood
165   A grove, with gleams of water through the trees
And over the tree-tops—nor did we want
Refreshment, strawberries and mellow cream—
And there through half an afternoon we played
On the smooth platform, and the shouts we sent
170   Made all the mountains ring. But ere the fall
Of night, when in our pinnace° we returned   *small boat*
Over the dusky lake, and to the beach
Of some small island steered our course, with one,
The minstrel of our troop, and left him there,
175   And rowed off gently, while he blew his flute
Alone upon the rock, oh, then the calm
And dead still water lay upon my mind
Even with a weight of pleasure, and the sky,
Never before so beautiful, sank down
180   Into my heart and held me like a dream.
Thus daily were my sympathies enlarged,
And thus the common range of visible things
Grew dear to me: already I began
To love the sun, a boy I loved the sun
185   Not as I since have loved him—as a pledge
And surety of our earthly life, a light
Which while we view we feel we are alive—
But for this cause, that I had seen him lay
His beauty on the morning hills, had seen
190   The western mountain touch his setting orb
In many a thoughtless hour, when from excess
Of happiness my blood appeared to flow
With its own pleasure, and I breathed with joy.
And from like feelings, humble though intense,
195   To patriotic and domestic love
Analogous, the moon to me was dear;
For I would dream away my purposes
Standing to look upon her, while she hung
Midway between the hills as if she knew
200   No other region but belonged to thee,
Yea, appertained by a peculiar right
To thee and thy grey huts,[3] my darling vale.

    Those incidental charms which first attached
My heart to rural objects, day by day

---

3. Cottages built of the gray local stone.

205 Grew weaker, and I hasten on to tell
How Nature, intervenient[4] till this time
And secondary, now at length was sought
For her own sake. But who shall[5] parcel out
His intellect by geometric rules,
210 Split like a province into round and square?
Who knows the individual hour in which
His habits were first sown even as a seed,
Who that shall point as with a wand, and say
'This portion of the river of my mind
215 Came from yon fountain'? Thou, my friend, art one
More deeply read in thy own thoughts; to thee
Science[6] appears but what in truth she is,
Not as our glory and our absolute boast,
But as a succedaneum,[7] and a prop
220 To our infirmity. Thou art no slave
Of that false secondary power by which
In weakness we create distinctions, then
Deem that our puny boundaries are things
Which we perceive, and not which we have made.
225 To thee, unblinded by these outward shows,
The unity of all has been revealed;
And thou wilt doubt with me, less aptly skilled
Than many are to class the cabinet
Of their sensations,[8] and in voluble phrase°   *fluent words*
230 Run through the history and birth of each
As of a single independent thing.
Hard task to analyse a soul, in which
Not only general habits and desires,
But each most obvious and particular thought—
Not in a mystical and idle sense,
235 But in the words of reason deeply weighed—
Hath no beginning.

        Blessed the infant babe—
For with my best conjectures I would trace
The progress of our being—blest the babe
240 Nursed in his mother's arms, the babe who sleeps
Upon his mother's breast, who, when his soul
Claims manifest kindred with an earthly soul,
Doth gather passion from his mother's eye.[9]
Such feelings pass into his torpid life
245 Like an awakening breeze, and hence his mind,
Even in the first trial of its powers,
Is prompt and watchful, eager to combine
In one appearance all the elements
And parts of the same object, else detached

---

4. I.e., entering only incidentally into his other
concerns.
5. I.e., who is able to.
6. In the older sense: learning.
7. In medicine a drug substituted for a different
drug. Wordsworth, however, uses the term to
signify a remedy.
8. To classify feelings as if they were exhibits in
a display case.
9. Like modern psychologists, Wordsworth recognized the importance of earliest infancy in the
development of the individual mind.

250 And loth to coalesce. Thus day by day
   Subjected to the discipline of love,
   His organs and recipient faculties
   Are quickened, are more vigorous; his mind spreads,
   Tenacious of° the forms which it receives   *holding fast to*
255 In one beloved presence—nay and more,
   In that most apprehensive habitude[1]
   And those sensations which have been derived
   From this beloved presence—there exists
   A virtue which irradiates and exalts
260 All objects through all intercourse of sense.
   No outcast he, bewildered and depressed;
   Along his infant veins are interfused
   The gravitation and the filial bond
   Of Nature that connect him with the world.[2]
265 Emphatically such a being lives,
   An inmate of° this *active* universe.   *dweller in*
   From Nature largely he receives, nor so
   Is satisfied, but largely gives again;
   For feeling has to him imparted strength,
270 And—powerful in all sentiments of grief,
   Of exultation, fear and joy—his mind,
   Even as an agent of the one great mind,
   Creates, creator and receiver both,
   Working but in alliance with the works
275 Which it beholds.[3] Such, verily, is the first
   Poetic spirit of our human life—
   By uniform controul of after years
   In most abated and suppressed, in some
   Through every change of growth or of decay
280 Preeminent till death.

                          From early days,
   Beginning not long after that first time
   In which, a babe, by intercourse of touch
   I held mute dialogues with my mother's heart,[4]
   I have endeavoured to display the means
285 Whereby the infant sensibility,
   Great birthright of our being, was in me
   Augmented and sustained. Yet is a path
   More difficult before me, and I fear
   That in its broken windings we shall need
290 The chamois'° sinews and the eagle's wing.   *mountain antelope's*
   For now a trouble came into my mind
   From unknown causes, I was left alone
   Seeking the visible world, nor knowing why.
   The props of my affections were removed,[5]

1. Relationship ("habitude") most suited to the apprehension of the world.
2. The infant, in the sense of security and love that is shed by his mother's presence, perceives what would otherwise be an alien world as a place to which he is connected, in a "filial bond" (line 263).
3. The mind partially creates, by altering, the world it seems simply to perceive.
4. I.e., both infant and mother feel the pulse of the other's heart.
5. Wordsworth's mother died the month before his eighth birthday.

295　　And yet the building stood, as if sustained
　　　By its own spirit. All that I beheld
　　　Was dear to me, and from this cause it came
　　　That now to Nature's finer influxes°　　　　　　　　　*influences*
　　　My mind lay open—to that more exact
300　　And intimate communion which our hearts
　　　Maintain with the minuter properties
　　　Of objects which already are beloved,
　　　And of those only.

　　　　　　　　　Many are the joys
　　　Of youth, but, oh, what happiness to live
305　　When every hour brings palpable access
　　　Of knowledge, when all knowledge is delight,
　　　And sorrow is not there. The seasons came,
　　　And every season to my notice brought
　　　A store of transitory qualities
310　　Which but for this most watchful power of love
　　　Had been neglected, left a register
　　　Of permanent relations else unknown.[6]
　　　Hence, life, and change, and beauty, solitude
　　　More active even than 'best society',[7]
315　　Society made sweet as solitude
　　　By silent inobtrusive sympathies,
　　　And gentle agitations of the mind
　　　From manifold distinctions, difference
　　　Perceived in things where to the common eye
320　　No difference is, and hence, from the same source,
　　　Sublimer joy. For I would walk alone
　　　In storm and tempest, or in starlight nights
　　　Beneath the quiet heavens, and at that time
　　　Have felt whate'er there is of power in sound
325　　To breathe an elevated mood, by form
　　　Or image unprofaned; and I would stand
　　　Beneath some rock, listening to sounds that are
　　　The ghostly° language of the ancient earth,　　　　*disembodied*
　　　Or make their dim abode in distant winds.
330　　Thence did I drink the visionary power.
　　　I deem not profitless those fleeting moods
　　　Of shadowy exultation; not for this,
　　　That they are kindred to our purer mind
　　　And intellectual life,[8] but that the soul—
335　　Remembering how she felt, but what she felt
　　　Remembering not—retains an obscure sense
　　　Of possible sublimity, to which
　　　With growing faculties she doth aspire,
　　　With faculties still growing, feeling still

6. I.e., had it not been for the "watchful power of love" (line 310), the "transitory qualities" (line 309) would have been neglected, and the "permanent relations" now recorded in his memory would have been unknown.

7. A partial quotation of a line spoken by Adam to Eve in *Paradise Lost* 9.249: "For solitude sometimes is best society."

8. I.e., not because they are related to the nonsensuous ("intellectual") aspect of life.

›340 That whatsoever point they gain they still
Have something to pursue.

* * *

[ADDRESS TO COLERIDGE]

Thou, my friend, wert reared
In the great city, 'mid far other scenes,[9]
But we by different roads at length have gained
The self-same bourne.° And for this cause to thee   *destination*
470 I speak unapprehensive of contempt,
The insinuated scoff of coward tongues,
And all that silent language which so oft
In conversation betwixt man and man
Blots from the human countenance all trace
475 Of beauty and of love. For thou hast sought
The truth in solitude, and thou art one
The most intense of Nature's worshippers,
In many things my brother, chiefly here
In this my deep devotion. Fare thee well.
480 Health and the quiet of a healthful mind
Attend thee, seeking oft the haunts of men—
And yet more often living with thyself,
And for thyself—so haply shall thy days
Be many, and a blessing to mankind.

From Book Fifth.

Books

[THE DREAM OF THE ARAB]

* * *

Thou also, man, hast wrought,
For commerce of thy nature with itself,[1]
Things worthy of unconquerable life;
20 And yet we feel—we cannot chuse but feel—
That these must perish. Tremblings of the heart
It gives, to think that the immortal being
No more shall need such garments;[2] and yet man,
As long as he shall be the child of earth,
25 Might almost 'weep to have' what he may lose[3]—
Nor be himself extinguished, but survive

---

9. A reminiscence of Coleridge's "Frost at Midnight," lines 51–52: "For I was reared / In the great city, pent 'mid cloisters dim." The two-part *Prelude* Wordsworth completed in 1799 ended with the address to Coleridge in lines 467–84.
1. From the works of God's creation, Nature, Wordsworth turns at this point in *The Prelude* to human creations. Man, as well as God, has created works by which to communicate with man ("commerce of thy nature with itself"): those creations are books, and the title of book 5 under-

lines their importance to Wordsworth's account of himself.
2. Wordsworth draws on the traditional image of the body as the garment of the soul, no longer needed at death and so discarded.
3. The quotation is from Shakespeare's sonnet 64, in which the thought that Time might come and take his love away is for the speaker "as a death, which cannot choose / But weep to have that which it fears to lose."

Abject, depressed, forlorn, disconsolate.
A thought is with me sometimes, and I say,
'Should earth by inward throes be wrenched throughout,
30 Or fire be sent from far to wither all
Her pleasant habitations, and dry up
Old Ocean in his bed, left singed and bare,
Yet would the living presence still subsist
Victorious; and composure would ensue,
35 And kindlings like the morning—presage sure,
Though slow perhaps, of a returning day.'
But all the meditations of mankind,
Yea, all the adamantine holds° of truth   *indestructible fortresses*
By reason built, or passion (which itself
40 Is highest reason in a soul sublime),
The consecrated works of bard and sage,
Sensuous or intellectual, wrought by men,
Twin labourers and heirs of the same hopes—
Where would they be? Oh, why hath not the mind
45 Some element to stamp her image on
In nature somewhat nearer to her own?
Why, gifted with such powers to send abroad
Her spirit, must it lodge in shrines so frail?

　　One day, when in the hearing of a friend
50 I had given utterance to thoughts like these,
He answered with a smile that in plain truth
'Twas going far to seek disquietude—
But on the front of his reproof confessed
That he at sundry seasons had himself
55 Yielded to kindred hauntings, and, forthwith,
Added that once upon a summer's noon
While he was sitting in a rocky cave
By the seaside, perusing as it chanced,
The famous history of the errant knight
60 Recorded by Cervantes,[4] these same thoughts
Came to him, and to height unusual rose
While listlessly he sate, and, having closed
The book, had turned his eyes towards the sea.
On poetry and geometric truth
65 (The knowledge that endures) upon these two,
And their high privilege of lasting life
Exempt from all internal injury,
He mused—upon these chiefly—and at length,
His senses yielding to the sultry air,
70 Sleep seized him and he passed into a dream.
He saw before him an Arabian waste,
A desart, and he fancied that himself
Was sitting there in the wide wilderness
Alone upon the sands. Distress of mind
75 Was growing in him when, behold, at once
To his great joy a man was at his side,

---

4. I.e., *Don Quixote*, the 17th-century novel about a man unable to distinguish between reality and books' romantic fictions.

Upon a dromedary° mounted high.   *camel*
He seemed an arab of the Bedouin tribes;[5]
A lance he bore, and underneath one arm
80   A stone, and in the opposite hand a shell
Of a surpassing brightness. Much rejoiced
The dreaming man that he should have a guide
To lead him through the desart; and he thought,
While questioning himself what this strange freight
85   Which the newcomer carried through the waste
Could mean, the arab told him that the stone—
To give it in the language of the dream—
Was *Euclid's Elements*.[6] 'And this', said he,
'This other', pointing to the shell, 'this book
90   Is something of more worth.' 'And, at the word,
The stranger', said my friend continuing,
'Stretched forth the shell towards me, with command
That I should hold it to my ear. I did so
And heard that instant in an unknown tongue,
95   Which yet I understood, articulate sounds,
A loud prophetic blast of harmony,
An ode in passion uttered, which foretold
Destruction to the children of the earth
By deluge now at hand. No sooner ceased
100   The song, but with calm look the arab said
That all was true, that it was even so
As had been spoken, and that he himself
Was going then to bury those two books—
The one that held acquaintance with the stars,
105   And wedded man to man by purest bond
Of nature, undisturbed by space or time;
Th' other that was a god, yea many gods,
Had voices more than all the winds, and was
A joy, a consolation, and a hope.'
110   My friend continued, 'Strange as it may seem
I wondered not, although I plainly saw
The one to be a stone, th' other a shell,
Nor doubted once but that they both were books,
Having a perfect faith in all that passed.
115   A wish was now engendered in my fear
To cleave unto this man, and I begged leave
To share his errand with him. On he passed
Not heeding me; I followed, and took note
That he looked often backward with wild look,
120   Grasping his twofold treasure to his side.
Upon a dromedary, lance in rest,
He rode, I keeping pace with him; and now
I fancied that he was the very knight
Whose tale Cervantes tells, yet not the knight,
125   But was an arab of the desert too,
Of these was neither, and was both at once.

---

5. Mathematics had flourished in Arabic culture—hence the Arab rider.
6. Celebrated book on geometry and the theory of numbers by the Greek mathematician Euclid (3rd century B.C.E.); it continued to be used as a textbook into the 19th century.

His countenance meanwhile grew more disturbed,
And looking backwards when he looked I saw
A glittering light, and asked him whence it came.
130 "It is", said he, "the waters of the deep
Gathering upon us." Quickening then his pace
He left me; I called after him aloud;
He heeded not, but with his twofold charge
Beneath his arm—before me full in view—
135 I saw him riding o'er the desart sands
With the fleet waters of the drowning world
In chace of him; whereat I waked in terror,
And saw the sea before me, and the book
In which I had been reading at my side.[7]

140   Full often, taking from the world of sleep
This arab phantom which my friend beheld,
This semi-Quixote, I to him have given
A substance, fancied him a living man—
A gentle dweller in the desart, crazed
145 By love, and feeling, and internal thought
Protracted among endless solitudes—
Have shaped him, in the oppression of his brain,
Wandering upon this quest and thus equipped.
And I have scarcely pitied him, have felt
150 A reverence for a being thus employed,
And thought that in the blind and awful lair
Of such a madness reason did lie couched.
Enow° there are on earth to take in charge   enough
Their wives, their children, and their virgin loves,
155 Or whatsoever else the heart holds dear—
Enow to think of these—yea, will I say,
In sober contemplation of the approach
Of such great overthrow, made manifest
By certain evidence, that I methinks
160 Could share that maniac's anxiousness, could go
Upon like errand. Oftentimes at least
Me hath such deep entrancement half-possessed
When I have held a volume in my hand—
Poor earthly casket of immortal verse—
165 Shakespeare or Milton, labourers divine.

*   *   *

[THE BOY OF WINANDER; THE DROWNED MAN]

There was a boy[8]—ye knew him well, ye cliffs
390   And islands of Winander—many a time

7. A late-17th-century biography reported that on a single night in 1619 three dreams troubled René Descartes, who believed them to be a supernatural visitation foretelling his future vocation as a philosopher. The third dream, which has had many interpreters, involved two books that appeared mysteriously to the dreamer and then vanished again, a dictionary and an anthology of poetry. Coleridge is usually thought to have told the story of that dream to Wordsworth, who in lines 56–139 reworks it brilliantly.
8. In an early manuscript version of lines 389–413, Wordsworth uses the first-person pronoun, suggesting the boy's experience was his own. Under the title "There was a Boy," the lines were published as a separate poem in Wordsworth's 1815 *Poems*. In the preface to that volume Wordsworth describes how the account of the boy's

At evening, when the stars had just begun
To move along the edges of the hills,
Rising or setting, would he stand alone
Beneath the trees or by the glimmering lake,
395 And there, with fingers interwoven, both hands
Pressed closely palm to palm, and to his mouth
Uplifted, he as through an instrument
Blew mimic hootings to the silent owls
That they might answer him. And they would shout
400 Across the wat'ry vale, and shout again,
Responsive to his call, with quivering peals
And long halloos, and screams, and echoes loud,
Redoubled and redoubled—concourse wild
Of mirth and jocund din. And when it chanced
405 That pauses of deep silence mocked his skill,
Then sometimes in that silence, while he hung
Listening, a gentle shock of mild surprize
Has carried far into his heart[9] the voice
Of mountain torrents; or the visible scene
410 Would enter unawares into his mind
With all its solemn imagery, its rocks,
Its woods, and that uncertain heaven, received
Into the bosom of the steady lake.

This boy was taken from his mates, and died
415 In childhood ere he was full ten years old.
Fair are the woods, and beauteous is the spot,
The vale where he was born; the churchyard hangs
Upon a slope above the village school,
And there, along that bank, when I have passed
420 At evening, I believe that oftentimes
A full half-hour together I have stood
Mute, looking at the grave in which he lies.
Even now methinks I have before my sight
That self-same village church: I see her sit—
425 The thronèd lady spoken of erewhile—
On her green hill, forgetful of this boy
Who slumbers at her feet, forgetful too
Of all her silent neighbourhood of graves,
And listening only to the gladsome sounds
430 That, from the rural school ascending, play
Beneath her and about her. May she long
Behold a race of young ones like to those
With whom I herded—easily, indeed,
We might have fed upon a fatter soil
435 Of Arts and Letters, but be that forgiven—
A race of real children, not too wise,

---

listening dramatizes a moment when internal
feelings cooperate with external accidents and
"plant, for immortality, images of sound and
sight, in the celestial soil of the Imagination."
9. Thomas De Quincey responded to this line in
Recollections of the Lakes and the Lake Poets:

"This very expression, 'far,' by which space and its
infinities are attributed to the human heart, and
to its capacities of re-echoing the sublimities of
nature, has always struck me as with a flash of
sublime revelation."

Too learned, or too good, but wanton, fresh,
And bandied up and down by love and hate;
Fierce, moody, patient, venturous, modest, shy,
440   Mad at their sports like withered leaves in winds;
Though doing wrong and suffering, and full oft
Bending beneath our life's mysterious weight
Of pain and fear, yet still in happiness
Not yielding to the happiest upon earth.
445   Simplicity in habit, truth in speech,
Be these the daily strengtheners of their minds!
May books and Nature be their early joy,
And knowledge, rightly honored with that name—
Knowledge not purchased with the loss of power!

450   Well do I call to mind the very week
When I was first entrusted to the care
Of that sweet valley[1]—when its paths, its shores
And brooks, were like a dream of novelty
To my half-infant thoughts—that very week,
455   While I was roving up and down alone
Seeking I knew not what, I chanced to cross
One of those open fields, which, shaped like ears,
Make green peninsulas on Esthwaite's Lake.
Twilight was coming on, yet through the gloom
460   I saw distinctly on the opposite shore
A heap of garments, left as I supposed
By one who there was bathing. Long I watched,
But no one owned them; meanwhile the calm lake
Grew dark, with all the shadows on its breast,
465   And now and then a fish up-leaping snapped
The breathless stillness. The succeeding day—
Those unclaimed garments telling a plain tale—
Went there a company, and in their boat
Sounded with grappling-irons and long poles:
470   At length, the dead man, 'mid that beauteous scene
Of trees and hills and water, bolt upright
Rose with his ghastly face, a spectre shape—
Of terror even. And yet no vulgar fear,
Young as I was, a child not nine years old,
475   Possessed me, for my inner eye had seen
Such sights before among the shining streams
Of fairyland, the forests of romance—
Thence came a spirit hallowing what I saw
With decoration and ideal grace,
480   A dignity, a smoothness, like the works
Of Grecian art and purest poesy.

*   *   *

---

1. At age nine Wordsworth was sent away from home to attend school at Hawkshead in the Esthwaite valley.

From Book Sixth.

Cambridge and the Alps

["HUMAN NATURE SEEMING BORN AGAIN"]

* * *

When the third summer brought its liberty[1]
A fellow student and myself, he too
340   A mountaineer, together sallied forth,
And, staff in hand on foot pursued our way
Towards the distant Alps. An open slight
Of college cares and study was the scheme,[2]
Nor entertained without concern for those
345   To whom my worldly interests were dear,
But Nature then was sovereign in my heart,
And mighty forms seizing a youthful fancy
Had given a charter[3] to irregular hopes.
In any age, without an impulse sent
350   From work of nations and their goings-on,
I should have been possessed by like desire;
But 'twas a time when Europe was rejoiced,
France standing on the top of golden hours,
And human nature seeming born again.
355   Bound, as I said, to the Alps, it was our lot
To land at Calais on the very eve
Of that great federal day;[4] and there we saw,
In a mean° city and among a few,   *lowly*
How bright a face is worn when joy of one
Is joy of tens of millions.

* * *

[CROSSING SIMPLON PASS]

'Tis not my present purpose to retrace
That variegated journey step by step;
A march it was of military speed,
And earth did change her images and forms
430   Before us fast as clouds are changed in heaven.
Day after day, up early and down late,
From vale to vale, from hill to hill we went,
From province on to province did we pass,
Keen hunters in a chace of fourteen weeks—
435   Eager as birds of prey, or as a ship

1. Wordsworth was a student at St. John's College, Cambridge University, from 1787 to 1791. Books 3 and 4 describe his first year there and the succeeding summer vacation. In this book, after reviewing briefly his second and third years at university, Wordsworth describes his trip through France and Switzerland with a college friend, Robert Jones, during the summer vacation of 1790. France was then in the "golden hours" of the early period of the Revolution; the fall of the Bastille had occurred on July 14 of the preceding year.
2. Undergraduates were expected to spend their third summer preparing for the final examinations that would determine their rank upon graduation and shape their career prospects.
3. Privileged freedom.
4. Wordsworth and Jones landed at the port of Calais in northeast France on July 13, 1790, just before the Festival of Federation, the ceremony, also marking the anniversary of the fall of the Bastille, in which King Louis XVI swore to be faithful to the nation's new, democratic constitution.

Upon the stretch when winds are blowing fair.
Sweet coverts did we cross of pastoral life,
Enticing vallies—greeted them, and left
Too soon, while yet the very flash and gleam
440　Of salutation were not passed away.
Oh, sorrow for the youth who could have seen
Unchastened, unsubdued, unawed, unraised
To patriarchal dignity of mind
And pure simplicity of wish and will,
445　Those sanctified abodes of peaceful man.
My heart leaped up when first I did look down
On that which was first seen of those deep haunts,
A green recess, an aboriginal° vale,　　　　　　　*primitive, untouched*
Quiet, and lorded over and possessed
450　By naked huts, wood-built, and sown like tents
Or Indian cabins over the fresh lawns
And by the river-side.

　　　　　　　　That day we first
Beheld the summit of Mount Blanc, and grieved
To have a soulless image on the eye
455　Which had usurped upon a living thought
That never more could be.[5] The wondrous Vale
Of Chamouny[6] did, on the following dawn,
With its dumb° cataracts and streams of ice—　　　*silent*
A motionless array of mighty waves,
460　Five rivers broad and vast—make rich amends,
And reconciled us to realities.
There small birds warble from the leafy trees,
The eagle soareth in the element,
There doth the reaper bind the yellow sheaf,
465　The maiden spread the haycock in the sun,
While Winter like a tamèd lion walks,
Descending from the mountain to make sport
Among the cottages by beds of flowers.

　　　　Whate'er in this wide circuit we beheld
470　Or heard was fitted to our unripe state
Of intellect and heart. By simple strains
Of feeling, the pure breath of real life,
We were not left untouched. With such a book
Before our eyes we could not chuse but read
475　A frequent lesson of sound tenderness,
The universal reason of mankind,
The truth of young and old. Nor, side by side
Pacing, two brother pilgrims, or alone
Each with his humour,° could we fail to abound—　*temperament*
480　Craft this which hath been hinted at before—
In dreams and fictions pensively composed:
Dejection taken up for pleasure's sake,

5. The "image" is the actual sight of Mont Blanc, as contrasted with what the poet has imagined the famous Swiss mountain to be.

6. Chamonix, a valley in eastern France, north of Mont Blanc.

And gilded sympathies, the willow wreath,[7]
Even among those solitudes sublime,
485 And sober posies of funereal flowers,
Culled from the gardens of the Lady Sorrow,
Did sweeten many a meditative hour.

Yet still in me, mingling with these delights,
Was something of stern mood, an under-thirst
490 Of vigour, never utterly asleep.
Far different dejection once was mine—
A deep and genuine sadness then I felt—
The circumstances I will here relate
Even as they were. Upturning with a band
495 Of travellers, from the Valais we had clomb°   *climbed*
Along the road that leads to Italy;[8]
A length of hours, making of these our guides,
Did we advance, and, having reached an inn
Among the mountains, we together ate
500 Our noon's repast, from which the travellers rose
Leaving us at the board. Erelong we followed,
Descending by the beaten road that led
Right to a rivulet's edge, and there broke off;
The only track now visible was one
505 Upon the further side, right opposite,
And up a lofty mountain. This we took,
After a little scruple° and short pause,   *hesitation*
And climbed with eagerness—though not, at length,
Without surprize and some anxiety
510 On finding that we did not overtake
Our comrades gone before. By fortunate chance,
While every moment now encreased our doubts,
A peasant met us, and from him we learned
That to the place which had perplexed us first
515 We must descend, and there should find the road
Which in the stony channel of the stream
Lay a few steps, and then along its banks—
And further, that thenceforward all our course
Was downwards with the current of that stream.
520 Hard of belief, we questioned him again,
And all the answers which the man returned
To our inquiries, in their sense and substance
Translated by the feelings which we had,
Ended in this—that we had crossed the Alps.[9]

525 Imagination!—lifting up itself
Before the eye and progress of my song°   *The Prelude* itself
Like an unfathered vapour,[1] here that power,

---

7. The mention of the "willow wreath" suggests that the poetry the two travelers composed to while away their time was conventionally sentimental. "Gilded": laid on like gilt; i.e., superficial.
8. Simplon Pass.
9. As Dorothy Wordsworth baldly put it later on, "The ambition of youth was disappointed at these tidings." The visionary experience that follows (lines 525–48) did not occur in the Alps; Wordsworth celebrates the creative power that he experiences at the time of writing this passage, fourteen years after the disappointment at Simplon Pass.
1. Vapor appearing suddenly from no apparent source.

In all the might of its endowments, came
Athwart me. I was lost as in a cloud,
530   Halted without a struggle to break through,
And now, recovering, to my soul I say
'I recognise thy glory'. In such strength
Of usurpation, in such visitings
Of awful° promise, when the light of sense   *awe-inspiring*
535   Goes out in flashes that have shewn to us
The invisible world, doth greatness make abode,
There harbours whether we be young or old.
Our destiny, our nature, and our home,
Is with infinitude—and only there;
540   With hope it is, hope that can never die,
Effort, and expectation, and desire,
And something evermore about to be.
The mind beneath such banners militant
Thinks not of spoils or trophies, nor of aught
545   That may attest its prowess, blest in thoughts
That are their own perfection and reward—
Strong in itself, and in the access of joy
Which hides it like the overflowing Nile.

The dull and heavy slackening which ensued
550   Upon those tidings by the peasant given
Was soon dislodged; downwards we hurried fast,
And entered with the road which we had missed
Into a narrow chasm. The brook and road
Were fellow-travellers in this gloomy pass,
555   And with them did we journey several hours
At a slow step. The immeasurable height
Of woods decaying, never to be decayed,
The stationary blasts of waterfalls,
And everywhere along the hollow rent
560   Winds thwarting winds, bewildered and forlorn,
The torrents shooting from the clear blue sky,
The rocks that muttered close upon our ears—
Black drizzling crags that spake by the wayside
As if a voice were in them—the sick sight
565   And giddy prospect of the raving stream,
The unfettered clouds and region of the heavens,
Tumult and peace, the darkness and the light,
Were all like workings of one mind, the features
Of the same face, blossoms upon one tree,
570   Characters of the great apocalypse,
The types and symbols of eternity,[2]
Of first, and last, and midst, and without end.[3]

*   *   *

2. The objects in this natural scene are like the
written words ("characters") of the Apocalypse—
i.e., of the Book of Revelation, concluding book of
the New Testament. "Types": signs foreshadowing
eternity.
3. See Revelation 1.8: "I am Alpha and Omega

[the first and last letters of the Greek alphabet],
the beginning and the ending, saith the Lord." In
Paradise Lost 5.153–65 Milton says that all God's
works declare their Creator, and call on all to
extol "him first, him last, him midst, and without
end."

From Book Seventh.

Residence in London

[THE BLIND BEGGAR; BARTHOLOMEW FAIR]

* * *

595 How often in the overflowing streets[1]
      Have I gone forwards with the crowd, and said
      Unto myself, 'The face of every one
      That passes by me is a mystery.'
      Thus have I looked, nor ceased to look, oppressed
600 By thoughts of what, and whither, when and how,
      Until the shapes before my eyes became
      A second-sight procession, such as glides
      Over still mountains, or appears in dreams,[2]
      And all the ballast of familiar life—
605 The present, and the past, hope, fear, all stays,°   *supports*
      All laws of acting, thinking, speaking man—
      Went from me, neither knowing me, nor known.
      And once, far travelled in such mood, beyond
      The reach of common indications, lost
610 Amid the moving pageant, 'twas my chance
      Abruptly to be smitten with the view
      Of a blind beggar, who, with upright face,
      Stood propped against a wall, upon his chest
      Wearing a written paper, to explain
615 The story of the man, and who he was.
      My mind did at this spectacle turn round
      As with the might of waters, and it seemed
      To me that in this label was a type
      Or emblem of the utmost that we know
620 Both of ourselves and of the universe,
      And on the shape of this unmoving man,
      His fixèd face and sightless eyes, I looked,
      As if admonished from another world.

      Though reared upon the base of outward things,
625 These chiefly are such structures as the mind
      Builds for itself. Scenes different there are—
      Full-formed—which take, with small internal help,
      Possession of the faculties: the peace
      Of night, for instance, the solemnity
630 Of Nature's intermediate hours of rest
      When the great tide of human life stands still,
      The business of the day to come unborn,
      Of that gone by locked up as in the grave;[3]
      The calmness, beauty, of the spectacle,
635 Sky, stillness, moonshine, empty streets, and sounds

1. Wordsworth spent a few unhappy months in London in 1791.
2. As though other people were seen in a vision or were optical illusions.
3. Wordsworth's sonnet "Composed upon Westminster Bridge" describes a similar response to London when its "mighty heart is lying still."

Unfrequent as in desarts;° at late hours   *wildernesses*
Of winter evenings when unwholesome rains
Are falling hard, with people yet astir,
The feeble salutation from the voice
640 Of some unhappy woman[4] now and then
Heard as we pass, when no one looks about,
Nothing is listened to. But these I fear
Are falsely catalogued:[5] things that are, are not,
Even as we give them welcome, or assist—
645 Are prompt, or are remiss. What say you then
To times when half the city shall break out
Full of one passion—vengeance, rage, or fear—
To executions,[6] to a street on fire,
Mobs, riots, or rejoicings? From those sights
650 Take one, an annual festival, the fair
Holden where martyrs suffered in past time,
And named of St Bartholomew,[7] there see
A work that's finished to our hands, that lays,
If any spectacle on earth can do,
655 The whole creative powers of man asleep.
For once the Muse's help will we implore,
And she shall lodge us—wafted on her wings
Above the press and danger of the crowd—
Upon some showman's platform. What a hell
600 For eyes and ears, what anarchy and din
Barbarian and infernal—'tis a dream
Monstrous in colour, motion, shape, sight, sound.
Below, the open space, through every nook
Of the wide area, twinkles, is alive
665 With heads; the midway region and above
Is thronged with staring pictures and huge scrolls,
Dumb proclamations of the prodigies;
And chattering monkeys dangling from their poles,
And children whirling in their roundabouts;°   *merry-go-rounds*
670 With those that stretch the neck, and strain the eyes,
And crack the voice in rivalship, the crowd
Inviting; with buffoons against buffoons
Grimacing, writhing, screaming; him who grinds
The hurdy-gurdy,[8] at the fiddle weaves,
675 Rattles the salt-box,[9] thumps the kettle-drum,
And him who at the trumpet puffs his cheeks,
The silver-collared negro with his timbrel,°   *tambourine*
Equestrians, tumblers, women, girls, and boys,
Blue-breeched, pink-vested, and with towering plumes.
680 All moveables of wonder from all parts
Are here, albinos, painted Indians, dwarfs,

4. Perhaps a prostitute.
5. Mistakenly classified, because what things are depends on the attitude with which they are perceived.
6. Executions were held in public in England until 1868.
7. This four-day-long fair was held every September in commemoration of the martyrdom of the Protestants burned at the stake during the reign of Catholic Queen Mary (1553–58).
8. A stringed instrument, used by street musicians, which is sounded by a turning wheel rather than a bow.
9. A crude musical instrument formed of a wooden box containing salt; it was rattled or beaten.

The horse of knowledge, and the learned pig,[1]
The stone-eater, the man that swallows fire,
Giants, ventriloquists, the invisible girl,
685   The bust that speaks and moves its goggling eyes,
The waxwork,[2] clockwork,° all the marvellous craft   robots
Of modern Merlins,[3] wild beasts, puppet-shows,
All out-o'-th'-way, far-fetched, perverted things,[4]
All freaks of Nature, all Promethean[5] thoughts,
690   Of man—his dulness, madness, and their feats,
All jumbled up together to make up
This parliament of monsters. Tents and booths
Meanwhile—as if the whole were one vast mill°—   factory
Are vomiting, receiving, on all sides,
495   Men, women, three-years' children, babes in arms.

       O, blank confusion, and a type° not false   image
Of what the mighty city is itself
To all, except a straggler here and there—
To the whole swarm of its inhabitants—
700   An undistinguishable world to men,
The slaves unrespited of low pursuits,
Living amid the same perpetual flow
Of trivial objects, melted and reduced
To one identity by differences
705   That have no law, no meaning, and no end—
Oppression under which even highest minds
Must labour, whence the strongest are not free.
But though the picture weary out the eye,
By nature an unmanageable sight,
710   It is not wholly so to him who looks
In steadiness, who hath among least things
An under-sense of greatest, sees the parts
As parts, but with a feeling of the whole.

                    *   *   *

735   This did I feel in that vast receptacle.[6]
The spirit of Nature was upon me here,
The soul of beauty and enduring life
Was present as a habit, and diffused—
Through meagre lines and colours, and the press
740   Of self-destroying, transitory things—
Composure and ennobling harmony.

---

1. Animals trained to tap out answers to arithmetic questions, etc.
2. Madame Tussaud brought her collection of wax figures of the leaders and victims of the French Revolution to London in 1802.
3. Merlin was the legendary magician in the court of King Arthur, but there was a modern Merlin: the Dutch inventor John Joseph Merlin, who in the late 18th century displayed ingenious contriv-

ances at Merlin's Mechanical Museum, a popular place of London entertainment.
4. Echoing Milton's description of how in Hell "Nature breeds / Perverse, all monstrous, all prodigious things" (*Paradise Lost* 2.624–25).
5. Daringly inventive. In Greek myth Prometheus made man out of clay and taught him the arts.
6. I.e., London.

From Book Tenth.

Residence in France and French Revolution

[REIGN OF TERROR][1]

* * *

Tyrants, strong before

310 In devilish pleas, were ten times stronger now,°   *i.e., in 1793*
And thus beset with foes on every side,
The goaded land waxed mad; the crimes of few
Spread into madness of the many; blasts
From hell came sanctified like airs from heaven.[2]
315 The sternness of the just,[3] the faith of those
Who doubted not that Providence had times
Of anger and of vengeance, theirs who throned
The human understanding paramount
And made of that their god,[4] the hopes of those
320 Who were content to barter short-lived pangs
For a paradise of ages, the blind rage
Of insolent tempers, the light vanity
Of intermeddlers, steady purposes
Of the suspicious, slips of the indiscreet,
325 And all the accidents of life, were pressed
Into one service, busy with one work.
The Senate was heart-stricken, not a voice
Uplifted, none to oppose or mitigate.
Domestic carnage now filled all the year
330 With feast-days:[5] the old man from the chimney-nook,
The maiden from the bosom of her love,
The mother from the cradle of her babe,
The warrior from the field—all perished, all—
Friends, enemies, of all parties, ages, ranks,
335 Head after head, and never heads enough
For those who bade them fall. They found their joy,
They made it, ever thirsty, as a child—
If light desires of innocent little ones
May with such heinous appetites be matched—
340 Having a toy, a windmill, though the air
Do of itself blow fresh and makes the vane
Spin in his eyesight, he is not content,
But with the plaything at arm's length he sets

---

1. Wordsworth visited France for the second time in 1791–92 and, as he explains in this book, became, initially, a passionate partisan of the Revolution. His lack of money forced him to return to England late in 1792. From there he looked on despairingly as the radicals, led by Robespierre, who ascended to power in France in the summer of 1793, undertook a campaign of mass arrests and executions in order to purge the new Republic of its enemies. This excerpt from book 10 begins with Wordsworth's account of the Terror.

2. Recalling the line in which Hamlet doubts whether the ghost resembling his father brings "airs from heaven, or blasts from hell" (*Hamlet* 1.4.441).

3. A punning allusion to Robespierre's ally with the ironic name, Louis Antoine de Saint-Just.

4. Catholic churches were turned into Temples of Reason in 1793.

5. I.e., festivals celebrated by human slaughter ("carnage"). Wordsworth alludes ironically to the patriotic festivals created to replace Catholic feast days within the new Republic's calendar. In 1794 a total of 1,376 people were guillotined in Paris in forty-nine days.

His front against the blast, and runs amain°   *full force*
345 To make it whirl the faster.

*   *   *

[RETROSPECT: FIRST IMPRESSION OF THE REVOLUTION][6]

*   *   *

O pleasant exercise of hope and joy,
690 For great were the auxiliars° which then stood   *allies*
Upon our side, we who were strong in love.
Bliss was it in that dawn to be alive,
But to be young was very heaven! O times,
In which the meagre, stale, forbidding ways
695 Of custom, law, and statute took at once
The attraction of a country in romance—
When Reason seemed the most to assert her rights
When most intent on making of herself
A prime enchanter to assist the work
700 Which then was going forwards in her name.
Not favored spots alone, but the whole earth,
The beauty wore of promise, that which sets
(To take an image which was felt, no doubt,
Among the bowers of Paradise itself)
705 The budding rose above the rose full-blown.
What temper° at the prospect did not wake   *temperament*
To happiness unthought of? The inert
Were rouzed, and lively natures rapt away.°   *enraptured*
They who had fed their childhood upon dreams—
710 The playfellows of fancy, who had made
All powers of swiftness, subtlety, and strength
Their ministers, used to stir in lordly wise
Among the grandest objects of the sense,
And deal with whatsoever they found there
715 As if they had within some lurking right
To wield it—they too, who, of gentle mood,
Had watched all gentle motions, and to these
Had fitted their own thoughts (schemers more mild,
And in the region of their peaceful selves),
720 Did now find helpers to their hearts' desire
And stuff at hand plastic° as they could wish,   *malleable*
Were called upon to exercise their skill
Not in Utopia—subterraneous fields,
Or some secreted island, heaven knows where—
725 But in the very world which is the world
Of all of us, the place in which, in the end,
We find our happiness, or not at all.

*   *   *

6. Wordsworth follows his account of Robespierre's rise and fall with a retrospect, a backward glance at the high hopes that the Revolution had raised at its start. He published lines 689–727 as a separate poem, first in Coleridge's journal *The Friend* in 1809, then in his own *Poems* of 1815, with the title "French Revolution as It Appeared to Enthusiasts at Its Commencement."

[CRISIS AND RECOVERY][7]

Time may come
When some dramatic story may afford
880 Shapes livelier to convey to thee, my friend,°   *i.e., Coleridge*
What then I learned—or think I learned—of truth,
And the errors into which I was betrayed
By present objects, and by reasonings false
From the beginning, inasmuch as drawn
885 Out of a heart which had been turned aside
From Nature by external accidents,
And which was thus confounded more and more,
Misguiding and misguided. Thus I fared,
Dragging all passions, notions, shapes of faith,
890 Like culprits to the bar,° suspiciously   *courtroom*
Calling the mind to establish in plain day
Her titles° and her honours, now believing,   *legal entitlements*
Now disbelieving, endlessly perplexed
With impulse, motive, right and wrong, the ground
895 Of moral obligation—what the rule,
And what the sanction—till, demanding proof,
And seeking it in every thing, I lost
All feeling of conviction, and, in fine,°   *in the end*
Sick, wearied out with contrarieties,
900 Yielded up moral questions in despair,
And for my future studies, as the sole
Employment of the inquiring faculty,
Turned towards mathematics, and their clear
And solid evidence.
Ah, then it was
905 That thou, most precious friend, about this time
First known to me, didst lend a living help
To regulate my soul. And then it was
That the belovèd woman in whose sight
Those days were passed—now speaking in a voice
910 Of sudden admonition like a brook
That does but cross a lonely road; and now
Seen, heard and felt, and caught at every turn,
Companion never lost through many a league—
Maintained for me a saving intercourse°   *communion*
915 With my true self (for, though impaired, and changed
Much, as it seemed, I was no further changed
Than as a clouded, not a waning moon);
She, in the midst of all, preserved me still
A poet, made me seek beneath that name
920 My office° upon earth, and nowhere else.[8]   *duty*
And lastly, Nature's self, by human love
Assisted, through the weary labyrinth
Conducted me again to open day,
Revived the feelings of my earlier life,

7. Wordsworth has been describing the crisis of
conscience he experienced when, in February
1793, war broke out between Britain and Revolutionary France. This section of book 7 describes
his suffering and the start of his recovery.
8. After a long separation Dorothy Wordsworth
came to live with her brother at Racedown in
1795.

925 Gave me that strength and knowledge full of peace,
    Enlarged, and never more to be disturbed,
    Which through the steps of our degeneracy,
    All degradation of this age, hath still
    Upheld me, and upholds me at this day
930 In the catastrophe° (for so they dream,   *dramatic climax*
    And nothing less), when, finally to close
    And rivet up the gains of France, a Pope
    Is summoned in to crown an Emperor⁹—
    This last opprobrium,° when we see the dog   *disgrace*
935 Returning to his vomit,¹ when the sun
    That rose in splendour, was alive, and moved
    In exultation among living clouds,
    Hath put his function and his glory off,
    And, turned into a gewgaw,° a machine,   *toy*
940 Sets like an opera phantom.²

*   *   *

From Book Eleventh.

Imagination, How Impaired and Restored

[SPOTS OF TIME]¹

*   *   *

    There are in our existence spots of time,
    Which with distinct preeminence retain
    A renovating virtue,° whence, depressed   *power of renewal*
260 By false opinion and contentious thought,
    Or aught of heavier or more deadly weight
    In trivial occupations and the round
    Of ordinary intercourse, our minds
    Are nourished and invisibly repaired—
265 A virtue, by which pleasure is enhanced,
    That penetrates, enables us to mount
    When high, more high, and lifts us up when fallen.
    This efficacious spirit chiefly lurks
    Among those passages of life in which
270 We have had deepest feeling that the mind
    Is lord and master, and that outward sense²
    Is but the obedient servant of her will.
    Such moments, worthy of all gratitude,
    Are scattered everywhere, taking their date
275 From our first childhood—in our childhood even

9. The ultimate blow to liberal hopes for France occurred when on December 2, 1804, Napoleon summoned the pope to officiate at the ceremony elevating him to emperor. At the last moment Napoleon grabbed the crown from the pope and donned it himself.
1. Allusion to Proverbs 26.11: "As a dog returneth to his vomit, a fool returneth to his folly."
2. Stage machinery used for theatrical effect.
1. Wordsworth's account in the lines that follow of two memories from childhood was originally drafted for the first book of the two-book *Prelude* of 1798. By transferring these early memories close to the end of his completed autobiography, rather than presenting them in its opening books alongside his other boyhood memories, he enacts his own theory about how remembrance of things past nourishes the imagination.
2. Perception of the external world.

Perhaps are most conspicuous. Life with me,
As far as memory can look back, is full
Of this beneficent influence.
At a time
When scarcely (I was then not six years old)
280   My hand could hold a bridle, with proud hopes
I mounted, and we rode towards the hills:
We were a pair of horsemen—honest James
Was with me, my encourager and guide,[3]
We had not travelled long ere some mischance
285   Disjoined me from my comrade, and, through fear
Dismounting, down the rough and stony moor
I led my horse, and stumbling on, at length
Came to a bottom° where in former times   valley
A murderer had been hung in iron chains.
290   The gibbet-mast[4] was mouldered down, the bones
And iron case were gone, but on the turf
Hard by, soon after that fell deed was wrought,
Some unknown hand had carved the murderer's name.
The monumental writing was engraven
295   In times long past, and still from year to year
By superstition of the neighbourhood
The grass is cleared away; and to this hour
The letters are all fresh and visible.
Faltering, and ignorant where I was, at length
300   I chanced to espy those characters° inscribed   letters
On the green sod: forthwith I left the spot,
And, reascending the bare common, saw
A naked pool that lay beneath the hills,
The beacon on the summit,[5] and more near,
305   A girl who bore a pitcher on her head
And seemed with difficult steps to force her way
Against the blowing wind. It was, in truth,
An ordinary sight, but I should need
Colours and words that are unknown to man
310   To paint the visionary dreariness
Which, while I looked all round for my lost guide,
Did at that time invest the naked pool,
The beacon on the lonely eminence,
The woman, and her garments vexed and tossed
315   By the strong wind. When, in blessèd season,
With those two dear ones[6]—to my heart so dear—
When, in the blessèd time of early love,
Long afterwards I roamed about
In daily presence of this very scene,
320   Upon the naked pool and dreary crags,
And on the melancholy beacon, fell

---

3. The 1850 *Prelude* refers to "an ancient Servant of my Father's house" (12.229).
4. The post with a projecting arm used for hanging criminals.

5. A signal beacon on a hill above Penrith.
6. His future wife, Mary Hutchinson, and his
sister, Dorothy.

The spirit of pleasure and youth's golden gleam—
And think ye not with radiance more divine
From these remembrances, and from the power
325 They left behind? So feeling comes in aid
Of feeling, and diversity of strength
Attends us, if but once we have been strong.

Oh mystery of man, from what a depth
Proceed thy honours! I am lost, but see
330 In simple childhood something of the base
On which thy greatness stands—but this I feel,
That from thyself it is that thou must give,
Else never canst receive. The days gone by
Come back upon me from the dawn almost
335 Of life; the hiding-places of my power
Seem open, I approach, and then they close;
I see by glimpses now, when age comes on
May scarcely see at all; and I would give
While yet we may, as far as words can give,
340 A substance and a life to what I feel:
I would enshrine the spirit of the past
For future restoration. Yet another
Of these to me affecting incidents,
With which we will conclude.

One Christmas-time,[7]
345 The day before the holidays began,
Feverish, and tired, and restless, I went forth
Into the fields, impatient for the sight
Of those two horses which should bear us home,
My brothers and myself. There was a crag,
350 An eminence,° which from the meeting-point   *elevated ground*
Of two highways ascending overlooked
At least a long half-mile of those two roads,
By each of which the expected steeds might come—
The choice uncertain. Thither I repaired
355 Up to the highest summit. 'Twas a day
Stormy, and rough, and wild, and on the grass
I sate half sheltered by a naked wall.
Upon my right hand was a single sheep,
A whistling hawthorn on my left, and there,
360 With those companions at my side, I watched,
Straining my eyes intensely as the mist
Gave intermitting prospect of the wood
And plain beneath. Ere I to school returned
That dreary time, ere I had been ten days
365 A dweller in my father's house, he died,
And I and my two brothers, orphans then,
Followed his body to the grave.[8] The event,
With all the sorrow which it brought, appeared

---

7. In 1783. Wordsworth, aged thirteen, was at
Hawkshead School with two of his brothers.

8. John Wordsworth died on December 30, 1783.
William's mother had died five years earlier.

A chastisement; and when I called to mind
370 That day so lately past, when from the crag
I looked in such anxiety of hope,
With trite reflections of morality,
Yet in the deepest passion, I bowed low
To God who thus corrected my desires.
375 And afterwards the wind and sleety rain,
And all the business[9] of the elements,
The single sheep, and the one blasted tree,
And the bleak music of that old stone wall,
The noise of wood and water, and the mist
380 Which on the line of each of those two roads
Advanced in such indisputable shapes[1]—
All these were spectacles and sounds to which
I often would repair, and thence would drink
As at a fountain. And I do not doubt
385 That in this later time, when storm and rain
Beat on my roof at midnight, or by day
When I am in the woods, unknown to me
The workings of my spirit thence are brought.

* * *

From Book Thirteenth.

Conclusion

[VISION ON MOUNT SNOWDON]

In one of these excursions, travelling then
Through Wales on foot and with a youthful friend,
I left Bethkelet's huts at couching-time,
And westward took my way to see the sun
5 Rise from the top of Snowdon.[1] Having reached
The cottage at the mountain's foot, we there
Rouzed up the shepherd who by ancient right
Of office is the stranger's usual guide,
And after short refreshment sallied forth.

10 It was a summer's night, a close warm night,
Wan, dull, and glaring,[2] with a dripping mist
Low-hung and thick that covered all the sky,
Half threatening storm and rain; but on we went
Unchecked, being full of heart and having faith

9. Busy-ness, motions.
1. I.e., shapes one did not dare question. Cf. Hamlet's declaration to the ghost of his father: "Thou com'st in such questionable shape / That I will speak to thee" (*Hamlet* 1.4.24–25).
1. Wordsworth climbed Mount Snowdon—the highest peak in Wales, some ten miles from the sea—with Robert Jones, the friend with whom he had also hiked through the Alps (book 6). The climb started from the village of Beddgelert

("Bethkelet") at "couching-time" (line 3), the time of night when the sheep lie down to sleep. This event took place in 1791 or possibly 1793; Wordsworth presents it out of its chronological order so as to introduce at this point the "perfect image" (line 69) for the mind, and especially for the activity of the imagination, whose "restoration" the previous books have described.
2. In the dialect of northern England, *glairie*, applied to the weather, means dull or rainy.

15   In our tried pilot. Little could we see,
Hemmed round on every side with fog and damp,
And, after ordinary travellers' chat
With our conductor, silently we sunk
Each into commerce with his private thoughts.

20   Thus did we breast the ascent, and by myself
Was nothing either seen or heard the while
Which took me from my musings, save that once
The shepherd's cur did to his own great joy
Unearth a hedgehog in the mountain-crags,

25   Round which he made a barking turbulent.
This small adventure—for even such it seemed
In that wild place and at the dead of night—
Being over and forgotten, on we wound
In silence as before. With forehead bent

30   Earthward, as if in opposition set
Against an enemy, I panted up
With eager pace, and no less eager thoughts,
Thus might we wear perhaps an hour away,
Ascending at loose distance each from each,

35   And I, as chanced, the foremost of the band—
When at my feet the ground appeared to brighten,
And with a step or two seemed brighter still;
Nor had I time to ask the cause of this,
For instantly a light upon the turf

40   Fell like a flash. I looked about, and lo,
The moon stood naked in the heavens at height
Immense above my head, and on the shore
I found myself of a huge sea of mist,
Which meek and silent rested at my feet.

45   A hundred hills their dusky backs upheaved
All over this still ocean,[3] and beyond,
Far, far beyond, the vapours shot themselves
In headlands, tongues, and promontory shapes,
Into the sea, the real sea, that seemed

50   To dwindle and give up its majesty,
Usurped upon as far as sight could reach.
Meanwhile, the moon looked down upon this shew
In single glory, and we stood, the mist
Touching our very feet; and from the shore

55   At distance not the third part of a mile
Was a blue chasm, a fracture in the vapour,
A deep and gloomy breathing-place, through which
Mounted the roar of waters, torrents, streams
Innumerable, roaring with one voice.

60   The universal spectacle throughout
Was shaped for admiration and delight,
Grand in itself alone, but in that breach
Through which the homeless voice of waters rose,
That dark deep thoroughfare, had Nature lodged

65   The soul, the imagination of the whole.

3. In Milton's description of God's creation of land from the waters, "the mountains huge appear / Emergent, and their broad bare backs upheave / Into the clouds" (*Paradise Lost* 7.285–87).

A meditation rose in me that night
Upon the lonely mountain when the scene
Had passed away, and it appeared to me
The perfect image of a mighty mind,
70 Of one that feeds upon infinity,
That is exalted by an under-presence,
The sense of God, or whatsoe'er is dim
Or vast in its own being—above all,
One function of such mind had Nature there
75 Exhibited by putting forth, and that
With circumstance most awful° and sublime: *awe-inspiring*
That domination which she oftentimes
Exerts upon the outward face of things,
So moulds them, and endues, abstracts, combines,
80 Or by abrupt and unhabitual influence
Doth make one object so impress itself
Upon all others, and pervades them so,
That even the grossest° minds must see and hear,   *dullest*
And cannot chuse but feel. The power which these
85 Acknowledge when thus moved, which Nature thus
Thrusts forth upon the senses, is the express
Resemblance—in the fullness of its strength
Made visible—a genuine counterpart
And brother of the glorious faculty
90 Which higher minds bear with them as their own.[4]
This is the very spirit in which they deal
With all the objects of the universe:
They from their native selves can send abroad
Like transformation, for themselves create
95 A like existence, and, when'er it is
Created for them, catch it by an instinct.
Them the enduring and the transient both
Serve to exalt. They build up greatest things
From least suggestions, ever on the watch,
100 Willing to work and to be wrought upon.
They need not extraordinary calls
To rouze them—in a world of life they live,
By sensible° impressions not enthralled,   *sensory*
But quickened, rouzed, and made thereby more fit
105 To hold communion with the invisible world.
Such minds are truly from the Deity,
For they are powers; and hence the highest bliss
That can be known is theirs—the consciousness
Of whom they are, habitually infused
110 Through every image,[5] and through every thought,
And all impressions; hence religion, faith,
And endless occupation for the soul,
Whether discursive or intuitive;[6]

4. The "glorious faculty" is the imagination, which transfigures and re-creates what is given to it, much as, in Wordsworth's account of the night on Snowdon, the moonlit mist, layering a metaphoric sea atop a "real sea," transfigures the familiar landscape.
5. I.e., through all they see.

6. An echo of Archangel Raphael's account to Adam of the soul's powers of reason (*Paradise Lost* 5.488–89). Discursive reason, mainly a human quality according to Raphael, undertakes to reach truths through a logical sequence of premises, observations, and conclusions; "intuitive" reason, mainly angelic, comprehends truth immediately.

Hence sovereignty within and peace at will,
115 Emotion which best foresight need not fear,
Most worthy then of trust when most intense;
Hence chearfulness in every act of life;
Hence truth in moral judgements; and delight
That fails not, in the external universe.

120   Oh, who is he that hath his whole life long
Preserved, enlarged, this freedom in himself?—
For this alone is genuine liberty.
Witness, ye solitudes, where I received
My earliest visitations (careless then
125 Of what was given me), and where now I roam,
A meditative, oft a suffering man,
And yet I trust with undiminished powers;
Witness—whatever falls my better mind,
Revolving with the accidents of life,
130 May have sustained—that, howsoe'er misled,
I never in the quest of right and wrong
Did tamper with myself° from private aims;   *my conscience*
Nor was in any of my hopes the dupe
Of selfish passions; nor did wilfully
135 Yield ever to mean cares and low pursuits;
But rather did with jealousy° shrink back   *vigilance*
From every combination that might aid
The tendency, too potent in itself,
Of habit to enslave the mind—I mean
140 Oppress it by the laws of vulgar° sense,   *commonplace*
And substitute a universe of death,
The falsest of all worlds, in place of that
Which is divine and true.[7]

*   *   *

[FINAL PROPHECY]

     Oh, yet a few short years of useful life,
And all will be complete—thy race be run,
430 Thy monument of glory will be raised.[8]
Then, though too weak to tread the ways of truth,
This age fall back to old idolatry,
Though men return to servitude as fast
As the tide ebbs, to ignominy and shame
435 By nations sink together,[9] we shall still
Find solace in the knowledge which we have,
Blessed with true happiness if we may be
United helpers forward of a day
Of firmer trust, joint labourers in the work—
440 Should Providence such grace to us vouchsafe°—   *grant*
Of their° redemption, surely yet to come.   *men's*

7. In *Paradise Lost* 2.622, the phrase "universe of death" is used to describe Hell. Wordsworth's Hell is a place in which individuals are enslaved by an unimaginative reliance on the senses and habitual perceptions.

8. In his conclusion, Wordsworth once again addresses Coleridge.
9. I.e., though men—whole nations of them together—sink to ignominy (disgrace) and shame.

Prophets of Nature, we to them will speak
A lasting inspiration, sanctified
By reason and by truth; what we have loved
445 Others will love, and we may teach them how:
Instruct them how the mind of man becomes
A thousand times more beautiful than the earth
On which he dwells, above this frame of things
(Which, 'mid all revolutions in the hopes
450 And fears of men, doth still remain unchanged)
In beauty exalted, as it is itself
Of substance and of fabric more divine.

1805   1926

DOROTHY WORDSWORTH
1771–1855

D orothy Wordsworth has an enduring place in English literature even though
she wrote almost nothing for publication. Not until long after her death did scholars gradually retrieve and print her letters, a few poems, and a series of journals that
she kept sporadically between 1798 and 1828 because, she wrote, "I shall give William pleasure by it." It has always been known, from tributes to her by her brother
and Coleridge, that she exerted an important influence on the lives and writings of
both these men. It is now apparent that she also possessed a power surpassing that of
the two poets for precise observation of people and the natural world, together with
a genius for terse, luminous, and delicately nuanced description in prose.

Dorothy was born on Christmas Day 1771, twenty-one months after William; she
was the only girl of five Wordsworth children. From her seventh year, when her mother
died, she lived with various relatives—some of them tolerant and affectionate, others
rigid and tyrannical—and saw William and her other brothers only occasionally, during the boys' summer vacations from school. In 1795, when she was twenty-four, an
inheritance that William received enabled her to carry out a long-held plan to join her
brother in a house at Racedown, and the two spent the rest of their long lives together,
first in Dorsetshire and Somersetshire, in the southwest of England, then in their
beloved Lake District. She uncomplainingly subordinated her own talents to looking
after her brother and his household. She also became William's secretary, tirelessly
copying and recopying the manuscripts of his poems to ready them for publication.
Despite the scolding of a great-aunt, who deemed "rambling about . . . on foot" unlady-
like, she accompanied her brother, too, in vigorous cross-country walks in which they
sometimes covered as much as thirty-three miles in a day.

All her adult life she was overworked; after a severe illness in 1835, she suffered a
physical and mental collapse. She spent the rest of her existence as an invalid. Hardest
for her family to endure was the drastic change in her temperament: from a high-
spirited and compassionate woman she became (save for brief intervals of lucidity)
bad-tempered, demanding, and at times violent. In this half-life she lingered for twenty
years, attended devotedly by William until his death five years before her own in 1855.

Our principal selections are from the journal Dorothy kept in 1798 at Alfoxden,
Somersetshire, where the Wordsworths had moved from Racedown to be near

Coleridge at Nether Stowey, as well as from her journals while at Grasmere (1800–1803), with Coleridge residing some thirteen miles away at Greta Hall, Keswick. Her records cover the period when both men emerged as major poets, and in their achievements Dorothy played an indispensable role. In book 10 of the 1805 *Prelude*, William says that in the time of his spiritual crisis, Dorothy "maintained for me a saving intercourse / With my true self" and "preserved me still / A Poet"; in a letter of 1797, Coleridge stressed the delicacy and tact in the responses of William's "exquisite sister" to the world of sense: "Her manners are simple, ardent, impressive. . . . Her information various—her eye watchful in minutest observation of nature—and her taste a perfect electrometer—it bends, protrudes, and draws in, at subtlest beauties & most recondite faults."

The verbal sketches of natural scenes given in the journal passages reprinted here are often echoed in Wordsworth's and Coleridge's poems. Of at least equal importance for Wordsworth was her chronicling of the busy wayfaring life of rural England. These were exceedingly hard times for country people, when the suffering caused by the displacement of small farms and of household crafts by large-scale farms and industries was aggravated by the economic distress caused by protracted Continental wars (see Wordsworth's comment in *The Ruined Cottage*, lines 133ff., p. 323). Peddlers, maimed war veterans, leech gatherers, adult and infant beggars, ousted farm families, fugitives, and women abandoned by husbands or lovers streamed along the rural roads and into William's brooding poetic imagination—often by way of Dorothy's prose records.

The journals also show the intensity of Dorothy's love for her brother. Inevitably in our era, the mutual devotion of the orphaned brother and sister has evoked psychoanalytic speculation. It is important to note that Mary Hutchinson, a gentle and openhearted young woman, had been Dorothy's closest friend since childhood, and that Dorothy encouraged William's courtship and marriage, even though she realized that it entailed her own displacement as a focus of her brother's life. All the evidence indicates that their lives in a single household never strained the affectionate relationship between the two women; indeed Dorothy, until she became an invalid, added to her former functions as William's chief support, housekeeper, and scribe a loving ministration to her brother's children.

In 1897 William Wordsworth's biographer William Knight published the first transcripts of Dorothy Wordsworth's Alfoxden and Grasmere journals, and those transcripts are the basis for the excerpts printed here. The exception is the entry from autumn 1802, in which Dorothy describes her distress on her brother's wedding day: because Knight excluded it from his edition, we rely there on Pamela Woof's edition of the Grasmere journals (Oxford University Press, 1991). Dorothy Wordsworth's poems, many of them originally written for the children in her brother's household, survived through the nineteenth and most of the twentieth centuries mainly as manuscripts in various family commonplace books. (William Wordsworth did, however, include three in his *Poems* of 1815, ascribing them to a "Female Friend.") Her poems were not collected until 1987, when Susan M. Levin edited thirty of them in an appendix ("The Collected Poems of Dorothy Wordsworth") to her *Dorothy Wordsworth and Romanticism*. The two poems included here are reprinted from that source.

From The Alfoxden Journal

Jan. 31, 1798. Set forward to Stowey[1] at half-past five. A violent storm in the wood; sheltered under the hollies. When we left home the moon immensely

---

1. I.e., to Coleridge's cottage at Nether Stowey, three miles from Alfoxden.

large, the sky scattered over with clouds. These soon closed in, contracting the dimensions of the moon without concealing her.[2] The sound of the pattering shower, and the gusts of wind, very grand. Left the wood when nothing remained of the storm but the driving wind, and a few scattering drops of rain. Presently all clear, Venus first showing herself between the struggling clouds; afterwards Jupiter appeared. The hawthorn hedges, black and pointed, glittering with millions of diamond drops; the hollies shining with broader patches of light. The road to the village of Holford glittered like another stream. On our return, the wind high—a violent storm of hail and rain at the Castle of Comfort.[3] All the Heavens seemed in one perpetual motion when the rain ceased; the moon appearing, now half veiled, and now retired behind heavy clouds, the stars still moving, the roads very dirty.

* * *

Feb. 3. A mild morning, the windows open at breakfast, the redbreasts singing in the garden. Walked with Coleridge over the hills. The sea at first obscured by vapour; that vapour afterwards slid in one mighty mass along the sea-shore; the islands and one point of land clear beyond it. The distant country (which was purple in the clear dull air), overhung by straggling clouds that sailed over it, appeared like the darker clouds, which are often seen at a great distance apparently motionless, while the nearer ones pass quickly over them, driven by the lower winds. I never saw such a union of earth, sky, and sea. The clouds beneath our feet spread themselves to the water, and the clouds of the sky almost joined them. Gathered sticks in the wood; a perfect stillness. The redbreasts sang upon the leafless boughs. Of a great number of sheep in the field, only one standing. Returned to dinner at five o'clock. The moonlight still and warm as a summer's night at nine o'clock.

Feb. 4. Walked a great part of the way to Stowey with Coleridge. The morning warm and sunny. The young lasses seen on the hill-tops, in the villages and roads, in their summer holiday clothes—pink petticoats and blue. Mothers with their children in arms, and the little ones that could just walk, tottering by their side. Midges or small flies spinning in the sunshine; the songs of the lark and redbreast; daisies upon the turf; the hazels in blossom; honeysuckles budding. I saw one solitary strawberry flower under a hedge. The furze[4] gay with blossom. The moss rubbed from the pailings by the sheep, that leave locks of wool, and the red marks with which they are spotted, upon the wood.[5]

* * *

Feb. 8. Went up the Park, and over the tops of the hills, till we came to a new and very delicious pathway, which conducted us to the Coombe.[6] Sat a considerable time upon the heath. Its surface restless and glittering with the motion of the scattered piles of withered grass, and the waving of the spiders' threads.[7] On our return the mist still hanging over the sea, but the opposite coast clear, and the rocky cliffs distinguishable. In the deep Coombe, as we

2. Cf. Coleridge's *Christabel*, lines 16–19 (p. 468).

3. A tavern halfway between Holford and Nether Stowey

4. Evergreen shrub with yellow flowers, sometimes called *gorse*.

5. Cf. Wordsworth's *The Ruined Cottage*, lines 330–36 (p. 327).

6. Hodder's Coombe is in the Quantock Hills, near Alfoxden. A coombe is a deep valley.

7. Cf. Coleridge's *The Rime of the Ancient Mariner*, line 184 (p. 453).

stood upon the sunless hill, we saw miles of grass, light and glittering, and the insects passing.

Feb. 9. William gathered sticks.

Feb. 10. Walked to Woodlands, and to the waterfall. The adder's-tongue and the ferns green in the low damp dell. These plants now in perpetual motion from the current of the air; in summer only moved by the drippings of the rocks. A cloudy day.[8]

* * *

Mar. 7. William and I drank tea at Coleridge's. A cloudy sky. Observed nothing particularly interesting—the distant prospect obscured. One only leaf upon the top of a tree—the sole remaining leaf—danced round and round like a rag blown by the wind.[9]

Mar. 8. Walked in the Park in the morning. I sate under the fir trees. Coleridge came after dinner, so we did not walk again. A foggy morning, but a clear sunny day.

Mar. 9. A clear sunny morning, went to meet Mr. and Mrs. Coleridge. The day very warm.

Mar. 10. Coleridge, Wm., and I walked in the evening to the top of the hill. We all passed the morning in sauntering about the park and gardens, the children playing about, the old man at the top of the hill gathering furze; interesting groups of human creatures, the young frisking and dancing in the sun, the elder quietly drinking in the life and soul of the sun and air.

Mar. 11. A cold day. The children went down towards the sea. William and I walked to the top of the hills above Holford. Met the blacksmith. Pleasant to see the labourer on Sunday jump with the friskiness of a cow upon a sunny day.

* * *

1798   1897

From The Grasmere Journals

1800

May 14, 1800.—Wm. and John set off into Yorkshire[1] after dinner at half-past two o'clock, cold pork in their pockets. I left them at the turning of the Lowwood bay under the trees. My heart was so full that I could hardly speak to W. when I gave him a farewell kiss. I sate a long time upon a stone at the margin of the lake, and after a flood of tears my heart was easier. The lake looked to me, I knew not why, dull and melancholy, and the weltering on the shores seemed a heavy sound. I walked as long as I could amongst the stones of the shore. The wood rich in flowers; a beautiful yellow (palish yellow) flower, that looked thick, round, and double—the smell very sweet (I supposed it was a ranunculus), crowfoot, the grassy-leaved rabbit-looking

8. Cf. the description of the dell in Coleridge's "This Lime-Tree Bower My Prison," lines 13–20 (p. 446).

9. Cf. *Christabel*, lines 49ff. (p. 469).

1. William and his younger brother John, on the way to visit Mary Hutchinson, whom William was to marry two and a half years later.

white flower, strawberries, geraniums, scentless violets, anemones, two kinds of orchises, primroses, the hackberry very beautiful, the crab coming out as a low shrub. Met an old man, driving a very large beautiful bull, and a cow. He walked with two sticks. Came home by Clappersgate. The valley very green; many sweet views up to Rydale, when I could juggle away the fine houses; but they disturbed me, even more than when I have been happier; one beautiful view of the bridge, without Sir Michael's.[2] Sate down very often, though it was cold. I resolved to write a journal of the time, till W. and J. return, and I set about keeping my resolve, because I will not quarrel with myself, and because I shall give William pleasure by it when he comes home again. At Rydale, a woman of the village, stout and well dressed, begged a half-penny. She had never she said done it before, but these hard times! Arrived at home, set some slips of privet, the evening cold, had a fire, my face now flame-coloured. It is nine o'clock. I shall now go to bed.

* * *

Friday, 3rd October. Very rainy all the morning. Wm. walked to Ambleside after dinner. I went with him part of the way. He talked much about the object of his essay for the second volume of "L. B."[3] * * *

N.B.—When William and I returned from accompanying Jones, we met an old man almost double.[4] He had on a coat, thrown over his shoulders, above his waistcoat and coat. Under this he carried a bundle, and had an apron on and a night-cap. His face was interesting. He had dark eyes and a long nose. John, who afterwards met him at Wytheburn, took him for a Jew. He was of Scotch parents, but had been born in the army. He had had a wife, and "she was a good woman, and it pleased God to bless us with ten children." All these were dead but one, of whom he had not heard for many years, a sailor. His trade was to gather leeches, but now leeches were scarce, and he had not strength for it. He lived by begging, and was making his way to Carlisle, where he should buy a few godly books to sell. He said leeches were very scarce, partly owing to this dry season, but many years they have been scarce. He supposed it owing to their being much sought after, that they did not breed fast, and were of slow growth. Leeches were formerly 2s. 6d.[5] per 100; they are now 30s. He had been hurt in driving a cart, his leg broken, his body driven over, his skull fractured. He felt no pain till he recovered from his first insensibility. It was then late in the evening, when the light was just going away.

* * *

Saturday, [Oct.] 11th. A fine October morning. Sat in the house working all the morning. William composing. * * * After dinner we walked up Greenhead Gill in search of a sheepfold.[6] We went by Mr. Olliff's, and through his woods. It was a delightful day, and the views looked excessively cheerful and beautiful, chiefly that from Mr. Olliff's field, where our own house is to be

2. Sir Michael le Fleming's estate, Rydal Hall. "Without": outside or beyond.
3. The Preface to the second edition of *Lyrical Ballads,* 1800.
4. William's "Resolution and Independence," composed one and a half years later, incorporated various details of Dorothy's description of

the leech gatherer. See May 4 and 7, 1802 (pp. 416 and 417), for William working on the poem he originally called "The Leech Gatherer."
5. Two shillings, six pence.
6. The sheepfold (pen for sheep) in William's "Michael." Lines 1–7 of the poem describe the walk up Greenhead Gill.

built. The colours of the mountains soft, and rich with orange fern; the cattle pasturing upon the hilltops; kites sailing in the sky above our heads; sheep bleating, and feeding in the water courses, scattered over the mountains. They come down and feed, on the little green islands in the beds of the torrents, and so may be swept away. The sheepfold is falling away. It is built nearly in the form of a heart unequally divided. Looked down the brook, and saw the drops rise upwards and sparkle in the air at the little falls. The higher sparkled the tallest. We walked along the turf of the mountain till we came to a track, made by the cattle which come upon the hills.

* * *

Sunday, October 12th. Sate in the house writing in the morning while Wm. went into the wood to compose. Wrote to John in the morning; copied poems for the L. B. In the evening wrote to Mrs. Rawson. Mary Jameson and Sally Ashburner dined. We pulled apples after dinner, a large basket full. We walked before tea by Bainriggs to observe the many-coloured foliage. The oaks dark green with yellow leaves, the birches generally still green, some near the water yellowish, the sycamore crimson and crimson-tufted, the mountain ash a deep orange, the common ash lemon-colour, but many ashes still fresh in their peculiar green, those that were discoloured chiefly near the water. Wm. composing in the evening. Went to bed at 12 o'clock.

1801

Tuesday, [Nov.] 24th * * * It was very windy, and we heard the wind everywhere about us as we went along the lane, but the walls sheltered us. John Green's house looked pretty under Silver How. As we were going along we were stopped at once, at the distance perhaps of 50 yards from our favourite birch tree. It was yielding to the gusty wind with all its tender twigs. The sun shone upon it, and it glanced in the wind like a flying sunshiny shower. It was a tree in shape, with stem and branches, but it was like a spirit of water. The sun went in, and it resumed its purplish appearance, the twigs still yielding to the wind, but not so visibly to us. The other birch trees that were near it looked bright and cheerful, but it was a creature by its own self among them. . . . We went through the wood. It became fair. There was a rainbow which spanned the lake from the island-house to the foot of Bainriggs. The village looked populous and beautiful. Catkins are coming out; palm trees budding; the alder, with its plum-coloured buds. We came home over the stepping-stones. The lake was foamy with white waves. I saw a solitary butter-flower in the wood. * * * Reached home at dinner time. Sent Peggy Ashburner some goose. She sent me some honey, with a thousand thanks. "Alas! the gratitude of men has," etc.[7] I went in to set her right about this, and sate a while with her. She talked about Thomas's having sold his land. "I," says she, "said many a time he's not come fra London to buy our land, however." Then she told me with what pains and industry they had made up their taxes, interest, etc. etc., how they all got up at 5 o'clock in the morning to spin and Thomas carded, and that they had paid off a hundred pounds of the interest. She said she used to take much pleasure in the cattle and sheep. "O how pleased I used to be when they fetched them down, and

---

7. A quotation from William's "Simon Lee." "Alas! the gratitude of men / Has oft'ner left me mourning."

when I had been a bit poorly I would gang out upon a hill and look over 't fields and see them, and it used to do me so much good you cannot think." Molly said to me when I came in, "Poor body! she's very ill, but one does not know how long she may last. Many a fair face may gang before her." We sate by the fire without work for some time, then Mary read a poem of Daniel.[8] * * * Wm. read Spenser, now and then, a little aloud to us. We were making his waistcoat. We had a note from Mrs. C., with bad news from poor C.—very ill. William went to John's Grove. I went to find him. Moonlight, but it rained. * * * He had been surprised, and terrified, by a sudden rushing of winds, which seemed to bring earth, sky, and lake together, as if the whole were going to enclose him in. He was glad he was in a high road.

In speaking of our walk on Sunday evening, the 22nd November, I forgot to notice one most impressive sight. It was the moon and the moonlight seen through hurrying driving clouds immediately behind the Stone-Man upon the top of the hill, on the forest side. Every tooth and every edge of rock was visible, and the Man stood like a giant watching from the roof of a lofty castle. The hill seemed perpendicular from the darkness below it. It was a sight that I could call to mind at any time, it was so distinct.

1802

Thursday [*Mar. 4*]. Before we had quite finished breakfast Calvert's man brought the horses for Wm.[9] We had a deal to do, pens to make, poems to put in order for writing, to settle for the press, pack up; and the man came before the pens were made, and he was obliged to leave me with only two. Since he left me at half-past 11 (it is now 2) I have been putting the drawers into order, laid by his clothes which he had thrown here and there and everywhere, filed two months' newspapers and got my dinner, 2 boiled eggs and 2 apple tarts. I have set Molly on to clean the garden a little, and I myself have walked. I transplanted some snowdrops—the Bees are busy. Wm. has a nice bright day. It was hard frost in the night. The Robins are singing sweetly. Now for my walk. I *will* be busy. I *will* look well, and be well when he comes back to me. O the Darling! Here is one of his bitten apples. I can hardly find it in my heart to throw it into the fire. * * * I walked round the two Lakes, crossed the stepping-stones at Rydale foot. Sate down where we always sit. I was full of thought about my darling. Blessings on him. I came home at the foot of our own hill under Lough-rigg. They are making sad ravages in the woods. Benson's wood is going, and the woods above the River. The wind has blown down a small fir tree on the Rock, that terminates John's path. I suppose the wind of Wednesday night. I read German after tea. I worked and read the L. B., enchanted with the *Idiot Boy*. Wrote to Wm. and then went to bed. It snowed when I went to bed.

* * *

Monday [*Mar. 22*]. A rainy day. William very poorly. 2 letters from Sara, and one from poor Annette. Wrote to my brother Richard. We talked a good deal about C. and other interesting things. We resolved to see Annette,

8. Identified as Samuel Daniel's poem *Muso-philes: Containing a General Defence of Learning* (1599).
9. For a journey to Keswick to visit Coleridge.

and that Wm. should go to Mary.[1] Wm. wrote to Coleridge not to expect us till Thursday or Friday.

Tuesday.—A mild morning. William worked at *The Cuckoo* poem.[2] I sewed beside him. After dinner he slept. I read German, and, at the closing-in of day, went to sit in the orchard. William came to me, and walked backwards and forwards. We talked about C. Wm. repeated the poem to me. I left him there, and in 20 minutes he came in, rather tired with attempting to write. He is now reading Ben Jonson. I am going to read German. It is about 10 o'clock, a quiet night. The fire flickers, and the watch ticks. I hear nothing save the breathing of my Beloved as he now and then pushes his book forward, and turns over a leaf. * * *

*   *   *

Thursday, [*Apr.*] *15th* It was a threatening, misty morning, but mild. We set off after dinner from Eusemere. Mrs. Clarkson went a short way with us, but turned back.[3] The wind was furious, and we thought we must have returned. We first rested in the large boathouse, then under a furze bush opposite Mr. Clarkson's. Saw the plough going in the field. The wind seized our breath. The lake was rough. There was a boat by itself floating in the middle of the bay below Water Millock. We rested again in the Water Millock Lane. The hawthorns are black and green, the birches here and there greenish, but there is yet more of purple to be seen on the twigs. We got over into a field to avoid some cows—people working. A few primroses by the roadside— woodsorrel flower, the anemone, scentless violets, strawberries, and that starry, yellow flower which Mrs. C. calls pile wort. When we were in the woods beyond Gowbarrow Park we saw a few daffodils close to the waterside.[4] We fancied that the sea had floated the seeds ashore, and that the little colony had so sprung up. But as we went along there were more and yet more; and at last, under the boughs of the trees, we saw that there was a long belt of them along the shore, about the breadth of a country turnpike road. I never saw daffodils so beautiful. They grew among the mossy stones about and above them; some rested their heads upon these stones, as on a pillow, for weariness; and the rest tossed and reeled and danced, and seemed as if they verily laughed with the wind, that blew upon them over the lake; they looked so gay, ever glancing, ever changing. This wind blew directly over the lake to them. There was here and there a little knot, and a few stragglers higher up; but they were so few as not to disturb the simplicity, unity, and life of that one busy highway. We rested again and again. The bays were stormy, and we heard the waves at different distances, and in the middle of the water, like the sea. Rain came on. * * * William was sitting by a good fire when I came downstairs. He soon made his way to the library, piled up in a corner of the window. He brought out a volume of Enfield's *Speaker*,[5] another miscellany, and an odd volume of Congreve's plays. We had a glass of warm rum

---

1. It had been arranged several months earlier that William was to marry Mary Hutchinson (Sara is Mary's sister, with whom Coleridge had fallen in love). Now the Wordsworths resolve to go to France to settle affairs with Annette Vallon, mother of William's daughter, Caroline. William did not conceal the facts of his early love affair from his family, or from Mary Hutchinson.
2. "To the Cuckoo."
3. Catherine Clarkson, the wife of the anti-slave-

trade campaigner Thomas Clarkson, was a neighbor and became one of Dorothy Wordsworth's closest friends.
4. William did not compose his poem on the daffodils, "I wandered lonely as a cloud," until two years later. Comparison with the poem will show how extensive was his use of Dorothy's prose description (p. 345).
5. William Enfield's *The Speaker* (1774), a volume of selections suitable for elocution.

and water. We enjoyed ourselves, and wished for Mary. It rained and blew, when we went to bed. * * *

Friday, 16th April (Good Friday).—When I undrew curtains in the morning, I was much affected by the beauty of the prospect, and the change. The sun shone, the wind had passed away, the hills looked cheerful, the river was very bright as it flowed into the lake. The church rises up behind a little knot of rocks, the steeple not so high as an ordinary three-story house. Trees in a row in the garden under the wall. The valley is at first broken by little woody knolls that make retiring places, fairy valleys in the vale, the river winds along under these hills, travelling, not in a bustle but not slowly, to the lake. We saw a fisherman in the flat meadow on the other side of the water. He came towards us, and threw his line over the two-arched bridge. It is a bridge of a heavy construction, almost bending inwards in the middle, but it is grey, and there is a look of ancientry in the architecture of it that pleased me. As we go on the vale opens out more into one vale, with somewhat of a cradle bed. Cottages, with groups of trees, on the side of the hills. We passed a pair of twin children, two years old. Sate on the next bridge which we crossed—a single arch. We rested again upon the turf, and looked at the same bridge. We observed arches in the water, occasioned by the large stones sending it down in two streams. A sheep came plunging through the river, stumbled up the bank, and passed close to us. It had been frightened by an insignificant little dog on the other side. Its fleece dropped a glittering shower under its belly. Primroses by the road-side, pile wort that shone like stars of gold in the sun, violets, strawberries, retired and half-buried among the grass. When we came to the foot of Brothers Water, I left William sitting on the bridge, and went along the path on the right side of the lake through the wood. I was delighted with what I saw. The water under the boughs of the bare old trees, the simplicity of the mountains, and the exquisite beauty of the path. There was one grey cottage. I repeated The Glow-worm,[6] as I walked along. I hung over the gate, and thought I could have stayed for ever. When I returned, I found William writing a poem descriptive of the sights and sounds we saw and heard. There was the gentle flowing of the stream, the glittering, lively lake, green fields without a living creature to be seen on them; behind us, a flat pasture with forty-two cattle feeding; to our left, the road leading to the hamlet. No smoke there, the sun shone on the bare roofs. The people were at work ploughing, harrowing, and sowing; . . . a dog barking now and then, cocks crowing, birds twittering, the snow in patches at the top of the highest hills, yellow palms, purple and green twigs on the birches, ashes with their glittering stems quite bare. The hawthorn a bright green, with black stems under the oak. The moss of the oak glossy. We went on. Passed two sisters at work (they first passed us), one with two pitchforks in her hand, the other had a spade. We had come to talk with them. They laughed long after we were gone, perhaps half in wantonness, half boldness. William finished his poem.[7] Before we got to the foot of Kirkstone, there were hundreds of cattle in the vale. * * *

Thursday, [Apr.] 29th. * * * After I had written down The Tinker, which William finished this morning,[8] Luff called. He was very lame, limped into the kitchen. He came on a little pony. We then went to John's Grove, sate a

6. William's poem beginning "Among all lovely things my Love had been," composed four days earlier; "my Love" in this line is Dorothy.

7. The short lyric "Written in March."
8. William never published his comic poem "The Tinkers." It was first printed in 1897.

while at first; afterwards William lay, and I lay, in the trench under the fence—he with his eyes shut, and listening to the waterfalls and the birds. There was no one waterfall above another—it was a sound of waters in the air—the voice of the air. William heard me breathing, and rustling now and then, but we both lay still, and unseen by one another. He thought that it would be so sweet thus to lie in the grave, to hear the peaceful sounds of the earth, and just to know that our dear friends were near. The lake was still; there was a boat out. Silver How reflected with delicate purple and yellowish hues, as I have seen spar; lambs on the island, and running races together by the half-dozen, in the round field near us. The copses greenish, hawthorns green, . . . cottages smoking. As I lay down on the grass, I observed the glittering silver line on the ridge of the backs of the sheep, owing to their situation respecting the sun, which made them look beautiful, but with something of strangeness, like animals of another kind, as if belonging to a more splendid world. * * *

                                                    * * *

Tuesday, May 4th. Though William went to bed nervous, and jaded in the extreme, he rose refreshed, wrote out *The Leech Gatherer*[9] for him, which he had begun the night before and of which he wrote several stanzas in bed this Monday morning. It was very hot. * * * We rested several times by the way,—read, and repeated *The Leech Gatherer.* * * * We saw Coleridge on the Wytheburn side of the water; he crossed the beck to us. Mr. Simpson was fishing there. William and I ate luncheon and then went on towards the waterfall. It is a glorious wild solitude under that lofty purple crag. It stood upright by itself; its own self, and its shadow below, one mass; all else was sunshine. We went on further. A bird at the top of the crag was flying round and round, and looked in thinness and transparency, shape and motion like a moth. We climbed the hill, but looked in vain for a shade, except at the foot of the great waterfall. We came down, and rested upon a moss-covered rock rising out of the bed of the river. There we lay, ate our dinner, and stayed there till about four o'clock or later. William and Coleridge repeated and read verses. I drank a little brandy and water, and was in heaven. The stag's horn is very beautiful and fresh, springing upon the fells; mountain ashes, green. We drank tea at a farm house. * * * We parted from Coleridge at Sara's crag, after having looked for the letters which C. carved in the morning. I missed them all. William deepened the T. with C.'s pen-knive.[1] We sate afterwards on the wall, seeing the sun go down, and the reflections in the still water. C. looked well, and parted from us cheerfully, hopping upon the side stones. On the Raise we met a woman with two little girls, one in her arms, the other, about four years old, walking by her side, a pretty little thing, but half-starved. * * * The mother, when we accosted her, told us how her husband had left her, and gone off with another woman, and how she "*pursued*" them. Then her fury kindled, and her eyes rolled about. She changed again to tears. She was a Cockermouth woman, thirty years of age—a child at Cockermouth when I was. I was moved, and gave her a shilling. . . . We had the

9. The poem that was published as "Resolution and Independence." For its origin see the entry for October 3, 1800 (p. 411).
1. The rock, which has since been blasted away to make room for a new road, contained the carved letters W. W., M. H., D. W., S. T. C., J. W., and S. H.: William Wordsworth, Mary Hutchinson, Dorothy Wordsworth, Samuel Taylor Coleridge, John Wordsworth, and Sara Hutchinson.

crescent moon with the "auld moon in her arms."[2] We rested often, always upon the bridges. Reached home at about ten o'clock. * * * We went soon to bed. I repeated verses to William while he was in bed; he was soothed, and I left him. "This is the spot"[3] over and over again.

* * *

Thursday, 6th May.—A sweet morning. We have put the finishing stroke to our bower, and here we are sitting in the orchard. It is one o'clock. We are sitting upon a seat under the wall, which I found my brother building up, when I came to him.—He had intended that it should have been done before I came. It is a nice, cool, shady spot. The small birds are singing, lambs bleating, cuckoos calling, the thrush sings by fits, Thomas Ashburner's axe is going quietly (without passion) in the orchard, hens are cackling, flies humming, the women talking together at their doors, plum and pear trees are in blossom—apple trees greenish—the opposite woods green, the crows are cawing, we have heard ravens, the ash trees are in blossom, birds flying all about us, the stitchwort is coming out, there is one budding lychnis, the primroses are passing their prime, celandine, violets, and wood sorrel for ever more, little geraniums and pansies on the wall. We walked in the evening to Tail End, to inquire about hurdles for the orchard shed. * * * When we came in we found a magazine, and review, and a letter from Coleridge, verses to Hartley, and Sara H. We read the review,[4] etc. The moon was a perfect boat, a silver boat, when we were out in the evening. The birch tree is all over green in *small* leaf, more light and elegant than when it is full out. It bent to the breezes, as if for the love of its own delightful motions. Sloe-thorns and hawthorns in the hedges.

Friday, 7th May.—William had slept uncommonly well, so, feeling himself strong, he fell to work at *The Leech Gatherer*; he wrote hard at it till dinner time, then he gave over, tired to death—he had finished the poem.[5] I was making Derwent's frocks. After dinner we sate in the orchard. It was a thick, hazy, dull air. The thrush sang almost continually; the little birds were more than usually busy with their voices. The sparrows are now full fledged. The nest is so full that they lie upon one another; they sit quietly in their nest with closed mouths. I walked to Rydale after tea, which we drank by the kitchen fire. The evening very dull; a terrible kind of threatening brightness at sunset above Easedale. The sloe-thorn beautiful in the hedges, and in the wild spots higher up among the hawthorns. No letters. William met me. He had been digging in my absence, and cleaning the well. We walked up beyond Lewthwaites. A very dull sky; coolish; crescent moon now and then. I had a letter brought me from Mrs. Clarkson while we were walking in the orchard. I observed the sorrel leaves opening at about nine o'clock. William went to bed tired with thinking about a poem.

* * *

[*July.*] On Thursday morning, 29th, we arrived in London.[6] Wm. left me at the Sun. * * * After various troubles and disasters, we left London on

2. From the "Ballad of Sir Patrick Spens." See p. 36.
3. William never completed this poem.
4. The *Monthly Review* for March 1802.
5. Later entries show, however, that William kept working on the manuscript until July 4.
6. On the way to France to visit Annette Vallon and Caroline (see the entry for March 22, 1802, p. 413).

Saturday morning at half-past five or six, the 31st of July. We mounted the Dover coach at Charing Cross. It was a beautiful morning. The city, St. Paul's, with the river, and a multitude of little boats, made a most beautiful sight as we crossed Westminster Bridge. The houses were not overhung by their cloud of smoke, and they were spread out endlessly, yet the sun shone so brightly, with such a fierce light, that there was even something like the purity of one of nature's own grand spectacles.[7]

We rode on cheerfully, now with the Paris diligence before us, now behind. We walked up the steep hills, a beautiful prospect everywhere, till we even reached Dover. * * * We arrived at Calais at four o'clock on Sunday morning, the 31st of July.[8] We stayed in the vessel till half-past seven; then William went for letters at about half-past eight or nine. We found out Annette and C. chez Madame Avril dans la Rue de la Tête d'or. We lodged opposite two ladies, in tolerably decent-sized rooms, but badly furnished. * * * The weather was very hot. We walked by the sea-shore almost every evening with Annette and Caroline, or William and I alone. I had a bad cold, and could not bathe at first, but William did. It was a pretty sight to see as we walked upon the sands when the tide was low, perhaps a hundred people bathing about a quarter of a mile distant from us. And we had delightful walks after the heat of the day was passed—seeing far off in the west the coast of England like a cloud crested with Dover castle, which was but like the summit of the cloud—the evening star and the glory of the sky, the reflections in the water were more beautiful than the sky itself, purple waves brighter than precious stones, for ever melting away upon the sands.

* * *

[*Sept. 24 and following.*] Mary first met us in the avenue. She looked so fat and well that we were made very happy by the sight of her—then came Sara, & last of all Joanna.[9] Tom was forking corn standing upon the corn cart. We dressed ourselves immediately & got tea—the garden looked gay with asters & sweet peas—I looked at everything with tranquillity & happiness but I was ill both on Saturday & Sunday & continued to be poorly most of the time of our stay. Jack & George came on Friday Evening 1st October. On Saturday 2nd we rode to Hackness, William Jack George & Sara single, I behind Tom. On Sunday 3rd Mary & Sara were busy packing. On Monday 4th October 1802, my Brother William was married to Mary Hutchinson. I slept a good deal of the night & rose fresh & well in the morning—at a little after 8 o'clock I saw them go down the avenue towards the Church. William had parted from me up stairs. I gave him the wedding ring—with how deep a blessing! I took it from my forefinger where I had worn it the whole of the night before—he slipped it again onto my finger and blessed me fervently. When they were absent my dear little Sara prepared the breakfast. I kept myself as quiet as I could, but when I saw the two men running up the walk, coming to tell us it was over, I could stand it no longer & threw myself on the bed where I lay in stillness, neither hearing or seeing any thing, till

7. Cf. William's sonnet "Composed upon Westminster Bridge" (p. 355).
8. The actual date was August 1. One of the walks by the sea that Dorothy goes on to describe was the occasion for William's sonnet "It is a beauteous evening."
9. The Wordsworths have come to Gallow Hill, Yorkshire, for the marriage of William and Mary. The people mentioned are Mary's sisters and brothers (Sara, Joanna, Tom, Jack, and George Hutchinson). Out of consideration for Dorothy's overwrought feelings, only Joanna, Jack, and Tom attended the ceremony at Brampton Church.

Sara came upstairs to me & said "They are coming." This forced me from the bed where I lay & I moved I knew not how straight forward, faster than my strength could carry me till I met my beloved William & fell upon his bosom. He & John Hutchinson led me to the house & there I stayed to welcome my dear Mary. As soon as we had breakfasted we departed.[1] It rained when we set off. Poor Mary was much agitated when she parted from her Brothers & Sisters & her home. Nothing particular occurred till we reached Kirby. We had sunshine & showers, pleasant talk, love & chearfulness. * * * It rained very hard when we reached Windermere. We sate in the rain at Wilcock's to change horses, & arrived at Grasmere at about 6 o'clock on Wednesday Evening, the 6th of October 1802. Molly was overjoyed to see us,—for my part I cannot describe what I felt, & our dear Mary's feelings would I dare say not be easy to speak of. We went by candle light into the garden & were astonished at the growth of the Brooms, Portugal Laurels, &c &c &—The next day, Thursday, we unpacked the Boxes. On Friday 8th we baked Bread, & Mary & I walked, first upon the Hill side, & then in John's Grove, then in view of Rydale, the first walk that I had taken with my Sister.

* * *

24th December.—Christmas Eve. William is now sitting by me, at half-past ten o'clock. I have been * * * repeating some of his sonnets to him, listening to his own repeating, reading some of Milton's, and the *Allegro* and *Penseroso*. It is a quick, keen frost. * * * Coleridge came this morning with Wedgwood. We all turned out * * * one by one, to meet him. He looked well. We had to tell him of the birth of his little girl, born yesterday morning at six o'clock. William went with them to Wytheburn in the chaise, and M. and I met W. on the Raise. It was not an unpleasant morning. * * * The sun shone now and then, and there was no wind, but all things looked cheerless and distinct; no meltings of sky into mountains, the mountains like stone work wrought up with huge hammers. Last Sunday was as mild a day as I ever remember. * * * Mary and I went round the lakes. There were flowers of various kinds—the topmost bell of a foxglove, geraniums, daisies, a buttercup in the water (but this I saw two or three days before), small yellow flowers (I do not know their name) in the turf. A large bunch of strawberry blossoms. * * * It is Christmas Day, Saturday, 25th December 1802. I am thirty-one years of age. It is a dull, frosty day.

* * *

Grasmere—A Fragment

> Peaceful our valley, fair and green,
> And beautiful her cottages,
> Each in its nook, its sheltered hold,
> Or underneath its tuft of trees.
>
> 5   Many and beautiful they are;
> But there is *one* that I love best,

---

1. Dorothy accompanied William and Mary on the three-day journey back to their cottage at Grasmere.

A lowly shed, in truth, it is,
A brother of the rest.

10 Yet when I sit on rock or hill,
Down looking on the valley fair,
That Cottage with its clustering trees
Summons my heart; it settles there.

Others there are whose small domain
Of fertile fields and hedgerows green
15 Might more seduce a wanderer's mind
To wish that *there* his home had been.

Such wish be his! I blame him not,
My fancies they perchance are wild
—I love that house because it is
20 The very Mountains' child.

Fields hath it of its own, green fields,
But they are rocky steep and bare;
Their fence is of the mountain stone,
And moss and lichen flourish there.

25 And when the storm comes from the North
It lingers near that pastoral spot,
And, piping through the mossy walls,
It seems delighted with its lot.

And let it take its own delight;
30 And let it range the pastures bare;
Until it reach that group of trees,
—It may not enter there!

A green unfading grove it is,
Skirted with many a lesser tree,
35 Hazel and holly, beech and oak,
A bright and flourishing company.

Precious the shelter of those trees;
They screen the cottage that I love;
The sunshine pierces to the roof,
40 And the tall pine-trees tower above.

When first I saw that dear abode,
It was a lovely winter's day:
After a night of perilous storm
The west wind ruled with gentle sway;

45 A day so mild, it might have been
The first day of the gladsome spring;
The robins warbled, and I heard
One solitary throstle sing.

A Stranger, Grasmere, in thy Vale,
50 All faces then to me unknown,
I left my sole companion-friend
To wander out alone.

Lured by a little winding path,
I quitted soon the public road,
55 A smooth and tempting path it was,
By sheep and shepherds trod.

Eastward, toward the lofty hills,
This pathway led me on
Until I reached a stately Rock,
60 With velvet moss o'ergrown.

With russet oak and tufts of fern
Its top was richly garlanded;
Its sides adorned with eglantine
Bedropp'd with hips of glossy red.

65 There, too, in many a sheltered chink
The foxglove's broad leaves flourished fair,
And silver birch whose purple twigs
Bend to the softest breathing air.

Beneath that Rock my course I stayed,
70 And, looking to its summit high,
"Thou wear'st," said I, "a splendid garb,
Here winter keeps his revelry.

"Full long a dweller on the Plains,
I griev'd when summer days were gone;
75 No more I'll grieve; for Winter here
Hath pleasure gardens of his own.

"What need of flowers? The splendid moss
Is gayer than an April mead;
More rich its hues of various green,
80 Orange, and gold, & glittering red."

—Beside that gay and lovely Rock
There came with merry voice
A foaming streamlet glancing by;
It seemed to say "Rejoice!"

85 My youthful wishes all fulfill'd,
Wishes matured by thoughtful choice,
I stood an Inmate of this vale
How *could* I but rejoice?

ca. 1802–1805   1892

Thoughts on My Sick-Bed[1]

And has the remnant of my life
Been pilfered of this sunny Spring?
And have its own prelusive sounds
Touched in my heart no echoing string?

5   Ah! say not so—the hidden life
Couchant° within this feeble frame   *lying*
Hath been enriched by kindred gifts,
That, undesired, unsought-for, came

With joyful heart in youthful days
10   When fresh each season in its Round
I welcomed the earliest Celandine
Glittering upon the mossy ground;

With busy eyes I pierced the lane
In quest of known and *un*known things,
15   —The primrose a lamp on its fortress rock,
The silent butterfly spreading its wings,

The violet betrayed by its noiseless breath,
The daffodil dancing in the breeze,
The carolling thrush, on his naked perch,
20   Towering above the budding trees.

Our cottage-hearth no longer our home,
Companions of Nature were we,
The Stirring, the Still, the Loquacious, the Mute—
To all we gave our sympathy.

25   Yet never in those careless days
When spring-time in rock, field, or bower
Was but a fountain of earthly hope
A promise of fruits & the *splendid* flower.

No! then I never felt a bliss
30   That might with *that* compare
Which, piercing to my couch of rest,
Came on the vernal air.

When loving Friends an offering brought,
The first flowers of the year,
35   Culled from the precincts of our home,
From nooks to Memory dear.

1. In a letter of May 25, 1832, William Wordsworth's daughter Dora mentions this as "an
affecting poem which she [her aunt Dorothy] has
written on the pleasure she received from the first
spring flowers that were carried up to her when
confined to her sick room." The lines refer to half
a dozen or more poems by William, including "I
wandered lonely as a cloud" (in line 18) and "Tintern Abbey" (lines 45–52).

With some sad thoughts the work was done,
Unprompted and unbidden,
But joy it brought to my *hidden* life,
40   To consciousness no longer hidden.

I felt a Power unfelt before,
Controlling weakness, languor, pain;
It bore me to the Terrace walk
I trod the Hills again;—

45   No prisoner in this lonely room,
I *saw* the green Banks of the Wye,
Recalling thy prophetic words,
Bard, Brother, Friend from infancy!

No need of motion, or of strength,
50   Or even the breathing air:
—I thought of Nature's loveliest scenes;
And with Memory I was there.

May 1832   1978

SIR WALTER SCOTT
1771–1832

Walter Scott was born in Edinburgh, but as a small boy, to improve his health, he lived for some years with his grandparents on their farm in the Scottish Border country (the part of southern Scotland lying immediately north of the border with England). This region was rich in ballad and folklore, much of it associated with the Border warfare between northern English and southern Scottish raiders. As a child Scott listened eagerly to stories about the past, especially to accounts of their experiences by survivors of the Jacobite rebellion of 1745, the last in a series of ill-fated attempts to restore to the throne of Britain the Stuart dynasty, who had been living in exile since 1688. The defeat of the ragtag army of Scottish Highland soldiers who had rallied around Charles Edward Stuart brought to an end not just the Jacobite cause but also the quasi-feudal power that the Highland chiefs had exercised over their clans. The Highlands' native traditions were suppressed by a government in London that was determined, to the point of brutality, to integrate all its Scottish subjects more fully into the United Kingdom. Ideally situated to witness these social and cultural transformations, Scott early acquired what he exploited throughout his work—a sense of history as associated with a specific place and a sense of the past that is kept alive, tenuously, in the oral traditions of the present.

Scott's father was a lawyer, and he himself was trained in the law, becoming in 1799 sheriff (local judge) of Selkirkshire, a Border county, and in 1806 clerk of session—that is, secretary to the highest civil court in Scotland—in Edinburgh. Scott viewed the law, in its development over the centuries, as embodying the changing social customs of the country and an important element in social history, and he often used it (as in *The Heart of Midlothian* and *Redgauntlet*) to give a special dimension to his fiction.

From early childhood Scott was an avid reader of ballads and poetic romances, which with his phenomenal memory he effortlessly memorized. He began his literary career as a poet, first as a translator of German ballad imitations and then as a writer of such imitations. In 1799 he set out on the collecting expedition that resulted in the *Minstrelsy of the Scottish Border* (1802–03), his compilation of Border ballads. Motivating the collection was Scott's belief that the authentic features of the Scottish character were "daily melting . . . into those of her . . . ally" (that is, England), but he had fewer compunctions than modern folklorists about "improving" the ballads he and assistants transcribed from the recitations of elderly peasant women and shepherds. Scott turned next to composing long narrative poems set in medieval times, the best-known of which are *The Lay of the Last Minstrel* (1805), *Marmion* (1808), and *The Lady of the Lake* (1810). (For an except from *Marmion* see the topic "Romantic Literature and Wartime" in the NAEL Archive.) Although these "metrical romances" were sensational best sellers (in 1830 Scott estimated that *The Lay* had sold thirty thousand copies) and helped establish nineteenth-century culture's vogue for medieval chivalry, Scott eventually gave up poetry for prose fiction. "Byron beat me," he explained, referring to the fact that his metrical romances ended up eclipsed by his rival's even more exotic "Eastern tales."

Scott continued to write lyric poems, which he inserted in his novels. Some of the lyrics, including "Proud Maisie," are based on the folk ballad and capture remarkably the terse suggestiveness of the oral form. *Waverley* (1814), which deals with the Jacobite defeat in 1745, introduced a motif that would remain central to Scott's fiction: the protagonist mediates between a heroic but violent old world that can no longer survive and an emerging new world that will be both safer than the old one—ensuring the security of property and the rule of law—and duller, allowing few opportunities for adventure. The novels negotiate between preserving the last traces of the traditional cultures whose disappearance they chronicle—for instance, the Scots superstitions and distinctive speech forms that feature in the ghost story that Wandering Willie recounts in *Redgauntlet* and the song, "Proud Maisie," that Madge Wildfire sings in *The Heart of Midlothian*—and representing, through the long views of the novels' impersonal narrators, the iron laws of historical development, as those were expounded in the emerging Scottish Enlightenment disciplines of political economy, sociology, and anthropology. This approach to representing change, one that acquiesces in the necessity of social progress but also nostalgically acknowledges the allure of the backward past, was timely. It appealed powerfully to a generation that, following the British victory at Waterloo, was both eager to think that a new period in its history had begun and yet reluctant to turn its back on the past, not least because devotion to its shared historical heritage might help reunify a fragmented nation. Scott did not invent the historical novel, and indeed was readier than most twentieth-century critics to acknowledge that he had been influenced by the women novelists who dominated the literary scene before his debut, but his example established the significance the form would henceforth claim.

Scott published all his novels anonymously, an index of how a gentleman-poet, even at the start of the nineteenth century, might find fiction a disreputable occupation. However, his authorship of "the Waverley Series" was an open secret, and Scott became the most internationally famous novelist as well as the most prolific writer of the day. In 1811 he started building his palatial country house at Abbotsford, a place that, characteristically, he both equipped with up-to-date indoor plumbing and gas lighting and stocked with antiquarian relics. There he enacted his vision of himself as a country gentleman of the old school. Though in 1820 he acquired the title of baronet and thus added a "Sir" to his name, this glamorous persona of the Scottish laird depended on his hardheaded, unromantic readiness to conceive of literature as a business. To support his expenditures at Abbotsford, Scott wrote (as Thomas Carlyle put it disapprovingly in 1838) "with the ardour of a steam-engine" and participated in a number of commercial ventures in printing and publishing. In the crash of 1826, as a result of the failure of the publishing firm of Constable, Scott was financially ruined. He insisted on working off his huge debts by his pen and exhausted himself in the effort to do so. Not until after his death were his creditors finally paid off in full with the proceeds of the continuing sale of his novels.

From The Lay of the Last Minstrel[1]

Introduction

The way was long, the wind was cold,
The Minstrel was infirm and old;
His withered cheek, and tresses gray,
Seemed to have known a better day;
5 The harp, his sole remaining joy,
Was carried by an orphan boy.
The last of all the Bards was he,
Who sung of Border chivalry;
For, well-a-day! their date was fled,
10 His tuneful brethren all were dead;
And he, neglected and oppressed,
Wished to be with them, and at rest.
No more, on prancing palfrey° borne,   *saddle horse*
He carolled, light as lark at morn;
15 No longer, courted and caressed,
High placed in hall, a welcome guest,
He poured, to lord and lady gay,
The unpremeditated lay;
Old times were changed, old manners gone,
20 A stranger[2] filled the Stuarts' throne;
The bigots of the iron time
Had called his harmless art a crime.
A wandering harper, scorned and poor,
He begged his bread from door to door;
25 And tuned, to please a peasant's ear,
The harp, a King had loved to hear.

He passed where Newark's[3] stately tower
Looks out from Yarrow's birchen bower:
The Minstrel gazed with wishful eye—
30 No humbler resting place was nigh.

1. Scott's first metrical romance interweaves two stories and boasts more than a hundred pages of historical notes. One story is set in the 16th century and combines the Border legend of the goblin Gilpin Horner with a story of the magic spells cast by the dowager lady of Branksome, who hopes to use a long-hidden book of black arts to avenge the death of her husband at the hands of a neighboring clan. In the second story, which unfolds across the introductions and endings of the poem's six cantos, the 17th-century minstrel who tells or sings the story of this witch's plot (a lay is a song) emerges as hero. In his prose preface Scott described this minstrel, who has "survived the Revolution" of 1688, as a figure of historical transition. He has caught "somewhat of the refinement of modern poetry without losing the simplicity of his original model"—a hint that the relationship between this figure and his 17th-century listeners mirrors Scott's relationship with his 19th-century audience. But in addition to allying his authorship with his minstrel's improvised vocal performance, Scott associates himself with the power of the written word: the "wondrous book" that the Lady of Branksome seeks is buried inside the grave of a wizard suggestively named "Michael Scott."
2. William III, who in 1688 ascended to the British throne after Parliament coerced the last Stuart monarch, the Catholic James II, into fleeing to France.
3. Newark Castle, located in the Border district, at a bend of the river Yarrow.

With hesitating step, at last,
The embattled portal-arch he passed,
Whose ponderous grate, and massy bar,
Had oft rolled back the tide of war,
35 But never closed the iron door
Against the desolate and poor.
The Duchess marked his weary pace,
His timid mien, and reverend face,
And bade her page the menials° tell,   *servants*
40 That they should tend the old man well:
For she had known adversity,
Though born in such a high degree;
In pride of power, in beauty's bloom,
Had wept o'er Monmouth's bloody tomb!⁴

45 When kindness had his wants supplied,
And the old man was gratified,
Began to rise his minstrel pride.
And he began to talk, anon,
Of good Earl Francis, dead and gone,
50 And of Earl Walter, rest him God!⁵
A braver ne'er to battle rode;
And how full many a tale he knew,
Of the old warriors of Buccleuch;
And, would the noble Duchess deign
55 To listen to an old man's strain,
Though stiff his hand, his voice though weak,
He thought even yet, the sooth° to speak,   *truth*
That, if she loved the harp to hear,
He could make music to her ear.

60 The humble boon was soon obtained;
The aged Minstrel audience gained.
But, when he reached the room of state,
Where she, with all her ladies, sate,
Perchance he wished his boon denied;
65 For, when to tune his harp he tried,
His trembling hand had lost the ease,
Which marks security to please;
And scenes, long past, of joy and pain,
Came wildering o'er his aged brain—
70 He tried to tune his harp in vain.
The pitying Duchess praised its chime,
And gave him heart, and gave him time,
Till every string's according glee
Was blended into harmony.
75 And then, he said, he would full fain
He could recall an ancient strain,
He never thought to sing again.

4. The duchess, identified in Scott's footnote as
Anne, duchess of Buccleuch, was, in addition to
being a descendant of the Lady of Branksome
whose black magic will figure in the minstrel's
story, the widow of the duke of Monmouth. A
bastard son of Charles II, Monmouth was executed in 1685 after his unsuccessful insurrection
against his uncle James II.
5. In footnotes Scott identifies Earl Francis and
Earl Walter as the father and grandfather of the
duchess.

It was not framed for village churls,
But for high dames and mighty earls;
80 He had played it to King Charles the Good
When he kept court at Holyrood;[6]
And much he wished, yet feared, to try
The long-forgotten melody.
Amid the strings his fingers strayed,
85 And an uncertain warbling made—
And oft he shook his hoary° head.   *gray with age*
But when he caught the measure wild,
The old man raised his face, and smiled;
And lightened up his faded eye,
90 With all a poet's extacy!
In varying cadence, soft or strong,
He swept the sounding chords along;
The present scene, the future lot,
His toils, his wants, were all forgot;
95 Cold diffidence, and age's frost,
In the full tide of song were lost.
Each blank, in faithless memory void,
The poet's glowing thought supplied;
And, while his harp responsive rung,
100 'Twas thus the LATEST MINSTREL sung.

1805

Proud Maisie[1]

Proud Maisie is in the wood
    Walking so early;
Sweet Robin sits on the bush,
    Singing so rarely.

5 "Tell me, thou bonny bird,
    When shall I marry me?"—
"When six braw° gentlemen   *fine*
    Kirkward shall carry ye."

"Who makes the bridal bed,
10   Birdie, say truly?"—
"The gray-headed sexton
    That delves the grave duly.

"The glowworm o'er grave and stone
    Shall light thee steady,
15 The owl from the steeple sing,
    'Welcome, proud lady.'"

1818

---

6. Having ascended to the throne of England in 1626, Charles I traveled to the palace of Holyrood in Edinburgh in 1633 to receive the crown of Scotland.

1. The "fragment" of a song heard by the characters in *The Heart of Midlothian* who attend the insane gypsy Madge Wildfire on her deathbed (chap. 40).

Wandering Willie's Tale "Wandering Willie's Tale" forms part of *Redgauntlet* (1824), Scott's most formally inventive novel and the last of his major fictions set in the Border Country. It is told by the blind fiddler Willie Steenson to a young gentleman of a romantic temperament, Darsie Latimer, who on a whim has joined him in his cross-country wandering and who subsequently writes down Willie's tale and sends it off in a letter to a friend in Edinburgh. (*Redgauntlet* begins, though after its first third does not continue, as a novel in letters, the eighteenth-century form that Scott revived for this book he called his "Tale of the Eighteenth Century.") Like most of Scott's fiction, then, "Wandering Willie's Tale" juxtaposes oral storytelling against written records, while also moving among several time frames: 1765, when Willie recounts to Darsie the tale he heard from his grandfather, the piper Steenie Steenson; the year—sometime in the early 1690s—when the events Steenie experienced occurred; and also the four decades before 1690, in which the central figure in the story, Sir Robert Redgauntlet, committed the wicked deeds for which, in the course of the tale, he will pay at last. The story likewise mixes fiction and history: Steenie's journey to the underworld, where he pursues the fictional Redgauntlet and thereby recovers a lost piece of his own past, gives Scott a device for making his reader acquainted with some central figures of seventeenth-century Scottish history.

We follow the text of the "Magnum Opus" edition of his works, which Scott prepared in 1832 and in which he officially acknowledged authorship of his novels; we omit, however, the long historical notes he added to that edition.

Scott's simulation of Willie's Scots dialect becomes easier to understand when one hears rather than reads it, so reading the tale aloud is advised.

From REDGAUNTLET

Wandering Willie's Tale

Ye maun[1] have heard of Sir Robert Redgauntlet of that Ilk, who lived in these parts before the dear years.[2] The country will lang mind him; and our fathers used to draw breath thick if ever they heard him named. He was out wi' the Hielandmen in Montrose's time; and again he was in the hills wi' Glencairn in the saxteen hundred and fifty-twa; and sae when King Charles the Second came in, wha was in sic[3] favour as the Laird of Redgauntlet?[4] He was knighted at Lonon court, wi' the King's ain sword; and being a redhot prelatist, he came down here, rampauging like a lion, with commissions of lieutenancy (and of lunacy, for what I ken[5]), to put down a' the Whigs and Covenanters in the country. Wild wark they made of it, for the Whigs were as

---

1. Must.
2. Years of famine at the end of the 1690s. "Of that ilk": from the estate that bears the same name as the family. Willie's story concerns Redgauntlet of Redgauntlet.
3. Such.
4. This opening establishes Redgauntlet's past as a "prelatist"—supporter of what was, for most of the 17th century, Scotland's established, Episcopal Church—and a royalist. For four decades he was the foe of the Covenanters—Presbyterians, often members of Scotland's middle and lower classes, who rejected episcopacy, the spiritual authority of the bishops, and supported "Covenants" to preserve the purity of their worship. The conflict between the royalists and Covenanters began during the Civil War of the 1640s,

when, on behalf of Charles I, the earl of Montrose and his Highland army battled the Presbyterian insurgents—known as the Whigs—who had sided in the war with Cromwell. In 1652, during the Interregnum that followed Charles's execution, the earl of Glencairn continued this battle: Redgauntlet, we are to understand, joined him. When Charles II was restored to the throne in 1660, the royalists and prelatists regained the upper hand. Their conflict with the Covenanters culminated, during the "killing years" of 1681–85, with massacres of the "hill folk," called this because Presbyterian ministers who after the Restoration had been ejected from their churches had taken to conducting religious services outdoors.
5. Know.

dour as the Cavaliers were fierce, and it was which should first tire the other. Redgauntlet was aye[6] for the strong hand; and his name is kend as wide in the country as Claverhouse's or Tarn Dalyell's.[7] Glen, nor dargle,[8] nor mountain, nor cave, could hide the puir hill-folk when Redgauntlet was out with bugle and bloodhound after them, as if they had been sae mony deer. And troth when they fand them, they didna mak muckle[9] mair ceremony than a Hielandman wi' a roebuck—It was just, "Will ye tak the test?"—if not, "Make ready—present—fire!"—and there lay the recusant.[1]

Far and wide was Sir Robert hated and feared. Men thought he had a direct compact with Satan—that he was proof against steel—and that bullets happed aff his buff-coat like hailstanes from a hearth—that he had a mear that would turn a hare on the side of Carrifra-gawns[2]—and muckle to the same purpose, of whilk mair anon. The best blessing they wared[3] on him was, "Deil scowp wi' Redgauntlet!"[4] He wasna a bad maister to his ain folk though, and was weel aneugh liked by his tenants; and as for the lackies and troopers that raid out wi' him to the persecutions, as the Whigs caa'd those killing times, they wad hae drunken themsells blind to his health at ony time.

Now you are to ken that my gudesire[5] lived on Redgauntlet's grund—they ca' the place Primrose-Knowe. We had lived on the grund, and under the Redgauntlets, since the riding days,[6] and lang before. It was a pleasant bit; and I think the air is callerer[7] and fresher there than ony where else in the country. It's a' deserted now; and I sat on the broken door-cheek three days since, and was glad I couldna see the plight the place was in; but that's a' wide o' the mark.[8] There dwelt my gudesire, Steenie Steenson, a rambling, rattling chiel[9] he had been in his young days, and could play weel on the pipes; he was famous at "Hoopers and Girders"—a' Cumberland couldna touch him at "Jockie Lattin"—and he had the finest finger for the back-lill[1] between Berwick and Carlisle. The like o' Steenie wasna the sort that they made Whigs o'. And so he became a Tory, as they ca' it, which we now ca' Jacobites,[2] just out of a kind of needcessity, that he might belang to some side or other. He had nae ill-will to the Whig bodies, and liked little to see the blude rin, though, being obliged to follow Sir Robert in hunting and hosting, watching and warding,[3] he saw muckle mischief, and maybe did some, that he couldna avoid.

Now Steenie was a kind of favourite with his master, and kend a' the folks about the castle, and was often sent for to play the pipes when they

6. Always.
7. Royalist aristocrats who led the persecutions of Covenanters in 1681–85. Folk legends held that both had diabolical powers, which Scott transfers to Redgauntlet in the following paragraph.
8. A word for river valley, perhaps of Scott's coining.
9. Much.
1. To take the Test is, according to the terms of the Test Act of 1681, to swear an oath recognizing the monarch's supremacy as head of the Church, something a Presbyterian, who recognized Christ alone as head, could not do. Redgauntlet and followers used this legal device to hunt down "recusants," i.e., those who did not conform to the Episcopal church.
2. Redgauntlet's supernaturally fleet-footed mare could turn a hare—i.e., get in front of it and change its course—while being ridden on Carrifra-

gawns, a steep slope.
3. Bestowed.
4. "Devil take Redgauntlet!"
5. Grandfather.
6. Period of Border warfare in the 16th century.
7. Cooler.
8. Beside the point.
9. Lad.
1. Thumbhole in the melody pipe of a bagpipe. The border between Scotland and England extends between Carlisle—chief city of the Northern English county of Cumberland (now known as Cumbria) on the west coast and Berwick on the east.
2. The Tory party in Scotland included most supporters of the Episcopal Church and, after 1688, the Jacobites—supporters of the exiled James Stuart and his heirs.
3. Guarding.

were at their merriment. Auld Dougal MacCallum, the butler, that had followed Sir Robert through gude and ill, thick and thin, pool and stream, was specially fond of the pipes, and aye gae[4] my gudesire his gude word wi' the Laird; for Dougal could turn his master round his finger.

Weel, round came the Revolution,[5] and it had like to have broken the hearts baith of Dougal and his master. But the change was not a'thegither sae great as they feared, and other folk thought for. The Whigs made an unco crawing[6] what they wad do with their auld enemies, and in special wi' Sir Robert Redgauntlet. But there were ower many great folks dipped in the same doings, to mak a spick and span new warld. So parliament passed it a' ower easy; and Sir Robert, bating[7] that he was held to hunting foxes instead of Covenanters, remained just the man he was. He revel was as loud, and his hall as weel lighted, as ever it had been, though maybe he lacked the fines of the nonconformists, that used to come to stock his larder and cellar; for it is certain he began to be keener about the rents than his tenants used to find him before, and they behoved to be[8] prompt to the rent-day, or else the Laird wasna pleased. And he was sic an awsome body, that naebody cared to anger him; for the oaths he swore, and the rage that he used to get into, and the looks that he put on, made men sometimes think him a devil incarnate.

Weel, my gudesire was nae manager—no that he was a very great misguider—but he hadna the saving gift, and he got twa terms' rent in arrear. He got the first brash at Whitsunday put ower wi' fair word and piping; but when Martinmas came, there was a summons from the grund-officer to come wi' the rent on a day preceese, or else Steenie behoved to flit.[9] Sair wark[1] he had to get the siller; but he was weel-freended, and at last he got the haill[2] scraped thegither—a thousand merks—the maist of it was from a neighbour they caa'd Laurie Lapraik—a sly tod.[3] Laurie had walth o' gear[4]— could hunt wi' the hound and rin wi' the hare—and be Whig or Tory, saunt or sinner, as the wind stood. He was a professor in this Revolution warld, but he liked an orra sough of this warld;[5] and a tune on the pipes weel aneugh at a bytime, and abune a',[6] he thought he had gude security for the siller he lent my gudesire ower the stocking at Primrose-Knowe.[7]

Away trots my gudesire to Redgauntlet Castle, wi' a heavy purse and a light heart, glad to be out of the Laird's danger. Weel, the first thing he learned at the Castle was, that Sir Robert had fretted himself into a fit of the gout, because he did not appear before twelve o'clock. It wasna a'thegither for sake of the money, Dougal thought; but because he didna like to part wi' my gudesire aff the grund. Dougal was glad to see Steenie, and brought him into the great oak parlour, and there sat the Laird his leesome lane, excepting that he had beside him a great, ill-favoured jackanape,[8] that was a spe-

---

4. Gave.
5. The Revolution of 1688, which expelled the Stuart dynasty from the British throne, and in Scotland reestablished Presbyterianism, ending the persecutions of the Covenanters. Jacobites continued to resist the Revolutionary Settlement until their last uprising in 1745.
6. Extraordinary crowing; i.e., much noise.
7. Except.
8. Were obliged to be.
9. To move house. Rents were due on "quarter days": Candlemas (February 2), Whitsunday (May 15), Lammas (August 1), and Martinmas (November 11).

1. Difficult work.
2. Whole.
3. Fox.
4. Lots of property.
5. I.e., in this post-Revolutionary world puritanical Laurie adheres to ("professes") his religion but still likes an occasional ("orra") worldly song ("sough").
6. Above all.
7. I.e., the security for the loan of the rent money is "the stocking"—cattle, farm implements, etc.—of Steenie's farm.
8. Monkey.

cial pet of his; a cankered beast it was, and mony an ill-natured trick it played—ill to please it was, and easily angered—ran about the haill castle, chattering and yowling, and pinching and biting folk, especially before ill weather, or disturbances in the state. Sir Robert caa'd it Major Weir, after the warlock that was burnt;[9] and few folk liked either the name or the conditions of the creature—they thought there was something in it by ordinar— and my gudesire was not just easy in his mind when the door shut on him, and he saw himself in the room wi' naebody but the Laird, Dougal Mac-Callum, and the Major, a thing that hadna chanced to him before.

Sir Robert sat, or, I should say, lay, in a great armed chair, wi' his grand velvet gown, and his feet on a cradle; for he had baith gout and gravel, and his face looked as gash and ghastly as Satan's. Major Weir sat opposite to him, in a red laced coat, and the Laird's wig[1] on his head; and aye as Sir Robert girned[2] wi' pain, the jackanape girned too, like a sheep's-head between a pair of tangs—an ill-faured,[3] fearsome couple they were. The Laird's buff-coat was hung on a pin behind him, and his broadsword and his pistols within reach; for he keepit up the auld fashion of having the weapons ready, and a horse saddled day and night, just as he used to do when he was able to loup on horseback, and away after ony of the hill-folk he could get speerings[4] of. Some said it was for fear of the Whigs taking vengeance, but I judge it was just his auld custom—he wasna gien to fear ony thing. The rental-book, wi' its black cover and brass clasps, was lying beside him; and a book of sculduddry sangs[5] was put betwixt the leaves, to keep it open at the place where it bore evidence against the Goodman of Primrose-Knowe, as behind the hand with his mails and duties.[6] Sir Robert gave my gudesire a look, as if he would have withered his heart in his bosom. Ye maun ken he had a way of bending his brows, that men saw the visible mark of a horse-shoe in his forehead, deep-dinted, as if it had been stamped there.

"Are ye come light-handed, ye son of a toom whistle?" said Sir Robert. "Zounds! if you are"—

My gudesire, with as gude a countenance as he could put on, made a leg,[7] and placed the bag of money on the table wi' a dash, like a man that does something clever. The Laird drew it to him hastily—"Is it all here, Steenie, man?"

"Your honour will find it right," said my gudesire.

"Here, Dougal," said the Laird, "gie Steenie a tass[8] of brandy down stairs, till I count the siller and write the receipt."

But they werena weel out of the room, when Sir Robert gied a yelloch that garr'd[9] the Castle rock! Back ran Dougal—in flew the livery-men—yell on yell gied the Laird, ilk ane mair awfu' than the ither. My gudesire knew not whether to stand or flee, but he ventured back into the parlour, where a' was gaun hirdy-girdie—naebody to say "come in," or "gae out." Terribly the Laird roared for cauld water to his feet, and wine to cool his throat; and hell, hell, hell, and its flames, was aye the word in his mouth. They brought

---

9. Major Weir, a historical figure who fought in the Covenanter cause in youth and in old age confessed to crimes that included wizardry, for which he was executed in 1670.
1. Gentlemen in the late 17th and the 18th centuries were in the custom of wearing wigs in public.
2. Grimaced.

3. Ugly.
4. News.
5. Obscene songs.
6. Rents.
7. I.e., he bowed.
8. Cup.
9. Made.

him water, and when they plunged his swoln feet into the tub, he cried out it was burning; and folk say that it *did* bubble and sparkle like a seething cauldron. He flung the cup at Dougal's head, and said he had given him blood instead of burgundy; and, sure aneugh, the lass washed clotted blood aff the carpet the neist day. The jackanape they caa'd Major Weir, it jibbered and cried as if it was mocking its master; my gudesire's head was like to turn—he forgot baith siller and receipt, and down stairs he banged; but as he ran, the shrieks came faint and fainter; there was a deep-drawn shivering groan, and word gaed through the Castle, that the Laird was dead.

Weel, away came my gudesire, wi' his finger in his mouth, and his best hope was, that Dougal had seen the money-bag, and heard the Laird speak of writing the receipt. The young Laird, now Sir John, came from Edinburgh, to see things put to rights. Sir John and his father never gree'd weel. Sir John had been bred an advocate, and afterwards sat in the last Scots Parliament and voted for the Union, having gotten, it was thought, a rug of the compensations[1]—if his father could have come out of his grave, he would have brained him for it on his awn hearthstane. Some thought it was easier counting with the auld rough Knight than the fair-spoken young ane—but mair of that anon.

Dougal MacCallum, poor body, neither grat[2] nor graned, but gaed about the house looking like a corpse, but directing, as was his duty, a' the order of the grand funeral. Now, Dougal looked aye waur and waur[3] when night was coming, and was aye the last to gang to his bed, whilk was in a little round just opposite the chamber of dais,[4] whilk his master occupied while he was living, and where he now lay in state, as they caa'd it, weel-a-day! The night before the funeral, Dougal could keep his awn counsel[5] nae langer; he came doun with his proud spirit, and fairly asked auld Hutcheon to sit in his room with him for an hour. When they were in the round, Dougal took ae tass of brandy to himself, and gave another to Hutcheon, and wished him all health and lang life, and said that, for himsell, he wasna lang for this world; for that, every night since Sir Robert's death, his silver call had sounded from the state chamber, just as it used to do at nights in his lifetime, to call Dougal to help to turn him in his bed. Dougal said, that being alone with the dead on that floor of the tower (for naebody cared to wake Sir Robert Redgauntlet like another corpse), he had never daured to answer the call, but that now his conscience checked him for neglecting his duty; for, "though death breaks service," said MacCallum, "it shall never break my service to Sir Robert; and I will answer his next whistle, so be you will stand by me, Hutcheon."

Hutcheon had nae will to the wark, but he had stood by Dougal in battle and broil, and he wad not fail him at this pinch; so down the carles[6] sat ower a stoup[7] of brandy, and Hutcheon, who was something of a clerk, would have read a chapter of the Bible; but Dougal would hear naething but a blaud[8] of Davie Lindsay, whilk was the waur preparation.

1. Sir John is eventually to hold a seat in the Scots Parliament that will make history in 1707 by passing the Act of Union that joins the kingdoms of England and Scotland and by this means voting itself out of existence. Like many of his peers, Sir John will take a cut ("rug") of the "compensations" offered the parliamentarians as a bribe.
2. Wept.
3. Always looked worse and worse.
4. Best bedroom.
5. Keep quiet.
6. Fellows.
7. Cup.
8. A selection: Lindsay was a 16th-century satirical poet.

When midnight came, and the house was quiet as the grave, sure aneugh the silver whistle sounded as sharp and shrill as if Sir Robert was blowing it, and up gat the twa auld serving-men, and tottered into the room where the dead man lay. Hutcheon saw aneugh at the first glance; for there were torches in the room, which showed him the foul fiend in his ain shape, sitting on the Laird's coffin! Over he cowped[9] as if he had been dead. He could not tell how lang he lay in a trance at the door, but when he gathered himself, he cried on his neighbour, and getting nae answer, raised the house, when Dougal was found lying dead within twa steps of the bed where his master's coffin was placed. As for the whistle, it was gaen anes and aye;[1] but mony a time was it heard at the top of the house on the bartizan,[2] and amang the auld chimneys and turrets, where the howlets have their nests. Sir John hushed the matter up, and the funeral passed over without mair bogle-wark.[3]

But when a' was ower, and the Laird was beginning to settle his affairs, every tenant was called up for his arrears, and my gudesire for the full sum that stood against him in the rental-book. Weel, away he trots to the Castle, to tell his story, and there he is introduced to Sir John, sitting in his father's chair, in deep mourning, with weepers and hanging cravat,[4] and a small walking rapier by his side, instead of the auld broadsword that had a hundredweight of steel about it, what with blade, chape, and basket-hilt. I have heard their communing so often tauld ower, that I almost think I was there mysell, though I couldna be born at the time. . . .

"I wuss ye joy, sir, of the head seat, and the white loaf, and the braid lairdship.[5] Your father was a kind man to friends and followers; muckle grace to you, Sir John, to fill his shoon—his boots, I suld say, for he seldom wore shoon, unless it were muils[6] when he had the gout."

"Ay, Steenie," quoth the Laird, sighing deeply, and putting his napkin to his een, "his was a sudden call, and he will be missed in the country; no time to set his house in order—weel prepared Godward, no doubt, which is the root of the matter—but left us behind a tangled hesp to wind,[7] Steenie.—Hem! hem! We maun go to business, Steenie; much to do, and little time to do it in."

Here he opened the fatal volume. I have heard of a thing they call Doomsday-book[8]—I am clear it has been a rental of back-ganging[9] tenants.

"Stephen," said Sir John, still in the same soft, sleekit tone of a voice—"Stephen Stevenson, or Steenson, ye are down here for a year's rent behind the hand—due at last term."

Stephen. "Please your honour, Sir John, I paid it to your father."

Sir John. "Ye took a receipt then, doubtless, Stephen; and can produce it?"

Stephen. "Indeed I hadna time, an it like your honour; for nae sooner had I set doun the siller, and just as his honour Sir Robert, that's gaen, drew it till him to count it, and write out the receipt, he was ta'en wi' the pains that removed him."

---

9. Tilted.
1. Once and always—i.e., forever.
2. Parapet atop a castle.
3. Ghostly occurrences.
4. Mourning dress included hat bands of white linen ("weepers") and a "hanging cravat" instead of the usual shirt frills.
5. A ceremonious speech wishing Sir John well in his new position as head of a great family: white bread ("white loaf") is mentioned as a delicacy

only the rich could afford; a "braid lairdship" is a large estate.
6. Slippers.
7. I.e., the deceased has left behind him a confused state of affairs that requires disentangling (winding). "Hesp": length of yarn.
8. The property survey of England ordered by William the Conqueror in 1086.
9. Behind in paying.

"That was unlucky," said Sir John, after a pause. "But ye maybe paid it in the presence of somebody. I want but a *talis qualis*[1] evidence, Stephen. I would go ower strictly to work with no poor man."

Stephen. "Troth, Sir John, there was naebody in the room but Dougal MacCallum, the butler. But, as your honour kens, he has e'en followed his auld master."

"Very unlucky again, Stephen," said Sir John, without altering his voice a single note. "The man to whom ye paid the money is dead—and the man who witnessed your payment is dead too—and the siller, which should have been to the fore, is neither seen nor heard tell of in the repositories. How am I to believe a' this?"

Stephen. "I dinna ken, your honour; but there is a bit memorandum note of the very coins; for, God help me! I had to borrow out of twenty purses; and I am sure that ilka[2] men there set down will take his grit oath for what purpose I borrowed the money."

Sir John. "I have little doubt that ye *borrowed* the money, Steenie. It is the *payment* to my father that I want to have some proof of."

Stephen. "The siller maun be about the house, Sir John. And since your honour never got it, and his honour that was canna have ta'en it wi' him, maybe some of the family may have seen it."

Sir John. "We will examine the servants, Stephen; that is but reasonable."

But lackey and lass, and page and groom, all denied stoutly that they had ever seen such a bag of money as my gudesire described. What was waur, he had unluckily not mentioned to any living soul of them his purpose of paying his rent. Ae quean[3] had noticed something under his arm, but she took it for the pipes.

Sir John Redgauntlet ordered the servants out of the room, and then said to my gudesire, "Now, Steenie, ye see you have fair play; and, as I have little doubt ye ken better where to find the siller than ony other body, I beg, in fair terms, and for your own sake, that you will end this fasherie;[4] for, Stephen, ye maun pay or flit."

"The Lord forgie your opinion," said Stephen, driven almost to his wit's end—"I am an honest man."

"So am I, Stephen," said his honour; "and so are all the folks in the house, I hope. But if there be a knave amongst us, it must be he that tells the story he cannot prove." He paused, and then added, mair sternly, "If I understand your trick, sir, you want to take advantage of some malicious reports concerning things in this family, and particularly respecting my father's sudden death, thereby to cheat me out of the money, and perhaps take away my character, by insinuating that I have received the rent I am demanding.— Where do you suppose this money to be?—I insist upon knowing."

My gudesire saw every thing look sae muckle against him that he grew nearly desperate—however, he shifted from one foot to another, looked to every corner of the room, and made no answer.

"Speak out, sirrah," said the Laird, assuming a look of his father's, a very particular ane, which he had when he was angry—it seemed as if the wrinkles of his frown made that selfsame fearful shape of a horse's shoe in

---

1. Of some kind (Latin); a legal term used for evidence that is acceptable only under special circumstances.
2. Every.
3. Young woman.
4. Annoyance.

the middle of his brow;—"Speak out, sir! I *will* know your thoughts;—do you suppose that I have this money?"

"Far be it frae me to say so," said Stephen.

"Do you charge any of my people with having taken it?"

"I wad be laith to charge them that may be innocent," said my gudesire; "and if there be any one that is guilty, I have nae proof."

"Somewhere the money must be, if there is a word of truth in your story," said Sir John; "I ask where you think it is—and demand a correct answer?"

"In hell, if you *will* have my thoughts of it," said my gudesire, driven to extremity, "in hell! with your father, his jackanape, and his silver whistle."

Down the stairs he ran (for the parlour was nae place for him after such a word), and he heard the Laird swearing blood and wounds behind him, as fast as ever did Sir Robert, and roaring for the bailie and the baron-officer.

Away rode my gudesire to his chief creditor (him they caa'd Laurie Lapraik), to try if he could make ony thing out of him; but when he tauld his story, he got but the warst word in his wame[5]—thief, beggar, and dyvour,[6] were the saftest terms; and to the boot of these hard terms, Laurie brought up the auld story of his dipping his hand in the blood of God's saunts, just as if a tenant could have helped riding with the Laird, and that a laird like Sir Robert Redgauntlet. My gudesire was, by this time, far beyond the bounds of patience, and while he and Laurie were at deil speed the liars, he was wanchancie[7] aneugh to abuse Lapraik's doctrine as weel as the man, and said things that garr'd folk's flesh grue[8] that heard them;—he wasna just himsell, and he had lived wi' a wild set in his day.

At last they parted, and my gudesire was to ride hame through the wood of Pitmurkie, that is a' fou of black firs, as they say.—I ken the wood, but the firs may be black or white for what I can tell.—At the entry of the wood there is a wild common, and on the edge of the common, a little lonely change-house, that was keepit then by an ostler-wife, they suld hae caa'd her Tibbie Faw,[9] and there puir Steenie cried for a mutchkin of brandy, for he had had no refreshment the haill day. Tibbie was earnest wi' him to take a bite of meat, but he couldna think o't, nor would he take his foot out of the stirrup, and took off the brandy wholely at twa draughts, and named a toast at each:—the first was, the memory of Sir Robert Redgauntlet, and might he never lie quiet in his grave till he had righted his poor bond-tenant; and the second was, a health to Man's Enemy, if he would but get him back the pock of siller, or tell him what came o't, for he saw the haill world was like to regard him as a thief and a cheat, and he took that waur than even the ruin of his house and hauld.[1]

On he rode, little caring where. It was a dark night turned, and the trees made it yet darker, and he let the beast take its ain road through the wood; when, all of a sudden, from tired and wearied that it was before, the nag began to spring, and flee, and stend, that my gudesire could hardly keep the saddle—Upon the whilk, a horseman, suddenly riding up beside him, said, "That's a mettle beast of yours, freend; will you sell him?"—So saying, he touched the horse's neck with his riding-wand, and it fell into its auld heigh-

---

5. Mind.
6. Good-for-nothing.
7. Unlucky.
8. Made people's flesh creep.

9. I.e., "I am told she was called Tibbie Faw." "Ostler-wife": female keeper of a hostelry (inn).
1. Home.

ho of a stumbling trot. "But his spunk's soon out of him, I think," continued the stranger, "and that is like mony a man's courage, that thinks he wad do great things till he came to the proof."

My gudesire scarce listened to this, but spurred his horse, with "Gude e'en to you, freend."

But it's like the stranger was ane that doesna lightly yield his point; for, ride as Steenie liked, he was aye beside him at the selfsame pace. At last my gudesire, Steenie Steenson, grew half angry; and, to say the truth, half feared.

"What is it that ye want with me, freend?" he said. "If ye be a robber, I have nae money; if ye be a leal[2] man, wanting company, I have nae heart to mirth or speaking; and if ye want to ken the road, I scarce ken it mysell."

"If you will tell me your grief," said the stranger, "I am one that, though I have been sair miscaa'd[3] in the world, am the only hand for helping my freends."

So my gudesire, to ease his ain heart, mair than from any hope of help, told him the story from beginning to end.

"It's a hard pinch," said the stranger; "but I think I can help you."

"If you could lend me the money, sir, and take a lang day[4]—I ken nae other help on earth," said my gudesire.

"But there may be some under the earth," said the stranger. "Come, I'll be frank wi' you; I could lend you the money on bond, but you would maybe scruple my terms. Now, I can tell you, that your auld Laird is disturbed in his grave by your curses, and the wailing of your family, and if ye daur venture to go to see him, he will give you the receipt."

My gudesire's hair stood on end at this proposal, but he thought his companion might be some humorsome chield that was trying to frighten him, and might end with lending him the money. Besides he was bauld wi' brandy, and desperate wi' distress; and he said, he had courage to go to the gate of hell, and a step farther, for that receipt.—The stranger laughed.

Weel, they rode on through the thickest of the wood, when, all of a sudden, the horse stopped at the door of a great house; and, but that he knew the place was ten miles off, my father would have thought he was at Redgauntlet Castle. They rode into the outer court-yard, through the muckle faulding yetts,[5] and aneath the auld portcullis; and the whole front of the house was lighted, and there were pipes and fiddles, and as much dancing and deray[6] within as used to be in Sir Robert's House at Pace and Yule,[7] and such high seasons. They lap off, and my gudesire, as seemed to him, fastened his horse to the very ring he had tied him to that morning, when he gaed to wait on the young Sir John.

"God!" said my gudesire, "if Sir Robert's death be but a dream!"

He knocked at the ha' door just as he was wont, and his auld acquaintance, Dougal MacCallum,—just after his wont, too,—came to open the door, and said, "Piper Steenie, are ye there, lad? Sir Robert has been crying for you."

My gudesire was like a man in a dream—he looked for the stranger, but he was gane for the time. At last he just tried to say, "Ha! Dougal Drive-ower,[8] are ye living? I thought ye had been dead."

---

2. Honest.
3. Much maligned.
4. Extend credit for a long time.
5. Great folding gates.

6. Disorderly revelry.
7. Easter and Christmas.
8. Nickname for an idler.

"Never fash[9] yoursell wi' me," said Dougal, "but look to yoursell; and see ye take naething frae onybody here, neither meat, drink, or siller, except just the receipt that is your ain."

So saying, he led the way out through halls and trances that were weel kend to my gudesire, and into the auld oak parlour; and there was as much singing of profane sangs, and birling[1] of red wine, and speaking blasphemy and sculduddry, as had ever been in Redgauntlet Castle when it was at the blithest.

But, Lord take us in keeping! what a set of ghastly revellers they were that sat round that table!—My gudesire kend mony that had long before gane to their place, for often had he piped to the most part in the hall of Redgauntlet. There was the fierce Middleton, and the dissolute Rothes, and the crafty Lauderdale; and Dalyell, with his bald head and a beard to his girdle; and Earlshall, with Cameron's blude on his hand; and wild Bonshaw, that tied blessed Mr Cargill's limbs till the blude sprung; and Dumbarton Douglas, the twice-turned traitor baith to country and king. There was the Bluidy Advocate MacKenyie, who, for his worldly wit and wisdom, had been to the rest as a god.[2] And there was Claverhouse, as beautiful as when he lived, with his long, dark, curled locks, streaming down over his laced buff-coat, and his left hand always on his right spule-blade, to hide the wound that the silver bullet had made.[3] He sat apart from them all, and looked at them with a melancholy, haughty countenance; while the rest hallooed, and sung, and laughed, that the room rang. But their smiles were fearfully contorted from time to time; and their laughter passed into such wild sounds, as made my gudesire's very nails grow blue, and chilled the marrow in his banes.

They that waited at the table were just the wicked serving-men and troopers, that had done their work and cruel bidding on earth. There was the Lang Lad of Nethertown, that helped to take Argyle; and the Bishop's summoner, that they called the Deil's Rattle-bag; and the wicked guardsmen, in their laced coats; and the savage Highland Amorites,[4] that shed blood like water; and many a proud serving-man, haughty of heart and bloody of hand, cringing to the rich, and making them wickeder than they would be; grinding the poor to powder, when the rich had broken them into fragments. And mony, mony mair were coming and ganging, a' as busy in their vocation as if they had been alive.

Sir Robert Redgauntlet, in the midst of a' this fearful riot, cried, wi' a voice like thunder, on Steenie Piper, to come to the board-head where he was sitting; his legs stretched out before him, and swathed up with flannel, with his holster pistols aside him, while the great broadsword rested against his chair, just as my gudesire had seen him the last time upon earth—the very cushion for the jackanape was close to him, but the creature itsell was not there—it wasna its hour, it's likely; for he heard them say as he came forward, "Is not the Major come yet?" And another answered, "The jackanape will be here betimes the morn." And when my gudesire came forward,

---

9. Trouble.
1. Pouring.
2. Willie's list identifies a number of the royalist aristocrats who, while alive, took the lead in persecuting the Covenanters.
3. John Graham of Claverhouse, another historical figure notorious for his ruthlessness during the killing years and the leader of the Highland army that fought for the cause of the exiled King James Stuart in 1689. He died in battle that year,

and legend reported that it took a silver bullet to kill him.
4. The "Highland host" sent into southwest Scotland in 1678 to enforce a law that legalized the evictions of people who attended Presbyterian conventicles rather than parish churches. Covenanter hymns compared this army to the Amorites, who in the Old Testament are the enemies of the Israelites.

Sir Robert, or his ghaist, or the deevil in his likeness, said, "Weel, piper, hae ye settled wi' my son for the year's rent?"

With much ado my father gat breath to say, that Sir John would not settle without his honour's receipt.

"Ye shall hae that for a tune of the pipes, Steenie," said the appearance of Sir Robert—"Play us up, 'Weel hoddled, Luckie.'"

Now this was a tune my gudesire learned frae a warlock, that heard it when they were worshipping Satan at their meetings; and my gudesire had sometimes played it at the ranting[5] suppers in Redgauntlet Castle, but never very willingly; and now he grew cauld at the very name of it, and said, for excuse, he hadna his pipes wi' him.

"MacCallum, ye limb of Beelzebub," said the fearfu' Sir Robert, "bring Steenie the pipes that I am keeping for him."

MacCallum brought a pair of pipes might have served the piper of Donald of the Isles.[6] But he gave my gudesire a nudge as he offered them; and looking secretly and closely, Steenie saw that the chanter[7] was of steel, and heated to a white heat; so he had fair warning not to trust his fingers with it. So he excused himself again, and said, he was faint and frightened, and had not wind aneugh to fill the bag.

"Then ye maun eat and drink, Steenie," said the figure; "for we do little else here; and it's ill speaking between a fou man and a fasting."[8]

Now these were the very words that the bloody Earl of Douglas said to keep the King's messenger in hand, while he cut the head off MacLellan of Bombie, at the Threave Castle;[9] and that put Steenie mair and mair on his guard. So he spoke up like a man, and said he came neither to eat, or drink, or make minstrelsy; but simply for his ain—to ken what was come o' the money he had paid, and to get a discharge for it; and he was so stout-hearted by this time, that he charged Sir Robert for conscience-sake—(he had no power to say the holy name)—and as he hoped for peace and rest, to spread no snares for him, but just to give him his ain.

The appearance gnashed its teeth and laughed, but it took from a large pocketbook the receipt, and handed it to Steenie. "There is your receipt, ye pitiful cur; and for the money, my dog-whelp of a son may go look for it in the Cat's Cradle."

My gudesire uttered mony thanks, and was about to retire, when Sir Robert roared aloud, "Stop though, thou sack-doudling son of a whore! I am not done with thee. HERE we do nothing for nothing; and you must return on this very day twelvemonth, to pay your master the homage that you owe me for my protection."

My father's tongue was loosed of a suddenty, and he said aloud, "I refer mysell to God's pleasure, and not to yours."

He had no sooner uttered the word than all was dark around him; and he sunk on the earth with such a sudden shock, that he lost both breath and sense.

How lang Steenie lay there, he could not tell; but when he came to himsell, he was lying in the auld kirkyard of Redgauntlet parochine,[1] just at the door

5. Merry.
6. A powerful chief of the Western Isles of Scotland.
7. Melody pipe of a bagpipe.
8. Proverb: a full man should not prevent a hungry man from eating.

9. In 1452 the earl of Douglas beheaded his prisoner MacLellan while the king's messenger bearing orders for his release was detained at the table refreshing himself after his journey.
1. Churchyard of Redgauntlet parish.

of the family aisle, and the scutcheon[2] of the auld knight, Sir Robert, hanging over his head. There was a deep morning fog on the grass and gravestane around him, and his horse was feeding quietly beside the minister's twa cows. Steenie would have thought the whole was a dream, but he had the receipt in his hand, fairly written and signed by the auld Laird; only the last letters of his name were a little disorderly, written like one seized with sudden pain.

Sorely troubled in his mind, he left that dreary place, rode through the mist to Redgauntlet Castle, and with much ado he got speech of the Laird.

"Well, you dyvour bankrupt," was the first word, "have you brought me my rent?"

"No," answered my gudesire, "I have not; but I have brought your honour Sir Robert's receipt for it."

"How, sirrah?—Sir Robert's receipt!—You told me he had not given you one."

"Will your honour please to see if that bit line is right?"

Sir John looked at every line, and at every letter, with much attention; and at last, at the date, which my gudesire had not observed,—*"From my appointed place,"* he read, *"this twenty-fifth of November.*—What!—That is yesterday!—Villain, thou must have gone to hell for this!"

"I got it from your honour's father—whether he be in heaven or hell, I know not," said Steenie.

"I will delate[3] you for a warlock to the Privy Council!" said Sir John. "I will send you to your master, the devil, with the help of a tar-barrel and a torch!"

"I intend to delate mysell to the Presbytery,"[4] said Steenie, "and tell them all I have seen last night, whilk are things fitter for them to judge of than a borrel[5] man like me."

Sir John paused, composed himsell, and desired to hear the full history; and my gudesire told it from point to point, as I have told it you—word for word, neither more nor less.

Sir John was silent again for a long time, and at last he said, very composedly, "Steenie, this story of yours concerns the honour of many a noble family besides mine; and if it be a leasing-making,[6] to keep yourself out of my danger, the least you can expect is to have a redhot iron driven through your tongue, and that will be as bad as scauding your fingers with a redhot chanter. But yet it may be true, Steenie; and if the money cast up, I shall not know what to think of it.—But where shall we find the Cat's Cradle? There are cats enough about the old house, but I think they kitten without the ceremony of bed or cradle."

"We were best ask Hutcheon," said my gudesire; "he kens a' the odd corners about as weel as—another serving-man that is now gane, and that I wad not like to name."

Aweel, Hutcheon, when he was asked, told them, that a ruinous turret, lang disused, next to the clock-house, only accessible by a ladder, for the opening was on the outside, and far above the battlements, was called of old the Cat's Cradle.

"There will I go immediately," said Sir John; and he took (with what purpose, Heaven kens) one of his father's pistols from the hall-table, where they had lain since the night he died, and hastened to the battlements.

2. Coat of arms.
3. Report.
4. Ecclesiastical court made up of ministers and

elders from the local parishes.
5. Simple.
6. Slander.

It was a dangerous place to climb, for the ladder was auld and frail, and wanted ane or twa rounds. However, up got Sir John, and entered at the turret door, where his body stopped the only little light that was in the bit turret. Something flees at him wi' a vengeance, maist dang him back ower—bang gaed the knight's pistol, and Hutcheon, that held the ladder, and my gudesire that stood beside him, hears a loud skelloch.[7] A minute after, Sir John flings the body of the jackanape down to them, and cries that the siller is fund, and that they should come up and help him. And there was the bag of siller sure aneugh, and mony orra things besides, that had been missing for mony a day. And Sir John, when he had riped[8] the turret weel, led my gudesire into the dining-parlour, and took him by the hand, and spoke kindly to him, and said he was sorry he should have doubted his word, and that he would hereafter be a good master to him, to make amends.

"And now, Steenie," said Sir John, "although this vision of yours tends, on the whole, to my father's credit, as an honest man, that he should, even after his death, desire to see justice done to a poor man like you, yet you are sensible that ill-dispositioned men might make bad constructions on it, concerning his soul's health. So, I think, we had better lay the haill dirdum[9] on that ill-deedie creature, Major Weir, and say naething about your dream in the wood of Pitmurkie. You had taken ower muckle brandy to be very certain about ony thing; and, Steenie, this receipt," (his hand shook while he held it out,)—"it's but a queer kind of document, and we will do best, I think, to put it quietly in the fire."

"Od, but for as queer as it is, it's a' the voucher I have for my rent," said my gudesire, who was afraid, it may be, of losing the benefit of Sir Robert's discharge.

"I will bear the contents to your credit in the rental-book, and give you a discharge under my own hand," said Sir John, "and that on the spot. And, Steenie, if you can hold your tongue about this matter, you shall sit, from this term downward, at an easier rent."

"Mony thanks to your honour," said Steenie, who saw easily in what corner the wind was; "doubtless I will be conformable to all your honour's commands; only I would willingly speak wi' some powerful minister on the subject, for I do not like the sort of soumons of appointment whilk your honour's father"—

"Do not call that phantom my father!" said Sir John, interrupting him.

"Weel, then, the thing that was so like him,"—said my gudesire; "he spoke of my coming back to him this time twelvemonth, and it's a weight on my conscience."

"Aweel, then," said Sir John, "if you be much distressed in mind, you may speak to our minister of the parish; he is a douce[1] man, regards the honour of our family, and the mair that he may look for some patronage from me."

Wi' that my gudesire readily agreed that the receipt should be burnt, and the Laird threw it into the chimney with his ain hand. Burn it would not for them, though; but away it flew up the lum,[2] wi' a lang train of sparks at its tail, and a hissing noise like a squib.[3]

My gudesire gaed down to the manse,[4] and the minister, when he had heard the story, said, it was his real opinion, that though my gudesire

---

7. Screech.
8. Searched.
9. Blame.
1. Respectable.

2. Chimney flue.
3. Firecracker.
4. Minister's house.

had gaen very far in tampering with such dangerous matters, yet, as he had refused the devil's arles[5] (for such was the offer of meat and drink,) and had refused to do homage by piping at his bidding, he hoped, that if he held a circumspect walk hereafter, Satan could take little advantage by what was come and gane. And, indeed, my gudesire, of his ain accord, lang forswore baith the pipes and the brandy—it was not even till the year was out, and the fatal day passed, that he would so much as take the fiddle, or drink usquebaugh or tippeny.[6]

Sir John made up his story about the jackanape as he liked himsell; and some believe till this day there was no more in the matter than the filching nature of the brute. Indeed, ye'll no hinder some to threap,[7] that it was nane o' the Auld Enemy that Dougal and my gudesire saw in the Laird's room, but only that wanchancy creature, the Major, capering on the coffin; and that as to the blawing on the Laird's whistle that was heard after he was dead, the filthy brute could do that as weel as the Laird himsell, if no better. But Heaven kens the truth, whilk first came out by the minister's wife, after Sir John and her ain gudeman[8] were baith in the moulds.[9] And then, my gudesire, wha was failed in his limbs, but not in his judgment or memory—at least nothing to speak of—was obliged to tell the real narrative to his freends, for the credit of his good name. He might else have been charged for a warlock.

The shades of evening were growing thicker around us as my conductor finished his long narrative with this moral—"Ye see, birkie,[1] it is nae chancy thing to tak a stranger traveller for a guide, when ye are in an uncouth[2] land."

1824

5. Money given to bind the bargain when a servant is hired.
6. Whiskey and weak beer that was sold for two pence. Cf. Burns's "Tam O'Shanter," lines 107–08; Steenie's adventure in some respects repeats Tam's.
7. Contend.
8. Husband.
9. Their graves.
1. Clever young man.
2. Strange.

SAMUEL TAYLOR COLERIDGE
1772–1834

In *The Prelude* Wordsworth, recording his gratitude to the mountains, lakes, and winds "that dwell among the hills where I was born," commiserates with Coleridge because "thou, my Friend! wert reared / In the great City, 'mid far other scenes." Samuel Taylor Coleridge had in fact been born in the small town of Ottery St. Mary, in rural Devonshire, but on the death of his father he had been sent to school at Christ's Hospital in London. He was a dreamy, enthusiastic, and extraordinarily precocious schoolboy. Charles Lamb, his schoolmate and lifelong friend, in an essay on Christ's Hospital gave a vivid sketch of Coleridge's loneliness, his learning, and his eloquence. When in 1791 Coleridge entered Jesus College, Cambridge, he was an accomplished scholar; but he found little intellectual stimulation at the university, fell into idleness, dissoluteness, and debt, then in despair fled to London and enlisted in the Light Dragoons under the alias of Silas Tomkyn Comberbache—one of the most inept cavalrymen in the long history of the British army. Although rescued by his brothers and sent back to Cambridge, he left the university in 1794 without a degree.

In June 1794 Coleridge met Robert Southey, then a student at Oxford who, like himself, had poetic aspirations, was a radical in religion and politics, and sympathized with the republican experiment in France. Together the two young men planned to establish an ideal democratic community in America for which Coleridge coined the name "Pantisocracy," signifying an equal rule by all. A plausible American real-estate agent persuaded them that the ideal location would be on the banks of the Susquehanna in Pennsylvania. Twelve men undertook to go; and because perpetuation of the scheme required offspring, hence wives, Coleridge dutifully became engaged to Sara Fricker, conveniently at hand as the sister of Southey's fiancée. The Pantisocracy scheme collapsed, but at Southey's insistence Coleridge went through with the marriage, "resolved," as he said, "but wretched." Later Coleridge's radicalism waned, and he became a conservative in politics—a highly philosophical one—and a staunch Anglican in religion.

In 1795 Coleridge met Wordsworth and at once judged him to be "the best poet of the age." When in 1797 Wordsworth brought his sister, Dorothy, to settle at Alfoxden, only three miles from the Coleridges at Nether Stowey, the period of intimate communication and poetic collaboration began that was the golden time of Coleridge's life. An annual allowance of £150, granted to Coleridge by Thomas and Josiah Wedgwood, sons of the founder of the famous pottery firm, came just in time to deflect him from assuming a post as a Unitarian minister. After their joint publication of *Lyrical Ballads* in 1798, Coleridge and the Wordsworths spent a winter in Germany, where Coleridge attended the University of Göttingen and began the lifelong study of German philosophers and critics—Kant, Schiller, Schelling, and Fichte—that helped alter profoundly his thinking about philosophy, religion, and aesthetics.

Back in England, Coleridge in 1800 followed the Wordsworths to the Lake District, settling at Greta Hall, Keswick. He had become gradually disaffected from his wife, and now he fell helplessly and hopelessly in love with Sara Hutchinson, whose sister, Mary, Wordsworth married in 1802. In accord with the medical prescription of that time, Coleridge had been taking laudanum (opium dissolved in alcohol) to ease the painful physical ailments from which he had suffered from an early age. In 1800–1801 heavy dosages during attacks of rheumatism made opium a necessity to him, and Coleridge soon recognized that the drug was a greater evil than the diseases it did not cure. "Dejection: An Ode," published in 1802, was Coleridge's despairing farewell to health, happiness, and poetic creativity. A two-year sojourn on the Mediterranean island of Malta, intended to restore his health, instead completed his decline. When he returned to England in the late summer of 1806, he was a broken man, a drug addict, estranged from his wife, suffering from agonies of remorse, and subject to terrifying nightmares of guilt and despair from which his own shrieks awakened him. By 1810, when he and Wordsworth quarreled bitterly, it must have seemed that he could not fall any lower.

Under these conditions Coleridge's literary efforts, however sporadic and fragmentary, were little short of heroic. In 1808 he debuted as a speaker at one of the new lecturing institutions that sprang up in British cities in the early nineteenth century. His lectures on poetry, like his later series on Shakespeare, became part of the social calendar for fashionable Londoners—women, excluded still from universities, particularly. He wrote for newspapers and single-handedly undertook to write, publish, and distribute a periodical, *The Friend*, which lasted for some ten months beginning in June 1809. A tragedy, *Remorse*, had in 1813 a successful run of twenty performances at the Drury Lane theater. In 1816 he took up residence at Highgate, a northern suburb of London, under the supervision of the excellent and endlessly forbearing physician James Gillman, who managed to control, although not to eliminate, Coleridge's consumption of opium. The next three years were Coleridge's most sustained period of literary activity. While continuing to lecture and to write for the newspapers on a variety of subjects, he published *Biographia Literaria, Zapolya* (a drama), a book consisting of the essays in *The Friend* (revised and greatly enlarged), two collections of poems, and several important treatises on philosophical and religious subjects. In these treatises and those that followed over the next fifteen years, he emerged as the heir to the conservatism of Edmund Burke, an opponent to secularism and a defender of the Anglican Church, and an unapologetic intellectual elitist with an ambitious account of the role elites might play in modern states, outlined in his discussions of national culture and of the "clerisy" who would take responsibility for preserving it.

The remaining years of his life, which he spent with Dr. and Mrs. Gillman, were quieter and happier than any he had known since the turn of the century. He came to a peaceful understanding with his wife and was reconciled with Wordsworth, with whom he toured the Rhineland in 1828. His rooms at Highgate became a center for friends, for the London literati, and for a steady stream of pilgrims from England and America. They came to hear one of the wonders of the age, the Sage of Highgate's conversation—or monologue—for even in his decline, Coleridge's talk never lost the almost hypnotic power that Hazlitt has immortalized in "My First Acquaintance with Poets." Mary Shelley appears to have been haunted by the memory of the evening when, a small child, she hid behind a sofa to listen to Coleridge, one of her father's visitors, recite *The Rime of the Ancient Mariner*, and a stanza from that poem of dark mystery found its way into *Frankenstein*, just as her recollections of that visitor's voice contributed to her depictions of the irresistible hold her novel's storytellers have over their auditors. When he died, Coleridge left his friends with the sense that an incomparable intellect had vanished from the world.

Coleridge's friends, however, abetted by his own merciless self-judgments, set current the opinion, still common, that he was great in promise but not in performance. Even in his buoyant youth he described his own character as "indolence capable of energies"; and it is true that while his mind was incessantly active and fertile, he lacked application and staying power. He also manifested early in life a profound sense of guilt and a need for public expiation. After drug addiction sapped his strength and will, he often adapted (or simply adopted) passages from other writers, with little or no acknowledgment, and sometimes in a context that seems designed to reveal that he relies on sources that he does not credit. Whatever the tangled motives for his procedure, Coleridge has repeatedly been charged with gross plagiarism, from his day to ours. After *The Ancient Mariner*, most of the poems he completed were written, like the first version of "Dejection: An Ode," in a spasm of intense effort. Writings that required sustained planning and application were either left unfinished or, like *Biographia Literaria*, made up of brilliant sections padded out with filler, sometimes lifted from other writers, in a desperate effort to meet a deadline. Many of his speculations Coleridge merely confided to his notebooks and the ears of his friends, incorporated in letters, and poured out in the margins of his own and other people's books.

Even so, it is only when measured against his own potentialities that Coleridge's achievements appear limited. In an 1838 essay the philosopher John Stuart Mill hailed the recently deceased Coleridge as one of "the two great seminal minds of England": according to Mill, Coleridge's conservatism had, along with the very different utilitarian philosophy of Jeremy Bentham (the other seminal mind identified in Mill's essay), revolutionized the political thought of the day. Coleridge was also one of the important and influential literary theorists of the nineteenth century. One of his major legacies is the notion that culture, the nation's artistic and spiritual heritage, represents a force with the power to combat the fragmentation of a modern, market-driven society and to restore a common, collective life. This was an idea that he worked out largely in opposition to Bentham's utilitarianism, the newly prestigious discipline of political economy, and the impoverished, soulless account of human nature that these systems of thought offered. And in *Biographia Literaria* and elsewhere, Coleridge raised the stakes for literary criticism, making it into a kind of writing that could address the most difficult and abstract questions—questions about, for instance, the relations between literary language and ordinary language, or between poetry and philosophy, or between perception and imagination. Above all, Coleridge's writings in verse—whether we consider the poetry of Gothic demonism in *Christabel* or the meditative conversation poems like "Frost at Midnight" or "This Lime-Tree Bower My Prison"—are the achievements of a remarkably innovative poet.

The Eolian Harp[1]

Composed at Clevedon, Somersetshire

My pensive Sara! thy soft cheek reclined
Thus on mine arm, most soothing sweet it is
To sit beside our cot, our cot o'ergrown
With white flowered jasmin, and the broad-leaved myrtle,
5　(Meet emblems they of Innocence and Love!)
And watch the clouds, that late were rich with light,
Slow saddening round, and mark the star of eve
Serenely brilliant (such should wisdom be)
Shine opposite! How exquisite the scents
10　Snatched from yon bean-field! and the world so hushed!
The stilly murmur of the distant sea
Tells us of silence.

　　　　　　And that simplest lute,
Placed length-ways in the clasping casement, hark!
How by the desultory breeze caressed,
15　Like some coy maid half yielding to her lover,
It pours such sweet upbraiding,° as must needs　　　　*scolding*
Tempt to repeat the wrong! And now, its strings
Boldlier swept, the long sequacious° notes　　　*regularly following*
Over delicious surges sink and rise,
20　Such a soft floating witchery of sound
As twilight Elfins make, when they at eve
Voyage on gentle gales from Fairy-Land,
Where Melodies round honey-dropping flowers,
Footless and wild, like birds of Paradise,[2]

1. Named for Aeolus, god of the winds, the harp has strings stretched over a rectangular sounding box. When placed in an opened window, the harp (also called "Eolian lute," "Eolian lyre," "wind harp") responds to the altering wind by sequences of musical chords. This instrument, which seems to voice nature's own music, was a favorite household furnishing in the period and was repeatedly alluded to in Romantic poetry. It served also as one of the recurrent Romantic images for the mind—either the mind in poetic inspiration, as in the last stanzas of Shelley's "Ode to the West Wind" (p. 806), or else the mind in perception, responding to an intellectual breeze by trembling into consciousness, as in this poem, lines 44–48.
　Coleridge wrote this poem to Sara Fricker, whom he married on October 4, 1795, and took to a cottage (the "cot" of lines 3 and 64) at Clevedon, overlooking the Bristol Channel. He later several times expanded and altered the original version; the famous lines 26–29, for example, were not added until 1817. Originally it was titled "Effusion XXXV" and was one of thirty-six such effusions that Coleridge included in a 1796 volume of verse; revised and retitled, it became what he called a "conversation poem"—the designation used since his day for a sustained blank-verse lyric of description and meditation, in the mode of conversation addressed to a silent auditor. This was the form that Coleridge perfected in "Frost at Midnight" and that Wordsworth adopted in "Tintern Abbey."

2. Brilliantly colored birds found in New Guinea and adjacent islands. The native practice of removing the legs when preparing the skin led Europeans to believe that the birds were footless and spent their lives hovering in the air and feeding on nectar.

25 Nor pause, nor perch, hovering on untamed wing!
O the one life within us and abroad,
Which meets all motion and becomes its soul,
A light in sound, a sound-like power in light,
Rhythm in all thought, and joyance[3] every where—
30 Methinks, it should have been impossible
Not to love all things in a world so filled;
Where the breeze warbles, and the mute still air
Is Music slumbering on her instrument.

And thus, my love! as on the midway slope
35 Of yonder hill I stretch my limbs at noon,
Whilst through my half-closed eye-lids I behold
The sunbeams dance, like diamonds, on the main,°   *ocean*
And tranquil muse upon tranquillity;
Full many a thought uncalled and undetained,
40 And many idle flitting phantasies,
Traverse my indolent and passive brain,
As wild and various as the random gales
That swell and flutter on this subject lute!

And what if all of animated nature
45 Be but organic harps diversely framed,
That tremble into thought, as o'er them sweeps
Plastic and vast, one intellectual breeze,
At once the Soul of each, and God of All?

But thy more serious eye a mild reproof
50 Darts, O beloved woman! nor such thoughts
Dim and unhallowed dost thou not reject,
And biddest me walk humbly with my God.
Meek daughter in the family of Christ!
Well hast thou said and holily dispraised
55 These shapings of the unregenerate[4] mind;
Bubbles that glitter as they rise and break
On vain Philosophy's aye-babbling° spring.   *ever babbling*
For never guiltless may I speak of him,
The Incomprehensible! save when with awe
60 I praise him, and with Faith that inly feels;
Who with his saving mercies healed me,
A sinful and most miserable man,
Wildered and dark, and gave me to possess
Peace, and this cot, and thee, heart-honored Maid!

1795   1796

3. An archaic term for enjoyment, coined in the 16th century by Spenser and reintroduced by Coleridge.
4. Spiritually unredeemed; not born again.

This Lime-Tree Bower My Prison

In the June of 1797, some long-expected Friends paid a visit to the author's cottage; and on the morning of their arrival, he met with an accident, which disabled him from walking during the whole time of their stay. One evening, when they had left him for a few hours, he composed the following lines in the garden-bower.[1]

Well, they are gone, and here must I remain,
This lime-tree bower my prison! I have lost
Beauties and feelings, such as would have been
Most sweet to my remembrance even when age
5   Had dimmed mine eyes to blindness! They, meanwhile,
Friends, whom I never more may meet again,
On springy[2] heath, along the hill-top edge,
Wander in gladness, and wind down, perchance,
To that still roaring dell, of which I told;
10   The roaring dell, o'erwooded, narrow, deep,
And only speckled by the mid-day sun;
Where its slim trunk the ash from rock to rock
Flings arching like a bridge;—that branchless ash,
Unsunned and damp, whose few poor yellow leaves
15   Ne'er tremble in the gale, yet tremble still,
Fanned by the water-fall! and there my friends
Behold the dark green file of long lank weeds,
That all at once (a most fantastic sight!)
Still nod and drip beneath the dripping edge
Of the blue clay-stone.[3]

20   Now, my friends emerge
Beneath the wide wide Heaven—and view again
The many-steepled tract magnificent
Of hilly fields and meadows, and the sea,
With some fair bark,° perhaps, whose sails light up   *boat*
25   The slip of smooth clear blue betwixt two Isles
Of purple shadow! Yes! they wander on
In gladness all; but thou, methinks, most glad,
My gentle-hearted Charles! for thou hast pined
And hungered after Nature, many a year,
30   In the great City pent,[4] winning thy way
With sad yet patient soul, through evil and pain
And strange calamity![5] Ah! slowly sink
Behind the western ridge, thou glorious sun!

1. The time was in fact July 1797. The visiting friends were William and Dorothy Wordsworth and Charles Lamb. The accident was the fault of Mrs. Coleridge—"dear Sara," Coleridge wrote, "accidentally emptied a skillet of boiling milk on my foot." The bower consisted of lime (i.e., linden) trees in the garden of Thomas Poole, next door to Coleridge's cottage at Nether Stowey. Coleridge related these facts in a letter to Robert Southey, July 17, 1797, in which he transcribed the first version of this poem. In the earliest printed text the title is followed by "Addressed to Charles Lamb, of the India-House, London."
2. *Elastic*, I mean [Coleridge's note].
3. Cf. Dorothy Wordsworth's description of the "low damp dell" in her *Alfoxden Journal*, February 10, 1798 (p. 410).
4. Despite Coleridge's claim, Charles Lamb eminently preferred London over what he called "dead Nature." For Lamb's love of city life, see his letter to Wordsworth in the NAEL Archive.
5. Some ten months earlier Charles Lamb's sister, Mary, had stabbed their mother to death in a fit of insanity.

    Shine in the slant beams of the sinking orb,
35 Ye purple heath-flowers! richlier burn, ye clouds!
    Live in the yellow light, ye distant groves!
    And kindle, thou blue ocean! So my Friend
    Struck with deep joy may stand, as I have stood,
    Silent with swimming sense; yea, gazing round
40 On the wide landscape, gaze till all doth seem
    Less gross than bodily; and of such hues
    As veil the Almighty Spirit, when yet he makes
    Spirits perceive his presence.

                  A delight
    Comes sudden on my heart, and I am glad
45 As I myself were there! Nor in this bower,
    This little lime-tree bower, have I not marked
    Much that has soothed me. Pale beneath the blaze
    Hung the transparent foliage; and I watched
    Some broad and sunny leaf, and loved to see
50 The shadow of the leaf and stem above
    Dappling its sunshine! And that walnut-tree
    Was richly tinged, and a deep radiance lay
    Full on the ancient ivy, which usurps
    Those fronting elms, and now, with blackest mass
55 Makes their dark branches gleam a lighter hue
    Through the late twilight: and though now the bat
    Wheels silent by, and not a swallow twitters,
    Yet still the solitary humble bee
    Sings in the bean-flower! Henceforth I shall know
60 That Nature ne'er deserts the wise and pure;
    No plot so narrow, be but Nature there,
    No waste so vacant, but may well employ
    Each faculty of sense, and keep the heart
    Awake to Love and Beauty! and sometimes
65 'Tis well to be bereft of promised good,
    That we may lift the Soul, and contemplate
    With lively joy the joys we cannot share.
    My gentle-hearted Charles! when the last rook
    Beat its straight path along the dusky air
70 Homewards, I blessed it! deeming its black wing
    (Now a dim speck, now vanishing in light)
    Had crossed the mighty orb's dilated glory,
    While thou stood'st gazing; or when all was still,
    Flew creeking o'er thy head, and had a charm
75 For thee, my gentle-hearted Charles, to whom
    No sound is dissonant which tells of Life.

1797   1800

The Rime of the Ancient Mariner[1]

IN SEVEN PARTS

Facile credo, plures esse Naturas invisibiles quam visibiles in rerum universitate. Sed horum [sic] omnium familiam quis nobis enar-rabit, et gradus et cognationes et discrimina et singulorum munera? Quid agunt? quae loca habitant? Harum rerum notitiam semper ambivit ingenium humanum, nunquam attigit. Juvat, interea, non diffiteor, quandoque in animo, tanquam in tabulâ, majoris et melioris mundi imaginem contemplari: ne mens assuefacta hodier-nae vitae minutiis se contrahat nimis, et tota subsidat in pusillas cogitationes. Sed veritati interea invigilandum est, modusque ser-vandus, ut certa ab incertis, diem a nocte, distinguamus.

T. BURNET, *Archaeol. Phil.* p. 68.[2]

Part 1

An ancient Mariner meeteth three gallants bidden to a wedding-feast, and detaineth one.

It is an ancient Mariner
And he stoppeth one of three.
"By thy long grey beard and glittering eye,
Now wherefore stopp'st thou me?

The Bridegroom's doors are opened wide,   5
And I am next of kin;
The guests are met, the feast is set:
May'st hear the merry din."

He holds him with his skinny hand,
"There was a ship," quoth he.   10
"Hold off! unhand me, grey-beard loon!"
Eftsoons[3] his hand dropt he.

The wedding guest is spellbound by the eye of the old sea-faring man, and con-strained to hear his tale.

He holds him with his glittering eye—
The wedding-guest stood still,
And listens like a three years' child: 15
The Mariner hath his will.[4]

1. Coleridge describes the origin of this poem in the opening section of chap. 14 of *Biographia Literaria.* In a comment made to the Reverend Alexander Dyce in 1835 and in a note on "We Are Seven" dictated in 1843, Wordsworth added some details. The poem, based on a dream of Coleridge's friend Cruikshank, was originally planned as a collaboration between Coleridge and Wordsworth, to pay the expense of a walking tour they took with Dorothy Wordsworth in November 1797. Before he dropped out of the enterprise, Wordsworth suggested the shooting of the alba-tross and the navigation of the ship by the dead men; he also contributed lines 13–16 and 226–27.
When printed in *Lyrical Ballads* (1798), this poem was titled "The Rime of the Ancyent Mari-nere" and contained many archaic words and spellings, which, Wordsworth believed, hurt the sales of their volume. In later editions Coleridge revised the poem, in part by pruning those archaisms. He also added the Latin epigraph and the marginal glosses written in the old-fashioned style of 17th-century learning.

2. "I readily believe that there are more invisible than visible Natures in the universe. But who will explain for us the family of all these beings, and the ranks and relations and distinguishing features and functions of each? What do they do? What places do they inhabit? The human mind has always sought the knowledge of these things, but never attained it. Meanwhile I do not deny that it is helpful sometimes to contemplate in the mind, as on a tablet, the image of a greater and better world, lest the intellect, habituated to the petty things of daily life, narrow itself and sink wholly into trivial thoughts. But at the same time we must be watchful for the truth and keep a sense of proportion, so that we may distinguish the certain from the uncertain, day from night." Adapted by Coleridge from Thomas Burnet, *Archaeologiae Philosophicae* (1692).
3. At once.
4. I.e., the Mariner has gained control of the will of the wedding guest by hypnosis or, as it was called in Coleridge's time, by "mesmerism."

The wedding-guest sat on a stone:
He cannot choose but hear;
And thus spake on that ancient man,
The bright-eyed Mariner.   20

"The ship was cheered, the harbor cleared,
Merrily did we drop
Below the kirk,[5] below the hill,
Below the light house top.

The Mariner tells how the ship sailed southward with a good wind and fair weather, till it reached the line.

The sun came up upon the left,   25
Out of the sea came he!
And he shone bright, and on the right
Went down into the sea.

Higher and higher every day,
Till over the mast at noon—"   30
The wedding-guest here beat his breast,
For he heard the loud bassoon.

The Wedding Guest heareth the bridal music; but the Mariner continueth his tale.

The bride hath paced into the hall,
Red as a rose is she;
Nodding their heads before her goes   35
The merry minstrelsy.

The wedding-guest he beat his breast,
Yet he cannot choose but hear;
And thus spake on that ancient man,
The bright-eyed Mariner.   40

The ship driven by a storm toward the south pole.

"And now the storm-blast came, and he
Was tyrannous and strong:
He struck with his o'ertaking wings,
And chased us south along.

With sloping masts and dipping prow,   45
As who pursued with yell and blow
Still treads the shadow of his foe,
And forward bends his head,
The ship drove fast, loud roared the blast,
And southward aye[6] we fled.   50

And now there came both mist and snow,
And it grew wondrous cold:
And ice, mast-high, came floating by,
As green as emerald.

The land of ice, and of fearful sounds where no living thing was to be seen.

And through the drifts the snowy clifts   55
Did send a dismal sheen:
Nor shapes of men nor beasts we ken[7]—
The ice was all between.

5. Church.
6. Always.

7. Knew.

The ice was here, the ice was there,
The ice was all around: 60
It cracked and growled, and roared and howled,
Like noises in a swound![8]

*Till a great sea-bird,
called the Albatross,
came through the
snow-fog, and was
received with great
joy and hospitality.*
At length did cross an Albatross,
Thorough the fog it came;
As if it had been a Christian soul,   65
We hailed it in God's name.

It ate the food it ne'er had eat,
And round and round it flew.
The ice did split with a thunder-fit;
The helmsman steered us through!   70

*And lo! the Albatross
proveth a bird of
good omen, and
followeth the ship as
it returned north-
ward through fog
and floating ice.*
And a good south wind sprung up behind;
The Albatross did follow,
And every day, for food or play,
Came to the mariners' hollo!

In mist or cloud, on mast or shroud,[9]   75
It perched for vespers nine;
Whiles all the night, through fog-smoke white,
Glimmered the white moon-shine."

*The ancient Mariner
inhospitably killeth
the pious bird of
good omen.*
"God save thee, ancient Mariner!
From the fiends, that plague thee thus!—   80
Why look'st thou so?"—With my cross-bow
I shot the Albatross.

Part 2

The Sun now rose upon the right:[1]
Out of the sea came he,
Still hid in mist, and on the left   85
Went down into the sea.

And the good south wind still blew behind,
But no sweet bird did follow,
Nor any day for food or play
Came to the mariners' hollo!   90

*His shipmates cry out
against the ancient
Mariner, for killing
the bird of good luck.*
And I had done a hellish thing,
And it would work 'em woe:
For all averred, I had killed the bird
That made the breeze to blow.
Ah wretch! said they, the bird to slay,   95
That made the breeze to blow!

---

8. Swoon.
9. Rope supporting the mast.

1. Having rounded Cape Horn, the ship heads
north into the Pacific.

But when the fog cleared off, they justify the same, and thus make themselves accomplices in the crime.

Nor dim nor red, like God's own head,
The glorious Sun uprist:
Then all averred, I had killed the bird
That brought the fog and mist. 100
'Twas right, said they, such birds to slay,
That bring the fog and mist.

The fair breeze con tinues; the ship enters the Pacific Ocean, and sails northward, even till it reaches the Line.[3]

The fair breeze blew, the white foam flew,
The furrow followed free;[2]
We were the first that ever burst 105
Into that silent sea.

The ship hath been suddenly becalmed.

Down dropt the breeze, the sails dropt down,
'Twas sad as sad could be;
And we did speak only to break
The silence of the sea! 110

All in a hot and copper sky,
The bloody Sun, at noon,
Right up above the mast did stand,
No bigger than the Moon.

Day after day, day after day, 115
We stuck, nor breath nor motion;
As idle as a painted ship
Upon a painted ocean.

And the Albatross begins to be avenged.

Water, water, every where,
And all the boards did shrink; 120
Water, water, every where,
Nor any drop to drink.

The very deep did rot: O Christ!
That ever this should be!
Yea, slimy things did crawl with legs 125
Upon the slimy sea.

About, about, in reel and rout
The death-fires[4] danced at night;
The water, like a witch's oils,
Burnt green, and blue and white. 130

2. In 1817 Coleridge wrote of this line, "I had not been long on board a ship, before I perceived that this was the image as seen by a spectator from the shore, or from another vessel. From the ship itself, the *Wake* appears like a brook flowing off from the stern." To better capture the Mariner's vision, he altered the line to "The furrow stream'd off free." Later editions reverted to the original words, as printed here.
3. I.e., the equator.
4. Usually glossed as St. Elmo's fire—an atmospheric electricity on a ship's mast or rigging—believed by superstitious sailors to portend disaster. Possibly the reference is instead to phosphorescence resulting from the decomposition of organic matter in the sea (see line 123).

A spirit had followed them; one of the invisible inhabitants of this planet, neither departed souls nor angels; concerning whom the learned

And some in dreams assured were
Of the spirit that plagued us so;
Nine fathom deep he had followed us
From the land of mist and snow.

Jew, Josephus, and the Platonic Constantinopolitan, Michael Psellus, may be consulted. They are very numerous, and there is no climate or element without one or more.

And every tongue, through utter drought,   135
Was withered at the root;
We could not speak, no more than if
We had been choked with soot.

The shipmates, in their sore distress, would fain throw the whole guilt on the ancient Mariner: in sign whereof they hang the dead sea bird round his neck.

Ah! well-a-day! what evil looks
Had I from old and young!   140
Instead of the cross, the Albatross
About my neck was hung.

Part 3

There passed a weary time. Each throat
Was parched, and glazed each eye.
A weary time! a weary time!   145
How glazed each weary eye,

The ancient Mariner beholdeth a sign in the element afar off.

When looking westward, I beheld
A something in the sky.

At first it seemed a little speck,
And then it seemed a mist;   150
It moved and moved, and took at last
A certain shape, I wist.[5]

A speck, a mist, a shape, I wist!
And still it neared and neared:
As if it dodged a water-sprite,[6]   155
It plunged and tacked and veered.

At its nearer approach, it seemeth him to be a ship; and at a dear ransom he freeth his speech from the bonds of thirst.

With throats unslaked, with black lips baked,
We could nor laugh nor wail;
Through utter drought all dumb we stood!
I bit my arm, I sucked the blood,   160
And cried, A sail! a sail!

With throats unslaked, with black lips baked,
Agape they heard me call:

A flash of joy;

Gramercy![7] they for joy did grin,
And all at once their breath drew in,   165
As they were drinking all.

5. Knew.
6. A supernatural being that supervises the nat-ural elements (but Coleridge may in fact have
been using the term to mean *water-spout*).
7. Great thanks; from the French *grand-merci*.

And horror follows.
For can it be a ship
that comes onward
without wind or tide?

See! see! (I cried) she tacks no more!
Hither to work us weal;[8]
Without a breeze, without a tide,
She steadies with upright keel!   170

The western wave was all a-flame.
The day was well nigh done!
Almost upon the western wave
Rested the broad bright Sun;
When that strange shape drove suddenly   175
Betwixt us and the Sun.

It seemeth him but
the skeleton of a
ship.

And straight the Sun was flecked with bars,
(Heaven's Mother send us grace!)
As if through a dungeon-grate he peered
With broad and burning face.   180

Alas! (thought I, and my heart beat loud)
How fast she nears and nears!
Are those her sails that glance in the Sun,
Like restless gossameres?[9]

And its ribs are seen
as bars on the face of
the setting Sun. The
specter-woman and
her death-mate, and
no other on board
the skeleton-ship.

Are those her ribs through which the Sun   185
Did peer, as through a grate?
And is that Woman all her crew?
Is that a Death? and are there two?
Is Death that woman's mate?

Like vessel, like
crew!

Her lips were red, her looks were free,   190
Her locks were yellow as gold:
Her skin was as white as leprosy,
The Night-mare Life-in-Death was she,
Who thicks man's blood with cold.

Death and Life-in-
death have diced for
the ship's crew, and
she (the latter)
winneth the ancient
Mariner.

The naked hulk[1] alongside came,   195
And the twain were casting dice;
"The game is done! I've won! I've won!"
Quoth she, and whistles thrice.

No twilight within
the courts of the sun.

The Sun's rim dips; the stars rush out:
At one stride comes the dark;   200
With far-heard whisper, o'er the sea,
Off shot the spectre-bark.[2]

At the rising of the
Moon,

We listened and looked sideways up!
Fear at my heart, as at a cup,
My life-blood seemed to sip!   205
The stars were dim, and thick the night,
The steersman's face by his lamp gleamed white;
From the sails the dew did drip—

8. Benefit.   1. Large ship.
9. Filmy cobwebs floating in the air.   2. Ghost ship.

Till clomb above the eastern bar
The horned Moon, with one bright star   210
Within the nether tip.[3]

One after another,   One after one, by the star-dogged Moon,
Too quick for groan or sigh,
Each turned his face with a ghastly pang,
And cursed me with his eye.   215

His shipmates drop   Four times fifty living men,
down dead.   (And I heard nor sigh nor groan)
With heavy thump, a lifeless lump,
They dropped down one by one.

But Life-in-Death   The souls did from their bodies fly,—   220
begins her work on   They fled to bliss or woe!
the ancient Mariner. And every soul, it passed me by,
Like the whizz of my cross-bow!

Part 4

The wedding guest   "I fear thee, ancient Mariner!
feareth that a spirit is I fear thy skinny hand!   225
talking to him.   And thou art long, and lank, and brown,
As is the ribbed sea-sand.

I fear thee and thy glittering eye,
And thy skinny hand, so brown."—
But the ancient Mar- Fear not, fear not, thou wedding-guest!   230
iner assureth him of This body dropt not down.
his bodily life, and
proceedeth to relate
his horrible penance. Alone, alone, all, all alone,
Alone on a wide wide sea!
And never a saint took pity on
My soul in agony.   235

He despiseth the   The many men, so beautiful!
creatures of the   And they all dead did lie:
calm,   And a thousand thousand slimy things
Lived on; and so did I.

And envieth that   I looked upon the rotting sea,   240
they should live, and And drew my eyes away;
so many lie dead.   I looked upon the rotting deck,
And there the dead men lay.

I looked to heaven, and tried to pray;
But or ever a prayer had gusht,   245
A wicked whisper came, and made
My heart as dry as dust.

---

3. An omen of impending evil.

I closed my lids, and kept them close,
And the balls like pulses beat;
For the sky and the sea, and the sea and the sky
Lay like a load on my weary eye,
And the dead were at my feet.   250

But the curse liveth
for him in the eye of
the dead men.

The cold sweat melted from their limbs,
Nor rot nor reek did they:
The look with which they looked on me
Had never passed away.   255

An orphan's curse would drag to hell
A spirit from on high;
But oh! more horrible than that
Is the curse in a dead man's eye!   260
Seven days, seven nights, I saw that curse,
And yet I could not die.

In his loneliness and
fixedness he yearneth
towards the journeying
Moon, and the
stars that still
sojourn, yet still
move onward; and

The moving Moon went up the sky,
And no where did abide:
Softly she was going up,
And a star or two beside—   265

everywhere the blue sky belongs to them, and is their appointed rest, and their native country and their
own natural homes, which they enter unannounced, as lords that are certainly expected and yet there
is a silent joy at their arrival.

Her beams bemocked the sultry main,
Like April hoar-frost spread;
But where the ship's huge shadow lay,
The charmed water burnt alway   270
A still and awful red.

By the light of the
Moon he beholdeth
God's creatures of
the great calm.

Beyond the shadow of the ship,
I watched the water-snakes:
They moved in tracks of shining white,
And when they reared, the elfish light   275
Fell off in hoary flakes.

Within the shadow of the ship
I watched their rich attire:
Blue, glossy green, and velvet black,
They coiled and swam; and every track   280
Was a flash of golden fire.

Their beauty and
their happiness.

O happy living things! no tongue
Their beauty might declare:
A spring of love gushed from my heart,

He blesseth them in
his heart.

And I blessed them unaware: 285
Sure my kind saint took pity on me,
And I blessed them unaware.

The spell begins to
break.

The selfsame moment I could pray;
And from my neck so free
The Albatross fell off, and sank   290
Like lead into the sea.

Part 5

Oh sleep! it is a gentle thing,
Beloved from pole to pole!
To Mary Queen the praise be given!
She sent the gentle sleep from Heaven,   295
That slid into my soul.

By grace of the holy
Mother, the ancient
Mariner is refreshed
with rain.

The silly[4] buckets on the deck,
That had so long remained,
I dreamt that they were filled with dew;
And when I awoke, it rained.   300

My lips were wet, my throat was cold,
My garments all were dank;
Sure I had drunken in my dreams,
And still my body drank.

I moved, and could not feel my limbs: 305
I was so light—almost
I thought that I had died in sleep,
And was a blessed ghost.

He heareth sounds
and seeth strange
sights and
commotions in the
sky and the element.

And soon I heard a roaring wind:
It did not come anear;   310
But with its sound it shook the sails,
That were so thin and sere.

The upper air burst into life!
And a hundred fire-flags sheen,[5]
To and fro they were hurried about!   315
And to and fro, and in and out,
The wan stars danced between.

And the coming wind did roar more loud,
And the sails did sigh like sedge;[6]
And the rain poured down from one black cloud;   320
The Moon was at its edge.

The thick black cloud was cleft, and still
The Moon was at its side:
Like waters shot from some high crag,
The lightning fell with never a jag,   325
A river steep and wide.

The bodies of the
ship's crew are
inspired, and the
ship moves on;

The loud wind never reached the ship,
Yet now the ship moved on!
Beneath the lightning and the moon
The dead men gave a groan.   330

---

4. Simple, homely.
5. Shone. These fire-flags are probably St. Elmo's
fire (see p. 451, n. 4), but Coleridge may be describing the Aurora Australis, or Southern Lights, and
possibly also lightning.
6. A rushlike plant growing in wet soil.

They groaned, they stirred, they all uprose,
Nor spake, nor moved their eyes;
It had been strange, even in a dream,
To have seen those dead men rise.

The helmsman steered, the ship moved on;   335
Yet never a breeze up blew;
The mariners all 'gan work the ropes,
Where they were wont to do;
They raised their limbs like lifeless tools—
We were a ghastly crew.   340

The body of my brother's son
Stood by me, knee to knee:
The body and I pulled at one rope,
But he said nought to me.

But not by the souls
of the men, nor by
dæmons⁷ of earth or
middle air, but by a
blessed troop of
angelic spirits,
sent down by the
invocation of the
guardian saint.

"I fear thee, ancient Mariner!"   345
Be calm, thou Wedding-Guest!
'Twas not those souls that fled in pain,
Which to their corses⁸ came again,
But a troop of spirits blest:

For when it dawned—they dropped their arms,   350
And clustered round the mast;
Sweet sounds rose slowly through their mouths,
And from their bodies passed.

Around, around, flew each sweet sound,
Then darted to the Sun;   355
Slowly the sounds came back again,
Now mixed, now one by one.

Sometimes a-dropping from the sky
I heard the sky-lark sing;
Sometimes all little birds that are,   360
How they seemed to fill the sea and air
With their sweet jargoning!⁹

And now 'twas like all instruments,
Now like a lonely flute;
And now it is an angel's song,   365
That makes the heavens be mute.

It ceased; yet still the sails made on
A pleasant noise till noon,
A noise like of a hidden brook
In the leafy month of June,   370
That to the sleeping woods all night
Singeth a quiet tune.

---

7. Supernatural beings halfway between mortals and gods (the type of spirit that Coleridge describes in the gloss beside lines 131–34).
8. Corpses.
9. Warbling (Middle English).

Till noon we quietly sailed on,
Yet never a breeze did breathe:
Slowly and smoothly went the ship,   375
Moved onward from beneath.

The lonesome spirit
from the south-pole
carries on the ship
as far as the line, in
obedience to the
angelic troop, but
still requireth
vengeance.

Under the keel nine fathom deep,
From the land of mist and snow,
The spirit slid: and it was he
That made the ship to go.   380
The sails at noon left off their tune,
And the ship stood still also.

The Sun, right up above the mast,
Had fixed her to the ocean:
But in a minute she 'gan stir,   385
With a short uneasy motion—
Backwards and forwards half her length
With a short uneasy motion.

Then like a pawing horse let go,
She made a sudden bound: 390
It flung the blood into my head,
And I fell down in a swound.

The Polar Spirit's
fellow dæmons, the
invisible inhabitants
of the element, take
part in his wrong;
and two of them
relate, one to the
other, that penance
long and heavy for
the ancient Mariner
hath been accorded
to the Polar Spirit,
who returneth
southward.

How long in that same fit I lay,
I have not[1] to declare;
But ere my living life returned,   395
I heard and in my soul discerned
Two voices in the air.

"Is it he?" quoth one, "Is this the man?
By him who died on cross,
With his cruel bow he laid full low   400
The harmless Albatross.

The spirit who bideth by himself
In the land of mist and snow,
He loved the bird that loved the man
Who shot him with his bow."   405

The other was a softer voice,
As soft as honey-dew:
Quoth he, "The man hath penance done,
And penance more will do."

Part 6

FIRST VOICE

"But tell me, tell me! speak again,   410
Thy soft response renewing—

---

1. I.e., have not the knowledge.

What makes that ship drive on so fast?
What is the ocean doing?"

SECOND VOICE

"Still as a slave before his lord,
The ocean hath no blast;
His great bright eye most silently   415
Up to the Moon is cast—

If he may know which way to go;
For she guides him smooth or grim.
See, brother, see! how graciously   420
She looketh down on him."

FIRST VOICE

*The Mariner hath
been cast into a
trance; for the
angelic power
causeth the vessel to
drive northward
faster than human
life could endure.*

"But why drives on that ship so fast,
Without or wave or wind?"

SECOND VOICE

"The air is cut away before,
And closes from behind.   425

Fly, brother, fly! more high, more high!
Or we shall be belated:
For slow and slow that ship will go,
When the Mariner's trance is abated."

*The supernatural
motion is retarded;
the Mariner awakes,
and his penance
begins anew.*

I woke, and we were sailing on   430
As in a gentle weather:
'Twas night, calm night, the moon was high;
The dead men stood together.

All stood together on the deck,
For a charnel-dungeon fitter: 435
All fixed on me their stony eyes,
That in the Moon did glitter.

The pang, the curse, with which they died,
Had never passed away:
I could not draw my eyes from theirs,   440
Nor turn them up to pray.

*The curse is finally
expiated.*

And now this spell was snapt: once more
I viewed the ocean green,
And looked far forth, yet little saw
Of what had else been seen—   445

Like one, that on a lonesome road
Doth walk in fear and dread,
And having once turned round walks on,
And turns no more his head;

Because he knows, a frightful fiend   450
Doth close behind him tread.

But soon there breathed a wind on me,
Nor sound nor motion made:
Its path was not upon the sea,
In ripple or in shade.   455

It raised my hair, it fanned my cheek
Like a meadow-gale of spring—
It mingled strangely with my fears,
Yet it felt like a welcoming.

Swiftly, swiftly flew the ship,   460
Yet she sailed softly too:
Sweetly, sweetly blew the breeze—
On me alone it blew.

And the ancient   Oh! dream of joy! is this indeed
Mariner beholdeth   The light-house top I see?   465
his native country.   Is this the hill? is this the kirk?
Is this mine own countree?

We drifted o'er the harbour-bar,
And I with sobs did pray—
O let me be awake, my God!   470
Or let me sleep alway.

The harbour-bay was clear as glass,
So smoothly it was strewn!
And on the bay the moonlight lay,
And the shadow of the moon.   475

The rock shone bright, the kirk no less,
That stands above the rock:
The moonlight steeped in silentness
The steady weathercock.

And the bay was white with silent light,   480
Till rising from the same,
The angelic spirits   Full many shapes, that shadows were,
leave the dead   In crimson colours came.
bodies,

And appear in their   A little distance from the prow
own forms of light.   Those crimson shadows were: 485
I turned my eyes upon the deck—
Oh, Christ! what saw I there!

Each corse lay flat, lifeless and flat,
And, by the holy rood!²

2. Cross.

A man all light, a seraph-man,[3]
On every corse there stood. 490

This seraph-band, each waved his hand:
It was a heavenly sight!
They stood as signals to the land,
Each one a lovely light; 495

This seraph-band, each waved his hand,
No voice did they impart—
No voice; but oh! the silence sank
Like music on my heart.

But soon I heard the dash of oars, 500
I heard the Pilot's cheer;
My head was turned perforce away,
And I saw a boat appear.

The Pilot and the Pilot's boy,
I heard them coming fast: 505
Dear Lord in Heaven! it was a joy
The dead men could not blast.

I saw a third—I heard his voice:
It is the Hermit good!
He singeth loud his godly hymns 510
That he makes in the wood.
He'll shrieve[4] my soul, he'll wash away
The Albatross's blood.

Part 7

The Hermit of the wood,

This Hermit good lives in that wood
Which slopes down to the sea. 515
How loudly his sweet voice he rears!
He loves to talk with marineres
That come from a far countree.

He kneels at morn, and noon, and eve—
He hath a cushion plump: 520
It is the moss that wholly hides
The rotted old oak-stump.

The skiff-boat neared: I heard them talk,
"Why, this is strange, I trow!
Where are those lights so many and fair, 525
That signal made but now?"

Approacheth the ship with wonder.

"Strange, by my faith!" the Hermit said—
"And they answered not our cheer!

3. A shining celestial being, highest in the ranks of the angels.
4. Absolve.

The planks looked warped! and see those sails,
How thin they are and sere!   530
I never saw aught like to them,
Unless perchance it were

Brown skeletons of leaves that lag
My forest-brook along;
When the ivy-tod[5] is heavy with snow,   535
And the owlet whoops to the wolf below,
That eats the she-wolf's young."

"Dear Lord! it hath a fiendish look"—
(The Pilot made reply)
"I am a-feared"—"Push on, push on!"   540
Said the Hermit cheerily.

The boat came closer to the ship,
But I nor spake nor stirred;
The boat came close beneath the ship,
And straight a sound was heard.   545

The ship suddenly sinketh.

Under the water it rumbled on,
Still louder and more dread:
It reached the ship, it split the bay;
The ship went down like lead.

The ancient Mariner is saved in the Pilot's boat.

Stunned by that loud and dreadful sound,   550
Which sky and ocean smote,
Like one that hath been seven days drowned
My body lay afloat;
But swift as dreams, myself I found
Within the Pilot's boat.   555

Upon the whirl, where sank the ship,
The boat spun round and round;
And all was still, save that the hill
Was telling of the sound.

I moved my lips—the Pilot shrieked   560
And fell down in a fit;
The holy Hermit raised his eyes,
And prayed where he did sit.

I took the oars: the Pilot's boy,
Who now doth crazy go,   565
Laughed loud and long, and all the while
His eyes went to and fro.
"Ha! ha!" quoth he, "full plain I see,
The Devil knows how to row."

And now, all in my own countree,   570
I stood on the firm land!

5. Clump of ivy.

The Hermit stepped forth from the boat,
And scarcely he could stand.

The ancient Mariner earnestly entreateth the Hermit to shrieve him; and the penance of life falls on him.

"O shrieve me, shrieve me,[6] holy man!"
The Hermit crossed his brow.[7]   575
"Say quick," quoth he, "I bid thee say—
What manner of man art thou?"

Forthwith this frame of mine was wrenched
With a woful agony,
Which forced me to begin my tale;   580
And then it left me free.

And ever and anon throughout his future life an agony constraineth him to travel from land to land.

Since then, at an uncertain hour,
That agony returns:
And till my ghastly tale is told,
This heart within me burns.   585

I pass, like night, from land to land;
I have strange power of speech;
That moment that his face I see,
I know the man that must hear me:
To him my tale I teach.   590

What loud uproar bursts from that door!
The wedding-guests are there:
But in the garden-bower the bride
And bride-maids singing are:
And hark the little vesper bell,   595
Which biddeth me to prayer!

O Wedding-Guest! this soul hath been
Alone on a wide wide sea:
So lonely 'twas, that God himself
Scarce seemed there to be.   600

O sweeter than the marriage-feast,
'Tis sweeter far to me,
To walk together to the kirk
With a goodly company!—

To walk together to the kirk,   605
And all together pray,
While each to his great Father bends,
Old men, and babes, and loving friends,
And youths and maidens gay!

And to teach, by his own example, love and reverence to all things that God made and loveth.

Farewell, farewell! but this I tell   610
To thee, thou Wedding-Guest!
He prayeth well, who loveth well
Both man and bird and beast.

---

6. Hear my confession and grant me absolution.
7. Made the sign of the cross on his forehead.

He prayeth best, who loveth best
All things both great and small; 615
For the dear God who loveth us,
He made and loveth all.[8]

The Mariner, whose eye is bright,
Whose beard with age is hoar,
Is gone: and now the Wedding-Guest 620
Turned from the bridegroom's door.

He went like one that hath been stunned,
And is of sense forlorn:[9]
A sadder and a wiser man,
He rose the morrow morn. 625

1797 1798, 1817

Kubla Khan

Or, A Vision in a Dream. A Fragment

In[1] the summer of the year 1797, the Author, then in ill health, had retired to a lonely farm house between Porlock and Linton, on the Exmoor confines of Somerset and Devonshire. In consequence of a slight indisposition, an anodyne had been prescribed, from the effect of which he fell asleep in his chair at the moment that he was reading the following sentence, or words of the same substance, in *Purchas's Pilgrimage*: "Here the Khan Kubla commanded a palace to be built, and a stately garden thereunto: and thus ten miles of fertile ground were inclosed with a wall."[2] The author continued for about three hours in a profound sleep, at least of the external senses,[3] during which time he has the most vivid confidence, that he could not have composed less than from two to three hundred lines; if that indeed can be called composition in which all the images rose up before him as things, with a parallel production of the correspondent expressions, without any sensation or consciousness of effort. On awaking he appeared to himself to have a distinct recollection of the whole, and taking his pen, ink, and paper, instantly and

8. Coleridge said in 1830, answering the objection of the poet Anna Barbauld that the poem "lacked a moral": "I told her that in my own judgment the poem had too much; and that the only, or chief fault, if I might say so, was the obtrusion of the moral sentiment so openly on the reader as a principle or cause of action in a work of pure imagination. It ought to have had no more moral than the *Arabian Nights'* tale of the merchant's sitting down to eat dates by the side of a well and throwing the shells aside, and lo! a genie starts up and says he *must* kill the aforesaid merchant *because* one of the date shells had, it seems, put out the eye of the genie's son."
9. Bereft.
1. In the texts of 1816–29, this note began with an additional short paragraph: "The following fragment is here published at the request of a poet of great and deserved celebrity, and, as far as the Author's own opinions are concerned, rather as a psychological curiosity, than on the ground of any

supposed *poetic* merits." The "poet of . . . celebrity" was Lord Byron.
2. "In Xamdu did Cublai Can build a stately Palace, encompassing sixteene miles of plaine ground with a wall, wherein are fertile Meddowes, pleasant Springs, delightfull Streames, and all sorts of beasts of chase and game, and in the middest thereof a sumptuous house of pleasure, which may be removed from place to place." From Samuel Purchas's book of travelers' tales, *Purchas his Pilgrimage* (1613). The historical Kublai Khan founded the Mongol dynasty in China in the 13th century.
3. In a note on a manuscript copy of "Kubla Khan," Coleridge gave a more precise account of the nature of this "sleep": "This fragment with a good deal more, not recoverable, composed, in a sort of reverie brought on by two grains of opium, taken to check a dysentery, at a farmhouse between Porlock and Linton, a quarter of a mile from Culbone Church, in the fall of the year, 1797."

eagerly wrote down the lines that are here preserved. At this moment he was unfortunately called out by a person on business from Porlock, and detained by him above an hour, and on his return to his room, found, to his no small surprise and mortification, that though he still retained some vague and dim recollection of the general purport of the vision, yet, with the exception of some eight or ten scattered lines and images, all the rest had passed away like the images on the surface of a stream into which a stone had been cast, but, alas! without the after restoration of the latter:

> Then all the charm
> Is broken—all that phantom-world so fair
> Vanishes, and a thousand circlets spread,
> And each mis-shape[s] the other. Stay awhile,
> Poor youth! who scarcely dar'st lift up thine eyes—
> The stream will soon renew its smoothness, soon
> The visions will return! And lo! he stays,
> And soon the fragments dim of lovely forms
> Come trembling back, unite, and now once more
> The pool becomes a mirror.
> [From Coleridge's *The Picture; or, the Lover's Resolution,*
> lines 91–100]

Yet from the still surviving recollections in his mind, the Author has frequently purposed to finish for himself what had been originally, as it were, given to him. Αὔριον ἄδιον ἄσω:[4] but the to-morrow is yet to come.

As a contrast to this vision, I have annexed a fragment of a very different character, describing with equal fidelity the dream of pain and disease.[5]—1816.

In Xanadu did Kubla Khan
A stately pleasure-dome decree:
Where Alph,[6] the sacred river, ran
Through caverns measureless to man
5   Down to a sunless sea.
So twice five miles of fertile ground
With walls and towers were girdled round:
And there were gardens bright with sinuous rills
Where blossomed many an incense-bearing tree;
10 And here were forests ancient as the hills,
Enfolding sunny spots of greenery.

But oh! that deep romantic chasm which slanted
Down the green hill athwart a cedarn cover!
A savage place! as holy and enchanted
15 As e'er beneath a waning moon was haunted
By woman wailing for her demon-lover!
And from this chasm, with ceaseless turmoil seething,

---

4. I shall sing a sweeter song tomorrow (Greek; recalled from Theocritus's *Idyls* 1.145).

A number of Coleridge's assertions in this preface have been debated by critics: whether the poem was written in 1797 or later, whether it was actually composed in a "dream" or opium reverie, even whether it is a fragment or in fact is complete. All critics agree, however, that this visionary poem of demonic inspiration is much more than a mere "psychological curiosity."

5. Coleridge refers to "The Pains of Sleep."

6. Derived probably from the Greek river Alpheus, which flows into the Ionian Sea. Its waters were fabled to rise again in Sicily as the fountain of Arethusa.

As if this earth in fast thick pants were breathing,
A mighty fountain momently was forced:
20 Amid whose swift half-intermitted burst
Huge fragments vaulted like rebounding hail,
Or chaffy grain beneath the thresher's flail:
And 'mid these dancing rocks at once and ever
It flung up momently the sacred river.
25 Five miles meandering with a mazy motion
Through wood and dale the sacred river ran,
Then reached the caverns measureless to man,
And sank in tumult to a lifeless ocean:
And 'mid this tumult Kubla heard from far
30 Ancestral voices prophesying war!

The shadow of the dome of pleasure
Floated midway on the waves;
Where was heard the mingled measure
From the fountain and the caves.
35 It was a miracle of rare device,
A sunny pleasure-dome with caves of ice!

A damsel with a dulcimer
In a vision once I saw:
It was an Abyssinian maid,
40 And on her dulcimer she played,
Singing of Mount Abora.[7]
Could I revive within me
Her symphony and song,
To such a deep delight 'twould win me,
45 That with music loud and long,
I would build that dome in air,
That sunny dome! those caves of ice!
And all who heard should see them there,
And all should cry, Beware! Beware!
50 His flashing eyes, his floating hair!
Weave a circle round him thrice,[8]
And close your eyes with holy dread,
For he on honey-dew hath fed,
And drunk the milk of Paradise.[9]

ca. 1797–98   1816

---

7. Apparently a reminiscence of Milton's *Paradise Lost* 4.280–82: "where Abassin Kings their issue guard / Mount Amara (though this by some supposed / True Paradise) under the Ethiop line."
8. A magic ritual, to protect the inspired poet from intrusion.

9. Lines 50ff. echo in part the description, in Plato's *Ion* 533–34, of inspired poets, who are "like Bacchic maidens who draw milk and honey from the rivers when they are under the influence of Dionysus but not when they are in their right mind."

Christabel[1]

Preface

The first part of the following poem was written in the year 1797, at Stowey, in the county of Somerset. The second part, after my return from Germany, in the year 1800, at Keswick, Cumberland. It is probable, that if the poem had been finished at either of the former periods, or if even the first and second part had been published in the year 1800, the impression of its originality would have been much greater than I dare at present expect. But for this, I have only my own indolence to blame. The dates are mentioned for the exclusive purpose of precluding charges of plagiarism or servile imitation from myself. For there is amongst us a set of critics, who seem to hold, that every possible thought and image is traditional; who have no notion that there are such things as fountains in the world, small as well as great; and who would therefore charitably derive every rill they behold flowing, from a perforation made in some other man's tank. I am confident, however, that as far as the present poem is concerned, the celebrated poets[2] whose writings I might be suspected of having imitated, either in particular passages, or in the tone and the spirit of the whole, would be among the first to vindicate me from the charge, and who, on any striking coincidence, would permit me to address them in this doggerel version of two monkish Latin hexameters.

> Tis mine and it is likewise yours;
> But an if this will not do;
> Let it be mine, good friend! for I
> Am the poorer of the two.

I have only to add, that the metre of the Christabel is not, properly speaking, irregular, though it may seem so from its being founded on a new principle: namely, that of counting in each line the accents, not the syllables.[3] Though the latter may vary from seven to twelve, yet in each line the accents will be found to be only four. Nevertheless this occasional variation in number of syllables is not introduced wantonly, or for the mere ends of convenience, but in correspondence with some transition, in the nature of the imagery or passion.

Part 1

'Tis the middle of night by the castle clock,
And the owls have awakened the crowing cock;
Tu—whit!——Tu—whoo!

1. Coleridge had planned to publish *Christabel* in the 2nd edition of *Lyrical Ballads* (1800) but had not been able to complete the poem. When *Christabel* was finally published in 1816 in its present fragmentary state, he still hoped to finish it, for the Preface contained this sentence (deleted in the edition of 1834): "But as, in my very first conception of the tale, I had the whole present to my mind, with the wholeness, no less than with the liveliness of a vision; I trust that I shall be able to embody in verse the three parts yet to come, in the course of the present year."
2. Sir Walter Scott and Lord Byron, who had read and admired *Christabel* while it circulated in manuscript. Coleridge has in mind Scott's *Lay of the Last Minstrel* (1805) and Byron's *Siege of Corinth* (1816), which showed the influence of *Christabel*, especially in their meter.
3. Much of the older English versification, following the example of Anglo-Saxon poetry, had been based on stress, or "accent," and some of it shows as much freedom in varying the number of syllables as does *Christabel*. The poem, however, is a radical departure from the theory and practice of versification in the 18th century, which had been based on a recurrent number of syllables in each line.

And hark, again! the crowing cock,
5   How drowsily it crew.

Sir Leoline, the Baron rich,
Hath a toothless mastiff bitch;
From her kennel beneath the rock
She maketh answer to the clock,
10   Four for the quarters, and twelve for the hour;
Ever and aye,° by shine and shower,   *always*
Sixteen short howls, not over loud;
Some say, she sees my lady's shroud.

Is the night chilly and dark?
15   The night is chilly, but not dark.
The thin gray cloud is spread on high,
It covers but not hides the sky.
The moon is behind, and at the full;
And yet she looks both small and dull.
20   The night is chill, the cloud is gray:
'Tis a month before the month of May,
And the Spring comes slowly up this way.

The lovely lady, Christabel,
Whom her father loves so well,
25   What makes her in the wood so late,
A furlong from the castle gate?
She had dreams all yesternight
Of her own betrothed knight;
And she in the midnight wood will pray
30   For the weal° of her lover that's far away.   *well-being*

She stole along, she nothing spoke,
The sighs she heaved were soft and low,
And naught was green upon the oak,
But moss and rarest mistletoe:[4]
35   She kneels beneath the huge oak tree,
And in silence prayeth she.

The lady sprang up suddenly,
The lovely lady, Christabel!
It moaned as near, as near can be,
40   But what it is, she cannot tell.—
On the other side it seems to be,
Of the huge, broad-breasted, old oak tree.

The night is chill; the forest bare;
Is it the wind that moaneth bleak?
45   There is not wind enough in the air
To move away the ringlet curl
From the lovely lady's cheek—
There is not wind enough to twirl

---

4. In Celtic Britain the mistletoe (a parasitic plant) had been held in veneration when it was found growing—as it rarely does—on an oak tree. (Its usual host is the apple tree.)

The one red leaf, the last of its clan,
50 That dances as often as dance it can,
Hanging so light, and hanging so high,
On the topmost twig that looks up at the sky.

Hush, beating heart of Christabel!
Jesu, Maria, shield her well!
55 She folded her arms beneath her cloak,
And stole to the other side of the oak.
        What sees she there?

There she sees a damsel bright,
Drest in a silken robe of white,
60 That shadowy in the moonlight shone:
The neck that made that white robe wan,
Her stately neck, and arms were bare;
Her blue-veined feet unsandal'd were,
And wildly glittered here and there
65 The gems entangled in her hair.
I guess, 'twas frightful there to see
A lady so richly clad as she—
Beautiful exceedingly!

"Mary mother, save me now!"
70 (Said Christabel,) "And who art thou?"

The lady strange made answer meet,°   *appropriate*
And her voice was faint and sweet:—
"Have pity on my sore distress,
I scarce can speak for weariness:
75 Stretch forth thy hand, and have no fear!"
Said Christabel, "How cam'st thou here?"
And the lady, whose voice was faint and sweet,
Did thus pursue her answer meet:—

"My sire is of a noble line,
80 And my name is Geraldine:
Five warriors seized me yestermorn,
Me, even me, a maid forlorn:
They choked my cries with force and fright,
And tied me on a palfrey white.
85 The palfrey was as fleet as wind,
And they rode furiously behind.
They spurred amain,° their steeds were white: *at top speed*
And once we crossed the shade of night.
As sure as Heaven shall rescue me,
90 I have no thought what men they be;
Nor do I know how long it is
(For I have lain entranced I wis[5])
Since one, the tallest of the five,
Took me from the palfrey's back,

---

5. I believe (Coleridge's misinterpretation of the Middle English adverb *ywis*, meaning "certainly").

95   A weary woman, scarce alive.
Some muttered words his comrades spoke:
He placed me underneath this oak;
He swore they would return with haste;
Whither they went I cannot tell—
100   I thought I heard, some minutes past,
Sounds as of a castle bell.
Stretch forth thy hand" (thus ended she),
"And help a wretched maid to flee."

Then Christabel stretched forth her hand
105   And comforted fair Geraldine:
"O well, bright dame! may you command
The service of Sir Leoline;
And gladly our stout chivalry
Will he send forth and friends withal
110   To guide and guard you safe and free
Home to your noble father's hall."

She rose: and forth with steps they passed
That strove to be, and were not, fast.
Her gracious stars the lady blest,
115   And thus spake on sweet Christabel:
"All our household are at rest,
The hall as silent as the cell;°   *of a monastery*
Sir Leoline is weak in health,
And may not well awakened be,
120   But we will move as if in stealth,
And I beseech your courtesy,
This night, to share your couch with me."

They crossed the moat, and Christabel
Took the key that fitted well;
125   A little door she opened straight,
All in the middle of the gate;
The gate that was ironed within and without,
Where an army in battle array had marched out.
The lady sank, belike through pain,
130   And Christabel with might and main
Lifted her up, a weary weight,
Over the threshold of the gate:[6]
Then the lady rose again,
And moved, as she were not in pain.

135   So free from danger, free from fear,
They crossed the court: right glad they were.
And Christabel devoutly cried
To the Lady by her side;
"Praise we the Virgin all divine
140   Who hath rescued thee from thy distress!"
"Alas, alas!" said Geraldine,

6. According to legend, a witch cannot cross the threshold by her own power because it has been blessed against evil spirits.

"I cannot speak for weariness."
So free from danger, free from fear,
They crossed the court: right glad they were.

145 Outside her kennel the mastiff old
Lay fast asleep, in moonshine cold.
The mastiff old did not awake,
Yet she an angry moan did make!
And what can ail the mastiff bitch?
150 Never till now she uttered yell
Beneath the eye of Christabel.
Perhaps it is the owlet's scritch:
For what can ail the mastiff bitch?

They passed the hall, that echoes still,
155 Pass as lightly as you will!
The brands were flat, the brands were dying,
Amid their own white ashes lying;
But when the lady passed, there came
A tongue of light, a fit of flame;
160 And Christabel saw the lady's eye,
And nothing else saw she thereby,
Save the boss of the shield of Sir Leoline tall,
Which hung in a murky old niche in the wall.
"O softly tread," said Christabel,
165 "My father seldom sleepeth well."

Sweet Christabel her feet doth bare,
And, jealous of the listening air,
They steal their way from stair to stair,
Now in glimmer, and now in gloom,
170 And now they pass the Baron's room,
As still as death with stifled breath!
And now have reached her chamber door;
And now doth Geraldine press down
The rushes[7] of the chamber floor.

175 The moon shines dim in the open air,
And not a moonbeam enters here.
But they without its light can see
The chamber carved so curiously,
Carved with figures strange and sweet,
180 All made out of the carver's brain,
For a lady's chamber meet:
The lamp with twofold silver chain
Is fastened to an angel's feet.

The silver lamp burns dead and dim;
185 But Christabel the lamp will trim.
She trimmed the lamp, and made it bright,
And left it swinging to and fro,

---

7. Often used as a floor covering in the Middle Ages.

While Geraldine, in wretched plight,
Sank down upon the floor below.

190   "O weary lady, Geraldine,
I pray you, drink this cordial wine!
It is a wine of virtuous powers;
My mother made it of wild flowers."

"And will your mother pity me,
195   Who am a maiden most forlorn?"
Christabel answered—"Woe is me!
She died the hour that I was born.
I have heard the grey-haired friar tell,
How on her death-bed she did say,
200   That she should hear the castle-bell
Strike twelve upon my wedding day.
O mother dear! that thou wert here!"
"I would," said Geraldine, "she were!"

But soon with altered voice, said she—
205   "Off, wandering mother! Peak and pine![8]
I have power to bid thee flee."
Alas! what ails poor Geraldine?
Why stares she with unsettled eye?
Can she the bodiless dead espy?
210   And why with hollow voice cries she,
"Off, woman, off! this hour is mine—
Though thou her guardian spirit be,
Off, woman, off! 'tis given to me."

Then Christabel knelt by the lady's side,
215   And raised to heaven her eyes so blue—
"Alas!" said she, "this ghastly ride—
Dear lady! it hath wildered you!"
The lady wiped her moist cold brow,
And faintly said, "'tis over now!"

220   Again the wild-flower wine she drank:
Her fair large eyes 'gan glitter bright,
And from the floor whereon she sank,
The lofty lady stood upright;
She was most beautiful to see,
225   Like a lady of a far countrée.

And thus the lofty lady spake—
"All they who live in the upper sky,
Do love you, holy Christabel!
And you love them, and for their sake
230   And for the good which me befell,
Even I in my degree will try,
Fair maiden, to requite you well.

8. Shakespeare's *Macbeth* 1.3.22. "Wandering": term that could designate a fit of hysteria.

But now unrobe yourself; for I
Must pray, ere yet in bed I lie."

235 Quoth Christabel, "So let it be!"
And as the lady bade, did she.
Her gentle limbs did she undress,
And lay down in her loveliness.

But through her brain of weal and woe
240 So many thoughts moved to and fro,
That vain it were her lids to close;
So half-way from the bed she rose,
And on her elbow did recline
To look at the lady Geraldine.

245 Beneath the lamp the lady bowed,
And slowly rolled her eyes around;
Then drawing in her breath aloud,
Like one that shuddered, she unbound
The cincture° from beneath her breast: *belt*
250 Her silken robe, and inner vest,
Dropt to her feet, and full in view,
Behold! her bosom and half her side——
A sight to dream of, not to tell!
O shield her! shield sweet Christabel![9]

255 Yet Geraldine nor speaks nor stirs;
Ah! what a stricken look was hers!
Deep from within she seems half-way
To lift some weight with sick assay,°   *attempt*
And eyes the maid and seeks delay;
260 Then suddenly as one defied
Collects herself in scorn and pride,
And lay down by the maiden's side!—
And in her arms the maid she took,
    Ah well-a-day!
265 And with low voice and doleful look
These words did say:
"In the touch of this bosom there worketh a spell,
Which is lord of thy utterance, Christabel!
Thou knowest to-night, and wilt know to-morrow
270 This mark of my shame, this seal of my sorrow;
    But vainly thou warrest,
      For this is alone in
    Thy power to declare,
    That in the dim forest
275   Thou heard'st a low moaning,
And found'st a bright lady, surpassingly fair:
And didst bring her home with thee in love and in charity,
To shield her and shelter her from the damp air."

9. In several manuscripts and the first printing, this line reads "And she is to sleep by [*or* with] Christabel."

The Conclusion to Part 1

It was a lovely sight to see
280 The lady Christabel, when she
Was praying at the old oak tree.
    Amid the jagged shadows
    Of mossy leafless boughs,
    Kneeling in the moonlight,
285   To make her gentle vows;
Her slender palms together prest,
Heaving sometimes on her breast;
Her face resigned to bliss or bale°—   *evil, sorrow*
Her face, oh call it fair not pale,
290 And both blue eyes more bright than clear,
Each about to have a tear.

With open eyes (ah woe is me!)
Asleep, and dreaming fearfully,
Fearfully dreaming, yet I wis,
295 Dreaming that alone, which is—
O sorrow and shame! Can this be she,
The lady, who knelt at the old oak tree?
And lo! the worker of these harms,
That holds the maiden in her arms,
300 Seems to slumber still and mild,
As a mother with her child.

A star hath set, a star hath risen,
O Geraldine! since arms of thine
Have been the lovely lady's prison.
305 O Geraldine! one hour was thine—
Thou'st had thy will! By tairn[1] and rill,
The night-birds all that hour were still.
But now they are jubilant anew,
From cliff and tower, tu—whoo! tu—whoo!
310 Tu—whoo! tu—whoo! from wood and fell![2]

And see! the lady Christabel
Gathers herself from out her trance;
Her limbs relax, her countenance
Grows sad and soft; the smooth thin lids
315 Close o'er her eyes; and tears she sheds—
Large tears that leave the lashes bright!
And oft the while she seems to smile
As infants at a sudden light!
Yea, she doth smile, and she doth weep,
320 Like a youthful hermitess,
Beauteous in a wilderness,
Who, praying always, prays in sleep.
And, if she move unquietly,
Perchance, 'tis but the blood so free,

---

1. Tarn, a mountain pool.
2. Elevated moor, or hill.

325 Comes back and tingles in her feet.
No doubt, she hath a vision sweet.
What if her guardian spirit 'twere?
What if she knew her mother near?
But this she knows, in joys and woes,
330 That saints will aid if men will call:
For the blue sky bends over all!

Part 2

"Each matin bell," the Baron saith,
"Knells us back to a world of death."
These words Sir Leoline first said,
335 When he rose and found his lady dead:
These words Sir Leoline will say,
Many a morn to his dying day!

And hence the custom and law began,
That still at dawn the sacristan,[3]
340 Who duly pulls the heavy bell,
Five and forty beads must tell[4]
Between each stroke—a warning knell,
Which not a soul can choose but hear
From Bratha Head to Wyndermere.[5]

345 Saith Bracy the bard, "So let it knell!
And let the drowsy sacristan
Still count as slowly as he can!
There is no lack of such, I ween,°   believe
As well fill up the space between.
350 In Langdale Pike° and Witch's Lair,   Peak
And Dungeon-ghyll[6] so foully rent,
With ropes of rock and bells of air
Three sinful sextons' ghosts are pent,
Who all give back, one after t'other,
355 The death-note to their living brother;
And oft too, by the knell offended,
Just as their one! two! three! is ended,
The devil mocks the doleful tale
With a merry peal from Borodale."

360 The air is still! through mist and cloud
That merry peal comes ringing loud;
And Geraldine shakes off her dread,
And rises lightly from the bed;
Puts on her silken vestments white,
365 And tricks her hair in lovely plight,°   plait
And nothing doubting of her spell

3. Church officer who digs the graves and rings
the bells.
4. Pray while "telling" (keeping count on) the
beads of a rosary.

5. These and the following names are of localities in the English Lake District.
6. Ravine forming the bed of a stream.

Awakens the lady Christabel.
"Sleep you, sweet lady Christabel?
I trust that you have rested well."

370 And Christabel awoke and spied
The same who lay down by her side—
O rather say, the same whom she
Raised up beneath the old oak tree!
Nay, fairer yet! and yet more fair!
375 For she belike hath drunken deep
Of all the blessedness of sleep!
And while she spake, her looks, her air
Such gentle thankfulness declare,
That (so it seemed) her girded vests
380 Grew tight beneath her heaving breasts.
"Sure I have sinned!" said Christabel,
"Now heaven be praised if all be well!"
And in low faltering tones, yet sweet,
Did she the lofty lady greet
385 With such perplexity of mind
As dreams too lively leave behind.

So quickly she rose, and quickly arrayed
Her maiden limbs, and having prayed
That He, who on the cross did groan,
390 Might wash away her sins unknown,
She forthwith led fair Geraldine
To meet her sire, Sir Leoline.

The lovely maid and the lady tall
Are pacing both into the hall,
395 And pacing on through page and groom,
Enter the Baron's presence room.

The Baron rose, and while he prest
His gentle daughter to his breast,
With cheerful wonder in his eyes
400 The lady Geraldine espies,
And gave such welcome to the same,
As might beseem so bright a dame!

But when he heard the lady's tale,
And when she told her father's name,
405 Why waxed Sir Leoline so pale,
Murmuring o'er the name again,
Lord Roland de Vaux of Tryermaine?

Alas! they had been friends in youth;
But whispering tongues can poison truth;
410 And constancy lives in realms above;
And life is thorny; and youth is vain;
And to be wroth with one we love,

Doth work like madness in the brain.
And thus it chanced, as I divine,
415 With Roland and Sir Leoline.
Each spake words of high disdain
And insult to his heart's best brother:
They parted—ne'er to meet again!
But never either found another
420 To free the hollow heart from paining—
They stood aloof, the scars remaining,
Like cliffs which had been rent asunder;
A dreary sea now flows between;—
But neither heat, nor frost, nor thunder,
425 Shall wholly do away, I ween,
The marks of that which once hath been.

Sir Leoline, a moment's space,
Stood gazing on the damsel's face:
And the youthful Lord of Tryermaine
430 Came back upon his heart again.

O then the Baron forgot his age,
His noble heart swelled high with rage;
He swore by the wounds in Jesu's side,
He would proclaim it far and wide
435 With trump and solemn heraldry,
That they who thus had wronged the dame,
Were base as spotted infamy!
"And if they dare deny the same,
My herald shall appoint a week,
440 And let the recreant traitors seek
My tourney court[7]—that there and then
I may dislodge their reptile souls
From the bodies and forms of men!"
He spake: his eye in lightning rolls!
445 For the lady was ruthlessly seized; and he kenned
In the beautiful lady the child of his friend!

And now the tears were on his face,
And fondly in his arms he took
Fair Geraldine, who met the embrace,
450 Prolonging it with joyous look.
Which when she viewed, a vision fell
Upon the soul of Christabel,
The vision of fear, the touch and pain!
She shrunk and shuddered, and saw again—
455 (Ah, woe is me! Was it for thee,
Thou gentle maid! such sights to see?)
Again she saw that bosom old,
Again she felt that bosom cold,
And drew in her breath with a hissing sound:

7. Arena for tournaments.

460 Whereat the Knight turned wildly round,
And nothing saw, but his own sweet maid
With eyes upraised, as one that prayed.

The touch, the sight, had passed away,
And in its stead that vision blest,
465 Which comforted her after-rest,
While in the lady's arms she lay,
Had put a rapture in her breast,
And on her lips and o'er her eyes
Spread smiles like light!
                                With new surprise,
470 "What ails then my beloved child?"
The Baron said—His daughter mild
Made answer, "All will yet be well!"
I ween, she had no power to tell
Aught else: so mighty was the spell.

475 Yet he, who saw this Geraldine,
Had deemed her sure a thing divine.
Such sorrow with such grace she blended,
As if she feared, she had offended
Sweet Christabel, that gentle maid!
480 And with such lowly tones she prayed,
She might be sent without delay
Home to her father's mansion.
                                "Nay!
Nay, by my soul!" said Leoline.
"Ho! Bracy, the bard, the charge be thine!
485 Go thou, with music sweet and loud,
And take two steeds with trappings proud,
And take the youth whom thou lov'st best
To bear thy harp, and learn thy song,
And clothe you both in solemn vest,
490 And over the mountains haste along,
Lest wandering folk, that are abroad,
Detain you on the valley road.
And when he has crossed the Irthing flood,
My merry bard! he hastes, he hastes
495 Up Knorren Moor, through Halegarth Wood,
And reaches soon that castle good
Which stands and threatens Scotland's wastes.

"Bard Bracy! bard Bracy! your horses are fleet,
Ye must ride up the hall, your music so sweet,
500 More loud than your horses' echoing feet!
And loud and loud to Lord Roland call,
Thy daughter is safe in Langdale hall!
Thy beautiful daughter is safe and free—
Sir Leoline greets thee thus through me.
505 He bids thee come without delay
With all thy numerous array;
And take thy lovely daughter home:

And he will meet thee on the way
With all his numerous array
510 White with their panting palfreys' foam:
And by mine honour! I will say,
That I repent me of the day
When I spake words of fierce disdain
To Roland de Vaux of Tryermaine!—
515 —For since that evil hour hath flown,
Many a summer's sun hath shone;
Yet ne'er found I a friend again
Like Roland de Vaux of Tryermaine."

The lady fell, and clasped his knees,
520 Her face upraised, her eyes o'erflowing;
And Bracy replied, with faltering voice,
His gracious hail on all bestowing!—
"Thy words, thou sire of Christabel,
Are sweeter than my harp can tell;
525 Yet might I gain a boon of thee,
This day my journey should not be,
So strange a dream hath come to me;
That I had vowed with music loud
To clear yon wood from thing unblest,
530 Warned by a vision in my rest!
For in my sleep I saw that dove,
That gentle bird, whom thou dost love,
And call'st by thy own daughter's name—
Sir Leoline! I saw the same
535 Fluttering, and uttering fearful moan,
Among the green herbs in the forest alone.
Which when I saw and when I heard,
I wonder'd what might ail the bird;
For nothing near it could I see,
540 Save the grass and green herbs underneath the old tree.

"And in my dream methought I went
To search out what might there be found;
And what the sweet bird's trouble meant,
That thus lay fluttering on the ground.
545 I went and peered, and could descry
No cause for her distressful cry;
But yet for her dear lady's sake
I stooped, methought, the dove to take,
When lo! I saw a bright green snake
550 Coiled around its wings and neck,
Green as the herbs on which it couched,
Close by the dove's its head it crouched;
And with the dove it heaves and stirs,
Swelling its neck as she swelled hers!
555 I woke; it was the midnight hour,
The clock was echoing in the tower;
But though my slumber was gone by,
This dream it would not pass away—

It seems to live upon my eye!
560 And thence I vowed this self-same day,
With music strong and saintly song
To wander through the forest bare,
Lest aught unholy loiter there."

Thus Bracy said: the Baron, the while,
565 Half-listening heard him with a smile;
Then turned to Lady Geraldine,
His eyes made up of wonder and love;
And said in courtly accents fine,
"Sweet maid, Lord Roland's beauteous dove,
570 With arms more strong than harp or song,
Thy sire and I will crush the snake!"
He kissed her forehead as he spake,
And Geraldine, in maiden wise,°   *manner*
Casting down her large bright eyes,
575 With blushing cheek and courtesy fine
She turned her from Sir Leoline;
Softly gathering up her train,
That o'er her right arm fell again;
And folded her arms across her chest,
580 And couched her head upon her breast,
And looked askance at Christabel—
Jesu Maria, shield her well!

A snake's small eye blinks dull and shy,
And the lady's eyes they shrunk in her head,
585 Each shrunk up to a serpent's eye,
And with somewhat of malice, and more of dread,
At Christabel she looked askance!—
One moment—and the sight was fled!
But Christabel in dizzy trance
590 Stumbling on the unsteady ground
Shuddered aloud, with a hissing sound;
And Geraldine again turned round,
And like a thing, that sought relief,
Full of wonder and full of grief,
595 She rolled her large bright eyes divine
Wildly on Sir Leoline.

The maid, alas! her thoughts are gone,
She nothing sees—no sight but one!
The maid, devoid of guile and sin,
600 I know not how, in fearful wise
So deeply had she drunken in
That look, those shrunken serpent eyes,
That all her features were resigned
To this sole image in her mind;
605 And passively did imitate
That look of dull and treacherous hate!
And thus she stood, in dizzy trance,
Still picturing that look askance
With forced unconscious sympathy

610 Full before her father's view——
    As far as such a look could be,
    In eyes so innocent and blue!
    And when the trance was o'er, the maid
    Paused awhile, and inly prayed:
615 Then falling at the Baron's feet,
    "By my mother's soul do I entreat
    That thou this woman send away!"
    She said: and more she could not say:
    For what she knew she could not tell,
620 O'er-mastered by the mighty spell.

    Why is thy cheek so wan and wild,
    Sir Leoline? Thy only child
    Lies at thy feet, thy joy, thy pride,
    So fair, so innocent, so mild;
625 The same, for whom thy lady died!
    O by the pangs of her dear mother
    Think thou no evil of thy child!
    For her, and thee, and for no other,
    She prayed the moment ere she died:
630 Prayed that the babe for whom she died,
    Might prove her dear lord's joy and pride!
        That prayer her deadly pangs beguiled,
            Sir Leoline!
        And wouldst thou wrong thy only child,
635   Her child and thine?

    Within the Baron's heart and brain
    If thoughts, like these, had any share,
    They only swelled his rage and pain,
    And did but work confusion there.
640 His heart was cleft with pain and rage,
    His cheeks they quivered, his eyes were wild,
    Dishonoured thus in his old age;
    Dishonoured by his only child,
    And all his hospitality
645 To the wrong'd daughter of his friend
    By more than woman's jealousy
    Brought thus to a disgraceful end—
    He rolled his eye with stern regard
    Upon the gentle minstrel bard,
650 And said in tones abrupt, austere—
    "Why, Bracy! dost thou loiter here?
    I bade thee hence!" The bard obeyed;
    And turning from his own sweet maid,
    The aged knight, Sir Leoline,
655 Led forth the lady Geraldine!

The Conclusion to Part 2

A little child, a limber elf,
Singing, dancing to itself,
A fairy thing with red round cheeks,

That always finds, and never seeks,
660 Makes such a vision to the sight
As fills a father's eyes with light;
And pleasures flow in so thick and fast
Upon his heart, that he at last
Must needs express his love's excess
665 With words of unmeant bitterness.
Perhaps 'tis pretty to force together
Thoughts so all unlike each other;
To mutter and mock a broken charm,
To dally with wrong that does no harm.
670 Perhaps 'tis tender too and pretty
At each wild word to feel within
A sweet recoil of love and pity.
And what, if in a world of sin
(O sorrow and shame should this be true!)
675 Such giddiness of heart and brain
Comes seldom save from rage and pain,
So talks as it's most used to do.

1798–1800   1816

Frost at Midnight[1]

temporally = present

The frost performs its secret ministry,
Unhelped by any wind. The owlet's cry   *enjambment*
caesura   Came loud—and hark, again! loud as before.
The inmates of my cottage, all at rest,
5   Have left me to that solitude, which suits   *enjamb.*
Abstruser musings: save that at my side   *meditation too*
My cradled infant slumbers peacefully.   *hard because*
'Tis calm indeed! so calm, that it disturbs   *too silent*
And vexes meditation with its strange
10   And extreme silentness. Sea, hill, and wood,
This populous village! Sea, and hill, and wood,
With all the numberless goings on of life,
Inaudible as dreams! the thin blue flame   — *shift to more*
Lies on my low burnt fire, and quivers not;   *formal line*
15   Only that film,[2] which fluttered on the grate,
Still flutters there, the sole unquiet thing.
Methinks, its motion in this hush of nature
Gives it dim sympathies with me who live,
Making it a companionable form,

1. The scene is Coleridge's cottage at Nether
Stowey; the infant in line 7 is his son Hartley,
then aged seventeen months.
2. In all parts of the kingdom these films are
called *strangers* and supposed to portend the
arrival of some absent friend [Coleridge's note].
The "film" is a piece of soot fluttering on the bar
of the grate. Cf. Cowper's *The Task* 4.292–95, in
which the poet describes how, dreaming before
the parlor fire, he watches "The sooty films that
play upon the bars, / Pendulous and foreboding,
in the view / Of superstition prophesying still, /
Though still deceived, some stranger's near
approach." Several editions of Cowper's poems
were advertised on the verso of the last page of
Coleridge's text in the 1798 volume in which
"Frost at Midnight" was first published.

20 Whose puny flaps and freaks the idling Spirit
By its own moods interprets, every where
Echo or mirror seeking of itself,
And makes a toy of Thought.

                    But O! how oft,
How oft, at school, with most believing mind,
25 Presageful, have I gazed upon the bars,
To watch that fluttering stranger! and as oft
With unclosed lids, already had I dreamt
Of my sweet birth-place,[3] and the old church-tower,
Whose bells, the poor man's only music, rang
30 From morn to evening, all the hot Fair-day,
So sweetly, that they stirred and haunted me
With a wild pleasure, falling on mine ear
Most like articulate sounds of things to come!
So gazed I, till the soothing things I dreamt
35 Lulled me to sleep, and sleep prolonged my dreams!
And so I brooded all the following morn,
Awed by the stern preceptor's[4] face, mine eye
Fixed with mock study on my swimming book:
Save if the door half opened, and I snatched
40 A hasty glance, and still my heart leaped up,
For still I hoped to see the stranger's face,
Townsman, or aunt, or sister more beloved,
My play-mate when we both were clothed alike![5]

        Dear Babe, that sleepest cradled by my side,
45 Whose gentle breathings, heard in this deep calm,
Fill up the interspersed vacancies
And momentary pauses of the thought!
My babe so beautiful! it thrills my heart
With tender gladness, thus to look at thee,
50 And think that thou shalt learn far other lore
And in far other scenes! For I was reared
In the great city, pent 'mid cloisters dim,
And saw nought lovely but the sky and stars.
But thou, my babe! shalt wander like a breeze
55 By lakes and sandy shores, beneath the crags
Of ancient mountain, and beneath the clouds,
Which image in their bulk both lakes and shores
And mountain crags: so shalt thou see and hear
The lovely shapes and sounds intelligible
60 Of that eternal language, which thy God
Utters, who from eternity doth teach
Himself in all, and all things in himself.
Great universal Teacher! he shall mould
Thy spirit, and by giving make it ask.

---

3. Coleridge was born at Ottery St. Mary, Devonshire, but went to school in London, beginning at the age of nine.
4. The Reverend James Boyer at Coleridge's school, Christ's Hospital.
5. I.e., when both Coleridge and his sister Ann still wore infant clothes, before he was deemed old enough to be breeched.

65 Therefore all seasons shall be sweet to thee,
Whether the summer clothe the general earth
With greenness, or the redbreast sit and sing
Betwixt the tufts of snow on the bare branch
Of mossy apple-tree, while the nigh thatch
70 Smokes in the sun-thaw; whether the eave-drops fall
Heard only in the trances of the blast,
Or if the secret ministry of frost
Shall hang them up in silent icicles,
Quietly shining to the quiet Moon.

Feb. 1798   *ends in silence + stillness*   1798

Dejection: An Ode[1]

Late, late yestreen I saw the new Moon,
With the old Moon in her arms;
And I fear, I fear, my Master dear!
We shall have a deadly storm.
            Ballad of Sir Patrick Spence

I

Well! If the Bard was weather-wise, who made
The grand old ballad of Sir Patrick Spence,
This night, so tranquil now, will not go hence
Unroused by winds, that ply a busier trade
5 Than those which mould yon cloud in lazy flakes,
Or the dull sobbing draft, that moans and rakes
Upon the strings of this Eolian lute,[2]
Which better far were mute.
For lo! the New-moon winter-bright!
10 And overspread with phantom light,
(With swimming phantom light o'erspread
But rimmed and circled by a silver thread)
I see the old Moon in her lap, foretelling
The coming on of rain and squally blast.
15 And oh! that even now the gust were swelling,
And the slant night-shower driving loud and fast!
Those sounds which oft have raised me, whilst they awed,
And sent my soul abroad,
Might now perhaps their wonted° impulse give,   *customary*
20 Might startle this dull pain, and make it move and live!

---

1. This poem originated in a verse letter of 340 lines, called "A Letter to————," that Coleridge wrote on the night of April 4, 1802, after hearing the opening stanzas of "Ode: Intimations of Immortality," which Wordsworth had just composed. The "Letter" was addressed to Sara Hutchinson (whom Coleridge sometimes called "Asra"), the sister of Wordsworth's fiancée, Mary. It picked up the theme of a loss in the quality of perceptual experience that Wordsworth had presented at the beginning of his "Ode." In his original poem Coleridge lamented at length his unhappy marriage and the hopelessness of his love for Sara Hutchinson. In the next six months Coleridge deleted more than half the original lines, revised and reordered the remaining passages, and so transformed a long verse confession into the compact and dignified "Dejection: An Ode." He published the "Ode," in substantially its present form, on October 4, 1802, Wordsworth's wedding day— and also the seventh anniversary of Coleridge's own disastrous marriage to Sara Flicker.

2. A stringed instrument played upon by the wind (see "The Eolian Harp," p. 444, n. 1.).

2

A grief without a pang, void, dark, and drear,
   A stifled, drowsy, unimpassioned grief,
   Which finds no natural outlet, no relief,
     In word, or sigh, or tear—
25 O Lady![3] in this wan and heartless mood,
To other thoughts by yonder throstle woo'd,
   All this long eve, so balmy and serene,
Have I been gazing on the western sky,
   And its peculiar tint of yellow green:
30 And still I gaze—and with how blank an eye!
And those thin clouds above, in flakes and bars,
That give away their motion to the stars;
Those stars, that glide behind them or between,
Now sparkling, now bedimmed, but always seen:
35 Yon crescent Moon as fixed as if it grew
In its own cloudless, starless lake of blue;
I see them all so excellently fair,
I see, not feel, how beautiful they are!

3

    My genial° spirits fail;   *creative*
40   And what can these avail
To lift the smothering weight from off my breast?
     It were a vain endeavour,
     Though I should gaze for ever
On that green light that lingers in the west:
45 I may not hope from outward forms to win
The passion and the life, whose fountains are within.

4

O Lady! we receive but what we give,
And in our life alone does nature live:
Ours is her wedding-garment, ours her shroud![4]
50   And would we aught° behold, of higher worth,   *anything*
Than that inanimate cold world allowed
To the poor loveless ever-anxious crowd,
    Ah! from the soul itself must issue forth,
A light, a glory,[5] a fair luminous cloud
55   Enveloping the Earth—
And from the soul itself must there be sent
    A sweet and potent voice, of its own birth,
Of all sweet sounds the life and element!

3. In the original version "Sara"—i.e., Sara Hutchinson. After intervening versions, in which the poem was addressed first to "William" (Wordsworth) and then to "Edmund," Coleridge introduced the noncommittal "Lady" in 1817.
4. I.e., nature's wedding garment and shroud are ours to give to her.
5. Halo. Coleridge often uses the term to identify in particular the phenomenon that occurs in the mountains when a walker sees his or her own figure projected by the sun in the mist, enlarged and with light encircling its head.

5

O pure of heart! thou need'st not ask of me
60   What this strong music in the soul may be!
What, and wherein it doth exist,
This light, this glory, this fair luminous mist,
This beautiful and beauty-making power.
   Joy, virtuous Lady! Joy that ne'er was given,
65   Save to the pure, and in their purest hour,
Life, and Life's effluence, cloud at once and shower,
Joy, Lady! is the spirit and the power,
Which wedding Nature to us gives in dower,
   A new Earth and new Heaven,[6]
70   Undreamt of by the sensual and the proud—
Joy is the sweet voice, Joy the luminous cloud—
     We in ourselves rejoice!
And thence flows all that charms or ear or sight,
   All melodies the echoes of that voice,
75   All colours a suffusion from that light.

6

There was a time when, though my path was rough,
   This joy within me dallied with distress,
And all misfortunes were but as the stuff
   Whence Fancy made me dreams of happiness:
80   For hope grew round me, like the twining vine,
And fruits, and foliage, not my own, seemed mine.
But now afflictions bow me down to earth:
Nor care I that they rob me of my mirth,
   But oh! each visitation°   *i.e., of affliction*
85   Suspends what nature gave me at my birth,
   My shaping spirit of Imagination.
For not to think of what I needs must feel,
   But to be still and patient, all I can;
And haply by abstruse research to steal
90   From my own nature all the natural man—
This was my sole resource, my only plan:
Till that which suits a part infects the whole,
And now is almost grown the habit of my soul.

7

Hence, viper thoughts, that coil around my mind,
95   Reality's dark dream!
I turn from you, and listen to the wind,
   Which long has raved unnoticed. What a scream
Of agony by torture lengthened out
That lute sent forth! Thou Wind, that ravest without,

6. The sense becomes clearer if line 68 is punctuated in the way that Coleridge punctuated it when quoting the passage in one of his essays: "Which, wedding Nature to us, gives in dower." I.e., Joy marries us to Nature and gives us, for our dowry, "a new Earth and a new Heaven," a phrase echoing Revelation 21.1.

100 Bare crag, or mountain-tairn,[7] or blasted tree,
Or pine-grove whither woodman never clomb,°   *climbed*
Or lonely house, long held the witches' home,
Methinks were fitter instruments for thee,
Mad Lutanist! who in this month of showers,
105 Of dark brown gardens, and of peeping flowers,
Mak'st Devils' yule,[8] with worse than wintry song,
The blossoms, buds, and timorous leaves among.
Thou Actor, perfect in all tragic sounds!
Thou mighty Poet, e'en to frenzy bold!
110   What tell'st thou now about?
'Tis of the rushing of a host in rout,
With groans of trampled men, with smarting wounds—
At once they groan with pain, and shudder with the cold!
But hush! there is a pause of deepest silence!
115 And all that noise, as of a rushing crowd,
With groans, and tremulous shudderings—all is over—
It tells another tale, with sounds less deep and loud!
A tale of less affright,
And tempered with delight,
120 As Otway's[9] self had framed the tender lay,
'Tis of a little child
Upon a lonesome wild,
Not far from home, but she hath lost her way:
And now moans low in bitter grief and fear,
125 And now screams loud, and hopes to make her mother hear.

8

'Tis midnight, but small thoughts have I of sleep:
Full seldom may my friend such vigils keep!
Visit her, gentle Sleep! with wings of healing,
And may this storm be but a mountain-birth,[1]
130 May all the stars hang bright above her dwelling,
Silent as though they watched the sleeping Earth!
With light heart may she rise,
Gay fancy, cheerful eyes,
Joy lift her spirit, joy attune her voice;
135 To her may all things live, from pole to pole,
Their life the eddying of her living soul!
O simple spirit, guided from above,
Dear Lady! friend devoutest of my choice,
Thus mayest thou ever, evermore rejoice.

Apr. 4, 1802   1802

---

7. Tarn, or mountain pool.
8. Christmas as, in a perverted form, it is celebrated by devils.
9. Thomas Otway (1652–1685), a dramatist noted
for the pathos of his tragic passages. The poet
originally named was "William," and the allusion

was probably to Wordsworth's "Lucy Gray."
1. Probably, "May this be a typical mountain
storm, short though violent," although Coleridge
might have intended an allusion to Horace's
phrase "the mountain labored and brought forth
a mouse."

The Pains of Sleep[1]

Ere on my bed my limbs I lay,
It hath not been my use° to pray   *custom*
With moving lips or bended knees;
But silently, by slow degrees,
5   My spirit I to Love compose,
In humble trust mine eye-lids close,
With reverential resignation,
No wish conceived, no thought exprest,
Only a sense of supplication;
10 A sense o'er all my soul imprest
That I am weak, yet not unblest,
Since in me, round me, every where
Eternal strength and wisdom are.

But yester-night I prayed aloud
15 In anguish and in agony,
Up-starting from the fiendish crowd
Of shapes and thoughts that tortured me:
A lurid light, a trampling throng,
Sense of intolerable wrong,
20 And whom I scorned, those only strong!
Thirst of revenge, the powerless will
Still baffled, and yet burning still!
Desire with loathing strangely mixed
On wild or hateful objects fixed.
25 Fantastic passions! maddening brawl!
And shame and terror over all!
Deeds to be hid which were not hid,
Which all confused I could not know,
Whether I suffered, or I did:
30 For all seemed guilt, remorse or woe,
My own or others still the same
Life-stifling fear, soul-stifling shame.

So two nights passed: the night's dismay
Saddened and stunned the coming day.
35 Sleep, the wide blessing, seemed to me
Distemper's worst calamity.
The third night, when my own loud scream
Had waked me from the fiendish dream,
O'ercome with sufferings strange and wild,
40 I wept as I had been a child;
And having thus by tears subdued

1. Coleridge included a draft of this poem in a letter to Robert Southey, September 11, 1803, in which he wrote that "my spirits are dreadful, owing entirely to the Horrors of every night—I truly dread to sleep. It is no shadow with me, but substantial Misery foot-thick, that makes me sit by my bedside of a morning, & cry—. I have abandoned all opiates except Ether be one; & that only in *fits*. . . ." The last sentence indicates what Coleridge did not know—that his guilty nightmares were probably withdrawal symptoms from opium. The dreams he describes are very similar to those that De Quincey represents as "The Pains of Opium" in his *Confessions of an English Opium-Eater*.

My anguish to a milder mood,
Such punishments, I said, were due
To natures deepliest stained with sin,—
45 For aye entempesting anew
The unfathomable hell within,
The horror of their deeds to view,
To know and loathe, yet wish and do!
Such griefs with such men well agree,
50 But wherefore, wherefore fall on me?
To be beloved is all I need,
And whom I love, I love indeed.

1803   1816

To William Wordsworth

Composed on the Night after His Recitation of a Poem on the
Growth of an Individual Mind[1]

Friend of the wise! and teacher of the good!
Into my heart have I received that lay°   song
More than historic, that prophetic lay
Wherein (high theme by thee first sung aright)
5 Of the foundations and the building up
Of a Human Spirit thou hast dared to tell
What may be told, to the understanding mind
Revealable; and what within the mind
By vital breathings secret as the soul
10 Of vernal° growth, oft quickens in the heart   springtime
Thoughts all too deep for words![2]—

                                          Theme hard as high!
Of smiles spontaneous, and mysterious fears
(The first-born they of Reason and twin birth),
Of tides obedient to external force,
15 And currents self-determined, as might seem,
Or by some inner power; of moments awful,°   awe-inspiring
Now in thy inner life, and now abroad,
When power streamed from thee, and thy soul received
The light reflected, as a light bestowed—
20 Of fancies fair, and milder hours of youth,
Hyblean[3] murmurs of poetic thought
Industrious in its joy, in vales and glens
Native or outland, lakes and famous hills!
Or on the lonely high-road, when the stars

1. This was the poem (later called *The Prelude*), addressed to Coleridge, that Wordsworth had completed in 1805. After Coleridge returned from Malta, very low in health and spirits, Wordsworth read the poem aloud to him during the evenings of almost two weeks. Coleridge wrote most of the present response immediately after the reading was completed, on January 7, 1807.

2. Wordsworth had described the effect on his mind of the animating breeze ("vital breathings") in *The Prelude* 1.1–47. "Thoughts . . . words" echoes the last line of Wordsworth's "Intimations" ode. Coleridge goes on to summarize the major themes and events of *The Prelude*.
3. Sweet. Hybla, in ancient Sicily, was famous for its honey.

25 Were rising; or by secret mountain-streams,
The guides and the companions of thy way!

      Of more than Fancy, of the Social Sense
Distending wide, and man beloved as man,
Where France in all her towns lay vibrating
30 Like some becalmed bark beneath the burst
Of Heaven's immediate thunder, when no cloud
Is visible, or shadow on the main.
For thou wert there, thine own brows garlanded,
Amid the tremor of a realm aglow,
35 Amid a mighty nation jubilant,
When from the general heart of human kind
Hope sprang forth like a full-born Deity!
——Of that dear Hope afflicted and struck down,
So summoned homeward, thenceforth calm and sure
40 From the dread watch-tower of man's absolute self,
With light unwaning on her eyes, to look
Far on—herself a glory to behold,
The Angel of the vision![4] Then (last strain)
Of Duty, chosen laws controlling choice,
45 Action and joy!—An Orphic song[5] indeed,
A song divine of high and passionate thoughts
To their own music chanted!

            O great Bard!
Ere yet that last strain dying awed the air,
With steadfast eye I viewed thee in the choir
50 Of ever-enduring men. The truly great
Have all one age, and from one visible space
Shed influence! They, both in power and act,
Are permanent, and Time is not with them,
Save as it worketh for them, they in it.
55 Nor less a sacred roll, than those of old,
And to be placed, as they, with gradual fame
Among the archives of mankind, thy work
Makes audible a linked lay of Truth,
Of Truth profound a sweet continuous lay,
60 Not learnt, but native, her own natural notes!
Ah! as I listened with a heart forlorn,
The pulses of my being beat anew:
And even as life returns upon the drowned,
Life's joy rekindling roused a throng of pains—
65 Keen pangs of Love, awakening as a babe
Turbulent, with an outcry in the heart;
And fears self-willed, that shunned the eye of hope;
And hope that scarce would know itself from fear;
Sense of past youth, and manhood come in vain,
70 And genius given, and knowledge won in vain;
And all which I had culled in wood-walks wild,

---

4. Probably alludes to "the great vision of the guarded mount" in Milton's "Lycidas," line 161.
5. As enchanting and oracular as the song of the legendary Orpheus. There may also be an allusion to the Orphic mysteries, involving spiritual death and rebirth (see lines 61–66).

And all which patient toil had reared, and all,
Commune with thee had opened out—but flowers
Strewed on my corse, and borne upon my bier,
75 In the same coffin, for the self-same grave!

That way no more! and ill beseems it me,
Who came a welcomer in herald's guise,
Singing of glory, and futurity,
To wander back on such unhealthful road,
80 Plucking the poisons of self-harm! And ill
Such intertwine beseems triumphal wreaths
Strewed before thy advancing!

Nor do thou,
Sage Bard! impair the memory of that hour
Of thy communion with my nobler mind[6]
85 By pity or grief, already felt too long!
Nor let my words import more blame than needs.
The tumult rose and ceased: for peace is nigh
Where wisdom's voice has found a listening heart.
Amid the howl of more than wintry storms,
90 The halcyon[7] hears the voice of vernal hours
Already on the wing.

Eve following eve,[8]
Dear tranquil time, when the sweet sense of Home
Is sweetest! moments for their own sake hailed
And more desired, more precious for thy song,
95 In silence listening, like a devout child,
My soul lay passive, by thy various strain
Driven as in surges now beneath the stars,
With momentary stars of my own birth,
Fair constellated foam, still darting off
100 Into the darkness; now a tranquil sea,
Outspread and bright, yet swelling to the moon.

And when—O Friend! my comforter and guide!
Strong in thyself, and powerful to give strength!—
Thy long sustained Song finally closed,
105 And thy deep voice had ceased—yet thou thyself
Wert still before my eyes, and round us both
That happy vision of beloved faces—
Scarce conscious, and yet conscious of its close
I sate, my being blended in one thought
110 (Thought was it? or aspiration? or resolve?)
Absorbed, yet hanging still upon the sound—
And when I rose, I found myself in prayer.

1807   1817

---

6. I.e., during the early association between the
two poets (1797–98).
7. A fabled bird, able to calm the sea where it

nested in winter.
8. The evenings during which Wordsworth read
his poem aloud.

Epitaph[1]

Stop, Christian Passer-by!—Stop, child of God,
And read with gentle breast. Beneath this sod
A poet lies, or that which once seem'd he.—
O, lift one thought in prayer for S. T. C.;
5 That he who many a year with toil of breath
Found death in life, may here find life in death!
Mercy for praise—to be forgiven for[2] fame
He ask'd, and hoped, through Christ. Do thou the same!

1833   1834

Biographia Literaria   In March 1815 Coleridge was preparing a collected
edition of his poems and planned to include "a general preface . . . on the principles
of philosophic and genial criticism." As was typical for Coleridge, the materials
developed as he worked on them until, on July 29, he declared that the preface had
expanded to become a book in its own right, an "Autobiographia Literaria." In a characteristic Romantic reinvention of autobiography, the work merged personal experience with philosophical speculation, as well as with what Coleridge identified as
"digression and anecdotes." It was to consist of two main parts, "my literary life and
opinions, as far as poetry and *poetical* criticism [are] concerned" and a critique of
Wordsworth's theory of poetic diction. This work was ready by September 17, 1815,
but the *Biographia Literaria*, in two volumes, was not published until July 1817. The
delay was caused by a series of miscalculations by his printer, which forced Coleridge
to add 150 pages of miscellaneous materials to pad out the length of the second
volume.

Coleridge had been planning a detailed critique of Wordsworth's theory of poetic
diction ever since 1802, when he had detected "a radical difference in our theoretical
opinions respecting poetry." In the selection from chapter 17, Coleridge agrees with
Wordsworth's general aim of reforming the artifices of current poetic diction, but he
sharply denies Wordsworth's claim that there is no essential difference between the
language of poetry and the language spoken by people in real life. The other selections printed here are devoted mainly to the central principle of Coleridge's own critical theory, the distinction between the mechanical "fancy" and the organic imagination,
which is tersely summarized in the conclusion to chapter 13. The definition of poetry
at the end of chapter 14 develops at greater length the nature of the "synthetic and
magical power . . . of imagination," which, for Coleridge, has the capacity to dissolve
the divisions (between, for instance, the perceiving human subject and his or her
objects of perception) that characterize human beings' fallen state.

For additional selections from *Biographia Literaria,* see "The Gothic and the
Development of a Mass Readership," p. 536, and "'Self-constituted judge of poesy':
Reviewer vs. Poet in the Romantic Period" in the NAEL Archive.

---

1. Written by Coleridge the year before he died.
One version that he sent in a letter had as a title:
"Epitaph on a Poet little known, yet better known
by the Initials of his name than by the Name

Itself."
2. "For" in the sense of "instead of" [Coleridge's
note].

From Biographia Literaria

From *Chapter 4*

[MR. WORDSWORTH'S EARLIER POEMS]

* * * During the last year of my residence at Cambridge, I became acquainted with Mr. Wordsworth's first publication, entitled *Descriptive Sketches*;[1] and seldom, if ever, was the emergence of an original poetic genius above the literary horizon more evidently announced. In the form, style, and manner of the whole poem, and in the structure of the particular lines and periods, there is a harshness and acerbity connected and combined with words and images all a-glow which might recall those products of the vegetable world, where gorgeous blossoms rise out of the hard and thorny rind and shell within which the rich fruit was elaborating. The language was not only peculiar and strong, but at times knotty and contorted, as by its own impatient strength; while the novelty and struggling crowd of images, acting in conjunction with the difficulties of the style, demanded always a greater closeness of attention than poetry (at all events than descriptive poetry) has a right to claim. It not seldom therefore justified the complaint of obscurity. In the following extract I have sometimes fancied that I saw an emblem of the poem itself and of the author's genius as it was then displayed:

'Tis storm; and hid in mist from hour to hour,
All day the floods a deepening murmur pour;
The sky is veiled, and every cheerful sight:
Dark is the region as with coming night;
And yet what frequent bursts of overpowering light!
Triumphant on the bosom of the storm,
Glances the fire-clad eagle's wheeling form;
Eastward, in long perspective glittering, shine
The wood-crowned cliffs that o'er the lake recline;
Wide o'er the Alps a hundred streams unfold,
At once to pillars turned that flame with gold;
Behind his sail the peasant strives to shun
The West, that burns like one dilated sun,
Where in a mighty crucible expire
The mountains, glowing hot, like coals of fire.[2]

The poetic Psyche, in its process to full development, undergoes as many changes as its Greek namesake, the butterfly.[3] And it is remarkable how soon genius clears and purifies itself from the faults and errors of its earliest products; faults which, in its earliest compositions, are the more obtrusive and confluent because, as heterogeneous elements which had only a temporary use, they constitute the very *ferment* by which themselves are carried off. Or we may compare them to some diseases, which must work on the humors and be thrown out on the surface in order to secure the patient from their future recurrence. I was in my twenty-fourth year when I had the happiness of know-

---

1. Published 1793, the year before Coleridge left Cambridge; a long descriptive-meditative poem in closed couplets, recounting Wordsworth's walking tour in the Alps in 1790. Wordsworth describes the same tour in *The Prelude*, book 6.
2. *Descriptive Sketches* (1815 version), lines 332ff.
3. In Greek, Psyche is the common name for the soul and the butterfly [Coleridge's note].

ing Mr. Wordsworth personally;[4] and, while memory lasts, I shall hardly forget the sudden effect produced on my mind by his recitation of a manuscript poem which still remains unpublished, but of which the stanza and tone of style were the same as those of *The Female Vagrant* as originally printed in the first volume of the *Lyrical Ballads*.[5] There was here no mark of strained thought or forced diction, no crowd or turbulence of imagery, and, as the poet hath himself well described in his lines on revisiting the Wye,[6] manly reflection and human associations had given both variety and an additional interest to natural objects which in the passion and appetite of the first love they had seemed to him neither to need or permit. The occasional obscurities, which had risen from an imperfect control over the resources of his native language, had almost wholly disappeared, together with that worse defect of arbitrary and illogical phrases, at once hackneyed and fantastic, which hold so distinguished a place in the *technique* of ordinary poetry and will, more or less, alloy the earlier poems of the truest genius, unless the attention has been specifically directed to their worthlessness and incongruity. I did not perceive anything particular in the mere style of the poem alluded to during its recitation, except indeed such difference as was not separable from the thought and manner; and the Spenserian stanza which always, more or less, recalls to the reader's mind Spenser's own style, would doubtless have authorized in my then opinion a more frequent descent to the phrases of ordinary life than could, without an ill effect, have been hazarded in the heroic couplet. It was not however the freedom from false taste, whether as to common defects or to those more properly his own, which made so unusual an impression on my feelings immediately, and subsequently on my judgment. It was the union of deep feeling with profound thought; the fine balance of truth in observing with the imaginative faculty in modifying the objects observed; and above all the original gift of spreading the tone, the *atmosphere*, and with it the depth and height of the ideal world, around forms, incidents, and situations of which, for the common view, custom had bedimmed all the luster, had dried up the sparkle and the dewdrops. "To find no contradiction in the union of old and new, to contemplate the Ancient of Days and all his works with feelings as fresh as if all had then sprang forth at the first creative fiat,[7] characterizes the mind that feels the riddle of the world and may help to unravel it. To carry on the feelings of childhood into the powers of manhood; to combine the child's sense of wonder and novelty with the appearances which every day for perhaps forty years had rendered familiar;

> With sun and moon and stars throughout the year,
> And man and woman;[8]

this is the character and privilege of genius, and one of the marks which distinguish genius from talents. And therefore it is the prime merit of genius, and its most unequivocal mode of manifestation, so to represent familiar objects as to awaken in the minds of others a kindred feeling concerning them, and that freshness of sensation which is the constant accompaniment of mental no less than of bodily convalescence. Who has not a thousand

4. The meeting occurred in September 1795.
5. *Salisbury Plain* (1793–94), which was left in manuscript until Wordsworth published a revised version in 1842 under the title "Guilt and Sorrow." An excerpt from *Salisbury Plain* was printed as "The Female Vagrant," in *Lyrical Ballads*

(1798).
6. Wordsworth's "Tintern Abbey," lines 76ff.
7. The first divine command: "Let there be light."
8. Altered from Milton's sonnet "To Mr. Cyriack Skinner upon His Blindness."

times seen snow fall on water? Who has not watched it with a new feeling from the time that he has read Burns' comparison of sensual pleasure

> To snow that falls upon a river
> A moment white—then gone forever![9]

In poems, equally as in philosophic disquisitions, genius produces the strongest impressions of novelty while it rescues the most admitted truths from the impotence caused by the very circumstance of their universal admission. Truths of all others the most awful and mysterious, yet being at the same time of universal interest, are too often considered as *so* true, that they lose all the life and efficiency of truth and lie bedridden in the dormitory of the soul side by side with the most despised and exploded errors." *The Friend*, p. 76, no. 5.[1]

[ON FANCY AND IMAGINATION—THE INVESTIGATION OF THE DISTINCTION IMPORTANT TO THE FINE ARTS]

This excellence, which in all Mr. Wordsworth's writings is more or less predominant and which constitutes the character of his mind, I no sooner felt than I sought to understand. Repeated meditations led me first to suspect (and a more intimate analysis of the human faculties, their appropriate marks, functions, and effects, matured my conjecture into full conviction) that fancy and imagination were two distinct and widely different faculties, instead of being, according to the general belief, either two names with one meaning, or at furthest the lower and higher degree of one and the same power. It is not, I own, easy to conceive a more apposite translation of the Greek *phantasia* than the Latin *imaginatio*; but it is equally true that in all societies there exists an instinct of growth, a certain collective unconscious good sense working progressively to desynonymize those words originally of the same meaning which the conflux of dialects had supplied to the more homogeneous languages, as the Greek and German: and which the same cause, joined with accidents of translation from original works of different countries, occasion in mixed languages like our own. The first and most important point to be proved is, that two conceptions perfectly distinct are confused under one and the same word, and (this done) to appropriate that word exclusively to one meaning, and the synonym (should there be one) to the other. But if (as will be often the case in the arts and sciences) no synonym exists, we must either invent or borrow a word. In the present instance the appropriation had already begun and been legitimated in the derivative adjective: Milton had a highly *imaginative*, Cowley a very *fanciful*, mind. If therefore I should succeed in establishing the actual existence of two faculties generally different, the nomenclature would be at once determined. To the faculty by which I had characterized Milton we should confine the term *imagination*; while the other would be contradistinguished as *fancy*. Now were it once fully ascertained that this division is no less grounded in nature than that of delirium from mania, or Otway's

> Lutes, lobsters, seas of milk, and ships of amber,[2]

9. Altered from Burns's "Tam o' Shanter," lines 61–62.
1. A periodical published by Coleridge (1809–10).

2. Thomas Otway, in *Venice Preserved* (1682), wrote "laurels" in place of "lobsters" (5.2.151).

from Shakespeare's

What! have his daughters brought him to this pass?[3]

or from the preceding apostrophe to the elements, the theory of the fine arts and of poetry in particular could not, I thought, but derive some additional and important light. It would in its immediate effects furnish a torch of guidance to the philosophical critic, and ultimately to the poet himself. In energetic minds truth soon changes by domestication into power; and from directing in the discrimination and appraisal of the product becomes influencive in the production. To admire on principle is the only way to imitate without loss of originality. * * *

From *Chapter 13*

[ON THE IMAGINATION, OR ESEMPLASTIC[4] POWER]

* * * The IMAGINATION, then, I consider either as primary, or secondary. The primary IMAGINATION I hold to be the living power and prime agent of all human perception, and as a repetition in the finite mind of the eternal act of creation in the infinite I AM. The secondary I consider as an echo of the former, coexisting with the conscious will, yet still as identical with the primary in the *kind* of its agency, and differing only in *degree*, and in the *mode* of its operation. It dissolves, diffuses, dissipates, in order to recreate; or where this process is rendered impossible, yet still, at all events, it struggles to idealize and to unify. It is essentially *vital*, even as all objects (*as* objects) are essentially fixed and dead.

FANCY, on the contrary, has no other counters to play with but fixities and definites. The fancy is indeed no other than a mode of memory emancipated from the order of time and space; and blended with, and modified by that empirical phenomenon of the will which we express by the word CHOICE. But equally with the ordinary memory it must receive all its materials ready made from the law of association.[5] * * *

Chapter 14

OCCASION OF THE *LYRICAL BALLADS*, AND THE OBJECTS ORIGINALLY PROPOSED—PREFACE TO THE SECOND EDITION—THE ENSUING CONTROVERSY, ITS CAUSES AND ACRIMONY—PHILOSOPHIC DEFINITIONS OF A POEM AND POETRY WITH SCHOLIA.[6]

During the first year that Mr. Wordsworth and I were neighbours,[7] our conversations turned frequently on the two cardinal points of poetry, the power of exciting the sympathy of the reader by a faithful adherence to the truth

---

3. *King Lear* 3.4.59.
4. Coleridge coined this word and used it to mean "molding into unity."
5. Coleridge conceives God's creation to be a continuing process, which has an analogy in the creative perception ("primary imagination") of all human minds. The creative process is repeated, or "echoed," on still a third level, by the "secondary imagination" of the poet, which dissolves the products of primary perception to shape them

into a new and unified creation—the imaginative passage or poem. The "fancy," on the other hand, can only manipulate "fixities and definites" that, linked by association, come to it ready-made from perception.
6. Additional remarks, after a philosophic demonstration.
7. At Nether Stowey and Alfoxden, Somerset, in 1797.

of nature, and the power of giving the interest of novelty by the modifying colors of imagination.[8] The sudden charm which accidents of light and shade, which moonlight or sunset diffused over a known and familiar landscape, appeared to represent the practicability of combining both. These are the poetry of nature. The thought suggested itself (to which of us I do not recollect) that a series of poems might be composed of two sorts. In the one, the incidents and agents were to be, in part at least, supernatural; and the excellence aimed at was to consist in the interesting of the affections by the dramatic truth of such emotions as would naturally accompany such situations, supposing them real. And real in *this* sense they have been to every human being who, from whatever source of delusion, has at any time believed himself under supernatural agency. For the second class, subjects were to be chosen from ordinary life; the characters and incidents were to be such as will be found in every village and its vicinity where there is a meditative and feeling mind to seek after them, or to notice them when they present themselves.

In this idea originated the plan of the *Lyrical Ballads*; in which it was agreed that my endeavours should be directed to persons and characters supernatural, or at least romantic; yet so as to transfer from our inward nature a human interest and a semblance of truth sufficient to procure for these shadows of imagination that willing suspension of disbelief for the moment, which constitutes poetic faith. Mr. Wordsworth, on the other hand, was to propose to himself as his object to give the charm of novelty to things of every day, and to excite a feeling analogous to the supernatural, by awakening the mind's attention from the lethargy of custom and directing it to the loveliness and the wonders of the world before us; an inexhaustible treasure, but for which, in consequence of the film of familiarity and selfish solicitude, we have eyes yet see not, ears that hear not, and hearts that neither feel nor understand.[9]

With this view I wrote *The Ancient Mariner*, and was preparing, among other poems, *The Dark Ladie*, and the *Christabel*, in which I should have more nearly realized my ideal than I had done in my first attempt. But Mr. Wordsworth's industry had proved so much more successful and the number of his poems so much greater, that my compositions, instead of forming a balance, appeared rather an interpolation of heterogeneous matter.[1] Mr. Wordsworth added two or three poems written in his own character, in the impassioned, lofty, and sustained diction which is characteristic of his genius. In this form the *Lyrical Ballads* were published; and were presented by him, as an *experiment*,[2] whether subjects which from their nature rejected the usual ornaments and extra-colloquial style of poems in general might not be so managed in the language of ordinary life as to produce the pleasurable interest which it is the peculiar business of poetry to impart. To the second edition[3] he added a preface of considerable length; in which, notwithstanding some passages of apparently a contrary import, he was understood to contend for the extension of this style to poetry of all kinds, and to reject as vicious and indefensible all phrases and forms of style that were not included in what he

8. Cf. Wordsworth's account in his Preface to *Lyrical Ballads* (p. 304).
9. Cf. Isaiah 6.9–10.
1. The first edition of *Lyrical Ballads*, published anonymously in 1798, contained nineteen poems by Wordsworth, four by Coleridge.
2. *Experiments* was the word used by Wordsworth in his *Advertisement* to the first edition.
3. Published in 1800.

(unfortunately, I think, adopting an equivocal expression) called the language of *real* life. From this preface, prefixed to poems in which it was impossible to deny the presence of original genius, however mistaken its direction might be deemed, arose the whole long-continued controversy.[4] For from the conjunction of perceived power with supposed heresy I explain the inveteracy[5] and in some instances, I grieve to say, the acrimonious passions with which the controversy has been conducted by the assailants.

Had Mr. Wordsworth's poems been the silly, the childish things which they were for a long time described as being; had they been really distinguished from the compositions of other poets merely by meanness[6] of language and inanity of thought; had they indeed contained nothing more than what is found in the parodies and pretended imitations of them; they must have sunk at once, a dead weight, into the slough of oblivion, and have dragged the preface along with them. But year after year increased the number of Mr. Wordsworth's admirers. They were found too not in the lower classes of the reading public, but chiefly among young men of strong sensibility and meditative minds; and their admiration (inflamed perhaps in some degree by opposition) was distinguished by its intensity, I might almost say, by its *religious* fervor. These facts, and the intellectual energy of the author, which was more or less consciously felt where it was outwardly and even boisterously denied, meeting with sentiments of aversion to his opinions and of alarm at their consequences, produced an eddy of criticism which would of itself have borne up the poems by the violence with which it whirled them round and round. With many parts of this preface, in the sense attributed to them and which the words undoubtedly seem to authorize, I never concurred; but, on the contrary objected to them as erroneous in principle, and as contradictory (in appearance at least) both to other parts of the same preface and to the author's own practice in the greater number of the poems themselves. Mr. Wordsworth in his recent collection[7] has, I find, degraded this prefatory disquisition to the end of his second volume, to be read or not at the reader's choice. But he has not, as far as I can discover, announced any change in his poetic creed. At all events, considering it as the source of a controversy in which I have been honored more than I deserve by the frequent conjunction of my name with his, I think it expedient to declare once for all in what points I coincide with his opinions, and in what points I altogether differ. But in order to render myself intelligible I must previously, in as few words as possible, explain my ideas, first, of a POEM; and secondly, of POETRY itself, in *kind* and in *essence*.

The office of philosophical *disquisition* consists in just *distinction;* while it is the privilege of the philosopher to preserve himself constantly aware that distinction is not division. In order to obtain adequate notions of any truth, we must intellectually separate its distinguishable parts; and this is the technical of philosophy. But having so done, we must then restore them in our conceptions to the unity in which they actually coexist; and this is the *result* of philosophy. A poem contains the same elements as a prose composition; the difference therefore must consist in a different combination of them, in consequence of a different object proposed. According to the

---

4. The controversy over Wordsworth's theory and poetical practice in the literary reviews of the day.

5. Deep-rooted prejudice.
6. Vulgarity.
7. *Poems*, 2 vols., 1815.

difference of the object will be the difference of the combination. It is possible that the object may be merely to facilitate the recollection of any given facts or observations by artificial arrangement; and the composition will be a poem, merely because it is distinguished from prose by meter, or by rhyme, or by both conjointly. In this, the lowest sense, a man might attribute the name of a poem to the well-known enumeration of the days in the several months:

> Thirty days hath September,
> April, June, and November, etc.

and others of the same class and purpose. And as a particular pleasure is found in anticipating the recurrence of sounds and quantities, all compositions that have this charm superadded, whatever be their contents, *may* be entitled poems.

So much for the superficial *form*. A difference of object and contents supplies an additional ground of distinction. The immediate purpose may be the communication of truths; either of truth absolute and demonstrable, as in works of science; or of facts experienced and recorded, as in history. Pleasure, and that of the highest and most permanent kind, may *result* from the *attainment* of the end; but it is not itself the immediate end. In other works the communication of pleasure may be the immediate purpose; and though truth, either moral or intellectual, ought to be the *ultimate* end, yet this will distinguish the character of the author, not the class to which the work belongs. Blessed indeed is that state of society in which the immediate purpose would be baffled by the perversion of the proper ultimate end; in which no charm of diction or imagery could exempt the Bathyllus even of an Anacreon, or the Alexis of Virgil,[8] from disgust and aversion!

But the communication of pleasure may be the immediate object of a work not metrically composed; and that object may have been in a high degree attained, as in novels and romances. Would then the mere superaddition of meter, with or without rhyme, entitle *these* to the name of poems? The answer is that nothing can permanently please which does not contain in itself the reason why it is so, and not otherwise. If meter be superadded, all other parts must be made consonant with it. They must be such as to justify the perpetual and distinct attention to each part which an exact correspondent recurrence of accent and sound are calculated to excite. The final definition then, so deduced, may be thus worded. A poem is that species of composition which is opposed to works of science by proposing for its *immediate object* pleasure, not truth; and from all other species (having *this* object in common with it) it is discriminated by proposing to itself such delight from the *whole* as is compatible with a distinct gratification from each component *part*.

Controversy is not seldom excited in consequence of the disputants attaching each a different meaning to the same word; and in few instances has this been more striking than in disputes concerning the present subject. If a man chooses to call every composition a poem which is rhyme, or measure, or both, I must leave his opinion uncontroverted. The distinction is at

---

8. The reference is to poems of same-sex love. Bathyllus was a beautiful boy praised by Anacreon, a Greek lyric poet (ca. 560–475 B.C.E.); Alexis was a young man loved by the shepherd Corydon in Virgil's *Eclogue* 2.

least competent to characterize the writer's intention. If it were subjoined that the whole is likewise entertaining or affecting as a tale or as a series of interesting reflections, I of course admit this as another fit ingredient of a poem and an additional merit. But if the definition sought for be that of a *legitimate* poem, I answer it must be one the parts of which mutually support and explain each other; all in their proportion harmonizing with, and supporting the purpose and known influences of metrical arrangement. The philosophic critics of all ages coincide with the ultimate judgment of all countries in equally denying the praises of a just poem on the one hand to a series of striking lines or distichs,[9] each of which absorbing the whole attention of the reader to itself disjoins it from its context and makes it a separate whole, instead of a harmonizing part; and on the other hand, to an unsustained composition, from which the reader collects rapidly the general result unattracted by the component parts. The reader should be carried forward, not merely or chiefly by the mechanical impulse of curiosity, or by a restless desire to arrive at the final solution; but by the pleasurable activity of mind excited by the attractions of the journey itself. Like the motion of a serpent, which the Egyptians made the emblem of intellectual power; or like the path of sound through the air; at every step he pauses and half recedes, and from the retrogressive movement collects the force which again carries him onward. *"Praecipitandus est* liber *spiritus,"*[1] says Petronius Arbiter most happily. The epithet *liber* here balances the preceding verb; and it is not easy to conceive more meaning condensed in fewer words.

But if this should be admitted as a satisfactory character of a poem, we have still to seek for a definition of poetry. The writings of Plato, and Bishop Taylor, and the *Theoria Sacra* of Burnet,[2] furnish undeniable proofs that poetry of the highest kind may exist without meter, and even without the contradistinguishing objects of a poem. The first chapter of Isaiah (indeed a very large proportion of the whole book) is poetry in the most emphatic sense; yet it would be not less irrational than strange to assert that pleasure, and not truth, was the immediate object of the prophet. In short, whatever *specific* import we attach to the word poetry, there will be found involved in it, as a necessary consequence, that a poem of any length neither can be, nor ought to be, all poetry. Yet if a harmonious whole is to be produced, the remaining parts must be preserved in *keeping*[3] with the poetry; and this can be no otherwise effected than by such a studied selection and artificial arrangement as will partake of *one*, though not a *peculiar*, property of poetry. And this again can be no other than the property of exciting a more continuous and equal attention than the language of prose aims at, whether colloquial or written.

My own conclusions on the nature of poetry, in the strictest use of the word, have been in part anticipated in the preceding disquisition on the fancy and imagination. What is poetry? is so nearly the same question with, what is a poet? that the answer to the one is involved in the solution of the other. For

---

9. Pairs of lines.
1. "The *free* spirit [of the poet] must be hurled onward." From the *Satyricon,* by the Roman satirist Petronius Arbiter (1st century C.E.).
2. Thomas Burnet (1635?–1715), author of *The Sacred Theory of the Earth.* Bishop Jeremy Taylor (1613–1667), author of *Holy Living* and *Holy*

Dying. Coleridge greatly admired the elaborate and sonorous prose of both these writers. He took from a work by Burnet the Latin motto for *The Rime of the Ancient Mariner.*
3. A term from the theory of painting for the maintenance of the harmony of a composition.

it is a distinction resulting from the poetic genius itself, which sustains and modifies the images, thoughts, and emotions of the poet's own mind.

The poet, described in *ideal* perfection, brings the whole soul of man into activity, with the subordination of its faculties to each other, according to their relative worth and dignity. He diffuses a tone and spirit of unity that blends and (as it were) *fuses*, each into each, by that synthetic and magical power to which we have exclusively appropriated the name of imagination. This power, first put in action by the will and understanding and retained under their irremissive,[4] though gentle and unnoticed, control (*laxis effertur habenis*)[5] reveals itself in the balance or reconciliation of opposite or discordant qualities:[6] of sameness, with difference; of the general, with the concrete; the idea, with the image; the individual, with the representative; the sense of novelty and freshness, with old and familiar objects; a more than usual state of emotion, with more than usual order; judgment ever awake and steady self-possession, with enthusiasm and feeling profound or vehement; and while it blends and harmonizes the natural and the artificial, still subordinates art to nature; the manner to the matter; and our admiration of the poet to our sympathy with the poetry. "Doubtless," as Sir John Davies observes of the soul (and his words may with slight alteration be applied, and even more appropriately, to the poetic IMAGINATION):

> Doubtless this could not be, but that she turns
>   Bodies to spirit by sublimation strange,
> As fire converts to fire the things it burns,
>   As we our food into our nature change.
>
> From their gross matter she abstracts their forms,
>   And draws a kind of quintessence from things;
> Which to her proper nature she transforms,
>   To bear them light on her celestial wings.
>
> Thus does she, when from individual states
>   She doth abstract the universal kinds;
> Which then reclothed in divers names and fates
>   Steal access through our senses to our minds.[7]

Finally, GOOD SENSE is the BODY of poetic genius, FANCY its DRAPERY,[8] MOTION its LIFE, and IMAGINATION the SOUL that is everywhere, and in each; and forms all into one graceful and intelligent whole.

From *Chapter 17*

[EXAMINATION OF THE TENETS PECULIAR TO MR. WORDSWORTH]

As far then as Mr. Wordsworth in his preface contended, and most ably contended, for a reformation in our poetic diction, as far as he has evinced the truth of passion, and the *dramatic* propriety of those figures and metaphors in the original poets which, stripped of their justifying reasons and

4. Continuous.
5. Driven with loosened reins (Latin).
6. Here Coleridge introduces the concept, which became central to the American New Critics of the mid-20th century, that the best poetry incorporates and reconciles opposite or discordant elements.
7. Adapted from John Davies's *Nosce Teipsum* ("Know Thyself"), a philosophical poem (1599).
8. Clothing.

converted into mere artifices of connection or ornament, constitute the characteristic falsity in the poetic style of the moderns; and as far as he has, with equal acuteness and clearness, pointed out the process by which this change was effected and the resemblances between that state into which the reader's mind is thrown by the pleasurable confusion of thought from an unaccustomed train of words and images and that state which is induced by the natural language of impassioned feeling, he undertook a useful task and deserves all praise, both for the attempt and for the execution. The provocations to this remonstrance in behalf of truth and nature were still of perpetual recurrence before and after the publication of this preface. * * *

My own differences from certain supposed parts of Mr. Wordsworth's theory ground themselves on the assumption that his words had been rightly interpreted, as purporting that the proper diction for poetry in general consists altogether in a language taken, with due exceptions, from the mouths of men in real life, a language which actually constitutes the natural conversation of men under the influence of natural feelings.[9] My objection is, first, that in *any* sense this rule is applicable only to *certain* classes of poetry; secondly, that even to these classes it is not applicable, except in such a sense as hath never by anyone (as far as I know or have read) been denied or doubted; and, lastly, that as far as, and in that degree in which it is *practicable*, yet as a *rule* it is useless, if not injurious, and therefore either need not or ought not to be practiced. * * *

[RUSTIC LIFE (ABOVE ALL, *LOW* AND RUSTIC LIFE) ESPECIALLY UNFAVORABLE
TO THE FORMATION OF A HUMAN DICTION—THE BEST PARTS OF LANGUAGE
THE PRODUCTS OF PHILOSOPHERS, NOT CLOWNS[1] OR SHEPHERDS]

As little can I agree with the assertion that from the objects with which the rustic hourly communicates the best part of language is formed. For first, if to communicate with an object implies such an acquaintance with it, as renders it capable of being discriminately reflected on; the distinct knowledge of an uneducated rustic would furnish a very scanty vocabulary. The few things, and modes of action, requisite for his bodily conveniences, would alone be individualized; while all the rest of nature would be expressed by a small number of confused general terms. Secondly, I deny that the words and combinations of words derived from the objects, with which the rustic is familiar, whether with distinct or confused knowledge, can be justly said to form the *best* part of language. It is more than probable that many classes of the brute creation possess discriminating sounds, by which they can convey to each other notices of such objects as concern their food, shelter, or safety. Yet we hesitate to call the aggregate of such sounds a language, otherwise than metaphorically. The best part of human language, properly so called, is derived from reflection on the acts of the mind itself. It is formed by a voluntary appropriation of fixed symbols to internal acts, to processes and results of imagination, the greater part of which have no place in the consciousness of uneducated man; though in civilized society, by imitation and passive remembrance of what they hear from their religious instructors and other superiors, the most uneducated share in the harvest which they neither sowed or reaped. * * *

9. Wordsworth's Preface to *Lyrical Ballads* (1800, 1802): "A selection of the real language of men in a state of vivid sensation. . . . Low and rustic life was generally chosen. . . . The language, too, of these men is adopted."
1. Rustic people.

[THE LANGUAGE OF MILTON AS MUCH THE LANGUAGE OF *REAL* LIFE, YEA,
INCOMPARABLY MORE SO THAN THAT OF THE COTTAGER]

Here let me be permitted to remind the reader that the positions which I
controvert are contained in the sentences—"a selection of the REAL language
of men"; "the language of these men (i.e., men in low and rustic life) I propose
to myself to imitate, and as far as possible to adopt the very language of men."
"Between the language of prose and that of metrical composition there neither is, nor can be any essential difference." It is against these exclusively that
my opposition is directed.

I object, in the very first instance, to an equivocation in the use of the word
"real." Every man's language varies according to the extent of his knowledge,
the activity of his faculties, and the depth or quickness of his feelings. Every
man's language has, first, its *individualities;* secondly, the common properties
of the *class* to which he belongs; and thirdly, words and phrases of *universal*
use. The language of Hooker, Bacon, Bishop Taylor, and Burke[2] differs from
the common language of the learned class only by the superior number and
novelty of the thoughts and relations which they had to convey. The language
of Algernon Sidney[3] differs not at all from that which every well-educated
gentleman would wish to write, and (with due allowances for the undeliber-
ateness and less connected train of thinking natural and proper to conversation) such as he would wish to talk. Neither one nor the other differ half
as much from the general language of cultivated society as the language of
Mr. Wordsworth's homeliest composition differs from that of a common
peasant. For "real" therefore we must substitute *ordinary*, or *lingua communis*.[4] And this, we have proved, is no more to be found in the phraseology of
low and rustic life than in that of any other class. Omit the peculiarities of
each, and the result of course must be common to all. And assuredly the
omissions and changes to be made in the language of rustics before it could
be transferred to any species of poem, except the drama or other professed
imitation, are at least as numerous and weighty as would be required
in adapting to the same purpose the ordinary language of tradesmen and
manufacturers. Not to mention that the language so highly extolled by Mr.
Wordsworth varies in every county, nay, in every village, according to the
accidental character of the clergyman, the existence or nonexistence of
schools; or even, perhaps, as the exciseman, publican, or barber happen to
be, or not to be, zealous politicians and readers of the weekly newspaper *pro
bono publico*.[5] Anterior to cultivation the *lingua communis* of every country,
as Dante has well observed, exists every where in parts and no where as a
whole.[6]

Neither is the case rendered at all more tenable by the addition of the words
"in a state of excitement."[7] For the nature of a man's words, when he is strongly
affected by joy, grief, or anger, must necessarily depend on the number and

---

2. Richard Hooker (1554–1600), author of *The
Laws of Ecclesiastical Polity*, Francis Bacon
(1561–1626), essayist and philosopher, and Jeremy Taylor were all, together with the late-18th-
century politician and opponent of the French
Revolution Edmund Burke (1729–1797), lauded
for their prose styles.
3. Republican soldier and statesman (1622–
1683), author of *Discourses Concerning Government*, executed for his part in the Rye House Plot

to assassinate Charles II.
4. The common language (Latin).
5. For the public welfare (Latin).
6. In *De Vulgari Eloquentia* ("On the Speech of
the people") Dante discusses—and affirms—the
fitness for poetry of the unlocalized Italian vernacular.
7. Wordsworth: "the manner in which we associate ideas in a state of excitement."

quality of the general truths, conceptions, and images, and of the words expressing them, with which his mind had been previously stored. For the property of passion is not to *create*, but to set in increased activity. At least, whatever new connections of thoughts or images, or (which is equally, if not more than equally, the appropriate effect of strong excitement) whatever generalizations of truth or experience the heat of passion may produce, yet the terms of their conveyance must have pre-existed in his former conversations, and are only collected and crowded together by the unusual stimulation. It is indeed very possible to adopt in a poem the unmeaning repetitions, habitual phrases, and other blank counters which an unfurnished or confused understanding interposes at short intervals in order to keep hold of his subject which is still slipping from him, and to give him time for recollection; or in mere aid of vacancy, as in the scanty companies of a country stage the same player pops backwards and forwards, in order to prevent the appearance of empty spaces, in the procession of *Macbeth* or *Henry VIIIth*. But what assistance to the poet or ornament to the poem these can supply, I am at a loss to conjecture. Nothing assuredly can differ either in origin or in mode more widely from the apparent tautologies of intense and turbulent feeling in which the passion is greater and of longer endurance than to be exhausted or satisfied by a single representation of the image or incident exciting it. Such repetitions I admit to be a beauty of the highest kind; as illustrated by Mr. Wordsworth himself from the song of Deborah. "At her feet he bowed, he fell, he lay down; at her feet he bowed, he fell; where he bowed, there he fell down dead."[8]

1815   1817

From Lectures on Shakespeare[1]

[FANCY AND IMAGINATION IN SHAKESPEARE'S POETRY]

In the preceding lecture we have examined with what armor clothed and with what titles authorized Shakespeare came forward as a poet to demand the throne of fame as the dramatic poet of England; we have now to observe and retrace the excellencies which compelled even his contemporaries to seat him on that throne, although there were giants in those days contending for the same honor. Hereafter we shall endeavor to make out the title of the English drama, as created by and existing in Shakespeare, and its right to the supremacy of dramatic excellence in general. I have endeavored to prove that he had shown himself a *poet*, previously to his appearance as a dramatic poet—and that had no *Lear*, no *Othello*, no *Henry the Fourth*, no *Twelfth Night* appeared, we must have admitted that Shakespeare possessed the chief if not all the requisites of a poet—namely, deep feeling and exqui-

8. Judges 5.27. Cited by Wordsworth in a note to *The Thorn* as an example of the natural repetitiousness of "impassioned feelings."
1. Although Coleridge's series of public lectures on Shakespeare and other poets contained much of his best criticism, he published none of this material, leaving only fragmentary remains of his lectures in notebooks, scraps of manuscript, and notes written in the margins of books. The fol-

lowing selections, which develop some of the principal ideas presented in *Biographia Literaria*, reproduce the text of T. M. Raysor's edition—based on Coleridge's manuscripts and on contemporary reports—of *Coleridge's Shakespearean Criticism* (1930); four minor corrections in wording have been taken from R. A. Foakes's edition of Coleridge's *Lectures 1808–1819: On Literature* (1987).

site sense of beauty, both as exhibited to the eye in combinations of form, and to the ear in sweet and appropriate melody (with the exception of Spenser he is [the sweetest of English poets]); that these feelings were under the command of *his own will*—that in his very first productions he projected his mind out of his own particular being, and felt and made others feel, on subjects [in] no way connected with himself, except by force of contemplation, and that sublime faculty, by which a great mind becomes that which it meditates on. To this we are to add the affectionate love of nature and natural objects, without which no man could have observed so steadily, or painted so truly and passionately the very minutest beauties of the external world. Next, we have shown that he possessed fancy, considered as the faculty of bringing together images dissimilar in the main by some one point or more of likeness distinguished.[2]

> Full gently now she takes him by the hand,
> A lily prisoned in a jail of snow,
> Or ivory in an alabaster band—
> So white a friend engirts so white a foe.

Still mounting, we find undoubted proof in his mind of imagination, or the power by which one image or feeling is made to modify many others and by a sort of *fusion to force many into one*—that which after showed itself in such might and energy in *Lear*, where the deep anguish of a father spreads the feeling of ingratitude and cruelty over the very elements of heaven. Various are the workings of this greatest faculty of the human mind—both passionate and tranquil. In its tranquil and purely pleasurable operation, it acts chiefly by producing out of many things, as they would have appeared in the description of an ordinary mind, described slowly and in unimpassioned succession, a oneness, even as nature, the greatest of poets, acts upon us when we open our eyes upon an extended prospect. Thus the flight of Adonis from the enamored goddess in the dusk of evening—

> Look how a bright star shooteth from the sky—
> So glides he in the night from Venus' eye.[3]

How many images and feelings are here brought together without effort and without discord—the beauty of Adonis—the rapidity of his flight—the yearning yet hopelessness of the enamored gazer—and a shadowy ideal character thrown over the whole.—Or it acts by impressing the stamp of humanity, of human feeling, over inanimate objects * * *

> Lo, here the gentle lark, weary of rest,
> From his moist cabinet mounts up on high
> And wakes the morning, from whose silver breast
> The sun ariseth in his majesty;
>   Who doth the world so gloriously behold
>   That cedar tops and hills seem burnished gold.[4]

And lastly, which belongs only to a great poet, the power of so carrying on the eye of the reader as to make him almost lose the consciousness of words—to make him *see* everything—and this without exciting any painful or laborious

---

2. Coleridge here applies the distinction between fancy and imagination presented in *Biographia Literaria*, chap. 13, to a passage from the narra- tive poem *Venus and Adonis* (lines 361–64).
3. *Venus and Adonis*, lines 815–16.
4. *Venus and Adonis*, lines 853–58.

attention, without any *anatomy* of description (a fault not uncommon in descriptive poetry) but with the sweetness and easy movement of nature.

Lastly, he previously to his dramas, gave proof of a most profound, energetic, and philosophical mind, without which he might have been a very delightful poet, but not the great dramatic poet. * * * But chance and his powerful instinct combined to lead him to his proper province—in the conquest of which we are to consider both the difficulties that opposed him, and the advantages.

1808   1930

[MECHANIC VS. ORGANIC FORM][5]

The subject of the present lecture is no less than a question submitted to your understandings, emancipated from national prejudice: Are the plays of Shakespeare works of rude uncultivated genius, in which the splendor of the parts compensates, if aught can compensate, for the barbarous shapelessness and irregularity of the whole? To which not only the French critics, but even his own English admirers, say [yes]. Or is the form equally admirable with the matter, the judgment of the great poet not less deserving of our wonder than his genius? Or to repeat the question in other words, is Shakespeare a great dramatic poet on account only of those beauties and excellencies which he possesses in common with the ancients, but with diminished claims to our love and honor to the full extent of his difference from them? Or are these very differences additional proofs of poetic wisdom, at once results and symbols of living power as contrasted with lifeless mechanism, of free and rival originality as contradistinguished from servile imitation, or more accurately, [from] a blind copying of effects instead of a true imitation of the essential principles? Imagine not I am about to oppose genius to rules. No! the comparative value of these rules is the very cause to be tried. The spirit of poetry, like all other living powers, must of necessity circumscribe itself by rules, were it only to unite power with beauty. It must embody in order to reveal itself; but a living body is of necessity an organized one—and what is organization but the connection of parts to a whole, so that each part is at once end and means! This is no discovery of criticism; it is a necessity of the human mind—and all nations have felt and obeyed it, in the invention of meter and measured sounds as the vehicle and involucrum[6] of poetry, itself a fellow growth from the same life, even as the bark is to the tree.

No work of true genius dare want its appropriate form; neither indeed is there any danger of this. As it must not, so neither can it, be lawless! For it is even this that constitutes its genius—the power of acting creatively under laws of its own origination. How then comes it that not only single Zoili,[7] but whole nations have combined in unhesitating condemnation of our great dramatist, as a sort of African nature, fertile in beautiful monsters, as a wild

5. Coleridge is opposing the view that because Shakespeare violates the critical "rules" based on classical drama—the unities, for instance—his dramatic successes are marred by his irregularities and reflect the work of an uncultivated genius that operates without artistry or judgment. His argument is based on a distinction between the "mechanical form" central to earlier critical assessments and "organic form." Mechanical form results from imposing a system of preexisting rules on the literary material. Shakespeare's organic form, on the other hand, evolves like a plant by an inner principle and according to the unique laws of its own growth, until it achieves an organic unity.

6. Outer covering of part of a plant.

7. Plural of "Zoilus," who in classical times was the standard example of a bad critic.

heath where islands of fertility look greener from the surrounding waste, where the loveliest plants now shine out among unsightly weeds and now are choked by their parasitic growth, so intertwined that we cannot disentangle the weed without snapping the flower. In this statement I have had no reference to the vulgar abuse of Voltaire,[8] save as far as his charges are coincident with the decisions of his commentators and (so they tell you) his almost idolatrous admirers. The true ground of the mistake, as has been well remarked by a continental critic,[9] lies in the confounding mechanical regularity with organic form. The form is mechanic when on any given material we impress a predetermined form, not necessarily arising out of the properties of the material, as when to a mass of wet clay we give whatever shape we wish it to retain when hardened. The organic form, on the other hand, is innate; it shapes as it develops itself from within, and the fullness of its development is one and the same with the perfection of its outward form. Such is the life, such the form. Nature, the prime genial[1] artist, inexhaustible in diverse powers, is equally inexhaustible in forms. Each exterior is the physiognomy of the being within, its true image reflected and thrown out from the concave mirror. And even such is the appropriate excellence of her chosen poet, of our own Shakespeare, himself a nature humanized, a genial understanding directing self-consciously a power and an implicit wisdom deeper than consciousness.

1812   1930

From The Statesman's Manual

[ON SYMBOL AND ALLEGORY][1]

The histories and political economy[2] of the present and preceding century partake in the general contagion of its mechanic philosophy, and are the *product* of an unenlivened generalizing Understanding. In the Scriptures they are the living *educts*[3] of the Imagination; of that reconciling and mediatory power, which incorporating the Reason in Images of the Sense, and organizing (as it were) the flux of the Senses by the permanence and self-circling energies of the Reason, gives birth to a system of symbols, harmonious in themselves, and consubstantial with the truths, of which they are the *conductors.* These are the Wheels which Ezekiel beheld, when the hand of the Lord was upon him, and he saw visions of God as he sat among the captives by the river of Chebar. *Whithersoever the Spirit was to go, the wheels went, and thither was their spirit to go: for the spirit of the living creature was*

8. The French writer Voltaire (1694–1778) vexed British nationalists with his description of Shakespeare as a barbarous, irregular, and sometimes indecent natural genius.
9. August Wilhelm Schlegel (1767–1845), German critic and literary historian, whose *Lectures on Dramatic Art and Literature* (1808–09) proposed the distinction between mechanical and organic form that Coleridge develops in this lecture.
1. Creative.
1. Coleridge published *The Statesman's Manual, or The Bible the Best Guide to Political Skill and Foresight* in 1816; it was intended to show that the Scriptures, properly interpreted, provide the uni-

versal principles that should guide lawmakers in meeting the political and economic emergencies of that troubled era. His discussion there of symbol, in contradistinction both to allegory and to metaphor, has been often cited and elaborated in treatments of symbolism in poetry. Coleridge's analysis, however, is directed not to poetry but to his view that the persons and events in biblical history signify timeless and universal, as well as particular and local, truths.
2. The increasingly prestigious intellectual discipline of economics.
3. Those things that are educed; i.e., brought forth, evolved.

in the wheels also.[4] The truths and the symbols that represent them move in conjunction and form the living chariot that bears up (for *us*) the throne of the Divine Humanity. Hence, by a derivative, indeed, but not a divided, influence, and though in a secondary yet in more than a metaphorical sense, the Sacred Book is worthily intitled *the* WORD OF GOD. Hence too, its contents present to us the stream of time continuous as Life and a symbol of Eternity, inasmuch as the Past and the Future are virtually contained in the Present. According therefore to our relative position on its banks the Sacred History becomes prophetic, the Sacred Prophecies historical, while the power and substance of both inhere in its Laws, its Promises, and its Comminations.[5] In the Scriptures therefore both Facts and Persons must of necessity have a twofold significance, a past and a future, a temporary and a perpetual, a particular and a universal application. They must be at once Portraits and Ideals.

Eheu! paupertina philosophia in paupertinam religionem ducit:[6]—A hunger-bitten and idea-less philosophy naturally produces a starveling and comfortless religion. It is among the miseries of the present age that it recognizes no medium between *Literal* and *Metaphorical.* Faith is either to be buried in the dead letter,[7] or its name and honors usurped by a counterfeit product of the mechanical understanding, which in the blindness of self-complacency confounds SYMBOLS with ALLEGORIES. Now an Allegory is but a translation of abstract notions into a picture-language which is itself nothing but an abstraction from objects of the senses; the principal being more worthless even than its phantom proxy, both alike unsubstantial, and the former shapeless to boot. On the other hand a Symbol (ὁ ἔστιν ἀεὶ ταυτηγόρικον)[8] is characterized by a translucence of the Special[9] in the Individual or of the General in the Especial or of the Universal in the General. Above all by the translucence of the Eternal through and in the Temporal. It always partakes of the Reality which it renders intelligible; and while it enunciates the whole, abides itself as a living part in that Unity, of which it is the representative. The other are but empty echoes which the fancy arbitrarily associates with apparitions of matter, less beautiful but not less shadowy than the sloping orchard or hillside pasture-field seen in the transparent lake below. Alas! for the flocks that are to be led forth to such pastures! *"It shall even be as when the hungry dreameth, and behold! he eateth; but he waketh and his soul is empty: or as when the thirsty dreameth, and behold he drinketh; but he awaketh and is faint!"*[1] * * *

* * * The fact therefore, that the mind of man in its own primary and constitutional forms represents the laws of nature, is a mystery which of itself should suffice to make us religious:[2] for it is a problem of which God is the only solution, God, the one before all, and of all, and through all!—True natural philosophy is comprised in the study of the science and language of *symbols.* The power delegated to nature is all in every part: and by a symbol I mean, not a metaphor or allegory or any other figure of speech or form of fancy, but an actual and essential part of that, the whole of which it represents. Thus our Lord speaks symbolically when he says that "the eye is the

---

4. Slightly altered from the prophet Ezekiel's vision of the Chariot of God, when he had been "among the captives by the river of Chebar" (Ezekiel 1.1–20). Ezekiel was among the Jews who had been taken into captivity in Babylonia by King Nebuchadnezzar in 597 B.C.E. He was put in a community of Jewish captives at Tel-Abib on the banks of the Chebar canal.
5. Divine threats of punishment for sins.
6. Alas! a poverty-stricken philosophy leads to a poverty-stricken religion (Latin).
7. I.e., the Scriptures read entirely literally.
8. Which is always tautegorical (Greek). Coleridge coined this word and elsewhere defined "*tautegorical*" as "expressing the *same* subject but with a difference."
9. That which pertains to the species.
1. Slightly altered from Isaiah 29.8.
2. This paragraph is from appendix C of *The Statesman's Manual.*

light of the body."[3] The genuine naturalist is a dramatic poet in his own line: and such as our myriad-minded Shakespeare is, compared with the Racines and Metastasios,[4] such and by a similar process of self-transformation would the man be, compared with the Doctors of the mechanic school,[5] who should construct his physiology on the heaven-descended, Know Thyself.[6]

[THE SATANIC HERO][7]

* * * In its state of immanence (or indwelling) in reason and religion, the WILL appears indifferently, as wisdom or as love. two names of the same power, the former more intelligential,[8] the latter more spiritual, the former more frequent in the Old, the latter in the New Testament. But in its utmost abstraction and consequent state of reprobation,[9] the Will becomes satanic pride and rebellious self-idolatry in the relations of the spirit to itself, and remorseless despotism relatively to others; the more hopeless as the more obdurate by its subjugation of sensual impulses, by its superiority to toil and pain and pleasure; in short, by the fearful resolve to find in itself alone the one absolute motive of action, under which all other motives from within and from without must be either subordinated or crushed.

This is the character which Milton has so philosophically as well as sublimely embodied in the Satan of his Paradise Lost. Alas! too often has it been embodied in *real* life! Too often has it given a dark and savage grandeur to the historic page! And wherever it has appeared, under whatever circumstances of time and country, the same ingredients have gone to its composition; and it has been identified by the same attributes. Hope in which there is no Cheerfulness; Steadfastness within and immovable Resolve, with outward Restlessness and whirling Activity; Violence with Guile; Temerity with Cunning; and, as the result of all, Interminableness of Object with perfect Indifference of Means; these are the qualities that have constituted the COMMANDING GENIUS! these are the Marks that have characterized the Masters of Mischief, the Liberticides, and mighty Hunters of Mankind, from NIMROD[1] to NAPOLEON. And from inattention to the possibility of such a character as well as from ignorance of its elements, even men of honest intentions too frequently become fascinated. Nay, whole nations have been so far duped by this want of insight and reflection as to regard with palliative admiration, instead of wonder and abhorrence, the Molochs[2] of human nature, who are indebted, for the far larger portion of their meteoric success, to their total want of principle, and who surpass the generality of their fellow creatures in one act of courage only, that of daring to say with their whole heart, "Evil, be thou my

---

3. Matthew 6.22: "The light of the body is the eye."
4. Pietro Metastasio (1698–1782), a minor Italian poet and author of opera librettos. Jean Racine (1639–1699), the great French author of verse tragedies. Set on dissociating himself from his youthful support for the Revolution, Coleridge enjoyed finding fault with French philosophy and culture. "Naturalist": one who studies natural science.
5. I.e., learned men who hold a mechanistic philosophy of nature.
6. The Roman Juvenal, in *Satires* 11.27 of Horace (Quintas Horatius Flaccus), had said, "From Heaven it descends, 'Know Thyself.'" The original saying, "Know Thyself," was attributed by classical authors to the Delphic oracle.
7. From *The Statesman's Manual*, appendix C. Coleridge analyzes the character of Milton's

Satan and goes on to recognize, and to warn his age against, the appeal of that type of Romantic hero (exemplified above all by the protagonists in Byron's romances and in his drama, *Manfred*), which was in large part modeled on the Satan of *Paradise Lost*.
8. Intellectual.
9. In its theological sense: rejection by God.
1. In Genesis 10.9 Nimrod is described as "a mighty hunter before the Lord." The passage was traditionally interpreted to signify that Nimrod hunted down men, hence that he was the prototype of all tyrants and bloody conquerors.
2. Molochs, monsters of evil. In the Old Testament Moloch is an idol to whom firstborn children are sacrificed. Milton adopted the name for the warlike fallen angel in Satan's company (see *Paradise Lost* 2.43–107).

good!"[3]—All *system* so far is power; and a *systematic* criminal, self-consistent and entire in wickedness, who entrenches villainy within villainy, and barricades crime by crime, has removed a world of obstacles by the mere decision, that he will have no obstacles, but those of force and brute matter.

1816

From Specimens of the Table Talk of Samuel Taylor Coleridge[1]

January 3. 1823.

MATERIALISM.

Either we have an immortal soul, or we have not. If we have not, we are beasts; the first and wisest of beasts, it may be; but still true beasts. We shall only differ in degree, and not in kind; just as the elephant differs from the slug. But by the concession of all the materialists of all the schools, or almost all, we are not of the same kind as beasts—and this also we say from our own consciousness. Therefore, methinks, it must be the possession of a soul within us that makes the difference.

———————

Read the first chapter of Genesis without prejudice, and you will be convinced at once. After the narrative of the creation of the earth and brute animals, Moses seems to pause, and says:—"And God said, Let us make man in *our image*, after *our likeness.*" And in the next chapter, he repeats the narrative:—"And the Lord God formed man of the dust of the ground, and breathed into his nostrils the breath of life;" and then he adds these words,—"*and man became a living soul.*"[2] Materialism will never explain those last words.

* * *

May 1. 1823.

DIFFERENCE BETWEEN STORIES OF DREAMS AND GHOSTS.

There is a great difference in the credibility to be attached to stories of dreams and stories of ghosts. Dreams have nothing in them which are absurd and nonsensical; and, though most of the coincidences may be readily explained by the diseased system of the dreamer, and the great and surprising power of association,[3] yet it is impossible to say whether an inner sense does not really exist in the mind, seldom developed, indeed, but which may have a power of presentiment. All the external senses have their correspondents in the mind; the eye can see an object before it is distinctly apprehended;—why may there not be a corresponding power in the soul? The power of prophecy

---

3. Spoken by Satan, *Paradise Lost* 4.110.
1. Around 1823 Coleridge's nephew Henry Nelson Coleridge conceived the project of preserving for posterity his uncle's wonderful talk, although from the outset he doubted his power to approximate the rushing cataract of his words or the encyclopedic range of the topics on which the "Sage of Highgate" was inclined to improvise. The resulting book, memorializing Henry's visits to his uncle's sickroom at the Gillmans' house, was

published in 1835, a year after Coleridge's death. In the 17th century, the term "table talk" came to designate books collecting fragments of the informal conversation of famous writers. In 1822 William Hazlitt had used the term as a title for a volume of his essays.
2. Genesis 1.26; 2.7.
3. I.e., the mind's automatic association of related ideas.

might have been merely a spiritual excitation of this dormant faculty. Hence you will observe that the Hebrew seers sometimes seem to have required music, as in the instance of Elisha before Jehoram—"But now bring me a minstrel. And it came to pass, when the minstrel played, that the hand of the Lord came upon him."[4] Every thing in nature has a tendency to move in cycles; and it would be a miracle if, out of such myriads of cycles moving concurrently, some coincidences did not take place. No doubt, many such take place in the daytime; but then our senses drive out the remembrance of them, and render the impression hardly felt; but when we sleep, the mind acts without interruption. Terror and the heated imagination will, even in the daytime, create all sorts of features, shapes, and colours out of a simple object possessing none of them in reality.

But ghost stories are absurd. Whenever a real ghost appears,—by which I mean some man or woman dressed up to frighten another,—if the supernatural character of the apparition has been for a moment believed, the effects on the spectator have always been most terrible,—convulsion, idiocy, madness, or even death on the spot. Consider the awful descriptions in the Old Testament of the effects of a spiritual presence on the prophets and seers of the Hebrews; the terror, the exceeding great dread, the utter loss of all animal power. But in our common ghost stories, you always find that the seer, after a most appalling apparition, as you are to believe, is quite well the next day. Perhaps, he may have a headache; but that is the outside of the effect produced. Alston,[5] a man of genius, and the best painter yet produced by America, when he was in England told me an anecdote which confirms what I have been saying. It was, I think, in the university of Cambridge, near Boston, that a certain youth took it into his wise head to endeavour to convert a Tom-Painish companion[6] of his by appearing as a ghost before him. He accordingly dressed himself up in the usual way, having previously extracted the ball from the pistol which always lay near the head of his friend's bed. Upon first awaking, and seeing the apparition, the youth who was to be frightened, A., very coolly looked his companion the ghost in the face, and said, "I know you. This is a good joke; but you see I am not frightened. Now you may vanish!" The ghost stood still. "Come," said A., "that is enough. I shall get angry. Away!" Still the ghost moved not. "By———," ejaculated A., "if you do not in three minutes go away, I'll shoot you." He waited the time, deliberately levelled the pistol, fired, and, with a scream at the immobility of the figure, became convulsed, and afterwards died. The very instant he believed it *to be* a ghost, his human nature fell before it.

* ⸪ *

June 24. 1827.

HAMLET.—PRINCIPLES AND MAXIMS.—LOVE.—.

* * *

Hamlet's character is the prevalence of the abstracting and generalizing habit over the practical. He does not want courage, skill, will, or opportunity;

---

4. Coleridge recalls the episode in 2 Kings 3.15 in which the prophet Elisha, called before King Jehoram, foretells the King's miraculous victory against his enemies.
5. Coleridge was a frequent visitor to the studio of the American painter Washington Allston

(1779–1843), who, following studies at Harvard, had traveled to England to enroll at the Royal Academy of Art.
6. A freethinker in matters of religion, like Thomas Paine in his book *Age of Reason* (1794).

but every incident sets him thinking; and it is curious, and at the same time strictly natural, that Hamlet, who all the play seems reason itself, should be impelled, at last, by mere accident to effect his object. I have a smack of Hamlet myself, if I may say so.

A Maxim is a conclusion upon observation of matters of fact, and is merely retrospective: an Idea, or, if you like, a Principle, carries knowledge within itself, and is prospective. Polonius is a man of maxims. Whilst he is descanting on matters of past experience, as in that excellent speech to Laertes before he sets out on his travels,[7] he is admirable; but when he comes to advise or project, he is a mere dotard. You see Hamlet, as the man of ideas, despises him.

A man of maxims only is like a Cyclops with one eye, and that eye placed in the back of his head.

---

* * *

Love is the admiration and cherishing of the amiable qualities of the beloved person, upon the condition of yourself being the object of their action. The qualities of the sexes correspond. The man's courage is loved by the woman, whose fortitude again is coveted by the man. His vigorous intellect is answered by her infallible tact. Can it be true, what is so constantly affirmed, that there is no sex in souls?—I doubt it, I doubt it exceedingly.

* * *

August 30. 1827.

PAINTING.

Painting is the intermediate somewhat between a thought and a thing.

* * *

July 27. 1830.

THELWALL

John Thelwall had something very good about him. We were once sitting in a beautiful recess, in the Quantocks, when I said to him, "Citizen John, this is a fine place to talk treason in!"—"Nay! Citizen Samuel," replied he, "it is rather a place to make a man forget that there is any necessity for treason!"[8]

---

7. Before his son leaves the court of Denmark to return to France, Polonius makes a long speech of advice to him: *Hamlet* 1.3.55–81.
8. As a spokesman in the 1790s for the radical London Corresponding Society, John Thelwall (1764–1834) won renown and the unwelcome attentions of government spies on the lookout for

sedition. Coleridge is remembering the visit that Thelwall, who was also a poet, paid him at Nether Stowey in July 1797. Thelwall, Coleridge, and William and Dorothy Wordsworth took long walks in the Quantock Hills, talked philosophy, and aroused local suspicions.

Thelwall thought it very unfair to influence a child's mind by inculcating any opinions before it should have come to years of discretion, and be able to choose for itself. I showed him my garden, and told him it was my botanical garden. "How so?" said he, "it is covered with weeds."—"Oh," I replied, "*that* is only because it has not yet come to its age of discretion and choice. The weeds, you see, have taken the liberty to grow, and I thought it unfair in me to prejudice the soil towards roses and strawberries."

* * *

September 22. 1830.

POETRY

A poet ought not to pick nature's pocket: let him borrow, and so borrow as to repay by the very act of borrowing. Examine nature accurately, but write from recollection; and trust more to your imagination than to your memory.

* * *

September 12. 1831.

MR. COLERIDGE'S SYSTEM OF PHILOSOPHY.

My system, if I may venture to give it so fine a name, is the only attempt I know, ever made to reduce all knowledges into harmony. It opposes no other system, but shows what was true in each; and how that which was true in the particular, in each of them became error, *because* it was only half the truth. I have endeavoured to unite the insulated fragments of truth, and therewith to frame a perfect mirror. I show to each system that I fully understand and rightfully appreciate what that system means; but then I lift up that system to a higher point of view, from which I enable it to see its former position, where it was, indeed, but under another light and with different relations;—so that the fragment of truth is not only acknowledged, but explained. Thus the old astronomers discovered and maintained much that was true; but, because they were placed on a false ground, and looked from a wrong point of view, they never did, they never could, discover the truth—that is, the whole truth. As soon as they left the earth, their false centre, and took their stand in the sun, immediately they saw the whole system in its true light, and their former station remaining, but remaining as a part of the prospect. I wish, in short, to connect by a moral *copula* natural history with political history; or, in other words, to make history scientific, and science historical—to take from history its accidentality, and from science its fatalism.

I never from a boy could, under any circumstances, feel the slightest dread of death as such. In all my illnesses I have ever had the most intense desire to be released from this life, unchecked by any but one wish, namely, to be able to finish my work on Philosophy. Not that I have any author's vanity on the subject: God knows that I should be absolutely glad, if I could hear that the thing had already been done before me.

* * *

The Gothic and the Development
of a Mass Readership

S trictly speaking, the Gothic is not "Gothic" at all, but a phenomenon that originates in the late eighteenth century, long after enlightened Europeans put the
era of Gothic cathedrals, chivalry, and superstition behind them—a phenomenon
that begins, in fact, as an embrace of a kind of counterfeit medievalism or as a "medieval revival." As a word they applied to a dark and distant past, Gothic gave Romantic-
period writers and readers a way to describe accounts of terrifying experiences in
ancient castles and ruined abbeys—experiences connected with subterranean dungeons, secret passageways, flickering lamps, screams, moans, ghosts, and graveyards.
In the long run Gothic became a label for the macabre, mysterious, supernatural, and
terrifying, especially the *pleasurably* terrifying, in literature generally; the link that
Romantic-period writers had forged between the Gothic and antiquated spaces was
eventually loosened. Even so, one has only to look, in post-Romantic literature, at the
fiction of the Brontës or Poe, or, in our own not-so-modern culture, at movies or com-
puter games to realize that the pleasures of regression the late-eighteenth-century
Gothic revival provided die hard. Readers continue to seek out opportunities to feel
haunted by pasts that will not let themselves be exorcised.

The Gothic revival appeared in later eighteenth-century English garden design
and architecture before it got into literature. In 1747 Horace Walpole (1717–1797),
younger son of the British prime minister, purchased Strawberry Hill, an estate on
the river Thames near London, and three years later set about remodeling it in what
he called a "Gothick" style. Adding towers, turrets, battlements, arched doors, windows, and ornaments of every description, he created the kind of spurious medieval
architecture that survives today mainly in churches and university buildings. Eventually tourists came from all over to see Strawberry Hill and went home to Gothicize
their own houses.

When the Gothic made its appearance in literature, Walpole was again a trail-
blazer. In 1764 he published *The Castle of Otranto*, a self-styled "Gothic story" featuring a haunted castle, an early, pre-Byronic version of the Byronic hero (suitably
named Manfred), mysterious deaths, a moaning ancestral portrait, damsels in distress, violent passions, and strange obsessions. Walpole's gamble—that the future of
the novel would involve the reclamation of the primitive emotions of fear and wonder
provided by the romances of a pre-Enlightened age—convinced many writers who
came after him. By the 1790s novels trading on horror, mystery, and faraway settings
flooded the book market; meanwhile in theaters new special effects were devised to
incarnate ghostly apparitions onstage. It is noteworthy that the best-selling author
of the terror school (Ann Radcliffe), the author of its most enduring novel (Mary
Shelley), and the author of its most effective send-up (Jane Austen) were all women.
Indeed, many of Radcliffe's numerous imitators (and, on occasion, downright plagia-
rizers) published under the auspices of the Minerva Press, a business whose very
name (that of the goddess of wisdom) acknowledged the centrality of female authors
and readers to this new lucrative trend in the book market. William Lane, the marketing genius who owned the press, also set up a cross-country network of circulating
libraries that stocked his ladies' volumes and made them available for hire at modest
prices.

This section offers extracts from some of the most celebrated works in the Gothic
mode: Walpole's *Otranto* as the initiating prototype; two extremely popular works
by Radcliffe, the "Queen of Terror," *The Romance of the Forest* (1791) and *The Mys-*

teries of Udolpho (1794); Matthew Lewis's concoction of devilry, sadism, and mob violence, *The Monk* (1796). We also include an essay of 1773 in which John and Anna Letitia Aikin provide justification after the fact for Walpole's rebellion against the critical orthodoxies. According to most early critics of novels, the only *moral* fiction was probable fiction; the Aikins, however, make the business of the novelist lie as much with the pleasures of the imagination as with moral edification and the representation of real life.

The Aikins' essay suggests why Gothic reading was appealing to so many Romantic poets—visionaries who in their own way dissented from critical rules that would, drearily, limit literature to the already known and recognizable. Signs of the poets' acquaintance with the terror school of novel writing show up in numerous well-known Romantic poems—from *The Rime of the Ancient Mariner* to *Manfred.* For instance, in Keats's *The Eve of St. Agnes*, a poem that in many respects represents an idealized tale of young love, Porphyro's invasion of Madeline's bedroom has some perturbing connections with the predatory overtones of the extract from *The Monk* reprinted here. And Keats's enigmatic fragment "This living hand" can be read as a brilliantly abbreviated version of the kind of tale of terror that aimed to make its reader's blood run cold.

Yet it simplifies matters to characterize the Gothic only as an influence on Romanticism. As the pieces by Coleridge in this section suggest, the poets had a love–hate relationship with Gothic writers and, even more so, with Gothic readers. Many contemporary commentators objected to the new school of novels on moral and technical grounds: they complained, for instance, about how plot driven they were and how cheaply they solved their mysteries. But questions about social class and literary taste were also important. In an era of revolution, in which newly literate workers were reading about "the rights of man" and crowds were starting to shape history, the very *popularity* of Gothic novels, the terror writers' capacity to move and manipulate whole crowds with their suspense and trickery, itself represented a source of anxiety. As the twentieth-century critic E. J. Clery explains, the "unprecedented capacity of the market to absorb at great speed large amounts of a particular type of literary product, the 'terrorist' novel, shook old certainties." Furthermore, terror had begun to seem a commodity produced on an assembly line.

Many of the Romantic poets comment, accordingly, on what is scary and pernicious *about* the Gothic as well as what is scary and pernicious *in* the Gothic. And throughout their writings, the tales of terror are invoked in ways that enable the writer to construct a divide between "high" and "low" culture and to play off the passive absorption associated with the reading of the crowds against the tasteful, active reading that is (according to the writer) practiced by the elite few. In the Preface to *Lyrical Ballads,* for instance, Wordsworth identifies as a cause of English culture's modern decline the "frenetic novels" that have blunted their consumers' powers of discrimination and reduced them "to a state of almost savage torpor" (a negative version of the regression that William Hazlitt, for instance, celebrates as he describes how Radcliffe "makes her readers twice children" while she "forces us to believe all that is strange and next to impossible"). Wordsworth follows a hint that he may have found three years earlier in Coleridge's review of *The Monk* (reprinted near the end of this section) and suggests that such readers inevitably need higher and higher doses of the "violent stimulants" that novelists—drug pushers of sorts—have supplied them. In this way the Preface pioneers an account of a mass readership addicted to what will kill it. In similar fashion our extract containing Coleridge's very funny tirade against the patrons of circulating libraries makes it seem that novels were objects of utterly mindless consumption (absorbed, imbibed, but not *read*). The selections with which we close this section register, in other words, a recoil from the Gothic. But Gothic themes frequently come back to haunt the critics of the mode. When they depict popular, commercialized culture's threat to individual autonomy and describe consumers as if they were zombies sunk in trances, the critics appear to rehearse nightmarish scenarios straight out of the tales of terror.

HORACE WALPOLE

Horace Walpole's landmark work *The Castle of Otranto* initially purported to be a translation from (as the title page of the first edition put it) "the original Italian of Onuphrio Muralto, Canon of the Church of St. Nicholas at Otranto." The events related in it were supposed to have occurred in the twelfth or thirteenth century. In the second edition, however, Walpole (1717–1797) renounced the hoax and confessed his authorship. Rather than presenting the narrative as a remarkable historical discovery, a manuscript from the lost barbaric past, he cast his "Gothic Story" as a novelty: an experiment in blending, he explained, "the ancient and modern" romance, and in combining the realism that was the hallmark of the up-to-date eighteenth-century novel with the imagination that had flourished in medieval romance and that this realism had suffocated.

When the story opens, the villainous Manfred, prince of Otranto, to get an heir to his estate, has arranged a marriage between his only son, Conrad, and the beautiful Isabella. But on his wedding day Conrad is mysteriously killed, victim of a giant helmet that falls from the sky and crushes him. Lest he should be left without male descendants, Manfred determines to divorce his present wife, Hippolita, who is past childbearing, and marry Isabella himself. In the extract reprinted here, Isabella learns of his intention and decides to flee the castle by night. The account of her flight suggests how the Gothic novelists, lavishing attention on architectural details, make experiences of terror inseparable from the walls, ceilings, floors, and doors enclosing them.

From The Castle of Otranto

From *Chapter 1*

As it was now evening, the servant who conducted Isabella bore a torch before her. When they came to Manfred, who was walking impatiently about the gallery, he started and said hastily, "Take away that light, and begone." Then shutting the door impetuously, he flung himself upon a bench against the wall, and bade Isabella sit by him. She obeyed trembling. "I sent for you, lady," said he,—and then stopped under great appearance of confusion. "My lord!"—"Yes, I sent for you on a matter of great moment," resumed he,—"Dry your tears, young lady—you have lost your bridegroom.— Yes, cruel fate! and I have lost the hopes of my race!—but Conrad was not worthy of your beauty."—"How! my lord," said Isabella; "sure you do not suspect me of not feeling the concern I ought. My duty and affection would have always—" "Think no more of him," interrupted Manfred; "he was a sickly puny child, and heaven has perhaps taken him away that I might not trust the honours of my house on so frail a foundation. The line of Manfred calls for numerous supports. My foolish fondness for that boy blinded the eyes of my prudence—but it is better as it is. I hope in a few years to have reason to rejoice at the death of Conrad."

Words cannot paint the astonishment of Isabella. At first she apprehended that grief had disordered Manfred's understanding. Her next thought suggested that this strange discourse was designed, to ensnare her: she feared

that Manfred had perceived her indifference for his son: and in consequence of that idea she replied, "Good my lord, do not doubt my tenderness:
my heart would have accompanied my hand. Conrad would have engrossed
all my care; and wherever fate shall dispose of me, I shall always cherish his
memory, and regard your highness and the virtuous Hippolita as my parents." "Curse on Hippolita!" cried Manfred: "forget her from this moment
as I do. In short, lady, you have missed a husband undeserving of your
charms: they shall now be better disposed of. Instead of a sickly boy, you
shall have a husband in the prime of his age, who will know how to value
your beauties, and who may expect a numerous offspring." "Alas! my lord,"
said Isabella, "my mind is too sadly engrossed by the recent catastrophe
in your family to think of another marriage. If ever my father returns, and
it shall be his pleasure, I shall obey, as I did when I consented to give my
hand to your son: but until his return, permit me to remain under your hospitable roof, and employ the melancholy hours in assuaging yours, Hippolita's, and the fair Matilda's affliction."

"I desired you once before," said Manfred angrily, "not to name that
woman: from this hour she must be a stranger to you, as she must be to
me;—in short, Isabella, since I cannot give you my son, I offer you myself."—
"Heavens!" cried Isabella, waking from her delusion, "what do I hear! You!
My lord! You! My father-in-law! the father of Conrad! the husband of the
virtuous and tender Hippolita!"—"I tell you," said Manfred imperiously,
"Hippolita is no longer my wife; I divorce her from this hour. Too long has
she cursed me by her unfruitfulness: my fate depends on having sons,—and
this night I trust will give a new date to my hopes." At those words he seized
the cold hand of Isabella, who was half-dead with fright and horror. She
shrieked and started from him. Manfred rose to pursue her, when the moon,
which was now up and gleamed in at the opposite casement, presented to
his sight the plumes of the fatal helmet, which rose to the height of the windows, waving backwards and forwards in a tempestuous manner, and accompanied with a hollow and rustling sound. Isabella, who gathered courage
from her situation, and who dreaded nothing so much as Manfred's pursuit
of his declaration, cried, "Look! my lord; see, heaven itself declares against
your impious intentions!"—"Heaven nor hell shall impede my designs," said
Manfred, advancing again to seize the princess. At that instant the portrait
of his grandfather, which hung over the bench where they had been sitting,
uttered a deep sigh, and heaved its breast. Isabella, whose back was turned
to the picture, saw not the motion, nor knew whence the sound came, but
started, and said, "Hark, my lord! What sound was that?" and at the same
time made towards the door. Manfred, distracted between the flight of Isabella, who had now reached the stairs, and yet unable to keep his eyes from
the picture, which began to move, had however advanced some steps after
her, still looking backwards on the portrait, when he saw it quit its panel,
and descend on the floor with a grave and melancholy air. "Do I dream?"
cried Manfred returning, "or are the devils themselves in league against me?
Speak, infernal spectre! or, if thou art my grandsire, why dost thou too con-
spire against thy wretched descendant, who too dearly pays for—" Ere he
could finish the sentence the vision sighed again, and made a sign to Manfred to follow him. "Lead on!" cried Manfred; "I will follow thee to the gulph
of perdition." The spectre marched sedately, but dejected, to the end of the
gallery, and turned into a chamber on the right hand. Manfred accompanied

him at a little distance, full of anxiety and horror, but resolved. As he would have entered the chamber, the door was clapped to with violence by an invisible hand. The prince, collecting courage from this delay, would have forcibly burst open the door with his foot, but found that it resisted his utmost efforts. "Since hell will not satisfy my curiosity," said Manfred, "I will use the human means in my power for preserving my race; Isabella shall not escape me."

That lady, whose resolution had given way to terror the moment she had quitted Manfred, continued her flight to the bottom of the principal staircase. There she stopped, not knowing whither to direct her steps, nor how to escape from the impetuosity of the prince. The gates of the castle she knew were locked, and guards placed in the court. Should she, as her heart prompted her, go and prepare Hippolita for the cruel destiny that awaited her, she did not doubt but Manfred would seek her there, and that his violence would incite him to double the injury he meditated, without leaving room for them to avoid the impetuosity of his passions. Delay might give him time to reflect on the horrid measures he had conceived, or produce some circumstance in her favour, if she could for that night at least avoid his odious purpose.—Yet where conceal herself? how avoid the pursuit he would infallibly make throughout the castle? As these thoughts passed rapidly through her mind, she recollected a subterraneous passage which led from the vaults of the castle to the church of St. Nicholas. Could she reach the altar before she was overtaken, she knew even Manfred's violence would not dare to profane the sacredness of the place; and she determined, if no other means of deliverance offered, to shut herself up for ever among the holy virgins, whose convent was contiguous to the cathedral. In this resolution, she seized a lamp that burned at the foot of the staircase, and hurried towards the secret passage. The lower part of the castle was hollowed into several intricate cloisters; and it was not easy for one under so much anxiety to find the door that opened into the cavern. An awful silence reigned throughout those subterraneous regions, except now and then some blasts of wind that shook the doors she had passed, and which, grating on the rusty hinges, were re-echoed through that long labyrinth of darkness. Every murmur struck her with new terror;—yet more she dreaded to hear the wrathful voice of Manfred urging his domestics[1] to pursue her. She trod as softly as impatience would give her leave,—yet frequently stopped and listened to hear if she was followed. In one of those moments she thought she heard a sigh. She shuddered, and recoiled a few paces. In a moment she thought she heard the step of some person. Her blood curdled; she concluded it was Manfred. Every suggestion that horror could inspire rushed into her mind. She condemned her rash flight, which had thus exposed her to his rage in a place where her cries were not likely to draw anybody to her assistance.—Yet the sound seemed not to come from behind,—if Manfred knew where she was, he must have followed her: she was still in one of the cloisters, and the steps she had heard were too distinct to proceed from the way she had come. Cheered with this reflection, and hoping to find a friend in whoever was not the prince, she was going to advance, when a door that stood ajar, at some distance to the left, was opened gently: but ere her lamp, which she held up, could discover who opened it, the person retreated precipitately on seeing the light.

1. Servants.

Isabella, whom every incident was sufficient to dismay, hesitated whether she should proceed. Her dread of Manfred soon outweighed every other terror. The very circumstance of the person avoiding her gave her a sort of courage. It could only be, she thought, some domestic belonging to the castle. Her gentleness had never raised her an enemy, and conscious innocence bade her hope that, unless sent by the prince's order to seek her, his servants would rather assist than prevent her flight. Fortifying herself with these reflections, and believing, by what she could observe, that she was near the mouth of the subterraneous cavern, she approached the door that had been opened; but a sudden gust of wind that met her at the door extinguished her lamp, and left her in total darkness.

1764

ANNA LETITIA AIKIN (LATER BARBAULD) AND JOHN AIKIN

In the following essay John Aikin (1747–1822) and his sister Anna Letitia (who appears earlier in this anthology as a poet and under her married name, Barbauld) engage a question philosophers and psychologists continue to debate: why do people who listen to ghost stories around the campfire, or read Gothic novels, or watch monster movies find such frightening experiences pleasing? The Aikins, members of a prominent family of religious dissenters and educators, begin by observing that it is easy to explain why we might feel satisfaction when we feel pity—that emotion is necessary for the well-being of the human community, which would fall apart were it not somehow in our own interest to feel for others. But it is by contrast more difficult to understand how morality is advanced when we delight in objects of terror. As they map out an alternative way of accounting for that amoral delight, the Aikins write an early Romantic description of the glory of the imagination; the reader's encounter with what is unknown and amazing elevates and expands the mind. The fragmentary story of a medieval knight errant that the Aikins appended to their essay was meant to give their readers a chance to test this thesis, but thanks to its handling of suspense "Sir Bertrand" soon came to be celebrated in its own right.

Published in 1773 in the Aikins' *Miscellaneous Pieces in Prose*, "On the Pleasure Derived from Objects of Terror" built on Walpole's innovation in *Otranto*. It gave the next generation of Gothic authors a critical justification for their engagement with the supernatural and for their swerve away from the didacticism that had valued fiction writers only when they seemed to be educating readers for real life. Family tradition ascribed the essay to Anna and "Sir Bertrand" to John.

On the Pleasure Derived from Objects of Terror; with Sir Bertrand, a Fragment

That the exercise of our benevolent feelings, as called forth by the view of human afflictions, should be a source of pleasure, cannot appear wonderful to one who considers that relation between the moral and natural system of man, which has connected a degree of satisfaction with every action or emotion productive of the general welfare. The painful sensation immediately arising from a scene of misery, is so much softened and alleviated by the reflex sense of self-approbation on attending virtuous sympathy, that we find, on the whole, a very exquisite and refined pleasure remaining, which makes us desirous of again being witnesses to such scenes, instead of flying from them with disgust and horror. It is obvious how greatly such a provision must conduce to the ends of mutual support and assistance. But the apparent delight with which we dwell upon objects of pure terror, where our moral feelings are not in the least concerned, and no passion seems to be excited but the depressing one of fear, is a paradox of the heart, much more difficult of solution.

The reality of this source of pleasure seems evident from daily observation. The greediness with which the tales of ghosts and goblins, of murders, earthquakes, fires, shipwrecks, and all the most terrible disasters attending human life, are devoured by every ear, must have been generally remarked. Tragedy, the most favourite work of fiction, has taken a full share of those scenes; "it has supt full with horrors"[1]—and has, perhaps, been more indebted to them for public admiration than to its tender and pathetic parts. The ghost of Hamlet, Macbeth descending into the witches' cave, and the tent scene in Richard, command as forcibly the attention of our souls as the parting of Jaffeir and Belvidera, the fall of Wolsey, or the death of Shore.[2] The inspiration of *terror* was by the antient critics assigned as the peculiar province of tragedy; and the Greek and Roman tragedians have introduced some extraordinary personages for this purpose: not only the shades of the dead, but the furies, and other fabulous inhabitants of the infernal regions. Collins, in his most poetical ode to Fear, has finely enforced this idea.

> Tho' gently Pity claim her mingled part,
> Yet all the thunders of the scene are thine.[3]

The old Gothic romance and the Eastern tale, with their genii, giants, enchantments, and transformations, however a refined critic may censure them as absurd and extravagant, will ever retain a most powerful influence on the mind, and interest the reader independently of all peculiarity of taste. Thus the great Milton, who had a strong bias to these wildnesses of the imagination, has with striking effect made the stories "of forests and enchantments drear," a favourite subject with his *Penseroso*; and had undoubtedly their awakening images strong upon his mind when he breaks out,

> Call up him that left half-told
> The story of Cambuscan bold; &c.[4]

How are we then to account for the pleasure derived from such objects? I have often been led to imagine that there is a deception in these cases; and that the avidity with which we attend is not a proof of our receiving real pleasure. The pain of suspense, and the irresistible desire of satisfying curi-

---

1. Shakespeare's *Macbeth* 5.5.13.
2. The mentions of Hamlet, Macbeth, and Richard III are followed by references to the doomed husband and wife in Thomas Otway's tragedy *Venice Preserv'd* (1681), the royal adviser whose fall from grace centers the action of Shakespeare's *Henry VIII*, and Jane Shore, title character of Nicholas Rowe's tragedy of 1714.

3. Lines 44–45 in William Collins's "Ode to Fear" (1746), slightly misquoted. The speaker of this poem anticipates the Aikins in marveling over the allure of fear and its potency as a source of art.
4. Quoting lines 119 and 109–10 of Milton's poem on the delights of studious melancholy. The story of Cambuscan was left half told in Chaucer's unfinished *Squire's Tale*.

osity, when once raised, will account for our eagerness to go quite through an adventure, though we suffer actual pain during the whole course of it. We rather chuse to suffer the smart pang of a violent emotion than the uneasy craving of an unsatisfied desire. That this principle, in many instances, may involuntarily carry us through what we dislike, I am convinced from experience. This is the impulse which renders the poorest and most insipid narrative interesting when once we get fairly into it; and I have frequently felt it with regard to our modern novels, which, if lying on my table, and taken up in an idle hour, have led me through the most tedious and disgusting pages, while, like Pistol eating his leek, I have swallowed and execrated to the end.[5] And it will not only force us through dullness, but through actual torture— through the relation of a Damien's execution, or an inquisitor's act of faith.[6] When children, therefore, listen with pale and mute attention to the frightful stories of apparitions, we are not, perhaps, to imagine that they are in a state of enjoyment, any more than the poor bird which is dropping into the mouth of the rattlesnake—they are chained by the ears, and fascinated by curiosity. This solution, however, does not satisfy me with respect to the well-wrought scenes of artificial terror which are formed by a sublime and vigorous imagination. Here, though we know before-hand what to expect, we enter into them with eagerness, in quest of a pleasure already experienced. This is the pleasure constantly attached to the excitement of surprise from new and wonderful objects. A strange and unexpected event awakens the mind, and keeps it on the stretch; and where the agency of invisible beings is introduced, of "forms unseen, and mightier far than we," our imagination, darting forth, explores with rapture the new world which is laid open to its view, and rejoices in the expansion of its powers. Passion and fancy cooperating elevate the soul to its highest pitch; and the pain of terror is lost in amazement.

Hence the more wild, fanciful, and extraordinary are the circumstance, of a scene of horror, the more pleasure we receive from it; and where they are too near common nature, though violently borne by curiosity through the adventure, we cannot repeat it or reflect on it, without an overbalance of pain. In the *Arabian Nights* are many most striking examples of the terrible joined with the marvellous: the story of Aladdin, and the travels of Sinbad are particularly excellent. The *Castle of Otranto* is a very spirited modern attempt upon the same plan of mixed terror, adapted to the model of Gothic romance. The best conceived, and most strongly worked-up scene of mere natural horror that I recollect, is in Smollett's *Ferdinand Count Fathom*;[7] where the hero, entertained in a lone house in a forest, finds a corpse just slaughtered in the room where he is sent to sleep, and the door of which is locked upon him. It may be amusing for the reader to compare his feelings upon these, and from thence form his opinion of the justness of my theory. The following fragment, in which both these manners are attempted to be in some degree united, is offered to entertain a solitary winter's evening.

---

5. Alluding to a comic scene of force-feeding in Shakespeare's *Henry V* (5.1.36–60).
6. Or *auto-da-fé*; the form of execution that the Spanish Inquisition inflicted on heretics: the condemned were burned alive. The brutality of the public torture and execution in 1757 of Robert-François Damiens, the would-be assassin of Louis XV of France, was commented on across Europe.
7. Tobias Smollett's 1753 novel of villainy and picaresque adventure.

Sir Bertrand, a Fragment

After this adventure, Sir Bertrand turned his steed towards the woulds,[8] hoping to cross these dreary moors before the curfew. But ere he had proceeded half his journey, he was bewildered by the different tracks, and not being able, as far as the eye could reach, to espy any object but the brown heath surrounding him, he was at length quite uncertain which way he should direct his course. Night overtook him in this situation. It was one of those nights when the moon gives a faint glimmering of light through the thick black clouds of a lowering sky. Now and then she suddenly emerged in full splendor from her veil; and then instantly retired behind it, having just served to give the forlorn Sir Bertrand a wide extended prospect over the desolate waste. Hope and native courage a while urged him to push forwards, but at length the increasing darkness and fatigue of body and mind overcame him; he dreaded moving from the ground he stood on, for fear of unknown pits and bogs, and alighting from his horse in despair, he threw himself on the ground. He had not long continued in that posture when the sullen toll of a distant bell struck his ears—he started up, and turning towards the sound discerned a dim twinkling light.

Instantly he seized his horse's bridle, and with cautious steps advanced towards it. After a painful march he was stopt by a moated ditch surrounding the place from whence the light proceeded; and by a momentary glimpse of moon-light he had a full view of a large antique mansion, with turrets at the corners, and an ample porch in the centre. The injuries of time were strongly marked on every thing about it. The roof in various places was fallen in, the battlements were half demolished, and the windows broken and dismantled. A drawbridge, with a ruinous gateway at each end, led to the court before the building—He entered, and instantly the light, which proceeded from a window in one of the turrets, glided along and vanished; at the same moment the moon sunk beneath a black cloud, and the night was darker than ever. All was silent—Sir Bertrand fastened his steed under a shed, and approaching the house traversed its whole front with light and slow footsteps—All was still as death—He looked in at the lower windows, but could not distinguish a single object through the impenetrable gloom. After a short parley with himself, he entered the porch, and seizing a massy iron knocker at the gate, lifted it up, and hesitating, at length struck a loud stroke. The noise resounded through the whole mansion with hollow echoes. All was still again—He repeated the strokes more boldly and louder—another interval of silence ensued—A third time he knocked, and a third time all was still. He then fell back to some distance that he might discern whether any light could be seen in the whole front—It again appeared in the same place and quickly glided away as before—at the same instant a deep sullen toll sounded from the turret. Sir Bertrand's heart made a fearful stop—He was a while motionless; then terror impelled him to make some hasty steps towards his steed—but shame stopt his flight; and urged by honour, and a resistless desire of finishing the adventure, he returned to the porch; and working up his soul to a full steadiness of resolution, he drew forth his sword with one hand, and with the other lifted up the latch of the gate. The heavy door, creaking upon its hinges, reluctantly yielded to his hand—he applied his shoulder to it and forced it open—he quit-

8. I.e., woulds: open, elevated ground.

ted it and stept forward—the door instantly shut with a thundering clap. Sir Bertrand's blood was chilled—he turned back to find the door, and it was long ere his trembling hands could seize it—but his utmost strength could not open it again. After several ineffectual attempts, he looked behind him, and beheld, across a hall, upon a large staircase, a pale bluish flame which cast a dismal gleam of light around. He again summoned forth his courage and advanced towards it—It retired. He came to the foot of the stairs, and after a moment's deliberation ascended. He went slowly up, the flame retiring before him, till he came to a wide gallery—The flame proceeded along it, and he followed in silent horror, treading lightly, for the echoes of his footsteps startled him. It led him to the foot of another staircase, and then vanished—At the same instant another toll sounded from the turret—Sir Bertrand felt it strike upon his heart. He was now in total darkness, and with his arms extended, began to ascend the second staircase. A dead cold hand met his left hand and firmly grasped it, drawing him forcibly forwards—he endeavoured to disengage himself, but could not—he made a furious blow with his sword, and instantly a loud shriek pierced his ears, and the dead hand was left powerless in his—He dropt it, and rushed forwards with a desperate valour. The stairs were narrow and winding, and interrupted by frequent breaches, and loose fragments of stone. The staircase grew narrower and narrower and at length terminated in a low iron grate. Sir Bertrand pushed it open—it led to an intricate winding passage, just large enough to admit a person upon his hands and knees. A faint glimmering of light served to show the nature of the place. Sir Bertrand entered—A deep hollow groan resounded from a distance through the vault—He went forwards, and proceeding beyond the first turning, he discerned the same blue flame which had before conducted him. He followed it. The vault, at length, suddenly opened into a lofty gallery, in the midst of which a figure appeared, compleatly armed, thrusting forwards the bloody stump of an arm, with a terrible frown and menacing gesture, and brandishing a sword in his hand. Sir Bertrand undauntedly sprung forwards; and aiming a fierce blow at the figure, it instantly vanished, letting fall a massy iron key. The flame now rested upon a pair of ample folding doors at the end of the gallery. Sir Bertrand went up to it, and applied the key to a brazen lock—with difficulty he turned the bolt—instantly the doors flew open, and discovered a large apartment, at the end of which was a coffin rested upon a bier, with a taper burning on each side of it. Along the room on both sides were gigantic statues of black marble, attired in the Moorish habit, and holding enormous sabres in their right hands. Each of them reared his arm, and advanced one leg forwards, as the knight entered; at the same moment the lid of the coffin flew open, and the bell tolled. The flame still glided forwards, and Sir Bertrand resolutely followed, till he arrived within six paces of the coffin. Suddenly, a lady in a shroud and black veil rose up in it, and stretched out her arms towards him—at the same time the statues clashed their sabres and advanced. Sir Bertrand flew to the lady and clasped her in his arms—she threw up her veil and kissed his lips; and instantly the whole building shook as with an earthquake, and fell asunder with a horrible crash. Sir Bertrand was thrown into a sudden trance, and on recovering, found himself seated on a velvet sofa, in the most magnificent room he had ever seen, lighted with innumerable tapers, in lustres of pure crystal. A sumptuous banquet was set in the middle. The doors opening to soft music, a lady of incomparable beauty, attired with amazing splendour entered, surrounded by a troop of gay nymphs far more fair than the Graces—She advanced to the knight, and falling on her knees thanked him as her deliverer. The nymphs placed a garland of laurel on his head, and the lady led him by the hand to the banquet, and sat beside him. The nymphs placed themselves at the table, and a numerous train of servants entering, served up the feast; delicious music playing all the time. Sir Bertrand could not speak for astonishment—he could only return their honours by courteous looks and gestures. After the banquet was finished, all retired but the lady, who leading back the knight to the sofa, addressed him in these words:—[9]

1773

9. The fragment ends here.

ANN RADCLIFFE

T he "Great Enchantress," Ann Radcliffe (1764–1823) published five novels between 1789 and 1797 and a sixth posthumously in 1826, most of them tremendously popular and influential on other writers for long afterward. She shunned fame and lived in seclusion; so little was known of her that, seeking to explain the long interval between *The Italian* in 1797 and *Gaston de Blondeville* in 1826, contemporaries gossiped that Radcliffe had at last gone mad from too much imagining and had spent her final decades confined in an asylum. The rumor was without basis, but the fate it assigned to Radcliffe is the fate most feared by her heroines, who cling valiantly to reason, but who are plunged into worlds of nightmarish mystery where nothing is as it seems and where reason, at least initially, does not get them very far. A Radcliffean heroine, like Radcliffe's reader, is kept on the rack of suspense by a succession of inexplicable sights and sounds that tempt her to believe that supernatural events really do happen. The ancient castle in which she is confined, the site of these mysteries, is often located in some wilderness that the forces of law have abandoned and that has become the haunt of mercenary soldiers and picaresque bandits. For all its strangeness, however, this place frequently turns out to be a version of the heroine's long-lost home, just as her tyrannical persecutors turn out to be closely allied with the fathers, uncles, and priests who are supposed to be a young lady's protectors.

The first extract is taken from Radcliffe's third novel, *The Romance of the Forest* (1791). In this episode, later remembered by Jane Austen as she recounted the story of the first eventful night that Catherine Morland spends as a guest at Northanger Abbey, the orphaned Adeline sets out, detectivelike, to solve a mystery. The second extract is from Radcliffe's masterpiece, *The Mysteries of Udolpho* (1794), one of her signature pieces of dreamy landscape description, representing Emily St. Aubert's reactions as she and her villainous guardian Montoni approach his castle high in the Italian Appenines.

From The Romance of the Forest

From *Chapter* 8

Adeline retired early to her room, which adjoined on one side to Madame La Motte's, and on the other to the closet formerly mentioned. It was spacious and lofty, and what little furniture it contained was falling to decay;

but, perhaps, the present tone of her spirits might contribute more than these circumstances to give that air of melancholy which seemed to reign in it. She was unwilling to go to bed, lest the dreams that had lately pursued her should return; and determined to sit up till she found herself oppressed by sleep, when it was probable her rest would be profound. She placed the light on a small table, and, taking a book, continued to read for above an hour, till her mind refused any longer to abstract itself from its own cares, and she sat for some time leaning pensively on her arm.

The wind was high, and as it whistled through the desolate apartment, and shook the feeble doors, she often started, and sometimes even thought she heard sighs between the pauses of the gust; but she checked these illusions, which the hour of the night and her own melancholy imagination conspired to raise. As she sat musing, her eyes fixed on the opposite wall, she perceived the arras, with which the room was hung, wave backwards and forwards; she continued to observe it for some minutes, and then rose to examine it farther. It was moved by the wind; and she blushed at the momentary fear it had excited: but she observed that the tapestry was more strongly agitated in one particular place than elsewhere, and a noise that seemed something more than that of the wind issued thence. The old bedstead, which La Motte had found in this apartment, had been removed to accommodate Adeline, and it was behind the place where this had stood that the wind seemed to rush with particular force: curiosity prompted her to examine still farther; she felt about the tapestry, and perceiving the wall behind shake under her hand, she lifted the arras, and discovered a small door, whose loosened hinges admitted the wind, and occasioned the noise she had heard.

The door was held only by a bolt, having undrawn which, and brought the light, she descended by a few steps into another chamber: she instantly remembered her dreams. The chamber was not much like that in which she had seen the dying Chevalier, and afterwards the bier; but it gave her a confused remembrance of one through which she had passed. Holding up the light to examine it more fully, she was convinced by its structure that it was part of the ancient foundation. A shattered casement, placed high from the floor, seemed to be the only opening to admit light. She observed a door on the opposite side of the apartment; and after some moments of hesitation, gained courage, and determined to pursue the inquiry. "A mystery seems to hang over these chambers," said she, "which it is, perhaps, my lot to develope;[1] I will, at least, see to what that door leads."

She stepped forward, and having unclosed it, proceeded with faltering steps along a suite of apartments resembling the first in style and condition, and terminating in one exactly like that where her dream had represented the dying person; the remembrance struck so forcibly upon her imagination that she was in danger of fainting; and looking round the room, almost expected to see the phantom of her dream.

Unable to quit the place, she sat down on some old lumber[2] to recover herself, while her spirits were nearly overcome by a superstitious dread, such as she had never felt before. She wondered to what part of the abbey these chambers belonged, and that they had so long escaped detection. The casements were all too high to afford any information from without. When she was sufficiently composed to consider the direction of the rooms, and the situ-

---

1. Unfold, reveal.
2. Disused furniture and the like.

ation of the abbey, there appeared not a doubt that they formed an interior part of the original building.

As these reflections passed over her mind, a sudden gleam of moonlight fell upon some object without the casement. Being now sufficiently composed to wish to pursue the inquiry, and believing this object might afford her some means of learning the situation of these rooms, she combated her remaining terrors, and, in order to distinguish it more clearly, removed the light to an outer chamber; but before she could return, a heavy cloud was driven over the face of the moon, and all without was perfectly dark: she stood for some moments waiting a returning gleam, but the obscurity continued. As she went softly back for the light, her foot stumbled over something on the floor, and while she stooped to examine it, the moon again shone, so that she could distinguish, through the casement, the eastern towers of the abbey. This discovery confirmed her former conjectures concerning the interior situation of these apartments. The obscurity of the place prevented her discovering what it was that had impeded her steps, but having brought the light forward, she perceived on the floor an old dagger: with a trembling hand she took it up, and upon a closer view perceived that it was spotted and stained with rust.

Shocked and surprised, she looked round the room for some object that might confirm or destroy the dreadful suspicion which now rushed upon her mind; but she saw only a great chair, with broken arms, that stood in one corner of the room, and a table in a condition equally shattered, except that in another part lay a confused heap of things, which appeared to be old lumber. She went up to it, and perceived a broken bedstead, with some decayed remnants of furniture, covered with dust and cobwebs, and which seemed, indeed, as if they had not been moved for many years. Desirous, however, of examining farther, she attempted to raise what appeared to have been part of the bedstead, but it slipped from her hand, and, rolling to the floor, brought with it some of the remaining lumber. Adeline started aside and saved herself, and when the noise it made had ceased, she heard a small rustling sound, and as she was about to leave the chamber, saw something falling gently among the lumber.

It was a small roll of paper, tied with a string, and covered with dust. Adeline took it up, and on opening it perceived an handwriting. She attempted to read it, but the part of the manuscript she looked at was so much obliterated that she found this difficult, though what few words were legible impressed her with curiosity and terror, and induced her to return immediately to her chamber.

1791

From The Mysteries of Udolpho

From *Volume 2, Chapter 5*

Towards the close of day, the road wound into a deep valley. Mountains, whose shaggy steeps appeared to be inaccessible, almost surrounded it. To the east, a vista opened, that exhibited the Apennines in their darkest horrors; and the long perspective of retiring summits, rising over each other, their ridges clothed with pines, exhibited a stronger image of grandeur, than any that Emily had yet seen. The sun had just sunk below the top of the mountains she was descending, whose long shadow stretched athwart the valley, but his sloping rays, shooting through an opening of the cliffs, touched with a yellow gleam the summits of the forest, that hung upon the opposite steeps, and streamed in full splendour upon the towers and battlements of a castle, that spread its extensive ramparts along the brow of a precipice above. The splendour of these illumined objects was heightened by the contrasted shade, which involved the valley below.

"There," said Montoni, speaking for the first time in several hours, "is Udolpho."

Emily gazed with melancholy awe upon the castle, which she understood to be Montoni's; for, though it was now lighted up by the setting sun, the gothic greatness of its features, and its mouldering walls of dark grey stone, rendered it a gloomy and sublime object. As she gazed, the light died away on its walls, leaving a melancholy purple tint, which spread deeper and deeper, as the thin vapour crept up the mountain, while the battlements above were still tipped with splendour. From those too, the rays soon faded, and the whole edifice was invested with the solemn duskiness of evening. Silent, lonely and sublime, it seemed to stand the sovereign of the scene, and to frown defiance on all who dared to invade its solitary reign. As the twilight deepened, its features became more awful in obscurity, and Emily continued to gaze, till its clustering towers were alone seen, rising over the tops of the woods, beneath whose thick shade the carriages soon after began to ascend.

The extent and darkness of these tall woods awakened terrific images in her mind, and she almost expected to see banditti start up from under the trees. At length, the carriages emerged upon a heathy rock, and, soon after, reached the castle gates, where the deep tone of the portal bell, which was struck upon to give notice of their arrival, increased the fearful emotions that had assailed Emily. While they waited till the servant within should come to open the gates, she anxiously surveyed the edifice: but the gloom that over-spread it allowed her to distinguish little more than a part of its outline, with the massy walls of the ramparts, and to know that it was vast, ancient and dreary. From the parts she saw, she judged of the heavy strength and extent of the whole. The gateway before her, leading into the courts, was of gigantic size, and was defended by two round towers, crowned by overhanging turrets, embattled, where instead of banners, now waved long grass and wild plants, that had taken root among the mouldering stones, and which seemed to sigh, as the breeze rolled past, over the desolation around them. The towers were united by a curtain, pierced and embattled also, below which appeared the pointed arch of an huge portcullis, surmounting the gates: from these, the walls of the ramparts extended to other towers, overlooking the precipice, whose shattered outline, appearing on a gleam that lingered in the west, told of the ravages of war.—Beyond these all was lost in the obscurity of evening.

While Emily gazed with awe upon the scene, footsteps were heard within the gates, and the undrawing of the bolts; after which an ancient servant of the castle appeared, forcing back the huge folds of the portal, to admit his lord. As the carriage-wheels rolled heavily under the portcullis, Emily's heart sunk, and she seemed as if she was going into her prison; the gloomy court into which she passed served to confirm the idea, and her imagination, ever awake to circumstance, suggested even more terrors than her reason could justify.

MATTHEW GREGORY LEWIS

Matthew Gregory Lewis's *The Monk*, published in 1796 when the author was twenty, is the most gory of the Gothic novels and one of the most vividly written (a combination guaranteed to produce a best seller). Lewis (1775–1818) appears to have been alarmed by the scandal that erupted when his authorship was revealed, but not so rattled as to alter his literary course. He went on to compose Gothic dramas for the stage and, finding new uses for the language skills honed during the education that was meant to have prepared him for a diplomatic career, played a major part in introducing German tales of terror to England.

In *The Monk* Ambrosio, abbot of a monastery in Madrid, goes from a pinnacle of self-satisfied saintliness to become one of the most depraved villains in all fiction, both an incestuous rapist and matricidal murderer. After being seduced by Matilda, a female demon who has entered his monastery disguised as a male novice named Rosario, Ambrosio, with the help of a talisman that Matilda provides, plots the rape of one of his penitents, Antonia. Within *The Monk* mob violence competes with Ambrosio's bloodlust as a source for horror, suggesting how Gothic stories, even when set in distant pasts and places, may have allowed the readers and writers of the 1790s to work through timely anxieties about the power of crowds and the threat of revolution.

In the first extract given here, Ambrosio exults in private after having delivered a spellbinding sermon to a packed church in Madrid. The second extract recounts his assault on Antonia and the discovery by her mother, Elvira, of the young woman's peril.

From The Monk

From *Chapter 2*

The monks having attended their abbot to the door of his cell, he dismissed them with an air of conscious superiority, in which humility's semblance combated with the reality of pride.

He was no sooner alone, than he gave free loose to the indulgence of his vanity. When he remembered the enthusiasm which his discourse had excited, his heart swelled with rapture, and his imagination presented him with splendid visions of aggrandizement. He looked round him with exultation; and pride told him loudly that he was superior to the rest of his fellow-creatures.

"Who," thought he, "who but myself has passed the ordeal of youth, yet sees no single stain upon his conscience? Who else has subdued the violence of strong passions and an impetuous temperament, and submitted even from the dawn of life to voluntary retirement? I seek for such a man in vain. I see no one but myself possessed of such resolution. Religion cannot boast Ambrosio's equal! How powerful an effect did my discourse produce upon its auditors! How they crowded round me! How they loaded me with benedictions, and pronounced me the sole uncorrupted pillar of the church! What then now is left for me to do? Nothing, but to watch as carefully over the conduct of my brethren, as I have hitherto watched over my own. Yet hold! May I not be tempted from those paths which till now I have pursued without one moment's wandering? Am I not a man whose nature is frail and prone to error? I must now abandon the solitude of my retreat; the fairest and noblest dames of Madrid continually present themselves at the abbey, and will use no other confessor. I must accustom my eyes to objects of temptation, and expose myself to the seduction of luxury and desire. Should I meet in that world which I am constrained to enter, some lovely female— lovely as you—Madona—!"

As he said this, he fixed his eyes upon a picture of the Virgin, which was suspended opposite to him: this for two years had been the object of his increasing wonder and adoration. He paused, and gazed upon it with delight.

"What beauty in that countenance!" he continued after a silence of some minutes; "how graceful is the turn of that head! what sweetness, yet what majesty in her divine eyes! how softly her cheek reclines upon her hand! Can the rose vie with the blush of that cheek? can the lily rival the white- ness of that hand? Oh! if such a creature existed, and existed but for me! were I permitted to twine round my fingers those golden ringlets, and press with my lips the treasures of that snowy bosom! gracious God, should I then resist the temptation? Should I not barter for a single embrace the reward of my sufferings for thirty years? Should I not abandon——Fool that I am! Whither do I suffer my admiration of this picture to hurry me? Away, impure ideas! Let me remember that woman is for ever lost to me. Never was mortal formed so perfect as this picture. But even did such exist, the trial might be too mighty for a common virtue; but Ambrosio's is proof against temptation. Temptation, did I say? To me it would be none. What charms me, when ideal and considered as a superior being, would disgust me, become woman and tainted with all the failings of mortality. It is not the woman's beauty that fills me with such enthusiasm: it is the painter's skill that I admire; it is the Divinity that I adore. Are not the passions dead in my bosom? have I not freed myself from the frailty of mankind? Fear not, Ambrosio! Take confidence in the strength of your virtue. Enter boldly into the world, to whose failings you are superior; reflect that you are now exempted from humanity's defects, and defy all the arts of the spirits of darkness. They shall know you for what you are!"

Here his reverie was interrupted by three soft knocks at the door of his cell. With difficulty did the abbot awake from his delirium. The knocking was repeated.

"Who is there?" said Ambrosio at length.

"It is only Rosario," replied a gentle voice.

From *Chapter 8*

It was almost two o'clock before the lustful monk ventured to bend his steps towards Antonia's dwelling. It has been already mentioned that the abbey was at no great distance from the strada di San Iago. He reached the house unob- served. Here he stopped, and hesitated for a moment. He reflected on the enormity of the crime, the consequences of a discovery, and the probability, after what had passed, of Elvira's suspecting him to be her daughter's rav- isher. On the other hand it was suggested that she could do no more than suspect; that no proofs of his guilt could be produced; that it would seem impossible for the rape to have been committed without Antonia's knowing when, where, or by whom; and finally, he believed that his fame was too firmly established to be shaken by the unsupported accusations of two unknown women. This latter argument was perfectly false. He knew not how uncertain is the air of popular applause, and that a moment suffices to make him to-day the detestation of the world, who yesterday was its idol. The result of the monk's deliberations was that he should proceed in his enterprise. He ascended the steps leading to the house. No sooner did he touch the door with the silver myrtle than it flew open, and presented him with a free passage. He entered, and the door closed after him of its own accord.

Guided by the moon-beams, he proceeded up the stair-case with slow and cautious steps. He looked round him every moment with apprehension and anxiety. He saw a spy in every shadow, and heard a voice in every murmur of the night-breeze. Consciousness of the guilty business on which he was employed appalled his heart, and rendered it more timid than a woman's. Yet still he proceeded. He reached the door of Antonia's chamber. He stopped, and listened. All was hushed within. The total silence persuaded him that his intended victim was retired to rest, and he ventured to lift up the latch. The door was fastened, and resisted his efforts. But no sooner was it touched by the talisman than the bolt flew back. The ravisher stepped on, and found himself in the chamber where slept the innocent girl, unconscious how dangerous a visitor was drawing near her couch. The door closed after him, and the bolt shot again into its fastening.

Ambrosio advanced with precaution. He took care that not a board should creak under his foot, and held in his breath as he approached the bed. His first attention was to perform the magic ceremony, as Matilda had charged him: he breathed thrice upon the silver myrtle, pronounced over it Antonia's name, and laid it upon her pillow. The effects which it had already produced permitted not his doubting its success in prolonging the slumbers of his devoted mistress. No sooner was the enchantment performed than he considered her to be absolutely in his power, and his eyes flashed with lust and impatience. He now ventured to cast a glance upon the sleeping beauty. A single lamp, burning before the statue of St. Rosolia, shed a faint light through the room, and permitted him to examine all the charms of the lovely object before him. The heat of the weather had obliged her to throw off part of the bed-clothes. Those which still covered her Ambrosio's insolent hand hastened to remove. She lay with her cheek reclining upon one ivory arm: the other rested on the side of the bed with graceful indolence. A few tresses of her hair had escaped from beneath the muslin which confined the rest, and fell carelessly over her bosom, as it heaved with slow and regular suspiration. The warm air had spread her cheek with a higher colour than usual. A smile inexpressibly sweet played round her ripe and coral lips, from which every now and then escaped a gentle sigh, or an half-pronounced sentence. An air of enchanting innocence and candour pervaded her whole form; and there was a sort of modesty in her very nakedness, which added fresh stings to the desires of the lustful monk.

He remained for some moments devouring those charms with his eyes which soon were to be subjected to his ill-regulated passions. Her mouth half-opened seem to solicit a kiss: he bent over her: he joined his lips to hers, and drew in the fragrance of her breath with rapture. This momentary pleasure increased his longing for still greater. His desires were raised to that frantic height by which brutes are agitated. He resolved not to delay for one instant longer the accomplishment of his wishes, and hastily proceeded to tear off those garments which impeded the gratification of his lust.

"Gracious God!" exclaimed a voice behind him: "Am I not deceived? Is not this an illusion?"

Terror, confusion, and disappointment accompanied these words, as they struck Ambrosio's hearing. He started, and turned towards it. Elvira stood at the door of the chamber, and regarded the monk with looks of surprise and detestation.

A frightful dream had represented to her Antonia on the verge of a precipice. She saw her trembling on the brink: every moment seemed to threaten her fall, and she heard her exclaim with shrieks, "Save me, mother! save me!—Yet a moment, and it will be too late." Elvira woke in terror. The vision had made too strong an impression upon her mind to permit her resting till assured of her daughter's safety. She hastily started from her bed, threw on a loose nightgown, and, passing through the closet in which slept the waiting-woman, reached Antonia's chamber just in time to rescue her from the grasp of the ravisher.

His shame and her amazement seemed to have petrified into statues both Elvira and the monk. They remained gazing upon each other in silence. The lady was the first to recover herself.

"It is no dream," she cried: "it is really Ambrosio who stands before me. It is the man whom Madrid esteems a saint that I find at this late hour near the couch of my unhappy child. Monster of hypocrisy! I already suspected your designs, but forbore your accusation in pity to human frailty. Silence would now be criminal. The whole city shall be informed of your incontinence. I will unmask you, villain, and convince the church what a viper she cherishes in her bosom."

Pale and confused, the baffled culprit stood trembling before her. He would fain have extenuated his offence, but could find no apology for his conduct. He could produce nothing but broken sentences, and excuses which contradicted each other. Elvira was too justly incensed to grant the pardon which he requested. She protested that she would raise the neighbourhood, and make him an example to all future hypocrites. Then hastening to the bed, she called to Antonia to wake; and finding that her voice had no effect, she took her arm, and raised her forcibly from the pillow. The charm operated too powerfully. Antonia remained insensible; and, on being released by her mother, sank back upon the pillow.

"This slumber cannot be natural," cried the amazed Elvira, whose indignation increased with every moment: "some mystery is concealed in it. But tremble, hypocrite! All your villainy shall soon be unravelled. Help! help!" she exclaimed aloud: "Within there! Flora! Flora!"

"Hear me for one moment, lady!" cried the monk, restored to himself by the urgency of the danger: "by all that is sacred and holy, I swear that your daughter's honour is still unviolated. Forgive my transgression! Spare me the shame of a discovery, and permit me to regain the abbey undisturbed. Grant me this request in mercy! I promise not only that Antonia shall be secure from me in future, but that the rest of my life shall prove—"

Elvira interrupted him abruptly.

"Antonia secure from you? *I* will secure her. You shall betray no longer the confidence of parents. Your iniquity shall be unveiled to the public eye.

Final Discovery & destruction of Count Rodolph the Skeleton Lover, on the bridal day.

"**Final Discovery . . .**" Frontispiece for a typical Gothic chapbook, the inexpensive form that Gothic fiction took as it became part of popular culture: *The Skeleton Lover: A Romantic Tale* (1830).

All Madrid shall shudder at your perfidy, your hypocrisy, and incontinence. What ho! there! Flora! Flora! I say."

While she spoke thus, the remembrance of Agnes struck upon his mind. Thus had she sued to him for mercy, and thus had he refused her prayer! It was now his turn to suffer, and he could not but acknowledge that his punishment was just. In the mean while Elvira continued to call Flora to her assistance; but her voice was so choaked with passion, that the servant, who was buried in profound slumber, was insensible to all her cries: Elvira dared not go towards the closet in which Flora slept, lest the monk should take that opportunity to escape. Such indeed was his intention: he trusted that, could he reach the abbey unobserved by any other than Elvira, her single testimony would not suffice to ruin a reputation so well established as his was in Madrid. With this idea he gathered up such garments as he had already thrown off, and hastened towards the door. Elvira was aware of his design: she followed him; and, ere he could draw back the bolt, seized him by the arm, and detained him.

"Attempt not to fly!" said she: "you quit not this room without witnesses of your guilt."

Ambrosio struggled in vain to disengage himself. Elvira quitted not her hold, but redoubled her cries for succour. The friar's danger grew more urgent. He expected every moment to hear people assembling at her voice;

and, worked up to madness by the approach of ruin, he adopted a resolution equally desperate and savage. Turning round suddenly, with one hand he grasped Elvira's throat so as to prevent her continuing her clamour, and with the other, dashing her violently upon the ground, he dragged her towards the bed. Confused by this unexpected attack, she scarcely had power to strive at forcing herself from his grasp: while the monk, snatching the pillow from beneath her daughter's head, covering with it Elvira's face, and pressing his knee upon her stomach with all his strength, endeavoured to put an end to her existence. He succeeded but too well. Her natural strength increased by the excess of anguish, long did the sufferer struggle to disengage herself, but in vain. The monk continued to kneel upon her breast, witnessed without mercy the convulsive trembling of her limbs beneath him, and sustained with inhuman firmness the spectacle of her agonies, when soul and body were on the point of separating. Those agonies at length were over. She ceased to struggle for life. The monk took off the pillow, and gazed upon her. Her face was covered with a frightful blackness: her limbs moved no more: the blood was chilled in her veins: her heart had forgotten to beat; and her hands were stiff and frozen. Ambrosio beheld before him that once noble and majestic form, now become a corse,[1] cold, senseless, and disgusting.

This horrible act was no sooner perpetrated, than the friar beheld the enormity of his crime. A cold dew flowed over his limbs: his eyes closed: he staggered to a chair, and sank into it almost as lifeless as the unfortunate who lay extended at his feet. From this state he was roused by the necessity of flight, and the danger of being found in Antonia's apartment. He had no desire to profit by the execution of his crime. Antonia now appeared to him an object of disgust. A deadly cold had usurped the place of that warmth which glowed in his bosom. No ideas offered themselves to his mind but those of death and guilt, of present shame and future punishment. Agitated by remorse and fear, he prepared for flight: yet his terrors did not so completely master his recollection as to prevent his taking the precautions necessary for his safety. He replaced the pillow upon the bed, gathered up his garments, and, with the fatal talisman in his hand, bent his unsteady steps towards the door. Bewildered by fear, he fancied that his flight was opposed by legions of phantoms. Wherever he turned, the disfigured corse seemed to lie in his passage, and it was long before he succeeded in reaching the door.

1795   1796

1. Corpse.

SAMUEL TAYLOR COLERIDGE

Many elements in Coleridge's poetry—the account of the skeleton ship in *The Rime of the Ancient Mariner*, for instance, or the atmosphere, setting, and fragmentary plot of witchery and seduction in *Christabel*—suggest how absorbing he found the novels of the "terrorist school." His letters from the 1790s sometimes reveal him sitting up all night, trembling, he says, "like an aspen leaf" as he turns their pages. But elsewhere Coleridge's writings indicate how complex and ambivalent the

Romantic poets' reaction to Gothic writing could be. As a first example we provide his scathing review, published in the *Critical Review* in February 1797, of *The Monk*. It should be noted that Coleridge's reaction to Matthew Lewis's novel is, for all its alarm, much more measured than those of most of his fellow critics.

From Review of *The Monk* by Matthew Lewis

The horrible and the preternatural have usually seized on the popular taste, at the rise and decline of literature. Most powerful stimulants, they can never be required except by the torpor of an unawakened, or the languor of an exhausted, appetite. The same phenomenon, therefore, which we hail as a favourable omen in the belles lettres[1] of Germany, impresses a degree of gloom in the compositions of our countrymen. We trust, however, that satiety will banish what good sense should have prevented; and that, wearied with fiends, incomprehensible characters, with shrieks, murders, and subterraneous dungeons, the public will learn, by the multitude of the manufacturers, with how little expense of thought or imagination this species of composition is manufactured. But, cheaply as we estimate romances in general, we acknowledge, in the work before us, the offspring of no common genius. The tale is similar to that of Santon Barsista in the Guardian.[2] Ambrosio, a monk, surnamed the Man of Holiness, proud of his own undeviating rectitude, and severe to the faults of others, is successfully assailed by the tempter of mankind, and seduced to the perpetration of rape and murder, and finally precipitated into a contract in which he consigns his soul to everlasting perdition.

The larger part of the three volumes is occupied by the underplot, which, however, is skilfully and closely connected with the main story, and is subservient to its development. The tale of the bleeding nun is truly terrific; and we could not easily recollect a bolder or more happy conception than that of the burning cross on the forehead of the wandering Jew (a mysterious character, which, though copied as to its more prominent features from Schiller's incomprehensible Armenian,[3] does, nevertheless, display great vigour of fancy). But the character of Matilda, the chief agent in the seduction of Antonio[4] appears to us to be the author's master-piece. It is, indeed, exquisitely imagined, and as exquisitely supported. The whole work is distinguished by the variety and impressiveness of its incidents; and the author everywhere discovers an imagination rich, powerful, and fervid. Such are the excellencies;—the errors and defects are more numerous, and (we are sorry to add) of greater importance.

All events are levelled into one common mass, and become almost equally probable, where the order of nature may be changed whenever the author's purposes demand it. No address is requisite to the accomplishment of any design; and no pleasure therefore can be received from the perception of *difficulty surmounted*. The writer may make us wonder, but he cannot surprise us. For the same reasons a romance is incapable of exemplifying a moral truth. No proud man, for instance, will be made less proud by being

---

1. Literature.
2. An Eastern tale published in 1713 and acknowledged by Lewis as one of his sources.

3. The mysterious villain of Friedrich Schiller's *The Ghost-seer* (English translation 1795).
4. Coleridge's mistake for Ambrosio.

told that Lucifer once seduced a presumptuous monk. *Incredulus odit.*[5] Or even if, believing the story, he should deem his virtue less secure, he would yet acquire no lessons of prudence, no feelings of humility. Human prudence can oppose no sufficient shield to the power and cunning of supernatural beings; and the privilege of being proud might be fairly conceded to him who could rise superior to all earthly temptations, and whom the strength of the spiritual world alone would be adequate to overwhelm. So falling, he would fall with glory, and might reasonably welcome his defeat with the haughty emotions of a conqueror. As far, therefore, as the story is concerned, the praise which a romance can claim, is simply that of having given pleasure during its perusal; and so many are the calamities of life, that he who has done this, has not written uselessly. The children of sickness and of solitude shall thank him. To this praise, however, our author has not entitled himself. The sufferings which he describes are so frightful and intolerable, that we break with abruptness from the delusion, and indignantly suspect the man of a species of brutality, who could find a pleasure in wantonly imagining them; and the abominations which he portrays with no hurrying pencil, are such as the observation of character by no means demanded, such as "no observation of character can justify, because no good man would willingly suffer them to pass, however transiently, through his own mind." The merit of a novelist is in proportion (not simply to the effect, but) to the *pleasurable* effect which he produces. Situations of torment, and images of naked horror, are easily conceived; and a writer in whose works they abound, deserves our gratitude almost equally with him who should drag us by way of sport through a military hospital, or force us to sit at the dissecting-table of a natural philosopher. To trace the nice[6] boundaries, beyond which terror and sympathy are deserted by the pleasurable emotions,—to reach those limits, yet never to pass them,—*hic labor, hic opus est.*[7] Figures that shock the imagination, and narratives that mangle the feelings, rarely discover *genius*, and always betray a low and vulgar *taste*. Nor has our author indicated less ignorance of the human heart in the management of the principal character. The wisdom and goodness of providence have ordered that the tendency of vicious actions to deprave the heart of the perpetrator, should diminish in proportion to the greatness of his temptations. Now, in addition to constitutional warmth and irresistible opportunity, the monk is impelled to incontinence by friendship, by compassion, by gratitude, by all that is amiable, and all that is estimable; yet in a few weeks after his first frailty, the man who had been described as possessing much general humanity, a keen and vigorous understanding, with habits of the most exalted piety, degenerates into an uglier fiend than the gloomy imagination of Dante would have ventured to picture. Again, the monk is described as feeling and acting under the influence of an appetite which could not co-exist with his other emotions. The romance-writer possesses an unlimited power over situations; but he must scrupulously make his characters act in congruity with them. Let him work *physical* wonders only, and we will be content to *dream* with him for a while; but the first *moral* miracle which he attempts, he disgusts and awakens us. Thus our judgment remains unoffended, when, announced by thunders and earthquakes, the spirit appears to Ambrosio involved in blue fires that increase

5. "To disbelieve is to dislike": Horace, *Art of Poetry* 1.188.

6. Subtle.

7. This is the effort, this is the work (Latin).

the cold of the cavern; and we acquiesce in the power of the silver myrtle which made gates and doors fly open at its touch, and charmed every eye into sleep. But when a mortal, fresh from the impression of that terrible appearance, and in the act of evincing for the first time the witching force of this myrtle, is represented as being at the same moment agitated by so fleeting an appetite as that of lust, our own feelings convince us that this is not improbable, but impossible; not preternatural, but contrary to nature. The extent of the powers that may exist, we can never ascertain; and therefore we feel no great difficulty in yielding a temporary belief to any, the strangest, situation of *things*. But that situation once conceived, how beings like ourselves would feel and act in it, our own feelings sufficiently instruct us; and we instantly reject the clumsy fiction that does not harmonise with them. These are the two *principal* mistakes in *judgment*, which the author has fallen into; but we cannot wholly pass over the frequent incongruity of his style with his subjects. It is gaudy where it should have been severely simple; and too often the mind is offended by phrases the most trite and colloquial, where it demands and had expected a sternness and solemnity of diction.

A more grievous fault remains, a fault for which no literary excellence can atone, a fault which all other excellence does but aggravate, as adding subtlety to a poison by the elegance of its preparation. Mildness of censure would here be criminally misplaced, and silence would make us accomplices. Not without reluctance then, but in full conviction that we are performing a duty, we declare it to be our opinion, that the Monk is a romance, which if a parent saw in the hands of a son or daughter, he might reasonably turn pale. The temptations of Ambrosio are described with a libidinous minuteness, which, we sincerely hope, will receive its best and only adequate censure from the offended conscience of the author himself. The shameless harlotry of Matilda, and the trembling innocence of Antonia, are seized with equal avidity, as vehicles of the most voluptuous images; and though the tale is indeed a tale of horror, yet the most painful impression which the work left on our minds was that of great acquirements and splendid genius employed to furnish a *mormo*[8] for children, a poison for youth, and a provocative for the debauchee. Tales of enchantments and witchcraft can never be *useful*: our author has contrived to make them *pernicious*, by blending, with an irreverent negligence, all that is most awfully true in religion with all that is most ridiculously absurd in superstition.

1797

From Biographia Literaria

From Chapter 3[1]

For as to the devotees of the circulating libraries, I dare not compliment their *pass-time*, or rather *kill-time*, with the name of *reading*. Call it rather a

---

8. Bogeyman, object of needless dread.
1. This paragraph makes up the first footnote to the third chapter of Coleridge's *Biographia Literaria*, the hybrid book in which he blended autobiography with philosophical speculations and favorite anecdotes. In the body of his text,

Coleridge refers to the frequency with which his name has been before the reading public; the footnote (the text given here) then goes on to identify the sort of people who for him do not count as bona fide members of that public.

sort of beggarly daydreaming, during which the mind of the dreamer furnishes for itself nothing but laziness and a little mawkish sensibility; while the whole *materiel* and imagery of the doze is supplied *ab extra*[2] by a sort of mental *camera obscura*[3] manufactured at the printing office, which *pro tempore*[4] fixes, reflects and transmits the moving phantasms of one man's delirium, so as to people the barrenness of an hundred other brains afflicted with the same trance or suspension of all common sense and all definite purpose. We should therefore transfer this species of *amusement* (if indeed those can be said to retire *a musis*,[5] who were never in their company, or relaxation be attributable to those, whose bows are never bent) from the genus, *reading*, to that comprehensive class characterized by the power of reconciling the two contrary yet co-existing propensities of human nature, namely indulgence of sloth, and hatred of vacancy. In addition to novels and tales of chivalry in prose or rhyme (by which last I mean neither rhythm nor metre) this genus comprises as its species, gaming; swinging or swaying on a chair or gate; spitting over a bridge; smoking; snuff-taking; tête-à-tête quarrels after dinner between husband and wife; conning word by word all the advertisements of the *Daily Advertiser* in a public house on a rainy day, etc. etc. etc.

1815   1817

2. From the outside (Latin).
3. A device (forerunner of the modern camera) creating a special optical effect: light passes through a pinhole into a darkened room and creates an inverted image of the world beyond the walls.
4. For the time being (Latin).
5. A pun linking "amusement" and *a musis*, "away from the Muses."

CHARLES LAMB
1775–1834

Charles Lamb was a near contemporary of Wordsworth and Coleridge. He numbered these two poets among his close friends, published his own early poems in combination with those of Coleridge in 1796 and 1797, and supported the *Lyrical Ballads* and some of the other new poetry of his time. Yet Lamb lacks almost all the traits and convictions we think of as characteristically "Romantic." He happily lived all his life in the city and its environs. He could not abide Shelley or his poetry, and he distrusted Coleridge's supernaturalism and Wordsworth's oracular sublimities and religion of nature, preferring those elements in their poems that were human and realistic. In an age when many of the important writers were fervent radicals and some became equally fervent reactionaries, Lamb remained uncommitted in both politics and religion, and although on intimate terms with such dedicated reformers as William Hazlitt, William Godwin, Thomas Holcroft, and Leigh Hunt, he chose them as friends, as he said, not for their opinions but "for some individuality of character which they manifested." In his own writings he shared Wordsworth's concern with memories' power to transform the present moment and, like him, interjected a sense of the ideal into his representations of the actual and everyday. "The streets of London," Hazlitt wrote, assessing the essays Lamb published under the pseudonym Elia in the *London Magazine*, "are his fairy-land, teeming with wonder, with life and interest to his retrospective glance, as it did to the eager eye of childhood."

Lamb was born in London at the Inner Temple, center of the English legal profession. His father, who began his working life as a footman, was assistant to a lawyer there. His paternal as well as maternal grandparents were servants. At the age of seven he entered Christ's Hospital, the school Coleridge also attended. Childhood ended early. He left the school before he was fifteen and soon thereafter became a clerk in the accounting department of the East India Company, a huge commercial house, where he remained for thirty-three years. His adult life was quiet and unadventurous, but under its calm surface lay great tragedy. When he was twenty-two his beloved sister, Mary, ten years his senior, exhausted by her labors as a dressmaker and the work of caring for her invalid parents, began to show signs of a breakdown. One day she turned in a manic rage on the little girl who was her apprentice. When Mrs. Lamb tried to intercede, her daughter stabbed her in the heart. The jury's verdict was lunacy, but the intercession of her father's former employer spared Mary permanent confinement in an asylum. Instead, she was remanded to the custody of Charles, who devoted the rest of his life to her and their common household. Mary's attacks of insanity recurred, and when the terribly familiar symptoms began to show themselves, Charles and Mary would walk arm in arm and weeping to the asylum, carrying a straitjacket with them.

Most of the time, however, Mary was her normally serene and gracious self, and shared her brother's love of company and genius for friendship. The evening gatherings at the Lambs' attracted a varied company that included many of the leading writers and artists of England. Charles drew furiously on a pipe of strong tobacco and drank copiously; as the alcohol eased his habitual stammer, his puns and practical jokes grew ever more outrageous. He had, in fact, a complex temperament, in which the playfulness overlay a somber melancholy and the eccentricity sometimes manifested a touch of malice.

To supplement his salary at the East India House, Lamb had early turned to writing in a variety of literary forms: sonnets; blank verse; a sentimental novel; a tragedy; and a farce, *Mr. H——*, which was hissed by the audience, including its honest author, when it was produced at Drury Lane (the uneasiness with the theater that informs his essay "On the Tragedies of Shakespeare" probably reflects this experience). He also collaborated with his sister, Mary, on a series of children's books, including the excellent *Tales from Shakespeare*, and wrote some brilliant critical commentaries in his anthology, important for the Elizabethan revival of that period, titled *Specimens of English Dramatic Poets Who Lived about the Time of Shakespeare*. Not until 1820, however, at the age of forty-five, did Lamb discover the form that would make his name, when he began to write essays for John Scott's new *London Magazine*.

Lamb's achievement in those contributions to the *London* was to accommodate the intimacies of the familiar essay, a genre dating back to Montaigne in the sixteenth century, to a modern world of magazine writing that aimed to reach a general public. The *Essays of Elia* make the magazine—an impersonal medium that contributed conspicuously to the information overload of the age—appear to be a forum in which a reader might really *know* an author. A sense of the paradoxes of that project—a sense that the illusions of personality in the personal essay might be easily debunked—is never far away in Lamb's writings, lending a fascinating edge to their charm and complicating the autobiographical impulse that seems to link them to the works of his contemporaries. Under the pseudonym Elia, which, Lamb said, was the name of an Italian clerk he had known briefly while employed in the South Sea House, Lamb projects in his essays the character of a man who is whimsical but strong-willed, self-deprecating yet self-absorbed, with strong likes and dislikes, a specialist in nostalgia and in that humor which balances delicately on the verge of pathos. But Elia is also, as Lamb noted, an anagram for "a lie": the essays' seemingly unguarded self-revelation is intertwined with the cunning of a deliberate and dedicated artist in prose. And to write about himself Lamb developed a prose style that was colored throughout by archaic words and expressions that continually alluded to literary precursors, including the works of other eccentrics such as Robert Burton and Laurence Sterne—as if he were suggesting that he was most distinctively himself when most immersed in his beloved old books.

From On the Tragedies of Shakespeare, Considered with Reference to Their Fitness for Stage Representation[1]

* * * [S]uch is the instantaneous nature of the impressions which we take in at the eye and ear at a play-house, compared with the slow apprehension oftentimes of the understanding in reading, that we are apt not only to sink the play-writer in the consideration which we pay to the actor, but even to identify in our minds, in a perverse manner, the actor with the character which he represents. It is difficult for a frequent play-goer to disembarrass the idea of Hamlet from the person and voice of Mr. K. We speak of Lady Macbeth, while we are in reality thinking of Mrs. S.[2] * * *

Never let me be so ungrateful as to forget the very high degree of satisfaction which I received some years back from seeing for the first time a tragedy of Shakespeare performed, in which these two great performers sustained the principal parts. It seemed to embody and realize conceptions which had hitherto assumed no distinct shape. But dearly do we pay all our life after for this juvenile pleasure, this sense of distinctness. When the novelty is past, we find to our cost that instead of realizing an idea, we have only materialized and brought down a fine vision to the standard of flesh and blood. We have let go a dream, in quest of an unattainable substance.

How cruelly this operates upon the mind, to have its free conceptions thus cramped and pressed down to the measure of a strait-lacing actuality, may be judged from that delightful sensation of freshness, with which we turn to those plays of Shakespeare which have escaped being performed. * * *

It may seem a paradox, but I cannot help being of opinion that the plays of Shakespeare are less calculated for performance on a stage than those of almost any other dramatist whatever. Their distinguished excellence is a reason that they should be so. There is so much in them, which comes not under the province of acting, with which eye, and tone, and gesture, have nothing to do.

The glory of the scenic art is to personate passion, and the turns of passion; and the more coarse and palpable the passion is, the more hold upon the eyes and ears of the spectators the performer obviously possesses. For this reason, scolding scenes, scenes where two persons talk themselves into a fit of fury, and then in a surprising manner talk themselves out of it again, have always been the most popular upon our stage. And the reason is plain, because the spectators are here most palpably appealed to, they are the proper judges in this war of words, they are the legitimate ring that should be formed round such "intellectual prize-fighters." Talking is the direct object of the imitation here. But in all the best dramas, and in Shakespeare above all, how obvious it is, that the form of *speaking*, whether it be in soliloquy or dialogue, is only a medium, and often a highly artificial one, for

---

1. Published under Lamb's name in the magazine *The Reflector* in 1811.

2. Acclaimed actors John Philip Kemble (1757–1823) and his sister Sarah Siddons (1755–1831).

putting the reader or spectator into possession of that knowledge of the inner structure and workings of a mind in a character, which he could otherwise never have arrived at *in that form of composition* by any gift short of intuition. We do here as we do with novels written in the *epistolary form*. How many improprieties, perfect solecisms in letter-writing, do we put up with in *Clarissa*³ and other books, for the sake of the delight which that form upon the whole gives us.

But the practice of stage representation reduces every thing to a controversy of elocution. Every character, from the boisterous blasphemings of Bajazet⁴ to the shrinking timidity of womanhood, must play the orator. * * *

The character of Hamlet is perhaps that by which, since the days of Betterton,⁵ a succession of popular performers have had the greatest ambition to distinguish themselves. The length of the part may be one of their reasons. But for the character itself, we find it in a play, and therefore we judge it a fit subject of dramatic representation. The play itself abounds in maxims and reflections beyond any other, and therefore we consider it as a proper vehicle for conveying moral instruction. But Hamlet himself—what does he suffer meanwhile by being dragged forth as a public schoolmaster, to give lectures to the crowd! Why, nine parts in ten of what Hamlet does, are transactions between himself and his moral sense, they are the effusions of his solitary musings, which he retires to holes and corners and the most sequestered parts of the palace to pour forth; or rather, they are the silent meditations with which his bosom is bursting, reduced to *words* for the sake of the reader, who must else remain ignorant of what is passing there. These profound sorrows, these light-and-noise-abhorring ruminations, which the tongue scarce dares utter to deaf walls and chambers, how can they be represented by a gesticulating actor, who comes and mouths them out before an audience, making four hundred people his confidants at once? I say not that it is the fault of the actor so to do; he must pronounce them *ore rotundo*,⁶ he must accompany them with his eye; he must insinuate them into his auditory by some trick of eye, tone, or gesture, or he fails. *He must be thinking all the while of his appearance, because he knows that all the while the spectators are judging of it.* And this is the way to represent the shy, negligent, retiring Hamlet.

It is true that there is no other mode of conveying a vast quantity of thought and feeling to a great portion of the audience, who otherwise would never earn it for themselves by reading, and the intellectual acquisition gained this way may, for aught I know, be inestimable; but I am not arguing that Hamlet should not be acted, but how much Hamlet is made another thing by being acted. * * *

The truth is, the Characters of Shakespeare are so much the objects of meditation rather than of interest or curiosity as to their actions, that while we are reading any of his great criminal characters,—Macbeth, Richard, even Iago,—we think not so much of the crimes which they commit, as of the ambition, the aspiring spirit, the intellectual activity, which prompts them to overleap those moral fences. * * * But when we see these things represented,

---

3. Samuel Richardson's novel in letters, published 1747–48, admired across Europe for its illumination of the mysteries of the human heart.
4. Ottoman sultan. More than one dramatic character is based on this historical figure, but Lamb likely refers to a performance of Nicholas

Rowe's *Tamerlane* (first staged 1701).
5. Thomas Betterton (1635?–1710), acclaimed tragedian.
6. With well-turned speech (Latin); literally, with rounded mouth.

the acts which they do are comparatively everything, their impulses nothing. The state of sublime emotion into which we are elevated by those images of night and horror which Macbeth is made to utter, that solemn prelude with which he entertains the time till the bell shall strike which is to call him to murder Duncan,[7]—when we no longer read it in a book, when we have given up that vantage-ground of abstraction which reading possesses over seeing, and come to see a man in his bodily shape before our eyes actually preparing to commit a murder, if the acting be true and impressive, as I have witnessed it in Mr. K.'s performance of that part, the painful anxiety about the act, the natural longing to prevent it while it yet seems unperpetrated, the too close pressing semblance of reality, give a pain and an uneasiness which totally destroy all the delight which the words in the book convey, where the deed doing never presses upon us with the painful sense of presence: it rather seems to belong to history,—to something past and inevitable, if it has any thing to do with time at all. The sublime images, the poetry alone, is that which is present to our minds in the reading.

So to see Lear acted,—to see an old man tottering about the stage with a walking-stick, turned out of doors by his daughters in a rainy night, has nothing in it but what is painful and disgusting. We want to take him into shelter and relieve him. That is all the feeling which the acting of Lear ever produced in me. But the Lear of Shakespeare cannot be acted. The contemptible machinery by which they mimic the storm which he goes out in, is not more inadequate to represent the horrors of the real elements, than any actor can be to represent Lear: they might more easily propose to personate the Satan of Milton upon a stage, or one of Michael Angelo's terrible figures. The greatness of Lear is not in corporal dimension, but in intellectual; the explosions of his passion are terrible as a volcano; they are storms turning up and disclosing to the bottom that sea, his mind, with all its vast riches. It is his mind which is laid bare. This case of flesh and blood seems too insignificant to be thought on; even as he himself neglects it. On the stage we see nothing but corporal infirmities and weakness, the impotence of rage; while we read it, we see not Lear, but we are Lear,—we are in his mind, we are sustained by a grandeur which baffles the malice of daughters and storms; in the aberrations of his reason, we discover a mighty irregular power of reasoning, immethodized from the ordinary purposes of life, but exerting its powers, as the wind bloweth where it listeth,[8] at will upon the corruptions and abuses of mankind. * * *

Lear is essentially impossible to be represented on a stage. But how many dramatic personages are there in Shakespeare, which, though more tractable and feasible (if I may so speak) than Lear, yet from some circumstance, some adjunct to their character, are improper to be shewn to our bodily eye. Othello for instance. Nothing can be more soothing, more flattering to the nobler parts of our natures, than to read of a young Venetian lady of highest extraction, through the force of love and from a sense of merit in him whom she loved, laying aside every consideration of kindred, and country, and colour, and wedding with a *coal-black Moor*—(for such he is represented, in the imperfect state of knowledge respecting foreign countries in those days, compared with our own, or in compliance with popular notions, though the

7. *Macbeth* 2.1.
8. Echo of Christ's discussion of the mysteries of spiritual rebirth in John 3.8.

Moors are now well enough known to be by many shades less unworthy of a white woman's fancy)—it is the perfect triumph of virtue over accidents,[9] of the imagination over the senses. She sees Othello's colour in his mind.[1] But upon the stage, when the imagination is no longer the ruling faculty, but we are left to our poor unassisted senses, I appeal to every one that has seen Othello played, whether he did not, on the contrary, sink Othello's mind in his colour; whether he did not find something extremely revolting in the courtship and wedded caresses of Othello and Desdemona; and whether the actual sight of the thing did not over-weigh all that beautiful compromise which we make in reading. And the reason it should do so is obvious, because there is just so much reality presented to our senses as to give a perception of disagreement, with not enough of belief in the internal motives,—all that which is unseen,—to overpower and reconcile the first and obvious prejudices. What we see upon a stage is body and bodily action; what we are conscious of in reading is almost exclusively the mind, and its movements: and this I think may sufficiently account for the very different sort of delight with which the same play so often affects us in the reading and the seeing.

1811   1811

Detached Thoughts on Books and Reading[1]

> To mind the inside of a book is to entertain one's self with the forced product of another man's brain. Now I think a man of quality and breeding may be much amused with the natural sprouts of his own.
>
> —Lord Foppington in *The Relapse*[2]

An ingenious acquaintance of my own was so much struck with this bright sally of his Lordship, that he has left off reading altogether, to the great improvement of his originality. At the hazard of losing some credit on this head, I must confess that I dedicate no inconsiderable portion of my time to other people's thoughts. I dream away my life in others' speculations. I love to lose myself in other men's minds. When I am not walking, I am reading; I cannot sit and think. Books think for me.

I have no repugnances. Shaftesbury is not too genteel for me, nor Jonathan Wild too low.[3] I can read any thing which I call a *book*. There are things in that shape which I cannot allow for such.

In this catalogue of *books which are no books—biblia a-biblia*—I reckon Court Calendars, Directories, Pocket Books, Draught Boards bound and

---

9. "Accidents" in the sense used for properties or qualities that are extraneous to—i.e., not of the essence of—an object.
1. *Othello* 1.3.247.
1. Published in the *London Magazine*, July 1822, and revised for *Last Essays of Elia* (1833), Lamb's essay, although often tongue in cheek, shrewdly challenges the hierarchies the era's reviewers and others used to rank different kinds of writing and sort out good, tasteful readers from bad. Elia's fondness for novels from circulating libraries is as unusual as his willingness to present himself as a

receptive reader first and an original author second. For a contrast to his bookishness, see Wordsworth's "Expostulation and Reply" and "The Tables Turned" (pp. 296–98).
2. The would-be man of fashion in Sir John Vanbrugh's comedy of 1696, *The Relapse*.
3. Two extremes in 18th-century prose: the third earl of Shaftesbury (1671–1713), philosopher and essayist, and the gang leader who inspired Henry Fielding's 1743 crime novel *Jonathan Wild the Great*.

lettered at the back, Scientific Treatises, Almanacks, Statutes at Large; the works of Hume, Gibbon, Robertson, Beattie, Soame Jenyns, and, generally, all those volumes which "no gentleman's library should be without":[4] the Histories of Flavius Josephus (that learned Jew), and Paley's *Moral Philosophy*.[5] With these exceptions, I can read almost any thing. I bless my stars for a taste so catholic, so unexcluding.

I confess that it moves my spleen to see these *things in books' clothing* perched upon shelves, like false saints, usurpers of true shrines, intruders into the sanctuary, thrusting out the legitimate occupants. To reach down a well-bound semblance of a volume, and hope it is some kind-hearted play-book, then, opening what "seem its leaves," to come bolt upon a withering Population Essay.[6] To expect a Steele, or a Farquhar, and find—Adam Smith.[7] To view a well-arranged assortment of blockheaded Encyclopaedias (Anglicanas or Metropolitanas) set out in an array of Russia, or Morocco,[8] when a tithe of that good leather would comfortably re-clothe my shivering folios; would renovate Paracelsus himself, and enable old Raymund Lully to look like himself again in the world.[9] I never see these impostors, but I long to strip them, to warm my ragged veterans in their spoils.

To be strong-backed and neat-bound is the desideratum of a volume. Magnificence comes after. This, when it can be afforded, is not to be lavished upon all kinds of books indiscriminately. I would not dress a set of Magazines, for instance, in full suit. The dishabille,[1] or half-binding (with Russia backs ever) is *our* costume. A Shakespeare, or a Milton (unless the first editions), it were mere foppery to trick out in gay apparel. The possession of them confers no distinction. The exterior of them (the things themselves being so common), strange to say, raises no sweet emotions, no tickling sense of property in the owner. Thomson's *Seasons*,[2] again, looks best (I maintain it) a little torn, and dog's-eared. How beautiful to a genuine lover of reading are the sullied leaves, and worn out appearance, nay, the very odour (beyond Russia), if we would not forget kind feelings in fastidiousness, of an old "Circulating Library" *Tom Jones*, or *Vicar of Wakefield*![3] How they speak of the thousand thumbs, that have turned over their pages with delight!—of the lone sempstress, whom they may have cheered (milliner, or harder-working mantuamaker[4]) after her long day's needle-toil, running far into midnight, when she has snatched an hour, ill spared from sleep, to steep her cares, as in some Lethean cup,[5] in spelling out their enchanting contents! Who would have them a whit less soiled? What better condition could we desire to see them in?

4. Elia's list begins with the types of books sold by stationers and ends with those authored by venerated and prolific moralists, philosophers, and historians of the 18th century.

5. William Paley (1743–1805), theologian and philosopher. Josephus (37–100 C.E.), historian of the Jewish people.

6. Thomas Malthus's *Essay on the Principle of Population*, first published 1798, had by 1822 been through several editions and prompted several responses, including ones by Lamb's friends Godwin and Hazlitt.

7. The early-18th-century dramatists Richard Steele and George Farquhar, contrasted with the author of *The Wealth of Nations* (1776).

8. Russia and Morocco are two varieties of leather used in bookbinding.

9. Paracelsus (1493–1541) and Ramon Lully (1235–1317), authors with connections to alchemy—the search for the philosopher's stone, which could transmute base metals into gold, and for the elixir of life.

1. Negligent or casual dress.

2. James Thomson's widely read poem of natural description, published in 1730.

3. Novels by Henry Fielding and Oliver Goldsmith, published in 1748 and 1766.

4. Dressmaker. "Milliner": bonnet maker. Mary Lamb, a great reader of novels borrowed from circulating libraries, was a mantua-maker.

5. The waters of the river Lethe, which flowed through Hades, caused forgetfulness.

In some respects the better a book is, the less it demands from binding. Fielding, Smollet, Sterne,[6] and all that class of perpetually self-reproductive volumes—Great Nature's Stereotypes[7]—we see them individually perish with less regret, because we know the copies of them to be "eterne."[8] But where a book is at once both good and rare—where the individual is almost the species, and when *that* perishes,

> We know not where is that Promethean torch
> That can its light relumine—[9]

such a book, for instance, as the *Life of the Duke of Newcastle*, by his Duchess[1]—no casket is rich enough, no casing sufficiently durable, to honour and keep safe such a jewel.

Not only rare volumes of this description, which seem hopeless ever to be reprinted; but old editions of writers, such as Sir Philip Sydney, Bishop Taylor,[2] Milton in his prose-works, Fuller[3]—of whom we *have* reprints, yet the books themselves, though they go about, and are talked of here and there, we know, have not endenizened themselves (nor possibly ever will) in the national heart, so as to become stock books—it is good to possess these in durable and costly covers. I do not care for a First Folio of Shakespeare. I rather prefer the common editions of Rowe and Tonson, without notes, and with *plates*, which, being so execrably bad, serve as maps, or modest remembrancers, to the text; and without pretending to any supposable emulation with it, are so much better than the Shakespeare gallery *engravings*, which *did*.[4] I have a community of feeling with my countrymen about his Plays, and I like those editions of him best, which have been oftenest tumbled about and handled.—On the contrary, I cannot read Beaumont and Fletcher but in Folio. The Octavo editions are painful to look at.[5] I have no sympathy with them. If they were as much read as the current editions of the other poet, I should prefer them in that shape to the older one. I do not know a more heartless sight than the reprint of the *Anatomy of Melancholy*.[6] What need was there of unearthing the bones of that fantastic old great man, to expose them in a winding-sheet of the newest fashion to modern censure? what hapless stationer could dream of Burton ever becoming popular?—The wretched Malone could not do worse, when he bribed the sexton of Stratford church to let him white-wash the painted effigy of old Shakespeare,[7]

6. The novelists Tobias Smollett (1721–1771) and Laurence Sterne (1713–1768).
7. Refers to the molds that at the start of the 19th century had begun to be employed in the printing process, considerably enhancing the speed and efficiency of book production.
8. Lady Macbeth, suggesting the killing of Banquo and Fleance: "in them nature's copy's not eterne" (Shakespeare, *Macbeth* 3.2.39).
9. Cf. Othello's words as he contemplates Desdemona's murder (Shakespeare, *Othello* 5.2.12–13).
1. The 1667 biography of her husband by the poet and playwright Margaret Cavendish.
2. Jeremy Taylor (1613–1667), author of *Holy Living* and *Holy Dying*.
3. Anglican clergyman and antiquarian Thomas Fuller (1608–1661).
4. Illustrations by leading English artists were provided for the deluxe edition of Shakespeare issued by the print seller John Boydell in 1802. Elia favors the editions that were prepared by Nicholas Rowe and his publisher Jacob Tonson

starting in 1709.
5. Francis Beaumont (1585?–1616) and John Fletcher (1579–1625), Elizabeth dramatists and collaborators. Lamb's folio edition of their works is also mentioned in "Old China." Folio editions are distinguished from octavo by size: folio is the largest format for books, produced when a full-sized printer's sheet is folded once, whereas an octavo book is sized for pages folded so that each is one-eighth the size of a full sheet. By Lamb's day, book formats were to an extent correlated with their contents: the more cultural authority granted the type of literature or the author, the larger the format.
6. Robert Burton's vast treatise from 1621; there was an 1800 reprint. Burton's unmethodical, motley prose, which seemingly broaches a thousand topics to take on one, gave Lamb a model for his style in the Elia essays.
7. Shakespeare editor Edmond Malone (1741–1812). The repainting of Shakespeare's bust occurred in 1793.

The Romantic Period
(1785–1832)

Sir Brooke Boothby, Joseph Wright of Derby, 1781

Many details combine here to portray Boothby, a Derbyshire landowner and intellectual, as a progressive man of his times: the soberly colored wool suit, one cuff casually unbuttoned, that he wears instead of the bright silks of court dress; the fact that he has taken philosophical contemplation outdoors, into an untamed woodland scene. Boothby's left hand caresses a book by Jean-Jacques Rousseau, the French philosopher whom Boothby had recently edited: the portrait seems an endorsement of Rousseau's argument for a return to nature. Offsetting Boothby's modern guise, in the reclining attitude Wright has chosen for his depiction there is a recollection of statuary depicting classical river gods.

Le triomphe de la Liberté en l'élargissement de la Bastille, engraving by James Gillray after a painting by James Northcote, 1790

Gillray's engraving, which reproduces a no longer extant painting, was published in time to commemorate the first anniversary of the Parisian people's capture of the Bastille, an event retrospectively recognized as the beginning of the French Revolution. Descending into the prison's dark depths, a rescue party has found a site out of gothic fiction, a place of unburied bodies and ghastly instruments of torture. The revolutionists lead a manacled figure grown old in captivity into the light of freedom.

Glad Day, or *The Dance of Albion,* William Blake, ca. 1793

Blake kept returning to this image of liberation. He first designed it in 1780, shortly after finishing his apprenticeship as an engraver, when the vision of a rising sun and a radiant human body may have expressed his own youthful sense of freedom. But later, in an age of revolution, he identified the figure as Albion—"Albion rose from where he labourd at the Mill with Slaves." For Blake the giant Albion represents the ancient form of Britain, a universal man who has fallen on evil, repressive times but is destined to awake and to unite all people in a dance of liberty, both political and spiritual. Eventually, in *Jerusalem* (ca. 1820), Blake's last great prophetic work, the figure of Albion merged with Jesus, risen from the tomb as an embodiment of "the human form divine"—immortal and perpetually creative.

Plate 1, Copy D, of *The Marriage of Heaven and Hell*, William Blake, 1790–93

This title page of a work composed in the early years of the French Revolution (p. 159) juxtaposes lighthearted activities (birds and humans soaring, strolling, playing music, dancing, embracing) with bleak and ominous surroundings (the leaflessness of the trees, the intensity of the flames). The larger reclining figures at the bottom of the page, sexy but genderless, are usually read as a devil and an angel whose embrace symbolizes the union ("marriage") of contraries running throughout the work.

The Sick Rose, William Blake, 1794

Blake's "illumination" (plate 39, copy C, of *Songs of Innocence and of Experience*; see p. 138) further complicates an already highly ambiguous poetic text. In the picture are two worms—one eating a leaf in the upper left corner, the other coming out of the fallen blossom at the bottom—and three female figures, two of which, situated on the thorny stems above the engraved text, appear to be in postures of despair. The third female figure, emerging from the blossom, has arms flung forward in an expression of either ecstasy or terror.

Interior of Tintern Abbey,
J. M. W. Turner, 1794

Turner painted this watercolor at the age of
nineteen, a year after Wordsworth made his
first visit to the abbey (1793) and four years
before the poet returned for a second visit
(1798), as recorded in the famous "Lines"
pondering the changes that have taken
place in both the speaker and the scene
(p. 299). In Turner's version—as, in a
different way, in Wordsworth's—the ruined
symbol of religion, towering above two tiny
human figures, presumably tourists, in the
lower left, is in the process of being taken
over (allegorically superseded) by the
more powerful force of nature.

Gordale Scar, James Ward, ca. 1812–14

Eroded over millennia by the River Aire, runoff of an ancient glacier, these limestone cliffs
were a popular destination for nineteenth-century sightseers in search of the sublime. One
such visitor, William Wordsworth, wrote a sonnet about this wild landscape's capacity to
overwhelm the viewer. Ward's enigmatic and vast painting—it measures twelve by fourteen
feet—manipulates the viewer's perspective so as to further emphasize the height of the
overhanging cliffs, which, along with the thunderclouds, dwarf the cattle and deer huddled on
the ground below.

The Nightmare, Henry Fuseli, ca. 1783–91

The first version of this painting created a sensation when the Swiss-born artist Fuseli exhibited it at London's Royal Academy in 1781. Even Horace Walpole, who had used his own nightmare of "a gigantic hand in armour" when composing his Gothic novel, *The Castle of Otranto,* found Fuseli's trademark blend of violence, eroticism, and the irrational excessively disturbing: "shockingly mad, madder than ever; quite mad" was Walpole's verdict on the witchcraft scene that Fuseli exhibited four years later. It is no surprise to learn that during the 1920s Sigmund Freud kept an engraving of *The Nightmare* on display.

A Philosopher in a Moonlit Churchyard, Phillipe de Louther- bourg, 1790

When, twenty years before this painting, de Loutherbourg first came to England from France, he assumed the job of scene designer for Drury Lane Theater. The atmospheric effects that he created for the theater's extravaganzas are recalled in this painting. The philosopher, looking up from his book, contemplates a painting of the risen Christ, while a grave housing the remains of a Norman knight lies at his feet. De Loutherbourg both gestures toward gothic mysteries and registers contemporary antiquarians' researches into the material remnants of medieval culture. The ruins are modeled on Tintern Abbey's.

The Sleep of Endymion, Anne-Louis Girodet, 1791

For this otherworldly love scene, the French painter Girodet draws on Greek mythology's legends of the love the goddess of the moon bore for a mortal, the shepherd Endymion, whom she visited while he slept. Girodet adds to the story a figure sometimes identified as Eros, sometimes as Zephyr, the personification of the breeze, who is shown on the left half-smiling as he parts the surrounding foliage, the better to enable the moonbeams to embrace the sleeper. The unconscious Endymion is, by contrast, a gorgeously passive figure, though he does appear to stir in his sleep (dreaming perhaps) and turn his face toward the silvery light. In some versions of the legend, the goddess arranges for Endymion to sleep eternally, preserving his physical perfection and making him immortal. "A thing of beauty is a joy for ever": in 1818, in his first long poem, which opens with this line, John Keats would also represent Endymion's story and, like Girodet, use it to think about pleasure, love, dream, arrested time, and their relations.

Lord Byron, Thomas Phillips, 1835
(after an original of 1813)

Garbed theatrically in an Albanian soldier's
dress that he had purchased while on his travels,
Byron appears in this portrait as one of his own
exotic heroes. The profits from his "Eastern"
tales *Lara* and *The Corsair* in fact helped pay
the painter's fees for the portrait, which Byron
commissioned in 1813, choosing to be pictured
not as a member of the British establishment but
as an outsider. The archives of London's
National Portrait Gallery record more than
forty portraits of Byron done during his lifetime, as well as a waxwork model from life
made by Madame Tussaud in 1816: a statistic
that suggests the poet's keen awareness of the
magnetism and marketability of his image.

Madeline After Prayer, Daniel
Maclise, 1868

Closely attending to Keats's words,
Maclise pictures the moment when,
"her vespers done," Madeline, the
heroine of *The Eve of Saint Agnes*,
frees her hair "of all its wreathed
pearls," illuminated all the while
by the moonlight shining through
the window Keats had also
described in detail. Missing from
the image is Porphyro, who in
the poem spies on this scene of
disrobing from his hiding place in
Madeline's closet. Maclise is one of
many nineteenth-century painters
who took inspiration from the
sumptuous sensory detail of Keats's
romance.

Disappointed Love, Francis Danby, 1821

In this, the first work he exhibited at the Royal Academy, the Anglo-Irish, Bristol-based painter Francis Danby adopted an unprecedented approach to the combination of figure and landscape that was increasingly central to nineteenth-century painting. *Disappointed Love* owes its power to its fusion of the general and the particularized. The depiction of the young woman, her face and individuality concealed from the viewer, allies her with allegorical representations of melancholy, mourning figures placed atop mortuary monuments, or even some of the female figures in Blake's illuminated books. The scene in which she is placed, by contrast, based on Danby's study of scenery along the River Frome on Bristol's outskirts, is rendered in minute, naturalistic detail. He depicts the plants around her with a botanist's eye.

which stood there, in rude but lively fashion depicted, to the very colour of the cheek, the eye, the eye-brow, hair, the very dress he used to wear—the only authentic testimony we had, however imperfect, of these curious parts and parcels of him. They covered him over with a coat of white paint. By——, if I had been a justice of peace for Warwickshire, I would have clapt both commentator and sexton fast in the stocks, for a pair of meddling sacrilegious varlets.

I think I see them at their work—these sapient trouble-tombs.

Shall I be thought fantastical, if I confess, that the names of some of our poets sound sweeter, and have a finer relish to the ear—to mine, at least—than that of Milton or of Shakespeare? It may be, that the latter are more staled and rung upon in common discourse. The sweetest names, and which carry a perfume in the mention, are, Kit Marlowe, Drayton, Drummond of Hawthornden, and Cowley.[8]

Much depends upon *when* and *where* you read a book. In the five or six impatient minutes, before the dinner is quite ready, who would think of taking up the *Fairy Queen* for a stopgap, or a volume of Bishop Andrewes' sermons?[9]

Milton almost requires a solemn service of music to be played before you enter upon him. But he brings his music, to which, who listens, had need bring docile thoughts, and purged ears.

Winter evenings—the world shut out—with less of ceremony the gentle Shakespeare enters. At such a season, the *Tempest*, or his own *Winter's Tale*—

These two poets you cannot avoid reading aloud—to yourself, or (as it chances) to some single person listening. More than one—and it degenerates into an audience.

Books of quick interest, that hurry on for incidents, are for the eye to glide over only. It will not do to read them out. I could never listen to even the better kind of modern novels without extreme irksomeness.

A newspaper, read out, is intolerable. In some of the Bank offices it is the custom (to save so much individual time) for one of the clerks—who is the best scholar—to commence upon the Times, or the Chronicle, and recite its entire contents aloud *pro bono publico*.[1] With every advantage of lungs and elocution, the effect is singularly vapid. In barbers' shops and public-houses a fellow will get up, and spell out a paragraph, which he communicates as some discovery. Another follows with *his* selection. So the entire journal transpires at length by piece-meal. Seldom-readers are slow readers, and, without this expedient no one in the company would probably ever travel through the contents of a whole paper.

Newspapers always excite curiosity. No one ever lays one down without a feeling of disappointment.

What an eternal time that gentleman in black, at Nando's,[2] keeps the paper! I am sick of hearing the waiter bawling out incessantly, "the Chronicle is in hand, Sir."

Coming in to an inn at night—having ordered your supper—what can be more delightful than to find lying in the window-seat, left there time out of mind by the carelessness of some former guest—two or three numbers of

8. Poet and dramatist Christopher Marlowe (1564–1593) and poets Michael Drayton (1563–1631), William Drummond of Hawthornden (1585–1649), and Abraham Cowley (1610–1667).

9. Launcelot Andrewes (1551–1626).
1. For the common good (Latin).
2. Coffeehouse in London's Fleet Street.

the old Town and Country Magazine, with its amusing *tête-à-tête* pictures—
"The Royal Lover and Lady G——"; "The Melting Platonic and the old
Beau,"—and such like antiquated scandal? Would you exchange it—at that
time, and in that place—for a better book?

Poor Tobin, who latterly fell blind, did not regret it so much for the
weightier kinds of reading—the *Paradise Lost*, or *Comus*, he could have *read*
to him—but he missed the pleasure of skimming over with his own eye a
magazine, or a light pamphlet.

I should not care to be caught in the serious avenues of some cathedral
alone, and reading *Candide*.[3]

I do not remember a more whimsical surprise than having been once
detected—by a familiar damsel—reclined at my ease upon the grass, on
Primrose Hill (her Cythera),[4] reading—*Pamela*.[5] There was nothing in the
book to make a man seriously ashamed at the exposure; but as she seated
herself down by me, and seemed determined to read in company, I could
have wished it had been—any other book. We read on very sociably for a
few pages; and, not finding the author much to her taste, she got up, and—
went away. Gentle casuist, I leave it to thee to conjecture, whether the
blush (for there was one between us) was the property of the nymph or the
swain in this dilemma. From me you shall never get the secret.

I am not much a friend to out-of-doors reading. I cannot settle my spirits to
it. I knew a Unitarian minister, who was generally to be seen upon Snowhill
(as yet Skinner's-street *was not*), between the hours of ten and eleven in the
morning, studying a volume of Lardner.[6] I own this to have been a strain of
abstraction beyond my reach. I used to admire how he sidled along, keeping
clear of secular contacts. An illiterate encounter with a porter's knot,[7] or a
bread basket, would have quickly put to flight all the theology I am master of,
and have left me worse than indifferent to the five points.[8]

There is a class of street-readers, whom I can never contemplate without
affection—the poor gentry, who, not having wherewithal to buy or hire a
book, filch a little learning at the open stalls—the owner, with his hard eye,
casting envious looks at them all the while, and thinking when they will have
done. Venturing tenderly, page after page, expecting every moment when he
shall interpose his interdict, and yet unable to deny themselves the gratification, they "snatch a fearful joy."[9] Martin B——,[1] in this way, by daily fragments, got through two volumes of *Clarissa*,[2] when the stallkeeper damped
his laudable ambition, by asking him (it was in his younger days) whether he
meant to purchase the work. M. declares, that under no circumstances of his
life did he ever peruse a book with half the satisfaction which he took in
those uneasy snatches. A quaint poetess of our day[3] has moralised upon this
subject in two very touching but homely stanzas.

3. Voltaire, the author of the satirical *Candide, or Optimism* (1759), was notorious for his free-thinking in religious matters.
4. Greek island sacred to the goddess of love. Primrose Hill is a green space in north London.
5. Samuel Richardson's 1740 novel in letters chronicling the failed seduction of a very virtuous maidservant.
6. Theologian Nathaniel Lardner (1684–1768).
7. The padded yoke a London market porter wore to help him carry his burden.
8. The five points of Calvinist belief: Original

Sin, Predestination, Irresistible Grace, Particular Redemption, and the Final Perseverance of the Saints.
9. Cf. the description of schoolboys' play in Thomas Gray's 1742 "Ode on a Distant Prospect of Eton College" (line 40).
1. The Lambs' friend Martin Burney, nephew of the novelist Frances Burney.
2. A million-word novel, Samuel Richardson's *Clarissa* (1747–48) took up seven volumes.
3. Mary Lamb. The poem had appeared earlier in the Lambs' *Poetry for Children* (1809).

I saw a boy with eager eye
Open a book upon a stall,
And read, as he'd devour it all;
Which when the stall-man did espy,
Soon to the boy I heard him call,
"You, Sir, you never buy a book,
Therefore in one you shall not look."
The boy pass'd slowly on, and with a sigh
He wish'd he never had been taught to read,
Then of the old churl's books he should have had no need.

Of sufferings the poor have many,
Which never can the rich annoy:
I soon perceiv'd another boy,
Who look'd as if he'd not had any
Food, for that day at least—enjoy
The sight of cold meat in a tavern larder.
This boy's case, then thought I, is surely harder,
Thus hungry, longing, thus without a penny,
Beholding choice of dainty-dressed meat:
No wonder if he wish he ne'er had learn'd to eat.

1822   1833

Old China

I have an almost feminine partiality for old china. When I go to see any great house, I inquire for the china closet, and next for the picture gallery. I cannot defend the order of preference, but by saying that we have all some taste or other, of too ancient a date to admit of our remembering distinctly that it was an acquired one. I can call to mind the first play, and the first exhibition, that I was taken to; but I am not conscious of a time when china jars and saucers were introduced into my imagination.

I had no repugnance then—why should I now have?—to those little, lawless, azure-tinctured grotesques, that under the notion of men and women float about, uncircumscribed by any element, in that world before perspective—a china teacup.

I like to see my old friends—whom distance cannot diminish—figuring up in the air (so they appear to our optics), yet on terra firma still—for so we must in courtesy interpret that speck of deeper blue, which the decorous artist, to prevent absurdity, had made to spring up beneath their sandals.

I love the men with women's faces, and the women, if possible, with still more womanish expressions.

Here is a young and courtly mandarin, handing tea to a lady from a salver—two miles off. See how distance seems to set off respect! And here the same lady, or another—for likeness is identity on teacups—is stepping into a little fairy boat, moored on the hither side of this calm garden river, with a dainty mincing foot, which in a right angle of incidence (as angles go in our world) must infallibly land her in the midst of a flowery mead—a furlong off on the other side of the same strange stream!

Farther on—if far or near can be predicated of their world—see horses, trees, pagodas, dancing the hays.[1]

Here—a cow and rabbit couchant,[2] and coextensive—so objects show, seen through the lucid atmosphere of fine Cathay.[3]

I was pointing out to my cousin last evening, over our Hyson[4] (which we are old-fashioned enough to drink unmixed still of an afternoon), some of these *speciosa miracula*[5] upon a set of extraordinary old blue china (a recent purchase) which we were now for the first time using; and could not help remarking how favorable circumstances had been to us of late years that we could afford to please the eye sometimes with trifles of this sort—when a passing sentiment seemed to overshade the brows of my companion. I am quick at detecting these summer clouds in Bridget.[6]

"I wish the good old times would come again," she said, "when we were not quite so rich. I do not mean that I want to be poor; but there was a middle state"—so she was pleased to ramble on—"in which I am sure we were a great deal happier. A purchase is but a purchase, now that you have money enough and to spare. Formerly it used to be a triumph. When we coveted a cheap luxury (and, O! how much ado I had to get you to consent in those times!)—we were used to have a debate two or three days before, and to weigh the *for* and *against*, and think what we might spare it out of, and what saving we could hit upon, that should be an equivalent. A thing was worth buying then, when we felt the money that we paid for it.

"Do you remember the brown suit, which you made to hang upon you, till all your friends cried shame upon you, it grew so threadbare—and all because of that folio Beaumont and Fletcher,[7] which you dragged home late at night from Barker's in Covent Garden? Do you remember how we eyed it for weeks before we could make up our minds to the purchase, and had not come to a determination till it was near ten o'clock of the Saturday night, when you set off from Islington,[8] fearing you should be too late—and when the old bookseller with some grumbling opened his shop, and by the twinkling taper (for he was setting bedwards) lighted out the relic from his dusty treasures—and when you lugged it home, wishing it were twice as cumbersome—and when you presented it to me—and when we were exploring the perfectness of it (*collating*, you called it)—and while I was repairing some of these loose leaves with paste, which your impatience would not suffer to be left till daybreak—was there no pleasure in being a poor man? or can those neat black clothes which you wear now, and are so careful to keep brushed, since we have become rich and finical, give you half the honest vanity with which you flaunted it about in that overworn suit—your old corbeau[9]—for four or five weeks longer than you should have done, to pacify your conscience for the mighty sum of fifteen—or sixteen shillings was it?—a great affair we thought it then—which you had lavished on the old folio. Now you can afford to buy any book that pleases you, but I do not see that you ever bring me home any nice old purchases now.

1. An English country dance.
2. Lying down with the head raised (term from heraldry).
3. The old European name for China.
4. A Chinese green tea.
5. Shining wonders (Latin).
6. In Lamb's essays, his name for his sister, Mary.

7. The Elizabethan dramatic collaborators, whose plays were first collected in a large folio volume in 1647.
8. In the north of London, where the Lambs had been living.
9. A dark green cloth, almost black (hence its name, the French for raven).

"When you came home with twenty apologies for laying out a less number of shillings upon that print after Leonardo,[1] which we christened the 'Lady Blanch'; when you looked at the purchase, and thought of the money—and thought of the money, and looked again at the picture—was there no pleasure in being a poor man? Now, you have nothing to do but to walk into Colnaghi's,[2] and buy a wilderness of Leonardos. Yet do you?

"Then, do you remember our pleasant walks to Enfield, and Potter's Bar, and Waltham,[3] when we had a holiday—holidays, and all other fun, are gone now we are rich—and the little hand-basket in which I used to deposit our day's fare of savory cold lamb and salad—and how you would pry about at noontide for some decent house, where we might go in and produce our store—only paying for the ale that you must call for—and speculate upon the looks of the landlady, and whether she was likely to allow us a tablecloth—and wish for such another honest hostess as Izaak Walton has described many a one on the pleasant banks of the Lea, when he went a-fishing—and sometimes they would prove obliging enough, and sometimes they would look grudgingly upon us—but we had cheerful looks still for one another, and would eat our plain food savorily, scarcely grudging Piscator[4] his Trout Hall? Now—when we go out a day's pleasuring, which is seldom, moreover, we *ride* part of the way—and go into a fine inn, and order the best of dinners, never debating the expense—which, after all, never has half the relish of those chance country snaps,[5] when we were at the mercy of uncertain usage and a precarious welcome.

"You are too proud to see a play anywhere now but in the pit. Do you remember where it was we used to sit, when we saw the *Battle of Hexham*, and the *Surrender of Calais*,[6] and Bannister and Mrs. Bland in the *Children in the Wood*[7]—when we squeezed out our shillings apiece to sit three or four times in a season in the one-shilling gallery—where you felt all the time that you ought not to have brought me—and more strongly I felt obligation to you for having brought me—and the pleasure was the better for a little shame—and when the curtain drew up, what cared we for our place in the house, or what mattered it where we were sitting, when our thoughts were with Rosalind in Arden, or with Viola at the Court of Ilyria.[8] You used to say that the gallery was the best place of all for enjoying a play socially—that the relish of such exhibitions must be in proportion to the infrequency of going—that the company we met there, not being in general readers of plays, were obliged to attend the more, and did attend, to what was going on, on the stage—because a word lost would have been a chasm, which it was impossible for them to fill up. With such reflections we consoled our pride then—and I appeal to you whether, as a woman, I met generally with less attention and accommodation than I have done since in more expensive situations in the house? The getting in indeed, and the crowding up those

1. Leonardo da Vinci (1452–1519), the great Italian painter. The painting is the one known as *Modesty and Vanity*.
2. Colnaghi was a London print seller. In the issue of the *London Magazine* in which "Old China" first appeared, the artist Thomas Griffiths Wainewright (using the signature "C. van Vinkboom") works some advice for Colnaghi into his essay: namely, to immediately "import a few impressions . . . of those beautiful plates from Da Vinci," including "Miss Lamb's favourite, 'Lady

Blanche,'" as he foresees that this issue "will occasion a considerable call for them."
3. All three are suburbs to the north of London.
4. The fisherman in Izaak Walton's *Complete Angler* (1653).
5. Snacks.
6. Comedies by George Colman (1762–1836).
7. By Thomas Morton (1764–1838).
8. Rosalind in Shakespeare's *As You Like It* and Viola in his *Twelfth Night*.

inconvenient staircases, was bad enough—but there was still a law of civility to woman recognized to quite as great an extent as we ever found in the other passages—and how a little difficulty overcome heightened the snug seat and the play, afterwards! Now we can only pay our money and walk in. You cannot see, you say, in the galleries now. I am sure we saw, and heard too, well enough then—but sight, and all, I think, is gone with our poverty.

"There was pleasure in eating strawberries, before they became quite common—in the first dish of peas, while they were yet dear—to have them for a nice supper, a treat. What treat can we have now? If we were to treat ourselves now—that is, to have dainties a little above our means, it would be selfish and wicked. It is the very little more that we allow ourselves beyond what the actual poor can get at that makes what I call a treat—when two people living together, as we have done, now and then indulge themselves in a cheap luxury, which both like; while each apologizes, and is willing to take both halves of the blame to his single share. I see no harm in people making much of themselves, in that sense of the word. It may give them a hint how to make much of others. But now—what I mean by the word—we never do make much of ourselves. None but the poor can do it. I do not mean the veriest poor of all, but persons as we were, just above poverty.

"I know what you were going to say, that it is mighty pleasant at the end of the year to make all meet—and much ado we used to have every Thirty-first Night of December to account for our exceedings—many a long face did you make over your puzzled accounts, and in contriving to make it out how we had spent so much—or that we had not spent so much—or that it was impossible we should spend so much next year—and still we found our slender capital decreasing—but then, betwixt ways, and projects, and com-promises of one sort or another, and talk of curtailing this charge, and doing without that for the future—and the hope that youth brings, and laughing spirits (in which you were never poor till now), we pocketed up our loss, and in conclusion, with 'lusty brimmers' (as you used to quote it out of *hearty cheerful Mr. Cotton*,[9] as you called him), we used to welcome in 'the coming guest.' Now we have no reckoning at all at the end of the old year—no flattering promises about the new year doing better for us."

Bridget is so sparing of her speech on most occasions that when she gets into a rhetorical vein, I am careful how I interrupt it. I could not help, how-ever, smiling at the phantom of wealth which her dear imagination had con-jured up out of a clear income of poor—— hundred pounds a year. "It is true we were happier when we were poorer, but we were also younger, my cousin. I am afraid we must put up with the excess, for if we were to shake the superflux into the sea, we should not much mend ourselves. That we had much to struggle with, as we grew up together, we have reason to be most thankful. It strengthened and knit our compact closer. We could never have been what we have been to each other, if we had always had the sufficiency which you now complain of. The resisting power—those natural dilations of the youthful spirit, which circumstances cannot straiten—with us are long since passed away. Competence to age is supplementary youth, a sorry supplement indeed, but I fear the best that is to be had. We must ride where we formerly walked: live better and lie softer—and shall be wise to do so—

---

9. Charles Cotton (1630–1687), a favorite poet of Lamb's. The quotations are from his poem "The New Year." "Lusty brimmers": glasses filled to the brim.

than we had means to do in those good old days you speak of. Yet could those days return—could you and I once more walk our thirty miles a day—could Bannister and Mrs. Bland again be young, and you and I be young to see them—could the good old one-shilling gallery days return—they are dreams, my cousin, now—but could you and I at this moment, instead of this quiet argument, by our well-carpeted fireside, sitting on this luxurious sofa—be once more struggling up those inconvenient staircases, pushed about, and squeezed, and elbowed by the poorest rabble of poor gallery scramblers—could I once more hear those anxious shrieks of yours—and the delicious *Thank God, we are safe*, which always followed when the topmost stair, conquered, let in the first light of the whole cheerful theater down beneath us—I know not the fathom line that ever touched a descent so deep as I would be willing to bury more wealth in than Croesus had, or the great Jew R——[1] is supposed to have, to purchase it. And now do just look at that merry little Chinese waiter holding an umbrella, big enough for a bed-tester,[2] over the head of that pretty insipid half Madonnaish chit of a lady in that very blue summerhouse."

1823   1823

1. Nathan Meyer Rothschild (1777–1836), founder of the English branch of the great Euro- pean banking house.
2. Bed canopy.

JANE AUSTEN
1775–1817

Although nowadays her portrait adorns coffee mugs and T-shirts, and journalists, making much of the movie adaptations of her novels, like to imagine her as the center of attention at Hollywood parties, Jane Austen spent her short, secluded life away from the spotlight. Other members of her large family—she was one of eight children born to an Anglican clergyman and his wife—appear to have lived more in the world and closer to this turbulent period's great events than she did. Two brothers fought as naval officers in the Napoleonic War; another became the banker to the flashy London set of the prince regent; her cousin Eliza, born in India, wed a captain in the French army who perished by the guillotine. Austen, however, spent most of her life in Hampshire, the same rural area of southern England in which she was born. Her formal education was limited to a short time at boarding school. Otherwise she and her beloved sister Cassandra had to scramble, like most girls of their class, into what education they could while at home and amid their father's books. As neither Austen daughter married, home was where these two remained the whole of their adult lives.

Jane Austen turned down a proposal of marriage in 1802, possibly intuiting how difficult it would be to combine authorship with life as a wife, mother, and gentry hostess. She had started writing at the age of twelve, for her family's amusement and her own, and in 1797 began sending work to publishers in London. At that stage they were for the most part unreceptive. In 1803 one paid £10 for the copyright of the novel we know as *Northanger Abbey*, but then declined to publish it, so that Austen had at last, after tangled negotiations, to buy it back. Finally she published *Sense and Sensibility* (1811) at her own expense, then *Pride and Prejudice* (1813) and *Mansfield Park* (1814). Next—by this time under the prestigious auspices of John Murray, who was also Byron's publisher—came *Emma* (1816) and, posthumously, after Austen's death at forty-one, *Persuasion* and a revised version of *Northanger Abbey* (both 1818). The Austen name was never publicly associated with any of these books, whose discreet title pages merely identified "a lady" as the author (though, as was also the case with Sir Walter Scott's Waverley novels, success made Austen's authorship an open secret). The modesty of that signature, however, is belied by the assurance of Austen's narrative voice, the confidence with which (to adapt the famous first sentence of *Pride and Prejudice*) it subjects "truths universally acknowledged" to witty critical scrutiny.

The six novels are all, in Austen's words, "pictures of domestic life in country villages." The world they depict might seem provincial and insular. For the most part the working classes are absent or present only as silent servants; the soldiers and sailors who were protecting England from Napoleon are presented mainly as welcome additions to a ball. Yet the novels also document with striking detail how, within those country villages, the boundaries that had formerly defined the category of "the gentleman" were becoming permeable under the influence of the changes wrought by revolution and war, and how competition for social status was becoming that much fiercer. Through their heroines, readers can see, as well, how harshly the hard facts of economic life bore down on gentlewomen during this period when a lady's security depended on her making a good marriage. The conundrum at the center of the fiction is whether such a marriage can be compatible with the independence of mind and moral integrity that Austen, like her heroines, cherishes.

Austen also wrote so as to explore what the novel form could be and do. Along with the reviewers of the time, she criticized the form, but unlike them, she did so to perfect it. With striking flexibility the new narrative voice that she introduced into novel writing shifts back and forth between a romantic point of view and an irony that reminds us of romance's limits—that reminds us that romance features its own sort of provincialism. At the same time Austen also distanced the novel form from the didactic agenda cultivated by her many contemporaries who were convinced that the only respectable fiction was the antiromance that weaned its readers of their romantic expectations. Her delight in mocking their preachy fictions is not only evident in the parodies that she wrote in the 1790s (including *Love and Friendship*, a forerunner of George Eliot's "Silly Novels by Lady Novelists") but is a feature of her mature novels, which as a rule conclude in ways that deviate quite flagrantly from the patterns of reward and punishment a moralist might prefer. "I leave it to be settled by whomsoever it may concern," the narrator of *Northanger Abbey* declares in a parting shot, and in characteristic epigrammatic style, "whether the tendency of this work be altogether to recommend parental tyranny, or reward filial disobedience." "[P]ictures of perfection," Austen wrote in a letter, "make me sick and wicked."

Austen's example is so central to what the novel as a form has become that it can be difficult from our present-day vantage point to recognize the iconoclasm in her depictions of the undervalued business of everyday life. It can be hard to see how much her originality—her creation of characters who are both ordinary and unforgettable, her accounts of how they change—challenged her contemporaries' expectations about novels' plots, settings, and characterizations. Her dissent from those expectations is palpable, however, in a "Plan of a Novel, According to Hints from Various Quarters," the satire Austen wrote after *Emma*, and which assembles the various "hints" she had received from well-wishers about what she should write next. The immediate occasion for the "Plan" was the series of letters Austen received from the Reverend James Stanier Clarke, librarian to the prince regent, who having conveyed to her the prince's wish that *Emma* should be dedicated to him, continued the correspondence so as to suggest topics that Austen should engage for the next novel—in particular, a historical romance about the royal house of Saxe Cobourg. Austen in reply affirmed the comic spirit of all her works: "I could not sit seriously down to write a serious Romance under any other motive than to save my Life, and if it were indispensable for me to keep it up and never relax into laughing at myself or other people, I am sure I should be hung before I had finished the first Chapter."

Love and Friendship   This work, an anarchic parody written when the author was fourteen, puts front and center Austen's gifts for ironic assassination and her sharp-eyed sense of the preachiness not simply of her period's moralists but more particularly of her period's rebels against orthodox morality. In this miniaturized novel in letters, Austen constructs a world whose inhabitants are absurdly faithful to codes of conduct they extract from their readings of novels in letters. The protagonists of *Love and Friendship* are energetic students of the clichés of fashionable sentimentalism. They adore Nature, like many poets favoring the romantic Scottish Highlands and picturesque Wales; they know that free spirits, true radicals, should elevate the dictates of the heart over the head. The young Austen calls attention to the messages about gender roles embedded in novel writers' celebrations of the strong feelings that make heroines swoon. She shares Wollstonecraft's impatience with how, as the latter put it in *A Vindication of the Rights of Woman,* the culture makes women slaves to their emotions—"blown about by every momentary gust of feeling." This work is usually classified among Austen's juvenilia, but it has the worldliness and bravado we expect from a much older author.

Our text modernizes the irregular spelling and, to a lesser extent, the punctuation of the manuscript, which Austen titled "Love and Freindship."

Love and Friendship

A Novel in a Series of Letters

"Deceived in Friendship & Betrayed in Love"

LETTER THE FIRST *From Isabel to Laura*

How often, in answer to my repeated entreaties that you would give my daughter a regular detail of the misfortunes and adventures of your life, have you said "No, my friend, never will I comply with your request till I may be no longer in danger of again experiencing such dreadful ones." Surely that time is now at hand. You are this day fifty-five. If a woman may ever be said to be in safety from the determined perseverance of disagreeable lovers and the cruel persecutions of obstinate fathers, surely it must be at such a time of life.

Isabel

LETTER THE SECOND *Laura to Isabel*

Although I cannot agree with you in supposing that I shall never again be exposed to misfortunes as unmerited as those I have already experienced, yet to avoid the imputation of obstinacy or ill nature, I will gratify the curiosity of your daughter; and may the fortitude with which I have suffered the many afflictions of my past life prove to her a useful lesson for the support of those which may befall her in her own.

Laura

LETTER THE THIRD *Laura to Marianne*

As the daughter of my most intimate friend I think you entitled to that knowledge of my unhappy story, which your mother has so often solicited me to give you. My father was a native of Ireland and an inhabitant of Wales; my mother was the natural daughter of a Scotch peer by an Italian opera-girl[1]—I was born in Spain and received my education at a convent in France.

When I had reached my eighteenth year I was recalled by my parents to my paternal roof in Wales. Our mansion was situated in one of the most romantic parts of the vale of Usk.[2] Though my charms are now considerably softened and somewhat impaired by the misfortunes I have undergone, I was once beautiful. But lovely as I was, the graces of my person were the least of my perfections. Of every accomplishment[3] accustomary to my sex, I was mistress. When in the convent, my progress had always exceeded my instructions, my acquirements had been wonderful for my age, and I had shortly surpassed my masters.

In my mind, every virtue that could adorn it was centered; it was the rendezvous of every good quality and of every noble sentiment.

A sensibility[4] too tremblingly alive to every affliction of my friends, my acquaintance, and particularly to every affliction of my own, was my only fault, if a fault it could be called. Alas! how altered now! Though indeed my own misfortunes do not make less impression on me than they ever did, yet now I never feel for those of an other. My accomplishments too, begin to fade—I can neither sing so well nor dance so gracefully as I once did—and I have entirely forgot the *Minuet Dela Cour.*[5]

Adieu.

Laura

LETTER THE FOURTH *Laura to Marianne*

Our neighbourhood was small, for it consisted only of your mother. She may probably have already told you that, being left by her parents in indigent circumstances, she had retired into Wales on economical motives. There it was our friendship first commenced. Isabel was then one and twenty— Though pleasing both in her person and manners (between ourselves) she never possessed the hundredth part of my beauty or accomplishments. Isabel had seen the world. She had passed two years at one of the first boarding

---

1. Illegitimate daughter of a Scottish nobleman and a woman who danced in the ballet corps of an opera company.
2. River valley in south Wales that had been celebrated by William Gilpin in his handbook for tourists in quest of picturesque scenes, *Observations on the River Wye* (1782). See "*Tintern Abbey*, Tourism, and Romantic Landscape" in the NAEL Archive.
3. Central to the curriculum of female education, "accomplishments" were the skills in music, dance, and drawing that were supposed to make young ladies better companions for their future husbands.

4. Sensibility, as a term designating the individual's capacity for sensitive emotional reaction, was celebrated in much late-18th-century literature at the same time that it was studied in medicine, investigations of the human nervous system especially. Sensibility was often linked to sympathy— the ability to enter into the feelings of another person—and hence to pity and benevolence, and was in this context assessed as a source of social harmony.
5. Literally, the court minuet—the stately formal dance that in the 18th century would begin a ball and be followed by livelier country dances.

schools in London, had spent a fortnight in Bath,[6] and had supped one night in Southampton.[7]

"Beware, my Laura, (she would often say) beware of the insipid vanities and idle dissipations of the metropolis of England; beware of the unmeaning luxuries of Bath and of the stinking fish of Southampton."

"Alas! (exclaimed I) how am I to avoid those evils I shall never be exposed to? What probability is there of my ever tasting the dissipations of London, the luxuries of Bath, or the stinking fish of Southampton? I who am doomed to waste my days of youth and beauty in an humble cottage in the vale of Usk."

Ah! little did I then think I was ordained so soon to quit that humble cottage for the deceitful pleasures of the world.

Adieu.

Laura

LETTER THE FIFTH *Laura to Marianne*

One evening in December as my father, my mother, and myself were arranged in social converse round our fireside, we were on a sudden greatly astonished by hearing a violent knocking on the outward door of our rustic cot.[8]

My father started—"What noise is that?" (said he.) "It sounds like a loud rapping at the door"—(replied my mother.) "It does indeed." (cried I.) "I am of your opinion; (said my father) it certainly does appear to proceed from some uncommon violence exerted against our unoffending door." "Yes, (exclaimed I) I cannot help thinking it must be somebody who knocks for admittance."

"That is another point (replied he;) We must not pretend to determine on what motive the person may knock—though that someone *does* rap at the door, I am partly convinced."

Here, a second tremendous rap interrupted my father in his speech and somewhat alarmed my mother and me.

"Had we not better go and see who it is? (said she) The servants are out." "I think we had." (replied I.) "Certainly, (added my father) by all means." "Shall we go now?" (said my mother.) "The sooner the better." (answered he). "Oh! let no time be lost." (cried I.)

A third more violent rap than ever again assaulted our ears. "I am certain there is somebody knocking at the door." (said my mother.) "I think there must," (replied my father) "I fancy the servants are returned; (said I) I think I hear Mary going to the door." "I'm glad of it (cried my father) for I long to know who it is."

I was right in my conjecture; for Mary instantly entering the room informed us that a young gentleman and his servant were at the door, who had lost their way, were very cold, and begged leave to warm themselves by our fire.

"Won't you admit them?" (said I) "You have no objection, my dear?" (said my Father.) "None in the world." (replied my mother.)

Mary, without waiting for any further commands, immediately left the room and quickly returned, introducing the most beauteous and amiable youth I had ever beheld. The servant, she kept to herself.

---

6. Fashionable spa town in the west of England.
7. Port town in the south of England, in Austen's home county of Hampshire.
8. Cottage.

My natural sensibility had already been greatly affected by the sufferings of the unfortunate stranger, and no sooner did I first behold him, than I felt that on him the happiness or misery of my future life must depend.

Adieu.

Laura

LETTER THE SIXTH *Laura to Marianne*

The noble youth informed us that his name was Lindsay—for particular reasons, however, I shall conceal it under that of Talbot. He told us that he was the son of an English baronet,[9] that his mother had been many years no more, and that he had a sister of the middle size. "My father (he continued) is a mean and mercenary wretch—it is only to such particular friends as this dear party that I would thus betray his failings. Your virtues, my amiable Polydore (addressing himself to my father), yours, dear Claudia, and yours, my charming Laura, call on me to repose in you my confidence." We bowed. "My Father, seduced by the false glare of fortune and the deluding pomp of title, insisted on my giving my hand to Lady Dorothea. No, never, exclaimed I. Lady Dorothea is lovely and engaging; I prefer no woman to her; but, know sir, that I scorn to marry her in compliance with your wishes. No! Never shall it be said that I obliged my father."

We all admired the noble manliness of his reply. He continued.

"Sir Edward was surprised; he had perhaps little expected to meet with so spirited an opposition to his will. 'Where, Edward, in the name of wonder (said he) did you pick up this unmeaning gibberish? You have been studying novels, I suspect.' I scorned to answer: it would have been beneath my dignity. I mounted my horse and, followed by my faithful William, set forwards for my aunt's."

"My father's house is situated in Bedfordshire, my aunt's in Middlesex, and, though I flatter myself with being a tolerable proficient in geography, I know not how it happened, but I found myself entering this beautiful vale, which I find is in South Wales, when I had expected to have reached my aunt's."[1]

"After having wandered some time on the banks of the Usk without knowing which way to go, I began to lament my cruel destiny in the bitterest and most pathetic manner. It was now perfectly dark, not a single star was there to direct my steps, and I know not what might have befallen me, had I not at length discerned through the solemn gloom that surrounded me a distant light, which, as I approached it, I discovered to be the cheerful blaze of your fire. Impelled by the combination of misfortunes under which I laboured, namely fear, cold, and hunger, I hesitated not to ask admittance, which at length I have gained; and now, my adorable Laura (continued he, taking my hand), when may I hope to receive that reward of all the painful sufferings I have undergone during the course of my attachment to you, to which I have ever aspired? Oh! when will you reward me with yourself?"

"This instant, dear and amiable Edward." (replied I.) We were immediately united by my father, who though he had never taken orders had been bred to the church.[2]

Adieu.

Laura

---

9. A baronet, a member of the lower aristocracy, is entitled to be called "Sir" and can pass on his title to his son.
1. Bedfordshire is in the eastern midlands of England. Middlesex is just northwest of London.

South Wales is many miles to the southwest of both.
2. Laura's father has never been ordained. This marriage is not legal.

LETTER THE SEVENTH *Laura to Marianne*

We remained but a few days after our marriage in the vale of Usk. After taking an affecting farewell of my father, my mother, and my Isabel, I accompanied Edward to his aunt's in Middlesex. Philippa received us both with every expression of affectionate love. My arrival was indeed a most agreeable surprise to her, as she had not only been totally ignorant of my marriage with her nephew, but had never even had the slightest idea of there being such a person in the world.

Augusta, the sister of Edward, was on a visit to her when we arrived. I found her exactly what her brother had described her to be—of the middle size. She received me with equal surprise, though not with equal cordiality, as Philippa. There was a disagreeable coldness and forbidding reserve in her reception of me which was equally distressing and unexpected. None of that interesting sensibility or amiable sympathy in her manners and address to me which should have distinguished our introduction to each other. Her language was neither warm, nor affectionate, her expressions of regard were neither animated nor cordial; her arms were not opened to receive me to her heart, though my own were extended to press her to mine.

A short conversation between Augusta and her brother, which I accidentally overheard, increased my dislike to her, and convinced me that her heart was no more formed for the soft ties of love than for the endearing intercourse of friendship.

"But do you think that my father will ever be reconciled to this imprudent connection?" (said Augusta.)

"Augusta (replied the noble youth) I thought you had a better opinion of me, than to imagine I would so abjectly degrade myself as to consider my father's concurrence in any of my affairs, either of consequence or concern to me. Tell me, Augusta, tell me with sincerity; did you ever know me consult his inclinations or follow his advice in the least trifling particular since the age of fifteen?"

"Edward (replied she) you are surely too diffident in your own praise. Since you were fifteen only!—My dear brother, since you were five years old, I entirely acquit you of ever having willingly contributed to the satisfaction of your father. But still I am not without apprehensions of your being shortly obliged to degrade yourself in your own eyes by seeking a support for your wife in the generosity of Sir Edward."

"Never, never, Augusta, will I so demean myself. (said Edward). Support! What support will Laura want which she can receive from him?"

"Only those very insignificant ones of victuals and drink." (answered she.)

"Victuals and drink! (replied my husband in a most nobly contemptuous manner) and dost thou then imagine that there is no other support for an exalted mind (such as is my Laura's) than the mean and indelicate employment of eating and drinking?"

"None that I know of so efficacious." (returned Augusta).

"And did you then never feel the pleasing pangs of love, Augusta? (replied my Edward). Does it appear impossible to your vile and corrupted palate to exist on love? Can you not conceive the luxury of living in every distress that poverty can inflict, with the object of your tenderest affection?"

"You are too ridiculous (said Augusta) to argue with; perhaps, however, you may in time be convinced that. . . ."

Here I was prevented from hearing the remainder of her speech, by the appearance of a very handsome young woman, who was ushered into the room at the door of which I had been listening. On hearing her announced by the name of "Lady Dorothea," I instantly quitted my post and followed her into the parlour, for I well remembered that she was the lady proposed as a wife for my Edward by the cruel and unrelenting baronet.

Although Lady Dorothea's visit was nominally to Philippa and Augusta, yet I have some reason to imagine that (acquainted with the marriage and arrival of Edward) to see me was a principal motive to it.

I soon perceived that, though lovely and elegant in her person and though easy and polite in her address, she was of that inferior order of beings with regard to delicate feeling, tender sentiments, and refined sensibility, of which Augusta was one.

She stayed but half an hour and neither, in the course of her visit, confided to me any of her secret thoughts, nor requested me to confide in her any of mine. You will easily imagine therefore, my dear Marianne, that I could not feel any ardent affection or very sincere attachment for Lady Dorothea.

Adieu.

Laura

LETTER THE EIGHTH *Laura to Marianne, in continuation*

Lady Dorothea had not left us long before another visitor, as unexpected a one as her Ladyship, was announced. It was Sir Edward, who, informed by Augusta of her brother's marriage, came doubtless to reproach him for having dared to unite himself to me without his knowledge. But Edward, foreseeing his design, approached him with heroic fortitude as soon as he entered the room, and addressed him in the following manner.

"Sir Edward, I know the motive of your journey here—You come with the base design of reproaching me for having entered into an indissoluble engagement with my Laura without your consent—But, Sir, I glory in the act—. It is my greatest boast that I have incurred the displeasure of my father!"

So saying, he took my hand and, whilst Sir Edward, Philippa, and Augusta were doubtless reflecting with admiration on his undaunted bravery, led me from the parlour to his father's carriage, which yet remained at the door and in which we were instantly conveyed from the pursuit of Sir Edward.

The postilions[3] had at first received orders only to take the London road; as soon as we had sufficiently reflected, however, we ordered them to drive to M——., the seat of Edward's most particular friend, which was but a few miles distant.

At M——. we arrived in a few hours; and on sending in our names were immediately admitted to Sophia, the wife of Edward's friend. After having been deprived during the course of three weeks of a real friend (for such I term your mother), imagine my transports at beholding one, most truly worthy of the name. Sophia was rather above the middle size; most elegantly formed. A soft languor spread over her lovely features, but increased their beauty.—It was the characteristic of her mind—. She was all sensibility and feeling. We flew into each other's arms and, after having exchanged vows of mutual friendship for the rest of our lives, instantly unfolded to each other

---

3. The servants mounted on and guiding the horses that draw a coach.

the most inward secrets of our hearts—. We were interrupted in this delightful employment by the entrance of Augustus (Edward's friend), who was just returned from a solitary ramble.

Never did I see such an affecting scene as was the meeting of Edward and Augustus.

"My life! my soul!" (exclaimed the former) "My adorable angel!" (replied the latter) as they flew into each other's arms. It was too pathetic for the feelings of Sophia and myself—We fainted alternately on a sofa.[4]

Adieu.

Laura

LETTER THE NINTH *From the same to the same*

Towards the close of the day we received the following letter from Philippa.

Sir Edward is greatly incensed by your abrupt departure; he has taken back Augusta with him to Bedfordshire. Much as I wish to enjoy again your charming society, I cannot determine to snatch you from that of such dear and deserving friends—When your visit to them is terminated, I trust you will return to the arms of your

Philippa

We returned a suitable answer to this affectionate note and, after thanking her for her kind invitation, assured her that we would certainly avail ourselves of it, whenever we might have no other place to go to. Though certainly nothing could, to any reasonable being, have appeared more satisfactory than so grateful a reply to her invitation, yet I know not how it was, but she was certainly capricious enough to be displeased with our behaviour and in a few weeks after, either to revenge our conduct, or relieve her own solitude, married a young and illiterate fortune-hunter. This imprudent step (though we were sensible[5] that it would probably deprive us of that fortune which Philippa had ever taught us to expect) could not on our own accounts excite from our exalted minds a single sigh; yet fearful lest it might prove a source of endless misery to the deluded bride, our trembling sensibility was greatly affected when we were first informed of the event. The affectionate entreaties of Augustus and Sophia that we would for ever consider their house as our home, easily prevailed on us to determine never more to leave them—. In the society of my Edward and this amiable pair, I passed the happiest moments of my life: Our time was most delightfully spent, in mutual protestations of friendship, and in vows of unalterable love, in which we were secure from being interrupted by intruding and disagreeable visitors, as Augustus and Sophia had, on their first entrance in the neighbourhood, taken due care to inform the surrounding families that, as their happiness centered wholly in themselves, they wished for no other society. But alas! my dear Marianne, such happiness as I then enjoyed was too perfect to be lasting. A most severe and unexpected blow at once destroyed every sensation of pleasure. Convinced as you must be from what I have already told you concerning Augustus and Sophia, that there never were a happier couple, I need

---

4. A stage direction in Richard Brinsley Sheridan's comedy *The Critic* (1779) directs the actors playing the mother and son to "faint alternately in each other's arms."
5. Conscious, aware.

not, I imagine, inform you that their union had been contrary to the inclinations of their cruel and mercenary parents, who had vainly endeavoured with obstinate perseverance to force them into a marriage with those whom they had ever abhorred, but, with an heroic fortitude worthy to be related and admired, they had both constantly refused to submit to such despotic power.

After having so nobly disentangled themselves from the shackles of parental authority by a clandestine marriage, they were determined never to forfeit the good opinion they had gained in the world in so doing, by accepting any proposals of reconciliation that might be offered them by their fathers—to this farther trial of their noble independence, however, they never were exposed.

They had been married but a few months when our visit to them commenced, during which time they had been amply supported by a considerable sum of money which Augustus had gracefully purloined from his unworthy father's escritoire,[6] a few days before his union with Sophia.

By our arrival their expenses were considerably increased, though their means for supplying them were then nearly exhausted. But they, exalted creatures! scorned to reflect a moment on their pecuniary distresses and would have blushed at the idea of paying their debts.—Alas! what was their reward for such disinterested behaviour? The beautiful Augustus was arrested and we were all undone. Such perfidious treachery in the merciless perpetrators of the deed will shock your gentle nature, dearest Marianne, as much as it then affected the delicate sensibility of Edward, Sophia, your Laura, and of Augustus himself. To complete such unparalleled barbarity, we were informed that an execution in the house would shortly take place.[7] Ah! what could we do but what we did! We sighed and fainted on the sofa.

Adieu.

Laura

LETTER THE TENTH *Laura in continuation*

When we were somewhat recovered from the overpowering effusions of our grief, Edward desired that we would consider what was the most prudent step to be taken in our unhappy situation, while he repaired to his imprisoned friend to lament over his misfortunes. We promised that we would, and he set forwards on his journey to town. During his absence we faithfully complied with his desire and, after the most mature deliberation, at length agreed that the best thing we could do was to leave the house of which we every moment expected the officers of justice to take possession. We waited therefore with the greatest impatience for the return of Edward, in order to impart to him the result of our deliberations—. But no Edward appeared—. In vain did we count the tedious moments of his absence—in vain did we weep—in vain even did we sigh—no Edward returned—. This was too cruel, too unexpected a blow to our gentle sensibility—we could not support it—we could only faint—. At length, collecting all the resolution I was mistress of, I arose and, after packing up some necessary apparel for Sophia and myself, I dragged her to a carriage I had ordered, and instantly we set out for London. As the habitation of Augustus was within twelve

6. Writing desk.
7. I.e., the goods in the house, as property of a debtor who has forfeited them, will be seized by a sheriff's officer.

miles of town, it was not long ere we arrived there, and no sooner had we entered Holborn[8] than, letting down one of the front glasses,[9] I enquired of every decent-looking person that we passed "If they had seen my Edward?"

But as we drove too rapidly to allow them to answer my repeated enquiries, I gained little, or indeed, no information concerning him. "Where am I to drive?" said the postilion. "To Newgate,[1] gentle youth (replied I), to see Augustus." "Oh! no, no, (exclaimed Sophia) I cannot go to Newgate; I shall not be able to support the sight of my Augustus in so cruel a confinement—my feelings are sufficiently shocked by the *recital* of his distress, but to behold it will overpower my sensibility." As I perfectly agreed with her in the justice of her sentiments, the postilion was instantly directed to return into the country. You may perhaps have been somewhat surprised, my dearest Marianne, that in the distress I then endured, destitute of any support, and unprovided with any habitation, I should never once have remembered my father and mother or my paternal cottage in the vale of Usk. To account for this seeming forgetfulness I must inform you of a trifling circumstance concerning them which I have as yet never mentioned—. The death of my parents a few weeks after my departure is the circumstance I allude to. By their decease I became the lawful inheritress of their house and fortune. But alas! the house had never been their own, and their fortune had only been an annuity[2] on their own lives. Such is the depravity of the world! To your mother I should have returned with pleasure, should have been happy to have introduced to her my charming Sophia, and should have with cheerfulness have passed the remainder of my life in their dear society in the vale of Usk, had not one obstacle to the execution of so agreeable a scheme intervened; which was the marriage and removal of your mother to a distant part of Ireland.

Adieu.

Laura

LETTER THE ELEVENTH *Laura in continuation*

"I have a relation in Scotland (said Sophia to me as we left London) who, I am certain, would not hesitate in receiving me." "Shall I order the boy to drive there?" said I—but instantly recollecting myself, exclaimed "Alas, I fear it will be too long a journey for the horses." Unwilling however to act only from my own inadequate knowledge of the strength and abilities of horses, I consulted the postilion, who was entirely of my opinion concerning the affair. We therefore determined to change horses at the next town and to travel post[3] the remainder of the journey—. When we arrived at the last inn we were to stop at, which was but a few miles from the house of Sophia's relation, unwilling to intrude our society on him unexpected and unthought of, we wrote a very elegant and well-penned note to him containing an account of our destitute and melancholy situation, and of our intention to spend some months with him in Scotland. As soon as we had dispatched this letter, we immediately prepared to follow it in person and were stepping

---

8. District in London.
9. Window of the coach.
1. A prison. That Augustus is thought to be there indicates he has been arrested as a thief

rather than as a debtor.
2. Annual payment of a set sum.
3. By speedy and expensive post coach.

into the carriage for that purpose, when our attention was attracted by the entrance of a coroneted coach and four[4] into the inn-yard. A gentleman considerably advanced in years descended from it—. At his first appearance my sensibility was wonderfully affected and ere I had gazed at him a second time, an instinctive sympathy whispered to my heart, that he was my grandfather.

Convinced that I could not be mistaken in my conjecture, I instantly sprang from the carriage I had just entered, and following the venerable stranger into the room he had been shewn to, I threw myself on my knees before him and besought him to acknowledge me as his grandchild.—He started, and, after having attentively examined my features, raised me from the ground and throwing his grandfatherly arms around my neck, exclaimed, "Acknowledge thee! Yes, dear resemblance of my Laurina and my Laurina's daughter, sweet image of my Claudia and my Claudia's mother, I do acknowledge thee as the daughter of the one and the granddaughter of the other." While he was thus tenderly embracing me, Sophia, astonished at my precipitate departure, entered the room in search of me—. No sooner had she caught the eye of the venerable peer, than he exclaimed with every mark of astonishment—"Another granddaughter ! Yes, yes, I see you are the daughter of my Laurina's eldest girl; your resemblance to the beauteous Matilda sufficiently proclaims it." "Oh!" replied Sophia, "when I first beheld you the instinct of nature whispered me that we were in some degree related—But whether grandfathers, or grandmothers, I could not pretend to determine." He folded her in his arms, and whilst they were tenderly embracing, the door of the apartment opened and a most beautiful young man appeared. On perceiving him Lord St. Clair started and, retreating back a few paces, with uplifted hands, said, "Another grandchild! What an unexpected happiness is this! to discover in the space of three minutes, as many of my descendants! This, I am certain, is Philander, the son of my Laurina's third girl, the amiable Bertha; there wants now but the presence of Gustavus to complete the union of my Laurina's grandchildren."

"And here he is; (said a graceful youth who that instant entered the room) here is the Gustavus you desire to see. I am the son of Agatha, your Laurina's fourth and youngest daughter." "I see you are indeed; replied Lord St. Clair— But tell me (continued he, looking fearfully towards the door) tell me, have I any other grandchildren in the house." "None, my Lord." "Then I will provide for you all without further delay—Here are four banknotes of 50£ each— Take them and remember I have done the duty of a grandfather—." He instantly left the room and immediately afterwards the house.

Adieu.

Laura

LETTER THE TWELFTH *Laura in continuation*

You may imagine how greatly we were surprised by the sudden departure of Lord St. Clair. "Ignoble grandsire!" exclaimed Sophia. "Unworthy grandfather!" said I, and instantly fainted in each other's arms. How long we remained in this situation I know not; but when we recovered we found

---

4. The coach, drawn by four horses, is adorned with the image of a crown, indicating its occupant's noble rank.

ourselves alone, without either Gustavus, Philander, or the banknotes. As we were deploring our unhappy fate, the door of the apartment opened and "Macdonald" was announced. He was Sophia's cousin. The haste with which he came to our relief so soon after the receipt of our note spoke so greatly in his favour that I hesitated not to pronounce him, at first sight, a tender and sympathetic friend. Alas! he little deserved the name—for though he told us that he was much concerned at our misfortunes, yet by his own account it appeared that the perusal of them had neither drawn from him a single sigh, nor induced him to bestow one curse on our vindictive stars—. He told Sophia that his daughter depended on her returning with him to Macdonald Hall, and that as his cousin's friend he should be happy to see me there also. To Macdonald Hall, therefore, we went, and were received with great kindness by Janetta, the daughter of Macdonald, and the mistress of the mansion. Janetta was then only fifteen; naturally well disposed, endowed with a susceptible heart, and a sympathetic disposition, she might, had these amiable qualities been properly encouraged, have been an ornament to human nature; but, unfortunately, her father possessed not a soul sufficiently exalted to admire so promising a disposition, and had endeavoured by every means in his power to prevent its increasing with her years. He had actually so far extinguished the natural noble sensibility of her heart, as to prevail on her to accept an offer from a young man of his recommendation. They were to be married in a few months, and Graham was in the house when we arrived. We soon saw through his character—. He was just such a man as one might have expected to be the choice of Macdonald. They said he was sensible, well-informed, and agreeable; we did not pretend to judge of such trifles, but, as we were convinced he had no soul, that he had never read the Sorrows of Werter,[5] and that his hair bore not the slightest resemblance to auburn, we were certain that Janetta could feel no affection for him, or at least that she ought to feel none. The very circumstance of his being her father's choice, too, was so much in his disfavour, that had he been deserving her in every other respect, yet that of itself ought to have been a sufficient reason in the eyes of Janetta for rejecting him. These considerations we were determined to represent to her in their proper light and doubted not of meeting with the desired success from one naturally so well disposed, whose errors in the affair had only arisen from a want of proper confidence in her own opinion, and a suitable contempt of her father's. We found her, indeed, all that our warmest wishes could have hoped for; we had no difficulty to convince her that it was impossible she could love Graham, or that it was her duty to disobey her father; the only thing at which she rather seemed to hesitate was our assertion that she must be attached to some other person. For some time, she persevered in declaring that she knew no other young man for whom she had the smallest affection; but upon explaining the impossibility of such a thing she said that she believed she did like Captain M'Kenzie better than anyone she knew besides. This confession satisfied us and, after having enumerated the good qualities of M'Kenzie and assured her that she was violently in love with him, we desired to know whether he had ever in anywise declared his affection to her.

5. Sorrows of Young Werther (1774), Goethe's novel in letters telling the story of the title character's hopeless love, was a hit in England when translated from its original German. It is often seen as a founding text of the European Romantic movement.

"So far from having ever declared it, I have no reason to imagine that he has ever felt any for me." said Janetta. "That he certainly adores you (replied Sophia) there can be no doubt—. The attachment must be reciprocal—. Did he never gaze on you with admiration—tenderly press your hand— drop an involuntary tear—and leave the room abruptly?" "Never (replied she) that I remember—he has always left the room indeed when his visit has been ended, but has never gone away particularly abruptly or without making a bow." "Indeed, my love (said I) you must be mistaken—: for it is absolutely impossible that he should ever have left you but with confusion, despair, and precipitation—. Consider but for a moment, Janetta, and you must be convinced how absurd it is to suppose that he could ever make a bow, or behave like any other person." Having settled this point to our satisfaction, the next we took into consideration was to determine in what manner we should inform M'Kenzie of the favourable opinion Janetta entertained of him—. We at length agreed to acquaint him with it by an anonymous letter which Sophia drew up in the following manner.

> Oh! happy lover of the beautiful Janetta; oh! enviable possessor of *her* heart whose hand is destined to another, why do you thus delay a confession of your attachment to the amiable object of it ? Oh! consider that a few weeks will at once put an end to every flattering hope that you may now entertain, by uniting the unfortunate victim of her father's cruelty to the execrable and detested Graham.
>
> Alas! why do you thus so cruelly connive at the projected misery of her and of yourself by delaying to communicate that scheme which had doubtless long possessed your imagination? A secret union will at once secure the felicity of both.

The amiable M'Kenzie, whose modesty, as he afterwards assured us, had been the only reason of his having so long concealed the violence of his affection for Janetta, on receiving this billet flew on the wings of love to Macdonald Hall and so powerfully pleaded his attachment to her who inspired it that, after a few more private interviews, Sophia and I experienced the satisfaction of seeing them depart for Gretna Green,[6] which they chose for the celebration of their nuptials, in preference to any other place, although it was at a considerable distance from Macdonald Hall.

Adieu.

Laura

LETTER THE THIRTEENTH *Laura in Continuation*

They had been gone nearly a couple of hours, before either Macdonald or Graham had entertained any suspicion of the affair—. And they might not even then have suspected it, but for the following little accident. Sophia, happening one day to open a private drawer in Macdonald's library with one of her own keys, discovered that it was the place where he kept his papers of consequence and amongst them some banknotes of considerable amount. This discovery she imparted to me; and having agreed together that it would be a proper treatment of so vile a wretch as Macdonald to deprive him of

---

6. A town in southern Scotland, in which marriages of minors could be quickly performed without questions being asked. It was for this reason the destination of many eloping couples during the period.

money, perhaps dishonestly gained, it was determined that the next time we should either of us happen to go that way, we would take one or more of the banknotes from the drawer. This well-meant plan we had often successfully put in execution; but alas! on the very day of Janetta's escape, as Sophia was majestically removing the fifth banknote from the drawer to her own purse, she was suddenly most impertinently interrupted in her employment by the entrance of Macdonald himself, in a most abrupt and precipitate manner. Sophia (who, though naturally all winning sweetness, could when occasions demanded it call forth the dignity of her sex) instantly put on a most forbidding look, and, darting an angry frown on the undaunted culprit, demanded in a haughty tone of voice "Wherefore her retirement was thus insolently broken in on?" The unblushing Macdonald, without even endeavouring to exculpate himself from the crime he was charged with, meanly endeavoured to reproach Sophia with ignobly defrauding him of his money. The dignity of Sophia was wounded; "Wretch (exclaimed she, hastily replacing the banknote in the drawer) how darest thou to accuse me of an act, of which the bare idea makes me blush?" The base wretch was still unconvinced and continued to upbraid the justly offended Sophia in such opprobrious language, that at length he so greatly provoked the gentle sweetness of her nature, as to induce her to revenge herself on him by informing him of Janetta's elopement, and of the active part we had both taken in the affair. At this period of their quarrel I entered the library and was, as you may imagine, equally offended as Sophia at the ill-grounded accusations of the malevolent and contemptible Macdonald. "Base miscreant (cried I) how canst thou thus undauntedly endeavour to sully the spotless reputation of such bright excellence? Why dost thou not suspect *my* innocence as soon?" "Be satisfied Madam (replied he) I *do* suspect it, and therefore must desire that you will both leave this house in less than half an hour."

"We shall go willingly; (answered Sophia) our hearts have long detested thee, and nothing but our friendship for thy daughter could have induced us to remain so long beneath thy roof."

"Your friendship for my daughter has indeed been most powerfully exerted by throwing her into the arms of an unprincipled fortune-hunter." (replied he.)

"Yes, (exclaimed I) amidst every misfortune, it will afford us some consolation to reflect that by this one act of friendship to Janetta, we have amply discharged every obligation that we have received from her father."

"It must indeed be a most grateful reflection, to your exalted minds." (said he.)

As soon as we had packed up our wardrobe and valuables, we left Macdonald Hall, and after having walked about a mile and a half we sat down by the side of a clear limpid stream to refresh our exhausted limbs. The place was suited to meditation—. A grove of full-grown elms sheltered us from the east—. A bed of full-grown nettles from the west—. Before us ran the murmuring brook and behind us ran the turnpike road. We were in a mood for contemplation and in a disposition to enjoy so beautiful a spot. A mutual silence, which had for some time reigned between us, was at length broke by my exclaiming—"What a lovely scene! Alas, why are not Edward and Augustus here to enjoy its beauties with us?"

"Ah! my beloved Laura (cried Sophia) for pity's sake, forbear recalling to my remembrance the unhappy situation of my imprisoned husband. Alas, what would I not give to learn the fate of my Augustus! to know if he is still in Newgate, or if he is yet hung. But never shall I be able so far to conquer my tender sensibility as to enquire after him. Oh! do not, I beseech you, ever let me again hear you repeat his beloved name—. It affects me too deeply—. I cannot bear to hear him mentioned; it wounds my feelings."

"Excuse me, my Sophia, for having thus unwillingly offended you—" replied I—and then changing the conversation, desired her to admire the noble grandeur of the elms which sheltered us from the eastern zephyr.[7] "Alas! my Laura (returned she) avoid so melancholy a subject, I entreat you.—Do not again wound my sensibility by observations on those elms. They remind me of Augustus—. He was like them, tall, majestic—he possessed that noble grandeur which you admire in them."

I was silent, fearful lest I might any more unwillingly distress her by fixing on any other subject of conversation which might again remind her of Augustus.

"Why do you not speak, my Laura?" (said she, after a short pause) "I cannot support this silence—you must not leave me to my own reflections; they ever recur to Augustus."

"What a beautiful sky! (said I) How charmingly is the azure varied by those delicate streaks of white!"

"Oh! my Laura (replied she, hastily withdrawing her eyes from a momentary glance at the sky) do not thus distress me by calling my attention to an object which so cruelly reminds me of my Augustus's blue satin waistcoat striped with white! In pity to your unhappy friend, avoid a subject so distressing." What could I do? The feelings of Sophia were at that time so exquisite, and the tenderness she felt for Augustus so poignant, that I had not the power to start any other topic, justly fearing that it might in some unforeseen manner again awaken all her sensibility by directing her thoughts to her husband.—Yet to be silent would be cruel; she had entreated me to talk.

From this dilemma I was most fortunately relieved by an accident truly apropos;[8] it was the lucky overturning of a gentleman's phaeton,[9] on the road which ran murmuring behind us. It was a most fortunate accident as it diverted the attention of Sophia from the melancholy reflections which she had been before indulging. We instantly quitted our seats and ran to the rescue of those who but a few moments before had been in so elevated a situation as a fashionably high phaeton, but who were now laid low and sprawling in the dust—. "What an ample subject for reflection on the uncertain enjoyments of this world, would not that phaeton and the life of Cardinal Wolsey afford a thinking mind!"[1] said I to Sophia as we were hastening to the field of action.

She had not time to answer me, for every thought was now engaged by the horrid spectacle before us. Two gentlemen, most elegantly attired but weltering in their blood, was what first struck our eyes—we approached—they were Edward and Augustus—Yes, dearest Marianne, they were our husbands. Sophia shrieked and fainted on the ground—I screamed and instantly ran mad—. We remained thus mutually deprived of our senses some min-

---

7. A breeze; usually one from the west.
8. Opportune.
9. Type of open carriage, named for the overadventurous charioteer of Greek mythology.
1. The reference is to Cardinal Wolsey's fall from

royal grace during the reign of Henry VIII. Laura, like any well-trained schoolgirl of the 18th century, knows how to moralize on topics from English history.

utes, and on regaining them were deprived of them again.—For an hour and a quarter did we continue in this unfortunate situation—Sophia fainting every moment and I running mad as often. At length a groan from the hapless Edward (who alone retained any share of life) restored us to ourselves—. Had we indeed before imagined that either of them lived, we should have been more sparing of our grief—but as we had supposed when we first beheld them that they were no more, we knew that nothing could remain to be done but what we were about—. No sooner therefore did we hear my Edward's groan than, postponing our lamentations for the present, we hastily ran to the dear youth and kneeling on each side of him implored him not to die—. "Laura (said he, fixing his now languid eyes on me) I fear I have been overturned."

I was overjoyed to find him yet sensible—.

"Oh! tell me, Edward (said I) tell me, I beseech you, before you die, what has befallen you since, that unhappy day in which Augustus was arrested and we were separated—"

"I will" (said he) and instantly fetching a deep sigh, expired—. Sophia immediately sunk again into a swoon—. *My* grief was more audible. My voice faltered, my eyes assumed a vacant stare, my face became as pale as death, and my senses were considerably impaired—.

"Talk not to me of phaetons (said I, raving in a frantic, incoherent manner)—give me a violin—. I'll play to him and soothe him in his melancholy hours—Beware, ye gentle nymphs, of Cupid's thunderbolts, avoid the piercing shafts of Jupiter—Look at that grove of firs—I see a leg of mutton—They told me Edward was not dead; but they deceived me—they took him for a cucumber—" Thus I continued, wildly exclaiming on my Edward's death—. For two hours did I rave thus madly and should not then have left off, as I was not in the least fatigued, had not Sophia, who was just recovered from her swoon, entreated me to consider that night was now approaching and that the damps began to fall. "And whither shall we go (said I) to shelter us from either?" "To that white cottage." (replied she, pointing to a neat building which rose up amidst the grove of elms and which I had not before observed—) I agreed, and we instantly walked to it—we knocked at the door—it was opened by an old woman; on being requested to afford us a night's lodging, she informed us that her house was but small, that she had only two bedrooms, but that however, we should be welcome to one of them. We were satisfied and followed the good woman into the house, where we were greatly cheered by the sight of a comfortable fire—. She was a widow and had only one daughter, who was then just seventeen—One of the best of ages; but alas! she was very plain and her name was Bridget. . . . . . Nothing therefore could be expected from her—she could not be supposed to possess either exalted ideas, delicate feelings, or refined sensibilities—She was nothing more than a mere good-tempered, civil, and obliging young woman; as such we could scarcely dislike her—she was only an object of contempt—.

Adieu.

Laura

LETTER THE FOURTEENTH *Laura in continuation*

Arm yourself, my amiable young friend, with all the philosophy you are mistress of; summon up all the fortitude you possess, for alas! in the perusal of the following pages your sensibility will be most severely tried. Ah! what were the misfortunes I had before experienced and which I have already related to you, to the one I am now going to inform you of. The death of my father, my mother, and my husband, though almost more than my gentle nature could support, were trifles in comparison to the misfortune I am now proceeding to relate. The morning after our arrival at the cottage, Sophia complained of a violent pain in her delicate limbs, accompanied with a disagreeable headache. She attributed it to a cold caught by her continued faintings in the open air as the dew was falling the evening before. This, I feared, was but too probably the case; since how could it be otherwise accounted for that I should have escaped the same indisposition, but by supposing that the bodily exertions I had undergone in my repeated fits of frenzy had so effectually circulated and warmed my blood as to make me proof against the chilling damps of night, whereas Sophia, lying totally inactive on the ground, must have been exposed to all their severity. I was most seriously alarmed by her illness, which, trifling as it may appear to you, a certain instinctive sensibility whispered me would in the end be fatal to her.

Alas! my fears were but too fully justified; she grew gradually worse, and I daily became more alarmed for her.—At length she was obliged to confine herself solely to the bed allotted us by our worthy landlady—. Her disorder turned to a galloping consumption[2] and in a few days carried her off. Amidst all my lamentations for her (and violent you may suppose they were) I yet received some consolation in the reflection of my having paid every attention to her that could be offered in her illness. I had wept over her every day— had bathed her sweet face with my tears and had pressed her fair hands continually in mine—. "My beloved Laura (said she to me, a few hours before she died) take warning from my unhappy end and avoid the imprudent conduct which has occasioned it . . . beware of fainting-fits . . . Though at the time they may be refreshing and agreeable, yet, believe me, they will in the end, if too often repeated and at improper seasons, prove destructive to your constitution. . . . . My fate will teach you this . . . I die a martyr to my grief for the loss of Augustus. . . . One fatal swoon has cost me my life. . . . Beware of swoons, dear Laura . . . A frenzy fit is not one quarter so pernicious; it is an exercise to the body and, if not too violent, is, I dare say, conducive to health in its consequences—Run mad as often as you choose; but do not faint—."

These were the last words she ever addressed to me . . . It was her dying advice to her afflicted Laura, who has ever most faithfully adhered to it.

After having attended my lamented friend to her early grave, I immediately (though late at night) left the detested village in which she died, and near which had expired my husband and Augustus. I had not walked many yards from it before I was overtaken by a stagecoach, in which I instantly took a place, determined to proceed in it to Edinburgh, where I hoped to find some kind pitying friend who would receive and comfort me in my afflictions.

It was so dark when I entered the coach that I could not distinguish the number of my fellow travellers; I could only perceive that they were many. Regardless, however, of any thing concerning them, I gave myself up to my own sad reflections. A general silence prevailed—a silence, which was by nothing interrupted but by the loud and repeated snores of one of the party.

2. A rapidly developing case of tuberculosis.

"What an illiterate villain must that man be! (thought I to myself) What a total want of delicate refinement must he have who can thus shock our senses by such a brutal noise! He must, I am certain, be capable of every bad action! There is no crime too black for such a character!" Thus reasoned I within myself, and doubtless such were the reflections of my fellow travellers.

At length, returning day enabled me to behold the unprincipled scoundrel who had so violently disturbed my feelings. It was Sir Edward, the father of my deceased husband. By his side sat Augusta, and on the same seat with me were your mother and Lady Dorothea. Imagine my surprise at finding myself thus seated amongst my old acquaintance. Great as was my astonishment, it was yet increased, when, on look[ing] out of [the] windows, I beheld the husband of Philippa, with Philippa by his side, on the coach-box,[3] and when, on looking behind, I beheld Philander and Gustavus in the basket.[4] "Oh! heavens, (exclaimed I) is it possible that I should so unexpectedly be surrounded by my nearest relations and connections?" These words roused the rest of the party, and every eye was directed to the corner in which I sat; "Oh! my Isabel (continued I, throwing myself across Lady Dorothea into her arms) receive once more to your bosom the unfortunate Laura. Alas! when we last parted in the vale of Usk, I was happy in being united to the best of Edwards; I had then a father and a mother, and had never known misfortunes—But now deprived of every friend but you—".

"What! (interrupted Augusta) is my brother dead then? Tell us, I entreat you, what is become of him?" "Yes, cold and insensible[5] nymph, (replied I) that luckless swain, your brother, is no more, and you may now glory in being the heiress of Sir Edward's fortune."

Although I had always despised her from the day I had overheard her conversation with my Edward, yet in civility I complied with hers and Sir Edward's entreaties that I would inform them of the whole melancholy affair. They were greatly shocked—Even the obdurate heart of Sir Edward and the insensible one of Augusta were touched with sorrow by the unhappy tale. At the request of your mother I related to them every other misfortune which had befallen me since we parted. Of the imprisonment of Augustus and the absence of Edward—of our arrival in Scotland—of our unexpected meeting with our grandfather and our cousins—of our visit to Macdonald Hall—of the singular service we there performed towards Janetta—of her father's ingratitude for it. . . . . of his inhuman behaviour, unaccountable suspicions, and barbarous treatment of us, in obliging us to leave the house. . . . . of our lamentations on the loss of Edward and Augustus and finally of the melancholy death of my beloved companion.

Pity and surprise were strongly depictured in your mother's countenance, during the whole of my narration, but I am sorry to say, that to the eternal reproach of her sensibility, the latter infinitely predominated. Nay, faultless as my conduct had certainly been during the whole course of my late misfortunes and adventures, she pretended to find fault with my behaviour in many of the situations in which I had been placed. As I was sensible myself, that I had always behaved in a manner which reflected honour on my feelings and refinement, I paid little attention to what she said, and desired her

---

3. Seat for the driver.
4. The overhanging back compartment on the outside of a stagecoach, where the passengers paying the cheapest fares were seated.
5. Incapable of feeling, callous.

to satisfy my curiosity by informing me how she came there, instead of wounding my spotless reputation with unjustifiable reproaches. As soon as she had complied with my wishes in this particular and had given me an accurate detail of everything that had befallen her since our separation (the particulars of which, if you are not already acquainted with, your mother will give you), I applied to Augusta for the same information respecting herself, Sir Edward, and Lady Dorothea.

She told me that, having a considerable taste for the beauties of nature, her curiosity to behold the delightful scenes it exhibited in that part of the world had been so much raised by Gilpin's tour to the Highlands,[6] that she had prevailed on her father to undertake a tour of Scotland and had persuaded Lady Dorothea to accompany them. That they had arrived at Edinburgh a few days before and from thence had made daily excursions into the country around in the stage-coach they were then in, from one of which excursions they were at that time returning. My next enquiries were concerning Philippa and her husband, the latter of whom, I learned, having spent all her fortune, had recourse for subsistence to the talent in which he had always most excelled, namely, driving, and that having sold everything which belonged to them, except their coach, had converted it into a stage, and in order to be removed from any of his former acquaintance, had driven it to Edinburgh from whence he went to Sterling[7] every other day; that Philippa, still retaining her affection for her ungrateful husband, had followed him to Scotland and generally accompanied him in his little excursions to Sterling. "It has only been to throw a little money into their pockets (continued Augusta) that my father has always travelled in their coach to view the beauties of the country since our arrival in Scotland—for it would certainly have been much more agreeable to us to visit the Highlands in a post-chaise[8] than merely to travel from Edinburgh to Sterling and from Sterling to Edinburgh, every other day in a crowded and uncomfortable stage." I perfectly agreed with her in her sentiments on the affair, and secretly blamed Sir Edward for thus sacrificing his daughter's pleasure for the sake of a ridiculous old woman, whose folly in marrying so young a man ought to be punished. His behaviour, however, was entirely of a piece with his general character; for what could be expected from a man who possessed not the smallest atom of sensibility, who scarcely knew the meaning of sympathy, and who actually snored—.

Adieu.

Laura

LETTER THE FIFTEENTH *Laura in continuation*

When we arrived at the town where we were to breakfast, I was determined to speak with Philander and Gustavus, and to that purpose as soon as I left the carriage, I went to the basket and tenderly enquired after their health, expressing my fears of the uneasiness of their situation. At first they seemed

---

6. Gilpin's *Observations, Relative Chiefly to Picturesque Beauty . . . On Several Parts of Great Britain; Particularly the High-Lands of Scotland* (1789).
7. Stirling, a town forty miles northeast of Edin-

burgh.
8. Augusta wishes that they had hired on their own a smaller, more comfortable carriage, rather than traveling in a public stagecoach that follows a predetermined route.

rather confused at my appearance, dreading no doubt that I might call them to account for the money which our grandfather had left me and which they had unjustly deprived me of, but finding that I mentioned nothing of the matter, they desired me to step into the basket, as we might there converse with greater ease. Accordingly I entered, and whilst the rest of the party were devouring green tea and buttered toast, we feasted ourselves in a more refined and sentimental manner by a confidential conversation. I informed them of everything which had befallen me during the course of my life, and at my request they related to me every incident of theirs.

"We are the sons, as you already know, of the two youngest daughters which Lord St. Clair had by Laurina, an Italian opera girl. Our mothers could neither of them exactly ascertain who were our fathers; though it is generally believed that Philander is the son of one Philip Jones, a bricklayer, and that my father was Gregory Staves, a stay-maker[9] of Edinburgh. This is, however, of little consequence, for as our mothers were certainly never married to either of them, it reflects no dishonour on our blood, which is of a most ancient and unpolluted kind. Bertha (the mother of Philander) and Agatha (my own mother) always lived together. They were neither of them very rich; their united fortunes had originally amounted to nine thousand pounds, but as they had always lived upon the principal of it, when we were fifteen it was diminished to nine hundred. This nine hundred, they always kept in a drawer in one of the tables which stood in our common sitting parlour, for the convenience of having it always at hand. Whether it was from this circumstance, of its being easily taken, or from a wish of being independent, or from an excess of sensibility (for which we were always remarkable), I cannot now determine, but certain it is that when we had reached our fifteenth year, we took the nine hundred pounds and ran away. Having obtained this prize we were determined to manage it with economy and not to spend it either with folly or extravagance. To this purpose we therefore divided it into nine parcels, one of which we devoted to victuals, the second to drink, the third to housekeeping, the fourth to carriages, the fifth to horses, the sixth to servants, the seventh to amusements, the eighth to clothes, and the ninth to silver buckles. Having thus arranged our expenses for two months (for we expected to make the nine hundred pounds last as long), we hastened to London and had the good luck to spend it in seven weeks and a day, which was six days sooner than we had intended. As soon as we had thus happily disencumbered ourselves from the weight of so much money, we began to think of returning to our mothers, but accidentally hearing that they were both starved to death, we gave over the design and determined to engage ourselves to some strolling company of players, as we had always a turn for the stage. Accordingly, we offered our services to one and were accepted; our company was indeed rather small, as it consisted only of the manager, his wife, and ourselves, but there were fewer to pay and the only inconvenience attending it was the scarcity of plays, which for want of people to fill the characters we could perform—. We did not mind trifles, however—. One of our most admired performances was *Macbeth*, in which we were truly great. The manager always played *Banquo* himself, his wife my *Lady Macbeth*. I did the *three witches*, and Philander acted *all the*

9. Maker of corsets.

rest. To say the truth, this tragedy was not only the best, but the only play we ever performed; and after having acted it all over England and Wales, we came to Scotland to exhibit it over the remainder of Great Britain. We happened to be quartered in that very town, where you came and met your grandfather—. We were in the inn-yard when his carriage entered and, perceiving by the arms[1] to whom it belonged, and, knowing that Lord St. Clair was our grandfather, we agreed to endeavour to get something from him by discovering the relationship—. You know how well it succeeded—. Having obtained the two hundred pounds, we instantly left the town, leaving our manager and his wife to act *Macbeth* by themselves, and took the road to Sterling, where we spent our little fortune with great *éclat.*[2] We are now returning to Edinburgh to get some preferment[3] in the acting way; and such, my dear cousin, is our history."

I thanked the amiable youth for his entertaining narration, and after expressing my wishes for their welfare and happiness, left them in their little habitation and returned to my other friends who impatiently expected me.

My adventures are now drawing to a close, my dearest Marianne; at least for the present.

When we arrived at Edinburgh, Sir Edward told me that, as the widow of his son, he desired I would accept from his hands of four hundred a year. I graciously promised that I would, but could not help observing that the unsympathetic baronet offered it more on account of my being the widow of Edward than in being the refined and amiable Laura.

I took up my residence in a romantic village in the Highlands of Scotland, where I have ever since continued, and where I can, uninterrupted by unmeaning visits, indulge, in a melancholy solitude, my unceasing lamentations for the death of my father, my mother, my husband, and my friend.

Augusta has been for several years united to Graham, the man of all others most suited to her; she became acquainted with him during her stay in Scotland.

Sir Edward, in hopes of gaining an heir to his title and estate, at the same time married Lady Dorothea—. His wishes have been answered.

Philander and Gustavus, after having raised their reputation by their performances in the theatrical line at Edinburgh, removed to Covent Garden, where they still exhibit under the assumed names of *Lewis and Quick.*[4]

Philippa has long paid the debt of nature;[5] her husband, however, still continues to drive the stage-coach from Edinburgh to Sterling:—

Adieu, my dearest Marianne.

Laura

1790   1922

---

1. The coat of arms painted on the side of a nobleman's or noblewoman's carriage.
2. Conspicuous success (French); literally, brilliant display.
3. Advancement.

4. William Thomas Lewis and John Quick were well-known actors of the late 18th century. Covent Garden was one of the two London theaters licensed by royal patent.
5. I.e., she has died.

Plan of a Novel, According to Hints from Various Quarters[1]

Scene to be in the country, heroine the daughter of a clergyman, one who after having lived much in the world had retired from it, and settled in a curacy,[2] with a very small fortune of his own.—He, the most excellent man that can be imagined, perfect in character, temper, and manners—without the smallest drawback or peculiarity to prevent his being the most delightful companion to his daughter from one year's end to the other.—Heroine a faultless character herself—, perfectly good, with much tenderness and sentiment, and not the least wit—very highly accomplished, understanding modern languages and (generally speaking) everything that the most accomplished young women learn, but particularly excelling in music—her favourite pursuit—and playing equally well on the piano forte and harp—and singing in the first stile. Her person, quite beautiful—dark eyes and plump cheeks.—Book to open with the description of father and daughter—who are to converse in long speeches, elegant language—and a tone of high, serious sentiment.—The father to be induced, at his daughter's earnest request, to relate to her the past events of his life. This narrative will reach through the greatest part of the first volume—as besides all the circumstances of his attachment to her mother and their marriage, it will comprehend his going to sea as chaplain to a distinguished naval character about the court, his going afterwards to court himself, which introduced him to a great variety of characters and involved him in many interesting situations, concluding with his opinion of the benefits to result from tythes being done away, and his having buried his own mother (heroine's lamented grandmother) in consequence of the high priest of the parish in which she died, refusing to pay her remains the respect due to them. The father to be of a very literary turn, an enthusiast in literature, nobody's enemy but his own[3]—at the same time most zealous in the discharge of his pastoral duties, the model of an exemplary parish priest.[4]—The heroine's friendship to be sought after by a young woman in the same neighbourhood, of talents and shrewdness, with light eyes and a fair skin, but having a considerable degree of wit, heroine shall shrink from the acquaintance.—From this outset, the story will proceed, and contain a striking variety of adventures. Heroine and her father never above a fortnight together in one place,[5] *he* being driven from his curacy by the vile arts of some totally unprincipled and heartless young man, desperately in love with the heroine, and pursuing her with unrelenting passion—no

1. Austen's teasing account of the novel she *would* write if she took to heart the advice people gave her about what her fiction ought to be is another manuscript preserved by her family. It was first published in her nephew James Austen-Leigh's *Memoir of Jane Austen* (1870). In the original manuscript, Austen supplied marginal glosses, mainly omitted here, indicating the source of each "hint" the "Plan" incorporates. Her would-be advisers included, in addition to the Reverend James Stanier Clarke (the librarian to the prince regent), neighbors; family members, most prominently her niece Fanny Knight; a parson, J. G. Sherer, who had been displeased, Austen reported, with her "pictures of clergymen"; and William Gifford, the editor of the *Quarterly Review* as well as the

adviser who had read *Emma* for the publisher John Murray.
2. I.e., settled in the position of curate, the assistant (often badly paid) to the incumbent priest of the parish.
3. For this summary of the clergyman's tale that will fill up her novel's projected first volume, Austen lifts a number of phrases directly from Clarke's letters. Clarke wished to see Austen address the benefits of the abolition of tithes (the taxes supporting the Anglican Church and clergy) and thought his own story of having buried his mother would make good material for her novel.
4. Mr. Sherer [Austen's note].
5. Many critics [Austen's note].

sooner settled in one country of Europe than they are necessitated to quit it and retire to another—always making new acquaintance, and always obliged to leave them.—This will of course exhibit a wide variety of characters—but there will be no mixture; the scene will be for ever shifting from one set of people to another—but all the good will be unexceptionable in every respect—and there will be no foibles or weaknesses but with the wicked, who will be completely depraved and infamous, hardly a resemblance of humanity left in them.—Early in her career, in the progress of her first removals, heroine must meet with the hero—all perfection of course—and only prevented from paying his addresses to her,[6] by some excess of refinement.—Wherever she goes, somebody falls in love with her, and she receives repeated offers of marriage—which she always refers wholly to her father, exceedingly angry that *he* should not be first applied to.—Often carried away by the anti-hero, but rescued either by her father or the hero—often reduced to support herself and her father by her talents and work for her bread;—continually cheated and defrauded of her hire,[7] worn down to a skeleton, and now and then starved to death—. At last, hunted out of civilized society, denied the poor shelter of the humblest cottage, they are compelled to retreat into Kamschatka[8] where the poor father, quite worn down, finding his end approaching, throws himself on the ground, and after four or five hours of tender advice and paternal admonition to his miserable child, expires in a fine burst of literary enthusiasm, intermingled with invectives again[st] holders of tythes.—Heroine inconsolable for some time—but afterwards crawls back towards her former country—having at least twenty narrow escapes of falling into the hands of anti-hero—and at last in the very nick of time, turning a corner to avoid him, runs into the arms of the hero himself, who having just shaken off the scruples which fetter'd him before, was at the very moment setting off in pursuit of her.—The tenderest and completest eclaircissement[9] takes place, and they are happily united.— Throughout the whole work, heroine to be in the most elegant society and living in high style. The name of the work *not* to be *Emma*—but of the same sort as S & S and P & P.

1816   1870

---

6. I.e., seeking her hand in marriage.
7. Wages.
8. Kamchatka; a peninsula on the eastern edge of Asia, extending into the Bering Sea, acquired by Russia in the 18th century. The novels of Austen's contemporaries tended to be cosmopolitan in setting and often did send heroines wandering across Europe. Austen, however, may be thinking particularly of Sophie de Cottin's *Elizabeth; or Exiles of Siberia* (1806; English translation, 1809).
9. The clarification of mysteries and misunderstandings that brings a narrative to closure (French).

WILLIAM HAZLITT
1778–1830

"I started in life," William Hazlitt wrote, "with the French Revolution, and I have lived, alas! to see the end of it. . . . Since then, I confess, I have no longer felt myself young, for with that my hopes fell." He was born into a radical circle, for the elder William Hazlitt, his father, was a Unitarian minister who declared from the pulpit his advocacy both of American independence and of the French Revolution. When young William was five years old, his father took the family to America in search of liberty and founded the first Unitarian church in Boston, but four years later he returned to settle at Wem, in Shropshire. Despite the persistent attacks of reviewers and the backsliding of his once-radical friends, Hazlitt never wavered in his loyalty to liberty, equality, and the principles behind the overthrow of the monarchy in France. His first literary production, at the age of thirteen, was a letter to a newspaper in indignant protest against the mob that sacked Joseph Priestley's house, when the scientist and preacher had celebrated publicly the second anniversary of the fall of the Bastille. His last book, published in the year he died, was a four-volume life of Napoleon, in which he expressed a vehement, but qualified, admiration of Napoleon as a man of heroic will and power in the service of the emancipation of mankind.

Hazlitt was a long time finding his vocation. When he attended the Hackney College, London, between the ages of fifteen and eighteen, he plunged into philosophical studies. In 1799 he took up the study of painting and did not relinquish the ambition to become a portraitist until 1812. His first books dealt with philosophy, economics, and politics; and his first job as a journalist was as parliamentary reporter for the *Morning Chronicle*. It was not until 1813, when he was thirty-six, that he began contributing dramatic criticism and miscellaneous essays to various periodicals and so discovered what he had been born to do. Years of wide reading and hard thinking had made him thoroughly ready: within the next decade he demonstrated himself to be a highly popular lecturer on Shakespeare, Elizabethan drama, and English poetry from Chaucer to his own day; a superb connoisseur of the theater and of painting; a master of the familiar essay; and with Coleridge, one of the two most important literary critics of his time. Coleridge elaborates his theory of poetry as part of a general philosophy of human imagination and human society. Hazlitt, on the other hand, disapproves of what he calls the "modern or metaphysical school of criticism." His distinctive critical gift is to communicate what he calls his "impressions"—that is, the immediacy of his firsthand responses to a passage or work of literature.

Unlike his contemporaries Coleridge, Lamb, and De Quincey, whose writings look back to the elaborate prose stylists of the earlier seventeenth century, Hazlitt developed a fast-moving, hard-hitting prose in a style that he called "plain, point-blank speaking." He wrote, indeed, nearly as fast as he talked, almost without correction and (despite the density of literary quotations) without reference to books or notes. This rapidity was possible only because his essays are relatively planless. Hazlitt characteristically lays down a topic, then piles up relevant observations and instances; the essay accumulates instead of developing; often, it does not round to a conclusion, but simply stops. Hazlitt's prose is unfailingly energetic, but his most satisfying essays, considered as works of literary art, are those that, like "My First Acquaintance with Poets," have a narrative subject matter to give him a principle of organization.

In demeanor Hazlitt was awkward and self-conscious; Coleridge described him in 1803 as "brow-hanging, shoe-contemplative, strange." He had grown up as a member of a highly unpopular minority, in both religion and politics; he found his friends deserting to the side of reaction; and his natural combativeness was exacerbated by the persistent abuse directed against him by writers in the conservative press and periodicals. In the course of his life, he managed to quarrel, in private and in print, with almost everyone whom he had once admired and liked, including Coleridge, Wordsworth, Leigh Hunt, and even his most intimate and enduring friend, Lamb. But what appealed to his admirers, as to modern readers of his essays, is his courage and uncompromising honesty, and above all his zest for life in its diversity—including even, as he announced in the title of an essay, "The Pleasure of Hating." He relished, and was able to convey completely, the particular qualities of things—a passage of poetry, a painting, a natural prospect, or a well-directed blow in a prize fight. Despite the recurrent frustrations of his fifty-two years of existence, he was able to say, with his last breath, "Well, I've had a happy life."

From Characters of Shakespeare's Plays

From Coriolanus[1]

Shakespear has in this play shewn himself well versed in history and state-affairs. *Coriolanus* is a store-house of political commonplaces. Any one who studies it may save himself the trouble of reading Burke's *Reflections*, or Paine's *Rights of Man*, or the Debates in both Houses of Parliament since the French Revolution or our own.[2] The arguments for and against aristocracy or democracy, on the privileges of the few and the claims of the many, on liberty and slavery, power and the abuse of it, peace and war, are here very ably handled, with the spirit of a poet and the acuteness of a philosopher. Shakespear himself seems to have had a leaning to the arbitrary side of the question,[3] perhaps from some feeling of contempt for his own origin; and to have spared no occasion of baiting the rabble. What he says of them is very true: what he says of their betters is also very true, though he dwells less upon it.—The cause of the people is indeed but little calculated as a subject for poetry: it admits of rhetoric, which goes into argument and explanation, but it presents no immediate or distinct images to the mind, "no jutting frieze, buttress, or coigne of vantage" for poetry "to make its pendant bed and procreant cradle in."[4] The language of poetry naturally falls in with the language of power. The imagination is an exaggerating and exclusive faculty: it takes from one thing to add to another: it accumulates circumstances together to give the greatest possible effect to a favourite object. The

---

1. In this chapter from Hazlitt's *Characters of Shakespeare's Plays* (1817), discussion of Shakespeare's tragedy *Coriolanus*, which Hazlitt had watched performed in 1816, occasions a provoking exploration of the poetic imagination's relationship to politics and political justice. The essay was fueled by Hazlitt's gloom over the repressive politics of the day and his disappointment with the poets, Wordsworth and Coleridge in particular, who appeared to have forsaken their commitment to the cause of liberty. Shakespeare's play had taken the political structures of classical Rome during its republican era and mapped them onto his own time and place. Hazlitt's essay does the same with *Coriolanus*, finding in the play a mirror of the political situation in Regency England, as well as probing the role that aesthetic

pleasure has played in upholding that situation.
2. I.e., Britain's Glorious Revolution of 1688, which expelled the Stuart dynasty from the throne. Edmund Burke's attack on the French people's pursuit of liberty in *Reflections on the Revolution in France*, from 1790, was followed in 1791 by Thomas Paine's defense of the Revolution in his pamphlet *Rights of Man*. For excerpts from their texts, see "The Revolution Controversy and the 'Spirit of the Age'" (p. 193).
3. I.e., Shakespeare favored despotism over democracy.
4. From *Macbeth* 1.6.6–8: Banquo, entering Macbeth's castle with King Duncan, describes how martins have made their nests in the castle walls.

understanding is a dividing and measuring faculty: it judges of things, not according to their immediate impression on the mind, but according to their relations to one another. The one is a monopolizing faculty, which seeks the greatest quantity of present excitement by inequality and disproportion; the other is a distributive faculty, which seeks the greatest quantity of ultimate good, by justice and proportion. The one is an aristocratical, the other a republican faculty. The principle of poetry is a very anti-levelling principle. It aims at effect, it exists by contrast. It admits of no medium. It is every thing by excess. It rises above the ordinary standard of sufferings and crimes. It presents a dazzling appearance. It shews its head turretted, crowned, and crested. Its front is gilt and bloodstained. Before it "it carries noise, and behind it tears."[5] It has its altars and its victims, sacrifices, human sacrifices.[6] Kings, priests, nobles, are its train-bearers, tyrants and slaves its executioners.—"Carnage is its daughter."[7]—Poetry is right-royal. It puts the individual for the species, the one above the infinite many, might before right. A lion hunting a flock of sheep or a herd of wild asses, is a more poetical object than they; and we even take part with the lordly beast, because our vanity or some other feeling makes us disposed to place ourselves in the situation of the strongest party. So we feel some concern for the poor citizens of Rome when they meet together to compare their wants and grievances, till Coriolanus comes in, and with blows and big words drives this set of "poor rats," this rascal scum, to their homes and beggary before him.[8] There is nothing heroical in a multitude of miserable rogues not wishing to be starved, or complaining that they are like to be so: but when a single man comes forward to brave their cries and to make them submit to the last indignities, from mere pride and self-will, our admiration of his prowess is immediately converted into contempt for their pusillanimity. The insolence of power is stronger than the plea of necessity. The tame submission to usurped authority or even the natural resistance to it has nothing to excite or flatter the imagination: it is the assumption of a right to insult or oppress others that carries an imposing air of superiority with it. We had rather be the oppressor than the oppressed. The love of power in ourselves and the admiration of it in others are both natural to man: the one makes him a tyrant, the other a slave. Wrong dressed out in pride, pomp, and circumstance has more attraction than abstract right.—Coriolanus complains of the fickleness of the people: yet the instant he cannot gratify his pride and obstinacy at their expense, he turns his arms against his country. If his country was not worth defending, why did he build his pride on its defence?

5. "Before him he carries noise, and behind him he leaves tears": lines from *Coriolanus* 2.1.144–45 applied to Shakespeare's protagonist on his triumphal return from military campaigning.
6. Hazlitt mimes Burke's syntax in a passage in *Reflections* in which Burke declares that, unlike the liberty of the French revolutionists, the liberty the English cherish "has a pedigree and illustrating ancestors": "It has its bearings and its ensigns armorial. It has its gallery of portraits; its monumental inscriptions; its records, evidences, and titles."
7. A strategically placed citation of Wordsworth's 1816 "Thanksgiving Ode" in which, celebrating the victory against Napoleon at Waterloo, Wordsworth seemed to announce also his new role as a defender of the political establishment. Wordsworth writes there that God's most dreaded instrument "in working out a pure intent / Is Man—arrayed for mutual slaughter— / Yes, Carnage is Thy Daughter."
8. Hazlitt refers to the opening scene of *Coriolanus*, in which Shakespeare's protagonist scornfully dismisses a mob of the Roman common people who have gathered to protest a food shortage. When this fierce veteran of Rome's wars is later convinced to run for a position as a Roman consul, he will prove catastrophically incapable of the maneuvering that would ensure his survival in the realm of politics. Banished, Coriolanus turns on the city he once served.

He is a conqueror and a hero; he conquers other countries, and makes this a plea for enslaving his own; and when he is prevented from doing so, he leagues with its enemies to destroy his country. He rates the people "as if he were a God to punish, and not a man of their infirmity."[9] He scoffs at one of their tribunes for maintaining their rights and franchises: "Mark you his absolute *shall*?"[1] not marking his own absolute *will* to take every thing from them, his impatience of the slightest opposition to his own pretensions being in proportion to their arrogance and absurdity. If the great and powerful had the beneficence and wisdom of Gods, then all this would have been well: if with a greater knowledge of what is good for the people, they had as great a care for their interest as they have themselves, if they were seated above the world, sympathising with the welfare, but not feeling the passions of men, receiving neither good nor hurt from them, but bestowing their benefits as free gifts on them, they might then rule over them like another Providence. But this is not the case. Coriolanus is unwilling that the senate should shew their "cares" for the people, lest their "cares" should be construed into "fears," to the subversion of all due authority; and he is no sooner disappointed in his schemes to deprive the people not only of the cares of the state, but of all power to redress themselves, than Volumnia is made madly to exclaim,

> "Now the red pestilence strike all trades in Rome, And occupations perish."[2]

This is but natural: it is but natural for a mother to have more regard for her son than for a whole city; but then the city should be left to take some care of itself. The care of the state cannot, we here see, be safely entrusted to maternal affection, or to the domestic charities of high life. The great have private feelings of their own, to which the interests of humanity and justice must courtesy. Their interests are so far from being the same as those of the community, that they are in direct and necessary opposition to them; their power is at the expense of *our* weakness; their riches of *our* poverty; their pride of *our* degradation; their splendour of *our* wretchedness; their tyranny of *our* servitude. If they had the superior knowledge ascribed to them (which they have not) it would only render them so much more formidable; and from Gods would convert them into Devils. The whole dramatic moral of *Coriolanus* is that those who have little shall have less, and that those who have much shall take all that others have left. The people are poor; therefore they ought to be starved. They are slaves; therefore they ought to be beaten. They work hard; therefore they ought to be treated like beasts of burden. They are ignorant; therefore they ought not to be allowed to feel that they want food, or clothing, or rest, that they are enslaved, oppressed, and miserable. This is the logic of the imagination and the passions; which seek to aggrandise what excites admiration and to heap contempt on misery, to raise power into tyranny, and to make tyranny absolute; to thrust down that which is low still lower, and to make wretches desperate: to exalt magistrates into kings, kings into gods; to degrade subjects to the rank of slaves, and slaves to the condition of brutes. The history of mankind is a romance,

---

9. *Coriolanus* 3.1.85–86.
1. *Coriolanus* 3.1.92–93.
2. *Coriolanus* 4.1.14–15: language with which

Coriolanus's mother curses Rome for banishing her son.

a mask, a tragedy, constructed upon the principles of *poetical justice*; it is a noble or royal hunt, in which what is sport to the few, is death to the many,[3] and in which the spectators halloo and encourage the strong to set upon the weak, and cry havoc in the chase, though they do not share in the spoil. We may depend upon it that what men delight to read in books, they will put in practice in reality.

* * *

1817

My First Acquaintance with Poets[1]

My father was a Dissenting Minister, at Wem, in Shropshire; and in the year 1798 (the figures that compose that date are to me like the "dreaded name of Demogorgon")[2] Mr. Coleridge came to Shrewsbury, to succeed Mr. Rowe in the spiritual charge of a Unitarian congregation there. He did not come till late on the Saturday afternoon before he was to preach; and Mr. Rowe, who himself went down to the coach, in a state of anxiety and expectation, to look for the arrival of his successor, could find no one at all answering the description but a round-faced man, in a short black coat (like a shooting jacket) which hardly seemed to have been made for him, but who seemed to be talking at a great rate to his fellow passengers. Mr. Rowe had scarce returned to give an account of his disappointment, when the round-faced man in black entered, and dissipated all doubts on the subject, by beginning to talk. He did not cease while he stayed; nor has he since, that I know of. He held the good town of Shrewsbury in delightful suspense for three weeks that he remained there, "fluttering the *proud Salopians*, like an eagle in a dovecote";[3] and the Welsh mountains that skirt the horizon with their tempestuous confusion, agree to have heard no such mystic sounds since the days of

High-born Hoel's harp or soft Llewellyn's lay![4]

As we passed along between Wem and Shrewsbury, and I eyed their blue tops seen through the wintry branches, or the red rustling leaves of the sturdy oak trees by the roadside, a sound was in my ears as of a Siren's song; I was stunned, startled with it, as from deep sleep; but I had no notion then that I should ever be able to express my admiration to others in motley imagery or quaint allusion, till the light of his genius shone into my soul, like the sun's rays glittering in the puddles of the road. I was at that time

3. Echoing a line from a fable of Aesop's, in which boys playing near a pond spot some frogs and begin pelting them with stones. One frog cries out for the boys to stop: "What is sport to you, is death to us."
1. This essay was written in 1823, a quarter century after the events it describes. By then Coleridge and Wordsworth had long given up their early radicalism, and both men had quarreled with Hazlitt; hence the essay's elegiac note in dealing with the genius of the two poets.
2. *Paradise Lost* 2.964–65. To mythographers of

the Renaissance, Demogorgon was a mysterious and terrifying demon, sometimes described as ancestor of all the gods. He plays a central role in Shelley's *Prometheus Unbound*.
3. Shakespeare's Roman general Coriolanus reminds his enemies that, in in his days of military glory, "like an eagle in a dove-cote, I / Fluttered your Volscians" (*Coriolanus* 5.6.115–16). "Salopians": inhabitants of Shropshire.
4. Thomas Gray's "The Bard," line 28—names of famous bards silenced by King Edward's conquest of Wales.

dumb, inarticulate, helpless, like a worm by the wayside, crushed, bleeding, lifeless; but now, bursting from the deadly bands that bound them,

With Styx nine times round them,[5]

my ideas float on winged words, and as they expand their plumes, catch the golden light of other years. My soul has indeed remained in its original bondage, dark, obscure, with longings infinite and unsatisfied; my heart, shut up in the prison house of this rude clay, has never found, nor will it ever find, a heart to speak to; but that my understanding also did not remain dumb and brutish, or at length found a language to express itself, I owe to Coleridge. But this is not to my purpose.

My father lived ten miles from Shrewsbury, and was in the habit of exchanging visits with Mr. Rowe, and with Mr. Jenkins of Whitechurch (nine miles farther on) according to the custom of Dissenting Ministers in each other's neighborhood. A line of communication is thus established, by which the flame of civil and religious liberty is kept alive, and nourishes its smoldering fire unquenchable, like the fires in the *Agamemnon* of Aeschylus, placed at different stations, that waited for ten long years to announce with their blazing pyramids the destruction of Troy. Coleridge had agreed to come over to see my father, according to the courtesy of the country, as Mr. Rowe's probable successor; but in the meantime, I had gone to hear him preach the Sunday after his arrival. A poet and a philosopher getting up into a Unitarian pulpit to preach the Gospel was a romance in these degenerate days, a sort of revival of the primitive spirit of Christianity, which was not to be resisted.

It was in January of 1798, that I rose one morning before daylight, to walk ten miles in the mud, and went to hear this celebrated person preach. Never, the longest day I have to live, shall I have such another walk as this cold, raw, comfortless one, in the winter of the year 1798. *Il y a des impressions que ni le temps ni les circonstances peuvent effacer. Dusse-je vivre des siècles entiers, le doux temps de ma jeunesse ne peut renaître pour moi, ni s'effacer jamais dans ma mémoire.*[6] When I got there, the organ was playing the 100th psalm, and when it was done, Mr. Coleridge rose and gave out his text, "And he went up into the mountain to pray, *himself, alone.*"[7] As he gave out this text, his voice "rose like a steam of rich distilled perfume,"[8] and when he came to the two last words, which he pronounced loud, deep, and distinct, it seemed to me, who was then young, as if the sounds had echoed from the bottom of the human heart, and as if that prayer might have floated in solemn silence through the universe. The idea of St. John came into my mind, "of one crying in the wilderness, who had his loins girt about, and whose food was locusts and wild honey."[9] The preacher then launched into his subject, like an eagle dallying with the wind. The sermon was upon peace and war; upon church and state—not their alliance but their separation—on the spirit of the world and the spirit of Christianity, not as the same, but as opposed to one another. He talked of those who had "inscribed the cross of

5. Adapted from Pope's "Ode on St. Cecilia's Day," lines 90–91.
6. There are some impressions that neither time nor circumstances can efface. Even if I lived whole centuries, the sweet time of my youth could not be reborn for me, nor ever erased from my memory (French). Based on Rousseau's novel in letters *La Nouvelle Héloïse* (1761), part 6, letter 7.
7. The text for Coleridge's sermon was perhaps Matthew 14.23 or John 6.15—both of which describe how Christ withdraws into the mountains to prevent the people from making him king.
8. Milton's *Comus*, line 556.
9. See Matthew 3.3–4 and Mark 1.3–6.

Christ on banners dripping with human gore." He made a poetical and pastoral excursion—and to show the fatal effects of war, drew a striking contrast between the simple shepherd boy, driving his team afield, or sitting under the hawthorn, piping to his flock, "as though he should never be old,"[1] and the same poor country lad, crimped,[2] kidnapped, brought into town, made drunk, at an alehouse, turned into a wretched drummer boy, with his hair sticking on end with powder and pomatum, a long cue[3] at his back, and tricked out in the loathsome finery of the profession of blood.

Such were the notes our once-loved poet sung.[4]

And for myself, I could not have been more delighted if I had heard the music of the spheres. Poetry and Philosophy had met together. Truth and Genius had embraced, under the eye and with the sanction of Religion. This was even beyond my hopes. I returned home well satisfied. The sun that was still laboring pale and wan through the sky, obscured by thick mists, seemed an emblem of the *good cause*;[5] and the cold dank drops of dew, that hung half melted on the beard of the thistle, had something genial and refreshing in them; for there was a spirit of hope and youth in all nature, that turned everything into good. The face of nature had not then the brand of *Jus Divinum*[6] on it:

Like to that sanguine flower inscribed with woe.[7]

On the Tuesday following, the half-inspired speaker came. I was called down into the room where he was, and went half-hoping, half-afraid. He received me very graciously, and I listened for a long time without uttering a word. I did not suffer in his opinion by my silence. "For those two hours," he afterwards was pleased to say, "he was conversing with W. H.'s forehead!" His appearance was different from what I had anticipated from seeing him before. At a distance, and in the dim light of the chapel, there was to me a strange wildness in his aspect, a dusky obscurity, and I thought him pitted with the smallpox. His complexion was at that time clear, and even bright—

As are the children of yon azure sheen.[8]

His forehead was broad and high, light as if built of ivory, with large projecting eyebrows, and his eyes rolling beneath them, like a sea with darkened luster. "A certain tender bloom his face o'erspread,"[9] a purple tinge as we see it in the pale thoughtful complexions of the Spanish portrait painters, Murillo and Velasquez. His mouth was gross, voluptuous, open, eloquent; his chin good-humored and round; but his nose, the rudder of the face, the index of the will, was small, feeble, nothing—like what he has done. It might seem that the genius of his face as from a height surveyed and projected him (with sufficient capacity and huge aspiration) into the world unknown of thought and imagination, with nothing to support or guide his veering purpose, as if Columbus had launched his adventurous course for

---

1. Sir Philip Sidney's *Arcadia* 1.2.
2. Tricked into enlisting in military service.
3. Pigtail. "Pomatum": perfumed hair oil.
4. The first line of Pope's "Epistle to Robert, Earl of Oxford."
5. The cause of liberty, i.e., the French Revolution.

6. The divine right (of kings).
7. I.e., the hyacinth, believed to be marked with the Greek letters "AI AI," a cry of grief. Hazlitt quotes Milton's "Lycidas," line 106.
8. Adapted from James Thomson's *The Castle of Indolence* 2.33.
9. See Thomson's *The Castle of Indolence* 1.57.

the New World in a scallop,[1] without oars or compass. So at least I comment on it after the event. Coleridge in his person was rather above the common size, inclining to the corpulent, or like Lord Hamlet, "somewhat fat and pursy."[2] His hair (now, alas! gray) was then black and glossy as the raven's, and fell in smooth masses over his forehead. This long pendulous hair is peculiar to enthusiasts, to those whose minds tend heavenward; and is traditionally inseparable (though of a different color) from the pictures of Christ. It ought to belong, as a character, to all who preach *Christ crucified*, and Coleridge was at that time one of those!

It was curious to observe the contrast between him and my father, who was a veteran in the cause, and then declining into the vale of years. He had been a poor Irish lad, carefully brought up by his parents, and sent to the University of Glasgow (where he studied under Adam Smith[3]) to prepare him for his future destination. It was his mother's proudest wish to see her son a Dissenting Minister. So if we look back to past generations (as far as eye can reach) we see the same hopes, fears, wishes, followed by the same disappointments, throbbing in the human heart; and so we may see them (if we look forward) rising up forever, and disappearing, like vaporish bubbles, in the human breast! After being tossed about from congregation to congregation in the heats of the Unitarian controversy, and squabbles about the American war,[4] he had been relegated to an obscure village, where he was to spend the last thirty years of his life, far from the only converse that he loved, the talk about disputed texts of Scripture and the cause of civil and religious liberty. Here he passed his days, repining but resigned, in the study of the Bible, and the perusal of the Commentators—huge folios, not easily got through, one of which would outlast a winter! Why did he pore on these from morn to night (with the exception of a walk in the fields or a turn in the garden to gather broccoli plants or kidney beans of his own rearing, with no small degree of pride and pleasure)? Here were "no figures nor no fantasies"[5]—neither poetry nor philosophy—nothing to dazzle, nothing to excite modern curiosity; but to his lackluster eyes there appeared, within the pages of the ponderous, unwieldy, neglected tomes, the sacred name of JEHOVAH in Hebrew capitals: pressed down by the weight of the style, worn to the last fading thinness of the understanding, there were glimpses, glimmering notions of the patriarchal wanderings, with palm trees hovering in the horizon, and processions of camels at the distance of three thousand years; there was Moses with the Burning Bush, the number of the Twelve Tribes, types, shadows,[6] glosses on the law and the prophets; there were discussions (dull enough) on the age of Methuselah, a mighty speculation! there were outlines, rude guesses at the shape of Noah's Ark and of the riches of Solomon's Temple; questions as to the date of the creation, predictions of the end of all things; the great lapses of time, the strange mutations of the globe were unfolded with the voluminous leaf,[7] as it turned over; and though the soul might slumber with an

1. Probably for *shallop*, a small boat.
2. Cf. Shakespeare's *Hamlet* 3.4.144, 5.2.230.
3. Scottish professor of moral philosophy, author of the *Theory of Moral Sentiments* (1759) and the great economic treatise *The Wealth of Nations* (1776).
4. The American Revolution, with which a number of radical Unitarian preachers were in sympathy.
5. In Shakespeare's *Julius Caesar* Brutus's

description of the carefree state of his sleeping servant, who knows nothing of his master's plotting (2.1.230).
6. Old Testament foreshadowings of later events, or symbols of moral and theological truths. "Types": characters and events in the Old Testament believed to prefigure analogous matters in the New Testament.
7. Page.

hieroglyphic veil of inscrutable mysteries drawn over it, yet it was in a slumber ill-exchanged for all the sharpened realities of sense, wit, fancy, or reason. My father's life was comparatively a dream; but it was a dream of infinity and eternity, of death, the resurrection, and a judgment to come!

No two individuals were ever more unlike than were the host and his guest. A poet was to my father a sort of nondescript: yet whatever added grace to the Unitarian cause was to him welcome. He could hardly have been more surprised or pleased if our visitor had worn wings. Indeed, his thoughts had wings; and as the silken sounds rustled round our little wainscoted parlor, my father threw back his spectacles over his forehead, his white hairs mixing with its sanguine hue; and a smile of delight beamed across his rugged cordial face, to think that Truth had found a new ally in Fancy! Besides, Coleridge seemed to take considerable notice of me, and that of itself was enough. He talked very familiarly, but agreeably, and glanced over a variety of subjects. At dinner time he grew more animated, and dilated in a very edifying manner on Mary Wollstonecraft and Mackintosh.[8] The last, he said, he considered (on my father's speaking of his *Vindiciae Gallicae* as a capital performance) as a clever scholastic[9] man—a master of the topics—or as the ready warehouseman of letters, who knew exactly where to lay his hand on what he wanted, though the goods were not his own. He thought him no match for Burke, either in style or matter. Burke was a metaphysician, Mackintosh a mere logician. Burke was an orator (almost a poet) who reasoned in figures, because he had an eye for nature: Mackintosh, on the other hand, was a rhetorician, who had only an eye to commonplaces. On this I ventured to say that I had always entertained a great opinion of Burke, and that (as far as I could find) the speaking of him with contempt might be made the test of a vulgar democratical mind. This was the first observation I ever made to Coleridge, and he said it was a very just and striking one. I remember the leg of Welsh mutton and the turnips on the table that day had the finest flavor imaginable. Coleridge added that Mackintosh and Tom Wedgwood[1] (of whom, however, he spoke highly) had expressed a very indifferent opinion of his friend Mr. Wordsworth, on which he remarked to them—"He strides on so far before you that he dwindles in the distance!" Godwin[2] had once boasted to him of having carried on an argument with Mackintosh for three hours with dubious success; Coleridge told him—"If there had been a man of genius in the room, he would have settled the question in five minutes." He asked me if I had ever seen Mary Wollstonecraft, and I said I had once for a few moments, and that she seemed to me to turn off Godwin's objections to something she advanced with quite a playful, easy air. He replied, that "this was only one instance of the ascendancy which people of imagination exercised over those of mere intellect." He did not rate Godwin very high[3] (this was caprice

8. Mary Wollstonecraft's *A Vindication of the Rights of Men* (1790) and the Scottish philosopher James Mackintosh's *Vindiciae Gallicae* ("Defense of France," 1791) were both written in opposition to Edmund Burke's *Reflections on the French Revolution* (1790). See p. 197.
9. The Scholastics, medieval philosophers and theologians, organized their thought systematically, often under various "topics"—standard headings, or "commonplaces."
1. Son of Josiah Wedgwood (1730–1795), who founded the great pottery firm.
2. William Godwin (1756–1836), radical philosopher and novelist, author of the influential *Inquiry Concerning Political Justice* (1793).
3. He complained in particular of the presumption of attempting to establish the future immortality of man "without" (as he said) "knowing what Death was or what Life was"—and the tone in which he pronounced these two words seemed to convey a complete image of both [Hazlitt's note].

or prejudice, real or affected) but he had a great idea of Mrs. Wollstone-craft's powers of conversation, none at all of her talent for book-making. We talked a little about Holcroft.[4] He had been asked if he was not much struck *with* him, and he said, he thought himself in more danger of being struck *by* him. I complained that he would not let me get on at all, for he required a definition of even the commonest word, exclaiming, "What do you mean by a *sensation*, sir? What do you mean by an *idea*?" This, Coleridge said, was barricadoing the road to truth: it was setting up a turnpike gate at every step we took. I forget a great number of things, many more than I remember; but the day passed off pleasantly, and the next morning Mr. Coleridge was to return to Shrewsbury. When I came down to breakfast, I found that he had just received a letter from his friend, T. Wedgwood, making him an offer of £150 a year if he chose to waive his present pursuit, and devote himself entirely to the study of poetry and philosophy. Coleridge seemed to make up his mind to close with this proposal in the act of tying on one of his shoes. It threw an additional damp on his departure. It took the way-ward enthusiast quite from us to cast him into Deva's winding vales,[5] or by the shores of old romance. Instead of living at ten miles' distance, of being the pastor of a Dissenting congregation at Shrewsbury, he was henceforth to inhabit the Hill of Parnassus, to be a Shepherd on the Delectable Mountains.[6] Alas! I knew not the way thither, and felt very little gratitude for Mr. Wedgwood's bounty. I was presently relieved from this dilemma; for Mr. Coleridge, asking for a pen and ink, and going to a table to write some-thing on a bit of card, advanced towards me with undulating step, and giv-ing me the precious document, said that that was his address, *Mr. Coleridge, Nether Stowey, Somersetshire;* and that he should be glad to see me there in a few weeks' time, and, if I chose, would come half-way to meet me. I was not less surprised than the shepherd boy (this simile is to be found in *Cassandra*[7]) when he sees a thunderbolt fall close at his feet. I stammered out my acknowledgments and acceptance of this offer (I thought Mr. Wedg-wood's annunity a trifle to it) as well as I could; and this mighty business being settled, the poet-preacher took leave, and I accompanied him six miles on the road. It was a fine morning in the middle of winter, and he talked the whole way. The scholar in Chaucer is described as going

————sounding on his way.[8]

So Coleridge went on his. In digressing, in dilating, in passing from subject to subject, he appeared to me to float in air, to slide on ice. He told me in confidence (going along) that he should have preached two sermons before he accepted the situation at Shrewsbury, one on Infant Baptism, the other on the Lord's Supper, showing that he could not administer either, which would have effectually disqualified him for the object in view. I observed

---

4. Thomas Holcroft (1749–1809), another radi-cal contemporary, author of plays and novels. Hazlitt completed his friend Holcroft's memoirs and published them in 1816.
5. In "Lycidas," line 55, Milton associates the "wizard stream" of Deva (the river Dee in Wales) with the ancient bards. Hazlitt's point is that Coleridge will henceforth inhabit the terrain of the poetic imagination.
6. In classical mythology Mount Parnassus was sacred to the muses. In John Bunyan's allegory

Pilgrim's Progress (1678–79), the pilgrim Chris-tian, on his journey to the Celestial City, passes through the Delectable Mountains, where he is entertained by the shepherds.
7. A romance by the 17th-century French writer La Calprenède.
8. *The Canterbury Tales,* "General Prologue," line 309: "Souning in moral vertu was his speeche" (in Chaucer the meaning of "souning in" is either "resounding in" or "consonant with").

that he continually crossed me on the way by shifting from one side of the footpath to the other. This struck me as an odd movement; but I did not at that time connect it with any instability of purpose or involuntary change of principle, as I have done since. He seemed unable to keep on in a straight line. He spoke slightingly of Hume[9] (whose *Essay on Miracles* he said was stolen from an objection started in one of South's sermons—*Credat Judaeus Appella!*[1]). I was not very much pleased at this account of Hume, for I had just been reading, with infinite relish, that completest of all metaphysical *choke-pears*,[2] his *Treatise on Human Nature*, to which the *Essays*, in point of scholastic subtlety and close reasoning, are mere elegant trifling, light summer reading. Coleridge even denied the excellence of Hume's general style, which I think betrayed a want of taste or candor. He however made me amends by the manner in which he spoke of Berkeley.[3] He dwelt particularly on his *Essay on Vision* as a masterpiece of analytical reasoning. So it undoubtedly is. He was exceedingly angry with Dr. Johnson for striking the stone with his foot, in allusion to this author's theory of matter and spirit, and saying, "Thus I confute him, sir."[4] Coleridge drew a parallel (I don't know how he brought about the connection) between Bishop Berkeley and Tom Paine.[5] He said the one was an instance of a subtle, the other of an acute mind, than which no two things could be more distinct. The one was a shop-boy's quality, the other the characteristic of a philosopher. He considered Bishop Butler[6] as a true philosopher, a profound and conscientious thinker, a genuine reader of nature and of his own mind. He did not speak of his *Analogy*, but of his *Sermons at the Rolls' Chapel*, of which I had never heard. Coleridge somehow always contrived to prefer the *unknown* to the *known*. In this instance he was right. The *Analogy* is a tissue of sophistry, of wire-drawn,[7] theological special-pleading; the *Sermons* (with the Preface to them) are in a fine vein of deep, matured reflection, a candid appeal to our observation of human nature, without pedantry and without bias. I told Coleridge I had written a few remarks, and was sometimes foolish enough to believe that I had made a discovery on the same subject (the *Natural Disinterestedness of the Human Mind*)[8]—and I tried to explain my view of it to Coleridge, who listened with great willingness, but I did not succeed in making myself understood. I sat down to the task shortly afterwards for the twentieth time, got new pens and paper, determined to make clear work of it, wrote a few meager sentences in the skeleton-style of a mathematical demonstration, stopped halfway down the second page; and, after trying in vain to pump up any words, images, notions, apprehensions, facts, or observations, from that gulf of abstraction in which I had plunged myself for four or five years preceding, gave up the attempt as labor in vain, and shed tears of helpless despondency on the blank unfinished paper. I can write fast enough now. Am I better than I was then? Oh no! One truth discovered,

9. David Hume, 18th-century Scottish philosopher.

1. From Horace's *Satires* 1.5.100: "Let Appella the Jew believe it" (Latin); implying that he himself does not. Robert South (1634–1716), Anglican divine.

2. A very sour variety of pear; hence anything hard to take in.

3. Bishop George Berkeley, 18th-century Irish idealist philosopher and author of *Essay toward a New Theory of Vision* (1709).

4. The anecdote is in James Boswell's *The Life of Samuel Johnson*.

5. Supporter of the American and French Revolutions and author of *Common Sense* and *Rights of Man* (see p. 209).

6. Joseph Butler, 18th-century theologian and moral philosopher, author of the *Analogy of Religion* (1736).

7. Drawn out to great length.

8. Published as *An Essay on the Principles of Human Action* (1805).

one pang of regret at not being able to express it, is better than all the fluency and flippancy in the world. Would that I could go back to what I then was! Why can we not revive past times as we can revisit old places? If I had the quaint Muse of Sir Philip Sidney to assist me, I would write a *Sonnet to the Road between Wem and Shrewsbury,* and immortalize every step of it by some fond enigmatical conceit. I would swear that the very milestones had ears, and that Harmer Hill stooped with all its pines, to listen to a poet, as he passed! I remember but one other topic of discourse in this walk. He mentioned Paley,[9] praised the naturalness and clearness of his style, but condemned his sentiments, thought him a mere time-serving casuist, and said that "the fact of his work on Moral and Political Philosophy being made a textbook in our universities was a disgrace to the national character." We parted at the six-mile stone; and I returned homeward pensive but much pleased. I had met with unexpected notice from a person whom I believed to have been prejudiced against me. "Kind and affable to me had been his condescension, and should be honored ever with suitable regard."[1] He was the first poet I had known, and he certainly answered to that inspired name. I had heard a great deal of his powers of conversation, and was not disappointed. In fact, I never met with anything at all like them, either before or since. I could easily credit the accounts which were circulated of his holding forth to a large party of ladies and gentlemen, an evening or two before, on the Berkeleian Theory, when he made the whole material universe look like a transparency of fine words; and another story (which I believe he has somewhere told himself)[2] of his being asked to a party at Birmingham, of his smoking tobacco and going to sleep after dinner on a sofa, where the company found him, to their no small surprise, which was increased to wonder when he started up of a sudden, and rubbing his eyes, looked about him, and launched into a three hours' description of the third heaven, of which he had had a dream, very different from Mr. Southey's *Vision of Judgment,* and also from that other *Vision of Judgment,* which Mr. Murray, the secretary of the Bridge Street Junto,[3] has taken into his especial keeping!

On my way back, I had a sound in my ears, it was the voice of Fancy: I had a light before me, it was the face of Poetry. The one still lingers there, the other has not quitted my side! Coleridge in truth met me half-way on the ground of philosophy, or I should not have been won over to his imaginative creed. I had an uneasy, pleasurable sensation all the time, till I was to visit him. During those months the chill breath of winter gave me a welcoming; the vernal air was balm and inspiration to me. The golden sunsets, the silver star of evening, lighted me on my way to new hopes and prospects.

9. William Paley, author of *Evidences of Christianity* (1794) and *Principles of Moral and Political Philosophy* (1785), which became a textbook for generations of Cambridge students. With its account of how individuals' calculations of their best interests provide an adequate foundation for Christian morality, Paley's utilitarian theology would have displeased Coleridge. A "casuist" uses reason in a slippery, deceptive manner.
1. Paraphrasing Adam's praise for the teaching offered to him by the archangel Raphael (*Paradise Lost* 8.648–50).
2. See Coleridge's *Biographia Literaria,* chap. 10.

3. Byron's *The Vision of Judgment* is a brilliant parody of Southey's poem (see p. 723). Charles Murray was solicitor to an association, located at New Bridge Street in London, that prosecuted John Hunt for publishing Byron's poem in 1822 in the first number of the journal *The Liberal.* Hazlitt's "My First Acquaintance with Poets" would appear in the pages of *The Liberal* the following year. Hazlitt derisively refers to Murray's Constitutional Association, founded to oppose "the progress of disloyal and seditious principles," as a "junto," i.e., a group formed for political intrigue.

I was to visit Coleridge in the spring. This circumstance was never absent from my thoughts, and mingled with all my feelings. I wrote to him at the time proposed, and received an answer postponing my intended visit for a week or two, but very cordially urging me to complete my promise then. This delay did not damp, but rather increased my ardor. In the meantime, I went to Llangollen Vale,[4] by way of initiating myself in the mysteries of natural scenery; and I must say I was enchanted with it. I had been reading Coleridge's description of England in his fine *Ode on the Departing Year*, and I applied it, *con amore*,[5] to the objects before me. That valley was to me (in a manner) the cradle of a new existence: in the river that winds through it, my spirit was baptized in the waters of Helicon![6]

I returned home, and soon after set out on my journey with unworn heart and untired feet. My way lay through Worcester and Gloucester, and by Upton, where I thought of Tom Jones and the adventure of the muff.[7] I remember getting completely wet through one day, and stopping at an inn (I think it was at Tewkesbury) where I sat up all night to read *Paul and Virginia*.[8] Sweet were the showers in early youth that drenched my body, and sweet the drops of pity that fell upon the books I read! I recollect a remark of Coleridge's upon this very book that nothing could show the gross indelicacy of French manners and the entire corruption of their imagination more strongly than the behavior of the heroine in the last fatal scene, who turns away from a person on board the sinking vessel, that offers to save her life, because he has thrown off his clothes to assist him in swimming. Was this a time to think of such a circumstance? I once hinted to Wordsworth, as we were sailing in his boat on Grasmere lake, that I thought he had borrowed the idea of his *Poems on the Naming of Places* from the local inscriptions of the same kind in *Paul and Virginia*. He did not own the obligation, and stated some distinction without a difference in defense to his claim to originality. Any the slightest variation would be sufficient for this purpose in his mind; for whatever he added or omitted would inevitably be worth all that any one else had done, and contain the marrow of the sentiment. I was still two days before the time fixed for my arrival, for I had taken care to set out early enough. I stopped these two days at Bridgewater, and when I was tired of sauntering on the banks of its muddy river, returned to the inn and read *Camilla*.[9] So have I loitered my life away, reading books, looking at pictures, going to plays, hearing, thinking, writing on what pleased me best. I have wanted only one thing to make me happy; but wanting that, have wanted everything!

I arrived, and was well received. The country about Nether Stowey is beautiful, green and hilly, and near the seashore. I saw it but the other day, after an interval of twenty years, from a hill near Taunton. How was the map of my life spread out before me, as the map of the country lay at my feet! In the afternoon, Coleridge took me over to Alfoxden, a romantic old family mansion of the St. Aubins, where Wordsworth lived. It was then in the possession of a friend of the poet's, who gave him the free use of it.[1] Somehow, that period (the time just after the French Revolution) was not a time when

---

4. In north Wales (about thirty-five miles from Wem)—a standard destination for lovers of picturesque landscapes.
5. "With love," fervently (Italian).
6. A mountain sacred to Apollo and the Muses.

7. Henry Fielding's *Tom Jones* 10.5ff.
8. A sentimental novel (1788) by the French writer Bernardin de Saint-Pierre.
9. A 1796 novel by Frances Burney.
1. A mistake; Wordsworth paid rent.

nothing was given for nothing. The mind opened and a softness might be perceived coming over the heart of individuals, beneath "the scales that fence" our self-interest. Wordsworth himself was from home, but his sister kept house, and set before us a frugal repast; and we had free access to her brother's poems, the *Lyrical Ballads*, which were still in manuscript, or in the form of *Sybilline Leaves.*[2] I dipped into a few of these with great satisfaction, and with the faith of a novice. I slept that night in an old room with blue hangings, and covered with the round-faced family portraits of the age of George I and II and from the wooded declivity of the adjoining park that overlooked my window, at the dawn of day, could

————hear the loud stag speak.[3]

In the outset of life (and particularly at this time I felt it so) our imagination has a body to it. We are in a state between sleeping and waking, and have indistinct but glorious glimpses of strange shapes, and there is always something to come better than what we see. As in our dreams the fullness of the blood gives warmth and reality to the coinage of the brain, so in youth our ideas are clothed, and fed, and pampered with our good spirits; we breathe thick with thoughtless happiness, the weight of future years presses on the strong pulses of the heart, and we repose with undisturbed faith in truth and good. As we advance, we exhaust our fund of enjoyment and of hope. We are no longer wrapped in *lamb's wool,* lulled in Elysium. As we taste the pleasures of life, their spirit evaporates, the sense palls; and nothing is left but the phantoms, the lifeless shadows of what *has been!*

That morning, as soon as breakfast was over, we strolled out into the park, and seating ourselves on the trunk of an old ash tree that stretched along the ground, Coleridge read aloud with a sonorous and musical voice, the ballad of *Betty Foy.*[4] I was not critically or skeptically inclined. I saw touches of truth and nature, and took the rest for granted. But in the *Thorn,* the *Mad Mother,* and the *Complaint of a Poor Indian Woman,* I felt that deeper power and pathos which have been since acknowledged,

In spite of pride, in erring reason's spite,[5]

as the characteristics of this author; and the sense of a new style and a new spirit in poetry came over me. It had to me something of the effect that arises from the turning up of the fresh soil, or of the first welcome breath of spring,

While yet the trembling year is unconfirmed.[6]

Coleridge and myself walked back to Stowey that evening, and his voice sounded high

Of Providence, foreknowledge, will, and fate,
Fixed fate, free will, foreknowledge absolute,[7]

as we passed through echoing grove, by fairy stream or waterfall, gleaming in the summer moonlight! He lamented that Wordsworth was not prone

---

2. I.e., prophetic writings in a scattered state. The phrase is used by Coleridge as the title for his published poems in 1817.
3. A pleasure of country life mentioned in Ben Jonson's 1616 poem "To Sir Robert Wroth" (line 22).

4. Wordsworth's *Idiot Boy.* Like the other poems mentioned, it was included in *Lyrical Ballads.*
5. Pope's *Essay on Man* 1.293.
6. James Thomson's *The Seasons: Spring,* line 18.
7. The topics debated by the fallen angels in *Paradise Lost* 2.559–60.

enough to believe in the traditional superstitions of the place, and that there was a something corporeal, a *matter-of-fact-ness*, a clinging to the palpable, or often to the petty, in his poetry, in consequence. His genius was not a spirit that descended to him through the air; it sprung out of the ground like a flower, or unfolded itself from a green spray, on which the goldfinch sang. He said, however (if I remember right), that this objection must be confined to his descriptive pieces, that his philosophic poetry had a grand and comprehensive spirit in it, so that his soul seemed to inhabit the universe like a palace, and to discover truth by intuition, rather than by deduction. The next day Wordsworth arrived from Bristol at Coleridge's cottage. I think I see him now. He answered in some degree to his friend's description of him, but was more gaunt and Don Quixote-like. He was quaintly dressed (according to the *costume* of that unconstrained period) in a brown fustian[8] jacket and striped pantaloons. There was something of a roll, a lounge in his gait, not unlike his own Peter Bell.[9] There was a severe, worn pressure of thought about his temples, a fire in his eye (as if he saw something in objects more than the outward appearance), an intense high narrow forehead, a Roman nose, cheeks furrowed by strong purpose and feeling, and a convulsive inclination to laughter about the mouth, a good deal at variance with the solemn, stately expression of the rest of his face. Chantry's bust wants the marking traits; but he was teased into making it regular and heavy; Haydon's[1] head of him, introduced into the *Entrance of Christ into Jerusalem*, is the most like his drooping weight of thought and expression. He sat down and talked very naturally and freely, with a mixture of clear gushing accents in his voice, a deep guttural intonation, and a strong tincture of the northern *burr*, like the crust on wine. He instantly began to make havoc of the half of a Cheshire cheese on the table, and said triumphantly that "his marriage with experience had not been so unproductive as Mr. Southey's in teaching him a knowledge of the good things of this life." He had been to see the *Castle Spectre* by Monk Lewis,[2] while at Bristol, and described it very well. He said "it fitted the taste of the audience like a glove." This *ad captandum*[3] merit was, however, by no means a recommendation of it, according to the severe principles of the new school, which reject rather than court popular effect. Wordsworth, looking out of the low, latticed window, said, "How beautifully the sun sets on that yellow bank!" I thought within myself, "With what eyes these poets see nature!" and ever after, when I saw the sunset stream upon the objects facing it, conceived I had made a discovery, or thanked Mr. Wordsworth for having made one for me! We went over to Alfoxden again the day following, and Wordsworth read us the story of *Peter Bell* in the open air; and the comment made upon it by his face and voice was very different from that of some later critics! Whatever might be thought of the poem, "his face was as a book where men might read strange matters,"[4] and he announced the fate of his hero in prophetic tones. There is a

---

8. A coarse and heavy cotton cloth.
9. The rough protagonist in Wordsworth's poem *Peter Bell* (1819).
1. Sir Francis Chantry's bust of Wordsworth was sculpted in 1820. In his large-scale history painting *Christ's Entry into Jerusalem* (1817), Benjamin Robert Haydon included likenesses of his friends Hazlitt, Keats, and Wordsworth among figures in the crowd surrounding Christ.

2. *The Castle Spectre* (staged in 1797) was a play of Gothic horrors by Matthew Gregory Lewis, nicknamed Monk Lewis in tribute to his most famous Gothic work, the novel *The Monk* (1795).
3. "For the sake of captivating" an audience (Latin).
4. Lady Macbeth's description of her husband as the two plot King Duncan's murder (Shakespeare, *Macbeth* 1.5.60–61).

chaunt in the recitation both of Coleridge and Wordsworth, which acts as a spell upon the hearer, and disarms the judgment. Perhaps they have deceived themselves by making habitual use of this ambiguous accompaniment. Coleridge's manner is more full, animated, and varied; Wordsworth's more equable, sustained, and internal. The one might be termed more *dramatic*, the other more *lyrical*. Coleridge has told me that he himself liked to compose in walking over uneven ground, or breaking through the straggling branches of a copse wood; whereas Wordsworth always wrote (if he could) walking up and down a straight gravel walk, or in some spot where the continuity of his verse met with no collateral interruption. Returning that same evening, I got into a metaphysical argument with Wordsworth, while Coleridge was explaining the different notes of the nightingale to his sister, in which we neither of us succeeded in making ourselves perfectly clear and intelligible. Thus I passed three weeks at Nether Stowey and in the neighborhood, generally devoting the afternoons to a delightful chat in an arbor made of bark by the poet's friend Tom Poole, sitting under two fine elm trees, and listening to the bees humming round us while we quaffed our flip.[5] It was agreed, among other things, that we should make a jaunt down the Bristol Channel, as far as Linton. We set off together on foot, Coleridge, John Chester, and I. This Chester was a native of Nether Stowey, one of those who were attracted to Coleridge's discourse as flies are to honey, or bees in swarming-time to the sound of a brass pan. He "followed in the chase like a dog who hunts, not like one that made up the cry."[6] He had on a brown cloth coat, boots, and corduroy breeches, was low in stature, bow-legged, had a drag in his walk like a drover, which he assisted by a hazel switch, and kept on a sort of trot by the side of Coleridge, like a running footman by a state coach, that he might not lose a syllable or sound that fell from Coleridge's lips. He told me his private opinion, that Coleridge was a wonderful man. He scarcely opened his lips, much less offered an opinion the whole way: yet of the three, had I to choose during that journey, I would be John Chester. He afterwards followed Coleridge into Germany, where the Kantean philosophers were puzzled how to bring him under any of their categories. When he sat down at table with his idol, John's felicity was complete; Sir Walter Scott's, or Mr. Blackwood's, when they sat down at the same table with the King,[7] was not more so. We passed Dunster on our right, a small town between the brow of a hill and the sea. I remember eying it wistfully as it lay below us: contrasted with the woody scene around, it looked as clear, as pure, as *embrowned* and ideal as any landscape I have seen since, of Gaspar Poussin's or Domenichino's. We had a long day's march—(our feet kept time to the echoes of Coleridge's tongue)—through Minehead and by the Blue Anchor, and on to Linton, which we did not reach till near midnight, and where we had some difficulty in making a lodgment. We however knocked the people of the house up at last, and we were repaid for our apprehensions and fatigue by some excellent rashers of fried bacon and eggs. The view in coming along had been splendid. We walked for miles and miles on dark brown heaths overlooking the channel, with the Welsh hills beyond, and at times descended into little sheltered valleys close

5. Spiced and sweetened ale.
6. See Shakespeare, *Othello* 2.3.337–38.
7. At a banquet given to George IV at Edinburgh in 1822. The publisher William Blackwood was, like his fellow Tory Sir Walter Scott (who had organized the king's visit), an ardent supporter of the unpopular monarchy.

by the seaside, with a smuggler's face scowling by us, and then had to ascend conical hills with a path winding up through a coppice to a barren top, like a monk's shaven crown, from one of which I pointed out to Coleridge's notice the bare masts of a vessel on the very edge of the horizon and within the red-orbed disk of the setting sun, like his own specter-ship in the *Ancient Mariner*. At Linton the character of the seacoast becomes more marked and rugged. There is a place called the Valley of Rocks (I suspect this was only the poetical name for it) bedded among precipices overhanging the sea, with rocky caverns beneath, into which the waves dash, and where the seagull forever wheels its screaming flight. On the tops of these are huge stones thrown transverse, as if an earthquake had tossed them there, and behind these is a fretwork of perpendicular rocks, something like the Giant's Causeway.[8] A thunderstorm came on while we were at the inn, and Coleridge was running out bareheaded to enjoy the commotion of the elements in the Valley of Rocks, but as if in spite, the clouds only muttered a few angry sounds, and let fall a few refreshing drops. Coleridge told me that he and Wordsworth were to have made this place the scene of a prose tale, which was to have been in the manner of, but far superior to, the *Death of Abel*,[9] but they had relinquished the design. In the morning of the second day, we breakfasted luxuriously in an old-fashioned parlor, on tea, toast, eggs, and honey, in the very sight of the beehives from which it had been taken, and a garden full of thyme and wild flowers that had produced it. On this occasion Coleridge spoke of Virgil's *Georgics*, but not well. I do not think he had much feeling for the classical or elegant. It was in this room that we found a little worn-out copy of the *Seasons*,[1] lying in a window seat, on which Coleridge exclaimed, "*That* is true fame!" He said Thomson was a great poet, rather than a good one; his style was as meretricious as his thoughts were natural. He spoke of Cowper as the best modern poet. He said the *Lyrical Ballads* were an experiment about to be tried by him and Wordsworth, to see how far the public taste would endure poetry written in a more natural and simple style than had hitherto been attempted; totally discarding the artifices of poetical diction, and making use only of such words as had probably been common in the most ordinary language since the days of Henry II. Some comparison was introduced between Shakespeare and Milton. He said "he hardly knew which to prefer. Shakespeare appeared to him a mere stripling in the art; he was as tall and as strong, with infinitely more activity than Milton, but he never appeared to have come to man's estate; or if he had, he would not have been a man, but a monster." He spoke with contempt of Gray, and with intolerance of Pope. He did not like the versification of the latter. He observed that "the ears of these couplet-writers might be charged with having short memories, that could not retain the harmony of whole passages." He thought little of Junius[2] as a writer; he had a dislike of Dr. Johnson; and a much higher opinion of Burke as an orator and politician, than of Fox or Pitt.[3] He however thought him very inferior in richness of style and imagery to some of our elder prose writers, particularly Jeremy Taylor.[4] He liked Richardson, but not

---

8. A mass of rocks on the northern Irish coast.
9. The "prose tale" exists as a fragment, *The Wanderings of Cain. The Death of Abel* (1758) is by the once celebrated Swiss poet Salomon Gessner.
1. By James Thomson, published in 1726–30.
2. The pseudonym of the author (whose identity

is still uncertain) of a series of attacks on George III and various politicians, 1769–72.
3. The liberal parliamentarian Charles James Fox (1749–1806) and the Conservative prime minister William Pitt (1759–1806).
4. The 17th-century divine, author of *Holy Living* (1650) and *Holy Dying* (1651).

Fielding; nor could I get him to enter into the merits of *Caleb Williams*.[5] In short, he was profound and discriminating with respect to those authors whom he liked, and where he gave his judgment fair play; capricious, perverse, and prejudiced in his antipathies and distastes. We loitered on the "ribbed sea-sands,"[6] in such talk as this, a whole morning, and I recollect met with a curious seaweed, of which John Chester told us the country name! A fisherman gave Coleridge an account of a boy that had been drowned the day before, and that they had tried to save him at the risk of their own lives. He said "he did not know how it was that they ventured, but, sir, we have a *nature* towards one another." This expression, Coleridge remarked to me, was a fine illustration of that theory of disinterestedness which I (in common with Butler) had adopted. I broached to him an argument of mine to prove that *likeness* was not mere association of ideas. I said that the mark in the sand put one in mind of a man's foot, not because it was part of a former impression of a man's foot (for it was quite new) but because it was like the shape of a man's foot. He assented to the justness of this distinction (which I have explained at length elsewhere, for the benefit of the curious) and John Chester listened; not from any interest in the subject, but because he was astonished that I should be able to suggest anything to Coleridge that he did not already know. We returned on the third morning, and Coleridge remarked the silent cottage-smoke curling up the valleys where, a few evenings before, we had seen the lights gleaming through the dark.

In a day or two after we arrived at Stowey, we set out, I on my return home, and he for Germany. It was a Sunday morning, and he was to preach that day for Dr. Toulmin of Taunton. I asked him if he had prepared anything for the occasion? He said he had not even thought of the text, but should as soon as we parted. I did not go to hear him—this was a fault—but we met in the evening at Bridgewater. The next day we had a long day's walk to Bristol, and sat down, I recollect, by a well-side on the road, to cool ourselves and satisfy our thirst, when Coleridge repeated to me some descriptive lines from his tragedy of *Remorse;* which I must say became his mouth and that occasion better than they, some years after, did Mr. Elliston's[7] and the Drury Lane boards,

> Oh memory! shield me from the world's poor strife,
> And give those scenes thine everlasting life.

I saw no more of him for a year or two, during which period he had been wandering in the Hartz Forest in Germany; and his return was cometary, meteorous, unlike his setting out. It was not till some time after that I knew his friends Lamb and Southey. The last always appears to me (as I first saw him) with a commonplace-book under his arm, and the first with a bon mot[8] in his mouth. It was at Godwin's that I met him with Holcroft and Coleridge, where they were disputing fiercely which was the best—*Man as he was, or man as he is to be*. "Give me," says Lamb, "man as he is *not* to be."

---

5. A 1794 novel by William Godwin. Samuel Richardson and Henry Fielding, the great 18th-century novelists.
6. Echoing *The Rime of the Ancient Mariner*, line 227.
7. Robert William Elliston, a well-known actor.

Coleridge's *Remorse* was produced at Drury Lane in 1813.
8. A witticism. "Commonplace-book": a manuscript notebook of personal reflections and favorite quotations culled from one's reading.

This saying was the beginning of a friendship between us, which I believe still continues.—Enough of this for the present.

> But there is matter for another rhyme,
> And I to this may add a second tale.[9]

1823

9. Wordsworth, *Hart-Leap Well*, lines 95–96.

THOMAS DE QUINCEY
1785–1859

Born in Manchester, the son of a wealthy merchant involved in the West Indian cotton trade, Thomas De Quincey was the fourth of eight children. Before his tenth birthday he experienced the deaths of a series of family members, his father included; the loss that more than any other haunted him his entire life was that of his favorite sister and "nursery playmate," Elizabeth, two years his senior, who died suddenly in 1792. Sent from home to school at seven, De Quincey was a precocious scholar, especially in Latin and Greek, and a gentle and bookish introvert; he found it difficult to adapt himself to discipline and routine and was thrown into panic by any emergency that called for decisive action. He ran away from Manchester Grammar School and, after a summer spent tramping through Wales, broke off completely from his family and guardians and went to London in the hope that he could obtain from moneylenders an advance on his prospective inheritance. There at the age of seventeen he spent a terrible winter of loneliness and poverty, befriended only by some kindly prostitutes. These early experiences with the sinister aspect of city life later became persistent elements in his dreams of terror.

After a reconciliation with his guardians, he entered Worcester College, Oxford, on an inadequate allowance. He spent the years 1803–08 in sporadic attendance, isolated as usual, then left abruptly in the middle of his examination for the A.B. with honors because he could not face the ordeal of an oral examination.

De Quincey had been an early admirer of Wordsworth and Coleridge. No sooner did he come of age and into his inheritance than, with his usual combination of generosity and recklessness, he made Coleridge an anonymous gift of £300. He became an intimate friend of the Wordsworths at Grasmere, and when they left Dove Cottage for Allan Bank, took up his own residence at Dove Cottage to be near them. For a time he lived the life of a rural scholar, but then fell in love with Margaret Simpson, the daughter of a minor local landholder and farmer and, after they had a son, married her in February 1817. This affair led to an estrangement from the Wordsworths and left him in severe financial difficulties. Worse still, De Quincey at this time became completely enslaved to opium. Following the ordinary medical practice of the time, he had been taking the drug for a variety of painful ailments; but now, driven by poverty and despair as well as pain, he indulged in huge quantities of laudanum (opium dissolved in alcohol) and was never thereafter able to free himself from addiction to what he called "the pleasures and pains of opium." It was during periods of maximum use, and especially in the recurrent agonies of cutting down his opium dosage, that he experienced the grotesque and terrifying reveries and nightmares that he wove into his literary fantasies.

Desperate for income, De Quincey at last turned to writing at the age of thirty-six. *Confessions of an English Opium-Eater*, which he contributed to the *London Magazine*, scored an immediate success and was at once reprinted as a book, but it earned him little money. In 1828 he moved with his three children to Edinburgh, to write for *Blackwood's Magazine*. For almost the rest of his life, he led a harried existence, beset by many physical ills, struggling with his indecisiveness and depression and the horrors of the opium habit, dodging his creditors and the constant threat of imprisonment for debt. All the while he ground out articles on any salable subject in a ceaseless struggle to keep his children, who ultimately numbered eight, from starving to death. Only after his mother died and left him a small income was he able, in his sixties, to live in comparative ease and freedom under the care of his devoted and practical-minded daughters. His last decade he spent mainly in gathering, revising, and expanding his essays for his "Collective Edition"; the final volume appeared in 1860, the year after his death.

De Quincey's life was chaotic, and in tone his best-known writings run the gamut from quirky wit to nightmarish sensationalism. Nonetheless, he was a conventional and conservative person—a rigid moralist, a Tory, and a faithful champion of the Church of England. Everybody who knew him testified to his gentleness, his courteous and musical speech, and his exquisite manners. Less obvious, under the surface timidity and irresolution, were the toughness and courage that sustained him through a long life of seemingly hopeless struggle.

A voracious reader (when he absconded from school, he was slowed down by a weighty trunk of books he was determined to take with him), De Quincey was a writer of encyclopedic intellectual interests and great versatility. A new twenty-one volume edition of his collected works encompasses the many essays he wrote on the philosophy and literature of Germany, as well as a book that explained the highly technical theories of value outlined by the economist David Ricardo. The collected works also include commentaries on politics and theology, numerous pieces of literary criticism (such as his "specimen of psychological criticism" "On the Knocking at the Gate in *Macbeth*"), and vivid biographical sketches of the many writers he knew personally, most notably Wordsworth, Coleridge, Southey, and Lamb. His most distinctive and impressive achievements, however, are the writings that start with fact and move into macabre fantasy ("On Murder Considered as One of the Fine Arts") and especially those that begin as quiet autobiography and develop into an elaborate construction made up from the materials of his reveries and dreams (*Confessions of an English Opium-Eater, Autobiographic Sketches, Suspiria de Profundis* ["Sighs from the depths"], and "The English Mail Coach"). In these achievements De Quincey opened up to English literature the nightside of human consciousness, with its grotesque strangeness, its angst, and its pervasive sense of guilt and alienation. "In dreams," he wrote, long before Sigmund Freud, "perhaps under some secret conflict of the midnight sleeper, lighted up to the consciousness at the time, but darkened to the memory as soon as all is finished, each several child of our mysterious race completes for himself the treason of the aboriginal fall." And for these dream writings he developed a mode of organization that is based on thematic statement, variation, and development in the art of music, in which he had a deep and abiding interest. Although by temperament a conservative, De Quincey was in his writings a radical innovator whose experiments look ahead to the materials and methods of later masters in prose and verse such as James Joyce, Franz Kafka, Virginia Woolf, and T. S. Eliot.

From Confessions of an English Opium-Eater[1]

From *Preliminary Confessions*[2]

[THE PROSTITUTE ANN]

* * * Another person there was at that time, whom I have since sought to trace with far deeper earnestness, and with far deeper sorrow at my failure. This person was a young woman, and one of that unhappy class who subsist upon the wages of prostitution. I feel no shame, nor have any reason to feel it, in avowing, that I was then on familiar and friendly terms with many women in that unfortunate condition. The reader needs neither smile at this avowal, nor frown. For, not to remind my classical readers of the old Latin proverb—"*Sine Cerere,*" &c.,[3] it may well be supposed that in the existing state of my purse, my connection with such women could not have been an impure one. But the truth is, that at no time of my life have I been a person to hold myself polluted by the touch or approach of any creature that wore a human shape: on the contrary, from my very earliest youth it has been my pride to converse familiarly, *more Socratico,*[4] with all human beings, man, woman, and child, that chance might fling in my way: a practice which is friendly to the knowledge of human nature, to good feelings, and to that frankness of address which becomes a man who would be thought a philosopher. For a philosopher should not see with the eyes of the poor limitary[5] creature, calling himself a man of the world, and filled with narrow and self-regarding prejudices of birth and education, but should look upon himself as a Catholic[6] creature, and as standing in an equal relation to high and low—to educated and uneducated, to the guilty and the innocent. Being myself at that time of necessity a peripatetic, or a walker of the street, I naturally fell in more frequently with those female peripatetics who are technically called street-walkers. Many of these women had occasionally taken my part against watchmen who wished to drive me off the

1. The *Confessions* were published anonymously in two issues of the *London Magazine,* September and October 1821, and were reprinted as a book in the following year. In 1856 De Quincey revised the book for the collected edition of his writings, expanding it to more than twice its original length. The author was over seventy years old at the time and privately expressed the judgment that the expanded edition lacks the immediacy and artistic economy of the original. The selections here are from the version of the *Confessions* printed in 1822.

The work is divided into three parts. The first part, "Preliminary Confessions," deals with De Quincey's early experiences—at school, in Wales, and in London—before taking opium. Part Two, "The Pleasures of Opium" (omitted here), describes the early effects on his perceptions and reveries of his moderate and occasional indulgence in the drug. Part Three, "The Pains of Opium," is an elaborate and artful representation of his fantastic nightmares; these, in modern medical opinion, are in part withdrawal symptoms, during periods when he tried to cut down his use of opium.

In De Quincey's own lifetime, and ever since, the charge has been brought that the reports of these dreams were largely fabricated by the author. But De Quincey always insisted that they

were substantially accurate; and both the fact and the content of such anguished nightmares are corroborated by the testimony of another laudanum addict, Samuel Taylor Coleridge, in his poem "The Pains of Sleep" (1803).
2. The seventeen-year-old De Quincey had run away from school and, although originally planning to head north from Manchester so as to introduce himself to Wordsworth (whose poetry he worshiped), had ended up taking refuge in London, his whereabouts unknown to his mother and his guardians. He had slept outdoors for two months but has now been permitted, by a disreputable and seedy lawyer, to sleep in an unoccupied, unfurnished, and rat-infested house. There he and a ten-year-old girl, nameless and of uncertain parentage, huddle together for warmth, eking out a famished existence on whatever scraps he can scavenge from his landlord's frugal breakfast. He goes on to describe his friendship with a young prostitute, Ann.
3. *Sine Cerere et Baccho friget Venus*—"without Ceres and Bacchus [food and wine], love grows cold."
4. In the manner of Socrates; i.e., by a dialogue of questions and answers.
5. Limited.
6. In the sense of "inclusive in tastes and understanding."

steps of houses where I was sitting. But one amongst them, the one on whose account I have at all introduced this subject—yet no! let me not class thee, oh noble-minded Ann——, with that order of women; let me find, if it be possible, some gentler name to designate the condition of her to whose bounty and compassion, ministering to my necessities when all the world had forsaken me, I owe it that I am at this time alive.—For many weeks I had walked at nights with this poor friendless girl up and down Oxford Street, or had rested with her on steps and under the shelter of porticos. She could not be so old as myself: she told me, indeed, that she had not completed her sixteenth year. By such questions as my interest about her prompted, I had gradually drawn forth her simple history. Hers was a case of ordinary occurrence (as I have since had reason to think), and one in which, if London beneficence had better adapted its arrangements to meet it, the power of the law might oftener be interposed to protect, and to avenge. But the stream of London charity flows in a channel which, though deep and mighty, is yet noiseless and underground; not obvious or readily accessible to poor houseless wanderers; and it cannot be denied that the outside air and framework of London society is harsh, cruel, and repulsive. In any case, however, I saw that part of her injuries might easily have been redressed; and I urged her often and earnestly to lay her complaint before a magistrate: friendless as she was, I assured her that she would meet with immediate attention; and that English justice, which was no respecter of persons, would speedily and amply avenge her on the brutal ruffian who had plundered her little property. She promised me often that she would; but she delayed taking the steps I pointed out from time to time: for she was timid and dejected to a degree which showed how deeply sorrow had taken hold of her young heart: and perhaps she thought justly that the most upright judge, and the most righteous tribunals, could do nothing to repair her heaviest wrongs. Something, however, would perhaps have been done: for it had been settled between us at length, but unhappily on the very last time but one that I was ever to see her, that in a day or two we should go together before a magistrate, and that I should speak on her behalf. This little service it was destined, however, that I should never realize. Meantime, that which she rendered to me, and which was greater than I could ever have repaid her, was this:—One night, when we were pacing slowly along Oxford Street, and after a day when I had felt more than usually ill and faint, I requested her to turn off with me into Soho Square: thither we went; and we sat down on the steps of a house, which, to this hour, I never pass without a pang of grief, and an inner act of homage to the spirit of that unhappy girl, in memory of the noble action which she there performed. Suddenly, as we sat, I grew much worse: I had been leaning my head against her bosom; and all at once I sank from her arms and fell backwards on the steps. From the sensations I then had, I felt an inner conviction of the liveliest kind that without some powerful and reviving stimulus, I should either have died on the spot—or should at least have sunk to a point of exhaustion from which all re-ascent under my friendless circumstances would soon have become hopeless. Then it was, at this crisis of my fate, that my poor orphan companion—who had herself met with little but injuries in this world—stretched out a saving hand to me. Uttering a cry of terror, but without a moment's delay, she ran off into Oxford Street, and in less time than could be imagined, returned to me with a glass of port wine and spices, that acted upon my empty stomach (which at that time would have rejected all solid food) with an instantaneous power of restoration: and for this glass the generous girl without a murmur paid out of her own humble purse at a time—be it remembered!—when she had scarcely wherewithal to purchase the bare necessaries of life, and when she could have no reason to expect that I should ever be able to reimburse her.——Oh! youthful benefactress! how often in succeeding years, standing in solitary places, and thinking of thee with grief of heart and perfect love, how often have I wished that, as in ancient times the curse of a father was believed to have a supernatural power, and to pursue its object with a fatal necessity of self-fulfillment— even so the benediction of a heart oppressed with gratitude, might have a like prerogative; might have power given to it from above to chase—to haunt—to waylay[7]—to overtake—to pursue thee into the central darkness of a London brothel, or (if it were possible) into the darkness of the grave— there to awaken thee with an authentic message of peace and forgiveness, and of final reconciliation!

I do not often weep: for not only do my thoughts on subjects connected with the chief interests of man daily, nay hourly, descend a thousand fathoms "too deep for tears";[8] not only does the sternness of my habits of thought present an antagonism to the feelings which prompt tears—wanting of necessity to those who, being protected usually by their levity from any tendency to meditative sorrow, would by that same levity be made incapable of resisting it on any casual access of such feelings:—but also, I believe that all minds which have contemplated such objects as deeply as I have done, must, for their own protection from utter despondency, have early encouraged and cherished some tranquilizing belief as to the future balances and the hieroglyphic meanings of human sufferings. On these accounts, I am cheerful to this hour; and, as I have said, I do not often weep. Yet some feelings, though not deeper or more passionate, are more tender than others; and often, when I walk at this time in Oxford Street by dreamy lamplight, and hear those airs played on a barrel-organ[9] which years ago solaced me and my dear companion (as I must always call her), I shed tears, and muse with myself at the mysterious dispensation which so suddenly and so critically separated us for ever.[1] * * *

From *Introduction to the Pains of Opium*[2]

[THE MALAY]

* * * I remember, about this time, a little incident, which I mention, because, trifling as it was, the reader will soon meet it again in my dreams, which it

---

7. From Wordsworth's "She was a phantom of delight," line 10: "To haunt, to startle, and way-lay." De Quincey was an early and enthusiastic admirer of Wordsworth's poetry.
8. From the last line of Wordsworth's "Ode: Intimations of Immortality."
9. Instrument played by an organ-grinder.
1. De Quincey goes on to narrate that, having been given some money by a family friend who recognized him in the street, he had traveled to Eton to ask a young nobleman whom he knew to stand security for a loan that De Quincey was soliciting from a moneylender. When he returned to London three days later, Ann had disappeared.

"If she lived," he writes, "doubtless we must have been sometimes in search of each other, at the very same moment, through the mighty labyrinths of London; perhaps, even within a few feet of each other—a barrier no wider in a London street, often amounting in the end to a separation for eternity!"
2. It is 1816. De Quincey is living at Dove Cottage, Grasmere, and for three years has been addicted to laudanum (i.e., opium dissolved in alcohol). At this time he has succeeded in reducing his daily dosage from eight thousand to one thousand drops, with a consequent improvement in health and energy.

influenced more fearfully than could be imagined. One day a Malay[3] knocked at my door. What business a Malay could have to transact amongst English mountains, I cannot conjecture: but possibly he was on his road to a seaport about forty miles distant.

The servant who opened the door to him was a young girl born and bred amongst the mountains, who had never seen an Asiatic dress of any sort: his turban, therefore, confounded her not a little: and, as it turned out that his attainments in English were exactly of the same extent as hers in the Malay, there seemed to be an impassable gulf fixed between all communication of ideas, if either party had happened to possess any. In this dilemma, the girl, recollecting the reputed learning of her master (and, doubtless, giving me credit for a knowledge of all the languages of the earth, besides, perhaps, a few of the lunar ones), came and gave me to understand that there was a sort of demon below, whom she clearly imagined that my art could exorcise from the house. I did not immediately go down: but, when I did, the group which presented itself, arranged as it was by accident, though not very elaborate, took hold of my fancy and my eye in a way that none of the statuesque attitudes exhibited in the ballets at the Opera House, though so ostentatiously complex, had ever done. In a cottage kitchen, but paneled on the wall with dark wood that from age and rubbing resembled oak, and looking more like a rustic hall of entrance than a kitchen, stood the Malay— his turban and loose trousers of dingy white relieved upon the dark paneling:[4] he had placed himself nearer to the girl than she seemed to relish; though her native spirit of mountain intrepidity contended with the feeling of simple awe which her countenance expressed as she gazed upon the tiger-cat before her. And a more striking picture there could not be imagined, than the beautiful English face of the girl, and its exquisite fairness, together with her erect and independent attitude, contrasted with the sallow and bilious skin of the Malay, enameled or veneered with mahogany, by marine air, his small, fierce, restless eyes, thin lips, slavish gestures and adorations. Half-hidden by the ferocious-looking Malay, was a little child from a neighboring cottage who had crept in after him, and was now in the act of reverting its head, and gazing upwards at the turban and the fiery eyes beneath it, whilst with one hand he caught at the dress of the young woman for protection. My knowledge of the Oriental tongues is not remarkably extensive, being indeed confined to two words—the Arabic word for barley, and the Turkish for opium (madjoon), which I have learnt from Anastasius.[5] And, as I had neither a Malay dictionary, nor even Adelung's *Mithridates*,[6] which might have helped me to a few words, I addressed him in some lines from the Iliad; considering that, of such languages as I possessed, Greek, in point of longitude, came geographically nearest to an Oriental one. He worshiped[7] me in a most devout manner, and replied in what I suppose was Malay. In this way I saved my reputation with my neighbors: for the Malay had no means of betraying the secret. He lay down upon the floor for about an hour, and then pursued his journey. On his departure, I presented him with a piece of

---

3. Native of the Malay peninsula in Southeast Asia.

4. I.e., his white clothing is cast in relief by the dark paneling.

5. *Anastasius, or Memoirs of a Greek*, was a novel published anonymously by Thomas Hope in 1819. It included a description of the physical effects of opium that De Quincey considered to be a "grievous misrepresentation."

6. *Mithridates, or The Universal Table of Languages*, by the German philologist J. C. Adelung (1732–1806).

7. Bowed down to.

opium. To him, as an Orientalist, I concluded that opium must be familiar: and the expression of his face convinced me that it was. Nevertheless, I was struck with some little consternation when I saw him suddenly raise his hand to his mouth, and (in the schoolboy phrase) bolt the whole, divided into three pieces, at one mouthful. The quantity was enough to kill three dragoons and their horses: and I felt some alarm for the poor creature: but what could be done? I had given him the opium in compassion for his solitary life, on recollecting that if he had traveled on foot from London, it must be nearly three weeks since he could have exchanged a thought with any human being. I could not think of violating the laws of hospitality, by having him seized and drenched with an emetic, and thus frightening him into a notion that we were going to sacrifice him to some English idol. No: there was clearly no help for it:—he took his leave: and for some days I felt anxious: but as I never heard of any Malay being found dead, I became convinced that he was used[8] to opium: and that I must have done him the service I designed, by giving him one night of respite from the pains of wandering.

This incident I have digressed to mention, because this Malay (partly from the picturesque exhibition he assisted to frame, partly from the anxiety I connected with his image for some days) fastened afterwards upon my dreams, and brought other Malays with him worse than himself, that ran "amuck"[9] at me, and led me into a world of troubles. * * *

From *The Pains of Opium*

[OPIUM REVERIES AND DREAMS]

I have thus described and illustrated my intellectual torpor, in terms that apply, more or less, to every part of the four years during which I was under the Circean[1] spells of opium. But for misery and suffering, I might, indeed, be said to have existed in a dormant state. I seldom could prevail on myself to write a letter; an answer of a few words, to any that I received, was the utmost that I could accomplish; and often *that* not until the letter had lain weeks, or even months, on my writing table. Without the aid of M.[2] all records of bills paid, or *to be* paid, must have perished: and my whole domestic economy, whatever became of Political Economy,[3] must have gone into irretrievable confusion.—I shall not afterwards allude to this part of the case: it is one, however, which the opium-eater will find, in the end, as oppressive and tormenting as any other, from the sense of incapacity and feebleness, from the direct embarrassments incident to the neglect or procrastination of each day's appropriate duties, and from the remorse which must often exasperate the stings of these evils to a reflective and conscientious mind. The opium-eater loses none of his moral sensibilities, or aspirations: he wishes and longs, as earnestly as ever, to realize what he believes

8. This, however, is not a necessary conclusion: the varieties of effect produced by opium on different constitutions are infinite [De Quincey's note].
9. See the common accounts in any Eastern traveller or voyager of the frantic excesses committed by Malays who have taken opium, or are reduced to desperation by ill luck at gambling [De Quincey's note]. "Amuck": also spelled "amok," as a term denoting frenzy, it entered English by way of travel literature and was used initially as a

generic designation for inhabitants of the Malay peninsula.
1. Like those of Circe, the enchantress in the *Odyssey* who turned Odysseus's men into swine.
2. Margaret Simpson, whom De Quincey had married in 1817.
3. Inspired by David Ricardo's *Principles of Political Economy* (1817), De Quincey had begun to write, but never completed, a work he called *Prolegomena to All Future Systems of Political Economy*.

possible, and feels to be exacted by duty; but his intellectual apprehension of what is possible infinitely outruns his power, not of execution only, but even of power to attempt. He lies under the weight of incubus and nightmare: he lies in sight of all that he would fain perform, just as a man forcibly confined to his bed by the mortal languor of a relaxing disease, who is compelled to witness injury or outrage offered to some object of his tenderest love:—he curses the spells which chain him down from motion:—he would lay down his life if he might get up and walk; but he is powerless as an infant, and cannot even attempt to rise.

I now pass to what is the main subject of these latter confessions, to the history and journal of what took place in my dreams; for these were the immediate and proximate cause of my acutest suffering.

The first notice I had of any important change going on in this part of my physical economy, was from the re-awakening of a state of eye generally incident to childhood, or exalted states of irritability. I know not whether my reader is aware that many children, perhaps most, have a power of painting, as it were, upon the darkness, all sorts of phantoms; in some, that power is simply a mechanic affection of the eye; others have a voluntary, or a semi-voluntary power to dismiss or to summon them; or, as a child once said to me when I questioned him on this matter, "I can tell them to go, and they go; but sometimes they come, when I don't tell them to come." Whereupon I told him that he had almost as unlimited a command over apparitions, as a Roman centurion[4] over his soldiers.—In the middle of 1817, I think it was, that this faculty became positively distressing to me: at night, when I lay awake in bed, vast processions passed along in mournful pomp; friezes of never-ending stories, that to my feelings were as sad and solemn as if they were stories drawn from times before Oedipus or Priam—before Tyre—before Memphis.[5] And, at the same time, a corresponding change took place in my dreams; a theater seemed suddenly opened and lighted up within my brain, which presented nightly spectacles of more than earthly splendor. And the four following facts may be mentioned, as noticeable at this time:

1. That, as the creative state of the eye increased, a sympathy seemed to arise between the waking and the dreaming states of the brain in one point—that whatsoever I happened to call up and to trace by a voluntary act upon the darkness was very apt to transfer itself to my dreams; so that I feared to exercise this faculty; for, as Midas turned all things to gold, that yet baffled his hopes and defrauded his human desires,[6] so whatsoever things capable of being visually represented I did but think of in the darkness, immediately shaped themselves into phantoms of the eye; and, by a process apparently no less inevitable, when thus once traced in faint and visionary colors, like writings in sympathetic ink,[7] they were drawn out by the fierce chemistry of my dreams, into insufferable splendor that fretted my heart.

2. For this, and all other changes in my dreams, were accompanied by deep-seated anxiety and gloomy melancholy, such as are wholly incommuni-

---

4. A Roman officer commanding a troop of a hundred soldiers (a "century").
5. De Quincey is calling the roll of great civilizations in the past. Oedipus was the king of Thebes. Priam was the king of Troy. Tyre was the chief city of Phoenicia. Memphis was the capital of ancient Egypt.
6. When granted his rash wish that all he touched should turn to gold, King Midas was horrified to discover that his food, drink, and beloved daughter all became gold at his touch.
7. Invisible ink.

cable by words. I seemed every night to descend, not metaphorically, but literally to descend, into chasms and sunless abysses, depths below depths, from which it seemed hopeless that I could ever reascend. Nor did I, by waking, feel that I *had* re-ascended. This I do not dwell upon; because the state of gloom which attended these gorgeous spectacles, amounting at least to utter darkness, as of some suicidal despondency, cannot be approached by words.

3. The sense of space, and in the end, the sense of time, were both powerfully affected. Buildings, landscapes, &c. were exhibited in proportions so vast as the bodily eye is not fitted to receive. Space swelled, and was amplified to an extent of unutterable infinity. This, however, did not disturb me so much as the vast expansion of time; I sometimes seemed to have lived for 70 or 100 years in one night; nay, sometimes had feelings representative of a millennium passed in that time, or, however, of a duration far beyond the limits of any human experience.

4. The minutest incidents of childhood, or forgotten scenes of later years, were often revived: I could not be said to recollect them; for if I had been told of them when waking, I should not have been able to acknowledge them as parts of my past experience. But placed as they were before me, in dreams like intuitions, and clothed in all their evanescent circumstances and accompanying feelings, I *recognized* them instantaneously. I was once told by a near relative[8] of mine, that having in her childhood fallen into a river, and being on the very verge of death but for the critical assistance which reached her, she saw in a moment her whole life, in its minutest incidents, arrayed before her simultaneously as in a mirror; and she had a faculty developed as suddenly for comprehending the whole and every part. This, from some opium experiences of mine, I can believe; I have, indeed, seen the same thing asserted twice in modern books, and accompanied by a remark which I am convinced is true; viz. that the dread book of account, which the Scriptures speak of,[9] is, in fact, the mind itself of each individual. Of this, at least, I feel assured, that there is no such thing as *forgetting* possible to the mind; a thousand accidents may, and will, interpose a veil between our present consciousness and the secret inscriptions on the mind; accidents of the same sort will also rend away this veil; but alike, whether veiled or unveiled, the inscription remains forever; just as the stars seem to withdraw before the common light of day, whereas, in fact, we all know that it is the light which is drawn over them as a veil—and that they are waiting to be revealed, when the obscuring daylight shall have withdrawn.

Having noticed these four facts as memorably distinguishing my dreams from those of health, I shall now cite a case illustrative of the first fact; and shall then cite any others that I remember, either in their chronological order, or any other that may give them more effect as pictures to the reader.

I had been in youth, and even since, for occasional amusement, a great reader of Livy,[1] whom, I confess, that I prefer, both for style and matter, to any of the Roman historians; and I had often felt as most solemn and appalling sounds, and most emphatically representative of the majesty of the

8. According to family report De Quincey's mother.
9. The book listing everyone's name at the Last Judgment (Revelation 20.12).
1. Titus Livius (59 B.C.E.–17 C.E.), author of a history of Rome in 142 books.

Roman people, the two words so often occurring in Livy—*Consul Romanus*;[2] especially when the consul is introduced in his military character. I mean to say, that the words king—sultan—regent, &c. or any other titles of those who embody in their own persons the collective majesty of a great people, had less power over my reverential feelings. I had also, though no great reader of history, made myself minutely and critically familiar with one period of English history, viz. the period of the Parliamentary War, having been attracted by the moral grandeur of some who figured in that day, and by the many interesting memoirs which survive those unquiet times. Both these parts of my lighter reading, having furnished me often with matter of reflection, now furnished me with matter for my dreams. Often I used to see, after painting upon the blank darkness a sort of rehearsal whilst waking, a crowd of ladies, and perhaps a festival, and dances. And I heard it said, or I said to myself, "These are English ladies from the unhappy times of Charles I. These are the wives and the daughters of those who met in peace, and sat at the same tables, and were allied by marriage or by blood; and yet, after a certain day in August, 1642,[3] never smiled upon each other again, nor met but in the field of battle; and at Marston Moor, at Newbury, or at Naseby,[4] cut asunder all ties of love by the cruel saber, and washed away in blood the memory of ancient friendship."—The ladies danced, and looked as lovely as the court of George IV.[5] Yet I knew, even in my dream, that they had been in the grave for nearly two centuries.—This pageant would suddenly dissolve: and at a clapping of hands, would be heard the heart-quaking sound of *Consul Romanus*; and immediately came "sweeping by," in gorgeous paludaments, Paulus or Marius,[6] girt round by a company of centurions, with the crimson tunic hoisted on a spear,[7] and followed by the *alalagmos*[8] of the Roman legions.

Many years ago, when I was looking over Piranesi's Antiquities of Rome, Mr. Coleridge, who was standing by, described to me a set of plates by that artist, called his *Dreams*,[9] and which record the scenery of his own visions during the delirium of a fever. Some of them (I describe only from memory of Mr. Coleridge's account) represented vast Gothic halls: on the floor of which stood all sorts of engines and machinery, wheels, cables, pulleys, levers, catapults, &c. &c. expressive of enormous power put forth, and resistance overcome. Creeping along the sides of the walls, you perceived a staircase; and upon it, groping his way upwards, was Piranesi himself: follow the stairs a little further, and you perceive it come to a sudden abrupt termination, without any balustrade, and allowing no step onwards to him who had reached the extremity, except into the depths below. Whatever is to become

---

2. Roman consul (Latin); one of two officials, elected annually, who wielded the chief military and judicial authority in Republican Rome.
3. The raising of the king's banner on Castle Hill, Nottingham, on August 22, 1642, signaled the beginning of the English Civil War.
4. Scenes of the defeat of King Charles's forces in the Civil War.
5. The reigning monarch at the time De Quincey was writing.
6. Lucius Paulus (d. 160 B.C.E.) and Caius Marius (d. 86 B.C.E.) were Roman generals who won famous victories. "Paludaments": the cloaks worn by Roman generals.

7. The signal which announced a day of battle [De Quincey's note in the revised edition].
8. A word expressing collectively the gathering of the Roman war-cries [De Quincey's note in the revised edition]. The word is Greek.
9. Giovanni Piranesi (1720–1778), a Venetian especially famed for his many etchings of ancient and modern Rome. He did not publish prints called *Dreams*; De Quincey doubtless refers to his series called *Carceri d'Invenzione*, "Imaginary prisons." The description that De Quincey recalls from Coleridge's conversation is remarkably apt for these terrifying architectural fantasies.

of poor Piranesi, you suppose, at least, that his labors must in some way terminate here. But raise your eyes, and behold a second flight of stairs still higher: on which again Piranesi is perceived, but this time standing on the very brink of the abyss. Again elevate your eye, and a still more aerial flight of stairs is beheld: and again is poor Piranesi busy on his aspiring labors: and so on, until the unfinished stairs and Piranesi both are lost in the upper gloom of the hall.—With the same power of endless growth and self-reproduction did my architecture proceed in dreams. In the early stage of my malady, the splendors of my dreams were indeed chiefly architectural: and I beheld such pomp of cities and palaces as was never yet beheld by the waking eye, unless in the clouds. From a great modern poet[1] I cite part of a passage which describes, as an appearance actually beheld in the clouds, what in many of its circumstances I saw frequently in sleep:

> The appearance, instantaneously disclosed,
> Was of a mighty city—boldly say
> A wilderness of building, sinking far
> And self-withdrawn into a wondrous depth,
> Far sinking into splendor—without end!
> Fabric[2] it seem'd of diamond, and of gold,
> With alabaster domes, and silver spires,
> And blazing terrace upon terrace, high
> Uplifted; here, serene pavilions bright
> In avenues disposed; there towers begirt
> With battlements that on their restless fronts
> Bore stars—illumination of all gems!
> By earthly nature had the effect been wrought
> Upon the dark materials of the storm
> Now pacified: on them, and on the coves,
> And mountain-steeps and summits, whereunto
> The vapors had receded,—taking there
> Their station under a cerulean sky, &c. &c.

The sublime circumstance—"battlements that on their *restless* fronts bore stars"—might have been copied from my architectural dreams, for it often occurred.—We hear it reported of Dryden, and of Fuseli[3] in modern times, that they thought proper to eat raw meat for the sake of obtaining splendid dreams: how much better for such a purpose to have eaten opium, which yet I do not remember that any poet is recorded to have done, except the dramatist Shadwell:[4] and in ancient days, Homer is, I think, rightly reputed to have known the virtues of opium.[5]

To my architecture succeeded dreams of lakes—and silvery expanses of water:—these haunted me so much, that I feared (though possibly it will appear ludicrous to a medical man) that some dropsical state or tendency of the brain[6] might thus be making itself (to use a metaphysical word) *objective*;

---

1. The quotation is from Wordsworth's *The Excursion*, book 2, lines 834ff. It describes a cloud structure after a storm.
2. I.e., building.
3. John Henry Fuseli (1741–1825) was born in Switzerland and painted in England. He was noted for his paintings of nightmarish fantasies.
4. Thomas Shadwell was a Restoration dramatist and poet. He is now better known as the target of Dryden's satire (in *Mac Flecknoe* and elsewhere)

than as a writer in his own right.
5. In the *Odyssey*, book 4, Homer praises nepenthe (which is probably opium) as a "drug to heal all pain and anger, and bring forgetfulness of every sorrow."
6. De Quincey's sister Elizabeth died at age nine of hydrocephalus, water on the brain. "Dropsical": afflicted with dropsy—an accumulation of fluid in the bodily tissues and cavities.

and the sentient organ *project* itself as its own object.—For two months I suffered greatly in my head—a part of my bodily structure which had hitherto been so clear from all touch or taint of weakness (physically, I mean), that I used to say of it, as the last Lord Orford[7] said of his stomach, that it seemed likely to survive the rest of my person.—Till now I had never felt a headache even, or any the slightest pain, except rheumatic pains caused by my own folly. However, I got over this attack, though it must have been verging on something very dangerous.

The waters now changed their character—from translucent lakes, shining like mirrors, they now became seas and oceans. And now came a tremendous change, which, unfolding itself slowly like a scroll, through many months, promised an abiding torment; and, in fact, it never left me until the winding up of my case. Hitherto the human face had mixed often in my dreams, but not despotically, nor with any special power of tormenting. But now that which I have called the tyranny of the human face began to unfold itself. Perhaps some part of my London life might be answerable for this. Be that as it may, now it was that upon the rocking waters of the ocean the human face began to appear: the sea appeared paved with innumerable faces, upturned to the heavens: faces, imploring, wrathful, despairing, surged upwards by thousands, by myriads, by generations, by centuries:—my agitation was infinite,—my mind tossed—and surged with the ocean.[8]

May 1818

The Malay has been a fearful enemy for months. I have been every night, through his means, transported into Asiatic scenes. I know not whether others share in my feelings on this point; but I have often thought that if I were compelled to forego England, and to live in China, and among Chinese manners and modes of life and scenery, I should go mad. The causes of my horror lie deep; and some of them must be common to others. Southern Asia, in general, is the seat of awful images and associations. As the cradle of the human race, it would alone have a dim and reverential feeling connected with it. But there are other reasons. No man can pretend that the wild, barbarous, and capricious superstitions of Africa, or of savage tribes elsewhere, affect him in the way that he is affected by the ancient, monumental, cruel, and elaborate religions of Indostan, &c. The mere antiquity of Asiatic things, of their institutions, histories, modes of faith, &c. is so impressive, that to me the vast age of the race and name overpowers the sense of youth in the individual. A young Chinese seems to me an antediluvian man[9] renewed. Even Englishmen, though not bred in any knowledge of such institutions, cannot but shudder at the mystic sublimity of *castes*[1] that have flowed apart, and refused to mix, through such immemorial tracts of time; nor can any man fail to be awed by the names of the Ganges, or the Euphrates. It contributes much to these feelings, that southern Asia is, and

7. Horace Walpole, 18th-century wit and letter writer, author of the Gothic novel *The Castle of Otranto* (1764).
8. Cf. De Quincey's earlier description of his repeated hunts through the London streets for his friend Ann: "I suppose that, in the literal and unrhetorical use of the word *myriad*, I may say that on my different visits to London, I have looked into many, many myriads of female faces, in the hope of meeting her."
9. A person who lived in the time before the great flood described in Genesis.
1. The reference is to the Hindu caste system of India, with its sharp divisions between four hereditary social classes.

has been for thousands of years, the part of the earth most swarming with human life; the great *officina gentium*.[2] Man is a weed in those regions. The vast empires also, into which the enormous population of Asia has always been cast, give a further sublimity to the feelings associated with all Oriental names or images. In China, over and above what it has in common with the rest of southern Asia, I am terrified by the modes of life, by the manners, and the barrier of utter abhorrence, and want of sympathy, placed between us by feelings deeper than I can analyze. I could sooner live with lunatics, or brute animals. All this, and much more than I can say, or have time to say, the reader must enter into before he can comprehend the unimaginable horror which these dreams of Oriental imagery, and mythological tortures, impressed upon me. Under the connecting feeling of tropical heat and vertical sunlights, I brought together all creatures, birds, beasts, reptiles, all trees and plants, usages and appearances, that are found in all tropical regions, and assembled them together in China or Indostan. From kindred feelings, I soon brought Egypt and all her gods under the same law. I was stared at, hooted at, grinned at, chattered at, by monkeys, by paroquets, by cockatoos. I ran into pagodas: and was fixed, for centuries, at the summit, or in secret rooms; I was the idol; I was the priest; I was worshiped; I was sacrificed. I fled from the wrath of Brama through all the forests of Asia: Vishnu hated me: Seeva[3] laid wait for me. I came suddenly upon Isis and Osiris: I had done a deed, they said, which the ibis and the crocodile[4] trembled at. I was buried, for a thousand years, in stone coffins, with mummies and sphinxes, in narrow chambers at the heart of eternal pyramids. I was kissed, with cancerous kisses, by crocodiles; and laid, confounded with all unutterable slimy things, amongst reeds and Nilotic mud.

I thus give the reader some slight abstraction of my Oriental dreams,[5] which always filled me with such amazement at the monstrous scenery, that horror seemed absorbed, for a while, in sheer astonishment. Sooner or later, came a reflux of feeling that swallowed up the astonishment, and left me, not so much in terror, as in hatred and abomination of what I saw. Over every form, and threat, and punishment, and dim sightless incarceration, brooded a sense of eternity and infinity that drove me into an oppression as of madness. Into these dreams only, it was, with one or two slight exceptions, that any circumstances of physical horror entered. All before had been moral and spiritual terrors. But here the main agents were ugly birds, or snakes, or crocodiles; especially the last. The cursed crocodile became to me the object of more horror than almost all the rest. I was compelled to live with him; and (as was always the case almost in my dreams) for centuries. I escaped sometimes, and found myself in Chinese houses, with cane tables, &c. All the feet of the tables, sofas, &c. soon became instinct with life: the abominable head of the crocodile, and his leering eyes, looked out at me, multiplied into a thousand repetitions: and I stood loathing and fascinated. And so often did this hideous reptile haunt my dreams, that many times the

2. Manufactory of populations (Latin).
3. Among the Hindu deities Brahma is the creative aspect of divine reality, Vishnu is its maintainer, and Shiva its destroyer.
4. The ibis (a long-legged wading bird) and the crocodile were considered sacred in ancient Egypt. Isis was the ancient Egyptian goddess of fertility. She was the sister and wife of Osiris, whose annual death and rebirth represented the seasonal cycle of nature.
5. For a discussion of the cultural context of De Quincey's "Oriental dreams," see "The Romantic Imagination and the 'Oriental Nations,'" p. 922.

very same dream was broken up in the very same way: I heard gentle voices speaking to me (I hear every thing when I am sleeping); and instantly I awoke: it was broad noon; and my children were standing, hand in hand, at my bedside; come to show me their colored shoes, or new frocks, or to let me see them dressed for going out. I protest that so awful was the transition from the damned crocodile, and the other unutterable monsters and abortions of my dreams, to the sight of innocent *human* natures and of infancy, that, in the mighty and sudden revulsion of mind, I wept, and could not forbear it, as I kissed their faces.

June 1819

I have had occasion to remark, at various periods of my life, that the deaths of those whom we love, and indeed the contemplation of death generally, is (*ceteris paribus*)[6] more affecting in summer than in any other season of the year. And the reasons are these three, I think: first, that the visible heavens in summer appear far higher, more distant, and (if such a solecism may be excused) more infinite; the clouds, by which chiefly the eye expounds the distance of the blue pavilion stretched over our heads, are in summer more voluminous, massed, and accumulated in far grander and more towering piles: secondly, the light and the appearances of the declining and the setting sun are much more fitted to be types and characters of the Infinite: and, thirdly (which is the main reason), the exuberant and riotous prodigality of life naturally forces the mind more powerfully upon the antagonist thought of death, and the wintry sterility of the grave. For it may be observed, generally, that wherever two thoughts stand related to each other by a law of antagonism, and exist, as it were, by mutual repulsion, they are apt to suggest each other. On these accounts it is that I find it impossible to banish the thought of death when I am walking alone in the endless days of summer; and any particular death, if not more affecting, at least haunts my mind more obstinately and besiegingly in that season. Perhaps this cause, and a slight incident which I omit, might have been the immediate occasions of the following dream; to which, however, a predisposition must always have existed in my mind; but having been once roused, it never left me, and split into a thousand fantastic varieties, which often suddenly reunited, and composed again the original dream.

I thought that it was a Sunday morning in May, that it was Easter Sunday, and as yet very early in the morning. I was standing, as it seemed to me, at the door of my own cottage. Right before me lay the very scene which could really be commanded from that situation, but exalted, as was usual, and solemnized by the power of dreams. There were the same mountains, and the same lovely valley at their feet; but the mountains were raised to more than Alpine height, and there was interspace far larger between them of meadows and forest lawns; the hedges were rich with white roses; and no living creature was to be seen, excepting that in the green churchyard there were cattle tranquilly reposing upon the verdant graves, and particularly round about the grave of a child whom I had tenderly loved,[7] just as I had really beheld them, a little before sunrise in the same summer, when that child died. I gazed upon the well-known scene, and I said aloud (as I

6. Other things being the same (Latin).
7. The child is Wordsworth's daughter Cathe-
rine, who died at the age of four. She is the subject of Wordsworth's sonnet "Surprised by joy."

thought) to myself, "It yet wants much of sunrise; and it is Easter Sunday; and that is the day on which they celebrate the first-fruits of resurrection. I will walk abroad; old griefs shall be forgotten today; for the air is cool and still, and the hills are high, and stretch away to heaven; and the forest-glades are as quiet as the churchyard; and, with the dew, I can wash the fever from my forehead, and then I shall be unhappy no longer." And I turned, as if to open my garden gate; and immediately I saw upon the left a scene far different; but which yet the power of dreams had reconciled into harmony with the other. The scene was an Oriental one; and there also it was Easter Sunday, and very early in the morning. And at a vast distance were visible, as a stain upon the horizon, the domes and cupolas of a great city—an image or faint abstraction, caught perhaps in childhood from some picture of Jerusalem. And not a bow-shot from me, upon a stone, and shaded by Judean palms, there sat a woman; and I looked; and it was—Ann! She fixed her eyes upon me earnestly; and I said to her at length: "So then I have found you at last." I waited: but she answered me not a word. Her face was the same as when I saw it last, and yet again how different! Seventeen years ago, when the lamp-light fell upon her face, as for the last time I kissed her lips (lips, Ann, that to me were not polluted), her eyes were streaming with tears: the tears were now wiped away; she seemed more beautiful than she was at that time, but in all other points the same, and not older. Her looks were tranquil, but with unusual solemnity of expression; and I now gazed upon her with some awe, but suddenly her countenance grew dim, and, turning to the mountains, I perceived vapors rolling between us; in a moment, all had vanished; thick darkness came on; and, in the twinkling of an eye, I was far away from mountains, and by lamplight in Oxford Street, walking again with Ann—just as we walked seventeen years before, when we were both children.

As a final specimen, I cite one of a different character, from 1820.

The dream commenced with a music which now I often heard in dreams—a music of preparation and of awakening suspense; a music like the opening of the Coronation Anthem,[8] and which, like *that*, gave the feeling of a vast march—of infinite cavalcades filing off—and the tread of innumerable armies. The morning was come of a mighty day—a day of crisis and of final hope for human nature, then suffering some mysterious eclipse, and laboring in some dread extremity. Somewhere, I knew not where—somehow, I knew not how—by some beings, I knew not whom—a battle, a strife, an agony, was conducting—was evolving like a great drama, or piece of music; with which my sympathy was the more insupportable from my confusion as to its place, its cause, its nature, and its possible issue. I, as is usual in dreams (where, of necessity, we make ourselves central to every movement), had the power, and yet had not the power, to decide it. I had the power, if I could raise myself, to will it; and yet again had not the power, for the weight of twenty Atlantics was upon me, or the oppression of inexpiable guilt. "Deeper than ever plummet sounded,"[9] I lay inactive. Then, like a chorus, the passion deepened. Some greater interest was at stake; some mightier cause than ever yet the sword

8. Composed by George Frideric Handel for the coronation of George II in 1727.
9. In Shakespeare's *The Tempest* guilt-ridden King Alonso, believing that his son has drowned, says he will "seek him deeper then e'er plummet sounded / And with him there lie mudded" (3.3.101–02).

had pleaded, or trumpet had proclaimed. Then came sudden alarms: hurryings to and fro: trepidations of innumerable fugitives, I knew not whether from the good cause or the bad: darkness and lights: tempest and human faces: and at last, with the sense that all was lost, female forms, and the features that were worth all the world to me, and but a moment allowed—and clasped hands, and heart-breaking partings, and then—everlasting farewells! and with a sigh, such as the caves of hell sighed when the incestuous mother uttered the abhorred name of death,[1] the sound was reverberated—everlasting farewells! and again, and yet again reverberated—everlasting farewells!

And I awoke in struggles, and cried aloud—"I will sleep no more!"[2]

1821   1821

1. The reference is to *Paradise Lost*, book 2, lines 777ff. The "incestuous mother" is Sin, who is doubly incestuous: she is the daughter of Satan, who begot Death upon her, and she was in turn raped by her son and gave birth to a pack of "yell-

ing Monsters."
2. Macbeth says: "Methought I heard a voice cry 'Sleep no more, / Macbeth does murder sleep'" (Shakespeare, *Macbeth* 2.2.33–34).

GEORGE GORDON, LORD BYRON
1788–1824

In his *History of English Literature*, written in the late 1850s, the French critic Hippolyte Taine gave only a few condescending pages to Wordsworth, Coleridge, Percy Shelley, and Keats and then devoted a long chapter to Lord Byron, "the greatest and most English of these artists; he is so great and so English that from him alone we shall learn more truths of his country and of his age than from all the rest together." This comment reflects the fact that Byron had achieved an immense European reputation during his own lifetime, while admirers of his English contemporaries were much more limited in number. Through much of the nineteenth century he continued to be rated as one of the greatest of English poets and the very prototype of literary Romanticism. His influence was manifested everywhere, among the major poets and novelists (Balzac and Stendhal in France, Pushkin and Dostoyevsky in Russia, and Melville in America), painters (especially Delacroix), and composers (including Beethoven and Berlioz).

Yet even as poets, painters, and composers across Europe and the Americas struck Byronic attitudes, Byron's place within the canon of English Romantic poetry was becoming insecure. The same Victorian critics who first described the Romantic period *as* a literary period warned readers against the immorality of Byron's poetry, finding in his voluptuous imagination and aristocratic disdain for the commonplace an affront to their own, middle-class values: "Close thy Byron; open thy Goethe," Thomas Carlyle urged in *Sartor Resartus* (1834), meaning to redirect the nation toward healthier reading matter. After getting a glimpse of the scandalous stuff recorded in Byron's journals, Felicia Hemans ceased to wear the brooch in which she had preserved a lock of the poet's hair: she could venerate him no longer. Indeed, Byron would have had qualms about being considered a representative figure of a period that also included Wordsworth (memorialized in Byron's *Don Juan* as "Wordy") or Keats (a shabby Cockney brat, Byron claimed) or scribbling women such as Hemans. These reservations were reciprocated. Of Byron's best-known male contemporaries, only Shelley thought highly of either the man or his work (although there are signs that, among the naysayers, the negative reactions were tinged with some resentment at Byron's success in developing a style that spoke to a popular audience). Byron in fact insisted that, measured against the poetic practice of Alexander Pope, he and his contemporaries were "all in the wrong, one as much as another. . . . We are upon a wrong revolutionary poetical system, or systems, not worth a damn in itself." Pope's Horatian satires, along with Laurence Sterne's novel *Tristram Shandy,* exerted a significant influence on the style that Byron developed for his epic survey of modern folly, *Don Juan.*

Still, even as he had recourse to old-fashioned eighteenth-century models, Byron cultivated a skepticism about established systems of belief that, in its restlessness and defiance, expressed the intellectual and social ferment of his era. And through much of his best poetry, he shared his contemporaries' fascination with the internal dramas of the individual mind (although Byron explored personality in an improvisatory and mercurial manner that could not have been more different from Wordsworth's autobiographical accounts of his psychological development). Readers marveled over the intensity of the feelings his verse communicated—"its force, fire, and thought," said the novelist Sydney Owenson—and the vividness of the sense of self they found in it. Byron's chief claim to be considered an arch-Romantic is that he provided the age with what Taine called its "ruling personage; that is, the model that contemporaries invest with their admiration and sympathy." This personage is the "Byronic hero." He is first sketched in the opening canto of *Childe Harold*, then recurs in various guises in the verse romances and dramas that followed. In his developed form, as we find it in *Manfred*, he is an alien, mysterious, and gloomy spirit, superior in his passions and powers to the common run of humanity, whom he regards with disdain. He harbors the torturing memory of an enormous, nameless guilt that drives him toward an inevitable doom. And he exerts an attraction on other characters that is the more compelling because it involves their terror at his obliviousness to ordinary human concerns and values. This figure, infusing the archrebel in a nonpolitical form with a strong erotic interest, was imitated in life as well as in art and helped shape the intellectual and the cultural history of the later nineteenth century. The literary descendants of the Byronic hero include Heathcliff in *Wuthering Heights*, Captain Ahab in *Moby-Dick*, and the hero of Pushkin's great poem *Eugene Onegin.* Byron also lived on in the guise of the Undead, thanks to the success of a novella by his former friend and traveling companion John Polidori, whose "The Vampyre" (1819) mischievously made Byron its model for the title character. Earlier Byron had in his writings helped introduce the English to the eastern Mediterranean's legends of bloodsucking evil spirits; it was left to Polidori, however, to portray the vampire as a habitué of England's most fashionable social circles. The fact that, for all their menace, vampires—from Bela Lugosi's Count Dracula to Anne Rice's L'Estat—remain models of well-dressed, aristocratic elegance represents yet another tribute to the staying power of Byron's image.

Byron's contemporaries insisted on identifying the author with his fictional characters, reading his writing as veiled autobiography even when it dealt with supernatural themes. (They also read other people's writing this way: to Polidori's chagrin, authorship of "The Vampyre" was attributed to Byron.) Byron's letters and the testimony of his friends show, however, that, except for recurrent moods of deep depression, his own temperament was in many respects opposite to that of his heroes. While he was passionate and willful, he was also a witty conversationalist capable of taking an ironic attitude toward his own activities as well as those of others. But although Byronism was largely a fiction, produced by a collaboration between Byron's imagination and that of his public, the fiction was historically more important than the actual person.

Byron was descended from two aristocratic families, both of them colorful, violent, and dissolute. His grandfather was an admiral nicknamed "Foulweather Jack"; his great-uncle was the fifth Baron Byron, known to his rural neighbors as the "Wicked Lord," who was tried by his peers for killing his kinsman William Chaworth in a drunken duel; his father, Captain John Byron, was a rake and fortune hunter who rapidly spent his way through the fortunes of two wealthy wives. Byron's mother was a Scotswoman, Catherine Gordon of Gight, the last descendant of a line of lawless Scottish lairds. After her husband died (Byron was then three), she brought up her son in near poverty in Aberdeen, where he was indoctrinated with the Calvinistic morality of Scottish Presbyterianism. Catherine Byron was an ill-educated and extremely irascible woman who nevertheless had an abiding love for her son; they fought violently when together, but corresponded affectionately enough when apart, until her death in 1811.

When Byron was ten the death of his great-uncle, preceded by that of more immediate heirs to the title, made him the sixth Lord Byron. In a fashion suitable to his new status, he was sent to Harrow School, then to Trinity College, Cambridge. He had a deformed foot, made worse by inept surgical treatment, about which he felt acute embarrassment. His lameness made him avid for athletic prowess; he played cricket and made himself an expert boxer, fencer, and horseman and a powerful swimmer. Both at Cambridge and at his ancestral estate of Newstead, he engaged with more than ordinary zeal in the expensive pursuits and fashionable dissipations of a young Regency lord. As a result, despite a sizable and increasing income, he got into financial difficulties from which he did not entirely extricate himself until late in his life. In the course of his schooling, he formed many close and devoted friendships, the most important with John Cam Hobhouse, a sturdy political liberal and commonsense moralist who exerted a steadying influence throughout Byron's turbulent life.

Despite his distractions at the university, Byron found time to try his hand at lyric verse, some of which was published in 1807 in a slim and conventional volume titled *Hours of Idleness*. This was treated so harshly by the *Edinburgh Review* that Byron was provoked to write in reply his first important poem, *English Bards and Scotch Reviewers*, a vigorous satire in which he incorporated brilliant ridicule (whose tactlessness he later came to regret) of important contemporaries, including Scott, Wordsworth, Coleridge, and the *Edinburgh* critics.

After attaining his M.A. degree and his legal independence from his guardians, Byron set out with Hobhouse in 1809 on a tour through Portugal and Spain to Malta, and then to little-known Albania, Greece, and Asia Minor. There, in the classic locale for Greek love, he encountered a culture that accepted sexual relations between older aristocratic men and beautiful boys, and he accumulated materials that, sometimes rather slyly, he incorporated into many of his important poems, including his last work, *Don Juan*. The first literary product was *Childe Harold*; he wrote the opening two cantos while on the tour that the poem describes; published them in 1812 soon after his return to England; and, in his own oft-quoted phrase, "awoke one morning and found myself famous." He became the celebrity of fashionable London and increased his literary success with a series of highly readable Eastern tales; in these the Byronic hero, represented against various exotic backdrops as a "Giaour" (an "infidel" within Muslim society), or a "Corsair" (a pirate), or in other forms, flaunts his misanthropy and undergoes violent and romantic adventures that current gossip attributed to the author. In his chronic shortage of money, Byron could well have used the huge income from these publications, but instead maintained his status as an aristocratic amateur by giving the royalties away. Occupying his inherited seat in the House of Lords, he also became briefly active on the liberal side of the Whig party and spoke courageously in defense of the Nottingham weavers who had resorted to smashing the newly invented textile machines that had thrown them out of work. He also supported other liberal measures, including that of Catholic Emancipation.

Byron was extraordinarily handsome—"so beautiful a countenance," Coleridge wrote, "I scarcely ever saw . . . his eyes the open portals of the sun—things of light, and for light." Because of a constitutional tendency to obesity, however, he was able to maintain his looks only by resorting again and again to a starvation diet of biscuits, soda water, and strong purgatives. Often as a result of female initiative rather than his own, Byron entered into a sequence of liaisons with ladies of fashion. One of these, the flamboyant and eccentric young Lady Caroline Lamb, caused him so much distress by her pursuit that Byron turned for relief to marriage with Anna-bella Milbanke, who was in every way Lady Caroline's opposite, for she was unworldly and intellectual (with a special passion for mathematics) and naively believed that she could reform her husband. This ill-starred marriage produced a daughter (Augusta Ada) and many scenes in which Byron, goaded by financial difficulties, behaved so frantically that his wife suspected his sanity; after only one year the union ended in a legal separation. The final blow came when Lady Byron discovered her husband's incestuous relations with his half-sister, Augusta Leigh. The two had been raised apart, so that they were almost strangers when they met as adults. Byron's affection for his sister, however guilty, was genuine and endured all through his life. This affair, enhanced by rumors about Byron's earlier liaisons with men, proved a delicious morsel even to the jaded palate of a public that was used to eating up stories of aristocratic vice. Byron was ostracized by all but a few friends and was finally forced to leave England forever on April 25, 1816.

Byron now resumed the travels incorporated in the third and fourth cantos of *Childe Harold*. At Geneva he lived for several months in close and intellectually fruitful relation to Percy and Mary Shelley, who were accompanied by Mary's stepsister, Claire Clairmont—a misguided seventeen-year-old who had had an affair with Byron while he was still in England and who in January 1817 bore him a daughter, Allegra. In the fall of 1817, Byron established himself in Venice, where he began a year and a half of debauchery that, he estimated, involved liaisons with more than two hundred women. This period, however, was also one of great literary creativity. Often working through the night, he finished his tragedy *Manfred*; wrote the fourth canto of *Childe Harold*; and then, feeling more and more trapped by the poetic modes that had won him his popularity, tested out an entirely new mode in *Beppo: A Venetian Story*, a comic verse tale about a deceived husband in which he previewed the playful narrative manner and the ottava rima stanzas of *Don Juan*. In December 1818 he began the composition of *Don Juan*.

Exhausted and bored by promiscuity, Byron in 1819 settled into a placid and relatively faithful relationship with Teresa Guiccioli, the young wife of the elderly Count Alessandro Guiccioli; according to the Italian upper-class mores of the times, having contracted a marriage of convenience, she could now with some propriety take Byron as her lover. Through the countess's nationalistic family, the Gambas, Byron became involved with a group of political conspirators seeking to end the Austrian Empire's control over northern Italy. When the Gambas were forced by the authorities to move to Pisa, Byron followed them there and, for the second time, joined the Shelleys. There grew up about them the "Pisan Circle," which in addition to the Gambas included their friends Thomas Medwin and Edward and Jane Williams, as well as the Greek nationalist leader Prince Mavrocordatos, the picturesque Irish Count Taaffe, and the adventurer Edward Trelawny, a great teller of tall tales who seems to have stepped out of one of Byron's romances. Leigh Hunt, the journalist and essayist, joined them, drawing Byron and Percy Shelley into his plan to make Italy the base for a radical political journal, *The Liberal*. This circle was gradually broken up, however, first by the Shelleys' anger over Byron's treatment of his daughter Allegra (Byron had sent the child to be brought up as a Catholic in an Italian convent, where she died of a fever in 1822); then by the expulsion of the Gambas, whom Byron followed to Genoa; and finally by the drowning of Percy Shelley and Edward Williams in July 1822.

Byron meanwhile had been steadily at work on a series of closet tragedies (including *Cain, Sardanapalus*, and *Marino Faliero*) and on his devastating satire on the life and death of George III, *The Vision of Judgment*. But increasingly he devoted himself to the continuation of *Don Juan*. He had always been diffident in his self-judgments and easily swayed by literary advice. But now, confident that he had at last found his true gifts as a poet, he kept on, in spite or persistent objections against the supposed immorality of the poem by the English public, by his publisher John Murray, by his friends and well-wishers, and by his extremely decorous lover, the Countess Guiccioli—by almost everyone, in fact, except the idealist Shelley, who thought *Juan* incomparably better than anything he himself could write and insisted "that every word of it is pregnant with immortality."

Byron finally broke off literature for action when he organized an expedition to assist in the Greek war for independence from the Ottoman Empire. He knew too well the conditions in Greece, and had too skeptical an estimate of human nature, to entertain hope of success; but, in part because his own writings had helped kindle European enthusiasm for the Greek cause, he now felt honor-bound to try what could be done. In the dismal, marshy town of Missolonghi, he lived a Spartan existence, training troops whom he had subsidized and exhibiting practical grasp and a power of leadership amid a chaos of factionalism, intrigue, and military ineptitude. Worn out, he succumbed to a series of feverish attacks and died just after he had reached his thirty-sixth birthday. To this day Byron is revered by the Greek people as a national hero.

Students of Byron still feel, as his friends had felt, the magnetism of his volatile temperament. As Mary Shelley wrote six years after his death, when she read Thomas Moore's edition of his *Letters and Journals:* "The Lord Byron I find there is our Lord Byron—the fascinating—faulty—childish—philosophical being—daring the world—docile to a private circle—impetuous and indolent—gloomy and yet more gay than any other." Of his contradictions Byron was well aware; he told his friend Lady Blessington: "I am so changeable, being everything by turns and nothing long—I am such a strange *mélange* of good and evil, that it would be difficult to describe me." Yet he remained faithful to his code: a determination to tell the truth as he saw it about the world and about himself (his refusal to suppress or conceal any of his moods is in part what made him seem so contradictory) and a dedication to the freedom of nations and individuals. As he went on to say to Lady Blessington: "There are but two sentiments to which I am constant—a strong love of liberty, and a detestation of cant."

The texts printed here are from *Byron's Poetry and Prose: A Norton Critical Edition*, edited by Alice Levine.

Written after Swimming from Sestos to Abydos[1]

May 9, 1810

1

If, in the month of dark December,
    Leander, who was nightly wont
(What maid will not the tale remember?)
    To cross thy stream, broad Hellespont!

2

5   If, when the wintry tempest roar'd,
    He sped to Hero, nothing loth,
And thus of old thy current pour'd,
    Fair Venus! how I pity both!

---

1. The Hellespont (now called the Dardanelles) is the narrow strait between Europe and Asia. In the ancient story, retold in Christopher Marlowe's *Hero and Leander*, young Leander of Abydos, on the Asian side, swam nightly to visit Hero, a priestess of the goddess Venus at Sestos, until he was drowned when he made the attempt in a storm. Byron and a young Lieutenant Ekenhead swam the Hellespont in the reverse direction on May 3, 1810. Byron alternated between complacency and humor in his many references to the event. In a note to the poem, he mentions that the distance was "upwards of four English miles, though the actual breadth is barely one. The rapidity of the current is such that no boat can row directly across. . . . The water was extremely cold, from the melting of the mountain snows."

3

For *me*, degenerate modern wretch,
10   Though in the genial month of May,
My dripping limbs I faintly stretch,
    And think I've done a feat to-day.

4

But since he cross'd the rapid tide,
    According to the doubtful story,
15 To woo,—and—Lord knows what beside,
    And swam for Love, as I for Glory;

5

'Twere hard to say who fared the best:
    Sad mortals! thus the Gods still plague you!
He lost his labour, I my jest:
20   For he was drown'd, and I've the ague.

1810   1812

She Walks in Beauty[1]

1

She walks in beauty, like the night
    Of cloudless climes and starry skies;
And all that's best of dark and bright
    Meet in her aspect and her eyes:
5 Thus mellow'd to that tender light
    Which heaven to gaudy day denies.

2

One shade the more, one ray the less,
    Had half impair'd the nameless grace
Which waves in every raven tress,
10   Or softly lightens o'er her face;
Where thoughts serenely sweet express
    How pure, how dear their dwelling-place.

1. From *Hebrew Melodies* (1815), a collection of lyrics on Old Testament themes that Byron composed to accompany the musician Isaac Nathan's settings of traditional synagogue chants. Byron wrote these lines about his beautiful cousin by marriage, Anne Wilmot, who at the ball where they first met wore a black mourning gown brightened with spangles. In their context as the opening poem of *Hebrew Melodies*, the lines praise any one of a number of Old Testament heroines.

3

And on that cheek, and o'er that brow,
So soft, so calm, yet eloquent,
15   The smiles that win, the tints that glow,
But tell of days in goodness spent,
A mind at peace with all below,
A heart whose love is innocent!

June 1814   1815

Darkness[1]

I had a dream, which was not all a dream.
The bright sun was extinguish'd, and the stars
Did wander darkling° in the eternal space,   *in the dark*
Rayless, and pathless, and the icy earth
5   Swung blind and blackening in the moonless air;
Morn came and went—and came, and brought no day,
And men forgot their passions in the dread
Of this their desolation; and all hearts
Were chill'd into a selfish prayer for light:
10   And they did live by watchfires—and the thrones,
The palaces of crowned kings—the huts,
The habitations of all things which dwell,
Were burnt for beacons; cities were consumed,
And men were gather'd round their blazing homes
15   To look once more into each other's face;
Happy were those who dwelt within the eye
Of the volcanos, and their mountain-torch:
A fearful hope was all the world contain'd;
Forests were set on fire—but hour by hour
20   They fell and faded—and the crackling trunks
Extinguish'd with a crash—and all was black.
The brows of men by the despairing light
Wore an unearthly aspect, as by fits
The flashes fell upon them; some lay down
And hid their eyes and wept; and some did rest
25   Their chins upon their clenched hands, and smiled;
And others hurried to and fro, and fed
Their funeral piles with fuel, and look'd up
With mad disquietude on the dull sky,
The pall of a past world; and then again
30   With curses cast them down upon the dust,
And gnash'd their teeth and howl'd: the wild birds shriek'd,
And, terrified, did flutter on the ground,
And flap their useless wings; the wildest brutes

---

1. A powerful blank-verse description of the end of life on earth. New geological sciences and an accompanying interest in what the fossil record indicated about the extinction of species made such speculations hardly less common in Byron's time than in ours. Mary Shelley would later take up the theme in her novel *The Last Man* (1826).

35 Came tame and tremulous; and vipers crawl'd
    And twined themselves among the multitude,
    Hissing, but stingless—they were slain for food:
    And War, which for a moment was no more,
    Did glut himself again;—a meal was bought
40 With blood, and each sate sullenly apart
    Gorging himself in gloom: no love was left;
    All earth was but one thought—and that was death,
    Immediate and inglorious; and the pang
    Of famine fed upon all entrails—men
45 Died, and their bones were tombless as their flesh;
    The meagre by the meagre were devour'd,
    Even dogs assail'd their masters, all save one,
    And he was faithful to a corse, and kept
    The birds and beasts and famish'd men at bay,
50 Till hunger clung° them, or the dropping dead   *withered*
    Lured their lank jaws; himself sought out no food,
    But with a piteous and perpetual moan,
    And a quick desolate cry, licking the hand
    Which answer'd not with a caress—he died.
55 The crowd was famish'd by degrees; but two
    Of an enormous city did survive,
    And they were enemies; they met beside
    The dying embers of an altar-place
    Where had been heap'd a mass of holy things
60 For an unholy usage; they raked up,
    And shivering scraped with their cold skeleton hands
    The feeble ashes, and their feeble breath
    Blew for a little life, and made a flame
    Which was a mockery; then they lifted up
65 Their eyes as it grew lighter, and beheld
    Each other's aspects—saw, and shriek'd, and died—
    Even of their mutual hideousness they died,
    Unknowing who he was upon whose brow
    Famine had written Fiend. The world was void,
70 The populous and the powerful—was a lump,
    Seasonless, herbless,° treeless, manless, lifeless—   *without vegetation*
    A lump of death—a chaos of hard clay.
    The rivers, lakes, and ocean all stood still,
    And nothing stirr'd within their silent depths;
75 Ships sailorless lay rotting on the sea,
    And their masts fell down piecemeal; as they dropp'd
    They slept on the abyss without a surge—
    The waves were dead; the tides were in their grave,
    The moon, their mistress, had expired before;
80 The winds were wither'd in the stagnant air,
    And the clouds perish'd; Darkness had no need
    Of aid from them—She was the Universe.

                              Diodati, July, 1816

                                              1816

So we'll go no more a roving[1]

So we'll go no more a roving
So late into the night,
Though the heart be still as loving,
And the moon be still as bright.

5 For the sword outwears its sheath,
And the soul wears out the breast,
And the heart must pause to breathe,
And Love itself have rest.

Though the night was made for loving,
10 And the day returns too soon,
Yet we'll go no more a roving
By the light of the moon.

1817   1830

From Childe Harold's Pilgrimage: A Romaunt[1]

From *Canto the First*

["SIN'S LONG LABYRINTH"]

1

Oh, thou! in Hellas° deem'd of heavenly birth,   *Greece*
Muse! form'd or fabled at the minstrel's will!
Since shamed full oft by later lyres on earth,
Mine dares not call thee from thy sacred hill:
5 Yet there I've wander'd by thy vaunted rill;
Yes! sigh'd o'er Delphi's long-deserted shrine,
Where, save that feeble fountain, all is still;
Nor mote° my shell awake the weary Nine[2]   *may*
To grace so plain a tale—this lowly lay° of mine.   *song*

2

10 Whilome[3] in Albion's° isle there dwelt a youth,   *England's*
Who ne in virtue's ways did take delight;
But spent his days in riot most uncouth,
And vex'd with mirth the drowsy ear of Night.
Ah, me! in sooth he was a shameless wight,°   *creature*

---

1. Composed in the Lenten aftermath of a period of late-night carousing during the Carnival season in Venice, and included in a letter to Thomas Moore, February 28, 1817. Byron wrote, "I find 'the sword wearing out the scabbard,' though I have but just turned the corner of twenty-nine." The poem is based on the refrain of a bawdy Scottish song, "The Jolly Beggar": "And we'll gang nae mair a roving / Sae late into the nicht."
1. A romance or narrative of adventure.
2. The Muses, whose "vaunted rill" (line 5) was the Castalian spring. "Shell": lyre. Hermes is fabled to have invented the lyre by stretching strings over the hollow of a tortoise shell.
3. Once upon a time; one of the many archaisms that Byron borrowed from Spenser.

15   Sore given to revel and ungodly glee;
      Few earthly things found favour in his sight
      Save concubines and carnal companie,
      And flaunting wassailers⁴ of high and low degree.

                              3

      Childe Harold was he hight:°—but whence his name   *called*
20   And lineage long, it suits me not to say;
      Suffice it, that perchance they were of fame,
      And had been glorious in another day:
      But one sad losel⁵ soils a name for aye,
      However mighty in the olden time;
25   Nor all that heralds rake from coffin'd clay,
      Nor florid prose, nor honied lies of rhyme,
      Can blazon evil deeds, or consecrate a crime.

                              4

      Childe Harold bask'd him in the noontide sun,
      Disporting there like any other fly;
30   Nor deem'd before his little day was done
      One blast might chill him into misery.
      But long ere scarce a third of his pass'd by,
      Worse than adversity the Childe befell;
      He felt the fulness of satiety:
35   Then loathed he in his native land to dwell,
      Which seem'd to him more lone than Eremite's⁶ sad cell.

                              5

      For he through Sin's long labyrinth had run,
      Nor made atonement when he did amiss,
      Had sigh'd to many though he loved but one,
40   And that loved one, alas! could ne'er be his.
      Ah, happy she! to 'scape from him whose kiss
      Had been pollution unto aught so chaste;
      Who soon had left her charms for vulgar bliss,
      And spoil'd her goodly lands to gild his waste,
45   Nor calm domestic peace had ever deign'd to taste.

                              6

      And now Childe Harold was sore sick at heart,
      And from his fellow bacchanals⁷ would flee;
      'Tis said, at times the sullen tear would start,
      But Pride congeal'd the drop within his ee:°   *eye*

---

4. Noisy, insolent drinkers (Byron is thought to refer to his own youthful carousing with friends at Newstead Abbey).
5. Rascal. Byron's great-uncle, the fifth Lord Byron, had killed a kinsman in a drunken duel.
6. A religious hermit.
7. Worshipers of Bacchus, ancient Roman god of wine and revelry.

50   Apart he stalk'd in joyless reverie,
         And from his native land resolved to go,
         And visit scorching climes beyond the sea;
         With pleasure drugg'd, he almost long'd for woe,
    And e'en for change of scene would seek the shades below.

From *Canto the Third*

["ONCE MORE UPON THE WATERS"]

1

      Is thy face like thy mothers, my fair child!
      ADA![8] sole daughter of my house and heart?
      When last I saw thy young blue eyes they smiled,
      And when we parted,—not as now we part,
      But with a hope.—
5   Awaking with a start,
      The waters heave around me; and on high
      The winds lift up their voices: I depart,
      Whither I know not; but the hour's gone by,
  When Albion's lessening shores could grieve or glad mine eye.

2

10   Once more upon the waters! yet once more!
      And the waves bound beneath me as a steed
      That knows his rider. Welcome, to their roar!
      Swift be their guidance, wheresoe'er it lead!
      Though the strain'd mast should quiver as a reed,
15   And the rent canvass fluttering strew the gale,
      Still must I on; for I am as a weed,
      Flung from the rock, on Ocean's foam, to sail
  Where'er the surge may sweep, or tempest's breath prevail.

3

      In my youth's summer[9] I did sing of One,
20   The wandering outlaw of his own dark mind;
      Again I seize the theme, then but begun,
      And bear it with me, as the rushing wind
      Bears the cloud onwards: in that Tale I find
      The furrows of long thought, and dried-up tears,
25   Which, ebbing, leave a sterile track behind,
      O'er which all heavily the journeying years
  Plod the last sands of life,—where not a flower appears.

8. Byron's daughter Augusta Ada, born in December 1815, a month before her parents separated. Byron's "hope" (line 5) had been for a reconciliation, but he was never to see Ada again.
9. Byron wrote canto 1 at age twenty-one; he is now twenty-eight.

4

Since my young days of passion—joy, or pain,
Perchance my heart and harp have lost a string,
30   And both may jar:[1] it may be, that in vain
I would essay as I have sung to sing.
Yet, though a dreary strain, to this I cling;
So that it wean me from the weary dream
Of selfish grief or gladness—so it fling
35   Forgetfulness around me—it shall seem
To me, though to none else, a not ungrateful theme.

5

He, who grown aged in this world of woe,
In deeds, not years, piercing the depths of life,
So that no wonder waits him; nor below
40   Can love, or sorrow, fame, ambition, strife,
Cut to his heart again with the keen knife
Of silent, sharp endurance: he can tell
Why thought seeks refuge in lone caves, yet rife
With airy images, and shapes which dwell
45 Still unimpair'd, though old, in the soul's haunted cell.

6

'Tis to create, and in creating live
A being more intense, that we endow
With form our fancy, gaining as we give
The life we image, even as I do now.
50   What am I? Nothing: but not so art thou,
Soul of my thought![2] with whom I traverse earth,
Invisible but gazing, as I glow
Mix'd with thy spirit, blended with thy birth,
And feeling still with thee in my crush'd feelings' dearth.

7

55   Yet must I think less wildly:—I *have* thought
Too long and darkly, till my brain became,
In its own eddy boiling and o'erwrought,
A whirling gulf of phantasy and flame:
And thus, untaught in youth my heart to tame,
60   My springs of life were poison'd. 'Tis too late!
Yet am I changed; though still enough the same
In strength to bear what time can not abate,
And feed on bitter fruits without accusing Fate.

---

1. Sound discordant.   2. I.e., Childe Harold, his literary creation.

8

Something too much of this:—but now 'tis past,
65   And the spell closes with its silent seal.[3]
Long absent HAROLD re-appears at last;
He of the breast which fain no more would feel,
Wrung with the wounds which kill not, but ne'er heal;
Yet Time, who changes all, had alter'd him
70   In soul and aspect as in age: years steal
Fire from the mind as vigour from the limb;
And life's enchanted cup but sparkles near the brim.

9

His had been quaff'd too quickly, and he found
The dregs were wormwood; but he fill'd again,
75   And from a purer fount, on holier ground,
And deem'd its spring perpetual; but in vain!
Still round him clung invisibly a chain
Which gall'd for ever, fettering though unseen,
And heavy though it clank'd not; worn with pain,
80   Which pined although it spoke not, and grew keen,
Entering with every step he took through many a scene.

10

Secure in guarded coldness, he had mix'd
Again in fancied safety with his kind,
And deem'd his spirit now so firmly fix'd
85   And sheathed with an invulnerable mind,
That, if no joy, no sorrow lurk'd behind;
And he, as one, might 'midst the many stand
Unheeded, searching through the crowd to find
Fit speculation; such as in strange land
90   He found in wonder-works of God and Nature's hand.

11

But who can view the ripen'd rose, nor seek
To wear it? who can curiously behold
The smoothness and the sheen of beauty's cheek,
Nor feel the heart can never all grow old?
95   Who can contemplate Fame through clouds unfold
The star which rises o'er her steep, nor climb?
Harold, once more within the vortex, roll'd
On with the giddy circle, chasing Time,
Yet with a nobler aim than in his youth's fond° prime.   *foolish*

3. I.e., he sets the seal of silence on his personal tale ("spell").

12

100 But soon he knew himself the most unfit
Of men to herd with Man; with whom he held
Little in common; untaught to submit
His thoughts to others, though his soul was quell'd
In youth by his own thoughts; still uncompell'd,
105 He would not yield dominion of his mind
To spirits against whom his own rebell'd;
Proud though in desolation; which could find
A life within itself, to breathe without mankind.

13

Where rose the mountains, there to him were friends;
110 Where roll'd the ocean, thereon was his home;
Where a blue sky, and glowing clime, extends,
He had the passion and the power to roam;
The desert, forest, cavern, breaker's foam,
Were unto him companionship; they spake
105 A mutual language, clearer than the tome°   *book*
Of his land's tongue, which he would oft forsake,
For Nature's pages glass'd° by sunbeams on the lake.   *made glassy*

14

Like the Chaldean,[4] he could watch the stars,
Till he had peopled them with beings bright
120 As their own beams; and earth, and earth-born jars,
And human frailties, were forgotten quite:
Could he have kept his spirit to that flight
He had been happy; but this clay will sink
Its spark immortal, envying it the light
125 To which it mounts, as if to break the link
That keeps us from yon heaven which woos us to its brink.

15

But in Man's dwellings he became a thing
Restless and worn, and stern and wearisome,
Droop'd as a wild-born falcon with clipt wing,
130 To whom the boundless air alone were home:
Then came his fit again, which to o'ercome,
As eagerly the barr'd-up bird will beat
His breast and beak against his wiry dome
Till the blood tinge his plumage, so the heat
135 Of his impeded soul would through his bosom eat.

---

4. A people of ancient Babylonia, expert in astronomy.

16

Self-exiled Harold wanders forth again,
With nought of hope left, but with less of gloom;
The very knowledge that he lived in vain,
That all was over on this side the tomb,
140   Had made Despair a smilingness assume,
Which, though 'twere wild,—as on the plunder'd wreck
When mariners would madly meet their doom
With draughts intemperate on the sinking deck,—
Did yet inspire a cheer, which he forebore to check.

[WATERLOO]

17

145   Stop!—for thy tread is on an Empire's dust!
An Earthquake's spoil is sepulchred below!
Is the spot mark'd with no colossal bust?
Nor column trophied for triumphal show?[5]
None; but the moral's truth tells simpler so,
150   As the ground was before, thus let it be;—
How that red rain hath made the harvest grow!
And is this all the world has gain'd by thee,
Thou first and last of fields! king-making Victory?

18

And Harold stands upon this place of skulls,
155   The grave of France, the deadly Waterloo;[6]
How in an hour the power which gave annuls
Its gifts, transferring fame as fleeting too!
In "pride of place" here last the eagle flew,[7]
Then tore with bloody talon the rent plain,
160   Pierced by the shaft of banded nations[8] through;
Ambitions life and labours all were vain;
He wears the shatter'd links of the world's broken chain.[9]

19

Fit retribution! Gaul[1] may champ the bit
And foam in fetters;—but is Earth more free?
165   Did nations combat to make *One* submit;
Or league to teach all kings true sovereignty?

5. Referring to the triumphal arches erected in ancient Rome to honor conquering generals, a custom Napoleon had revived.
6. Napoleon's defeat at Waterloo, near Brussels, had occurred only the year before, on June 18, 1815. The battlefield, where almost fifty thousand English, Prussian, and French soldiers were killed in a single day, quickly became a gruesome tourist attraction. See "Romantic Literature and Wartime," p. 741.
7. "Pride of place," is a term of falconry, and

means the highest pitch of flight [Byron's note, which continues by referring to the use of the term in Shakespeare's *Macbeth* 2.4]. The eagle was the symbol of Napoleon.
8. The Grand Alliance formed in opposition to Napoleon.
9. Napoleon was then a prisoner at St. Helena.
1. France. Byron, like other liberals, saw the defeat of the Napoleonic tyranny as a victory for tyrannical kings and the forces of reaction throughout Europe.

What! shall reviving Thraldom again be
The patch'd-up idol of enlighten'd days?
Shall we, who struck the Lion down, shall we
170   Pay the Wolf homage? proffering lowly gaze
And servile knees to thrones? No; *prove*[2] before ye praise!

20

If not, o'er one fallen despot boast no more!
In vain fair cheeks were furrow'd with hot tears
For Europe's flowers long rooted up before
175   The trampler of her vineyards; in vain years
Of death, depopulation, bondage, fears,
Have all been borne, and broken by the accord
Of roused-up millions: all that most endears
Glory, is when the myrtle wreathes a sword
180   Such as Harmodius drew on Athens' tyrant lord.[3]

*   *   *

[NAPOLEON]

36

There sunk the greatest, nor the worst of men,[4]
Whose spirit antithetically mixt
One moment of the mightiest, and again
On little objects with like firmness fixt,
320   Extreme in all things! hadst thou been betwixt,
Thy throne had still been thine, or never been;
For daring made thy rise as fall: thou seek'st
Even now to re-assume the imperial mien,°   character
And shake again the world, the Thunderer of the scene!

37

325   Conqueror and captive of the earth art thou!
She trembles at thee still, and thy wild name
Was ne'er more bruited in men's minds than now
That thou art nothing, save the jest of Fame,
Who woo'd thee once, thy vassal, and became
330   The flatterer of thy fierceness, till thou wert
A god unto thyself; nor less the same
To the astounded kingdoms all inert,
Who deem'd thee for a time whate'er thou didst assert.

38

Oh, more or less than man—in high or low,
335   Battling with nations, flying from the field;
Now making monarchs' necks thy footstool, now

2. Await the test (proof) of experience.
3. In 514 B.C.E. Harmodius and Aristogeiton,
hiding their daggers in myrtle (symbol of love),
killed Hipparchus, tyrant of Athens.
4. Napoleon, here portrayed with many characteristics of the Byronic hero.

More than thy meanest° soldier taught to yield;   *lowest*
An empire thou couldst crush, command, rebuild,
But govern not thy pettiest passion, nor,
340   However deeply in men's spirits skill'd,
Look through thine own, nor curb the lust of war,
Nor learn that tempted Fate will leave the loftiest star.

39

Yet well thy soul hath brook'd the turning tide
With that untaught innate philosophy,
345   Which, be it wisdom, coldness, or deep pride,
Is gall and wormwood to an enemy.
When the whole host of hatred stood hard by,
To watch and mock thee shrinking, thou hast smiled
With a sedate and all-enduring eye;—
350   When Fortune fled her spoil'd and favourite child,
He stood unbow'd beneath the ills upon him piled.

40

Sager than in thy fortunes; for in them
Ambition steel'd thee on too far to show
That just habitual scorn which could contemn
355   Men and their thoughts; 'twas wise to feel, not so
To wear it ever on thy lip and brow,
And spurn the instruments thou wert to use
Till they were turn'd unto thine overthrow;
'Tis but a worthless world to win or lose;
360   So hath it proved to thee, and all such lot who choose.[5]

41

If, like a tower upon a headlong rock,
Thou hadst been made to stand or fall alone,
Such scorn of man had help'd to brave the shock;
But men's thoughts were the steps which paved thy
    throne,
365   *Their* admiration thy best weapon shone;
The part of Philip's son[6] was thine, not then
(Unless aside thy purple had been thrown)
Like stern Diogenes[7] to mock at men;
For sceptred cynics earth were far too wide a den.

5. An inversion: "all who choose such lot" (i.e., who choose to play such a game of chance).
6. Alexander the Great, son of Philip of Macedon.
7. The Greek philosopher of Cynicism, contemporary of Alexander. It is related that Alexander was so struck by his independence of mind that he said, "If I were not Alexander, I should wish to be Diogenes."

42

370   But quiet to quick bosoms is a hell,
And *there* hath been thy bane; there is a fire
And motion of the soul which will not dwell
In its own narrow being, but aspire
Beyond the fitting medium of desire;
375   And, but once kindled, quenchless evermore,
Preys upon high adventure, nor can tire
Of aught but rest; a fever at the core,
Fatal to him who bears, to all who ever bore.

43

This makes the madmen who have made men mad
380   By their contagion; Conquerors and Kings,
Founders of sects and systems, to whom add
Sophists,[8] Bards, Statesmen, all unquiet things
Which stir too strongly the soul's secret springs,
And are themselves the fools to those they fool;
385   Envied, yet how unenviable! what stings
Are theirs! One breast laid open were a school
Which would unteach mankind the lust to shine or rule:

44

Their breath is agitation, and their life
A storm whereon they ride, to sink at last,
390   And yet so nursed and bigoted to strife,
That should their days, surviving perils past,
Melt to calm twilight, they feel overcast
With sorrow and supineness, and so die;
Even as a flame unfed, which runs to waste
395   With its own flickering, or a sword laid by,
Which eats into itself, and rusts ingloriously.

45

He who ascends to mountain-tops, shall find
The loftiest peaks most wrapt in clouds and snow;
He who surpasses or subdues mankind,
400   Must look down on the hate of those below.
Though high *above* the sun of glory glow,
And far *beneath* the earth and ocean spread,
Round him are icy rocks, and loudly blow
Contending tempests on his naked head,
405   And thus reward the toils which to those summits led.[9]

*   *   *

---

8. Learned men. But the term often carries a derogatory sense—thinkers with a penchant for tricky reasoning.

9. In the stanzas here omitted, Harold is sent sailing up the Rhine, meditating on the "thousand battles" that "have assailed thy banks."

52

460 Thus Harold inly said, and pass'd along,
Yet not insensibly to all which here
Awoke the jocund birds to early song
In glens which might have made even exile dear:
Though on his brow were graven lines austere,
465 And tranquil sternness which had ta'en the place
Of feelings fierier far but less severe,
Joy was not always absent from his face,
But o'er it in such scenes would steal with transient trace.

53

Nor was all love shut from him, though his days
470 Of passion had consumed themselves to dust.
It is in vain that we would coldly gaze
On such as smile upon us; the heart must
Leap kindly back to kindness, though disgust
Hath wean'd it from all worldlings: thus he felt,
475 For there was soft remembrance, and sweet trust
In one fond breast,[1] to which his own would melt,
And in its tenderer hour on that his bosom dwelt.

54

And he had learn'd to love,—I know not why,
For this in such as him seems strange of mood,—
480 The helpless looks of blooming infancy,
Even in its earliest nurture; what subdued,
To change like this, a mind so far imbued
With scorn of man, it little boots to know;
But thus it was; and though in solitude
485 Small power the nipp'd affections have to grow,
In him this glow'd when all beside had ceased to glow.

55

And there was one soft breast, as hath been said,
Which unto his was bound by stronger ties
Than the church links withal; and, though unwed,
490 *That* love was pure, and, far above disguise,
Had stood the test of mortal enmities
Still undivided, and cemented more
By peril, dreaded most in female eyes;
But this was firm, and from a foreign shore
495 Well to that heart might his these absent greetings pour!

* * *

---

1. Commentators agree that the reference is to Byron's half-sister, Augusta Leigh.

[SWITZERLAND]²

68

Lake Leman° woos me with its crystal face,⠀⠀⠀⠀⠀⠀⠀⠀⠀*Geneva*
645⠀⠀The mirror where the stars and mountains view
⠀⠀⠀⠀The stillness of their aspect in each trace
⠀⠀⠀⠀Its clear depth yields of their far height and hue:
⠀⠀⠀⠀There is too much of man here, to look through
⠀⠀⠀⠀With a fit mind the might which I behold;
650⠀⠀But soon in me shall Loneliness renew
⠀⠀⠀⠀Thoughts hid, but not less cherish'd than of old,
⠀Ere mingling with the herd had penn'd me in their fold.

69

⠀⠀⠀⠀To fly from, need not be to hate, mankind:
⠀⠀⠀⠀All are not fit with them to stir and toil,
655⠀⠀Nor is it discontent to keep the mind
⠀⠀⠀⠀Deep in its fountain, lest it overboil
⠀⠀⠀⠀In the hot throng, where we become the spoil
⠀⠀⠀⠀Of our infection, till too late and long
⠀⠀⠀⠀We may deplore and struggle with the coil,°⠀⠀⠀⠀⠀⠀⠀*tumult*
660⠀⠀In wretched interchange of wrong for wrong
⠀Midst a contentious world, striving where none are strong.

70

⠀⠀⠀⠀There, in a moment, we may plunge our years
⠀⠀⠀⠀In fatal penitence, and in the blight
⠀⠀⠀⠀Of our own soul turn all our blood to tears,
665⠀⠀And colour things to come with hues of Night;
⠀⠀⠀⠀The race of life becomes a hopeless flight
⠀⠀⠀⠀To those that walk in darkness: on the sea,
⠀⠀⠀⠀The boldest steer but where their ports invite,
⠀⠀⠀⠀But there are wanderers o'er Eternity
670⠀Whose bark drives on and on, and anchor'd ne'er shall be.

71

⠀⠀⠀⠀Is it not better, then, to be alone,
⠀⠀⠀⠀And love Earth only for its earthly sake?
⠀⠀⠀⠀By the blue rushing of the arrowy Rhone,³
⠀⠀⠀⠀Or the pure bosom of its nursing lake,
675⠀⠀Which feeds it as a mother who doth make
⠀⠀⠀⠀A fair but froward infant her own care,

2. Byron with his traveling companion and physician, John Polidori, spent the gloomy summer of 1816 near Geneva, in a villa rented for its proximity to the household that Percy Shelley, Mary Wollstonecraft Godwin (who would marry Shelley at the end of the year), and her half-sister Claire Clairmont had set up there. The famous ghost-story-telling contest in which these five participated, and which saw the genesis of both *Frankenstein* and Polidori's "The Vampyre," took place that June. The Shelley household's involvement in *Childe Harold* is extensive. The fair copy of this canto was in fact written out by Claire, and Percy would eventually deliver it to Byron's publisher in London.

3. River rising in Switzerland and flowing through France into the Mediterranean.

Kissing its cries away as these awake;—
Is it not better thus our lives to wear,
Than join the crushing crowd, doom'd to inflict or bear?

72

680   I live not in myself, but I become
Portion of that around me; and to me
High mountains are a feeling, but the hum
Of human cities torture: I can see
Nothing to loathe in nature, save to be
685   A link reluctant in a fleshly chain,
Class'd among creatures, when the soul can flee,
And with the sky, the peak, the heaving plain
Of ocean, or the stars, mingle, and not in vain.[4]

73

And thus I am absorb'd, and this is life:
690   I look upon the peopled desert past,
As on a place of agony and strife,
Where, for some sin, to sorrow I was cast,
To act and suffer, but remount at last
With a fresh pinion; which I feel to spring,
695   Though young, yet waxing vigorous, as the blast
Which it would cope with, on delighted wing,
Spurning the clay-cold bonds which round our being cling.

74

And when, at length, the mind shall be all free
From what it hates in this degraded form,
700   Reft of its carnal life, save what shall be
Existent happier in the fly and worm,—
When elements to elements conform,
And dust is as it should be, shall I not
Feel all I see, less dazzling, but more warm?
705   The bodiless thought? the Spirit of each spot?
Of which, even now, I share at times the immortal lot?

75

Are not the mountains, waves, and skies, a part
Of me and of my soul, as I of them?
Is not the love of these deep in my heart
710   With a pure passion? should I not contemn
All objects, if compared with these? and stem
A tide of suffering, rather than forego

---

4. During the tour around Lake Geneva that they took in late June 1816, Percy Shelley introduced Byron to the poetry of Wordsworth and Wordsworth's concepts of nature. Those ideas are reflected in canto 3, but the voice is Byron's own.

Such feelings for the hard and worldly phlegm
Of those whose eyes are only turn'd below,
Gazing upon the ground, with thoughts which dare not
715   glow?

*   *   *

85

Clear, placid Leman! thy contrasted lake,
With the wild world I dwelt in, is a thing
Which warns me, with its stillness, to forsake
800 Earth's troubled waters for a purer spring.
This quiet sail is as a noiseless wing
To waft me from distraction; once I loved
Torn ocean's roar, but thy soft murmuring
Sounds sweet as if a Sister's voice reproved,
805 That I with stern delights should e'er have been so moved.

86

It is the hush of night, and all between
Thy margin and the mountains, dusk, yet clear,
Mellow'd and mingling, yet distinctly seen,
Save darken'd Jura,[5] whose capt heights appear
810 Precipitously steep; and drawing near,
There breathes a living fragrance from the shore,
Of flowers yet fresh with childhood; on the ear
Drops the light drip of the suspended oar,
Or chirps the grasshopper one good-night carol more;

87

815 He is an evening reveller, who makes
His life an infancy, and sings his fill;
At intervals, some bird from out the brakes°   *thickets*
Starts into voice a moment, then is still.
There seems a floating whisper on the hill,
820 But that is fancy, for the starlight dews
All silently their tears of love instil,
Weeping themselves away, till they infuse
Deep into Nature's breast the spirit of her hues.

88

Ye stars! which are the poetry of heaven!
825 If in your bright leaves we would read the fate
Of men and empires,—'tis to be forgiven,
That in our aspirations to be great,
Our destinies o'erleap their mortal state,
And claim a kindred with you; for ye are

5. The mountain range between Switzerland and France, visible from Lake Geneva.

830   A beauty and a mystery, and create
      In us such love and reverence from afar,
That fortune, fame, power, life, have named themselves a
        star,

89

    All heaven and earth are still—though not in sleep,
    But breathless, as we grow when feeling most;
835   And silent, as we stand in thoughts too deep:—
    All heaven and earth are still: From the high host
    Of stars, to the lull'd lake and mountain-coast,
    All is concenter'd in a life intense,
    Where not a beam, nor air, nor leaf is lost,
840   But hath a part of being, and a sense
Of that which is of all Creator and defence.

90

    Then stirs the feeling infinite, so felt
    In solitude, where we are *least* alone;
    A truth, which through our being then doth melt
845   And purifies from self: it is a tone,
    The soul and source of music, which makes known
    Eternal harmony, and sheds a charm,
    Like to the fabled Cytherea's zone,[6]
    Binding all things with beauty;—'twould disarm
850 The spectre Death, had he substantial power to harm.

91

    Not vainly did the early Persian make
    His altar the high places and the peak
    Of earth-o'ergazing mountains, and thus take[7]
    A fit and unwall'd temple, there to seek
855   The Spirit, in whose honour shrines are weak,
    Uprear'd of human hands. Come, and compare
    Columns and idol-dwellings, Goth or Greek,
    With Nature's realms of worship, earth and air,
Nor fix on fond abodes to circumscribe thy prayer!

92

860   Thy sky is changed!—and such a change! Oh night,
    And storm, and darkness, ye are wondrous strong,
    Yet lovely in your strength, as is the light
    Of a dark eye in woman! Far along,
    From peak to peak, the rattling crags among
865   Leaps the live thunder! Not from one lone cloud,

6. The sash of Venus, which conferred the power to attract love.
7. It is to be recollected, that the most beautiful and impressive doctrines of the Founder of Christianity were delivered, not in the *Temple*, but on the *Mount* [Byron's note].

> But every mountain now hath found a tongue,
> And Jura answers, through her misty shroud,
> Back to the joyous Alps, who call to her aloud!

93

> And this is in the night:—Most glorious night!
> 870 Thou wert not sent for slumber! let me be
> A sharer in thy fierce and far delight,—
> A portion of the tempest and of thee!
> How the lit lake shines, a phosphoric sea,
> And the big rain comes dancing to the earth!
> 875 And now again 'tis black,—and now, the glee
> Of the loud hills shakes with its mountain-mirth,
> As if they did rejoice o'er a young earthquake's birth.

94

> Now, where the swift Rhone cleaves his way between
> Heights which appear as lovers who have parted
> 880 In hate, whose mining depths so intervene,
> That they can meet no more, though broken-hearted:
> Though in their souls, which thus each other thwarted,
> Love was the very root of the fond rage
> Which blighted their life's bloom, and then departed—
> 885 Itself expired, but leaving them an age
> Of years all winters,—war within themselves to wage.

95

> Now, where the quick Rhone thus hath cleft his way,
> The mightiest of the storms hath ta'en his stand:
> For here, not one, but many, make their play,
> 890 And fling their thunder-bolts from hand to hand,
> Flashing and cast around: of all the band,
> The brightest through these parted hills hath fork'd
> His lightnings,—as if he did understand,
> That in such gaps as desolation work'd,
> 895 There the hot shaft should blast whatever therein lurk'd.

96

> Sky, mountains, river, winds, lake, lightnings! ye!
> With night, and clouds, and thunder, and a soul
> To make these felt and feeling, well may be
> Things that have made me watchful; the far roll
> 900 Of your departing voices, is the knoll[8]
> Of what in me is sleepless,—if I rest.
> But where of ye, oh tempests! is the goal?
> Are ye like those within the human breast?
> Or do ye find, at length, like eagles, some high nest?

8. Old form of knell: the sound of a bell.

97

905 Could I embody and unbosom now
That which is most within me,—could I wreak
My thoughts upon expression, and thus throw
Soul, heart, mind, passions, feelings, strong or weak,
All that I would have sought, and all I seek,
910 Bear, know, feel, and yet breathe—into *one* word,
And that one word were Lightning, I would speak;
But as it is, I live and die unheard,
With a most voiceless thought, sheathing it as a sword.

98

The morn is up again, the dewy morn,
915 With breath all incense, and with cheek all bloom,
Laughing the clouds away with playful scorn,
And living as if earth contain'd no tomb,—
And glowing into day: we may resume
The march of our existence: and thus I,
920 Still on thy shores, fair Leman! may find room
And food for meditation, nor pass by
Much, that may give us pause, if ponder'd fittingly.

* * *

113

I have not loved the world, nor the world me;
1050 I have not flatter'd its rank breath, nor bow'd
To its idolatries a patient knee,—
Nor coin'd my cheek to smiles,—nor cried aloud
In worship of an echo; in the crowd
They could not deem me one of such; I stood
1055 Among them, but not of them; in a shroud
Of thoughts which were not their thoughts, and still
    could,
Had I not filed[9] my mind, which thus itself subdued.

114

I have not loved the world, nor the world me,—
But let us part fair foes; I do believe,
1060 Though I have found them not, that there may be
Words which are things,—hopes which will not deceive,
And virtues which are merciful, nor weave
Snares for the failing: I would also deem
O'er others' griefs that some sincerely grieve;
1065 That two, or one, are almost what they seem,
That goodness is no name, and happiness no dream.

---

9. Defiled. In a note Byron refers to *Macbeth* 3.1.66 ("For Banquo's issue have I filed my mind").

115

My daughter! with thy name this song begun—
My daughter! with thy name thus much shall end—
I see thee not,—I hear thee not,—but none
1070 Can be so wrapt in thee; thou art the friend
To whom the shadows of far years extend:
Albeit my brow thou never should'st behold,
My voice shall with thy future visions blend,
And reach into thy heart,—when mine is cold,—
1075 A token and a tone, even from thy father's mould.

116

To aid thy mind's development,—to watch
Thy dawn of little joys,—to sit and see
Almost thy very growth,—to view thee catch
Knowledge of objects,—wonders yet to thee!
1080 To hold thee lightly on a gentle knee,
And print on thy soft cheek a parent's kiss,—
This, it should seem, was not reserved for me;
Yet this was in my nature:—as it is,
I know not what is there, yet something like to this.

117

1085 Yet, though dull Hate as duty should be taught,
I know that thou wilt love me; though my name
Should be shut from thee, as a spell still fraught
With desolation,—and a broken claim:
Though the grave closed between us,—'twere the same,
1090 I know that thou wilt love me; though to drain
My blood from out thy being were an aim,
And an attainment,—all would be in vain,—
Still thou would'st love me, still that more than life retain.

118

The child of love,—though born in bitterness
1095 And nurtured in convulsion,—of thy sire
These were the elements,—and thine no less.
As yet such are around thee,—but thy fire
Shall be more temper'd, and thy hope far higher.
Sweet be thy cradled slumbers! O'er the sea,
1100 And from the mountains where I now respire,
Fain would I waft such blessing upon thee,
As, with a sigh, I deem thou might'st have been to me!

1812, 1816

Manfred *Manfred* is Byron's first dramatic work. As its subtitle, "A Dramatic Poem," indicates, it was not intended to be produced on the stage; Byron also referred to it as a "metaphysical" drama—that is, a drama of ideas. He began writing it in the autumn of 1816 while living in the Swiss Alps, whose grandeur stimulated his imagination; he finished the drama the following year in Italy.

Manfred's literary forebears include the villains of Gothic fiction (another Manfred can be found in Horace Walpole's *Castle of Otranto*; see p. 516) and of the Gothic dramas Byron had encountered during his time on the board of managers of London's Drury Lane Theatre. Manfred also shares traits with the Greek Titan Prometheus, rebel against Zeus, ruler of the gods; Milton's Satan; Ahasuerus, the legendary Wandering Jew who, having ridiculed Christ as he bore the Cross to Calvary, is doomed to live until Christ's Second Coming; and Faust, who yielded his soul to the devil in exchange for superhuman powers. Byron denied that he had ever heard of Marlowe's *Doctor Faustus*, and because he knew no German he had not read Goethe's *Faust*, of which part I had been published in 1808. But during an August 1816 visit to Byron and the Shelley household, Matthew Lewis (author of the Gothic novel *The Monk*; see p. 528) had read parts of *Faust* to him aloud, translating as he went, and Byron worked memories of this oral translation into his own drama in a way that evoked Goethe's admiration.

Like Byron's earlier heroes, Childe Harold and the protagonists of some of his Eastern tales, Manfred is hounded by remorse—in this instance, for a transgression that (it is hinted but never quite specified) is incest with his sister Astarte; it is also hinted that Astarte has taken her own life. While this element in the drama is often regarded as Byron's veiled confession of his incestuous relations with his half-sister, Augusta, and while Byron, ever the attention-seeker, in some ways courted this interpretation, the theme of incest was a common one in Gothic and Romantic writings. It features in *The Monk* and Walpole's closet drama *The Mysterious Mother* (1768), and, at about the time Byron was composing his drama, it was also being explored by Mary and Percy Shelley.

The character of Manfred is its author's most impressive representation of the Byronic Hero. Byron's invention is to have Manfred, unlike Faust, disdainfully reject the offer of a pact with the powers of darkness. He thereby sets himself up as the totally autonomous man, independent of any external authority or power, whose own mind, as he says in the concluding scene (3.4.127–40), generates the values by which he lives "in sufferance or in joy," and by reference to which he judges, requites, and finally destroys himself. In his work *Ecce Homo*, the German philosopher Friedrich Nietzsche, recognizing Byron's anticipation of his own *Übermensch* (the "superman" who posits for himself a moral code beyond all traditional standards of good and evil), asserted that the character of Manfred was greater than that of Goethe's Faust.

For more information on the context of *Manfred*, see "The Satanic and Byronic Hero" in the NAEL Archive.

Manfred

A DRAMATIC POEM

There are more things in heaven and earth, Horatio,
Than are dreamt of in your philosophy.[1]

DRAMATIS PERSONAE

MANFRED	WITCH OF THE ALPS
CHAMOIS HUNTER	ARIMANES
ABBOT OF ST. MAURICE	NEMESIS
MANUEL	THE DESTINIES
HERMAN	SPIRITS, &C.

*The Scene of the Drama is amongst the Higher Alps—partly
in the Castle of Manfred, and partly in the Mountains.*

Act 1

SCENE 1

MANFRED *alone.—Scene, a Gothic Gallery.*[2]*—Time, Midnight.*

MAN.   The lamp must be replenish'd, but even then
It will not burn so long as I must watch:
My slumbers—if I slumber—are not sleep,
But a continuance of enduring thought,
5 Which then I can resist not: in my heart
There is a vigil, and these eyes but close
To look within; and yet I live, and bear
The aspect and the form of breathing men.
But grief should be the instructor of the wise;
10 Sorrow is knowledge: they who know the most
Must mourn the deepest o'er the fatal truth,
The Tree of Knowledge is not that of Life.
Philosophy and science, and the springs
Of wonder, and the wisdom of the world,
15 I have essay'd, and in my mind there is
A power to make these subject to itself—
But they avail not: I have done men good,
And I have met with good even among men—
But this avail'd not: I have had my foes,
20 And none have baffled, many fallen before me—
But this avail'd not:—Good, or evil, life,
Powers, passions, all I see in other beings,
Have been to me as rain unto the sands,
Since that all-nameless hour. I have no dread,
25 And feel the curse to have no natural fear,
Nor fluttering throb, that beats with hopes or wishes,

---

1. Hamlet's comment after having seen his father's ghost (Shakespeare, *Hamlet* 1.5.168–69).

2. A large chamber built in the medieval Gothic style with high, pointed arches.

Or lurking love of something on the earth.—
Now to my task.—
     Mysterious Agency!
Ye spirits of the unbounded Universe!
30 Whom I have sought in darkness and in light—
Ye, who do compass earth about, and dwell
In subtler essence—ye, to whom the tops
Of mountains inaccessible are haunts,
And earth's and ocean's caves familiar things—
35 I call upon ye by the written charm
Which gives me power upon you—Rise! appear!
        [*A pause.*]
They come not yet.—Now by the voice of him
Who is the first among you[3]—by this sign,
Which makes you tremble—by the claims of him
40 Who is undying,[4]—Rise! appear!—Appear!
        [*A pause.*]
If it be so.—Spirits of earth and air,
Ye shall not thus elude me: by a power,
Deeper than all yet urged, a tyrant-spell,
Which had its birthplace in a star condemn'd,
45 The burning wreck of a demolish'd world,
A wandering hell in the eternal space;
By the strong curse which is upon my soul,
The thought which is within me and around me,
I do compel ye to my will.—Appear!
  [*A star is seen at the darker end of the gallery: it is stationary; and
  voice is heard singing.*]

      FIRST SPIRIT.[5]
50 Mortal! to thy bidding bow'd,
From my mansion in the cloud,
Which the breath of twilight builds,
And the summer's sunset gilds
With the azure and vermilion,
55 Which is mix'd for my pavilion;
Though thy quest may be forbidden,
On a star-beam I have ridden;
To thine adjuration° bow'd,   *summons*
Mortal—be thy wish avow'd!

    Voice of the SECOND SPIRIT.
60 Mont Blanc[6] is the monarch of mountains;
  They crown'd him long ago
On a throne of rocks, in a robe of clouds,
  With a diadem of snow.
Around his waist are forests braced,
65 The Avalanche in his hand;

3. Arimanes, who appears in 2.4.
4. Probably God, to whom traditional magic conjurations often allude.
5. The Spirits, successively, are those of the Air, Mountain, Ocean, Earth, Winds, Night, and

Manfred's guiding Star.
6. The highest mountain in the Alps. Percy Shelley paid tribute to it in a poem published in the same year as *Manfred*.

But ere it fall, that thundering ball
   Must pause for my command.
The Glacier's cold and restless mass
   Moves onward day by day;
70   But I am he who bids it pass,
   Or with its ice delay.
I am the spirit of the place,
   Could make the mountain bow
And quiver to his cavern'd base—
75   And what with me wouldst *Thou?*

       Voice of the THIRD SPIRIT.
In the blue depth of the waters,
   Where the wave hath no strife,
Where the wind is a stranger,
   And the sea-snake hath life,
80   Where the Mermaid is decking
   Her green hair with shells;
Like the storm on the surface
   Came the sound of thy spells;
O'er my calm Hall of Coral
85   The deep echo roll'd—
To the Spirit of Ocean
   Thy wishes unfold!

       FOURTH SPIRIT.
Where the slumbering earthquake
   Lies pillow'd on fire,
90   And the lakes of bitumen°   *tar*like mineral
   Rise boilingly higher;
Where the roots of the Andes
   Strike deep in the earth,
As their summits to heaven
95   Shoot soaringly forth;
I have quitted my birthplace,
   Thy bidding to bide—
Thy spell hath subdued me,
   Thy will be my guide!

       FIFTH SPIRIT.
100   I am the Rider of the wind,
   The Stirrer of the storm;
The hurricane I left behind
   Is yet with lightning warm;
To speed to thee, o'er shore and sea
105   I swept upon the blast:
The fleet I met sail'd well, and yet
   'Twill sink ere night be past.

       SIXTH SPIRIT.
My dwelling is the shadow of the night,
Why doth thy magic torture me with light?

SEVENTH SPIRIT.

110 The star which rules thy destiny
Was ruled, ere earth began, by me:
It was a world as fresh and fair
As e'er revolved round sun in air;
Its course was free and regular,
115 Space bosom'd not a lovelier star.
The hour arrived—and it became
A wandering mass of shapeless flame,
A pathless comet, and a curse,
The menace of the universe;
120 Still rolling on with innate force,
Without a sphere, without a course,
A bright deformity on high,
The monster of the upper sky!
And thou! beneath its influence born—
125 Thou worm! whom I obey and scorn—
Forced by a power (which is not thine,
And lent thee but to make thee mine)
For this brief moment to descend,
Where these weak spirits round thee bend
130 And parley with a thing like thee—
What wouldst thou, Child of Clay! with me?

The SEVEN SPIRITS.

Earth, ocean, air, night, mountains, winds, thy star,
Are at thy beck and bidding, Child of Clay!
Before thee at thy quest their spirits are—
135 What wouldst thou with us, son of mortals—say?

MAN. Forgetfulness—
FIRST SPIRIT. Of what—of whom—and why?
MAN. Of that which is within me; read it there—
Ye know it, and I cannot utter it.
SPIRIT. We can but give thee that which we possess:
140 Ask of us subjects, sovereignty, the power
O'er earth, the whole, or portion, or a sign
Which shall control the elements, whereof
We are the dominators, each and all,
These shall be thine.
MAN. Oblivion, self-oblivion—
145 Can ye not wring from out the hidden realms
Ye offer so profusely what I ask?
SPIRIT. It is not in our essence, in our skill;
But—thou mayst die.
MAN. Will death bestow it on me?
SPIRIT. We are immortal, and do not forget;
150 We are eternal; and to us the past
Is, as the future, present. Art thou answer'd?
MAN. Ye mock me—but the power which brought ye here
Hath made you mine. Slaves, scoff not at my will!

The mind, the spirit, the Promethean spark,[7]
155 The lightning of my being, is as bright,
Pervading, and far darting as your own,
And shall not yield to yours, though coop'd in clay!
Answer, or I will teach you what I am.
SPIRIT.   We answer as we answer'd; our reply
Is even in thine own words.
160 MAN.   Why say ye so?
SPIRIT.   If, as thou say'st, thine essence be as ours,
We have replied in telling thee, the thing
Mortals call death hath nought to do with us.
MAN.   I then have call'd ye from your realms in vain;
Ye cannot, or ye will not, aid me.
165 SPIRIT.   Say;
What we possess we offer; it is thine:
Bethink ere thou dismiss us, ask again—
Kingdom, and sway, and strength, and length of days—
MAN.   Accursed! what have I to do with days?
170 They are too long already.—Hence—begone!
SPIRIT.   Yet pause: being here, our will would do thee service;
Bethink thee, is there then no other gift
Which we can make not worthless in thine eyes?
MAN.   No, none: yet stay—one moment, ere we part—
175 I would behold ye face to face. I hear
Your voices, sweet and melancholy sounds,
As music on the waters; and I see
The steady aspect of a clear large star;
But nothing more. Approach me as ye are,
180 Or one, or all, in your accustom'd forms.
SPIRIT.   We have no forms, beyond the elements
Of which we are the mind and principle:
But choose a form—in that we will appear.
MAN.   I have no choice; there is no form on earth
185 Hideous or beautiful to me. Let him,
Who is most powerful of ye, take such aspect
As unto him may seem most fitting—Come!
SEVENTH SPIRIT. (*Appearing in the shape of a beautiful female figure.*)[8]
                                        Behold!
MAN.   Oh God! if it be thus, and *thou*
Art not a madness and a mockery,
190 I yet might be most happy. I will clasp thee,
And we again will be——   [*The figure vanishes.*]
                              My heart is crush'd!
                                        [MANFRED *falls senseless.*]
(*A Voice is heard in the Incantation*[9] *which follows.*)

---

7. In Greek myth Prometheus molded man from
clay and stole fire from heaven to give it to
humans.
8. This shape may be an image of Astarte, whose
phantom appears in 2.3.97.

9. Byron had published this "incantation"—a
magical spell—as a separate poem six months
before *Manfred*, with a note explaining that the
poem was "a Chorus in an unfinished Witch
drama began some years ago."

When the moon is on the wave,
　　And the glow-worm in the grass,
And the meteor on the grave,
195　　And the wisp on the morass;
When the falling stars are shooting,
And the answer'd owls are hooting,
And the silent leaves are still
In the shadow of the hill,
200　Shall my soul be upon thine,
With a power and with a sign.

Though thy slumber may be deep,
Yet thy spirit shall not sleep;
There are shades which will not vanish,
205　There are thoughts thou canst not banish;
By a power to thee unknown,
Thou canst never be alone;
Thou art wrapt as with a shroud,
Thou art gather'd in a cloud;
210　And for ever shalt thou dwell
In the spirit of this spell.

Though thou seest me not pass by,
Thou shalt feel me with thine eye
As a thing that, though unseen,
215　Must be near thee, and hath been;
And when in that secret dread
Thou hast turn'd around thy head,
Thou shalt marvel I am not
As thy shadow on the spot,
220　And the power which thou dost feel
Shall be what thou must conceal.

And a magic voice and verse
Hath baptized thee with a curse;
And a spirit of the air
225　Hath begirt thee with a snare;
In the wind there is a voice
Shall forbid thee to rejoice;
And to thee shall Night deny
All the quiet of her sky;
230　And the day shall have a sun,
Which shall make thee wish it done.

From thy false tears I did distil
An essence which hath strength to kill;
From thy own heart I then did wring
235　The black blood in its blackest spring;
From thy own smile I snatched the snake,
For there it coil'd as in a brake;°　　　　　　　　*thicket*
From thy own lip I drew the charm

Which gave all these their chiefest harm;
240 In proving every poison known,
I found the strongest was thine own.

By thy cold breast and serpent smile,
By thy unfathom'd gulfs of guile,
By that most seeming virtuous eye,
245 By thy shut soul's hypocrisy;
By the perfection of thine art
Which pass'd for human thine own heart;
By thy delight in others' pain,
And by thy brotherhood of Cain,[1]
250 I call upon thee! and compel
Thyself to be thy proper Hell![2]

And on thy head I pour the vial
Which doth devote thee to this trial;
Nor to slumber, nor to die,
255 Shall be in thy destiny;
Though thy death shall still seem near
To thy wish, but as a fear;
Lo! the spell now works around thee,
And the clankless chain hath bound thee;
260 O'er thy heart and brain together
Hath the word been pass'd—now wither!

SCENE 2

The Mountain of the Jungfrau.[3]*—Time, Morning.—*
MANFRED *alone upon the Cliffs.*

MAN.   The spirits I have raised abandon me—
The spells which I have studied baffle me—
5 The remedy I reck'd of° tortured me;   *considered*
I lean no more on super-human aid,
It hath no power upon the past, and for
The future, till the past be gulf'd in darkness,
It is not of my search.—My mother Earth!
And thou fresh breaking Day, and you, ye Mountains,
Why are ye beautiful? I cannot love ye.
10 And thou, the bright eye of the universe,
That openest over all, and unto all
Art a delight—thou shin'st not on my heart.
And you, ye crags, upon whose extreme edge
I stand, and on the torrent's brink beneath
15 Behold the tall pines dwindled as to shrubs
In dizziness of distance; when a leap,
A stir, a motion, even a breath, would bring

1. I.e., by your kinship with Cain, who murdered his brother, Abel.
2. Cf. Satan's words in Milton's *Paradise Lost*

4.75: "Which way I fly is Hell; my self am Hell."
3. A high Alpine mountain in south-central Switzerland.

My breast upon its rocky bosom's bed
To rest for ever—wherefore do I pause?
20   I feel the impulse—yet I do not plunge;
I see the peril—yet do not recede;
And my brain reels—and yet my foot is firm:
There is a power upon me which withholds,
And makes it my fatality to live;
25   If it be life to wear within myself
This barrenness of spirit, and to be
My own soul's sepulchre, for I have ceased
To justify my deeds unto myself—
The last infirmity of evil.⁴ Ay,
30   Thou winged and cloud-cleaving minister,

[*An eagle passes.*]

Whose happy flight is highest into heaven,
Well may'st thou swoop so near me—I should be
Thy prey, and gorge thine eaglets; thou art gone
Where the eye cannot follow thee; but thine
35   Yet pierces downward, onward, or above,
With a pervading vision.—Beautiful!
How beautiful is all this visible world!
How glorious in its action and itself!
But we, who name ourselves its sovereigns, we,
40   Half dust, half deity, alike unfit
To sink or soar, with our mix'd essence make
A conflict of its elements, and breathe
The breath of degradation and of pride,
Contending with low wants and lofty will,
45   Till our mortality predominates,
And men are—what they name not to themselves,
And trust not to each other. Hark! the note,
        [*The Shepherd's pipe in the distance is heard.*]
The natural music of the mountain reed—
For here the patriarchal days⁵ are not
50   A pastoral fable—pipes in the liberal° air,   *free-moving*
Mix'd with the sweet bells of the sauntering herd;
My soul would drink those echoes.—Oh, that I were
The viewless° spirit of a lovely sound,   *invisible*
A living voice, a breathing harmony,
55   A bodiless enjoyment—born and dying
With the blest tone which made me!

        Enter from below a CHAMOIS⁶ HUNTER.
CHAMOIS HUNTER.   Even so
This way the chamois leapt: her nimble feet
Have baffled me; my gains to-day will scarce
Repay my break-neck travail.—What is here?

---

4. An echo of Milton's "Lycidas," where fame is
identified as "That last infirmity of a noble
mind" (line 71).
5. The days of the Old Testament partriarchs,

who were shepherds.
6. A goatlike antelope found in the European
mountains.

60   Who seems not of my trade, and yet hath reach'd
       A height which none even of our mountaineers,
       Save our best hunters, may attain: his garb
       Is goodly, his mien° manly, and his air   *appearance*
       Proud as a free-born peasant's, at this distance.—
       I will approach him nearer.

65 MAN. (*not perceiving the other*).   To be thus—
       Grey-hair'd with anguish, like these blasted pines,
       Wrecks of a single winter, barkless, branchless,
       A blighted trunk upon a cursed root,
       Which but supplies a feeling to decay—
70   And to be thus, eternally but thus,
       Having been otherwise! Now furrow'd o'er
       With wrinkles, plough'd by moments, not by years
       And hours—all tortured into ages—hours
       Which I outlive!—Ye toppling crags of ice!
75   Ye avalanches, whom a breath draws down
       In mountainous o'erwhelming, come and crush me—
       I hear ye momently above, beneath,
       Crash with a frequent conflict; but ye pass,
       And only fall on things that still would live;
80   On the young flourishing forest, or the hut
       And hamlet of the harmless villager.
     C. HUN.   The mists begin to rise from up the valley;
       I'll warn him to descend, or he may chance
       To lose at once his way and life together.
85 MAN.   The mists boil up around the glaciers; clouds
       Rise curling fast beneath me, white and sulphury,
       Like foam from the roused ocean of deep Hell,
       Whose every wave breaks on a living shore,
       Heap'd with the damn'd like pebbles.—I am giddy.
90 C. HUN.   I must approach him cautiously; if near,
       A sudden step will startle him, and he
       Seems tottering already.
     MAN.   Mountains have fallen,
       Leaving a gap in the clouds, and with the shock
       Rocking their Alpine brethren; filling up
95   The ripe green valleys with destruction's splinters;
       Damming the rivers with a sudden dash,
       Which crush'd the waters into mist, and made
       Their fountains find another channel—thus,
       Thus, in its old age, did Mount Rosenberg[7]—
       Why stood I not beneath it?
100 C. HUN.   Friend! have a care,
       Your next step may be fatal!—for the love
       Of him who made you, stand not on that brink!
     MAN. (*not hearing him*).   Such would have been for me a fitting
         tomb;

---

7. In 1806, ten years before the composition of *Manfred*, a huge landslide on Mount Rossberg ("Rosen-berg") had destroyed four villages and killed 457 people.

My bones had then been quiet in their depth;
105 They had not then been strewn upon the rocks
For the wind's pastime—as thus—thus they shall be—
In this one plunge.—Farewell, ye opening heavens!
Look not upon me thus reproachfully—
Ye were not meant for me—Earth! take these atoms!
　　　　[As MANFRED is in act to spring from the cliff, the CHAMOIS
　　　　HUNTER seizes and retains him with a sudden grasp.]
110 C. HUN.　Hold, madman!—though aweary of thy life,
Stain not our pure vales with thy guilty blood—
Away with me——I will not quit my hold.
MAN.　I am most sick at heart—nay, grasp me not—
I am all feebleness—the mountains whirl
115 Spinning around me——I grow blind——What art thou?
C. HUN.　I'll answer that anon.—Away with me——
The clouds grow thicker—there—now lean on me—
Place your foot here—here, take this staff, and cling
A moment to that shrub—now give me your hand,
120 And hold fast by my girdle—softly—well—
The Chalet will be gain'd within an hour—
Come on, we'll quickly find a surer footing,
And something like a pathway, which the torrent
Hath wash'd since winter.—Come, 'tis bravely done—
125 You should have been a hunter.—Follow me.
　　　　[As they descend the rocks with difficulty, the scene closes.]

Act 2

SCENE 1

A Cottage amongst the Bernese Alps.[8]

MANFRED *and the* CHAMOIS HUNTER.

C. HUN.　No, no—yet pause—thou must not yet go forth:
Thy mind and body are alike unfit
To trust each other, for some hours, at least;
When thou art better, I will be thy guide—
But whither?
5 MAN.　　　　It imports not: I do know
My route full well, and need no further guidance.
C. HUN.　Thy garb and gait bespeak thee of high lineage—
One of the many chiefs, whose castled crags
Look o'er the lower valleys—which of these
10 May call thee lord? I only know their portals;
My way of life leads me but rarely down
To bask by the huge hearths of those old halls,
Carousing with the vassals; but the paths,
Which step from out our mountains to their doors,
15 I know from childhood—which of these is thine?
MAN.　No matter.

---

8. A mountain range in south-central Switzerland.

C. HUN.   Well, sir, pardon me the question,
    And be of better cheer. Come, taste my wine;
    'Tis of an ancient vintage; many a day
    'T has thawed my veins among our glaciers, now
20   Let it do thus for thine—Come, pledge me fairly.
    MAN.   Away, away! there's blood upon the brim!
    Will it then never—never sink in the earth?
    C. HUN.   What dost thou mean? thy senses wander from thee.
    MAN.   I say 'tis blood—my blood! the pure warm stream
25   Which ran in the veins of my fathers, and in ours
    When we were in our youth, and had one heart,
    And loved each other as we should not love,
    And this was shed: but still it rises up,
    Colouring the clouds, that shut me out from heaven,
30   Where thou art not—and I shall never be.
    C. HUN.   Man of strange words, and some half-maddening sin,
    Which makes thee people° vacancy, whate'er   *populate*
    Thy dread and sufferance be, there's comfort yet—
    The aid of holy men, and heavenly patience——
35   MAN.   Patience and patience! Hence—that word was made
    For brutes of burthen, not for birds of prey;
    Preach it to mortals of a dust like thine,—
    I am not of thine order.
    C. HUN.   Thanks to heaven!
    I would not be of thine for the free fame
40   Of William Tell;[9] but whatsoe'er thine ill,
    It must be borne, and these wild starts are useless.
    MAN.   Do I not bear it?—Look on me—I live.
    C. HUN.   This is convulsion, and no healthful life.
    MAN.   I tell thee, man! I have lived many years,
45   Many long years, but they are nothing now
    To those which I must number: ages—ages—
    Space and eternity—and consciousness,
    With the fierce thirst of death—and still unslaked!
    C. HUN.   Why, on thy brow the seal of middle age
50   Hath scarce been set; I am thine elder far.
    MAN.   Think'st thou existence doth depend on time?
    It doth; but actions are our epochs: mine
    Have made my days and nights imperishable,
    Endless, and all alike, as sands on the shore,
55   Innumerable atoms, and one desert,
    Barren and cold, on which the wild waves break,
    But nothing rests, save carcasses and wrecks,
    Rocks, and the salt-surf weeds of bitterness.
    C. HUN.   Alas! he's mad—but yet I must not leave him.
60   MAN.   I would I were—for then the things I see
    Would be but a distemper'd° dream.   *disturbed*
    C. HUN.   What is it
    That thou dost see, or think thou look'st upon?
    MAN.   Myself, and thee—a peasant of the Alps—

---

9. The hero who, according to legend, liberated Switzerland from Austrian oppression in the 14th century.

Thy humble virtues, hospitable home,
65 And spirit patient, pious, proud, and free;
Thy self-respect, grafted on innocent thoughts;
Thy days of health, and nights of sleep; thy toils,
By danger dignified, yet guiltless; hopes
Of cheerful old age and a quiet grave,
70 With cross and garland over its green turf,
And thy grandchildren's love for epitaph;
This do I see—and then I look within—
It matters not—my soul was scorch'd already!
C. HUN.   And would'st thou then exchange thy lot for mine?
75 MAN.   No, friend! I would not wrong thee, nor exchange
My lot with living being: I can bear—
However wretchedly, 'tis still to bear—
In life what others could not brook to dream,
But perish in their slumber.
C. HUN.   And with this—
80 This cautious feeling for another's pain,
Canst thou be black with evil?—say not so.
Can one of gentle thoughts have wreak'd revenge
Upon his enemies?
MAN.   Oh! no, no, no!
My injuries came down on those who loved me—
85 On those whom I best loved; I never quell'd°   killed
An enemy, save in my just defence—
My wrongs were all on those I should have cherished
But my embrace was fatal.
C. HUN.   Heaven give thee rest!
And penitence restore thee to thyself;
My prayers shall be for thee.
90 MAN.   I need them not,
But can endure thy pity. I depart—
'Tis time—farewell!—Here's gold, and thanks for thee—
No words—it is thy due.—Follow me not—
I know my path—the mountain peril's past:
95 And once again, I charge thee, follow not!
                                        [*Exit* MANFRED.]

SCENE 2

A lower Valley in the Alps.—A Cataract.

Enter MANFRED.

It is not noon—the sunbow's rays still arch[1]
The torrent with the many hues of heaven,
And roll the sheeted silver's waving column
O'er the crag's headlong perpendicular,
5 And fling its lines of foaming light along,
And to and fro, like the pale courser's tail,

---

1. This iris is formed by the rays of the sun over the lower part of the Alpine torrents: it is exactly like a rainbow come to pay a visit, and so close that you may walk into it: this effect lasts until noon [Byron's note].

The Giant steed, to be bestrode by Death,
As told in the Apocalypse.[2] No eyes
But mine now drink this sight of loveliness;
10 I should be sole in this sweet solitude,
And with the Spirit of the place divide
The homage of these waters.—I will call her.
    [MANFRED *takes some of the water into the palm of his hand, and*
    flings it into the air, muttering the adjuration. After a pause, the
    WITCH OF THE ALPS *rises beneath the arch of the sunbow of the*
    torrent.]
Beautiful Spirit! with thy hair of light,
And dazzling eyes of glory, in whose form
15 The charms of Earth's least mortal daughters grow
To an unearthly stature, in an essence
Of purer elements; while the hues of youth,—
Carnation'd like a sleeping infant's cheek,
Rock'd by the beating of her mother's heart,
20 Or the rose tints, which summer's twilight leaves
Upon the lofty glacier's virgin snow,
The blush of earth embracing with her heaven,—
Tinge thy celestial aspect, and make tame
The beauties of the sunbow which bends o'er thee.
25 Beautiful Spirit! in thy calm clear brow,
Wherein is glass'd° serenity of soul,   *reflected*
Which of itself shows immortality,
I read that thou wilt pardon to a Son
Of Earth, whom the abstruser powers permit
30 At times to commune with them—if that he
Avail him of his spells—to call thee thus,
And gaze on thee a moment.
WITCH.   Son of Earth!
I know thee, and the powers which give thee power;
I know thee for a man of many thoughts,
35 And deeds of good and ill, extreme in both,
Fatal and fated in thy sufferings.
I have expected this—what would'st thou with me?
MAN.   To look upon thy beauty—nothing further.
The face of the earth hath madden'd me, and I
40 Take refuge in her mysteries, and pierce
To the abodes of those who govern her—
But they can nothing aid me. I have sought
From them what they could not bestow, and now
I search no further.
WITCH.   What could be the quest
45 Which is not in the power of the most powerful,
The rulers of the invisible?
MAN.   A boon;
But why should I repeat it? 'twere in vain.

---

2. Revelation 6.8: "And I looked, and behold a pale horse: and his name that sat on him was Death, and
Hell followed with him."

WITCH. I know not that; let thy lips utter it.
MAN. Well, though it torture me, 'tis but the same;
50   My pang shall find a voice. From my youth upwards
        My spirit walk'd not with the souls of men,
        Nor look'd upon the earth with human eyes;
        The thirst of their ambition was not mine,
        The aim of their existence was not mine;
55   My joys, my griefs, my passions, and my powers,
        Made me a stranger; though I wore the form,
        I had no sympathy with breathing flesh,
        Nor midst the creatures of clay that girded me
        Was there but one who—but of her anon.
60   I said, with men, and with the thoughts of men,
        I held but slight communion; but instead,
        My joy was in the Wilderness, to breathe
        The difficult air of the iced mountain's top,
        Where the birds dare not build, nor insect's wing
65   Flit o'er the herbless granite; or to plunge
        Into the torrent, and to roll along
        On the swift whirl of the new breaking wave
        Of river-stream, or ocean, in their flow.
        In these my early strength exulted; or
70   To follow through the night the moving moon,
        The stars and their development; or catch
        The dazzling lightnings till my eyes grew dim;
        Or to look, list'ning, on the scatter'd leaves,
        While Autumn winds were at their evening song.
75   These were my pastimes, and to be alone;
        For if the beings, of whom I was one,—
        Hating to be so,—cross'd me in my path,
        I felt myself degraded back to them,
        And was all clay again. And then I dived,
80   In my lone wanderings, to the caves of death,
        Searching its cause in its effect; and drew
        From wither'd bones, and skulls, and heap'd up dust,
        Conclusions most forbidden.[3] Then I pass'd
        The nights of years in sciences untaught,
85   Save in the old time; and with time and toil,
        And terrible ordeal, and such penance
        As in itself hath power upon the air,
        And spirits that do compass air and earth,
        Space, and the peopled infinite, I made
90   Mine eyes familiar with Eternity,
        Such as, before me, did the Magi,[4] and
        He who from out their fountain dwellings raised
        Eros and Anteros, at Gadara,[5]

---

3. Cf. passages from Victor Frankenstein's account of his scientific investigations. "To examine the causes of life, we must first have recourse to death"; "Who shall conceive the horrors of my secret toil, as I dabbled among the unhallowed damps of the grave . . . ?" (chap. 4).

4. Masters of occult knowledge (plural of *magus*).
5. Byron's note to lines 92–93 identifies this figure as Iamblicus, the 4th-century Neoplatonic philosopher, who called up Eros, god of love, and Anteros, god of unrequited love, from the hot springs named after them at Gadara, in Syria.

As I do thee:—and with my knowledge grew
95   The thirst of knowledge, and the power and joy
Of this most bright intelligence; until——
WITCH.   Proceed.
MAN.   Oh! I but thus prolong'd my words,
Boasting these idle attributes, because
As I approach the core of my heart's grief—
100   But to my task. I have not named to thee
Father or mother, mistress, friend, or being,
With whom I wore the chain of human ties;
If I had such, they seem'd not such to me—
Yet there was one— —
WITCH.   Spare not thyself—proceed.
105   MAN.   She was like me in lineaments—her eyes,
Her hair, her features, all, to the very tone
Even of her voice, they said were like to mine;
But soften'd all, and temper'd into beauty;
She had the same lone thoughts and wanderings,
110   The quest of hidden knowledge, and a mind
To comprehend the universe: nor these
Alone, but with them gentler powers than mine,
Pity, and smiles, and tears—which I had not;
And tenderness—but that I had for her;
115   Humility—and that I never had.
Her faults were mine—her virtues were her own—
I loved her, and destroy'd her!
WITCH.   With thy hand?
MAN.   Not with my hand, but heart—which broke her heart—
It gazed on mine, and wither'd. I have shed
120   Blood, but not hers—and yet her blood was shed—
I saw—and could not stanch it.
WITCH.   And for this—
A being of the race thou dost despise,
The order which thine own would rise above,
Mingling with us and ours, thou dost forego
125   The gifts of our great knowledge, and shrink'st back
To recreant mortality——Away!
MAN.   Daughter of Air! I tell thee, since that hour—
But words are breath—look on me in my sleep,
Or watch my watchings—Come and sit by me!
130   My solitude is solitude no more,
But peopled with the Furies;—I have gnash'd
My teeth in darkness till returning morn,
Then cursed myself till sunset;—I have pray'd
For madness as a blessing—'tis denied me.
135   I have affronted death—but in the war
Of elements the waters shrunk from me,
And fatal things pass'd harmless—the cold hand
Of an all-pitiless demon held me back,
Back by a single hair, which would not break.
140   In fantasy, imagination, all

The affluence of my soul—which one day was
A Croesus in creation[6]—I plunged deep,
But, like an ebbing wave, it dash'd me back
Into the gulf of my unfathom'd thought.

145   I plunged amidst mankind—Forgetfulness
I sought in all, save where 'tis to be found,
And that I have to learn—my sciences,[7]
My long pursued and super-human art,
Is mortal here—I dwell in my despair—
And live—and live for ever.

150 WITCH.   It may be
That I can aid thee.

MAN.   To do this thy power
Must wake the dead, or lay me low with them.
Do so—in any shape—in any hour—
With any torture—so it be the last.

155 WITCH.   That is not in my province; but if thou
Wilt swear obedience to my will, and do
My bidding, it may help thee to thy wishes.

MAN.   I will not swear—Obey! and whom? the spirits
Whose presence I command, and be the slave
Of those who served me—Never!

160 WITCH.   Is this all?
Hast thou no gentler answer?—Yet bethink thee,
And pause ere thou rejectest.

MAN.   I have said it.

WITCH.   Enough!—I may retire then—say!

MAN.   Retire!

[*The* WITCH *disappears.*]

MAN. (*alone*).   We are the fools of time and terror: Days

165   Steal on us and steal from us; yet we live,
Loathing our life, and dreading still to die.
In all the days of this detested yoke—
This heaving burthen, this accursed breath,
This vital weight upon the struggling heart,

170   Which sinks with sorrow, or beats quick with pain,
Or joy that ends in agony or faintness—
In all the days of past and future, for
In life there is no present, we can number
How few—how less than few—wherein the soul

175   Forbears to pant for death, and yet draws back
As from a stream in winter, though the chill
Be but a moment's. I have one resource
Still in my science—I can call the dead,
And ask them what it is we dread to be:

180   The sternest answer can but be the Grave,
And that is nothing—if they answer not—

6. I.e., my imagination had at one time been, in its creative powers, as rich as King Croesus (the legendary monarch famed for his wealth). Manfred's self-description in this passage, as longing for a death that is denied him, is modeled on the legend, often treated in Romantic literature, of the Wandering Jew.
7. Occult bodies of knowledge.

The buried Prophet answered to the Hag
Of Endor;[8] and the Spartan Monarch drew
From the Byzantine maid's unsleeping spirit
185 An answer and his destiny—he slew
That which he loved, unknowing what he slew,
And died unpardon'd—though he call'd in aid
The Phyxian Jove, and in Phigalia roused
The Arcadian Evocators to compel
190 The indignant shadow to depose her wrath,[9]
Or fix her term of vengeance—she replied
In words of dubious import, but fulfill'd.
If I had never lived, that which I love
Had still been living; had I never loved,
195 That which I love would still be beautiful—
Happy and giving happiness. What is she?
What is she now?—a sufferer for my sins—
A thing I dare not think upon—or nothing.
Within few hours I shall not call in vain—
200 Yet in this hour I dread the thing I dare:
Until this hour I never shrunk to gaze
On spirit, good or evil—now I tremble,
And feel a strange cold thaw upon my heart.
But I can act even what I most abhor,
205 And champion human fears.—The night approaches.
                                        [*Exit.*]

SCENE 3

The Summit of the Jungfrau Mountain.

Enter FIRST DESTINY.[1]
The moon is rising broad, and round, and bright;
And here on snows, where never human foot
Of common mortal trod, we nightly tread,
And leave no traces; o'er the savage sea,
5   The glassy ocean of the mountain ice,
We skim its rugged breakers, which put on
The aspect of a tumbling tempest's foam,
Frozen in a moment—a dead whirlpool's image.
And this most steep fantastic pinnacle,
10   The fretwork of some earthquake—where the clouds
Pause to repose themselves in passing by—
Is sacred to our revels, or our vigils;

8. The Woman of Endor, at the behest of King Saul, summoned up the spirit of the dead prophet Samuel, who foretold that in an impending battle the Philistines would conquer the Israelites and kill Saul and his sons (1 Samuel 28.7–19).
9. Plutarch relates that King Pausanias ("the Spartan Monarch") had accidentally killed Cleonice ("the Byzantine maid"), whom he desired as his mistress. Her ghost haunted him until he called up her spirit to beg her forgiveness. She told him, enigmatically, that he would quickly be freed from his troubles; soon after that, he was killed. Another Pausanias, author of the *Description of Greece,* adds the details that King Pausanias, in the vain attempt to purge his guilt, had called for aid from Jupiter Phyxius and consulted the Evocators at Phigalia, in Arcadia, who had the power to call up the souls of the dead.
1. The three Destinies are modeled on both the witches of Shakespeare's *Macbeth* and the three Fates of classical mythology, who, in turn, spin, measure, and then cut the thread of an individual's life.

Here do I wait my sisters, on our way
To the Hall of Arimanes,[2] for to-night
15 Is our great festival—'tis strange they come not.

A Voice without, singing.
The Captive Usurper,[3]
  Hurl'd down from the throne,
Lay buried in torpor,
  Forgotten and lone;
20 I broke through his slumbers,
  I shiver'd his chain,
I leagued him with numbers—
  He's Tyrant again!
With the blood of a million he'll answer my care,
25 With a nation's destruction—his flight and despair.

Second Voice, without.
The ship sail'd on, the ship sail'd fast,
But I left not a sail, and I left not a mast;
There is not a plank of the hull or the deck,
And there is not a wretch to lament o'er his wreck;
30 Save one, whom I held, as he swam, by the hair,
And he was a subject well worthy my care;
A traitor on land, and a pirate at sea—
But I saved him to wreak further havoc for me!

First Destiny, *answering.*
The city lies sleeping;
35   The morn, to deplore it,
May dawn on it weeping:
   Sullenly, slowly,
The black plague flew o'er it—
   Thousands lie lowly;
40 Tens of thousands shall perish—
   The living shall fly from
The sick they should cherish;
   But nothing can vanquish
The touch that they die from.
45   Sorrow and anguish,
And evil and dread,
   Envelope a nation—
The blest are the dead,
Who see not the sight
50   Of their own desolation—
This work of a night—
This wreck of a realm—this deed of my doing—
For ages I've done, and shall still be renewing!

2. The name is derived from Ahriman, who in the dualistic Zoroastrian religion was the principle of darkness and evil.
3. Napoleon. The song of the first Voice alludes to Napoleon's escape from his captivity on the island of Elba in March 1815. After his defeat at the Battle of Waterloo he was imprisoned on another island, St. Helena, in October 1815.

Enter the SECOND *and* THIRD DESTINIES.

The Three.
Our hands contain the hearts of men,
55   Our footsteps are their graves;
We only give to take again
        The spirits of our slaves!

FIRST DES.   Welcome!—Where's Nemesis?[4]
SECOND DES.   At some great work;
  But what I know not, for my hands were full.
THIRD DES.   Behold she cometh.

Enter NEMESIS.
60 FIRST DES.   Say, where hast thou been?
  My sisters and thyself are slow to-night.
NEM.   I was detain'd repairing shatter'd thrones,
  Marrying fools, restoring dynasties,[5]
  Avenging men upon their enemies,
65 And making them repent their own revenge;
  Goading the wise to madness; from the dull
  Shaping out oracles to rule the world
  Afresh, for they were waxing out of date,
  And mortals dared to ponder for themselves,
70 To weigh kings in the balance, and to speak
  Of freedom, the forbidden fruit.—Away!
  We have outstay'd the hour—mount we our clouds!
                          [*Exeunt.*]

SCENE 4

*The Hall of Arimanes—Arimanes on his Throne, a Globe
of Fire, surrounded by the Spirits.*

Hymn of the SPIRITS.
Hail to our Master!—Prince of Earth and Air!
  Who walks the clouds and waters—in his hand
The sceptre of the elements, which tear
  Themselves to chaos at his high command!
5 He breatheth—and a tempest shakes the sea;
  He speaketh—and the clouds reply in thunder;
He gazeth—from his glance the sunbeams flee;
  He moveth—earthquakes rend the world asunder.
Beneath his footsteps the volcanoes rise;
10 His shadow is the Pestilence; his path
The comets herald through the crackling skies;
  And planets turn to ashes at his wrath.
To him War offers daily sacrifice;
  To him Death pays his tribute; Life is his,

---

4. The Greek and Roman goddess of vengeance, particularly of the sin of hubris, overweening presumption against the gods.

5. Alluding to Byron's marriage and to the restoration of monarchies across Europe that followed the battle of Waterloo.

15   With all its infinite of agonies—
     And his the spirit of whatever is!

       Enter the DESTINIES *and* NEMESIS.
FIRST DES. Glory to Arimanes! on the earth
 His power increaseth—both my sisters did
 His bidding, nor did I neglect my duty!
20 SECOND DES. Glory to Arimanes! we who bow
 The necks of men, bow down before his throne!
 THIRD DES. Glory to Arimanes! we await
 His nod!
 NEM. Sovereign of Sovereigns! we are thine,
 And all that liveth, more or less, is ours,
25 And most things wholly so; still to increase
 Our power, increasing thine, demands our care,
 And we are vigilant—Thy late commands
 Have been fulfill'd to the utmost.

       Enter MANFRED.
A SPIRIT.   What is here?
 A mortal!—Thou most rash and fatal wretch,
 Bow down and worship!
30 SECOND SPIRIT.   I do know the man—
 A Magian° of great power, and fearful skill!   *magus*
 THIRD SPIRIT. Bow down and worship, slave!—
             What, know'st thou not
 Thine and our Sovereign?—Tremble, and obey!
 ALL THE SPIRITS. Prostrate thyself, and thy condemned clay,
 Child of the Earth! or dread the worst.
35 MAN.   I know it;
 And yet ye see I kneel not.
 FOURTH SPIRIT.   'Twill be taught thee.
 MAN. 'Tis taught already;—many a night on the earth,
 On the bare ground, have I bow'd down my face,
 And strew'd my head with ashes; I have known
40 The fulness of humiliation, for
 I sunk before my vain despair, and knelt
 To my own desolation.
 FIFTH SPIRIT.   Dost thou dare
 Refuse to Arimanes on his throne
 What the whole earth accords, beholding not
45 The terror of his Glory?—Crouch! I say.
 MAN. Bid *him* bow down to that which is above him,
 The overruling Infinite—the Maker
 Who made him not for worship—let him kneel,
 And we will kneel together.
 THE SPIRITS.   Crush the worm!
 Tear him in pieces!—
50 FIRST DES.   Hence! Avaunt!—he's mine.
 Prince of the Powers invisible! This man
 Is of no common order, as his port

And presence here denote; his sufferings
Have been of an immortal nature, like
55 Our own; his knowledge, and his powers and will,
As far as is compatible with clay,
Which clogs the ethereal essence, have been such
As clay hath seldom borne; his aspirations
Have been beyond the dwellers of the earth,
60 And they have only taught him what we know—
That knowledge is not happiness, and science
But an exchange of ignorance for that
Which is another kind of ignorance.
This is not all—the passions, attributes
65 Of earth and heaven, from which no power, nor being,
Nor breath from the worm upwards is exempt,
Have pierced his heart; and in their consequence
Made him a thing, which I, who pity not,
Yet pardon those who pity. He is mine,
70 And thine, it may be—be it so, or not,
No other Spirit in this region hath
A soul like his—or power upon his soul.
NEM.　What doth he here then?
FIRST DES.　　　　　　　Let him answer that.
MAN.　Ye know what I have known; and without power
75 I could not be amongst ye: but there are
Powers deeper still beyond—I come in quest
Of such, to answer unto what I seek.
NEM.　What would'st thou?
MAN.　　　　　　　Thou canst not reply to me.
Call up the dead—my question is for them.
80 NEM.　Great Arimanes, doth thy will avouch°　　　　　　　*confirm*
The wishes of this mortal?
ARI.　　　　　　　Yea.
NEM.　　　　　　　Whom would'st thou
Uncharnel?
MAN.　　One without a tomb—call up Astarte.[6]

　　　　　　NEMESIS.
　　　Shadow! or Spirit!
　　　　Whatever thou art,
85　　Which still doth inherit
　　　　The whole or a part
　　　Of the form of thy birth,
　　　　Of the mould of thy clay,
　　　Which return'd to the earth,
90　　Re-appear to the day!
　　　Bear what thou borest,
　　　　The heart and the form,
　　　And the aspect thou worest

6. Byron applies to Manfred's beloved the name of Astarte (also known as Ashtoreth), goddess of love and fertility, the Eastern equivalent of the Greek goddess Aphrodite.

Redeem from the worm.

95   Appear!—Appear!—Appear!

Who sent thee there requires thee here!

[The Phantom of ASTARTE *rises and stands in the midst.]*

MAN.   Can this be death? there's bloom upon her cheek;
    But now I see it is no living hue,
    But a strange hectic°—like the unnatural red   *feverish flush*
100   Which Autumn plants upon the perish'd leaf.
    It is the same! Oh, God! that I should dread
    To look upon the same—Astarte!—No,
    I cannot speak to her—but bid her speak—
    Forgive me or condemn me.

NEMESIS.

105   By the power which hath broken
      The grave which enthrall'd thee,
    Speak to him who hath spoken,
      Or those who have call'd thee!

MAN.   She is silent,
110   And in that silence I am more than answer'd.
NEM.   My power extends no further. Prince of air!
    It rests with thee alone—command her voice.
ARI.   Spirit—obey this sceptre!
NEM.   Silent still!
    She is not of our order, but belongs
115   To the other powers. Mortal! thy quest is vain,
    And we are baffled also.
MAN.   Hear me, hear me—
    Asarte! my beloved! speak to me:
    I have so much endured—so much endure—
    Look on me! the grave hath not changed thee more
120   Than I am changed for thee. Thou lovedst me
    Too much, as I loved thee: we were not made
    To torture thus each other, though it were
    The deadliest sin to love as we have loved.
    Say that thou loath'st me not—that I do bear
125   This punishment for both—that thou wilt be
    One of the blessed—and that I shall die;
    For hitherto all hateful things conspire
    To bind me in existence—in a life
    Which makes me shrink from immortality—
130   A future like the past. I cannot rest.
    I know not what I ask, nor what I seek:
    I feel but what thou art—and what I am;
    And I would hear yet once before I perish
    The voice which was my music—Speak to me!
135   For I have call'd on thee in the still night,
    Startled the slumbering birds from the hush'd boughs,
    And woke the mountain wolves, and made the caves
    Acquainted with thy vainly echoed name,
    Which answer'd me—many things answer'd me—

140 Spirits and men—but thou wert silent all.
Yet speak to me! I have outwatch'd the stars,
And gazed o'er heaven in vain in search of thee.
Speak to me! I have wander'd o'er the earth,
And never found thy likeness—Speak to me!
145 Look on the fiends around—they feel for me:
I fear them not, and feel for thee alone—
Speak to me! though it be in wrath;—but say—
I reck not what—but let me hear thee once—
This once—once more!
PHANTOM OF ASTARTE.   Manfred!
MAN.   Say on, say on—
150 I live but in the sound—it is thy voice!
PHAN.   Manfred! To-morrow ends thine earthly ills.
Farewell!
MAN.   Yet one word more—am I forgiven?
PHAN.   Farewell!
MAN.   Say, shall we meet again?
PHAN.   Farewell!
MAN.   One word for mercy! Say, thou lovest me.
PHAN.   Manfred!
          [*The Spirit of* ASTARTE *disappears.*]
155 NEM.   She's gone, and will not be recall'd;
Her words will be fulfill'd. Return to the earth.
A SPIRIT.   He is convulsed—This is to be a mortal
And seek the things beyond mortality.
ANOTHER SPIRIT.   Yet, see, he mastereth himself, and makes
160 His torture tributary to his will.
Had he been one of us, he would have made
An awful spirit.
NEM.   Hast thou further question
Of our great sovereign, or his worshippers?
MAN.   None.
NEM.   Then for a time farewell.
MAN.   We meet then—
Where? On the earth?
165 NEM.   That will be seen hereafter.
MAN.   Even as thou wilt: and for the grace accorded
I now depart a debtor. Fare ye well!
                                        [*Exit* MANFRED.]
                    (*Scene closes.*)

Act 3

SCENE 1

A Hall in the Castle of Manfred.

MANFRED *and* HERMAN.

MAN.   What is the hour?
HER.   It wants but one till sunset,
And promises a lovely twilight.

MAN.   Say,
    Are all things so disposed of in the tower
    As I directed?
HER.   All, my lord, are ready:
    Here is the key and casket.
5   MAN.   It is well:
    Thou may'st retire.   [*Exit* HERMAN.]
MAN. (*alone*).   There is a calm upon me—
    Inexplicable stillness! which till now
    Did not belong to what I knew of life.
    If that I did not know philosophy
10   To be of all our vanities the motliest,[7]
    The merest word that ever fool'd the ear
    From out the schoolman's jargon, I should deem
    The golden secret, the sought "Kalon,"[8] found,
    And seated in my soul. It will not last,
15   But it is well to have known it, though but once:
    It hath enlarged my thoughts with a new sense,
    And I within my tablets would note down
    That there is such a feeling. Who is there?

Re-enter HERMAN.

HER.   My lord, the abbot of St. Maurice[9] craves
    To greet your presence.

Enter the ABBOT OF ST. MAURICE.

20   ABBOT.   Peace be with Count Manfred!
MAN.   Thanks, holy father! welcome to these walls;
    Thy presence honours them, and blesseth those
    Who dwell within them.
ABBOT.   Would it were so, Count!—
    But I would fain confer with thee alone.
25   MAN.   Herman, retire.—What would my reverend guest?
                [*Exit* HERMAN.]
ABBOT.   Thus, without prelude:—Age and zeal, my office,[1]
    And good intent, must plead my privilege;
    Our near, though not acquainted neighbourhood,
    May also be my herald. Rumours strange,
30   And of unholy nature, are abroad,
    And busy with thy name; a noble name
    For centuries: may he who bears it now
    Transmit it unimpaired!
MAN.   Proceed,—I listen.
ABBOT.   'Tis said thou holdest converse with the things
35   Which are forbidden to the search of man;
    That with the dwellers of the dark abodes,
    The many evil and unheavenly spirits

7. "The most diverse" or, possibly, "the most foolish" (*motley* was the multicolored suit worn by a court jester).
8. Greek for both "the Beautiful" and "the Good."
9. In the Rhone Valley in Switzerland.
1. Position in the church.

Which walk the valley of the shade of death,
Thou communest. I know that with mankind,
40   Thy fellows in creation, thou dost rarely
Exchange thy thoughts, and that thy solitude
Is as an anchorite's,[2] were it but holy.
MAN.   And what are they who do avouch these things?
ABBOT.   My pious brethren—the scared peasantry—
45   Even thy own vassals—who do look on thee
With most unquiet eyes. Thy life's in peril.
MAN.   Take it.
ABBOT.   I come to save, and not destroy—
I would not pry into thy secret soul;
But if these things be sooth, there still is time
50   For penitence and pity: reconcile thee
With the true church, and through the church to heaven.
MAN.   I hear thee. This is my reply: whate'er
I may have been, or am, doth rest between
Heaven and myself.—I shall not choose a mortal
55   To be my mediator. Have I sinn'd
Against your ordinances? prove and punish!
ABBOT.   My son! I did not speak of punishment,
But penitence and pardon;—with thyself
The choice of such remains—and for the last,
60   Our institutions and our strong belief
Have given me power to smooth the path from sin
To higher hope and better thoughts; the first
I leave to heaven,—"Vengeance is mine alone!"
So saith the Lord,[3] and with all humbleness
65   His servant echoes back the awful word.
MAN.   Old man! there is no power in holy men,
Nor charm in prayer—nor purifying form
Of penitence—nor outward look—nor fast—
Nor agony—nor, greater than all these,
70   The innate tortures of that deep despair,
Which is remorse without the fear of hell,
But all in all sufficient to itself
Would make a hell of heaven—can exorcise
From out the unbounded spirit the quick sense
75   Of its own sins, wrongs, sufferance, and revenge
Upon itself; there is no future pang
Can deal that justice on the self-condemn'd
He deals on his own soul.
ABBOT.   All this is well;
For this will pass away, and be succeeded
80   By an auspicious hope, which shall look up
With calm assurance to that blessed place,
Which all who seek may win, whatever be

2. A person who, for religious reasons, lives in seclusion.

3. Romans 12.19: "Vengeance is mine; I will repay, saith the Lord."

Their earthly errors, so they be atoned:
And the commencement of atonement is
85 The sense of its necessity.—Say on—
And all our church can teach thee shall be taught;
And all we can absolve thee shall be pardon'd.
MAN.　When Rome's sixth emperor[4] was near his last,
The victim of a self-inflicted wound,
90 To shun the torments of a public death
From senates once his slaves, a certain soldier,
With show of loyal pity, would have stanch'd
The gushing throat with his officious robe;
The dying Roman thrust him back, and said—
95 Some empire still in his expiring glance—
"It is too late—is this fidelity?"
ABBOT.　And what of this?
MAN.　　　　　　　　I answer with the Roman—
"It is too late!"
ABBOT.　　　　It never can be so,
To reconcile thyself with thy own soul,
100 And thy own soul with heaven. Hast thou no hope?
'Tis strange—even those who do despair above,
Yet shape themselves some fantasy on earth,
To which frail twig they cling, like drowning men.
MAN.　Ay—father! I have had those earthly visions
105 And noble aspirations in my youth,
To make my own the mind of other men,
The enlightener of nations; and to rise
I knew not whither—it might be to fall;
But fall, even as the mountain-cataract,
110 Which having leapt from its more dazzling height,
Even in the foaming strength of its abyss
(Which casts up misty columns that become
Clouds raining from the re-ascended skies),
Lies low but mighty still.—But this is past,
My thoughts mistook themselves.
115 ABBOT.　　　　　　　　　And wherefore so?
MAN.　I could not tame my nature down; for he
Must serve who fain would sway—and soothe—and sue—
And watch all time—and pry into all place—
And be a living lie—who would become
120 A mighty thing amongst the mean, and such
The mass are; I disdain'd to mingle with
A herd, though to be leader—and of wolves.
The lion is alone, and so am I.
ABBOT.　And why not live and act with other men?
125 MAN.　Because my nature was averse from life;
And yet not cruel; for I would not make,
But find a desolation:—like the wind,

---

4. Byron transfers to Otho, the sixth emperor, a story that the historian Suetonius tells about the death of an earlier emperor, Nero.

The red-hot breath of the most lone Simoom,[5]
Which dwells but in the desert, and sweeps o'er
130   The barren sands which bear no shrubs to blast,
And revels o'er their wild and arid waves,
And seeketh not, so that it is not sought,
But being met is deadly; such hath been
The course of my existence; but there came
Things in my path which are no more.

135 ABBOT.   Alas!
I 'gin to fear that thou art past all aid
From me and from my calling; yet so young,
I still would——

MAN.   Look on me! there is an order
Of mortals on the earth, who do become
140   Old in their youth, and die ere middle age,
Without the violence of warlike death;
Some perishing of pleasure—some of study—
Some worn with toil—some of mere weariness—
Some of disease—and some insanity—
145   And some of wither'd, or of broken hearts;
For this last is a malady which slays
More than are number'd in the lists of Fate,
Taking all shapes, and bearing many names.
Look upon me! for even of all these things
150   Have I partaken; and of all these things,
One were enough; then wonder not that I
Am what I am, but that I ever was,
Or having been, that I am still on earth.

ABBOT.   Yet, hear me still——

MAN.   Old man! I do respect
155   Thine order, and revere thine years; I deem
Thy purpose pious, but it is in vain:
Think me not churlish; I would spare thyself,
Far more than me, in shunning at this time
All further colloquy—and so—farewell.

                             [*Exit* MANFRED.]

160 ABBOT.   This should have been a noble creature: he
Hath all the energy which would have made
A goodly frame of glorious elements,
Had they been wisely mingled; as it is,
It is an awful chaos—light and darkness—
165   And mind and dust—and passions and pure thoughts
Mix'd, and contending without end or order,
All dormant or destructive: he will perish,
And yet he must not; I will try once more,
For such are worth redemption; and my duty
170   Is to dare all things for a righteous end.
I'll follow him—but cautiously, though surely.

                             [*Exit* ABBOT.]

---

5. A hot, sand-laden wind in the Sahara and Arabian deserts.

SCENE 2

Another Chamber.

MANFRED *and* HERMAN.

HER.   My lord, you bade me wait on you at sunset:
    He sinks behind the mountain.
MAN.   Doth he so?
    I will look on him.
[MANFRED advances to the Window of the Hall.]
Glorious Orb! the idol
    Of early nature, and the vigorous race
5   Of undiseased mankind, the giant sons
    Of the embrace of angels, with a sex
    More beautiful than they, which did draw down
    The erring spirits[6] who can ne'er return.—
    Most glorious orb! that wert a worship, ere
10   The mystery of thy making was reveal'd!
    Thou earliest minister of the Almighty,
    Which gladden'd, on their mountain tops, the hearts
    Of the Chaldean° shepherds, till they pour'd   *Babylonian*
    Themselves in orisons!° Thou material God!   *prayers*
15   And representative of the Unknown—
    Who chose thee for his shadow! Thou chief star!
    Centre of many stars! which mak'st our earth
    Endurable, and temperest the hues
    And hearts of all who walk within thy rays!
20   Sire of the seasons! Monarch of the climes,
    And those who dwell in them! for near or far,
    Our inborn spirits have a tint of thee,
    Even as our outward aspects;—thou dost rise,
    And shine, and set in glory. Fare thee well!
25   I ne'er shall see thee more. As my first glance
    Of love and wonder was for thee, then take
    My latest look: thou wilt not beam on one
    To whom the gifts of life and warmth have been
    Of a more fatal nature. He is gone:
30   I follow.
[Exit MANFRED.]

SCENE 3

*The Mountains—The Castle of Manfred at some distance—
A Terrace before a Tower.—Time, Twilight.*

HERMAN, MANUEL, *and other Dependants of* MANFRED.

HER.   'Tis strange enough; night after night, for years,
    He hath pursued long vigils in this tower,
    Without a witness. I have been within it,—

---

6. Genesis 6.4: "There were giants in the earth in those days; and also after that, when the sons of God came in unto the daughters of men, and they bare children to them, the same became mighty men which were of old, men of renown." Byron interprets "the sons of God" as denoting disobedient angels.

So have we all been oft-times; but from it,
5   Or its contents, it were impossible
To draw conclusions absolute, of aught
His studies tend to. To be sure, there is
One chamber where none enter: I would give
The fee° of what I have to come these three years,   *ownership*
10   To pore upon its mysteries.
MANUEL.   'Twere dangerous;
Content thyself with what thou know'st already.
HER.   Ah! Manuel! thou art elderly and wise,
And couldst say much; thou hast dwelt within the castle—
How many years is't?
MANUEL.   Ere Count Manfred's birth,
15   I served his father, whom he nought resembles.
HER.   There be more sons in like predicament.
But wherein do they differ?
MANUEL.   I speak not
Of features or of form, but mind and habits;
Count Sigismund was proud,—but gay and free,—
20   A warrior and a reveller; he dwelt not
With books and solitude, nor made the night
A gloomy vigil, but a festal time,
Merrier than day; he did not walk the rocks
And forests like a wolf, nor turn aside
25   From men and their delights.
HER.   Beshrew[7] the hour,
But those were jocund times! I would that such
Would visit the old walls again; they look
As if they had forgotten them.
MANUEL.   These walls
Must change their chieftain first. Oh! I have seen
Some strange things in them, Herman.
30 HER.   Come, be friendly;
Relate me some to while away our watch:
I've heard thee darkly speak of an event
Which happen'd hereabouts, by this same tower.
MANUEL.   That was a night indeed! I do remember
35   'Twas twilight, as it may be now, and such
Another evening;—yon red cloud, which rests
On Eigher's[8] pinnacle, so rested then,—
So like that it might be the same; the wind
Was faint and gusty, and the mountain snows
40   Began to glitter with the climbing moon;
Count Manfred was, as now, within his tower,—
How occupied, we knew not, but with him
The sole companion of his wanderings
And watchings—her, whom of all earthly things
45   That lived, the only thing he seem'd to love,—
As he, indeed, by blood was bound to do,

7. Curse (used jokingly).   8. A peak a few miles north of the Jungfrau.

The lady Astarte, his——
                Hush! who comes here?
Enter the ABBOT.
ABBOT.   Where is your master?
HER.   Yonder, in the tower.
ABBOT.   I must speak with him.
MANUEL.   'Tis impossible;

50   He is most private, and must not be thus
Intruded on.
ABBOT.   Upon myself I take
The forfeit of my fault, if fault there be—
But I must see him.
HER.   Thou hast seen him once
This eve already.
ABBOT.   Sirrah! I command thee,

55   Knock, and apprize the Count of my approach.
HER.   We dare not.
ABBOT.   Then it seems I must be herald
Of my own purpose.
MANUEL.   Reverend father, stop—
I pray you pause.
ABBOT.   Why so?
MANUEL.   But step this way,
And I will tell you further.
                            [*Exeunt.*]

SCENE 4

Interior of the Tower.

MANFRED *alone.*
The stars are forth, the moon above the tops
Of the snow-shining mountains.—Beautiful!
I linger yet with Nature, for the night
Hath been to me a more familiar face

5   Than that of man; and in her starry shade
Of dim and solitary loveliness,
I learn'd the language of another world.
I do remember me, that in my youth,
When I was wandering,—upon such a night

10   I stood within the Coliseum's wall,
Midst the chief relics of almighty Rome;
The trees which grew along the broken arches
Waved dark in the blue midnight, and the stars
Shone through the rents of ruin; from afar

15   The watchdog bay'd beyond the Tiber;[9] and
More near from out the Caesars' palace[1] came
The owl's long cry, and, interruptedly,
Of distant sentinels the fitful song

9. The river that flows through Rome.
1. The palace of the Roman emperors. It stands   on the Palatine hill, immediately southwest of the Coliseum.

Begun and died upon the gentle wind.
20 Some cypresses beyond the time-worn breach
Appear'd to skirt the horizon, yet they stood
Within a bowshot—where the Caesars dwelt,
And dwell the tuneless birds of night amidst
A grove which springs through levell'd battlements
25 And twines its roots with the imperial hearths.
Ivy usurps the laurel's place of growth;—
But the gladiators' bloody Circus[2] stands,
A noble wreck in ruinous perfection!
While Caesar's chambers, and the Augustan halls,
30 Grovel on earth in indistinct decay.—
And thou didst shine, thou rolling moon, upon
All this, and cast a wide and tender light,
Which soften'd down the hoar austerity
Of rugged desolation, and fill'd up,
35 As 'twere anew, the gaps of centuries;
Leaving that beautiful which still was so,
And making that which was not, till the place
Became religion, and the heart ran o'er
With silent worship of the great of old!—
40 The dead, but sceptred sovereigns, who still rule
Our spirits from their urns.—
                           'Twas such a night!
'Tis strange that I recall it at this time;
But I have found our thoughts take wildest flight
Even at the moment when they should array
Themselves in pensive order.
           Enter the ABBOT.
45 ABBOT.   My good lord!
I crave a second grace for this approach;
But yet let not my humble zeal offend
By its abruptness—all it hath of ill
Recoils on me; its good in the effect
50 May light upon your head—could I say *heart*—
Could I touch *that*, with words or prayers, I should
Recall a noble spirit which hath wander'd
But is not yet all lost.
MAN.   Thou know'st me not;
My days are number'd, and my deeds recorded:
55 Retire, or 'twill be dangerous—Away!
ABBOT.   Thou dost not mean to menace me?
MAN.   Not I;
I simply tell thee peril is at hand,
And would preserve thee.
ABBOT.   What dost thou mean?
MAN.   Look there!
What dost thou see?

---

2. The circular arena within the Coliseum where professional gladiators fought to the death as public entertainment.

ABBOT.   Nothing.

MAN.   Look there, I say,

60   And steadfastly;—now tell me what thou seest?

ABBOT.   That which should shake me,—but I fear it not—
      I see a dusk and awful figure rise
      Like an infernal god from out the earth;
      His face wrapt in a mantle, and his form

65   Robed as with angry clouds: he stands between
      Thyself and me—but I do fear him not.

MAN.   Thou hast no cause—he shall not harm thee—but
      His sight may shock thine old limbs into palsy.
      I say to thee—Retire!

ABBOT.   And I reply—

70   Never—till I have battled with this fiend:—
      What doth he here?

MAN.   Why—ay—what doth he here?
      I did not send for him,—he is unbidden.

ABBOT.   Alas! lost mortal! what with guests like these
      Hast thou to do? I tremble for thy sake:

75   Why doth he gaze on thee, and thou on him?
      Ah! he unveils his aspect: on his brow
      The thunder-scars are graven; from his eye
      Glares forth the immortality of hell—
      Avaunt!——

MAN.   Pronounce—what is thy mission?

SPIRIT.   Come!

80   ABBOT.   What art thou, unknown being? answer!—speak!

SPIRIT.   The genius[3] of this mortal.—Come! 'tis time.

MAN.   I am prepared for all things, but deny
      The power which summons me. Who sent thee here?

SPIRIT.   Thou'lt know anon—Come! come!

MAN.   I have commanded

85   Things of an essence greater far than thine,
      And striven with thy masters. Get thee hence!

SPIRIT.   Mortal! thine hour is come—Away! I say.

MAN.   I knew, and know my hour is come, but not
      To render up my soul to such as thee:

90   Away! I'll die as I have lived—alone.

SPIRIT.   Then I must summon up my brethren.—Rise!
                    [Other Spirits rise up.]

ABBOT.   Avaunt! ye evil ones!—Avaunt! I say,—
      Ye have no power where piety hath power,
      And I do charge ye in the name—

SPIRIT.   Old man!

95   We know ourselves, our mission, and thine order;
      Waste not thy holy words on idle uses,
      It were in vain: this man is forfeited.
      Once more I summon him—Away! away!

MAN.   I do defy ye,—though I feel my soul

---

3. The spirit or deity presiding over a human being from birth.

100 Is ebbing from me, yet I do defy ye;
Nor will I hence, while I have earthly breath
To breathe my scorn upon ye—earthly strength
To wrestle, though with spirits; what ye take
Shall be ta'en limb by limb.

SPIRIT.   Reluctant mortal!
105 Is this the Magian who would so pervade
The world invisible, and make himself
Almost our equal?—Can it be that thou
Art thus in love with life? the very life
Which made thee wretched!

MAN.   Thou false fiend, thou liest!
110 My life is in its last hour,—*that* I know,
Nor would redeem a moment of that hour;
I do not combat against death, but thee
And thy surrounding angels; my past power
Was purchased by no compact with thy crew,
115 But by superior science—penance—daring—
And length of watching—strength of mind—and skill
In knowledge of our fathers—when the earth
Saw men and spirits walking side by side,
And gave ye no supremacy: I stand
120 Upon my strength—I do defy—deny—
Spurn back, and scorn ye!—

SPIRIT.   But thy many crimes
Have made thee——

MAN.   What are they to such as thee?
Must crimes be punish'd but by other crimes,
And greater criminals?—Back to thy hell!
125 Thou hast no power upon me, *that* I feel;
Thou never shalt possess me, *that* I know:
What I have done is done; I bear within
A torture which could nothing gain from thine:
The mind which is immortal makes itself
130 Requital for its good or evil thoughts—
Is its own origin of ill and end—
And its own place and time[4]—its innate sense,
When stripp'd of this mortality, derives
No colour from the fleeting things without,
135 But is absorb'd in sufferance or in joy,
Born from the knowledge of its own desert.
Thou didst not tempt me, and thou couldst not tempt me;
I have not been thy dupe, nor am thy prey—
But was my own destroyer, and will be
140 My own hereafter.—Back, ye baffled fiends!
The hand of death is on me—but not yours!
        [*The Demons disappear.*]

---

4. The last of several echoes by Manfred of Satan's claim that "The mind is its own place, and in itself / Can make a Heaven of Hell, and a Hell of Heaven" (*Paradise Lost* 1.254–55). See also lines 1.1.251 (p. 641) and 3.1.70–73 (p. 659).

ABBOT.   Alas! how pale thou art—thy lips are white—
    And thy breast heaves—and in thy gasping throat
    The accents rattle—Give thy prayers to heaven—
145 Pray—albeit but in thought,—but die not thus.
MAN.   'Tis over—my dull eyes can fix thee not;
    But all things swim around me, and the earth
    Heaves as it were beneath me. Fare thee well—
    Give me thy hand.
ABBOT.   Cold—cold—even to the heart—
150 But yet one prayer—Alas! how fares it with thee?
MAN.   Old man! 'tis not so difficult to die.[5]
          [MANFRED *expires.*]
ABBOT.   He's gone—his soul hath ta'en its earthless flight—
    Whither? I dread to think—but he is gone.

1816–17   1817

Don Juan

Don Juan   Byron began his masterpiece (pronounced in the English fashion,
Don Joó-un) in July 1818, published it in installments beginning with cantos 1 and
2 in 1819, and continued working on it almost until his death. Initially he improvised the poem from episode to episode. "I *have* no plan," he said, "I *had* no plan;
but I had or have materials." The work was composed with remarkable speed (the
888 lines of canto 13, for example, were dashed off within a week), and it aims at
the effect of improvisation rather than of artful compression; it asks to be read rapidly, at a conversational pace.

   The poem breaks off with the sixteenth canto, but even in its unfinished state *Don
Juan* is the longest satirical poem, and indeed one of the longest poems of any kind, in
English. Its hero, the Spanish libertine, had in the original legend been superhuman
in his sexual energy and wickedness. Throughout Byron's version the unspoken but
persistent joke is that this archetypal lady-killer of European legend is in fact more
acted upon than active. Unfailingly amiable and well intentioned, he is guilty largely
of youth, charm, and a courteous and compliant spirit. The women do all the rest.

   The chief models for the poem were the Italian seriocomic versions of medieval
chivalric romances; the genre had been introduced by Pulci in the fifteenth century
and was adopted by Ariosto in his *Orlando Furioso* (1532). From these writers Byron
caught the mixed moods and violent oscillations between the sublime and the ridiculous as well as the colloquial management of the complex ottava rima—an eight-
line stanza in which the initial interlaced rhymes (*ababab*) build up to the comic turn
in the final couplet (*cc*). Byron was influenced in the English use of this Italian form
by a mildly amusing poem published in 1817, under the pseudonym of "Whistle-
craft," by his friend John Hookham Frere. Other recognizable antecedents of *Don
Juan* are Jonathan Swift's *Gulliver's Travels* and Samuel Johnson's *Rasselas*, both of
which had employed the naive traveler as a satiric device, and Laurence Sterne's
novel *Tristram Shandy*, with its comic exploitation of a narrative medium blatantly
subject to the whimsy of the author. But even the most original literary works play
variations on inherited conventions. Shelley at once recognized his friend's poem as
"something wholly new and relative to the age."

   Byron's literary advisers thought the poem unacceptably immoral, and John Murray took the precaution of printing the first two installments (cantos 1–2, then 3–5)

5. When this line was dropped in the printing of
the first edition, Byron wrote angrily to his publisher: "You have destroyed the whole effect and
moral of the poem by omitting the last line of
Manfred's speaking."

without identifying Byron as the author or himself as the publisher. The eleven completed cantos that followed were, because of Murray's continuing jitters, brought out in 1823–24 by the radical publisher John Hunt. In those cantos Byron's purpose deepened. He set out to create a comic yet devastatingly critical history of the Europe of his own age, sending the impressionable Juan from west to east and back again, from his native Spain to a Russian court (by way of a primitive Greek island and the 1790 siege of the Turkish town of Ismail) and then into the English gentry's country manors. These journeys, which facilitated Byron's satire on almost all existing forms of political organization, would, according to the scheme that he projected for the poem as a whole, ultimately have taken Juan to a death by guillotining in Revolutionary France.

Yet the controlling element of *Don Juan* is not the narrative but the narrator. His running commentary on Juan's misadventures, his reminiscences, and his opinionated remarks on the epoch of political reaction in which he is actually telling Juan's story together add another level to the poem's engagement with history. The narrator's reflections also at the same time lend unity to *Don Juan*'s effervescent variety. Tellingly, the poem opens with the first-person pronoun and immediately lets us into the storyteller's predicament: "I want a hero. . . ." The voice then goes on, for almost two thousand stanzas, with effortless volubility and shifts of mood. The poet, who in his brilliant successful youth created the gloomy Byronic hero, in his later and sadder life created a character (not the hero, but the narrator of *Don Juan*) who is one of the great comic inventions in English literature.

From Don Juan

Fragment[1]

On the back of the Poet's MS. of Canto I

I would to heaven that I were so much clay,
    As I am blood, bone, marrow, passion, feeling—
Because at least the past were pass'd away—
    And for the future—(but I write this reeling,
Having got drunk exceedingly to-day,
    So that I seem to stand upon the ceiling)
I say—the future is a serious matter—
And so—for God's sake—hock° and soda-water!   *German wine*

From Cante the First

[JUAN AND DONNA JULIA]

1

I want a hero: an uncommon want,
    When every year and month sends forth a new one,
Till, after cloying the gazettes with cant,

---

1. This stanza was written on the back of a page of the manuscript of canto 1. For the author's revisions while composing two stanzas of *Don Juan*, see "Poems in Process" in the NAEL Archive.

    The age discovers he is not the true one;
5 Of such as these I should not care to vaunt,
      I'll therefore take our ancient friend Don Juan—
    We all have seen him, in the pantomime,[1]
    Sent to the devil somewhat ere his time.

*   *   *

5

    Brave men were living before Agamemnon[2]
      And since, exceeding valorous and sage,
35 A good deal like him too, though quite the same none;
      But then they shone not on the poet's page,
    And so have been forgotten:—I condemn none,
      But can't find any in the present age
    Fit for my poem (that is, for my new one);
40 So, as I said, I'll take my friend Don Juan.

6

    Most epic poets plunge "in medias res"[3]
      (Horace makes this the heroic turnpike road),[4]
    And then your hero tells, whene'er you please,
      What went before—by way of episode,
45 While seated after dinner at his ease,
      Beside his mistress in some soft abode,
    Palace, or garden, paradise, or cavern,
    Which serves the happy couple for a tavern.

7

    That is the usual method, but not mine—
50   My way is to begin with the beginning;
    The regularity of my design
      Forbids all wandering as the worst of sinning,
    And therefore I shall open with a line
      (Although it cost me half an hour in spinning)
55 Narrating somewhat of Don Juan's father,
    And also of his mother, if you'd rather.

8

    In Seville was he born, a pleasant city,
      Famous for oranges and women—he
    Who has not seen it will be much to pity,
60   So says the proverb—and I quite agree;
    Of all the Spanish towns is none more pretty,

---

1. The Juan of legend was a popular subject in English pantomime.
2. In Homer's *Iliad* the king commanding the Greeks in the siege of Troy. This line is translated from a Latin ode by Horace.
3. Into the middle of things (Latin; Horace's *Art of Poetry* 148).
4. I.e., the smoothest road for heroic poetry.

Cadiz perhaps—but that you soon may see:—
Don Juan's parents lived beside the river,
A noble stream, and call'd the Guadalquivir.

9

65 His father's name was Jóse[5]—*Don*, of course,
A true Hidalgo,° free from every stain   nobleman
Of Moor or Hebrew blood, he traced his source
Through the most Gothic gentlemen of Spain;
A better cavalier ne'er mounted horse,
70 Or, being mounted, e'er got down again,
Than Jóse, who begot our hero, who
Begot—but that's to come—Well, to renew:

10

His mother was a learned lady, famed
For every branch of every science known—
75 In every Christian language ever named,
With virtues equall'd by her wit alone,
She made the cleverest people quite ashamed,
And even the good with inward envy groan,
Finding themselves so very much exceeded
80 In their own way by all the things that she did.

11

Her memory was a mine: she knew by heart
All Calderon and greater part of Lopé,[6]
So that if any actor miss'd his part
She could have served him for the prompter's copy;
85 For her Feinagle's[7] were an useless art,
And he himself obliged to shut up shop—he
Could never make a memory so fine as
That which adorn'd the brain of Donna Inez.

12

Her favourite science was the mathematical,
90 Her noblest virtue was her magnanimity,
Her wit (she sometimes tried at wit) was Attic[8] all,
Her serious sayings darken'd to sublimity;
In short, in all things she was fairly what I call
A prodigy—her morning dress was dimity,°   cotton
95 Her evening silk, or, in the summer, muslin,
And other stuffs, with which I won't stay puzzling.

---

5. Normally "José"; Byron transferred the accent
to keep his meter.
6. Calderón de la Barca and Lope de Vega, the
great Spanish dramatists of the early 17th century.
7. Gregor von Feinagle, a German expert on the
art of memory who had lectured in England in
1811.
8. Athenian. *Attic salt* is a term for the famed
wit of the Athenians.

13

She knew the Latin—that is, "the Lord's prayer,"
    And Greek—the alphabet—I'm nearly sure;
She read some French romances here and there,
100   Although her mode of speaking was not pure;
For native Spanish she had no great care,
    At least her conversation was obscure;
Her thoughts were theorems, her words a problem,
As if she deem'd that mystery would ennoble 'em.

*   *   *

22

'Tis pity learned virgins ever wed
170   With persons of no sort of education,
Or gentlemen, who, though well born and bred,
    Grow tired of scientific conversation:
I don't choose to say much upon this head,
    I'm a plain man, and in a single station,
175 But—Oh! ye lords of ladies intellectual,
Inform us truly, have they not hen-peck'd you all?

23

Don Jóse and his lady quarrell'd—*why*,
    Not any of the many could divine,
Though several thousand people chose to try,
180   'Twas surely no concern of theirs nor mine;
I loathe that low vice—curiosity;
    But if there's any thing in which I shine,
'Tis in arranging all my friends' affairs,
Not having, of my own, domestic cares.

24

185 And so I interfered, and with the best
    Intentions, but their treatment was not kind;
I think the foolish people were possess'd,
    For neither of them could I ever find,
Although their porter afterwards confess'd—
190   But that's no matter, and the worst's behind,
For little Juan o'er me threw, down stairs,
A pail of housemaid's water unawares.

25

A little curly-headed, good-for-nothing,
    And mischief-making monkey from his birth;
195 His parents ne'er agreed except in doting
    Upon the most unquiet imp on earth;

Instead of quarrelling, had they been but both in
    Their senses, they'd have sent young master for
To school, or had him soundly whipp'd at home,
200 To teach him manners for the time to come.

26

Don Jóse and the Donna Inez led
    For some time an unhappy sort of life,
Wishing each other, not divorced, but dead;
    They lived respectably as man and wife,
205 Their conduct was exceedingly well-bred,
    And gave no outward signs of inward strife,
Until at length the smother'd fire broke out,
And put the business past all kind of doubt.

27

For Inez call'd some druggists, and physicians,
210   And tried to prove her loving lord was *mad*,[9]
But as he had some lucid intermissions,
    She next decided he was only *bad*;
Yet when they ask'd her for her depositions,
    No sort of explanation could be had,
215 Save that her duty both to man and God
Required this conduct—which seem'd very odd.

28

She kept a journal, where his faults were noted,
    And open'd certain trunks of books and letters,
All which might, if occasion served, be quoted;
220   And then she had all Seville for abettors,
Besides her good old grandmother (who doted);
    The hearers of her case became repeaters,
Then advocates, inquisitors, and judges,
Some for amusement, others for old grudges.

29

225 And then this best and meekest woman bore
    With such serenity her husband's woes,
Just as the Spartan ladies did of yore,
    Who saw their spouses kill'd, and nobly chose
Never to say a word about them more——
230   Calmly she heard each calumny that rose,
And saw *his* agonies with such sublimity,
That all the world exclaim'd, "What magnanimity!

*   *   *

9. Lady Byron had thought her husband might be insane and sought medical advice on the matter. This and other passages obviously allude to his wife, although Byron insisted that Donna Inez was not intended to be a caricature of Lady Byron. In her determination to preserve her son's innocence, Donna Inez also shares traits with Byron's mother.

32

Their friends had tried at reconciliation,
   Then their relations, who made matters worse:
('Twere hard to say upon a like occasion
   To whom it may be best to have recourse—
I can't say much for friend or yet relation):
   The lawyers did their utmost for divorce,
255   But scarce a fee was paid on either side
Before, unluckily, Don Jóse died.

33

He died: and most unluckily, because,
   According to all hints I could collect
From counsel learned in those kinds of laws,
260   (Although their talk's obscure and circumspect)
His death contrived to spoil a charming cause;°   *lawsuit*
   A thousand pities also with respect
To public feeling, which on this occasion
Was manifested in a great sensation.

*   *   *

37

Dying intestate,° Juan was sole heir   *without a will*
290   To a chancery suit, and messuages,[1] and lands,
Which, with a long minority and care,
   Promised to turn out well in proper hands:
Inez became sole guardian, which was fair,
   And answer'd but to nature's just demands;
295   An only son left with an only mother
Is brought up much more wisely than another.

38

Sagest of women, even of widows, she
   Resolved that Juan should be quite a paragon,
And worthy of the noblest pedigree:
300   (His sire was of Castile, his dam from Aragon.)
Then for accomplishments of chivalry,
   In case our lord the king should go to war again,
He learn'd the arts of riding, fencing, gunnery,
And how to scale a fortress—or a nunnery.

39

305   But that which Donna Inez most desired,
   And saw into herself each day before all

---

1. Houses and the adjoining lands. "Chancery suit": a case in what was then the highest English court, notorious for its delays.

The learned tutors whom for him she hired,
 Was, that his breeding should be strictly moral:
Much into all his studies she enquired,
310 And so they were submitted first to her, all,
Arts, sciences, no branch was made a mystery
To Juan's eyes, excepting natural history.[2]

40

The languages, especially the dead,
 The sciences, and most of all the abstruse,
315 The arts, at least all such as could be said
  To be the most remote from common use,
In all these he was much and deeply read;
  But not a page of any thing that's loose,
Or hints continuation of the species,
320 Was ever suffer'd, lest he should grow vicious.

41

His classic studies made a little puzzle,
 Because of filthy loves of gods and goddesses,
Who in the earlier ages made a bustle,
  But never put on pantaloons or bodices;
325 His reverend tutors had at times a tussle,
  And for their Aeneids, Iliads, and Odysseys,
Were forced to make an odd sort of apology,
For Donna Inez dreaded the Mythology.

42

Ovid's a rake, as half his verses show him,
330 Anacreon's morals are a still worse sample,
Catullus scarcely has a decent poem,
  I don't think Sappho's Ode a good example,
Although Longinus[3] tells us there is no hymn
  Where the sublime soars forth on wings more ample;
335 But Virgil's songs are pure, except that horrid one
Beginning with "Formosum Pastor Corydon."[4]

43

Lucretius' irreligion[5] is too strong
 For early stomachs, to prove wholesome food;
I can't help thinking Juvenal[6] was wrong,

2. Includes biology, physiology, and particularly botany, popular in the era in part because study of plants' stamens and pistils offered a form of surreptitious sex education.
3. In *On the Sublime* 10, the Greek rhetorician Longinus praises a passage of erotic longing from one of Sappho's odes.
4. Virgil's *Eclogue* 2 begins: "The shepherd, Corydon, burned with love for the handsome Alexis."
5. In *De Rerum Natura* (*On the Nature of Things*), Lucretius argues that the universe can be explained in entirely materialist terms without reference to any god.
6. The Latin satires of Juvenal attacked the corruption of Roman society in the 1st century C.E. and displayed its vices.

340   Although no doubt his real intent was good,
      For speaking out so plainly in his song,
        So much indeed as to be downright rude;
      And then what proper person can be partial
      To all those nauseous epigrams of Martial?

44

345   Juan was taught from out the best edition,
      Expurgated by learned men, who place,
      Judiciously, from out the schoolboy's vision,
        The grosser parts; but fearful to deface
      Too much their modest bard by this omission,
350   And pitying sore his mutilated case,
      They only add them all in an appendix,[7]
      Which saves, in fact, the trouble of an index;

                    *   *   *

52

    For my part I say nothing—nothing—but
410   *This* I will say—my reasons are my own—
      That if I had an only son to put
        To school (as God be praised that I have none),
      'Tis not with Donna Inez I would shut
        Him up to learn his catechism alone,
415   No—no—I'd send him out betimes to college,
      For there it was I pick'd up my own knowledge.

53

    For there one learns—'tis not for me to boast,
      Though I acquired—but I pass over *that,*
      As well as all the Greek I since have lost:
420   I say that there's the place—but *"Verbum sat,"*[8]
      I think I pick'd up too, as well as most,
        Knowledge of matters—but no matter *what—*
      I never married—but, I think, I know
      That sons should not be educated so.

54

425   Young Juan now was sixteen years of age,
      Tall, handsome, slender, but well knit: he seem'd
      Active, though not so sprightly, as a page;
        And every body but his mother deem'd
      Him almost man; but she flew in a rage

---

7. Fact! There is, or was, such an edition, with all the obnoxious epigrams of Martial placed by themselves at the end [Byron's note]. Martial, another Latin poet, was a contemporary of Juvenal.

8. A word [to the wise] is sufficient (Latin).

430   And bit her lips (for else she might have scream'd)
       If any said so, for to be precocious
       Was in her eyes a thing the most atrocious.

55

       Amongst her numerous acquaintance, all
         Selected for discretion and devotion,
435   There was the Donna Julia, whom to call
         Pretty were but to give a feeble notion
       Of many charms in her as natural
         As sweetness to the flower, or salt to ocean,
       Her zone to Venus,[9] or his bow to Cupid,
440   (But this last simile is trite and stupid.)

56

       The darkness of her Oriental eye
         Accorded with her Moorish origin;
       (Her blood was not all Spanish, by the by;
         In Spain, you know, this is a sort of sin.)
445   When proud Granada fell, and, forced to fly,
         Boabdil wept,[1] of Donna Julia's kin
       Some went to Africa, some stay'd in Spain,
       Her great great grandmamma chose to remain.

57

       She married (I forget the pedigree)
450   With an Hidalgo, who transmitted down
       His blood less noble than such blood should be;
         At such alliances his sires would frown,
       In that point so precise in each degree
         That they bred *in and in*, as might be shown,
455   Marrying their cousins—nay, their aunts, and nieces,
       Which always spoils the breed, if it increases.

58

       This heathenish cross restored the breed again,
         Ruin'd its blood, but much improved its flesh;
       For from a root the ugliest in Old Spain
460   Sprung up a branch as beautiful as fresh;
       The sons no more were short, the daughters plain:
         But there's a rumour which I fain would hush,
       'Tis said that Donna Julia's grandmamma
       Produced her Don more heirs at love than law.

---

9. The belt ("zone") of Venus made its wearer sexually irresistible.
1. The Moorish king of Granada (the last Islamic enclave in Spain) wept when his capital fell and he and his people were forced to emigrate to Africa (1492).

59

465 However this might be, the race° went on   *family line*
    Improving still through every generation,
Until it centred in an only son,
    Who left an only daughter; my narration
May have suggested that this single one
470   Could be but Julia (whom on this occasion
I shall have much to speak about), and she
Was married, charming, chaste,[2] and twenty-three.

60

Her eye (I'm very fond of handsome eyes)
    Was large and dark, suppressing half its fire
475 Until she spoke, then through its soft disguise
    Flash'd an expression more of pride than ire,
And love than either; and there would arise
    A something in them which was not desire,
But would have been, perhaps, but for the soul
480   Which struggled through and chasten'd down the whole.

61

Her glossy hair was cluster'd o'er a brow
    Bright with intelligence, and fair, and smooth;
Her eyebrow's shape was like th' aërial bow,
    Her cheek all purple with the beam of youth,
485 Mounting, at times, to a transparent glow,
    As if her veins ran lightning; she, in sooth,
Possess'd an air and grace by no means common:
Her stature tall—I hate a dumpy woman.

62

Wedded she was some years, and to a man
490   Of fifty, and such husbands are in plenty;
And yet, I think, instead of such a ONE
    'Twere better to have two of five-and-twenty,
Especially in countries near the sun:
    And now I think on't, "mi vien in mente,"[3]
495 Ladies even of the most uneasy virtue
Prefer a spouse whose age is short of thirty.

63

'Tis a sad thing, I cannot choose but say,
    And all the fault of that indecent sun,
Who cannot leave alone our helpless clay,
500   But will keep baking, broiling, burning on,

---

2. I.e., faithful to her husband.   3. It comes to my mind (Italian).

That howsoever people fast and pray,
　　The flesh is frail, and so the soul undone:
What men call gallantry, and gods adultery,
　　Is much more common where the climate's sultry.

64

505　Happy the nations of the moral North!
　　Where all is virtue, and the winter season
Sends sin, without a rag on, shivering forth
　　('Twas snow that brought St. Francis back to reason);
Where juries cast up what a wife is worth,
510　By laying whate'er sum, in mulct,[4] they please on
The lover, who must pay a handsome price,
Because it is a marketable vice.

65

Alfonso was the name of Julia's lord,
　　A man well looking for his years, and who
515　Was neither much beloved nor yet abhorr'd:
　　They lived together, as most people do,
Suffering each other's foibles by accord,
　　And not exactly either *one* or *two*;
Yet he was jealous, though he did not show it,
520　For jealousy dislikes the world to know it.

* * *

69

545　Juan she saw, and, as a pretty child,
　　Caress'd him often—such a thing might be
Quite innocently done, and harmless styled,
　　When she had twenty years, and thirteen he;
But I am not so sure I should have smiled
550　When he was sixteen, Julia twenty-three;
These few short years make wondrous alterations,
Particularly amongst sun-burnt nations.

70

Whate'er the cause might be, they had become
　　Changed; for the dame grew distant, the youth shy,
555　Their looks cast down, their greetings almost dumb,
　　And much embarrassment in either eye;
There surely will be little doubt with some
　　That Donna Julia knew the reason why,
But as for Juan, he had no more notion
560　Than he who never saw the sea of ocean.

---

4. By way of a fine or legal penalty.

71

Yet Julia's very coldness still was kind,
   And tremulously gentle her small hand
Withdrew itself from his, but left behind
   A little pressure, thrilling, and so bland
565 And slight, so very slight, that to the mind
   'Twas but a doubt; but ne'er magician's wand
Wrought change with all Armida's[5] fairy art
Like what this light touch left on Juan's heart.

72

And if she met him, though she smiled no more,
570   She look'd a sadness sweeter than her smile,
As if her heart had deeper thoughts in store
   She must not own, but cherish'd more the while
For that compression in its burning core;
   Even innocence itself has many a wile,
575 And will not dare to trust itself with truth,
   And love is taught hypocrisy from youth.

*   *   *

75

Poor Julia's heart was in an awkward state;
   She felt it going, and resolved to make
595 The noblest efforts for herself and mate,
   For honour's, pride's, religion's, virtue's sake;
Her resolutions were most truly great,
   And almost might have made a Tarquin[6] quake:
She pray'd the Virgin Mary for her grace,
600 As being the best judge of a lady's case.

76

She vow'd she never would see Juan more,
   And next day paid a visit to his mother,
And look'd extremely at the opening door,
   Which, by the Virgin's grace, let in another;
605 Grateful she was, and yet a little sore—
   Again it opens, it can be no other,
'Tis surely Juan now—No! I'm afraid
That night the Virgin was no further pray'd.

---

5. The sorceress in Torquato Tasso's *Jerusalem Delivered* (1581) who seduces Rinaldo into forgetting his vows as a crusader.
6. A member of a legendary family of Roman kings noted for tyranny and cruelty; perhaps a reference specifically to Lucius Tarquinus, the villain of Shakespeare's *The Rape of Lucrece*.

77

She now determined that a virtuous woman
610   Should rather face and overcome temptation,
That flight was base and dastardly, and no man
    Should ever give her heart the least sensation;
That is to say, a thought beyond the common
    Preference, that we must feel upon occasion,
615 For people who are pleasanter than others,
But then they only seem so many brothers.

78

And even if by chance—and who can tell?
    The devil's so very sly—she should discover
That all within was not so very well,
620   And, if still free, that such or such a lover
Might please perhaps, a virtuous wife can quell
    Such thoughts, and be the better when they're over;
And if the man should ask, 'tis but denial:
I recommend young ladies to make trial.

79

625 And then there are such things as love divine,
    Bright and immaculate, unmix'd and pure,
Such as the angels think so very fine,
    And matrons, who would be no less secure,
Platonic, perfect, "just such love as mine:"
630   Thus Julia said—and thought so, to be sure;
And so I'd have her think, were I the man
On whom her reveries celestial ran.

*   *   *

86

So much for Julia. Now we'll turn to Juan,
    Poor little fellow! he had no idea
Of his own case, and never hit the true one;
    In feelings quick as Ovid's Miss Medea,[7]
685 He puzzled over what he found a new one,
    But not as yet imagined it could be a
Thing quite in course, and not at all alarming,
Which, with a little patience, might grow charming.

*   *   *

7. In *Metamorphoses* 7 Ovid tells the story of Medea's mad infatuation for Jason.

90

Young Juan wander'd by the glassy brooks
    Thinking unutterable things; he threw
715 Himself at length within the leafy nooks
    Where the wild branch of the cork forest grew;
There poets find materials for their books,
    And every now and then we read them through,
So that their plan and prosody are eligible,
720 Unless, like Wordsworth, they prove unintelligible.

91

He, Juan, (and not Wordsworth) so pursued
    His self-communion with his own high soul,
Until his mighty heart, in its great mood,
    Had mitigated part, though not the whole
725 Of its disease; he did the best he could
    With things not very subject to control,
And turn'd, without perceiving his condition,
Like Coleridge, into a metaphysician.

92

He thought about himself, and the whole earth,
730   Of man the wonderful, and of the stars,
And how the deuce they ever could have birth;
    And then he thought of earthquakes, and of wars,
How many miles the moon might have in girth,
    Of air-balloons, and of the many bars
735 To perfect knowledge of the boundless skies;—
And then he thought of Donna Julia's eyes.

93

In thoughts like these true wisdom may discern
    Longings sublime, and aspirations high,
Which some are born with, but the most part learn
740   To plague themselves withal, they know not why:
'Twas strange that one so young should thus concern
    His brain about the action of the sky;
Do *you* think 'twas philosophy that this did,
I can't help thinking puberty assisted.

94

745 He pored upon the leaves, and on the flowers,
    And heard a voice in all the winds; and then
He thought of wood-nymphs and immortal bowers,
    And how the goddesses came down to men:
He miss'd the pathway, he forgot the hours,
750   And when he look'd upon his watch again,

He found how much old Time had been a winner—
He also found that he had lost his dinner.

* * *

103

'Twas on a summer's day—the sixth of June:—
    I like to be particular in dates,
Not only of the age, and year, but moon;
820   They are a sort of post-house, where the Fates
Change horses, making history change its tune,
    Then spur away o'er empires and o'er states,
Leaving at last not much besides chronology,
Excepting the post-obits[8] of theology.

104

825   'Twas on the sixth of June, about the hour
    Of half-past six—perhaps still nearer seven—
When Julia sate within as pretty a bower
    As e'er held houri in that heathenish heaven
Described by Mahomet, and Anacreon Moore,[9]
830   To whom the lyre and laurels have been given,
With all the trophies of triumphant song—
He won them well, and may he wear them long!

105

She sate, but not alone; I know not well
    How this same interview had taken place,
835   And even if I knew, I should not tell—
    People should hold their tongues in any case;
No matter how or why the thing befell,
    But there were she and Juan, face to face—
When two such faces are so, 'twould be wise,
840   But very difficult, to shut their eyes.

106

How beautiful she look'd! her conscious[1] heart
    Glow'd in her cheek, and yet she felt no wrong.
Oh Love! how perfect is thy mystic art,
    Strengthening the weak, and trampling on the strong,
845   How self-deceitful is the sagest part
    Of mortals whom thy lure hath led along—

---

8. I.e., postobit bonds (*post obitum*, "after death"
[Latin]): loans to an heir that fall due after the
death of the person whose estate he or she is to
inherit. Byron's meaning is probably that only
theology purports to tell us what rewards are due
in heaven.
9. Byron's friend the poet Thomas Moore, who

in 1800 had translated the *Odes* of the ancient
Greek Anacreon and whose popular Orientalist
poem *Lalla Rookh* (1817) had portrayed the "hea-
thenish heaven" of Islam as populated by "houris," beautiful maidens who in the afterlife will
give heroes their reward.
1. Secretly aware (of her feelings).

The precipice she stood on was immense,
So was her creed° in her own innocence.   *belief*

107

She thought of her own strength, and Juan's youth
850   And of the folly of all prudish fears,
Victorious virtue, and domestic truth,
     And then of Don Alfonso's fifty years:
I wish these last had not occurr'd, in sooth,
     Because that number rarely much endears,
855 And through all climes, the snowy and the sunny,
Sounds ill in love, whate'er it may in money.

*   *   *

113

The sun set, and up rose the yellow moon:
     The devil's in the moon for mischief; they
Who call'd her CHASTE, methinks, began too soon
900   Their nomenclature; there is not a day,
The longest, not the twenty-first of June,
     Sees half the business in a wicked way
On which three single hours of moonshine smile—
And then she looks so modest all the while.

114

905 There is a dangerous silence in that hour,
     A stillness, which leaves room for the full soul
To open all itself, without the power
     Of calling wholly back its self-control;
The silver light which, hallowing tree and tower,
910   Sheds beauty and deep softness o'er the whole,
Breathes also to the heart, and o'er it throws
A loving languor, which is not repose.

115

And Julia sate with Juan, half embraced
     And half retiring from the glowing arm,
915 Which trembled like the bosom where 'twas placed;
     Yet still she must have thought there was no harm,
Or else 'twere easy to withdraw her waist;
     But then the situation had its charm,
And then——God knows what next—I can't go on;
920 I'm almost sorry that I e'er begun.

116

Oh Plato! Plato! you have paved the way,
     With your confounded fantasies, to more

Immoral conduct by the fancied sway
　　Your system feigns o'er the controulless core
925 Of human hearts, than all the long array
　　Of poets and romancers:—You're a bore,
A charlatan, a coxcomb—and have been,
At best, no better than a go-between.

117

And Julia's voice was lost, except in sighs,
930 　　Until too late for useful conversation;
The tears were gushing from her gentle eyes,
　　I wish, indeed, they had not had occasion,
But who, alas! can love, and then be wise?
　　Not that remorse did not oppose temptation,
935 A little still she strove, and much repented,
And whispering "I will ne'er consent"—consented.

*　*　*

126

'Tis sweet to win, no matter how, one's laurels,
　　By blood or ink; 'tis sweet to put an end
To strife; 'tis sometimes sweet to have our quarrels,
　　Particularly with a tiresome friend:
1005 Sweet is old wine in bottles, ale in barrels;
　　Dear is the helpless creature we defend
Against the world; and dear the schoolboy spot
We ne'er forget, though there we are forgot.

127

But sweeter still than this, than these, than all,
1010 　　Is first and passionate love—it stands alone,
Like Adam's recollection of his fall;
　　The tree of knowledge has been pluck'd—all's known—
And life yields nothing further to recall
　　Worthy of this ambrosial sin, so shown,
1015 No doubt in fable, as the unforgiven
Fire which Prometheus[2] filch'd for us from heaven.

*　*　*

133

Man's a phenomenon, one knows not what,
　　And wonderful beyond all wondrous measure;
'Tis pity though, in this sublime world, that
1060 　　Pleasure's a sin, and sometimes sin's a pleasure;
Few mortals know what end they would be at,

2. The Titan Prometheus incurred the wrath of Zeus by stealing fire from heaven for humans.

But whether glory, power, or love, or treasure,
The path is through perplexing ways, and when
The goal is gain'd, we die, you know—and then——

134

1065 What then?—I do not know, no more do you—
  And so good night.—Return we to our story:
'Twas in November, when fine days are few,
  And the far mountains wax a little hoary,
And clap a white cape on their mantles blue;
1070 And the sea dashes round the promontory,
And the loud breaker boils against the rock,
And sober suns must set at five o'clock.

135

'Twas, as the watchmen say, a cloudy night;
  No moon, no stars, the wind was low or loud
1075 By gusts, and many a sparkling hearth was bright
  With the piled wood, round which the family crowd;
There's something cheerful in that sort of light,
  Even as a summer sky's without a cloud:
I'm fond of fire, and crickets, and all that,
1080 A lobster salad, and champagne, and chat.

136

'Twas midnight—Donna Julia was in bed,
  Sleeping, most probably,—when at her door
Arose a clatter might awake the dead,
  If they had never been awoke before,
1085 And that they have been so we all have read,
  And are to be so, at the least, once more;—
The door was fasten'd, but with voice and fist
First knocks were heard, then "Madam—Madam—hist!

137

"For God's sake, Madam—Madam—here's my master,
1090 With more than half the city at his back—
Was ever heard of such a curst disaster!
  'Tis not my fault—I kept good watch—Alack!
Do pray undo the bolt a little faster—
  They're on the stair just now, and in a crack°   *moment*
1095 Will all be here; perhaps he yet may fly—
Surely the window's not so *very* high!"

138

By this time Don Alfonso was arrived,
  With torches, friends, and servants in great number;

The major part of them had long been wived,
1100　　And therefore paused not to disturb the slumber
Of any wicked woman, who contrived
　　By stealth her husband's temples to encumber:[3]
Examples of this kind are so contagious.
Were *one* not punish'd, *all* would be outrageous.

139

1105　I can't tell how, or why, or what suspicion
　　　Could enter into Don Alfonso's head;
But for a cavalier of his condition°　　　　　　　　　　*rank*
　　　It surely was exceedingly ill-bred,
Without a word of previous admonition,
1110　　To hold a levee[4] round his lady's bed,
And summon lackeys, arm'd with fire and sword,
To prove himself the thing he most abhorr'd.

140

Poor Donna Julia! starting as from sleep,
　　　(Mind—that I do not say—she had not slept)
1115　Began at once to scream, and yawn, and weep;
　　　Her maid Antonia, who was an adept,
Contrived to fling the bed-clothes in a heap,
　　　As if she had just now from out them crept:
I can't tell why she should take all this trouble
1120　To prove her mistress had been sleeping double.

141

But Julia mistress, and Antonia maid,
　　　Appear'd like two poor harmless women, who
Of goblins, but still more of men afraid,
　　　Had thought one man might be deterr'd by two,
1125　And therefore side by side were gently laid,
　　　Until the hours of absence should run through,
And truant husband should return, and say,
"My dear, I was the first who came away."

142

Now Julia found at length a voice, and cried,
1130　　"In heaven's name, Don Alfonso, what d' ye mean?
Has madness seized you? would that I had died
　　　Ere such a monster's victim I had been!
What may this midnight violence betide,
　　　A sudden fit of drunkenness or spleen?
1135　Dare you suspect me, whom the thought would kill?
Search, then, the room!"—Alfonso said, "I will."

3. I.e., with horns that, growing on the forehead,　　husband.
were the traditional emblem of the cuckolded　　4. Morning reception.

143

He search'd, *they* search'd, and rummaged every where,
  Closet and clothes' press, chest and window-seat,
And found much linen, lace, and several pair
1140   Of stockings, slippers, brushes, combs, complete,
With other articles of ladies fair,
  To keep them beautiful, or leave them neat:
Arras[5] they prick'd and curtains with their swords,
And wounded several shutters, and some boards.

144

1145 Under the bed they search'd, and there they found[6]—
  No matter what—it was not that they sought;
They open'd windows, gazing if the ground
  Had signs or footmarks, but the earth said nought;
And then they stared each others' faces round:
1150   'T is odd, not one of all these seekers thought,
And seems to me almost a sort of blunder,
Of looking *in* the bed as well as under.

145

During this inquisition, Julia's tongue
  Was not asleep—"Yes, search and search," she cried,
1155 "Insult on insult heap, and wrong on wrong!
  It was for this that I became a bride!
For this in silence I have suffer'd long
  A husband like Alfonso at my side;
But now I'll bear no more, nor here remain,
1160 If there be law, or lawyers, in all Spain.

146

"Yes, Don Alfonso! husband now no more,
  If ever you indeed deserved the name,
Is't worthy of your years?—you have threescore—
  Fifty, or sixty, it is all the same—
1165 Is't wise or fitting, causeless to explore
  For facts against a virtuous woman's fame?
Ungrateful, perjured, barbarous Don Alfonso,
How dare you think your lady would go on so?"

*   *   *

159

1265 The Senhor Don Alfonso stood confused;
  Antonia bustled round the ransack'd room,
And, turning up her nose, with looks abused

---

5. A tapestry hanging on a wall.   6. Perhaps a chamber pot.

Her master, and his myrmidons,[7] of whom
Not one, except the attorney, was amused;
1270   He, like Achates,[8] faithful to the tomb,
So there were quarrels, cared not for the cause,
Knowing they must be settled by the laws.

160

With prying snub-nose, and small eyes, he stood,
    Following Antonia's motions here and there,
1275 With much suspicion in his attitude;
    For reputations he had little care;
So that a suit or action were made good,
    Small pity had he for the young and fair,
And ne'er believed in negatives, till these
1280 Were proved by competent false witnesses.

161

But Don Alfonso stood with downcast looks,
    And, truth to say, he made a foolish figure;
When, after searching in five hundred nooks,
    And treating a young wife with so much rigour,
1285 He gain'd no point, except some self-rebukes,
    Added to those his lady with such vigour
Had pour'd upon him for the last half-hour,
Quick, thick, and heavy—as a thunder-shower.

162

At first he tried to hammer an excuse,
1290   To which the sole reply was tears, and sobs,
And indications of hysterics, whose
    Prologue is always certain throes, and throbs,
Gasps, and whatever else the owners choose:
    Alfonso saw his wife, and thought of Job's;[9]
1295 He saw too, in perspective, her relations,
And then he tried to muster all his patience.

163

He stood in act to speak, or rather stammer,
    But sage Antonia cut him short before
The anvil of his speech received the hammer,
1300   With "Pray, sir, leave the room, and say no more,
Or madam dies."—Alfonso mutter'd, "D—n her,"
    But nothing else, the time of words was o'er;

---

7. Servants, so named for the followers Achilles led to the Trojan War.
8. The *fidus Achates* ("faithful Achates") of Virgil's *Aeneid*, whose loyalty to Aeneas has become proverbial.

9. Job's wife advised her afflicted husband to "curse God, and die." He replied, "Thou speakest as one of the foolish women speaketh" (Job 2.9–10).

He cast a rueful look or two, and did,
He knew not wherefore, that which he was bid.

164

1305 With him retired his *"posse comitatus,"*[1]
　　　The attorney last, who linger'd near the door,
Reluctantly, still tarrying there as late as
　　　Antonia let him—not a little sore
At this most strange and unexplain'd *"hiatus"*
1310　　In Don Alfonso's facts, which just now wore
An awkward look; as he revolved the case,
The door was fasten'd in his legal face.

165

No sooner was it bolted, than—Oh shame!
　　　Oh sin! Oh sorrow! and Oh womankind!
1315 How can you do such things and keep your fame,
　　　Unless this world, and t'other too, be blind?
Nothing so dear as an unfilch'd good name!
　　　But to proceed—for there is more behind:
With much heartfelt reluctance be it said,
1320 Young Juan slipp'd, half-smother'd, from the bed.

166

He had been hid—I don't pretend to say
　　　How, nor can I indeed describe the where—
Young, slender, and pack'd easily, he lay,
　　　No doubt, in little compass, round or square;
1325 But pity him I neither must nor may
　　　His suffocation by that pretty pair;
'Twere better, sure, to die so, than be shut
With maudlin Clarence in his Malmsey butt.[2]

* * *

169

1345 What's to be done? Alfonso will be back
　　　The moment he has sent his fools away.
Antonia's skill was put upon the rack,
　　　But no device could be brought into play—
And how to parry the renew'd attack?
1350　　Besides, it wanted but few hours of day:
Antonia puzzled; Julia did not speak,
But press'd her bloodless lip to Juan's cheek.

1. The complete form of the modern word *posse* (*posse comitatus* means literally "power of the county" [Latin], i.e., the body of citizens summoned by a sheriff to preserve order in the county).

2. Clarence, brother of Edward IV and of the future Richard III, was reputed to have been assassinated by being drowned in a cask ("butt") of malmsey, a sweet and aromatic wine.

170

He turn'd his lip to hers, and with his hand
    Call'd back the tangles of her wandering hair;
1355   Even then their love they could not all command,
    And half forgot their danger and despair:
Antonia's patience now was at a stand—
    "Come, come, 'tis no time now for fooling there,"
She whisper'd, in great wrath—"I must deposit
1360   This pretty gentleman within the closet:"

       *   *   *

173

Now, Don Alfonso entering, but alone,
    Closed the oration of the trusty maid:
She loiter'd, and he told her to be gone,
1380   An order somewhat sullenly obey'd;
However, present remedy was none,
    And no great good seem'd answer'd if she staid:
Regarding both with slow and sidelong view,
She snuff'd the candle, curtsied, and withdrew.

174

1385   Alfonso paused a minute—then begun
    Some strange excuses for his late proceeding;
He would not justify what he had done,
    To say the best, it was extreme ill-breeding;
But there were ample reasons for it, none
1390   Of which he specified in this his pleading:
His speech was a fine sample, on the whole,
Of rhetoric, which the learn'd call *"rigmarole."*

       *   *   *

180

Alfonso closed his speech, and begg'd her pardon,
    Which Julia half withheld, and then half granted,
1435   And laid conditions, he thought, very hard on,
    Denying several little things he wanted:
He stood like Adam lingering near his garden,
    With useless penitence perplex'd and haunted,
Beseeching she no further would refuse,
1440   When, lo! he stumbled o'er a pair of shoes.

181

A pair of shoes!—what then? not much, if they
    Are such as fit with ladies' feet, but these

(No one can tell how much I grieve to say)
  Were masculine; to see them, and to seize,
1445 Was but a moment's act.—Ah! well-a-day!
  My teeth begin to chatter, my veins freeze—
Alfonso first examined well their fashion,
And then flew out into another passion.

182

He left the room for his relinquish'd sword,
1450   And Julia instant to the closet flew.
"Fly, Juan, fly! for heaven's sake—not a word—
  The door is open—you may yet slip through
The passage you so often have explored—
  Here is the garden-key—Fly—fly—Adieu!
1455 Haste—haste! I hear Alfonso's hurrying feet—
Day has not broke—there's no one in the street."

183

None can say that this was not good advice,
  The only mischief was, it came too late;
Of all experience 'tis the usual price,
1460   A sort of income-tax laid on by fate:
Juan had reach'd the room-door in a trice,
  And might have done so by the garden-gate,
But met Alfonso in his dressing-gown,
Who threaten'd death—so Juan knock'd him down.

184

1465 Dire was the scuffle, and out went the light;
  Antonia cried out "Rape!" and Julia "Fire!"
But not a servant stirr'd to aid the fight.
  Alfonso, pommell'd to his heart's desire,
Swore lustily he'd be revenged this night;
1470   And Juan, too, blasphemed an octave higher;
His blood was up: though young, he was a Tartar,[3]
And not at all disposed to prove a martyr.

185

Alfonso's sword had dropp'd ere he could draw it,
  And they continued battling hand to hand,
1475 For Juan very luckily ne'er saw it;
  His temper not being under great command,
If at that moment he had chanced to claw it,
  Alfonso's days had not been in the land
Much longer.—Think of husbands', lovers' lives!
1480 And how ye may be doubly widows—wives!

---

3. A formidable opponent.

186

Alfonso grappled to detain the foe,
　　And Juan throttled him to get away,
And blood ('twas from the nose) began to flow;
　　At last, as they more faintly wrestling lay,
1485　Juan contrived to give an awkward blow,
　　And then his only garment quite gave way;
He fled, like Joseph,[4] leaving it; but there,
I doubt, all likeness ends between the pair.

187

Lights came at length, and men, and maids, who found
1490　An awkward spectacle their eyes before;
Antonia in hysterics, Julia swoon'd,
　　Alfonso leaning, breathless, by the door;
Some half-torn drapery scatter'd on the ground,
　　Some blood, and several footsteps, but no more:
1495　Juan the gate gain'd, turn'd the key about,
And liking not the inside, lock'd the out.

188

Here ends this canto.—Need I sing, or say,
　　How Juan, naked, favour'd by the night,
Who favours what she should not, found his way,
1500　And reach'd his home in an unseemly plight?
The pleasant scandal which arose next day,
　　The nine days' wonder which was brought to light,
And how Alfonso sued for a divorce,
Were in the English newspapers, of course.

189

1505　If you would like to see the whole proceedings,
　　The depositions, and the cause at full,
The names of all the witnesses, the pleadings
　　Of counsel to nonsuit,[5] or to annul,
There's more than one edition, and the readings
1510　Are various, but they none of them are dull;
The best is that in short-hand ta'en by Gurney,[6]
Who to Madrid on purpose made a journey.

190

But Donna Inez, to divert the train
　　Of one of the most circulating scandals

---

4. In Genesis 39.7ff. the chaste Joseph flees from the advances of Potiphar's wife, leaving "his garment in her hand."
5. Judgment against the plaintiff for failure to establish his case.
6. William B. Gurney (1777–1855), official short-hand writer for the houses of Parliament and a famous court reporter.

1515 That had for centuries been known in Spain,
    Since Roderic's Goths, or older Genseric's Vandals,[7]
First vow'd (and never had she vow'd in vain)
    To Virgin Mary several pounds of candles;
And then, by the advice of some old ladies,
1520 She sent her son to be embark'd at Cadiz.

191

She had resolved that he should travel through
    All European climes, by land or sea,
To mend his former morals, or get new,
    Especially in France and Italy
1525 (At least this is the thing most people do).
    Julia was sent into a nunnery
And there, perhaps, her feelings may be better
Shown in the following copy of her letter:—

192

"They tell me 'tis decided; you depart:
1530   'Tis wise—'tis well, but not the less a pain;
I have no further claim on your young heart,
    Mine is the victim, and would be again;
To love too much has been the only art
    I used;—I write in haste, and if a stain
1535 Be on this sheet, 'tis not what it appears;
My eyeballs burn and throb, but have no tears.

193

"I loved, I love you, for that love have lost
    State, station, heaven, mankind's, my own esteem,
And yet can not regret what it hath cost,
1540   So dear is still the memory of that dream;
Yet, if I name my guilt, 'tis not to boast,
    None can deem harshlier of me than I deem:
I trace this scrawl because I cannot rest—
I've nothing to reproach, nor to request.

194

1545 "Man's love is of his life a thing apart,
    'Tis woman's whole existence; man may range
The court, camp, church, the vessel, and the mart,
    Sword, gown, gain, glory, offer in exchange
Pride, fame, ambition, to fill up his heart,
1550   And few there are whom these can not estrange;
Men have all these resources, we but one,
To love again, and be again undone.

7. The Germanic tribes that overran Spain and other parts of southern Europe in the 5th through 8th centuries, notorious for rape and violence.

195

"My breast has been all weakness, is so yet;
　　I struggle, but cannot collect my mind;
1555　My blood still rushes where my spirit's set,
　　As roll the waves before the settled wind;
My brain is feminine, nor can forget—
　　To all, except your image, madly blind;
As turns the needle[8] trembling to the pole
1560　It ne'er can reach, so turns to you, my soul.

196

"You will proceed in beauty, and in pride,
　　Beloved and loving many; all is o'er
For me on earth, except some years to hide
　　My shame and sorrow deep in my heart's core;
1565　These I could bear, but cannot cast aside
　　The passion which still rages as before,—
And so farewell—forgive me, love me—No,
That word is idle now—but let it go.

197

"I have no more to say, but linger still,
1570　　And dare not set my seal upon this sheet,
And yet I may as well the task fulfil,
　　My misery can scarce be more complete:
I had not lived till now, could sorrow kill;
　　Death flies the wretch who fain the blow would meet,
1575　And I must even survive this last adieu,
And bear with life, to love and pray for you!"

198

This note was written upon gilt-edged paper
　　With a neat crow-quill, rather hard, but new;
Her small white fingers scarce could reach the taper,[9]
1580　　But trembled as magnetic needles do,
And yet she did not let one tear escape her;
　　The seal a sun-flower; *"Elle vous suit partout,"*[1]
The motto, cut upon a white cornelian;
The wax was superfine, its hue vermilion.

199

1585　This was Don Juan's earliest scrape; but whether
　　I shall proceed with his adventures is

8. Of a compass.
9. The candle (to melt wax to seal the letter).
1. She follows you everywhere (French). Byron himself owned a seal inscribed with this motto, as well as a cornelian gemstone, given him by John Edleston, the boy with whom he had a romantic friendship while at Cambridge. Byron's 1807 poem "The Cornelian" memorializes this relationship.

Dependent on the public altogether;
   We'll see, however, what they say to this,
Their favour in an author's cap's a feather,
1590   And no great mischief's done by their caprice;
And if their approbation we experience,
Perhaps they'll have some more about a year hence.

200

My poem's epic, and is meant to be
   Divided in twelve books; each book containing,
1595 With love, and war, a heavy gale at sea,
   A list of ships, and captains, and kings reigning,
New characters; the episodes are three:
   A panoramic view of hell's in training,
After the style of Virgil and of Homer,
1600 So that my name of Epic's no misnomer.

201

All these things will be specified in time,
   With strict regard to Aristotle's rules,
The *Vade Mecum*[2] of the true sublime,
   Which makes so many poets, and some fools:
1605 Prose poets like blank-verse, I'm fond of rhyme,
   Good workmen never quarrel with their tools;
I've got new mythological machinery,[3]
And very handsome supernatural scenery.

202

There's only one slight difference between
1610   Me and my epic brethren gone before,
And here the advantage is my own, I ween;
   (Not that I have not several merits more,
But this will more peculiarly be seen;)
   They so embellish, that 'tis quite a bore
1615 Their labyrinth of fables to thread through,
Whereas this story's actually true.

203

If any person doubt it, I appeal
   To history, tradition, and to facts,
To newspapers, whose truth all know and feel,
1620   To plays in five, and operas in three acts;
All these confirm my statement a good deal,
   But that which more completely faith exacts

---

2. Go with me (Latin, literal trans.); handbook. Byron is deriding the neoclassical view that Aristotle's *Poetics* proposes "rules" for writing epic and tragedy.

3. The assemblage of supernatural personages and incidents introduced into a literary work.

Is, that myself, and several now in Seville,
Saw Juan's last elopement with the devil.[4]

204

1625   If ever I should condescend to prose,
    I'll write poetical commandments, which
Shall supersede beyond all doubt all those
    That went before; in these I shall enrich
My text with many things that no one knows,
1630   And carry precept to the highest pitch:
I'll call the work "Longinus o'er a Bottle,
Or, Every Poet his *own* Aristotle."

205

Thou shalt believe in Milton, Dryden, Pope;[5]
    Thou shalt not set up Wordsworth, Coleridge, Southey;
1635   Because the first is crazed beyond all hope,
    The second drunk, the third so quaint and mouthy:
With Crabbe[6] it may be difficult to cope,
    And Campbell's Hippocrene[7] is somewhat drouthy:
Thou shalt not steal from Samuel Rogers, nor
1640   Commit—flirtation with the muse of Moore.[8]

206

Thou shalt not covet Mr. Sotheby's[9] Muse,
    His Pegasus,[1] nor any thing that's his;
Thou shalt not bear false witness like "the Blues"[2]—
    (There's one, at least, is very fond of this);
1645   Thou shalt not write, in short, but what I choose:
    This is true criticism, and you may kiss—
Exactly as you please, or not,—the rod;
But if you don't, I'll lay it on, by G—d![3]

207

If any person should presume to assert
1650   This story is not moral, first, I pray,

4. The usual plays on the Juan legend ended with Juan in hell; an early-20th-century version is George Bernard Shaw's *Man and Superman*.
5. This is one of many passages, in prose and verse, in which Byron vigorously defends Dryden and Pope against his Romantic contemporaries.
6. George Crabbe, whom Byron admired, was the author of *The Village* and other realistic poems of rural life.
7. Fountain on Mount Helicon whose waters supposedly gave inspiration.
8. Thomas Campbell, Samuel Rogers, and Thomas Moore were lesser poets of the Romantic period; the last two were close friends of Byron and members of London's liberal Whig circles.
9. The wealthy William Sotheby, minor poet and translator, is satirized, as Botherby, in Byron's *Beppo*.
1. The winged horse symbolizing poetic inspiration.
2. I.e., Bluestockings, a contemporary term for female intellectuals, among whom Byron numbered his wife (line 1644).
3. Byron's parody of the Ten Commandments seemed blasphemous to some commentators. In 1817 the radical publisher William Hone was put on trial for the ostensible blasphemy of a political satire that had used the form of the Anglican Church's creed and catechism.

That they will not cry out before they're hurt,
  Then that they'll read it o'er again, and say,
(But, doubtless, nobody will be so pert)
  That this is not a moral tale, though gay;
1655 Besides, in Canto Twelfth, I mean to show
The very place where wicked people go.

*   *   *

213

But now at thirty years my hair is grey—
  (I wonder what it will be like at forty?
I thought of a peruke° the other day—)   *wig*
1700   My heart is not much greener; and, in short, I
Have squander'd my whole summer while 'twas May,
  And feel no more the spirit to retort; I
Have spent my life, both interest and principal,
And deem not, what I deem'd, my soul invincible.

214

1705 No more—no more—Oh! never more on me
  The freshness of the heart can fall like dew,
Which out of all the lovely things we see
  Extracts emotions beautiful and new,
Hived in our bosoms like the bag o' the bee:
1710   Think'st thou the honey with those objects grew?
Alas! 'twas not in them, but in thy power
To double even the sweetness of a flower.

215

No more—no more—Oh! never more, my heart,
  Canst thou be my sole world, my universe!
1715 Once all in all, but now a thing apart,
  Thou canst not be my blessing or my curse:
The illusion's gone for ever, and thou art
  Insensible, I trust, but none the worse,
And in thy stead I've got a deal of judgment,
1720 Though heaven knows how it ever found a lodgement.

216

My days of love are over; me no more
  The charms of maid, wife, and still less of widow,
Can make the fool of which they made before,—
  In short, I must not lead the life I did do;
1725 The credulous hope of mutual minds is o'er,
  The copious use of claret is forbid too,
So for a good old-gentlemanly vice,
I think I must take up with avarice.

217

Ambition was my idol, which was broken
1730   Before the shrines of Sorrow, and of Pleasure;
And the two last have left me many a token
    O'er which reflection may be made at leisure:
Now, like Friar Bacon's brazen head, I've spoken,
    "Time is, Time was, Time's past:"[4]—a chymic treasure[5]
1735 Is glittering youth, which I have spent betimes—
My heart in passion, and my head on rhymes.

218

What is the end of Fame? 'tis but to fill
    A certain portion of uncertain paper:
Some liken it to climbing up a hill,
1740   Whose summit, like all hills, is lost in vapour;
For this men write, speak, preach, and heroes kill,
    And bards burn what they call their "midnight taper,"
To have, when the original is dust,
A name, a wretched picture, and worse bust.[6]

219

1745 What are the hopes of man? Old Egypt's King
    Cheops erected the first pyramid
And largest, thinking it was just the thing
    To keep his memory whole, and mummy hid;
But somebody or other rummaging,
1750   Burglariously broke his coffin's lid:
Let not a monument give you or me hopes,
Since not a pinch of dust remains of Cheops.

220

But I being fond of true philosophy,
    Say very often to myself, "Alas!
1755 All things that have been born were born to die,
    And flesh (which Death mows down to hay) is grass;[7]
You've pass'd your youth not so unpleasantly,
    And if you had it o'er again—'twould pass—
So thank your stars that matters are no worse,
1760 And read your Bible, sir, and mind your purse."

---

4. Spoken by a bronze bust in Robert Greene's *Friar Bacon and Friar Bungay* (1594). This comedy was based on legends about the magical power of Roger Bacon, the 13th-century Franciscan monk who was said to have built with diabolical assistance a brazen head capable of speech.
5. "Chymic": alchemic. I.e., the "treasure" is counterfeit gold.
6. Byron was unhappy with the portrait bust of him recently made by the Danish sculptor Thorwaldsen.
7. An echo of Isaiah 40.6 and 1 Peter 1.24: "All flesh is grass."

221

But for the present, gentle reader! and
   Still gentler purchaser! the bard—that's I—
Must, with permission, shake you by the hand,
   And so your humble servant, and good-b'ye!
1765   We meet again, if we should understand
   Each other; and if not, I shall not try
Your patience further than by this short sample—
'Twere well if others follow'd my example.

222

"Go, little book, from this my solitude!
1770   I cast thee on the waters—go thy ways!
And if, as I believe, thy vein be good,
   The world will find thee after many days."
When Southey's read, and Wordsworth understood,
   I can't help putting in my claim to praise—
1775   The four first rhymes are Southey's every line:[8]
For God's sake, reader! take them not for mine.

From Canto the Second

*   *   *

[THE SHIPWRECK]

11

Juan embark'd—the ship got under way,
   The wind was fair, the water passing rough:
A devil of a sea rolls in that bay,
   As I, who've cross'd it oft, know well enough;
85   And, standing upon deck, the dashing spray
   Flies in one's face, and makes it weather-tough:
And there he stood to take, and take again,
His first—perhaps his last—farewell of Spain.

12

I can't but say it is an awkward sight
90   To see one's native land receding through
The growing waters; it unmans one quite,
   Especially when life is rather new:
I recollect Great Britain's coast looks white,
   But almost every other country's blue,
95   When gazing on them, mystified by distance,
We enter on our nautical existence.

*   *   *

---

8. The lines are part of the last stanza of Southey's "Epilogue to the Lay of the Laureate."

17

And Juan wept, and much he sigh'd and thought,
130   While his salt tears dropp'd into the salt sea,
"Sweets to the sweet" (I like so much to quote;
    You must excuse this extract, 'tis where she,
The Queen of Denmark, for Ophelia brought
    Flowers to the grave);[1] and, sobbing often, he
135 Reflected on his present situation,
And seriously resolved on reformation.

18

"Farewell, my Spain! a long farewell!" he cried,
    "Perhaps I may revisit thee no more,
But die, as many an exiled heart hath died,
140   Of its own thirst to see again thy shore:
Farewell, where Guadalquivir's waters glide!
    Farewell, my mother! and, since all is o'er,
Farewell, too, dearest Julia!—(Here he drew
Her letter out again, and read it through.)

19

145 "And, oh! if e'er I should forget, I swear—
    But that's impossible, and cannot be—
Sooner shall this blue ocean melt to air,
    Sooner shall earth resolve itself to sea,
Than I resign thine image, oh, my fair!
150   Or think of any thing excepting thee;
A mind diseased no remedy can physic
(Here the ship gave a lurch, and he grew sea-sick).

20

"Sooner shall heaven kiss earth (here he fell sicker),
    Oh, Julia! what is every other woe?
155 (For God's sake let me have a glass of liquor,
    Pedro, Battista, help me down below.)
Julia, my love! (you rascal, Pedro, quicker)—
    Oh, Julia! (this curst vessel pitches so)—
Beloved Julia, hear me still beseeching!"
160 (Here he grew inarticulate with retching)

21

He felt that chilling heaviness of heart,
    Or rather stomach, which, alas! attends,
Beyond the best apothecary's art,
    The loss of love, the treachery of friends,

1. *Hamlet* 5.1.227.

165   Or death of those we dote on, when a part
      Of us dies with them as each fond hope ends:
    No doubt he would have been much more pathetic,
    But the sea acted as a strong emetic.[2]

*   *   *

52

    Then rose from sea to sky the wild farewell—
410   Then shriek'd the timid, and stood still the brave,—
    Then some leap'd overboard with dreadful yell,
      As eager to anticipate their grave;
    And the sea yawn'd around her like a hell,
      And down she suck'd with her the whirling wave,
415   Like one who grapples with his enemy,
    And strives to strangle him before he die.

53

    And first one universal shriek there rush'd,
      Louder than the loud ocean, like a crash
    Of echoing thunder; and then all was hush'd,
420   Save the wild wind and the remorseless dash
    Of billows; but at intervals there gush'd,
      Accompanied with a convulsive splash,
    A solitary shriek, the bubbling cry
    Of some strong swimmer in his agony.

*   *   *

56

    Juan got into the long-boat, and there
      Contrived to help Pedrillo[3] to a place;
    It seem'd as if they had exchanged their care,
      For Juan wore the magisterial face
445   Which courage gives, while poor Pedrillo's pair
      Of eyes were crying for their owner's case:
    Battista, though (a name call'd shortly Tita)
    Was lost by getting at some aqua-vita.°   *brandy*

57

    Pedro, his valet, too, he tried to save,
450   But the same cause, conducive to his loss,
    Left him so drunk, he jump'd into the wave
      As o'er the cutter's edge he tried to cross,

---

2. In stanzas 22–51 (here omitted) the ship, bound for Leghorn in Italy, runs into a storm and is battered into a helpless, sinking wreck.
3. Juan's tutor.

And so he found a wine-and-watery grave;
   They could not rescue him although so close,
455 Because the sea ran higher every minute,
And for the boat—the crew kept crowding in it.

* * *

66

'Tis thus with people in an open boat,
   They live upon the love of life, and bear
More than can be believed, or even thought,
   And stand like rocks the tempest's wear and tear;
525 And hardship still has been the sailor's lot,
   Since Noah's ark went cruising here and there;
She had a curious crew as well as cargo,
Like the first old Greek privateer, the Argo.[4]

67

But man is a carnivorous production,
530   And must have meals, at least one meal a day;
He cannot live, like woodcocks, upon suction,[5]
   But, like the shark and tiger, must have prey;
Although his anatomical construction
   Bears vegetables, in a grumbling way,
535 Your labouring people think beyond all question,
Beef, veal, and mutton, better for digestion.

68

And thus it was with this our hapless crew,
   For on the third day there came on a calm,
And though at first their strength it might renew,
540   And lying on their weariness like balm,
Lull'd them like turtles sleeping on the blue
   Of ocean, when they woke they felt a qualm,
And fell all ravenously on their provision,
Instead of hoarding it with due precision.

* * *

72

The seventh day,[6] and no wind—the burning sun
570   Blister'd and scorch'd, and, stagnant on the sea,
They lay like carcasses; and hope was none,

---

4. In the Greek myth the *Argo* is the ship on which Jason set out in quest of the Golden Fleece. Byron ironically calls it a "privateer" (a private ship licensed by a government in wartime to attack and pillage enemy vessels).

5. Woodcocks probe the turf with their long flexible bills, seeming to suck air as they feed.
6. On the fourth day the crew had killed and eaten Juan's pet spaniel. Byron based the episode of cannibalism that follows on various historical

Save in the breeze that came not; savagely
They glared upon each other—all was done,
Water, and wine, and food,—and you might see
575   The longings of the cannibal arise
(Although they spoke not) in their wolfish eyes.

73

At length one whisper'd his companion, who
Whisper'd another, and thus it went round,
And then into a hoarser murmur grew,
580   An ominous, and wild, and desperate sound;
And when his comrade's thought each sufferer knew,
'Twas but his own, suppress'd till now, he found:
And out they spoke of lots for flesh and blood,
And who should die to be his fellow's food.

74

585   But ere they came to this, they that day shared
Some leathern caps, and what remain'd of shoes;
And then they look'd around them, and despair'd,
And none to be the sacrifice would choose;
At length the lots were torn up, and prepared,
590   But of materials that much shock the Muse—
Having no paper, for the want of better,
They took by force from Juan Julia's letter.

75

The lots were made, and mark'd, and mix'd, and handed,
In silent horror, and their distribution
595   Lull'd even the savage hunger which demanded,
Like the Promethean vulture,[7] this pollution;
None in particular had sought or plann'd it,
'Twas nature gnaw'd them to this resolution,
By which none were permitted to be neuter—
600   And the lot fell on Juan's luckless tutor.

76

He but requested to be bled to death:
The surgeon had his instruments, and bled
Pedrillo, and so gently ebb'd his breath,
You hardly could perceive when he was dead.
605   He died as born, a Catholic in faith,
Like most in the belief in which they're bred,

---

accounts of disasters at sea, including his grandfather Admiral Byron's 1768 narrative of his mis-
adventure off the coast of Patagonia.
7. Because Prometheus had stolen fire from

heaven to give to humans, Zeus punished him by
chaining him to a mountain peak, where an
eagle fed on his ever-renewing liver.

And first a little crucifix he kiss'd,
And then held out his jugular and wrist.

77

The surgeon, as there was no other fee,
610   Had his first choice of morsels for his pains;
But being thirstiest at the moment, he
    Preferr'd a draught from the fast-flowing veins:
Part was divided, part thrown in the sea,
    And such things as the entrails and the brains
615 Regaled two sharks, who follow'd o'er the billow—
The sailors ate the rest of poor Pedrillo.

78

The sailors ate him, all save three or four,
    Who were not quite so fond of animal food;
To these was added Juan, who, before
620   Refusing his own spaniel, hardly could
Feel now his appetite increased much more;
    'Twas not to be expected that he should,
Even in extremity of their disaster,
Dine with them on his pastor and his master.

79

625 'Twas better that he did not; for, in fact,
    The consequence was awful in the extreme;
For they, who were most ravenous in the act,
    Went raging mad—Lord! how they did blaspheme!
And foam and roll, with strange convulsions rack'd,
630   Drinking salt-water like a mountain-stream,
Tearing, and grinning, howling, screeching, swearing,
And, with hyaena-laughter, died despairing.

*   *   *

103

As they drew nigh the land, which now was seen
    Unequal in its aspect here and there,
They felt the freshness of its growing green,
820   That waved in forest-tops, and smooth'd the air,
And fell upon their glazed eyes like a screen
    From glistening waves, and skies so hot and bare—
Lovely seem'd any object that should sweep
Away the vast, salt, dread, eternal deep.

104

825 The shore look'd wild, without a trace of man,
    And girt by formidable waves; but they

Were mad for land, and thus their course they ran,
　　Though right ahead the roaring breakers lay:
A reef between them also now began
830　　To show its boiling surf and bounding spray,
But finding no place for their landing better,
They ran the boat for shore,—and overset her.

105

But in his native stream, the Guadalquivir,
　　Juan to lave° his youthful limbs was wont;　　　　　　　*bathe*
835　And having learnt to swim in that sweet river,
　　Had often turn'd the art to some account:
A better swimmer you could scarce see ever,
　　He could, perhaps, have pass'd the Hellespont,
As once (a feat on which ourselves we prided)
840　Leander, Mr. Ekenhead, and I did.[8]

106

So here, though faint, emaciated, and stark,
　　He buoy'd his boyish limbs, and strove to ply
With the quick wave, and gain, ere it was dark,
　　The beach which lay before him, high and dry:
845　The greatest danger here was from a shark,
　　That carried off his neighbour by the thigh;
As for the other two, they could not swim,
So nobody arrived on shore but him.

107

Nor yet had he arrived but for the oar,
850　　Which, providentially for him, was wash'd
Just as his feeble arms could strike no more,
　　And the hard wave o'erwhelm'd him as 'twas dash'd
Within his grasp; he clung to it, and sore
　　The waters beat while he thereto was lash'd;
855　At last, with swimming, wading, scrambling, he
Roll'd on the beach, half senseless, from the sea:

108

There, breathless, with his digging nails he clung
　　Fast to the sand, lest the returning wave,
From whose reluctant roar his life he wrung,
860　　Should suck him back to her insatiate grave:
And there he lay, full length, where he was flung,
　　Before the entrance of a cliff-worn cave,
With just enough of life to feel its pain,
And deem that it was saved, perhaps, in vain.

8. Like Leander in the myth, Byron and Lieutenant Ekenhead had swum the Hellespont, on May 3, 1810. See "Written after Swimming from Sestos to Abydos" (p. 612).

109

865 With slow and staggering effort he arose,
But sunk again upon his bleeding knee
And quivering hand; and then he look'd for those
Who long had been his mates upon the sea;
But none of them appear'd to share his woes,
870 Save one, a corpse from out the famish'd three,
Who died two days before, and now had found
An unknown barren beach for burial ground.

110

And as he gazed, his dizzy brain spun fast,
And down he sunk; and as he sunk, the sand
875 Swam round and round, and all his senses pass'd:
He fell upon his side, and his stretch'd hand
Droop'd dripping on the oar (their jury-mast),[9]
And, like a wither'd lily, on the land
His slender frame and pallid aspect lay,
880 As fair a thing as e'er was form'd of clay.

[JUAN AND HAIDEE]

111

How long in his damp trance young Juan lay
He knew not, for the earth was gone for him,
And Time had nothing more of night nor day
For his congealing blood, and senses dim;
885 And how this heavy faintness pass'd away
He knew not, till each painful pulse and limb,
And tingling vein, seem'd throbbing back to life,
For Death, though vanquish'd, still retired with strife.

112

His eyes he open'd, shut, again unclosed,
890 For all was doubt and dizziness; he thought
He still was in the boat, and had but dozed,
And felt again with his despair o'erwrought,
And wish'd it death in which he had reposed,
And then once more his feelings back were brought,
895 And slowly by his swimming eyes was seen
A lovely female face of seventeen.

113

'Twas bending close o'er his, and the small mouth
Seem'd almost prying into his for breath;
And chafing him, the soft warm hand of youth

---

9. A mast put up in the place of one that has been carried away or broken.

900   Recall'd his answering spirits back from death;
And, bathing his chill temples, tried to soothe
    Each pulse to animation, till beneath
Its gentle touch and trembling care, a sigh
To these kind efforts made a low reply.

114

905   Then was the cordial pour'd, and mantle flung
    Around his scarce-clad limbs; and the fair arm
Raised higher the faint head which o'er it hung;
    And her transparent cheek, all pure and warm,
Pillow'd his death-like forehead; then she wrung
910   His dewy curls, long drench'd by every storm;
And watch'd with eagerness each throb that drew
A sigh from his heaved bosom—and hers, too.

115

And lifting him with care into the cave,
    The gentle girl, and her attendant,—one
915 Young, yet her elder, and of brow less grave,
    And more robust of figure,—then begun
To kindle fire, and as the new flames gave
    Light to the rocks that roof'd them, which the sun
Had never seen, the maid, or whatsoe'er
920 She was, appear'd distinct, and tall, and fair.

116

Her brow was overhung with coins of gold,
    That sparkled o'er the auburn of her hair,
Her clustering hair, whose longer locks were roll'd
    In braids behind, and though her stature were
925 Even of the highest for a female mould,
    They nearly reach'd her heel; and in her air
There was a something which bespoke command,
As one who was a lady in the land.

117

Her hair, I said, was auburn; but her eyes
930   Were black as death, their lashes the same hue,
Of downcast length, in whose silk shadow lies
    Deepest attraction, for when to the view
Forth from its raven fringe the full glance flies,
    Ne'er with such force the swiftest arrow flew;
935 'Tis as the snake late coil'd, who pours his length,
And hurls at once his venom and his strength.

*   *   *

123

And these two tended him, and cheer'd him both
　　With food and raiment, and those soft attentions,
Which are—(as I must own)—of female growth,
980　　And have ten thousand delicate inventions:
They made a most superior mess of broth,
　　A thing which poesy but seldom mentions,
But the best dish that e'er was cook'd since Homer's
Achilles order'd dinner for new comers.[1]

124

985　I'll tell you who they were, this female pair,
　　Lest they should seem princesses in disguise;
Besides, I hate all mystery, and that air
　　Of clap-trap, which your recent poets prize;
And so, in short, the girls they really were
990　　They shall appear before your curious eyes,
Mistress and maid; the first was only daughter
Of an old man, who lived upon the water.

125

A fisherman he had been in his youth,
　　And still a sort of fisherman was he;
995　But other speculations were, in sooth,
　　Added to his connection with the sea,
Perhaps not so respectable, in truth:
　　A little smuggling, and some piracy,
Left him, at last, the sole of many masters
1000　Of an ill-gotten million of piastres.[2]

126

A fisher, therefore, was he,—though of men,
　　Like Peter the Apostle,[3]—and he fish'd
For wandering merchant-vessels, now and then,
　　And sometimes caught as many as he wish'd;
1005　The cargoes he confiscated, and gain
　　He sought in the slave-market too, and dish'd
Full many a morsel for that Turkish trade,
By which, no doubt, a good deal may be made.

127

He was a Greek, and on his isle had built
1010　　(One of the wild and smaller Cyclades)[4]

---

1. A reference to the lavish feast with which Achilles entertained Ajax, Phoenix, and Ulysses (*Iliad* 9.193ff.).
2. Near Eastern coins.
3. Christ's words to Peter and Andrew, both fishermen: "Follow me, and I will make you fishers of men" (Matthew 4.19).
4. A group of islands in the Aegean Sea.

A very handsome house from out his guilt,
    And there he lived exceedingly at ease;
Heaven knows, what cash he got, or blood he spilt,
    A sad[5] old fellow was he, if you please;
1015   But this I know, it was a spacious building,
Full of barbaric carving, paint, and gilding.

128

He had an only daughter, call'd Haidee,
    The greatest heiress of the Eastern Isles;
Besides, so very beautiful was she,
1020   Her dowry was as nothing to her smiles:
Still in her teens, and like a lovely tree
    She grew to womanhood, and between whiles
Rejected several suitors, just to learn
How to accept a better in his turn.

129

1025 And walking out upon the beach, below
    The cliff, towards sunset, on that day she found,
Insensible,° not dead, but nearly so,—   *unconscious*
    Don Juan, almost famish'd, and half drown'd;
But being naked, she was shock'd, you know,
1030   Yet deem'd herself in common pity bound,
As far as in her lay, "to take him in,
A stranger"[6] dying, with so white a skin.

130

But taking him into her father's house
    Was not exactly the best way to save,
1035 But like conveying to the cat the mouse,
    Or people in a trance into their grave;
Because the good old man had so much "γους,"[7]
    Unlike the honest Arab thieves so brave,
He would have hospitably cured the stranger,
1040 And sold him instantly when out of danger.

131

And therefore, with her maid, she thought it best
    (A virgin always on her maid relies)
To place him in the cave for present rest:
    And when, at last, he open'd his black eyes,
1045   Their charity increased about their guest;
    And their compassion grew to such a size,

---

5. In the playful sense: wicked.
6. Cf. Matthew 25.35: "I was a stranger, and ye took me in."

7. *Nous*, intelligence (Greek); in England pronounced so as to rhyme with *mouse*.

It open'd half the turnpike-gates to heaven—
(St. Paul says, 'tis the toll which must be given.)[8]

*   *   *

141

And Haidee met the morning face to face;
  Her own was freshest, though a feverish flush
Had dyed it with the headlong blood, whose race
  From heart to cheek is curb'd into a blush,
1125 Like to a torrent which a mountain's base,
  That overpowers some Alpine river's rush,
Checks to a lake, whose waves in circles spread;
Or the Red Sea—but the sea is not red.

142

And down the cliff the island virgin came,
1130   And near the cave her quick light footsteps drew,
While the sun smiled on her with his first flame,
  And young Aurora° kiss'd her lips with dew,   *dawn*
Taking her for a sister; just the same
  Mistake you would have made on seeing the two,
1135 Although the mortal, quite as fresh and fair,
Had all the advantage, too, of not being air.

143

And when into the cavern Haidee stepp'd
  All timidly, yet rapidly, she saw
That like an infant Juan sweetly slept;
1140   And then she stopp'd, and stood as if in awe
(For sleep is awful°), and on tiptoe crept   *awe-inspiring*
  And wrapt him closer, lest the air, too raw,
Should reach his blood, then o'er him still as death
Bent, with hush'd lips, that drank his scarce-drawn breath.

*   *   *

148

And she bent o'er him, and he lay beneath,
  Hush'd as the babe upon its mother's breast,
Droop'd as the willow when no winds can breathe,
1180   Lull'd like the depth of ocean when at rest,
Fair as the crowning rose of the whole wreath,
  Soft as the callow cygnet° in its nest;   *young swan*

8. 1 Corinthians 13.13: "And now abideth faith, hope, charity, these three; but the greatest of these is charity."

In short, he was a very pretty fellow,
Although his woes had turn'd him rather yellow.

149

1185   He woke and gazed, and would have slept again,
     But the fair face which met his eyes forbade
Those eyes to close, though weariness and pain
     Had further sleep a further pleasure made;
For woman's face was never form'd in vain
1190   For Juan, so that even when he pray'd
He turn'd from grisly saints, and martyrs hairy,
To the sweet portraits of the Virgin Mary.

150

And thus upon his elbow he arose,
     And look'd upon the lady, in whose cheek
1195 The pale contended with the purple rose,
     As with an effort she began to speak;
Her eyes were eloquent, her words would pose,
     Although she told him, in good modern Greek,
With an Ionian accent, low and sweet,
1200 That he was faint, and must not talk, but eat.

*   *   *   *

168

And every day by daybreak—rather early
     For Juan, who was somewhat fond of rest—
She came into the cave, but it was merely
1340   To see her bird reposing in his nest;
And she would softly stir his locks so curly,
     Without disturbing her yet slumbering guest,
Breathing all gently o'er his cheek and mouth,
As o'er a bed of roses the sweet south.[9]

169

1345 And every morn his colour freshlier came,
     And every day help'd on his convalescence;
'Twas well, because health in the human frame
     Is pleasant, besides being true love's essence,
For health and idleness to passion's flame
1350   Are oil and gunpowder; and some good lessons
Are also learnt from Ceres and from Bacchus,[1]
Without whom Venus will not long attack us.

---

9. The south wind.
1. God of wine and revelry. Ceres was the goddess of grain.

170

While Venus fills the heart (without heart really
    Love, though good always, is not quite so good,)
1355 Ceres presents a plate of vermicelli,—
    For love must be sustain'd like flesh and blood,—
While Bacchus pours out wine, or hands a jelly:
    Eggs, oysters, too, are amatory food;
But who is their purveyor from above
1360 Heaven knows,—it may be Neptune, Pan, or Jove.

171

When Juan woke he found some good things ready,
    A bath, a breakfast, and the finest eyes
That ever made a youthful heart less steady,
    Besides her maid's, as pretty for their size;
1365 But I have spoken of all this already—
    And repetition's tiresome and unwise,—
Well—Juan, after bathing in the sea,
Came always back to coffee and Haidee.

172

Both were so young, and one so innocent,
1370   That bathing pass'd for nothing; Juan seem'd
To her, as 'twere, the kind of being sent,
    Of whom these two years she had nightly dream'd,
A something to be loved, a creature meant
    To be her happiness, and whom she deem'd
1375 To render happy; all who joy would win
Must share it,—Happiness was born a twin.

173

It was such pleasure to behold him, such
    Enlargement of existence to partake
Nature with him, to thrill beneath his touch,
1380   To watch him slumbering, and to see him wake:
To live with him for ever were too much;
    But then the thought of parting made her quake:
He was her own, her ocean-treasure, cast
Like a rich wreck—her first love, and her last.

174

1385 And thus a moon° roll'd on, and fair Haidee   *month*
    Paid daily visits to her boy, and took
Such plentiful precautions, that still he
    Remain'd unknown within his craggy nook;
At last her father's prows put out to sea,
1390   For certain merchantmen upon the look,

Not as of yore to carry off an Io,[2]
But three Ragusan vessels, bound for Scio.[3]

175

Then came her freedom, for she had no mother,
    So that, her father being at sea, she was
1395 Free as a married woman, or such other
    Female, as where she likes may freely pass,
Without even the incumbrance of a brother,
    The freest she that ever gazed on glass:°   *in a mirror*
I speak of Christian lands in this comparison,
1400 Where wives, at least, are seldom kept in garrison.

176

Now she prolong'd her visits and her talk
    (For they must talk), and he had learnt to say
So much as to propose to take a walk,—
    For little had he wander'd since the day
1405 On which, like a young flower snapp'd from the stalk,
    Drooping and dewy on the beach he lay,—
And thus they walk'd out in the afternoon,
And saw the sun set opposite the moon.

177

It was a wild and breaker-beaten coast,
1410   With cliffs above, and a broad sandy shore,
Guarded by shoals and rocks as by an host,
    With here and there a creek, whose aspect wore
A better welcome to the tempest-tost;
    And rarely ceased the haughty billow's roar,
1415 Save on the dead long summer days, which make
The outstretch'd ocean glitter like a lake.

178

And the small ripple spilt upon the beach
    Scarcely o'erpass'd the cream of your champagne,
When o'er the brim the sparkling bumpers reach,
1420   That spring-dew of the spirit! the heart's rain!
Few things surpass old wine; and they may preach
    Who please,—the more because they preach in vain,—
Let us have wine and women, mirth and laughter,
Sermons and soda-water the day after.

---

2. A mistress of Zeus who was persecuted by his jealous wife, Hera, and kidnapped by Phoenician merchants.

3. The Italian name for Chios, an island near Turkey. "Ragusan": from Ragusa (or Dubrovnik), an Adriatic port located in what is now Croatia.

179

₁₄₂₅ Man, being reasonable, must get drunk;
    The best of life is but intoxication:
Glory, the grape, love, gold, in these are sunk
    The hopes of all men, and of every nation;
Without their sap, how branchless were the trunk
₁₄₃₀   Of life's strange tree, so fruitful on occasion:
But to return,—Get very drunk; and when
You wake with headach, you shall see what then.

180

Ring for your valet—bid him quickly bring
    Some hock° and soda-water, then you'll know   *German wine*
₁₄₃₅ A pleasure worthy Xerxes[4] the great king;
    For not the blest sherbet, sublimed with snow,
Nor the first sparkle of the desert-spring,
    Nor Burgundy in all its sunset glow,
After long travel, ennui, love, or slaughter,
₁₄₄₀ Vie with that draught of hock and soda-water.

181

The coast—I think it was the coast that I
    Was just describing—Yes, it *was* the coast—
Lay at this period quiet as the sky,
    The sands untumbled, the blue waves untost,
₁₄₄₅ And all was stillness, save the sea-bird's cry,
    And dolphin's leap, and little billow crost
By some low rock or shelve, that made it fret
Against the boundary it scarcely wet.

182

And forth they wander'd, her sire being gone,
₁₄₅₀   As I have said, upon an expedition;
And mother, brother, guardian, she had none,
    Save Zoe, who, although with due precision
She waited on her lady with the sun,
    Thought daily service was her only mission,
₁₄₅₅ Bringing warm water, wreathing her long tresses,
And asking now and then for cast-off dresses.

183

It was the cooling hour, just when the rounded
    Red sun sinks down behind the azure hill,
Which then seems as if the whole earth it bounded,

---

4. The 5th-century Persian king was said to have offered a reward to anyone who could discover a new kind of pleasure.

1460   Circling all nature, hush'd, and dim, and still,
With the far mountain-crescent half surrounded
    On one side, and the deep sea calm and chill
Upon the other, and the rosy sky,
With one star sparkling through it like an eye.

184

1465   And thus they wander'd forth, and hand in hand,
    Over the shining pebbles and the shells,
Glided along the smooth and harden'd sand,
    And in the worn and wild receptacles
Work'd by the storms, yet work'd as it were plann'd,
1470   In hollow halls, with sparry roofs and cells,
They turn'd to rest; and, each clasp'd by an arm,
Yielded to the deep twilight's purple charm.

185

They look'd up to the sky, whose floating glow
    Spread like a rosy ocean, vast and bright;
1475   They gazed upon the glittering sea below,
    Whence the broad moon rose circling into sight;
They heard the wave's splash, and the wind so low,
    And saw each other's dark eyes darting light
Into each other—and, beholding this,
1480   Their lips drew near, and clung into a kiss;

186

A long, long kiss, a kiss of youth and love
    And beauty, all concentrating like rays
Into one focus, kindled from above;
    Such kisses as belong to early days,
1485   Where heart, and soul, and sense, in concert move,
    And the blood's lava, and the pulse a blaze,
Each kiss a heart-quake,—for a kiss's strength,
I think, it must be reckon'd by its length.

187

By length I mean duration; theirs endured
1490   Heaven knows how long—no doubt they never reckon'd;
And if they had, they could not have secured
    The sum of their sensations to a second:
They had not spoken; but they felt allured,
    As if their souls and lips each other beckon'd,
1495   Which, being join'd, like swarming bees they clung—
Their hearts the flowers from whence the honey sprung.

188

They were alone, but not alone as they
    Who shut in chambers think it loneliness;
The silent ocean, and the starlight bay,
1500   The twilight glow, which momently grew less,
The voiceless sands, and dropping caves, that lay
    Around them, made them to each other press,
As if there were no life beneath the sky
Save theirs, and that their life could never die.

189

1505 They fear'd no eyes nor ears on that lone beach,
    They felt no terrors from the night, they were
All in all to each other: though their speech
    Was broken words, they *thought* a language there,—
And all the burning tongues the passions teach
1510   Found in one sigh the best interpreter
Of nature's oracle—first love,—that all
Which Eve has left her daughters since her fall.

190

Haidee[5] spoke not of scruples, ask'd no vows,
    Nor offer'd any; she had never heard
1515 Of plight and promises to be a spouse,
    Or perils by a loving maid incurr'd;
She was all which pure ignorance allows,
    And flew to her young mate like a young bird;
And, never having dreamt of falsehood, she
1520 Had not one word to say of constancy.

191

She loved, and was beloved—she adored,
    And she was worshipp'd; after nature's fashion,
Their intense souls, into each other pour'd,
    If souls could die, had perish'd in that passion,—
1525 But by degrees their senses were restored,
    Again to be o'ercome, again to dash on;
And, beating 'gainst *his* bosom, Haidee's heart
Felt as if never more to beat apart.

192

Alas! they were so young, so beautiful,
1530   So lonely, loving, helpless, and the hour

---

5. According to the countess of Blessington, who published *Conversations with Lord Byron* in 1834, Byron said, with reference to Haidee: "I was, and am, penetrated with the conviction that women only know evil from men, whereas men have no criterion to judge of purity or goodness but woman."

Was that in which the heart is always full,
 And, having o'er itself no further power,
Prompts deeds eternity can not annul,
 But pays off moments in an endless shower
1535 Of hell-fire—all prepared for people giving
Pleasure or pain to one another living.

193

Alas! for Juan and Haidee! they were
 So loving and so lovely—till then never,
Excepting our first parents, such a pair
1540 Had run the risk of being damn'd for ever;
And Haidee, being devout as well as fair,
 Had, doubtless, heard about the Stygian river,[6]
And hell and purgatory—but forgot
 Just in the very crisis she should not.

194

1545 They look upon each other, and their eyes
 Gleam in the moonlight; and her white arm clasps
Round Juan's head, and his around hers lies
 Half buried in the tresses which it grasps;
She sits upon his knee, and drinks his sighs,
1550 He hers, until they end in broken gasps;
And thus they form a group that's quite antique,
Half naked, loving, natural, and Greek.

195

And when those deep and burning moments pass'd,
 And Juan sunk to sleep within her arms,
1555 She slept not, but all tenderly, though fast,
 Sustain'd his head upon her bosom's charms;
And now and then her eye to heaven is cast,
 And then on the pale cheek her breast now warms,
Pillow'd on her o'erflowing heart, which pants
1560 With all it granted, and with all it grants.

196

An infant when it gazes on a light,
 A child the moment when it drains the breast,
A devotee when soars the Host[7] in sight,
 An Arab with a stranger for a guest,
1565 A sailor when the prize has struck[8] in fight,
 A miser filling his most hoarded chest,

---

6. The Styx, which flows through Hades.
7. The bread or wafer that a priest consecrates to celebrate Mass.

8. When a captured vessel (a "prize") lowers its flag in token of surrender.

Feel rapture; but not such true joy are reaping
As they who watch o'er what they love while sleeping.

197

For there it lies so tranquil, so beloved,
1570   All that it hath of life with us is living;
So gentle, stirless, helpless, and unmoved,
    And all unconscious of the joy 'tis giving;
All it hath felt, inflicted, pass'd, and proved,
    Hush'd into depths beyond the watcher's diving;
1575 There lies the thing we love with all its errors
And all its charms, like death without its terrors.

198

The lady watch'd her lover—and that hour
    Of Love's, and Night's, and Ocean's solitude,
O'erflow'd her soul with their united power;
1580   Amidst the barren sand and rocks so rude
She and her wave-worn love had made their bower,
    Where nought upon their passion could intrude,
And all the stars that crowded the blue space
Saw nothing happier than her glowing face.

199

1585 Alas! the love of women! it is known
    To be a lovely and a fearful thing;
For all of theirs upon that die is thrown,
    And if 'tis lost, life hath no more to bring
To them but mockeries of the past alone,
1590   And their revenge is as the tiger's spring,
Deadly, and quick, and crushing; yet, as real
Torture is theirs, what they inflict they feel.

200

They are right; for man, to man so oft unjust,
    Is always so to women; one sole bond
1595 Awaits them, treachery is all their trust;
    Taught to conceal, their bursting hearts despond
Over their idol, till some wealthier lust
    Buys them in marriage—and what rests beyond?
A thankless husband, next a faithless lover,
1600 Then dressing, nursing, praying, and all's over.

201

Some take a lover, some take drams° or prayers,   *drink*
    Some mind their household, others dissipation,
Some run away, and but exchange their cares,

Losing the advantage of a virtuous station;
1605　　Few changes e'er can better their affairs,
　　Theirs being an unnatural situation,
From the dull palace to the dirty hovel:
Some play the devil, and then write a novel.[9]

202

Haidee was Nature's bride, and knew not this;
1610　　Haidee was Passion's child, born where the sun
Showers triple light, and scorches even the kiss
　　Of his gazelle-eyed daughters; she was one
Made but to love, to feel that she was his
　　Who was her chosen: what was said or done
1615　Elsewhere was nothing.—She had nought to fear,
Hope, care, nor love, beyond, her heart beat *here*.

203

And oh! that quickening of the heart, that beat!
　　How much it costs us! yet each rising throb
Is in its cause as its effect so sweet,
1620　　That Wisdom, ever on the watch to rob
Joy of its alchymy and to repeat
　　Fine truths, even Conscience, too, has a tough job
To make us understand each good old maxim,
So good—I wonder Castlereagh[1] don't tax 'em.

204

1625　And now 'twas done—on the lone shore were plighted
　　Their hearts; the stars, their nuptial torches, shed
Beauty upon the beautiful they lighted:
　　Ocean their witness, and the cave their bed,
By their own feelings hallow'd and united,
1630　　Their priest was Solitude, and they were wed:
And they were happy, for to their young eyes
Each was an angel, and earth paradise.[2]

* * *

9. The impetuous Lady Caroline Lamb, having thrown herself at Byron and been after a time rejected, incorporated incidents from the affair in her novel *Glenarvon* (1816).
1. Robert Stewart, Viscount Castlereagh, detested by Byron for the ruthlessness he had shown in 1798 as the government's chief secretary for Ireland and for the foreign policy he later pursued as foreign secretary (1812–22). His bel-
ligerence with political opponents contributed to his unpopularity. Byron refers to a famously testy speech in which Castlereagh complained of "an ignorant impatience of taxation."
2. This episode rewrites *Aeneid* 4, in which, influenced by the malicious goddess Juno's love spells, the hero Aeneas and Dido, queen of Carthage, consummate their union in the cave in which they have taken refuge from a storm.

208

But Juan! had he quite forgotten Julia?
   And should he have forgotten her so soon?
I can't but say it seems to me most truly a
1660   Perplexing question; but, no doubt, the moon
Does these things for us, and whenever newly a
   Palpitation rises, 'tis her boon,
Else how the devil is it that fresh features
Have such a charm for us poor human creatures?

209

1665 I hate inconstancy—I loathe, detest,
   Abhor, condemn, abjure the mortal made
Of such quicksilver clay that in his breast
   No permanent foundation can be laid;
Love, constant love, has been my constant guest,
1670   And yet last night, being at a masquerade,
I saw the prettiest creature, fresh from Milan,
Which gave me some sensations like a villain.

210

But soon Philosophy came to my aid,
   And whisper'd, "Think of every sacred tie!"
1675 "I will, my dear Philosophy!" I said,
   "But then her teeth, and then, oh, Heaven! her eye!
I'll just enquire if she be wife or maid,
   Or neither—out of curiosity."
"Stop!" cried Philosophy, with air so Grecian,
1680 (Though she was masqued then as a fair Venetian).

211

"Stop!" so I stopp'd.—But to return: that which
   Men call inconstancy is nothing more
Than admiration due where nature's rich
   Profusion with young beauty covers o'er
1685 Some favour'd object; and as in the niche
   A lovely statue we almost adore,
This sort of adoration of the real
Is but a heightening of the "beau ideal."[3]

212

'Tis the perception of the beautiful,
1690   A fine extension of the faculties,
Platonic, universal, wonderful,
   Drawn from the stars, and filter'd through the skies,

3. Ideal beauty (French), a common phrase in discussions of aesthetics.

Without which life would be extremely dull;
  In short, it is the use of our own eyes,
1695 With one or two small senses added, just
To hint that flesh is form'd of fiery dust.

213

Yet 'tis a painful feeling, and unwilling,
  For surely if we always could perceive
In the same object graces quite as killing
1700   As when she rose upon us like an Eve,
'Twould save us many a heartache, many a shilling
  (For we must get them any how, or grieve),
Whereas if one sole lady pleased for ever,
How pleasant for the heart, as well as liver!

* * *

216

In the mean time, without proceeding more
  In this anatomy, I've finish'd now
Two hundred and odd stanzas as before,
  That being about the number I'll allow
1725 Each canto of the twelve, or twenty-four;
  And, laying down my pen, I make my bow,
Leaving Don Juan and Haidee to plead
For them and theirs with all who deign to read.[4]

1818–19   1819

The Vision of Judgment

The Vision of Judgment Byron's brilliant, buoyant satire shares its title with another *Vision of Judgment,* which, as Byron stated, it also "reverses." In 1821, just after the death of George III in the eighty-first year of his life, and sixty-first year of his reign, the former advocate of revolution and current poet laureate Robert Southey published his poem *Vision of Judgment:* a dream-vision in which a reverent Southey is vouchsafed a ring-side seat from which to behold the late king's ascent to heaven, his beatification, and the shaming of the radicals who had been his political enemies. In the preface to his *Vision* Southey defended its unusual prosody—the poem adopted the dactylic hexameters of classical Greek and Latin

4. Haidee and Juan's tryst is brought to an abrupt end by the unexpected return of her pirate father, who erupts in rage when he discovers the two together. Haidee dies of a broken heart, but Juan's adventures continue. Her father's crew wound him in a fight and then ship him off as a slave. In the slave market of Constantinople, he is bought by an enamored sultana, who disguises him as a girl and adds him to her husband's harem for convenience of access. Juan escapes, joins the Russian army that is besieging Ismail, and distinguishes himself so well in the capture of the town that he is sent with dispatches to the Russian capital. (For Byron's account of the siege, see "Romantic Literature and Wartime," p. 756.) In Russia, Juan becomes "man-mistress" to the insatiable empress, Catherine the Great. As a result of her attentions, he falls into a physical decline and in the hope that a change of scene will restore his health is sent on a diplomatic mission to England. In canto 16, the last that Byron finished, Juan is in the middle of an amorous adventure while a guest in the haunted mansion of an English nobleman and his beautiful wife, the "fair most fatal Juan ever met."

verse—and then launched digressively into a lament about the current state of English poetry. Poetry had declined into lewdness, Southey complained. Throwing down the gauntlet to Byron in particular, he ascribed that decline to a "Satanic school" of poets, "characterised by a Satanic spirit of pride and audacious impiety." When he first read this, Byron thought of challenging Southey to a duel. But in the end his rejoinder to all this "'skimble scamble stuff' about 'Satanic' and so forth," as he put it in a preface, took the form of this witty burlesque. Byron's *Vision* preserves the basic plot outline of Southey's original: it too depicts the king's arrival at heaven's gate and arraignment of his accusers. At the same time it deflates Southey's epic pretensions and unsettles his moral certitude. The angels and demons of this *Vision*'s heaven and hell, for instance, are more like diligent office workers than embodiments of good and evil. Fearing legal repercussions, Byron's publisher John Murray backed off from publishing his star author's free-wheeling satire, and it appeared in *The Liberal*, the short-lived journal Byron edited with Leigh Hunt.

From The Vision of Judgment

1

Saint Peter sat by the celestial° gate: *heaven's*
 His keys were rusty, and the lock was dull,
So little trouble had been given of late;
 Not that the place by any means was full,
5 But since the Gallic° era "eighty-eight"[1]   *French*
 The devils had ta'en a longer, stronger pull,
And "a pull altogether," as they say
At sea—which drew most souls another way.

2

The angels all were singing out of tune,
10 And hoarse with having little else to do,
Excepting to wind up the sun and moon,
 Or curb a runaway young star or two,
Or wild colt of a comet, which too soon
 Broke out of bounds o'er the ethereal blue,
15 Splitting some planet with its playful tail,
As boats are sometimes by a wanton whale.

3

The guardian seraphs had retired on high,
 Finding their charges past all care below;
Terrestrial business fill'd nought in the sky
20 Save the recording angel's black bureau;[2]
 Who found, indeed, the facts to multiply

---

1. 1788, when the political agitation leading to the French Revolution began, also the year of Byron's birth.

2. The account book in which the angel keeps the list of damned souls.

With such rapidity of vice and woe,
That he had stripp'd off both his wings in quills,°   quill pens
And yet was in arrear of human ills.

4

25 His business so augmented of late years,
    That he was forced, against his will, no doubt,
(Just like those cherubs, earthly ministers,)
    For some resource to turn himself about
And claim the help of his celestial peers,
30   To aid him ere he should be quite worn out
By the increased demand for his remarks;
Six angels and twelve saints were named his clerks.

5

This was a handsome board—at least for heaven;
    And yet they had even then enough to do,
35 So many conquerors' cars were daily driven,
    So many kingdoms fitted up anew;
Each day too slew its thousands six or seven,
    Till at the crowning carnage, Waterloo,
They threw their pens down in divine disgust—
40 The page was so besmear'd with blood and dust.[3]

6

This by the way; 'tis not mine to record
    What angels shrink from: even the very devil
On this occasion his own work abhorr'd,
    So surfeited° with the infernal revel: overindulged
45 Though he himself had sharpen'd every sword,
    It almost quench'd his innate thirst of evil.
(Here Sathan's sole good work deserves insertion—
'Tis, that he has both generals in reversion.)[4]

7

Let's skip a few short years of hollow peace,
50   Which peopled earth no better, hell as wont,
And heaven none—they° form the tyrant's lease,   the years
    With nothing but new names subscribed upon't;
'Twill one day finish: meantime they° increase,   the new names
    "With seven heads and ten horns," and all in front,
55 Like Saint John's foretold beast;[5] but ours are born
Less formidable in the head than horn.

---

3. At the Battle of Waterloo in June 1815 fifty
thousand soldiers died in a single day.
4. I.e., Sathan (Byron's name throughout for
Satan) is legally guaranteed future possession of
the souls of both Napoleon and Wellington, the
commanders whose forces met at Waterloo.
5. In Revelation 13.1 Saint John beholds a
dragon "having seven heads, and ten horns, and
upon his horns ten crowns, and upon his heads
the name of blasphemy."

8

In the first year of freedom's second dawn
    Died George the Third;[6] although no tyrant, one
Who shielded tyrants, till each sense withdrawn
60   Left him nor mental nor external sun:[7]
A better farmer[8] ne'er brush'd dew from lawn,
    A weaker king ne'er left a realm undone!
He died—but left his subjects still behind,
One half as mad—and t' other no less blind.

9

65 He died!—his death made no great stir on earth;
    His burial made some pomp; there was profusion
Of velvet, gilding, brass, and no great dearth
    Of aught but tears—save those shed by collusion.
For these things may be bought at their true worth;
70   Of elegy there was the due° infusion—   *appropriate*
Bought also; and the torches, cloaks, and banners,
Heralds, and relics of old Gothic manners,

10

Form'd a sepulchral melodrame. Of all
    The fools who flock'd to swell or see the show,
75 Who cared about the corpse? The funeral
    Made the attraction, and the black the woe.
There throbb'd not there a thought which pierced the pall;
    And when the gorgeous coffin was laid low,
It seem'd the mockery of hell to fold
80 The rottenness of eighty years in gold.

       *   *   *

16

Saint Peter sat by the celestial gate,
    And nodded o'er his keys; when, lo! there came
A wondrous noise he had not heard of late—
    A rushing sound of wind, and stream, and flame;
125 In short, a roar of things extremely great,
    Which would have made aught save a saint exclaim;
But he, with first a start and then a wink,
Said, "There's another star gone out, I think!"

6. George III died January 29, 1820, a year that saw liberal revolutions in Spain, Portugal, and the kingdom of Naples in southern Italy.
7. The king was insane and blind when he died.
8. To the delight of cartoonists such as James Gillray, who portrayed him as "Farmer George," the king had taken a keen interest in agriculture, particularly on the crown estates of Windsor and Richmond.

17

But ere he could return to his repose,
130   A cherub flapp'd his right wing o'er his eyes—
At which Saint Peter yawn'd, and rubb'd his nose:
    "Saint porter," said the Angel, "prithee rise!"
Waving a goodly wing, which glow'd, as glows
    An earthly peacock's tail, with heavenly dyes:
135 To which the Saint replied, "Well, what's the matter?
"Is Lucifer come back with all this clatter?"

18

"No," quoth the Cherub: "George the Third is dead."
    "And who *is* George the Third?" replied the apostle:
"*What George? what Third?*" "The king of England," said
140 The Angel. "Well! he won't find kings to jostle
Him on his way; but does he wear his head?
    Because the last we saw here had a tussle,
And ne'er would have got into heaven's good graces,
Had he not flung his head in all our faces.[9]

19

145 "He was, if I remember, king of France;
    That head of his, which could not keep a crown
On earth, yet ventured in my face to advance
    A claim to those° of martyrs—like my own: *i.e., the crowns*
If I had had my sword, as I had once
150 When I cut ears off, I had cut him down;
    But having but my *keys*, and not my brand,°   *sword*
I only knock'd his head from out his hand.[1]

20

"And then he set up such a headless howl,
    That all the saints came out and took him in;
155 And there he sits by Saint Paul, cheek by jowl;
    That fellow Paul—the parvenù!° The skin   *social climber*
Of Saint Bartholomew, which makes his cowl
    In heaven, and upon earth redeem'd his sin
So as to make a martyr,[2] never sped
160 Better than did this weak and wooden head.

9. Saint Peter remembers that the last monarch to arrive at heaven's gate was Louis XVI of France, executed by guillotine in 1793.
1. In John 18.10 the apostle Peter, seeking to save Jesus from the group of priests and Pharisees who have come to arrest him, takes his sword and cuts off the ear of the high priest's servant. In Matthew 16.19 Jesus tells Peter that he will be given "the keys of the kingdom of heaven."
2. The apostle Bartholomew was martyred, and earned his sainthood, by being skinned alive.

21

"But had it come up here upon its shoulders,
   There would have been a different tale to tell:
The fellow-feeling in the saint's beholders
   Seems to have acted on them like a spell;
165 And so this very foolish head heaven solders
   Back on its trunk: it may be very well,
And seems the custom here to overthrow
Whatever has been wisely done below."

22

The Angel answer'd, "Peter! do not pout:
170   The king who comes has head and all entire,
And never knew much what it was about—
   He did as doth the puppet—by its wire,
And will be judged like all the rest, no doubt:
   My business and your own is not to enquire
175 Into such matters, but to mind our cue—
Which is to act as we are bid to do."

23

While thus they spake, the angelic caravan,
   Arriving like a rush of mighty wind,
Cleaving the fields of space, as doth the swan
180   Some silver stream (say Ganges, Nile, or Inde,
Or Thames, or Tweed), and 'midst them an old man
   With an old soul, and both extremely blind,
Halted before the gate, and in his shroud
Seated their fellow-traveller on a cloud.

24

185 But bringing up the rear of this bright host
   A Spirit of a different aspect waved
His wings, like thunder-clouds above some coast
   Whose barren beach with frequent wrecks is paved;
His brow was like the deep when tempest-toss'd;
190   Fierce and unfathomable thoughts engraved
Eternal wrath on his immortal face,
And *where* he gazed a gloom pervaded space.[3]

3. This stanza introduces Sathan and in terms that playfully stress his resemblance to semiautobiographical Byronic heroes such as the Giaour and Manfred. See also the description of Satan as fallen angel in *Paradise Lost* 1.600–603: "his face / Deep scars of thunder had intrenched, and care / Sat on his faded cheek, but under brows / Of dauntless courage."

25

As he drew near, he gazed upon the gate
    Ne'er to be enter'd more by him or sin,
195 With such a glance of supernatural hate,
    As made Saint Peter wish himself within;
He patter'd with his keys at a great rate,
    And sweated through his apostolic skin:
Of course his perspiration was but ichor,[4]
200 Or some such other spiritual liquor.

26

The very cherubs huddled all together,
    Like birds when soars the falcon; and they felt
A tingling to the tip of every feather,
    And form'd a circle like Orion's belt
205 Around their poor old charge; who scarce knew whither
    His guards had led him, though they gently dealt
With royal manes° (for by many stories,   *souls*
And true, we learn the angels all are Tories).

27

As things were in this posture, the gate flew
210   Asunder, and the flashing of its hinges
Flung over space an universal hue
    Of many-colour'd flame, until its tinges
Reach'd even our speck of earth, and made a new
    Aurora borealis spread its fringes
215 O'er the North Pole; the same seen, when ice-bound,
By Captain Parry's crews, in "Melville's Sound."[5]

28

And from the gate thrown open issued beaming
    A beautiful and mighty Thing of Light,
Radiant with glory, like a banner streaming
220   Victorious from some world-o'erthrowing fight:
My poor comparisons must needs be teeming
    With earthly likenesses, for here the night
Of clay obscures our best conceptions, saving
Johanna Southcote,[6] or Bob Southey raving.

---

4. Ethereal fluid flowing in the veins of gods.
5. In his *Journal of a Voyage for the Discovery of a North-west Passage* (1821), Parry reported on the northern lights ("aurora borealis").
6. Joanna Southcott, the maidservant who in the early 19th century went public as a prophetess, publishing spiritual communications and apocalyptic predictions with the assistance of her many followers. Byron's speaker puns on *conceptions* when, in line 223, he makes his mock apology for not matching Southcott's or Southey's resources for speaking of spiritual matters. In 1814 Southcott, then sixty-four, announced she was pregnant with Shiloh, the prince of peace, whose arrival on earth she had been foretelling. She died soon after.

29

225 'Twas the archangel Michael: all men know
  The make of angels and archangels, since
There's scarce a scribbler has not one to show,
  From the fiends' leader to the angels' prince.
There also are some altar-pieces, though
230   I really can't say that they much evince
One's inner notions of immortal spirits;
But let the connoisseurs explain *their* merits.

30

Michael flew forth in glory and in good;
  A goodly work of him from whom all glory
235 And good arise; the portal past—he stood;
  Before him the young cherubs and saints hoary°—   *ancient*
(I say *young*, begging to be understood
  By looks, not years; and should be very sorry
To state, they were not older than Saint Peter,
240 But merely that they seem'd a little sweeter).

31

The cherubs and the saints bow'd down before
  That arch-angelic Hierarch, the first
Of essences angelical, who wore
  The aspect of a god; but this ne'er nursed°   *fostered*
245 Pride in his heavenly bosom, in whose core
  No thought, save for his Maker's service, durst
Intrude, however glorified and high;
He knew him but the viceroy of the sky.

32

He and the sombre silent Spirit met—
250   They knew each other both for good and ill;
Such was their power, that neither could forget
  His former friend and future foe; but still
There was a high, immortal, proud regret
  In either's eye, as if 'twere less their will
255 Than destiny to make the eternal years
Their date of war, and their "champ clos" the spheres.[7]

33

But here they were in neutral space: we know
  From Job, that Sathan hath the power to pay
A heavenly visit thrice a year or so;

---

7. In Ptolemaic astronomy, the entirety of the universe. "Champ clos": enclosed field used for a tournament or duel (French).

260   And that "the sons of God," like those of clay,
           Must keep him company;[8] and we might show,
              From the same book, in how polite a way
           The dialogue is held between the Powers
           Of Good and Evil—but 'twould take up hours.

34

265   And this is not a theologic tract,
           To prove with Hebrew and with Arabic
           If Job be allegory or a fact,
              But a true narrative; and thus I pick
           From out the whole but such and such an act
270   As sets aside the slightest thought of trick.
           'Tis every tittle[9] true, beyond suspicion,
           And accurate as any other vision.

35

       The spirits were in neutral space, before
           The gate of heaven; like eastern thresholds is
275   The place where Death's grand cause is argued o'er,[1]
           And souls despatch'd to that world or to this;
           And therefore Michael and the other wore
              A civil aspect: though they did not kiss,
           Yet still between his Darkness and his Brightness
280   There pass'd a mutual glance of great politeness.

36

       The Archangel bow'd, not like a modern beau,
           But with a graceful oriental bend,
           Pressing one radiant arm just where below
              The heart in good men is supposed to tend.
285   He turn'd as to an equal, not too low,
           But kindly; Sathan met his ancient friend
           With more hauteur,° as might an old Castilian°   *haughtiness / Spanish*
           Poor noble meet a mushroom° rich civilian.   *upstart*

37

       He merely bent his diabolic brow
290   An instant; and then raising it, he stood
           In act to assert his right or wrong, and show
              Cause why King George by no means could or should
           Make out a case to be exempt from woe
              Eternal, more than other kings, endued
295   With better sense and hearts, whom history mentions,
           Who long have "paved hell with their good intentions."

---

8. Cf. Job 1.6: "Now there was a day when the sons of God came to present themselves before the Lord, and Satan came also among them."
9. I.e., a tiny amount. Also a term for the small-est sort of written mark, for instance, the dot over the letter *i*.
1. In the Middle East in Byron's time justice was administered at cities' gates.

38

Michael began: "What wouldst thou with this man,
    Now dead, and brought before the Lord? What ill
Hath he wrought since his mortal race began,
300   That thou canst claim him? Speak! and do thy will,
If it be just: if in his earthly span°   *lifetime*
    He hath been greatly failing to fulfil
His duties as a king and mortal, say,
And he is thine; if not, let him have way."

39

305 "Michael!" replied the Prince of Air,° "even here,   *i.e., Sathan*
    Before the gate of him thou servest, must
I claim my subject: and will make appear
    That as he was my worshipper in dust,
So shall he be in spirit, although dear
310   To thee and thine, because nor wine nor lust
Were of his weaknesses; yet on the throne
He reign'd o'er millions to serve me alone.

40

"Look to *our* earth, or rather *mine*; it was,
    Once, more thy master's: but I triumph not
315 In this poor planet's conquest; nor, alas!
    Need he thou servest envy me my lot:
With all the myriads of bright worlds which pass
    In worship round him, he may have forgot
Yon weak creation of such paltry things:
320   I think few worth damnation save their kings,—

41

"And these but as a kind of quit-rent,[2] to
    Assert my right as lord; and even had
I such an inclination, 'twere (as you
    Well know) superfluous; they are grown so bad,
325 That hell has nothing better left to do
    Than leave them to themselves: so much more mad
And evil by their own internal curse,
Heaven cannot make them better, nor I worse.

42

"Look to the earth, I said, and say again:
330   When this old, blind, mad, helpless, weak, poor worm[3]
Began in youth's first bloom and flush to reign,

---

2. A small, nominal payment. Sathan claims the souls of earth's kings only, as a way to assert his rightful sovereignty over the earth.

3. Echoing the first line of Percy Shelley's "England in 1819": "An old, mad, blind, despised, and dying King" (see p. 805).

The world and he both wore a different form,
And much of earth and all the watery plain
Of ocean call'd him king: through many a storm
335   His isles had floated on the abyss of time;
For the rough virtues chose them for their clime.

43

"He came to his sceptre young; he leaves it old:
Look to the state in which he found his realm,
And left it; and his annals too behold,
340   How to a minion first he gave the helm;[4]
How grew upon his heart a thirst for gold,
The beggar's vice, which can but overwhelm
The meanest° hearts; and for the rest, but glance   shabbiest
Thine eye along America and France.

44

345   "'Tis true, he was a tool from first to last
(I have the workmen safe); but as a tool
So let him be consumed. From out the past
Of ages, since mankind have known the rule
Of monarchs—from the bloody rolls amass'd
350   Of sin and slaughter—from the Caesars' school,
Take the worst pupil; and produce a reign
More drench'd with gore, more cumber'd with the slain.

45

"He ever warr'd with freedom and the free:
Nations as men, home subjects, foreign foes,
355   So that they utter'd the word 'Liberty!'
Found George the Third their first opponent. Whose
History was ever stain'd as his will be
With national and individual woes?
I grant his household abstinence; I grant
360   His neutral virtues, which most monarchs want;°   i.e., lack

46

"I know he was a constant consort; own
He was a decent sire, and middling lord.
All this is much, and most upon a throne;
As temperance, if at Apicius'[5] board,°   dining table
365   Is more than at an anchorite's° supper shown.   hermit's
I grant him all the kindest can accord;
And this was well for him, but not for those
Millions who found him what oppression chose.

---

4. George III's first prime minister was the earl
of Bute, who had been his tutor.

5. Famous gourmet in ancient Rome.

47

"The New World° shook him off; the Old yet groans   *i.e., America*
370   Beneath what he and his prepared, if not
Completed: he leaves heirs on many thrones
      To all his vices, without what begot
Compassion for him—his tame virtues; drones
      Who sleep, or despots who have now forgot
375   A lesson which shall be re-taught them, wake
Upon the thrones of earth; but let them quake![6]

*   *   *

85

At length with jostling, elbowing, and the aid
      Of cherubim appointed to that post,
675   The devil Asmodeus to the circle made
      His way, and look'd as if his journey cost
Some trouble. When his burden down he laid,
      "What's this?" cried Michael; "why, 'tis not a ghost?"
"I know it," quoth the incubus; "but he
680   Shall be one, if you leave the affair to me.

86

"Confound the Renegado![7] I have sprain'd
      My left wing, he's so heavy; one would think
Some of his works about his neck were chain'd.
      But to the point; while hovering o'er the brink
685   Of Skiddaw[8] (where as usual it still rain'd),
      I saw a taper, far below me, wink,
And stooping, caught this fellow at a libel—
No less on History than the Holy Bible.

87

"The former is the devil's scripture, and
690   The latter yours, good Michael; so the affair
Belongs to all of us, you understand.
      I snatch'd him up just as you see him there,
And brought him off for sentence out of hand:

6. In the omitted section, stanzas 48–84, Sathan summons witnesses to support his claim that King George should be damned. Chief among these opponents to George are the radical politician John Wilkes and the mysterious 18th-century political commentator who is still known, despite efforts to discover his true identity, only by the pseudonym Junius: the books collecting Junius's writings of 1768–73 carried instead of an author's name the Latin phrase "*Stat nominis umbra*" (the shadow of a name stands here). To Sathan's chagrin Junius melts away into shadow and smoke, refusing to elabo-rate on the testimony given in that book. At that point the trial is interrupted.
7. Southey is named the Renegado—a turncoat or traitor—because his political beliefs had fluctuated immensely since his literary debut in the 1790s. He was very prolific: William Hazlitt's portrait in *The Spirit of the Age* (1825) represents Southey passing "from verse to prose, from history to poetry, from reading to writing, by a stopwatch." As the demon suggests, his collected works would weigh a substantial amount.
8. Mountain near Southey's home in the Lake District.

I've scarcely been ten minutes in the air—
695 At least a quarter it can hardly be:
I dare say that his wife is still at tea."

88

Here Sathan said, "I know this man of old,
    And have expected him for some time here;
A sillier fellow you will scarce behold,
700   Or more conceited in his petty sphere:
But surely it was not worth while to fold
    Such trash below your wing, Asmodeus dear:
We had the poor wretch safe (without being bored
With carriage) coming of his own accord.

89

705 "But since he's here, let's see what he has done."
    "Done!" cried Asmodeus, "he anticipates
The very business you are now upon,
    And scribbles as if head clerk to the Fates.
Who knows to what his ribaldry° may run,   *indecency*
710   When such an ass as this, like Balaam's, prates?"⁹
"Let's hear," quoth Michael, "what he has to say;
You know we're bound to that in every way."

90

Now the Bard, glad to get an audience, which
    By no means often was his case below,
715 Began to cough, and hawk, and hem, and pitch
    His voice into that awful note of woe
To all unhappy hearers within reach
    Of poets when the tide of rhyme's in flow;
But stuck fast with his first hexameter,
720 Not one of all whose gouty feet would stir.

91

But ere the spavin'd° dactyls could be spurr'd   *lame*
    Into recitative, in great dismay
Both cherubim and seraphim were heard
    To murmur loudly through their long array;
725 And Michael rose ere he could get a word
    Of all his founder'd verses under way,
And cried, "For God's sake stop, my friend! 'twere best
*Non Di, non homines*¹—you know the rest."

9. In Numbers 22, the ass on which Balaam, disobedient to God's will, has been riding is miraculously given the power of speech to make him aware of his fault.

1. Neither gods, nor men (Latin). Archangel Michael cites the Latin poet Horace's *Art of Poetry*, lines 372–73: "Neither men nor gods nor booksellers can tolerate mediocre poetry."

92

A general bustle spread throughout the throng,
730   Which seem'd to hold all verse in detestation;
The angels had of course enough of song
    When upon service; and the generation
Of ghosts had heard too much in life, not long
    Before, to profit by a new occasion;
735 The Monarch, mute till then, exclaim'd, "What! what!
Pye² come again? No more—no more of that!"

93

The tumult grew; an universal cough
    Convulsed the skies, as during a debate,
When Castlereagh has been up long enough³
740   (Before he was first minister of state,
I mean—the slaves hear now); some cried "Off, off!"
    As at a farce; till, grown quite desperate,
The Bard Saint Peter pray'd to interpose
(Himself an author)⁴ only for his prose.

94

745 The varlet° was not an ill-favour'd knave;   i.e., Southey
    A good deal like a vulture in the face,
With a hook nose and a hawk's eye, which gave
    A smart and sharper-looking sort of grace
To his whole aspect, which, though rather grave,
750   Was by no means so ugly as his case;
But that indeed was hopeless as can be,
Quite a poetic felony "de se."⁵

95

Then Michael blew his trump, and still'd the noise
    With one still greater, as is yet the mode
755 On earth besides; except some grumbling voice,
    Which now and then will make a slight inroad
Upon decorous silence, few will twice
    Lift up their lungs when fairly overcrow'd;°   overpowered
And now the bard could plead his own bad cause,
760 With all the attitudes of self-applause.

2. Henry James Pye, the mediocre poet who had been poet laureate before Southey.
3. Robert Stewart, Viscount Castlereagh, a Tory cabinet minister much loathed by Byron, was a poor public speaker.
4. I.e., author of two chapters in the New Testament.
5. Poetic self-murder, i.e., suicide.

96

He said—(I only give the heads°)—he said,   *headings*
   He meant no harm in scribbling; 'twas his way
Upon all topics; 'twas, besides, his bread,
   Of which he butter'd both sides; 'twould delay
765 Too long the assembly (he was pleased to dread),
   And take up rather more time than a day,
To name his works—he would but cite a few—
"Wat Tyler"—"Rhymes on Blenheim"—"Waterloo."[6]

97

He had written praises of a regicide;[7]
770   He had written praises of all kings whatever;
He had written for republics far and wide,
   And then against them bitterer than ever;
For pantisocracy he once had cried[8]
   Aloud, a scheme less moral than 'twas clever;
775 Then grew a hearty anti-jacobin[9]
Had turn'd his coat—and would have turn'd his skin.

98

He had sung against all battles, and again
   In their high praise and glory; he had call'd
Reviewing "the ungentle craft,"[1] and then
780   Become as base a critic as e'er° crawl'd—   *ever*
Fed, paid, and pamper'd by the very men
   By whom his muse and morals had been maul'd:
He had written much blank verse, and blanker prose,
And more of both than any body knows.

99

785 He had written Wesley's life:[2]—here turning round
   To Sathan, "Sir, I'm ready to write yours,
In two octavo volumes, nicely bound,
   With notes and preface, all that most allures
The pious purchaser; and there's no ground
790   For fear, for I can choose my own reviewers:
So let me have the proper documents,
That I may add you to my other saints."

6. Works by Southey: his dramatic tragedy about a medieval peasants' revolt, *Wat Tyler* (written in 1794, and published in a pirated edition in 1817, somewhat to the middle-aged Southey's embarrassment); "The Battle of Blenheim" (1798); *The Poet's Pilgrimage to Waterloo* (1816).
7. Southey's "Inscription for the Apartment in Chepstow Castle" (1797), about Henry Marten, an organizer of the trial and execution in 1649 of Charles I.
8. In 1794–96 Southey and Coleridge had planned to establish "pantisocracy"—a community in which all would be equal and all would rule—in the American wilderness.
9. Opponent of the French Revolution and its British supporters.
1. See "Life of Henry Kirke White" [Byron's note, quoting Southey's 1807 biography of a working-class poet he had befriended before the young man's tragically early death].
2. A biography in 1820 of John Wesley, the 18th-century founder of the Methodist movement within the Church of England.

100

Sathan bow'd, and was silent. "Well, if you,
  With amiable modesty, decline
795 My offer, what says Michael? There are few
  Whose memoirs could be render'd more divine.
Mine is a pen of all work; not so new
  As it was once, but I would make you shine
Like your own trumpet. By the way, my own
800 Has more of brass in it, and is as well blown.

101

"But talking about trumpets, here's my Vision!
  Now you shall judge, all people; yes, you shall
Judge with my judgment! and by my decision
  Be guided who shall enter heaven or fall.
805 I settle all these things by intuition,
  Times present, past, to come, heaven, hell, and all,
Like King Alfonso.³ When I thus see double,
I save the Deity some worlds of trouble."

102

He ceased, and drew forth an MS.;° and no   *manuscript*
810   Persuasion on the part of devils, or saints,
Or angels, now could stop the torrent; so
  He read the first three lines of the contents;
But at the fourth, the whole spiritual show
  Had vanish'd, with variety of scents,
815 Ambrosial and sulphureous, as they sprang,
Like lightning, off from his "melodious twang."⁴

103

Those grand heroics acted as a spell;
  The angels stopp'd their ears and plied their pinions;
The devils ran howling, deafen'd, down to hell;
820   The ghosts fled, gibbering, for their own dominions—
(For 'tis not yet decided where they dwell,
  And I leave every man to his opinions);
Michael took refuge in his trump—but, lo!
His teeth were set on edge, he could not blow!

---

3. King Alphonso, speaking of the Ptolemean system, said, that "had he been consulted at the creation of the world, he would have spared the Maker some absurdities" [Byron's note; Alfonso was a 13th-century king of Castile and Léon in Spain].
4. See Aubrey's account of the apparition, which disappeared "with a curious perfume and a melodious twang"; or see *Antiquary*, vol. 1 [Byron's note, referring to a report on ghost-seeing in John Aubrey's *Miscellanies*, 1696, and an episode involving a haunted chamber in Sir Walter Scott's 1816 novel *The Antiquary*].

104

825 Saint Peter, who has hitherto been known
　　　For an impetuous saint, upraised his keys,
　　And at the fifth line knock'd the Poet down;
　　　Who fell like Phaeton,[5] but more at ease,
　　Into his lake, for there he did not drown;
830　　A different web being by the Destinies
　　Woven for the Laureate's final wreath, whene'er
　　Reform shall happen either here or there.

105

　　He first sank to the bottom—like his works,
　　　But soon rose to the surface—like himself;
835 For all corrupted things are buoy'd like corks,[6]
　　　By their own rottenness, light as an elf,
　　Or wisp that flits o'er a morass: he lurks,
　　　It may be, still, like dull books on a shelf,
　　In his own den, to scrawl some "Life" or "Vision,"
840 As Welborn says—"the devil turn'd precisian."[7]

106

　　As for the rest, to come to the conclusion
　　　Of this true dream, the telescope is gone
　　Which kept my optics free from all delusion,
　　　And show'd me what I in my turn have shown;
845 All I saw farther, in the last confusion,
　　　Was, that King George slipp'd into heaven for one;
　　And when the tumult dwindled to a calm,
　　I left him practising the hundredth psalm.[8]

1821   1822

---

5. In classical mythology, the reckless boy who, when he tries to drive the chariot of the sun, nearly burns up creation. To stop him, Zeus, king of the gods, sends a thunderbolt that casts Phaeton down from the chariot to his death in a river below.
6. A drowned body lies at the bottom till rotten; it then floats, as most people know [Byron's note].
7. Puritan. Citing Philip Massinger's 1633 comedy *A New Way to Pay Old Debts* 1.1.5–7: the protagonist's words to the barman who has refused to serve him.
8. The psalm beginning "Make a joyful noise unto the Lord."

On This Day I Complete My Thirty-Sixth Year

Missolonghi, Jan. 22, 1824.

1

'Tis time this heart should be unmoved,
   Since others it hath ceased to move,
Yet though I cannot be beloved,
      Still let me love!

2

5 My days are in the yellow leaf;
   The flowers and fruits of Love are gone;
The worm, the canker, and the grief
      Are mine alone!

3

The fire that on my bosom preys
10   Is lone as some volcanic isle;
No torch is kindled at its blaze—
      A funeral pile!

4

The hope, the fear, the jealous care,
   The exalted portion of the pain
15 And power of Love I cannot share,
      But wear the chain.

5

But 'tis not *thus*—and 'tis not *here*
   Such thoughts should shake my Soul, nor *now*,
Where Glory decks the hero's bier
20   Or binds his brow.

6

The Sword—the Banner—and the Field—
   Glory and Greece around us see!
The Spartan borne upon his shield
      Was not more free!

7

25   Awake! (not Greece—she *is* awake!)
      Awake, my Spirit! think through *whom*
      Thy life-blood tracks its parent lake
          And then strike home!

8

      Tread those reviving passions down,
30   Unworthy Manhood;—unto thee
      Indifferent should the smile or frown
          Of Beauty be.

9

      If thou regret'st thy youth, *why live?*
      The land of honourable Death
35   Is here:—up to the Field! and give
          Away thy Breath.

10

      Seek out—less often sought than found—
      A Soldier's Grave, for thee the best;
      Then look around and choose thy ground
40   And take thy Rest.

Jan. 1824   1824

Romantic Literature and Wartime

B y birth British Romantic authors were the fortunate inhabitants, as Shakespeare's John of Gaunt had declared, of a "sceptered isle" moated about by the sea. Home for them was at a safe distance from battlefields on the European continent, in the Americas, or in the West and East Indian colonies: since 1745–46, the years witnessing the quelling of the last of the Jacobite Rebellions, military conflict had almost by definition been something that did not take place on British ground. Nonetheless, the sense that no peace could or should be found in that home shaped in important ways Romantic authors' understanding of literature's public role. Romanticism was a wartime phenomenon. Between the outbreak of hostilities in 1793, which followed hard on the heels of Jacobin France's trial and execution of its former king, and the Duke of Wellington's victory over Napoleon at the Battle of Waterloo in 1815, Britain and France waged an almost unremitting war.

Invasion by France, much feared by inhabitants of the southeast of England particularly, never came to pass, but there were extended periods, in 1798 and 1803–04, when Napoleon's armies encamped on the Channel coast, only twenty-one miles from Dover, their flotillas of invasion barges readied. At these moments of high alert, cartoonists on the government payroll, such as James Gillray, did their gory best to evoke "the Promis'd Horrors of the French Invasion" and so ensure that those out of reach of the artillery were nonetheless bombarded with images of French atrocity. As William Wordsworth's "Discharged Soldier" suggests, for many civilians the distant conflicts also became more immediate whenever they encountered, "linger[ing] in the public ways," the numerous wounded veterans who survived their military duty but were reduced to vagrancy and beggary upon their return home. The sense of foreboding aroused by the nameless soldier in Wordsworth's 1798 poem, survivor of "war and battle and . . . pestilence" in "the tropical isles," may register Wordsworth's fearful awareness that English rural society could not escape being affected by the militarism his government was exporting across the globe. This topic is meant to suggest, through examples like these, the many ways in which, between 1793 and 1815, war's violence came home to Englishmen and women's imaginations.

This intractable, twenty-two-year conflict represented a new kind of warfare. Certainly Britain had repeatedly been on a war footing during the eighteenth century, the most recent hostilities being those terminated by the Treaty of Versailles in 1783. Britons' nationalism had developed in concert with their francophobia since the sixteenth century: as Catholic Other and rival for trade and later colonies, France had long occupied the role of Britain's archenemy. The conflict with the new French republic that began in 1793 was, however, unprecedented in both scale and intensity—a dress rehearsal, historians say, for the "total war" of the twentieth century. It spanned the globe. It involved huge portions of the British population: the navy expanded by a factor of eight during these years, the army by a factor of six, and measures for civil defense adopted following the first invasion scare involved the formation of huge auxiliary forces of civilian volunteers. Ultimately one-sixth to one-fifth of the nation's adult men were enrolled in the armed forces. This level of mobilization would remain unmatched until World War I.

"The people became a participant in war; instead of governments and armies as heretofore, the full weight of the nation was thrown into the balance": the Prussian general Carl von Clausewitz's retrospect on how the French republic changed history by altering the conduct of war also applies to Britain, despite Britain's official opposition to the political innovations happening across the Channel. Though the wars Britain waged between 1793 and 1815 did enrich the empire with new overseas possessions (many former French colonies), the prospect of territorial expansion was not the principal reason that this warfare had come to command "the full weight of the nation." The support that ordinary people voluntarily lent to the war effort (not least by paying the high taxes that it required) instead demonstrated (or so loyalist propaganda proposed) Britons' attachment to the constitution, or their wish to redeem the national character, which had become effete or addicted to luxury, or their hatred of Napoleonic tyranny.

The British Crown was quick to realize that the defense of the realm would also necessarily involve the management of public opinion. The government invested in an intensive campaign of communal festivity and patriotic pageantry—witness the five days of ceremonies, attended by tens of thousands, held when Admiral Horatio Nelson was laid to rest at St. Paul's Cathedral, following his death at Trafalgar. Few people in British towns would have been able to remain aloof from this particular campaign, to feel that they could count on being left alone in peace or, for that matter, in quiet. Church bells were rung for victories; patriotic choruses of "God save the king" sometimes erupted, mid-performance, from the stalls of theaters; recruiting sergeants beat their drums as they trawled the streets looking to lure the local poor with enlistment bounties and promises of escape. ("I hate that drum's discordant sound / Parading round and round and round," John Scott's much-reprinted poem on recruitment began; that drum beat is echoed in the opening of Anna Letitia Barbauld's anti-war *Eighteen Hundred and Eleven.*) An additional way in which the warfare that stepped forth in 1793 differed from wars of the past was that the hostilities with France both coincided with and fueled a rapid expansion of the newspaper industry. News of fleet movements, generals' strategies, casualties, victories, and defeats was more intensely disseminated and reported than in previous conflicts, a fact that made the management of public opinion at once more urgent and more difficult. Battles waged in distant climes became news stories that were consumed in British parlors, amid middle-class families' daily routines. "Boys and girls, / And women . . . all read of war, / the best amusement for our morning meal!" Coleridge observed with consternation in "Fears of Solitude."

Of course, Romantic poetry and fiction were themselves part of this media blitz—war sold books as well as newspapers—though poems and novels did not so much broadcast war news as provide instruction as to how readers should feel about that news. That instruction changed over the course of the period. In the eighteenth century some thinkers had decried war as an absurd, archaic dueling that vainglorious monarchs engaged in at the expense of their subjects. (William Godwin repeats in *Political Justice* some biting lines from Jonathan Swift: "Sometimes the quarrel between two princes is to decide which of them shall possess a third of his dominions, where neither of them pretends to any right. Sometimes one prince quarrels with another, for fear the other should quarrel with him.") Critiques in this vein continued to circulate after 1793: profiling current war poetry in 1799 the reviewers for the *Anti-Jacobin Review* accused contemporary poets of keeping victory out of sight so as to emphasize war's pains, stating that "we are presented with nothing but contusions and amputations, plundered peasants and deserted looms." But anti-war poetry was soon overshadowed by the new accounts construing the battle against the French as a crusade for a holy cause or as a purifying ordeal that might bring about individual and national regeneration. Many nineteenth-century writers and readers reembraced the epic, a genre with a legacy of bloodlust, emphasizing war's glories and the opportunities for virile heroism battle afforded. Sir Walter Scott was at the forefront of this abandonment of what a reviewer called "the mild pacific tone" of modern poetry, for in his works, this reviewer said, he had assumed "the ancient function of a bard, to celebrate military prowess, and set off pride, ferocity, and revenge." Modern war was becoming a matter of mechanically drilled mass armies, each side aiming to dominate the other through sheer force of numbers, but in poems engaging a picturesque, premodern past—be they Scott's *Marmion* (1808) or Robert Southey's *Roderick, the Last of the Goths* (1814)—martial might could step forth once again as a gloriously individual and impassioned thing.

WILLIAM GODWIN

With its faith in the perfectibility of our political arrangements, the *Enquiry Concerning Political Justice* (1793) is now recognized as the exemplary statement of the utopianism of the 1790s: according to William Hazlitt, with this text William Godwin (1756–1836) "carried with him all the most sanguine and fearless understandings of the time." The *Enquiry* distills an Enlightenment tradition of anti-war arguments as it traces how government, "once intended to suppress injustice," now gives rise to "oppression, despotism, war, and conquest."

From Enquiry Concerning Political Justice and Its Influence on General Virtue and Happiness

From *Of the Causes of War*

* * *

One of the most essential principles of political justice is diametrically the reverse of that which impostors and patriots have too frequently agreed to recommend. Their perpetual exhortation has been, "Love your country. Sink the personal existence of individuals in the existence of the community. Make little account of the particular men of whom the society consists, but aim at the general wealth, prosperity and glory. Purify your mind from the gross ideas of sense, and elevate it to the single contemplation of that abstract individual of which particular men are so many detached members, valuable only for the place they fill."[1]

The lessons of reason on this head are precisely opposite. "Society is an ideal existence, and not on its own account entitled to the smallest regard. The wealth, prosperity and glory of the whole are unintelligible chimeras. Set no value on any thing, but in proportion as you are convinced of its tendency to make individual men happy and virtuous. Benefit by every practicable mode man wherever he exists; but be not deceived by the specious idea of affording services to a body of men, for which no individual man is the better. Society was instituted, not for the sake of glory, not to furnish splendid materials for the page of history, but for the benefit of its members. The love of our country, if we would speak accurately, is another of those specious illusions, which have been invented by impostors in order to render the multitude the blind instruments of their crooked designs."

---

1. Here Godwin footnotes Jean-Jacques Rousseau's *The Social Contract* (1762).

Meanwhile let us beware of passing from one injurious extreme to another. Much of what has been usually understood by the love of our country is highly excellent and valuable, though perhaps nothing that can be brought within the strict interpretation of the phrase. A wise man will not fail to be the votary of liberty and equality. He will be ready to exert himself in their defence wherever they exist. It cannot be a matter of indifference to him, when his own liberty and that of other men with whose excellence and capabilities he has the best opportunity of being acquainted, are involved in the event of the struggle to be made. But his attachment will be to the cause, and not to the country. Wherever there are men who understand the value of political justice and are prepared to assert it, that is his country. Wherever he can most contribute to the diffusion of these principles and the real happiness of mankind, that is his country. Nor does he desire for any country any other benefit than justice.

* * *

Because individuals were liable to error, and suffered their apprehensions of justice to be perverted by a bias in favour of themselves, government was instituted. Because nations were susceptible of a similar weakness, and could find no sufficient umpire to whom to appeal, war was introduced. Men were induced deliberately to seek each other's lives, and to adjudge the controversies between them, not according to the dictates of reason and justice, but as either should prove most successful in devastation and murder. This was no doubt in the first instance the extremity of exasperation and rage. But it has since been converted into a trade. One part of the nation pays another part to murder and be murdered in their stead; and the most trivial causes, a supposed insult or a sally of youthful ambition, have sufficed to deluge provinces with blood.

We can have no adequate idea of this evil, unless we visit, at least in imagination, a field of battle. Here men deliberately destroy each other by thousands without any resentment against or even knowledge of each other. The plain is strewed with death in all its various forms. Anguish and wounds display the diversified modes in which they can torment the human frame. Towns are burned, ships are blown up in the air while the mangled limbs descend on every side, the fields are laid desolate, the wives of the inhabitants exposed to brutal insult, and their children driven forth to hunger and nakedness. It would be despicable to mention, along with these scenes of horror, and the total subversion of all ideas of moral justice they must occasion in the auditors and spectators, the immense treasures which are wrung in the form of taxes from those inhabitants whose residence is at a distance from the scene.

1793

WILLIAM WORDSWORTH

This haunting poem, which Wordsworth composed in early 1798 (at around the time he was also working on "The Ruined Cottage"), was left unpublished during Wordsworth's lifetime, though he eventually incorporated the lines into *The Prelude*, Book 4. There this disquieting meeting with a returned veteran of foreign wars interrupts the poet's account of his first summer vacation from college. Pestilence (line 139) afflicted many soldiers and sailors, especially those unlucky enough to see service in the West Indies. Epidemics of yellow fever, dysentery, and other diseases are estimated to have killed more servicemen than military encounters.

The Discharged Soldier

              I love to walk
Along the public way when for the night,
Deserted in its silence, it assumes
A character of deeper quietness
5   Than pathless solitudes. At such a time
I slowly mounted up a steep ascent
Where the road's watry surface to the ridge
Of that sharp rising glittered in the moon
And seemed before my eyes another stream
10   Stealing with silent lapse to join the brook
That murmured in the valley. On I passed
Tranquil, receiving in my own despite
Amusement, as I slowly passed along,
From such near objects as from time to time
15   Perforce disturbed the slumber of the sense
Quiescent, and disposed to sympathy,
With an exhausted mind worn out by toil
And all unworthy of the deeper joy
Which waits on distant prospect, cliff or sea,
20   The dark blue vault, and universe of stars.
Thus did I steal along that silent road,
My body from the stillness drinking in
A restoration like the calm of sleep
But sweeter far. Above, before, behind,
25   Around me, all was peace and solitude:
I looked not round, nor did the solitude
Speak to my eye, but it was heard and felt.
Oh happy state! What beauteous pictures now
Rose in harmonious imagery—they rose
30   As from some distant region of my soul
And came along like dreams, yet such as left
Obscurely mingled with their passing forms
A consciousness of animal delight,
A self-possession felt in every pause
35   And every gentle movement of my frame.

"John Bull's glorious Return."
The ironically titled final panel of John Gillray's 1793 print "John Bull's Progress" images a British soldier, wounded and disfigured, coming home to his impoverished family.

     While thus I wandered, step by step led on,
It chanced a sudden turning of the road
Presented to my view an uncouth shape
So near that, stepping back into the shade
40   Of a thick hawthorn, I could mark him well,
Myself unseen. He was in stature tall,
A foot above man's common measure tall,
And lank, and upright. There was in his form
A meagre stiffness. You might almost think
45   That his bones wounded him. His legs were long,
So long and shapeless that I looked at them
Forgetful of the body they sustained.
His arms were long and lean; his hands were bare;
His visage, wasted though it seemed, was large
50   In feature; his cheeks sunken; and his mouth
Shewed ghastly in the moonlight. From behind
A mile-stone propped him, and his figure seemed
Half-sitting and half-standing. I could mark
That he was clad in military garb,
55   Though faded yet entire. His face was turned
Towards the road, yet not as if he sought
For any living thing. He appeared
Forlorn and desolate, a man cut off
From all his kind, and more than half detached
60   From his own nature.
                He was alone,
Had no attendant, neither dog, nor staff,
Nor knapsack—in his very dress appeared
A desolation, a simplicity
That appertained to solitude. I think
65   If but a glove had dangled in his hand
It would have made him more akin to man.
Long time I scanned him with a mingled sense
Of fear and sorrow. From his lips meanwhile
There issued murmuring sounds as if of pain
70   Or of uneasy thought; yet still his form
Kept the same fearful steadiness. His shadow

Lay at his feet and moved not. In a glen
Hard by a village stood, whose silent doors
Were visible among the scattered trees,
75   Scarce distant from the spot an arrow's flight.
I wished to see him move, but he remained
Fixed to his place, and still from time to time
Sent forth a murmuring voice of dead complaint,
A groan scarce audible. Yet all the while
80   The chained mastiff in his wooden house
Was vexed, and from among the village trees
Howled never ceasing. Not without reproach
Had I prolonged my watch, and now confirmed,
And my heart's specious cowardice subdued,
85   I left the shady nook where I had stood
And hailed the Stranger. From his resting-place
He rose, and with his lean and wasted arm
In measured gesture lifted to his head
Returned my salutation. A short while
90   I held discourse on things indifferent
And casual matter. He meanwhile had ceased
From all complaint—his station had resumed,
Propped by the mile stone as before, and when erelong
I asked his history, he in reply
95   Was neither slow nor eager, but unmoved,
And with a quiet uncomplaining voice,
A stately air of mild indifference,
He told a simple fact: that he had been
A Soldier, to the tropic isles had gone,
100   Whence he had landed now some ten days past;
That on his landing he had been dismissed,
And with the little strength he yet had left
Was travelling to regain his native home.
At this I turned and through the trees looked down
105   Into the village—all were gone to rest,
Nor smoke nor any taper light appeared,
But every silent window to the moon
Shone with a yellow glitter. 'No one there,'
Said I, 'is waking; we must measure back
110   The way which we have come. Behind yon wood
A labourer dwells, an honest man and kind;
He will not murmur should we break his rest,
And he will give you food if food you need,
And lodging for the night.' At this he stooped,
115   And from the ground took up an oaken staff
By me yet unobserved, a traveller's staff,
Which I suppose from his slack hand had dropped,
And, such the languor of the weary man,
Had lain till now neglected in the grass,
120   But not forgotten. Back we turned and shaped
Our course toward the cottage. He appeared
To travel without pain, and I beheld
With ill-suppressed astonishment his tall
And ghostly figure moving at my side.

125 As we advanced I asked him for what cause
He tarried there, nor had demanded rest
At inn or cottage. He replied, 'In truth
My weakness made me loth to move, and here
I felt myself at ease and much relieved,
130 But that the village mastiff fretted me,
And every second moment rang a peal
Felt at my very heart. There was no noise,
Nor any foot abroad—I do not know
What ailed him, but it seemed as if the dog
135 Were howling to the murmur of the stream.'
While thus we travelled on I did not fail
To question him of what he had endured
From war and battle and the pestilence.
He all the while was in demeanor calm,
140 Concise in answer: solemn and sublime
He might have seemed, but that in all he said
There was a strange half-absence and a tone
Of weakness and indifference, as of one
Remembering the importance of his theme,
145 But feeling it no longer. We advanced
Slowly, and ere we to the wood were come
Discourse had ceased. Together on we passed
In silence through the shades gloomy and dark,
Then turning up along an open field
150 We gained the cottage. At the door I knocked,
And called aloud, 'My Friend, here is a man
By sickness overcome; beneath your roof
This night let him find rest, and give him food—
The service if need be I will requite.'
155 Assured that now my comrade would repose
In comfort, I entreated that henceforth
He would not linger in the public ways
But at the door of cottage or of inn
Demand the succour which his state required,
160 And told him, feeble as he was 'twere fit
He asked relief or alms. At this reproof
With the same ghastly mildness in his look
He said, 'My trust is in the God of heaven,
And in the eye of him that passes me.'
165 By this the labourer had unlocked the door,
And now my comrade touched his hat again
With his lean hand, and in a voice that seemed
To speak with a reviving interest
Till then unfelt, he thanked me. I returned
170 The blessing of the poor unhappy man,
And so we parted.

1798

SAMUEL TAYLOR COLERIDGE

"He now read with listless unconcern of events which, but a very few years ago, would have filled all Europe with astonishment," Coleridge wrote in the newspaper *The Morning Post*, an insight into public apathy that he develops at length in this poem of crisis. "Fears in Solitude" (1798; first published in the same volume as "Frost at Midnight") is often read as documenting a pivotal moment in Coleridge's political allegiances: here the radical, known for his enthusiasm for the French Revolution and opposition to war, presents himself as patriot.

From Fears in Solitude

Written in April 1798, during the Alarm of an Invasion

A green and silent spot, amid the hills,
A small and silent dell! O'er stiller place
No singing sky-lark ever poised himself.
The hills are heathy, save that swelling slope,
5   Which hath a gay and gorgeous covering on,
All golden with the never-bloomless furze,
Which now blooms most profusely: but the dell,
Bathed by the mist, is fresh and delicate
As vernal corn-field, or the unripe flax,
10 When, through its half-transparent stalks, at eve,
The level sunshine glimmers with green light.
Oh! 'tis a quiet spirit-healing nook!
Which all, methinks, would love; but chiefly he,
The humble man, who, in his youthful years,
15 Knew just so much of folly, as had made
His early manhood more securely wise!
Here he might lie on fern or withered heath,
While from the singing lark (that sings unseen
The minstrelsy that solitude loves best),
20 And from the sun, and from the breezy air,
Sweet influences trembled o'er his frame;
And he, with many feelings, many thoughts,
Made up a meditative joy, and found
Religious meanings in the forms of nature!
25 And so, his senses gradually wrapt
In a half sleep, he dreams of better worlds,
And dreaming hears thee still, O singing lark,
That singest like an angel in the clouds!

    My God! It is a melancholy thing
30 For such a man, who would full fain preserve
His soul in calmness, yet perforce must feel
For all his human brethren—O my God!
It weighs upon the heart, that he must think
What uproar and what strife may now be stirring

35 This way or that way o'er these silent hills—
    Invasion, and the thunder and the shout,
    And all the crash of onset; fear and rage,
    And undetermined conflict—even now,
    Even now, perchance, and in his native isle;
40 Carnage and groans beneath this blessed sun!
    We have offended, Oh! My countrymen!
    We have offended very grievously
    And been most tyrannous.

                            *   *   *

                            Thankless too for peace,
    (Peace long preserved by fleets and perilous seas)
    Secure from actual warfare, we have loved
    To swell the war-whoop, passionate for war!
90 Alas! for ages ignorant of all
    Its ghastlier workings, (famine or blue plague,
    Battle, or siege, or flight through wintry snows,)
    We, this whole people, have been clamorous
    For war and bloodshed; animating sports,
95 The which we pay for as a thing to talk of,
    Spectators and not combatants! No guess
    Anticipative of a wrong unfelt,
    No speculation on contingency,
    However dim and vague, too vague and dim
100 To yield a justifying cause; and forth,
    (Stuffed out with big preamble, holy names,
    And adjurations of the God in Heaven,)
    We send our mandates for the certain death
    Of thousands and ten thousands! Boys and girls,
105 And women, that would groan to see a child
    Pull off an insect's leg, all read of war,
    The best amusement for our morning meal!
    The poor wretch, who has learnt his only prayers
    From curses, who knows scarcely words enough
110 To ask a blessing from his Heavenly Father,
    Becomes a fluent phraseman, absolute
    And technical in victories and defeats,
    And all our dainty terms for fratricide;
    Terms which we trundle smoothly o'er our tongues
115 Like mere abstractions, empty sounds to which
    We join no feeling and attach no form!
    As if the soldier died without a wound;
    As if the fibres of this godlike frame
    Were gored without a pang; as if the wretch,
120 Who fell in battle, doing bloody deeds,
    Passed off to Heaven, translated and not killed;
    As though he had no wife to pine for him,
    No God to judge him! Therefore, evil days
    Are coming on us, O my countrymen!
125 And what if all-avenging Providence,
    Strong and retributive, should make us know
    The meaning of our words, force us to feel
    The desolation and the agony

Of our fierce doings?

                 Spare us yet awhile,
130 Father and God! O! spare us yet awhile!
     Oh! Let not English women drag their flight
     Fainting beneath the burthen of their babes,
     Of the sweet infants, that but yesterday
     Laughed at the breast! Sons, brothers, husbands, all
135 Who ever gazed with fondness on the forms
     Which grew up with you round the same fire-side,
     And all who ever heard the sabbath-bells
     Without the infidel's scorn, make yourselves pure!
     Stand forth! be men! repel an impious foe,
140 Impious and false, a light yet cruel race,
     Who laugh away all virtue, mingling mirth
     With deeds of murder; and still promising
     Freedom, themselves too sensual to be free,
     Poison life's amities, and cheat the heart
145 Of faith and quiet hope, and all that soothes,
     And all that lifts the spirit! Stand we forth;
     Render them back upon the insulted ocean,
     And let them toss as idly on its waves
     As the vile sea-weed, which some mountain-blast
150 Swept from our shores! And oh! may we return
     Not with a drunken triumph, but with fear,
     Repenting of the wrongs with which we stung
     So fierce a foe to frenzy!

                    *   *   *

                                               1798

ROBERT SOUTHEY

Anti-war verse of the 1790s often pits collective celebration against individual mourning in the manner of "The Victory," which Robert Southey (1744–1843), at that point still a political radical, published in his *Poems* of 1799. The devastation of the war widow who learns only belatedly of her husband's death, having listened at first to the tidings "with dreadful hope," also appears frequently in poetry from this decade.

The Victory

     Hark—how the church-bells thundering harmony
     Stuns the glad ear! tidings of joy have come,
     Good tidings of great joy! two gallant ships
     Met on the element,—they met, they fought
5 A desperate fight!—good tidings of great joy!
     Old England triumphed! yet another day
     Of glory for the ruler of the waves!
     For those who fell, 'twas in their country's cause,
     They have their passing paragraphs of praise

10   And are forgotten.
                        There was one who died
     In that day's glory, whose obscurer name
     No proud historian's page will chronicle.
     Peace to his honest soul! I read his name,
     'Twas in the list of slaughter, and blest God
15   The sound was not familiar to mine ear.
     But it was told me after that this man
     Was one whom lawful violence[1] had forced
     From his own home and wife and little ones,
     Who by his labour lived; that he was one
20   Whose uncorrupted heart could keenly feel
     A husband's love, a father's anxiousness,
     That from the wages of his toil he fed
     The distant dear ones, and would talk of them
     At midnight when he trod the silent deck
25   With him he valued, talk of them, of joys
     That he had known—oh God! and of the hour
     When they should meet again, till his full heart
     His manly heart at last would overflow
     Even like a child's with very tenderness.
30   Peace to his honest spirit! Suddenly
     It came, and merciful the ball of death,
     For it came suddenly and shattered him,
     And left no moment's agonizing thought
     On those he loved so well.
                                He ocean deep
35   Now lies at rest. Be Thou her comforter
     Who art the widow's friend. Man does not know
     What a cold sickness made her blood run back
     When first she heard the tidings of the fight;
     Man does not know with what a dreadful hope
40   She listened to the names of those who died,
     Man does not know, or knowing will not heed,
     With what an agony of tenderness
     She gazed upon her children, and beheld
     His image who was gone. Oh God! be thou
45   Her comforter who art the widow's friend!

                                                          1799

1. The person alluded to was pressed into the service [Southey's footnote].

MARY ROBINSON

On July 18, 1800, in a ceremony lasting three hours and attracting numerous civilian spectators, George III inspected the thirty-two thousand troops assembled near his royal residence at Windsor. Twelve days later, in the newspaper *The Morning Post*, Mary Robinson (1757?–1800) published this poetic catalog memorializing the "hurly-burly" of the day. The poem was reprinted in 1804 with the title "Winkfield Plain: or a Description of a Camp in the Year 1800." In her novel *Pride and Prejudice* (published 1813, but drafted in the late 1790s) Jane Austen would also turn her satiric gaze on the social and sexual disruptions engendered by the wartime economy. She might have had Robinson's poem in view as she detailed the daydreams the novel's irrepressible flirt Lydia Bennet indulges about Brighton, site of another military encampment: "She saw all the glories of the camp; its tents stretched forth in beauteous uniformity of lines, crowded with the young and the gay, and dazzling with scarlet; and to complete the view, she saw herself seated beneath a tent, tenderly flirting with at least six officers at once."

The Camp

     Tents, *marquees*, and baggage waggons;
     Suttling houses,[1] beer in flaggons;
     Drums and trumpets, singing, firing;
     Girls seducing, *beaux* admiring;
5   Country lasses gay and smiling,
     City lads their hearts beguiling;
     Dusty roads, and horses frisky;
     Many an *Eton boy* in whisky,[2]
     Tax'd carts full of farmer's daughters;
10   Brutes condemn'd, and man—who slaughters!
     Public-houses, booths, and castles;
     Belles of fashion, serving vassals;
     Lordly Gen'rals fiercely staring,
     Weary soldiers, sighing, swearing!
15   *Petit maitres*° always dressing—   *fops*
     In the glass themselves caressing;
     Perfum'd, painted, patch'd and blooming
     Ladies—manly airs assuming!
     Dowagers of fifty, simp'ring
20   Misses, for a lover whimp'ring—
     Husbands drill'd to household tameness;
     Dames heart sick of wedded sameness.
     Princes setting girls a-madding—
     Wives for ever fond of gadding—
25   Princesses with lovely faces,
     Beauteous children of the Graces!
     Britain's pride and Virtue's treasure,
     Fair and gracious, beyond measure!
     Aid de Camps, and youthful pages—
30   Prudes, and vestals° of all ages!—   *virgins*
     Old coquets, and matrons surly,
     Sounds of distant *hurly burly*!
     Mingled voices uncouth singing;
     Carts, full laden, forage bringing;
35   Sociables,[3] and horses weary;
     Houses warm, and dresses airy;
     Loads of fatten'd poultry; pleasure

1. Establishments selling provisions to soldiers.
2. Besides being a drink, a whisky was a fashionable two-wheeled carriage. Eton, the famous public school, is in Windsor.
3. Carriages with facing seats.

Serv'd (TO NOBLES) without measure.
Doxies[4] who the waggons follow;
40   Beer, for thirsty hinds° to swallow;   *farm boys*
Washerwomen, fruit-girls cheerful,
ANTIENT LADIES—*chaste* and *fearful*!
Tradesmen, leaving shops, and seeming
More of *war* than profit dreaming;
45   Martial sounds, and braying asses;
Noise, that ev'ry noise surpasses!
All confusion, din, and riot—
NOTHING CLEAN—and NOTHING QUIET.

1800

4. Mistresses, perhaps prostitutes.

ANNA LETITIA BARBAULD

Barbauld's bitter poem on the moral and economic condition of England in the year 1811, written at a moment when it seemed that the nation's wars with France might be protracted interminably, concludes by imagining the end of the British Empire. The historian of the future will see "Europe sit in dust, as Asia now" (line 126), and England will at that future moment be a mere memory, at best representing for America what Greece and Rome in the nineteenth century represent for England. The poem, published in 1812, was both one of the most widely reviewed of Barbauld's works and the most reviled: the reviewer for the Tory *Quarterly Review* sniped, "We had hoped . . . that the empire might have been saved without the intervention of a lady-author . . . we must take the liberty of warning her to desist from satire, which indeed is satire on herself alone."

From Eighteen Hundred and Eleven, a Poem

Still the loud death drum, thundering from afar,
O'er the vext nations pours the storm of war:
To the stern call still Britain bends her ear,
Feeds the fierce strife, the alternate hope and fear;
5   Bravely, though vainly, dares to strive with Fate,
And seeks by turns to prop each sinking state.
Colossal Power with overwhelming force
Bears down each fort of Freedom in its course;
Prostrate she lies beneath the Despot's[1] sway,
10   While the hushed nations curse him—and obey.
    Bounteous in vain, with frantic man at strife,
Glad Nature pours the means—the joys of life;
In vain with orange blossoms scents the gale,
The hills with olives clothes, with corn the vale;
15   Man calls to Famine, nor invokes in vain,
Disease and Rapine follow in her train;
The tramp of marching hosts disturbs the plough,
The sword, not sickle, reaps the harvest now,

1. Napoleon's.

And where the Soldier gleans the scant supply,
20 The helpless Peasant but retires to die;
No laws his hut from licensed outrage shield,
And war's least horror is the ensanguined field.
    Fruitful in vain, the matron counts with pride
The blooming youths that grace her honoured side;
25 No son returns to press her widow'd hand,
Her fallen blossoms strew a foreign strand.
—Fruitful in vain, she boasts her virgin race,
Whom cultured arts adorn and gentlest grace;
Defrauded of its homage, Beauty mourns,
30 And the rose withers on its virgin thorns.
Frequent, some stream obscure, some uncouth name
By deeds of blood is lifted into fame;
Oft o'er the daily page some soft-one bends
To learn the fate of husband, brothers, friends,
35 Or the spread map with anxious eye explores,
Its dotted boundaries and penciled shores,
Asks *where* the spot that wrecked her bliss is found,
And learns its name but to detest the sound.
    And thinks't thou, Britain, still to sit at ease,
40 An island Queen amidst thy subject seas,
While the vext billows, in their distant roar,
But soothe thy slumbers, and but kiss thy shore?
To sport in wars, while danger keeps aloof,
Thy grassy turf unbruised by hostile hoof?
45 So sing thy flatterers; but, Britain, know,
Thou who hast shared the guilt must share the woe.
Nor distant is the hour; low murmurs spread,
And whispered fears, creating what they dread;
Ruin, as with an earthquake shock, is here,
50 There, the heart-witherings of unuttered fear,
And that sad death, whence most affection bleeds,
Which sickness, only of the soul, precedes.
Thy baseless wealth dissolves in air away,
Like mists that melt before the morning ray:
55 No more on crowded mart or busy street
Friends, meeting friends, with cheerful hurry greet;
Sad, on the ground thy princely merchants bend
Their altered looks, and evil days portend,
And fold their arms, and watch with anxious breast
60 The tempest blackening in the distant West.[2]
    Yes, thou must droop; thy Midas dream is o'er;
The golden tide of Commerce leaves thy shore,
Leaves thee to prove the alternate ills that haunt
Enfeebling Luxury and ghastly Want;
65 Leaves thee, perhaps, to visit distant lands,
And deal the gifts of Heaven with equal hands.

1812

2. War with the United States was imminent.

GEORGE GORDON, LORD BYRON

I n Canto 8 (1823) of *Don Juan*, following an escape from the Turkish harem into which he was sold in the fifth canto, the fictional hero's fortunes take him into a real theater of war. He joins the Russian army and participates in the conquest of Ismail (1790): the Turkish forces defending that city had been ordered to stand their ground, and 40,000 of them are thought to have been killed in the siege. These military adventures, Byron's narrator suggests, perhaps with excessive candor, fulfill the generic contract that he, as participant in a literary tradition begun by Homer, made with his reader back in Canto 1: as these adventures have been "all very accurate, you must allow / And *Epic*" (stanza 138), the poet has kept his side of the bargain. But the epic premise that "glory's a great thing" (stanza 14) appears to hold truer in Canto 8 for bards who sing of battlefields (and win government pensions by doing so) than for troops who fight and die on them.

From Don Juan, Canto 8

12

    Three hundred cannon threw up their emetic,
90   And thirty thousand muskets flung their pills
    Like hail to make a bloody diuretic.
        Mortality, thou hast thy monthly bills.
    Thy plagues, thy famines, thy physicians yet tick
        Like the deathwatch within our ears the ills
95   Past, present, and to come, but all may yield
    To the true portrait of one battlefield.

13

    There the still varying pangs, which multiply
        Until their very number makes men hard
    By the infinities of agony,
100   Which meet the gaze, whate'er it may regard—
    The groan, the roll in dust, the all-white eye
        Turned back within its socket—these reward
    Your rank and file by thousands, while the rest
    May win perhaps a ribbon at the breast!

14

105   Yet I love glory—glory's a great thing.
        Think what it is to be in your old age
    Maintained at the expense of your good king.
        A moderate pension shakes full many a sage,
    And heroes are but made for bards to sing,
110   Which is still better. Thus in verse to wage

Your wars eternally, besides enjoying
Half-pay for life, makes mankind worth destroying.

15

The troops already disembarked pushed on
   To take a battery on the right; the others
115 Who landed lower down, their landing done,
   Had set to work as briskly as their brothers.
Being grenadiers they mounted one by one,
   Cheerful as children climb the breasts of mothers,
O'er the entrenchment and the palisade,
120 Quite orderly, as if upon parade.

16

And this was admirable, for so hot
   The fire was, that were red Vesuvius loaded,
Besides its lava, with all sorts of shot
   And shells or hells, it could not more have goaded.
125 Of officers a third fell on the spot,
   A thing which victory by no means boded
To gentlemen engaged in the assault.
Hounds, when the huntsman tumbles, are at fault.

17

But here I leave the general concern,
130 To track our hero on his path of fame.
He must his laurels separately earn;
   For fifty thousand heroes, name by name,
Though all deserving equally to turn
   A couplet, or an elegy to claim,
135 Would form a lengthy lexicon of glory
And what is worse still, a much longer story.

18

And therefore we must give the greater number
   To the *Gazette*, which doubtless fairly dealt
By the deceased, who lie in famous slumber
140 In ditches, fields, or wheresoe'er they felt
Their clay for the last time their souls encumber.
   Thrice happy he whose name has been well spelt
In the dispatch; I knew a man whose loss
Was printed Grove, although his name was Grose.

19

145 Juan and Johnson joined a certain corps
   And fought away with might and main, not knowing

758 | ROMANTIC LITERATURE AND WARTIME

The way, which they had never trod before,
   And still less guessing where they might be going,
But on they marched, dead bodies trampling o'er,
150 Firing and thrusting, slashing, sweating, glowing,
But fighting thoughtlessly enough to win
To their *two* selves *one* whole bright bulletin.

20

Thus on they wallowed in the bloody mire
   Of dead and dying thousands, sometimes gaining
155 A yard or two of ground, which brought them nigher
   To some odd angle for which all were straining;
At other times, repulsed by the close fire,
   Which really poured as if all hell were raining,
Instead of heaven, they stumbled backwards o'er
160 A wounded comrade, sprawling in his gore.

21

Though 'twas Don Juan's first of fields, and though
   The nightly muster and the silent march
In the chill dark, when courage does not glow
   So much as under a triumphal arch,
165 Perhaps might make him shiver, yawn, or throw
   A glance on the dull clouds (as thick as starch,
Which stiffened heaven) as if he wished for day;
Yet for all this he did not run away.

*   *   *

1823

THOMAS DE QUINCEY

This section of De Quincey's nostalgic essay of 1849, in which he reminisces about his youthful experiences of travel and deplores the changes brought by the advent of the railway, celebrates the mail coaches' awe-inspiring "political mission." In bringing news of battles to the civilian public, the mail-coach system became a medium of nationalism; in the early nineteenth century, through the shared celebration of the nation's military successes, class antagonisms were dissolved, or so De Quincey proposes.

The English Mail-Coach, or the Glory of Motion

From Going Down with Victory

But the grandest chapter of our experience, within the whole mail-coach service, was on those occasions when we went down from London with the news of victory. A period of about ten years stretched from Trafalgar to Waterloo: the second and third years of which period (1806 and 1807) were comparatively sterile; but the rest, from 1805 to 1815 inclusively, furnished a long succession of victories; the least of which, in a contest of that portentous nature, had an inappreciable value of position—partly for its absolute interference with the plans of our enemy, but still more from its keeping alive in central Europe the sense of a deep-seated vulnerability in France. Even to tease the coasts of our enemy, to mortify them by continual blockades, to insult them by capturing if it were but a baubling schooner under the eyes of their arrogant armies, repeated from time to time a sullen proclamation of power lodged in a quarter to which the hopes of Christendom turned in secret. How much more loudly must this proclamation have spoken in the audacity of having bearded the *élite* of their troops, and having beaten them in pitched battles! Five years of life it was worth paying down for the privilege of an outside place on a mail-coach, when carrying down the first tidings of any such event. And it is to be noted that, from our insular situation, and the multitude of our frigates disposable for the rapid transmission of intelligence, rarely did any unauthorized rumour steal away a prelibation from the aroma of the regular despatches. The government official news was generally the first news.

From eight P.M. to fifteen or twenty minutes later, imagine the mails assembled on parade in Lombard Street, where, at that time, was seated the General Post-Office. In what exact strength we mustered I do not remember; but, from the length of each separate *attelage*,[1] we filled the street, though a long one, and though we were drawn up in double file. On *any* night the spectacle was beautiful. The absolute perfection of all the appointments about the carriages and the harness, and the magnificence of the horses, were what might first have fixed the attention. Every carriage, on every morning in the year, was taken down to an inspector for examination—wheels, axles, linchpins, pole, glasses, &c., were all critically probed and tested. Every part of every carriage had been cleaned, every horse had been groomed, with as much rigour as if they belonged to a private gentleman; and that part of the spectacle offered itself always. But the night before us is a night of victory; and behold! to the ordinary display, what a heart-shaking addition!—horses, men, carriages—all are dressed in laurels and flowers, oak leaves and ribbons. The guards, who are his Majesty's servants, and the coachmen, who are within the privilege of the Post-Office, wear the royal liveries of course; and as it is summer (for all the *land* victories were won in summer,) they wear, on this fine evening, these liveries exposed to view, without any covering of upper coats. Such a costume, and the elaborate arrangement of the laurels in their hats, dilated their hearts, by giving to them openly an *official*

1. Team of horses.

connection with the great news, in which already they have the general interest of patriotism. That great national sentiment surmounts and quells all sense of ordinary distinctions. Those passengers who happen to be gentlemen are now hardly to be distinguished as such except by dress. The usual reserve of their manner in speaking to the attendants has on this night melted away. One heart, one pride, one glory, connects every man by the transcendant bond of his English blood. The spectators, who are numerous beyond precedent, express their sympathies with these fervent feelings by continual hurrahs. Every moment are shouted aloud by the Post-Office servants the great ancestral names of cities known to history through a thousand years,—Lincoln, Winchester, Portsmouth, Gloucester, Oxford, Bristol, Manchester, York, Newcastle, Edinburgh, Perth, Glasgow—expressing the grandeur of the empire by the antiquity of its towns, and the grandeur of the mail establishment by the diffusive radiation of its separate missions. Every moment you hear the thunder of lids locked down upon the mail-bags. That sound to each individual mail is the signal for drawing off, which process is the finest part of the entire spectacle. Then come the horses into play;—horses! can these be horses that (unless powerfully reined in) would bound off with the action and gestures of leopards? What stir!—what sea-like ferment!—what a thundering of wheels, what a trampling of horses!—what farewell cheers—what redoubling peals of brotherly congratulation, connecting the name of the particular mail—"Liverpool for ever!"—with the name of the particular victory—"Badajoz for ever!" or "Salamanca for ever!" The half-slumbering consciousness that, all night long and all the next day—perhaps for even a longer period—many of these mails, like fire racing along a train of gunpowder, will be kindling at every instant new successions of burning joy, has an obscure effect of multiplying the victory itself, by multiplying to the imagination into infinity the stages of its progressive diffusion. A fiery arrow seems to be let loose, which from that moment is destined to travel, almost without intermission, westwards for three hundred miles—northwards for six hundred; and the sympathy of our Lombard Street friends at parting is exalted a hundredfold by a sort of visionary sympathy with the approaching sympathies, yet unborn, which we were going to evoke.

Liberated from the embarrassments of the city, and issuing into the broad uncrowded avenues of the northen suburbs, we begin to enter upon our natural pace of ten miles an hour. In the broad light of the summer evening, the sun perhaps only just at the point of setting, we are seen from every storey of every house. Heads of every age crowd to the windows—young and old understand the language of our victorious symbols—and rolling volleys of sympathizing cheers run along behind and before our course. The beggar, rearing himself against the wall, forgets his lameness—real or assumed—thinks not of his whining trade, but stands erect, with bold exulting smiles, as we pass him. The victory has healed him, and says—Be thou whole! Women and children, from garrets alike and cellars, look down or look up with loving eyes upon our gay ribbons and our martial laurels—sometimes kiss their hands, sometimes hang out, as signals of affection, pocket handkerchiefs, aprons, dusters, anything that lies ready to their hands. On the London side of Barnet, to which we drew near within a few minutes after nine, observe that private carriage which is approaching us. The weather being so warm, the glasses are all down; and one may read, as on the stage of a theatre, everything that goes on within the carriage. It contains three ladies, one likely to be "mama," and two of seventeen or eighteen, who are probably her daughters. What lovely animation, what beautiful unpremeditated pantomime, explaining to us every syllable that passes, in these ingenuous girls! By the sudden start and raising of the hands, on first discovering our laurelled equipage—by the sudden movement and appeal to the elder lady from both of them—and by the heightened colour on their animated countenances, we can almost hear them saying—"See, see! Look at their laurels. Oh, mama! there has been a great battle in Spain: and it has been a great victory." In a moment we are on the point of passing them. We passengers—I on the box, and the two on the roof behind me—raise our hats, the coachman makes his professional salute with the whip; the guard even, though punctilious on the matter of his dignity as an officer under the crown, touches his hat. The ladies move to us, in return, with a winning graciousness of gesture: all smile on each side in a way that nobody could misunderstand, and that nothing short of a grand national sympathy could so instantaneously prompt. Will these ladies say that we are nothing to *them*? Oh, no; they will not say *that*. They cannot deny—they do not deny—that for this night they are our sisters: gentle or simple, scholar or illiterate servant, for twelve hours to come—we on the outside have the honour to be their brothers. Those poor women again, who stop to gaze upon us with delight at the entrance of Barnet, and seem by their air of weariness to be returning from labour—do you mean to say that they are washerwomen and charwomen? Oh, my poor friend, you are quite mistaken; they are nothing of the kind. I assure you, they stand in a higher rank: for this one night they feel themselves by birthright to be daughters of England, and answer to no humbler title.

Every joy, however, even rapturous joy—such is the sad law of earth—may carry with it grief, or fear of grief, to some. Three miles beyond Barnet, we see approaching us another private carriage, nearly repeating the circumstances of the former case. Here also the glasses are all down—here also is an elderly lady seated; but the two amiable daughters are missing; for the single young person, sitting by the lady's side, seems to be an attendant—so I judge from her dress, and her air of respectful reserve. The lady is in mourning; and her countenance expresses sorrow. At first she does not look up; so that I believe she is not aware of our approach, until she hears the measured beating of our horses's hoofs. Then she raises her eyes to settle them painfully on our triumphal equipage. Our decorations explain the case to her at once; but she beholds them with apparent anxiety, or even with terror. Some time before this, I, finding it difficult to hit a flying mark, when embarrassed by the coachman's person and reins intervening, had given to the guard a *Courier* evening paper, containing the gazette, for the next carriage that might pass. Accordingly he tossed it in so folded that the huge capitals expressing some such legend as—GLORIOUS VICTORY, might catch the eye at once. To see the paper, however, at all, interpreted as it was by our ensigns of triumph, explained everything; and, if the guard were right in thinking the lady to have received it with a gesture of horror, it could not be doubted that she had suffered some deep personal affliction in connexion with this Spanish war.

Here now was the case of one who, having formerly suffered, might, erroneously perhaps, be distressing herself with anticipations of another similar suffering. That same night, and hardly three hours later, occurred the reverse case. A poor woman, who too probably would find herself, in a day or two, to have suffered the heaviest of afflictions by the battle, blindly allowed herself to express an exultation so unmeasured in the news, and its details, as gave to her the appearance which amongst Celtic Highlanders is called *fey*. This was at some little town, I forget what, where we happened to change horses near midnight. Some fair or wake had kept the people up out of their beds. We saw many lights moving about as we drew near; and perhaps the most impressive scene on our route was our reception at this place. The flashing of torches and the beautiful radiance of blue lights (technically Bengal lights) upon the heads of our horses; the fine effect of such a showery and ghostly illumination falling upon flowers and glittering laurels, whilst all around the massy darkness seemed to invest us with walls of impenetrable blackness, together with the prodigious enthusiasm of the people, composed a picture at once scenical and affecting. As we staid for three or four minutes, I alighted. And immediately from a dismantled stall in the street, where perhaps she had been presiding at some part of the evening, advanced eagerly a middle-aged woman. The sight of my newspaper it was that had drawn her attention upon myself. The victory which we were carrying down to the provinces on *this* occasion was the imperfect one of Talavera.[2] I told her the main outline of the battle. But her agitation, though not the agitation of fear, but of exultation rather, and enthusiasm, had been so conspicuous when listening, and when first applying for information, that I could not but ask her if she had not some relation in the Peninsular army. Oh! yes: her only son was there. In what regiment? He was a trooper in the 23rd Dragoons. My heart sank within me as she made that answer. This sublime regiment, which an Englishman should never mention without raising his hat to their memory, had made the most memorable and effective charge recorded in military annals. They leaped their horse—*over* a trench, where they could: *into* it, and with the result of death or mutilation when they could *not*. What proportion cleared the trench is nowhere stated. Those who *did*, closed up and went down upon the enemy with such divinity of fervour—(I use the word *divinity* by design: the inspiration of God must have prompted this movement to those whom even then he was calling to his presence)—that two results followed. As regarded the enemy, this 23rd Dragoons, not, I believe, originally 350 strong, paralysed a French column, 6000 strong, then ascending the hill, and fixed the gaze of the whole French army. As regarded themselves, the 23rd were supposed at first to have been all but annihilated; but eventually, I believe, not so many as one in four survived. And this, then, was the regiment—a regiment already for some hours known to myself and all London as stretched, by a large majority, upon one bloody aceldama[3]—in which the young trooper served whose mother was now talking with myself in a spirit of such hopeful enthusiasm. Did I tell her the truth? Had I the heart to break up her dream? No. I said to myself, Tomorrow, or the next day, she will hear the worst. For this night, wherefore should she not sleep in peace? After tomorrow, the chances are too many that peace will forsake her pillow. This brief respite, let her owe this to *my* gift and *my* forbearance. But, if I told her not of the bloody price that had been paid, there was no reason for suppressing the contributions from her son's regiment to the service and glory of the day. For the very

---

2. The Battle of Talavera, July 27–28, 1809, an important English victory in the Peninsular War, was fought for control of the Iberian peninsula following the Napoleonic conquest of Portugal in 1807 and then of Spain, France's former ally, in 1808. Casualties on both sides were immense.
3. Field of blood; Acts 1.19.

few words that I had time for speaking, I governed myself accordingly. I showed her not the funeral banners under which the noble regiment was sleeping. I lifted not the overshadowing laurels from the bloody trench in which horse and rider lay mangled together. But I told her how these dear children of England, privates and officers, had leaped their horses over all obstacles as gaily as hunters to the morning's chase. I told her how they rode their horses into the mists of death, (saying to myself, but not saying to *her*,) and laid down their young lives for thee, O mother England! as willingly— poured out their noble blood as cheerfully—as ever, after a long day's sport, when infants, they had rested their wearied heads upon their mother's knees, or had sunk to sleep in her arms. It is singular that she seemed to have no fears, even after this knowledge that the 23rd Dragoons had been conspicuously engaged, for her son's safety: but so much was she enraptured by the knowledge that *his* regiment, and therefore *he*, had rendered eminent service in the trying conflict—a service which had actually made them the foremost topic of conversation in London—that in the mere simplicity of her fervent nature, she threw her arms round my neck, and, poor woman, kissed me.

* * *

1849

PERCY BYSSHE SHELLEY
1792–1822

Percy Bysshe Shelley, radical in every aspect of his life and thought, emerged from a solidly conservative background. His ancestors had been Sussex aristocrats since early in the seventeenth century; his grandfather, Sir Bysshe Shelley, made himself the richest man in Horsham, Sussex; his father, Timothy Shelley, was a hardheaded and conventional member of Parliament. Percy Shelley was in line for a baronetcy and, as befitted his station, was sent to be educated at Eton and Oxford. As a youth he was slight of build, eccentric in manner, and unskilled in sports or fighting and, as a consequence, was mercilessly bullied by older and stronger boys. He later said that he saw the petty tyranny of schoolmasters and schoolmates as representative of man's general inhumanity to man, and dedicated his life to a war against injustice and oppression. As he described the experience in the Dedication to *Laon and Cythna*:

> So without shame, I spake:—"I will be wise,
> And just, and free, and mild, if in me lies
> Such power, for I grow weary to behold
> The selfish and the strong still tyrannise
> Without reproach or check." I then controuled
> My tears, my heart grew calm, and I was meek and bold.

At Oxford in the autumn of 1810, Shelley's closest friend was Thomas Jefferson Hogg, a self-centered, self-confident young man who shared Shelley's love of philosophy and scorn of orthodoxy. Shelley at this early date had already published, anonymously, two Gothic novels and three slim volumes of verse, including his recently rediscovered *Poetical Essay on the Existing State of Things*, an antiwar poem in heroic couplets. With Hogg he collaborated on a pamphlet, *The Necessity of Atheism*, which claimed that God's existence cannot be proved on empirical grounds, and, provocatively, the co-authors mailed it to the bishops and heads of the colleges at Oxford. Shelley refused to repudiate the document and, to his shock and grief, was peremptorily expelled, terminating a university career that had lasted only six months. This event opened a breach between Shelley and his father that widened over the years.

Shelley went to London, where he took up the cause of Harriet Westbrook, the pretty and warmhearted daughter of a well-to-do tavern keeper, whose father, Shelley wrote to Hogg, "has persecuted her in a most horrible way by endeavoring to compel her to go to school." Harriet threw herself on Shelley's protection, and "gratitude and admiration," he wrote, "all demand that I shall love her *forever*." He eloped with Harriet to Edinburgh and married her, against his conviction that marriage was a tyrannical and degrading social institution. He was then eighteen years of age; his bride, sixteen. The couple moved restlessly from place to place, living on a small allowance granted reluctantly by their families. In February 1812, accompanied by Harriet's sister Eliza, they traveled to Dublin to distribute Shelley's *Address to the Irish People* and otherwise take part in the movement for Catholic emancipation and for the amelioration of that oppressed and poverty-stricken people.

Back in London Shelley eagerly sought the acquaintance of the radical novelist and philosopher William Godwin, author of *Enquiry Concerning Political Justice* (1794), and in 1813 he published his first important work, *Queen Mab, A Philosophical Poem*, which owes much to Godwin's optimistic conviction in *Political Justice* that the regeneration of the human species was at hand and that in these modern times "the phalanx of reason" would prove "invulnerable" in its advance. In Shelley's long poem, which he printed at his own expense, so as to maneuver around blasphemy and sedition laws, the fairy Queen Mab reveals to a journeying soul visions of the woeful past, a dreadful present, and a utopian future. Queen Mab's denunciations of institutional religion, aristocracy, and monarchy are elaborated at length in the poem's many endnotes. These atheistic and revolutionary sentiments made Shelley infamous for the rest of his life. They also, somewhat to his embarrassment in later life, came to the attention of the radical press, which kept *Queen Mab* in print, in cheap, pirated editions, for the rest of the century.

In the following spring Shelley, who had drifted away from Harriet, fell in love with Godwin's and the late Mary Wollstonecraft's beautiful and intelligent daughter, Mary. Convinced that cohabitation without love was immoral, he abandoned Harriet, fled to France with Mary (taking along her stepsister, Claire Clairmont), and—in accordance with his belief in nonexclusive love—invited Harriet to come live with them as another sister. Shelley's elopement with Mary outraged her father, even though his own views of marriage had once been, on the testimony of *Political Justice*, no less radical than Shelley's and even though Shelley, despite his own financial difficulties, had earlier taken over Godwin's substantial debts. When he returned to London, Shelley found that the public, his family, and many friends regarded him as not only an atheist and a revolutionist but also a libertine. When two years later Harriet, pregnant by an unknown lover, drowned herself in a fit of despair, the courts denied Shelley the custody of their two children. (His first child with Mary Godwin had died earlier, only twelve days after her birth in February 1815.) Percy and Mary married in December 1816, and in spring 1818 they moved to Italy.

In Italy Shelley resumed his restless way of life, evading the people to whom he owed money by moving from town to town and house to house. His health was usually bad. Although the death of his grandfather in 1815 had provided a substantial income, he dissipated so much of it by his warmhearted but imprudent support of Godwin and other needy acquaintances that he was constantly short of funds.

Within nine months of their arrival in Italy, both Clara and William, the children Mary had borne in 1815 and 1817, died. Grief over these deaths destroyed the earlier harmony of the Shelleys' marriage; the birth in November 1819 of another son, Percy Florence (their only child to survive to adulthood), was not enough to mend the rift.

In these circumstances Shelley wrote his greatest works. Exile from England prompted him, on the one hand, to envision himself as an alien and outcast, bereft of an audience, and rejected by the human race to whose welfare he had dedicated his powers. It also prompted him, on the other hand, to imagine and, to a lesser extent, initiate new kinds of intellectual alliances and forms of ethical and political community, ambitions manifested in his friendship with Lord Byron and in the invitations to join him in Italy that he extended to Keats, Leigh Hunt, Thomas Peacock, and others. The poems of 1819–21, so rich and complex in part because they often seek to reconcile these conflicting accounts of the poetic self in relation to community, include (from 1819 alone) *Prometheus Unbound*, an epic-scale "closet-drama" about the Greek Titan's survival and transcendence of oppression; his Jacobean-style revenge tragedy of incest and parricide, *The Cenci*; his visionary call for revolution, *The Mask of Anarchy*; a witty satire on Wordsworth, *Peter Bell the Third*; a penetrating, proto-Marxist essay, "A Philosophical View of Reform"; and numerous lyric poems. Later came "A Defence of Poetry"; *Epipsychidion*, a rhapsodic view of love as a spiritual union beyond earthly limits; *Adonais*, his elegy on Keats, representing the younger poet as a victim of a politicized review culture; and *Hellas*, a lyrical drama inspired by the Greek war for liberation from the Turks.

These writings are enriched by Shelley's omnivorous reading, in the natural sciences, ancient and modern philosophy, Dante, Milton, the Bible—reading that he carried on, as his friend Hogg said, "in season and out of season, at table, in bed, and especially during a walk" until he became one of the most erudite of the English poets. In particular the late works often evince Shelley's study of Plato (whose *Ion* and *Symposium* he translated) and of the Neoplatonists. The Platonic division of the cosmos into two worlds—the ordinary world of change, mortality, evil, and suffering, which is contrasted with the ideal world of perfect and eternal forms, of which the world of sense experience is only a distant and illusory reflection—was immensely attractive to Shelley. His *Adonais* set out that contrast memorably: "Life like a dome of many-coloured glass / Stains the white radiance of eternity" (lines 462–63). At the same time, however, the idealism these lines register as they evoke a beauty that is offset by the "stain" of temporal existence was often, within Shelley's late writings, tempered by his enthusiastic study of British empiricist philosophy, which limits knowledge to what is given in sense experience, and tempered, especially, by the affinities he felt for the radical skepticism of David Hume. Works such as "Mont Blanc" are shaped by his sense that there are narrow limits to what human beings can know with certainty. Out of this divided intellectual inheritance, Shelley developed, some critics have proposed, a "skeptical idealism," an attitude that also colors the hopes for radical social and political reform that he retained even at a historical moment that seemed (with the restoration of the old autocratic monarchies after 1815, with the suffering of the poor in the economic depression that followed the end of the war) to have delivered an insurmountable setback to the cause of liberty. For him such hopes were moral obligations, more than they were expressions of intellectual certainty. We must continue to hope because, by keeping open the possibility of a better future, hope releases the imaginative and creative powers that are the only means of achieving that end. Shelley had a motto in Italian inscribed on a ring that he often wore: "Il buon tempo verra" ("the good time will come").

When in 1820 the Shelleys settled finally at Pisa, he came closer to finding contentment than at any other time in his adult life. A group of friends, Shelley's "Pisan Circle," gathered around them, including for a while Byron and the swashbuckling Cornishman Edward Trelawny. Chief in Shelley's affections were Edward Williams, a retired lieutenant of a cavalry regiment serving in India, and his common-law wife Jane, with whom Shelley became infatuated and to whom he addressed some of his best lyrics and verse letters. The end came suddenly, and in a way prefigured uncannily in the last stanza of *Adonais*, in which he had described his spirit as a ship driven by a violent storm out into the dark unknown. On July 8, 1822, Shelley and Edward Williams were sailing their open boat, the *Don Juan*, on the Gulf of Spezia. A violent squall swamped the boat. When several days later the bodies were washed ashore, they were cremated, and Shelley's ashes were buried in the Protestant Cemetery at Rome, near the graves of John Keats and William Shelley, the poet's young son.

Shelley's character has been the subject of heated and contradictory estimates, and commentators have also disagreed, analogously, in their assessments of his success at mixing politics and poetry. The actions that he justified to himself because they were true to his convictions often led to disastrous consequences for those near him, especially women; and even recent scholars, while repudiating the vicious attacks made by Shelley's contemporaries, attribute some of those actions to a self-assured egotism that masked itself as idealism. Yet Byron, who knew Shelley intimately, and did not readily pay compliments, wrote to his publisher John Murray, in response to attacks on Shelley at the time of his death: "You are all brutally mistaken about Shelley, who was, without exception, the *best* and least selfish man I ever knew." Vilified by the Tory press during his lifetime, Shelley's politics recommended his poetry to many later political radicals: the Chartists in the middle of the nineteenth century, Marx and Engels at the end, and at the start of the twentieth century, Mahatma Gandhi and many guiding lights of the British Labour Party. And, despite their ideological differences, Wordsworth recognized early on the extent to which Shelley in that poetry had expanded English versification's metrical and stanzaic resources: "Shelley," Wordsworth said, "is one of the best *artists* of us all."

The texts here are those prepared by Donald H. Reiman and Neil Fraistat for *Shelley's Poetry and Prose: A Norton Critical Edition*, 2nd ed. (2001); Reiman has also edited for this anthology a few poems not included in that edition.

Mutability

We are as clouds that veil the midnight moon;
    How restlessly they speed, and gleam, and quiver,
Streaking the darkness radiantly!—yet soon
    Night closes round, and they are lost for ever:

5 Or like forgotten lyres,° whose dissonant strings   *wind harps*
    Give various response to each varying blast,
To whose frail frame no second motion brings
    One mood or modulation like the last.

We rest.—A dream has power to poison sleep;
10   We rise.—One wandering thought pollutes the day;
We feel, conceive or reason, laugh or weep;
    Embrace fond woe, or cast our cares away:

It is the same!—For, be it joy or sorrow,
    The path of its departure still is free:
15 Man's yesterday may ne'er be like his morrow;
    Nought may endure but Mutability.

ca. 1814–15   1816

To Wordsworth[1]

Poet of Nature, thou hast wept to know
That things depart which never may return:
Childhood and youth, friendship and love's first glow,
Have fled like sweet dreams, leaving thee to mourn.
5 These common woes I feel. One loss is mine
Which thou too feel'st, yet I alone deplore.
Thou wert as a lone star, whose light did shine
On some frail bark° in winter's midnight roar: *small ship*
Thou hast like to a rock-built refuge stood
10 Above the blind and battling multitude:
In honoured poverty thy voice did weave
Songs consecrate to truth and liberty,[2]—
Deserting these, thou leavest me to grieve,
Thus having been, that thou shouldst cease to be.

ca. 1814–15   1816

Alastor; or, The Spirit of Solitude

Shelley wrote *Alastor* in the fall and early winter of 1815 and published it in March 1816. According to his friend Thomas Love Peacock, the poet was "at a loss for a title, and I proposed that which he adopted: Alastor, or the Spirit of Solitude. The Greek word *Alastor* is an evil genius. . . . I mention the true meaning of the word because many have supposed *Alastor* to be the name of the hero" (*Memoirs of Shelley*). Peacock's definition of an *alastor* as "an *evil* genius" has compounded the problems in interpreting this work: the term *evil* does not seem to fit the attitude expressed within the poem toward the protagonist's solitary quest, the poem seems to clash with statements in Shelley's preface, and the first and second paragraphs of the preface seem inconsistent with each other. These problems, however, may be largely resolved if we recognize that, in this early achievement (he was only twenty-three when he wrote *Alastor*), Shelley established his characteristic procedure of working with multiple perspectives. Both preface and poem explore alternative and conflicting possibilities in what Shelley calls "doubtful knowledge"—matters that are humanly essential but in which no certainty is humanly possible.

By the term *allegorical* in the opening sentence of his preface, Shelley seems to mean that his poem, like medieval and Renaissance allegories such as Dante's *Divine Comedy* and Spenser's *Faerie Queene*, represents an aspiration in the spiritual realm by the allegorical vehicle of a journey and quest in the material world. As Shelley's first paragraph outlines, the poem's protagonist, for whom objects in the natural world "cease to suffice," commits himself to the search for a female Other who will fulfill his intellectual, imaginative, and sensuous needs. The second paragraph of the preface, by contrast, passes judgment on the visionary protagonist in terms of the values of "actual men"—that is, the requirements of human and social life in this world. From this point of view, the visionary has been "avenged" (punished) for turning away from community in pursuit of his individual psychic needs. The diversity of attitudes expressed within the poem becomes easier to understand

---

1. Shelley's grieved comment on the poet of nature and of social radicalism after his views had become conservative.
2. Perhaps an allusion to "Sonnets Dedicated to Liberty," the title that Wordsworth gave to the section of sonnets such as "London, 1802" when he republished them in his *Poems* of 1807.

if, on the basis of the many echoes of Wordsworth in the opening invocation, we identify the narrator of the story as a Wordsworthian poet for whom the natural world is sufficient to satisfy both the demands of his imagination and his need for community. This narrative poet, it can be assumed, undertakes to tell compassionately, but from his own perspective, the history of a nameless visionary who has surrendered everything in the quest for a goal beyond possibility.

In this early poem, Shelley establishes a form, a conceptual frame, and the imagery for the Romantic quest that he reiterated in his later poems and that also served as a paradigm for many other poems, from Byron's *Manfred* and Keats's *Endymion* to the quest poems of Shelley's later admirer William Butler Yeats. At the same time, in presenting a protagonist who journeys farther and farther east, from Greece onward to Jerusalem and then India, *Alastor* also prefigures story lines that Victorian adventure novels would construct for their empire-building heroes.

Alastor; or, The Spirit of Solitude

Preface

The poem entitled "ALASTOR," may be considered as allegorical of one of the most interesting situations of the human mind. It represents a youth of uncorrupted feelings and adventurous genius led forth by an imagination inflamed and purified through familiarity with all that is excellent and majestic, to the contemplation of the universe. He drinks deep of the fountains of knowledge, and is still insatiate. The magnificence and beauty of the external world sinks profoundly into the frame of his conceptions, and affords to their modifications a variety not to be exhausted. So long as it is possible for his desires to point towards objects thus infinite and unmeasured, he is joyous, and tranquil, and self-possessed. But the period arrives when these objects cease to suffice. His mind is at length suddenly awakened and thirsts for intercourse with an intelligence similar to itself. He images to himself the Being whom he loves. Conversant with speculations of the sublimest and most perfect natures, the vision in which he embodies his own imaginations unites all of wonderful, or wise, or beautiful, which the poet, the philosopher, or the lover could depicture. The intellectual faculties, the imagination, the functions of sense, have their respective requisitions on the sympathy of corresponding powers in other human beings. The Poet is represented as uniting these requisitions, and attaching them to a single image.[1] He seeks in vain for a prototype of his conception. Blasted by his disappointment, he descends to an untimely grave.

The picture is not barren of instruction to actual men. The Poet's self-centred seclusion was avenged by the furies of an irresistible passion pursuing him to speedy ruin. But that Power which strikes the luminaries of the world with sudden darkness and extinction, by awakening them to too exquisite a perception of its influences, dooms to a slow and poisonous decay those meaner spirits that dare to abjure its dominion. Their destiny is more abject and inglorious as their delinquency is more contemptible and pernicious. They who, deluded by no generous error, instigated by no sacred thirst of doubtful knowledge, duped by no illustrious superstition, loving nothing on

---

1. For Shelley's expansion of this account of love as an idealized projection of all that is best in the self, cf. his essay "On Love," p. 791.

this earth, and cherishing no hopes beyond, yet keep aloof from sympathies with their kind, rejoicing neither in human joy nor mourning with human grief; these, and such as they, have their apportioned curse. They languish, because none feel with them their common nature. They are morally dead. They are neither friends, nor lovers, nor fathers, nor citizens of the world, nor benefactors of their country. Among those who attempt to exist without human sympathy, the pure and tender-hearted perish through the intensity and passion of their search after its communities, when the vacancy of their spirit suddenly makes itself felt. All else, selfish, blind, and torpid, are those unforeseeing multitudes who constitute, together with their own, the lasting misery and loneliness of the world. Those who love not their fellow-beings live unfruitful lives, and prepare for their old age a miserable grave.

> "The good die first,
> And those whose hearts are dry as summer dust,
> Burn to the socket!"[2]

December 14, 1815

Alastor; or, The Spirit of Solitude

Nondum amabam, et amare amabam, qæurebam quid amarem, amans amare.—Confess. St. August.[3]

Earth, ocean, air, beloved brotherhood!
If our great Mother[4] has imbued my soul
With aught of natural piety[5] to feel
Your love, and recompense the boon° with mine;[6]   *gift*
5   If dewy morn, and odorous noon, and even,°   *evening*
With sunset and its gorgeous ministers,[7]
And solemn midnight's tingling silentness;
If autumn's hollow sighs in the sere wood,
And winter robing with pure snow and crowns
10 Of starry ice the grey grass and bare boughs;
If spring's voluptuous pantings when she breathes
Her first sweet kisses, have been dear to me;
If no bright bird, insect, or gentle beast
I consciously have injured, but still loved
15 And cherished these my kindred; then forgive
This boast, beloved brethren, and withdraw
No portion of your wonted° favour now!   *customary*

Mother of this unfathomable world!
Favour my solemn song, for I have loved
20 Thee ever, and thee only; I have watched

2. Wordsworth's *The Excursion* 1.519–21; the passage occurs also in *The Ruined Cottage* 96–98, which Wordsworth reworked into the first book of *The Excursion* (1814).
3. St. Augustine's *Confessions* 3.1: "Not yet did I love, though I loved to love, seeking what I might love, loving to love." Augustine thus describes his state of mind when he was addicted to illicit sexual love; the true object of his desire, which compels the tortuous spiritual journey of his life, he later discovered to be the infinite and tran-

scendent God.
4. Nature, invoked as common mother to both the elements and the poet.
5. Wordsworth, "My heart leaps up," lines 8–9: "And I could wish my days to be / Bound each to each by natural piety." Wordsworth also used these lines as the epigraph to his "Ode: Intimations of Immortality."
6. I.e., with my love.
7. The sunset colors.

Thy shadow, and the darkness of thy steps,
And my heart ever gazes on the depth
Of thy deep mysteries. I have made my bed
In charnels and on coffins, where black death
25   Keeps record of the trophies won from thee,
Hoping to still these obstinate questionings[8]
Of thee and thine, by forcing some lone ghost,
Thy messenger, to render up the tale
Of what we are. In lone and silent hours,
30   When night makes a weird sound of its own stillness,
Like an inspired and desperate alchymist
Staking his very life on some dark hope,
Have I mixed awful talk and asking looks
With my most innocent love, until strange tears
35   Uniting with those breathless kisses, made
Such magic as compels the charmed night
To render up thy charge: . . . and, though ne'er yet
Thou hast unveil'd thy inmost sanctuary,
Enough from incommunicable dream,
40   And twilight phantasms, and deep noonday thought,
Has shone within me, that serenely now
And moveless,° as a long-forgotten lyre   *motionless*
Suspended in the solitary dome
Of some mysterious and deserted fane,°   *temple*
45   I wait thy breath, Great Parent, that my strain
May modulate with murmurs of the air, [9]
And motions of the forests and the sea,
And voice of living beings, and woven hymns
Of night and day, and the deep heart of man.[1]

50   There was a Poet whose untimely tomb
No human hands with pious reverence reared,
But the charmed eddies of autumnal winds
Built o'er his mouldering bones a pyramid
Of mouldering leaves in the waste wilderness:—
55   A lovely youth,—no mourning maiden decked
With weeping flowers, or votive cypress[2] wreath,
The lone couch of his everlasting sleep:—
Gentle, and brave, and generous,—no lorn° bard   *abandoned*
Breathed o'er his dark fate one melodious sigh:
60   He lived, he died, he sung, in solitude.
Strangers have wept to hear his passionate notes,
And virgins, as unknown he past, have pined
And wasted for fond love of his wild eyes.
The fire of those soft orbs has ceased to burn,
65   And Silence, too enamoured of that voice,
Locks its mute music in her rugged cell.

8. Wordsworth, "Ode: Intimations of Immortality," lines 141–42: "those obstinate questionings / Of sense and outward things."
9. The narrator calls on the Mother, his natural muse, to make him her wind harp.
1. Cf. Wordsworth, "Tintern Abbey," lines 94ff.:
"A presence . . . / Whose dwelling is . . . the round ocean and the living air, / And the blue sky, and in the mind of man: / A motion and a spirit."
2. The cypress represented mourning. "Votive": offered to fulfill a vow to the gods.

By solemn vision, and bright silver dream,
His infancy was nurtured. Every sight
And sound from the vast earth and ambient air,
70 Sent to his heart its choicest impulses.
The fountains of divine philosophy
Fled not his thirsting lips, and all of great
Or good, or lovely, which the sacred past
In truth or fable consecrates, he felt
75 And knew. When early youth had past, he left
His cold fireside and alienated home
To seek strange truths in undiscovered lands.
Many a wide waste and tangled wilderness
Has lured his fearless steps; and he has bought
80 With his sweet voice and eyes, from savage men,
His rest and food. Nature's most secret steps
He like her shadow has pursued, where'er
The red volcano overcanopies
Its fields of snow and pinnacles of ice
85 With burning smoke, or where bitumen lakes[3]
On black bare pointed islets ever beat
With sluggish surge, or where the secret caves
Rugged and dark, winding among the springs
Of fire and poison, inaccessible
90 To avarice or pride, their starry domes
Of diamond and of gold expand above
Numberless and immeasurable halls,
Frequent° with crystal column, and clear shrines   *crowded*
Of pearl, and thrones radiant with chrysolite.[4]
95 Nor had that scene of ampler majesty
Than gems or gold, the varying roof of heaven
And the green earth lost in his heart its claims
To love and wonder; he would linger long
In lonesome vales, making the wild his home,
100 Until the doves and squirrels would partake
From his innocuous hand his bloodless food,[5]
Lured by the gentle meaning of his looks,
And the wild antelope, that starts whene'er
The dry leaf rustles in the brake,° suspend   *thicket*
105 Her timid steps to gaze upon a form
More graceful than her own.

                    His wandering step
Obedient to high thoughts, has visited
The awful° ruins of the days of old: *awe-inspiring*
Athens, and Tyre, and Balbec,[6] and the waste
110 Where stood Jerusalem, the fallen towers
Of Babylon, the eternal pyramids,
Memphis and Thebes,[7] and whatsoe'er of strange
Sculptured on alabaster obelisk,

---

3. Lakes of pitch, flowing from a volcano.
4. An olive-green semiprecious stone.
5. Shelley was himself a vegetarian.
6. An ancient city in what is now Lebanon. Tyre

was once an important commercial city on the
Phoenician coast.
7. The ancient capital of Upper Egypt. Memphis
is the ruined capital of Lower Egypt.

Or jasper tomb, or mutilated sphinx,
115 Dark Æthiopia in her desert hills
Conceals. Among the ruined temples there,
Stupendous columns, and wild images
Of more than man, where marble daemons[8] watch
The Zodiac's[9] brazen mystery, and dead men
120 Hang their mute thoughts on the mute walls around,[1]
He lingered, poring on memorials
Of the world's youth, through the long burning day
Gazed on those speechless shapes, nor, when the moon
Filled the mysterious halls with floating shades
125 Suspended he that task, but ever gazed
And gazed, till meaning on his vacant mind
Flashed like strong inspiration, and he saw
The thrilling secrets of the birth of time.

Meanwhile an Arab maiden brought his food,
130 Her daily portion, from her father's tent,
And spread her matting for his couch, and stole
From duties and repose to tend his steps:—
Enamoured, yet not daring for deep awe
To speak her love:—and watched his nightly sleep,
135 Sleepless herself, to gaze upon his lips
Parted in slumber, whence the regular breath
Of innocent dreams arose: then, when red morn
Made paler the pale moon, to her cold home
Wildered,° and wan, and panting, she returned.   *bewildered*

140 The Poet wandering on, through Arabie
And Persia, and the wild Carmanian waste,[2]
And o'er the aërial mountains which pour down
Indus and Oxus[3] from their icy caves,
In joy and exultation held his way;
145 Till in the vale of Cashmire,[4] far within
Its loneliest dell, where odorous plants entwine
Beneath the hollow rocks a natural bower,
Beside a sparkling rivulet he stretched
His languid limbs. A vision on his sleep
150 There came, a dream of hopes that never yet
Had flushed his cheek. He dreamed a veiled maid
Sate near him, talking in low solemn tones.
Her voice was like the voice of his own soul
Heard in the calm of thought; its music long,
155 Like woven sounds of streams and breezes, held

8. In Greek mythology, not evil spirits but minor deities or attendant spirits.
9. In the temple of Isis at Denderah, Egypt, the Zodiac is represented on the ceiling. Journeying among the great civilizations of the past has taken the Poet backward in time to older and older cultures—from the Greeks to the Phoenicians, the Jews, the Babylonians, and the Egyptians. Finally he reaches Ethiopia (line 115), which had been described as the "cradle of the sciences."
1. I.e., by quotations inscribed in the stone.
2. A desert in southern Persia.
3. Rivers in Asia.
4. Now known as Kashmir, an Indian state bordered on the northeast by the Himalayas. In this choice of setting, Shelley was influenced by *The Missionary*, the 1811 novel by Sydney Owenson. See "The Romantic Imagination and the 'Oriental Nations'" on p. 922.

His inmost sense suspended in its web
Of many-coloured woof° and shifting hues.   *weave*
Knowledge and truth and virtue were her theme,
And lofty hopes of divine liberty,
160 Thoughts the most dear to him, and poesy,
Herself a poet. Soon the solemn mood
Of her pure mind kindled through all her frame
A permeating fire: wild numbers° then   *verse*
She raised, with voice stifled in tremulous sobs
165 Subdued by its own pathos: her fair hands
Were bare alone, sweeping from some strange harp
Strange symphony, and in their branching veins
The eloquent blood told an ineffable tale.
The beating of her heart was heard to fill
170 The pauses of her music, and her breath
Tumultuously accorded with those fits
Of intermitted song. Sudden she rose,
As if her heart impatiently endured
Its bursting burthen: at the sound he turned,
175 And saw by the warm light of their own life
Her glowing limbs beneath the sinuous veil
Of woven wind, her outspread arms now bare,
Her dark locks floating in the breath of night,
Her beamy bending eyes, her parted lips
180 Outstretched, and pale, and quivering eagerly.
His strong heart sunk and sickened with excess
Of love. He reared his shuddering limbs and quelled
His gasping breath, and spread his arms to meet
Her panting bosom: . . . she drew back a while,
185 Then, yielding to the irresistible joy,
With frantic gesture and short breathless cry
Folded his frame in her dissolving arms.
Now blackness veiled his dizzy eyes, and night
Involved° and swallowed up the vision; sleep,   *wrapped up*
190 Like a dark flood suspended in its course,
Rolled back its impulse on his vacant brain.

Roused by the shock he started from his trance—
The cold white light of morning, the blue moon
Low in the west, the clear and garish hills,
195 The distinct valley and the vacant woods,
Spread round him where he stood. Whither have fled
The hues of heaven that canopied his bower
Of yesternight? The sounds that soothed his sleep,
The mystery and the majesty of Earth,
200 The joy, the exultation? His wan eyes
Gaze on the empty scene as vacantly
As ocean's moon looks on the moon in heaven.
The spirit of sweet human love has sent
A vision to the sleep of him who spurned
205 Her choicest gifts. He eagerly pursues
Beyond the realms of dream that fleeting shade;°   *phantom*
He overleaps the bounds. Alas! alas!
Were limbs, and breath, and being intertwined

Thus treacherously? Lost, lost, for ever lost,
210 In the wide pathless desart of dim sleep,
That beautiful shape! Does the dark gate of death
Conduct to thy mysterious paradise,
O Sleep?[5] Does the bright arch of rainbow clouds,
And pendent° mountains seen in the calm lake,   *jutting, overhanging*
215 Lead only to a black and watery depth,
While death's blue vault, with loathliest vapours hung,
Where every shade which the foul grave exhales
Hides its dead eye from the detested day,
Conduct, O Sleep, to thy delightful realms?
220 This doubt with sudden tide flowed on his heart,
The insatiate hope which it awakened, stung
His brain even like despair.   While day-light held
The sky, the Poet kept mute conference
With his still soul. At night the passion came,
225 Like the fierce fiend of a distempered dream,
And shook him from his rest, and led him forth
Into the darkness.—As an eagle grasped
In folds of the green serpent, feels her breast
Burn with the poison, and precipitates°   *hastens*
230 Through night and day, tempest, and calm, and cloud,
Frantic with dizzying anguish, her blind flight
O'er the wide aëry wilderness:[6] thus driven
By the bright shadow of that lovely dream,
Beneath the cold glare of the desolate night,
235 Through tangled swamps and deep precipitous dells,
Startling with careless step the moon-light snake,
He fled. Red morning dawned upon his flight,
Shedding the mockery of its vital hues
Upon his cheek of death. He wandered on
240 Till vast Aornos seen from Petra's steep[7]
Hung o'er the low horizon like a cloud;
Through Balk,[8] and where the desolated tombs
Of Parthian kings[9] scatter to every wind
Their wasting dust, wildly he wandered on,
245 Day after day, a weary waste of hours,
Bearing within his life the brooding care
That ever fed on its decaying flame.
And now his limbs were lean; his scattered hair
Sered by the autumn of strange suffering
250 Sung dirges in the wind; his listless hand
Hung like dead bone within its withered skin;
Life, and the lustre that consumed it, shone
As in a furnace burning secretly
From his dark eyes alone. The cottagers,

---

5. I.e., is death the only access to this maiden of his dream?
6. The eagle and serpent locked in mortal combat is a recurrent image in Shelley's poems (see *Prometheus Unbound* 3.1.72–73).
7. A mountain stronghold in the northern part of ancient Arabia. Aornos is a high mountain. "Petra": the rock (literal trans.).
8. Bactria, in ancient Persia, is now part of Afghanistan.
9. The Parthians inhabited northern Persia.

255　Who ministered with human charity
　　His human wants, beheld with wondering awe
　　Their fleeting visitant. The mountaineer,
　　Encountering on some dizzy precipice
　　That spectral form, deemed that the Spirit of wind
260　With lightning eyes, and eager breath, and feet
　　Disturbing not the drifted snow, had paused
　　In its career: the infant would conceal
　　His troubled visage in his mother's robe
　　In terror at the glare of those wild eyes,
265　To remember their strange light in many a dream
　　Of after-times; but youthful maidens, taught
　　By nature, would interpret half the woe
　　That wasted him, would call him with false° names　　*mistaken*
　　Brother, and friend, would press his pallid hand
270　At parting, and watch, dim through tears, the path
　　Of his departure from their father's door.

　　　　At length upon the lone Chorasmian shore[1]
　　He paused, a wide and melancholy waste
　　Of putrid marshes. A strong impulse urged
275　His steps to the sea-shore. A swan was there,
　　Beside a sluggish stream among the reeds.
　　It rose as he approached, and with strong wings
　　Scaling the upward sky, bent its bright course
　　High over the immeasurable main.
280　His eyes pursued its flight.—"Thou hast a home,
　　Beautiful bird; thou voyagest to thine home,
　　Where thy sweet mate will twine her downy neck
　　With thine, and welcome thy return with eyes
　　Bright in the lustre of their own fond joy.
285　And what am I that I should linger here,
　　With voice far sweeter than thy dying notes,
　　Spirit more vast than thine, frame more attuned
　　To beauty, wasting these surpassing powers
　　In the deaf air, to the blind earth, and heaven
290　That echoes not my thoughts?" A gloomy smile
　　Of desperate hope convulsed his curling lips
　　For sleep, he knew, kept most relentlessly
　　Its precious charge,[2] and silent death exposed,
　　Faithless perhaps as sleep, a shadowy lure,
295　With doubtful smile mocking its own strange charms.

　　　　Startled by his own thoughts he looked around.
　　There was no fair fiend[3] near him, not a sight
　　Or sound of awe but in his own deep mind.
　　A little shallop° floating near the shore　　*small open boat*
300　Caught the impatient wandering of his gaze.
　　It had been long abandoned, for its sides

1. The shore of Lake Aral, about 175 miles east of the Caspian Sea.
2. I.e., the maiden in the sleeper's dream.
3. Apparently he suspects there may have been an external agent luring him to the death described in the preceding lines.

Gaped wide with many a rift, and its frail joints
Swayed with the undulations of the tide.
A restless impulse urged him to embark
305 And meet lone Death on the drear ocean's waste;
For well he knew that mighty Shadow loves
The slimy caverns of the populous deep.

    The day was fair and sunny; sea and sky
Drank its inspiring radiance, and the wind
310 Swept strongly from the shore, blackening the waves.
Following his eager soul, the wanderer
Leaped in the boat, he spread his cloak aloft
On the bare mast, and took his lonely seat,
And felt the boat speed o'er the tranquil sea
315 Like a torn cloud before the hurricane.[4]

    As one that in a silver vision floats
Obedient to the sweep of odorous winds
Upon resplendent clouds, so rapidly
Along the dark and ruffled waters fled
320 The straining boat.—A whirlwind swept it on,
With fierce gusts and precipitating force,
Through the white ridges of the chafed sea.
The waves arose. Higher and higher still
Their fierce necks writhed beneath the tempest's scourge
325 Like serpents struggling in a vulture's grasp.
Calm and rejoicing in the fearful war
Of wave ruining° on wave, and blast on blast   *crashing*
Descending, and black flood on whirlpool driven
With dark obliterating course, he sate:
330 As if their genii were the ministers
Appointed to conduct him to the light
Of those beloved eyes, the Poet sate
Holding the steady helm. Evening came on,
The beams of sunset hung their rainbow hues
335 High 'mid the shifting domes of sheeted spray
That canopied his path o'er the waste deep;
Twilight, ascending slowly from the east,
Entwin'd in duskier wreaths her braided locks
O'er the fair front and radiant eyes of day;
340 Night followed, clad with stars. On every side
More horribly the multitudinous streams
Of ocean's mountainous waste to mutual war
Rushed in dark tumult thundering, as to mock
The calm and spangled sky. The little boat
345 Still fled before the storm; still fled, like foam
Down the steep cataract of a wintry river;

4. If the Poet's boat is being carried upstream on the Oxus River from the Aral Sea to the river's headwaters in the Hindu Kush Mountains (the "Indian Caucasus" that is the setting for *Prometheus Unbound*), then the journey is taking him to a region that the naturalist Buffon (whom Shelley often read) had identified as the cradle of the human race. But it is also possible that the starting point for this journey is the Caspian Sea, in which case the journey would end near the traditional site of the Garden of Eden.

Now pausing on the edge of the riven° wave;   *torn asunder*
Now leaving far behind the bursting mass
That fell, convulsing ocean. Safely fled—
350   As if that frail and wasted human form,
Had been an elemental god.[5]
                   At midnight
The moon arose: and lo! the etherial cliffs[6]
Of Caucasus, whose icy summits shone
Among the stars like sunlight, and around
355   Whose cavern'd base the whirlpools and the waves
Bursting and eddying irresistibly
Rage and resound for ever.—Who shall save?—
The boat fled on,—the boiling torrent drove,—
The crags closed round with black and jagged arms,
360   The shattered mountain overhung the sea,
And faster still, beyond all human speed,
Suspended on the sweep of the smooth wave,
The little boat was driven. A cavern there
Yawned, and amid its slant and winding depths
365   Ingulphed the rushing sea. The boat fled on
With unrelaxing speed.—"Vision and Love!"
The Poet cried aloud, "I have beheld
The path of thy departure. Sleep and death
Shall not divide us long!"

                The boat pursued
370   The winding of the cavern. Day-light shone
At length upon that gloomy river's flow;
Now, where the fiercest war among the waves
Is calm, on the unfathomable stream
The boat moved slowly. Where the mountain, riven,
375   Exposed those black depths to the azure sky,
Ere yet the flood's enormous volume fell
Even to the base of Caucasus, with sound
That shook the everlasting rocks, the mass
Filled with one whirlpool all that ample chasm;
380   Stair above stair the eddying waters rose,
Circling immeasurably fast, and laved°   *washed*
With alternating dash the knarled roots
Of mighty trees, that stretched their giant arms
In darkness over it. I' the midst was left,
385   Reflecting, yet distorting every cloud,
A pool of treacherous and tremendous calm.
Seized by the sway of the ascending stream,
With dizzy swiftness, round, and round, and round,
Ridge after ridge the straining boat arose,
390   Till on the verge of the extremest curve,
Where, through an opening of the rocky bank,
The waters overflow, and a smooth spot
Of glassy quiet mid those battling tides

---

5. A god of one of the natural elements (see line 1).
6. I.e., cliffs high in the air.

Is left, the boat paused shuddering.—Shall it sink
395 Down the abyss? Shall the reverting stress
Of that resistless gulph embosom it?
Now shall it fall?—A wandering stream of wind,
Breathed from the west, has caught the expanded sail,
And, lo! with gentle motion, between banks
400 Of mossy slope, and on a placid stream,
Beneath a woven grove it sails, and, hark!
The ghastly torrent mingles its far roar,
With the breeze murmuring in the musical woods.
Where the embowering trees recede, and leave
405 A little space of green expanse, the cove
Is closed by meeting banks, whose yellow flowers
For ever gaze on their own drooping eyes,
Reflected in the crystal calm. The wave
Of the boat's motion marred their pensive task,
410 Which nought but vagrant bird, or wanton wind,
Or falling spear-grass, or their own decay
Had e'er disturbed before. The Poet longed
To deck with their bright hues his withered hair,
But on his heart its solitude returned,
415 And he forbore.[7] Not the strong impulse hid
In those flushed cheeks, bent eyes, and shadowy frame,
Had yet performed its ministry: it hung
Upon his life, as lightning in a cloud
Gleams, hovering ere it vanish, ere the floods
Of night close over it.
420   The noonday sun
Now shone upon the forest, one vast mass
Of mingling shade, whose brown magnificence
A narrow vale embosoms. There, huge caves,
Scooped in the dark base of their aëry rocks
425 Mocking[8] its moans, respond and roar for ever.
The meeting boughs and implicated° leaves   *intertwined*
Wove twilight o'er the Poet's path, as led
By love, or dream, or god, or mightier Death,
He sought in Nature's dearest haunt, some bank,
430 Her cradle, and his sepulchre. More dark
And dark the shades accumulate. The oak,
Expanding its immense and knotty arms,
Embraces the light beech. The pyramids
Of the tall cedar overarching, frame
435 Most solemn domes within, and far below.
Like clouds suspended in an emerald sky,
The ash and the acacia floating hang
Tremulous and pale. Like restless serpents, clothed
In rainbow and in fire, the parasites,
440 Starred with ten thousand blossoms, flow around

---

7. The "yellow flowers" overhanging their own reflection (lines 406–8), probably narcissus, may signify the narcissistic temptation of the Poet to be satisfied with a projection of his own self. But his need for an unearthly Other revives, and "the strong impulse" (line 415) drives him on.
8. As often in Shelley, "mocking" has a double sense: mimicking as well as ridiculing the sounds of the forest (line 421).

The grey trunks, and, as gamesome infants' eyes,
With gentle meanings, and most innocent wiles,
Fold their beams round the hearts of those that love,
These twine their tendrils with the wedded boughs
445 Uniting their close union; the woven leaves
Make net-work of the dark blue light of day,
And the night's noontide clearness, mutable
As shapes in the weird clouds. Soft mossy lawns
Beneath these canopies extend their swells,
450 Fragrant with perfumed herbs, and eyed with blooms
Minute yet beautiful. One darkest glen
Sends from its woods of musk-rose, twined with jasmine,
A soul-dissolving odour, to invite
To some more lovely mystery. Through the dell,
455 Silence and Twilight here, twin-sisters, keep
Their noonday watch, and sail among the shades,
Like vaporous shapes half seen; beyond, a well,
Dark, gleaming, and of most translucent wave,
Images all the woven boughs above,
460 And each depending leaf, and every speck
Of azure sky, darting between their chasms;
Nor aught else in the liquid mirror laves
Its portraiture, but some inconstant star
Between one foliaged lattice twinkling fair,
465 Or, painted bird, sleeping beneath the moon,
Or gorgeous insect floating motionless,
Unconscious of the day, ere yet his wings
Have spread their glories to the gaze of noon.

Hither the Poet came. His eyes beheld
470 Their own wan light through the reflected lines
Of his thin hair, distinct in the dark depth
Of that still fountain; as the human heart,
Gazing in dreams over the gloomy grave,
Sees its own treacherous likeness there. He heard
475 The motion of the leaves, the grass that sprung
Startled and glanced and trembled even to feel
An unaccustomed presence, and the sound
Of the sweet brook that from the secret springs
Of that dark fountain rose. A Spirit seemed
480 To stand beside him—clothed in no bright robes
Of shadowy silver or enshrining light,
Borrowed from aught the visible world affords
Of grace, or majesty, or mystery;—
But, undulating woods, and silent well,
485 And leaping rivulet, and evening gloom
Now deepening the dark shades, for speech assuming
Held commune with him, as if he and it
Were all that was,—only . . . when his regard
Was raised by intense pensiveness, . . . two eyes,
490 Two starry eyes, hung in the gloom of thought,
And seemed with their serene and azure smiles
To beckon him.

Obedient to the light
That shone within his soul, he went, pursuing
The windings of the dell.—The rivulet
495 Wanton and wild, through many a green ravine
Beneath the forest flowed. Sometimes it fell
Among the moss with hollow harmony
Dark and profound. Now on the polished stones
It danced; like childhood laughing as it went:
500 Then, through the plain in tranquil wanderings crept,
Reflecting every herb and drooping bud
That overhung its quietness.—"O stream!
Whose source is inaccessibly profound,
Whither do thy mysterious waters tend?
505 Thou imagest my life. Thy darksome stillness,
Thy dazzling waves, thy loud and hollow gulphs,
Thy searchless° fountain, and invisible course   *undiscoverable*
Have each their type in me: and the wide sky,
And measureless ocean may declare as soon
510 What oozy cavern or what wandering cloud
Contains thy waters, as the universe
Tell where these living thoughts reside, when stretched
Upon thy flowers my bloodless limbs shall waste
I' the passing wind!"

Beside the grassy shore
515 Of the small stream he went; he did impress
On the green moss his tremulous step, that caught
Strong shuddering from his burning limbs. As one
Roused by some joyous madness from the couch
Of fever, he did move; yet, not like him,
520 Forgetful of the grave, where, when the flame
Of his frail exultation shall be spent,
He must descend. With rapid steps he went
Beneath the shade of trees, beside the flow
Of the wild babbling rivulet; and now
525 The forest's solemn canopies were changed
For the uniform and lightsome° evening sky.   *luminous*
Grey rocks did peep from the spare moss, and stemmed
The struggling brook: tall spires of windlestrae[9]
Threw their thin shadows down the rugged slope,
530 And nought but knarled roots[1] of antient pines
Branchless and blasted, clenched with grasping roots
The unwilling soil. A gradual change was here,
Yet ghastly. For, as fast years flow away,
The smooth brow gathers, and the hair grows thin
535 And white, and where irradiate° dewy eyes   *illumined*
Had shone, gleam stony orbs:—so from his steps
Bright flowers departed, and the beautiful shade
Of the green groves, with all their odorous winds
And musical motions. Calm, he still pursued
540 The stream, that with a larger volume now
Rolled through the labyrinthine dell; and there

9. Windlestraw (Scottish dial.); tall, dried stalks of grass.
1. Probably an error for "stumps" or "trunks."

Fretted a path through its descending curves
With its wintry speed. On every side now rose
Rocks, which, in unimaginable forms,
545   Lifted their black and barren pinnacles
In the light of evening, and its precipice[2]
Obscuring the ravine, disclosed above,
Mid toppling stones, black gulphs and yawning caves,
Whose windings gave ten thousand various tongues
550   To the loud stream. Lo! where the pass expands
Its stony jaws, the abrupt mountain breaks,
And seems, with its accumulated crags,
To overhang the world: for wide expand
Beneath the wan stars and descending moon
555   Islanded seas, blue mountains, mighty streams,
Dim tracts and vast, robed in the lustrous gloom
Of leaden-coloured even, and fiery hills
Mingling their flames with twilight, on the verge
Of the remote horizon. The near° scene,   *nearby*
560   In naked and severe simplicity,
Made contrast with the universe. A pine,[3]
Rock-rooted, stretched athwart the vacancy
Its swinging boughs, to each inconstant blast
Yielding one only response, at each pause
565   In most familiar cadence, with the howl
The thunder and the hiss of homeless streams
Mingling its solemn song, whilst the broad river,
Foaming and hurrying o'er its rugged path,
Fell into that immeasurable void
570   Scattering its waters to the passing winds.

      Yet the grey precipice and solemn pine
And torrent, were not all;—one silent nook
Was there. Even on the edge of that vast mountain,
Upheld by knotty roots and fallen rocks,
575   It overlooked in its serenity
The dark earth, and the bending vault of stars.
It was a tranquil spot, that seemed to smile
Even in the lap of horror. Ivy clasped
The fissured stones with its entwining arms,
580   And did embower with leaves for ever green,
And berries dark, the smooth and even space
Of its inviolated floor, and here
The children of the autumnal whirlwind bore,
In wanton sport, those bright leaves, whose decay,
585   Red, yellow, or etherially pale,
Rivals the pride of summer. 'Tis the haunt
Of every gentle wind, whose breath can teach
The wilds to love tranquillity. One step,
One human step alone, has ever broken
590   The stillness of its solitude:—one voice
Alone inspired its echoes,—even that voice

2. Headlong fall (of the stream, line 540).
3. Pine trees in Shelley often signify persistence and steadfastness amid change and vicissitudes.

Which hither came, floating among the winds,
And led the loveliest among human forms
To make their wild haunts the depository
595 Of all the grace and beauty that endued
Its motions, render up its majesty,
Scatter its music on the unfeeling storm,
And to the damp leaves and blue cavern mould,
Nurses of rainbow flowers and branching moss,
600 Commit the colours of that varying cheek,
That snowy breast, those dark and drooping eyes.

The dim and horned[4] moon hung low, and poured
A sea of lustre on the horizon's verge
That overflowed its mountains. Yellow mist
605 Filled the unbounded atmosphere, and drank
Wan moonlight even to fulness: not a star
Shone, not a sound was heard; the very winds,
Danger's grim playmates, on that precipice
Slept, clasped in his embrace.—O, storm of death!
610 Whose sightless[5] speed divides this sullen night:
And thou, colossal Skeleton,° that, still   *Death*
Guiding its irresistible career
In thy devastating omnipotence,
Art king of this frail world, from the red field
615 Of slaughter, from the reeking hospital,
The patriot's sacred couch, the snowy bed
Of innocence, the scaffold and the throne,
A mighty voice invokes thee. Ruin calls
His brother Death. A rare and regal prey
620 He hath prepared, prowling around the world;
Glutted with which thou mayst repose, and men
Go to their graves like flowers or creeping worms,
Nor ever more offer at thy dark shrine
The unheeded tribute of a broken heart.

625   When on the threshold of the green recess
The wanderer's footsteps fell, he knew that death
Was on him. Yet a little, ere it fled,
Did he resign his high and holy soul
To images of the majestic past,
630 That paused within his passive being now,
Like winds that bear sweet music, when they breathe
Through some dim latticed chamber. He did place
His pale lean hand upon the rugged trunk
Of the old pine. Upon an ivied stone
635 Reclined his languid head, his limbs did rest,
Diffused and motionless, on the smooth brink
Of that obscurest° chasm;—and thus he lay,   *darkest*
Surrendering to their final impulses
The hovering powers of life. Hope and despair,
640 The torturers, slept; no mortal pain or fear

---

4. The moon is crescent shaped with the points rising, as in Coleridge's "Dejection: An Ode": "the new Moon / With the old Moon in her arms."
5. Invisible, or perhaps "unseeing."

Marred his repose, the influxes of sense,
And his own being unalloyed by pain,
Yet feebler and more feeble, calmly fed
The stream of thought, till he lay breathing there
645 At peace, and faintly smiling:—his last sight
Was the great moon, which o'er the western line
Of the wide world her mighty horn suspended,
With whose dun° beams inwoven darkness seemed   *darkened*
To mingle. Now upon the jagged hills
650 It rests, and still as the divided frame
Of the vast meteor[6] sunk, the Poet's blood,
That ever beat in mystic sympathy
With nature's ebb and flow, grew feebler still:
And when two lessening points of light alone
655 Gleamed through the darkness, the alternate gasp
Of his faint respiration scarce did stir
The stagnate night:[7]—till the minutest ray
Was quenched, the pulse yet lingered in his heart.
It paused—it fluttered. But when heaven remained
660 Utterly black, the murky shades involved
An image, silent, cold, and motionless,
As their own voiceless earth and vacant air.
Even as a vapour° fed with golden beams   *cloud*
That ministered on[8] sunlight, ere the west
665 Eclipses it, was now that wonderous frame—
No sense, no motion, no divinity—
A fragile lute, on whose harmonious strings
The breath of heaven did wander—a bright stream
Once fed with many-voiced waves—a dream
670 Of youth, which night and time have quenched for ever,
Still, dark, and dry, and unremembered now.

     O, for Medea's wondrous alchemy,
Which wheresoe'er it fell made the earth gleam
With bright flowers, and the wintry boughs exhale
675 From vernal blooms fresh fragrance![9] O, that God,
Profuse of poisons, would concede the chalice
Which but one living man[1] has drained, who now,
Vessel of deathless wrath, a slave that feels
No proud exemption in the blighting curse
680 He bears, over the world wanders for ever,
Lone as incarnate death! O, that the dream
Of dark magician in his visioned cave,[2]
Raking the cinders of a crucible
For life and power, even when his feeble hand

---

6. I.e., the moon. The word *meteor* was once used for any phenomenon in the skies, as our modern term "meteorology" suggests.
7. The ebbing of the Poet's life parallels the descent of the "homed moon," to the moment when only the two "points of light"—its horns—show above the hills.
8. Attended, acted as a servant to.
9. Medea brewed a magic potion to rejuvenate the dying Aeson; where some of the potion spilled on the ground, flowers sprang up (Ovid,

Metamorphoses 7.275ff.).
1. The Wandering Jew. According to a medieval legend, he had taunted Christ on the way to the crucifixion and was condemned to wander the world, deathless, until Christ's second coming.
2. Cave in which he has visions. "Dark magician": an alchemist attempting to produce the elixir of enduring life. Alchemy intrigued both Shelleys. See Mary Shelley's "The Mortal Immortal" (p. 1036).

685 Shakes in its last decay, were the true law
Of this so lovely world! But thou art fled
Like some frail exhalation;° which the dawn   *mist*
Robes in its golden beams,—ah! thou hast fled!
The brave, the gentle, and the beautiful,
690 The child of grace and genius. Heartless things
Are done and said i' the world, and many worms
And beasts and men live on, and mighty Earth
From sea and mountain, city and wilderness,
In vesper³ low or joyous orison,°   *prayer*
695 Lifts still its solemn voice:—but thou art fled—
Thou canst no longer know or love the shapes
Of this phantasmal scene, who have to thee
Been purest ministers, who are, alas!
Now thou art not. Upon those pallid lips
700 So sweet even in their silence, on those eyes
That image sleep in death, upon that form
Yet safe from the worm's outrage, let no tear
Be shed—not even in thought. Nor, when those hues
Are gone, and those divinest lineaments,
705 Worn by the senseless° wind, shall live alone   *unfeeling*
In the frail pauses of this simple strain,
Let not high verse, mourning the memory
Of that which is no more, or painting's woe
Or sculpture, speak in feeble imagery
710 Their own cold powers. Art and eloquence,
And all the shews o' the world are frail and vain
To weep a loss that turns their lights to shade.
It is a woe too "deep for tears,"⁴ when all
Is reft at once, when some surpassing Spirit,
715 Whose light adorned the world around it, leaves
Those who remain behind, not sobs or groans,
The passionate tumult of a clinging hope;
But pale despair and cold tranquillity,
Nature's vast frame, the web of human things,
720 Birth and the grave, that are not as they were.

1815   1816

Mont Blanc¹

Lines Written in the Vale of Chamouni

I

The everlasting universe of things
Flows through the mind, and rolls its rapid waves,
Now dark—now glittering—now reflecting gloom—

3. Evening prayer.
4. From the last line of Wordsworth's "Ode: Intimations of Immortality": "Thoughts that do often lie too deep for tears."

1. This poem, in which Shelley both echoes and argues with the poetry of natural description written by Wordsworth and Coleridge, was first-published as the conclusion to the *History of a*

Now lending splendour, where from secret springs
5 The source of human thought its tribute brings
Of waters,—with a sound but half its own,
Such as a feeble brook will oft assume
In the wild woods, among the mountains lone,
Where waterfalls around it leap forever,
10 Where woods and winds contend, and a vast river
Over its rocks ceaselessly bursts and raves.

2

Thus thou, Ravine of Arve—dark, deep Ravine—
Thou many-coloured, many-voiced vale,
Over whose pines, and crags, and caverns sail
15 Fast cloud shadows and sunbeams: awful° scene,   *awe-inspiring*
Where Power in likeness of the Arve comes down
From the ice gulphs that gird his secret throne,
Bursting through these dark mountains like the flame
Of lightning through the tempest;—thou dost lie,
20 Thy giant brood of pines around thee clinging,
Children of elder° time, in whose devotion   *earlier, ancient*
The chainless winds still come and ever came
To drink their odours, and their mighty swinging
To hear—an old and solemn harmony;
25 Thine earthly rainbows stretched across the sweep
Of the etherial waterfall, whose veil
Robes some unsculptured[2] image; the strange sleep
Which when the voices of the desart fail
Wraps all in its own deep eternity;—
30 Thy caverns echoing to the Arve's commotion,
A loud, lone sound no other sound can tame;
Thou art pervaded with that ceaseless motion,
Thou art the path of that unresting sound—
Dizzy Ravine! and when I gaze on thee
35 I seem as in a trance sublime and strange
To muse on my own separate phantasy,

Six Weeks' Tour. This was a book that Percy and Mary Shelley wrote together detailing the excursion that they and Claire Clairmont took in July 1816 to the valley of Chamonix, in what is now southeastern France. That valley lies at the foot of Mont Blanc, the highest mountain in the Alps and in all Europe.

In the *History* Percy Shelley commented on his poem: "It was composed under the immediate impression of the deep and powerful feelings excited by the objects it attempts to describe; and, as an indisciplined overflowing of the soul rests its claim to approbation on an attempt to imitate the untamable wildness and inaccessible solemnity from which those feelings sprang." He was inspired to write the poem while standing on a bridge spanning the river Arve, which flows through the valley of Chamonix and is fed from above by the meltoff of the glacier, the Mer de Glace.

In a letter to Thomas Love Peacock drafted in the same week as "Mont Blanc," Shelley had recalled that the count de Buffon, a French pioneer of the science we now know as geology, had proposed a "sublime but gloomy theory—that this globe which we inhabit will at some future period be changed to a mass of frost." This sense, which Shelley takes from Buffon, of a Nature that is utterly alien and indifferent to human beings (and whose history takes shape on a timescale of incomprehensible immensity) is counterposed throughout "Mont Blanc" with Shelley's interest, fueled by his reading of 18th-century skeptics such as David Hume, in questions about the human mind, its powers, and the limits of knowledge. "All things exist as they are perceived: at least in relation to the percipient," Shelley would later write in "A Defence of Poetry" (p. 881). In "Mont Blanc" the priority that this statement gives to the mind over the external world is challenged by the sheer destructive power of the mountain.

2. I.e., not formed by humans.

My own, my human mind, which passively
Now renders and receives fast influencings,
Holding an unremitting interchange
40 With the clear universe of things around;
One legion of wild thoughts, whose wandering wings
Now float above thy darkness, and now rest
Where that° or thou° art no unbidden guest,   *thy darkness / the ravine*
In the still cave of the witch Poesy,[3]
45 Seeking among the shadows that pass by
Ghosts of all things that are, some shade of thee,
Some phantom, some faint image; till the breast
From which they fled recalls them, thou art there![4]

3

Some say that gleams of a remoter world
50 Visit the soul in sleep,—that death is slumber,
And that its shapes the busy thoughts outnumber
Of those who wake and live.—I look on high;
Has some unknown omnipotence unfurled
The veil of life and death? or do I lie
55 In dream, and does the mightier world of sleep
Spread far around and inaccessibly
Its circles? For the very spirit fails,
Driven like a homeless cloud from steep to steep
That vanishes among the viewless° gales!   *invisible*
60 Far, far above, piercing the infinite sky,
Mont Blanc appears,—still, snowy, and serene—
Its subject mountains their unearthly forms
Pile around it, ice and rock; broad vales between
Of frozen floods, unfathomable deeps,
65 Blue as the overhanging heaven, that spread
And wind among the accumulated steeps;
A desart peopled by the storms alone,
Save° when the eagle brings some hunter's bone,   *except*
And the wolf tracts° her there—how hideously   *tracks*
70 Its shapes are heaped around! rude, bare, and high,
Ghastly, and scarred, and riven.°—Is this the scene   *split*
Where the old Earthquake-dæmon[5] taught her young
Ruin? Were these their toys? or did a sea
Of fire, envelope once this silent snow?
75 None can reply—all seems eternal now.
The wilderness has a mysterious tongue
Which teaches awful doubt,[6] or faith so mild,

3. I.e., in the part of the mind that creates poetry.
4. In these difficult lines (41–48) Shelley seems to be recalling Plato's allegory in the *Republic* of the mind as cave. Plato describes human beings' sense of reality as if it were based only on the shadows cast by firelight on the walls and we remained ignorant of the light of reality outside the cave. The syntax in the passage blurs the distinction between what is inside the human viewer's mind and outside in the world that he views: the thoughts (line 41) seek in the poet's creative faculty ("the still cave of the witch

Poesy") some "shade," "phantom," or "faint image" of the ravine of the Arve, and when the ravine is thereby remembered (when "the breast" from which the images has fled "recalls them"), then the ravine exists.
5. A supernatural being, halfway between mortals and the gods. Here it represents the force that makes earthquakes. Shelley views this landscape as the product of violent geological upheavals in the past.
6. Awe-filled open-mindedness.

So solemn, so serene, that man may be
But for such faith[7] with nature reconciled;
80   Thou hast a voice, great Mountain, to repeal
Large codes of fraud and woe; not understood
By all, but which[8] the wise, and great, and good
Interpret, or make felt, or deeply feel.

4

The fields, the lakes, the forests, and the streams,
85   Ocean, and all the living things that dwell
Within the dædal[9] earth; lightning, and rain,
Earthquake, and fiery flood, and hurricane,
The torpor of the year when feeble dreams
Visit the hidden buds, or dreamless sleep
90   Holds every future leaf and flower;—the bound
With which from that detested trance they leap;
The works and ways of man, their death and birth,
And that of him and all that his may be;
All things that move and breathe with toil and sound
95   Are born and die; revolve, subside and swell.
Power dwells apart in its tranquillity
Remote, serene, and inaccessible:
And *this*, the naked countenance of earth,
On which I gaze, even these primæval mountains
100   Teach the adverting° mind. The glaciers creep   *observant*
Like snakes that watch their prey, from their far fountains,
Slow rolling on; there, many a precipice,
Frost and the Sun in scorn of mortal power
Have piled: dome, pyramid, and pinnacle,
105   A city of death, distinct with many a tower
And wall impregnable of beaming ice.
Yet not a city, but a flood of ruin
Is there, that from the boundaries of the sky
Rolls its perpetual stream; vast pines are strewing
110   Its destined path, or in the mangled soil
Branchless and shattered stand: the rocks, drawn down
From yon remotest waste, have overthrown
The limits of the dead and living world,
Never to be reclaimed. The dwelling-place
115   Of insects, beasts, and birds, becomes its spoil;
Their food and their retreat for ever gone,
So much of life and joy is lost. The race
Of man, flies far in dread; his work and dwelling
Vanish, like smoke before the tempest's stream,
120   And their place is not known. Below, vast caves
Shine in the rushing torrents' restless gleam,
Which from those secret chasms in tumult welling[1]

Meet in the vale, and one majestic River,[2]
The breath and blood of distant lands, for ever
125   Rolls its loud waters to the ocean waves,
Breathes its swift vapours to the circling air.

5

Mont Blanc yet gleams on high:—the power is there,
The still and solemn power of many sights,
And many sounds, and much of life and death.
130   In the calm darkness of the moonless nights,
In the lone glare of day, the snows descend
Upon that Mountain; none beholds them there,
Nor when the flakes burn in the sinking sun,
Or the star-beams dart through them:—Winds contend
135   Silently there, and heap the snow with breath
Rapid and strong, but silently! Its home
The voiceless lightning in these solitudes
Keeps innocently, and like vapour broods
Over the snow. The secret strength of things
140   Which governs thought, and to the infinite dome
Of heaven is as a law, inhabits thee!
And what were thou,° and earth, and stars, and sea,   *Mont Blanc*
If to the human mind's imaginings
Silence and solitude were vacancy?

1816   1817

Hymn to Intellectual Beauty[1]

I

The awful shadow of some unseen Power
    Floats though unseen amongst us,—visiting
    This various world with as inconstant wing
As summer winds that creep from flower to flower.—
5   Like moonbeams that behind some piny mountain shower,[2]
        It visits with inconstant glance
        Each human heart and countenance;
    Like hues and harmonies of evening,—
        Like clouds in starlight widely spread,—
10   Like memory of music fled,—
        Like aught that for its grace may be
Dear, and yet dearer for its mystery.

2

Spirit of BEAUTY, that dost consecrate
    With thine own hues all thou dost shine upon

2. The Arve, which flows into Lake Geneva. Nearby the river Rhone flows out of Lake Geneva to begin its course through France and into the Mediterranean.
1. "Intellectual": nonmaterial, that which is beyond access to the human senses. In this poem intellectual beauty is something postulated to account for occasional states of awareness that lend splendor, grace, and truth both to the natural world and to people's moral consciousness.
2. Used as a verb.

15 Of human thought or form,—where art thou gone?
 Why dost thou pass away and leave our state,
 This dim vast vale of tears, vacant and desolate?
  Ask why the sunlight not forever
  Weaves rainbows o'er yon mountain river,
20 Why aught° should fail and fade that once is shewn,   *anything*
  Why fear and dream and death and birth
  Cast on the daylight of this earth
  Such gloom,—why man has such a scope
 For love and hate, despondency and hope?

3

25 No voice from some sublimer world hath ever
  To sage or poet these responses given—
  Therefore the name of God and ghosts and Heaven,
 Remain the records of their vain endeavour,[3]
 Frail spells—whose uttered charm might not avail to sever,
30 From all we hear and all we see,
  Doubt, chance, and mutability.
 Thy light alone—like mist o'er mountains driven,
  Or music by the night wind sent
  Through strings of some still instrument,
35 Or moonlight on a midnight stream,
 Gives grace and truth to life's unquiet dream.

4

 Love, Hope, and Self-esteem, like clouds depart
  And come, for some uncertain moments lent.
  Man were immortal, and omnipotent,
40 Didst thou, unknown and awful as thou art,
 Keep with thy glorious train firm state within his heart.[4]
  Thou messenger of sympathies,
  That wax and wane in lovers' eyes—
 Thou—that to human thought art nourishment,
45 Like darkness to a dying flame![5]
  Depart not as thy shadow came,
  Depart not—lest the grave should be,
 Like life and fear, a dark reality.

5

 While yet a boy I sought for ghosts, and sped
50 Through many a listening chamber, cave and ruin,
  And starlight wood, with fearful steps pursuing
 Hopes of high talk with the departed dead.
 I called on poisonous names with which our youth is fed;[6]

---

3. The names (line 27) represent nothing better than the feeble guesses that philosophers and poets have made in attempting to answer the questions posed in stanza 2, but these guesses also delude us as though they were magic spells.
4. I.e., "man would be immortal . . . if thou didst keep."
5. Darkness may be said to nourish the dying flame by providing the contrast that offsets its light.
6. Lines 49–52 refer to Shelley's youthful experiments with magic and conjuring. In one manuscript version this line reads "I called on that false name with which our youth is fed"; the next line continues, "He answered not." This version would have clinched Shelley's scandalous reputation for atheism.

I was not heard—I saw them not—
55 When musing deeply on the lot
Of life, at that sweet time when winds are wooing
        All vital things that wake to bring
        News of buds and blossoming,—
        Sudden, thy shadow fell on me;
60 I shrieked, and clasped my hands in extacy!

6

I vowed that I would dedicate my powers
    To thee and thine—have I not kept the vow?
    With beating heart and streaming eyes, even now
I call the phantoms of a thousand hours
65 Each from his voiceless grave: they have in visioned bowers
        Of studious zeal or love's delight
        Outwatched with me the envious night[7]—
They know that never joy illumed my brow
        Unlinked with hope that thou wouldst free
70   This world from its dark slavery,
        That thou—O awful LOVELINESS,
Wouldst give whate'er these words cannot express.

7

The day becomes more solemn and serene
    When noon is past—there is a harmony
75   In autumn, and a lustre in its sky,
Which through the summer is not heard or seen,
As if it could not be, as if it had not been!
        Thus let thy power, which like the truth
        Of nature on my passive youth
80 Descended, to my onward life supply
        Its calm—to one who worships thee,
        And every form containing thee,
        Whom, SPIRIT fair, thy spells did bind
To fear[8] himself, and love all human kind.

1816   1817

Ozymandias[1]

I met a traveller from an antique land,
Who said—"Two vast and trunkless° legs of stone   *without a torso*
Stand in the desert. . . . Near them, on the sand,
Half sunk a shattered visage lies, whose frown,
5   And wrinkled lip, and sneer of cold command,

---

7. I.e., stayed up until the night, envious of their
delight, had reluctantly departed.
8. Probably in the old sense: "to stand in awe of."
1. According to Diodorus Siculus, Greek historian of the 1st century B.C.E., the largest statue
in Egypt had the inscription "I am Ozymandias,
king of kings; if anyone wishes to know what
I am and where I lie, let him surpass me in some
of my exploits." Ozymandias was the Greek
name for Ramses II of Egypt, 13th century B.C.E.

Tell that its sculptor well those passions read
Which yet survive,° stamped on these lifeless things,   *outlive*
The hand that mocked them, and the heart that fed;[2]
And on the pedestal, these words appear:
10   My name is Ozymandias, King of Kings,
Look on my Works, ye Mighty, and despair!
Nothing beside remains. Round the decay
Of that colossal Wreck, boundless and bare
The lone and level sands stretch far away."

1817   1818

On Love[1]

What is Love? Ask him who lives what is life; ask him who adores what is God.

I know not the internal constitution of other men, nor even of thine whom I now address. I see that in some external attributes they resemble me, but when, misled by that appearance, I have thought to appeal to something in common and unburthen my inmost soul to them, I have found my language misunderstood, like one in a distant and savage land. The more opportunities they have afforded me for experience, the wider has appeared the interval between us, and to a greater distance have the points of sympathy been withdrawn. With a spirit ill-fitted to sustain such proof, trembling and feeble through its tenderness, I have every where sought, and have found only repulse and disappointment.

Thou demandest what is Love. It is that powerful attraction towards all we conceive, or fear, or hope beyond ourselves, when we find within our own thoughts the chasm of an insufficient void, and seek to awaken in all things that are, a community with what we experience within ourselves. If we reason, we would be understood; if we imagine, we would that the airy children of our brain were born anew within another's; if we feel, we would that another's nerves should vibrate to our own, that the beams of their eyes should kindle at once and mix and melt into our own; that lips of motionless ice should not reply to lips quivering and burning with the heart's best blood:— this is Love. This is the bond and the sanction which connects not only man with man, but with every thing which exists. We are born into the world, and there is something within us, which from the instant that we live, more and more thirsts after its likeness. It is probably in correspondence with this law that the infant drains milk from the bosom of its mother; this propensity develops itself with the development of our nature. We dimly see within our intellectual nature, a miniature as it were of our entire self, yet deprived of all

---

2. "The hand" is the sculptor's, who had "mocked" (both imitated and satirized) the sculptured passions; "the heart" is the king's, which has "fed" his passions.
1. Shelley's essay, likely composed in the summer of 1818 just after he translated Plato's *Symposium*, first appeared in print in *The Keepsake for 1829*—a miscellany of poems, stories, and engravings, edited by Frederick Mansel Reynolds. The *Keep-*

sake belonged to the group of publications that, debuting in Britain in the 1820s, were known as the literary annuals: sumptuously produced, bound in silk, these books were promoted as especially appropriate and tasteful gifts to be given to young women. Mary Shelley, who supplied Reynolds with her late husband's manuscript, was herself a frequent contributor to *The Keepsake*: see "The Mortal Immortal," p. 1036.

that we condemn or despise, the ideal prototype of every thing excellent and lovely that we are capable of conceiving as belonging to the nature of man. Not only the portrait of our external being, but an assemblage of the minutest particles of which our nature is composed:[2] a mirror whose surface reflects only the forms of purity and brightness: a soul within our own soul that describes a circle around its proper Paradise, which pain and sorrow and evil dare not overleap. To this we eagerly refer all sensations, thirsting that they should resemble and correspond with it. The discovery of its antitype; the meeting with an understanding capable of clearly estimating our own; an imagination which should enter into and seize upon the subtle and delicate peculiarities which we have delighted to cherish and unfold in secret, with a frame, whose nerves, like the chords of two exquisite lyres, strung to the accompaniment of one delightful voice, vibrate with the vibrations of our own; and a combination of all these in such proportion as the type within demands: this is the invisible and unattainable point to which Love tends; and to attain which, it urges forth the powers of man to arrest the faintest shadow of that, without the possession of which, there is no rest nor respite to the heart over which it rules. Hence in solitude, or that deserted state when we are surrounded by human beings and yet they sympathize not with us, we love the flowers, the grass, the waters, and the sky. In the motion of the very leaves of spring, in the blue air, there is then found a secret correspondence with our heart. There is eloquence in the tongueless wind, and a melody in the flowing brooks and the rustling of the reeds beside them, which by their inconceivable relation to something within the soul awaken the spirits to dance of breathless rapture, and bring tears of mysterious tenderness to the eyes, like the enthusiasm of patriotic success, or the voice of one beloved singing to you alone. Sterne says that if he were in a desert he would love some cypress.[3] So soon as this want or power is dead, man becomes a living sepulchre of himself, and what yet survives is the mere husk of what once he was.

1818   1829

Stanzas Written in Dejection— December 1818, near Naples[1]

The Sun is warm, the sky is clear,
The waves are dancing fast and bright,
Blue isles and snowy mountains wear
The purple noon's transparent might,
5   The breath of the moist earth is light
Around its unexpanded buds;
Like many a voice of one delight
The winds, the birds, the Ocean-floods;
The City's voice itself is soft, like Solitude's.

2. These words are ineffectual and metaphorical. Most words are so,—no help! [Shelley's note].
3. Paraphrase of a passage in Sterne's *A Sentimental Journey through France and Italy* (1768), in which the narrator contrasts his approach to traveling with that of travelers less easily pleased: "was I in a desert, I would find out wherewith in it

to call forth my affections."
1. Shelley's first wife, Harriet, had drowned herself; Clara, his baby daughter with Mary Shelley, had just died; and he was plagued by ill health, pain, financial worries, and the sense that he had failed as a poet.

<pre>
10   I see the Deep's untrampled floor
        With green and purple seaweeds strown;
        I see the waves upon the shore
        Like light dissolved in star-showers, thrown;
        I sit upon the sands alone;
15   The lightning of the noontide Ocean
        Is flashing round me, and a tone
        Arises from its measured motion,
    How sweet! did any heart now share in my emotion.

        Alas, I have nor hope nor health
20   Nor peace within nor calm around,
        Nor that content surpassing wealth
        The sage² in meditation found,
        And walked with inward glory crowned;
        Nor fame nor power nor love nor leisure—
25   Others I see whom these surround,
        Smiling they live and call life pleasure:
    To me that cup has been dealt in another measure.

        Yet now despair itself is mild,
        Even as the winds and waters are;
30   I could lie down like a tired child
        And weep away the life of care
        Which I have borne and yet must bear
        Till Death like Sleep might steal on me,
        And I might feel in the warm air
35   My cheek grow cold, and hear the Sea
    Breathe o'er my dying brain its last monotony.

        Some might lament that I were cold,
        As I, when this sweet day is gone,³
        Which my lost heart, too soon grown old,
40   Insults with this untimely moan—
        They might lament,—for I am one
        Whom men love not, and yet regret;
        Unlike this day, which, when the Sun
        Shall on its stainless glory set,
45   Will linger though enjoyed, like joy in Memory yet.
</pre>

1818   1824

Sonnet [Lift not the painted veil]

Lift not the painted veil which those who live
Call Life; though unreal shapes be pictured there
And it but mimic all we would believe
With colours idly spread,—behind, lurk Fear

---

2. Probably the Roman emperor Marcus Aurelius (2nd century C.E.), Stoic philosopher who wrote twelve books of *Meditations*.

3. I.e., as I will lament this sweet day when it has gone.

5   And Hope, twin Destinies, who ever weave
    Their shadows o'er the chasm, sightless and drear.
    I knew one who had lifted it. . . . he sought,
    For his lost heart was tender, things to love
    But found them not, alas; nor was there aught
10   The world contains, the which he could approve.
    Through the unheeding many he did move,
    A splendour among shadows—a bright blot
    Upon this gloomy scene—a Spirit that strove
    For truth, and like the Preacher, found it not.[1]

1818–20   1824

The Mask of Anarchy On August 16, 1819, a crowd of sixty thousand, men, women, and children, gathered on St. Peter's Field in Manchester to support reform of the system of political representation. The event had been in preparation for months: the organizers aimed to make the gathering a display not just of the people's numerical strength but also their discipline. On the day, the magistrates sent in the local militia, backed up by a force of saber-wielding cavalry, to arrest one of the speakers, Henry "Orator" Hunt, and to disperse the peaceable, unarmed crowd. In the mayhem, eleven died, and hundreds were injured. The opposition press quickly circulated eyewitness accounts of the events, which came to be known as the Peterloo Massacre. The name invited a comparison to the Battle of Waterloo: that had been viewed as a national glory, but this was a national shame.

    Shelley began this protest poem shortly after the news reached him in Italy, writing, as he reported, in a "torrent" of "indignation." In September he sent it to Leigh Hunt for publication in Hunt's journal *The Examiner*. Justifiably fearful that he would be charged with libel, Hunt postponed its publication until 1832. At that point, with the passage, at last, of a bill reforming Parliament, the concluding vision (in Hunt's words) of the "rise and growth of the Public Enlightenment" seemed prophetic, and the poem read as a call for peaceable reform, not violent revolution. In the 1832 printing the title was *The Masque of Anarchy*. That allusion to the masque, the performance genre celebrating aristocrats' class identity and authority, compounds the poem's ironies. Through the pageantry of the court-masque, seventeenth-century aristocrats had enacted their transcendence of the disorder personified by the vulgar performers of the anti-masque. In the upside-down world of role reversals that Shelley envisions, Anarchy—a term the British government used to stigmatize democratic reform—plays host to aristocratic revels.

The Mask of Anarchy

Written on the Occasion of the Massacre at Manchester

    As I lay asleep in Italy
    There came a voice from over the Sea,
    And with great power it forth led me
    To walk in the visions of Poesy.

---

1. Cf. Ecclesiastes 1.2: "Vanity of vanities, saith the Preacher, vanity of vanities; all is vanity."

5   I met Murder on the way—
He had a mask like Castlereagh—
Very smooth he looked, yet grim;[1]
Seven bloodhounds followed him:

All were fat; and well they might
10   Be in admirable plight,
For one by one, and two by two,
He tossed them human hearts to chew
Which from his wide cloak he drew.

Next came Fraud, and he had on,
15   Like Eldon, an ermined gown;[2]
His big tears, for he wept well,
Turned to mill-stones as they fell.

And the little children, who
Round his feet played to and fro,
20   Thinking every tear a gem,
Had their brains knocked out by them.

Clothed with the Bible, as with light,
And the shadows of the night,
Like Sidmouth, next, Hypocrisy
25   On a crocodile rode by.[3]

And many more Destructions played
In this ghastly masquerade,
All disguised, even to the eyes,
Like Bishops, lawyers, peers° or spies.   *nobles*

30   Last came Anarchy: he rode
On a white horse, splashed with blood;
He was pale even to the lips,
Like Death in the Apocalypse.[4]

And he wore a kingly crown,
35   And in his grasp a sceptre shone;
On his brow this mark I saw—
"I AM GOD, AND KING, AND LAW!"

---

1. Viscount Castlereagh, foreign secretary and parliamentary leader of the governing Tory party. His bloody suppression of rebellion in Ireland in 1798 and his role, following the peace of 1815, in engineering the restoration of Europe's autocrats made him a hated figure for liberals.
2. Baron Eldon, the Lord Chancellor, head of the judiciary, who in the court of Chancery denied Shelley access to Ianthe and Charles, the children born to Shelley's first wife. Fraud sports the ermine-trimmed gown customary for chief justices.
3. Henry Addington, Viscount Sidmouth, England's home secretary, responsible for policing and internal security and so overseer of a network of spies who infiltrated radical organizations and betrayed their members to the forces of the law. Hypocrisy rides a crocodile, an animal legendarily said to weep over its human prey before devouring it. With the mention of the Bible, these lines may also allude to the huge investment in church building that in 1818 Parliament made at Sidmouth's instigation: a project of pacification targeting the industrial towns that were hotbeds of political unrest.
4. Cf. Saint John in Revelation 6.8: "And I looked and behold a pale horse: and his name that sat on him was Death, and Hell followed with him." Benjamin West's apocalyptic painting *Death on a Pale Horse,* which Shelley could have seen in London in 1817, may inform his description of Anarchy's destructive army in the next four stanzas.

With a pace stately and fast,
Over English land he past,
40 Trampling to a mire of blood
The adoring multitude.

And a mighty troop around,
With their trampling shook the ground,
Waving each a bloody sword,
45 For the service of their Lord.

And with glorious triumph, they
Rode through England proud and gay,
Drunk as with intoxication
Of the wine of desolation.

50 O'er fields and towns, from sea to sea,
Passed the Pageant swift and free,
Tearing up, and trampling down;
Till they came to London town.

And each dweller, panic-stricken,
55 Felt his heart with terror sicken
Hearing the tempestuous cry
Of the triumph of Anarchy.

For with pomp to meet him came
Clothed in arms like blood and flame,
60 The hired Murderers,[5] who did sing
"Thou art God, and Law, and King.

"We have waited, weak and lone
For thy coming, Mighty One!
Our purses are empty, our swords are cold,
65 Give us glory, and blood, and gold."

Lawyers and priests, a motley crowd,
To the earth their pale brows bowed;
Like a bad prayer not over loud,
Whispering—"Thou art Law and God."—

70 Then all cried with one accord;
"Thou art King, and God, and Lord;
Anarchy, to Thee we bow,
Be thy name made holy now!"

And Anarchy, the Skeleton,
75 Bowed and grinned to every one,
As well as if his education
Had cost ten millions to the Nation.[6]

---

5. I.e., British soldiers, who wear red coats ("Clothed in arms like blood and flame").
6. Anarchy shares his expensive education with the Prince Regent, who during his youth ran up enormous debts that Parliament repeatedly paid off. The allusion might also be to the ballooning of the national debt that occurred as a consequence of Britain's military expenditures.

For he knew the Palaces
Of our Kings were rightly his;
80 His the sceptre, crown, and globe,[7]
And the gold-inwoven robe.

So he sent his slaves before
To seize upon the Bank and Tower,[8]
And was proceeding with intent
85 To meet his pensioned[9] Parliament

When one fled past, a maniac maid,
And her name was Hope, she said:
But she looked more like Despair,
And she cried out in the air:

90 "My father Time is weak and grey
With waiting for a better day;
See how idiot-like he stands,
Fumbling with his palsied hands!

"He has had child after child
95 And the dust of death is piled
Over every one but me—
Misery, oh, Misery!"

Then she lay down in the street,
Right before the horses' feet,
100 Expecting, with a patient eye,
Murder, Fraud and Anarchy.

When between her and her foes
A mist, a light, an image rose,
Small at first, and weak, and frail
105 Like the vapour of a vale:[1]

Till as clouds grow on the blast,
Like tower-crowned giants striding fast
And glare with lightnings as they fly,
And speak in thunder to the sky,

110 It grew—a Shape arrayed in mail°   *armor*
Brighter than the Viper's scale,
And upborne on wings whose grain°   *color*
Was as the light of sunny rain.

On its helm, seen far away,
115 A planet, like the Morning's, lay;[2]

---

7. Symbols of royal authority: the globe is the golden orb the monarch carries, with the scepter, on occasions of state.
8. The Bank of England, the nation's central bank, and the Tower of London, a military arsenal where the crown jewels were safeguarded.
9. "Pensioned": receiving annuities for services rendered. Parliament has been bribed.
1. Cf. 1 Kings 18.44 when the prophet Elijah, to demonstrate God's might to King Ahab, alerts him that his land is about to be relieved from drought: "Behold, there ariseth a little cloud out of the sea, like a man's hand."
2. Venus, as the morning star.

And those plumes its light rained through
Like a shower of crimson dew.

With step as soft as wind it past
O'er the heads of men—so fast
120　That they knew the presence there,
And looked,—but all was empty air.

As flowers beneath May's footstep waken
As stars from Night's loose hair are shaken
As waves arise when loud winds call
125　Thoughts sprung where'er that step did fall.

And the prostrate multitude
Looked—and ankle-deep in blood,
Hope that maiden most serene
Was walking with a quiet mien:

130　And Anarchy, the ghastly birth,
Lay dead earth upon the earth—
The Horse of Death tameless as wind
Fled, and with his hoofs did grind
To dust, the murderers thronged behind.

135　A rushing light of clouds and splendour,
A sense awakening and yet tender
Was heard and felt—and at its close
These words of joy and fear arose

As if their own indignant Earth
140　Which gave the sons of England birth
Had felt their blood upon her brow,
And shuddering with a mother's throe°　　　　　*labor pain*

Had turned every drop of blood
By which her face had been bedewed
145　To an accent unwithstood,—
As if her heart had cried aloud:

"Men of England, heirs of Glory,
Heroes of unwritten story,
Nurslings of one mighty Mother,
150　Hopes of her, and one another;

"Rise like Lions after slumber
In unvanquishable number
Shake your chains to Earth like dew
Which in sleep had fallen on you—
155　Ye are many—they are few.

"What is Freedom?—ye can tell
That which slavery is, too well—
For its very name has grown
To an echo of your own.

160   "'Tis to work and have such pay
     As just keeps life from day to day
     In your limbs, as in a cell
     For the tyrants' use to dwell

     "So that ye for them are made
165   Loom, and plough, and sword, and spade,
     With or without your own will bent
     To their defence and nourishment.

     "'Tis to see your children weak
     With their mothers pine and peak,°   *waste away*
170   When the winter winds are bleak,—
     They are dying whilst I speak.

     "'Tis to hunger for such diet
     As the rich man in his riot
     Casts to the fat dogs that lie
175   Surfeiting beneath his eye;

     "'Tis to let the Ghost of Gold
     Take from Toil a thousand fold
     More than e'er its substance could
     In the tyrannies of old.[3]

180   "Paper coin—that forgery
     Of the title deeds, which ye
     Hold to something of the worth
     Of the inheritance of Earth.

     "'Tis to be a slave in soul
185   And to hold no strong controul
     Over your own wills, but be
     All that others make of ye.

     "And at length when ye complain
     With a murmur weak and vain
190   'Tis to see the Tyrant's crew
     Ride over your wives and you—
     Blood is on the grass like dew.

     "Then it is to feel revenge
     Fiercely thirsting to exchange
195   Blood for blood—and wrong for wrong—
     Do not thus when ye are strong.

3. In 1797 the Bank of England was granted the power to refuse to convert paper notes presented to it to gold coin; fearing a run on the bank's gold reserves, the government meant through this measure to safeguard the gold that it required in order to wage its war with France. This Bank Restriction Act was the precondition for the launch of England's first official paper currency ("the Ghost of Gold"). By the war's end, with the money system severed from its backing in gold, the English currency depreciated in value to a drastic extent, and with harmful effects, the purchasing power of working-class wages, which did not rise, was correspondingly diminished. In describing the authorities as perpetrating "forgery" in creating "paper coin" (line 180), Shelley alludes to the many capital prosecutions that the bank undertook of malefactors who forged its paper notes. His lines, however, make the criminality that of the bank itself.

"Birds find rest, in narrow nest
When weary of their winged quest;
Beasts find fare, in woody lair

200 When storm and snow are in the air.

"Asses, swine, have litter spread
And with fitting food are fed;
All things have a home but one—
Thou, Oh, Englishman, hast none!⁴

205 "This is Slavery—savage men,
Or wild beasts within a den
Would endure not as ye do—
But such ills they never knew.

"What art thou Freedom? O! could slaves

210 Answer from their living graves
This demand—tyrants would flee
Like a dream's dim imagery:

"Thou art not, as impostors say,
A shadow soon to pass away,

215 A superstition, and a name
Echoing from the cave of Fame.°   rumor

"For the labourer thou art bread,
And a comely table spread
From his daily labour come

220 In a neat and happy home.

"Thou art clothes, and fire, and food
For the trampled multitude—
No—in countries that are free
Such starvation cannot be

225 As in England now we see.

"To the rich thou art a check,
When his foot is on the neck
Of his victim, thou dost make
That he treads upon a snake.⁵

230 "Thou art Justice—ne'er for gold
May thy righteous laws be sold
As laws are in England—thou
Shield'st alike the high and low.

"Thou art Wisdom—Freemen never

235 Dream that God will damn for ever
All who think those things untrue
Of which Priests make such ado.

---

4. Cf. Jesus's warning in Matthew 8.20 to the scribe who wishes to join his followers: "The foxes have holes, and the birds of the air have nests; but the Son of man hath not where to lay his head."

5. Perhaps recalling the coiled snake, with the caption "Don't tread on me," that became an emblem of the American Revolution.

"Thou art Peace—never by thee
Would blood and treasure wasted be
240   As tyrants wasted them, when all
Leagued to quench thy flame in Gaul.°   *revolutionary France*

"What if English toil and blood
Was poured forth, even as a flood?
It availed, Oh, Liberty!
245   To dim, but not extinguish thee.

"Thou art Love—the rich have kist
Thy feet, and like him following Christ,
Give their substance to the free
And through the rough world follow thee[6]

250   "Or turn their wealth to arms, and make
War for thy beloved sake
On wealth, and war, and fraud—whence they
Drew the power which is their prey.

"Science, Poetry and Thought
255   Are thy lamps; they make the lot
Of the dwellers in a cot°   *cottage*
So serene, they curse it not.

"Spirit, Patience, Gentleness,
All that can adorn and bless
260   Art thou—let deeds not words express
Thine exceeding loveliness.

"Let a great Assembly be
Of the fearless and the free
On some spot of English ground
265   Where the plains stretch wide around.

"Let the blue sky overhead,
The green earth on which ye tread,
All that must eternal be
Witness the solemnity.

270   "From the corners uttermost
Of the bounds of English coast,
From every hut, village and town
Where those who live and suffer moan
For others' misery or their own,

275   "From the workhouse[7] and the prison
Where pale as corpses newly risen,
Women, children, young and old
Groan for pain, and weep for cold—

6. Cf. Jesus's advice to a rich man: "If thou wilt
be perfect, go and sell that thou hast, and give to
the poor, and thou shalt have treasure in heaven;
and come and follow me" (Matthew 19.21).

7. Institution conceptualized as an alternative to
traditional forms of charity, in which poor people
who applied for help would be confined and set to
work for meager wages.

"From the haunts of daily life
280   Where is waged the daily strife
With common wants and common cares
Which sows the human heart with tares[8]—

"Lastly from the palaces
Where the murmur of distress
285   Echoes, like the distant sound
Of a wind alive around

"Those prison halls of wealth and fashion
Where some few feel such compassion
For those who groan, and toil, and wail
290   As must make their brethren pale—

"Ye who suffer woes untold,
Or° to feel, or to behold   *either*
Your lost country bought and sold
With a price of blood and gold—

295   "Let a vast assembly be,
And with great solemnity
Declare with measured words that ye
Are, as God has made ye, free—

"Be your strong and simple words
300   Keen to wound as sharpened swords,
And wide as targes° let them be   *shields*
With their shade to cover ye.

"Let the tyrants pour around
With a quick and startling sound,
305   Like the loosening of a sea
Troops of armed emblazonry.

"Let the charged artillery drive
Till the dead air seems alive
With the clash of clanging wheels,
310   And the tramp of horses' heels.

"Let the fixed bayonet
Gleam with sharp desire to wet
Its bright point in English blood
Looking keen as one for food.

315   "Let the horsemen's scimitars
Wheel and flash, like sphereless stars
Thirsting to eclipse their burning
In a sea of death and mourning.

8. Harmful weeds. Cf. Jesus's parable of the wheat and the tares, which grow together in a single field but which at harvest time will be separated (Matthew 13.24–30).

"Stand ye calm and resolute,
320 Like a forest close and mute,
With folded arms and looks which are
Weapons of unvanquished war,

"And let Panic, who outspeeds
The career of armed steeds
325 Pass, a disregarded shade
Through your phalanx undismayed.

"Let the Laws of your own land,
Good or ill, between ye stand
Hand to hand, and foot to foot,
330 Arbiters of the dispute,

"The old laws of England—they
Whose reverend heads with age are grey,
Children of a wiser day;
And whose solemn voice must be
335 Thine own echo—Liberty!

"On those who first should violate
Such sacred heralds in their state
Rest the blood that must ensue,
And it will not rest on you.

340 "And if then the tyrants dare
Let them ride among you there,
Slash, and stab, and maim, and hew,—
What they like, that let them do.

"With folded arms and steady eyes,
345 And little fear, and less surprise
Look upon them as they slay
Till their rage has died away.

"Then they will return with shame
To the place from which they came
350 And the blood thus shed will speak
In hot blushes on their cheek.

"Every woman in the land
Will point at them as they stand—
They will hardly dare to greet
355 Their acquaintance in the street.

"And the bold, true warriors
Who have hugged Danger in wars
Will turn to those who would be free,
Ashamed of such base company.

360 "And that slaughter to the Nation
Shall steam up like inspiration,

Memorializing the Peterloo Massacre. Detail from an illustration
by George Cruikshank for William Hone's *A Slap at Slop and the
Bridge-Street Gang* (1821), a stinging attack on the conservative
press that had attempted to justify the soldiers' brutality.

> Eloquent, oracular;
> A volcano heard afar.
>
> "And these words shall then become
> 365 Like oppression's thundered doom
> Ringing through each heart and brain,
> Heard again—again—again—
>
> "Rise like lions after slumber
> In unvanquishable number—
> 370 Shake your chains to earth like dew
> Which in sleep had fallen on you—
> Ye are many—they are few."

1819   1832

England in 1819[1]

An old, mad, blind, despised, and dying King;[2]
Princes, the dregs of their dull race, who flow
Through public scorn,—mud from a muddy spring;
Rulers who neither see nor feel nor know,
5   But leechlike to their fainting country cling
Till they drop, blind in blood, without a blow.
A people starved and stabbed in th' untilled field;[3]
An army, whom liberticide[4] and prey
Makes as a two-edged sword to all who wield;
10   Golden and sanguine laws[5] which tempt and slay;
Religion Christless, Godless—a book sealed;
A senate, Time's worst statute, unrepealed—
Are graves from which a glorious Phantom[6] may
Burst, to illumine our tempestuous day.

1819   1839

To Sidmouth and Castlereagh[1]

As from their ancestral oak
   Two empty ravens wind their clarion,
Yell by yell, and croak by croak,
When they scent the noonday smoke
5   Of fresh human carrion:—

As two gibbering night-birds flit
   From their bowers of deadly yew
Through the night to frighten it—
When the moon is in a fit,
10   And the stars are none, or few:—

As a shark and dogfish wait
   Under an Atlantic isle
For the Negro-ship, whose freight

---

1. Knowing full well that this sonnet on a turbulent time of injustice and unrest would read as sedition, Shelley, when he sent it to Leigh Hunt, his friend and the editor of *The Examiner*, wrote, "I don't expect you to publish it, but you may show it to whom you wish." Shelley also planned to include it in a book of political poetry, "a little volume of popular songs . . . destined to awaken and direct the imagination of the reformers," but that plan came to nothing. The sonnet finally appeared as a part of a grouping of "Poems of 1819" in Mary Shelley's 1839 edition of her late husband's work.
2. George III, who had been declared insane in 1811. He died in 1820.
3. Alluding to the Peterloo Massacre on August 16, 1819. In St. Peter's field, near Manchester, a troop of cavalry had charged into a crowd attending a peaceful rally in support of parliamentary reform.

4. The killing of liberty.
5. Laws bought with gold and leading to bloodshed.
6. I.e., a revolution.
1. Shelley's powerful satire is directed against Viscount Castlereagh, foreign secretary during 1812–22, who took a leading part in the European settlement after the Battle of Waterloo, and Viscount Sidmouth (1757–1844), the home secretary, whose cruelly coercive measures (supported by Castlereagh) against unrest in the laboring classes were in large part responsible for the Peterloo Massacre.

When this poem was reprinted by Mary Shelley in 1839, it was given the title "Similes for Two Political Characters of 1819."

Is the theme of their debate,
15   Wrinkling their red gills the while—

Are ye—two vultures sick for battle,
    Two scorpions under one wet stone,
    Two bloodless wolves whose dry throats rattle,
    Two crows perched on the murrained[2] cattle,
20   Two vipers tangled into one.

1819   1832

Ode to the West Wind[1]

I

O wild West Wind, thou breath of Autumn's being,
Thou, from whose unseen presence the leaves dead
Are driven, like ghosts from an enchanter fleeing,

Yellow, and black, and pale, and hectic[2] red,
5   Pestilence-stricken multitudes: O Thou,
Who chariotest to their dark wintry bed

The winged seeds, where they lie cold and low,
Each like a corpse within its grave, until
Thine azure sister of the Spring[3] shall blow

10   Her clarion[4] o'er the dreaming earth, and fill
(Driving sweet buds like flocks to feed in air)
With living hues and odours plain and hill:

Wild Spirit, which art moving everywhere;
Destroyer and Preserver;[5] hear, O hear!

2

15   Thou on whose stream, 'mid the steep sky's commotion,
Loose clouds like Earth's decaying leaves are shed,
Shook from the tangled boughs of Heaven and Ocean,

2. A *murrain* is a malignant disease of domestic animals.

1. This poem was conceived and chiefly written in a wood that skirts the Arno, near Florence, and on a day when that tempestuous wind, whose temperature is at once mild and animating, was collecting the vapours which pour down the autumnal rains [Shelley's note]. As in other major Romantic poems—e.g., the opening of Wordsworth's *Prelude,* Coleridge's "Dejection: An Ode," and the conclusion to Shelley's *Adonais*— the rising wind, linked with the cycle of the seasons, is presented as the correspondent in the external world to an inner change, a burst of creative power. In many languages the words for *wind, breath, soul,* and *inspiration* are identical or related. Thus Shelley's west wind is a "spirit" (the Latin *spiritus:* "wind," "breath," "soul," and the root word for *inspiration*), the "breath of Autumn's being," which on earth, sky, and sea destroys in autumn to revive in the spring. In some philosophical histories written in Shelley's period, the spirit of liberty was said to have deserted Europe for the Americas. In blowing from the west, the wind may carry liberty back again.

Shelley's sonnet-length stanza, developed from the interlaced three-line units of the Italian *terza rima (aba bcb cdc,* etc.), consists of a set of four such tercets, closed by a couplet rhyming with the middle line of the preceding tercet: *aba bcb cdc ded ee.*

2. Referring to the kind of fever that occurs in tuberculosis.

3. The west wind that will blow in the spring.

4. A high, shrill trumpet.

5. Refers to the Hindu gods Siva the Destroyer and Vishnu the Preserver.

Angels[6] of rain and lightning: there are spread
On the blue surface of thine aery surge,
20　Like the bright hair uplifted from the head

Of some fierce Mænad,[7] even from the dim verge
Of the horizon to the zenith's height,
The locks of the approaching storm. Thou Dirge

Of the dying year, to which this closing night
25　Will be the dome of a vast sepulchre,
Vaulted with all thy congregated might

Of vapours,° from whose solid atmosphere　　　　　　　clouds
Black rain and fire and hail will burst: O hear!

3

Thou who didst waken from his summer dreams
30　The blue Mediterranean, where he lay,
Lulled by the coil of his chrystalline streams,[8]

Beside a pumice isle in Baiæ's bay,[9]
And saw in sleep old palaces and towers
Quivering within the wave's intenser day,

35　All overgrown with azure moss and flowers
So sweet, the sense faints picturing them! Thou
For whose path the Atlantic's level powers

Cleave themselves into chasms, while far below
The sea-blooms and the oozy woods which wear
40　The sapless foliage of the ocean, know

Thy voice, and suddenly grow grey with fear,
And tremble and despoil themselves:[1] O hear!

4

If I were a dead leaf thou mightest bear;
If I were a swift cloud to fly with thee;
45　A wave to pant beneath thy power, and share

The impulse of thy strength, only less free
Than thou, O Uncontrollable! If even
I were as in my boyhood, and could be

6. In the old sense of messengers.
7. A female worshiper who danced frenziedly in the worship of Dionysus (Bacchus), the Greek god of wine and vegetation. As vegetation god he was fabled to die in the fall and to be resurrected in the spring.
8. The currents that flow in the Mediterranean Sea, sometimes with a visible difference in color.
9. West of Naples, the locale of imposing villas built in the glory days of imperial Rome. Their ruins are reflected in the waters of the bay, a sight Mary Shelley also describes in the Introduction to *The Last Man* (see p. 1032).
1. The vegetation at the bottom of the sea . . . sympathizes with that of the land in the change of seasons, and is consequently influenced by the winds which announce it [Shelley's note].

The comrade of thy wanderings over Heaven,
50 As then, when to outstrip thy skiey speed
Scarce seemed a vision; I would ne'er have striven

As thus with thee in prayer in my sore need.
Oh! lift me as a wave, a leaf, a cloud!
I fall upon the thorns of life! I bleed!

55 A heavy weight of hours has chained and bowed
One too like thee: tameless, and swift, and proud.

5

Make me thy lyre,[2] even as the forest is:
What if my leaves are falling like its own!
The tumult of thy mighty harmonies

60 Will take from both a deep, autumnal tone,
Sweet though in sadness. Be thou, Spirit fierce,
My spirit! Be thou me, impetuous one!

Drive my dead thoughts over the universe
Like withered leaves to quicken a new birth![3]
65 And, by the incantation of this verse,

Scatter, as from an unextinguished hearth
Ashes and sparks, my words among mankind!
Be through my lips to unawakened Earth

The trumpet of a prophecy! O Wind,
70 If Winter comes, can Spring be far behind?

1819   1820

Prometheus Unbound   Shelley composed this work in Italy between the
autumn of 1818 and the close of 1819 and published it the following summer. Upon
its completion he wrote in a letter, "It is a drama, with characters and mechanism
of a kind yet unattempted; and I think the execution is better than any of my former
attempts." It is based on the *Prometheus Bound* of Aeschylus, which dramatizes the
sufferings of Prometheus, unrepentant champion of humanity, who, because he had
stolen fire from heaven, was condemned by Zeus to be chained to Mount Caucasus
and to be tortured by a vulture feeding on his liver; in a lost sequel Aeschylus reconciled Prometheus with his oppressor. Shelley continued Aeschylus's story but
transformed it into a symbolic drama about the origin of evil and the possibility of
overcoming it. In such early writings as *Queen Mab*, Shelley had expressed his
belief that injustice and suffering could be eliminated by an external revolution
that would wipe out or radically reform the causes of evil, attributed to existing
social, political, and religious institutions. Implicit in *Prometheus Unbound*, on the
other hand, is the view that both evil and the possibility of reform are the moral

2. The Eolian lyre, which responds to the wind with rising and falling musical chords.
3. This line may play on the secondary sense of "leaves" as pages in a book.

responsibility of men and women. Social chaos and wars are a gigantic projection of human moral disorder and inner division and conflict; tyrants are the outer representatives of the tyranny of our baser over our better elements; hatred for others is a product of self-contempt; and external political reform is impossible unless we have first reformed our own nature at its roots, by substituting selfless love for divisive hatred. Shelley thus incorporates into his secular myth—of universal regeneration by a triumph of humanity's moral imagination—the ethical teaching of Christ on the Mount, together with the classical morality represented in the *Prometheus* of Aeschylus.

FROM PROMETHEUS UNBOUND

A Lyrical Drama in Four Acts

Audisne hæc Amphiarae, sub terram abdite?[1]

Preface

The Greek tragic writers, in selecting as their subject any portion of their national history or mythology, employed in their treatment of it a certain arbitrary discretion. They by no means conceived themselves bound to adhere to the common interpretation or to imitate in story as in title their rivals and predecessors. Such a system would have amounted to a resignation of those claims to preference over their competitors which incited the composition. The Agamemnonian story was exhibited on the Athenian theatre with as many variations as dramas.

I have presumed to employ a similar licence.—The *Prometheus Unbound* of Æschylus, supposed the reconciliation of Jupiter with his victim as the price of the disclosure of the danger threatened to his empire by the consummation of his marriage with Thetis. Thetis, according to this view of the subject, was given in marriage to Peleus, and Prometheus by the permission of Jupiter delivered from his captivity by Hercules.[2]—Had I framed my story on this model I should have done no more than have attempted to restore the lost drama of Æschylus; an ambition, which, if my preference to this mode of treating the subject had incited me to cherish, the recollection of the high comparison such an attempt would challenge, might well abate. But in truth I was averse from a catastrophe so feeble as that of reconciling the Champion with the Oppressor of mankind. The moral interest of the fable which is so powerfully sustained by the sufferings and endurance of Prometheus, would be annihilated if we could conceive of him as unsaying his high language, and quailing before his successful and perfidious adversary. The only imaginary being resembling in any degree Prometheus, is

1. Cicero, *Tusculan Disputations* 2.60: "Do you hear this, O Amphiaraus, concealed under the earth?" In Greek myth Amphiaraus was a seer. Fleeing from an unsuccessful assault on Thebes, he was saved from his pursuers by Zeus, who by a thunderbolt opened a cleft in the earth that swallowed him up.

In his *Disputations* Cicero is arguing for the Stoic doctrine of the need to master pain and suffering. He quotes this line (a Latin translation from Aeschylus's lost drama *Epigoni*) in the

course of an anecdote about Dionysius of Heraclea, who, tormented by kidney stones, abjures the doctrine of his Stoic teacher Zeno that pain is not an evil. By way of reproof his fellow-Stoic Cleanthes strikes his foot on the ground and utters this line. Cicero interprets it as an appeal to Zeno the Stoic master (under the name of Amphiaraus).
2. Shelley's description of the subject of Aeschylus's lost drama, *Prometheus Unbound*, is a speculation based on surviving fragments.

Satan; and Prometheus is, in my judgement, a more poetical character than Satan because, in addition to courage and majesty and firm and patient opposition to omnipotent force, he is susceptible of being described as exempt from the taints of ambition, envy, revenge, and a desire for personal aggrandisement, which in the Hero of *Paradise Lost*, interfere with the interest. The character of Satan engenders in the mind a pernicious casuistry[3] which leads us to weigh his faults with his wrongs and to excuse the former because the latter exceed all measure. In the minds of those who consider that magnificent fiction with a religious feeling, it engenders something worse. But Prometheus is, as it were, the type of the highest perfection of moral and intellectual nature, impelled by the purest and the truest motives to the best and noblest ends.

This Poem was chiefly written upon the mountainous ruins of the Baths of Caracalla, among the flowery glades, and thickets of odoriferous blossoming trees which are extended in ever winding labyrinths upon its immense platforms and dizzy arches suspended in the air. The bright blue sky of Rome, and the effect of the vigorous awakening of spring in that divinest climate, and the new life with which it drenches the spirits even to intoxication, were the inspiration of this drama.

The imagery which I have employed will be found in many instances to have been drawn from the operations of the human mind, or from those external actions by which they are expressed. This is unusual in modern Poetry; although Dante and Shakespeare are full of instances of the same kind: Dante indeed more than any other poet and with greater success. But the Greek poets, as writers to whom no resource of awakening the sympathy of their contemporaries was unknown, were in the habitual use of this power, and it is the study of their works (since a higher merit would probably be denied me) to which I am willing that my readers should impute this singularity.

One word is due in candour to the degree in which the study of contemporary writings may have tinged my composition, for such has been a topic of censure with regard to poems far more popular, and indeed more deservedly popular than mine. It is impossible that any one who inhabits the same age with such writers as those who stand in the foremost ranks of our own, can conscientiously assure himself, that his language and tone of thought may not have been modified by the study of the productions of those extraordinary intellects. It is true, that, not the spirit of their genius, but the forms in which it has manifested itself, are due, less to the peculiarities of their own minds, than to the peculiarity of the moral and intellectual condition of the minds among which they have been produced. Thus a number of writers possess the form, whilst they want the spirit of those whom, it is alleged, they imitate; because the former is the endowment of the age in which they live, and the latter must be the uncommunicated lightning of their own mind.

The peculiar style of intense and comprehensive imagery which distinguishes the modern literature of England, has not been, as a general power, the product of the imitation of any particular writer. The mass of capabilities remains at every period materially the same; the circumstances which awaken it to action perpetually change. If England were divided into forty republics, each equal in population and extent to Athens, there is no reason

3. Slippery reasoning.

to suppose but that, under institutions not more perfect than those of Athens, each would produce philosophers and poets equal to those who (if we except Shakespeare) have never been surpassed. We owe the great writers of the golden age of our literature to that fervid awakening of the public mind which shook to dust the oldest and most oppressive form of the Christian Religion. We owe Milton to the progress and developement of the same spirit; the sacred Milton was, let it ever be remembered, a Republican,[4] and a bold enquirer into morals and religion. The great writers of our own age are, we have reason to suppose, the companions and forerunners of some unimagined change in our social condition or the opinions which cement it. The cloud of mind is discharging its collected lightning, and the equilibrium between institutions and opinions is now restoring, or is about to be restored.[5]

As to imitation; Poetry is a mimetic art. It creates, but it creates by combination and representation. Poetical abstractions are beautiful and new, not because the portions of which they are composed had no previous existence in the mind of man or in nature, but because the whole produced by their combination has some intelligible and beautiful analogy with those sources of emotion and thought, and with the contemporary condition of them: one great poet is a masterpiece of nature, which another not only ought to study but must study. He might as wisely and as easily determine that his mind should no longer be the mirror of all that is lovely in the visible universe, as exclude from his contemplation the beautiful which exists in the writings of a great contemporary. The pretence of doing it would be a presumption in any but the greatest; the effect, even in him, would be strained, unnatural and ineffectual. A Poet, is the combined product of such internal powers as modify the nature of others, and of such external influences as excite and sustain these powers; he is not one, but both. Every man's mind is in this respect modified by all the objects of nature and art, by every word and every suggestion which he ever admitted to act upon his consciousness; it is the mirror upon which all forms are reflected, and in which they compose one form. Poets, not otherwise than philosophers, painters, sculptors and musicians, are in one sense the creators and in another the creations of their age. From this subjection the loftiest do not escape. There is a similarity between Homer and Hesiod, between Æschylus and Euripides, between Virgil and Horace, between Dante and Petrarch, between Shakespeare and Fletcher, between Dryden and Pope; each has a generic resemblance under which their specific distinctions are arranged. If this similarity be the result of imitation, I am willing to confess that I have imitated.

Let this opportunity be conceded to me of acknowledging that I have, what a Scotch philosopher characteristically terms, "a passion for reforming the world:"[6] what passion incited him to write and publish his book, he omits to explain. For my part I had rather be damned with Plato and Lord Bacon, than go to Heaven with Paley and Malthus.[7] But it is a mistake to suppose

---

4. I.e., Milton hoped that the overthrow of the monarchy during the Civil War would lead to England's rebirth as a republic.
5. See Shelley's similar tribute to his great contemporaries in the concluding paragraph of his "Defence of Poetry" (p. 883).
6. This is the title of chap. 16 in *The Principles of Moral Science* (1805), by the Scottish writer Robert Forsyth.

7. Thomas Malthus's *An Essay on the Principle of Population* (1798) argued that the rate of increase in population will soon exceed the rate of increase in the food supply necessary to sustain it. William Paley wrote *Evidences of Christianity* (1794), which undertakes to prove that the design apparent in natural phenomena, and especially in the human body, entails the existence of God as the great Designer. Shelley ironically expresses his

that I dedicate my poetical compositions solely to the direct enforcement of reform, or that I consider them in any degree as containing a reasoned system on the theory of human life. Didactic poetry is my abhorrence; nothing can be equally well expressed in prose that is not tedious and supererogatory in verse. My purpose has hitherto been simply to familiarise the highly refined imagination of the more select classes of poetical readers with beautiful idealisms of moral excellence; aware that until the mind can love, and admire, and trust, and hope, and endure, reasoned principles of moral conduct are seeds cast upon the highway of life which the unconscious passenger tramples into dust, although they would bear the harvest of his happiness. Should I live to accomplish what I purpose, that is, produce a systematical history of what appear to me to be the genuine elements of human society,[8] let not the advocates of injustice and superstition flatter themselves that I should take Æschylus rather than Plato as my model.

The having spoken of myself with unaffected freedom will need little apology with the candid; and let the uncandid consider that they injure me less than their own hearts and minds by misrepresentation. Whatever talents a person may possess to amuse and instruct others, be they ever so inconsiderable, he is yet bound to exert them: if his attempt be ineffectual, let the punishment of an unaccomplished purpose have been sufficient; let none trouble themselves to heap the dust of oblivion upon his efforts; the pile they raise will betray his grave which might otherwise have been unknown.

Prometheus Unbound

Act 1

SCENE: *A Ravine of Icy Rocks in the Indian Caucasus.* PROMETHEUS *is discovered bound to the Precipice.* PANTHEA *and* IONE[1] *are seated at his feet. Time, Night. During the Scene, Morning slowly breaks.*

PROMETHEUS   Monarch of Gods and Dæmons,[2] and all Spirits
    But One,[3] who throng those bright and rolling Worlds
    Which Thou and I alone of living things
    Behold with sleepless eyes! regard this Earth
5   Made multitudinous with thy slaves, whom thou
    Requitest for knee-worship, prayer and praise,
    And toil, and hecatombs[4] of broken hearts,
    With fear and self contempt and barren hope;
    Whilst me, who am thy foe, eyeless° in hate,   *blinded*
10   Hast thou made reign and triumph, to thy scorn,
    O'er mine own misery and thy vain revenge.—
    Three thousand years of sleep-unsheltered hours
    And moments—aye° divided by keen pangs   *always*
    Till they seemed years, torture and solitude,

contempt for the doctrines of both these thinkers, which he conceives as arguments for accepting uncomplainingly the present state of the world.
8. Shelley did not live to write this history.
1. Ione, Panthea, and Asia (introduced in the following scene) are sisters and Oceanids; i.e.,

daughters of Oceanus.
2. Supernatural beings, intermediaries between gods and mortals.
3. Demogorgon (see 2.4). Prometheus is addressing Jupiter.
4. Large sacrificial offerings.

15   Scorn and despair,—these are mine empire:—
More glorious far than that which thou surveyest
From thine unenvied throne, O Mighty God!
Almighty, had I deigned[5] to share the shame
Of thine ill tyranny, and hung not here
20   Nailed to this wall of eagle-baffling mountain,
Black, wintry, dead, unmeasured; without herb,°   *vegetation*
Insect, or beast, or shape or sound of life.
Ah me, alas, pain, pain ever, forever!

No change, no pause, no hope!—Yet I endure.
25   I ask the Earth, have not the mountains felt?
I ask yon Heaven—the all-beholding Sun,
Has it not seen? The Sea, in storm or calm,
Heaven's ever-changing Shadow, spread below—
Have its deaf waves not heard my agony?
30   Ah me, alas, pain, pain ever, forever!

The crawling glaciers pierce me with the spears
Of their moon-freezing chrystals; the bright chains
Eat with their burning cold into my bones.
Heaven's winged hound, polluting from thy lips
35   His beak in poison not his own, tears up
My heart;[6] and shapeless sights come wandering by,
The ghastly people of the realm of dream,
Mocking me: and the Earthquake-fiends are charged
To wrench the rivets from my quivering wounds
40   When the rocks split and close again behind;
While from their loud abysses howling throng
The genii of the storm, urging the rage
Of whirlwind, and afflict me with keen hail.
And yet to me welcome is Day and Night,
45   Whether one breaks the hoar frost of the morn,
Or starry, dim, and slow, the other climbs
The leaden-coloured East; for then they lead
Their wingless, crawling Hours,[7] one among whom
—As some dark Priest hales° the reluctant victim—   *drags*
50   Shall drag thee, cruel King, to kiss the blood
From these pale feet,[8] which then might trample thee
If they disdained not such a prostrate slave.
Disdain? Ah no! I pity thee.[9]—What Ruin
Will hunt thee undefended through wide Heaven!
55   How will thy soul, cloven to its depth with terror,
Gape like a Hell within! I speak in grief,
Not exultation, for I hate no more,
As then, ere misery made me wise.—The Curse

5. I.e., you would have been all-powerful, if I had deigned.
6. The vulture, tearing daily at Prometheus's heart, was kissed by Jupiter by way of reward.
7. The Hours were represented in Greek myth and art by human figures with wings.
8. One of a number of implied parallels between the agony of Prometheus and the passion of Christ.
9. At this early point occurs the crisis of the action: the beginning of Prometheus's change of heart from hate to compassion, consummated in lines 303–05.

Once breathed on thee I would recall.[1] Ye Mountains,
60 Whose many-voiced Echoes, through the mist
Of cataracts, flung the thunder of that spell!
Ye icy Springs, stagnant with wrinkling frost,
Which vibrated to hear me, and then crept
Shuddering through India! Thou serenest Air,
65 Through which the Sun walks burning without beams!
And ye swift Whirlwinds, who on poised wings
Hung mute and moveless o'er yon hushed abyss,
As thunder louder than your own made rock
The orbed world! If then my words had power
70 —Though I am changed so that aught evil wish
Is dead within, although no memory be
Of what is hate—let them not lose it now![2]
What was that curse? for ye all heard me speak.

FIRST VOICE: *from the Mountains*
Thrice three hundred thousand years
75   O'er the Earthquake's couch we stood;
Oft as men convulsed with fears
   We trembled in our multitude.

SECOND VOICE: *from the Springs*
Thunderbolts had parched out water,
   We had been stained with bitter blood,
80 And had run mute 'mid shrieks of slaughter
   Through a city and a solitude!

THIRD VOICE: *from the Air*
I had clothed since Earth uprose
   Its wastes in colours not their own,
And oft had my serene repose
85   Been cloven by many a rending groan.

FOURTH VOICE: *from the Whirlwinds*
We had soared beneath these mountains
   Unresting ages;—nor had thunder
Nor yon Volcano's flaming fountains
   Nor any power above or under
90   Ever made us mute with wonder!

FIRST VOICE
   But never bowed our snowy crest
   As at the voice of thine unrest.

SECOND VOICE
Never such a sound before
To the Indian waves we bore.—
95 A pilot asleep on the howling sea
Leaped up from the deck in agony

---

1. I.e., remember. But the word's alternative sense, "revoke," will later become crucial.
2. Let my words not lose their power now.

And heard, and cried, "Ah, woe is me!"
And died as mad as the wild waves be.

THIRD VOICE

By such dread words from Earth to Heaven
100   My still realm was never riven;
When its wound was closed, there stood
Darkness o'er the Day, like blood.

FOURTH VOICE

And we shrank back—for dreams of ruin
To frozen caves our flight pursuing
105   Made us keep silence—thus—and thus—
Though silence is as hell to us.

THE EARTH

The tongueless Caverns of the craggy hills
Cried "Misery!" then; the hollow Heaven replied,
"Misery!" And the Ocean's purple waves,
110   Climbing the land, howled to the lashing winds.
And the pale nations heard it,—"Misery!"

PROMETHEUS

I hear a sound of voices—not the voice
Which I gave forth.—Mother,° thy sons and thou   *Earth*
Scorn him, without whose all-enduring will
115   Beneath the fierce omnipotence of Jove
Both they and thou had vanished like thin mist
Unrolled on the morning wind!—Know ye not me,
The Titan, he who made his agony
The barrier to your else all-conquering foe?
120   O rock-embosomed lawns and snow-fed streams
Now seen athwart frore vapours[3] deep below,
Through whose o'er-shadowing woods I wandered once
With Asia, drinking life from her loved eyes;
Why scorns the spirit which informs ye, now
125   To commune with me? me alone, who checked—
As one who checks a fiend-drawn charioteer—
The falshood and the force of Him who reigns
Supreme, and with the groans of pining slaves
Fills your dim glens and liquid wildernesses?
Why answer ye not, still? brethren!

THE EARTH

130   They dare not.

PROMETHEUS

Who dares? for I would hear that curse again. . . .
Ha, what an awful whisper rises up!
'Tis scarce like sound, it tingles through the frame
As lightning tingles, hovering ere it strike.—
135   Speak, Spirit! from thine inorganic voice

3. Through frosty vapors.

I only know that thou art moving near
And love. How cursed I him?

THE EARTH
How canst thou hear
Who knowest not the language of the dead?

PROMETHEUS
Thou art a living spirit—speak as they.

THE EARTH
140 I dare not speak like life, lest Heaven's fell° King   cruel
Should hear, and link me to some wheel of pain
More torturing than the one whereon I roll.—
Subtle thou art and good, and though the Gods
Hear not this voice—yet thou art more than God
145 Being wise and kind—earnestly hearken now.—

PROMETHEUS
Obscurely through my brain like shadows dim
Sweep awful° thoughts, rapid and thick.—I feel   awe-inspiring
Faint, like one mingled in entwining love,
Yet 'tis not pleasure.

THE EARTH
No, thou canst not hear:
150 Thou art immortal, and this tongue is known
Only to those who die . . .

PROMETHEUS
And what art thou,
O melancholy Voice?

THE EARTH
I am the Earth,
Thy mother, she within whose stony veins
To the last fibre of the loftiest tree
155 Whose thin leaves trembled in the frozen air
Joy ran, as blood within a living frame,
When thou didst from her bosom, like a cloud
Of glory, arise, a spirit of keen joy!
And at thy voice her pining sons uplifted
160 Their prostrate brows from the polluting dust
And our almighty Tyrant with fierce dread
Grew pale—until his thunder chained thee here.—
Then—see those million worlds which burn and roll
Around us: their inhabitants beheld
165 My sphered light wane in wide Heaven; the sea
Was lifted by strange tempest, and new fire
From earthquake-rifted mountains of bright snow
Shook its portentous hair beneath Heaven's frown;
Lightning and Inundation vexed the plains;
170 Blue thistles bloomed in cities; foodless toads

Within voluptuous chambers panting crawled,
When Plague had fallen on man and beast and worm,
And Famine,—and black blight on herb and tree,
And in the corn and vines and meadow-grass
175 Teemed ineradicable poisonous weeds
Draining their growth, for my wan breast was dry
With grief,—and the thin air, my breath, was stained
With the contagion of a mother's hate
Breathed on her child's destroyer—aye, I heard
180 Thy curse, the which if thou rememberest not
Yet my innumerable seas and streams,
Mountains and caves and winds, and yon wide Air
And the inarticulate people of the dead
Preserve, a treasured spell. We meditate
185 In secret joy and hope those dreadful words
But dare not speak them.

PROMETHEUS
Venerable Mother!
All else who live and suffer take from thee
Some comfort; flowers and fruits and happy sounds
And love, though fleeting; these may not be mine.
190 But mine own words, I pray, deny me not.

THE EARTH
They shall be told.—Ere Babylon was dust,
The Magus Zoroaster,[4] my dead child,
Met his own image walking in the garden.
That apparition, sole of men, he saw.
195 For know there are two worlds of life and death:
One that which thou beholdest, but the other
Is underneath the grave, where do inhabit
The shadows of all forms that think and live
Till death unite them, and they part no more;
200 Dreams and the light imaginings of men
And all that faith creates, or love desires,
Terrible, strange, sublime and beauteous shapes.
There thou art, and dost hang, a writhing shade
'Mid whirlwind-peopled mountains; all the Gods
205 Are there, and all the Powers of nameless worlds,
Vast, sceptred Phantoms; heroes, men, and beasts;
And Demogorgon,[5] a tremendous Gloom;
And he, the Supreme Tyrant,[6] on his throne
Of burning Gold. Son, one of these shall utter

4. Zoroaster founded in ancient Persia a dualistic religion that worshiped fire and light in opposition to the evil principle of darkness. Priests of the religion were called Magi (singular: Magus).
5. In a note to the name in a poem published in 1817, Thomas Love Peacock alludes to Milton's mention of Demogorgon (*Paradise Lost*, 2.965) and explains: "He was the Genius of the Earth, and the Sovereign Power of the Terrestrial Dæmons. He dwelt originally with Eternity and Chaos, till, becoming weary of inaction, he organised the chaotic elements, and surrounded the earth with the heavens. In addition to Pan and the Fates, his children were Uranus, Titæa, Pytho, Eris, and Erebus." Thus, in Peacock's account, Demogorgon is the father of the Sky, the Earth, and the Underworld, as well as the Fates.
6. The shade or simulacrum of Jupiter.

210   The curse which all remember. Call at will
Thine own ghost, or the ghost of Jupiter,
Hades or Typhon,[7] or what mightier Gods
From all-prolific Evil, since thy ruin
Have sprung, and trampled on my prostrate sons.—
215   Ask and they must reply—so the revenge
Of the Supreme may sweep through vacant shades
As rainy wind through the abandoned gate
Of a fallen palace.

PROMETHEUS

         Mother, let not aught
Of that which may be evil, pass again
220   My lips, or those of aught resembling me.—
Phantasm of Jupiter, arise, appear!

IONE

    My wings are folded o'er mine ears,
My wings are crossed over mine eyes,
Yet through their silver shade appears
225   And through their lulling plumes arise
      A Shape, a throng of sounds:
        May it be, no ill to thee[8]
      O thou of many wounds!
Near whom for our sweet sister's sake
230   Ever thus we watch and wake.

PANTHEA

    The sound is of whirlwind underground,
Earthquake and fire, and mountains cloven,—
The Shape is awful like the sound,
Clothed in dark purple, star-inwoven.
235   A sceptre of pale gold
      To stay steps proud, o'er the slow cloud
       His veined hand doth hold.
Cruel he looks but calm and strong
Like one who does, not suffers wrong.

PHANTASM OF JUPITER

240   Why have the secret powers of this strange world
Driven me, a frail and empty phantom, hither
On direst storms? What unaccustomed sounds
Are hovering on my lips, unlike the voice
With which our pallid race hold ghastly talk
245   In darkness? And, proud Sufferer, who art thou?

PROMETHEUS

   Tremendous Image! as thou art must be
He whom thou shadowest forth. I am his foe

---

7. Typhon, a hundred-headed giant, imprisoned beneath volcanic Mount Aetna. Hades (Pluto), king of the underworld.

8. Shelley uses the comma in the middle of lines like these to emphasize the internal rhymes.

The Titan. Speak the words which I would hear,
Although no thought inform thine empty voice.

THE EARTH

250 Listen! and though your echoes must be mute,
Grey mountains and old woods and haunted springs,
Prophetic caves and isle-surrounding streams
Rejoice to hear what yet ye cannot speak.

PHANTASM

A spirit seizes me, and speaks within:
255 It tears me as fire tears a thunder-cloud!

PANTHEA

See how he lifts his mighty looks, the Heaven
Darkens above.

IONE

He speaks! O shelter me—

PROMETHEUS

I see the curse on gestures proud and cold,
And looks of firm defiance, and calm hate,
260 And such despair as mocks itself with smiles,
Written as on a scroll . . . yet speak—O speak!

PHANTASM

Fiend, I defy thee! with a calm, fixed mind,
    All that thou canst inflict I bid thee do;
Foul Tyrant both of Gods and Humankind,
265   One only being shalt thou not subdue.
        Rain then thy plagues upon me here,
        Ghastly disease and frenzying fear;
        And let alternate frost and fire
        Eat into me, and be thine ire
270 Lightning and cutting hail and legioned forms
Of furies, driving by upon the wounding storms.

Aye, do thy worst. Thou art Omnipotent.
    O'er all things but thyself I gave thee power,
And my own will. Be thy swift mischiefs sent
275   To blast mankind, from yon etherial tower.
        Let thy malignant spirit move
        Its darkness over those I love:
        On me and mine I imprecate°   *call down*
        The utmost torture of thy hate
280 And thus devote to sleepless agony
This undeclining head while thou must reign on high.

But thou who art the God and Lord—O thou
    Who fillest with thy soul this world of woe,
To whom all things of Earth and Heaven do bow
285   In fear and worship—all-prevailing foe!

I curse thee! let a sufferer's curse
Clasp thee, his torturer, like remorse,
Till thine Infinity shall be
A robe of envenomed agony;[9]
290　And thine Omnipotence a crown of pain
To cling like burning gold round thy dissolving brain.

Heap on thy soul by virtue of this Curse
　Ill deeds, then be thou damned, beholding good,
Both infinite as is the Universe,
295　　And thou, and thy self-torturing solitude.
　　An awful Image of calm power
　　Though now thou sittest, let the hour
　　Come, when thou must appear to be
　　That which thou art internally.
300　And after many a false and fruitless crime
Scorn track thy lagging fall through boundless space and time.

　　　　　　　　　　　　　　　　　[*The Phantasm vanishes.*]

PROMETHEUS　Were these my words, O Parent?
THE EARTH　　　　　　　　　　　　　　They were thine.
PROMETHEUS　It doth repent me: words are quick and vain;
　　Grief for awhile is blind, and so was mine.
305　　I wish no living thing to suffer pain.

　　　　　　　　　　　THE EARTH
　　Misery, O misery to me,
　　That Jove at length should vanquish thee.
　　Wail, howl aloud, Land and Sea,
　　The Earth's rent heart shall answer ye.
310　Howl, Spirits of the living and the dead,
Your refuge, your defence lies fallen and vanquished.

　　　　　　　　　　FIRST ECHO
Lies fallen and vanquished?

　　　　　　　　　SECOND ECHO
　　Fallen and vanquished!

　　　　　　　　　　IONE
　　Fear not—'tis but some passing spasm,
315　　The Titan is unvanquished still.
But see, where through the azure chasm
　　Of yon forked and snowy hill,
Trampling the slant winds on high
　　With golden-sandalled feet, that glow
320　Under plumes of purple dye
Like rose-ensanguined[1] ivory,
　　A Shape comes now,

---

9. Like the poisoned shirt of the centaur Nessus, which consumed Hercules's flesh when he put it on. The next two lines allude to the mock crown-ing of Christ with a crown of thorns.
1. Stained blood color.

Stretching on high from his right hand
  A serpent-cinctured[2] wand.

PANTHEA

325 'Tis Jove's world-wandering Herald, Mercury.

IONE

And who are those with hydra tresses[3]
  And iron wings that climb the wind,
Whom the frowning God represses
  Like vapours steaming up behind,
330 Clanging loud, an endless crowd—

PANTHEA

These are Jove's tempest-walking hounds,[4]
  Whom he gluts with groans and blood,
When charioted on sulphurous cloud
  He bursts Heaven's bounds.

IONE

335 Are they now led, from the thin dead
On new pangs to be fed?

PANTHEA

The Titan looks as ever, firm, not proud.

FIRST FURY

Ha! I scent life!

SECOND FURY

Let me but look into his eyes!

THIRD FURY

The hope of torturing him smells like a heap
340 Of corpses to a death-bird after battle!

FIRST FURY

Darest thou delay, O Herald! take cheer, Hounds
Of Hell—what if the Son of Maia° soon   *Mercury*
Should make us food and sport? Who can please long
The Omnipotent?

MERCURY

Back to your towers of iron
345 And gnash, beside the streams of fire, and wail
Your foodless teeth! . . . Geryon, arise! and Gorgon,[5]
Chimæra,[6] and thou Sphinx, subtlest of fiends,

2. Mercury carries a caduceus, a staff encircled by two snakes with their heads facing each other, a symbol of peace befitting the role of Hermes/Mercury as the messenger of the Gods.
3. Locks of hair resembling the many-headed snake, the hydra.
4. I.e., the Furies, avengers of crimes committed against the gods.

5. The Gorgons were three mythical personages, with snakes for hair, who turned beholders into stone. Geryon was a monster with three heads and three bodies.
6. The Chimera, a fabled fire-breathing monster of Greek mythology with three heads (lion, goat, and dragon), the body of a lion and a goat, and a dragon's tail.

Who ministered to Thebes Heaven's poisoned wine,
Unnatural love and more unnatural hate:[7]
These shall perform your task.

FIRST FURY

350   O mercy! mercy!
We die with our desire—drive us not back!

MERCURY

Crouch then in silence.—
              Awful° Sufferer!   *awe-inspiring*
To thee unwilling, most unwillingly
I come, by the great Father's will driven down
355 To execute a doom of new revenge.
Alas! I pity thee, and hate myself
That I can do no more.—Aye from thy sight
Returning, for a season, Heaven seems Hell,
So thy worn form pursues me night and day,
360 Smiling reproach. Wise art thou, firm and good,
But vainly wouldst stand forth alone in strife
Against the Omnipotent, as yon clear lamps
That measure and divide the weary years
From which there is no refuge, long have taught
365 And long must teach.—Even now thy Torturer arms
With the strange might of unimagined pains
The powers who scheme slow agonies in Hell,
And my commission is, to lead them here,
Or what more subtle,° foul or savage fiends   *artful*
370 People° the abyss, and leave them to their task.   *populate*
Be it not so! . . . There is a secret known
To thee and to none else of living things
Which may transfer the sceptre of wide Heaven,
The fear of which perplexes the Supreme . . .
375 Clothe it in words, and bid it clasp his throne
In intercession; bend thy soul in prayer
And like a suppliant in some gorgeous fane°   *temple*
Let the will kneel within thy haughty heart;
For benefits and meek submission tame
The fiercest and the mightiest.

PROMETHEUS

380   Evil minds
Change good to their own nature. I gave all
He has; and in return he chains me here
Years, ages, night and day: whether the Sun
Split my parched skin, or in the moony night
385 The chrystal-winged snow cling round my hair—
Whilst my beloved race is trampled down
By his thought-executing ministers.

---

7. The Sphinx, a monster with the body of a lion, wings, and the face and breasts of a woman, besieged Thebes by devouring those who could not answer her riddle. Oedipus solved the riddle (causing the Sphinx to kill herself), only to marry his mother ("unnatural love"), leading to the tragic events depicted in the Greek Theban plays.

Such is the tyrant's recompense—'tis just:
He who is evil can receive no good;
390 And for a world bestowed, or a friend lost,
He can feel hate, fear, shame—not gratitude:
He but requites me for his own misdeed.
Kindness to such is keen reproach, which breaks
With bitter stings the light sleep of Revenge.
395 Submission, thou dost know, I cannot try:
For what submission but that fatal word,
The death-seal of mankind's captivity—
Like the Sicilian's hair-suspended sword[8]
Which trembles o'er his crown—would he accept,
400 Or could I yield?—which yet I will not yield.
Let others flatter Crime where it sits throned
In brief Omnipotence; secure are they:
For Justice when triumphant will weep down
Pity not punishment on her own wrongs,
405 Too much avenged by those who err. I wait,
Enduring thus the retributive hour[9]
Which since we spake is even nearer now.—
But hark, the hell-hounds clamour. Fear delay!
Behold! Heaven lowers° under thy Father's frown.   *cowers*

MERCURY

410 O that we might be spared—I to inflict
And thou to suffer! Once more answer me:
Thou knowest not the period[1] of Jove's power?

PROMETHEUS

I know but this, that it must come.

MERCURY
Alas!
Thou canst not count thy years to come of pain?

PROMETHEUS

415 They last while Jove must reign, nor more nor less
Do I desire or fear.

MERCURY
Yet pause, and plunge
Into Eternity, where recorded time,
Even all that we imagine, age on age,
Seems but a point, and the reluctant mind
420 Flags wearily in its unending flight
Till it sink, dizzy, blind, lost, shelterless;
Perchance it has not numbered the slow years
Which thou must spend in torture, unreprieved.

---

8. I.e., the sword of Damocles, suspended by a
single hair above the throne of Damocles, ruler
of Syracuse in Sicily.

9. Time of retribution.
1. The end or conclusion.

PROMETHEUS

Perchance no thought can count them—yet they pass.

MERCURY

425 If thou might'st dwell among the Gods the while
Lapped in voluptuous joy?—

PROMETHEUS

          I would not quit
This bleak ravine, these unrepentant pains.

MERCURY

Alas! I wonder at, yet pity thee.

PROMETHEUS

Pity the self-despising slaves of Heaven,
430 Not me, within whose mind sits peace serene
As light in the sun, throned. . . . How vain is talk!
Call up the fiends.

IONE

         O sister, look! White fire
Has cloven to the roots yon huge snow-loaded Cedar;
How fearfully God's thunder howls behind!

MERCURY

435 I must obey his words and thine—alas!
Most heavily remorse hangs at my heart!

PANTHEA

See where the child of Heaven with winged feet
Runs down the slanted sunlight of the dawn.

IONE

Dear sister, close thy plumes over thine eyes
440 Lest thou behold and die—they come, they come
Blackening the birth of day with countless wings,
And hollow underneath, like death.

FIRST FURY

         Prometheus!

SECOND FURY

Immortal Titan!

THIRD FURY

        Champion of Heaven's slaves!

PROMETHEUS

He whom some dreadful voice invokes is here,
445 Prometheus, the chained Titan.—Horrible forms,
What and who are ye? Never yet there came
Phantasms° so foul through monster-teeming Hell   *apparitions*
From the all-miscreative brain of Jove;

Whilst I behold such execrable shapes,
450 Methinks I grow like what I contemplate
And laugh and stare in loathsome sympathy.

FIRST FURY

We are the ministers of pain and fear
And disappointment and mistrust and hate
And clinging° crime; and as lean dogs pursue   *clasping*
455 Through wood and lake some struck and sobbing fawn,
We track all things that weep and bleed and live
When the great King betrays them to our will.

PROMETHEUS

O many fearful natures in one name!
I know ye, and these lakes and echoes know
460 The darkness and the clangour of your wings.
But why more hideous than your loathed selves
Gather ye up in legions from the deep?

SECOND FURY

We knew not that—Sisters, rejoice, rejoice!

PROMETHEUS

Can aught exult in its deformity?

SECOND FURY

465 The beauty of delight makes lovers glad
Gazing on one another—so are we.
As from the rose which the pale priestess kneels
To gather for her festal° crown of flowers   *festive*
The aerial crimson falls, flushing her cheek—
470 So from our victim's destined agony
The shade which is our form invests us round,
Else we are shapeless as our Mother Night.

PROMETHEUS

I laugh° your power and his who sent you here   *mock*
To lowest scorn.—Pour forth the cup of pain.

FIRST FURY

475 Thou thinkest we will rend thee bone from bone?
And nerve from nerve, working like fire within?

PROMETHEUS

Pain is my element as hate is thine;
Ye rend me now: I care not.

SECOND FURY
                        Dost imagine
We will but laugh into thy lidless eyes?

PROMETHEUS

480 I weigh° not what ye do, but what ye suffer   *consider*

Being evil. Cruel was the Power which called
You, or aught else so wretched, into light.

THIRD FURY

Thou think'st we will live through thee, one by one,
Like animal life, and though we can obscure not
485　The soul which burns within, that we will dwell
Beside it, like a vain loud multitude
Vexing the self-content of wisest men—
That we will be dread thought beneath thy brain
And foul desire round thine astonished heart
490　And blood within thy labyrinthine veins
Crawling like agony.

PROMETHEUS

Why, ye are thus now;
Yet am I king over myself, and rule
The torturing and conflicting throngs within
As Jove rules you when Hell grows mutinous.

CHORUS OF FURIES

495　From the ends of the Earth, from the ends of the Earth,
Where the night has its grave and the morning its birth,
　　　Come, Come, Come!
O yet who shake hills with the scream of your mirth
When cities sink howling in ruin, and ye
500　Who with wingless footsteps trample the Sea,
And close upon Shipwreck and Famine's track
Sit chattering with joy on the foodless wrack;
　　　Come, Come, Come!
　　Leave the bed, low, cold and red,
505　　Strewed beneath a nation dead;
　　Leave the hatred—as in ashes
　　　Fire is left for future burning,—
　　It will burst in bloodier flashes
　　　When ye stir it, soon returning;
510　　Leave the self-contempt implanted
　　In young spirits sense-enchanted,
　　　Misery's yet unkindled fuel;
　　Leave Hell's secrets half-unchanted
　　　To the maniac dreamer: cruel
515　　More than ye can be with hate,
　　　Is he with fear.
　　　Come, Come, Come!
We are steaming up from Hell's wide gate
And we burthen the blasts of the atmosphere,
520　But vainly we toil till ye come here.

IONE

Sister, I hear the thunder of new wings.

PANTHEA

These solid mountains quiver with the sound

Even as the tremulous air:—their shadows make
The space within my plumes more black than night.

FIRST FURY

525   Your call was as a winged car°   *chariot*
     Driven on whirlwinds fast and far;
     It rapt° us from red gulphs of war—   *carried*

SECOND FURY

From wide cities, famine-wasted—

THIRD FURY

Groans half heard, and blood untasted—

FOURTH FURY

530   Kingly conclaves, stern and cold,
     Where blood with gold is bought and sold—

FIFTH FURY

From the furnace, white and hot,
In which—

A FURY

        Speak not—whisper not!
I know all that ye would tell,
535   But to speak might break the spell
Which must bend the Invincible,
     The stern of thought;
He yet defies the deepest power of Hell.

A FURY

Tear the veil!—

ANOTHER FURY

     It is torn!

CHORUS

        The pale stars of the morn
540 Shine on a misery dire to be borne.
Dost thou faint, mighty Titan? We laugh thee to scorn.
Dost thou boast the clear knowledge thou waken'dst for man?
Then was kindled within him a thirst which outran
Those perishing waters: a thirst of fierce fever,
545 Hope, love, doubt, desire—which consume him forever.
     One° came forth, of gentle worth,   *Christ*
     Smiling on the sanguine earth;
     His words outlived him, like swift poison
        Withering up truth, peace and pity.
550   Look! where round the wide horizon
        Many a million-peopled city
     Vomits smoke in the bright air.—
     Hark that outcry of despair!
     'Tis his mild and gentle ghost

555   Wailing for the faith he kindled.
                Look again,—the flames almost
                  To a glow-worm's lamp have dwindled:
                The survivors round the embers
                  Gather in dread.
560   Joy, Joy, Joy!
Past ages crowd on thee, but each one remembers,
And the future is dark, and the present is spread
Like a pillow of thorns for thy slumberless head.

SEMICHORUS I
                Drops of bloody agony flow
565   From his white and quivering brow.
                Grant a little respite now—
                See! a disenchanted Nation[2]
                Springs like day from desolation;
                To truth its state, is dedicate,
570   And Freedom leads it forth, her mate;
                A legioned band of linked brothers
                Whom Love calls children—

SEMICHORUS II
                            'Tis another's—
                See how kindred murder kin!
                'Tis the vintage-time for Death and Sin:
575   Blood, like new wine, bubbles within
                  Till Despair smothers
The struggling World—which slaves and tyrants win.
                      [*All the* Furies *vanish, except one.*]

IONE
Hark, sister! what a low yet dreadful groan
Quite unsuppressed is tearing up the heart
580 Of the good Titan—as storms tear the deep
And beasts hear the Sea moan in inland caves.
Darest thou observe how the fiends torture him?

PANTHEA
Alas, I looked forth twice, but will no more.

IONE
What didst thou see?

PANTHEA
                A woeful sight—a youth°   *Christ*
585 With patient looks nailed to a crucifix.

IONE
What next?

PANTHEA
                The Heaven around, the Earth below
Was peopled with thick shapes of human death,

2. Usually identified as France, breaking the spell of monarchy at the time of the Revolution.

All horrible, and wrought by human hands,
And some appeared the work of human hearts,
590 For men were slowly killed by frowns and smiles:
And other sights too foul to speak and live
Were wandering by. Let us not tempt worse fear
By looking forth—those groans are grief enough.

FURY   Behold, an emblem—those who do endure
595 Deep wrongs for man, and scorn and chains, but heap
Thousand-fold torment on themselves and him.
PROMETHEUS   Remit the anguish of that lighted stare—
Close those wan lips—let that thorn-wounded brow
Stream not with blood—it mingles with thy tears!
600 Fix, fix those tortured orbs in peace and death
So thy sick throes shake not that crucifix,
So those pale fingers play not with thy gore.—
O horrible! Thy name I will not speak,
It hath become a curse.[3] I see, I see
605 The wise, the mild, the lofty and the just,
Whom thy slaves hate for being like to thee,
Some hunted by foul lies from their heart's home,
An early-chosen, late-lamented home,
As hooded ounces[4] cling to the driven hind,°   *doe*
610 Some linked to corpses in unwholesome cells:
Some—hear I not the multitude laugh loud?—
Impaled in lingering fire: and mighty realms
Float by my feet like sea-uprooted isles
Whose sons are kneaded down in common blood
615 By the red light of their own burning homes.
FURY   Blood thou canst see, and fire; and canst hear groans;
Worse things, unheard, unseen, remain behind.
PROMETHEUS   Worse?
FURY   In each human heart terror survives
The ravin it has gorged:[5] the loftiest fear
620 All that they would disdain to think were true:
Hypocrisy and custom make their minds
The fanes° of many a worship, now outworn.   *temples*
They dare not devise good for man's estate
And yet they know not that they do not dare.
625 The good want power, but to weep barren tears.[6]
The powerful goodness want: worse need for them.
The wise want love, and those who love want wisdom;
And all best things are thus confused to ill.
Many are strong and rich,—and would be just,—
630 But live among their suffering fellow men
As if none felt: they know not what they do.[7]

---

3. I.e., the name "Christ" has become, literally, a curse word, and metaphorically, a curse to humankind, in that His religion of love is used to justify religious wars and bloody oppression.
4. Cheetahs, or leopards, used in hunting (hoods were sometimes placed over their eyes to make them easier to control).

5. The prey that it has greedily devoured.
6. I.e., the good lack ("want") power except to weep "barren tears."
7. The Fury ironically echoes Christ's plea for forgiveness of his crucifiers: "Father, forgive them: for they know not what they do" (Luke 23.34).

PROMETHEUS   Thy words are like a cloud of winged snakes
    And yet, I pity those they torture not.
FURY   Thou pitiest them? I speak no more!   [*Vanishes.*]
PROMETHEUS   Ah woe!
635   Ah woe! Alas! pain, pain ever, forever!
    I close my tearless eyes, but see more clear
    Thy works within my woe-illumed mind,
    Thou subtle Tyrant![8] . . . Peace is in the grave—
    The grave hides all things beautiful and good—
640   I am a God and cannot find it there,
    Nor would I seek it: for, though dread revenge,
    This is defeat, fierce King, not victory.
    The sights with which thou torturest gird my soul
    With new endurance, till the hour arrives
645   When they shall be no types of things which are.
PANTHEA   Alas! what sawest thou?
PROMETHEUS   There are two woes:
    To speak and to behold; thou spare me one.[9]
    Names are there, Nature's sacred watchwords—they
    Were borne aloft in bright emblazonry.[1]
650   The nations thronged around, and cried aloud
    As with one voice, "Truth, liberty and love!"
    Suddenly fierce confusion fell from Heaven
    Among them—there was strife, deceit and fear;
    Tyrants rushed in, and did divide the spoil.
655   This was the shadow of the truth I saw.
THE EARTH   I felt thy torture, Son, with such mixed joy
    As pain and Virtue give.—To cheer thy state
    I bid ascend those subtle and fair spirits
    Whose homes are the dim caves of human thought
660   And who inhabit, as birds wing the wind,
    Its world-surrounding ether;[2] they behold
    Beyond that twilight realm, as in a glass,°   mirror
    The future—may they speak comfort to thee!

                        PANTHEA
    Look, Sister, where a troop of spirits gather
665   Like flocks of clouds in spring's delightful weather,
    Thronging in the blue air!

                        IONE
                    And see! more come
    Like fountain-vapours when the winds are dumb,
    That climb up the ravine in scattered lines.
    And hark! is it the music of the pines?
670   Is it the lake? is it the waterfall?

                        PANTHEA
    'Tis something sadder, sweeter far than all.

---

8. Jupiter (also addressed as "fierce King," line
642).
9. I.e., spare me the woe of speaking (about
what I have beheld).

1. As in a brilliant display of banners.
2. A medium, weightless and infinitely elastic,
once supposed to permeate the universe.

CHORUS OF SPIRITS[3]
From unremembered ages we
Gentle guides and guardians be
Of Heaven-oppressed mortality—
675 And we breathe, and sicken not,
The atmosphere of human thought:
Be it dim and dank and grey
Like a storm-extinguished day
Travelled o'er by dying gleams;
680   Be it bright as all between
Cloudless skies and windless streams,
        Silent, liquid and serene—
As the birds within the wind,
        As the fish within the wave,
685 As the thoughts of man's own mind
        Float through all above the grave,
We make there, our liquid lair,
Voyaging cloudlike and unpent°   *unconfined*
Through the boundless element—
690 Thence we bear the prophecy
Which begins and ends in thee!

IONE
More yet come, one by one: the air around them
Looks radiant as the air around a star.

FIRST SPIRIT
On a battle-trumpet's blast
695 I fled hither, fast, fast, fast,
Mid the darkness upward cast—
From the dust of creeds outworn,
From the tyrant's banner torn,
Gathering round me, onward borne,
700 There was mingled many a cry—
Freedom! Hope! Death! Victory!
Till they faded through the sky
And one sound—above, around,
One sound beneath, around, above,
705 Was moving; 'twas the soul of love;
'Twas the hope, the prophecy,
Which begins and ends in thee.

SECOND SPIRIT
A rainbow's arch stood on the sea,
Which rocked beneath, immoveably;
710 And the triumphant Storm did flee,
Like a conqueror swift and proud
Between, with many a captive cloud
A shapeless, dark and rapid crowd,
Each by lightning riven in half.—
715 I heard the thunder hoarsely laugh.—

3. Identified by Earth at lines 658–63.

Mighty fleets were strewn like chaff
And spread beneath, a hell of death
O'er the white waters. I alit
On a great ship lightning-split
720 And speeded hither on the sigh
Of one who gave an enemy
His plank—then plunged aside to die.

THIRD SPIRIT

I sate beside a sage's bed
And the lamp was burning red
725 Near the book where he had fed,
When a Dream with plumes of flame
To his pillow hovering came,
And I knew it was the same
Which had kindled long ago
730 Pity, eloquence and woe;
And the world awhile below
Wore the shade its lustre made.
It has borne me here as fleet
As Desire's lightning feet:
735 I must ride it back ere morrow,
Or the sage will wake in sorrow.

FOURTH SPIRIT

On a Poet's lips I slept
Dreaming like a love-adept
In the sound his breathing kept;
740 Nor seeks nor finds he mortal blisses
But feeds on the aerial kisses
Of shapes that haunt thought's wildernesses.
He will watch from dawn to gloom
The lake-reflected sun illume
745 The yellow bees i' the ivy-bloom
Nor heed nor see, what things they be;
But from these create he can
Forms more real than living man,
Nurslings° of immortality!—   *children*
750 One of these awakened me
And I sped to succour thee.

IONE

Behold'st thou not two shapes from the East and West
Come, as two doves to one beloved nest,
Twin nurslings of the all-sustaining air,
755 On swift still wings glide down the atmosphere?
And hark! their sweet, sad voices! 'tis despair
Mingled with love, and then dissolved in sound.—

PANTHEA

Canst thou speak, sister? all my words are drowned.

IONE

Their beauty gives me voice. See how they float

760   On their sustaining wings of skiey grain,
Orange and azure, deepening into gold:
Their soft smiles light the air like a star's fire.

CHORUS OF SPIRITS

Hast thou beheld the form of Love?

FIFTH SPIRIT

As over wide dominions

I sped, like some swift cloud that wings the wide air's wildernesses.
765   That planet-crested Shape swept by on lightning-braided
       pinions,°   *wings*
   Scattering the liquid joy of life from his ambrosial° tresses: *heavenly*
His footsteps paved the world with light—but as I past 'twas fading
   And hollow Ruin yawned behind. Great Sages bound in madness
And headless patriots and pale youths who perished unupbraiding,[4]
770   Gleamed in the Night I wandered o'er—till thou, O King of sadness,
Turned by thy smile the worst I saw to recollected gladness.

SIXTH SPIRIT

Ah, sister! Desolation is a delicate thing:
It walks not on the Earth, it floats not on the air,
But treads with silent footstep, and fans with silent wing
775   The tender hopes which in their hearts the best and gentlest bear,
Who, soothed to false repose by the fanning plumes above
And the music-stirring motion of its soft and busy feet,
Dreams visions of aerial joy, and call the monster, Love,
And wake, and find the shadow Pain—as he whom now we greet.

CHORUS

780   Though Ruin now Love's shadow be,
Following him destroyingly
   On Death's white and winged steed,
Which the fleetest cannot flee—
   Trampling down both flower and weed,
785   Man and beast and foul and fair,
Like a tempest through the air;
Thou shalt quell this Horseman grim,
Woundless though in heart or limb.—

PROMETHEUS

Spirits! how know ye this shall be?

CHORUS

790   In the atmosphere we breathe—
As buds grow red when snow-storms flee
From spring gathering up beneath,
Whose mild winds shake, the elder brake°   *thicket*
And the wandering herdsmen know
795   That the white-thorn soon will blow°—   *blossom*
Wisdom, Justice, Love and Peace,
When they struggle to increase,

---

4. Without uttering reproaches.

Are to us as soft winds be
To shepherd-boys—the prophecy
800   Which begins and ends in thee.

IONE

Where are the Spirits fled?

PANTHEA

          Only a sense
Remains of them, like the Omnipotence
Of music when the inspired voice and lute
Languish, ere yet the responses are mute
805   Which through the deep and labyrinthine soul,
Like echoes through long caverns, wind and roll.

PROMETHEUS

How fair these air-born shapes! and yet I feel
Most vain all hope but love, and thou art far,
Asia! who when my being overflowed
810   Wert like a golden chalice to bright wine
Which else had sunk into the thirsty dust.
All things are still—alas! how heavily
This quiet morning weighs upon my heart;
Though I should dream, I could even sleep with grief
815   If slumber were denied not . . . I would fain
Be what it is my destiny to be,
The saviour and the strength of suffering man,
Or sink into the original gulph of things. . . .
There is no agony and no solace left;
820   Earth can console, Heaven can torment no more.

PANTHEA

Hast thou forgotten one who watches thee
The cold dark night, and never sleeps but when
The shadow of thy spirit falls on her?

PROMETHEUS

I said all hope was vain but love—thou lovest . . .

PANTHEA

825   Deeply in truth—but the Eastern star looks white,
And Asia waits in that far Indian vale,
The scene of her sad exile—rugged once
And desolate and frozen like this ravine;
But now invested with fair flowers and herbs
830   And haunted by sweet airs and sounds, which flow
Among the woods and waters, from the ether°   *purer air*
Of her transforming presence—which would fade
If it were mingled not with thine.—Farewell!

From *Act 2*

SCENE 4—*The Cave of* DEMOGORGON. ASIA *and* PANTHEA.[1]

PANTHEA   What veiled form sits on that ebon throne?

ASIA   The veil has fallen! . . .

PANTHEA   I see a mighty Darkness
Filling the seat of power; and rays of gloom
Dart round, as light from the meridian Sun,
5   Ungazed upon and shapeless—neither limb
Nor form—nor outline;[2] yet we feel it is
A living Spirit.

DEMOGORGON   Ask what thou wouldst know.

ASIA   What canst thou tell?

DEMOGORGON   All things thou dar'st demand.

ASIA   Who made the living world?

DEMOGORGON   God.

ASIA   Who made all
10   That it contains—thought, passion, reason, will,
Imagination?

DEMOGORGON   God, Almighty God.

ASIA   Who made that sense[3] which, when the winds of Spring
In rarest visitation, or the voice
Of one beloved heard in youth alone,
15   Fills the faint eyes with falling tears, which dim
The radiant looks of unbewailing flowers,
And leaves this peopled earth a solitude
When it returns no more?

DEMOGORGON   Merciful God.

ASIA   And who made terror, madness, crime, remorse,
20   Which from the links of the great chain of things
To every thought within the mind of man
Sway and drag heavily—and each one reels
Under the load towards the pit of death;
Abandoned hope, and love that turns to hate;
25   And self-contempt, bitterer to drink than blood;
Pain whose unheeded and familiar speech
Is howling and keen shrieks, day after day;
And Hell, or the sharp fear of Hell?[4]

DEMOGORGON   He reigns.

ASIA   Utter his name—a world pining in pain
30   Asks but his name; curses shall drag him down.

DEMOGORGON   He reigns.

---

1. Act 2 has opened with Asia—the feminine principle and embodiment of love, who was separated from Prometheus at the moment of his fall into divisive hate—in a lovely Indian valley at the first hour of the dawn of the spring season of redemption. Asia and her sister Panthea have been led, by a sweet and irresistible compulsion, first to the portal and then down into the depths of the cave of Demogorgon—the central enigma of Shelley's poem.

As the father of all that exists, Demogorgon may represent the ultimate reason for the way things are. As such, Shelley appears to argue, Demogorgon must be a mystery inaccessible to knowledge and must be ignorant of the principle controlling him. In this scene Demogorgon can give only riddling answers to Asia's questions about the "why" of creation, good, and evil.

2. Echoing Milton's description of Death, *Paradise Lost* 2.666–73.

3. Presumably the sense by which one is aware of the "unseen Power" that Shelley calls "Intellectual Beauty" (see "Hymn to Intellectual Beauty," stanza 2, p. 788).

4. The nouns "hope," "love," etc. (lines 24–28) are all objects of the verb "made" (line 19).

ASIA   I feel, I know it—who?

DEMOGORGON   He reigns.

ASIA   Who reigns? There was the Heaven and Earth at first
And Light and Love;—then Saturn,[5] from whose throne
Time fell, an envious shadow; such the state
35   Of the earth's primal spirits beneath his sway
As the calm joy of flowers and living leaves
Before the wind or sun has withered them
And semivital worms; but he refused
The birthright of their being, knowledge, power,
40   The skill which wields the elements, the thought
Which pierces this dim Universe like light,
Self-empire and the majesty of love,
For thirst of which they fainted. Then Prometheus
Gave wisdom, which is strength, to Jupiter
45   And with this law alone: "Let man be free,"
Clothed him with the dominion of wide Heaven.
To know nor faith nor love nor law, to be
Omnipotent but friendless, is to reign;
And Jove now reigned; for on the race of man
50   First famine, and then toil, and then disease,
Strife, wounds, and ghastly death unseen before,
Fell; and the unseasonable seasons drove,
With alternating shafts of frost and fire,
Their shelterless, pale tribes to mountain caves;
55   And in their desart° hearts fierce wants he sent   *empty*
And mad disquietudes, and shadows idle
Of unreal good, which levied mutual war,
So ruining the lair wherein they raged.
Prometheus saw, and waked the legioned hopes
60   Which sleep within folded Elysian flowers,
Nepenthe, Moly, Amaranth,[6] fadeless blooms;
That they might hide with thin and rainbow wings
The shape of Death; and Love he sent to bind
The disunited tendrils of that vine
65   Which bears the wine of life, the human heart;
And he tamed fire which, like some beast of prey,
Most terrible, but lovely, played beneath
The frown of man, and tortured to his will
Iron and gold, the slaves and signs of power,
70   And gems and poisons, and all subtlest forms,
Hidden beneath the mountains and the waves.
He gave man speech, and speech created thought,
Which is the measure of the Universe;
And Science struck the thrones of Earth and Heaven
75   Which shook, but fell not; and the harmonious mind
Poured itself forth in all-prophetic song,
And music lifted up the listening spirit

5. In Greek myth Saturn's reign was the golden age. In Shelley's version Saturn refused to grant mortals knowledge and science, so that it was an age of ignorant innocence in which the deepest human needs remained unfulfilled.

6. In Greek myth, medicinal drugs and flowers. Asia is describing (lines 59–97) the various sciences and arts given to humans by Prometheus, the culture bringer.

Until it walked, exempt from mortal care,
Godlike, o'er the clear billows of sweet sound;
80 And human hands first mimicked and then mocked[7]
With moulded limbs more lovely than its own
The human form, till marble grew divine,
And mothers, gazing, drank the love men see
Reflected in their race, behold, and perish.[8]—
85 He told the hidden power of herbs and springs,
And Disease drank and slept—Death grew like sleep.—
He taught the implicated° orbits woven   *intertwined*
Of the wide-wandering stars, and how the Sun
Changes his lair, and by what secret spell
90 The pale moon is transformed, when her broad eye
Gazes not on the interlunar[9] sea;
He taught to rule, as life directs the limbs,
The tempest-winged chariots of the Ocean,
And the Celt knew the Indian.[1] Cities then
95 Were built, and through their snow-like columns flowed
The warm winds, and the azure æther shone,
And the blue sea and shadowy hills were seen . . .
Such the alleviations of his state
Prometheus gave to man—for which he hangs
100 Withering in destined pain—but who rains down
Evil, the immedicable plague, which while
Man looks on his creation like a God
And sees that it is glorious, drives him on,
The wreck of his own will, the scorn of Earth,
105 The outcast, the abandoned, the alone?—
Not Jove: while yet his frown shook Heaven, aye when
His adversary from adamantine° chains   *unbreakable*
Cursed him, he trembled like a slave. Declare
Who is his master? Is he too a slave?
110 DEMOGORGON   All spirits are enslaved which serve things evil:
Thou knowest if Jupiter be such or no.
ASIA   Whom calledst thou God?
DEMOGORGON   I spoke but as ye speak—
For Jove is the supreme of living things.
ASIA   Who is the master of the slave?
DEMOGORGON   —If the Abysm
115 Could vomit forth its secrets:—but a voice
Is wanting, the deep truth is imageless;
For what would it avail to bid thee gaze
On the revolving world? what to bid speak
Fate, Time, Occasion, Chance and Change? To these
120 All things are subject but eternal Love.
ASIA   So much I asked before, and my heart gave
The response thou hast given; and of such truths

---

7. I.e., sculptors first merely reproduced but later improved on and heightened the beauty of the human form, so that the original was inferior to, and hence "mocked" by, the copy.
8. Expectant mothers looked at the beautiful statues so that their children might, by prenatal influence, be born with the beauty that makes beholders die of love.
9. The phase between old and new moons, when the moon is invisible.
1. A reference to the ships in which the Celtic (here, non-Greco-Roman) races of Europe were able to sail to India.

Each to itself must be the oracle.—
One more demand . . . and do thou answer me
125   As my own soul would answer, did it know
That which I ask.—Prometheus shall arise
Henceforth the Sun of this rejoicing world:
When shall the destined hour arrive?
DEMOGORGON   Behold!²
ASIA   The rocks are cloven, and through the purple night
130   I see Cars drawn by rainbow-winged steeds
Which trample the dim winds—in each there stands
A wild-eyed charioteer, urging their flight.
Some look behind, as fiends pursued them there
And yet I see no shapes but the keen stars:
135   Others with burning eyes lean forth, and drink
With eager lips the wind of their own speed,
As if the thing they loved fled on before,
And now—even now they clasped it; their bright locks
Stream like a comet's flashing hair: they all
Sweep onward.—
140 DEMOGORGON   These are the immortal Hours
Of whom thou didst demand.—One waits for thee.
ASIA   A Spirit with a dreadful countenance
Checks its dark chariot by the craggy gulph.
Unlike thy brethren, ghastly charioteer,
145   What art thou? whither wouldst thou bear me? Speak!
SPIRIT   I am the shadow of a destiny
More dread than is my aspect—ere yon planet
Has set, the Darkness which ascends with me
Shall wrap in lasting night Heaven's kingless throne.
ASIA   What meanest thou?
150 PANTHEA   That terrible shadow³ floats
Up from its throne, as may the lurid° smoke   *red-glaring*
Of earthquake-ruined cities o'er the sea.—
Lo! it ascends the Car . . . the coursers fly
Terrified; watch its path among the stars
Blackening the night!
155 ASIA   Thus I am answered—strange!
PANTHEA   See, near the verge° another chariot stays;   *horizon*
An ivory shell inlaid with crimson fire
Which comes and goes within its sculptured rim
Of delicate strange tracery—the young Spirit
160   That guides it, has the dovelike eyes of hope.
How its soft smiles attract the soul!—as light
Lures winged insects⁴ through the lampless air.

SPIRIT
My coursers are fed with the lightning,
They drink of the whirlwind's stream
165   And when the red morning is brightning

---

2. Demogorgon's answer is a gesture: he points
to the approaching chariots ("Cars").
3. Demogorgon (the "Darkness" of line 148), who
is ascending (lines 150–55) to dethrone Jupiter.

4. The ancient image of the soul, or *psyche*, was
a moth. The chariot described here will carry
Asia to a reunion with Prometheus.

They bathe in the fresh sunbeam;
They have strength for their swiftness, I deem:
Then ascend with me, daughter of Ocean.

I desire—and their speed makes night kindle;
170   I fear—they outstrip the Typhoon;
Ere the cloud piled on Atlas[5] can dwindle
We encircle the earth and the moon:
We shall rest from long labours at noon:
Then ascend with me, daughter of Ocean.

SCENE 5—*The Car pauses within a Cloud on the Top of a snowy Mountain.*
ASIA, PANTHEA, *and the* SPIRIT OF THE HOUR.

SPIRIT
On the brink of the night and the morning
My coursers are wont to respire,[6]
But the Earth has just whispered a warning
That their flight must be swifter than fire:
5   They shall drink the hot speed of desire!

ASIA   Thou breathest on their nostrils—but my breath
Would give them swifter speed.
SPIRIT   Alas, it could not.
PANTHEA   O Spirit! pause and tell whence is the light
Which fills the cloud? the sun is yet unrisen.
10   SPIRIT   The sun will rise not until noon.[7]—Apollo
Is held in Heaven by wonder—and the light
Which fills this vapour, as the aerial hue
Of fountain-gazing roses fills the water,
Flows from thy mighty sister.
PANTHEA   Yes, I feel . . .
15   ASIA   What is it with thee, sister? Thou art pale.
PANTHEA   How thou art changed! I dare not look on thee;
I feel, but see thee not. I scarce endure
The radiance of thy beauty.[8] Some good change
Is working in the elements which suffer
20   Thy presence thus unveiled.—The Nereids tell
That on the day when the clear hyaline°   *glassy sea*
Was cloven at thy uprise, and thou didst stand
Within a veined shell,[9] which floated on
Over the calm floor of the chrystal sea,
25   Among the Ægean isles, and by the shores
Which bear thy name, love, like the atmosphere
Of the sun's fire filling the living world,
Burst from thee, and illumined Earth and Heaven

5. A mountain in North Africa that the Greeks regarded as so high that it supported the heavens.
6. Catch their breath.
7. The time of the reunion of Prometheus and Asia.
8. In an earlier scene Panthea had envisioned in a dream the radiant and eternal inner form of Prometheus emerging through his "wound-worn limbs." The corresponding transfiguration of Asia, prepared for by her descent to the underworld to question Demogorgon, now takes place.
9. The story told by the Nereids (sea nymphs) serves to associate Asia with Aphrodite, goddess of love, emerging (as in Botticelli's painting) from the Mediterranean on a seashell.

And the deep ocean and the sunless caves,
30 And all that dwells within them; till grief cast
Eclipse upon the soul from which it came:
Such art thou now, nor is it I alone,
Thy sister, thy companion, thine own chosen one,
But the whole world which seeks thy sympathy.
35 Hearest thou not sounds i' the air which speak the love
Of all articulate beings? Feelest thou not
The inanimate winds enamoured of thee?—List!   [*Music.*]
ASIA   Thy words are sweeter than aught else but his
Whose echoes they are—yet all love is sweet,
40 Given or returned; common as light is love
And its familiar voice wearies not ever.
Like the wide Heaven, the all-sustaining air,
It makes the reptile equal to the God . . .
They who inspire it most are fortunate
45 As I am now; but those who feel it most
Are happier still, after long sufferings
As I shall soon become.
PANTHEA   List! Spirits speak.

VOICE (*in the air, singing*)[1]
Life of Life! thy lips enkindle
    With their love the breath between them
And thy smiles before they dwindle
50   Make the cold air fire; then screen them
In those looks where whoso gazes
Faints, entangled in their mazes.

Child of Light! thy limbs are burning
55   Through the vest which seems to hide them
As the radiant lines of morning
    Through the clouds ere they divide them,
And this atmosphere divinest
Shrouds thee wheresoe'er thou shinest.

60 Fair are others;—none beholds thee
    But thy voice sounds low and tender
Like the fairest, for it folds thee
    From the sight, that liquid splendour,
And all feel, yet see thee never
65 As I feel now, lost forever!

Lamp of Earth! where'er thou movest
    Its dim shapes are clad with brightness
And the souls of whom thou lovest
    Walk upon the winds with lightness
70 Till they fail, as I am failing,
Dizzy, lost . . . yet unbewailing!

1. The voice attempts to describe, in a dizzying whirl of optical paradoxes, what it feels like to look on the naked essence of love and beauty.

ASIA

My soul is an enchanted Boat
Which, like a sleeping swan, doth float
Upon the silver waves of thy sweet singing,
75   And thine doth like an Angel sit
Beside the helm conducting it
Whilst all the winds with melody are ringing.
It seems to float ever—forever—
Upon that many winding River
80   Between mountains, woods, abysses,
A Paradise of wildernesses,
Till like one in slumber bound
Borne to the Ocean, I float down, around,
Into a Sea profound, of ever-spreading sound.

85   Meanwhile thy spirit lifts its pinions°   *wings*
In Music's most serene dominions,
Catching the winds that fan that happy Heaven.
And we sail on, away, afar,
Without a course—without a star—
90 But by the instinct of sweet Music driven
Till, through Elysian garden islets
By thee, most beautiful of pilots,
Where never mortal pinnace° glided,   *small boat*
The boat of my desire is guided—
95 Realms where the air we breathe is Love
Which in the winds and on the waves doth move,
Harmonizing this Earth with what we feel above.

We have past Age's icy caves,
And Manhood's dark and tossing waves
100 And Youth's smooth ocean, smiling to betray;
Beyond the glassy gulphs we flee
Of shadow-peopled Infancy,
Through Death and Birth to a diviner day,[2]
A Paradise of vaulted bowers
105   Lit by downward-gazing flowers
And watery paths that wind between
Wildernesses calm and green,
Peopled by shapes too bright to see,
And rest, having beheld—somewhat like thee,
110 Which walk upon the sea, and chaunt melodiously!

From *Act 3*

SCENE 1—*Heaven,* JUPITER *on his Throne;* THETIS *and the other Deities assembled.*

JUPITER   Ye congregated Powers of Heaven who share
The glory and the strength of him ye serve,

---

2. Asia is describing what it feels like to be transfigured—in the image of moving backward in the stream of time, through youth and infancy and birth, in order to die to this life and be born again to a "diviner" existence.

Rejoice! henceforth I am omnipotent.
All else had been subdued to me—alone
5 The soul of man, like unextinguished fire,
Yet burns towards Heaven with fierce reproach and doubt
And lamentation and reluctant prayer,
Hurling up insurrection, which might make
Our antique empire insecure, though built
10 On eldest faith, and Hell's coeval,[1] fear.
And though my curses through the pendulous° air   *overhanging*
Like snow on herbless peaks, fall flake by flake
And cling to it[2]—though under my wrath's night
It climb the crags of life, step after step,
15 Which wound it, as ice wounds unsandalled feet,
It yet remains supreme o'er misery,
Aspiring . . . unrepressed; yet soon to fall:
Even now have I begotten a strange wonder,
That fatal Child,[3] the terror of the Earth,
20 Who waits but till the destined Hour arrive,
Bearing from Demogorgon's vacant throne
The dreadful might of ever living limbs
Which clothed that awful spirit unbeheld—
To redescend, and trample out the spark[4] . . .

25 Pour forth Heaven's wine, Idæan Ganymede,
And let it fill the dædal[5] cups like fire
And from the flower-inwoven soil divine
Ye all triumphant harmonies arise
As dew from Earth under the twilight stars;
30 Drink! be the nectar circling through your veins
The soul of joy, ye everliving Gods,
Till exultation burst in one wide voice
Like music from Elysian winds.—
                   And thou
Ascend beside me, veiled in the light
35 Of the desire which makes thee one with me,
Thetis, bright Image of Eternity!—
When thou didst cry, "Insufferable might![6]
God! spare me! I sustain not the quick flames,
The penetrating presence; all my being,
40 Like him whom the Numidian seps[7] did thaw
Into a dew with poison, is dissolved,
Sinking through its foundations"—even then
Two mighty spirits, mingling, made a third
Mightier than either—which unbodied now

1. Of the same age.
2. I.e., "the soul of man" (line 5), as also in lines 14 and 16.
3. The son of Jupiter and Thetis. Jupiter believes that he has begotten a child who will assume the bodily form of the conquered Demogorgon and then return to announce his victory and the defeat of the resistance of Prometheus.
4. Of Prometheus's defiance.

5. Skillfully wrought (from the name of the Greek craftsman Daedalus). Ganymede (line 25) had been seized on Mount Ida by an eagle and carried to heaven to be Jupiter's cupbearer.
6. This description of Jupiter's rape of Thetis is a grotesque parody of the reunion of Prometheus and Asia.
7. A serpent of Numidia (North Africa) whose bite was thought to cause putrefaction.

45 Between us, floats, felt although unbeheld,
Waiting the incarnation, which ascends—
Hear ye the thunder of the fiery wheels
Griding[8] the winds?—from Demogorgon's throne.—
Victory! victory! Feel'st thou not, O World,
50 The Earthquake of his chariot thundering up
Olympus?
        [*The Car of the* HOUR *arrives.* DEMOGORGON *descends and moves*
        toward the Throne of JUPITER.]
        Awful Shape, what art thou? Speak!
DEMOGORGON   Eternity—demand no direr name.
Descend, and follow me down the abyss;
I am thy child,[9] as thou wert Saturn's child,
55 Mightier than thee; and we must dwell together
Henceforth in darkness.—Lift thy lightnings not.
The tyranny of Heaven none may retain,
Or reassume, or hold succeeding thee . . .
Yet if thou wilt—as 'tis the destiny
60 Of trodden worms to writhe till they are dead—
Put forth thy might.
JUPITER   Detested prodigy!
Even thus beneath the deep Titanian prisons[1]
I trample thee! . . . thou lingerest?
                    Mercy! mercy!
No pity—no release, no respite! . . . Oh,
65 That thou wouldst make mine enemy my judge.
Even where he hangs, seared by my long revenge
On Caucasus—he would not doom me thus.—
Gentle and just and dreadless, is he not
The monarch of the world? what then art thou? . . .
No refuge! no appeal— . . .
70   Sink with me then—
We two will sink in the wide waves of ruin
Even as a vulture and a snake outspent
Drop, twisted in inextricable fight,[2]
Into a shoreless sea.—Let Hell unlock
75 Its mounded Oceans of tempestuous fire,
And whelm on them° into the bottomless void   *wash them*
The desolated world and thee and me,
The conqueror and the conquered, and the wreck
Of that for which they combated.
                    Ai! Ai![3]
80 The elements obey me not . . . I sink . . .
Dizzily down—ever, forever, down—
And, like a cloud, mine enemy above
Darkens my fall with victory!—Ai! Ai!

---

8. Cutting with a rasping sound.
9. Ironically, and in a figurative sense: Demogorgon's function follows from Jupiter's actions.
1. After they overthrew the Titans, Jupiter and
the Olympian gods imprisoned them in Tartarus,

deep beneath the earth.
2. The eagle (or vulture) and the snake locked in
equal combat—a favorite Shelleyan image (cf.
Alastor, lines 227–32, p. 774).
3. Traditional Greek cry of sorrow.

From SCENE 4—*A Forest. In the Background a Cave.* PROMETHEUS, ASIA, PANTHEA, IONE, *and the* SPIRIT OF THE EARTH.[4]

* * *

[*The* SPIRIT OF THE HOUR *enters.*]

PROMETHEUS   We feel what thou hast heard and seen—yet speak.

SPIRIT OF THE HOUR   Soon as the sound had ceased whose thunder filled
The abysses of the sky, and the wide earth,
100   There was a change . . . the impalpable thin air
And the all-circling sunlight were transformed
As if the sense of love dissolved in them
Had folded itself round the sphered world.
My vision then grew clear and I could see
105   Into the mysteries of the Universe.[5]
Dizzy as with delight I floated down,
Winnowing the lightsome air with languid plumes,
My coursers sought their birthplace in the sun
Where they henceforth will live exempt from toil,
110   Pasturing flowers of vegetable fire—
And where my moonlike car will stand within
A temple, gazed upon by Phidian forms,[6]
Of thee, and Asia and the Earth, and me
And you fair nymphs, looking the love we feel,
115   In memory of the tidings it has borne,
Beneath a dome fretted with graven flowers,
Poised on twelve columns of resplendent stone
And open to the bright and liquid sky.
Yoked to it by an amphisbænic snake[7]
120   The likeness of those winged steeds will mock[8]
The flight from which they find repose.—Alas,
Whither has wandered now my partial[9] tongue
When all remains untold which ye would hear!—
As I have said, I floated to the Earth:
125   It was, as it is still, the pain of bliss
To move, to breathe, to be; I wandering went
Among the haunts and dwellings of mankind
And first was disappointed not to see
Such mighty change as I had felt within
130   Expressed in outward things; but soon I looked,
And behold! thrones were kingless, and men walked
One with the other even as spirits do,
None fawned, none trampled; hate, disdain or fear,
Self-love or self-contempt on human brows

---

4. After Jupiter's annihilation (described in scene 2), Hercules unbinds Prometheus, who is reunited with Asia and retires to a cave "where we will sit and talk of time and change / . . . ourselves unchanged." In the speech that concludes the act (included here) the Spirit of the Hour describes what happened in the human world when he sounded the apocalyptic trumpet.

5. I.e., the earth's atmosphere clarifies, no longer refracting the sunlight, and so allows the Spirit of the Hour to see what is happening on earth.

6. The crescent-shaped ("moonlike") chariot, its

apocalyptic mission accomplished, will be frozen to stone and will be surrounded by the sculptured forms of other agents in the drama. Phidias (5th century B.C.E.) was the noblest of Greek sculptors.

7. A mythical snake with a head at each end; it serves here as a symbolic warning that a reversal of the process is always possible.

8. "Imitate" and also, in their immobility, "mock at" the flight they represent.

9. Biased or, possibly, telling only part of the story.

135　No more inscribed, as o'er the gate of hell,
　　　"All hope abandon, ye who enter here";[1]
　　　None frowned, none trembled, none with eager fear
　　　Gazed on another's eye of cold command
　　　Until the subject of a tyrant's will
140　Became, worse fate, the abject of his own[2]
　　　Which spurred him, like an outspent° horse, to death.　　　*exhausted*
　　　None wrought his lips in truth-entangling lines
　　　Which smiled the lie his tongue disdained to speak;
　　　None with firm sneer trod out in his own heart
145　The sparks of love, and hope, till there remained
　　　Those bitter ashes, a soul self-consumed,
　　　And the wretch crept, a vampire among men,
　　　Infecting all with his own hideous ill.
　　　None talked that common, false, cold, hollow talk
150　Which makes the heart deny the *yes* it breathes
　　　Yet question that unmeant hypocrisy
　　　With such a self-mistrust as has no name.
　　　And women too, frank, beautiful and kind
　　　As the free Heaven which rains fresh light and dew
155　On the wide earth, past: gentle, radiant forms,
　　　From custom's evil taint exempt and pure;
　　　Speaking the wisdom once they could not think,
　　　Looking emotions once they feared to feel
　　　And changed to all which once they dared not be,
160　Yet being now, made Earth like Heaven—nor pride
　　　Nor jealousy nor envy nor ill shame,
　　　The bitterest of those drops of treasured gall,
　　　Spoilt the sweet taste of the nepenthe,[3] love.

　　　Thrones, altars, judgement-seats and prisons; wherein
165　And beside which, by wretched men were borne
　　　Sceptres, tiaras, swords and chains, and tomes
　　　Of reasoned wrong glozed on° by ignorance,　　　*annotated, explained*
　　　Were like those monstrous and barbaric shapes,
　　　The ghosts of a no more remembered fame,
170　Which from their unworn obelisks[4] look forth
　　　In triumph o'er the palaces and tombs
　　　Of those who were their conquerors, mouldering round.
　　　Those imaged to the pride of Kings and Priests
　　　A dark yet mighty faith, a power as wide
175　As is the world it wasted, and are now
　　　But an astonishment; even so the tools
　　　And emblems of its last captivity
　　　Amid the dwellings of the peopled Earth,
　　　Stand, not o'erthrown, but unregarded now.
180　And those foul shapes, abhorred by God and man—

---

1. The inscription over the gate of hell in Dante's
Inferno 3.9.
2. I.e., he was so abjectly enslaved that his own
will accorded with the tyrant's will.
3. A drug (probably opium) that brings forgetfulness of pain and sorrow.

4. The Egyptian obelisks (tapering shafts of
stone), brought to Rome by its conquering armies,
included hieroglyphs that—because they were
still undeciphered in Shelley's time—seemed
"monstrous and barbaric shapes" (line 168).

Which under many a name and many a form
Strange, savage, ghastly, dark and execrable
Were Jupiter,[5] the tyrant of the world;
And which the nations panic-stricken served

185   With blood, and hearts broken by long hope, and love
        Dragged to his altars soiled and garlandless
        And slain amid men's unreclaiming tears,
        Flattering the thing they feared, which fear was hate—
        Frown, mouldering fast, o'er their abandoned shrines.

190   The painted veil, by those who were, called life,[6]
        Which mimicked, as with colours idly spread,
        All men believed and hoped, is torn aside—
        The loathsome mask has fallen, the man remains
        Sceptreless, free, uncircumscribed—but man:

195   Equal, unclassed, tribeless, and nationless,
        Exempt from awe, worship, degree,—the King
        Over himself; just, gentle, wise—but man:
        Passionless? no—yet free from guilt or pain
        Which were, for his will made, or suffered them,

200   Nor yet exempt, though ruling them like slaves,
        From chance and death and mutability,
        The clogs of that which else might oversoar
        The loftiest star of unascended Heaven
        Pinnacled dim in the intense inane.[7]

From Act 4[1]

SCENE—*A Part of the Forest near the Cave of* PROMETHEUS.

*   *   *

DEMOGORGON

    This is the Day which down the void Abysm
555   At the Earth-born's spell[2] yawns for Heaven's Despotism,
        And Conquest is dragged Captive through the Deep;[3]
    Love from its awful° throne of patient power   *awesome*
    In the wise heart, from the last giddy hour

---

5. The "foul shapes" (line 180) were statues of the gods who, whatever their names, were all really manifestations of Jupiter.

6. I.e., which was thought to be life by humans as they were before their regeneration.

7. I.e., a dim point in the extreme of empty space. The sense of lines 198–204 is if regenerate man were to be released from all earthly and biological impediments ("clogs"), he would become what even the stars are not—a pure ideal.

1. The original drama, completed in the spring of 1819, consisted of three acts. Later that year Shelley added a jubilant fourth act. In Revelation 21 the apocalyptic replacement of the old world by "a new heaven and new earth" had been symbolized by the marriage of the Lamb with the New Jerusalem. Shelley's fourth act, somewhat like the conclusion of Blake's *Jerusalem*, expands this figure into a cosmic epithalamion, representing a union of divided elements that enacts everywhere the reunion of Prometheus and Asia taking place offstage.

Shelley's model is the Renaissance court-

masque, which combines song and dance with spectacular displays. Panthea and Ione serve as commentators on the action, which is divided into three episodes. In the first episode the purified "Spirits of the human mind" unite in a ritual dance with the Hours of the glad new day. In the second episode (lines 194–318), there appear emblematic representations of the moon and the earth, each bearing an infant whose hour has come round at last. Shelley based this description in part on Ezekiel 1, the vision of the chariot of divine glory, which had traditionally been interpreted as a portent of apocalypse. The third episode (lines 319–502) is the bacchanalian dance of the love-intoxicated Moon around her brother and paramour, the rejuvenescent Earth.

2. Prometheus's spell—the magically effective words of pity, rather than vengefulness, that he spoke in act 1.

3. Ephesians 4.8: "When [Christ] ascended up on high, he led captivity captive."

Of dread endurance, from the slippery, steep,
560 And narrow verge of crag-like Agony, springs
And folds over the world its healing wings.

Gentleness, Virtue, Wisdom and Endurance,—
These are the seals of that most firm assurance
        Which bars the pit over Destruction's strength;
565 And if, with infirm hand, Eternity,
Mother of many acts and hours, should free
        The serpent that would clasp her with his length[4]—
These are the spells by which to reassume
An empire o'er the disentangled Doom.[5]

570 To suffer woes which Hope thinks infinite;
To forgive wrongs darker than Death or Night;
        To defy Power which seems Omnipotent;
To love, and bear; to hope, till Hope creates
From its own wreck the thing it contemplates;
575   Neither to change nor falter nor repent:
This, like thy glory, Titan! is to be
Good, great and joyous, beautiful and free;
This is alone Life, Joy, Empire and Victory.

1818–19   1820

The Cloud

    I bring fresh showers for the thirsting flowers,
        From the seas and streams;
    I bear light shade for the leaves when laid
        In their noon-day dreams.
5   From my wings are shaken the dews that waken
        The sweet buds every one,
    When rocked to rest on their mother's° breast,   *earth's*
        As she dances about the Sun.
    I wield the flail[1] of the lashing hail,
10   And whiten the green plains under,
    And then again I dissolve it in rain,
        And laugh as I pass in thunder.

    I sift the snow on the mountains below,
        And their great pines groan aghast;
15   And all the night 'tis my pillow white,
        While I sleep in the arms of the blast.
    Sublime on the towers of my skiey bowers,
        Lightning my pilot sits;

---

4. A final reminder that the serpent incessantly struggles to break loose and start the cycle of humanity's fall all over again.
5. Shelley's four cardinal virtues (line 562), which seal the serpent in the pit, also constitute the magic formulas ("spells") by which to remaster him, should he again break loose.
1. Either a weapon fashioned as a ball and chain or a tool for threshing grain.

In a cavern under is fettered the thunder,
20 It struggles and howls at fits;°   *fitfully*
Over Earth and Ocean, with gentle motion,
  This pilot is guiding me,
Lured by the love of the genii that move
  In the depths of the purple sea;[2]
25 Over the rills, and the crags, and the hills,
  Over the lakes and the plains,
Wherever he dream, under mountain or stream,
  The Spirit he loves remains;
And I all the while bask in Heaven's blue smile,[3]
30 Whilst he is dissolving in rains.

The sanguine Sunrise, with his meteor eyes,[4]
  And his burning plumes outspread,[5]
Leaps on the back of my sailing rack,[6]
  When the morning star shines dead;
35 As on the jag of a mountain crag,
  Which an earthquake rocks and swings,
An eagle alit one moment may sit
  In the light of its golden wings.
And when Sunset may breathe, from the lit Sea beneath,
40 Its ardours of rest and of love,
And the crimson pall° of eve may fall   *rich coverlet*
  From the depth of Heaven above,
With wings folded I rest, on mine aëry nest,
  As still as a brooding dove.[7]

45 That orbed maiden with white fire laden
  Whom mortals call the Moon,
Glides glimmering o'er my fleece-like floor,
  By the midnight breezes strewn;
And wherever the beat of her unseen feet,
50 Which only the angels hear,
May have broken the woof,° of my tent's thin roof,   *texture*
  The stars peep behind her, and peer;
And I laugh to see them whirl and flee,
  Like a swarm of golden bees,
55 When I widen the rent in my wind-built tent,
  Till the calm rivers, lakes, and seas,
Like strips of the sky fallen through me on high,
  Are each paved with the moon and these.[8]

I bind the Sun's throne with a burning zone°   *belt, sash*
60 And the Moon's with a girdle of pearl;
The volcanos are dim and the stars reel and swim
  When the whirlwinds my banner unfurl.

---

2. I.e., atmospheric electricity, guiding the cloud (line 18), discharges as lightning when "lured" by the attraction of an opposite charge.
3. The upper part of the cloud remains exposed to the sun.
4. As bright as a burning meteor.
5. The sun's corona.

6. High, broken clouds, driven by the wind.
7. An echo of Milton's description of his Muse, identified with the Holy Spirit, who "with mighty wings outspread / Dove-like sat'st brooding on the vast abyss" (*Paradise Lost* 1.20–21).
8. The stars reflected in the water.

From cape to cape, with a bridge-like shape,
    Over a torrent sea,
65 Sunbeam-proof, I hang like a roof—
    The mountains its columns be!
The triumphal arch, through which I march
    With hurricane, fire, and snow,
When the Powers of the Air, are chained to my chair,°   *chariot*
70 Is the million-coloured Bow;
The sphere-fire° above its soft colours wove   *sunlight*
    While the moist Earth was laughing below.

I am the daughter of Earth and Water,
    And the nursling of the Sky;
75 I pass through the pores, of the ocean and shores;
    I change, but I cannot die—
For after the rain, when with never a stain
    The pavilion of Heaven is bare,
And the winds and sunbeams, with their convex gleams,
80 Build up the blue dome of Air[9]—
I silently laugh at my own cenotaph,[1]
    And out of the caverns of rain,
Like a child from the womb, like a ghost from the tomb,
    I arise, and unbuild it again.—

1820   1820

To a Sky-Lark[1]

Hail to thee, blithe Spirit!
    Bird thou never wert—
That from Heaven, or near it,
    Pourest thy full heart
5 In profuse strains of unpremeditated art.

Higher still and higher
    From the earth thou springest
Like a cloud of fire;
    The blue deep thou wingest,
10 And singing still dost soar, and soaring ever singest.

In the golden lightning
    Of the sunken Sun—
O'er which clouds are brightning,
    Thou dost float and run;
15 Like an unbodied joy whose race is just begun.

9. The blue color of the sky. The phenomenon, as Shelley indicates, results from the way "sunbeams" are filtered by the earth's atmosphere.
1. The memorial monument of the dead cloud is the cloudless blue dome of the sky. (The point is that a cenotaph is a monument that does not contain a corpse.)
1. The European skylark is a small bird that sings only in flight, often when it is too high to be visible.

The pale purple even°   *evening*
   Melts around thy flight,
Like a star of Heaven
   In the broad day-light
20 Thou art unseen,—but yet I hear thy shrill delight,

Keen as are the arrows
   Of that silver sphere,²
Whose intense lamp narrows
   In the white dawn clear
25 Until we hardly see—we feel that it is there.

All the earth and air
   With thy voice is loud,
As when Night is bare
   From one lonely cloud
30 The moon rains out her beams—and Heaven is overflowed.

What thou art we know not;
   What is most like thee?
From rainbow clouds there flow not
   Drops so bright to see
35 As from thy presence showers a rain of melody.

Like a Poet hidden
   In the light of thought,
Singing hymns unbidden,
   Till the world is wrought
40 To sympathy with hopes and fears it heeded not:

Like a high-born maiden
   In a palace-tower,
Soothing her love-laden
   Soul in secret hour,
45 With music sweet as love—which overflows her bower:

Like a glow-worm golden
   In a dell of dew,
Scattering unbeholden
   Its aerial hue
50 Among the flowers and grass which screen it from the view:

Like a rose embowered
   In its own green leaves—
By warm winds deflowered—
   Till the scent, it gives
55 Makes faint with too much sweet those heavy-winged thieves:³

Sound of vernal° showers   *springtime*
   On the twinkling grass,
Rain-awakened flowers,

2. The morning star, Venus.
3. The "warm winds," line 53.

All that ever was
60 Joyous, and clear and fresh, thy music doth surpass.

Teach us, Sprite° or Bird,   *spirit*
What sweet thoughts are thine;
I have never heard
Praise of love or wine
65 That panted forth a flood of rapture so divine:

Chorus Hymeneal[4]
Or triumphal chaunt
Matched with thine would be all
But an empty vaunt,
70 A thing wherein we feel there is some hidden want.

What objects are the fountains
Of thy happy strain?
What fields or waves or mountains?
What shapes of sky or plain?
75 What love of thine own kind? what ignorance of pain?

With thy clear keen joyance
Languor cannot be—
Shadow of annoyance
Never came near thee;
80 Thou lovest—but ne'er knew love's sad satiety.

Waking or asleep,
Thou of death must deem
Things more true and deep
Than we mortals dream,
85 Or how could thy notes flow in such a chrystal stream?

We look before and after,
And pine for what is not—
Our sincerest laughter
With some pain is fraught—
90 Our sweetest songs are those that tell of saddest thought.

Yet if we could scorn
Hate and pride and fear;
If we were things born
Not to shed a tear,
95 I know not how thy joy we ever should come near.

Better than all measures
Of delightful sound—
Better than all treasures
That in books are found—
100 Thy skill to poet were, thou Scorner of the ground!

4. Marital (from Hymen, Greek god of marriage).

Teach me half the gladness
That thy brain must know,
Such harmonious madness
From my lips would flow
105 The world should listen then—as I am listening now.

1820   1820

To Night

Swiftly walk o'er the western wave,
    Spirit of Night!
Out of the misty eastern cave
Where, all the long and lone daylight
5 Thou wovest dreams of joy and fear,
Which make thee terrible and dear,
    Swift be thy flight!

Wrap thy form in a mantle grey,
    Star-inwrought!
10 Blind with thine hair the eyes of day,
Kiss her until she be wearied out—
Then wander o'er City and sea and land,
Touching all with thine opiate wand—
    Come, long-sought!

15 When I arose and saw the dawn
    I sighed for thee;
When Light rode high, and the dew was gone,
And noon lay heavy on flower and tree,
And the weary Day[1] turned to his rest,
20 Lingering like an unloved guest,
    I sighed for thee.

Thy brother Death came, and cried,
    Wouldst thou me?
Thy sweet child Sleep, the filmy-eyed,
25 Murmured like a noontide bee,
Shall I nestle near thy side?
Wouldst thou me? and I replied,
    No, not thee!

Death will come when thou art dead,
30   Soon, too soon—
Sleep will come when thou art fled;
Of neither would I ask the boon
I ask of thee, beloved Night—
Swift be thine approaching flight,
35   Come soon, soon!

1820   1824

1. Here the "Day" is the male sun, not the female "day" with whom the Spirit of Night dallies in the
preceding stanza.

To ——— [Music, when soft voices die][1]

Music, when soft voices die,
Vibrates in the memory.—
Odours, when sweet violets sicken,
Live within the sense they quicken.°—   enliven

5   Rose leaves, when the rose is dead,
Are heaped for the beloved's bed[2]—
And so thy thoughts,[3] when thou art gone,
Love itself shall slumber on.

1821   1824

O World, O Life, O Time[1]

O World, O Life, O Time,
On whose last steps I climb,
Trembling at that where I had stood before,
When will return the glory of your prime?
5   No more, O never more!

Out of the day and night
A joy has taken flight—
Fresh spring and summer [   ] and winter hoar
Move my faint heart with grief, but with delight
10   No more, O never more!

1824

Chorus from *Hellas*[1]

The world's great age[2]

The world's great age begins anew,
The golden years[3] return,

---

1. This poem was first published under the title "Memory" in Mary Shelley's edition of her husband's *Posthumous Poems* in 1824, with the two stanzas in the reverse order from what we give here. Our text is based on a version found in a notebook of Percy Shelley's now housed in the Bodleian Library at Oxford. The square brackets in line 8 mark blank spaces left unfilled in the manuscript.
2. The bed of the dead rose.
3. I.e., my thoughts of thee.
1. For the author's revisions while composing this poem, see "Poems in Process," in the NAEL Archive.
1. *Hellas*, a closet drama written in the autumn of 1821, was inspired by the Greek war for independence against the Turks. ("Hellas" is another name for Greece.) In his preface Shelley declared that he viewed this revolution as foretelling the final overthrow of all tyranny. The choruses

throughout are sung by enslaved Greek women. We give the chorus that concludes the drama.
2. Prophecies of wars, and rumours of wars, etc., may safely be made by poet or prophet in any age, but to anticipate however darkly a period of regeneration and happiness is a more hazardous exercise of the faculty which bards possess or fain. It will remind the reader . . . of Isaiah and Virgil, whose ardent spirits . . . saw the possible and perhaps approaching state of society in which the "lion shall lie down with the lamb," and *"omnis feret omnia tellus."* Let these great names be my authority and excuse [Shelley's note]. The quotations are from Isaiah's millennial prophecy (e.g., chaps. 25, 45), and Virgil's prediction, in *Eclogue* 4, of a return of the golden age, when "all the earth will produce all things."
3. In Greek myth the first period of history, when Saturn reigned.

The earth doth like a snake renew
    Her winter weeds[4] outworn;
5 Heaven smiles, and faiths and empires gleam
    Like wrecks of a dissolving dream.

A brighter Hellas rears its mountains
    From waves serener far,
A new Peneus[5] rolls his fountains
10   Against the morning-star,
Where fairer Tempes bloom, there sleep
Young Cyclads[6] on a sunnier deep.

A loftier Argo[7] cleaves the main,
    Fraught with a later prize;
15 Another Orpheus[8] sings again,
    And loves, and weeps, and dies;
A new Ulysses leaves once more
Calypso[9] for his native shore.

O, write no more the tale of Troy,
20   If earth Death's scroll must be!
Nor mix with Laian[1] rage the joy
    Which dawns upon the free;
Although a subtler Sphinx renew
Riddles of death Thebes never knew.

25 Another Athens shall arise,
    And to remoter time
Bequeath, like sunset to the skies,
    The splendour of its prime,
And leave, if nought so bright may live,
30 All earth can take or Heaven can give.

Saturn and Love their long repose
    Shall burst, more bright and good
Than all who fell, than One who rose,
    Than many unsubdued;[2]
35 Not gold, not blood their altar dowers°   *gifts*
But votive tears and symbol flowers.

O cease! must hate and death return?
    Cease! must men kill and die?
    Cease! drain not to its dregs the urn

4. Clothes (especially mourning garments) as well as dead vegetation.
5. The river in northeast Greece that flows through the beautiful vale of Tempe (line 11).
6. The Cyclades, islands in the Aegean Sea.
7. On which Jason sailed in his quest for the Golden Fleece.
8. The legendary player on the lyre who was torn to pieces by the frenzied Thracian women while he was mourning the death of his wife, Eurydice.
9. The nymph deserted by Ulysses on his voyage back from the Trojan War to his native Ithaca.
1. King Laius of Thebes was killed in a quarrel by his son Oedipus, who did not recognize his father. Shortly thereafter Oedipus delivered Thebes from the ravages of the Sphinx by answering its riddle (lines 23–24).
2. Saturn and Love were among the deities of a real or imaginary state of innocence and happiness. "All" those "who fell" [are] the Gods of Greece, Asia, and Egypt; the "One who rose" [is] Jesus Christ . . . and the "many unsubdued" [are] the monstrous objects of the idolatry of China, India, the Antarctic islands, and the native tribes of America [Shelley's note].

40   Of bitter prophecy.
       The world is weary of the past,
       O might it die or rest at last!

1821   1822

Adonais.   John Keats died in Rome on February 23, 1821, and was buried there in the Protestant Cemetery. In the Preface to *Adonais*, his elegy for Keats, Percy Shelley, who had buried his three-year-old son William in that "romantic and lonely cemetery" a year and a half earlier, describes the site as "an open space among the ruins covered in winter with violets and daisies." "It might make one in love with death," he adds, "to think that one should be buried in so sweet a place." In fact, after his drowning in 1822, Shelley's ashes would be interred in that sweet place also.

Shelley had met Keats, had invited him to be his guest at Pisa in Italy (an invitation Keats did not live to accept), and had gradually come to realize that Keats was, as the Preface to *Adonais* states, "among the writers of the highest genius who have adorned our age." In his elegy, which he began writing in April 1821, almost immediately after hearing of Keats's death, Shelley mourns Keats, honors him, and also pursues a case against the reviewers of Keats's poems—in particular the anonymous critic for the influential *Quarterly Review* (now known to be the Tory civil servant John Wilson Croker), who had written a grossly insulting review of Keats's *Endymion*. Shelley believed, wrongly, that Keats's disappointment over the review had caused his illness and death: Keats's "genius," he stated in the Preface, "was not less delicate and fragile than it was beautiful. . . . The savage criticism . . . produced the most violent effect on his susceptible mind." Shelley's readiness to believe the exaggerated rumors about Keats's reaction to his bad reviews is the more understandable when one remembers that he had been savaged by reviewers on several occasions himself. It is also true that in this period of fierce political enmities rancorous book reviews were very near being the norm rather than the exception. (Those antagonisms, which helped define Romantic understandings of the modern author, are explored at length in "'Self-constituted judge of poesy': Reviewer vs. Poet in the Romantic Period," found in the NAEL Archive.)

Shelley in a letter described *Adonais* as a "highly wrought piece of art." Its artistry consists in part in the care with which it follows the conventions of the pastoral elegy, the literary form established more than two thousand years earlier by the Greek poets Bion, Moschus, and Theocritus—Shelley had translated into English Bion's *Lament for Adonis* and Moschus's *Lament for Bion*. Those conventions include an invocation to a muse; descriptions of nature's sympathetic participation in the grieving and of the procession of mourners; and most important, the final turn from despair to consolation in the discovery that, paradoxically, the grave is the gate to a higher existence. The name that Shelley gives to Keats in this pastoral elegy, "Adonais," likely derives from Adonis, the name of the beautiful mortal who was beloved by the goddess Venus. Slain by a wild boar while hunting, Adonis was restored to life and a kind of immortality on the condition that he spend only part of the year with Venus, and the remaining part with Proserpine in the underworld. This cycle of rebirth and death, symbolic of the alternate return of summer and winter, suggests why Adonis was central to ancient fertility myths. This cycle is also an integral element of *Adonais*.

Published first in Pisa in 1821, *Adonais* was not issued in England until 1829, in an edition sponsored by the so-called Cambridge Apostles, a group including the poets Alfred Tennyson and A. H. Hallam. The appearance of this edition marked the beginning of Keats's posthumous emergence from obscurity.

Adonais

An Elegy on the Death of John Keats, Author of Endymion, Hyperion, etc.

[Thou wert the morning star among the living,
Ere thy fair light had fled—
Now, having died, thou art as Hesperus, giving
New splendour to the dead.]¹

1

I weep for Adonais—he is dead!
O, weep for Adonais! though our tears
Thaw not the frost which binds so dear a head!
And thou, sad Hour,² selected from all years
5   To mourn our loss, rouse thy obscure compeers,°   companions
And teach them thine own sorrow, say: with me
Died Adonais; till the Future dares
Forget the Past, his fate and fame shall be
An echo and a light unto eternity!

2

10   Where wert thou mighty Mother,³ when he lay,
When thy Son lay, pierced by the shaft which flies
In darkness?⁴ where was lorn° Urania   forlorn
When Adonais died? With veiled eyes,
'Mid listening Echoes, in her Paradise
15   She sate, while one,⁵ with soft enamoured breath,
Rekindled all the fading melodies,
With which, like flowers that mock the corse° beneath,   corpse
He had adorned and hid the coming bulk of death.

3

O, weep for Adonais—he is dead!
20   Wake, melancholy Mother, wake and weep!
Yet wherefore? Quench within their burning bed
Thy fiery tears, and let thy loud heart keep
Like his, a mute and uncomplaining sleep;
For he is gone, where all things wise and fair
25   Descend;—oh, dream not that the amorous Deep°   abyss
Will yet restore him to the vital air;
Death feeds on his mute voice, and laughs at our despair.

---

1. Shelley prefixed to *Adonais* a Greek epigraph
attributed to Plato; this is Shelley's translation of
the Greek. The planet Venus appears both as the
morning star, Lucifer, and as the evening star,
Hesperus or Vesper. Shelley makes of this phenomenon a key symbol for Adonais's triumph
over death, in stanzas 44–46.
2. Shelley follows the classical mode of personi-
fying the hours, which mark the passage of time

and turn of the seasons.
3. Urania. She had originally been the Muse of
astronomy, but the name was also an epithet for
Venus. Shelley converts Venus Urania, who in
Greek myth had been the lover of Adonis, into
the mother of Adonais.
4. Alludes to the anonymity of the review of
Endymion.
5. I.e., one of the Echoes (line 14).

4

Most musical of mourners, weep again!
Lament anew, Urania!—He[6] died,
30   Who was the Sire of an immortal strain,
Blind, old, and lonely, when his country's pride,
The priest, the slave, and the liberticide,
Trampled and mocked with many a loathed rite
Of lust and blood; he went, unterrified,
35   Into the gulph of death; but his clear Sprite°   *spirit*
Yet reigns o'er earth; the third among the sons of light.[7]

5

Most musical of mourners, weep anew!
Not all to that bright station dared to climb;
And happier they their happiness who knew,
40   Whose tapers° yet burn through that night of time   *candles*
In which suns perished; others more sublime,
Struck by the envious wrath of man or God,
Have sunk, extinct in their refulgent° prime;   *radiant*
And some yet live, treading the thorny road,
45   Which leads, through toil and hate, to Fame's serene abode.

6

But now, thy youngest, dearest one, has perished—
The nursling of thy widowhood, who grew,
Like a pale flower by some sad maiden cherished,
And fed with true love tears, instead of dew;[8]
50   Most musical of mourners, weep anew!
Thy extreme° hope, the loveliest and the last,   *last; highest*
The bloom, whose petals nipt before they blew°   *bloomed*
Died on the promise of the fruit, is waste;
The broken lily lies—the storm is overpast.

7

55   To that high Capital,° where kingly Death   *Rome*
Keeps his pale court in beauty and decay,
He came; and bought, with price of purest breath,
A grave among the eternal.—Come away!
Haste, while the vault of blue Italian day
60   Is yet his fitting charnel-roof! while still
He lies, as if in dewy sleep he lay;
Awake him not! surely he takes his fill
Of deep and liquid rest, forgetful of all ill.

6. Milton, regarded as precursor of the great poetic tradition in which Keats wrote. He had adopted Urania as the muse of *Paradise Lost*. Lines 31–35 describe Milton's life during the restoration of the Stuart monarchy.

7. In "A Defence of Poetry," Shelley says that Milton was the third great epic poet, along with Homer and Dante. The following stanza describes the fate of other poets, up to Shelley's own time.
8. An allusion to an incident in Keats's *Isabella*.

8

He will awake no more, oh, never more!—
65 Within the twilight chamber spreads apace,
The shadow of white Death, and at the door
Invisible Corruption waits to trace
His extreme way to her dim dwelling-place;
The eternal Hunger sits, but pity and awe
70 Soothe her pale rage, nor dares she to deface
So fair a prey, till darkness, and the law
Of change, shall o'er his sleep the mortal curtain draw.

9

O, weep for Adonais!—The quick° Dreams,   living
The passion-winged Ministers of thought,
75 Who were his flocks,⁹ whom near the living streams
Of his young spirit he fed, and whom he taught
The love which was its music, wander not,—
Wander no more, from kindling brain to brain,
But droop there, whence they sprung; and mourn their lot
80 Round the cold heart, where, after their sweet pain,
They ne'er will gather strength, or find a home again.

10

And one¹ with trembling hands clasps his cold head,
And fans him with her moonlight wings, and cries;
"Our love, our hope, our sorrow, is not dead;
85 See, on the silken fringe of his faint eyes,
Like dew upon a sleeping flower, there lies
A tear some Dream has loosened from his brain."
Lost Angel of a ruined Paradise!
She knew not 'twas her own; as with no stain
90 She faded, like a cloud which had outwept its rain.

11

One from a lucid° urn of starry dew   luminous
Washed his light limbs as if embalming them;
Another clipt her profuse locks, and threw
The wreath upon him, like an anadem,°   rich garland
95 Which frozen tears instead of pearls begem;
Another in her wilful grief would break
Her bow and winged reeds,° as if to stem   arrows
A greater loss with one which was more weak;
And dull the barbed fire against his frozen cheek.

12

100 Another Splendour on his mouth alit,
That mouth, whence it was wont° to draw the breath   accustomed

---

9. The products of Keats's imagination, figuratively represented (according to the conventions
of the pastoral elegy) as his sheep.
1. One of the Dreams (line 73).

Which gave it strength to pierce the guarded wit,[2]
And pass into the panting heart beneath
With lightning and with music: the damp death
105 Quenched its caress upon his icy lips;
And, as a dying meteor stains a wreath
Of moonlight vapour, which the cold night clips,°   clasps
It flushed through his pale limbs, and past to its eclipse.

13

And others came . . . Desires and Adorations,
110 Winged Persuasions and veiled Destinies,
Splendours, and Glooms, and glimmering Incarnations
Of hopes and fears, and twilight Phantasies;
And Sorrow, with her family of Sighs,
And Pleasure, blind with tears, led by the gleam
115 Of her own dying smile instead of eyes,
Came in slow pomp;—the moving pomp might seem
Like pageantry of mist on an autumnal stream.

14

All he had loved, and moulded into thought,
From shape, and hue, and odour, and sweet sound,
120 Lamented Adonais. Morning sought
Her eastern watchtower, and her hair unbound,
Wet with the tears which should adorn the ground,
Dimmed the aerial eyes that kindle day;
Afar the melancholy thunder moaned,
125 Pale Ocean in unquiet slumber lay,
And the wild winds flew round, sobbing in their dismay.

15

Lost Echo sits amid the voiceless mountains,
And feeds her grief with his remembered lay,°   song
And will no more reply to winds or fountains,
130 Or amorous birds perched on the young green spray,
Or herdsman's horn, or bell at closing day;
Since she can mimic not his lips, more dear
Than those for whose disdain she pined away
Into a shadow of all sounds:[3]—a drear
135 Murmur, between their songs, is all the woodmen hear.

16

Grief made the young Spring wild, and she threw down
Her kindling buds, as if she Autumn were,
Or they dead leaves; since her delight is flown
For whom should she have waked the sullen year?

2. The cautious intellect (of the listener).
3. Because of her unrequited love for Narcissus, who was enamored of his own reflection (line 141), the nymph Echo pined away until she was only a reflected sound.

140 To Phoebus was not Hyacinth so dear[4]
    Nor to himself Narcissus, as to both
    Thou Adonais: wan they stand and sere°   *dried, withered*
    Amid the faint companions of their youth,
With dew all turned to tears; odour, to sighing ruth.°   *pity*

17

145 Thy spirit's sister, the lorn nightingale[5]
    Mourns not her mate with such melodious pain;
    Not so the eagle, who like thee could scale
    Heaven, and could nourish in the sun's domain
    Her mighty youth with morning,[6] doth complain,°   *lament*
150 Soaring and screaming round her empty nest,
    As Albion° wails for thee: the curse of Cain   *England*
    Light on his head[7] who pierced thy innocent breast,
And scared the angel soul that was its earthly guest!

18

    Ah woe is me! Winter is come and gone,
155 But grief returns with the revolving year;
    The airs and streams renew their joyous tone;
    The ants, the bees, the swallows reappear;
    Fresh leaves and flowers deck the dead Seasons' bier;
    The amorous birds now pair in every brake,°   *thicket*
160 And build their mossy homes in field and brere;°   *briar*
    And the green lizard, and the golden snake,
Like unimprisoned flames, out of their trance awake.

19

    Through wood and stream and field and hill and Ocean
    A quickening life from the Earth's heart has burst
165 As it has ever done, with change and motion,
    From the great morning of the world when first
    God dawned on Chaos; in its stream immersed
    The lamps of Heaven flash with a softer light;
    All baser things pant with life's sacred thirst;
170 Diffuse themselves; and spend in love's delight,
The beauty and the joy of their renewed might.

20

    The leprous corpse touched by this spirit tender
    Exhales itself in flowers of gentle breath;
    Like incarnations of the stars, when splendour
175 Is changed to fragrance, they illumine death
    And mock the merry worm that wakes beneath;
    Nought we know, dies. Shall that alone which knows

---

4. Young Hyacinthus was loved by Phoebus Apollo, who accidentally killed him in a game of quoits. Apollo made the hyacinth flower spring from his blood.
5. To whom Keats had written "Ode to a Nightingale."
6. In the legend the aged eagle, to renew his youth, flies toward the sun until his old plumage is burned off and the film cleared from his eyes.
7. The reviewer of *Endymion*.

Be as a sword consumed before the sheath[8]
By sightless° lightning?—th' intense atom glows   *invisible*
180   A moment, then is quenched in a most cold repose.

21

Alas! that all we loved of him should be,
But for our grief, as if it had not been,
And grief itself be mortal! Woe is me!
Whence are we, and why are we? of what scene
185   The actors or spectators? Great and mean°   *low*
Meet massed in death, who lends what life must borrow.
As long as skies are blue, and fields are green,
Evening must usher night, night urge the morrow,
Month follow month with woe, and year wake year to sorrow.

22

190   *He* will awake no more, oh, never more!
"Wake thou," cried Misery, "childless Mother, rise
Out of thy sleep, and slake,° in thy heart's core,   *assuage*
A wound more fierce than his with tears and sighs."
And all the Dreams that watched Urania's eyes,
195   And all the Echoes whom their sister's song[9]
Had held in holy silence, cried: "Arise!"
Swift as a Thought by the snake Memory stung,
From her ambrosial rest the fading Splendour° sprung.   *Urania*

23

She rose like an autumnal Night, that springs
200   Out of the East, and follows wild and drear
The golden Day, which, on eternal wings,
Even as a ghost abandoning a bier,
Had left the Earth a corpse. Sorrow and fear
So struck, so roused, so rapt Urania;
205   So saddened round her like an atmosphere
Of stormy mist; so swept her on her way
Even to the mournful place where Adonais lay.

24

Out of her secret Paradise she sped,
Through camps and cities rough with stone, and steel,
210   And human hearts, which to her aery tread
Yielding not, wounded the invisible
Palms of her tender feet where'er they fell:
And barbed tongues, and thoughts more sharp than they
Rent° the soft Form they never could repel,   *tore*
215   Whose sacred blood, like the young tears of May,
Paved with eternal flowers that undeserving way.

---

8. The "sword" is the mind that knows; the "sheath" is its vehicle, the material body.
9. I.e., the Echo in line 127.

25

In the death chamber for a moment Death
Shamed by the presence of that living Might
Blushed to annihilation, and the breath
220   Revisited those lips, and life's pale light
Flashed through those limbs, so late her dear delight.
"Leave me not wild and drear and comfortless,
As silent lightning leaves the starless night!
Leave me not!" cried Urania: her distress
225   Roused Death: Death rose and smiled, and met her vain caress.

26

"Stay yet awhile! speak to me once again;
Kiss me, so long but as a kiss may live;
And in my heartless[1] breast and burning brain
That word, that kiss shall all thoughts else survive
230   With food of saddest memory kept alive,
Now thou art dead, as if it were a part
Of thee, my Adonais! I would give
All that I am to be as thou now art!
But I am chained to Time, and cannot thence depart!

27

235   "Oh gentle child, beautiful as thou wert,
Why didst thou leave the trodden paths of men
Too soon, and with weak hands though mighty heart
Dare° the unpastured dragon in his den?[2]   *challenge*
Defenceless as thou wert, oh where was then
240   Wisdom the mirrored shield, or scorn the spear?[3]
Or hadst thou waited the full cycle, when
Thy spirit should have filled its crescent sphere,[4]
The monsters of life's waste had fled from thee like deer.

28

"The herded wolves, bold only to pursue;
245   The obscene ravens, clamorous o'er the dead;
The vultures to the conqueror's banner true
Who feed where Desolation first has fed,
And whose wings rain contagion;—how they fled,
When like Apollo, from his golden bow,
250   The Pythian of the age[5] one arrow sped
And smiled!—The spoilers tempt no second blow,
They fawn on the proud feet that spurn them lying low.

1. Because her heart had been given to Adonais.
2. I.e., the hostile reviewers.
3. The allusion is to Perseus, who had cut off Medusa's head while avoiding the direct sight of her (which would have turned him to stone) by looking only at her reflection in his shield.
4. I.e., when thy spirit, like the full moon, should

have reached its maturity.
5. Byron, who had directed against critics of the age his satiric poem *English Bards and Scotch Reviewers* (1809). The allusion is to Apollo, called "the Pythian" because he had slain the dragon Python.

29

"The sun comes forth, and many reptiles spawn;
He sets, and each ephemeral insect[6] then
255   Is gathered into death without a dawn,
And the immortal stars awake again;
So is it in the world of living men:
A godlike mind soars forth, in its delight
Making earth bare and veiling heaven,[7] and when
260   It sinks, the swarms that dimmed or shared its light
Leave to its kindred lamps[8] the spirit's awful night."

30

Thus ceased she: and the mountain shepherds came,
Their garlands sere, their magic mantles° rent;   *cloaks*
The Pilgrim of Eternity,[9] whose fame
265   Over his living head like Heaven is bent,
An early but enduring monument,
Came, veiling all the lightnings of his song
In sorrow; from her wilds Ierne sent
The sweetest lyrist[1] of her saddest wrong,
270   And love taught grief to fall like music from his tongue.

31

Midst others of less note, came one frail Form,[2]
A phantom among men; companionless
As the last cloud of an expiring storm
Whose thunder is its knell;° he, as I guess,   *funeral bell*
275   Had gazed on Nature's naked loveliness,
Actæon-like, and now he fled astray
With feeble steps o'er the world's wilderness,
And his own thoughts, along that rugged way,
Pursued, like raging hounds, their father and their prey.[3]

32

280   A pardlike° Spirit beautiful and swift—   *leopardlike*
A Love in desolation masked;—a Power
Girt round with weakness;—it can scarce uplift
The weight of the superincumbent hour;[4]
It is a dying lamp, a falling shower,
285   A breaking billow;—even whilst we speak
Is it not broken? On the withering flower
The killing sun smiles brightly: on a cheek
The life can burn in blood, even while the heart may break.

---

6. I.e., an insect that lives and dies in a single day.
7. As the sun reveals the earth but veils the other stars.
8. The other stars (i.e., creative minds), of lesser brilliance than the sun.
9. Byron, who had referred to his Childe Harold as one of the "wanderers o'er Eternity" (3.669).
1. Thomas Moore (1779–1852), from Ireland ("Ierne"), who had written poems about the oppression of his native land.
2. Shelley, represented in one of his aspects— such as the Poet in *Alastor*, rather than the author of *Prometheus Unbound*.
3. Actaeon, while hunting, came upon the naked Diana bathing and, as a punishment, was turned into a stag and torn to pieces by his own hounds.
4. The heavy, overhanging hour of Keats's death.

33

His head was bound with pansies overblown,
290 And faded violets, white, and pied, and blue;
And a light spear topped with a cypress cone,
Round whose rude shaft dark ivy tresses grew[5]
Yet dripping with the forest's noonday dew,
Vibrated, as the ever-beating heart
295 Shook the weak hand that grasped it; of that crew
He came the last, neglected and apart;
A herd-abandoned deer struck by the hunter's dart.

34

All stood aloof, and at his partial moan
Smiled through their tears; well knew that gentle band
300 Who in another's fate now wept his own;
As in the accents of an unknown land,
He sung new sorrow; sad Urania scanned
The Stranger's mien, and murmured: "who art thou?"
He answered not, but with a sudden hand
305 Made bare his branded and ensanguined° brow,   *bloodied*
Which was like Cain's or Christ's[6]—Oh! that it should be so!

35

What softer voice is hushed over the dead?
Athwart what brow is that dark mantle thrown?
What form leans sadly o'er the white death-bed,
310 In mockery of monumental stone,[7]
The heavy heart heaving without a moan?
If it be He,[8] who, gentlest of the wise,
Taught, soothed, loved, honoured the departed one;
Let me not vex, with inharmonious sighs
315 The silence of that heart's accepted sacrifice.

36

Our Adonais has drunk poison—oh!
What deaf and viperous murderer could crown
Life's early cup with such a draught of woe?
The nameless worm[9] would now itself disown:
320 It felt, yet could escape the magic tone
Whose prelude held all envy, hate, and wrong,
But what was howling in one breast alone,
Silent with expectation of the song,[1]
Whose master's hand is cold, whose silver lyre unstrung.

5. Like the thyrsus, the leaf-entwined and cone-topped staff carried by Dionysus, to whom leopards (see line 280) are sacred. The pansies, which are "overblown," i.e., past their bloom, are emblems of sorrowful thought. The cypress is an emblem of mourning.

6. His bloody ("ensanguined") brow bore a mark like that with which God had branded Cain for murdering Abel—or like that left by Christ's crown of thorns.

7. In imitation of a memorial statue.

8. Leigh Hunt, close friend of both Keats and Shelley.

9. Snake; i.e., the anonymous reviewer.

1. The promise of later greatness in Keats's early poems "held . . . silent" the expression of "all envy, hate, and wrong" except the reviewer's.

37

325 Live thou, whose infamy is not thy fame!
Live! fear no heavier chastisement from me,
Thou noteless blot on a remembered name!
But be thyself, and know thyself to be!
And ever at thy season be thou free
330 To spill the venom when thy fangs o'erflow:
Remorse and Self-contempt shall cling to thee;
Hot Shame shall burn upon thy secret brow,
And like a beaten hound tremble thou shalt—as now.

38

Nor let us weep that our delight is fled
335 Far from these carrion kites[2] that scream below;
He wakes or sleeps with the enduring dead;
Thou canst not soar where he is sitting now.—
Dust to the dust! but the pure spirit shall flow
Back to the burning fountain whence it came,
340 A portion of the Eternal,[3] which must glow
Through time and change, unquenchably the same,
Whilst thy cold embers choke the sordid hearth of shame.

39

Peace, peace! he is not dead, he doth not sleep—
He hath awakened from the dream of life—
345 'Tis we, who lost in stormy visions, keep
With phantoms an unprofitable strife,
And in mad trance, strike with our spirit's knife
Invulnerable nothings.—*We* decay
Like corpses in a charnel; fear and grief
350 Convulse us and consume us day by day,
And cold hopes swarm like worms within our living clay.

40

He has outsoared the shadow of our night;[4]
Envy and calumny° and hate and pain,   *slander*
And that unrest which men miscall delight,
355 Can touch him not and torture not again;
From the contagion of the world's slow stain
He is secure, and now can never mourn
A heart grown cold, a head grown grey in vain;
Nor, when the spirit's self has ceased to burn,
360 With sparkless ashes load an unlamented urn.

---

2. A species of hawk that feeds on dead flesh.
3. Shelley adopts for this poem the Neoplatonic view that all life and all forms emanate from the Absolute, the eternal One. The Absolute is imaged as both a radiant light source and an over-flowing fountain, which circulates continuously through the dross of matter (stanza 43) and back to its source.
4. He has soared beyond the shadow cast by the earth as it intercepts the sun's light.

41

He lives, he wakes—'tis Death is dead, not he;
Mourn not for Adonais.—Thou young Dawn
Turn all thy dew to splendour, for from thee
The spirit thou lamentest is not gone;
365   Ye caverns and ye forests, cease to moan!
Cease ye faint flowers and fountains, and thou Air
Which like a mourning veil thy scarf hadst thrown
O'er the abandoned Earth, now leave it bare
Even to the joyous stars which smile on its despair![5]

42

370   He is made one with Nature: there is heard
His voice in all her music, from the moan
Of thunder, to the song of night's sweet bird;[6]
He is a presence to be felt and known
In darkness and in light, from herb and stone,
375   Spreading itself where'er that Power may move
Which has withdrawn his being to its own;
Which wields the world with never wearied love,
Sustains it from beneath, and kindles it above.

43

He is a portion of the loveliness
380   Which once he made more lovely: he doth bear
His part, while the one Spirit's plastic° stress   *formative, shaping*
Sweeps through the dull dense world, compelling there,
All new successions to the forms they wear;
Torturing th' unwilling dross that checks its flight
385   To its own likeness, as each mass may bear;[7]
And bursting in its beauty and its might
From trees and beasts and men into the Heaven's light.

44

The splendours of the firmament of time
May be eclipsed, but are extinguished not;
390   Like stars to their appointed height they climb
And death is a low mist which cannot blot
The brightness it may veil.[8] When lofty thought
Lifts a young heart above its mortal lair,
And love and life contend in it, for what°   *whatever*
395   Shall be its earthly doom,° the dead live there[9]   *destiny*
And move like winds of light on dark and stormy air.

5. Shelley's science is accurate: it is the envelope of air around the earth that, by diffusing and reflecting sunlight, veils the stars so that they are invisible during the day.
6. The nightingale, in allusion to Keats's "Ode to a Nightingale."
7. I.e., to the degree that a particular substance will permit.
8. The radiance of stars (i.e., of poets) persists, even when they are temporarily "eclipsed" by another heavenly body, or obscured by the veil of the earth's atmosphere.
9. I.e., in the thought of the "young heart."

45

The inheritors of unfulfilled renown[1]
Rose from their thrones, built beyond mortal thought,
Far in the Unapparent. Chatterton
400 Rose pale, his solemn agony had not
Yet faded from him; Sidney, as he fought
And as he fell and as he lived and loved
Sublimely mild, a Spirit without spot,
Arose; and Lucan, by his death approved:°   *justified*
405 Oblivion as they rose shrank like a thing reproved.

46

And many more, whose names on Earth are dark
But whose transmitted effluence cannot die
So long as fire outlives the parent spark,
Rose, robed in dazzling immortality.
410 "Thou art become as one of us," they cry,
"It was for thee yon kingless sphere has long
Swung blind in unascended majesty,
Silent alone amid an Heaven of song.
Assume thy winged throne, thou Vesper of our throng!"[2]

47

415 Who mourns for Adonais? oh come forth
Fond° wretch! and know thyself and him aright.   *foolish*
Clasp with thy panting soul the pendulous[3] Earth;
As from a centre, dart thy spirit's light
Beyond all worlds, until its spacious might°   *power*
420 Satiate the void circumference: then shrink
Even to a point within our day and night;[4]
And keep thy heart light lest it make thee sink
When hope has kindled hope, and lured thee to the brink.

48

Or go to Rome, which is the sepulchre
425 O, not of him, but of our joy: 'tis nought
That ages, empires, and religions there
Lie buried in the ravage they have wrought;
For such as he can lend,—they[5] borrow not
Glory from those who made the world their prey;
430 And he is gathered to the kings of thought

1. Poets who (like Keats) died young, before achieving their full measure of fame: The seventeen-year-old Thomas Chatterton (1752–1770) was believed to have committed suicide out of despair over his poverty and lack of recognition. Sir Philip Sidney (1554–1586) died in battle at thirty-two. The Roman poet Lucan (39–65 C.E.) killed himself at twenty-six to escape a sentence of death for having plotted against the tyrant Nero.
2. Adonais assumes his place in the sphere of Vesper, the evening star, hitherto unoccupied ("kingless"), hence also "silent" amid the music of the other spheres.
3. Suspended, floating in space.
4. The poet bids the mourner to stretch his imagination so as to reach the poet's own cosmic viewpoint and then allow it to contract ("shrink") back to its ordinary vantage point on Earth—where, unlike Adonais in his heavenly place, we have an alternation of day and night.
5. Poets such as Keats.

Who waged contention with their time's decay,
And of the past are all that cannot pass away.

49

Go thou to Rome,—at once the Paradise,
The grave, the city, and the wilderness;
435 And where its wrecks° like shattered mountains rise,   *ruins*
And flowering weeds, and fragrant copses[6] dress
The bones of Desolation's nakedness
Pass, till the Spirit of the spot shall lead
Thy footsteps to a slope of green access[7]
440 Where, like an infant's smile,[8] over the dead,
A light of laughing flowers along the grass is spread.

50

And grey walls moulder round,[9] on which dull Time
Feeds, like slow fire upon a hoary brand;[1]
And one keen pyramid with wedge sublime,[2]
445 Pavilioning the dust of him who planned
This refuge for his memory, doth stand
Like flame transformed to marble; and beneath,
A field is spread, on which a newer band
Have pitched in Heaven's smile their camp of death[3]
450 Welcoming him we lose with scarce extinguished breath.

51

Here pause: these graves are all too young as yet
To have outgrown the sorrow which consigned
Its charge to each; and if the seal is set,
Here, on one fountain of a mourning mind,[4]
455 Break it not thou! too surely shalt thou find
Thine own well full, if thou returnest home,
Of tears and gall. From the world's bitter wind
Seek shelter in the shadow of the tomb.
What Adonais is, why fear we to become?

52

460 The One remains, the many change and pass;
Heaven's light forever shines, Earth's shadows fly;
Life, like a dome of many-coloured glass,
Stains the white radiance of Eternity,
Until Death tramples it to fragments.[5]—Die,

---

6. Undergrowth. In Shelley's time the ruins of ancient Rome were overgrown with weeds and shrubs, almost as if the ground were returning to its natural state.
7. The Protestant Cemetery, Keats's burial place.
8. A glancing allusion to Shelley's three-year-old son, William, also buried there.
9. The wall of ancient Rome formed one boundary of the cemetery.
1. A burning log, white with ash.
2. The tomb of Caius Cestius, a Roman tribune, just outside the cemetery.

3. A common name for a cemetery in Italy is *camposanto*, "holy camp or ground." Shelley is punning on the Italian word.
4. Shelley's mourning for his son.
5. Earthly life colors ("stains") the pure white light of the One, which is the source of all light (see lines 339–40, n. 3). The azure sky, flowers, etc., of lines 466–68 exemplify earthly colors that, however beautiful, fall far short of the "glory" of the pure Light that they transmit but also refract ("transfuse").

465 If thou wouldst be with that which thou dost seek!
Follow where all is fled!—Rome's azure sky,
Flowers, ruins, statues, music, words, are weak
The glory they transfuse with fitting truth to speak.

53

Why linger, why turn back, why shrink, my Heart?
470 Thy hopes are gone before; from all things here
They have departed; thou shouldst now depart!
A light is past° from the revolving year,   *passed*
And man, and woman; and what still is dear
Attracts to crush, repels to make thee wither.
475 The soft sky smiles,—the low wind whispers near:
'Tis Adonais calls! oh, hasten thither,
No more let Life divide what Death can join together.

54

That Light whose smile kindles the Universe,
That Beauty in which all things work and move,
480 That Benediction which the eclipsing Curse
Of birth can quench not, that sustaining Love
Which through the web of being blindly wove
By man and beast and earth and air and sea,
Burns bright or dim, as each are mirrors of[6]
485 The fire for which all thirst;[7] now beams on me,
Consuming the last clouds of cold mortality.

55

The breath whose might I have invoked in song[8]
Descends on me; my spirit's bark is driven,
Far from the shore, far from the trembling throng
490 Whose sails were never to the tempest given;
The massy earth and sphered skies are riven![9]
I am borne darkly, fearfully, afar;
Whilst burning through the inmost veil of Heaven,
The soul of Adonais, like a star,
495 Beacons from the abode where the Eternal are.

1821   1821

6. I.e., according to the degree that each reflects.
7. The "thirst" of the human spirit is to return to the fountain and fire (the "burning fountain," line 339) that are its source.
8. Two years earlier Shelley had "invoked" (prayed to, and also asked for) "the breath of Autumn's being" in his "Ode to the West Wind" (p. 806).
9. In her 1839 edition of her husband's works, Mary Shelley, thinking of the manner of Percy's death, asked: "who but will regard as a prophecy the last stanza of the 'Adonais'?"

When the lamp is shattered

When the lamp is shattered
The light in the dust lies dead—
When the cloud is scattered
The rainbow's glory is shed—
When the lute is broken   5
Sweet tones are remembered not—
When the lips have spoken
Loved accents are soon forgot.

As music and splendour
Survive not the lamp and the lute,   10
The heart's echoes render
No song when the spirit is mute—
No song—but sad dirges
Like the wind through a ruined cell
Or the mournful surges   15
That ring the dead seaman's knell.

When hearts have once mingled
Love first leaves the well-built nest—
The weak one is singled
To endure what it once possest.   20
O Love! who bewailest
The frailty of all things here,
Why choose you the frailest
For your cradle, your home and your bier?

Its passions will rock thee   25
As the storms rock the ravens on high—
Bright Reason will mock thee
Like the Sun from a wintry sky—
From thy nest every rafter
Will rot, and thine eagle home   30
Leave thee naked to laughter
When leaves fall and cold winds come.

1822   1824

A Defence of Poetry   In 1820 Shelley's friend Thomas Love Peacock published an ironic essay, "The Four Ages of Poetry," implicitly directed against the towering claims for poetry and the poetic imagination made by his Romantic contemporaries. In this essay, available in the NAEL Archive, Peacock adopted the premise of Wordsworth and other Romantic critics—that poetry in its origin was a primitive use of language and mind—but from this premise he proceeded to conclude that poetry had become a useless anachronism in his own Age of Bronze, a time defined by new sciences (including economics and political theory) and technologies that had the potential to improve the world. Peacock was a poet as well as an excellent prose satirist, and Shelley saw the joke; but he also recognized that the view that Peacock, as a satirist, had assumed was very close to that actually held in his day by Utilitarian philosophers and the material-minded public, which either attacked or contemptuously ignored the imaginative faculty and its achievements. He therefore undertook, as he good-humoredly wrote to Peacock, "to break a lance with you . . . in honor of my mistress Urania" (giving the cause for which he battled the name that Milton had used for the muse inspiring *Paradise Lost*), even though he was only "the knight of the shield of shadow and the lance of gossamere." The result was "A Defence of Poetry," planned to consist of three parts. The last two parts were never written, and even the existing section, written in 1821, remained unpublished until 1840, eighteen years after Shelley's death.

Shelley's emphasis in this essay is not on the particularity of individual poems but on the universal and permanent qualities and values that, he believes, all great poems, as products of imagination, have in common. Shelley in addition extends the term *poet* to include all creative minds that break out of the conditions of their historical time and place in order to envision such values. This category includes not only writers in prose as well as verse but also artists, legislators, prophets, and the founders of new social and religious institutions.

The "Defence" is an eloquent and enduring claim for the indispensability of the visionary and creative imagination in all the great human concerns. Few later social critics have equaled the cogency of Shelley's attack on our acquisitive society and its narrowly material concepts of utility and progress. Such a bias has opened the way to enormous advances in the physical sciences and our material well-being, but without a proportionate development of our "poetic faculty," the moral imagination. The result, Shelley says, is that "man, having enslaved the elements, remains himself a slave."

From A Defence of Poetry

or Remarks Suggested by an Essay Entitled "The Four Ages of Poetry"

According to one mode of regarding those two classes of mental action, which are called reason and imagination, the former may be considered as mind contemplating the relations borne by one thought to another, however produced; and the latter, as mind acting upon those thoughts so as to colour them with its own light, and composing from them, as from elements, other thoughts, each containing within itself the principle of its own integrity. The one[1] is the *to poiein*,[2] or the principle of synthesis, and has for its objects those forms which are common to universal nature and existence itself; the other is the *to logizein*,[3] or principle of analysis, and its action regards the relations of things, simply as relations; considering thoughts, not in their integral unity, but as the algebraical representations which conduct to certain general results. Reason is the enumeration of quantities already known; imagination is the perception of the value of those quantities, both separately and as a whole. Reason respects the differences, and imagination the similitudes of things. Reason is to Imagination as the instrument to the agent, as the body to the spirit, as the shadow to the substance.

Poetry, in a general sense, may be defined to be "the expression of the Imagination": and poetry is connate with the origin of man. Man is an instrument over which a series of external and internal impressions are driven, like the alternations of an ever-changing wind over an Æolian lyre,[4] which move it by their motion to ever-changing melody. But there is a prin-

---

1. The imagination. "The other" (later in the sentence) is the reason.
2. Making. The Greek word from which the English term *poet* derives means "maker," and the word *maker* was often used as equivalent to "poet" by Renaissance critics such as Sir Philip

Sidney in his *Defence of Poesy*, which Shelley had carefully studied.
3. Calculating, reasoning.
4. A wind harp (see Coleridge, "The Eolian Harp," p. 444).

ciple within the human being, and perhaps within all sentient beings, which acts otherwise than in the lyre, and produces not melody, alone, but harmony, by an internal adjustment of the sounds or motions thus excited to the impressions which excite them. It is as if the lyre could accommodate its chords to the motions of that which strikes them, in a determined proportion of sound; even as the musician can accommodate his voice to the sound of the lyre. A child at play by itself will express its delight by its voice and motions; and every inflexion of tone and every gesture will bear exact relation to a corresponding antitype in the pleasurable impressions which awakened it; it will be the reflected image of that impression; and as the lyre trembles and sounds after the wind has died away, so the child seeks, by prolonging in its voice and motions the duration of the effect, to prolong also a consciousness of the cause. In relation to the objects which delight a child, these expressions are, what poetry is to higher objects. The savage (for the savage is to ages what the child is to years) expresses the emotions produced in him by surrounding objects in a similar manner; and language and gesture, together with plastic[5] or pictorial imitation, become the image of the combined effect of those objects, and of his apprehension of them. Man in society, with all his passions and his pleasures, next becomes the object of the passions and pleasures of man; an additional class of emotions produces an augmented treasure of expressions; and language, gesture, and the imitative arts, become at once the representation and the medium, the pencil and the picture, the chisel and the statue, the chord and the harmony. The social sympathies, or those laws from which as from its elements society results, begin to develope themselves from the moment that two human beings coexist; the future is contained within the present as the plant within the seed; and equality, diversity, unity, contrast, mutual dependence, become the principles alone capable of affording the motives according to which the will of a social being is determined to action, inasmuch as he is social; and constitute pleasure in sensation, virtue in sentiment, beauty in art, truth in reasoning, and love in the intercourse of kind. Hence men, even in the infancy of society, observe a certain order in their words and actions, distinct from that of the objects and the impressions represented by them, all expression being subject to the laws of that from which it proceeds. But let us dismiss those more general considerations which might involve an enquiry into the principles of society itself, and restrict our view to the manner in which the imagination is expressed upon its forms.

In the youth of the world, men dance and sing and imitate natural objects, observing[6] in these actions, as in all others, a certain rhythm or order. And, although all men observe a similar, they observe not the same order, in the motions of the dance, in the melody of the song, in the combinations of language, in the series of their imitations of natural objects. For there is a certain order or rhythm belonging to each of these classes of mimetic representation, from which the hearer and the spectator receive an intenser and purer pleasure than from any other: the sense of an approximation to this order has been called taste, by modern writers. Every man in the infancy of art, observes an order which approximates more or less closely to that from which this highest delight results: but the diversity is not sufficiently marked,

5. Sculptural.
6. Following, obeying.

as that its gradations should be sensible,[7] except in those instances where the predominance of this faculty of approximation to the beautiful (for so we may be permitted to name the relation between this highest pleasure and its cause) is very great. Those in whom it exists in excess are poets, in the most universal sense of the word; and the pleasure resulting from the manner in which they express the influence of society or nature upon their own minds, communicates itself to others, and gathers a sort of reduplication from that community. Their language is vitally metaphorical; that is, it marks the before unapprehended relations of things, and perpetuates their apprehension, until the words which represent them, become through time signs for portions or classes of thoughts[8] instead of pictures of integral thoughts; and then if no new poets should arise to create afresh the associations which have been thus disorganized, language will be dead to all the nobler purposes of human intercourse. These similitudes or relations are finely said by Lord Bacon to be "the same footsteps of nature impressed upon the various subjects of the world"[9]—and he considers the faculty which perceives them as the storehouse of axioms common to all knowledge. In the infancy of society every author is necessarily a poet, because language itself is poetry; and to be a poet is to apprehend the true and the beautiful, in a word the good which exists in the relation, subsisting, first between existence and perception, and secondly between perception and expression. Every original language near to its source is in itself the chaos of a cyclic poem:[1] the copiousness of lexicography and the distinctions of grammar are the works of a later age, and are merely the catalogue and the form of the creations of Poetry.

But Poets, or those who imagine and express this indestructible order, are not only the authors of language and of music, of the dance and architecture and statuary and painting: they are the institutors of laws, and the founders of civil society and the inventors of the arts of life and the teachers, who draw into a certain propinquity with the beautiful and the true that partial apprehension of the agencies of the invisible world which is called religion.[2] Hence all original religions are allegorical, or susceptible of allegory, and like Janus[3] have a double face of false and true. Poets, according to the circumstances of the age and nation in which they appeared, were called in the earlier epochs of the world legislators or prophets:[4] a poet essentially comprises and unites both these characters. For he not only beholds intensely the present as it is, and discovers those laws according to which present things ought to be ordered, but he beholds the future in the present, and his thoughts are the germs of the flower and the fruit of latest time. Not that I assert poets to be prophets in the gross sense of the word, or that they can foretell the form as surely as they foreknow the spirit of events: such is the pretence of superstition which would make poetry an attribute of prophecy, rather than prophecy an attribute of poetry. A Poet participates in the eternal, the infinite, and the one; as far as relates to his conceptions, time and place and number are not. The grammatical forms which express the moods

7. Discernible.
8. I.e., abstract concepts.
9. Francis Bacon's *The Advancement of Learning* 3.1.
1. A group of poems (e.g., "the Arthurian cycle") that deal with the same subject.
2. Here Shelley enlarges the scope of the term *poetry* to denote all the creative achievements,

or imaginative breakthroughs, of humankind, including noninstitutional religious insights.
3. Roman god of beginnings and endings, often represented by two heads facing opposite directions.
4. Sir Philip Sidney had pointed out, in his *Defence of Poesy*, that *vates*, the Roman term for "poet," signifies "a diviner, fore-seer, or Prophet."

of time, and the difference of persons and the distinction of place are convertible with respect to the highest poetry without injuring it as poetry, and the choruses of Æschylus, and the book of Job, and Dante's Paradise would afford, more than any other writings, examples of this fact, if the limits of this essay did not forbid citation. The creations of sculpture, painting, and music, are illustrations still more decisive.

Language, colour, form, and religious and civil habits of action are all the instruments and materials of poetry; they may be called poetry by that figure of speech which considers the effect as a synonime of the cause. But poetry in a more restricted sense[5] expresses those arrangements of language, and especially metrical language, which are created by that imperial faculty, whose throne is curtained within the invisible nature of man. And this springs from the nature itself of language, which is a more direct representation of the actions and passions of our internal being, and is susceptible of more various and delicate combinations, than colour, form, or motion, and is more plastic and obedient to the controul of that faculty of which it is the creation. For language is arbitrarily produced by the Imagination and has relation to thoughts alone; but all other materials, instruments and conditions of art, have relations among each other, which limit and interpose between conception and expression. The former[6] is as a mirror which reflects, the latter as a cloud which enfeebles, the light of which both are mediums of communication. Hence the fame of sculptors, painters and musicians, although the intrinsic powers of the great masters of these arts, may yield in no degree to that of those who have employed language as the hieroglyphic of their thoughts, has never equalled that of poets in the restricted sense of the term; as two performers of equal skill will produce unequal effects from a guitar and a harp. The fame of legislators and founders of religions, so long as their institutions last, alone seems to exceed that of poets in the restricted sense; but it can scarcely be a question whether, if we deduct the celebrity which their flattery of the gross opinions of the vulgar usually conciliates, together with that which belonged to them in their higher character of poets, any excess will remain.

We have thus circumscribed the meaning of the word Poetry within the limits of that art which is the most familiar and the most perfect expression of the faculty itself. It is necessary however to make the circle still narrower, and to determine the distinction between measured and unmeasured language;[7] for the popular division into prose and verse is inadmissible in accurate philosophy.

Sounds as well as thoughts have relation both between each other and towards that which they represent, and a perception of the order of those relations has always been found connected with a perception of the order of the relations of thoughts. Hence the language of poets has ever affected a certain uniform and harmonious recurrence of sound, without which it were not poetry, and which is scarcely less indispensable to the communication of its influence, than the words themselves, without reference to that peculiar order. Hence the vanity of translation; it were as wise to cast a violet into a crucible that you might discover the formal principle of its colour and odour, as seek to transfuse from one language into another the creations of a poet.

---

5. I.e., restricted to specifically verbal poetry, as against the inclusive sense in which Shelley has been applying the term.

6. I.e., language, as opposed to the media of sculpture, painting, and music.

7. I.e., in meter versus in prose.

The plant must spring again from its seed or it will bear no flower—and this is the burthen of the curse of Babel.[8]

An observation of the regular mode of the recurrence of this harmony in the language of poetical minds, together with its relation to music, produced metre, or a certain system of traditional forms of harmony of language. Yet it is by no means essential that a poet should accommodate his language to this traditional form, so that the harmony which is its spirit, be observed. The practise is indeed convenient and popular, and to be preferred, especially in such composition as includes much form and action: but every great poet must inevitably innovate upon the example of his predecessors in the exact structure of his peculiar versification. The distinction between poets and prose writers is a vulgar error. The distinction between philosophers and poets has been anticipated.[9] Plato was essentially a poet—the truth and splendour of his imagery and the melody of his language is the most intense that it is possible to conceive. He rejected the measure of the epic, dramatic, and lyrical forms, because he sought to kindle a harmony in thoughts divested of shape and action, and he forbore to invent any regular plan of rhythm which would include, under determinate forms, the varied pauses of his style. Cicero[1] sought to imitate the cadence of his periods but with little success. Lord Bacon was a poet.[2] His language has a sweet and majestic rhythm, which satisfies the sense, no less than the almost superhuman wisdom of his philosophy satisfies the intellect; it is a strain which distends, and then bursts the circumference of the hearer's mind, and pours itself forth together with it into the universal element with which it has perpetual sympathy. All the authors of revolutions in opinion are not only necessarily poets as they are inventors, nor even as their words unveil the permanent analogy of things by images which participate in the life of truth; but as their periods are harmonious and rhythmical and contain in themselves the elements of verse; being the echo of the eternal music. Nor are those supreme poets, who have employed traditional forms of rhythm on account of the form and action of their subjects, less capable of perceiving and teaching the truth of things, than those who have omitted that form. Shakespeare, Dante, and Milton (to confine ourselves to modern writers) are philosophers of the very loftiest power.

A poem is the very image of life expressed in its eternal truth. There is this difference between a story and a poem, that a story is a catalogue of detached facts, which have no other bond of connexion than time, place, circumstance, cause and effect; the other is the creation of actions according to the unchangeable forms of human nature, as existing in the mind of the creator, which is itself the image of all other minds. The one is partial, and applies only to a definite period of time, and a certain combination of events which can never again recur; the other is universal, and contains within itself the germ of a relation to whatever motives or actions have place in the possible varieties of human nature. Time, which destroys the beauty and the use of the story of particular facts, stript of the poetry which should invest them,

8. When the descendants of Noah, who spoke a single language, undertook to build the Tower of Babel, which would reach heaven, God cut short the attempt by multiplying languages so that the builders could no longer communicate (see Genesis 11.1–9).

9. I.e., in what Shelley has already said.
1. Marcus Tullius Cicero, the great Roman orator of the 1st century B.C.E.
2. See the *Filium Labyrinthi* and the *Essay on Death* particularly [Shelley's note].

augments that of Poetry, and for ever develops new and wonderful applications of the eternal truth which it contains. Hence epitomes[3] have been called the moths of just history;[4] they eat out the poetry of it. The story of particular facts is as a mirror which obscures and distorts that which should be beautiful: Poetry is a mirror which makes beautiful that which is distorted.

The parts of a composition may be poetical, without the composition as a whole being a poem. A single sentence may be considered as a whole though it be found in a series of unassimilated portions; a single word even may be a spark of inextinguishable thought. And thus all the great historians, Herodotus, Plutarch, Livy,[5] were poets; and although the plan of these writers, especially that of Livy, restrained them from developing this faculty in its highest degree, they make copious and ample amends for their subjection, by filling all the interstices of their subjects with living images.

Having determined what is poetry, and who are poets, let us proceed to estimate its effects upon society.

Poetry is ever accompanied with pleasure: all spirits on which it falls, open themselves to receive the wisdom which is mingled with its delight. In the infancy of the world, neither poets themselves nor their auditors are fully aware of the excellence of poetry: for it acts in a divine and unapprehended manner, beyond and above consciousness; and it is reserved for future generations to contemplate and measure the mighty cause and effect in all the strength and splendour of their union. Even in modern times, no living poet ever arrived at the fulness of his fame; the jury which sits in judgement upon a poet, belonging as he does to all time, must be composed of his peers: it must be impanelled by Time from the selectest of the wise of many generations. A Poet is a nightingale, who sits in darkness and sings to cheer its own solitude with sweet sounds: his auditors are as men entranced by the melody of an unseen musician, who feel that they are moved and softened, yet know not whence or why. The poems of Homer and his contemporaries were the delight of infant Greece; they were the elements of that social system which is the column upon which all succeeding civilization has reposed. Homer embodied the ideal perfection of his age in human character; nor can we doubt that those who read his verses were awakened to an ambition of becoming like to Achilles, Hector and Ulysses: the truth and beauty of friendship, patriotism and persevering devotion to an object, were unveiled to the depths in these immortal creations: the sentiments of the auditors must have been refined and enlarged by a sympathy with such great and lovely impersonations, until from admiring they imitated, and from imitation they identified themselves with the objects of their admiration. Nor let it be objected, that these characters are remote from moral perfection, and that they can by no means be considered as edifying patterns for general imitation. Every epoch under names more or less specious has deified its peculiar errors; Revenge is the naked Idol of the worship of a semi-barbarous age; and Self-deceit is the veiled Image of unknown evil before which luxury and satiety lie prostrate. But a poet considers the vices of his contemporaries as the temporary dress in which his creations must be arrayed, and which cover without concealing

---

3. Abstracts, summaries.
4. By Bacon in *The Advancement of Learning* 2.2.4.
5. Titus Livius (59 B.C.E.–17 C.E.) wrote an immense history of Rome. Herodotus (ca. 480–ca. 425 B.C.E.) wrote the first systematic history of Greece. Plutarch (ca. 46–ca. 120 C.E.) wrote *Parallel Lives* (of eminent Greeks and Romans).

the eternal proportions of their beauty. An epic or dramatic personage is understood to wear them around his soul, as he may the antient armour or the modern uniform around his body; whilst it is easy to conceive a dress more graceful than either. The beauty of the internal nature cannot be so far concealed by its accidental vesture, but that the spirit of its form shall communicate itself to the very disguise, and indicate the shape it hides from the manner in which it is worn. A majestic form and graceful motions will express themselves through the most barbarous and tasteless costume. Few poets of the highest class have chosen to exhibit the beauty of their conceptions in its naked truth and splendour; and it is doubtful whether the alloy of costume, habit, etc., be not necessary to temper this planetary music[6] for mortal ears.

The whole objection, however, of the immorality of poetry[7] rests upon a misconception of the manner in which poetry acts to produce the moral improvement of man. Ethical science[8] arranges the elements which poetry has created, and propounds schemes and proposes examples of civil and domestic life: nor is it for want of admirable doctrines that men hate, and despise, and censure, and deceive, and subjugate one another. But Poetry acts in another and diviner manner. It awakens and enlarges the mind itself by rendering it the receptacle of a thousand unapprehended combinations of thought. Poetry lifts the veil from the hidden beauty of the world, and makes familiar objects be as if they were not familiar; it reproduces[9] all that it represents, and the impersonations clothed in its Elysian light stand thenceforward in the minds of those who have once contemplated them, as memorials of that gentle and exalted content[1] which extends itself over all thoughts and actions with which it coexists. The great secret of morals is Love; or a going out of our own nature, and an identification of ourselves with the beautiful which exists in thought, action, or person, not our own. A man, to be greatly good, must imagine intensely and comprehensively; he must put himself in the place of another and of many others; the pains and pleasures of his species must become his own. The great instrument of moral good is the imagination;[2] and poetry administers to the effect by acting upon the cause. Poetry enlarges the circumference of the imagination by replenishing it with thoughts of ever new delight, which have the power of attracting and assimilating to their own nature all other thoughts, and which form new intervals and interstices whose void for ever craves fresh food. Poetry strengthens that faculty which is the organ of the moral nature of man, in the same manner as exercise strengthens a limb. A Poet therefore would do ill to embody his own conceptions of right and wrong, which are usually those of his place and time, in his poetical creations, which participate in neither. By this assumption of the inferior office of interpreting the effect, in which perhaps after all he might acquit himself but imperfectly, he would resign the glory in a participation in the cause.[3] There was little danger that Homer, or any of the

6. The music made by the revolving crystalline spheres of the planets, inaudible to human ears.
7. In the preceding paragraph Shelley has been implicitly dealing with the charge, voiced by Plato in his *Republic*, that poetry is immoral because it represents evil characters acting evilly.
8. Moral philosophy.
9. Produces anew, re-creates.
1. Contentment.
2. Central to Shelley's theory is the concept (developed by 18th-century philosophers) of the

sympathetic imagination—the faculty by which an individual is enabled to identify with the thoughts and feelings of others. Shelley insists that the faculty in poetry that enables us to share the joys and sufferings of invented characters is also the basis of all morality, for it compels us to feel for others as we feel for ourselves.
3. The "effect," or the explicit moral standards into which imaginative insights are translated at a particular time or place, is contrasted to the "cause" of all morality, the imagination itself.

eternal Poets, should have so far misunderstood themselves as to have abdicated this throne of their widest dominion. Those in whom the poetical faculty, though great, is less intense, as Euripides, Lucan, Tasso,[4] Spenser, have frequently affected[5] a moral aim, and the effect of their poetry is diminished in exact proportion to the degree in which they compel us to advert to this purpose.[6]

* * *

It is difficult to define pleasure in its highest sense; the definition involving a number of apparent paradoxes. For, from an inexplicable defect of harmony in the constitution of human nature, the pain of the inferior is frequently connected with the pleasures of the superior portions of our being. Sorrow, terror, anguish, despair itself are often the chosen expressions of an approximation to the highest good. Our sympathy in tragic fiction depends on this principle; tragedy delights by affording a shadow of the pleasure which exists in pain. This is the source also of the melancholy which is inseparable from the sweetest melody. The pleasure that is in sorrow is sweeter than the pleasure of pleasure itself. And hence the saying, "It is better to go to the house of mourning, than to the house of mirth."[7] Not that this highest species of pleasure is necessarily linked with pain. The delight of love and friendship, the ecstasy of the admiration of nature, the joy of the perception and still more of the creation of poetry is often wholly unalloyed.

The production and assurance of pleasure in this highest sense is true utility. Those who produce and preserve this pleasure are Poets or poetical philosophers.

The exertions of Locke, Hume, Gibbon, Voltaire, Rousseau,[8] and their disciples, in favour of oppressed and deluded humanity, are entitled to the gratitude of mankind. Yet it is easy to calculate the degree of moral and intellectual improvement which the world would have exhibited, had they never lived. A little more nonsense would have been talked for a century or two; and perhaps a few more men, women, and children, burnt as heretics. We might not at this moment have been congratulating each other on the abolition of the Inquisition in Spain.[9] But it exceeds all imagination to conceive what would have been the moral condition of the world if neither Dante, Petrarch, Boccaccio, Chaucer, Shakespeare, Calderon, Lord Bacon, nor Milton, had ever existed; if Raphael and Michael Angelo had never been born; if the Hebrew poetry had never been translated; if a revival of the study of Greek literature had never taken place; if no monuments of antient sculpture had been handed down to us; and if the poetry of the religion of the antient world had been extinguished together with its belief. The human mind could never, except by the intervention of these excitements, have been

4. Tasso Torquato (1544–1595), Italian poet, author of *Jerusalem Delivered*, an epic poem about a crusade. Euripides (ca. 484–406 B.C.E.), Greek writer of tragedies. Lucan (39–65 C.E.), Roman poet, author of the *Pharsalia*.
5. Assumed, adopted.
6. In the following, omitted, passage Shelley reviews the history of drama and poetry in relation to civilization and morality and proceeds to refute the charge that poets are less useful than "reasoners and merchants." He begins by defining *utility* in terms of pleasure and then distinguishes between the lower (physical and material) and the higher (imaginative) pleasures.
7. Ecclesiastes 7.2.
8. I follow the classification adopted by the author of Four Ages of Poetry. But Rousseau was essentially a poet. The others, even Voltaire, were mere reasoners [Shelley's note].
9. The Inquisition had been suspended following the Spanish Revolution of 1820, the year before Shelley wrote this essay; it was not abolished permanently until 1834.

awakened to the invention of the grosser sciences, and that application of analytical reasoning to the aberrations of society, which it is now attempted to exalt over the direct expression of the inventive and creative faculty itself.

We have more moral, political and historical wisdom, than we know how to reduce into practice; we have more scientific and economical knowledge than can be accommodated to the just distribution of the produce which it multiplies. The poetry in these systems of thought, is concealed by the accumulation of facts and calculating processes. There is no want of knowledge respecting what is wisest and best in morals, government, and political economy, or at least, what is wiser and better than what men now practise and endure. But we let "*I dare not* wait upon *I would*, like the poor cat i' the adage."[1] We want[2] the creative faculty to imagine that which we know; we want the generous impulse to act that which we imagine; we want the poetry of life: our calculations have outrun conception; we have eaten more than we can digest. The cultivation of those sciences which have enlarged the limits of the empire of man over the external world, has, for want of the poetical faculty, proportionally circumscribed those of the internal world; and man, having enslaved the elements, remains himself a slave. To what but a cultivation of the mechanical arts in a degree disproportioned to the presence of the creative faculty, which is the basis of all knowledge, is to be attributed the abuse of all invention for abridging and combining labour, to the exasperation of the inequality of mankind? From what other cause has it arisen that these inventions which should have lightened, have added a weight to the curse imposed on Adam?[3] Poetry, and the principle of Self, of which money is the visible incarnation, are the God and Mammon of the world.[4]

The functions of the poetical faculty are two-fold; by one it creates new materials of knowledge, and power and pleasure; by the other it engenders in the mind a desire to reproduce and arrange them according to a certain rhythm and order which may be called the beautiful and the good. The cultivation of poetry is never more to be desired than at periods when, from an excess of the selfish and calculating principle, the accumulation of the materials of external life exceed the quantity of the power of assimilating them to the internal laws of human nature. The body has then become too unwieldy for that which animates it.

Poetry is indeed something divine. It is at once the centre and circumference of knowledge; it is that which comprehends all science, and that to which all science must be referred. It is at the same time the root and blossom of all other systems of thought; it is that from which all spring, and that which adorns all; and that which, if blighted, denies the fruit and the seed, and withholds from the barren world the nourishment and the succession of the scions of the tree of life. It is the perfect and consummate surface and bloom of things; it is as the odour and the colour of the rose to the texture of the elements which compose it, as the form and the splendour of unfaded beauty to the secrets of anatomy and corruption. What were Virtue, Love, Patriotism, Friendship etc.—what were the scenery of this beautiful Uni-

---

1. The words with which Lady Macbeth encourages her husband's ambition (Shakespeare, *Macbeth* 1.7.44–45).
2. Lack.
3. God says to Adam: "cursed is the ground for thy sake. . . . Thorns also and thistles shall it

bring forth. . . . In the sweat of thy face shalt thou eat bread, till thou return unto the ground" (Genesis 3.17–19).
4. Matthew 6.24: "Ye cannot serve God and Mammon."

verse which we inhabit—what were our consolations on this side of the grave—and what were our aspirations beyond it—if Poetry did not ascend to bring light and fire from those eternal regions where the owl-winged faculty of calculation dare not ever soar? Poetry is not like reasoning, a power to be exerted according to the determination of the will. A man cannot say, "I will compose poetry." The greatest poet even cannot say it: for the mind in creation is as a fading coal which some invisible influence, like an inconstant wind, awakens to transitory brightness: this power arises from within, like the colour of a flower which fades and changes as it is developed, and the conscious portions of our natures are unprophetic either of its approach or its departure. Could this influence be durable in its original purity and force, it is impossible to predict the greatness of the results; but when composition begins, inspiration is already on the decline, and the most glorious poetry that has ever been communicated to the world is probably a feeble shadow of the original conception of the poet. I appeal to the greatest Poets of the present day, whether it be not an error to assert that the finest passages of poetry are produced by labour and study. The toil and the delay recommended by critics can be justly interpreted to mean no more than a careful observation of the inspired moments, and an artificial connexion of the spaces between their suggestions by the intertexture of conventional expressions; a necessity only imposed by the limitedness of the poetical faculty itself. For Milton conceived the Paradise Lost as a whole before he executed it in portions. We have his own authority also for the Muse having "dictated" to him the "unpremeditated song,"[5] and let this be an answer to those who would allege the fifty-six various readings of the first line of the Orlando Furioso.[6] Compositions so produced are to poetry what mosaic is to painting. This instinct and intuition of the poetical faculty is still more observable in the plastic and pictorial arts: a great statue or picture grows under the power of the artist as a child in the mother's womb; and the very mind which directs the hands in formation is incapable of accounting to itself for the origin, the gradations, or the media of the process.

Poetry is the record of the best and happiest[7] moments of the happiest and best minds. We are aware of evanescent visitations of thought and feeling sometimes associated with place or person, sometimes regarding our own mind alone, and always arising unforeseen and departing unbidden, but elevating and delightful beyond all expression: so that even in the desire and the regret they leave, there cannot but be pleasure, participating as it does in the nature of its object. It is as it were the interpenetration of a diviner nature through our own; but its footsteps are like those of a wind over a sea, where the coming calm erases, and whose traces remain only as on the wrinkled sand which paves it. These and corresponding conditions of being are experienced principally by those of the most delicate sensibility[8] and the most enlarged imagination; and the state of mind produced by them is at war with every base desire. The enthusiasm of virtue, love, patriotism, and friendship is essentially linked with these emotions; and whilst they last, self appears as what it is, an atom to a Universe. Poets are not only subject to these experiences as spirits of the most refined organization, but they can colour all that they combine with the evanescent hues of this etherial world;

5. *Paradise Lost* 9.21–24.
6. The epic poem by the 16th-century Italian poet Ariosto, noted for his care in composition.

7. In the double sense of "most joyous" and "most apt or felicitous in invention."
8. Sensitivity, capacity for sympathetic feeling.

a word, or a trait in the representation of a scene or a passion, will touch the enchanted chord, and reanimate, in those who have ever experienced these emotions, the sleeping, the cold, the buried image of the past. Poetry thus makes immortal all that is best and most beautiful in the world; it arrests the vanishing apparitions which haunt the interlunations[9] of life, and veiling them or in language or in form sends them forth among mankind, bearing sweet news of kindred joy to those with whom their sisters abide—abide, because there is no portal of expression from the caverns of the spirit which they inhabit into the universe of things. Poetry redeems from decay the visitations of the divinity in man.

Poetry turns all things to loveliness; it exalts the beauty of that which is most beautiful, and it adds beauty to that which is most deformed; it marries exultation and horror, grief and pleasure, eternity and change; it subdues to union under its light yoke all irreconcilable things. It transmutes all that it touches, and every form moving within the radiance of its presence is changed by wondrous sympathy to an incarnation of the spirit which it breathes; its secret alchemy turns to potable gold[1] the poisonous waters which flow from death through life; it strips the veil of familiarity from the world, and lays bare the naked and sleeping beauty which is the spirit of its forms.

All things exist as they are perceived: at least in relation to the percipient. "The mind is its own place, and of itself can make a heaven of hell, a hell of heaven."[2] But poetry defeats the curse which binds us to be subjected to the accident of surrounding impressions. And whether it spreads its own figured curtain or withdraws life's dark veil from before the scene of things, it equally creates for us a being within our being. It makes us the inhabitants of a world to which the familiar world is a chaos. It reproduces the common universe of which we are portions and percipients, and it purges from our inward sight the film of familiarity which obscures from us the wonder of our being. It compels us to feel that which we perceive, and to imagine that which we know. It creates anew the universe after it has been annihilated in our minds by the recurrence of impressions blunted by reiteration.[3] It justifies that bold and true word of Tasso: *Non merita nome di creatore, se non Iddio ed il Poeta.*[4]

A Poet, as he is the author to others of the highest wisdom, pleasure, virtue and glory, so he ought personally to be the happiest, the best, the wisest, and the most illustrious of men. As to his glory, let Time be challenged to declare whether the fame of any other institutor of human life be comparable to that of a poet. That he is the wisest, the happiest, and the best, inasmuch as he is a poet, is equally incontrovertible: the greatest poets have been men of the most spotless virtue, of the most consummate prudence, and, if we could look into the interior of their lives, the most fortunate of men: and the exceptions, as they regard those who possessed the poetic faculty in a high yet inferior degree, will be found on consideration to confirm rather than destroy the rule. Let us for a moment stoop to the arbitration of popular breath, and

9. The dark intervals between the old and new moons.
1. Alchemists aimed to produce a drinkable ("potable") form of gold that would be an elixir of life, curing all diseases.
2. Satan's speech, *Paradise Lost* 1.254–55.
3. Shelley's version of a widespread Romantic doctrine that the poetic imagination transforms the familiar into the miraculous and re-creates the old world into a new world. See, e.g., Coleridge's

Biographia Literaria, chap. 4 (p. 495): "To carry on the feelings of childhood into the powers of manhood; to combine the child's sense of wonder and novelty with the appearances which every day for perhaps forty years has rendered familiar; . . . this is the character and privilege of genius."
4. "No one merits the name of Creator except God and the Poet." Quoted by Pierantonio Serassi in his *Life of Torquato Tasso* (1785).

usurping and uniting in our own persons the incompatible characters of accuser, witness, judge and executioner, let us decide without trial, testimony, or form that certain motives of those who are "there sitting where we dare not soar"[5] are reprehensible. Let us assume that Homer was a drunkard, that Virgil was a flatterer, that Horace was a coward, that Tasso was a madman, that Lord Bacon was a peculator, that Raphael was a libertine, that Spenser was a poet laureate.[6] It is inconsistent with this division of our subject to cite living poets, but Posterity has done ample justice to the great names now referred to. Their errors have been weighed and found to have been dust in the balance; if their sins "were as scarlet, they are now white as snow";[7] they have been washed in the blood of the mediator and the redeemer Time. Observe in what a ludicrous chaos the imputations of real or fictitious crime have been confused in the contemporary calumnies against poetry and poets;[8] consider how little is, as it appears—or appears, as it is; look to your own motives, and judge not, lest ye be judged.[9]

Poetry, as has been said, in this respect differs from logic, that it is not subject to the controul of the active powers of the mind, and that its birth and recurrence has no necessary connexion with consciousness or will. It is presumptuous to determine that these[1] are the necessary conditions of all mental causation, when mental effects are experienced insusceptible of being referred to them. The frequent recurrence of the poetical power, it is obvious to suppose, may produce in the mind an habit of order and harmony correlative with its own nature and with its effects upon other minds. But in the intervals of inspiration, and they may be frequent without being durable, a poet becomes a man, and is abandoned to the sudden reflux of the influences under which others habitually live. But as he is more delicately organized than other men, and sensible[2] to pain and pleasure, both his own and that of others, in a degree unknown to them, he will avoid the one and pursue the other with an ardour proportioned to this difference. And he renders himself obnoxious to calumny,[3] when he neglects to observe the circumstances under which these objects of universal pursuit and flight have disguised themselves in one another's garments.

But there is nothing necessarily evil in this error, and thus cruelty, envy, revenge, avarice, and the passions purely evil, have never formed any portion of the popular imputations on the lives of poets.

I have thought it most favourable to the cause of truth to set down these remarks according to the order in which they were suggested to my mind, by a consideration of the subject itself, instead of following that of the treatise that excited me to make them public.[4] Thus although devoid of the formality of a polemical reply; if the view they contain be just, they will be

5. Satan's scornful words to the angels who discover him after he has surreptitiously entered Eden: "Ye knew me once no mate / For you, sitting where ye durst not soar" (*Paradise Lost* 4.828–29).
6. Charges that had in fact been made against these men. The use of "poet laureate" as a derogatory term was a dig at Robert Southey, who held that honor at the time Shelley was writing. "Peculator": an embezzler of public money. Raphael is the 16th-century Italian painter.
7. Isaiah 1.18.
8. Shelley alludes especially to the charges of immorality by contemporary reviewers against Lord Byron and himself.

9. Christ's warning in Matthew 7.1.
1. I.e., consciousness or will. Shelley again proposes that some mental processes are unconscious—outside our control or awareness.
2. I.e., sensitive to, conscious of. Cf. Wordsworth's Preface to *Lyrical Ballads* (p. 310): "What is a poet? . . . He is a man speaking to men: a man, it is true, endued with more lively sensibility, more enthusiasm, and tenderness, who has a greater knowledge of human nature, and a more comprehensive soul, than are supposed to be common among mankind."
3. Exposed to slander.
4. Peacock's "Four Ages of Poetry."

found to involve a refutation of the doctrines of the Four Ages of Poetry, so far at least as regards the first division of the subject. I can readily conjecture what should have moved the gall of the learned and intelligent author of that paper; I confess myself, like him, unwilling to be stunned by the Theseids of the hoarse Codri of the day. Bavius and Maevius[5] undoubtedly are, as they ever were, insufferable persons. But it belongs to a philosophical critic to distinguish rather than confound.

The first part of these remarks has related to Poetry in its elements and principles; and it has been shewn, as well as the narrow limits assigned them would permit, that what is called poetry, in a restricted sense, has a common source with all other forms of order and of beauty according to which the materials of human life are susceptible of being arranged, and which is poetry in an universal sense.

The second part[6] will have for its object an application of these principles to the present state of the cultivation of Poetry, and a defence of the attempt to idealize the modern forms of manners and opinions, and compel them into a subordination to the imaginative and creative faculty. For the literature of England, an energetic developement of which has ever preceded or accompanied a great and free developement of the national will, has arisen as it were from a new birth. In spite of the low-thoughted envy which would undervalue contemporary merit, our own will be a memorable age in intellectual achievements, and we live among such philosophers and poets as surpass beyond comparison any who have appeared since the last national struggle for civil and religious liberty.[7] The most unfailing herald, companion, and follower of the awakening of a great people to work a beneficial change in opinion or institution, is Poetry. At such periods there is an accumulation of the power of communicating and receiving intense and impassioned conceptions respecting man and nature. The persons in whom this power resides, may often, as far as regards many portions of their nature, have little apparent correspondence with that spirit of good of which they are the ministers. But even whilst they deny and abjure, they are yet compelled to serve, the Power which is seated upon the throne of their own soul. It is impossible to read the compositions of the most celebrated writers of the present day without being startled with the electric life which burns within their words. They measure the circumference and sound the depths of human nature with a comprehensive and all-penetrating spirit, and they are themselves perhaps the most sincerely astonished at its manifestations, for it is less their spirit than the spirit of the age. Poets are the hierophants[8] of an unapprehended inspiration, the mirrors of the gigantic shadows which futurity casts upon the present, the words which express what they understand not; the trumpets which sing to battle, and feel not what they inspire: the influence which is moved not, but moves.[9] Poets are the unacknowledged legislators of the World.

1821   1840

---

5. Would-be poets satirized by Virgil and Horace. "Theseids": epic poems about Theseus. Codrus (plural "Codri") was the Roman author of a long, dull *Theseid* attacked by Juvenal and others. In 1794 and 1795 the conservative critic William Gifford had borrowed from Virgil and Horace and published the *Baviad* and the *Maeviad*, hard-hitting and highly influential satires on popular poetry and drama.
6. Shelley, however, completed only the first part.
7. In the age of Milton and the English Civil Wars.
8. Priests who are expositors of sacred mysteries.
9. Aristotle had said that God is the "Unmoved Mover" of the universe.

JOHN CLARE
1793–1864

S ince the mid-eighteenth century, when critics had begun to worry that the
authentic vigor of poetry was being undermined in their age of modern learning
and refinement, they had looked for untaught primitive geniuses among the nation's
peasantry. In the early-nineteenth-century literary scene, John Clare was the nearest thing to a "natural poet" there was. An earlier peasant poet, Robert Burns, had
managed to acquire a solid liberal education. Clare, however, was born at Helpston,
a Northamptonshire village, the son of a field laborer and a mother who was entirely
illiterate, and he obtained only enough schooling to enable him to read and write.
Although he was a sickly and fearful child, he had to work hard in the field, where
he found himself composing verse "for downright pleasure in giving vent to my feelings." The fragments of an autobiography that he wrote later in life describe mov-
ingly, and with humor, the stratagems that as a young man he devised to find the
time and the materials for writing. A blank notebook could cost him a week's wages.
In 1820 publication of his *Poems Descriptive of Rural Life and Scenery* attracted
critical attention, and on a trip to London, he was made much of by leading writers
of the day. But his celebrity soon dimmed, and his three later books of verse were
financial failures. Under these and other disappointments his mind gave way in 1837,
and he spent almost all the rest of his life in an asylum. The place was for him a
refuge as well as a confinement, for he was treated kindly, allowed to wander about
the countryside, and encouraged to go on writing his verses. Some of his best achievements are the poems composed during his madness.

Clare did not, of course, write independently of literary influences, for he had studied the poetry of James Thomson, William Cowper, Burns, Milton, Wordsworth, and
Coleridge. But he stayed true to his own experience of everyday country sights and
customs. His nightingale poem, written in a long-established literary tradition, has
many more particulars of nature than any of those by his predecessors, and his
homely mouse, in the "nest poem" reprinted here, is a bit of pure rustic impressionism
in a way that even Burns's moralized mouse is not (see "To a Mouse," p. 177). Some of
Clare's introspective asylum poems achieve so haunting a poignancy and are spoken
in so quietly distinctive a voice that they have made the great mass of manuscripts he
left at his death an exciting place of discovery for scholars.

Those same manuscripts have been, however, a site of contention among Clare
critics. Words are spelled erratically, and there is almost no punctuation: the pages
are cluttered with revisions and erasures. In his own day Clare was respelled, punctuated, and generally tidied up by his publisher, John Taylor. (Taylor had done the same
for John Keats, another of his poets who took a casual view of such matters.) Clare
had mixed feelings about the transformation his writings underwent as they became
printed books. Sometimes it felt like meddling. Critics and editors who propose that
Clare's works should now be published without such emendation often cite a letter he
sent to Taylor in 1822. "Grammer in learning is like Tyranny in government," Clare
wrote: "confound the bitch, I'll never be her slave." As the analogy suggests, the standardization of his language that Taylor promoted, as he tried to broaden the poems'
appeal and bring them into line with the expectations of a middle-class readership,
could to the poet feel like an instance of class oppression. (Clare's aristocratic patrons
in Northamptonshire certainly felt free to warn their protégé away from vulgarity and
rebelliousness.) On the other hand, Clare actively sought assistance in preparing his
work for the press and often acknowledged that the work was better for that assis-

tance: "If I cannot hear from John Taylor now and then I cannot rhyme." And Taylor took to print himself to dispute readers' objections to Clare's unconventional diction and their wish (as he put it) that Clare "would *thresh* and not *thump* the corn."

Between 1984 and 2003 Eric Robinson, David Powell, and P. M. S. Dawson, who number among those modern critics who believe that Clare's work should be presented without editors' emendations, took on the monumental task of transcribing Clare's thirty-five hundred manuscript poems for a nine-volume edition for Oxford University Press. Their edition aims for the utmost fidelity to the manuscripts. But in that form, however authentic, the poems can be difficult reading for an audience that is not already familiar with Clare's voice. The texts printed here are therefore presented as "reading" versions of Clare's lines and employ modern punctuation and spelling.

Life, Death, and Eternity

A shadow moving by one's side,
  That would a substance seem—
That is, yet is not,—though descried—
  Like skies beneath the stream;
5 A tree that's ever in the bloom,
  Whose fruit is never rife°;   plentiful
A wish for joys that never come—
  Such are the hopes of Life.

A dark, inevitable night,
10   A blank that will remain;
A waiting for the morning light,
  Where waiting is in vain;
A gulph, where pathway never led
  To show the depth beneath;
15 A thing we know not, yet we dread—
  That dreaded thing is Death.

The vaulted void of purple sky
  That every where extends,
That stretches from the dazzled eye,
20   In space that never ends;
A morning whose uprisen sun
  No setting e'er shall see;
A day that comes without a noon—
  Such is Eternity.

1827

The Nightingale's Nest

Up this green woodland ride° let's softly rove,   riding path
And list° the nightingale—she dwelleth here.   listen to
Hush! let the wood gate softly clap, for fear
The noise may drive her from her home of love;

5 For here I've heard her many a merry year—
 At morn and eve, nay, all the livelong day,
 As though she lived on song. This very spot,
 Just where that old man's beard[1] all wildly trails
 Rude arbours o'er the road and stops the way—
10 And where that child its blue-bell flowers hath got,
 Laughing and creeping through the mossy rails°—   *fence rails*
 There have I hunted like a very boy,
 Creeping on hands and knees through matted thorns
 To find her nest and see her feed her young.
15 And vainly did I many hours employ:
 All seemed as hidden as a thought unborn.
 And where these crimping° fern leaves ramp° among *curling / shoot up*
 The hazel's under-boughs, I've nestled down
 And watched her while she sung; and her renown
20 Hath made me marvel that so famed a bird[2]
 Should have no better dress than russet brown.
 Her wings would tremble in her ecstasy,
 And feathers stand on end, as 'twere with joy,
 And mouth wide open to release her heart
25 Of its out-sobbing songs. The happiest part
 Of summer's fame she shared, for so to me
 Did happy fancies shapen her employ;[3]
 But if I touched a bush or scarcely stirred,
 All in a moment stopt. I watched in vain:
30 The timid bird had left the hazel bush,
 And at a distance hid to sing again.
 Lost in a wilderness of listening leaves,
 Rich ecstasy would pour its luscious strain,
 Till envy spurred the emulating thrush
35 To start less wild and scarce inferior songs;
 For cares with him for half the year remain,
 To damp the ardour of his speckled breast,
 While nightingales to summer's life belongs,
 And naked trees and winter's nipping wrongs
40 Are strangers to her music and her rest.
 Her joys are evergreen, her world is wide—
 Hark! there she is as usual—let's be hush—
 For in this black-thorn clump, if rightly guessed,
 Her curious house is hidden. Part aside
45 These hazel branches in a gentle way,
 And stoop right cautious 'neath the rustling boughs,
 For we will have another search to-day,
 And hunt this fern-strewn thorn clump round and round;
 And where this seeded wood grass idly bows,
50 We'll wade right through, it is a likely nook:
 In such like spots, and often on the ground,
 They'll build where rude boys never think to look—

---

1. *Clematis vitalba*, a vine.
2. The nightingale had been celebrated by, among others, Chaucer, Spenser, Shakespeare, Milton, and, closer to Clare's time, William Cowper, Charlotte Smith, Mary Robinson, Coleridge, Wordsworth, and Keats. In lines 22, 24–25, and 33, Clare echoes lines 57–58 of Keats's "Ode to a Nightingale."
3. Give shape to her (the nightingale's) regular activities.

Aye, as I live! her secret nest is here,
Upon this whitethorn stulp°—I've searched about   *stump*
55 For hours in vain. There! put that bramble by—
Nay, trample on its branches and get near.
How subtle is the bird! she started out
And raised a plaintive note of danger nigh,
Ere we were past the brambles; and now, near
60 Her nest, she sudden stops—as° choking fear   *as if*
That might betray her home. So even now
We'll leave it as we found it: safety's guard
Of pathless solitude shall keep it still.
See, there she's sitting on the old oak bough,
65 Mute in her fears; our presence doth retard
Her joys, and doubt turns all her rapture chill.

Sing on, sweet bird! may no worse hap° befall   *fate*
Thy visions, than the fear that now deceives.
We will not plunder music of its dower,°   *dowry, gift*
70 Nor turn this spot of happiness to thrall;°   *misery*
For melody seems hid in every flower,
That blossoms near thy home. These harebells all
Seem bowing with the beautiful in song;
And gaping cuckoo° with its spotted leaves   *a spring flower*
75 Seems blushing of the singing it has heard.
How curious is the nest; no other bird
Uses such loose materials, or weaves
Their dwellings in such spots: dead oaken leaves
Are placed without, and velvet moss within,
80 And little scraps of grass, and, scant and spare,
Of what seems scarce materials, down and hair;
For from man's haunts she seemeth nought to win.
Yet nature is the builder and contrives
Homes for her children's comfort even here;
85 Where solitude's disciples spend their lives
Unseen save when a wanderer passes near
That loves such pleasant places. Deep adown,
The nest is made an hermit's mossy cell.
Snug lie her curious eggs, in number five,
90 Of deadened green, or rather olive brown;
And the old prickly thorn-bush guards them well.
And here we'll leave them, still unknown to wrong,
As the old woodland's legacy of song.

1825–30   1835

Insects

These tiny loiterers on the barley's beard
And happy units of a numerous herd
Of playfellows, the laughing Summer brings,
Mocking° the sunshine on their glittering wings.   *mimicking*

5 How merrily they creep, and run, and fly!
 No kin they bear to labour's drudgery,
 Smoothing the velvet of the pale hedge-rose,
 And where they fly for dinner no one knows—
 The dew-drops feed them not—they love the shine
10 Of noon, whose suns may bring them golden wine.
 All day they're playing in their Sunday dress—
 When night reposes, for they can do no less;
 Then, to the heath-bell's purple hood they fly,
 And like to princes in their slumbers lie,
15 Secure from rain, and dropping dews, and all,
 In silken beds and roomy painted hall.
 So merrily they spend their summer-day,
 Now in the corn-fields, now the new-mown hay,
 One almost fancies that such happy things,
20 With coloured hoods and richly burnished wings,
 Are fairy folk, in splendid masquerade
 Disguised, as if of mortal folk afraid,
 Keeping their joyous pranks a mystery still,
 Lest glaring day should do their secrets ill.

1835

The Yellowhammer's Nest

 Just by the wooden bridge a bird flew up,
 Frit° by the cowboy,° as he scrambled down   *frightened / cattle herd*
 To reach the misty dewberry[1]—Let us stoop,
 And seek its nest. The brook we need not dread—
5 'Tis scarcely deep enough a bee to drown,
 As it sings harmless o'er its pebbly bed.
 —Aye, here it is! stuck close beside the bank,
 Beneath the bunch of grass, that spindles rank
 Its husk-seeds tall and high:—'tis rudely planned
10 Of bleachèd stubbles, and the withered fare
 That last year's harvest left upon the land—
 Lined thinly with the horse's sable hair.
 Five eggs, pen-scribbled o'er with ink their shells,
 Resembling writing-scrawls, which Fancy reads
15 As Nature's poesy, and pastoral spells—
 They are the Yellowhammer's; and she dwells,
 Most poet-like, where brooks and flowery weeds
 As sweet as Castaly her fancy deems;[2]
 And that old mole-hill is Parnassus' hill,
20 On which her partner haply sits and dreams
 O'er all his joys of song. Let's leave it still
 A happy home of sunshine, flowers, and streams.

1. Species of blackberry.
2. Castaly fountain, on Mount Parnassus, the
Greek mountain sacred to the muses. Its waters
inspired those who drank them with the power
of poetry.

Yet is the sweetest place exposed to ill,
A noisome weed, that burthens every soil;
25   For snakes are known, with chill and deadly coil,
To watch such nests, and seize the helpless young;
And like as if the plague became a guest,
To leave a houseless home, a ruined nest:
Aye: mournful hath the little warbler sung
30   When such like woes have rent his gentle breast.

1825–26   1835

Pastoral Poesy

True poesy is not in words,
But images that thoughts express,
By which the simplest hearts are stirred
To elevated happiness.

5   Mere books would be but useless things
Where none had taste or mind to read,
Like unknown lands where beauty springs
And none are there to heed.

But poesy is a language meet,°   *suitable, proper*
10   And fields are every one's employ;°   *concern*
The wild flower 'neath the shepherd's feet
Looks up and gives him joy;

A language that is ever green,
That feelings unto all impart,
15   As hawthorn blossoms, soon as seen,
Give May to every heart.

The pictures that our summer minds
In summer's dwellings meet;
The fancies that the shepherd finds
20   To make his leisure sweet;

The dust mills that the cowboy delves
In banks for dust to run,[1]
Creates a summer in ourselves—
He does as we have done.

25   An image to the mind is brought,
Where happiness enjoys
An easy thoughtlessness of thought
And meets excess of joys.

---

1. The boy tending the cows has (as an amusement) dug miniature millstreams in the dirt.

The world is in that little spot
30 With him—and all beside
Is nothing, all a life forgot,
In feelings satisfied.

And such is poesy; its power
May varied lights employ,
35 Yet to all minds it gives the dower
Of self-creating joy.

And whether it be hill or moor,
I feel where'er I go
A silence that discourses more
40 That any tongue can do.

Unruffled quietness hath made
A peace in every place,
And woods are resting in their shade
Of social loneliness.

45 The storm, from which the shepherd turns
To pull his beaver° down,   *beaver hat*
While he upon the heath sojourns,
Which autumn bleaches brown,

Is music, aye, and more indeed
50 To those of musing mind
Who through the yellow woods proceed
And listen to the wind.

The poet in his fitful glee
And fancy's many moods
55 Meets it as some strange melody,
And poem of the woods.

It sings and whistles in his mind,
And then it talks aloud,
While by some leaning tree reclined
60 He shuns a coming cloud,

That sails its bulk against the sun,
A mountain in the light—
He heeds not for the storm begun
But dallies with delight.

65 And now a harp that flings around
The music of the wind,
The poet often hears the sound
When beauty fills the mind.

The morn with saffron° strips and gray,   *orange-yellow*
70 Or blushing to the view,
Like summer fields when run away
In weeds of crimson hue,

Will simple shepherds' hearts imbue
With nature's poesy,
75 Who inly fancy while they view
How grand must heaven be.

With every musing mind she steals
Attendance[2] on their way;
The simplest thing her heart reveals
80 Is seldom thrown away.

The old man, full of leisure hours,
Sits cutting at his door
Rude fancy sticks to tie his flowers
—They're sticks and nothing more

85 With many passing by his door—
But pleasure has its bent;°   *inclination*
With him 'tis happiness and more,
Heart satisfied content.

Those box-edged borders that impart
90 Their fragrance near his door
Hath been the comfort of his heart
For sixty years and more.

That mossy thatch above his head
In winter's drifting showers
95 To him and his old partner made
A music many hours.

It patted to their hearts a joy[3]
That humble comfort made—
A little fire to keep them dry
100 And shelter over head.

And such no matter what they call
Each all are nothing less
Than poesy's power that gives to all
A cheerful blessedness.

105 So would I my own mind employ,
And my own heart impress,
That poesy's self's a dwelling joy
Of humble quietness.

So would I for the biding° joy   *abiding, lasting*
110 That to such thoughts belong,
That I life's errand may employ
As harmless as a song.

1824–32   1935

2. She (nature) demands attention (to her beauties).
3. The patter of the rain on the thatch (lines 93–94) enhanced the comfort of the fire and shelter indoors.

[The Lament of Swordy Well][1]

Petitioners are full of prayers
To fall in pity's way,
But if her hand the gift forbears
They'll sooner swear than pray.
5   They're not the worst to want who lurch
On plenty with complaints,
No more than those who go to church
Are e'er the better saints.

I hold no hat to beg a mite
10   Nor pick it up when thrown,
Nor limping leg I hold in sight
But pray to keep me own.
Where profit gets his clutches in
There's little he will leave;
15   Gain stooping for a single pin
Will stick it on his sleeve.

For passers-by I never pin
No troubles to my breast,
Nor carry round some names to win,
20   More money from the rest.
I'm Swordy Well, a piece of land
That's fell upon the town,
Who worked me till I couldn't stand
And crush me now I'm down.

25   In parish bonds I well may wail,
Reduced to every shift;
Pity may grieve at trouble's tale,
But cunning shares the gift.
Harvests with plenty on his brow
30   Leaves losses' taunts with me,
Yet gain comes yearly with the plough
And will not let me be.

Alas, dependence thou'rt a brute
Want° only understands;   *poverty*
35   His feelings wither branch and root
That falls in parish hands.
The muck that clouts the ploughman's shoe,
The moss that hides the stone,

1. Located near Clare's native village, Helpston, Swordy Well, also known as Swaddywell, was an ancient stone quarry first used by the Romans. During Clare's youth, waste grounds like these, formerly places where poor families gathered fuel or found pasturage for their cows or horses, were, through Acts of Parliament, enclosed—converted to private property and fenced off from the community. As part of this enclosures movement, Swordy Well was handed over to overseers of the parish roads to be used for mending-stone. Clare's poem, unpublished and untitled during his lifetime, gives this piece of land a voice with which to lament its misfortunes. Swordy Well speaks in the tones of a laboring man who hates how enclosure has made him a charity case.

Now I'm become the parish due
40 Is more than I can own.

Though I'm no man yet any wrong
Some sort of right may seek;
And I am glad if e'en a song
Gives me the room to speak.
45 I've got among such grubbling gear[2]
And such a hungry pack,
If I brought harvests twice a year,
They'd bring me nothing back.

When war their tyrant prices got,
50 I trembled with alarms;
They fell and saved my little spot,
Or towns had turned to farms.
Let profit keep an humble place
That gentry may be known;
55 Let pedigrees their honours trace
And toil enjoy its own.

The silver springs grown naked dykes
Scarce own a bunch of rushes;
When grain got high the tasteless tykes°   country bumpkins
60 Grubbed up trees, banks, and bushes,
And me, they turned me inside out
For sand and grit and stones
And turned my old green hills about
And picked my very bones.

65 These things that claim my own as theirs
Were born but yesterday,
But ere I fell to town affairs
I were as proud as they.
I kept my horses, cows, and sheep
70 And built the town below
Ere they had cat or dog to keep—
And then to use me so.

Parish allowance, gaunt and dread,
Had it the earth to keep
75 Would even pine° the bees to dead   torment
To save an extra keep.
Pride's workhouse[3] is a place that yields
From poverty its gains
And mine's a workhouse for the fields
80 A-starving the remains.

The bees fly round in feeble rings
And find no blossom by,

___

2. I.e., people digging for wealth, money-grubbers.
3. An institution where the able-bodied poor who sought help from the parish were confined and set to work.

Then thrum° their almost weary wings   *beat*
Upon the moss and die.
85   Rabbits that find my hills turned o'er
Forsake my poor abode;
They dread a workhouse like the poor
And nibble on the road.

If with a clover bottle now
90   Spring dares to lift her head,
The next day brings the hasty plough
And makes me misery's bed.
The butterflies may whir and come,
I cannot keep 'em now,
95   Nor can they bear my parish home
That withers on my brow.

No, now not e'en a stone can lie,
I'm just what e'er they like;
My hedges like the winter fly
100   And leave me but the dyke;
My gates are thrown from off the hooks,
The parish thoroughfare:
Lord, he that's in the parish books
Has little wealth to spare.

105   I couldn't keep a dust of grit
Nor scarce a grain of sand,
But bags and carts claimed every bit,
And now they've got the land.
I used to bring the summer's life
110   To many a butterfly,
But in oppression's iron strife
Dead tussocks° bow and sigh.   *tufts of grass*

I've scarce a nook to call my own
For things that creep or fly;
115   The beetle hiding 'neath a stone
Does well to hurry by;
Stock⁴ eats my struggles every day
As bare as any road;
He's sure to be in something's way
120   If e'er he stirs abroad.

I am no man to whine and beg,
But fond of freedom still,
I hing° no lies on pity's peg   *hang*
To bring a grist to mill;
125   On pity's back I needn't jump,
My looks speak loud alone:
My only tree they've left a stump
And nought remains my own.

---

4. Generic term for a stupid person.

My mossy hills gain's greedy hand,
130 And more than greedy mind,
Levels into a russet land,
Nor leaves a bent° behind.   *blade of grass*
In summers gone I bloomed in pride,
Folks came for miles to prize
135 My flowers that bloomed nowhere beside
And scarce believed their eyes.

Yet worried with a greedy pack,
They rend and delve and tear
The very grass from off my back—
140 I've scarce a rag to wear.
Gain takes my freedom all away
Since its dull suit I wore,
And yet scorn vows I never pay
And hurts me more and more.

145 And should the price of grain get high—
Lord help and keep it low—
I shan't possess a single fly
Or get a weed to grow;
I shan't possess a yard of ground
150 To bid a mouse to thrive,
For gain has put me in a pound,
I scarce can keep alive.

I own I'm poor like many more,
But then the poor mun° live,   *must*
155 And many came for miles before
For what I had to give;
But since I fell upon the town
They pass me with a sigh;
I've scarce the room to say sit down
160 And so they wander by.

Though now I seem so full of clack,°   *chatter*
Yet when yer' riding by
The very birds upon my back
Are not more fain to fly.
165 I feel so lorn° in this disgrace,   *forlorn*
God send the grain to fall;
I am the oldest in the place
And the worst served of all.

Lord bless ye, I was kind to all,
170 And poverty in me
Could always find a humble stall,
A rest and lodging free.
Poor bodies with an hungry ass
I welcomed many a day,
175 And gave him tether, room, and grass,
And never said him nay.

There was a time my bit of ground
Made freemen of the slave;
The ass no pindar'd[5] dare to pound
180 When I his supper gave.
The gypsies' camp was not afraid,
I made his dwelling free,
Till vile enclosure came and made
A parish slave of me.

185 The gypsies further on sojourn,
No parish bounds they like.
No sticks I own, and would earth burn,
I shouldn't own a dyke.
I am no friend to lawless work,
190 Nor would a rebel be,
And why I call a Christian Turk[6]
Is they are Turks to me.

And if I could but find a friend
With no deceit to sham,
195 Who'd send me some few sheep to tend,
And leave me as I am,
To keep my hills from cart and plough
And strife of mongrel men,
And as spring found me find me now,
200 I should look up again.

And save his Lordship's woods that past
The day of danger dwell,
Of all the fields I am the last
That my own face can tell.
205 Yet what with stone pits' delving holes
And strife to buy and sell,
My name will quickly be the whole,
That's left of Swordy Well.

1832–37   1935

[Mouse's Nest]

I found a ball of grass among the hay
And progged° it as I passed and went away;   *prodded*
And when I looked I fancied something stirred,
And turned again and hoped to catch the bird—
5   When out an old mouse bolted in the wheat
With all her young ones hanging at her teats;
She looked so odd and so grotesque to me,
I ran and wondered what the thing could be,

---

5. A pindar is a person in charge of impounding stray animals.
6. Common designation for a cruel and barbaric person.

And pushed the knapweed[1] bunches where I stood,
10 When the mouse hurried from the crawling brood.
The young ones squeaked, and when I went away
She found her nest again among the hay.
The water o'er the pebbles scarce could run
And broad old cesspools[2] glittered in the sun.

1835–37   1935

[The Badger]

The badger grunting on his woodland track
With shaggy hide and sharp nose scrowed° with black   *marked, scratched*
Roots in the bushes and the woods, and makes
A great huge burrow in the ferns and brakes.°   *bracken*
5   With nose on ground he runs an awkward pace,
And anything will beat him in the race.
The shepherd's dog will run him to his den
Followed and hooted by the dogs and men.
The woodman when the hunting comes about
10 Goes round at night to stop the foxes out[1]
And hurrying through the bushes, ferns, and brakes
Nor sees the many holes the badger makes,
And often through the bushes to the chin
Breaks the old holes, and tumbles headlong in.

15 When midnight comes a host of dogs and men
Go out and track the badger to his den,
And put a sack within the hole and lie
Till the old grunting badger passes by.[2]
He comes and hears—they let the strongest loose.
20 The old fox hears the noise[3] and drops the goose.
The poacher shoots and hurries from the cry,
And the old hare half wounded buzzes by.
They get a forkèd stick to bear him down
And clap° the dogs and bear him to the town,   *urge on*
25 And bait him all the day with many dogs,[4]
And laugh and shout and fright the scampering hogs.
He runs along and bites at all he meets;
They shout and hollo° down the noisy streets.   *holler*

1. A plant with knobs of purple flowers.
2. Rainwater pools on the surface of a peat bog (a "cess"). In the manuscript Clare in fact spelled this word "sexpools," perhaps deliberately testing readers' tolerance.
1. To ensure that there will be foxes for the hunters to pursue on the day of the hunt, the woodman blocks up, or *stops*, the mouths of the animals' dens the night before.
2. By letting loose the dog, the badger hunters mean to force their quarry to bolt into its hole, where it will get entangled in the sack that they have placed there.
3. In a manuscript on natural history, Clare commented on the horror that a badger's screams—"like those of a woman under the agonys of murder"—could induce in listeners.
4. In Clare's lifetime, middle- and upper-class commentators were increasingly vocal in their condemnations of badger baiting, a sport in which human beings would set their dogs on a badger and watch the ensuing battle. Parliament in 1835 passed laws that made it a misdemeanor to arrange such fights, doing so in spite of this blood sport's undiminished popularity among men of the rural working class. Fox hunting, a blood sport enjoyed by the aristocracy, was not banned until 2004.

He turns about to face the loud uproar
30 And drives the rebels to their very doors.
The frequent stone is hurled where'er they go;
When badgers fight, and every one's a foe.
The dogs are clapped and urged to join the fray,
The badger turns and drives them all away.
35 Though scarcely half as big, dimute and small,
He fights with dogs for hours and beats them all.
The heavy mastiff, savage in the fray,
Lies down and licks his feet and turns away.
The bulldog knows his match and waxes cold,
40 The badger grins and never leaves his hold.
He drives the crowd and follows at their heels
And bites them through—the drunkard swears and reels.

The frighted women take the boys away,
The blackguard° laughs and hurries on the fray.   *despicable fellow*
45 He tries to reach the woods, an awkward race,
But sticks and cudgels quickly stop the chase.
He turns again and drives the noisy crowd
And beats the many dogs in noises loud.
He drives away and beats them every one,
50 And then they loose them all and set them on.
He falls as dead and kicked by boys and men,
Then starts and grins and drives the crowd again,
Till kicked and torn and beaten out he lies
And leaves his hold and cackles, groans, and dies.

55 Some keep a baited badger tame as hog[5]
And tame him till he follows like the dog.
They urge him on like dogs and show fair play.
He beats and scarcely wounded goes away.
Lapt up as if asleep, he scorns to fly
60 And seizes any dog that ventures nigh.
Clapped like a dog, he never bites the men,
But worries dogs and hurries to his den.
They let him out and turn a barrow° down   *barrel*
And there he fights the host of all the town.
65 He licks the patting hand, and tries to play
And never tries to bite or run away,
And runs away from the noise in hollow trees
Burnt by the boys to get a swarm of bees.

1832–37   1920

---

5. The baited badger would sometimes be pursued through the village streets by dogs and people, as in lines 29–54, but this concluding sonnet in Clare's sequence describes an alternative form of baiting, according to David Perkins (*Romanticism* *and Animal Rights* [Cambridge UP, 2003], p. 168, n. 31). Here a semi-tamed badger is placed in a barrel and various dog owners compete to see whose dog can drag it out.

A Vision

1

I lost the love of heaven above;
I spurn'd the lust of earth below;
I felt the sweets of fancied love,—
And hell itself my only foe.

2

5   I lost earth's joys but felt the glow
Of heaven's flame abound in me:
Till loveliness and I did grow
The bard of immortality.

3

I loved, but woman fell away;
10   I hid me from her faded fame:
I snatch'd the sun's eternal ray,—
And wrote till earth was but a name.

4

In every language upon earth,
On every shore, o'er every sea,
15   I gave my name immortal birth,
And kept my spirit with the free.

Aug. 2, 1844   1924

I Am

1

I am—yet what I am, none cares or knows;
    My friends forsake me like a memory lost:—
I am the self-consumer of my woes;—
    They rise and vanish in oblivion's host,
5   Like shadows in love's frenzied stifled throes:—
And yet I am, and live—like vapours tossed

2

Into the nothingness of scorn and noise,—
    Into the living sea of waking dreams,
Where there is neither sense of life or joys,
10   But the vast shipwreck of my life's esteems;
Even the dearest that I love the best
Are strange—nay, rather, stranger than the rest.

3

I long for scenes where man hath never trod,
   A place where woman never smiled or wept,
15 There to abide with my Creator, God,
   And sleep as I in childhood sweetly slept,
Untroubling and untroubled where I lie,
The grass below—above, the vaulted sky.

1842–46   1848

An Invite to Eternity

1

Wilt thou go with me, sweet maid,
Say maiden, wilt thou go with me
Through the valley depths of shade,
Of night and dark obscurity,
5 Where the path hath lost its way,
Where the sun forgets the day,
Where there's nor life nor light to see,
Sweet maiden, wilt thou go with me?

2

Where stones will turn to flooding streams,
10 Where plains will rise like ocean waves,
Where life will fade like visioned dreams
And mountains darken into caves,
Say maiden, wilt thou go with me
Through this sad non-identity,
15 Where parents live and are forgot
And sisters live and know us not?

3

Say maiden, wilt thou go with me
In this strange death of life to be,
To live in death and be the same
20 Without this life, or home, or name,
At once to be and not to be,
That was and is not—yet to see
Things pass like shadows—and the sky
Above, below, around us lie?

4

25 The land of shadows wilt thou trace
And look—nor know each other's face,
The present mixed with reasons gone
And past and present all as one?
Say maiden, can thy life be led
30 To join the living with the dead?

Then trace thy footsteps on with me—
We're wed to one eternity.

1847   1848

Clock a Clay[1]

1

In the cowslip's peeps I lie,[2]
Hidden from the buzzing fly,
While green grass beneath me lies,
Pearled wi' dew like fishes' eyes;
5   Here I lie, a Clock a Clay,
Waiting for the time o' day.

2

While grassy forests quake surprise,
And the wild wind sobs and sighs,
My gold home rocks as like to fall
10   On its pillars green and tall;
When the pattering rain drives by
Clock a Clay keeps warm and dry.

3

Day by day and night by night,
All the week I hide from sight;
15   In the cowslip's peeps I lie,
In rain and dew still warm and dry;
Day and night and night and day,
Red black-spotted Clock a Clay.

4

My home it shakes in wind and showers,
20   Pale green pillar topped wi' flowers,
Bending at the wild wind's breath,
Till I touch the grass beneath;
Here still I live, lone Clock a Clay,
Watching for the time of day.

ca. 1848   1873

---

1. The ladybird, or ladybug. The sixth and last
lines allude to the children's game of telling the
hour by the number of taps it takes to make the
ladybird fly away home.
2. Cf. the opening lines of Ariel's song in act 5 of

Shakespeare's *The Tempest*: "Where the bee
sucks, there suck I: / In a cowslip's bell I lie."
"Cowslip": a yellow primrose. "Peeps": i.e., pips—
single blossoms of flowers growing in a cluster.

The Peasant Poet

He loved the brook's soft sound,
The swallow swimming by;
He loved the daisy-covered ground,
The cloud-bedappled sky.
5   To him the dismal storm appeared
The very voice of God,
And where the evening rack° was reared   *mass of clouds*
Stood Moses with his rod.
And everything his eyes surveyed,
10 The insects i' the brake,
Were creatures God Almighty made—
He loved them for his sake:
A silent man in life's affairs,
A thinker from a boy,
15 A peasant in his daily cares—
The poet in his joy.

1842–64   1920

FELICIA DOROTHEA HEMANS
1793–1835

Born in Liverpool and brought up in Wales, Felicia Hemans published her first two volumes—*Poems* and *England and Spain, or Valour and Patriotism*—when she was fifteen. She followed these four years later with *The Domestic Affections and Other Poems* (1812) and from 1816 on into the 1830s produced new books of poetry almost annually: short sentimental lyrics, tales and "historic scenes," translations, songs for music, sketches of women, hymns for children. She also published literary criticism in magazines and wrote three plays. Her work was widely read, anthologized, memorized, and set to music throughout the nineteenth century and was especially popular and influential in the United States, where the first of many collected editions of her poems appeared in 1825. When she died she was eulogized by many poets, including William Wordsworth, Letitia Landon, and Elizabeth Barrett—a sign of the high regard in which she was held by her contemporaries.

    A tablet erected by her brothers in the cathedral of St. Asaph, in north Wales, reads in part, "In memory of Felicia Hemans, whose character is best pourtrayed in her writings." But there are several characters in her poems, and some of them seem not entirely compatible with some of the others. She is frequently thought of as the poet (in the nineteenth century as "the poetess") of domestic affections, at the center of a cult of domesticity in which the home is conceptualized as a haven apart from the stresses of the public world, to which only men are suited. Her poems have been viewed as celebrations of a feminine ethic founded on women's— especially mothers'—capacities for forbearance, piety, and long suffering. Among her most popular pieces in this vein, "Evening Prayer, at a Girls' School" depicts the happy ignorance of schoolgirls whose enjoyment of life will end when they reach womanhood, and "Indian Woman's Death-Song" is the lament of a Native American woman whose husband has abandoned her, sung as she plunges in her canoe over a cataract to suicide with an infant in her arms.

Many of Hemans's longer narratives, by contrast, recount the exploits of women warriors who, to avenge personal, family, or national injustice or insult, destroy enemies in a manner not conventionally associated with female behavior. In *The Widow of Crescentius*, Stephania stalks and poisons the German emperor Otho, the murderer of her husband; in "The Wife of Asdrubal," a mother publicly kills her own children and herself to show contempt for her husband, a betrayer of the Carthaginians whom he governed; the heroine of "The Bride of the Greek Isle," boarding the ship of the pirates who have killed her husband, annihilates them (and herself) in a conflagration rivaling the monumental explosion described in "Casabianca." Among the numerous themes of her work, patriotism and military action recur frequently; there may be a biographical basis for these motifs, given that her two oldest brothers distinguished themselves in the Peninsular War and her military husband (who deserted her and their five sons in 1818) had also served in Spain. But some of her most famous patriotic and military poems are now being viewed as critiques of the virtues and ideologies they had been thought by earlier readers to inculcate. "The Homes of England," for example, has been read as both asserting and undermining the idea that all homes are equal, ancestral estates and cottages alike; and in "Casabianca," the boy's automatic steadfastness has been interpreted as empty obedience rather than admirable loyalty.

Hemans was the highest paid writer in *Blackwood's Magazine* during her day. Her books sold more copies than those of any other contemporary poet except Byron and Walter Scott. She was a shrewd calculator of the literary marketplace and a genius in her negotiations with publishers (which she carried on entirely through the mails). Her self-abasing women of the domestic affections and her scimitar-wielding superwomen of the revenge narratives exist side by side throughout her works. These and other seeming dissonances clearly enhanced the strong appeal of her poems to a wide range of readers, men as well as women.

England's Dead

Son of the ocean isle!
Where sleep your mighty dead?
Show me what high and stately pile
Is rear'd o'er Glory's bed.

5   Go, stranger! track the deep,
Free, free the white sail spread!
Wave may not foam, nor wild wind sweep,
Where rest not England's dead.

On Egypt's burning plains,
10   By the pyramid o'ersway'd,
With fearful power the noonday reigns,
And the palm trees yield no shade.[1]

---

1. English forces defeated the French at Alexandria in the spring of 1801. The rest of the references—to 18th- and early-19th-century battles in India (lines 17–24), America (lines 25–32), Spain (lines 33–40), and on the sea (lines 41–48)—are more general.

But let the angry sun
From heaven look fiercely red,
15   Unfelt by those whose task is done!—
There slumber England's dead.

The hurricane hath might
Along the Indian shore,
And far by Ganges' banks at night,
20   Is heard the tiger's roar.

But let the sound roll on!
It hath no tone of dread,
For those that from their toils are gone;—
There slumber England's dead.

25   Loud rush the torrent floods
The western wilds among,
And free, in green Columbia's woods,
The hunter's bow is strung.

But let the floods rush on!
30   Let the arrow's flight be sped!
Why should *they* reck whose task is done?—
There slumber England's dead!

The mountain storms rise high
In the snowy Pyrenees,
35   And toss the pine boughs through the sky,
Like rose leaves on the breeze.

But let the storm rage on!
Let the fresh wreaths be shed!
For the Roncesvalles' field[2] is won,—
40   *There* slumber England's dead.

On the frozen deep's repose
'Tis a dark and dreadful hour,
When round the ship the ice-fields close,
And the northern night clouds lower.

45   But let the ice drift on!
Let the cold-blue desert spread!
Their course with mast and flag is done,—
Even there sleep England's dead.

The warlike of the isles,
50   The men of field and wave!
Are not the rocks their funeral piles,
The seas and shores their grave?

---

2. Roncesvalles, the mountain pass in the Pyrenees between France and Spain, was a scene of action
during the Peninsular War (1808–14).

Go, stranger! track the deep,
 Free, free the white sail spread!
55 Wave may not foam, nor wild wind sweep,
 Where rest not England's dead.

1822

Casabianca[1]

The boy stood on the burning deck
 Whence all but he had fled;
The flame that lit the battle's wreck
 Shone round him o'er the dead.

5 Yet beautiful and bright he stood,
 As born to rule the storm;
A creature of heroic blood,
 A proud, though childlike form.

The flames roll'd on—he would not go
10 Without his Father's word;
That Father, faint in death below,
 His voice no longer heard.

He call'd aloud:—"Say, Father, say
 If yet my task is done?"
15 He knew not that the chieftain lay
 Unconscious of his son.

"Speak, Father!" once again he cried,
 "If I may yet be gone!
And"—but the booming shots replied,
20 And fast the flames roll'd on.

Upon his brow he felt their breath,
 And in his waving hair,
And look'd from that lone post of death
 In still, yet brave despair.

25 And shouted but once more aloud,
 "My Father! must I stay?"
While o'er him fast, through sail and shroud,
 The wreathing fires made way.

They wrapt the ship in splendour wild,
30 They caught the flag on high,
And stream'd above the gallant child,
 Like banners in the sky.

1. Young Casabianca, a boy about thirteen years old, son to the Admiral of the *Orient*, remained at his post (in the Battle of the Nile) after the ship had taken fire, and all the guns had been abandoned; and perished in the explosion of the vessel, when the flames had reached the powder [Hemans's note]. The Battle of the Nile, in which Nelson captured and destroyed the French fleet in Aboukir Bay, took place on August 1, 1798. Admiral Casabianca and his son (who was in fact only ten) were among those killed by the British forces.

There came a burst of thunder sound—
The boy—oh! where was he?
35 Ask of the winds that far around
With fragments strew'd the sea!—

With mast, and helm, and pennon fair,
That well had borne their part,
But the noblest thing which perish'd there
40 Was that young faithful heart!

1826

Corinne at the Capitol[1]

Les femmes doivent penser qu'il est dans cette carrière bien peu
de sorte qui puissent valoir la plus obscure vie d'une femme
aimée et d'une mère heureuse.

MADAME DE STAEL[2]

Daughter of th' Italian heaven!
Thou, to whom its fires are given,
Joyously thy car° hath roll'd   chariot
Where the conqueror's pass'd of old;
5 And the festal sun that shone,
O'er three[3] hundred triumphs gone,
Makes thy day of glory bright,
With a shower of golden light.

Now thou tread'st th'ascending road,
10 Freedom's foot so proudly trode;
While, from tombs of heroes borne,
From the dust of empire shorn,
Flowers upon thy graceful head,
Chaplets° of all hues, are shed,   wreaths
15 In a soft and rosy rain,
Touch'd with many a gemlike stain.

Thou hast gain'd the summit now!
Music hails thee from below;—
Music, whose rich notes might stir
20 Ashes of the sepulchre;
Shaking with victorious notes

1. Hemans's poem comments on one of the most famous and controversial novels of early-19th-century Europe, *Corinne, or Italy* (1807), by the Swiss-French writer Germaine de Staël, and particularly on its second book, in which Staël's heroine, an *improvisatrice* (a poet who speaks from rhapsodic inspiration rather than texts) is crowned at the Capitol in Rome in recognition of her genius, as Petrarch had been crowned in the 14th century. Corinne's triumph is short-lived, and at the novel's close, abandoned by her Scottish lover, she dies of a broken heart. Hemans confessed in a letter that some passages in *Corinne* "seem to give me back my own thoughts and feel-ings, my whole inner being, with a mirror more true than ever friend could hold up."
2. "Women must recognize that very little in this career equals in value the most obscure life of a beloved wife and happy mother." From Staël's *De l'Influence des Passions sur le Bonheur des Individus et des Nations* (*On the Influence of the Passions on the Happiness of Individuals and Nations*; 1796).
3. The trebly hundred triumphs—BYRON [Hemans's note]. From a stinging account in *Childe Harold* (4.731) of the celebrations that greeted imperial Rome's victorious heroes.

All the bright air as it floats.
Well may woman's heart beat high
Unto that proud harmony!

25 Now afar it rolls—it dies—
And thy voice is heard to rise
With a low and lovely tone
In its thrilling power alone;
And thy lyre's deep silvery string,
30 Touch'd as by a breeze's wing,
Murmurs tremblingly at first,
Ere the tide of rapture burst.

All the spirit of thy sky
Now hath lit thy large dark eye,
35 And thy cheek a flush hath caught
From the joy of kindled thought;
And the burning words of song
From thy lip flow fast and strong,
With a rushing stream's delight
40 In the freedom of its might.

Radiant daughter of the sun!
Now thy living wreath is won.
Crown'd of Rome!—Oh! art thou not
Happy in that glorious lot?—
45 Happier, happier far than thou,
With the laurel[4] on thy brow,
She that makes the humblest hearth
Lovely but to one on earth!

1827   1827

The Homes of England

> Where's the coward that would not dare
> To fight for such a land?
> —*Marmion*[1]

The stately Homes of England,
    How beautiful they stand!
Amidst their tall ancestral trees,
    O'er all the pleasant land.
5 The deer across their greensward bound
    Through shade and sunny gleam,
And the swan glides past them with the sound
    Of some rejoicing stream.

4. Wreaths of laurel were bestowed on honored poets in classical antiquity.
1. From Sir Walter Scott's long poem *Marmion* (1808), 4.633–34, a tale of betrayal and bloody conflict between the English and the Scots. When she first published the poem, in *Blackwood's*, April 1827, Hemans used as epigraph a passage from the work of another Scottish author, Joanna Baillie's *Ethwald: A Tragedy*, part 2 (1802), 1.2.76–82.

The merry Homes of England!
10   Around their hearths by night,
What gladsome looks of household love
    Meet in the ruddy light!
There woman's voice flows forth in song,
    Or childhood's tale is told,
15 Or lips move tunefully along
    Some glorious page of old.

The blessed Homes of England!
    How softly on their bowers
Is laid the holy quietness
20   That breathes from Sabbath-hours!
Solemn, yet sweet, the church-bell's chime
    Floats through their woods at morn;
All other sounds, in that still time,
    Of breeze and leaf are born.

25 The Cottage Homes of England!
    By thousands on her plains,
They are smiling o'er the silvery brooks,
    And round the hamlet-fanes.°   *village churches*
Through glowing orchards forth they peep,
30   Each from its nook of leaves,
And fearless there the lowly sleep,
    As the bird beneath their eaves.

The free, fair Homes of England!
    Long, long, in hut and hall,
35 May hearts of native proof be rear'd
    To guard each hallow'd wall!
And green for ever be the groves,
    And bright the flowery sod,
Where first the child's glad spirit loves
40   Its country and its God!

1827

Properzia Rossi

Properzia Rossi, a celebrated female sculptor of Bologna, possessed also of talents for poetry and music, died in consequence of an unrequited attachment.—A painting by Ducis represents her showing her last work, a basso-relievo of Ariadne, to a Roman Knight, the object of her affection, who regards it with indifference.[1]

> ————Tell me no more, no more
> Of my soul's lofty gifts! Are they not vain
> To quench its haunting thirst for happiness?
> Have I not lov'd, and striven, and fail'd to bind
> One true heart unto me, whereon my own
> Might find a resting-place, a home for all
> Its burden of affections? I depart,
> Unknown, tho' Fame goes with me; I must leave
> The earth unknown. Yet it may be that death
> Shall give my name a power to win such tears
> As would have made life precious.[2]

I

One dream of passion and of beauty more!
And in its bright fulfilment let me pour
My soul away! Let earth retain a trace
Of that which lit my being, tho' its race
5   Might have been loftier far.—Yet one more dream!
From my deep spirit one victorious gleam
Ere I depart! For thee alone, for thee!
May this last work, this farewell triumph be,
Thou, lov'd so vainly! I would leave enshrined
10   Something immortal of my heart and mind,
That yet may speak to thee when I am gone,
Shaking thine inmost bosom with a tone
Of lost affection;—something that may prove
What she hath been, whose melancholy love
15   On thee was lavish'd; silent pang and tear,
And fervent song, that gush'd when none were near,
And dream by night, and weary thought by day,
Stealing the brightness from her life away,—
While thou————Awake! not yet within me die.
20   Under the burden and the agony
Of this vain tenderness,—my spirit, wake!
Ev'n for thy sorrowful affection's sake,
Live! in thy work breathe out!—that he may yet,
Feeling sad mastery there, perchance regret
25   Thine unrequited gift.

1. Establishing her poem's connection to a tradition of ecphrastic verse, Hemans's initial note refers to two visual artists: Properzia de Rossi (ca. 1490–1530), the female sculptor active in early-16th-century Italy, whose life was recounted in Giorgio Vasari's *Lives of the Artists* (1550; 2nd ed., 1568); and Louis Ducis (1775–1847), the French painter who between 1818 and 1822 had exhibited at the Louvre a series of allegorical paintings representing the various arts "under the influence of love." The painting that Ducis devotes to the art of sculpture depicts Properzia de Rossi as she unveils her bas-relief sculpture of Ariadne to a man in Renaissance dress. He has that man regard her work, or perhaps Properzia herself, with evident admiration, however. The "indifference" that Hemans mentions in this note is her addition.
2. The blank verse epigraph is by Hemans.

II

It comes,—the power
Within me born, flows back; my fruitless dower°   *gift*
That could not win me love. Yet once again
I greet it proudly, with its rushing train
30   Of glorious images:—they throng—they press—
A sudden joy lights up my loneliness,—
I shall not perish all!
                    The bright work grows
Beneath my hand, unfolding, as a rose,
35   Leaf after leaf, to beauty; line by line,
I fix my thought, heart, soul, to burn, to shine,
Thro' the pale marble's veins. It grows—and now
I give my own life's history to thy brow,
Forsaken Ariadne![3] thou shalt wear
40   My form, my lineaments; but oh! more fair,
Touch'd into lovelier being by the glow
    Which in me dwells, as by the summer-light
All things are glorified. From thee my woe
    Shall yet look beautiful to meet his sight,
45   When I am pass'd away. Thou art the mould
Wherein I pour the fervent thoughts, th' untold,
The self-consuming! Speak to him of me,
Thou, the deserted by the lonely sea,
With the soft sadness of thine earnest eye,
50   Speak to him, lorn° one, deeply, mournfully,   *forlorn*
Of all my love and grief! Oh! could I throw
Into thy frame a voice, a sweet, and low,
And thrilling voice of song! when he came nigh,
To send the passion of its melody
55   Thro' his pierced bosom—on its tones to bear
My life's deep feeling, as the southern air
Wafts the faint myrtle's breath,—to rise, to swell,
To sink away in accents of farewell,
Winning but one, *one* gush of tears, whose flow
60   Surely my parted spirit yet might know,
If love be strong as death!

III

Now fair thou art,
Thou form, whose life is of my burning heart!
Yet all the vision that within me wrought,
65   I cannot make thee! Oh! I might have given
Birth to creations of far nobler thought,
    I might have kindled, with the fire of heaven,
Things not of such as die! But I have been
Too much alone; a heart, whereon to lean,
70   With all these deep affections that o'erflow

3. In Greek mythology, Ariadne, daughter of King Minos of Crete, in love with the Greek prince Theseus, helped Theseus defeat the monstrous Minotaur by teaching him how to find his way out of the labyrinth in which he had been imprisoned as a sacrifice to the monster. Theseus married Ariadne, but then deserted her on the island of Naxos, where, in some versions of the myth, she pined away.

My aching soul, and find no shore below;
An eye to be my star, a voice to bring
Hope o'er my path, like sounds that breathe of spring,
These are denied me—dreamt of still in vain,—
75 Therefore my brief aspirings from the chain,
Are ever but as some wild fitful song,
Rising triumphantly, to die ere long
In dirge-like echoes.

IV

Yet the world will see
80 Little of this, my parting work, in thee,
    Thou shalt have fame! Oh, mockery! give the reed
From storms a shelter,—give the drooping vine
Something round which its tendrils may entwine,—
    Give the parch'd flower a rain-drop, and the meed°   reward
85 Of love's kind words to woman! Worthless fame!
That in *his* bosom wins not for my name
Th' abiding place it asked! Yet how my heart,
In its own fairy world of song and art,
Once beat for praise! Are those high longings o'er?
90 That which I have been can I be no more?—
Never, oh! never more; tho' still thy sky
Be blue as then, my glorious Italy!
And tho' the music, whose rich breathings fill
Thine air with soul, be wandering past me still,
95 And tho' the mantle of thy sunlight streams
Unchang'd on forms instinct with° poet-dreams;   animated by
Never, oh! never more! Where'er I move,
The shadow of this broken-hearted love
Is on me and around! Too well *they* know,
100   Whose life is all within, too soon and well,
When there the blight hath settled;—but I go
    Under the silent wings of Peace to dwell;
From the slow wasting, from the lonely pain,
The inward burning of those words—*"in vain,"*
105   Sear'd on the heart—I go. 'Twill soon be past.
Sunshine, and song, and bright Italian heaven,
    And thou, oh! thou, on whom my spirit cast
Unvalued wealth,—who know'st not what was given
In that devotedness,—the sad, and deep,
110 And unrepaid—farewell! If I could weep
Once, only once, belov'd one! on thy breast,
Pouring my heart forth ere I sink to rest!
But that were happiness, and unto me
Earth's gift is *fame*. Yet I was form'd to be
115 So richly blest! With thee to watch the sky,
Speaking not, feeling but that thou wert nigh;
With thee to listen, while the tones of song
Swept ev'n as part of our sweet air along,
To listen silently;—with thee to gaze
120 On forms, the deified of olden days,—
This had been joy enough;—and hour by hour,

From its glad well-springs drinking life and power,
How had my spirit soar'd, and made its fame
   A glory for thy brow!—Dreams, dreams!—the fire
125 Burns faint within me. Yet I leave my name—
   As a deep thrill° may linger on the lyre   *vibration*
When its full chords are hush'd—awhile to live,
And one day haply in thy heart revive
Sad thoughts of me:—I leave it, with a sound,
130 A spell o'er memory, mournfully profound,
I leave it, on my country's air to dwell,—
Say proudly yet—"'Twas hers who lov'd me well!"

1828

Indian Woman's Death Song

An Indian woman, driven to despair by her husband's desertion of her for another
wife, entered a canoe with her children, and rowed it down the Mississippi towards
a cataract. Her voice was heard from the shore singing a mournful death-song,
until overpowered by the sound of the waters in which she perished. The tale is
related in Long's *Expedition to the Source of St Peter's River.*[1]

> *Non, je ne puis vivre avec un coeur brisé. Il faut que je retrouve la
> joie, et que je m'unisse aux esprits libres de l'air.*
> > Bride of Messina,
> > Translated by Madame de Staël[2]

> *Let not my child be a girl, for very sad is the life of a woman.*
> > The Prairie[3]

Down a broad river of the western wilds,
Piercing thick forest glooms, a light canoe
Swept with the current: fearful was the speed
5 Of the frail bark, as by a tempest's wing
Borne leaf-like on to where the mist of spray
Rose with the cataract's thunder.—Yet within,
Proudly, and dauntlessly, and all alone,
Save that a babe lay sleeping at her breast,
A woman stood: upon her Indian brow
10 Sat a strange gladness, and her dark hair wav'd
As if triumphantly. She press'd her child,
In its bright slumber, to her beating heart,
And lifted her sweet voice, that rose awhile
Above the sound of waters, high and clear,
15 Wafting a wild proud strain, her song of death.

---

1. William Hippolytus Keating, *Narrative of an
Expedition to the Source of St. Peter's River*
(1824), which compiles notes taken by Stephen
Harriman Long and other members of an 1823
expedition that traveled up the Minnesota River
(then called St. Peter's River) to the northern
Great Plains.
2. "No, I cannot live with a broken heart. I must

regain joy and join the free spirits of the air":
Staël cites Friedrich Schiller's tragedy *The Bride
of Messina*, which she discusses in her book on
German culture, *Germany* (1810).
3. From the last of James Fenimore Cooper's
series of Leatherstocking novels, *The Prairie*
(1827), spoken by a Sioux woman.

Roll swiftly to the Spirit's land, thou mighty stream and free!
Father of ancient waters,[4] roll! and bear our lives with thee!
The weary bird that storms have toss'd, would seek the sunshine's calm,
And the deer that hath the arrow's hurt, flies to the woods of balm.

20 Roll on!—my warrior's eye hath look'd upon another's face,
And mine hath faded from his soul, as fades a moonbeam's trace;
My shadow comes not o'er his path, my whisper to his dream,
He flings away the broken reed—roll swifter yet, thou stream!

The voice that spoke of other days is hush'd within *his* breast,
25 But *mine* its lonely music haunts, and will not let me rest;
It sings a low and mournful song of gladness that is gone,
I cannot live without that light—Father of waves! roll on!

Will he not miss the bounding step that met him from the chase?°   hunt
The heart of love that made his home an ever sunny place?
30 The hand that spread the hunter's board, and deck'd his couch of yore?—
He will not!—roll, dark foaming stream, on to the better shore!

Some blessed fount amidst the woods of that bright land must flow,
Whose waters from my soul may lave the memory of this woe;
Some gentle wind must whisper there, whose breath may waft away
35 The burden of the heavy night, the sadness of the day.

And thou, my babe! tho' born, like me, for woman's weary lot,
Smile!—to that wasting of the heart, my own! I leave thee not;
Too bright a thing art *thou* to pine in aching love away,
Thy mother bears thee far, young Fawn! from sorrow and decay.

40 She bears thee to the glorious bowers where none are heard to weep,
And where th' unkind one hath no power again to trouble sleep;
And where the soul shall find its youth, as wakening from a dream,—
One moment, and that realm is ours—On, on, dark rolling stream!

1828

An Hour of Romance

> ——I come
> To this sweet place for quiet. Every tree,
> And bush, and fragrant flower, and hilly path,
> And thymy mound that flings unto the winds
> Its morning incense, is my friend.
> BARRY CORNWALL.[1]

There were thick leaves above me and around,
    And low sweet sighs, like those of childhood's sleep,
Amidst their dimness, and a fitful sound
    As of soft showers on water;—dark and deep

---

4. "Father of waters," the Indian name for the Mississippi [Hemans's note].
1. From "A Haunted Stream," an 1819 poem by

Barry Cornwall, pseudonym of Bryan Waller Proctor.

5 Lay the oak shadows o'er the turf, so still,
They seem'd but pictur'd glooms: a hidden rill
Made music, such as haunts us in a dream,
Under the fern-tufts; and a tender gleam
Of soft green light, as by the glow-worm shed,
10 Came pouring thro' the woven beech-boughs down,
And steep'd the magic page wherein I read
  Of royal chivalry and old renown,
A tale of Palestine.[2]—Meanwhile the bee
  Swept past me with a tone of summer hours,
15 A drowsy bugle, wafting thoughts of flowers,
Blue skies and amber sunshine : brightly free,
On filmy wings the purple dragon-fly
Shot glancing like a fairy javelin by;
And a sweet voice of sorrow told the dell
20 Where sat the lone wood-pigeon:
        But ere long,
All sense of these things faded, as the spell
  Breathing from that high gorgeous tale grew strong
On my chain'd soul :—'twas not the leaves I heard—
25 A Syrian wind the Lion-banner stirr'd,[3]
Thro' its proud floating folds :—'twas not the brook,
  Singing in secret thro' its grassy glen—
  A wild shrill trumpet of the Saracen[4]
Peal'd from the desert's lonely heart, and shook
30 The burning air.—Like clouds when winds are high,
O'er glittering sands flew steeds of Araby,
And tents rose up, and sudden lance and spear
Flash'd where a fountain's diamond wave lay clear,
Shadow'd by graceful palm-trees. Then the shout
35 Of merry England's joy swell'd freely out,
Sent thro' an Eastern heaven, whose glorious hue
Made shields dark mirrors to its depths of blue;
And harps were there—I heard their sounding strings,
As the waste° echoed to the mirth of kings.—   *desert*
40 The bright masque faded.—Unto life's worn track,
What call'd me from its flood of glory, back?
A voice of happy childhood!—and they pass'd,
Banner, and harp, and Paynim° trumpet's blast;   *pagan or Muslim*
Yet might I scarce bewail the splendours gone,
45 My heart so leap'd to that sweet laughter's tone.

                   1828

---

2. The Talisman—Tales of the Crusaders [Hemans's note]. The "magic page" entrancing Hemans's speaker is from Sir Walter's Scott historical novel from 1825. Set in 12th-century Palestine, *The Talisman* dramatizes the infighting among the British knights involved in the Third Crusade and an unlikely friendship between the Scotsman Sir Kenneth and the mysterious figure who turns out to be the sultan Saladin (Salah ad-Din Yusuf), the Muslim conqueror of Jerusalem.
3. Banner of the English king Richard I (1157–1199), called the "Lion-hearted."
4. European designation for the Muslim forces arrayed against the Crusaders.

The Image in Lava[1]

Thou thing of years departed!
    What ages have gone by,
Since here the mournful seal was set
    By love and agony!

5   Temple and tower have moulder'd,
    Empires from earth have pass'd,—
And woman's heart hath left a trace
    Those glories to outlast!

And childhood's fragile image
10   Thus fearfully enshrin'd,
Survives the proud memorials rear'd
    By conquerors of mankind.

Babe! wert thou brightly slumbering
    Upon thy mother's breast,
15   When suddenly the fiery tomb
    Shut round each gentle guest?

A strange dark fate o'ertook you,
    Fair babe and loving heart!
One moment of a thousand pangs—
20   Yet better than to part!

Haply of that fond bosom,
    On ashes here impress'd,
Thou wert the only treasure, child!
    Whereon a hope might rest.

25   Perchance all vainly lavish'd,
    Its other love had been,
And where it trusted, nought remain'd
    But thorns on which to lean.

Far better then to perish,
30   Thy form within its clasp,
Than live and lose thee, precious one!
    From that impassion'd grasp.

Oh! I could pass all relics
    Left by the pomps of old,
35   To gaze on this rude monument,
    Cast in affection's mould.

---

1. The impression of a woman's form, with an infant clasped to the bosom, found at the uncovering of Herculaneum [Hemans's note]. When the poem was first printed in 1827 in the *New Monthly Magazine* this note referenced not Herculaneum but Pompeii; Paula Feldman, Hemans's modern editor, proposes in fact that the "image" the poem addresses recalls the petrified skeletons of a mother and child unearthed in Pompeii in 1812. Both these Roman towns, buried (mainly under volcanic ash, not lava) by the castastrophic eruption of Vesuvius in 79 C.E. had been lost to history until brought back to light by 18th- and 19th-century archaeology.

Love, human love! what art thou?
  Thy print upon the dust
Outlives the cities of renown
40   Wherein the mighty trust!

Immortal, oh! immortal
  Thou art, whose earthly glow
Hath given these ashes holiness—
  It must, it *must* be so!

1827/28

A Spirit's Return

"This is to be a mortal,
And seek the things beyond mortality!"
—MANFRED[1]

Thy voice prevails—dear friend, my gentle friend!
This long-shut heart for thee shall be unsealed,
And though thy soft eye mournfully will bend
Over the troubled stream, yet once revealed
5   Shall its freed waters flow; then rocks must close
For evermore, above their dark repose.

Come while the gorgeous mysteries of the sky
Fused in the crimson sea of sunset lie;
Come to the woods, where all strange wandering sound
10   Is mingled into harmony profound;
Where the leaves thrill with spirit, while the wind
Fills with a viewless° being, unconfined,   *invisible*
The trembling reeds and fountains—our own dell,
With its green dimness and Aeolian° breath,   *wind-blown*
15   Shall suit th' unveiling of dark records well—
Hear me in tenderness and silent faith!

Thou knew'st me not in life's fresh vernal morn—
I would thou hadst!—for then my heart on thine
Had poured a worthier love; now, all o'erworn
20   By its deep thirst for something too divine,
It hath but fitful music to bestow,
Echoes of harp-strings broken long ago.

Yet even in youth companionless I stood,
As a lone forest-bird 'midst ocean's foam;
25   For me the silver cords of brotherhood
Were early loosed; the voices from my home

1. A spirit's verdict on Manfred's quest, spoken just after Manfred is convulsed by the disappearance of the Phantom of his beloved Astarte (*Manfred* 2.4.158–59; see p. 657). Hemans's poem can be read as commentary on Byron's play, Percy Shelley's *Alastor*, and Keats's *Endymion* (see the note to lines 216–17), all of which depict a protagonist's problems in communicating with an otherworldly lover.

Passed one by one and melody and mirth
Left me a dreamer by a silent hearth.

But, with the fulness of a heart that burned
30   For the deep sympathies of mind, I turned
From that unanswering spot, and fondly sought
In all wild scenes with thrilling murmurs fraught,
In every still small voice and sound of power,
And flute-note of the wind through cave and bower,
35   A perilous delight!—for then first woke
My life's lone passion, the mysterious quest
Of secret knowledge; and each tone that broke
From the wood-arches or the fountain's breast,
Making my quick soul vibrate as a lyre,
40   But ministered to that strange inborn fire.
'Midst the bright silence of the mountain dells,
In noon-tide hours or golden summer-eves,
My thoughts have burst forth as a gale that swells
Into a rushing blast, and from the leaves
45   Shakes out response. O thou rich world unseen!
Thou curtained realm of spirits!—thus my cry
Hath troubled air and silence—dost thou lie
Spread all around, yet by some filmy screen
Shut from us ever? The resounding woods,
50   Do their depths teem with marvels?—and the floods,
And the pure fountains, leading secret veins
Of quenchless melody through rock and hill,
Have they bright dwellers?—are their lone domains
Peopled with beauty, which may never still
55   *Our* weary thirst of soul?—Cold, weak and cold,
Is earth's vain language, piercing not one fold
Of our deep being! Oh, for gifts more high!
For a seer's glance to rend mortality!
For a charmed rod, to call from each dark shrine
60   The oracles divine!

I woke from those high fantasies, to know
My kindred with the earth—I woke to love:
O gentle friend! to love in doubt and woe,
Shutting the heart the worshipped name above,
65   Is to love deeply—and *my* spirit's dower
Was a sad gift, a melancholy power
Of so adoring—with a buried care,
And with the o'erflowing of a voiceless prayer,
And with a deepening dream, that day by day,
70   In the still shadow of its lonely sway,
Folded me closer, till the world held nought
Save the *one* being to my centred thought.

There was no music but his voice to hear,
No joy but such as with *his* step drew near;
75   Light was but where he looked—life where he moved;
Silently, fervently, thus, thus I loved.

Oh! but such love is fearful!—and I knew
Its gathering doom:—the soul's prophetic sight
Even then unfolded in my breast, and threw
80   O'er all things round a full, strong, vivid light,
Too sorrowfully clear!—an undertone
Was given to Nature's harp, for me alone
Whispering of grief.—Of grief?—be strong, awake,
Hath not thy love been victory, O, my soul?
85   Hath not its conflict won a voice to shake
Death's fastnesses?—a magic to control
Worlds far removed?—from o'er the grave to thee
Love hath made answer; and *thy* tale should be
Sung like a lay of triumph!—Now return,
90   And take thy treasure from its bosomed urn,[2]
And lift it once to light!

            In fear, in pain,
I said I loved—but yet a heavenly strain
Of sweetness floated down the tearful stream,
A joy flashed through the trouble of my dream!
95   I knew myself beloved!—we breathed no vow,
No mingling visions might our fate allow,
As unto happy hearts; but still and deep,
Like a rich jewel gleaming in a grave,
Like golden sand in some dark river's wave,
100   So did my soul that costly knowledge keep
So jealously!°—a thing o'er which to shed,   *watchfully*
When stars alone beheld the drooping head,
Lone tears! yet ofttimes burdened with the excess
Of our strange nature's quivering happiness.

105   But, oh! sweet friend! we dream not of love's might
Till death has robed with soft and solemn light
The image we enshrine!—Before *that* hour,
We have but glimpses of the o'ermastering power
Within us laid!—*then* doth the spirit-flame
110   With sword-like lightning rend its mortal frame;
The wings of that which pants to follow fast
Shake their clay-bars, as with a prisoned blast—
The sea is in our souls!

            He died—*he* died
On whom my lone devotedness was cast!
115   I might not keep one vigil by his side,
I, whose wrung heart watched with him to the last!
I might not once his fainting head sustain,
Nor bathe his parched lips in the hour of pain,
Nor say to him, "Farewell!"—He passed away—
120   Oh! had *my* love been there, its conquering sway
Had won him back from death! but thus removed,
Borne o'er the abyss no sounding-line hath proved,

2. Suggests an urn in which funerary ashes are kept.

Joined with the unknown, the viewless—he became
Unto my thoughts another, yet the same—
125 Changed—hallowed—glorified!—and his low grave
Seemed a bright mournful altar—mine, all mine:—
Brother and friend soon left me *that* sole shrine,
The birthright of the faithful!—*their* world's wave
Soon swept them from its brink.—Oh! deem thou not
130 That on the sad and consecrated spot
My soul grew weak!—I tell thee that a power
There kindled heart and lip—a fiery shower
My words were made—a might was given to prayer,
And a strong grasp to passionate despair,
135 And a dead triumph!—Know'st thou what I sought?
For what high boon my struggling spirit wrought?—
Communion with the dead!—I sent a cry,
Through the veiled empires of eternity,
A voice to cleave them! By the mournful truth,
140 By the lost promise of my blighted youth,
By the strong chain a mighty love can bind
On the beloved, the spell of mind o'er mind;
By words, which in themselves are magic high,
Armed and inspired, and winged with agony;
145 By tears, which comfort not, but burn, and seem
To bear the heart's blood in their passion stream;
I summoned, I adjured!°—with quickened sense,   *entreated*
With the keen vigil of a life intense,
I watched, an answer from the winds to wring,
150 I listened, if perchance the stream might bring
Token from worlds afar: I taught *one* sound
Unto a thousand echoes—one profound
Imploring accent to the tomb, the sky—
One prayer to night—"Awake, appear, reply!"
155 Hast thou been told that from the viewless bourne,°   *invisible region*
The dark way never hath allowed return?
That all, which tears can move, with life is fled—
That earthly love is powerless on the dead?
Believe it not!—there is a large lone star
160 Now burning o'er yon western hill afar,
And under its clear light there lies a spot
Which well might utter forth—Believe it not!
I sat beneath that planet—I had wept
My woe to stillness, every night-wind slept;
165 A hush was on the hills; the very streams
Went by like clouds, or noiseless founts in dreams,
And the dark tree o'ershadowing me that hour,
Stood motionless, even as the gray church-tower
Whereon I gazed unconsciously:—there came
170 A low sound, like the tremor of a flame,
Or like the light quick shiver of a wing,
Flitting through twilight woods, across the air;
And I looked up!—Oh! for strong words to bring
Conviction o'er thy thought!—Before me there,
175 He, the departed, stood!—Ay, face to face,

So near, and yet how far!—his form, his mien,
Gave to remembrance back each burning trace
Within:—Yet something awfully serene,
Pure, sculpture-like, on the pale brow, that wore
180   Of the once-beating heart no token more;
And stillness on the lip—and o'er the hair
A gleam, that trembled through the breathless air;
And an unfathomed calm, that seemed to lie
In the grave sweetness of the illumined eye;
185   Told of the gulfs between our beings set,
And, as that unsheathed spirit-glance I met,
Made my soul faint:—with *fear*? Oh! *not* with fear!
With the sick feeling that in *his* far sphere
My love could be as nothing! But he spoke—
190   How shall I tell thee of the startling thrill
In that low voice, whose breezy tones could fill
My bosom's infinite? O, friend! I woke
Then first to heavenly life!—Soft, solemn, clear
Breathed the mysterious accents on mine ear,
195   Yet strangely seemed as if the while they rose
From depths of distance, o'er the wide repose
Of slumbering waters wafted, or the dells
Of mountains, hollow with sweet-echo cells;
But, as they murmured on, the mortal chill
200   Passed from me, like a mist before the morn,
And, to that glorious intercourse upborne
By slow degrees, a calm, divinely still,
Possessed my frame: I sought that lighted eye—
From its intense and searching purity
205   I drank in *soul*!—I questioned of the dead—
Of the hushed, starry shores their footsteps tread,
And I was answered:—if remembrance there,
With dreamy whispers fill the immortal air;
If thought, here piled from many a jewel-heap,
210   Be treasure in that pensive land to keep;
If love, o'ersweeping change, and blight, and blast
Find *there* the music of his home at last;
I asked, and I was answered:—Full and high
Was that communion with eternity,
215   Too rich for aught so fleeting!—Like a knell
Swept o'er my sense its closing words, "Farewell,
On earth we meet no more!"[3]—and all was gone—
The pale bright settled brow—the thrilling tone,
The still and shining eye! and never more
220   May twilight gloom or midnight hush restore
That radiant guest! One full-fraught hour of heaven,
To earthly passion's wild implorings given,
Was made my own—the ethereal fire hath shivered
The fragile censer[4] in whose mould it quivered

3. This is the answer to Manfred's question to the Phantom of Astarte (2.4.154): "Say, shall we meet again?" Astarte vanishes, and Nemesis says, "She's gone, and will not be recall'd." Hemans's lines also echo Endymion's renunciation of his dream goddess at a crucial moment in Keats's *Endymion* (4.657–59): "The hour may come / When we shall meet in pure elysium. / On earth I may not love thee."
4. Container in which incense is burned.

225 Brightly, consumingly! What now is left?
A faded world, of glory's hues bereft—
A void, a chain!—I dwell 'midst throngs, apart,
In the cold silence of the stranger's heart;
A fixed, immortal shadow stands between
230 My spirit and life's fast receding scene;
A gift hath severed me from human ties,
A power is gone from all earth's melodies,
Which never may return: their chords are broken,
The music of another land hath spoken—
235 No after-sound is sweet!—this weary thirst!
And I have heard celestial fountains burst!—
What *here* shall quench it?
                                        Dost thou not rejoice,
When the spring sends forth an awakening voice
Through the young woods?—Thou dost!—And in the birth
240 Of early leaves, and flowers, and songs of mirth,
Thousands, like thee, find gladness!—Couldst thou know
How every breeze then summons *me* to go!
How all the light of love and beauty shed
By those rich hours, but woos me to the dead!
245 The *only* beautiful that change no more—
The only loved!—the dwellers on the shore
Of spring fulfilled!—The dead!—*whom* call we so?
They that breathe purer air, that feel, that know
Things wrapt from us!—Away!—within me pent,
250 That which is barred from its own element
Still droops or struggles!—But the day *will* come—
Over the deep the free bird finds its home,
And the stream lingers 'midst the rocks, yet greets
The sea at last; and the winged flower-seed meets
255 A soil to rest in:—shall not *I*, too, be,
My spirit-love! upborne to dwell with thee?
Yes! by the power whose conquering anguish stirred
The tomb, whose cry beyond the stars was heard,
Whose agony of triumph won thee back
260 Through the dim pass no mortal step may track,
Yet shall we meet!—that glimpse of joy divine
Proved thee for ever and for ever mine!

1830

The Romantic Imagination
and the "Oriental Nations"

A significant proportion of the poems, novels, and plays written in Britain during the Romantic period are set thousands of miles away from the British Isles, in terrain stretching from the eastern Mediterranean to the Indian Ocean—contested territory that for much of the nineteenth century would be squabbled over by the British, Russian, and Ottoman Empires. In *Beppo* (1818), Lord Byron's narrator commented on the public's fascination with the strangeness of these distant lands and the salability of the English literature repackaging it for domestic consumption: "How quickly would I print (the world delighting) / A Grecian, Syrian, or Assyrian tale; / And sell you, mix'd with western sentimentalism / Some samples of the finest Orientalism." Byron evidences some bad faith in these flippant lines. In poetry published between 1813 and 1816 he had himself turned regularly to the Islamic world, making locales in the Ottoman Empire the standard backdrop for his stories of glamorous outsiders. Byron's series of "Turkish tales" joined other best sellers that traded in like manner on the magnificence, marvel, and horror that the European imagination had come to associate with "Oriental" climes (a nebulous geographical term that concealed, needless to say, the cultural and religious differences that divided the many nations located beyond the eastern margins of Europe). There was, for instance, Thomas Moore's *Lalla Rookh: An Oriental Romance* (1817), composed of separate long poems that Moore presented as entertainments produced for the court of the seventeenth-century Mughal emperor Aurangzeb. In 1819 and 1824 there were the Crusader novels by Sir Walter Scott, fictions set during the medieval moment when Europeans' desire to conquer Jerusalem for Christendom first brought them into sustained contact with the civilizations of the Arab-Muslim world. To look eastward for one's themes became in Romantic-period literature a primary way to examine cultural identity and difference and examine the tensions and longings dividing and connecting devotee and infidel, friend and enemy, self and other.

The popularity of these examinations registered geopolitical developments that had begun early in the eighteenth century: first, the chipping away of Mughal dominion over the Indian subcontinent, followed by the slow crumbling of the Ottoman Empire; the territorial gains the British Empire made at both those empires' expense, especially during its wars with Napoleonic France; and most of all, in the words of the critic Nigel Leask, "the transformation of India and parts of the Middle East from sources of tribute and producers of luxury goods to real or potential subject states, sources of raw material and consumer markets for [British] home manufactures." By the 1820s the British East India Company controlled almost the whole of the Indian subcontinent. The end of the Romantic period also saw Britain at last managing to exploit for its own advantage the mighty Chinese Empire, as it had long sought to do; China's autonomy began to be undermined when, to finance its military enterprises, the East India Company took to smuggling opium out of India for export there.

In other respects, though, the decisive event in the history of the Romantic imagination was not the advent of new revenue streams from the empire's Asian colonies or dependencies but the import of new stories. At the start of the eighteenth century, the course of European cultural development had been decisively redirected by the translation, first into French (1704), then English (1706), of the *Alf layla wa layl*, the *Arabian Nights Entertainment*. The tales included in this collection are supposed to have been told over 1,001 nights by the wily heroine, Scheherazade, who uses her narrative skills to awaken her cruel husband's curiosity and so postpone the execution that all the sultan's previous wives have suffered follow-ing their wedding nights. Western audiences went wild for this collection of stories from the Arabic heartland of Iraq and Syria. Coleridge reported that when he was a child *The Arabian Nights* made so deep an impression that he had been "a dreamer" ever since. Cued by the stories of evil magicians, wish-granting genii, and artful storytellers that filled *The Arabian Nights*, as they also filled the faux-Oriental tales that succeeded it in their libraries, English writers increasingly identified the East as the imagination's own territory. Sometimes it was even heralded as the place where fictionality (make believe) had begun.

The encounter with the traditions of the east was also valued, to different effect, for how it opened up new vistas for the Western literary imagination—how it offered an escape route from an overfamiliar classical and biblical heritage. The Calcutta-based jurist Sir William Jones was celebrated accordingly for how his imitations of medieval Sanskrit verse (founded, unlike most of the faux-Oriental writing of his compatriots, on deep linguistic knowledge) had expanded English literature's stock of poetical imagery. "Where can we find so much beauty as in the *Eastern* poems, which turn chiefly upon the loveliest objects in nature?" Jones asked. He conjured for read-ers back home in damp, smoky England a sunlit Eden, where the breezes carried murmurs of song and the fragrances of spices and flowers.

Jones's Orient, like that of *The Arabian Nights*, was good to dream with, if in a different way. At the same time, however, Jones was one of the first to insist that the Orient was also good to study. His founding of the Asiatick Society in Calcutta in 1784 heralded a new determination to supplement delicious fantasy with serious linguistic, historical, and scientific research. This scholarship, not incidentally, would also broaden the knowledge base from which colonial administrators might draw.

The representations of the East generated out of this compound of make-believe and empirical, factual study were not easy to resolve into a single picture. (Many Romantic authors seem in fact to have actively cultivated the irresolution. They tended to highlight, rather than play down, the discrepancy in tone between their tales of Eastern wonders and the scholarly notes with which they conventionally surrounded those tales. Absorption in otherness needed to be countered, it appears, by distance and detachment.) The literary image of the Oriental nations was thus full of contradiction. Idealization often, and increasingly, went hand in hand with vilification. Stories of the harems of the Ottoman Empire and the *zenana* of India, for instance, tended to project, from one moment to the next, both a region of beauty and sensual pleasure and a region defined by a cruel sexual slavery, in which women were denied any measure of autonomy and even denied souls.

English observers who had internalized the French political theorist Montesquieu's account of Asiatic countries as despotism's natural milieu thus counterpointed Jones's pictures of "felix Arabia" (happy Arabia) with stories of the fearfulness and grief that defined life in a region where civil liberty lacked a foothold. The political theorist Judith Shklar explains that, within Montesquieu's discussion of despotism in *The Spirit of the Laws*, "the East is not so much a geographic area as a nightmare ter-ritory of the mind in which all the worst human impulses govern." Nonetheless, Mon-tesquieu's tendency to look eastward for his examples of unchecked, arbitrary, self-indulging tyrants had real historical effects. He and European commentators writing in his wake made it appear that there was something inherently "Asiatic" about tyranny. Such representations could be used to alibi the increasing interven-tionism of the imperial powers. They helped repackage economic and political domi-nation as civilizational uplift—as a rescue of populations who needed to be saved from their own slavish propensities.

Several visions of the Oriental nations contended in the public sphere, in other words, and underwrote diverging accounts of what Englishmen and women them-selves might be in relationship to these cultural others. Arrayed chronologically, the writings excerpted in this section do suggest that the farther one progresses into the nineteenth century, the less likely one is to encounter the belief, held by William Jones, that Britain could learn from Hindu and Islamic cultures. Fewer writers gave voice to the feeling that the English heroine of Phebe Gibbes's *Hartly House, Calcutta* (1789) celebrates when dazzled by her first view of Indian splendor: "the European world faded before my eyes, and I became *orientalised* at all points." Plots driven by cross-cultural identification and sympathy (Gibbes's, Sydney Owenson's in *The Missionary*) gave way over time to plots driven by antipathy, resentment, and fear.

As twenty-first-century postcolonial critics have observed, the often degrading images of the Middle Eastern and South Asian cultures manufactured in the Romantic period bolstered the English sense of moral superiority. They helped naturalize Western rule over these regions. But just as the *Arabian Nights'* Scheherazade might have foreseen, the European appetite for stories of the marvelous East remained insatiable all the same.

BARON DE MONTESQUIEU (CHARLES-LOUIS DE SECONDAT)

The French aristocrat the Baron de Montesquieu (1689–1755) is famous for his influence on the American constitution, whose architects derived the principle of checks and balances from the political philosopher's survey of "the laws, the various customs, and manners, of all the nations of the earth." *The Spirit of the Laws* also shaped Anglo-American understandings of Asia. According to its deterministic account (founded in part on reports by European travelers), the peoples of Asia were condemned both by the sultry climate and by their nature to suffer under the yoke of despotic government: "Here they have no limitations or restrictions . . . [and] man is a creature that blindly submits to the absolute will of the sovereign."

From The Spirit of the Laws

Book V, Chapter 13: An Idea of Despotic Power

When the savages of Louisiana are desirous of fruit, they cut the tree to the root, and gather the fruit. This is an emblem of despotic government.

From Book V, Chapter 14: In What Manner the Laws Are Relative to the Principles of Despotic Government

The principle of despotic government is fear: but a timid, ignorant, and faint-spirited people have no occasion for a great number of laws.

Every thing ought to depend here on two or three ideas: hence there is no necessity that any new notions should be added. When we want to break a horse, we take care not to let him change his master, his lesson, or his pace. Thus an impression is made on his brain by two or three motions, and no more.

If a prince is shut up in a seraglio,[1] he cannot leave his voluptuous abode without alarming those who keep him confined. They will not bear that his person and power should pass into other hands. He seldom, therefore, wages war in person, and hardly ventures to intrust the command to his generals.

A prince of this stamp, unaccustomed to resistance in his palace, is enraged to see his will opposed by armed force: hence he is generally governed by wrath or vengeance. Besides, he can have no notion of true glory. War, therefore, is carried on, under such a government, in its full natural fury, and less extent is given to the law of nations than in other states.

Such a prince has so many imperfections, that they are afraid to expose his natural stupidity to public view. He is concealed in his palace, and the people are ignorant of his situation. It is lucky for him that the inhabitants of those countries need only the name of a prince to govern them.

When Charles XII was at Bender, he met with some opposition from the senate of Sweden:[2] upon which he wrote word home that he would send one of his boots to command them. This boot would have governed like a despotic prince.

If the prince is a prisoner, he is supposed to be dead, and another mounts the throne. The treaties made by the prisoner are void; his successor will not ratify them. And, indeed (as he is the law, the state, and the prince), when he is no longer a prince, he is nothing: were he not, therefore, deemed to be deceased, the state would be subverted.

One thing which chiefly determined the Turks to conclude a separate peace with Peter I was the Muscovites telling the vizir,[3] that, in Sweden, another prince had been set upon the throne.

The preservation of the state is only the preservation of the prince, or rather of the palace where he is confined. Whatever does not directly menace this palace, or the capital, makes no impression on ignorant, proud, and prejudiced minds; and, as for the concatenation of events, they are unable to trace, to foresee, or even to conceive it. Politics, with its several springs and laws, must here be very much limited; the political government is as simple as the civil.

The whole is reduced to reconciling the political and civil administration to the domestic government, the officers of state to those of the seraglio.

Such a state is happiest when it can look upon itself as the only one in the world, when it is environed with deserts, and separated from those people whom they call barbarians. Since it cannot depend on the militia, it is proper it should destroy a part of itself.

As fear is the principle of despotic government, its end is tranquillity: but this tranquillity cannot be called a peace; no, it is only the silence of those towns which the enemy is ready to invade.

* * *

1748/1777

---

1. Harem; the apartments in the sovereign's palace in which his wives and concubines were secluded.
2. After Swedish forces were routed by the army of the Russian czar in 1709 (in the battle that kicks off Lord Byron's 1819 poem *Mazeppa*), the Swedish king Charles XII began a five-year exile in Bender, then a town in the Ottoman Empire.
3. The Ottoman sultan's chief minister.

SIR WILLIAM JONES

A formidably talented linguist and legal scholar, Sir William Jones (1746–1794) spearheaded the Oriental Renaissance of the late eighteenth century. His translations of Arabic, Farsi, and Sanskrit poetry, some of which he began while an undergraduate at Oxford, had a tremendous impact on European literature. The excitement his writing generated was not so different from that greeting the humanists of quattrocento Italy when they rediscovered long-forgotten texts from classical antiquity. Jones's identification of the affinity between Sanskrit and classical Greek and Latin laid the foundation for historical linguistics: the idea of an Indo-European common grammar originates with an address he gave to the Asiatick Society of Calcutta in 1784. While serving as high court judge in Bengal from 1783 until his death, Jones cooperated with a group of Brahmin scholars on a massive digest of Hindu law that became the basis for courtroom practice throughout British India.

The essay excerpted here—a celebration of the fertility of the "Eastern" imagination that proceeds through a survey of Arab, Persian, Turkish, and Mughal poetry—appeared in Jones's *Poems Consisting Chiefly of Translations from the Asiatick Languages*. In linking the reinvigoration of modern Western poetry to a rejection of familiar neoclassical examples, it is sometimes seen as prophesying Wordsworth's Preface to *Lyrical Ballads*. We reprint its final paragraph.

From On the Poetry of Eastern Nations

* * *

I must once more request, that in bestowing these praises on the writings of Asia, I may not be thought to derogate from the merit of the Greek and Latin poems, which have justly been admired in every age: yet I cannot but think that our European poetry has subsisted too long on the perpetual repetition of the same images, and incessant allusions to the same fables: and it has been my endeavour for several years to inculcate this truth, 'That, if the principal writings of the Asiaticks, which are reposited in our public libraries, were printed with the usual advantage of notes and illustrations; and if the languages of the Eastern nations were studied in our places of education, where every other branch of useful knowledge is taught to perfection; a new and ample field would be open for speculation; we should have a more extensive insight into the history of the human mind, we should be furnished with a new set of images and similitudes, and a number of excellent compositions would be brought to light, which future scholars might explain, and future poets might imitate.'

1772

JAMES BEATTIE

"On Fable and Romance," a 1783 essay by an influential Scottish poet and philosopher, represents an early attempt to assess and contextualize the rapid expansion of novel writing and novel reading in eighteenth-century Britain. Also a reluctant attempt, in as much as James Beattie (1735–1803) ends his investigation of "modern romances," as he calls the new genre, by repudiating his topic: "Let not the usefulness of romance be estimated by the length of my discourse upon it," he writes. "Romances are a dangerous recreation." Some hint of that anxiety about fiction's allure is audible even in this early passage in the essay, where Beattie turns to "the Oriental nations" to trace the origins of the romance and, in doing so, registers the high profile that *The Thousand and One Nights* and the many English-language books that imitated its tales of marvels and magic enjoyed in his moment. Here Beattie insinuates that there is something Eastern—exotic, un-British—about the appetite for fantastic stories; he seems to associate the very concept of fictionality or make-believe ("fable") with the hedonistic landscape of Oriental despotism.

From On Fable and Romance

* * *

[T]he Oriental nations have long been famous for fabulous narrative. The indolence peculiar to the genial climates of Asia, and the luxurious life which the kings and other great men, of those countries, lead in their seraglios, have made them seek for this sort of amusement, and set a high value upon it. When an Eastern prince happens to be idle, as he commonly is, and at a loss for expedients to kill the time, he commands his Grand Visir, or his favourite, to tell him stories. Being ignorant, and consequently credulous; having no passion for moral improvement, and little knowledge of nature; he does not desire, that they should be probable, or of an instructive tendency: it is enough if they be astonishing. And hence it is, no doubt, that those oriental tales are so extravagant. Every thing is carried on by inchantment and prodigy; by fairies, genii, and demons, and wooden horses, which, on turning a peg, fly through the air with inconceivable swiftness.

Another thing remarkable in these eastern tales, is, that their authors expatiate, with peculiar delight, in the description of magnificence; rich robes, gaudy furniture, sumptuous entertainments, and palaces shining in gold, or sparkling with diamonds. This too is conformable to the character and circumstances of the people. Their great men, whose taste has never been improved by studying the *simplicity* of nature and art, pique themselves chiefly on the *splendour* of their equipage, and the vast quantities of gold, jewels, and curious things, which they can heap together in their repositories.

* * *

1783

SIR WILLIAM JONES

William Jones's (1746–1794) poem "Hymn to Camdeo," the first of nine "hymns" he wrote for the deities of the Hindu pantheon, amalgamates exotic content with the familiar classical form of the Pindaric ode. Even so, the "Hymn" was for a couple of decades understood to be Jones's translation rather than his original composition. Camdeo, Jones explains in a preface, is the same as the Romans' Cupid, a god of love; but, he continues, "the *Indian* description of his person and arms, his family, attendants, and attributes has new and peculiar beauties."

Hymn to Camdeo

What potent God from Agra's[1] orient bow'rs
Floats through the lucid air, whilst living flow'rs
With sunny twine the vocal arbours wreathe,
And gales enamour'd heavenly fragrance breathe?
5   Hail, power unknown! for at thy beck
    Vales and groves their bosoms deck,
    And every laughing blossom dresses
    With gems of dew his musky tresses.
I feel, I feel thy genial flame divine,
10   And hallow thee, and kiss thy shrine.

'Know'st thou not me?' Celestial sounds I hear!
'Know'st thou not me?' Ah, spare a mortal ear!
'Behold'—My swimming eyes entranc'd I raise,
But oh! they sink before the' excessive blaze.
15   Yes, son of Maya,[2] yes, I know
    Thy bloomy shafts and cany[3] bow,
    Cheeks with youthful glory beaming,
    Locks in braids ethereal streaming,
Thy scaly standard,[4] thy mysterious arms,
20   And all thy pains and all thy charms.

God of each lovely sight, each lovely sound,
Soul-kindling, world-inflaming, star-ycrown'd,
Eternal Cama! Or doth Smara bright,
Or proud Ananga[5] give thee more delight?
25   Whate'er thy seat, whate'er thy name,
    Seas, Earth, and Air, thy reign proclaim:
    Wreathy smiles and roseate pleasures

---

1. City in northern India and location of the Taj Mahal.
2. In the Vedic tradition that feeds into modern Hinduism, Maya names the power of illusion, the appearances concealing reality.
3. I.e., made from sugarcane.

4. In his prefatory remarks, Jones mentions that Camdeo's attendants carry his flag, which shows "a fish on a red ground."
5. "Cáma" (love), "Smara" (remembrance), and "Ananga" (bodiless one) are alternative names for this deity.

Are thy richest, sweetest treasures.
All animals to thee their tribute bring,
30 And hail thee universal king.

Thy consort mild, Affection ever true,[6]
Graces thy side, her vest of glowing hue,
And in her train twelve blooming girls advance,
Touch golden strings and knit the mirthful dance.
35   Thy dreaded implements they bear,
         And wave them in the scented air,
         Each with pearls her neck adorning,
         Brighter than the tears of morning.
Thy crimson ensign, which before them flies,
40 Decks with new stars the sapphire skies.

God of the flowery shafts and flowery bow,
Delight of all above and all below!
Thy lov'd companion, constant from his birth,
In heaven clep'd° Bessent, and gay Spring on earth,   *called*
45   Weaves thy green robe and flaunting bow'rs,
         And from thy clouds draws balmy show'rs,
         He with fresh arrows fills thy quiver,
         (Sweet the gift, and sweet the giver!)
And bids the many-plumed warbling throng
50 Burst the pent blossoms with their song.

He bends the luscious cane, and twists the string
With bees, how sweet! but ah, how keen their sting!
He with five flowerets tips thy ruthless darts,
Which through five senses pierce enraptur'd hearts:
55   Strong Chumpa, rich in odorous gold,
         Warm Amer, nurs'd in heavenly mould,
         Dry Nagkeser in silver smiling,
         Hot Kiticum our sense beguiling,
And last, to kindle fierce the scorching flame,
60 Loveshaft, which gods bright Bela name.[7]

Can men resist thy power, when Krishen yields,
Krishen, who still in Matra's holy fields
Tunes harps immortal, and to strains divine
Dances by moonlight with the Gopia nine?[8]
65   But, when thy daring arm untam'd
         At Mahadeo a loveshaft aim'd,
         Heaven shook, and, smit with stony wonder,
         Told his deep dread in bursts of thunder,

6. Jones's modern editor, Michael Franklin, remarks on how with this line's reference to the god's "consort," Jones manages to "convey a type of marital fidelity" that is ill-suited to both Western and Eastern notions of Eros.
7. Lines 55–60 identify the various species of Indian flowers that form part of the love god's weaponry. Banks was a keen botanist, sending seeds and roots of India's native plants back to the Royal Society in England.
8. Jones refers to the story, told in the poet Jayadeva's *The Song of Góvinda*, of the god Krishna's love for Rhapa, one of the nine gopi (milkmaids) with whom the deity liked to play. Jones's 1792 translation of this 12th-century Sanskrit epic, whose manuscript he rediscovered with the help of a Brahmin friend, was acclaimed throughout western Europe.

Whilst on thy beauteous limbs an azure fire
70   Blaz'd forth, which never must expire.[9]

O thou for ages born, yet ever young,
For ages may thy Bramin's lay be sung!
And, when thy lory° spreads his emerald wings   *parrot*
To waft thee high above the towers of Kings,
75   Whilst o'er thy throne the moon's pale light
Pours her soft radiance through the night,
And to each floating cloud discovers
The haunts of bless'd or joyless lovers,
Thy mildest influence to thy bard impart,
80   To warm, but not consume his heart.

1784

9. "The seventh stanza," Jones states in his preface, "alludes to the bold attempt" Camdeo made "to wound the great god *Mahadeo* [also known as *Siva*], for which he was punished by a flame consuming his corporeal nature and reducing him to a mental essence; and hence his chief dominion is over the *minds* of mortals."

WILLIAM BECKFORD

Thanks to his inherited fortune, founded on his family's Jamaican estates, William Beckford (1760–1844) was for a time famous mainly as "England's wealthiest son." But in the wake of the public scandal sparked by his love affairs with, simultaneously, his cousin's wife and with William Courtenay, the sixteen-year-old in line to be the next earl of Devon, Beckford was also a social outcast. *Vathek* was completed not long after Beckford fled disgrace in England to begin an exile of eleven years on the European continent. He originally composed the book in French, during a "single sitting," his biographer reports, "of three days and two nights." This account suggests something of the intensity of Beckford's relation to the dark and glamorous fantasy world that his book assembles out of materials found in texts like *The Arabian Nights*—and the urgency of the escape from Englishness and English norms that the book's composition facilitated. In some measure, the story of the caliph Vathek's lust for power and this sensual tyrant's fatal deception at the hands of an even greater villain, a mysterious Indian magician known as the Giaour, was an intensely personal document: Beckford all but invited his readers to regard this Oriental despot's story as authorial autobiography.

However, on *Vathek*'s debut in English in 1786 some readers lit on alternative ways to understand the book, prompted by the 122 pages of scholarly notes on the customs of the Islamic world that Beckford's English translator, Samuel Henley, thought the story required. Henley's annotations to a book that was then known under the title *An Arabian Tale from an Unpublished Manuscript* were praised with enthusiasm for their accuracy, despite the evidence that many had been cribbed from a seventeenth-century French encyclopedia.

The clash between those two ways of reading and valuing *Vathek* suggests the duality in late-eighteenth-century accounts of the Middle East. It suggests how the Arabia of Beckford's tale could represent at once an object of ethnographic investigation—an investigation that could be made to serve the English nation's geopolitical interests—and a site of fantasy and refuge from workaday English reality.

From The History of the Caliph Vathek

Vathek, ninth *caliph* of the race of the Abassides, was the son of Motassem, and the grandson of Haroun Al Raschid.[1] From an early accession to the throne, and the talents he possessed to adorn it; his subjects were induced to expect that his reign would be long, and happy. His figure was pleasing, and majestick; but when he was angry, one of his eyes became so terrible, that no person could bear to behold it; and the wretch upon whom it was fixed, instantly fell backward and, sometimes, expired. For fear, however, of depopulating his dominions, and making his palace desolate, he but rarely gave way to his anger.

Being much addicted to women, and the pleasures of the table, he sought, by his affability, to procure agreeable companions; and he succeeded the better, as his generosity was unbounded; and his indulgences unrestrained: for he was by no means scrupulous: nor did he think, with the Caliph, Omar Ben Abdalaziz, that it was necessary to make a hell of this world, to enjoy Paradise in the next.

He surpassed in magnificence all his predecessors. The palace of Alkoremmi, which his father Motassem had erected, on the hill of Pied Horses and which commanded the whole city of Samarah,[2] was, in his idea, far too scanty: he added, therefore, five wings, or rather, other palaces, which he destined for the particular gratification of each of his senses.

In the first of these were tables continually covered, with the most exquisite dainties, which were supplied, both by night and by day, according to their constant consumption, whilst the most delicious wines, and the choicest cordials, flowed forth from a hundred fountains that were never exhausted. This Palace was called THE ETERNAL or UNSATIATING BANQUET.

The second was styled THE TEMPLE OF MELODY, or THE NECTAR OF THE SOUL. It was inhabited by the most skilful musicians and admired poets of the time, who not only displayed their talents within, but, dispersing in bands without, caused every surrounding scene to reverberate their songs, which were continually varied in the most delightful succession.

The palace named THE DELIGHT OF THE EYES, or THE SUPPORT OF MEMORY was one entire enchantment. Rarities collected from every corner of the earth were there found in such profusion, as to dazzle and confound, but for the order in which they were arranged. One gallery exhibited the pictures of the celebrated Mani:[3] and statues that seemed to be alive. Here, a well-managed perspective attracted the sight; there, the magick of opticks agreeably deceived it: whilst the Naturalist, on his part, exhibited, in their several classes, the various gifts that Heaven had bestowed on our globe. In a word, Vathek omitted nothing in this palace that might gratify the curiosity of those who resorted to it; although he was not able to satisfy his own, for, he was, of all men, the most curious.

THE PALACE OF PERFUMES, which was termed likewise, THE INCENTIVE TO PLEASURE, consisted of various halls where the different perfumes which

1. The names ground Beckford's tale in the history of Islamic civilization. In the 8th century, Haroun Al Raschid ruled a territory extending from northern Africa, through Iraq and Iran, all the way to modern Pakistan. "Caliph": from the Arabic *khalifa,* designating God's deputy on earth.
2. A real city, located in modern-day Jordan.
3. The Iranian founder of the sect of Manicheans.

the earth produces, were kept perpetually burning in censers of gold. Flam-beaus[4] and aromatick lamps were here lighted in open day. But the too powerful effects of this agreeable delirium might be avoided, by descending into an immense garden, where an assemblage of every fragrant flower diffused through the air the purest odours.

The fifth palace, denominated THE RETREAT OF JOY, or THE DANGEROUS, was frequented by troops of young females, beautiful as the Houris, and not less seducing, who never failed to receive, with caresses, all whom the Caliph allowed to approach them: for, he was by no means disposed to be jealous, as his own women were secluded within the palace he inhabited himself.

Notwithstanding the sensuality in which Vathek indulged, he experienced no abatement in the love of his people, who thought, that a sovereign immersed in pleasure was not less tolerable to his subjects, than one that employed himself in creating them foes. But the unquiet and impetuous disposition of the Caliph, would not allow him to rest there. He had studied so much for his amusement in the life-time of his father as to acquire a great deal of knowledge; though not a sufficiency to satisfy himself, for, he wished to know everything, even sciences that did not exist. He was fond of engaging in disputes with the learned, but liked them not to push their opposition with warmth. He stopped the mouths of those, with presents, whose mouths could be stopped, whilst others, whom his liberality was unable to subdue, he sent to prison to cool their blood, a remedy that often succeeded.

Vathek discovered also a predilection for theological controversy; but it was not with the orthodox that he usually held. By this means he induced the zealots to oppose him, and then persecuted them in return; for, he resolved, at any rate, to have reason on his side.

The great prophet Mahomet, whose Vicars the Caliphs are, beheld with indignation from his abode in the seventh heaven, the irreligious conduct of such a viceregent. "Let us leave him to himself," said he to the Genii, who are always ready to receive his commands: "let us see to what lengths his folly and impiety will carry him: if he run into excess, we shall know how to chastise him. Assist him, therefore, to complete the tower which, in imitation of Nimrod,[5] he hath begun; not, like that great warriour, to escape being drowned, but from the insolent curiosity of penetrating the secrets of Heaven:—he will not divine the fate that awaits him."

The Genii obeyed; and when the workmen had raised their structure a cubit, in the day-time, two cubit more were added in the night. The expedition with which the fabrick arose was not a little flattering to the vanity of Vathek. He fancied that even insensible matter shewed a forwardness to subserve his designs; not considering that the successes of the foolish and wicked form the first rod of their chastisement.

His pride arrived at its height, when having ascended, for the first time, the eleven thousand stairs of his tower, he cast his eyes below, and beheld men not larger than pismires;[6] mountains, than shells; and cities, than bee-hives. The idea which such an elevation inspired of his own grandeur completely bewildered him; he was almost ready to adore himself; till, lifting his eyes

4. Torches.
5. He figures in the book of Genesis and the Chronicles. Biblical commentaries often identified him with the building of the Tower of Babel.
6. Ants.

upward, he saw the stars, as high above him, as they appeared, when he stood on the surface of the earth. He consoled himself, however, for this transient perception of his littleness, with the thought of being great in the eyes of others; and flattered himself, that the light of his mind would extend beyond the reach of his sight, and transfer to the stars the decrees of his destiny.

* * *

1782–85   1786

THOMAS DANIELL

Thomas Daniell (1759–1840) journeyed to India in 1784, accompanied by his nephew William Daniell (1769–1837), also a landscape painter. The pair would spend eight years traveling throughout the Indian subcontinent recording landscapes hitherto unseen by British eyes. While they traveled, the British dominance over India was consolidated, as the emphasis on trade that had defined East India Company policy gave way to an emphasis on the military conquest of new territories. Daniell's introduction, written more than a decade after the painters' return home to England, announces this transformation and proposes that it is now the turn of the artist to take possession of India, in an act of "guiltless spoliation." The Daniells' watercolors, reproduced as aquatints and collected in their books, familiarized the British public with their distant empire. They were very popular, with some images from A Picturesque Voyage showing up on the china dishes of people of fashion.

From A Picturesque Voyage to India by the Way of China

Introduction

From the earliest era of history the attention of Europe has been drawn to the East; whose fastidious people, vainly disclaiming kindred with other families of mankind, have been implicated in the fate of distant nations, and compelled to endure their unwelcome alliance, or to enhance their suspicious friendship. By a series of political changes, in other quarters of the globe, these countries have been rendered subservient to the feeling or policy of Europe. Curiosity has penetrated the veil of mystery that so long enveloped their civil and religious systems; and their pompous pretensions to antiquity, their venerable laws and institutions, are now exposed to the sacrilegious scrutiny of strangers.

It was an honourable feature in the late century, that the passion for discovery, originally kindled by the thirst for gold, was exalted to higher and nobler aims than commercial speculations. Since this new era of civilization, a liberal spirit of curiosity has prompted undertakings to which avarice lent no incentive, and fortune annexed no reward: associations have been formed, not for piracy, but humanity: science has had her adventurers, and philanthropy her achievements: the shores of Asia have been invaded by a race of students with no rapacity but for lettered relics; by naturalists, whose cruelty extends not to one human inhabitant; by philosophers, ambitious only for the extirpation of error, and the diffusion of truth. It remains for the artist to claim his part in these guiltless spoliations and to transport to Europe the picturesque beauties of these favoured regions. The contemplation of oriental scenery is interesting to the philosophic eye, from the number of monuments and other venerable objects which still exist in those ever-celebrated countries; and which cast a gleam of traditionary light on the obscurity of departed ages. Happily for curiosity, these vestiges are often elucidated by the manners of the present inhabitants, who with unexampled fidelity have preserved their primitive customs unimpaired by time or conquest; and in their domestic institutions still present the image of a remote and almost obsolete antiquity. There are other associations of sentiment, which in this country must lend to oriental scenery peculiar attractions: a large part of Hindoostan is now annexed to the British empire; and it cannot but afford gratification to our public feelings to become familiar with a country to which we are now attached by the ties of consanguinity and affection. There are, perhaps, few of us who have not been impelled by stronger motives than curiosity to trace the progress of an Indian voyage; and to acquire some local ideas of those distant regions which it has been the fortune of our friends or relatives to explore. To assist the imagination in this erratic flight is the object of the following work: delineation is the only medium by which a faithful description can be given of sensible images: the pencil is narrative to the eye; and however minute in its relations, can scarcely become tedious: its representations are not liable to the omissions of memory, or the misconceptions of fancy; whatever it communicates is a transcript from nature.

1810

ROBERT SOUTHEY

I nspired by a formative childhood encounter with Bernard Picart and Jean Frédéric Bernard's monumental survey the *Religious Ceremonies and Customs of the World* (1723), Robert Southey (1774–1843) as a young man intended to write a series of epics that would one after another, on an annual basis, engage all the belief systems of the globe—"the Persian, the Runic, the Keltic, the Greek, the Jewish, the Roman Catholick, and the Japanese," as he outlined in 1808. The grandiose scheme was not realized, but in 1801 Southey did publish *Thalaba the Destroyer*, set in Islamic Arabia, and then the following year set to transposing his Arabian epic's tale of sorcery and revenge into a new setting, that of Hindu India. *The Curse of Kehama*, a poem of twenty-four books and more than a hundred pages of notes, was eventually published in 1810 (so many books, one guesses, because Southey was emulating Homer, and so many notes, because he was emulating Beckford and Henley).

The poem begins with the curse that the cruel Brahmin priest Kehama pronounces on Ladurlad, the peasant who has killed Kehama's heir in the effort to save

Kailyal, a fellow peasant, from rape at his hands. Much of the narrative of *The Curse of Kehama* tracks Kehama's vengeful pursuit of Ladurlad and Kailyal, until, in a last-minute reversal of fortunes, his curse redounds on the tyrant's own head, and he is doomed to eternal suffering in hell. Here we pick up the story at an earlier moment, in Book 14, when the virtuous maiden Kailyal is on the verge of being forced into a ritual marriage of death with the god of the Juggernaut, an avatar of Krishna and the seven-headed god referred to in the following lines. Though the episode, titled "Jaga-Naut," has some of the flavor of the Gothic novels of Southey's day (and would be replayed in an even more lurid idiom in Charles Maturin's 1824 novel *Melmoth the Wanderer*), Southey's notes refer the reader to several factual sources, including early writing by Claudius Buchanan.

Jaga-Naut

    Joy in the City of great Jaga-Naut!
    Joy in the seven-headed Idol's shrine!
A virgin-bride his ministers have brought,
    A mortal maid, in form and face divine,
5   Peerless among all daughters of mankind;
Search'd they the world again from East to West,
        In endless quest,
        Seeking the fairest and the best,
No maid so lovely might they hope to find; . .
10   For she hath breath'd celestial air,
    And heavenly food hath been her fare,
And heavenly thoughts and feelings give her face
        That heavenly grace.
    Joy in the City of great Jaga-Naut,
15   Joy in the seven-headed Idol's shrine!
The fairest Maid his Yoguees[1] sought,
A fairer than the fairest have they brought,
A maid of charms surpassing human thought,
        A maid divine.

20   Now bring ye forth the Chariot of the God!
        Bring him abroad,
That through the swarming City he may ride;
        And by his side
Place ye the Maid of more than mortal grace,
25   The Maid of perfect form and heavenly face!
      Set her aloft in triumph, like a bride
        Upon the bridal car,°   *chariot*
And spread the joyful tidings wide and far, . .
        Spread it with trump and voice
30   That all may hear, and all who hear rejoice, . .
The Mighty One hath found his mate! the God
        Will ride abroad!

1. I.e., yogis. In an 1811 letter to the publisher John Murray, Southey offered a definition of *yoguee*: "Hindoo Devotee."

To-night will he go forth from his abode!
   Ye myriads who adore him,
35   Prepare the way before him!

   Uprear'd on twenty wheels elate,
Huge as a Ship, the bridal car appear'd;
Loud creak its ponderous wheels, as through the gate
A thousand Bramins° drag the enormous load.   *Hindu priests*
40   There, thron'd aloft in state,
   The Image of the seven-headed God
Came forth from his abode; and at his side
     Sate Kailyal like a bride;
A bridal statue rather might she seem,
45   For she regarded all things like a dream,
Having no thought, nor fear, nor will, nor aught
Save hope and faith, that liv'd within her still.

   O silent Night, how have they startled thee
     With the brazen trumpet's blare!
50   And thou, O Moon! whose quiet light serene
Filleth wide heaven, and bathing hill and wood,
   Spreads o'er the peaceful valley like a flood,
How have they dimm'd thee with the torches glare,
Which round yon moving pageant flame and flare,
55   As the wild rout, with deafening song and shout,
     Fling their long flashes out,
   That, like infernal lightnings, fire the air.

   A thousand pilgrims strain
Arm, shoulder, breast and thigh, with might and main,
60   To drag that sacred wain,°   *wagon*
And scarce can draw along the enormous load.
Prone fall the frantic votaries° in its road,   *worshipers*
     And, calling on the God,
Their self-devoted bodies there they lay
65   To pave his chariot-way.
     On Jaga-Naut they call,
The ponderous Car rolls on, and crushes all.
Through blood and bones it ploughs its dreadful path.
   Groans rise unheard; the dying cry,
70   And death and agony
Are trodden under foot by yon mad throng,
Who follow close, and thrust the deadly wheels along.

   Pale grows the Maid at this accursed sight;
     The yells which round her rise
75   Have rous'd her with affright,
And fear hath given to her dilated eyes
     A wilder light.
Where shall those eyes be turn'd? she knows not where!
   Downward they dare not look, for there
80   Is death, and horror, and despair;
Nor can her patient looks to Heaven repair,

For the huge Idol over her, in air,
Spreads his seven hideous heads, and wide
Extends their snaky necks on every side;
85   And all around, behind, before,
The bridal Car, is the raging rout,
With frantic shout, and deafening roar,
Tossing the torches' flames about.
And the double double peals of the drum are there,
90   And the startling burst of the trumpet's blare;
And the gong, that seems, with its thunders dread,
To stun the living, and waken the dead.
The ear-strings throb as if they were broke,
And the eye-lids drop at the weight of its stroke.
95   Fain would the Maid have kept them fast,
But open they start at the crack of the blast.

* * *

1801–10   1810

CLAUDIUS BUCHANAN

Between 1797 and 1808, Claudius Buchanan (1766–1815) served as an Anglican chaplain with the East India Company. Even before he returned to England, he began campaigning for the Christianization of India, a goal that set him at loggerheads with established Company policy. Since the eighteenth century, the Company had thought it wise to permit the populations it governed to practice their religions undisturbed; it had prohibited missionary activity (Buchanan was bound by the Company code to minister to fellow employees only); and emulating a practice of the Mughal Empire that it had displaced, it had even derived revenue from a scheme that involved taxing the pilgrims attending Hindu festivals. However, in 1805 Buchanan, who loathed this pilgrim tax, asked his countrymen whether they were indeed willing "to receive the riches of the East on the terms of chartering immoral superstition."

In *Christian Researches in Asia*, Buchanan used the record of his travels in India to persuade Britons that their answer must be no. The book's sensationalized reporting, and especially its lurid account of the annual festival of Juggernaut, galvanized British and American readers. It went through nine editions in two years. Extracts even appeared in the *Lady's Magazine*. By portraying Hinduism as a religion of death, Buchanan helped transform British attitudes toward their Indian empire; when the East India Company charter was revised in 1813, it was so as to register the new consensus that India had to be ruled by British cultural codes, not its own. The glorious image of India cultivated by men like Sir William Jones faded from view.

From Christian Researches in Asia

From The Author's Journal in His Tour to the Temple of Juggernaut[1]

Juggernaut, 18th of June.

I have returned home from witnessing a scene which I shall never forget. At twelve o'clock of this day, being the great day of the feast, the Moloch of Hindoostan[2] was brought out of his temple amidst the acclamations of hundreds of thousands of his worshippers. When the idol was placed on his throne, a shout was raised, by the multitude, such as I had never heard before. It continued equable for a few minutes, and then gradually died away. After a short interval of silence, a murmur was heard at a distance; all eyes were turned towards the place, and, behold, a *grove* advancing. A body of men, having green branches, or palms, in their hands, approached with great celerity. The people opened a way for them; and when they had come up to the throne, they fell down before him that sat thereon, and worshipped. And the multitude again sent forth a voice 'like the sound of a great thunder.'[3]—But the voices I now heard, were not those of melody or of joyful acclamation; for there is no harmony in the praise of Moloch's worshippers. Their number indeed brought to my mind the countless multitude of the Revelations; but their voices gave no tuneful Hosanna or Hallelujah; but rather a yell of approbation, united with a kind of *hissing* applause.[4]—I was at a loss how to account for this latter noise, until I was directed to notice the women; who emitted a sound like that of *whistling*, with the lips circular and the tongue vibrating: as if a serpent would speak by their organs, uttering human sounds.

The throne of the idol was placed on a stupendous car or tower about sixty feet in height, resting on wheels which indented the ground deeply, as they turned slowly under the ponderous machine. Attached to it were six cables, of the size and length of a ship's cable, by which the people drew it along. Upon the tower were the priests and satellites of the idol, surrounding his throne. The idol is a block of wood, having a frightful visage painted black, with a distended mouth of a bloody colour. His arms are of gold, and he is dressed in gorgeous apparel. The other two idols are of a white and yellow colour.—Five elephants preceded the three towers, bearing towering flags, dressed in crimson caparisons, and having bells hanging to their caparisons, which sounded musically as they moved.

I went on in the procession, close by the tower of Moloch; which, as it was drawn with difficulty, grated on its many wheels harsh thunder. After a few minutes it stopped; and now the worship of the God began.—A high priest mounted the car in front of the idol, and pronounced his obscene stanzas in the ears of the people; who responded at intervals in the same strain. 'These

---

1. This temple, in the eastern state of Odisha, remains the site of a popular annual festival in which gigantic chariots carrying the statues of the gods are paraded through crowds of pilgrims. From the Middle Ages on, European travelers had reported that some of those devotees deliberately threw themselves under the chariot wheels as religious sacrifices. Because of those reports, now often disputed, the word *Juggernaut* (Jagannath), at first a name for an avatar of Krishna, has in English become a term for any sort of institution or practice that demands blind, senseless devotion.

2. In the Old Testament, Moloch is the god the Canaanites worship through the practice of child sacrifice.

3. Buchanan quotes Revelation 14.2.

4. See *Milton's Pandemonium*, Book X [Buchanan's note]. As Buchanan remembers, in *Paradise Lost* Milton has Satan return to hell after the successful temptation of Adam and Eve and present himself to the convened devils to receive their congratulations, "when contrary he hears / On all sides from innumerable tongues / A dismal universal hiss, the sound / Of public scorn" (10.506–09). All have been metamorphosed into serpents, Satan included.

songs,' said he, 'are the delight of the God. His car can only move when he is pleased with the song.'—The car moved on a little way and then stopped. A boy of about twelve years was then brought forth to attempt something yet more lascivious, if peradventure the God would move. The 'child perfected the praise' of his idol with such ardent expression and gesture, that the God was pleased,[5] and the multitude, emitting a sensual yell of delight, urged the car along.—After a few minutes it stopped again. An aged minister of the idol then stood up, and with a long rod in his hand, which he moved with indecent action, completed the variety of this disgusting exhibition.—I felt a consciousness of doing wrong in witnessing it. I was also somewhat appalled at the magnitude and horror of the spectacle; I felt like a guilty person, on whom all eyes were fixed, and I was about to withdraw. But a scene of a different kind was now to be presented. The characteristics of Moloch's worship are obscenity and blood. We have seen the former. Now comes the blood.

After the tower had proceeded some way, a pilgrim announced that he was ready to offer himself a sacrifice to the idol. He laid himself down in the road before the tower as it was moving along, lying on his face, with his arms stretched forwards. The multitude passed round him, leaving the space clear, and he was crushed to death by the wheels of the tower. A shout of joy was raised to the God. He is said to *smile* when the libation of the blood is made. The People threw cowries, or small money, on the body of the victim, in approbation of the deed. He was left to view a considerable time, and was then carried by the *Hurries* to the Golgotha,[6] where I have just been viewing his remains. How much I wished that the Proprietors of India Stock could have attended the wheels of Juggernaut, and seen this peculiar source of their revenue.

1806   1811

5. Buchanan's ironic citation of Matthew 21.16 in which the children worship Jesus in defiance of the priests of the Temple. When the latter challenge Jesus, he responds "have ye never read, Out of the mouths of babes and sucklings thou hast perfected praise?" For Buchanan the worship the Hindu boy offers his god is disgusting by contrast with this scene from early Christianity; in India, he implies, worship is mingled with sexuality ("something yet more lascivious"). 6. The site outside Jerusalem where Christ was crucified. *Hurries*: servants (Bengali).

SYDNEY OWENSON

S et in seventeenth-century India, and using that setting to comment on what colonialism would become two centuries later, *The Missionary* narrates the doomed love between Hilarion, a Portuguese Franciscan monk, and Luxima, the Hindu priestess whose conversion he had aimed to secure. Throughout her career, the Anglo-Irish Sydney Owenson (1778?–1859) used her trademark blend of sentimental fiction and travel narrative to probe the relations between colonized and colonizer and query the possibility of cross-cultural understanding. *The Missionary* continues an investigation begun in Owenson's runaway success, *The Wild Irish Girl* (1806)—in part about Irish resistance to English rule—and continued in her *Ida of Athens* (1809)—in part about Greece's rebellion against the Ottoman Empire.

In 1810 Southey had used the *The Curse of Kehama*—partially intended as his demonstration that, as he put it, Hinduism was "of all false religions . . . the most monstrous in its fables, and the most fatal in its effects"—to endorse the interventionism and proselytizing that were in this moment becoming key elements of British imperial policy. Owenson by contrast tells a story in which tragedy arises from religious dogmatism. As in the passages reprinted here, which record Hilarion's first encounter with Luxima, Owenson's protagonists suffer because they and their communities, Brahmin and Catholic, have internalized the prejudices making it impossible for them to love. Percy Shelley pressed *The Missionary* on friends after reading it in 1812 and wrote, "Since I have read it I have read no other—but I have thought strangely." In 1816 he turned that mental dislocation to account in *Alastor*, whose veiled maiden is a new version of Luxima.

From The Missionary: An Indian Tale[1]

* * *

The religious attendants of the Guru, mounted on Arabian horses, led the van;[2] followed by the Ramganny, or dancing priestesses of the temple, who sung, as they proceeded, the histories of their gods, while incarnate upon earth. Their movements were slow, languid, and graceful; and their hymns, accompanied by the tamboora, the seringa, and other instruments, whose deep, soft, and solemn tones, seem consecrated to the purposes of a tender and fanciful religion, excited in the soul of their auditors, emotions which belonged not all to Heaven.

This group, which resembled, in form and movement, the personfication of the first hours of Love and Youth, was succeeded by the Guru, mounted on an elephant, which moved with a majestic pace; his howdah,[3] of pure gold, sparkling to the radiance of the rising day. Disciples of the Brahman surrounded his elephant, and were immediately followed by a palanquin, which from its simplicity formed a striking contrast to the splendid objects that had preceded it. Its drapery, composed of the snowy muslin of the country, shone like the fleecy vapour on which the sun's first light reposes: its delicate shafts were entwined with the caressing fibres of the camalata, the flower of the Indian heaven, dedicated to Camdeo, the god of 'mystic love,' whose crimson blossoms breathed of odours which soothed, rather than intoxicated the senses.

The acclamations which had rent the air on the appearance of the Guru, died softly away as the palanquin approached. An awe more profound, a feeling more pure, more sublimated, seemed to take possession of the multitude; for, indistinctly seen through the transparent veil of the palanquin, appeared the most sacred of vestals, the Prophetess and Brachmachira of Cashmire. Her perfect form, thus shrouded, caught, from the circumstance, a mysterious charm, and seemed like one of the splendid illusions, with which the enthusiasm of religion brightens the holy dream of its votarist, like the spirit which descends amidst the shadows of night upon the slumbers of the blessed. Considered as the offspring of Brahma, as a ray of the divine excellence, the Indians of the most distinguished rank drew back as she approached, lest their very breath should pollute that reigion of purity her respiration conse-

1. Hilarion has decided, counseled by the Brahmin philosopher who tutors him in the native languages, to launch his evangelizing by participating in the theological debates held to mark the arrival in the city of Lahore of the guru of Cashmire. The first of the excerpts here describes the guru's entrance into the city, along with his granddaughter Luxima. A "brachmachira," or nun, she is devoted, like her grandfather, to the Vedanti sect, which Hilarion's adviser describes as a faith centered on the notion that "a passionate and exclusive love of Heaven is that feeling only, which offers no illusion to the soul, and secures its eternal felicity." This description intrigues Hilarion. The next morning he follows Luxima when she visits the shrine of Camdeo, the god of love. The second excerpt traces his response to what he witnesses there.
2. Procession.
3. Canopied seat used for riding on an elephant's back.

crated; and the odour of the sacred flowers, by which she was adorned, was inhaled with an eager devotion, as if it purified the soul it almost seemed to penetrate. The venerated palanquin was guarded by a number of pilgrim women, and the chief casts of the inhabitants of Lahore; while a band of the native troops closed the procession, which proceeded to the Pagoda of Crishna.

From the contemplation of a spectacle so new, so unexpected, the Missionary retired within his solitary tent, with that feeling of horror and disgust, which a profanation of the sentiment and purposes of religion might be supposed to excite, in a mind so pure, so zealous, so far above all the pomp and passions of life, and hitherto so ignorant of all the images connected with their representation. The music, the perfumes, the women, the luxury, and the splendour of the extraordinary procession, offended his piety, and almost disordered his imagination. He thought, for a moment, of the perils of an enterprise, undertaken in a country where the very air was unfavourable to virtue, and where all breathed a character of enjoyment, even over the awful[4] sanctity of religion; a species of enjoyment, to whose very existence he had been, hitherto, almost a stranger; but the genius of his zeal warmed in proportion to the obstacles he found he had to encounter.

* * *

The sibyl Priestess stood at the foot of the shrine of her tutelar deity, and the superstitious multitude fell prostrate at the feet of the Prophetess. They invoked her intercession with the god she served: mothers held up their infants to her view; fathers inquired from her the fate of their absent sons; and many addressed her on the future events of their lives; while she, not more deceiving than deceived, became the victim of her own imposition, and stood in the midst of her votarists, in all the imposing charm of holy illusion. Her enthusiasm once kindled, her imagination became disordered: believing herself inspired, she looked the immortality she fancied, and uttered rhapsodies in accents so impressive and so tender, and with emotions so wild, and yet so touching, that the mind no longer struggled against the imposition of the senses, and the spirit of fanatical zeal confirmed the influence of human loveliness.

Hitherto, curiosity had induced the Missionary to follow the procession; but he now turned back, horror-struck. Too long had the apostle of Christianity been the witness of those impious rites, offered by the idolaters to the idolatress; and the indignation he felt at all he had seen, at all he had heared, produced an irritability of feeling, new to a mind so tranquil, and but little consonant to a character so regulated, so subdued, so far above even the laudable weakness of human nature. He considered the false Prophetess as the most fatal opponent to his intentions, and he looked to her conversion as the most effectual means to accomplish the success of his enterprise. He shuddered to reflect on the weakness and frailty of man, who is so often led to truth by the allurements which belong to error; and he devoted the remainder of the day to the consideration of those pious plans, by which he hoped, one day, to shade the brow of the Heathen Priestess with the sacred veil of the Christian Nun.

* * *

1811

---

4. Awe-inspiring.

GEORGE GORDON, LORD BYRON

"The public are orientalizing," Byron wrote to Thomas Moore in August 1813, counseling his brother poet to engage with the East, that most salable of literary themes. Byron assiduously followed his own advice. He had already launched his line of "Turkish tales" with *The Giaour*, first published in June 1813 and then in longer and longer versions, over the next two years. Between 1813 and 1816, he followed up this narrative poem with similar, and similarly best-selling, tales: *The Bride of Abydos*, *The Corsair*, *Lara*, and *The Siege of Corinth*.

The Giaour originated, Byron said, in a story he had heard sung in a Levantine coffeehouse he had visited by chance during his travels of 1809–10. It is a purposefully fragmentary narrative, divided between multiple narrators and vantage points on the action, and supplemented, in the manner of earlier literary reports from the eastern edge of Christian Europe, with notes about this foreign land's customs and topography, notes mainly omitted from the excerpt reprinted here. In prefatory remarks affixed to one edition, Byron gave the general outline of what his story would have been "when entire": it *"contained the adventures of a female slave, who was thrown, in the Mussulman* [Mohammedan] *manner, into the sea for infidelity, and avenged by a young Venetian."* That slave is Leila, the favorite among the concubines whom the Turkish lord Hassan keeps in his harem. Her lover, the Venetian, is the poem's "Giaour." (Byron possibly encountered in Beckford's *Vathek* this exotic word for "foreigner" or "infidel"—pronounced, we think, so as to rhyme with "power.") The poem concludes with the narrative of the Christian friar who listens to the Giaour's confession in the monastery to which he has retreated to repent his sins. In the section presented here, the primary voice is also that of a bystander to the action, here a Turkish fisherman, who reports the "strange rumours" circulating in his city following Leila's disappearance. This excerpt is drawn from *The Giaour's* fifth edition.

The Giaour. The translations of Byron's Turkish tales fired the imaginations of many visual artists in France, including Théodore Géricault. This 1823 lithograph, part of a suite of images Géricault devoted to the tales, pictures the Giaour.

From The Giaour: A Fragment of a Turkish Tale

* * *

Black Hassan from the Haram flies,
440 Nor bends on woman's face his eyes,
The unwonted chase° each hour employs,   *hunt*
Yet shares he not the hunter's joys.
Not thus was Hassan wont to fly
When Leila dwelt in his Serai.°   *harem*
445 Doth Leila there no longer dwell?
That tale can only Hassan tell:
Strange rumours in our city say
Upon that eve she fled away;
When Rhamazan's last sun was set,
450 And flashing from each minaret
Millions of lamps proclaim'd the feast
Of Bairam[1] through the boundless East.
'Twas then she went as to the bath,
Which Hassan vainly search'd in wrath,
455 But she was flown her master's rage
In likeness of a Georgian page;
And far beyond the Moslem's power
Had wrong'd him with the faithless Giaour.
Somewhat of this had Hassan deem'd,
460 But still so fond, so fair she seem'd,
Too well he trusted to the slave
Whose treachery deserv'd a grave:
And on that eve had gone to mosque,
And thence to feast in his kiosk.[2]
465 Such is the tale his Nubians[3] tell,
Who did not watch their charge too well;
But others say, that on that night,
By pale Phingari's° trembling light,   *moon's*
The Giaour upon his jet black steed
470 Was seen—but seen alone to speed
With bloody spur along the shore,
Nor maid nor page behind him bore.

• • • • • • • • • •

Her eye's dark charm 'twere vain to tell,
But gaze on that of the Gazelle,
475 It will assist thy fancy well,
As large, as languishingly dark,
But Soul beam'd forth in every spark
That darted from beneath the lid,
Bright as the ruby of Giamschid.[4]

1. Feast day that in the Islamic calendar ends Ramadan (or Rhamazan), the month of fasting.
2. Pavilion.
3. Men from Sudan. European accounts often identified them as the guards placed over the harem women.

4. The celebrated fabulous ruby of Sultan Giamschid, the embellisher of Ishtakhar [Byron's note, which continues several lines further, tracing, as though in parody of the era's philological researchers, the pronunciation of *Giamschid*].

480 Yea, *Soul*, and should our prophet say
     That form was nought but breathing clay,
     By Alla! I would answer nay;
     Though on Al-Sirat's arch I stood,[5]
     Which totters o'er the fiery flood,
485 With Paradise within my view,
     And all his Houris° beckoning through.   beautiful women
     Oh! who young Leila's glance could read
     And keep that portion of his creed[6]
     Which saith, that woman is but dust,
490 A soulless toy for tyrant's lust?
     On her might Muftis[7] gaze, and own
     That through her eye the Immortal shone—
     On her fair cheek's unfading hue,
     The young pomegranate's blossoms strew
495 Their bloom in blushes ever new—
     Her hair in hyacinthine flow
     When left to roll its folds below;
     As midst her handmaids in the hall
     She stood superior to them all,
500 Hath swept the marble where her feet
     Gleamed whiter than the mountain sleet
     Ere from the cloud that gave it birth,
     It fell, and caught one stain of earth.
     The cygnet nobly walks the water—
505 So moved on earth Circassia's[8] daughter—
     The loveliest bird of Franguestan!
     As rears her crest the ruffled Swan,
          And spurns the wave with wings of pride,
     When pass the steps of stranger man
510   Along the banks that bound her tide;
     Thus rose fair Leila's whiter neck:—
     Thus armed with beauty would she check
     Intrusion's glance, till Folly's gaze
     Shrunk from the charms it meant to praise.
515 Thus high and graceful was her gait;
     Her heart as tender to her mate—
     Her mate—stern Hassan, who was he?
     Alas! that name was not for thee!

          • • • • • • • • • • • • •

          Stern Hassan hath a journey ta'en
520 With twenty vassals in his train,
     Each arm'd as best becomes a man
     With arquebuss° and ataghan;°   gun / sword

---

5. Al-Sirat, the bridge of breadth less than the thread of a famished spider, over which the Mussulmans must *skate* into Paradise, to which it is the only entrance . . . [Byron's note, which continues, quite jokily, with comments on the hellish region underneath the bridge].
6. Here Byron's long note records, and rejects as popular misconception, the belief that Islamic doctrine denied that women had souls.
7. Administrators of Sharia law.
8. Circassia, also called Franguestan (line 506), is a region in the Caucasus mountains, considered the border between Europe and Asia.

The chief before, as deck'd for war,
Bears in his belt the scimitar
525 Stain'd with the best of Arnaut° blood,   *Albanian*
When in the pass the rebels stood,
And few return'd to tell the tale
Of what befell in Parne's vale.[9]
The pistols which his girdle bore
Were those that once a pasha wore,
530 Which still, though gemm'd and boss'd with gold,
Even robbers tremble to behold.—
'Tis said he goes to woo a bride
More true than her who left his side;
The faithless slave that broke her bower,
535 And, worse than faithless, for a Giaour!—

• • • • • • • • • • • • •

The sun's last rays are on the hill,
And sparkle in the fountain rill,
Whose welcome waters cool and clear,
540 Draw blessings from the mountaineer;
Here may the loitering merchant Greek
Find that repose 'twere vain to seek
In cities lodg'd too near his lord,
And trembling for his secret hoard—
545 Here may he rest where none can see,
In crowds a slave, in deserts free;
And with forbidden wine may stain
The bowl a Moslem must not drain.—

• • • • • • • • • • •

The foremost Tartar's in the gap,
550 Conspicuous by his yellow cap,
The rest in lengthening line the while
Wind slowly through the long defile;°   *narrow passage*
Above, the mountain rears a peak,
Where vultures whet the thirsty beak,
555 And their's may be a feast to-night,
Shall tempt them down ere morrow's light.
Beneath, a river's wintry stream
Has shrunk before the summer beam,
And left a channel bleak and bare,
560 Save shrubs that spring to perish there.
Each side the midway path there lay
Small broken crags of granite gray,
By time or mountain lightning riven,
From summits clad in mists of heaven;

9. Valley beside Mount Parnitha, a densely forested mountain north of Athens. *The Giaour* is set in Turkish-occupied Greece, contested territory that in the early 18th century, when these adventures are meant to have taken place, was also coveted by the Venetian Empire.

565 For where is he that hath beheld
The peak of Liakura[1] unveil'd?

• • • • • • • • • • •

They reach the grove of pine at last,
"Bismillah!° now the peril's past;   *in Allah's name*
For yonder view the opening plain,
570 And there we'll prick our steeds amain:"
The Chiaus° spake, and as he said,   *Turkish sergeant*
A bullet whistled o'er his head;
The foremost Tartar bites the ground!
Scarce had they time to check the rein
575 Swift from their steeds the riders bound,
But three shall never mount again,
Unseen the foes that gave the wound,
The dying ask revenge in vain.
With steel unsheath'd, and carbines° bent,   *firearms*
580 Some o'er their courser's harness leant,
Half shelter'd by the steed,
Some fly behind the nearest rock,
And there await the coming shock,
Nor tamely stand to bleed
585 Beneath the shaft of foes unseen,
Who dare not quit their craggy screen.
Stern Hassan only from his horse
Disdains to light, and keeps his course,
Till fiery flashes in the van°   *front*
590 Proclaim too sure the robber-clan
Have well secur'd the only way
Could now avail the promis'd prey;
Then curl'd his very beard with ire,
And glared his eye with fiercer fire.
595 "Though far and near the bullets hiss,
I've scaped a bloodier hour than this."
And now the foe their covert quit,
And call his vassals to submit;
But Hassan's frown and furious word
600 Are dreaded more than hostile sword,
Nor of his little band a man
Resign'd carbine or ataghan—
Nor raised the craven cry, Amaun!°   *pardon*
In fuller sight, more near and near,
605 The lately ambush'd foes appear,
And issuing from the grove advance,
Some who on battle charger prance.—
Who leads them on with foreign brand,
Far flashing in his red right hand?
610 "'Tis he—'tis he—I know him now,
I know him by his pallid brow;
I know him by the evil eye

1. A mountain in Greece.

That aids his envious treachery;
I know him by his jet-black barb,
615 Though now array'd in Arnaut garb,
Apostate from his own vile faith,[2]
It shall not save him from the death;
'Tis he, well met in any hour,
Lost Leila's love—accursed Giaour!"

620 As rolls the river into ocean,
In sable torrent wildly streaming;
As the sea-tide's opposing motion
In azure column proudly gleaming,
Beats back the current many a rood,
625 In curling foam and mingling flood;
While eddying whirl, and breaking wave,
Roused by the blast of winter rave,
Through sparkling spray in thundering clash,
The lightnings of the waters flash
630 In aweful whiteness o'er the shore,
That shines and shakes beneath the roar;
Thus—as the stream and ocean greet,
With waves that madden as they meet—
Thus join the bands whom mutual wrong,
635 And fate and fury drive along.
The bickering sabres' shivering jar,
    And pealing wide—or ringing near
    Its echoes on the throbbing ear
The deathshot hissing from afar—
640 The shock—the shout—the groan of war—
    Reverberate along that vale,
    More suited to the shepherd's tale:
Though few the numbers—their's the strife,
That neither spares nor speaks for life!
645 Ah! fondly youthful hearts can press,
To seize and share the dear caress;
But Love itself could never pant
For all that Beauty sighs to grant,
With half the fervour Hate bestows
650 Upon the last embrace of foes,
When grappling in the fight they fold
Those arms that ne'er shall lose their hold.
Friends meet to part—Love laughs at faith;—
True foes, once met, are joined till death!

* * *

1813

---

2. As leader of a band of Albanian (Arnaut) mercenaries, the Giaour betrays his own faith, Christianity.

LETITIA ELIZABETH LANDON

This much reprinted poem was originally published in the annual giftbook *Fisher's Drawing Room Scrapbook*, which Landon edited between 1832 and 1838. (For more about the poet, see p. 1045.) On its first appearance, the poem was presented as her literary accompaniment to an aquatint the *Scrapbook* had reprinted from an Indian travelogue by the infantry officer and amateur artist Robert Melville Grindlay.

Suttee or *sati*, the Hindu practice in which widows were immolated on their husbands' funeral pyres, focused much of the early-nineteenth-century controversy over whether the British ought to intervene into the culture of their colony. An anti-sati movement also grew up at this time among native social reformers, led by Raja Ram Mohan Roy (1772–1833). The practice was finally banned by the British government in 1829. Long after, however, English literature—not least literature by women—continued to gravitate toward sati as source material, both exploiting it as an occasion for Gothic horror and idealizing the dying widow as a willing martyr to altruistic love. Landon herself wrote about sati multiple times, before and after the ban.

"Preparations for a Suttee": one of the aquatint views included in Robert Melville Grindlay's lavish picture book *Scenery, Costumes, and Architecture Chiefly on the Western Side of India* (published in six parts between 1826 and 1830). Grindlay went to India as a teenager and served in the East India Company's army from 1804 to 1820.

Immolation of a Hindoo Widow

Gather her raven hair in one rich cluster,
Let the white champac° light it, as a star   *magnolia*
Gives to the dusky night a sudden lustre,
                 Shining afar.

5   Shed fragrant oils upon her fragrant bosom,
Until the breathing air around grows sweet;
Scatter the languid jasmine's yellow blossom
                 Beneath her feet.

Those small white feet are bare—too soft are they
10   To tread on aught but flowers; and there is roll'd
Round the slight ankle, meet for such display,
                 The band of gold.

Chains and bright stones are on her arms and neck;
What pleasant vanities are linked with them,
15   Of happy hours, which youth delights to deck
                 With gold and gem.

She comes! So comes the Moon, when she has found
A silvery path wherein thro' heaven to glide.
Fling the white veil—a summer cloud—around;
20   She is a bride!

And yet the crowd that gather at her side
Are pale, and every gazer holds his breath.
Eyes fill with tears unbidden, for the bride—
                 The bride of Death!

25   She gives away the garland from her hair,
She gives the gems that she will wear no more;
All the affections, whose love-signs they were,
                 Are gone before.

The red pile blazes—let the bride ascend,
30   And lay her head upon her husband's heart,
Now in a perfect unison to blend—
                 No more to part.

1836

JOHN KEATS
1795–1821

John Keats's father was head stableman at a London livery stable; he married his employer's daughter and inherited the business. The poet's mother, by all reports, was an affectionate but negligent parent to her children; remarrying almost immediately after a fall from a horse killed her first husband, she left the eight-year-old John (her firstborn), his brothers, and a sister with their grandmother and did not reenter their lives for four years. The year before his father's death, Keats had been sent to the Reverend John Clarke's private school at Enfield, famous for its progressive curriculum, where he was a noisy, high-spirited boy; despite his small stature (when full-grown, he was barely over five feet in height), he distinguished himself in sports and fistfights. Here he had the good fortune to have as a mentor Charles Cowden Clarke, son of the headmaster, who later became a writer and an editor; he encouraged Keats's passion for reading and, both at school and in the course of their later friendship, introduced him to Spenser and other poets, to music, and to the theater.

When Keats's mother returned to her children, she was already ill, and in 1810 she died of tuberculosis. Although the livery stable had prospered, and £8,000 had been left in trust to the children by Keats's grandmother, the estate remained tied up in the law courts for all of Keats's lifetime. The children's guardian, Richard Abbey, an unimaginative and practical-minded businessman, took Keats out of school at the age of fifteen and bound him apprentice to Thomas Hammond, a surgeon and apothecary at Edmonton. In 1815 Keats carried on his medical studies at Guy's Hospital, London, and the next year qualified to practice as an apothecary-surgeon—but almost immediately, over his guardian's protests, he abandoned medicine for poetry.

This decision was influenced by Keats's friendship with Leigh Hunt, then editor of the *Examiner* and a leading political radical, poet, and prolific writer of criticism and periodical essays. Hunt, the first successful author of Keats's acquaintance, added his enthusiastic encouragement of Keats's poetic efforts to that of Clarke. More important, he introduced him to writers greater than Hunt himself—William Hazlitt, Charles Lamb, and Percy Shelley—as well as to Benjamin Robert Haydon, painter of grandiose historical and religious canvases. Through Hunt, Keats also met John Hamilton Reynolds and then Charles Wentworth Dilke and Charles Brown, who became his intimate friends and provided him with an essential circumstance for a fledgling poet: a sympathetic and appreciative audience.

The rapidity and sureness of Keats's development has no match. Although he did not begin writing poetry until his eighteenth year, by 1816 in the bold sonnet "On First Looking into Chapman's Homer" he had found his voice. Later that same year he wrote "Sleep and Poetry," in which he laid out for himself a program deliberately modeled on the careers of the greatest poets, asking only

> for ten years, that I may overwhelm
> Myself in poesy; so I may do the deed
> That my own soul has to itself decreed.

For even while his health was good, Keats felt a foreboding of early death and applied himself to his art with a desperate urgency. In 1817 he went on to compose *Endymion*, an ambitious undertaking of more than four thousand lines. It is a rich allegory of a mortal's quest for an ideal feminine counterpart and a flawless happiness beyond earthly possibility; in a number of passages, it already exhibits the sure movement and phrasing of his mature poetic style. But Keats's critical judgment and aspiration exceeded his achievement: long before he completed it, he declared impatiently that he carried on with the "slipshod" *Endymion* only as a "trial of invention" and began to block out *Hyperion*, conceived on the model of Milton's *Paradise Lost* in that most demanding of forms, the epic poem. His success in achieving the Miltonic manner is one of the reasons why Keats abandoned *Hyperion* before it was finished, for he recognized that he was uncommonly susceptible to poetic influences and regarded this as a threat to his individuality. "I will write independently," he insisted. "The Genius of Poetry must work out its own salvation in a man." He had refused the chance of intimacy with Shelley "that I might have my own unfettered scope"; he had broken away from Leigh Hunt's influence lest he get "the reputation of Hunt's *élève* [pupil]"; now he shied away from domination by Milton's powerfully infectious style.

In sentimental, later nineteenth-century accounts of "poor Keats," 1818 was cast as the year in which this rising genius, already frail and sensitive, was mortally crushed by vicious reviews. Percy Shelley helped initiate this myth in *Adonais*, which describes Keats as "a pale flower." Byron, who did not like Keats's verse, put it unsentimentally: Keats, he wrote, was "snuffed out by an article." It is true that the critics were brutal to Keats, those associated with the Tory journals especially. (On the new power and hostility of the reviewers in Keats's day, see "'Self-constituted judge of poesy': Reviewer vs. Poet in the Romantic Period" in the NAEL Archive.) For these critics his poetry proved an irresistible target precisely because it had been promoted by the radical Hunt. *Endymion* was mauled in the *Quarterly Review*, and one of the articles on "the Cockney School of Poetry" that appeared in *Blackwood's Magazine* condemned Keats as hopelessly vulgar, a writer who wanted to be a poet of nature but thought, as a social-climbing, undereducated Londoner would, that nature was "flowers seen in window-pots." "It is a better and wiser thing to be a starved apothecary than a starved poet," the reviewer scolded, "so back to the shop Mr John." Keats had for his own part the good sense to recognize that the attacks were motivated by political prejudice and class snobbery, and he had already passed his own severe judgment on *Endymion*: "My own domestic criticism," he said, "has given me pain without comparison beyond what *Blackwood* or the *Quarterly* could possibly inflict." More important was the financial distress of his brother George and his young bride, who emigrated to Kentucky and lost their money in an ill-advised investment. Keats, short of funds and needing to supplement the family income, had now to find ways to make money from his writing: he turned to journalism and began planning plays. His brother Tom contracted tuberculosis, and the poet, in devoted attendance, helplessly watched him waste away until his death that December. In the summer of that year, Keats had taken a strenuous walking tour in the English Lake District, Scotland, and Ireland. It was a glorious adventure but a totally exhausting one in wet, cold weather, and he returned in August with a chronically ulcerated throat made increasingly ominous by the shadow of the tuberculosis that had killed his mother and brother. And in the late fall of that same year, Keats fell unwillingly but deeply in love with Fanny Brawne, the eighteen-year-old girl next door. They became engaged, knowing, though, that Keats's poverty and worsening health might well make their marriage impossible.

In this period of turmoil, Keats achieved the culmination of his brief poetic career. Between January and September of 1819, masterpiece followed masterpiece in astonishing succession: *The Eve of St. Agnes*, "La Belle Dame sans Merci," all of the "great odes," *Lamia*, and a sufficient number of fine sonnets to make him, with Wordsworth, the major Romantic craftsman in that form. All of these poems possess the distinctive qualities of the work of Keats's maturity: a slow-paced, gracious movement; a concreteness of description in which all the senses—tactile, gustatory, kinetic, visceral, as well as visual and auditory—combine to give the total apprehension of an experience; a delight at the sheer existence of things outside himself, the poet seeming to lose his own identity in a total identification with the object he contemplates; and a concentrated felicity of phrasing that reminded his friends, as it has many critics since, of the language of Shakespeare. Under the richly sensuous surface, we find Keats's characteristic presentation of all experience as a tangle of inseparable but irreconcilable opposites. He finds melancholy in delight and pleasure in pain; he feels the highest intensity of love as an approximation to death; he inclines equally toward a life of indolence and "sensation" and toward a life of thought; he is aware both of the attraction of an imaginative dream world without "disagreeables" and the remorseless pressure of the actual; he aspires at the same time to aesthetic detachment and to social responsibility.

His letters, hardly less remarkable than his poetry, show that Keats felt on his pulses the conflicts he dramatized in his major poems. Above all, they reveal him wrestling with the problem of evil and suffering—what to make of our lives in the discovery that "the world is full of misery and heartbreak, pain, sickness and oppression." To the end of his life, he refused to seek solace for the complexity and contradictions of experience either in the abstractions of inherited philosophical doctrines or in the absolutes of a religious creed. At the close of his poetic career, in the latter part of 1819, Keats began to rework the epic *Hyperion* into the form of a dream vision that he called *The Fall of Hyperion*. In the introductory section of this fragment the poet is told by the prophetess Moneta that he has hitherto been merely a dreamer; he must know that

> The poet and the dreamer are distinct,
> Diverse, sheer opposite, antipodes,

and that the height of poetry can be reached only by

> those to whom the miseries of the world
> Are misery, and will not let them rest.

He was seemingly planning to undertake a new direction and subject matter, when illness and death intervened.

On the night of February 3, 1820, he coughed up blood. As a physician he refused to evade the truth: "I cannot be deceived in that colour; that drop of blood is my death warrant. I must die." That spring and summer a series of hemorrhages rapidly weakened him. In the autumn he allowed himself to be persuaded to seek the milder climate of Italy in the company of Joseph Severn, a young painter, but these last months were only what he called "a posthumous existence." He died in Rome on February 23, 1821, and was buried in the Protestant Cemetery, where Mary and Percy Shelley had already interred their little son William, and where Percy's ashes, too, would be deposited in 1822. At times the agony of his disease, the seeming frustration of his hopes for great poetic achievement, and the despair of his passion for Fanny Brawne compelled even Keats's brave spirit to bitterness and jealousy, but he always recovered his gallantry. His last letter, written to Charles Brown, concludes: "I can scarcely bid you good bye even in a letter. I always made an awkward bow. God bless you! John Keats."

No one can read Keats's poems and letters without sensing the tragic waste of an extraordinary intellect and genius cut off so early. What he might have done is beyond conjecture; what we do know is that his poetry, when he stopped writing at the age of twenty-four, exceeds the accomplishment at the same age of Chaucer, Shakespeare, and Milton.

The texts reprinted here are based on Jack Stillinger's edition, *The Poems of John Keats* (1978).

On First Looking into Chapman's Homer[1]

Greekian influence

Much have I travell'd in the realms of gold,
   And many goodly states and kingdoms seen;
   Round many western islands have I been
Which bards in fealty to Apollo hold.
5   Oft of one wide expanse had I been told
   That deep-brow'd Homer ruled as his demesne;[2]
   Yet did I never breathe its pure serene[3]
Till I heard Chapman speak out loud and bold:
Then felt I like some watcher of the skies
10   When a new planet swims into his ken;°   *view*
   Or like stout Cortez when with eagle eyes
   He star'd at the Pacific—and all his men
Look'd at each other with a wild surmise—
   Silent, upon a peak in Darien.

Oct. 1816   1816

From Sleep and Poetry[1]

["O FOR TEN YEARS"]

O for ten years, that I may overwhelm
Myself in poesy; so I may do the deed
That my own soul has to itself decreed.
Then will I pass the countries that I see
100   In long perspective, and continually
Taste their pure fountains. First the realm I'll pass
Of Flora, and old Pan:[2] sleep in the grass,
Feed upon apples red, and strawberries,
And choose each pleasure that my fancy sees;
105   Catch the white-handed nymphs in shady places,
To woo sweet kisses from averted faces,—
Play with their fingers, touch their shoulders white
Into a pretty shrinking with a bite

1. Keats's mentor Charles Cowden Clarke introduced him to Homer in the robust translation by the Elizabethan poet and dramatist George Chapman. They read through the night, and Keats walked home at dawn. This sonnet reached Clarke by the ten o'clock mail that same morning. Readers have often assumed Keats got history wrong in this sonnet's sestet and confused Balboa, the first European explorer to see the Pacific, with Cortez, the conqueror of Mexico. But as Charles Rzepka pointed out in 2002, there is strictly speaking no reason to suppose Keats is concerned with original discoveries here (his Cortez stares at, rather than discovers, the Pacific): the sonnet overall is centrally concerned with sublime ambitions that are poignantly belated, and Cortez, who reached the Pacific two decades after Balboa did, is an apt vehicle for that concern.
2. Realm, feudal possession.
3. Clear expanse of air.

1. At the age of twenty-one, Keats set himself a regimen of poetic training modeled on the course followed by the greatest poets. Virgil had established the pattern of beginning with pastoral writing and proceeding gradually to the point at which he was ready to undertake the epic, and this pattern had been deliberately followed by Spenser and Milton. Keats's version of this program, as he describes it here, is to begin with the realm "of Flora, and old Pan" (line 102) and, within ten years, to climb up to the level of poetry dealing with "the agonies, the strife / Of human hearts" (lines 124–25). The program Keats set himself is illuminated by his analysis of Wordsworth's progress in his letter to J. H. Reynolds of May 3, 1818 (p. 1019).
2. I.e., the carefree pastoral world. Flora was the Roman goddess of flowers. Pan was the Greek god of pastures, woods, and animal life.

As hard as lips can make it: till agreed,
110 A lovely tale of human life we'll read.
And one will teach a tame dove how it best
May fan the cool air gently o'er my rest;
Another, bending o'er her nimble tread,
Will set a green robe floating round her head,
115 And still will dance with ever varied ease,
Smiling upon the flowers and the trees:
Another will entice me on, and on
Through almond blossoms and rich cinnamon;
Till in the bosom of a leafy world
120 We rest in silence, like two gems upcurl'd
In the recesses of a pearly shell.

    And can I ever bid these joys farewell?
Yes, I must pass them for a nobler life,
Where I may find the agonies, the strife
125 Of human hearts: for lo! I see afar,
O'er sailing the blue cragginess, a car°   *chariot*
And steeds with streamy manes—the charioteer[3]
Looks out upon the winds with glorious fear:
And now the numerous tramplings quiver lightly
130 Along a huge cloud's ridge; and now with sprightly
Wheel downward come they into fresher skies,
Tipt round with silver from the sun's bright eyes.
Still downward with capacious whirl they glide;
And now I see them on a green-hill's side
135 In breezy rest among the nodding stalks.
The charioteer with wond'rous gesture talks
To the trees and mountains; and there soon appear
Shapes of delight, of mystery, and fear,
Passing along before a dusky space
140 Made by some mighty oaks: as they would chase
Some ever-fleeting music on they sweep.
Lo! how they murmur, laugh, and smile, and weep:
Some with upholden hand and mouth severe;
Some with their faces muffled to the ear
145 Between their arms; some, clear in youthful bloom,
Go glad and smilingly athwart° the gloom;   *against*
Some looking back, and some with upward gaze;
Yes, thousands in a thousand different ways
Flit onward—now a lovely wreath of girls
150 Dancing their sleek hair into tangled curls;
And now broad wings. Most awfully intent,
The driver of those steeds is forward bent,
And seems to listen: O that I might know
All that he writes with such a hurrying glow.

155   The visions all are fled—the car is fled
Into the light of heaven, and in their stead

---

3. The description that follows recalls the traditional portrayal of Apollo, god of the sun and
poetry, and represents the higher poetic imagination, which bodies forth the matters "of delight, of
mystery, and fear" (line 138) that characterize the
grander poetic genres.

A sense of real things comes doubly strong,
And, like a muddy stream, would bear along
My soul to nothingness: but I will strive
160 Against all doubtings, and will keep alive
The thought of that same chariot, and the strange
Journey it went.

Oct.–Dec. 1816   1817

* * *

On Seeing the Elgin Marbles[1]

My spirit is too weak—mortality
Weighs heavily on me like unwilling sleep,
And each imagined pinnacle and steep
Of godlike hardship tells me I must die
5 Like a sick eagle looking at the sky.
Yet 'tis a gentle luxury to weep
That I have not the cloudy winds to keep
Fresh for the opening of the morning's eye.
Such dim-conceived glories of the brain
10 Bring round the heart an undescribable feud;
So do these wonders a most dizzy pain,
That mingles Grecian grandeur with the rude
Wasting of old time—with a billowy main°—   ocean
A sun—a shadow of a magnitude.

Mar. 1 or 2, 1817   1817

From Endymion: A Poetic Romance[1]

"The stretchèd metre of an antique song"

INSCRIBED TO THE MEMORY OF THOMAS CHATTERTON

Preface

Knowing within myself the manner in which this Poem has been produced,
it is not without a feeling of regret that I make it public.

1. Lord Elgin had brought to England in 1806 many of the marble statues and friezes that adorned the Parthenon at Athens. In 1817 Keats, along with his artist friend Haydon, viewed the marbles at the British Museum, which had just purchased them, an acquisition that was and remains controversial. Keats's sonnet first appeared on the same day in both Leigh Hunt's *Examiner* and, through Keats's friend Reynolds, *The Champion*, and then was reprinted in Haydon's magazine *Annals of the Fine Arts*.

1. This poem of more than four thousand lines (based on the classical myth of a mortal beloved by the goddess of the moon) tells of Endymion's long and agonized search for an immortal goddess whom he had seen in several visions. In the course of his wanderings, he comes upon an

Indian maid who had been abandoned by the followers of Bacchus, god of wine and revelry. To his utter despair, he succumbs to a sensual passion for her, in apparent betrayal of his love for his heavenly ideal. The conclusion to Keats's "romance" offers a way of resolving this opposition, which runs throughout the poem, between the inevitably mortal pleasures of this world and the possibility of delights that would be eternal: the Indian maid reveals that she is herself Cynthia (Diana), goddess of the moon, the celestial subject of his earlier visions.

The verse epigraph is adapted from Shakespeare's Sonnet 17, line 12: "And stretchèd metre of an antique song." Thomas Chatterton (1752–1770), to whom *Endymion* is dedicated, and who is the "marvellous Boy" of Wordsworth's "Resolu-

What manner I mean, will be quite clear to the reader, who must soon perceive great inexperience, immaturity, and every error denoting a feverish attempt, rather than a deed accomplished. The two first books, and indeed the two last, I feel sensible are not of such completion as to warrant their passing the press; nor should they if I thought a year's castigation would do them any good;—it will not: the foundations are too sandy. It is just that this youngster should die away: a sad thought for me, if I had not some hope that while it is dwindling I may be plotting, and fitting myself for verses fit to live.

This may be speaking too presumptuously, and may deserve a punishment: but no feeling man will be forward to inflict it: he will leave me alone, with the conviction that there is not a fiercer hell than the failure in a great object. This is not written with the least atom of purpose to forestall criticisms of course, but from the desire I have to conciliate men who are competent to look, and who do look with a zealous eye, to the honour of English literature.

The imagination of a boy is healthy, and the mature imagination of a man is healthy; but there is a space of life between, in which the soul is in a ferment, the character undecided, the way of life uncertain, the ambition thick-sighted: thence proceeds mawkishness, and all the thousand bitters which those men I speak of must necessarily taste in going over the following pages.

I hope I have not in too late a day touched the beautiful mythology of Greece,[2] and dulled its brightness: for I wish to try once more,[3] before I bid it farewell.

Teignmouth, April 10, 1818

From *Book 1*

["A THING OF BEAUTY"]

A thing of beauty is a joy for ever:
Its loveliness increases; it will never
Pass into nothingness; but still will keep
A bower quiet for us, and a sleep
5   Full of sweet dreams, and health, and quiet breathing.
Therefore, on every morrow, are we wreathing
A flowery band to bind us to the earth,
Spite° of despondence, of the inhuman dearth   *despite*
Of noble natures, of the gloomy days,
10   Of all the unhealthy and o'er-darkened ways
Made for our searching: yes, in spite of all,
Some shape of beauty moves away the pall
From our dark spirits. Such the sun, the moon,
Trees old, and young sprouting a shady boon

---

tion and Independence," wrote a number of brilliant pseudoarchaic poems that he attributed to an imaginary 15th-century poet, Thomas Rowley. Keats described him as "the most English of poets except Shakespeare."

2. In 1820 an anonymous reviewer of Keats's final volume of poems cited this phrase and, in a complaint that suggests the political charge that the poetic use of classical mythology could carry at this time, wrote disparagingly of "the nonsense

that Mr. Keats . . . and Mr. Percy Bysshe Shelley, and some of the poets about town, have been talking of 'the beautiful mythology of Greece'"; "To some persons . . . that mythology comes recommended chiefly by its grossness—its alliance to the sensitive pleasures which belong to the animal."

3. In *Hyperion*, which Keats was already planning.

15   For simple sheep; and such are daffodils
     With the green world they live in; and clear rills°   *small streams*
     That for themselves a cooling covert make
     'Gainst the hot season; the mid forest brake,°   *thicket*
     Rich with a sprinkling of fair musk-rose blooms:
20   And such too is the grandeur of the dooms°   *judgments*
     We have imagined for the mighty dead;
     All lovely tales that we have heard or read:
     An endless fountain of immortal drink,
     Pouring unto us from the heaven's brink.

25   Nor do we merely feel these essences
     For one short hour; no, even as the trees
     That whisper round a temple become soon
     Dear as the temple's self, so does the moon,
     The passion poesy, glories infinite,
30   Haunt us till they become a cheering light
     Unto our souls, and bound to us so fast,
     That, whether there be shine, or gloom o'ercast,
     They alway must be with us, or we die.

        Therefore, 'tis with full happiness that I
35   Will trace the story of Endymion.
     The very music of the name has gone
     Into my being, and each pleasant scene
     Is growing fresh before me as the green
     Of our own vallies. * * *

[THE "PLEASURE THERMOMETER"]

        "Peona!⁴ ever have I long'd to slake
770 My thirst for the world's praises: nothing base,
     No merely slumberous phantasm, could unlace
     The stubborn canvas for my voyage prepar'd—
     Though now 'tis tatter'd; leaving my bark bar'd
     And sullenly drifting: yet my higher hope
775 Is of too wide, too rainbow-large a scope,
     To fret at myriads of earthly wrecks.
     Wherein lies happiness? In that which becks°   *beckons*
     Our ready minds to fellowship divine,
     A fellowship with essence; till we shine,
780 Full alchemiz'd,⁵ and free of space. Behold
     The clear religion of heaven! Fold
     A rose leaf round thy finger's taperness,
     And soothe thy lips: hist,° when the airy stress   *listen*

4. The sister to whom Endymion confides his troubles. Of lines 769–857 Keats said to his publisher, John Taylor: "When I wrote it, it was the regular stepping of the Imagination towards a Truth. My having written that Argument will perhaps be of the greatest Service to me of anything I ever did—It set before me at once the gradations of Happiness even like a kind of Pleasure Thermometer, and is my first step towards the chief attempt in the Drama—the playing of different Natures with Joy and Sorrow." The gradations on this "Pleasure Thermometer" mark the stages on the way to what Keats calls "happiness" (line 777)—his secular version of the religious concept of "felicity" that, in the orthodox view, is to be achieved by a surrender of oneself to God. For Keats the way to happiness lies through a fusion of ourselves, first sensuously, with the lovely objects of nature and art (lines 781–97), then on a higher level, with other human beings through "love and friendship" (line 801) and, ultimately, sexual love.
5. Transformed by alchemy from a base to a precious metal.

Of music's kiss impregnates the free winds,
785   And with a sympathetic touch unbinds
Eolian[6] magic from their lucid wombs:
Then old songs waken from enclouded tombs;
Old ditties sigh above their father's grave;
Ghosts of melodious prophecyings rave
790   Round every spot where trod Apollo's foot;
Bronze clarions awake, and faintly bruit,[7]
Where long ago a giant battle was;
And, from the turf, a lullaby doth pass
In every place where infant Orpheus[8] slept.
795   Feel we these things?—that moment have we stept
Into a sort of oneness, and our state
Is like a floating spirit's. But there are
Richer entanglements, enthralments far
More self-destroying, leading, by degrees,
800   To the chief intensity: the crown of these
Is made of love and friendship, and sits high
Upon the forehead of humanity.
All its more ponderous and bulky worth
Is friendship, whence there ever issues forth
805   A steady splendour; but at the tip-top
There hangs by unseen film, an orbed drop
Of light, and that is love: its influence,
Thrown in our eyes, genders° a novel sense,   *engenders*
At which we start and fret; till in the end,
810   Melting into its radiance, we blend,
Mingle, and so become a part of it,—
Nor with aught else can our souls interknit
So wingedly: when we combine therewith,
Life's self is nourish'd by its proper pith,[9]
815   And we are nurtured like a pelican brood.[1]
Aye, so delicious is the unsating food,[2]
That men, who might have tower'd in the van°   *forefront*
Of all the congregated world, to fan
And winnow from the coming step of time
820   All chaff of custom, wipe away all slime
Left by men-slugs and human serpentry,
Have been content to let occasion die,
Whilst they did sleep in love's elysium.°   *heaven*
And, truly, I would rather be struck dumb,
825   Than speak against this ardent listlessness:
For I have ever thought that it might bless
The world with benefits unknowingly;
As does the nightingale, upperched high,
And cloister'd among cool and bunched leaves—
830   She sings but to her love, nor e'er conceives

6. From Aeolus, god of winds.
7. Make a sound.
8. The musician of Greek legend, whose beautiful music could move even inanimate things.
9. Its own elemental substance.
1. Young pelicans were once thought to feed on

their mother's flesh. In a parallel way our life is
nourished by another's life, with which it fuses
in love.
2. Food that never satiates, that never ceases to
satisfy.

How tiptoe Night holds back her dark-grey hood.[3]
Just so may love, although 'tis understood
The mere commingling of passionate breath,
Produce more than our searching witnesseth:
835   What I know not: but who, of men, can tell
That flowers would bloom, or that green fruit would swell
To melting pulp, that fish would have bright mail,
The earth its dower of river, wood, and vale,
The meadows runnels, runnels pebble-stones,
840   The seed its harvest, or the lute its tones,
Tones ravishment, or ravishment its sweet,
If human souls did never kiss and greet?

    "Now, if this earthly love has power to make
Men's being mortal, immortal; to shake
845   Ambition from their memories, and brim
Their measure of content; what merest whim,
Seems all this poor endeavour after fame,
To one, who keeps within his stedfast aim
A love immortal, an immortal too.
850   Look not so wilder'd; for these things are true,
And never can be born of atomies°   *mites*
That buzz about our slumbers, like brain-flies,
Leaving us fancy-sick. No, no, I'm sure,
My restless spirit never could endure
855   To brood so long upon one luxury,
Unless it did, though fearfully, espy
A hope beyond the shadow of a dream."

Apr.–Nov. 1817   1818

On Sitting Down to Read *King Lear* Once Again[1]

O golden-tongued Romance, with serene lute!
    Fair plumed syren,[2] queen of far-away!
    Leave melodizing on this wintry day,
Shut up thine olden pages, and be mute.
5   Adieu! for, once again, the fierce dispute
    Betwixt damnation and impassion'd clay
    Must I burn through; once more humbly assay°   *test*
The bitter-sweet of this Shakespearean fruit.
Chief Poet! and ye clouds of Albion,[3]
10   Begetters of our deep eternal theme!
When through the old oak forest I am gone,
    Let me not wander in a barren dream:

---

3. I.e., in order to hear better.
1. Keats pauses, while revising *Endymion: A Poetic Romance*, to read again Shakespeare's great tragedy. The word *syren* (line 2) indicates Keats's feeling that "Romance" was enticing him from the poet's prime duty, to deal with "the ago-

nies, the strife / Of human hearts" (*Sleep and Poetry*, lines 124–25).
2. Syrens (sirens) were sea nymphs whose singing lured listeners to their deaths.
3. Old name for England. *King Lear* is set in Celtic Britain.

But, when I am consumed in the fire,
Give me new phoenix[4] wings to fly at my desire.

Jan. 22, 1818   1838

When I have fears that I may cease to be[1]

When I have fears that I may cease to be
   Before my pen has glean'd my teeming brain,
Before high piled books, in charactry,[2]
   Hold like rich garners the full ripen'd grain;
5 When I behold, upon the night's starr'd face,
   Huge cloudy symbols of a high romance,
And think that I may never live to trace
   Their shadows, with the magic hand of chance;
And when I feel, fair creature of an hour,
10   That I shall never look upon thee more,
Never have relish in the faery power
   Of unreflecting love;—then on the shore
Of the wide world I stand alone, and think
Till love and fame to nothingness do sink.

Jan. 1818   1848

To Homer

Standing aloof in giant ignorance,
   Of thee I hear and of the Cyclades,[1]
As one who sits ashore and longs perchance
   To visit dolphin-coral in deep seas.
5 So wast thou blind;—but then the veil was rent,
   For Jove uncurtain'd heaven to let thee live,
And Neptune made for thee a spumy tent,
   And Pan made sing for thee his forest-hive;
Aye on the shores of darkness there is light,
10   And precipices show untrodden green,
There is a budding morrow in midnight,
   There is a triple sight in blindness keen;
Such seeing hadst thou, as it once befel
To Dian, Queen of Earth, and Heaven, and Hell.[2]

1818   1848

---

4. The fabulous bird that periodically burns itself to death to rise anew from the ashes.
1. The first, and one of the most successful, of Keats's attempts at the sonnet in the Shakespearean rhyme scheme.
2. Characters; printed letters of the alphabet.
1. A group of islands in the Aegean Sea, off Greece. Keats's allusion is to his ignorance of the Greek language. Schooling in Greek was a badge

of gentlemanly identity in the period.
2. In late pagan cults Diana was worshiped as a three-figured goddess, the deity of nature and of the moon as well as the queen of hell. The "triple sight" that blind Homer paradoxically commands is of these three regions and also of heaven, sea, and earth (the realms of Jove, Neptune, and Pan, lines 6–8).

The Eve of St. Agnes[1]

I

St. Agnes' Eve—Ah, bitter chill it was!
The owl, for all his feathers, was a-cold;
The hare limp'd trembling through the frozen grass,
And silent was the flock in woolly fold:
5   Numb were the Beadsman's[2] fingers, while he told
His rosary, and while his frosted breath,
Like pious incense from a censer old,
Seem'd taking flight for heaven, without a death,
Past the sweet Virgin's picture, while his prayer he saith.

2

10   His prayer he saith, this patient, holy man;
Then takes his lamp, and riseth from his knees,
And back returneth, meagre,° barefoot, wan,   *lean*
Along the chapel aisle by slow degrees:
The sculptur'd dead, on each side, seem to freeze,
15   Emprison'd in black, purgatorial rails:
Knights, ladies, praying in dumb° orat'ries,°   *silent / chapels*
He passeth by; and his weak spirit fails
To think[3] how they may ache in icy hoods and mails.

3

Northward he turneth through a little door,
20   And scarce three steps, ere Music's golden tongue
Flatter'd° to tears this aged man and poor;   *charmed*
But no—already had his deathbell rung;
The joys of all his life were said and sung:
His was harsh penance on St. Agnes' Eve:
25   Another way he went, and soon among
Rough ashes sat he for his soul's reprieve,°   *salvation*
And all night kept awake, for sinners' sake to grieve.

4

That ancient Beadsman heard the prelude soft;
And so it chanc'd, for many a door was wide,
30   From hurry to and fro. Soon, up aloft,
The silver, snarling trumpets 'gan to chide:
The level chambers, ready with their pride,°   *ostentation*
Were glowing to receive a thousand guests:

1. St. Agnes, martyred ca. 303 at the age of thirteen, is the patron saint of virgins. Legend has it that if a chaste young woman performs the proper ritual, she will dream of her future husband on the evening before St. Agnes's Day, January 21. Keats combines this superstition with the Romeo and Juliet theme of young love thwarted by feuding families and tells the story in a sequence of evolving Spenserian stanzas. The poem is Keats's first complete success in sustained narrative romance. For the author's revisions while composing stanzas 26 and 30 of *The Eve of St. Agnes*, see "Poems in Process," in the NAEL Archive.
2. One who is paid to pray for his benefactor. He "tells" (counts) the beads of his rosary to keep track of his prayers.
3. I.e., when he thinks.

The carved angels, ever eager-eyed,
35   Star'd, where upon their heads the cornice rests,
With hair blown back, and wings put cross-wise on their breasts.

5

At length burst in the argent revelry,[4]
With plume, tiara, and all rich array,
Numerous as shadows haunting fairily
40   The brain, new stuff'd, in youth, with triumphs gay
Of old romance.° These let us wish away,   *stories*
And turn, sole-thoughted, to one Lady there,
Whose heart had brooded, all that wintry day,
On love, and wing'd St. Agnes' saintly care,
45 As she had heard old dames full many times declare.

6

They told her how, upon St. Agnes' Eve,
Young virgins might have visions of delight,
And soft adorings from their loves receive
Upon the honey'd middle of the night,
50   If ceremonies due they did aright;
As, supperless to bed they must retire,
And couch supine their beauties, lily white;
Nor look behind, nor sideways, but require
Of heaven with upward eyes for all that they desire.

7

55 Full of this whim was thoughtful Madeline:
The music, yearning like a god in pain,
She scarcely heard: her maiden eyes divine,
Fix'd on the floor, saw many a sweeping train[5]
Pass by—she heeded not at all: in vain
60   Came many a tiptoe, amorous cavalier,
And back retir'd, not cool'd by high disdain;
But she saw not: her heart was otherwhere:
She sigh'd for Agnes' dreams, the sweetest of the year.

8

She danc'd along with vague, regardless eyes,
65   Anxious her lips, her breathing quick and short:
The hallow'd hour was near at hand: she sighs
Amid the timbrels,° and the throng'd resort   *tambourines*
Of whisperers in anger, or in sport;
'Mid looks of love, defiance, hate, and scorn,
70   Hoodwink'd[6] with faery fancy; all amort,
Save to St. Agnes[7] and her lambs unshorn,[8]
And all the bliss to be before to-morrow morn.

---

4. Silver-adorned revelers.
5. Skirts sweeping along the ground.
6. Covered by a hood or blindfolded.
7. Entirely oblivious or dead ("amort") to everything except St. Agnes.
8. On St. Agnes's Day it was the custom to offer
lambs' wool at the altar, to be made into cloth by
nuns.

9

So, purposing each moment to retire,
She linger'd still. Meantime, across the moors,
75   Had come young Porphyro, with heart on fire
For Madeline. Beside the portal doors,
Buttress'd from moonlight,[9] stands he, and implores
All saints to give him sight of Madeline,
But for one moment in the tedious hours,
80   That he might gaze and worship all unseen;
Perchance speak, kneel, touch, kiss—in sooth such things have been.

10

He ventures in: let no buzz'd whisper tell:
All eyes be muffled, or a hundred swords
Will storm his heart, Love's fev'rous citadel:
85   For him, those chambers held barbarian hordes,
Hyena foemen, and hot-blooded lords,
Whose very dogs would execrations howl
Against his lineage: not one breast affords
Him any mercy, in that mansion foul,
90   Save one old beldame,[1] weak in body and in soul.

11

Ah, happy chance! the aged creature came,
Shuffling along with ivory-headed wand,°   staff
To where he stood, hid from the torch's flame,
Behind a broad hall-pillar, far beyond
95   The sound of merriment and chorus bland:°   soft
He startled her; but soon she knew his face,
And grasp'd his fingers in her palsied hand,
Saying, "Mercy, Porphyro! hie thee from this place;
They are all here to-night, the whole blood-thirsty race!

12

100   "Get hence! get hence! there's dwarfish Hildebrand;
He had a fever late, and in the fit
He cursed thee and thine, both house and land:
Then there's that old Lord Maurice, not a whit
More tame for his gray hairs—Alas me! flit!
105   Flit like a ghost away."—"Ah, Gossip[2] dear,
We're safe enough; here in this arm-chair sit,
And tell me how"—"Good Saints! not here, not here;
Follow me, child, or else these stones will be thy bier."°   tomb

9. Sheltered from the moonlight by the buttresses (the supports projecting from the wall).
1. Old (and, usually, homely) woman; an ironic

development in English from the French meaning, "lovely lady."
2. In the old sense: godmother or old friend.

13

He follow'd through a lowly arched way,
110   Brushing the cobwebs with his lofty plume,
And as she mutter'd "Well-a—well-a-day!"
He found him in a little moonlight room,
Pale, lattic'd, chill, and silent as a tomb.
"Now tell me where is Madeline," said he,
115   "O tell me, Angela, by the holy loom
Which none but secret sisterhood may see,
When they St. Agnes' wool are weaving piously."

14

"St. Agnes! Ah! it is St. Agnes' Eve—
Yet men will murder upon holy days:
120   Thou must hold water in a witch's sieve,[3]
And be liege-lord of all the Elves and Fays,
To venture so: it fills me with amaze
To see thee, Porphyro!—St. Agnes' Eve!
God's help! my lady fair the conjuror plays[4]
125   This very night: good angels her deceive!
But let me laugh awhile, I've mickle° time to grieve."   *much*

15

Feebly she laugheth in the languid moon,
While Porphyro upon her face doth look,
Like puzzled urchin on an aged crone
130   Who keepeth clos'd a wond'rous riddle-book,
As spectacled she sits in chimney nook.
But soon his eyes grew brilliant, when she told
His lady's purpose; and he scarce could brook°   *restrain*
Tears, at the thought of those enchantments cold,
135 And Madeline asleep in lap of legends old.

16

Sudden a thought came like a full-blown rose,
Flushing his brow, and in his pained heart
Made purple riot: then doth he propose
A stratagem, that makes the beldame start:
140   "A cruel man and impious thou art:
Sweet lady, let her pray, and sleep, and dream
Alone with her good angels, far apart
From wicked men like thee. Go, go!—I deem
Thou canst not surely be the same that thou didst seem."

17

145   "I will not harm her, by all saints I swear,"
Quoth Porphyro: "O may I ne'er find grace

---

3. A sieve made to hold water by witchcraft.
4. I.e., uses magic in her attempt to evoke the vision of her lover.

When my weak voice shall whisper its last prayer,
If one of her soft ringlets I displace,
Or look with ruffian passion in her face:
150   Good Angela, believe me by these tears;
Or I will, even in a moment's space,
Awake, with horrid shout, my foemen's ears,
And beard° them, though they be more fang'd than wolves and   *confront*
    bears."

18

"Ah! why wilt thou affright a feeble soul?
155   A poor, weak, palsy-stricken, churchyard thing,
Whose passing-bell° may ere the midnight toll;   *death knell*
Whose prayers for thee, each morn and evening,
Were never miss'd."—Thus plaining,° doth she bring   *complaining*
A gentler speech from burning Porphyro;
160   So woful, and of such deep sorrowing,
That Angela gives promise she will do
Whatever he shall wish, betide her weal or woe.[5]

19

Which was, to lead him, in close secrecy,
Even to Madeline's chamber, and there hide
165   Him in a closet, of such privacy
That he might see her beauty unespied,
And win perhaps that night a peerless bride,
While legion'd fairies pac'd the coverlet,
And pale enchantment held her sleepy-eyed.
170   Never on such a night have lovers met,
Since Merlin paid his Demon all the monstrous debt.[6]

20

"It shall be as thou wishest," said the Dame:
"All cates° and dainties shall be stored there   *delicacies*
Quickly on this feast-night: by the tambour frame[7]
175   Her own lute thou wilt see: no time to spare,
For I am slow and feeble, and scarce dare
On such a catering trust my dizzy head.
Wait here, my child, with patience; kneel in prayer
The while: Ah! thou must needs the lady wed,
180   Or may I never leave my grave among the dead."

21

So saying, she hobbled off with busy fear.
The lover's endless minutes slowly pass'd;
The dame return'd, and whisper'd in his ear
To follow her; with aged eyes aghast

5. I.e., whether good or ill befalls her.
6. Probably the episode in the Arthurian legends in which Merlin, the magician, lost his life
when the wily Vivien turned one of his own spells against him.
7. A drum-shaped embroidery frame.

185　From fright of dim espial. Safe at last,
　　　Through many a dusky gallery, they gain°　　　　　　*arrive at*
　　　The maiden's chamber, silken, hush'd, and chaste;
　　　Where Porphyro took covert, pleas'd amain.°　　　　*mightily*
　　　His poor guide hurried back with agues° in her brain.　*shivering*

22

190　Her falt'ring hand upon the balustrade,
　　　Old Angela was feeling for the stair,
　　　When Madeline, St. Agnes' charmed maid,
　　　Rose, like a mission'd spirit,[8] unaware:
　　　With silver taper's light, and pious care,
195　She turn'd, and down the aged gossip led
　　　To a safe level matting. Now prepare,
　　　Young Porphyro, for gazing on that bed;
　　　She comes, she comes again, like ring-dove fray'd° and fled.　*frightened*

23

　　　Out went the taper as she hurried in;
200　Its little smoke, in pallid moonshine, died:
　　　She clos'd the door, she panted, all akin
　　　To spirits of the air, and visions wide:
　　　No uttered syllable, or, woe betide!
　　　But to her heart, her heart was voluble,
205　Paining with eloquence her balmy side;
　　　As though a tongueless nightingale[9] should swell
　　　Her throat in vain, and die, heart-stifled, in her dell.

24

　　　A casement° high and triple-arch'd there was,　　　　*window*
　　　All garlanded with carven imag'ries
210　Of fruits, and flowers, and bunches of knot-grass,
　　　And diamonded with panes of quaint device,
　　　Innumerable of stains and splendid dyes,
　　　As are the tiger-moth's deep-damask'd wings;
　　　And in the midst, 'mong thousand heraldries,
215　And twilight saints, and dim emblazonings,
　　　A shielded scutcheon blush'd with blood of queens and kings.[1]

25

　　　Full on this casement shone the wintry moon,
　　　And threw warm gules° on Madeline's fair breast,　　*red (heraldry)*
　　　As down she knelt for heaven's grace and boon;°　　*gift, blessing*
220　Rose-bloom fell on her hands, together prest,

8. I.e., like an angel sent on a mission.
9. An allusion to Ovid's story, in the *Metamorphoses*, of Philomel, who was raped by Tereus, her sister's husband. He cut out Philomel's tongue to prevent her from speaking of his crime, but she managed to weave her story and make herself understood to her sister, Procne. Just as Tereus was about to kill both women, Philomel and Procne were metamorphosed into a nightingale and a swallow.
1. I.e., among the genealogical emblems ("heraldries") and other devices ("emblazonings"), a heraldic shield signified by its colors that the family was of royal blood.

And on her silver cross soft amethyst,
And on her hair a glory,° like a saint: *halo*
She seem'd a splendid angel, newly drest,
Save wings, for heaven:—Porphyro grew faint:
225   She knelt, so pure a thing, so free from mortal taint.

26

Anon his heart revives: her vespers done,
Of all its wreathed pearls her hair she frees;[2]
Unclasps her warmed jewels one by one;
Loosens her fragrant boddice; by degrees
230   Her rich attire creeps rustling to her knees:
Half-hidden, like a mermaid in sea-weed,
Pensive awhile she dreams awake, and sees,
In fancy, fair St. Agnes in her bed,
But dares not look behind, or all the charm is fled.

27

235   Soon, trembling in her soft and chilly nest,
In sort of wakeful swoon, perplex'd[3] she lay,
Until the poppied warmth of sleep oppress'd
Her soothed limbs, and soul fatigued away;
Flown, like a thought, until the morrow-day;
240   Blissfully haven'd both from joy and pain;
Clasp'd like a missal where swart Paynims pray;[4]
Blinded alike from sunshine and from rain,
As though a rose should shut, and be a bud again.

28

Stol'n to this paradise, and so entranced,
245   Porphyro gazed upon her empty dress,
And listen'd to her breathing, if it chanced
To wake into a slumberous tenderness;
Which when he heard, that minute did he bless,
And breath'd himself: then from the closet crept,
250   Noiseless as fear in a wide wilderness,
And over the hush'd carpet, silent, stept,
And 'tween the curtains peep'd, where, lo!—how fast she slept.

29

Then by the bed-side, where the faded moon
Made a dim, silver twilight, soft he set
255   A table, and, half anguish'd, threw thereon
A cloth of woven crimson, gold, and jet:—
O for some drowsy Morphean amulet!°   *sleep-producing charm*

2. The Pre-Raphaelite-inspired painter Daniel
Maclise represented this moment in Keats's
romance in his painting of 1868, *Madeline after
Prayer.*
3. In a confused state between waking and sleeping.

4. Variously interpreted; perhaps: held tightly,
cherished (or else kept shut, fastened with a
clasp), like a Christian prayer book ("missal") in
a land where the religion is that of dark-skinned
pagans ("swart Paynims").

The boisterous, midnight, festive clarion,°   *high-pitched trumpet*
The kettle-drum, and far-heard clarionet,
260   Affray° his ears, though but in dying tone:—   *frighten*
The hall door shuts again, and all the noise is gone.

30

And still she slept an azure-lidded sleep,
In blanched linen, smooth, and lavender'd,
While he from forth the closet brought a heap
265   Of candied apple, quince, and plum, and gourd;°   *melon*
With jellies soother than the creamy curd,
And lucent syrops, tinct with cinnamon;
Manna and dates, in argosy transferr'd
From Fez,[5] and spiced dainties, every one,
270 From silken Samarcand to cedar'd Lebanon.

31

These delicates he heap'd with glowing hand
On golden dishes and in baskets bright
Of wreathed silver: sumptuous they stand
In the retired quiet of the night,
275   Filling the chilly room with perfume light.—
"And now, my love, my seraph[6] fair, awake!
Thou art my heaven, and I thine eremite:[7]
Open thine eyes, for meek St. Agnes' sake,
Or I shall drowse beside thee, so my soul doth ache."

32

280 Thus whispering, his warm, unnerved° arm   *unmanned, weak*
Sank in her pillow. Shaded was her dream
By the dusk curtains:—'twas a midnight charm
Impossible to melt as iced stream:
The lustrous salvers° in the moonlight gleam;   *trays*
285   Broad golden fringe upon the carpet lies:
It seem'd he never, never could redeem
From such a stedfast spell his lady's eyes;
So mus'd awhile, entoil'd in woofed phantasies.[8]

33

Awakening up, he took her hollow lute,—
290 Tumultuous,—and, in chords that tenderest be,
He play'd an ancient ditty, long since mute,
In Provence call'd, "La belle dame sans mercy":[9]
Close to her ear touching the melody;—
Wherewith disturb'd, she utter'd a soft moan:

5. I.e., jellies softer ("soother") than the curds of cream, clear ("lucent") syrups tinged with cinnamon, and sweet gums ("manna") and dates transported in a great merchant ship ("argosy") from Fez, in Morocco.
6. One of the highest orders of angels.

7. Hermit, religious solitary.
8. Entangled in a weave of fantasies.
9. "The Lovely Lady without Pity," title of a work by the medieval poet Alain Chartier. Keats later adopted the title for his own ballad.

295 He ceased—she panted quick—and suddenly
Her blue affrayed eyes wide open shone:
Upon his knees he sank, pale as smooth-sculptured stone.

34

Her eyes were open, but she still beheld,
Now wide awake, the vision of her sleep:
300 There was a painful change, that nigh° expell'd   *nearly*
The blisses of her dream so pure and deep:
At which fair Madeline began to weep,
And moan forth witless words with many a sigh;
While still her gaze on Porphyro would keep;
305 Who knelt, with joined hands and piteous eye,
Fearing to move or speak, she look'd so dreamingly.

35

"Ah, Porphyro!" said she, "but even now
Thy voice was at sweet tremble in mine ear,
Made tuneable with every sweetest vow;
310 And those sad eyes were spiritual and clear:
How chang'd thou art! how pallid, chill, and drear!
Give me that voice again, my Porphyro,
Those looks immortal, those complainings dear!
Oh leave me not in this eternal woe,
315 For if thou diest, my love, I know not where to go."

36

Beyond a mortal man impassion'd far
At these voluptuous accents, he arose,
Ethereal, flush'd, and like a throbbing star
Seen mid the sapphire heaven's deep repose;
320 Into her dream he melted, as the rose
Blendeth its odour with the violet,—
Solution° sweet: meantime the frost-wind blows   *fusion*
Like Love's alarum pattering the sharp sleet
Against the window-panes; St. Agnes' moon hath set.

37

325 'Tis dark: quick pattereth the flaw-blown° sleet: *gust-blown*
"This is no dream, my bride, my Madeline!"
'Tis dark: the iced gusts still rave and beat:
"No dream, alas! alas! and woe is mine!
Porphyro will leave me here to fade and pine.—
330 Cruel! what traitor could thee hither bring?
I curse not, for my heart is lost in thine,
Though thou forsakest a deceived thing;—
A dove forlorn and lost with sick unpruned wing."

38

"My Madeline! sweet dreamer! lovely bride!
335 Say, may I be for aye thy vassal blest?
Thy beauty's shield, heart-shap'd and vermeil° dyed?   *vermilion, bright red*
Ah, silver shrine, here will I take my rest
After so many hours of toil and quest,
A famish'd pilgrim,—saved by miracle.
340 Though I have found, I will not rob thy nest
Saving of thy sweet self; if thou think'st well
To trust, fair Madeline, to no rude infidel.

39

"Hark! 'tis an elfin-storm from faery land,
Of haggard[1] seeming, but a boon indeed:
345 Arise—arise! the morning is at hand;—
The bloated wassaillers° will never heed:—   *drunken carousers*
Let us away, my love, with happy speed;
There are no ears to hear, or eyes to see,—
Drown'd all in Rhenish and the sleepy mead:[2]
350 Awake! arise! my love, and fearless be,
For o'er the southern moors I have a home for thee."

40

She hurried at his words, beset with fears,
For there were sleeping dragons all around,
At glaring watch, perhaps, with ready spears—
355 Down the wide stairs a darkling° way they found.—   *in the dark*
In all the house was heard no human sound.
A chain-droop'd lamp was flickering by each door;
The arras,° rich with horseman, hawk, and hound,   *tapestry*
Flutter'd in the besieging wind's uproar;
360 And the long carpets rose along the gusty floor.

41

They glide, like phantoms, into the wide hall;
Like phantoms, to the iron porch, they glide;
Where lay the Porter, in uneasy sprawl,
With a huge empty flaggon by his side:
365 The wakeful bloodhound rose, and shook his hide,
But his sagacious eye an inmate owns:[3]
By one, and one, the bolts full easy slide:—
The chains lie silent on the footworn stones;—
The key turns, and the door upon its hinges groans.

---

1. Wild, untamed (originally, a wild hawk).
2. Rhine wine and the sleep-producing mead (a
heavy fermented drink made with honey).
3. Acknowledges a member of the household.

42

370 And they are gone: ay, ages long ago
These lovers fled away into the storm.
That night the Baron dreamt of many a woe,
And all his warrior-guests, with shade and form
Of witch, and demon, and large coffin-worm,
375 Were long be-nightmar'd. Angela the old
Died palsy-twitch'd, with meagre face deform;
The Beadsman, after thousand aves[4] told,
For aye° unsought for slept among his ashes cold.   *ever*

Jan.–Feb. 1819   1820

Why did I laugh tonight? No voice will tell[1]

Why did I laugh tonight? No voice will tell:
No god, no demon of severe response,
Deigns to reply from heaven or from hell.
Then to my human heart I turn at once—
5 Heart! thou and I are here sad and alone;
Say, wherefore did I laugh? O mortal pain!
O darkness! darkness! ever must I moan,
To question heaven and hell and heart in vain!
Why did I laugh? I know this being's lease—
10 My fancy to its utmost blisses spreads:
Yet could I on this very midnight cease,
And the world's gaudy ensigns° see in shreds.   *banners*
Verse, fame, and beauty are intense indeed,
But death intenser—death is life's high meed.°   *reward*

Mar. 1819   1848

Bright star, would I were stedfast as thou art[1]

Bright star, would I were stedfast as thou art—
Not in lone splendor hung aloft the night,
And watching, with eternal lids apart,
Like nature's patient, sleepless eremite,[2]
5 The moving waters at their priestlike task
Of pure ablution[3] round earth's human shores,

4. The prayers beginning *Ave Maria* ("Hail Mary").
1. In the letter to his brother and sister-in-law, George and Georgiana Keats, into which he copied this sonnet, March 19, 1819, Keats wrote: "Though the first steps to it were through my human passions, they went away, and I wrote with my Mind— and perhaps I must confess a little bit of my heart. . . . I went to bed, and enjoyed an uninterrupted sleep. Sane I went to bed and sane I arose." 1. While on a tour of the Lake District in 1818, Keats had said that the austere scenes "refine one's sensual vision into a sort of north star which can never cease to be open lidded and steadfast over the wonders of the great Power." The thought developed into this sonnet, which Keats drafted in 1819, then copied into his volume of Shakespeare's poems at the end of September or the beginning of October 1820, while on his way to Italy, where he died.
2. Hermit, religious solitary.
3. Washing, as part of a religious rite.

Or gazing on the new soft-fallen masque
   Of snow upon the mountains and the moors;
No—yet still stedfast, still unchangeable,
10   Pillow'd upon my fair love's ripening breast,
To feel for ever its soft swell and fall,
   Awake for ever in a sweet unrest,
Still, still to hear her tender-taken breath,
And so live ever—or else swoon to death.[4]

1819   1838

La Belle Dame sans Merci: A Ballad[1]

1

O what can ail thee, knight-at-arms,
   Alone and palely loitering?
The sedge° has wither'd from the lake,   *rushes*
   And no birds sing.

2

5 O what can ail thee, knight-at-arms,
   So haggard and so woe-begone?
The squirrel's granary is full,
   And the harvest's done.

3

I see a lily on thy brow
10   With anguish moist and fever dew,
And on thy cheeks a fading rose
   Fast withereth too.

4

I met a lady in the meads,
   Full beautiful, a fairy's child;
15 Her hair was long, her foot was light,
   And her eyes were wild.

5

I made a garland for her head,
   And bracelets too, and fragrant zone;[2]
She look'd at me as she did love,
20   And made sweet moan.

4. In the earlier version: "Half passionless, and so swoon on to death."
1. The title, though not the subject, was taken from a medieval poem by Alain Chartier and means "The Lovely Lady without Pity." The story of a mortal destroyed by his love for a supernatural femme fatale has been told repeatedly in myth, fairy tale, and ballad. The text printed here is Keats's earlier version of the poem, as transcribed by Charles Brown. The version published in 1820 begins, "Ah, what can ail thee, wretched wight."

Keats imitates a frequent procedure of folk ballads by casting the poem into the dialogue form. The first three stanzas are addressed to the knight, and the rest of the poem is his reply.
2. Belt (of flowers).

6

I set her on my pacing steed,
 And nothing else saw all day long,
For sidelong would she bend, and sing
 A fairy's song.

7

25 She found me roots of relish° sweet,   *flavor*
 And honey wild, and manna dew,
And sure in language strange she said—
 "I love thee true."

8

She took me to her elfin grot°   *cave*
30 And there she wept, and sigh'd full sore,
And there I shut her wild wild eyes
 With kisses four.[3]

9

And there she lulled me asleep,
 And there I dream'd—Ah! woe betide!
35 The latest° dream I ever dream'd   *last*
 On the cold hill's side.

10

I saw pale kings, and princes too,
 Pale warriors, death pale were they all;
They cried—"La belle dame sans merci
40 Hath thee in thrall!"

11

I saw their starv'd lips in the gloom°   *twilight*
 With horrid warning gaped wide,
And I awoke and found me here
 On the cold hill's side.

12

45 And this is why I sojourn here,
 Alone and palely loitering,
Though the sedge is wither'd from the lake,
 And no birds sing.

Apr. 1819   1820

3. Keats commented in a letter to his brother and sister-in-law, "Why four kisses—you will say—why four because I wish to restrain the headlong impetuosity of my Muse—she would have fain said 'score' without hurting the rhyme—but we must temper the Imagination as the Critics say with Judgment. I was obliged to choose an even number that both eyes might have fair play."

On Fame

Fame, like a wayward girl, will still be coy
    To those who woo her with too slavish knees,
But makes surrender to some thoughtless boy,
    And dotes the more upon a heart at ease;
5   She is a gipsey, will not speak to those
    Who have not learnt to be content without her;
A jilt, whose ear was never whisper'd close,
    Who thinks they scandal her who talk about her;
A very gipsey is she, Nilus born,[1]
10   Sister-in-law to jealous Potiphar;[2]
Ye love-sick bards, repay her scorn for scorn;
    Ye lovelorn artists, madmen that ye are!
Make your best bow to her and bid adieu;
    Then, if she likes it, she will follow you.

Apr. 1819   1838

Sonnet to Sleep

O soft embalmer of the still midnight,
    Shutting with careful fingers and benign
Our gloom-pleas'd eyes, embower'd from the light,
    Enshaded in forgetfulness divine:
5   O soothest° Sleep! if so it please thee, close,   *softest*
    In midst of this thine hymn, my willing eyes,
Or wait the Amen ere thy poppy[1] throws
    Around my bed its lulling charities.
Then save me or the passed day will shine
10   Upon my pillow, breeding many woes:
Save me from curious° conscience, that still hoards   *scrupulous*
    Its strength for darkness, burrowing like the mole;
Turn the key deftly in the oiled wards,[2]
    And seal the hushed casket of my soul.

Apr. 1819   1838

1. I.e., born near the Nile, in Egypt, where gypsies were thought to have originated.
2. In Genesis 39, the wife of Potiphar, an Egyptian soldier, does her best to seduce Joseph, the handsome slave her husband has bought. When she fails, she falsely accuses Joseph of rape, and Potiphar casts him into prison.

1. Opium is made from the dried juice of the opium poppy.
2. The ridges in a lock that correspond to the notches of the key.

Ode to Psyche[1]

O Goddess! hear these tuneless numbers,° wrung   *verses*
  By sweet enforcement and remembrance dear,
And pardon that thy secrets should be sung
  Even into thine own soft-conched[2] ear:
5 Surely I dreamt to-day, or did I see
  The winged Psyche with awaken'd eyes?
I wander'd in a forest thoughtlessly,
  And, on the sudden, fainting with surprise,
Saw two fair creatures, couched side by side
10   In deepest grass, beneath the whisp'ring roof
  Of leaves and trembled blossoms, where there ran
    A brooklet, scarce espied:
'Mid hush'd, cool-rooted flowers, fragrant-eyed,
  Blue, silver-white, and budded Tyrian,[3]
15 They lay calm-breathing on the bedded grass;
  Their arms embraced, and their pinions° too;   *wings*
  Their lips touch'd not, but had not bade adieu,
As if disjoined by soft-handed slumber,
And ready still past kisses to outnumber
20   At tender eye-dawn of aurorean love:[4]
    The winged boy I knew;
But who wast thou, O happy, happy dove?
    His Psyche true!

O latest born and loveliest vision far
25   Of all Olympus' faded hierarchy![5]
Fairer than Phoebe's sapphire-region'd star,[6]
  Or Vesper,° amorous glow-worm of the sky;   *evening star*
Fairer than these, though temple thou hast none,
    Nor altar heap'd with flowers;
30 Nor virgin-choir to make delicious moan
    Upon the midnight hours;
No voice, no lute, no pipe, no incense sweet

1. This poem initiated the sequence of great odes that Keats wrote in the spring of 1819. It is copied into the same journal-letter that included the "Sonnet to Sleep" and several other sonnets as well as a comment about "endeavoring to discover a better sonnet stanza than we have." It is therefore likely that Keats's experiments with sonnet schemes led to the development of the intricate and varied stanzas of his odes and that he abandoned the sonnet on discovering the richer possibilities of the more spacious form.

Psyche, which gives us our modern term *psychology*, means "mind" or "soul" (and also "butterfly") in Greek. In the story told by the Roman author Apuleius in the 2nd century, Psyche was a lovely mortal beloved by Cupid, the "winged boy" (line 21), son of Venus. To keep their love a secret from his mother, who envied Psyche's beauty, he visited his lover only in the dark of night, and had her promise never to try to discover his identity. After Psyche broke the promise, she endured various tribulations as a penance and then was finally wedded to Cupid and translated to heaven as an immortal. To this goddess, added to the pantheon of pagan gods too late to have been the center of a cult, Keats in the last two stanzas promises to establish a place of worship within his own mind, with himself as poet-priest and prophet.

2. Soft and shaped like a seashell.
3. The purple dye once made in ancient Tyre.
4. Aurora was the goddess of the dawn.
5. The ranks of the gods who lived on Mount Olympus, according to the classical mythology now eclipsed (made "faded") by Christianity. "You must recollect that Psyche was not embodied as a goddess before the time of Apuleius the Platonist who lived after the Augustan age, and consequently the Goddess was never worshipped or sacrificed to with any of the ancient fervour—and perhaps never thought of in the old religion—I am more orthodox tha[n] to let a hethen Goddess be so neglected" (Keats, in a long letter written over several months to George and Georgiana Keats in America, April 30, 1819).
6. The moon, supervised by the goddess Phoebe (Diana).

From chain-swung censer teeming;
No shrine, no grove, no oracle, no heat
35   Of pale-mouth'd prophet dreaming.

O brightest! though too late for antique vows,[7]
    Too, too late for the fond believing lyre,
When holy were the haunted° forest boughs,   *spirit-filled*
    Holy the air, the water, and the fire;
40 Yet even in these days so far retir'd
        From happy pieties, thy lucent fans,°   *shining wings*
        Fluttering among the faint Olympians,
I see, and sing, by my own eyes inspired.
So let me be thy choir, and make a moan
45   Upon the midnight hours;
Thy voice, thy lute, thy pipe, thy incense sweet
    From swinged censer teeming;
Thy shrine, thy grove, thy oracle, thy heat
    Of pale-mouth'd prophet dreaming.

50 Yes, I will be thy priest, and build a fane°   *temple*
    In some untrodden region of my mind,
Where branched thoughts, new grown with pleasant pain,
    Instead of pines shall murmur in the wind:
Far, far around shall those dark-cluster'd trees
55   Fledge the wild-ridged mountains steep by steep;[8]
And there by zephyrs,° streams, and birds, and bees,   *breezes*
    The moss-lain Dryads° shall be lull'd to sleep;   *wood nymphs*
And in the midst of this wide quietness
A rosy sanctuary will I dress
60 With the wreath'd trellis of a working brain,
    With buds, and bells, and stars without a name,
With all the gardener Fancy e'er could feign,
    Who breeding flowers, will never breed the same:
And there shall be for thee all soft delight
65   That shadowy thought can win,
A bright torch, and a casement ope at night,
    To let the warm Love[9] in!

Apr. 1819   1820

---

7. I.e., of worshipers.   like layers of feathers.
8. I.e., the trees shall stand, rank against rank,   9. I.e., Cupid, god of love.

Ode to a Nightingale[1]

My heart aches, and a drowsy numbness pains
  My sense, as though of hemlock[2] I had drunk,
Or emptied some dull opiate to the drains
  One minute past, and Lethe[3]-wards had sunk:
5 'Tis not through envy of thy happy lot,
  But being too happy in thine happiness,—
    That thou, light-winged Dryad of the trees,
      In some melodious plot
  Of beechen green, and shadows numberless,
10   Singest of summer in full-throated ease.

O, for a draught of vintage!° that hath been
  Cool'd a long age in the deep-delved earth,
Tasting of Flora[4] and the country green,
Dance, and Provençal song,[5] and sunburnt mirth!
15 O for a beaker full of the warm South,
  Full of the true, the blushful Hippocrene,[6]
    With beaded bubbles winking at the brim,
      And purple-stained mouth;
That I might drink, and leave the world unseen,
20   And with thee fade away into the forest dim:

3

Fade far away, dissolve, and quite forget
  What thou among the leaves hast never known,
The weariness, the fever, and the fret
  Here, where men sit and hear each other groan;
25 Where palsy shakes a few, sad, last gray hairs,
  Where youth grows pale, and spectre-thin, and dies;[7]
    Where but to think is to be full of sorrow
      And leaden-eyed despairs,
  Where Beauty cannot keep her lustrous eyes,
30   Or new Love pine at them beyond to-morrow.

1. Charles Brown, with whom Keats was then living in Hampstead, wrote: "In the spring of 1819 a nightingale had built her nest near my house. Keats felt a tranquil and continual joy in her song; and one morning he took his chair from the breakfast table to the grass plot under a plum tree, where he sat for two or three hours. When he came into the house, I perceived he had some scraps of paper in his hand, and these he was quietly thrusting behind the books. On inquiry, I found those scraps, four or five in number, contained his poetic feeling on the song of our nightingale."
2. A poisonous herb, not the North American evergreen tree; a sedative if taken in small doses.
3. River in Hades whose waters cause forgetfulness.
4. The Roman goddess of flowers or the flowers themselves.
5. Provence, in southern France, was in the late Middle Ages renowned for its troubadours—writers and singers of love songs.
6. Fountain of the Muses on Mount Helicon, hence the waters of inspiration, here applied metaphorically to a beaker of wine.
7. Keats's brother Tom, wasted by tuberculosis, had died the preceding winter.

4

Away! away! for I will fly to thee,
   Not charioted by Bacchus and his pards,
But on the viewless wings of Poesy,[8]
   Though the dull brain perplexes and retards:

35 Already with thee! tender is the night,
   And haply the Queen-Moon is on her throne,
     Cluster'd around by all her starry Fays;°   *fairies*
        But here there is no light,
   Save what from heaven is with the breezes blown
40   Through verdurous° glooms and winding mossy ways.   *green-foliaged*

5

I cannot see what flowers are at my feet,
   Nor what soft incense hangs upon the boughs,
But, in embalmed° darkness, guess each sweet   *perfumed*
   Wherewith the seasonable month endows
45 The grass, the thicket, and the fruit-tree wild;
   White hawthorn, and the pastoral eglantine;[9]
     Fast fading violets cover'd up in leaves;
       And mid-May's eldest child,
   The coming musk-rose, full of dewy wine,
50   The murmurous haunt of flies on summer eves.

6

Darkling° I listen; and, for many a time   *in darkness*
   I have been half in love with easeful Death,
Call'd him soft names in many a mused° rhyme,   *meditated*
   To take into the air my quiet breath;
55 Now more than ever seems it rich to die,
   To cease upon the midnight with no pain,
     While thou art pouring forth thy soul abroad
       In such an ecstasy!
   Still wouldst thou sing, and I have ears in vain—
60   To thy high requiem° become a sod.   *mass for the dead*

7

Thou wast not born for death, immortal Bird!
   No hungry generations tread thee down;
The voice I hear this passing night was heard
   In ancient days by emperor and clown:°   *peasant*
65 Perhaps the self-same song that found a path
   Through the sad heart of Ruth,[1] when, sick for home,
     She stood in tears amid the alien corn;°   *wheat*
       The same that oft-times hath

8. I.e., by getting drunk not on wine (the "vintage" of stanza 2) but on the invisible ("viewless") wings of the poetic imagination. (Bacchus, god of wine, was sometimes represented in a chariot drawn by "pards"—leopards.)
9. Sweetbrier or honeysuckle.
1. The young widow in the biblical Book of Ruth.

Charm'd magic casements,° opening on the foam   *windows*
70   Of perilous seas, in faery lands forlorn.

8

Forlorn! the very word is like a bell
To toll me back from thee to my sole self!
Adieu! the fancy[2] cannot cheat so well
As she is fam'd to do, deceiving elf.
75 Adieu! adieu! thy plaintive anthem° fades   *hymn*
Past the near meadows, over the still stream,
Up the hill-side; and now 'tis buried deep
In the next valley-glades:
Was it a vision, or a waking dream?
80   Fled is that music:—Do I wake or sleep?

May 1819   1819

[handwritten annotations: bird stops singing, flies away, song fades into background; return to beginning; resolution found through meditation]

Ode on a Grecian Urn[1]

[handwritten annotations: each stanza takes you to a diff part of the urn; indicative of virginity; urn is feminized; pivoted from a sonnet to an ode; irregular ode; reckoning w/ his longevity]

Thou still unravish'd bride of quietness,
Thou foster-child of silence and slow time,
Sylvan[2] historian, who canst thus express
A flowery tale more sweetly than our rhyme:
5   What leaf-fring'd legend haunts about thy shape
Of deities or mortals, or of both,
In Tempe or the dales of Arcady?[3]
What men or gods are these? What maidens loth?
What mad pursuit? What struggle to escape?
10   What pipes and timbrels? What wild ecstasy?

2

Heard melodies are sweet, but those unheard
Are sweeter; therefore, ye soft pipes, play on;
Not to the sensual ear,[4] but, more endear'd,
Pipe to the spirit ditties of no tone:
15 Fair youth, beneath the trees, thou canst not leave
Thy song, nor ever can those trees be bare;
Bold lover, never, never canst thou kiss,

2. I.e., imagination, "the viewless wings of Poesy" of line 33.
1. Another poem that Keats published in Haydon's *Annals of the Fine Arts*. This urn, with its sculptured reliefs of revelry and panting young lovers in chase and in flight, of a pastoral piper under spring foliage, and of the quiet procession of priest and townspeople, resembles parts of various vases, sculptures, and paintings, but it existed in all its particulars only in Keats's imagination. In the urn—which captures moments of intense experience in attitudes of grace and immobilizes them in marble—Keats found the perfect correlative for his concern with the long-

ing for permanence in a world of change. The interpretation of the details with which he develops this concept, however, is hotly disputed. The disputes begin with the opening phrase: is "still" an adverb ("as yet"), or is it an adjective ("motionless"), as the punctuation of the *Annals* version, which adds a comma after "still," suggests?
2. Rustic, representing a woodland scene.
3. The valleys of Arcadia, a state in ancient Greece often used as a symbol of the pastoral ideal. Tempe is a beautiful valley in Greece that has come to represent rural beauty.
4. The ear of sense (as opposed to that of the "spirit," or imagination).

Though winning near the goal—yet, do not grieve;
　　She cannot fade, though thou hast not thy bliss,
20　For ever wilt thou love, and she be fair!

3

Ah, happy, happy boughs! that cannot shed
　　Your leaves, nor ever bid the spring adieu;
And, happy melodist, unwearied,
　　For ever piping songs for ever new;
25　More happy love! more happy, happy love!
　　For ever warm and still to be enjoy'd,
　　　For ever panting, and for ever young;
All breathing human passion far above,
　　That leaves a heart high-sorrowful and cloy'd,
30　　A burning forehead, and a parching tongue.

4

Who are these coming to the sacrifice?
　　To what green altar, O mysterious priest,
Lead'st thou that heifer lowing at the skies,
　　And all her silken flanks with garlands drest?
35　What little town by river or sea shore,
　　Or mountain-built with peaceful citadel,
　　　Is emptied of this folk, this pious morn?
And, little town, thy streets for evermore
　　Will silent be; and not a soul to tell
40　　Why thou art desolate, can e'er return.

5

O Attic[5] shape! Fair attitude![6] with brede
　　Of marble men and maidens overwrought,[7]
With forest branches and the trodden weed;
　　Thou, silent form, dost tease us out of thought
45　As doth eternity: Cold Pastoral!
　　When old age shall this generation waste,
　　　Thou shalt remain, in midst of other woe
Than ours, a friend to man, to whom thou say'st,
"Beauty is truth, truth beauty,"[8]—that is all
50　　Ye know on earth, and all ye need to know.

1819　　　　　　　　　　　　　　　　　　　　　　　　1820

---

5. Greek. Attica was the region of Greece in which Athens was located.
6. Probably used in its early, technical sense: the pose struck by a figure in statuary or painting.
7. Ornamented all over ("overwrought") with an interwoven pattern ("brede"). The adjective "overwrought" might also modify "maidens" and even "men" and so hint at the emotional anguish of the figures portrayed on the urn.
8. The quotation marks around this phrase are found in the volume of poems Keats published in 1820, but there are no quotation marks in the version printed in *Annals of the Fine Arts* that same year or in the transcripts of the poem made by

Keats's friends. This discrepancy has multiplied the diversity of critical interpretations of the last two lines. Critics disagree whether the whole of these lines is said by the urn, or "Beauty is truth, truth beauty" by the urn and the rest by the lyric speaker; whether the "ye" in the last line is addressed to the lyric speaker, to the readers, to the urn, or to the figures on the urn; whether "all ye know" is that beauty is truth, or this plus the statement in lines 46–48; and whether "beauty is truth" is a profound metaphysical proposition or an overstatement representing the limited point of view of the urn.

Ode on Melancholy   This is Keats's best-known statement of his recurrent theme of the mingled contrarieties of life. The remarkable last stanza, in which Melancholy becomes a veiled goddess worshiped in secret religious rites, implies that it is the tragic human destiny that beauty, joy, and life itself owe not only their quality but their value to the fact that they are transitory and turn into their opposites. Melancholy—a synonym for depression, involving a paralyzing self-consciousness engendered by an excess of thought—is a highly literary and even bookish ailment, as Keats knew. Shakespeare's Hamlet and Milton's speaker in "Il Penseroso" are the disorder's most famous sufferers. Keats was also an admirer of Robert Burton's encyclopedic *Anatomy of Melancholy* (1621).

The poem once had the following initial stanza, which Keats canceled in manuscript:

> Though you should build a bark of dead men's bones,
>   And rear a phantom gibbet for a mast,
> Stitch creeds together for a sail, with groans
>   To fill it out, bloodstained and aghast;
> Although your rudder be a Dragon's tail,
>   Long sever'd, yet still hard with agony,
>   Your cordage large uprootings from the skull
> Of bald Medusa: certes you would fail
>   To find the Melancholy, whether she
>   Dreameth in any isle of Lethe dull.

Ode on Melancholy

I

No, no, go not to Lethe,[1] neither twist
    Wolf's-bane, tight-rooted, for its poisonous wine;
Nor suffer thy pale forehead to be kiss'd
    By nightshade, ruby grape of Proserpine;[2]
5   Make not your rosary of yew-berries,[3]
    Nor let the beetle,[4] nor the death-moth be
        Your mournful Psyche,[5] nor the downy owl
A partner in your sorrow's mysteries;°   *secret rituals*
    For shade to shade will come too drowsily,
10   And drown the wakeful anguish of the soul.[6]

2

But when the melancholy fit shall fall
    Sudden from heaven like a weeping cloud,
That fosters the droop-headed flowers all,
    And hides the green hill in an April shroud;
15 Then glut thy sorrow on a morning rose,

---

1. The waters of forgetfulness in Hades.
2. The wife of Pluto and queen of the underworld. "Nightshade" and "wolf's-bane" (line 2) are poisonous plants.
3. A symbol of death.
4. A reference to replicas of the large black beetle, the scarab, which were often placed by Egyptians in their tombs as a symbol of resurrection.

5. In ancient times Psyche (the soul) was sometimes represented as a butterfly or moth, fluttering out of the mouth of a dying man. The allusion may also be to the death's-head moth, which has skull-like markings on its back.
6. I.e., sorrow needs contrast to sustain its intensity.

Or on the rainbow of the salt sand-wave,
　　Or on the wealth of globed peonies;
Or if thy mistress some rich anger shows,
　　Emprison her soft hand, and let her rave,
20　　　And feed deep, deep upon her peerless eyes.

3

She[7] dwells with Beauty—Beauty that must die;
　　And Joy, whose hand is ever at his lips
Bidding adieu; and aching Pleasure nigh,
　　Turning to poison while the bee-mouth sips:
25　Ay, in the very temple of Delight
　　Veil'd Melancholy has her sovran shrine,
　　　　Though seen of none save him whose strenuous tongue
　　Can burst Joy's grape against his palate fine;[8]
His soul shall taste the sadness of her might,
30　　　And be among her cloudy trophies hung.[9]

1819　　　　　　　　　　　　　　　　　　　　　　　　　　1820

Ode on Indolence[1]

"They toil not, neither do they spin."[2]

I

One morn before me were three figures seen,
　　With bowed necks, and joined hands, side-faced;
And one behind the other stepp'd serene,
　　In placid sandals, and in white robes graced:
5　They pass'd, like figures on a marble urn,
　　When shifted round to see the other side;
　　　They came again: as when the urn once more
Is shifted round, the first seen shades return;
　　And they were strange to me, as may betide
10　　　With vases, to one deep in Phidian[3] lore.

2

How is it, shadows, that I knew ye not?
　　How came ye muffled in so hush a masque?
Was it a silent deep-disguised plot

---

7. Usually taken to refer to Melancholy rather than to "thy mistress" in line 18.
8. Sensitive, refined.
9. A reference to the Greek and Roman practice of hanging trophies in the temples of the gods.
1. On March 19, 1819, Keats wrote to George and Georgiana Keats: "This morning I am in a sort of temper indolent and supremely careless. . . . Neither Poetry, nor Ambition, nor Love have any alertness of countenance as they pass by me: they seem rather like three figures on a greek vase—a Man and two women—whom no one but myself could distinguish in their disguisement. This is

the only happiness; and is a rare instance of advantage in the body overpowering the Mind." The ode was probably written soon after this time, but was not published until 1848, long after the poet's death.
2. Matthew 6.28. Christ's comment on the lilies of the field—a parable justifying those who trust to God rather than worry about how they will feed or clothe themselves.
3. Phidias was the great Athenian sculptor of the 5th century B.C.E. who designed the marble sculptures for the Parthenon.

To steal away, and leave without a task
15　My idle days? Ripe was the drowsy hour;
　　　The blissful cloud of summer-indolence
　　　　　Benumb'd my eyes; my pulse grew less and less;
　　Pain had no sting, and pleasure's wreath no flower.
　　　O, why did ye not melt, and leave my sense
20　　　Unhaunted quite of all but—nothingness?

3

A third time pass'd they by, and, passing, turn'd
　　Each one the face a moment whiles to me;
Then faded, and to follow them I burn'd
　　And ached for wings, because I knew the three:
25　The first was a fair maid, and Love her name;
　　　The second was Ambition, pale of cheek,
　　　　　And ever watchful with fatigued eye;
　　The last, whom I love more, the more of blame
　　　Is heap'd upon her, maiden most unmeek,—
30　　　I knew to be my demon[4] Poesy.

4

They faded, and, forsooth! I wanted wings:
　　O folly! What is Love? and where is it?
And for that poor Ambition—it springs
　　From a man's little heart's short fever-fit;
35　For Poesy!—no,—she has not a joy,—
　　　At least for me,—so sweet as drowsy noons,
　　　　　And evenings steep'd in honied indolence;
　　O, for an age so shelter'd from annoy,
　　　That I may never know how change the moons,
40　　　Or hear the voice of busy common-sense!

5

A third time came they by;—alas! wherefore?
　　My sleep had been embroider'd with dim dreams;
My soul had been a lawn besprinkled o'er
　　With flowers, and stirring shades, and baffled beams:
45　The morn was clouded, but no shower fell,
　　　Though in her lids hung the sweet tears of May;
　　　　　The open casement° press'd a new-leaved vine,　　　*window*
　　Let in the budding warmth and throstle's lay;°　　　*thrush's song*
　　O shadows! 'twas a time to bid farewell!
50　　　Upon your skirts had fallen no tears of mine.

6

So, ye three ghosts, adieu! Ye cannot raise
　　My head cool-bedded in the flowery grass;
For I would not be dieted with praise,

4. Meaning both devil and, as in Greek myth,　　individual.
the spirit that attends constantly on the human

A pet-lamb in a sentimental farce![5]
55 Fade softly from my eyes, and be once more
    In masque-like figures on the dreamy urn;
        Farewell! I yet have visions for the night,
    And for the day faint visions there is store;
        Vanish, ye phantoms, from my idle spright,°   spirit
60 Into the clouds, and never more return!

Spring 1819   1848

Lamia   In a note printed at the end of the poem, Keats cited as his source the following story in Robert Burton's *Anatomy of Melancholy* (1621):

> One Menippus Lycius, a young man twenty-five years of age, that going betwixt Cenchreas and Corinth, met such a phantasm in the habit of a fair gentlewoman, which, taking him by the hand, carried him home to her house, in the suburbs of Corinth. . . . The young man, a philosopher, otherwise staid and discreet, able to moderate his passions, though not this of love, tarried with her a while to his great content, and at last married her, to whose wedding, amongst other guests, came Apollonius; who, by some probable conjectures, found her out to be a serpent, a lamia; and that all her furniture was, like Tantalus's gold, described by Homer, no substance but mere illusions. When she saw herself descried, she wept, and desired Apollonius to be silent, but he would not be moved, and thereupon she, plate, house, and all that was in it, vanished in an instant: many thousands took notice of this fact, for it was done in the midst of Greece.

In ancient demonology a lamia was a monster in woman's form who preyed on human beings. Several passages of Keats's romance seem, however, to call on readers to sympathize with this monster, as one might with Coleridge's Geraldine or Landon's Fairy of the Fountains. In the contest between Lamia and Apollonius it is hard to know what side to take.

The poem, written between late June and early September 1819, is a return, after the Spenserian stanzas of *The Eve of St. Agnes*, to the pentameter couplets Keats had used in *Endymion* and other early poems. Keats's friends Charles Armitage Brown and Richard Woodhouse commented in letters on how *Lamia* was influenced by the characteristic meter of the Restoration poet John Dryden.

Lamia

Part 1

    Upon a time, before the faery broods
    Drove Nymph and Satyr[1] from the prosperous woods,
    Before King Oberon's bright diadem,
    Sceptre, and mantle, clasp'd with dewy gem,
5   Frighted away the Dryads and the Fauns
    From rushes green, and brakes,° and cowslip'd lawns,[2]   thickets

---

5. In a letter of June 9, 1819, Keats wrote: "I have been very idle lately, very averse to writing; both from the overpowering idea of our dead poets and from abatement of my love of fame. I hope I am a little more of a Philosopher than I was, consequently a little less of a versifying Pet-lamb. . . . You will judge of my 1819 temper when I tell you that the thing I have most enjoyed this year has been writing an ode to Indolence."

1. Nymphs and satyrs—like the dryads and fauns in line 5—were minor classical deities of the woods and fields, said here to have been driven off by Oberon, king of the fairies, who were supernatural beings of the postclassical era.

2. Cowslips are primroses, here blooming amid the grass.

The ever smitten Hermes[3] empty left
His golden throne, bent warm on amorous theft:
From high Olympus had he stolen light,

10 On this side of Jove's clouds, to escape the sight
Of his great summoner, and made retreat
Into a forest on the shores of Crete.
For somewhere in that sacred island dwelt
A nymph, to whom all hoofed Satyrs knelt;

15 At whose white feet the languid Tritons[4] poured
Pearls, while on land they wither'd and adored.
Fast by the springs where she to bathe was wont,°   *accustomed*
And in those meads where sometime she might haunt,
Were strewn rich gifts, unknown to any Muse,

20 Though Fancy's casket were unlock'd to choose.
Ah, what a world of love was at her feet!
So Hermes thought, and a celestial heat
Burnt from his winged heels to either ear,
That from a whiteness, as the lily clear,

25 Blush'd into roses 'mid his golden hair,
Fallen in jealous curls about his shoulders bare.[5]

    From vale to vale, from wood to wood, he flew,
Breathing upon the flowers his passion new,
And wound with many a river to its head,

30 To find where this sweet nymph prepar'd her secret bed:
In vain; the sweet nymph might nowhere be found,
And so he rested, on the lonely ground,
Pensive, and full of painful jealousies
Of the Wood-Gods, and even the very trees.

35 There as he stood, he heard a mournful voice,
Such as once heard, in gentle heart, destroys
All pain but pity: thus the lone voice spake:
"When from this wreathed tomb shall I awake!
When move in a sweet body fit for life,

40 And love, and pleasure, and the ruddy strife
Of hearts and lips! Ah, miserable me!"
The God, dove-footed,[6] glided silently
Round bush and tree, soft-brushing, in his speed,
The taller grasses and full-flowering weed,

45 Until he found a palpitating snake,
Bright, and cirque-couchant[7] in a dusky brake.

    She was a gordian[8] shape of dazzling hue,
Vermilion-spotted, golden, green, and blue;
Striped like a zebra, freckled like a pard,°   *leopard*

50 Eyed like a peacock,[9] and all crimson barr'd;

---

3. Or Mercury; wing-footed messenger at the summons of Jove (line 11), Hermes was notoriously amorous.
4. Minor sea gods.
5. I.e., the curls clung jealously to his bare shoulders. This line is the first of a number of Alexandrines, a six-foot line, used to vary the metrical movement—a device that Keats learned from Dryden. Another such device is the triplet, occurring first in lines 61–63.
6. I.e., quietly as a dove.
7. Lying in a circular coil. Keats borrows the language of heraldry.
8. Intricately twisted, like the knot tied by King Gordius, which no one could undo.
9. Having multicolored spots, like the "eyes" in a peacock's tail.

And full of silver moons, that, as she breathed,
Dissolv'd, or brighter shone, or interwreathed
Their lustres with the gloomier tapestries—
So rainbow-sided, touch'd with miseries,
55 She seem'd, at once, some penanced lady elf,
Some demon's mistress, or the demon's self.
Upon her crest she wore a wannish° fire   rather dark
Sprinkled with stars, like Ariadne's tiar:[1]
Her head was serpent, but ah, bitter-sweet!
60 She had a woman's mouth with all its pearls[2] complete:
And for her eyes: what could such eyes do there
But weep, and weep, that they were born so fair?
As Proserpine still weeps for her Sicilian air.[3]
Her throat was serpent, but the words she spake
65 Came, as through bubbling honey, for Love's sake,
And thus; while Hermes on his pinions° lay,   wings
Like a stoop'd falcon[4] ere he takes his prey.

        "Fair Hermes, crown'd with feathers, fluttering light,
I had a splendid dream of thee last night:
70 I saw thee sitting, on a throne of gold,
Among the Gods, upon Olympus old,
The only sad one; for thou didst not hear
The soft, lute-finger'd Muses chaunting clear,
Nor even Apollo when he sang alone,
75 Deaf to his throbbing throat's long, long melodious moan.
I dreamt I saw thee, robed in purple flakes,
Break amorous through the clouds, as morning breaks,
And, swiftly as a bright Phœbean dart,[5]
Strike for the Cretan isle; and here thou art!
80 Too gentle Hermes, hast thou found the maid?"
Whereat the star of Lethe[6] not delay'd
His rosy eloquence, and thus inquired:
"Thou smooth-lipp'd serpent, surely high inspired!
Thou beauteous wreath, with melancholy eyes,
85 Possess whatever bliss thou canst devise,
Telling me only where my nymph is fled,—
Where she doth breathe!" "Bright planet, thou hast said,"
Return'd the snake, "but seal with oaths, fair God!"
"I swear," said Hermes, "by my serpent rod,
90 And by thine eyes, and by thy starry crown!"
Light flew his earnest words, among the blossoms blown.
Then thus again the brilliance feminine:
"Too frail of heart! for this lost nymph of thine,
Free as the air, invisibly, she strays

1. Ariadne's jeweled wedding crown, or tiara ("tiar"), was given to her by the god Bacchus, who took her as his wife after she was abandoned by her faithless mortal lover Theseus. The crown, transformed into a constellation of stars in the sky, is represented in Titian's *Bacchus and Ariadne*, which Keats had seen when the painting was exhibited in London in 1816. Keats's memories of this painting may also inform his reference to Bacchus's chariot and leopards in "Ode to a Nightingale," line 32.

2. "Pearls" had become almost a synonym for teeth in Elizabethan love poems.
3. Proserpine had been carried off to Hades by Pluto from the field of Enna, in Sicily.
4. *Stoop* is the term for the plunge of a falcon on his prey.
5. A ray of Phoebus Apollo, god of the sun.
6. Hermes, when he appeared like a star on the banks of Lethe, in the darkness of Hades. (One of Hermes' offices was to guide the souls of the dead to the lower regions.)

95 About these thornless wilds; her pleasant days
  She tastes unseen; unseen her nimble feet
  Leave traces in the grass and flowers sweet;
  From weary tendrils, and bow'd branches green,
  She plucks the fruit unseen, she bathes unseen:
100 And by my power is her beauty veil'd
  To keep it unaffronted, unassail'd
  By the love-glances of unlovely eyes,
  Of Satyrs, Fauns, and blear'd Silenus'[7] sighs.
  Pale grew her immortality, for woe
105 Of all these lovers, and she grieved so
  I took compassion on her, bade her steep
  Her hair in weïrd° syrops, that would keep   *magical*
  Her loveliness invisible, yet free
  To wander as she loves, in liberty.
110 Thou shalt behold her, Hermes, thou alone,
  If thou wilt, as thou swearest, grant my boon!"
  Then, once again, the charmed God began
  An oath, and through the serpent's ears it ran
  Warm, tremulous, devout, psalterian.[8]
115 Ravish'd, she lifted her Circean[9] head,
  Blush'd a live damask,[1] and swift-lisping said,
  "I was a woman, let me have once more
  A woman's shape, and charming as before.
  I love a youth of Corinth—O the bliss!
120 Give me my woman's form, and place me where he is.
  Stoop, Hermes, let me breathe upon thy brow,
  And thou shalt see thy sweet nymph even now."
  The God on half-shut feathers sank serene,
  She breath'd upon his eyes, and swift was seen
125 Of both the guarded nymph near-smiling on the green.
  It was no dream; or say a dream it was,
  Real are the dreams of Gods, and smoothly pass
  Their pleasures in a long immortal dream.
  One warm, flush'd moment, hovering, it might seem
130 Dash'd by the wood-nymph's beauty, so he burn'd;
  Then, lighting on the printless verdure, turn'd
  To the swoon'd serpent, and with languid arm,
  Delicate, put to proof the lythe Caducean charm.[2]
  So done, upon the nymph his eyes he bent
135 Full of adoring tears and blandishment,
  And towards her stept: she, like a moon in wane,
  Faded before him, cower'd, nor could restrain
  Her fearful sobs, self-folding like a flower
  That faints into itself at evening hour:
140 But the God fostering her chilled hand,
  She felt the warmth, her eyelids open'd bland,°   *softly*
  And, like new flowers at morning song of bees,
  Bloom'd, and gave up her honey to the lees.°   *dregs*

---

7. Satyr, a tutor of Bacchus, usually represented as a fat, jolly drunkard.
8. Either "like a psalm" or "like the sound of the psaltery" (an ancient stringed instrument).
9. Like that of Circe, the enchantress in the *Odyssey.*
1. The color of a damask rose (large and fragrant pink rose).
2. I.e., put to the test the magic of the flexible Caduceus (the name given to Hermes' wand).

Into the green-recessed woods they flew;
145 Nor grew they pale, as mortal lovers do.

    Left to herself, the serpent now began
To change; her elfin blood in madness ran,
Her mouth foam'd, and the grass, therewith besprent,°   *sprinkled*
Wither'd at dew so sweet and virulent;
150 Her eyes in torture fix'd, and anguish drear,
Hot, glaz'd, and wide, with lid-lashes all sear,
Flash'd phosphor and sharp sparks, without one cooling tear.
The colours all inflam'd throughout her train,
She writh'd about, convuls'd with scarlet pain:
155 A deep volcanian yellow took the place
Of all her milder-mooned body's grace;[3]
And, as the lava ravishes the mead,
Spoilt all her silver mail, and golden brede;[4]
Made gloom of all her frecklings, streaks and bars,
160 Eclips'd her crescents, and lick'd up her stars:
So that, in moments few, she was undrest
Of all her sapphires, greens, and amethyst,
And rubious-argent:° of all these bereft,   *silvery red*
Nothing but pain and ugliness were left.
165 Still shone her crown; that vanish'd, also she
Melted and disappear'd as suddenly;
And in the air, her new voice luting soft,
Cried, "Lycius! gentle Lycius!"—Borne aloft
With the bright mists about the mountains hoar°   *white*
170 These words dissolv'd: Crete's forests heard no more.

    Whither fled Lamia, now a lady bright,
A full-born beauty new and exquisite?
She fled into that valley they pass o'er
Who go to Corinth from Cenchreas' shore;[5]
175 And rested at the foot of those wild hills,
The rugged founts of the Peæran rills,
And of that other ridge whose barren back
Stretches, with all its mist and cloudy rack,
South-westward to Cleone. There she stood
180 About a young bird's flutter from a wood,
Fair, on a sloping green of mossy tread,
By a clear pool, wherein she passioned[6]
To see herself escap'd from so sore ills,
While her robes flaunted with the daffodils.

185   Ah, happy Lycius!—for she was a maid
More beautiful than ever twisted braid,
Or sigh'd, or blush'd, or on spring-flowered lea°   *meadow*
Spread a green kirtle° to the minstrelsy: *gown*
A virgin purest lipp'd, yet in the lore

---

3. I.e., the yellow of sulfur (thrown up by a volcano) replaced her former silvery moon color.
4. Embroidery, interwoven pattern. "Mail": interlinked rings, as in a coat of armor.

5. Cenchrea (Keats's "Cenchreas") was a harbor of Corinth, in southern Greece.
6. Felt intense excitement.

190 Of love deep learned to the red heart's core:
Not one hour old, yet of sciential brain
To unperplex bliss from its neighbour pain;
Define their pettish limits, and estrange
Their points of contact, and swift counterchange;[7]
195 Intrigue with the specious chaos,[8] and dispart
Its most ambiguous atoms with sure art;
As though in Cupid's college she had spent
Sweet days a lovely graduate, still unshent,°   unspoiled
And kept his rosy terms[9] in idle languishment.

200   Why this fair creature chose so fairily
By the wayside to linger, we shall see;
But first 'tis fit to tell how she could muse
And dream, when in the serpent prison-house,
Of all she list,° strange or magnificent: wished
205 How, ever, where she will'd, her spirit went;
Whether to faint Elysium,[1] or where
Down through tress-lifting waves the Nereids[2] fair
Wind into Thetis' bower by many a pearly stair;
Or where God Bacchus drains his cups divine,
210 Stretch'd out, at ease, beneath a glutinous pine;
Or where in Pluto's gardens palatine°   palatial
Mulciber's columns gleam in far piazzian line.[3]
And sometimes into cities she would send
Her dream, with feast and rioting to blend;
215 And once, while among mortals dreaming thus,
She saw the young Corinthian Lycius
Charioting foremost in the envious race,
Like a young Jove with calm uneager face,
And fell into a swooning love of him.
220 Now on the moth-time of that evening dim
He would return that way, as well she knew,
To Corinth from the shore; for freshly blew
The eastern soft wind, and his galley now
Grated the quaystones with her brazen prow
225 In port Cenchreas, from Egina isle
Fresh anchor'd; whither he had been awhile
To sacrifice to Jove, whose temple there
Waits with high marble doors for blood and incense rare.
Jove heard his vows, and better'd his desire;
230 For by some freakful chance he made retire
From his companions, and set forth to walk,
Perhaps grown wearied of their Corinth talk:
Over the solitary hills he fared,

---

7. I.e., of knowledgeable ("sciential") brain to disentangle ("unperplex") bliss from its closely related pain, to define their quarreled-over ("pettish") limits, and to separate out ("estrange") their points of contact and the swift changes of each condition into its opposite. Cf. Keats's "Ode on Melancholy," lines 21–26 (p. 982).
8. I.e., turn to her own artful purpose the seeming ("specious") chaos.

9. The terms spent studying in "Cupid's college."
1. Region inhabited by the virtuous after death.
2. Sea nymphs, of whom Thetis (line 208, the mother of Achilles) was one.
3. I.e., columns made by Mulciber (Vulcan, god of fire and metalworking) gleam in long lines around open courts (piazzas).

Thoughtless at first, but ere eve's star appeared
235 His phantasy was lost, where reason fades,
In the calm'd twilight of Platonic shades.[4]
Lamia beheld him coming, near, more near—
Close to her passing, in indifference drear,
His silent sandals swept the mossy green;
240 So neighbour'd to him, and yet so unseen
She stood: he pass'd, shut up in mysteries,
His mind wrapp'd like his mantle, while her eyes
Follow'd his steps, and her neck regal white
Turn'd—syllabling thus, "Ah, Lycius bright,
245 And will you leave me on the hills alone?
Lycius, look back! and be some pity shown."
He did; not with cold wonder fearingly,
But Orpheus-like at an Eurydice;[5]
For so delicious were the words she sung,
250 It seem'd he had lov'd them a whole summer long:
And soon his eyes had drunk her beauty up,
Leaving no drop in the bewildering cup,
And still the cup was full,—while he, afraid
Lest she should vanish ere his lip had paid
255 Due adoration, thus began to adore;
Her soft look growing coy, she saw his chain so sure:
"Leave thee alone! Look back! Ah, Goddess, see
Whether my eyes can ever turn from thee!
For pity do not this sad heart belie°—   betray
260 Even as thou vanishest so I shall die.
Stay! though a Naiad of the rivers, stay!
To thy far wishes will thy streams obey:
Stay! though the greenest woods be thy domain,
Alone they can drink up the morning rain:
265 Though a descended Pleiad,[6] will not one
Of thine harmonious sisters keep in tune
Thy spheres, and as thy silver proxy shine?
So sweetly to these ravish'd ears of mine
Came thy sweet greeting, that if thou shouldst fade
270 Thy memory will waste me to a shade:—
For pity do not melt!"—"If I should stay,"
Said Lamia, "here, upon this floor of clay,
And pain my steps upon these flowers too rough,
What canst thou say or do of charm enough
275 To dull the nice[7] remembrance of my home?
Thou canst not ask me with thee here to roam
Over these hills and vales, where no joy is,—
Empty of immortality and bliss!
Thou art a scholar, Lycius, and must know
280 That finer spirits cannot breathe below

---

4. I.e., he was absorbed in musing about the obscurities of Plato's philosophy.
5. As Orpheus looked at Eurydice in Hades. Orpheus was allowed by Pluto to lead Eurydice back to Earth on condition that he not look back at her, but he could not resist doing so and hence lost her once more.

6. One of the seven sisters composing the constellation Pleiades. The lines that follow allude to the ancient belief that the planets traveled inside crystalline spheres whose movements produced heavenly music.
7. Detailed, minutely accurate.

In human climes, and live: Alas! poor youth,
What taste of purer air hast thou to soothe
My essence? What serener palaces,
Where I may all my many senses please,
285 And by mysterious sleights a hundred thirsts appease?
It cannot be—Adieu!" So said, she rose
Tiptoe with white arms spread. He, sick to lose
The amorous promise of her lone complain,
Swoon'd, murmuring of love, and pale with pain.
290 The cruel lady, without any show
Of sorrow for her tender favourite's woe,
But rather, if her eyes could brighter be,
With brighter eyes and slow amenity,°   *pleasure*
Put her new lips to his, and gave afresh
295 The life she had so tangled in her mesh:
And as he from one trance was wakening
Into another, she began to sing,
Happy in beauty, life, and love, and every thing,
A song of love, too sweet for earthly lyres,
300 While, like held breath, the stars drew in their panting fires.
And then she whisper'd in such trembling tone,
As those who, safe together met alone
For the first time through many anguish'd days,
Use other speech than looks; bidding him raise
305 His drooping head, and clear his soul of doubt,
For that she was a woman, and without
Any more subtle fluid in her veins
Than throbbing blood, and that the self-same pains
Inhabited her frail-strung heart as his.
310 And next she wonder'd how his eyes could miss
Her face so long in Corinth, where, she said,
She dwelt but half retir'd, and there had led
Days happy as the gold coin could invent
Without the aid of love; yet in content
315 Till she saw him, as once she pass'd him by,
Where 'gainst a column he leant thoughtfully
At Venus' temple porch, 'mid baskets heap'd
Of amorous herbs and flowers, newly reap'd
Late on that eve, as 'twas the night before
320 The Adonian feast;[8] whereof she saw no more,
But wept alone those days, for why should she adore?
Lycius from death awoke into amaze,
To see her still, and singing so sweet lays;
Then from amaze into delight he fell
325 To hear her whisper woman's lore so well;
And every word she spake entic'd him on
To unperplex'd delight[9] and pleasure known.
Let the mad poets say whate'er they please
Of the sweets of Fairies, Peris,[1] Goddesses,
330 There is not such a treat among them all,

---

8. The feast of Adonis, beloved by Venus.   (see line 192).
9. I.e., delight not mixed with its neighbor, pain   1. Fairylike creatures in Persian mythology.

Haunters of cavern, lake, and waterfall,
As a real woman, lineal indeed
From Pyrrha's pebbles[2] or old Adam's seed.
Thus gentle Lamia judg'd, and judg'd aright,
335 That Lycius could not love in half a fright,
So threw the goddess off, and won his heart
More pleasantly by playing woman's part,
With no more awe than what her beauty gave,
That, while it smote, still guaranteed to save.
340 Lycius to all made eloquent reply,
Marrying to every word a twinborn sigh;
And last, pointing to Corinth, ask'd her sweet,
If 'twas too far that night for her soft feet.
The way was short, for Lamia's eagerness
345 Made, by a spell, the triple league decrease
To a few paces; not at all surmised
By blinded Lycius, so in her comprized.[3]
They pass'd the city gates, he knew not how,
So noiseless, and he never thought to know.

350   As men talk in a dream, so Corinth all,
Throughout her palaces imperial,
And all her populous streets and temples lewd,[4]
Mutter'd, like tempest in the distance brew'd,
To the wide-spreaded night above her towers.
355 Men, women, rich and poor, in the cool hours,
Shuffled their sandals o'er the pavement white,
Companion'd or alone; while many a light
Flared, here and there, from wealthy festivals,
And threw their moving shadows on the walls,
360 Or found them cluster'd in the corniced shade
Of some arch'd temple door, or dusky colonnade.

    Muffling his face, of greeting friends in fear,
Her fingers he press'd hard, as one came near
With curl'd gray beard, sharp eyes, and smooth bald crown,
365 Slow-stepp'd, and robed in philosophic gown:
Lycius shrank closer, as they met and past,
Into his mantle, adding wings to haste,
While hurried Lamia trembled: "Ah," said he,
"Why do you shudder, love, so ruefully?
370 Why does your tender palm dissolve in dew?"—
"I'm wearied," said fair Lamia: "tell me who
Is that old man? I cannot bring to mind
His features:—Lycius! wherefore did you blind
Yourself from his quick eyes?" Lycius replied,
375 "'Tis Apollonius sage, my trusty guide
And good instructor; but to-night he seems
The ghost of folly haunting my sweet dreams."

2. Descended from the pebbles with which, in
Greek myth, Pyrrha and Deucalion repeopled
the earth after the flood.
3. Bound up, absorbed.

4. Temples of Venus, whose worship sometimes
involved ritual prostitution. The city of Corinth
was notorious in antiquity as a site of commerce
and prostitution.

While yet he spake they had arrived before
A pillar'd porch, with lofty portal door,
380 Where hung a silver lamp, whose phosphor glow
Reflected in the slabbed steps below,
Mild as a star in water; for so new,
And so unsullied was the marble hue,
So through the crystal polish, liquid fine,
385 Ran the dark veins, that none but feet divine
Could e'er have touch'd there. Sounds Æolian[5]
Breath'd from the hinges, as the ample span
Of the wide doors disclos'd a place unknown
Some time to any, but those two alone,
390 And a few Persian mutes, who that same year
Were seen about the markets: none knew where
They could inhabit; the most curious
Were foil'd, who watch'd to trace them to their house:
And but the flitter-winged verse must tell,
395 For truth's sake, what woe afterwards befel,
'Twould humour many a heart to leave them thus,
Shut from the busy world of more incredulous.

Part 2

Love in a hut, with water and a crust,
Is—Love, forgive us!—cinders, ashes, dust;
Love in a palace is perhaps at last
More grievous torment than a hermit's fast:—
5 That is a doubtful tale from faery land,
Hard for the non-elect to understand.
Had Lycius liv'd to hand his story down,
He might have given the moral a fresh frown,
Or clench'd it quite: but too short was their bliss
10 To breed distrust and hate, that make the soft voice hiss.
Besides, there, nightly, with terrific glare,
Love, jealous grown of so complete a pair,
Hover'd and buzz'd his wings, with fearful roar,
Above the lintel of their chamber door,
15 And down the passage cast a glow upon the floor.

For all this came a ruin: side by side
They were enthroned, in the even tide,
Upon a couch, near to a curtaining
Whose airy texture, from a golden string,
20 Floated into the room, and let appear
Unveil'd the summer heaven, blue and clear,
Betwixt two marble shafts:—there they reposed,
Where use had made it sweet, with eyelids closed,
Saving a tythe which love still open kept,
25 That they might see each other while they almost slept;
When from the slope side of a suburb hill,
Deafening the swallow's twitter, came a thrill

5. Like sounds from the wind harp (Aeolus is god of winds), which responds musically to a current of air.

Of trumpets—Lycius started—the sounds fled,
But left a thought, a buzzing in his head.
30 For the first time, since first he harbour'd in
That purple-lined palace of sweet sin,
His spirit pass'd beyond its golden bourn°   boundary
Into the noisy world almost forsworn.
The lady, ever watchful, penetrant,
35 Saw this with pain, so arguing a want
Of something more, more than her empery°   empire
Of joys; and she began to moan and sigh
Because he mused beyond her, knowing well
That but a moment's thought is passion's passing bell.°   death knell
40 "Why do you sigh, fair creature?" whisper'd he:
"Why do you think?" return'd she tenderly:
"You have deserted me;—where am I now?
Not in your heart while care weighs on your brow:
No, no, you have dismiss'd me; and I go
45 From your breast houseless: ay, it must be so."
He answer'd, bending to her open eyes,
Where he was mirror'd small in paradise,
"My silver planet, both of eve and morn!⁶
Why will you plead yourself so sad forlorn,
50 While I am striving how to fill my heart
With deeper crimson, and a double smart?
How to entangle, trammel up and snare
Your soul in mine, and labyrinth you there
Like the hid scent in an unbudded rose?
55 Ay, a sweet kiss—you see your mighty woes.⁷
My thoughts! shall I unveil them? Listen then!
What mortal hath a prize, that other men
May be confounded and abash'd withal,
But lets it sometimes pace abroad majestical,
60 And triumph, as in thee I should rejoice
Amid the hoarse alarm of Corinth's voice.
Let my foes choke, and my friends shout afar,
While through the thronged streets your bridal car°   chariot
Wheels round its dazzling spokes."—The lady's cheek
65 Trembled; she nothing said, but, pale and meek,
Arose and knelt before him, wept a rain
Of sorrows at his words; at last with pain
Beseeching him, the while his hand she wrung,
To change his purpose. He thereat was stung,
70 Perverse, with stronger fancy to reclaim
Her wild and timid nature to his aim:
Besides, for all his love, in self despite,
Against his better self, he took delight
Luxurious in her sorrows, soft and new.
75 His passion, cruel grown, took on a hue
Fierce and sanguineous as 'twas possible
In one whose brow had no dark veins to swell.

6. The planet Venus, which is both the morning and the evening star.

7. Playfully: "You see how great your troubles were!"

Fine was the mitigated fury, like
Apollo's presence when in act to strike
80 The serpent—Ha, the serpent! certes, she
Was none. She burnt, she lov'd the tyranny,
And, all subdued, consented to the hour
When to the bridal he should lead his paramour.
Whispering in midnight silence, said the youth,
85 "Sure some sweet name thou hast, though, by my truth,
I have not ask'd it, ever thinking thee
Not mortal, but of heavenly progeny,
As still I do. Hast any mortal name,
Fit appellation for this dazzling frame?
90 Or friends or kinsfolk on the citied earth,
To share our marriage feast and nuptial mirth?"
"I have no friends," said Lamia, "no, not one;
My presence in wide Corinth hardly known:
My parents' bones are in their dusty urns
95 Sepulchred, where no kindled incense burns,
Seeing all their luckless race are dead, save me,
And I neglect the holy rite for thee.
Even as you list° invite your many guests;   choose
But if, as now it seems, your vision rests
100 With any pleasure on me, do not bid
Old Apollonius—from him keep me hid."
Lycius, perplex'd at words so blind and blank,
Made close inquiry; from whose touch she shrank,
Feigning a sleep; and he to the dull shade
105 Of deep sleep in a moment was betray'd.

    It was the custom then to bring away,
The bride from home at blushing shut of day,
Veil'd, in a chariot, heralded along
By strewn flowers, torches, and a marriage song,
110 With other pageants: but this fair unknown
Had not a friend. So being left alone,
(Lycius was gone to summon all his kin)
And knowing surely she could never win
His foolish heart from its mad pompousness,
115 She set herself, high-thoughted, how to dress
The misery in fit magnificence.
She did so, but 'tis doubtful how and whence
Came, and who were her subtle servitors.
About the halls, and to and from the doors,
120 There was a noise of wings, till in short space
The glowing banquet-room shone with wide-arched grace.
A haunting music, sole perhaps and lone
Supportress of the faery-roof, made moan
Throughout, as fearful the whole charm might fade.
125 Fresh carved cedar, mimicking a glade
Of palm and plantain, met from either side,
High in the midst, in honour of the bride:
Two palms and then two plantains, and so on,
From either side their stems branch'd one to one

130 All down the aisled place; and beneath all
There ran a stream of lamps straight on from wall to wall.
So canopied, lay an untasted feast
Teeming with odours. Lamia, regal drest,
Silently paced about, and as she went,
135 In pale contented sort of discontent,
Mission'd her viewless° servants to enrich   invisible
The fretted⁸ splendour of each nook and niche.
Between the tree-stems, marbled plain at first,
Came jasper pannels; then, anon, there burst
140 Forth creeping imagery of slighter trees,
And with the larger wove in small intricacies.
Approving all, she faded at self-will,
And shut the chamber up, close, hush'd and still,
Complete and ready for the revels rude,
145 When dreadful° guests would come to spoil her solitude.   terrifying

     The day appeared, and all the gossip rout.
O senseless Lycius! Madman! wherefore flout
The silent-blessing fate, warm cloister'd hours,
And show to common eyes these secret bowers?
150 The herd approach'd; each guest, with busy brain,
Arriving at the portal, gaz'd amain,°   intently
And enter'd marveling: for they knew the street,
Remember'd it from childhood all complete
Without a gap, yet ne'er before had seen
155 That royal porch, that high-built fair demesne;°   estate
So in they hurried all, maz'd, curious and keen:
Save one, who look'd thereon with eye severe,
And with calm-planted steps walk'd in austere;
'Twas Apollonius: something too he laugh'd,
160 As though some knotty problem, that had daft°   baffled
His patient thought, had now begun to thaw,
And solve and melt:—'twas just as he foresaw.

     He met within the murmurous vestibule
His young disciple. "'Tis no common rule,
165 Lycius," said he, "for uninvited guest
To force himself upon you, and infest
With an unbidden presence the bright throng
Of younger friends; yet must I do this wrong,
And you forgive me." Lycius blush'd, and led
170 The old man through the inner doors broad-spread;
With reconciling words and courteous mien°   appearance
Turning into sweet milk the sophist's° spleen.   scholar's

     Of wealthy lustre was the banquet-room,
Fill'd with pervading brilliance and perfume:
175 Before each lucid pannel fuming stood
A censer fed with myrrh and spiced wood,

---

8. Adorned with fretwork (interlaced patterns).

Each by a sacred tripod held aloft,
Whose slender feet wide-swerv'd upon the soft
Wool-woofed° carpets: fifty wreaths of smoke   *woven*
180 From fifty censers their light voyage took
To the high roof, still mimick'd as they rose
Along the mirror'd walls by twin-clouds odorous.
Twelve sphered tables, by silk seats insphered,
High as the level of a man's breast rear'd
185 On libbard's° paws, upheld the heavy gold   *leopard's*
Of cups and goblets, and the store thrice told
Of Ceres' horn,[9] and, in huge vessels, wine
Come from the gloomy tun with merry shine.
Thus loaded with a feast the tables stood,
190 Each shrining in the midst the image of a God.

When in an antichamber every guest
Had felt the cold full sponge to pleasure press'd,
By minist'ring slaves, upon his hands and feet,
And fragrant oils with ceremony meet°   *suitable*
195 Pour'd on his hair, they all mov'd to the feast
In white robes, and themselves in order placed
Around the silken couches, wondering
Whence all this mighty cost and blaze of wealth could spring.

Soft went the music the soft air along,
200 While fluent Greek a vowel'd undersong
Kept up among the guests, discoursing low
At first, for scarcely was the wine at flow;
But when the happy vintage touch'd their brains,
Louder they talk, and louder come the strains
205 Of powerful instruments:—the gorgeous dyes,
The space, the splendour of the draperies,
The roof of awful richness, nectarous cheer,
Beautiful slaves, and Lamia's self, appear,
Now, when the wine has done its rosy deed,
210 And every soul from human trammels freed,
No more so strange; for merry wine, sweet wine,
Will make Elysian shades not too fair, too divine.

Soon was God Bacchus at meridian height;
Flush'd were their cheeks, and bright eyes double bright:
215 Garlands of every green, and every scent
From vales deflower'd, or forest-trees branch-rent,
In baskets of bright osier'd[1] gold were brought
High as the handles heap'd, to suit the thought
Of every guest; that each, as he did please,
220 Might fancy-fit his brows, silk-pillow'd at his ease.

What wreath for Lamia? What for Lycius?
What for the sage, old Apollonius?

9. The horn of plenty, overflowing with the products of Ceres, goddess of grain.
1. Plaited. An "osier" is a strip of willow used in weaving baskets.

Upon her aching forehead be there hung
The leaves of willow and of adder's tongue;[2]
225 And for the youth, quick, let us strip for him
The thyrsus,[3] that his watching eyes may swim
Into forgetfulness; and, for the sage,
Let spear-grass and the spiteful thistle wage
War on his temples. Do not all charms fly
230 At the mere touch of cold philosophy?[4]
There was an awful° rainbow once in heaven: *awe-inspiring*
We know her woof, her texture; she is given
In the dull catalogue of common things.
Philosophy will clip an Angel's wings,
235 Conquer all mysteries by rule and line,
Empty the haunted air, and gnomed mine[5]—
Unweave a rainbow, as it erewhile made
The tender-person'd Lamia melt into a shade.

By her glad Lycius sitting, in chief place,
240 Scarce saw in all the room another face,
Till, checking his love trance, a cup he took
Full brimm'd, and opposite sent forth a look
'Cross the broad table, to beseech a glance
From his old teacher's wrinkled countenance,
245 And pledge° him. The bald-head philosopher   *drink a toast to*
Had fix'd his eye, without a twinkle or stir
Full on the alarmed beauty of the bride,
Brow-beating her fair form, and troubling her sweet pride.
Lycius then press'd her hand, with devout touch,
250 As pale it lay upon the rosy couch:
'Twas icy, and the cold ran through his veins;
Then sudden it grew hot, and all the pains
Of an unnatural heat shot to his heart.
"Lamia, what means this? Wherefore dost thou start?
255 Know'st thou that man?" Poor Lamia answer'd not.
He gaz'd into her eyes, and not a jot
Own'd° they the lovelorn piteous appeal: *acknowledged*
More, more he gaz'd: his human senses reel:
Some hungry spell that loveliness absorbs;
260 There was no recognition in those orbs.
"Lamia!" he cried—and no soft-toned reply.
The many heard, and the loud revelry
Grew hush; the stately music no more breathes;
The myrtle[6] sicken'd in a thousand wreaths.
265 By faint degrees, voice, lute, and pleasure ceased;
A deadly silence step by step increased,
Until it seem'd a horrid presence there,

2. A fern whose spikes resemble a serpent's tongue.
3. The vine-covered staff of Bacchus, used to signify drunkenness.
4. In the sense of "natural philosophy," or science. Benjamin Haydon tells in his *Autobiography* how, at a hard-drinking and high-spirited dinner party, Keats had agreed with Charles Lamb (to what extent jokingly, it is not clear) that Newton's *Optics* "had destroyed all the poetry of the rainbow by reducing it to the prismatic colors."
5. Gnomes were guardians of mines.
6. Sacred to Venus, hence an emblem of love.

And not a man but felt the terror in his hair.
"Lamia!" he shriek'd; and nothing but the shriek
270 With its sad echo did the silence break.
"Begone, foul dream!" he cried, gazing again
In the bride's face, where now no azure vein
Wander'd on fair-spaced temples; no soft bloom
Misted the cheek; no passion to illume
275 The deep-recessed vision:—all was blight;
Lamia, no longer fair, there sat a deadly white.
"Shut, shut those juggling⁷ eyes, thou ruthless man!
Turn them aside, wretch! or the righteous ban
Of all the Gods, whose dreadful images
280 Here represent their shadowy presences,
May pierce them on the sudden with the thorn
Of painful blindness; leaving thee forlorn,
In trembling dotage to the feeblest fright
Of conscience, for their long offended might,
285 For all thine impious proud-heart sophistries,
Unlawful magic, and enticing lies.
Corinthians! look upon that gray-beard wretch!
Mark how, possess'd, his lashless eyelids stretch
Around his demon eyes! Corinthians, see!
290 My sweet bride withers at their potency."
"Fool!" said the sophist, in an under-tone
Gruff with contempt; which a death-nighing moan
From Lycius answer'd, as heart-struck and lost,
He sank supine beside the aching ghost.
295 "Fool! Fool!" repeated he, while his eyes still
Relented not, nor mov'd; "from every ill
Of life have I preserv'd thee to this day,
And shall I see thee made a serpent's prey?"
Then Lamia breath'd death breath; the sophist's eye,
300 Like a sharp spear, went through her utterly,
Keen, cruel, perceant,° stinging: she, as well   *piercing*
As her weak hand could any meaning tell,
Motion'd him to be silent; vainly so,
He look'd and look'd again a level—No!
305 "A Serpent!" echoed he; no sooner said,
Than with a frightful scream she vanished:
And Lycius' arms were empty of delight,
As were his limbs of life, from that same night.
On the high couch he lay!—his friends came round—
310 Supported him—no pulse, or breath they found,
And, in its marriage robe, the heavy body wound.

July–Aug. 1819   1820

---

7. Deceiving, full of trickery.

To Autumn[1]

1

Season of mists and mellow fruitfulness,
　　Close bosom-friend of the maturing sun;
Conspiring with him how to load and bless
　　With fruit the vines that round the thatch-eves run;
5　To bend with apples the moss'd cottage-trees,
　　And fill all fruit with ripeness to the core;
　　　　To swell the gourd, and plump the hazel shells
　　With a sweet kernel; to set budding more,
And still more, later flowers for the bees,
10　Until they think warm days will never cease,
　　　　For summer has o'er-brimm'd their clammy cells.

2

Who hath not seen thee oft amid thy store?
　　Sometimes whoever seeks abroad may find
Thee sitting careless on a granary floor,
15　　Thy hair soft-lifted by the winnowing[2] wind;
Or on a half-reap'd furrow sound asleep,
　　Drows'd with the fume of poppies, while thy hook°　　　　scythe
　　　　Spares the next swath and all its twined flowers:
And sometimes like a gleaner thou dost keep
20　Steady thy laden head across a brook;
　　Or by a cyder-press, with patient look,
　　　　Thou watchest the last oozings hours by hours.

3

Where are the songs of spring? Ay, where are they?
　　Think not of them, thou hast thy music too,—
25　While barred clouds bloom the soft-dying day,
　　And touch the stubble-plains with rosy hue;
Then in a wailful choir the small gnats mourn
　　Among the river sallows,° borne aloft　　　　willows
　　　　Or sinking as the light wind lives or dies;
30　And full-grown lambs loud bleat from hilly bourn;°　　　　region
　　Hedge-crickets sing; and now with treble soft
　　The red-breast whistles from a garden-croft;[3]
　　　　And gathering swallows twitter in the skies.

Sept. 19, 1819　　　　　　　　　　　　　　　　　　　　　1820

---

1. Two days after this ode was composed, Keats wrote to J. H. Reynolds: "I never liked stubble fields so much as now—Aye, better than the chilly green of the spring. Somehow a stubble plain looks warm—in the same way that some pictures look warm—this struck me so much in my Sun- day's walk that I composed upon it." For the author's revisions while composing "To Autumn," see "Poems in Process," in the NAEL Archive.
2. To "winnow" is to fan the chaff from the grain.
3. An enclosed plot of farmland.

The Fall of Hyperion: A Dream

Late in 1818, while he was serving as nurse to his dying brother Tom, Keats planned to undertake an epic poem, modeled on *Paradise Lost*, that he called *Hyperion*. Greek mythology gave Keats its subject— the displacement of Saturn and his fellow Titans by a new generation of gods, Zeus and the other Olympians. But in engaging this topic Keats addressed the epic question at the center of *Paradise Lost*: how did evil come into the world and why? The Titans had been fair and benign gods, and their rule had been a golden age of happiness. Yet at the beginning of the poem all the Titans except Hyperion, god of the sun, have been dethroned; and the uncomprehending Saturn again and again raises the question of how this injustice could have come to be.

In book 3 of the original *Hyperion*, the scenes among the Titans are supplemented by the experience of the Olympian Apollo, still a youth but destined to displace Hyperion as the sun god among the heavenly powers. He lives in "aching ignorance" of the universe and its processes but thirsts for knowledge. Suddenly Apollo reads in the face of his tutor Mnemosyne—goddess of memory, who will be mother of the Muses and so of all the arts—the silent record of the defeat of the Titans and at once soars to the knowledge that he seeks. Apollo cries out:

> Knowledge enormous makes a God of me.
> Names, deeds, gray legends, dire events, rebellions,
> Majesties, sovran voices, agonies,
> Creations and destroyings, all at once
> Pour into the wide hollows of my brain,
> And deify me. . . .

This opening out of Apollo's awareness to the tragic nature of life is what the Titans lacked. As the fragment breaks off, Apollo is transfigured—not only into one who has earned the right to displace Hyperion as god of the sun, but also into the god of the highest poetry.

Keats abandoned this extraordinary fragment in April 1819. Late that summer, however, he took up the theme again, under the title *The Fall of Hyperion: A Dream*. This time his primary model is Dante. In Dante's *Divine Comedy* all the narrated events are represented as a vision granted to the poet. In the same way, Keats begins *The Fall of Hyperion* with a frame story whose central event is that the poet-protagonist, in a dream, falls from a paradisal landscape into a wasteland and there earns the right to a vision. That vision reincorporates the events narrated in the first *Hyperion*: Moneta (her Latin name suggests "the Admonisher"), who stands in the same relationship to the poet as, in the earlier tale, Mnemosyne stood to Apollo, permits, or challenges, this protagonist to remember, with her, her own memories of the fall of the Titans. By devising this frame story, Keats shifted his center of poetic concern from the narration of epic action to an account of the evolving consciousness of the epic poet.

Keats abandoned this attempt at *The Fall of Hyperion* at the sixty-first line of the second canto. (A fragment was published, against his wishes, in his 1820 volume of poems.) He wrote to Reynolds on September 21, 1819:

> I have given up Hyperion. . . . Miltonic verse cannot be written but in an artful or rather artist's humour. I wish to give myself up to other sensations.

In the same letter Keats mentions having composed two days earlier the ode "To Autumn." In this, the poet had envisaged the circumstance of the cycle of life and death, and had articulated his experience in his own poetic voice.

The Fall of Hyperion: A Dream

Canto 1

Fanatics have their dreams, wherewith they weave
A paradise for a sect; the savage too
From forth the loftiest fashion of his sleep
Guesses at heaven: pity these have not
5   Trac'd upon vellum° or wild Indian leaf   *parchment*
The shadows of melodious utterance.
But bare of laurel[1] they live, dream, and die;
For Poesy alone can tell her dreams,
With the fine spell of words alone can save
10   Imagination from the sable charm
And dumb° enchantment. Who alive can say   *mute*
"Thou art no poet; mayst not tell thy dreams"?
Since every man whose soul is not a clod
Hath visions, and would speak, if he had lov'd
15   And been well nurtured in his mother tongue.
Whether the dream now purposed to rehearse
Be poet's or fanatic's will be known
When this warm scribe my hand is in the grave.

Methought I stood where trees of every clime,
20   Palm, myrtle, oak, and sycamore, and beech,
With plantane, and spice blossoms, made a screen;
In neighbourhood of fountains, by the noise
Soft showering in mine ears, and, by the touch
Of scent, not far from roses. Turning round,
25   I saw an arbour with a drooping roof
Of trellis vines, and bells, and larger blooms,
Like floral-censers swinging light in air;
Before its wreathed doorway, on a mound
Of moss, was spread a feast of summer fruits,
30   Which, nearer seen, seem'd refuse of a meal
By angel tasted, or our mother Eve;[2]
For empty shells were scattered on the grass,
And grape stalks but half bare, and remnants more,
Sweet smelling, whose pure kinds I could not know.
35   Still was more plenty than the fabled horn[3]
Thrice emptied could pour forth, at banqueting
For Proserpine return'd to her own fields,[4]
Where the white heifers low. And appetite
More yearning than on earth I ever felt
40   Growing within, I ate deliciously;
And, after not long, thirsted, for thereby
Stood a cool vessel of transparent juice,
Sipp'd by the wander'd bee, the which I took,

---

1. The laurel, associated with Apollo, is the emblem of poetic fame.
2. In *Paradise Lost* 5.321ff Eve serves the visiting angel Raphael with a meal of fruits and fruit juices.

3. The cornucopia, or horn of plenty.
4. When Proserpine each year is released by her husband, Pluto, god of the underworld, for a sojourn on Earth, it is the beginning of spring.

And, pledging all the mortals of the world,
45 And all the dead whose names are in our lips,
Drank. That full draught is parent of my theme.[5]
No Asian poppy,° nor elixir fine   *opium*
Of the soon fading jealous caliphat;[6]
No poison gender'd in close monkish cell
50 To thin the scarlet conclave of old men,[7]
Could so have rapt unwilling life away.
Among the fragrant husks and berries crush'd,
Upon the grass I struggled hard against
The domineering potion; but in vain:
55 The cloudy swoon came on, and down I sunk
Like a Silenus[8] on an antique vase.
How long I slumber'd 'tis a chance to guess.
When sense of life return'd, I started up
As if with wings; but the fair trees were gone,
60 The mossy mound and arbour were no more;
I look'd around upon the carved sides
Of an old sanctuary with roof august,
Builded so high, it seem'd that filmed clouds
Might spread beneath, as o'er the stars of heaven;
65 So old the place was, I remembered none
The like upon the earth; what I had seen
Of grey cathedrals, buttress'd walls, rent towers,
The superannuations° of sunk realms,   *ruins*
Or nature's rocks toil'd hard in waves and winds,
70 Seem'd but the faulture° of decrepit things   *defects*
To° that eternal domed monument.   *compared to*
Upon the marble at my feet there lay
Store of strange vessels, and large draperies,
Which needs had been of dyed asbestus wove,
75 Or in that place the moth could not corrupt,[9]
So white the linen; so, in some, distinct
Ran imageries from a sombre loom.
All in a mingled heap confus'd there lay
Robes, golden tongs, censer, and chafing dish,
80 Girdles, and chains, and holy jewelries.[1]

    Turning from these with awe, once more I rais'd
My eyes to fathom the space every way;
The embossed roof, the silent massy range
Of columns north and south, ending in mist
85 Of nothing, then to eastward, where black gates
Were shut against the sunrise evermore.
Then to the west I look'd, and saw far off
An image, huge of feature as a cloud,

5. The drink puts the poet to sleep and effects
the dream within a dream that constitutes the
remainder of the fragment.
6. A council of caliphs, Muslim rulers, who plot
to kill each other with a poisonous drink ("elixir").
7. The College of Cardinals. This scenario of
poisoning, like the preceding Orientalist reference to intrigue among the caliphs, recalls a
stock setting of the period's Gothic novels.
8. An elderly satyr, usually represented as drunk.
9. Matthew 6.20: "Lay up for yourselves treasures in heaven, where neither moth nor rust
doth corrupt."
1. Offerings to the gods were spread on the floor
of Greek temples.

At level of whose feet an altar slept,
90　To be approach'd on either side by steps,
And marble balustrade,° and patient travail   *banister*
To count with toil the innumerable degrees.
Towards the altar sober-pac'd I went,
Repressing haste, as too unholy there;
95　And, coming nearer, saw beside the shrine
One minist'ring;[2] and there arose a flame.
When in mid-May the sickening east wind
Shifts sudden to the south, the small warm rain
Melts out the frozen incense from all flowers,
100　And fills the air with so much pleasant health
That even the dying man forgets his shroud;
Even so that lofty sacrificial fire,
Sending forth Maian[3] incense, spread around
Forgetfulness of every thing but bliss,
105　And clouded all the altar with soft smoke,
From whose white fragrant curtains thus I heard
Language pronounc'd. "If thou canst not ascend
These steps,[4] die on that marble where thou art.
Thy flesh, near cousin to the common dust,
110　Will parch for lack of nutriment—thy bones
Will wither in few years, and vanish so
That not the quickest eye could find a grain
Of what thou now art on that pavement cold.
The sands of thy short life are spent this hour,
115　And no hand in the universe can turn
Thy hour glass, if these gummed° leaves be burnt   *aromatic*
Ere thou canst mount up these immortal steps."
I heard, I look'd: two senses both at once
So fine, so subtle, felt the tyranny
120　Of that fierce threat, and the hard task proposed.
Prodigious seem'd the toil; the leaves were yet
Burning,—when suddenly a palsied chill
Struck from the paved level up my limbs,
And was ascending quick to put cold grasp
125　Upon those streams° that pulse beside the throat: *arteries*
I shriek'd; and the sharp anguish of my shriek
Stung my own ears—I strove hard to escape
The numbness; strove to gain the lowest step.
Slow, heavy, deadly was my pace: the cold
130　Grew stifling, suffocating, at the heart;
And when I clasp'd my hands I felt them not.
One minute before death, my iced foot touch'd
The lowest stair; and as it touch'd, life seem'd
To pour in at the toes: I mounted up,
135　As once fair angels on a ladder flew
From the green turf to heaven.[5]—"Holy Power,"

2. Who identifies herself in line 226 as Moneta.
3. Maia was one of the Pleiades, a daughter of Atlas and (by Zeus) the mother of Hermes. She was the goddess of the month of May.
4. These steps that the poet must ascend were probably suggested by the stairs going up the steep side of the purgatorial mount in Dante's *Purgatorio.*
5. The ladder by which, in a dream, Jacob saw angels passing between heaven and Earth (Genesis 28.12 and *Paradise Lost* 3.510–15).

Cried I, approaching near the horned shrine,[6]
"What am I that should so be sav'd from death?
What am I that another death come not
140   To choke my utterance sacrilegious here?"
Then said the veiled shadow—"Thou hast felt
What 'tis to die and live again before
Thy fated hour. That thou hadst power to do so
Is thy own safety; thou hast dated on
145   Thy doom."[7]—"High Prophetess," said I, "purge off
Benign, if so it please thee, my mind's film."[8]
"None can usurp this height," return'd that shade,
"But those to whom the miseries of the world
Are misery, and will not let them rest.
150   All else who find a haven in the world,
Where they may thoughtless sleep away their days,
If by a chance into this fane° they come,   *temple*
Rot on the pavement where thou rotted'st half."[9]—
"Are there not thousands in the world," said I,
155   Encourag'd by the sooth[1] voice of the shade,
"Who love their fellows even to the death;
Who feel the giant agony of the world;
And more, like slaves to poor humanity,
Labour for mortal good? I sure should see
160   Other men here: but I am here alone."
"They whom thou spak'st of are no vision'ries,"
Rejoin'd that voice—"They are no dreamers weak,
They seek no wonder but the human face;
No music but a happy-noted voice—
165   They come not here, they have no thought to come—
And thou art here, for thou art less than they.
What benefit canst thou do, or all thy tribe,
To the great world? Thou art a dreaming thing;
A fever of thyself—think of the earth;
170   What bliss even in hope is there° for thee?   *on Earth*
What haven? Every creature hath its home;
Every sole man hath days of joy and pain,
Whether his labours be sublime or low—
The pain alone; the joy alone; distinct:
175   Only the dreamer venoms all his days,
Bearing more woe than all his sins deserve.
Therefore, that happiness be somewhat shar'd,
Such things as thou art are admitted oft
Into like gardens thou didst pass erewhile,
180   And suffer'd in° these temples; for that cause   *allowed to enter*
Thou standest safe beneath this statue's knees."

6. As, e.g., in Exodus 27.2, "And thou shalt make the horns of [the altar] upon the four corners thereof." In his description of the temple and its accoutrements, Keats deliberately mingles Hebrew, Christian, and pagan elements to represent the poet's passage through the stage represented by all religions, which are "dreams" made into the creed for "a sect" (lines 1–18).
7. I.e., you have postponed the time when you will be judged.
8. Cf. Milton's plea, following his account of his blindness, for a celestial light that might "Shine inward": "Irradiate, there plant eyes, all mist from thence / Purge and disperse, that I may see and tell / Of things invisible to mortal sight" (*Paradise Lost* 3.52–54).
9. I.e., where you halfway rotted.
1. Soothing, also truth-telling.

"That I am favored for unworthiness,
By such propitious parley medicin'd
In sickness not ignoble, I rejoice,
185   Aye, and could weep for love of such award."
So answer'd I, continuing, "If it please,
Majestic shadow, tell me: sure not all[2]
Those melodies sung into the world's ear
Are useless: sure a poet is a sage;
190   A humanist, physician to all men.
That I am none I feel, as vultures feel
They are no birds when eagles are abroad.
What am I then? Thou spakest of my tribe:
What tribe?"—The tall shade veil'd in drooping white
195   Then spake, so much more earnest, that the breath
Mov'd the thin linen folds that drooping hung
About a golden censer from the hand
Pendent.—"Art thou not of the dreamer tribe?
The poet and the dreamer are distinct,
200   Diverse, sheer opposite, antipodes.
The one pours out a balm upon the world,
The other vexes it." Then shouted I
Spite of myself, and with a Pythia's spleen,[3]
"Apollo! faded, far flown Apollo!
205   Where is thy misty pestilence[4] to creep
Into the dwellings, through the door crannies,
Of all mock lyrists, large self worshipers,
And careless hectorers in proud bad verse.[5]
Though I breathe death with them it will be life
210   To see them sprawl before me into graves.[6]
Majestic shadow, tell me where I am:
Whose altar this; for whom this incense curls:
What image this, whose face I cannot see,
For the broad marble knees; and who thou art,
215   Of accent feminine, so courteous."
Then the tall shade in drooping linens veil'd
Spake out, so much more earnest, that her breath
Stirr'd the thin folds of gauze that drooping hung
About a golden censer from her hand
220   Pendent; and by her voice I knew she shed

2. Keats's friend Richard Woodhouse, whose manuscript copy of the poem is our principal source of the text, crossed out lines 187–210 with the marginal comment next to lines 197–99: "K. seems to have intended to erase this & the next 21 lines." Probably the basis for his opinion is the partial repetition of lines 187 and 194–98 in lines 211 and 216–20.
3. With the anger ("spleen") of the Pythia, the priestess who served at Delphi as the oracle of Apollo, the god of poetry.
4. Apollo was a sender of plagues as well as the inspirer of prophecy and poetry. He was also the god of medicine. Keats's medical studies gave him special reason to be interested in this figure and the roles he combined.
5. This has been thought to refer to Byron, or else to several contemporaries, including Shelley

and Wordsworth. But the poetic types, not individuals, are what matter to Keats's argument.
6. In lines 147–210 we find a series of progressive distinctions: (1) between humanitarians who feel for "the miseries of the world" and people who are "thoughtless" sleepers (lines 147–53); (2) within the class of humanitarians, between those who actively "benefit . . . the great world" and the poets who are "vision'ries" and "dreamers" (lines 161–69); (3) and within the class of poets, between those who are merely dreamers and those who are sages and healers (lines 187–202). As in the colloquy between Asia and Demogorgon (see Shelley's *Prometheus Unbound* 2.4.1–128, pp. 835–38), the interchange here may be taken to represent, in dramatized form, a process of inner analysis and self-discovery on the part of the questing poet.

Long treasured tears. "This temple sad and lone
Is all spar'd from the thunder of a war
Foughten long since by giant hierarchy
Against rebellion: this old image here,
225   Whose carved features wrinkled as he fell,
Is Saturn's;[7] I, Moneta, left supreme
Sole priestess of his desolation."—
I had no words to answer; for my tongue,
Useless, could find about its roofed home
230   No syllable of a fit majesty
To make rejoinder to Moneta's mourn.
There was a silence while the altar's blaze
Was fainting for sweet food: I look'd thereon
And on the paved floor, where nigh were pil'd
235   Faggots of cinnamon, and many heaps
Of other crisped spice-wood—then again
I look'd upon the altar and its horns
Whiten'd with ashes, and its lang'rous flame,
And then upon the offerings again;
240   And so by turns—till sad Moneta cried,
"The sacrifice is done, but not the less
Will I be kind to thee for thy good will.
My power, which to me is still a curse,
Shall be to thee a wonder; for the scenes
245   Still swooning vivid through my globed brain
With an electral changing misery
Thou shalt with those dull mortal eyes behold,
Free from all pain, if wonder pain thee not."
As near as an immortal's sphered words
250   Could to a mother's soften, were these last:
But yet I had a terror of her robes,
And chiefly of the veils, that from her brow
Hung pale, and curtain'd her in mysteries
That made my heart too small to hold its blood.
255   This saw that Goddess, and with sacred hand
Parted the veils. Then saw I a wan face,
Not pin'd° by human sorrows, but bright blanch'd   *exhausted*
By an immortal sickness which kills not;
It works a constant change, which happy death
260   Can put no end to; deathwards progressing
To no death was that visage; it had pass'd
The lily and the snow; and beyond these
I must not think now, though I saw that face—
But for her eyes I should have fled away.
265   They held me back, with a benignant light,
Soft mitigated by divinest lids
Half closed, and visionless° entire they seem'd   *blind*
Of all external things—they saw me not,
But in blank splendor beam'd like the mild moon,
270   Who comforts those she sees not, who knows not
What eyes are upward cast. As I had found

7. Cf. the "shattered visage" of the fallen statue in Shelley's "Ozymandias" (p. 790).

A grain of gold upon a mountain's side,
And twing'd with avarice strain'd out my eyes
To search its sullen entrails rich with ore,
275   So at the view of sad Moneta's brow,
I ached to see what things the hollow brain
Behind enwombed: what high tragedy
In the dark secret chambers of her skull
Was acting, that could give so dread a stress
280   To her cold lips, and fill with such a light
Her planetary eyes; and touch her voice
With such a sorrow. "Shade of Memory!"
Cried I, with act adorant at her feet,
"By all the gloom hung round thy fallen house,
285   By this last temple, by the golden age,
By great Apollo, thy dear foster child,
And by thy self, forlorn divinity,
The pale Omega[8] of a wither'd race,
Let me behold, according as thou said'st,
290   What in thy brain so ferments to and fro."—
No sooner had this conjuration pass'd
My devout lips, than side by side we stood,
(Like a stunt bramble by a solemn pine)
Deep in the shady sadness of a vale,[9]
295   Far sunken from the healthy breath of morn,
Far from the fiery noon, and eve's one star.
Onward I look'd beneath the gloomy boughs,
And saw, what first I thought an image huge,
Like to the image pedestal'd so high
300   In Saturn's temple. Then Moneta's voice
Came brief upon mine ear,—"So Saturn sat
When he had lost his realms."—Whereon there grew
A power within me of enormous ken,°   *range of vision*
To see as a God sees, and take the depth
305   Of things as nimbly as the outward eye
Can size and shape pervade. The lofty theme
At those few words hung vast before my mind,
With half unravel'd web. I set myself
Upon an eagle's watch, that I might see,
310   And seeing ne'er forget. No stir of life
Was in this shrouded vale, not so much air
As in the zoning° of a summer's day   *course*
Robs not one light seed from the feather'd grass,
But where the deaf leaf fell there did it rest:
315   A stream went voiceless by, still deaden'd more
By reason of the fallen divinity
Spreading more shade: the Naiad° mid her reeds   *water nymph*
Press'd her cold finger closer to her lips.
Along the margin sand large footmarks went
320   No farther than to where old Saturn's feet

8. The final letter of the Greek alphabet.
9. This had been the opening line of the original *Hyperion*. The rest of the poem is a revised version of part of that first narrative, with the poet now represented as allowed to envision the course of events that Moneta recalls in her memory (lines 282, 289–90).

Had rested, and there slept, how long a sleep!
Degraded, cold, upon the sodden ground
His old right hand lay nerveless, listless, dead,
Unsceptred; and his realmless[1] eyes were clos'd,
325   While his bow'd head seem'd listening to the Earth,
His antient mother,[2] for some comfort yet.

          It seem'd no force could wake him from his place;
But there came one who with a kindred hand
Touch'd his wide shoulders, after bending low
330   With reverence, though to one who knew it not.
Then came the griev'd voice of Mnemosyne,[3]
And griev'd I hearken'd. "That divinity
Whom thou saw'st step from yon forlornest wood,
And with slow pace approach our fallen King,
335   Is Thea,[4] softest-natur'd of our brood."
I mark'd the goddess in fair statuary
Surpassing wan Moneta by the head,[5]
And in her sorrow nearer woman's tears.
There was a listening fear in her regard,
340   As if calamity had but begun;
As if the vanward clouds[6] of evil days
Had spent their malice, and the sullen rear
Was with its stored thunder labouring up.
One hand she press'd upon that aching spot
345   Where beats the human heart; as if just there,
Though an immortal, she felt cruel pain;
The other upon Saturn's bended neck
She laid, and to the level of his hollow ear
Leaning, with parted lips, some words she spake
350   In solemn tenor and deep organ tune;
Some mourning words, which in our feeble tongue
Would come in this-like accenting; how frail
To that large utterance of the early Gods!—
"Saturn! look up—and for what, poor lost King?[7]
355   I have no comfort for thee, no—not one:
I cannot cry, *Wherefore thus sleepest thou?*
For heaven is parted from thee, and the earth
Knows thee not, so afflicted, for a God;
And ocean too, with all its solemn noise,
360   Has from thy sceptre pass'd, and all the air
Is emptied of thine hoary majesty.
Thy thunder, captious° at the new command,   quarrelsome
Rumbles reluctant o'er our fallen house;
And thy sharp lightning in unpracticed hands

---

1. Saturn's eyes, when open, express the fact
that he has lost his realm.
2. Saturn and the other Titans were the children of heaven and Earth.
3. As in 2.50, Keats substitutes for "Moneta" the
"Mnemosyne" of the first *Hyperion*. This may be
a slip but more likely indicates an alternative
name for Moneta, in her role as participant in, as
well as commentator on, the tragic action.

4. Sister and wife of Hyperion.
5. I.e., Thea was a head taller than Moneta.
6. The front line of clouds.
7. Keats several times recalls King Lear in representing the condition of Saturn. Keats's contemporaries may have thought, too, of George
III, mad, blind, and dethroned by his son, who
had become prince regent.

365 Scorches and burns our once serene domain.
With such remorseless speed still come new woes
That unbelief has not a space to breathe.[8]
Saturn, sleep on:—Me thoughtless,[9] why should I
Thus violate thy slumbrous solitude?
370 Why should I ope thy melancholy eyes?
Saturn, sleep on, while at thy feet I weep."

    As when, upon a tranced summer night,
Forests, branch-charmed by the earnest stars,[1]
Dream, and so dream all night, without a noise,
375 Save from one gradual solitary gust,
Swelling upon the silence; dying off;
As if the ebbing air had but one wave;
So came these words, and went; the while in tears
She press'd her fair large forehead to the earth,
380 Just where her fallen hair might spread in curls,
A soft and silken mat for Saturn's feet.
Long, long, those two were postured motionless,
Like sculpture builded up upon the grave
Of their own power. A long awful time
385 I look'd upon them; still they were the same;
The frozen God still bending to the earth,
And the sad Goddess weeping at his feet;
Moneta silent. Without stay or prop
But my own weak mortality, I bore
390 The load of this eternal quietude,
The unchanging gloom, and the three fixed shapes
Ponderous upon my senses a whole moon.
For by my burning brain I measured sure
Her silver seasons shedded on the night,
395 And every day by day methought I grew
More gaunt and ghostly. Oftentimes I pray'd
Intense, that death would take me from the vale
And all its burthens. Gasping with despair
Of change, hour after hour I curs'd myself:
400 Until old Saturn rais'd his faded eyes,
And look'd around, and saw his kingdom gone,
And all the gloom and sorrow of the place,
And that fair kneeling Goddess at his feet.
As the moist scent of flowers, and grass, and leaves
405 Fills forest dells with a pervading air
Known to the woodland nostril, so the words
Of Saturn fill'd the mossy glooms around,
Even to the hollows of time-eaten oaks,
And to the windings in the foxes' hole,
410 With sad low tones, while thus he spake, and sent
Strange musings to the solitary Pan.
    "Moan, brethren, moan; for we are swallow'd up

8. That disbelief has not an instant to catch its breath.
9. I.e., how thoughtless I am!
1. The grander version in the first *Hyperion*, 1.72ff., reads: "As when, upon a tranced summer-night / Those green-rob'd senators of mighty woods, / Tall oaks, branch-charmed by the earnest stars, / Dream."

And buried from all godlike exercise
Of influence benign on planets pale,

415 And peaceful sway above man's harvesting,
And all those acts which deity supreme
Doth ease its heart of love in. Moan and wail.
Moan, brethren, moan; for lo! the rebel spheres
Spin round, the stars their antient courses keep,

420 Clouds still with shadowy moisture haunt the earth,
Still suck their fill of light from sun and moon,
Still buds the tree, and still the sea-shores murmur.
There is no death in all the universe,
No smell of death—there shall be death²—Moan, moan,

425 Moan, Cybele,³ moan, for thy pernicious babes
Have chang'd a God into a shaking palsy.
Moan, brethren, moan; for I have no strength left,
Weak as the reed—weak—feeble as my voice—
O, O, the pain, the pain of feebleness.

430 Moan, moan; for still I thaw—or give me help:
Throw down those imps⁴ and give me victory.
Let me hear other groans, and trumpets blown
Of triumph calm, and hymns of festival
From the gold peaks of heaven's high piled clouds;

435 Voices of soft proclaim,° and silver stir   *proclamation*
Of strings in hollow shells; and let there be
Beautiful things made new for the surprize
Of the sky children."—So he feebly ceas'd,
With such a poor and sickly sounding pause,

440 Methought I heard some old man of the earth
Bewailing earthly loss; nor could my eyes
And ears act with that pleasant unison of sense
Which marries sweet sound with the grace of form,
And dolorous accent from a tragic harp

445 With large limb'd visions.⁵ More I scrutinized:
Still fix'd he sat beneath the sable trees,
Whose arms spread straggling in wild serpent forms,
With leaves all hush'd: his awful presence there
(Now all was silent) gave a deadly lie

450 To what I erewhile heard: only his lips
Trembled amid the white curls of his beard.
They told the truth, though, round, the snowy locks
Hung nobly, as upon the face of heaven
A midday fleece of clouds. Thea arose

455 And stretch'd her white arm through the hollow dark,
Pointing some whither: whereat he too rose
Like a vast giant seen by men at sea
To grow pale from the waves at dull midnight.⁶
They melted from my sight into the woods:

2. The passing of the Saturnian golden age (paralleled by Keats with the fable of the loss of Eden) has introduced suffering, and will also introduce death.
3. The wife of Saturn and mother of the Olympian gods, who have overthrown their parents.
4. I.e., his rebellious children, the Titans.
5. I.e., the narrator could not attach this speech, like that of a feebly complaining old mortal, to the visible form of the large-limbed god who uttered it.
6. I.e., like a giant who is seen at sea to emerge, pale, from the waves.

460 Ere I could turn, Moneta cried—"These twain
Are speeding to the families of grief,
Where roof'd in by black rocks they waste in pain
And darkness for no hope."—And she spake on,
As ye may read who can unwearied pass
465 Onward from the antichamber° of this dream,   *entry room*
Where even at the open doors awhile
I must delay, and glean my memory
Of her high phrase: perhaps no further dare.

Canto 2

"Mortal, that thou may'st understand aright,
I humanize my sayings to thine ear,
Making comparisons of earthly things;[7]
Or thou might'st better listen to the wind,
5 Whose language is to thee a barren noise,
Though it blows legend-laden through the trees.
In melancholy realms big tears are shed,
More sorrow like to this, and such-like woe,
Too huge for mortal tongue, or pen of scribe.
10 The Titans fierce, self-hid, or prison-bound,
Groan for the old allegiance once more,
Listening in their doom for Saturn's voice.
But one of our whole eagle-brood still keeps
His sov'reignty, and rule, and majesty;
15 Blazing Hyperion on his orbed fire
Still sits, still snuffs the incense teeming up
From man to the Sun's God: yet unsecure;
For as upon the earth dire prodigies°   *terrifying omens*
Fright and perplex, so also shudders he:
20 Nor at dog's howl, or gloom-bird's even screech,
Or the familiar visitings of one
Upon the first toll of his passing bell:[8]
But horrors portion'd° to a giant nerve   *proportioned*
Make great Hyperion ache. His palace bright,
25 Bastion'd with pyramids of glowing gold,
And touch'd with shade of bronzed obelisks,
Glares a blood red through all the thousand courts,
Arches, and domes, and fiery galeries:
And all its curtains of Aurorian clouds
30 Flush angerly: when he would taste the wreaths
Of incense breath'd aloft from sacred hills,
Instead of sweets, his ample palate takes
Savour of poisonous brass, and metals sick.
Wherefore when harbour'd in the sleepy west,

7. Cf. the angel Raphael's words as he begins to recount to Adam the history of the rebellion in heaven: "what surmounts the reach / Of human sense, I shall delineate so, / By lik'ning spiritual to corporal forms" (*Paradise Lost* 5.571–73).
8. Lines 20–22 might be paraphrased: "Not, however, at such portents as a dog's howl or the evening screech of the owl or with the well-known feelings ['visitings'] of someone when he hears the first stroke of his own death knell." It had been the English custom to ring the church bell when a person was close to death, to invite hearers to pray for his departing soul.

35 After the full completion of fair day,
    For rest divine upon exalted couch
    And slumber in the arms of melody,
    He paces through the pleasant hours of ease,
    With strides colossal, on from hall to hall;
40 While, far within each aisle and deep recess,
    His winged minions° in close clusters stand   *followers*
    Amaz'd, and full of fear; like anxious men
    Who on a wide plain gather in sad troops,
    When earthquakes jar their battlements and towers.
45 Even now, while Saturn, rous'd from icy trance,
    Goes, step for step, with Thea from yon woods,
    Hyperion, leaving twilight in the rear,
    Is sloping to the threshold of the west.
    Thither we tend."—Now in clear light I stood,
50 Reliev'd from the dusk vale. Mnemosyne
    Was sitting on a square edg'd polish'd stone,
    That in its lucid depth reflected pure
    Her priestess-garments. My quick eyes ran on
    From stately nave to nave, from vault to vault,
55 Through bowers of fragrant and enwreathed light,
    And diamond paved lustrous long arcades.
    Anon rush'd by the bright Hyperion;
    His flaming robes stream'd out beyond his heels,
    And gave a roar, as if of earthly fire,
60 That scar'd away the meek ethereal hours
    And made their dove-wings tremble: on he flared[9]

July–Sept. 1819   1857

This living hand, now warm and capable[1]

    This living hand, now warm and capable
    Of earnest grasping, would, if it were cold
    And in the icy silence of the tomb,
    So haunt thy days and chill thy dreaming nights
5   That thou would wish thine own heart dry of blood,
    So in my veins red life might stream again,
    And thou be conscience-calm'd—see, here it is—
    I hold it towards you—

1819   1898

---

9. The manuscript breaks off at this point.
1. These lines, first published in H. B. Forman's edition of Keats's poems in 1898, were written on a sheet that later formed part of the draft of Keats's unfinished satire *The Jealousies*. They have been a key text in late-20th-century critical and theoretical discussions of interpretation. Readings range from the personal and autobiographical— Keats addressing a loved one (Fanny Brawne) or

his posthumous readers (e.g., users of this Norton anthology)—to the fictionalized and dramatic (e.g., a fragment of a speech intended for the deranged Ludolph toward the end of Keats's and Charles Brown's never-produced tragedy *Otho the Great*). In their lyric character the lines are included in anthologies of love poetry. In their dramatic character they are described by critics as, for example, "ghoulishly aggressive."

Letters   Keats's letters serve as a running commentary on his life, reading, thinking, and writing. They are, in his career, the equivalent of the essays, prefaces, and defenses of poetry produced by his contemporaries. His early reputation as a poet of pure luxury, sensation, and art for art's sake has undergone a radical change since, in the twentieth century, critics began to pay close attention to the letters. For Keats thought hard and persistently about life and art, and any seed of an ethical or critical idea that he picked up from his contemporaries (in particular, Hazlitt, Coleridge, Wordsworth) instantly germinated and flourished in the rich soil of his imagination. What T. S. Eliot said about the Metaphysical poets applies to Keats in his letters: his "mode of feeling was directly and freshly altered by [his] reading and thought." And like Donne, he looked not only into the heart but, literally, "into the cerebral cortex, the nervous system, and the digestive tract." A number of Keats's casual comments on the poet and on poetry included here—especially those dealing with "negative capability" and the kind of imaginative identification with someone or something outside ourselves that we now call empathy—have become standard points of reference in aesthetic theory. But Keats regarded nothing that he said as final; each statement constituted only a stage in his continuing exploration into what he called "the mystery."

The texts here are from the edition of the *Letters* by Hyder E. Rollins (1958), which reproduces the original manuscripts precisely.

LETTERS

To Benjamin Bailey[1]

["THE AUTHENTICITY OF THE IMAGINATION"]

[November 22, 1817]

My dear Bailey,

* * * O I wish I was as certain of the end of all your troubles as that of your momentary start about the authenticity of the Imagination. I am certain of nothing but of the holiness of the Heart's affections and the truth of Imagination—What the imagination seizes as Beauty must be truth[2]—whether it existed before or not—for I have the same Idea of all our Passions as of Love they are all in their sublime, creative of essential Beauty—In a Word, you may know my favorite Speculation by my first Book and the little song[3] I sent in my last—which is a representation from the fancy of the probable mode of operating in these Matters—The Imagination may be compared to Adam's dream[4]—he awoke and found it truth. I am the more zealous in this affair, because I have never yet been able to perceive how any thing can be known for truth by consequitive reasoning[5]—and yet it must be—Can it be that even the greatest Philosopher ever ~~when~~ arrived at his goal without

---

1. One of Keats's closest friends. Keats had stayed with him the month before at Oxford, where Bailey was an undergraduate.
2. At the close of "Ode on a Grecian Urn," Keats also grapples with these categories. Where Keats uses "truth" we might substitute the words *real* or *reality*.
3. The song was "O Sorrow," from book 4 of

Endymion.
4. In Milton's *Paradise Lost* 8.452–90 Adam dreams that Eve has been created and awakes to find her real. Adam also describes an earlier prefigurative dream in the same work, 8.283–311.
5. Consecutive reasoning—reasoning that moves by logical steps.

putting aside numerous objections—However it may be, O for a Life of Sensations[6] rather than of Thoughts! It is "a Vision in the form of Youth" a Shadow of reality to come—and this consideration has further conv[i]nced me for it has come as auxiliary to another favorite Speculation of mine, that we shall enjoy ourselves here after by having what we called happiness on Earth repeated in a finer tone and so repeated[7]—And yet such a fate can only befall those who delight in sensation rather than hunger as you do after Truth—Adam's dream will do here and seems to be a conviction that Imagination and its empyreal[8] reflection is the same as human Life and its spiritual repetition. But as I was saying—the simple imaginative Mind may have its rewards in the repeti[ti]on of its own silent Working coming continually on the spirit with a fine suddenness—to compare great things with small—have you never by being surprised with an old Melody—in a delicious place—by a delicious voice, fe[l]t over again your very speculations and surmises at the time it first operated on your soul—do you not remember forming to yourself the singer's face more beautiful [than] it was possible and yet with the elevation of the Moment you did not think so—even then you were mounted on the Wings of Imagination so high—that the Prototype must be here after—that delicious face you will see—What a time! I am continually running away from the subject—sure this cannot be exactly the case with a complex Mind—one that is imaginative and at the same time careful of its fruits—who would exist partly on sensation partly on thought—to whom it is necessary that years should bring the philosophic Mind[9]—such an one I consider your's and therefore it is necessary to your eternal Happiness that you not only drink this old Wine of Heaven which I shall call the redigestion of our most ethereal Musings on Earth; but also increase in knowledge and know all things. I am glad to hear you are in a fair Way for Easter—you will soon get through your unpleasant reading and then!—but the world is full of troubles and I have not much reason to think myself pesterd with many—I think Jane or Marianne has a better opinion of me than I deserve—for really and truly I do not think my Brothers illness connected with mine—you know more of the real Cause than they do—nor have I any chance of being rack'd as you have been[1]—you perhaps at one time thought there was such a thing as Worldly Happiness to be arrived at, at certain periods of time marked out—you have of necessity from your disposition been thus led away—I scarcely remember counting upon any Happiness—I look not for it if it be not in the present hour—nothing startles me beyond the Moment. The setting sun will always set me to rights—or if a Sparrow come before my Window I take part in its existence and pick about the Gravel. The first thing that strikes me on hea[r]ing a Misfortune having befallen another is this. "Well it cannot be helped.—he will have the pleasure of trying the resourses of his spirit, and I beg now my dear Bailey that hereafter should you observe any thing cold in me not to [put] it to the account of heartlessness but abstraction—for I assure you I sometimes feel not the influence of a Passion or Affection during a

6. Probably not only sense experiences but also the intuitive perceptions of truths, as opposed to truth achieved by consecutive reasoning.
7. Cf. the "Pleasure Thermometer" in *Endymion* 1.777ff. (p. 957).
8. Heavenly.
9. An echo of Wordsworth, "Ode: Intimations of Immortality," line 187.
1. Keats's friends Jane and Mariane Reynolds feared that his ill health at this time threatened tuberculosis, from which his brother Tom was suffering. Bailey had recently experienced pain (been "racked") because of an unsuccessful love affair.

whole week—and so long this sometimes continues I begin to suspect myself and the genuiness of my feelings at other times—thinking them a few barren Tragedy-tears. * * *

Your affectionate friend
John Keats—

To George and Thomas Keats

["NEGATIVE CAPABILITY"]

[December 21, 27 (?), 1817]

My dear Brothers

I must crave your pardon for not having written ere this. * * * I spent Friday evening with Wells[1] & went the next morning to see *Death on the Pale horse*. It is a wonderful picture, when West's[2] age is considered; But there is nothing to be intense upon; no women one feels mad to kiss; no face swelling into reality. the excellence of every Art is its intensity, capable of making all disagreeables evaporate, from their being in close relationship with Beauty & Truth[3]—Examine King Lear & you will find this examplified throughout; but in this picture we have unpleasantness without any momentous depth of speculation excited, in which to bury its repulsiveness—The picture is larger than Christ rejected—I dined with Haydon[4] the sunday after you left, & had a very pleasant day, I dined too (for I have been out too much lately) with Horace Smith & met his two Brothers with Hill & Kingston & one Du Bois,[5] they only served to convince me, how superior humour is to wit in respect to enjoyment—These men say things which make one start, without making one feel, they are all alike; their manners are alike; they all know fashionables; they have a mannerism in their very eating & drinking, in their mere handling a Decanter—They talked of Kean[6] & his low company—Would I were with that company instead of yours said I to myself! I know such like acquaintance will never do for me & yet I am going to Reynolds, on Wednesday—Brown & Dilke[7] walked with me & back from the Christmas pantomime.[8] I had not a dispute but a disquisition with Dilke, on various subjects; several things dovetailed in my mind, & at once it struck me, what quality went to form a Man of Achievement especially in

---

1. Charles Wells, a former schoolmate of Tom Keats.
2. Benjamin West (1738–1820), painter of historical pictures, was an American who moved to England and became president of the Royal Academy. The *Christ Rejected* mentioned a few sentences farther on is also by West.
3. Keats's solution to a problem at least as old as Aristotle's *Poetics*: why do we take pleasure in the aesthetic representation of a subject that in life would be ugly or painful?
4. Keats's close friend Benjamin Haydon, painter of large-scale historical and religious pictures.
5. Smith was one of the best-known literary wits

of the day; the others mentioned were men of letters or of literary interests.
6. Edmund Kean, noted Shakespearean actor. His popularity in the early 19th century was contentious because he made no secret of his humble class origins. Keats had written an article on Kean for the *Champion*.
7. Charles Armitage Brown, John Hamilton Reynolds, and Charles Wentworth Dilke were all writers and friends of Keats. Keats interrupted the writing of this letter after the dash; beginning with "Brown & Dilke" he is writing several days after the preceding sentences.
8. Christmas pantomimes were performed each year at Drury Lane and Covent Garden theaters.

Literature & which Shakespeare possessed so enormously—I mean *Negative Capability*,[9] that is when man is capable of being in uncertainties, Mysteries, doubts, without any irritable reaching after fact & reason—Coleridge, for instance, would let go by a fine isolated verisimilitude caught from the Penetralium[1] of mystery, from being incapable of remaining content with half knowledge. This pursued through Volumes would perhaps take us no further than this, that with a great poet the sense of Beauty overcomes every other consideration, or rather obliterates all consideration.

Shelley's poem[2] is out & there are words about its being objected too, as much as Queen Mab was. Poor Shelley I think he has his Quota of good qualities, in sooth la!! Write soon to your most sincere friend & affectionate Brother

John

To John Hamilton Reynolds[1]

[WORDSWORTH'S POETRY]

[February 3, 1818]

My dear Reynolds,

* * * It may be said that we ought to read our Contemporaries, that Wordsworth &c should have their due from us but for the sake of a few fine imaginative or domestic passages, are we to be bullied into a certain Philosophy engendered in the whims of an Egotist—Every man has his speculations, but every man does not brood and peacock over them till he makes a false coinage and deceives himself—Many a man can travel to the very bourne[2] of Heaven, and yet want confidence to put down his halfseeing. Sancho[3] will invent a Journey heavenward as well as any body. We hate poetry that has a palpable design upon us—and if we do not agree, seems to put its hand in its breeches pocket.[4] Poetry should be great & unobtrusive, a thing which enters into one's soul, and does not startle it or amaze it with itself but with its subject.—How beautiful are the retired flowers! how would they lose their beauty were they to throng into the highway crying out, "admire me I am a violet! dote upon me I am a primrose! Modern poets differ from the Elizabethans in this. Each of the moderns like an Elector of Hanover governs his petty state, & knows how many straws are swept daily from the Causeways in all his dominions & has a continual itching that all the Housewives should have their coppers well scoured: the antients were ~~Emperors of large~~ Emper-

9. This famous and elusive phrase has been much discussed. Keats coins it so as to distinguish between, on the one hand, a poetry that is evidently shaped by the writer's personal interests and beliefs and, on the other hand, a poetry of impersonality that records the writer's receptivity to the "uncertainties" of experience. This second kind of poetry, in which a sense of beauty overcomes considerations of truth versus falsehood, is that produced by the poet of "negative capability." Cf. Keats's dislike, in his letter to John Hamilton Reynolds, February 3, 1818, of "poetry that has a palpable design upon us."
1. The Latin *penetralia* signified the innermost and most secret parts of a temple.

2. *Laon and Cythna* (1817), whose treatment of incest created scandal and which had to be withdrawn by the author. Shelley revised and republished it as *The Revolt of Islam* (1818). In *Queen Mab* (1813) Shelley had presented a radical program for the achievement of a millennial earthly state through the elimination of "kings, priests, and statesmen."
1. A close friend who was at this time an insurance clerk and also an able poet and man of letters.
2. Boundary.
3. Sancho Panza, the earthy squire in Cervantes's *Don Quixote*.
4. I.e., sulks and refuses to interact with us.

ors of vast Provinces, they had only heard of the remote ones and scarcely cared to visit them.—I will cut all this—I will have no more of Wordsworth or Hunt[5] in particular—Why should we be of the tribe of Manasseh, when we can wander with Esau?[6] why should we kick against the Pricks, when we can walk on Roses? Why should we be owls, when we can be Eagles? Why be teased with "nice Eyed wagtails," when we have in sight "the Cherub Contemplation"?[7]—Why with Wordsworths "Matthew with a bough of wilding in his hand" when we can have Jacques "under an oak &c"[8]—The secret of the Bough of Wilding will run through your head faster than I can write it—Old Matthew spoke to him some years ago on some nothing, & because he happens in an Evening Walk to imagine the figure of the old man—he must stamp it down in black & white, and it is henceforth sacred—I don't mean to deny Wordsworth's grandeur & Hunt's merit, but I mean to say we need not be teazed with grandeur & merit—when we can have them uncontaminated & unobtrusive. Let us have the old Poets, & robin Hood[9] Your letter and its sonnets gave me more pleasure than will the 4th Book of Childe Harold[1] & the whole of any body's life & opinions. * * *

Y[r] sincere friend and Coscribbler
John Keats.

To John Taylor[1]

[KEATS'S AXIOMS IN POETRY]

[February 27, 1818]

My dear Taylor,

Your alteration strikes me as being a great improvement—the page, looks much better. * * * It is a sorry thing for me that any one should have to overcome Prejudices in reading my Verses—that affects me more than any hypercriticism on any particular Passage. In *Endymion* I have most likely but moved into the Go-cart from the leading strings.[2] In Poetry I have a few Axioms, and you will see how far I am from their Centre. 1st I think Poetry should surprise by a fine excess and not by Singularity—it should strike the Reader as a wording of his own highest thoughts, and appear almost a Remembrance—2nd Its touches of Beauty should never be half way therby making the reader breathless instead of content: the rise, the progress, the setting of imagery should like the Sun come natural natural too him—shine over him and set soberly although in magnificence leaving him in the Luxury of twilight—but it is easier to think what Poetry should be than to write

5. Leigh Hunt, a poet who earlier had strongly influenced Keats's style.
6. I.e., why should we carry on a conventional way of life (as did the tribe of Manasseh in Old Testament history) when we can become adventurers (like Esau, who sold his birthright in Genesis 25.29–34 and became an outlaw).
7. Milton, "Il Penseroso," line 54. "Nice Eyed wagtails": from Hunt's *Nymphs*.
8. Shakespeare's *As You Like It* 2.1.31. The Wordsworth phrase is from his poem "The Two April Mornings." "Wilding": is a wild apple tree.
9. A reference to two sonnets on Robin Hood,

written by Reynolds, which he had sent to Keats.
1. Canto 4 of Byron's *Childe Harold's Pilgrimage* was being eagerly awaited by English readers.
1. Partner in the publishing firm of Taylor and Hessey, to whom Keats wrote this letter while *Endymion* was being put through the press.
2. Go-carts were the wheeled walkers in which 19th-century toddlers learned to walk. Leadingstrings were the harnesses with which they were guided and supported while they learned. Keats's point appears to be that as a poet he has not advanced and may even have regressed in *Endymion*.

it—and this leads me on to another axiom. That if Poetry comes not as naturally as the Leaves to a tree it had better not come at all. However it may be with me I cannot help looking into new countries with "O for a Muse of fire to ascend!"[3]—If Endymion serves me as a Pioneer perhaps I ought to be content. I have great reason to be content, for thank God I can read and perhaps understand Shakspeare to his depths, and I have I am sure many friends, who, if I fail, will attribute any change in my Life and Temper to Humbleness rather than to Pride—to a cowering under the Wings of great Poets rather than to a Bitterness that I am not appreciated. I am anxious to get Endymion printed that I may forget it and proceed. * * *

Your sincere and oblig^d friend
John Keats—

P.S. You shall have a sho[r]t *Preface* in good time—

To John Hamilton Reynolds

[MILTON, WORDSWORTH, AND THE CHAMBERS OF HUMAN LIFE]

[May 3, 1818]

My dear Reynolds.

* * * Were I to study physic or rather Medicine again,—I feel it would not make the least difference in my Poetry; when the Mind is in its infancy a Bias is in reality a Bias, but when we have acquired more strength, a Bias becomes no Bias. Every department of knowledge we see excellent and calculated towards a great whole. I am so convinced of this, that I am glad at not having given away my medical Books, which I shall again look over to keep alive the little I know thitherwards; and moreover intend through you and Rice to become a sort of Pip-civilian.[1] An extensive knowledge is needful to thinking people—it takes away the heat and fever; and helps, by widening speculation, to ease the Burden of the Mystery:[2] a thing I begin to understand a little, and which weighed upon you in the most gloomy and true sentence in your Letter. The difference of high Sensations with and without knowledge appears to me this—in the latter case we are falling continually ten thousand fathoms deep and being blown up again without wings[3] and with all [the] horror of a ~~Case~~ bare shoulderd Creature—in the former case, our shoulders are fledged[4] and we go thro' the same ~~Fir~~ air and space without fear. * * *

You say "I fear there is little chance of any thing else in this life." You seem by that to have been going through with a more painful and acute ~~test~~ zest the same labyrinth that I have—I have come to the same conclusion thus far. My Branchings out therefrom have been numerous: one of them is the consideration of Wordsworth's genius and as a help, in the manner of gold being the meridian Line of worldly wealth,—how he differs from Milton.[5]—And

---

3. Altered from Shakespeare's *Henry V*, Prologue, line 1.
1. Apparently "a small-scale layman." James Rice, a lawyer, was one of Keats's favorite friends.
2. Wordsworth, "Tintern Abbey," line 38.
3. Recalls the description of Satan's flight through Chaos (Milton, *Paradise Lost* 2.933–34).

4. Grow wings.
5. I.e., as gold is the standard of material wealth (in the way that the meridian line of Greenwich Observatory, England, is the reference for measuring degrees of longitude), so Milton is the standard of poetic value, by which we may measure Wordsworth.

here I have nothing but surmises, from an uncertainty whether Miltons apparently less anxiety for Humanity proceeds from his seeing further or no than Wordsworth: And whether Wordsworth has in truth epic passions, and martyrs himself to the human heart, the main region of his song[6]—In regard to his genius alone—we find what he says true as far as we have experienced and we can judge no further but by larger experience—for axioms in philosophy are not axioms until they are proved upon our pulses: We read fine—— things but never feel them to [the] full until we have gone the same steps as the Author.—I know this is not plain; you will know exactly my meaning when I say, that now I shall relish Hamlet more than I ever have done—Or, better—You are sensible no man can set down Venery[7] as a bestial or joyless thing until he is sick of it and therefore all philosophizing on it would be mere wording. Until we are sick, we understand not;—in fine, as Byron says, "Knowledge is Sorrow";[8] and I go on to say that "Sorrow is Wisdom"—and further for aught we can know for certainty! "Wisdom is folly." * * *

I will return to Wordsworth—whether or no he has an extended vision or a circumscribed grandeur—whether he is an eagle in his nest, or on the wing—And to be more explicit and to show you how tall I stand by the giant, I will put down a simile of human life as far as I now perceive it; that is, to the point to which I say we both have arrived at—Well—I compare human life to a large Mansion of Many Apartments, two of which I can only describe, the doors of the rest being as yet shut upon me—The first we step into we call the infant or thoughtless Chamber, in which we remain as long as we do not think—We remain there a long while, and notwithstanding the doors of the second Chamber remain wide open, showing a bright appearance, we care not to hasten to it; but are at length imperceptibly impelled by the awakening of the thinking principle—within us—we no sooner get into the second Chamber, which I shall call the Chamber of Maiden-Thought,[9] than we become intoxicated with the light and the atmosphere, we see nothing but pleasant wonders, and think of delaying there for ever in delight: However among the effects this breathing is father of is that tremendous one of sharpening one's vision into the ~~head~~ heart and nature of Man—of convincing ones nerves that the World is full of Misery and Heartbreak, Pain, Sickness and oppression—whereby This Chamber of Maiden Thought becomes gradually darken'd and at the same time on all sides of it many doors are set open—but all dark—all leading to dark passages—We see not the ballance of good and evil. We are in a Mist—We are now in that state—We feel the "burden of the Mystery," To this point was Wordsworth come, as far as I can conceive when he wrote "Tintern Abbey" and it seems to me that his Genius is explorative of those dark Passages. Now if we live, and go on thinking, we too shall explore them. he is a Genius and superior [to] us, in so far as he can, more than we, make discoveries, and shed a light in them—Here I must think Wordsworth is deeper than Milton—though I think it has depended more upon the general and gregarious advance of intellect, than individual greatness of Mind—From the Paradise Lost and the other Works of Milton, I hope it is not too presuming, even between ourselves to say, his Philosophy, human and divine, may be tolerably understood by one not much advanced

---

6. In the Prospectus to *The Recluse*, Wordsworth, laying out his poetic program, had identified "the Mind of Man" as "My haunt, and the main region of my song" (lines 40–41).

7. Sexual indulgence.
8. *Manfred* 1.1.10: "Sorrow is knowledge."
9. I.e., innocent thought, with the implication (as in "maiden voyage") of a first undertaking.

in years, In his time englishmen were just emancipated from a great superstition—and Men had got hold of certain points and resting places in reasoning which were too newly born to be doubted, and too much ~~oppressed~~ opposed by the Mass of Europe not to be thought etherial and authentically divine—who could gainsay his ideas on virtue, vice, and Chastity in Comus, just at the time of the dismissal of Codpieces[1] and a hundred other disgraces? who would not rest satisfied with his hintings at good and evil in the Paradise Lost, when just free from the inquisition and burrning in Smithfield?[2] The Reformation produced such immediate and great benefits, that Protestantism was considered under the immediate eye of heaven, and its own remaining Dogmas and superstitions, then, as it were, regenerated, constituted those resting places and seeming sure points of Reasoning—from that I have mentioned, Milton, whatever he may have thought in the sequel,[3] appears to have been content with these by his writings—He did not think into the human heart, as Wordsworth has done—Yet Milton as a Philosop[h]er, had sure as great powers as Wordsworth—What is then to be inferr'd? O many things—It proves there is really a grand march of intellect—, It proves that a mighty providence subdues the mightiest Minds to the service of the time being, whether it be in human Knowledge or Religion— * * * Tom[4] has spit a leetle blood this afternoon, and that is rather a damper—but I know—the truth is there is something real in the World Your third Chamber of Life shall be a lucky and a gentle one—stored with the wine of love—and the Bread of friendship— * * *

> Your affectionate friend
> John Keats.

To Richard Woodhouse[1]

["A POET HAS NO IDENTITY"]

[October 27, 1818]

My dear Woodhouse,

Your Letter gave me a great satisfaction; more on account of its friendliness, than any relish of that matter in it which is accounted so acceptable in the "genus irritabile"[2] The best answer I can give you is in a clerklike manner to make some observations on two principle points, which seem to point like indices into the midst of the whole pro and con, about genius, and views and atchievements and ambition and cœtera. 1st As to the poetical Character itself, (I mean that sort of which, if I am any thing, I am a Member; that sort distinguished from the wordsworthian or egotistical sublime; which is a thing per se and stands alone) it is not itself—it has no self—it is every

1. In the 15th and 16th centuries, the codpiece was a flap, often ornamental, that covered an opening in the front of men's breeches. In Milton's masque the chastity of a young lady is put to the proof by the evil enchanter Comus.
2. An open place northwest of the walls of the City of London where, in the 16th century, heretics were burned.
3. Later on.

4. Keats's younger brother, then eighteen, who was dying of tuberculosis.
1. A young lawyer with literary interests who early recognized Keats's talents and prepared, or preserved, manuscript copies of many of his poems and letters.
2. "The irritable race," a phrase Horace had applied to poets (Epistles 2.2.102).

thing and nothing—It has no character—it enjoys light and shade; it lives in gusto,[3] be it foul or fair, high or low, rich or poor, mean or elevated—It has as much delight in conceiving an Iago as an Imogen.[4] What shocks the virtuous philosop[h]er, delights the camelion[5] Poet. It does no harm from its relish of the dark side of things any more than from its taste for the bright one; because they both end in speculation.[6] A Poet is the most unpoetical of any thing in existence; because he has no Identity—he is continually in for[7]—and filling some other Body—The Sun, the Moon, the Sea and Men and Women who are creatures of impulse are poetical and have about them an unchangeable attribute—the poet has none; no identity—he is certainly the most unpoetical of all God's Creatures. If then he has no self, and if I am a Poet, where is the Wonder that I should say I would write no more? Might I not at that very instant [have] been cogitating on the Characters of saturn and Ops?[8] It is a wretched thing to confess; but is a very fact that not one word I ever utter can be taken for granted as an opinion growing out of my identical nature—how can it, when I have no nature? When I am in a room with People if I ever am free from speculating on creations of my own brain, then not myself goes home to myself: but the identity of every one in the room begins to to press upon me[9] that, I am in a very little time an[ni]hilated—not only among Men; it would be the same in a Nursery of children: I know not whether I make myself wholly understood: I hope enough so to let you see that no dependence is to be placed on what I said that day.

In the second place I will speak of my views, and of the life I purpose to myself—I am ambitious of doing the world some good: if I should be spared that may be the work of maturer years—in the interval I will assay to reach to as high a summit in Poetry as the nerve bestowed upon me will suffer. The faint conceptions I have of Poems to come brings the blood frequently into my forehead—All I hope is that I may not lose all interest in human affairs—that the solitary indifference I feel for applause even from the finest Spirits, will not blunt any acuteness of vision I may have. I do not think it will—I feel assured I should write from the mere yearning and fondness I have for the Beautiful even if my night's labours should be burnt every morning and no eye ever shine upon them. But even now I am perhaps not speaking from myself; but from some character in whose soul I now live. I am sure however that this next sentence is from myself. I feel your anxiety, good opinion and friendliness in the highest degree, and am

Your's most sincerely
John Keats

3. Hazlitt had defined gusto in an 1816 essay as "power or passion."
4. Iago is the villain in Shakespeare's *Othello* and Imogen the virtuous heroine in his *Cymbeline*.
5. The chameleon is a lizard that camouflages itself by changing its color to match its surroundings.
6. I.e., without affecting our practical judgment or actions. Cf. Keats's discussion of "negative capability" in his letter to George and Thomas Keats begun on December 21, 1817 (p. 1016).
7. Instead of "in for," Keats may have intended to write "informing."
8. Characters in Keats's *Hyperion*. Woodhouse had recently written Keats to express concern at a remark by the poet that, because former writers had preempted the best poetic materials and styles, there was nothing new left for the modern poet.
9. Perhaps "*so* to press upon me."

To George and Georgiana Keats[1]

["THE VALE OF SOUL-MAKING"]

[February 14–May 3, 1819]

My dear Brother & Sister—

* * * I have this moment received a note from Haslam[2] in which he expects the death of his Father who has been for some time in a state of insensibility—his mother bears up he says very well—I shall go to [town] tommorrow to see him. This is the world—thus we cannot expect to give way many hours to pleasure—Circumstances are like Clouds continually gathering and bursting—While we are laughing the seed of some trouble is put into he the wide arable land of events—while we are laughing it sprouts [it] grows and suddenly bears a poison fruit which we must pluck—Even so we have leisure to reason on the misfortunes of our friends; our own touch us too nearly for words. Very few men have ever arrived at a complete disinterestedness[3] of Mind: very few have been influenced by a pure desire of the benefit of others—in the greater part of the Benefactors of & to Humanity some meretricious motive has sullied their greatness—some melodramatic scenery has facinated them—From the manner in which I feel Haslam's misfortune I perceive how far I am from any humble standard of disinterestedness—Yet this feeling ought to be carried to its highest pitch, as there is no fear of its ever injuring society—which it would do I fear pushed to an extremity—For in wild nature the Hawk would loose his Breakfast of Robins and the Robin his of Worms The Lion must starve as well as the swallow—The greater part of Men make their way with the same instinctiveness, the same unwandering eye from their purposes, the same animal eagerness as the Hawk—The Hawk wants a Mate, so does the Man—look at them both they set about it and procure on[e] in the same manner—They want both a nest and they both set about one in the same manner—they get their food in the same manner—The noble animal Man for his amusement smokes his pipe—the Hawk balances about the Clouds—that is the only difference of their leisures. This it is that makes the Amusement of Life—to a speculative Mind. I go among the Feilds and catch a glimpse of a stoat[4] or a fieldmouse peeping out of the withered grass—the creature hath a purpose and its eyes are bright with it—I go amongst the buildings of a city and I see a Man hurrying along—to what? The Creature has a purpose and his eyes are bright with it. But then as Wordsworth says, "we have all one human heart"[5]—there is an ellectric fire in human nature tending to purify—so that among these human creature[s] there is continually some birth of new heroism—The pity is that we must wonder at it: as we should at finding a pearl in rubbish—I have no doubt that thousands of people never heard of have had hearts completely disinterested: I can remember but two—Socrates and Jesus—their Histories evince it—What I

---

1. Keats's brother and his wife, who had emigrated to Louisville, Kentucky, in 1818. This is part of a long letter that Keats wrote over a period of several months, and into which he transcribed several of his poems, including "Ode to Psyche." The date of this first extract is March 19.

2. William Haslam, a young businessman and close friend.
3. Transcendence of self-interest, of one's selfish instincts.
4. A weasel.
5. "The Old Cumberland Beggar," line 153.

heard a little time ago, Taylor observe with respect to Socrates, may be said of Jesus—That he was so great as man that though he transmitted no writing of his own to posterity, we have his Mind and his sayings and his greatness handed to us by others. It is to be lamented that the history of the latter was written and revised by Men interested in the pious frauds of Religion. Yet through all this I see his splendour. Even here though I myself am pursueing the same instinctive course as the veriest human animal you can think of—I am however young writing at random—straining at particles of light in the midst of a great darkness—without knowing the bearing of any one assertion of any one opinion. Yet may I not in this be free from sin? May there not be superior beings amused with any graceful, though instinctive attitude my mind [may] fall into, as I am entertained with the alertness of a Stoat or the anxiety of a Deer? Though a quarrel in the streets is a thing to be hated, the energies displayed in it are fine; the commonest Man shows a grace in his quarrel—By a superior being our reasoning[s] may take the same tone—though erroneous they may be fine—This is the very thing in which consists poetry; and if so it is not so fine a thing as philosophy—For the same reason that an eagle is not so fine a thing as a truth—Give me this credit—Do you not think I strive—to know myself? Give me this credit—and you will not think that on my own accou[n]t I repeat Milton's lines

> "How charming is divine Philosophy
> Not harsh and crabbed as dull fools suppose
> But musical as is Apollo's lute"—[6]

No—no for myself—feeling grateful as I do to have got into a state of mind to relish them properly—Nothing ever becomes real till it is experienced—Even a Proverb is no proverb to you till your Life has illustrated it— * * * * * * I have been reading lately two very different books Robertson's America and Voltaire's Siecle De Louis xiv[7] It is like walking arm and arm between Pizarro and the great-little Monarch.[8] In How lementabl[e] a case do we see the great body of the people in both instances: in the first, where Men might seem to inherit quiet of Mind from unsophisticated senses; from uncontamination of civilisation; and especially from their being as it were estranged from the mutual helps of Society and its mutual injuries—and thereby more immediately under the Protection of Providence—even there they had mortal pains to bear as bad; or even worse than Baliffs,[9] Debts and Poverties of civilised Life—The whole appears to resolve into this—that Man is originally "a poor forked creature"[1] subject to the same mischances as the beasts of the forest, destined to hardships and disquietude of some kind or other. If he improves by degrees his bodily accommodations and comforts—at each stage, at each accent there are waiting for him a fresh set of annoyances—he is mortal and there is still a heaven with its Stars abov[e] his head. The most interesting question that can come before us is, How far by the persevering endeavours of a seldom appearing Socrates Mankind may be made happy—I

---

6. *Comus*, lines 475–77.
7. Two books of history, Voltaire's *Le Siècle de Louis XIV* (1751) and William Robertson's *The History of America* (1777). In this second extract from the journal-letter, Keats is writing toward the end of April (on the 21st or 28th).
8. Louis XIV of France. Francisco Pizarro, the

Spanish explorer whose exploits are described in Robertson's *America*.
9. Officers of the law whose duties included making arrests for bad debts.
1. Shakespeare's *King Lear* 3.4.95–97. Lear says of "Poor Tom," "Unaccommodated man is no more but such a poor, bare, forked animal as thou art."

can imagine such happiness carried to an extreme—but what must it end in?—Death—and who could in such a case bear with death—the whole troubles of life which are now frittered away in a series of years, would the[n] be accumulated for the last days of a being who instead of hailing its approach, would leave this world as Eve left Paradise—But in truth I do not at all believe in this sort of perfectibility—the nature of the world will not admit of it—the inhabitants of the world will correspond to itself—Let the fish philosophise the ice away from the Rivers in winter time and they shall be at continual play in the tepid delight of summer. Look at the Poles and at the sands of Africa, Whirlpools and volcanoes—Let men exterminate them and I will say that they may arrive at earthly Happiness—The point at which Man may arrive is as far as the paralel state in inanimate nature and no further—For instance suppose a rose to have sensation, it blooms on a beautiful morning it enjoys itself—but there comes a cold wind, a hot sun—it can not escape it, it cannot destroy its annoyances—they are as native to the world as itself: no more can man be happy in spite, the world[l]y elements will prey upon his nature—The common cognomen of this world among the misguided and superstitious is "a vale of tears" from which we are to be redeemed by a certain arbitrary interposition of God and taken to Heaven—What a little circumscribe[d] straightened notion! Call the world if you Please "The vale of Soul-making" Then you will find out the use of the world (I am speaking now in the highest terms for human nature admitting it to be immortal which I will here take for granted for the purpose of showing a thought which has struck me concerning it) I say "*Soul making*" Soul as distinguished from an Intelligence—There may be intelligences or sparks of the divinity in millions—but they are not Souls the till they acquire identities, till each one is personally itself. I[n]telligences are atoms of perception—they know and they see and they are pure, in short they are God—how then are Souls to be made? How then are these sparks which are God to have identity given them—so as ever to possess a bliss peculiar to each ones individual existence? How, but by the medium of a world like this? This point I sincerely wish to consider because I think it a grander system of salvation than the chrystean religion—or rather it is a system of Spirit-creation[2]—This is effected by three grand materials acting the one upon the other for a series of years—These three Materials are the *Intelligence*—the *human heart* (as distinguished from intelligence or Mind) and the *World* or *Elemental space* suited for the proper action of *Mind and Heart* on each other for the purpose of forming the *Soul* or *Intelligence destined to possess the sense of Identity.* I can scarcely express what I but dimly perceive—and yet I think I perceive it—that you may judge the more clearly I will put it in the most homely form possible—I will call the *world* a School instituted for the purpose of teaching little children to read—I will call the *human heart* the *horn Book*[3] used in that School—and I will call the *Child able to read, the Soul* made from that *school* and its *hornbook.* Do you not see how necessary a World of Pains

2. Keats is struggling for an analogy that will embody his solution to the ancient riddle of evil, as an alternative to what he understands to be the Christian view: that evil exists as a test of the individual's worthiness of salvation in heaven, and this world is only a proving ground for a later and better life. Keats proposes that the function of the human experience of sorrow and pain is to feed and discipline the formless and unstocked "intelligence" that we possess at birth and thus to shape it into a rich and coherent "identity," or "soul." This result provides a justification ("salvation") for our suffering in terms of our earthly life: i.e., experience is its own reward.

3. A child's primer, which used to consist of a sheet of paper mounted on thin wood, protected by a sheet of transparent horn.

and troubles is to school an Intelligence and make it a soul? A Place where the heart must feel and suffer in a thousand diverse ways! Not merely is the Heart a Hornbook, It is the Minds Bible, it is the Minds experience, it is the teat from which the Mind or intelligence sucks its identity—As various as the Lives of Men are—so various become their souls, and thus does God make individual beings, Souls, Identical Souls of the sparks of his own essence— This appears to me a faint sketch of a system of Salvation which does not affront our reason and humanity—I am convinced that many difficulties which christians labour under would vanish before it—There is one wh[i]ch even now Strikes me—the Salvation of Children—In them the Spark or intelligence returns to God without any identity—it having had no time to learn of, and be altered by, the heart—or seat of the human Passions—It is pretty generally suspected that the chr[i]stian scheme has been coppied from the ancient persian and greek Philosophers. Why may they not have made this simple thing even more simple for common apprehension by introducing Mediators and Personages in the same manner as in the hethen mythology abstractions are personified—Seriously I think it probable that this System of Soulmaking—may have been the Parent of all the more palpable and personal Schemes of Redemption, among the Zoroastrians the Christians and the Hindoos. For as one part of the human species must have their carved Jupiter; so another part must have the palpable and named Mediatior and saviour, their Christ their Oromanes and their Vishnu[4]—If what I have said should not be plain enough, as I fear it may not be, I will [put] you in the place where I began in this series of thoughts—I mean, I began by seeing how man was formed by circumstances—and what are circumstances?—but touchstones of his heart—? and what are touch stones?—but proovings of his hearrt?[5]—and what are proovings of his heart but fortifiers or alterers of his nature? and what is his altered nature but his soul?—and what was his soul before it came into the world and had These provings and alterations and perfectionings?—An intelligences—without Identity—and how is this Identity to be made? Through the medium of the Heart? And how is the heart to become this Medium but in a world of Circumstances?—There now I think what with Poetry and Theology you may thank your Stars that my pen is not very long winded— * * *

This is the 3d of May & every thing is in delightful forwardness; the violets are not withered, before the peeping of the first rose; You must let me know every thing, how parcels go & come, what papers you have, & what Newspapers you want, & other things—God bless you my dear Brother & Sister

Your ever Affectionate Brother
John Keats—

4. The deity who creates and preserves the world, in Hindu belief. Oromanes (Ahriman) was the principle of evil, locked in a persisting struggle with Ormazd, the principle of good, in the Zoroastrian religion of ancient Persia.
5. I.e., experiences by which the human heart is put to the test.

To Fanny Brawne

[FANNY BRAWNE AS KEATS'S "FAIR STAR"]

[July 25, 1819]

My sweet Girl,

I hope you did not blame me much for not obeying your request of a Letter on Saturday: we have had four in our small room playing at cards night and morning leaving me no undisturb'd opportunity to write. Now Rice and Martin are gone I am at liberty. Brown to my sorrow confirms the account you give of your ill health. You cannot conceive how I ache to be with you: how I would die for one hour——for what is in the world? I say you cannot conceive; it is impossible you should look with such eyes upon me as I have upon you: it cannot be. Forgive me if I wander a little this evening, for I have been all day employ'd in a very abstr[a]ct Poem[1] and I am in deep love with you—two things which must excuse me. I have, believe me, not been an age in letting you take possession of me; the very first week I knew you I wrote myself your vassal; but burnt the Letter as the very next time I saw you I thought you manifested some dislike to me. If you should ever feel for Man at the first sight what I did for you, I am lost. Yet I should not quarrel with you, but hate myself if such a thing were to happen—only I should burst if the thing were not as fine as a Man as you are as a Woman. Perhaps I am too vehement, then fancy me on my knees, especially when I mention a part of your Letter which hurt me; you say speaking of Mr. Severn[2] "but you must be satisfied in knowing that I admired you much more than your friend." My dear love, I cannot believe there ever was or ever could be any thing to admire in me especially as far as sight goes—I cannot be admired, I am not a thing to be admired. You are, I love you; all I can bring you is a swooning admiration of your Beauty. I hold that place among Men which snub-nos'd brunettes with meeting eyebrows do among women—they are trash to me—unless I should find one among them with a fire in her heart like the one that burns in mine. You absorb me in spite of myself—you alone: for I look not forward with any pleasure to what is call'd being settled in the world; I tremble at domestic cares—yet for you I would meet them, though if it would leave you the happier I would rather die than do so. I have two luxuries to brood over in my walks, your Loveliness and the hour of my death. O that I could have possession of them both in the same minute. I hate the world: it batters too much the wings of my self-will, and would I could take a sweet poison from your lips to send me out of it. From no others would I take it. I am indeed astonish'd to find myself so careless of all cha[r]ms but yours—remembring as I do the time when even a bit of ribband was a matter of interest with me. What softer words can I find for you after this—what it is I will not read. Nor will I say more here, but in a Postscript answer any thing else you may have mentioned in your Letter in so many words—for I am distracted with a thousand thoughts. I will imagine you Venus tonight and pray, pray, pray to your star like a Hethen.[3]

Your's ever, fair Star,
John Keats.

---

1. Probably *The Fall of Hyperion*.
2. Joseph Severn, who later looked after Keats in Rome during his final illness.

3. See Keats's sonnet "Bright star" (p. 971) for parallels to this and other remarks in the present letter.

To Percy Bysshe Shelley[1]

["LOAD EVERY RIFT" WITH ORE]

[August 16, 1820]

My dear Shelley,

I am very much gratified that you, in a foreign country, and with a mind almost over occupied, should write to me in the strain of the Letter beside me. If I do not take advantage of your invitation it will be prevented by a circumstance I have very much at heart to prophesy[2]—There is no doubt that an english winter would put an end to me, and do so in a lingering hateful manner, therefore I must either voyage or journey to Italy as a soldier marches up to a battery. My nerves at present are the worst part of me, yet they feel soothed when I think that come what extreme may, I shall not be destined to remain in one spot long enough to take a hatred of any four particular bedposts. I am glad you take any pleasure in my poor Poem;[3]— which I would willingly take the trouble to unwrite, if possible, did I care so much as I have done about Reputation. I received a copy of the Cenci,[4] as from yourself from Hunt. There is only one part of it I am judge of; the Poetry, and dramatic effect, which by many spirits now a days is considered the mammon.[5] A modern work it is said must have a purpose,[6] which may be the God—*an artist* must serve Mammon—he must have "self concentration" selfishness perhaps. You I am sure will forgive me for sincerely remarking that you might curb your magnanimity and be more of an artist, and "load every rift"[7] of your subject with ore. The thought of such discipline must fall like cold chains upon you, who perhaps never sat with your wings furl'd for six Months together. And is not this extraordinary talk for the writer of Endymion? whose mind was like a pack of scattered cards—I am pick'd up and sorted to a pip.[8] My Imagination is a Monastry and I am its Monk—you must explain my metap[cs][9] to yourself. I am in expectation of Prometheus[1] every day. Could I have my own wish for its interest effected you would have it still in manuscript—or be but now putting an end to the second act. I remember you advising me not to publish my first-blights, on Hampstead heath—I am returning advice upon your hands. Most of the Poems in the volume I send you[2] have been written above two years, and would never have been publish'd but from a hope of gain; so you see I am inclined enough to take your advice now. I must exp[r]ess once more my deep sense of your kindness, adding my sincere thanks and respects for M[rs] Shelley. In the hope of soon seeing you I remain

most sincerely yours,
John Keats—

1. Written in reply to a letter urging Keats (who was ill) to spend the winter with the Shelleys in Pisa.
2. His own death.
3. Keats's *Endymion*, Shelley had written, contains treasures, "though treasures poured forth, with indistinct profusion." Keats here responds with advice in kind.
4. Shelley's blank-verse tragedy, *The Cenci*, had been published in the spring of 1820.
5. See Matthew 6.24 and Luke 16.13: "Ye cannot serve God and mammon."
6. Wordsworth had said this in his Preface to *Lyrical Ballads*.
7. From Spenser's description of the Cave of Mammon in *The Faerie Queene* 2.7.28: "With rich metall loaded every rifte."
8. Perfectly ordered; all the suits in the deck matched up ("pips" are the conventional spots on playing cards).
9. Metaphysics.
1. *Prometheus Unbound*, of which Shelley had promised Keats a copy.
2. Keats's volume of 1820, including *Lamia, The Eve of St. Agnes*, and the odes. When Shelley drowned he had this small book in his pocket.

To Charles Brown[1]

[KEATS'S LAST LETTER]

Rome. 30 November 1820.

My dear Brown,

'Tis the most difficult thing in the world to me to write a letter. My stomach continues so bad, that I feel it worse on opening any book,—yet I am much better than I was in Quarantine.[2] Then I am afraid to encounter the proing and conning of any thing interesting to me in England. I have an habitual feeling of my real life having past, and that I am leading a posthumous existence. God knows how it would have been—but it appears to me—however, I will not speak of that subject. I must have been at Bedhampton nearly at the time you were writing to me from Chichester[3]—how unfortunate—and to pass on the river too! There was my star predominant![4] I cannot answer any thing in your letter, which followed me from Naples to Rome, because I am afraid to look it over again. I am so weak (in mind) that I cannot bear the sight of any hand writing of a friend I love so much as I do you. Yet I ride the little horse,—and, at my worst, even in Quarantine, summoned up more puns, in a sort of desperation, in one week than in any year of my life. There is one thought enough to kill me—I have been well, healthy, alert &c, walking with her[5]—and now—the knowledge of contrast, feeling for light and shade, all that information (primitive sense) necessary for a poem are great enemies to the recovery of the stomach. There, you rogue, I put you to the torture,—but you must bring your philosophy to bear—as I do mine, really—or how should I be able to live? Dr Clarke is very attentive to me; he says, there is very little the matter with my lungs, but my stomach, he says, is very bad. I am well disappointed in hearing good news from George,—for it runs in my head we shall all die young. I have not written to x x x x x yet,[6] which he must think very neglectful; being anxious to send him a good account of my health, I have delayed it from week to week. If I recover, I will do all in my power to correct the mistakes made during sickness; and if I should not, all my faults will be forgiven. I shall write to x x x to-morrow, or next day. I will write to x x x x x in the middle of next week. Severn is very well, though he leads so dull a life with me. Remember me to all friends, and tell x x x x I should not have left London without taking leave of him, but from being so low in body and mind. Write to George as soon as you receive this, and tell him how I am, as far as you can guess;—and also a note to my sister—who walks about my imagination like a ghost—she is so like Tom.[7] I can scarcely bid you good bye even in a letter. I always made an awkward bow.

God bless you!
John Keats.

1. Written to Keats's friend Charles Armitage Brown from the house on the Spanish Steps, in the Piazza di Spagna, where Keats was being tended in his mortal illness by the devoted Joseph Severn.
2. When it landed at Naples, Keats's ship had been quarantined for ten miserably hot days.
3. Bedhampton and Chichester are both near the harbor town of Portsmouth, where Keats had embarked for Naples two months before.
4. I.e., that was my usual luck. Cf. Shakespeare's

The Winter's Tale 1.2.202–3: "It is a bawdy planet, that will strike / Where 'tis predominant."
5. Fanny Brawne.
6. Charles Brown, whose manuscript transcription is the only text for this letter, substituted crosses for the names of Keats's friends to conceal their identities.
7. Keats's youngest brother, whom Fanny, his only sister, closely resembled, had died of tuberculosis on December 1, 1818. George was John Keats's younger brother.

MARY WOLLSTONECRAFT SHELLEY
1797–1851

Percy Shelley wrote of his young wife, in the Dedication to *Laon and Cythna*:

> They say that thou wert lovely from thy birth,
> Of glorious parents, thou aspiring Child.

The "glorious parents" were William Godwin, the leading reformer and radical philosopher of the time, and Mary Wollstonecraft, famed as the author of A *Vindication of the Rights of Woman*. Wollstonecraft had died from childbed fever when she gave birth to Mary. Four years later Godwin married a widow, Mary Jane Clairmont, who soon had more than she could cope with trying to manage a family of five children of diverse parentage, amid increasing financial difficulties. Mary bitterly resented her stepmother but adored her father, who, she later said, "was my God—and I remember many childish instances of the excess of attachment I bore for him."

To ease the situation Mary was sent at the age of fourteen to live in Dundee, Scotland, with the family of William Baxter, an admirer of Godwin. After two pleasant years roaming the countryside, daydreaming, and writing stories (which have been lost), she returned in 1814 to her father's house in London. There, at the age of sixteen, she encountered the twenty-one-year-old poet Percy Bysshe Shelley, a devotee of Godwin's and an almost daily visitor, who had become estranged from his wife, Harriet. The young people fell in love; within a few months Mary was pregnant. On July 28 they ran off to Europe, taking with them her stepsister Jane Clairmont, who later changed her name to Claire. Mary described their happy though heedless wanderings through France, Switzerland, and Germany in her first book, *History of a Six Weeks' Tour*, published anonymously in 1817.

Back in England she gave premature birth to a daughter who lived only twelve days; a year later, in 1816, she bore a son, William. Shelley was usually in financial difficulties and often had to hide from his creditors to avoid arrest. Nonetheless, he contributed substantial sums (borrowed against his expectations as heir to his father, Sir Timothy) to Godwin's support, even though Godwin, despite his earlier advocacy of free love, refused to countenance Shelley's liaison with his daughter. Claire Clairmont meanwhile sought out and had a brief affair with Byron, who left her pregnant. In the spring of 1816, the Shelleys went abroad again with Claire, and at the latter's behest settled in Geneva, where Byron, accompanied by his physician and friend John William Polidori, set up residence in the nearby Villa Diodati. Mary Shelley tells us, in the introduction to *Frankenstein*, how her imagination was fired by their animated conversations during many social evenings. Encouraged and assisted by Shelley, she wrote *Frankenstein, or The Modern Prometheus*, her story of the man of science who, with catastrophic consequences, seeks to conquer nature, rival the divinity, and make new life, and who then withholds love from the life he has made. Since its anonymous publication in 1818, the novel has never been out of print. As the basis for innumerable plays (beginning in 1823) and movies (beginning in 1910), the story has become a central myth of modern Western culture.

The last six years of Mary's life with her husband, spent first in England and then in Italy, were filled with disasters. In October 1816 her sensitive and moody half-sister, Fanny Imlay, feeling herself an unloved burden on the Godwin household, committed suicide by an overdose of laudanum. Two months later Shelley's abandoned wife, Harriet, pregnant by an unknown lover, drowned herself in the Serpentine lake at Hyde Park in London. Shelley at once married Mary, but the courts denied him custody of Harriet's two children on the grounds that he was morally unfit to rear them. In September 1818 came the death of Mary's third baby, Clara, followed less than nine months later by the death from malaria, rampant in Rome at the time, of her adored son, William: "We came to Italy thinking to do Shelley's health good," Mary wrote bitterly, "but the Climate is not [by] any means warm enough to be of benefit to him & yet it is that that has destroyed my two children." These tragedies and her own ill health threw her into a depression that was only partly relieved by the birth of a second son, Percy Florence, in November 1819, and was deepened again the next spring by a miscarriage, as well as by the death of Claire's daughter, Allegra, whom Byron had placed in an Italian convent. Mary Shelley's habitual reserve, which masked the depth of her feelings, now became an apathy that caused her to withdraw, emotionally, from her husband. He became distant in turn, giving their friend Jane Williams the affection he denied his wife. When he was drowned in the Gulf of Spezia in July 1822, Mary was left with a persisting sense that she had failed her husband when he most needed her.

An impoverished widow of twenty-four, she returned to England with two ambitions. One was to disseminate the poetry and to rescue the character of Shelley, whom she idolized in memory; the other was to support by her writings her surviving son. Her only financial assistance was a small allowance given her by Sir Timothy Shelley, which he threatened to cut off if she wrote a biography of his radical and scandal-haunted son. In the remaining quarter century of her life, Mary Shelley became a notable success as a professional woman of letters, publishing as "The Author of 'Frankenstein'" to comply with Sir Timothy's demand that she never use the Shelley name. After *Frankenstein* she wrote first a novella and then five more novels, of which the first two are the best. The novella, *Matilda*, written in 1819 but left in manuscript and not published until 1959, deals with the disastrous results of a father's incestuous passion for a daughter who resembles his dead wife. *Valperga* (1823), set in the Italian Middle Ages, is a historical romance about a quasi-Napoleonic figure who sacrifices his love and humanity to his lust for political power and about the two women whom he betrays. *The Last Man* (1826), set in the twenty-first century, tracing the progress of a plague that destroys all of humankind except for one survivor, the novel's narrator, almost equals *Frankenstein* in its analysis of human isolation. This novel also served Shelley as a forum in which to write autobiographically, for as she reflected in a diary entry, her own companions, like her ever-mourning narrator's, were gone, become "the people of the grave." She in fact arranged to endow two characters in the novel, her narrator's associates, with traits recognizably those of Percy Shelley and Byron, whose death in Greece occurred as she began writing.

Shelley all this while also contributed short stories to the gift books and literary annuals that were a publishing phenomenon during the 1820s and 1830s: deluxe volumes, gorgeously bound and lavishly illustrated, whose literary selections mingled pieces by esteemed authors—Scott, Hemans, Wordsworth, Coleridge—with contributions by the most fashionable members of the aristocracy. (All writers, however, were by the makers of gift books deemed less important than the visual artists: the stories or poems were often commissioned to accompany preexisting illustrations.) In 1835–39 she contributed to the *Cabinet Cyclopedia* five volumes of admirable biographical and critical studies of continental authors. She also published several separate editions of her husband's writings in verse and prose. In accordance with what was then standard editorial procedure, she altered and emended Shelley's texts; she also added prefaces and notes, relating Shelley's writings to the circumstances of his life and thought, that have been an important resource for scholars of Romantic literature.

Not until old Sir Timothy died in 1844, leaving his title and estate to her son, did she find herself in comfortable circumstances. Her last years were cheered by the devotion of her son—who was an amiable man but entirely lacked the genius of his parents—and by her close friendship with Jane St. John, an admirer of Shelley's poetry, whom Sir Percy Florence married in 1848. Mary Shelley died three years later, at the age of fifty-three.

During her widowhood she craved social acceptance and status and, although she maintained liberal principles, tried hard, by adapting herself to conventional standards in her writings and her life, to work free from the onus of what her contemporaries regarded as the scandalous careers of her mother, father, and husband. In later life she wrote an apologia in her journal, dated October 21, 1838, that reveals the stresses of a life spent trying to measure up to the example, yet escape the bad reputations, of her parents and husband.

> In the first place, with regard to "the good cause"—the cause of the advancement of freedom and knowledge, of the rights of women, etc.—I am not a person of opinions. . . . Some have a passion for reforming the world; others do not cling to particular opinions. That my parents and Shelley were of the former class, makes me respect it. . . . For myself, I earnestly desire the good and enlightenment of my fellow creatures, and see all, in the present course, tending to the same, and rejoice; but I am not for violent extremes, which only brings on an injurious reaction. . . .
>
> To hang back, as I do, brings a penalty. I was nursed and fed with a love of glory. To be something great and good was the precept given me by my father; Shelley reiterated it. . . . But Shelley died, and I was alone. . . . My total friendlessness, my horror of pushing, and inability to put myself forward unless led, cherished and supported—all this has sunk me in a state of loneliness no other human being ever before, I believe, endured—except Robinson Crusoe. . . .
>
> But I have never crouched to society—never sought it unworthily. If I have never written to vindicate the rights of women, I have ever defended women when oppressed. At every risk I have befriended and supported victims to the social system; but I make no boast, for in truth it is simple justice I perform; and so am I still reviled for being worldly. . . .
>
> Such as I have written appears to me the exact truth.

From The Last Man

Introduction[1]

I visited Naples in the year 1818. On the 8th of December of that year, my companion and I crossed the Bay, to visit the antiquities which are scattered on the shores of Baiae.[2] The translucent and shining waters of the calm sea covered fragments of old Roman villas, which were interlaced by sea-weed, and received diamond tints from the chequering of the sun-beams; the blue and pellucid element was such as Galatea[3] might have skimmed in her car of mother of pearl; or Cleopatra, more fitly than the Nile, have chosen as the path of her magic ship.[4] Though it was winter, the atmosphere seemed more

---

1. A contribution to Romantic-period investigations of the nature of creativity, Shelley's Introduction to The Last Man (composed 1824 and published at the start of 1826) enigmatically identifies the novel that follows as a strange blend of creative work, transcription, and translation, in which biography (Shelley's personal history of suffering) is subsumed by history and myth. Playing with the convention of Gothic romances that involves the protagonist's discovery of a decaying, all but illegible, manuscript from the past, Shelley

leaves it an open question whether she is the editor or author of her "sibylline leaves."
2. Shelley begins with an actual event—the visit she and Percy paid in December 1818 to the ancient Roman resort of Baiae near Naples. See "Ode to the West Wind," lines 32–34 (p. 806).
3. Name given to a sea nymph in Greek mythology.
4. See Enobarbus's description of Cleopatra's ship in Shakespeare's Antony and Cleopatra 2.2.197–203.

appropriate to early spring; and its genial warmth contributed to inspire those sensations of placid delight, which are the portion of every traveller, as he lingers, loath to quit the tranquil bays and radiant promontories of Baiae.

We visited the so called Elysian Fields and Avernus:[5] and wandered through various ruined temples, baths, and classic spots; at length we entered the gloomy cavern of the Cumaean Sibyl.[6] Our Lazzeroni[7] bore flaring torches, which shone red, and almost dusky, in the murky subterranean passages, whose darkness thirstily surrounding them, seemed eager to imbibe more and more of the element of light. We passed by a natural archway, leading to a second gallery, and enquired, if we could not enter there also. The guides pointed to the reflection of their torches on the water that paved it, leaving us to form our own conclusion; but adding it was a pity, for it led to the Sibyl's Cave. Our curiosity and enthusiasm were excited by this circumstance, and we insisted upon attempting the passage. As is usually the case in the prosecution of such enterprizes, the difficulties decreased on examination. We found, on each side of the humid pathway, "dry land for the sole of the foot."[8] At length we arrived at a large, desert, dark cavern, which the Lazzeroni assured us was the Sibyl's Cave. We were sufficiently disappointed—Yet we examined it with care, as if its blank, rocky walls could still bear trace of celestial visitant. On one side was a small opening. Whither does this lead? we asked: can we enter here?—"*Questo poi, no*,"[9]—said the wild looking savage, who held the torch; "you can advance but a short distance, and nobody visits it."

"Nevertheless, I will try it," said my companion; "it may lead to the real cavern. Shall I go alone, or will you accompany me?"

I signified my readiness to proceed, but our guides protested against such a measure. With great volubility, in their native Neapolitan dialect, with which we were not very familiar, they told us that there were spectres, that the roof would fall in, that it was too narrow to admit us, that there was a deep hole within, filled with water, and we might be drowned. My friend shortened the harangue, by taking the man's torch from him; and we proceeded alone.

The passage, which at first scarcely admitted us, quickly grew narrower and lower; we were almost bent double; yet still we persisted in making our way through it. At length we entered a wider space, and the low roof heightened; but, as we congratulated ourselves on this change, our torch was extinguished by a current of air, and we were left in utter darkness. The guides bring with them materials for renewing the light, but we had none—our only resource was to return as we came. We groped round the widened space to find the entrance, and after a time fancied that we had succeeded. This proved however to be a second passage, which evidently ascended. It terminated like the former; though something approaching to a ray, we could not tell whence, shed a very doubtful twilight in the space. By degrees, our eyes grew somewhat accustomed to this dimness, and we perceived that there was no direct passage leading us further; but that it was possible to climb one side

5. Sites near Naples named for places in mythology: the fields thought to be inhabited after death by those favored by the gods and the entrance to the underworld, by tradition located at Lake Avernus.
6. The prophetess, inspired by the god Apollo, whose mad frenzies and cryptic accounts of future history are most famously described in the *Aeneid*, book 6. Other accounts describe how the sibyl wrote her prophecies on leaves, which she placed at the entrance to her cave; when the wind

dispersed them, they became unintelligible. Coleridge had titled his 1817 collection of poems *Sibylline Leaves* so as to allude, he said, "to the fragmentary and widely scattered state in which [the poems] have been long suffered to remain."
7. Generic term for the poor of Naples, here employed as guides.
8. Allusion to Genesis 8.9: the dove sent by Noah from the ark finds "no rest for the sole of her foot."
9. Definitely not! (Italian).

of the cavern to a low arch at top, which promised a more easy path, from whence we now discovered that this light proceeded. With considerable difficulty we scrambled up, and came to another passage with still more of illumination, and this led to another ascent like the former.

After a succession of these, which our resolution alone permitted us to surmount, we arrived at a wide cavern with an arched dome-like roof. An aperture in the midst let in the light of heaven; but this was overgrown with brambles and underwood, which acted as a veil, obscuring the day, and giving a solemn religious hue to the apartment. It was spacious, and nearly circular, with a raised seat of stone, about the size of a Grecian couch, at one end. The only sign that life had been here, was the perfect snow-white skeleton of a goat, which had probably not perceived the opening as it grazed on the hill above, and had fallen headlong. Ages perhaps had elapsed since this catastrophe; and the ruin it had made above, had been repaired by the growth of vegetation during many hundred summers.

The rest of the furniture of the cavern consisted of piles of leaves, fragments of bark, and a white filmy substance, resembling the inner part of the green hood which shelters the grain of the unripe Indian corn. We were fatigued by our struggles to attain this point, and seated ourselves on the rocky couch, while the sounds of tinkling sheep-bells, and shout of shepherd-boy, reached us from above.

At length my friend, who had taken up some of the leaves strewed about, exclaimed, "This *is* the Sibyl's cave; these are Sibylline leaves." On examination, we found that all the leaves, bark, and other substances were traced with written characters. What appeared to us more astonishing, was that these writings were expressed in various languages: some unknown to my companion, ancient Chaldee,[1] and Egyptian hieroglyphics, old as the Pyramids. Stranger still, some were in modern dialects, English and Italian. We could make out little by the dim light, but they seemed to contain prophecies, detailed relations of events but lately passed; names, now well known, but of modern date; and often exclamations of exultation or woe, of victory or defeat, were traced on their thin scant pages. This was certainly the Sibyl's Cave; not indeed exactly as Virgil describes it; but the whole of this land had been so convulsed by earthquake and volcano, that the change was not wonderful, though the traces of ruin were effaced by time; and we probably owed the preservation of these leaves, to the accident which had closed the mouth of the cavern, and the swift-growing vegetation which had rendered its sole opening impervious to the storm. We made a hasty selection of such of the leaves, whose writing one at least of us could understand; and then, laden with our treasure, we bade adieu to the dim hypaethric[2] cavern, and after much difficulty succeeded in rejoining our guides.

During our stay at Naples, we often returned to this cave, sometimes alone, skimming the sun-lit sea, and each time added to our store. Since that period, whenever the world's circumstance has not imperiously called me away, or the temper of my mind impeded such study, I have been employed in deciphering these sacred remains. Their meaning, wondrous and eloquent, has often repaid my toil, soothing me in sorrow, and exciting my imagination to daring flights, through the immensity of nature and the mind of man. For awhile my

1. Language of ancient Babylon, famed for its astronomical and astrological knowledge.
2. Open to the sky.

labours were not solitary; but that time is gone, and, with the selected and matchless companion of my toils, their dearest reward is also lost to me—

> Di mie tenere frondi altro lavoro
> Credea mostrarte; e qual fero pianeta
> Ne' nvidiò insieme, o mio nobil tesoro?[3]

I present the public with my latest discoveries in the slight Sibylline pages. Scattered and unconnected as they were, I have been obliged to add links, and model the work into a consistent form. But the main substance rests on the truths contained in these poetic rhapsodies, and the divine intuition which the Cumaean damsel obtained from heaven.

I have often wondered at the subject of her verses, and at the English dress of the Latin poet. Sometimes I have thought that, obscure and chaotic as they are, they owe their present form to me, their decipherer. As if we should give to another artist, the painted fragments which form the mosaic copy of Raphael's Transfiguration in St. Peter's; he would put them together in a form, whose mode would be fashioned by his own peculiar mind and talent.[4] Doubtless the leaves of the Cumaean Sibyl have suffered distortion and diminution of interest and excellence in my hands. My only excuse for thus transforming them, is that they were unintelligible in their pristine condition.

My labours have cheered long hours of solitude, and taken me out of a world, which has averted its once benignant face from me, to one glowing with imagination and power. Will my readers ask how I could find solace from the narration of misery and woeful change? This is one of the mysteries of our nature, which holds full sway over me, and from whose influence I cannot escape. I confess, that I have not been unmoved by the development of the tale; and that I have been depressed, nay, agonized, at some parts of the recital, which I have faithfully transcribed from my materials. Yet such is human nature, that the excitement of mind was dear to me, and that the imagination, painter of tempest and earthquake, or, worse, the stormy and ruin-fraught passions of man, softened my real sorrows and endless regrets, by clothing these fictitious ones in that ideality, which takes the mortal sting from pain.

I hardly know whether this apology is necessary. For the merits of my adaptation and translation must decide how far I have well bestowed my time and imperfect powers, in giving form and substance to the frail and attenuated Leaves of the Sibyl.

1824   1826

---

3. Quoted from the Italian of a sonnet by Petrarch (1304–1374): "From my tender leaves, I thought to show you a different work, and what fierce planet ended our being together, oh, my noble treasure?"

4. The Italian Renaissance artist Raphael's painting of the transfiguration of Christ is copied in mosaic on the altarpiece of the Cappella Clementina of St. Peter's in Rome.

The Mortal Immortal[1]

A Tale

JULY 16, 1833.—This is a memorable anniversary for me; on it I complete my three hundred and twenty-third year!

The Wandering Jew?[2]—certainly not. More than eighteen centuries have passed over his head. In comparison with him, I am a very young Immortal.

Am I, then, immortal? This is a question which I have asked myself, by day and night, for now three hundred and three years, and yet cannot answer it. I detected a gray hair amidst my brown locks this very day—that surely signifies decay. Yet it may have remained concealed there for three hundred years—for some persons have become entirely white-headed before twenty years of age.

I will tell my story, and my reader shall judge for me. I will tell my story, and so contrive to pass some few hours of a long eternity, become so wearisome to me. For ever! Can it be? to live for ever! I have heard of enchantments, in which the victims were plunged into a deep sleep, to wake, after a hundred years, as fresh as ever: I have heard of the Seven Sleepers[3]—thus to be immortal would not be so burthensome: but, oh! the weight of never-ending time—the tedious passage of the still-succeeding hours! How happy was the fabled Nourjahad![4]——But to my task.

All the world has heard of Cornelius Agrippa.[5] His memory is as immortal as his arts have made me. All the world has also heard of his scholar, who, unawares, raised the foul fiend during his master's absence, and was destroyed by him.[6] The report, true or false, of this accident, was attended with many inconveniences to the renowned philosopher. All his scholars at once deserted him—his servants disappeared. He had no one near him to put coals on his ever-burning fires while he slept, or to attend to the changeful colours of his medicines while he studied. Experiment after experiment failed, because one pair of hands was insufficient to complete them: the dark spirits laughed at him for not being able to retain a single mortal in his service.

I was then very young—very poor—and very much in love. I had been for about a year the pupil of Cornelius, though I was absent when this accident took place. On my return, my friends implored me not to return to the alchymist's abode. I trembled as I listened to the dire tale they told; I required no

1. Cf. Keats's *Endymion* 1.843–44: "if this earthly love has power to make / Men's being mortal, immortal." "The Mortal Immortal" is one of the sixteen stories Shelley during her career contributed to *The Keepsake*, a gift book published annually between 1828 and 1857. This tale shares its first-person narrative form and interest in the consequences of scientific ambition with Shelley's best-known novel. With a certain irony, given its original setting in a volume that its publisher marketed as a lasting memento of affection that might be purchased for a loved one, "The Mortal Immortal" also examines the question of whether love can survive time's ravages if beauty does not.
2. The man who, according to legend, taunted Christ on the road to the crucifixion and was therefore condemned to wander the earth until Judgment Day.
3. Legendary Christian youths who took refuge in a cave in Ephesus to escape their pagan persecutors and slept for 187 years.
4. Title character of Frances Sheridan's Oriental tale of 1767, who is tricked into believing that he has become immortal and that, when he sleeps, he does so for several years at a time.
5. The 16th-century German researcher of the occult and the alchemical sciences. Agrippa's works are among the books that Victor Frankenstein reads when young and that prompt him to begin "the search of the philosopher's stone" (which had the power to transmute base metal into gold) and of "the elixir of life"; his "favourite authors" also promise to teach the "raising of ghosts or devils."
6. The story was told by Robert Southey in a 1798 poem titled "Cornelius Agrippa: A Ballad of a Young Man That Would Read Unlawful Books."

second warning; and when Cornelius came and offered me a purse of gold if I would remain under his roof, I felt as if Satan himself tempted me. My teeth chattered—my hair stood on end:—I ran off as fast as my trembling knees would permit.

My failing steps were directed whither for two years they had every evening been attracted,—a gently bubbling spring of pure living waters, beside which lingered a dark-haired girl, whose beaming eyes were fixed on the path I was accustomed each night to tread. I cannot remember the hour when I did not love Bertha; we had been neighbours and playmates from infancy—her parents, like mine, were of humble life, yet respectable—our attachment had been a source of pleasure to them. In an evil hour, a malignant fever carried off both her father and mother, and Bertha became an orphan. She would have found a home beneath my paternal roof, but, unfortunately, the old lady of the near castle, rich, childless, and solitary, declared her intention to adopt her. Henceforth Bertha was clad in silk—inhabited a marble palace—and was looked on as being highly favoured by fortune. But in her new situation among her new associates, Bertha remained true to the friend of her humbler days; she often visited the cottage of my father, and when forbidden to go thither, she would stray towards the neighbouring wood, and meet me beside its shady fountain.

She often declared that she owed no duty to her new protectress equal in sanctity to that which bound us. Yet still I was too poor to marry, and she grew weary of being tormented on my account. She had a haughty but an impatient spirit, and grew angry at the obstacles that prevented our union. We met now after an absence, and she had been sorely beset while I was away; she complained bitterly, and almost reproached me for being poor. I replied hastily,—

"I am honest, if I am poor!—were I not, I might soon become rich!" This exclamation produced a thousand questions. I feared to shock her by owning the truth, but she drew it from me; and then, casting a look of disdain on me, she said—

"You pretend to love, and you fear to face the Devil for my sake!"

I protested that I had only dreaded to offend her;—while she dwelt on the magnitude of the reward that I should receive. Thus encouraged—shamed by her—led on by love and hope, laughing at my late fears, with quick steps and a light heart, I returned to accept the offers of the alchymist, and was instantly installed in my office.

A year passed away. I became possessed of no insignificant sum of money. Custom had banished my fears. In spite of the most painful vigilance, I had never detected the trace of a cloven foot; nor was the studious silence of our abode ever disturbed by demoniac howls. I still continued my stolen interviews with Bertha, and Hope dawned on me—Hope—but not perfect joy; for Bertha fancied that love and security were enemies, and her pleasure was to divide them in my bosom. Though true of heart, she was somewhat of a coquette in manner; and I was jealous as a Turk. She slighted me in a thousand ways, yet would never acknowledge herself to be in the wrong. She would drive me mad with anger, and then force me to beg her pardon. Sometimes she fancied that I was not sufficiently submissive, and then she had some story of a rival, favoured by her protectress. She was surrounded by silk-clad youths—the rich and gay—What chance had the sad-robed scholar of Cornelius compared with these?

On one occasion, the philosopher made such large demands upon my time, that I was unable to meet her as I was wont. He was engaged in some mighty work, and I was forced to remain, day and night, feeding his furnaces and watching his chemical preparations. Bertha waited for me in vain at the fountain. Her haughty spirit fired at this neglect; and when at last I stole out during the few short minutes allotted to me for slumber, and hoped to be consoled by her, she received me with disdain, dismissed me in scorn, and vowed that any man should possess her hand rather than he who could not be in two places at once for her sake. She would be revenged!—And truly she was. In my dingy retreat I heard that she had been hunting, attended by Albert Hoffer. Albert Hoffer was favoured by her protectress, and the three passed in cavalcade before my smoky window. Methought that they mentioned my name—it was followed by a laugh of derision, as her dark eyes glanced contemptuously towards my abode.

Jealousy, with all its venom, and all its misery, entered my breast. Now I shed a torrent of tears, to think that I should never call her mine; and, anon, I imprecated a thousand curses on her inconstancy. Yet, still I must stir the fires of the alchymist, still attend on the changes of his unintelligible medicines.

Cornelius had watched for three days and nights, nor closed his eyes. The progress of his alembics[7] was slower than he expected: in spite of his anxiety, sleep weighed upon his eyelids. Again and again he threw off drowsiness with more than human energy; again and again it stole away his senses. He eyed his crucibles wistfully. "Not ready yet," he murmured; "will another night pass before the work is accomplished? Winzy,[8] you are vigilant—you are faithful—you have slept, my boy—you slept last night. Look at that glass vessel. The liquid it contains is of a soft rose-colour: the moment it begins to change its hue, awaken me—till then I may close my eyes. First, it will turn white, and then emit golden flashes; but wait not till then; when the rose-colour fades, rouse me." I scarcely heard the last words, muttered, as they were, in sleep. Even then he did not quite yield to nature. "Winzy, my boy," he again said, "do not touch the vessel—do not put it to your lips; it is a philter[9]—a philter to cure love; you would not cease to love your Bertha—beware to drink!"

And he slept. His venerable head sunk on his breast, and I scarce heard his regular breathing. For a few minutes I watched the vessel—the rosy hue of the liquid remained unchanged. Then my thoughts wandered—they visited the fountain, and dwelt on a thousand charming scenes never to be renewed—never! Serpents and adders were in my heart as the word "Never!" half formed itself on my lips. False girl!—false and cruel! Never more would she smile on me as that evening she smiled on Albert. Worthless, detested woman! I would not remain unrevenged—she should see Albert expire at her feet—she should die beneath my vengeance. She had smiled in disdain and triumph—she knew my wretchedness and her power. Yet what power had she?—the power of exciting my hate—my utter scorn—my—oh, all but indifference! Could I attain that—could I regard her with careless eyes, transferring my rejected love to one fairer and more true, that were indeed a victory!

7. Distilling apparatuses that Agrippa uses in his alchemical investigations.
8. The narrator's name suggests the Scots *winze*, meaning "curse."
9. Magic potion.

A bright flash darted before my eyes. I had forgotten the medicine of the adept; I gazed on it with wonder: flashes of admirable beauty, more bright than those which the diamond emits when the sun's rays are on it, glanced from the surface of the liquid; an odour the most fragrant and grateful stole over my sense; the vessel seemed one globe of living radiance, lovely to the eye, and most inviting to the taste. The first thought, instinctively inspired by the grosser sense, was, I will—I must drink. I raised the vessel to my lips. "It will cure me of love—of torture!" Already I had quaffed half of the most delicious liquor ever tasted by the palate of man, when the philosopher stirred. I started—I dropped the glass—the fluid flamed and glanced along the floor, while I felt Cornelius's gripe at my throat, as he shrieked aloud, "Wretch! you have destroyed the labour of my life!"

The philosopher was totally unaware that I had drunk any portion of his drug. His idea was, and I gave a tacit assent to it, that I had raised the vessel from curiosity, and that, frighted at its brightness, and the flashes of intense light it gave forth, I had let it fall. I never undeceived him. The fire of the medicine was quenched—the fragrance died away—he grew calm, as a philosopher should under the heaviest trials, and dismissed me to rest.

I will not attempt to describe the sleep of glory and bliss which bathed my soul in paradise during the remaining hours of that memorable night. Words would be faint and shallow types of my enjoyment, or of the gladness that possessed my bosom when I woke. I trod air—my thoughts were in heaven. Earth appeared heaven, and my inheritance upon it was to be one trance of delight. "This it is to be cured of love," I thought; "I will see Bertha this day, and she will find her lover cold and regardless; too happy to be disdainful, yet how utterly indifferent to her!"

The hours danced away. The philosopher, secure that he had once succeeded, and believing that he might again, began to concoct the same medicine once more. He was shut up with his books and drugs, and I had a holiday. I dressed myself with care; I looked in an old but polished shield, which served me for a mirror; methought my good looks had wonderfully improved. I hurried beyond the precincts of the town, joy in my soul, the beauty of heaven and earth around me. I turned my steps towards the castle—I could look on its lofty turrets with lightness of heart, for I was cured of love. My Bertha saw me afar off, as I came up the avenue. I know not what sudden impulse animated her bosom, but at the sight, she sprung with a light fawn-like bound down the marble steps, and was hastening towards me. But I had been perceived by another person. The old high-born hag, who called herself her protectress, and was her tyrant, had seen me, also; she hobbled, panting, up the terrace; a page, as ugly as herself, held up her train, and fanned her as she hurried along, and stopped my fair girl with a "How, now, my bold mistress? whither so fast? Back to your cage—hawks are abroad!"[1]

Bertha clasped her hands—her eyes were still bent on my approaching figure. I saw the contest. How I abhorred the old crone who checked the kind impulses of my Bertha's softening heart. Hitherto, respect for her rank had caused me to avoid the lady of the castle; now I disdained such trivial considerations. I was cured of love, and lifted above all human fears; I hastened forwards, and soon reached the terrace. How lovely Bertha looked! her eyes flashing fire, her cheeks glowing with impatience and anger, she

---

1. In the *Keepsake* volume this is the scene that the artist and engraver picture.

was a thousand times more graceful and charming than ever—I no longer loved—Oh! no, I adored—worshipped—idolized her!

She had that morning been persecuted, with more than usual vehemence, to consent to an immediate marriage with my rival. She was reproached with the encouragement that she had shown him—she was threatened with being turned out of doors with disgrace and shame. Her proud spirit rose in arms at the threat; but when she remembered the scorn that she had heaped upon me, and how, perhaps, she had thus lost one whom she now regarded as her only friend, she wept with remorse and rage. At that moment I appeared. "O, Winzy!" she exclaimed, "take me to your mother's cot; swiftly let me leave the detested luxuries and wretchedness of this noble dwelling—take me to poverty and happiness."

I clasped her in my arms with transport. The old lady was speechless with fury, and broke forth into invective only when we were far on our road to my natal cottage. My mother received the fair fugitive, escaped from a gilt cage to nature and liberty, with tenderness and joy; my father, who loved her, welcomed her heartily; it was a day of rejoicing, which did not need the addition of the celestial potion of the alchymist to steep me in delight.

Soon after this eventful day, I became the husband of Bertha. I ceased to be the scholar of Cornelius, but I continued his friend. I always felt grateful to him for having, unawares, procured me that delicious draught of a divine elixir, which, instead of curing me of love (sad cure! solitary and joyless remedy for evils which seem blessings to the memory), had inspired me with courage and resolution, thus winning for me an inestimable treasure in my Bertha.

I often called to mind that period of trance-like inebriation with wonder. The drink of Cornelius had not fulfilled the task for which he affirmed that it had been prepared, but its effects were more potent and blissful than words can express. They had faded by degrees, yet they lingered long—and painted life in hues of splendour. Bertha often wondered at my lightness of heart and unaccustomed gaiety; for, before, I had been rather serious, or even sad, in my disposition. She loved me the better for my cheerful temper, and our days were winged by joy.

Five years afterwards I was suddenly summoned to the bedside of the dying Cornelius. He had sent for me in haste, conjuring my instant presence. I found him stretched on his pallet, enfeebled even to death; all of life that yet remained animated his piercing eyes, and they were fixed on a glass vessel, full of a roseate liquid.

"Behold," he said, in a broken and inward voice, "the vanity of human wishes! a second time my hopes are about to be crowned, a second time they are destroyed. Look at that liquor—you remember five years ago I had prepared the same, with the same success;—then, as now, my thirsting lips expected to taste the immortal elixir—you dashed it from me! and at present it is too late."

He spoke with difficulty, and fell back on his pillow. I could not help saying,—

"How, revered master, can a cure for love restore you to life?"

A faint smile gleamed across his face as I listened earnestly to his scarcely intelligible answer.

"A cure for love and for all things—the Elixir of Immortality. Ah! if now I might drink, I should live for ever!"

As he spoke, a golden flash gleamed from the fluid; a well remembered fragrance stole over the air; he raised himself, all weak as he was—strength seemed miraculously to re-enter his frame—he stretched forth his hand—a loud explosion startled me—a ray of fire shot up from the elixir, and the glass vessel which contained it was shivered to atoms! I turned my eyes towards the philosopher; he had fallen back—his eyes were glassy—his features rigid—he was dead!

But I lived, and was to live for ever! So said the unfortunate alchymist, and for a few days I believed his words. I remembered the glorious drunkenness that had followed my stolen draught. I reflected on the change I had felt in my frame—in my soul. The bounding elasticity of the one—the buoyant lightness of the other. I surveyed myself in a mirror, and could perceive no change in my features during the space of the five years which had elapsed. I remembered the radiant hues and grateful scent of that delicious beverage—worthy the gift it was capable of bestowing——I was, then, IMMORTAL!

A few days after I laughed at my credulity. The old proverb, that "a prophet is least regarded in his own country," was true with respect to me and my defunct master. I loved him as a man—I respected him as a sage—but I derided the notion that he could command the powers of darkness, and laughed at the superstitious fears with which he was regarded by the vulgar. He was a wise philosopher, but had no acquaintance with any spirits but those clad in flesh and blood. His science was simply human; and human science, I soon persuaded myself, could never conquer nature's laws so far as to imprison the soul for ever within its carnal habitation. Cornelius had brewed a soul-refreshing drink—more inebriating than wine—sweeter and more fragrant than any fruit: it possessed probably strong medicinal powers, imparting gladness to the heart and vigor to the limbs; but its effects would wear out; already were they diminished in my frame. I was a lucky fellow to have quaffed health and joyous spirits, and perhaps long life, at my master's hands; but my good fortune ended there: longevity was far different from immortality.

I continued to entertain this belief for many years. Sometimes a thought stole across me—Was the alchymist indeed deceived? But my habitual credence was, that I should meet the fate of all the children of Adam at my appointed time—a little late, but still at a natural age. Yet it was certain that I retained a wonderfully youthful look. I was laughed at for my vanity in consulting the mirror so often, but I consulted it in vain—my brow was untrenched—my cheeks—my eyes—my whole person continued as untarnished as in my twentieth year.

I was troubled. I looked at the faded beauty of Bertha—I seemed more like her son. By degrees our neighbours began to make similar observations, and I found at last that I went by the name of the Scholar bewitched. Bertha herself grew uneasy. She became jealous and peevish, and at length she began to question me. We had no children; we were all in all to each other; and though, as she grew older, her vivacious spirit became a little allied to ill-temper, and her beauty sadly diminished, I cherished her in my heart as the mistress I had idolized, the wife I had sought and won with such perfect love.

At last our situation became intolerable: Bertha was fifty—I twenty years of age. I had, in very shame, in some measure adopted the habits of a more advanced age; I no longer mingled in the dance among the young and gay, but my heart bounded along with them while I restrained my feet; and a sorry figure I cut among the Nestors[2] of our village. But before the time I mention, things were altered—we were universally shunned; we were—at least, I was—reported to have kept up an iniquitous acquaintance with some of my former master's supposed friends. Poor Bertha was pitied, but deserted. I was regarded with horror and detestation.

What was to be done? we sat by our winter fire—poverty had made itself felt, for none would buy the produce of my farm; and often I had been forced to journey twenty miles, to some place where I was not known, to dispose of our property. It is true we had saved something for an evil day—that day was come.

We sat by our lone fireside—the old-hearted youth and his antiquated wife. Again Bertha insisted on knowing the truth; she recapitulated all she had ever heard said about me, and added her own observations. She conjured me to cast off the spell; she described how much more comely gray hairs were than my chestnut locks; she descanted on the reverence and respect due to age—how preferable to the slight regard paid to mere children: could I imagine that the despicable gifts of youth and good looks outweighed disgrace, hatred, and scorn? Nay, in the end I should be burnt as a dealer in the black art, while she, to whom I had not deigned to communicate any portion of my good fortune, might be stoned as my accomplice. At length she insinuated that I must share my secret with her, and bestow on her like benefits to those I myself enjoyed, or she would denounce me—and then she burst into tears.

Thus beset, methought it was the best way to tell the truth. I revealed it as tenderly as I could, and spoke only of a *very long life*, not of immortality—which representation, indeed, coincided best with my own ideas. When I ended, I rose and said,

"And now, my Bertha, will you denounce the lover of your youth?—You will not, I know. But it is too hard, my poor wife, that you should suffer from my ill-luck and the accursed arts of Cornelius. I will leave you—you have wealth enough, and friends will return in my absence. I will go; young as I seem, and strong as I am, I can work and gain my bread among strangers, unsuspected and unknown. I loved you in youth; God is my witness that I would not desert you in age, but that your safety and happiness require it."

I took my cap and moved towards the door; in a moment Bertha's arms were round my neck, and her lips were pressed to mine. "No, my husband, my Winzy," she said, "you shall not go alone—take me with you; we will remove from this place, and, as you say, among strangers we shall be unsuspected and safe. I am not so very old as quite to shame you, my Winzy; and I dare say the charm will soon wear off, and, with the blessing of God, you will become more elderly-looking, as is fitting; you shall not leave me."

I returned the good soul's embrace heartily. "I will not, my Bertha; but for your sake I had not thought of such a thing. I will be your true, faithful husband while you are spared to me, and do my duty by you to the last."

The next day we prepared secretly for our emigration. We were obliged to make great pecuniary sacrifices—it could not be helped. We realised a sum sufficient, at least, to maintain us while Bertha lived; and, without saying adieu to anyone, quitted our native country to take refuge in a remote part of western France.

2. Village elders. In the *Iliad* Nestor is the old and battle-scarred advisor to the Greek army.

It was a cruel thing to transport poor Bertha from her native village, and the friends of her youth, to a new country, new language, new customs. The strange secret of my destiny rendered this removal immaterial to me; but I compassionated her deeply, and was glad to perceive that she found compensation for her misfortunes in a variety of little ridiculous circumstances. Away from all tell-tale chroniclers, she sought to decrease the apparent disparity of our ages by a thousand feminine arts—rouge, youthful dress, and assumed juvenility of manner. I could not be angry—Did not I myself wear a mask? Why quarrel with hers, because it was less successful? I grieved deeply when I remembered that this was my Bertha, whom I had loved so fondly, and won with such transport—the dark-eyed, dark-haired girl, with smiles of enchanting archness and a step like a fawn—this mincing, simpering, jealous old woman. I should have revered her gray locks and withered cheeks; but thus!— —It was my work, I knew; but I did not the less deplore this type of human weakness.

Her jealousy never slept. Her chief occupation was to discover that, in spite of outward appearances, I was myself growing old. I verily believe that the poor soul loved me truly in her heart, but never had woman so tormenting a mode of displaying fondness. She would discern wrinkles in my face and decrepitude in my walk, while I bounded along in youthful vigour, the youngest looking of twenty youths. I never dared address another woman: on one occasion, fancying that the belle of the village regarded me with favouring eyes, she bought me a gray wig. Her constant discourse among her acquaintances was, that though I looked so young, there was ruin at work within my frame; and she affirmed that the worst symptom about me was my apparent health. My youth was a disease, she said, and I ought at all times to prepare, if not for a sudden and awful death, at least to awake some morning white-headed, and bowed down with all the marks of advanced years. I let her talk—I often joined in her conjectures. Her warnings chimed in with my never-ceasing speculations concerning my state, and I took an earnest, though painful, interest in listening to all that her quick wit and excited imagination could say on the subject.

Why dwell on these minute circumstances? We lived on for many long years. Bertha became bed-rid and paralytic: I nursed her as a mother might a child. She grew peevish, and still harped upon one string—of how long I should survive her. It has ever been a source of consolation to me, that I performed my duty scrupulously towards her. She had been mine in youth, she was mine in age, and at last, when I heaped the sod over her corpse, I wept to feel that I had lost all that really bound me to humanity.

Since then how many have been my cares and woes, how few and empty my enjoyments! I pause here in my history—I will pursue it no further. A sailor without rudder or compass, tossed on a stormy sea—a traveller lost on a widespread heath, without landmark or star to guide him—such have I been: more lost, more hopeless than either. A nearing ship, a gleam from some far cot, may save them; but I have no beacon except the hope of death.

Death! mysterious, ill-visaged friend of weak humanity! Why alone of all mortals have you cast me from your sheltering fold? O, for the peace of the grave! the deep silence of the iron-bound tomb! that thought would cease to work in my brain, and my heart beat no more with emotions varied only by new forms of sadness!

Am I immortal? I return to my first question. In the first place, is it not more probable that the beverage of the alchymist was fraught rather with longevity than eternal life? Such is my hope. And then be it remembered, that I only drank *half* of the potion prepared by him. Was not the whole necessary to complete the charm? To have drained half the Elixir of Immortality is but to be half immortal—my For-ever is thus truncated and null.

But again, who shall number the years of the half of eternity? I often try to imagine by what rule the infinite may be divided. Sometimes I fancy age advancing upon me. One gray hair I have found. Fool! do I lament? Yes, the fear of age and death often creeps coldly into my heart; and the more I live, the more I dread death, even while I abhor life. Such an enigma is man—born to perish—when he wars, as I do, against the established laws of his nature.

But for this anomaly of feeling surely I might die: the medicine of the alchymist would not be proof against fire—sword—and the strangling waters. I have gazed upon the blue depths of many a placid lake, and the tumultuous rushing of many a mighty river, and have said, peace inhabits those waters; yet I have turned my steps away, to live yet another day. I have asked myself, whether suicide would be a crime in one to whom thus only the portals of the other world could be opened. I have done all, except presenting myself as a soldier or duellist, an object of destruction to my—no, *not* my fellow-mortals, and therefore I have shrunk away. They are not my fellows. The inextinguishable power of life in my frame, and their ephemeral existence, place us wide as the poles asunder. I could not raise a hand against the meanest or the most powerful among them.

Thus I have lived on for many a year—alone, and weary of myself—desirous of death, yet never dying—a mortal immortal. Neither ambition nor avarice can enter my mind, and the ardent love that gnaws at my heart, never to be returned—never to find an equal on which to expend itself—lives there only to torment me.

This very day I conceived a design by which I may end all—without self-slaughter, without making another man a Cain—an expedition, which mortal frame can never survive, even endued with the youth and strength that inhabits mine. Thus I shall put my immortality to the test, and rest for ever—or return, the wonder and benefactor of the human species.[3]

Before I go, a miserable vanity has caused me to pen these pages. I would not die, and leave no name behind. Three centuries have passed since I quaffed the fatal beverage: another year shall not elapse before, encountering gigantic dangers—warring with the powers of frost in their home—beset by famine, toil, and tempest—I yield this body, too tenacious a cage for a soul which thirsts for freedom, to the destructive elements of air and water—or, if I survive, my name shall be recorded as one of the most famous among the sons of men; and, my task achieved, I shall adopt more resolute means, and, by scattering and annihilating the atoms that compose my frame, set at liberty the life imprisoned within, and so cruelly prevented from soaring from this dim earth to a sphere more congenial to its immortal essence.

1833   1834

3. Cf. Walton in *Frankenstein*, who describes his expedition to the North Pole as conferring "inestimable benefit . . . on all mankind to the last generation," or Frankenstein, who likewise anticipates the gratitude of posterity: "A new species would bless me as its creator and source."

LETITIA ELIZABETH LANDON
1802–1838

Letitia Elizabeth Landon, whose initials became one of the most famous literary pseudonyms of nineteenth-century Britain, was born and educated in Chelsea, London. She published her first poem in the weekly *Literary Gazette* in March 1820, when she was seventeen, and soon thereafter became a principal writer and reviewer for the magazine. Her first important collection of poems, published in 1824, was *The Improvisatrice*—a work that suggests Landon's fascination with Germaine de Staël's *Corinne* and with the Italy that she never visited but encountered in the pages of Staël, the Shelleys, and Byron. It went through six editions in its first year and was followed by *The Troubadour, Catalogue of Pictures, and Historical Sketches* (1825), which went through four. She quickly followed these with *The Golden Violet* (1827), the first of many editions of her *Poetical Works* (1827), and *The Venetian Bracelet* (1829). She also wrote essays, short fiction, children's stories, several novels, and a play; and she edited—and contributed hundreds of poems to—the albums, gift books, and annual anthologies that became a staple of British literary production of the 1820s and 1830s. All this highly remunerative work appeared from the pen of "L.E.L.," the pseudonym that she first used in the *Literary Gazette* and that attracted increasing numbers of readers and also poetic responses, as it was disclosed by stages that the author behind the initials was female, young, and a great beauty. To this day many of Landon's books continue to be cataloged under the pseudonym, and one "feminist companion" to literature in English has an entry for "L.E.L." but none for "Landon."

Landon and Felicia Hemans, as "L.E.L." and "Mrs. Hemans," were the two best-selling poets of their time—the decade and a half following the deaths of Keats, Percy Shelley, and Byron in the early 1820s—and were major inspirations to subsequent writers such as Elizabeth Barrett and Christina Rossetti. Unlike Hemans, Landon attracted scandal, partly because of her casual social relations with men and partly because of her principal subject matter, the joys and especially the sorrows of female passion. (In her preface to *The Venetian Bracelet*, she attempted wittily, but without success, to forestall this biographical reading of her poems: "With regard to the frequent application of my works to myself, considering that I sometimes portrayed love unrequited, then betrayed, and again destroyed by death—may I hint the conclusions are not quite logically drawn, as assuredly the same mind cannot have suffered such varied modes of misery. However, if I must have an unhappy passion, I can only console myself with my own perfect unconsciousness of so great a misfortune.") There were rumors of affairs with, among others, William Jerdan, who was editor of the *Literary Gazette*, the journalist William Maginn, and the artist Daniel Maclise. She was engaged to the editor John Forster, future biographer of Dickens, but had to break the engagement because of these rumors. In 1838 she married someone she had known for only a short time, George Maclean, governor of the British settlement at Cape Coast Castle, west Africa (in what is now Ghana). She arrived with Maclean at Cape Coast in August 1838 and two months later was dead, reportedly from an overdose of prussic acid. Wild rumors—of suicide or of murder (at the hands, some speculated, of Maclean's jealous African mistress or mistresses)—began circulating when news of Landon's death reached England. They appear now to have been unfounded. The nineteenth-century public insisted, however, on using Landon's poetic personas to interpret the circumstances of her death.

Landon perfected, and reviewers helped maintain, several of these personas: the pseudonymous, therefore anonymous, writer of passionate love lyrics; the Romantic "improvisatrice" jotting down verses in the interstices of an intense social life; the renowned beauty who constantly fails in love and, in lamenting her crushed feelings, becomes the female equivalent of the Byronic hero; and an early version of the Victorian "poetess" composing songs to appeal to a burgeoning cult of domesticity. As in Hemans's poetry, some of these personas are not wholly compatible with some of the others. But their variety and vitality captivated readers.

From The Improvisatrice

Sappho's Song[1]

Farewell, my lute!—and would that I
    Had never waked thy burning chords!
Poison has been upon thy sigh,
    And fever has breathed in thy words.

5   Yet wherefore, wherefore should I blame
    Thy power, thy spell, my gentlest lute?
I should have been the wretch I am,
    Had every chord of thine been mute.

It was my evil star above,
10   Not my sweet lute, that wrought me wrong;
It was not song that taught me love,
    But it was love that taught me song.

If song be past, and hope undone,
    And pulse, and head, and heart, are flame;
15   It is thy work, thou faithless one!
    But, no!—I will not name thy name!

Sun-god, lute, wreath, are vowed to thee!
    Long be their light upon my grave—
My glorious grave—yon deep blue sea:
20   I shall sleep calm beneath its wave!

1824

---

1. From Landon's long poem *The Improvisatrice*, which she described in a prefatory comment as "an attempt to illustrate that species of inspiration common in Italy, where the mind is warmed from earliest childhood by all that is beautiful in Nature and glorious in Art." In this song, however, Landon's heroine, an artist and a poet who performs her compositions, looks to Greece and to the legends that had grown up around Sappho (7th century B.C.E.), founder of the lyric tradition, whose poems have survived only in fragmentary form. Presented as a renunciation of song, and even as a suicide note of sorts, this poem draws particularly on the legend that tells of how Sappho drowned herself in the Aegean Sea, distraught over the handsome boatman Phaon's refusal to reciprocate her love.

Lines

Written under a Picture of a Girl Burning a Love-Letter

The lines were filled with many a tender thing,
All the impassioned heart's fond communing.

I took the scroll: I could not brook
    An eye to gaze on it, save mine;
I could not bear another's look
    Should dwell upon one thought of thine.
5 My lamp was burning by my side,
    I held thy letter to the flame,
I marked the blaze swift o'er it glide,
    It did not even spare thy name.
Soon the light from the embers past,
10   I felt so sad to see it die,
So bright at first, so dark at last,
    I feared it was love's history.

1824

Love's Last Lesson

"Teach it me, if you can,—forgetfulness![1]
I surely shall forget, if you can bid me;
I who have worshipped thee, my god on earth,
I who have bow'd me at thy lightest word.
5 Your last command, 'Forget me,' will it not
Sink deeply down within my inmost soul?
Forget thee!—ay, forgetfulness will be
A mercy to me. By the many nights
When I have wept for that I dared not sleep,—
10 A dream had made me live my woes again,
Acting my wretchedness, without the hope
My foolish heart still clings to, though that hope
Is like the opiate which may lull a while,
Then wake to double torture; by the days
15 Pass'd in lone watching and in anxious fears,
When a breath sent the crimson to my cheek,
Like the red gushing of a sudden wound;
By all the careless looks and careless words
Which have to me been like the scorpion's stinging;
20 By happiness blighted, and by thee, for ever;
By thy eternal work of wretchedness;
By all my wither'd feelings, ruin'd health,
Crush'd hopes, and rifled heart, I will forget thee!

---

1. An allusion to Byron's *Manfred* 1.1.135–36: "What wouldst thou with us, son of mortals— say?"—to which Manfred replies, "Forgetfulness." Other Byronic echoes in lines 14–15, 18–23, 85– 86, and 95–98 further link Landon's speaker to the protagonists of *Childe Harold* and *Manfred*.

Alas! my words are vanity. Forget thee!
25 Thy work of wasting is too surely done.
The April shower may pass and be forgotten,
The rose fall and one fresh spring in its place,
And thus it may be with light summer love.
It was not thus with mine: it did not spring,
30 Like the bright colour on an evening cloud,
Into a moment's life, brief, beautiful;
Not amid lighted halls, when flatteries
Steal on the ear like dew upon the rose,
As soft, as soon dispersed, as quickly pass'd;
35 But you first call'd my woman's feelings forth,
And taught me love ere I had dream'd love's name.
I loved unconsciously: your name was all
That seem'd in language, and to me the world
Was only made for you; in solitude,
40 When passions hold their interchange together,
Your image was the shadow of my thought;
Never did slave, before his Eastern lord,
Tremble as I did when I met your eye,
And yet each look was counted as a prize;
45 I laid your words up in my heart like pearls
Hid in the ocean's treasure-cave. At last
I learn'd my heart's deep secret: for I hoped,
I dream'd you loved me; wonder, fear, delight,
Swept my heart like a storm; my soul, my life,
50 Seem'd all too little for your happiness;
Had I been mistress of the starry worlds
That light the midnight, they had all been yours,
And I had deem'd such boon but poverty.
As it was, I gave all I could—my love,
55 My deep, my true, my fervent, faithful love;
And now you bid me learn forgetfulness:
It is a lesson that I soon shall learn.
There is a home of quiet for the wretched,
A somewhat dark, and cold, and silent rest,
60 But still it is rest,—for it is the grave."

    She flung aside the scroll, as it had part
In her great misery. Why should she write?
What could she write? Her woman's pride forbade
To let him look upon her heart, and see
65 It was an utter ruin;—and cold words,
And scorn and slight, that may repay his own,
Were as a foreign language, to whose sound
She might not frame her utterance. Down she bent
Her head upon an arm so white that tears
70 Seem'd but the natural melting of its snow,
Touch'd by the flush'd cheek's crimson; yet life-blood
Less wrings in shedding than such tears as those.

    And this then is love's ending! It is like
The history of some fair southern clime.
75 Hot fires are in the bosom of the earth,

And the warm'd soil puts forth its thousand flowers,
Its fruits of gold, summer's regality,
And sleep and odours float upon the air:
At length the subterranean element
80 Breaks from its secret dwelling-place, and lays
All waste before it; the red lava stream
Sweeps like the pestilence; and that which was
A garden in its colours and its breath,
Fit for the princess of a fairy tale,
85 Is as a desert, in whose burning sands,
And ashy waters, who is there can trace
A sign, a memory of its former beauty?
It is thus with the heart; love lights it up
With hopes like young companions, and with joys
90 Dreaming deliciously of their sweet selves.

This is at first; but what is the result?
Hopes that lie mute in their own sullenness,
For they have quarrell'd even with themselves;
And joys indeed like birds of Paradise:[2]
95 And in their stead despair coils scorpion-like
Stinging itself;[3] and the heart, burnt and crush'd
With passion's earthquake, scorch'd and wither'd up,
Lies in its desolation,—this is love.

What is the tale that I would tell? Not one
100 Of strange adventure, but a common tale
Of woman's wretchedness; one to be read
Daily in many a young and blighted heart.
The lady whom I spake of rose again
From the red fever's couch, to careless eyes
105 Perchance the same as she had ever been.
But oh, how alter'd to herself! She felt
That bird-like pining for some gentle home
To which affection might attach itself,
That weariness which hath but outward part
110 In what the world calls pleasure, and that chill
Which makes life taste the bitterness of death.

And he she loved so well,—what opiate
Lull'd consciousness into its selfish sleep?—
He said he loved her not; that never vow
115 Or passionate pleading won her soul for him;
And that he guess'd not her deep tenderness.

Are words, then, only false? are there no looks,
Mute but most eloquent; no gentle cares
That win so much upon the fair weak things
120 They seem to guard? And had he not long read
Her heart's hush'd secret in the soft dark eye

2. In Eastern tales, the bird of Paradise never
rests on the earth [Landon's note].
3. In *The Giaour: A Fragment of a Turkish Tale*

(1813), Byron had written of how "The Mind, that
broods o'er guilty woes, / Is like the Scorpion girt
by fire" (lines 423–24).

Lighted at his approach, and on the cheek
Colouring all crimson at his lightest look?
This is the truth; his spirit wholly turn'd
125　To stern ambition's dream, to that fierce strife
Which leads to life's high places, and reck'd° not　　　　　　*cared*
What lovely flowers might perish in his path.

　　And here at length is somewhat of revenge:
For man's most golden dreams of pride and power
130　Are vain as any woman-dreams of love;
Both end in weary brow and wither'd heart,
And the grave closes over those whose hopes
Have lain there long before.

　　　　　　　　　　　　　　　　　　　　　　　　1827

Lines of Life

> Orphan in my first years, I early learnt
> To make my heart suffice itself, and seek
> Support and sympathy in its own depths.[1]

Well, read my cheek, and watch my eye, —
　　Too strictly school'd are they,
One secret of my soul to show,
　　One hidden thought betray.

5　I never knew the time my heart
　　Look'd freely from my brow;
It once was check'd by timidness,
　　'Tis taught by caution now.

I live among the cold, the false,
10　　And I must seem like them;
And such I am, for I am false
　　As those I most condemn.

I teach my lip its sweetest smile,
　　My tongue its softest tone;
15　I borrow others' likeness, till
　　Almost I lose my own.

I pass through flattery's gilded sieve,
　　Whatever I would say;
In social life, all, like the blind,
20　　Must learn to feel their way.

I check my thoughts like curbed steeds
　　That struggle with the rein;

1. The epigraph is by Landon herself. Her title may reference Shakespeare's sonnet 16, in which the speaker, questioning the power of art to bestow immortality, promotes the "lines of life" (line 9), i.e., the family lines engendered through the begetting of children, over the lines of poets and painters.

I bid my feelings sleep, like wrecks
    In the unfathom'd main.

25 I hear them speak of love, the deep,
    The true, and mock the name;
Mock at all high and early truth,
    And I too do the same.

I hear them tell some touching tale,
30   I swallow down the tear;
I hear them name some generous deed,
    And I have learnt to sneer.

I hear the spiritual, the kind,
    The pure, but named in mirth;
35 Till all of good, ay, even hope,
    Seems exiled from our earth.

And one fear, withering ridicule,
    Is all that I can dread;
A sword hung by a single hair
40   For ever o'er the head.

We bow to a most servile faith,
    In a most servile fear;
While none among us dares to say
    What none will choose to hear.

45 And if we dream of loftier thoughts,
    In weakness they are gone;
And indolence and vanity
    Rivet our fetters on.

Surely I was not born for this!
50   I feel a loftier mood
Of generous impulse, high resolve,
    Steal o'er my solitude!

I gaze upon the thousand stars
    That fill the midnight sky;
55 And wish, so passionately wish,
    A light like theirs on high.

I have such eagerness of hope
    To benefit my kind;
And feel as if immortal power
60   Were given to my mind.

I think on that eternal fame,
    The sun of earthly gloom,
Which makes the gloriousness of death,
    The future of the tomb —

65 That earthly future, the faint sign
    Of a more heavenly one;

— A step, a word, a voice, a look, —
Alas! my dream is done.

And earth, and earth's debasing stain,
70   Again is on my soul;
And I am but a nameless part
    Of a most worthless whole.

Why write I this? because my heart
    Towards the future springs,
75 That future where it loves to soar
    On more than eagle wings.

The present, it is but a speck
    In that eternal time,
In which my lost hopes find a home,
80   My spirit knows its clime.

Oh! not myself, — for what am I? —
    The worthless and the weak,
Whose every thought of self should raise
    A blush to burn my cheek.

85 But song has touch'd my lips with fire,
    And made my heart a shrine;
For what, although alloy'd, debased,
    Is in itself divine.

I am myself but a vile link
90   Amid life's weary chain;
But I have spoken hallow'd words,
    Oh do not say in vain!

My first, my last, my only wish,
    Say will my charmed chords
95 Wake to the morning light of fame,
    And breathe again my words?

Will the young maiden, when her tears
    Alone in moonlight shine —
Tears for the absent and the loved —
100   Murmur some song of mine?

Will the pale youth by his dim lamp,
    Himself a dying flame,
From many an antique scroll beside,
    Choose that which bears my name?

105 Let music make less terrible
    The silence of the dead;
I care not, so my spirit last
    Long after life has fled.

1829

The Fairy of the Fountains[1]

The Legend, on which this story is founded, is immediately taken from Mr. Thoms's most interesting collection. I have allowed myself some licence, in my arrangement of the story: but fairy tales have an old-established privilege of change; at least, if we judge by the various shapes which they assume in the progress of time, and by process of translation.

Why did she love her mother so?
It hath wrought her wondrous woe

Once she saw an armed knight
In the pale sepulchral night;
5   When the sullen starbeams throw
Evil spells on earth below;
And the moon is cold and pale,
And a voice is on the gale,
Like a lost soul's heavenward cry,
10   Hopeless in its agony.

He stood beside the castle gate,
The hour was dark, the hour was late;
With the bearing of a king
Did he at the portal ring,
15   And the loud and hollow bell
Sounded like a Christian's knell.
That pale child stood on the wall,
Watching there, and saw it all.
Then she was a child as fair
20   As the opening blossoms are:
But with large black eyes, whose light
Spoke of mystery and might.

The stately stranger's head was bound
With a bright and golden round;
25   Curiously inlaid, each scale
Shone upon his glittering mail;
His high brow was cold and dim,
And she felt she hated him.

1. From 1832 until her departure for Africa, Landon edited *Fisher's Drawing-Room Scrapbook*, a lavishly produced literary annual marketed, as its title suggests, as a stylish ornament for the homes of English people of taste. She wrote nearly all the verse that appeared in this annual, much of it on topics suggested by the books' pictures. "The Fairy of the Fountains" was first published in the *Drawing-Room Scrapbook*, but this poem, about forbidden sights, was not written to accompany a picture. Instead, Landon's source, as her headnote explains, was a book by the scholar who is now known mainly for being the coiner in 1846 of the term *folklore*, William J. Thoms. In Thoms's *Lays and Legends of France* (1834), one volume in his collection of romances and folktales from across Europe, he retold the story of the accursed fairy Mesuline. The legend had been part of European literature since the 14th century: then, Jean D'Arras wrote it down in French as part of his history of the Castle of Lusignan, which Melusine is said to have built for her husband. (The same legend also underlies Hans Christian Andersen's "The Little Mermaid" and the opera and ballet "Undine.") In "The Fairy of the Fountains" Landon retells the story in her turn. Her enigmatic account of this fatal woman and her haunted family history invites comparison with works such as Keats's *Lamia* and "La Belle Dame Sans Merci" and Coleridge's "Christabel."

Then she heard her mother's voice,
30 Saying, "'Tis not at my choice!
Woe for ever, woe the hour,
When you sought my secret bower,
Listening to the word of fear,
Never meant for human ear.
35 Thy suspicion's vain endeavour,
Woe! woe! parted us for ever."

Still the porter of the hall
Heeded not that crown'd knight's call,
When a glittering shape there came,
40 With a brow of starry flame;
And he led that knight again
O'er the bleak and barren plain.
He flung, with an appealing cry,
His dark and desperate arms on high;
45 And from Melusina's sight
Fled away through thickest night.
    Who has not, when but a child,
Treasured up some vision wild;
Haunting them with nameless fear,
50 Filling all they see or hear,
In the midnight's lonely hour,
With a strange mysterious power?
So a terror undefined
Entered in that infant mind;—
55 A fear that haunted her alone,
For she told her thought to none.

        Years passed on, and each one threw
O'er those walls a deeper hue;
Large and old the ivy leaves
60 Heavy hung around the caves,
Till the darksome rooms within,
Daylight never entered in.
And the spider's silvery line
Was the only thing to shine.
65   Years past on,—the fair child now
Wore maiden beauty on her brow—
Beauty such as rarely flowers
In a fallen world like ours.
She was tall;—a queen might wear
70 Such a proud imperial air;
She was tall, yet when unbound,
Swept her bright hair to the ground,
Glittering like the gold you see
On a young laburnum tree.
75 Yet her eyes were dark as night,
Melancholy as moonlight,
With the fierce and wilder ray
Of a meteor on its way.
Lonely was her childhood's time,
80 Lonelier was her maiden prime;

And she wearied of the hours
Wasted in those gloomy towers;
Sometimes through the sunny sky
She would watch the swallows fly,
85 Making of the air a bath,
    In a thousand joyous rings;
She would ask of them their path,
    She would ask of them their wings.
Once her stately mother came,
90 With her dark eye's funeral flame,
And her cheek as pale as death,
And her cold and whispering breath;
With her sable garments bound
By a mystic girdle° round,   *belt*
95 Which, when to the east she turned.
With a sudden lustre burned.
Once that ladye, dark and tall,
Stood upon the castle wall;
And she marked her daughter's eyes
100 Fix'd upon the glad sunrise,
With a sad yet eager look,
Such as fixes on a book
Which describes some happy lot,
Lit with joys that we have not.
105 And the thought of what has been,
    And the thought of what might be,
Makes us crave the fancied scene,
    And despise reality.
'Twas a drear and desert° plain   *lonely, barren*
110 Lay around their own domain;
But, far off, a world more fair
Outlined on the sunny air;
Hung amid the purple clouds,
With which early morning shrouds
115 All her blushes, brief and bright,
Waking up from sleep and night,
In a voice so low and dread,
As a voice that wakes the dead;
Then that stately lady said:
120 "Daughter of a kingly line,—
Daughter, too, of race like mine,—
Such a kingdom had been thine;
For thy father was a king,
Whom I wed with word and ring.
125 But in an unhappy hour,
Did he pass my secret bower,—
Did he listen to the word,
Mortal ear hath never heard;
From that hour of grief and pain
130 Might we never meet again.
    "Maiden, listen to my rede,°   *advice*
Punished for thy father's deed;
Here, an exile, I must stay,
While he sees the light of day.

135 Child, his race is mixed in thee,
With mine own more high degree.
Hadst thou at Christ's altar stood,
Bathed in His redeeming flood;
Thou of my wild race had known
140 But its loveliness alone.
Now thou hast a mingled dower,
Human passion—fairy power.
But forefend thee from° the last: *keep away from*
Be its gifts behind thee cast.
145 Many tears will wash away
Mortal sin from mortal clay.
Keep thou then a timid eye
On the hopes that fill yon sky;
Bend thou with a suppliant knee,
150 And thy soul yet saved may be;—
Saved by Him who died to save
Man from death beyond the grave."

Easy 'tis advice to give,
    Hard it is advice to take.
155 Years that lived—and years to live,
    Wide and weary difference make.
To that elder ladye's mood,
Suited silent solitude:
For her lorn° heart's wasted soil   *forlorn*
160 Now repaid not hope's sweet toil.
Never more could spring-flowers grow,
On the worn-out soil below;
But to the young Melusine,
Earth and heaven were yet divine.
165 Still illusion's purple light
    Was upon the morning tide,
And there rose before her sight
    The loveliness of life untried.
Three sweet genii,—Youth, Love, Hope,—
170 Drew her future horoscope.
Must such lights themselves consume?
Must she be her own dark tomb?
But far other thoughts than these—
Life's enchanted phantasies,
175 Were, with Melusina now,
Stern and dark, contracts her brow;
And her bitten lip is white,
As with passionate resolve.
Muttered she,—"It is my right;
180 On me let the task devolve:
Since such blood to me belongs;
    It shall seek its own bright sphere;
I will well avenge the wrongs
    Of my mother exiled here."

• • • • • •

185   Two long years are come and past,
     And the maiden's lot is cast;—
     Cast in mystery and power,
     Work'd out by the watching hour,
     By the word that spirits tell,
190   By the sign and by the spell.
     Two long years have come and gone,
     And the maiden dwells alone.
     For the deed which she hath done,
     Is she now a banished one;—
195   Banished from her mother's arms,
     Banished by her mother's charms,
     With a curse of grief and pain,
     Never more to meet again.
     Great was the revenge she wrought,
200   Dearly that revenge was bought.

     When the maiden felt her powers,
     Straight she sought her father's towers.
     With a sign, and with a word,
     Passed she on unseen, unheard.
205   One, a pallid minstrel born
     On Good Friday's mystic morn,[2]
     Said he saw a lady there,
     Tall and stately, strange and fair,
     With a stern and glittering eye,
210   Like a shadow gliding by.
     All was fear and awe next day,
     For the king had passed away.
     He had pledged his court at night,
     In the red grape's flowing light.
215   All his pages saw him sleeping;
     Next day there was wail and weeping.
     Halls and lands were wandered o'er,
     But they saw their king no more.
       Strange it is, and sad to tell,
220   What the royal knight befell.
     Far upon a desert land,
     Does a mighty mountain stand;
     On its summit there is snow,
     While the bleak pines moan below;
225   And within there is a cave
     Opened for a monarch's grave.
     Bound in an enchanted sleep
     She hath laid him still and deep.
     She, his only child, has made
230   That strange tomb where he is laid:
     Nothing more of earth to know,
     Till the final trumpet blow.
     Mortal lip nor mortal ear,
     Were not made to speak nor hear

2. People born on Good Friday supposedly had the power to see spirits.

235   That accursed word which sealed,—
      All those gloomy depths concealed.
        With a look of joy and pride,
      Then she sought her mother's side.
      Whispering, on her bended knee,
240   "Oh! my mother, joyous be;
      For the mountain torrents spring
      O'er that faithless knight and king."
      Not another word she spoke,
      For her speech a wild shriek broke;
245   For the widowed queen upsprung,
      Wild her pale thin hands she wrung.
      With her black hair falling round,
      Flung her desperate on the ground;
      While young Melusine stood by,
250   With a fixed and fearful eye.
        When her agony was past,
      Slowly rose the queen at last;
      With her black hair, like a shroud,
      And her bearing high and proud;
255   With the marble of her brow,
      Colder than its custom now;
      And her eye with a strange light,
      Seemed to blast her daughter's sight.
      And she felt her whole frame shrink,
260   And her young heart's pulses sink;
      And the colour left her mouth,
        As she saw her mother signing,
      One stern hand towards the south,
        Where a strange red star was shining.
265   With a muttered word and gaze,
      Fixed upon its vivid rays;
      Then she spoke, but in a tone,
      Her's, yet all alike her own.—
      "Spirit of our spirit-line,
270   Curse for me this child of mine.
      Six days yield not to our powers,
      But the seventh day is ours.
      By yon star, and by our line,
      Be thou cursed, maiden mine."
275   Then the maiden felt hot pain
      Run through every burning vein.
      Sudden, with a fearful cry,
      Writhes she in her agony;
      Burns her cheek as with a flame,
280   For the maiden knows her shame.

Part II

      By a lovely river's side,
      Where the water-lilies glide,
      Pale, as if with constant care

Of the treasures which they bear;
285 For those ivory vases hold
Each a sunny gift of gold.
And blue flowers on the banks,
Grow in wild and drooping ranks,
Bending mournfully above,
290 O'er the waters which they love;
But which bear off, day by day,
Their shadow and themselves away.
Willows by that river grow
With their leaves half green, half snow,
295 Summer never seems to be
Present all with that sad tree.
With its bending boughs are wrought
Tender and associate thought,
Of the wreaths that maidens wear
300 In their long-neglected hair.
Of the branches that are thrown
On the last, the funeral stone.
And of those torn wreaths that suit
Youthful minstrel's wasted lute.
305   But the stream is gay to-night
With the full moon's golden light,
And the air is sweet with singing;
And the joyous horn is ringing,
While fair groups of dancers round
310 Circle the enchanted ground.
And a youthful warrior stands
Gazing not upon those bands,
Not upon the lovely scene,
But upon its lovelier queen,
315 Who with gentle word and smile
Courteous prays his stay awhile.
    The fairy of the fountains, she
A strange and lovely mystery,
She of whom wild tales have birth,
320 When beside a winter hearth,
By some aged crone is told,
Marvel new or legend old.
But the ladye fronts° him there,   *faces*
He but sees she is so fair,
325 He but hears that in her tone
Dwells a music yet unknown;
He but feels that he could die
For the sweetness of her sigh.
But how many dreams take flight
330 With the dim enamoured night;
Cold the morning light has shone,
And the fairy train are gone,
Melted in the dewy air,
Lonely stands young Raymond there.
335 Yet not all alone, his heart

Hath a dream that will not part
From that beating heart's recess;
What that dream that lovers guess.

Yet another year hath flown
340 In a stately hall alone,
Like an idol in a shrine,
Sits the radiant Melusine.
It is night, yet o'er the walls,
Light, but light unearthly, falls.
345 Not from lamp nor taper thrown,
But from many a precious stone,
With whose variegated shade
Is the azure roof inlaid,
And whose coloured radiance throws
350 Hues of violet, and rose.
Sixty pillars, each one shining
With a wreath of rubies twining,
Bear the roof—the snow-white floor
Is with small stars studded o'er.
355 Sixty vases stand between,
Filled with perfumes for a queen;
And a silvery cloud exhales
Odours like those fragrant gales,
Which at eve float o'er the sea
360 From the purple Araby.
Nothing stirs the golden gloom
Of that dim enchanted room.
Not a step is flitting round,
Not a noise, except the sound.
365 Of the distant fountains falling,
With a soft perpetual calling,
To the echoes which reply
Musical and mournfully.

Sits the fairy ladye there,
370 Like a statue, pale and fair;
From her cheek the rose has fled,
Leaving deeper charms instead.
On that marble brow are wrought
Traces of impassioned thought;
375 Such as without shade or line,
Leave their own mysterious sign.
While her eyes, they are so bright,
Dazzle with imperious light.
Wherefore doth the maiden bend?
380 Wherefore doth the blush ascend,
Crimson even to her brow,
Sight nor step are near her now?
Hidden by her sweeping robe,
Near her stands a crystal globe,
385 Gifted with strange power to show
All that she desires to know.

First she sees her palace gate,
With its steps of marble state;
Where two kneeling forms seem weeping
390 O'er the watch which they are keeping.
While around the dusky boughs
Of a gloomy forest close,
Not for those that blush arose.
But she sees beside the gate,
395 A young and anxious palmer° wait;   *pilgrim*
Well she knows it is for her,
He has come a worshipper.
For a year and for a day,
Hath he worn his weary way;
400 Now a sign from that white hand,
And the portals open stand.
But a moment, and they meet,
Raymond kneels him at her feet;
Reading in her downcast eye,
405 All that woman can reply.
 Weary, weary had the hours
Passed within her fairy bowers;
She was haunted with a dream
Of the knight beside the stream.
410 Who hath never felt the sense
Of such charmed influence,
When the shapes of midnight sleep
One beloved object keep,
Which amid the cares of day
415 Never passes quite away?
Guarded for the sweetest mood
Of our happy solitude,
Linked with every thing we love,
Flower below or star above:
420 Sweet spell after sweet spell thrown
Till the wide world is its own.
 Turned the ladye deadly pale,
As she heard her lover's tale,
"Yes," she said, oh! low sweet word,
425 Only in a whisper heard.
"Yes, if my true heart may be
Worthy, Christian knight, of thee,
By the love that makes thee mine
I am deeply dearly thine.
430 But a spell is on me thrown,
Six days may each deed be shown,
But the seventh day must be
Mine, and only known to me.
Never must thy step intrude
435 On its silent solitude.
Hidden from each mortal eye
Until seven years pass by.
When these seven years are flown,
All my secret may be known.

440　But if, with suspicious eye,
　　Thou on those dark hours wilt pry,
　　Then farewell, beloved in vain,
　　Never might we meet again."
　　Gazing on one worshipped brow,
445　When hath lover spared a vow?
　　With an oath and with a prayer
　　Did he win the prize he sought,
　　Never was a bride so fair,
　　As the bride that Raymond brought
450　From the wood's enchanted bowers
　　To his old ancestral towers.
　　——— Oh, sweet love, could thy first prime
　　Linger on the steps of time,
　　Man would dream the unkind skies
455　Sheltered still a Paradise.
　　But, alas, the serpent's skill
　　Is amid our gardens still.
　　　Soon a dark inquiring thought
　　On the baron's spirit wrought:
460　She, who seemed to love him so,
　　Had she aught he might not know?
　　Was it woe, how could she bear
　　Grief he did not soothe nor share?
　　Was it guilt? no—heaven's own grace
465　Lightened in that loveliest face.
　　Then his jealous fancies rose,
　　(Our Lady keep the mind from those!)
　　Like a fire within the brain,
　　Maddens that consuming pain.
470　Henceforth is no rest by night,
　　Henceforth day has no delight.
　　Life hath agonies that tell
　　Of their late left native hell.
　　But mid their despair is none
475　Like that of the jealous one.
　　　'Tis again the fatal day,
　　When the ladye must away,
　　To her lonely palace made
　　Far within the forest shade,
480　Where the mournful fountains sweep
　　With a voice that seems to weep.
　　On that morn Lord Raymond's bride
　　Ere the daybreak leaves his side.
　　Never does the ladye speak,
485　But her tears are on his cheek,
　　And he hears a stifled moan
　　As she leaves him thus alone.
　　Hath she then complaint to make,
　　Is there yet some spell to break?
490　Come what will, of weal or woe,
　　'Tis the best the worst to know.

He hath followed—woe, for both,
That the knight forgot his oath.
   Where the silvery fountains fall,
495 Stands no more the charmed hall;
But the dismal yew trees droop,
And the pines above them stoop,
While the gloomy branches spread,
As they would above the dead,
500 In some church-yard large and drear
Haunted with perpetual fear.
Dark and still like some vast grave,
Near there yawns a night-black cave.
O'er its mouth wild ivy twines
505 There the daylight never shines.
Beast of prey or dragon's lair,
Yet the knight hath entered there.
   Dimly doth the distant day
Scatter an uncertain ray,
510 While strange shapes and ghastly eyes
Mid the spectral darkness rise.
But he hurries on, and near
He sees a sudden light appear,
Wan and cold like that strange lamp
515 Which amid the charnel's damp
Shows but brightens not the gloom
Of the corpse and of the tomb.
With a cautious step he steals
To the cave that light reveals.
520 'Tis such grotto as might be,
Nereïd's[3] home beneath the sea.
Crested with the small bright stars
Of a thousand rainbow spars.
And a fountain from the side
525 Pours beneath its crystal tide,
In a white and marble bath
Singing on its silvery path;
While a meteor's emerald rays
O'er the lucid water plays.—
530 Close beside, with wild flowers laid,
Is a couch of green moss made.
There he sees his lady lie;
Pain is in her languid eye,
And amid her hair the dew
535 Half obscures its golden hue;
Damp and heavy, and unbound,
Its wan clusters sweep around.
On her small hand leans her head,—
See the fevered cheek is red,
540 And the fiery colour rushes
To her brow in hectic blushes.—

---

3. In classical mythology, a sea nymph inhabiting an underwater cave.

What strange vigil is she keeping!
He can hear that she is weeping.—
He will fling him at her feet,
545   He will kiss way her tears.
Ah, what doth his wild eyes meet,
    What below that form appears?
Downwards from that slender waist,
By a golden zone° embraced,   *belt*
550 Do the many folds escape,
Of the subtle serpent's shape.—
Bright with many-coloured dyes
All the glittering scales arise,
With a red and purple glow
555 Colouring the waves below!
At the strange and fearful sight,
Stands in mute despair the knight,—
Soon to feel a worse despair,
Melusina sees him there!
560 And to see him is to part
With the idol of her heart,
Part as just the setting sun
Tells the fatal day is done.
Vanish all those serpent rings,
565 To her feet the lady springs,
And the shriek rings thro' the cell,
Of despairing love's farewell,—
Hope and happiness are o'er,
They can meet on earth no more.

     • • • • • •

570 Years have past since this wild tale—
Still is heard that lady's wail,
Ever round that ancient tower,
Ere its lord's appointed hour.
With a low and moaning breath
575 She must mark approaching death,
While remains Lord Raymond's line
Doomed to wander and to pine.
Yet, before the stars are bright,
On the evening's purple light,
580 She beside the fountain stands
Wringing sad her shadowy hands.
May our Lady, as long years
Pass with their atoning tears,
Pardon with her love divine
585 The fountain fairy—Melusine![4]

1835

4. Raymond, first Lord of Lusignan, died as a hermit, at Monserrat. Melusina's was a yet harsher doom: fated to flit over the earth, in pain and sorrow, as a spectre. Only when one of the race of Lusignan were about to die, does she become visible,—and wanders wailing around the Castle. Tradition also represents her shadow as hovering over the Fountain of Thirst.—*Thoms's Lays and Legends* [Landon's note].

APPENDIXES

General Bibliography

This bibliography consists of a list of suggested general readings on English literature. Bibliographies for the authors in *The Norton Anthology of English Literature* are available online in the NAEL Archive (digital.wwnorton.com/englishlit10abc and digital.wwnorton.com/englishlit10def).

Suggested General Readings

Histories of England and of English Literature

Even the most distinguished of the comprehensive general histories written in past generations have come to seem outmoded. Innovative research in social, cultural, and political history has made it difficult to write a single coherent account of England from the Middle Ages to the present, let alone to accommodate in a unified narrative the complex histories of Scotland, Ireland, Wales, and the other nations where writing in English has flourished. Readers who wish to explore the historical matrix out of which the works of literature collected in this anthology emerged are advised to consult the studies of particular periods listed in the appropriate sections of this bibliography. The multivolume *Oxford History of England* and *New Oxford History of England* are useful, as are the three-volume *Peoples of the British Isles: A New History*, ed. Stanford Lehmberg, 1992; the nine-volume *Cambridge Cultural History of Britain*, ed. Boris Ford, 1992; the three-volume *Cambridge Social History of Britain, 1750–1950*, ed. F. M. L. Thompson, 1992; and the multivolume *Penguin History of Britain*, gen. ed. David Cannadine, 1996–. For Britain's imperial history, readers can consult the five-volume *Oxford History of the British Empire*, ed. Roger Louis, 1998–99, as well as *Gender and Empire*, ed. Philippa Levine, 2004. Given the cultural centrality of London, readers may find particular interest in *The London Encyclopaedia*, ed. Ben Weinreb et al., 3rd ed., 2008; Roy Porter, *London: A Social History*, 1994; and Jerry White, *London in the Nineteenth Century: "A Human Awful Wonder of God,"* 2007, and *London in the Twentieth Century: A City and Its People*, 2001.

Similar observations may be made about literary history. In the light of such initiatives as women's studies, new historicism, and postcolonialism, the range of authors deemed significant has expanded, along with the geographical and conceptual boundaries of literature in English. Attempts to capture in a unified account the great sweep of literature from *Beowulf* to the early twenty-first century have largely given way to studies of individual genres, carefully delimited time periods, and specific authors. For these more focused accounts, see the listings by period. Among the large-scale literary surveys, *The Cambridge Guide to Literature in English*, 3rd ed., 2006, is useful, as is the nine-volume *Penguin History of Literature*, 1993–94. *The Feminist Companion to Literature in English*, ed. Virginia Blain, Isobel Grundy, and Patricia Clements, 1990, is an important resource, and the editorial materials in *The Norton Anthology of Literature by Women*, 3rd ed., 2007, eds. Sandra M. Gilbert and Susan Gubar, constitute a concise history and set of biographies of women authors since the Middle Ages. *Annals of English Literature, 1475–1950*, rev. 1961, lists important publications year by year, together with the significant literary events for each year. Six volumes have been published in the *Oxford English Literary History*, gen. ed. Jonathan Bate, 2002–: Laura Ashe, *1000–1350: Conquest and Transformation*;

James Simpson, *1350–1547: Reform and Cultural Revolution*; Philip Davis, *1830–1880: The Victorians*; Chris Baldick, *1830–1880: The Modern Movement*; Randall Stevenson, *1960–2000: The Last of England?*; and Bruce King, *1948–2000: The Internationalization of English Literature*. See also *The Cambridge History of Medieval English Literature*, ed. David Wallace, 1999; *The Cambridge History of Early Medieval English Literature*, ed. Clare E. Lees, 2012; *The Cambridge History of Early Modern English Literature*, ed. David Loewenstein and Janel Mueller, 2003; *The Cambridge History of English Literature, 1660–1780*, ed. John Richetti, 2005; *The Cambridge History of English Romantic Literature*, ed. James Chandler, 2009; *The Cambridge History of Victorian Literature*, ed. Kate Flint, 2012; and *The Cambridge History of Twentieth-Century English Literature*, ed. Laura Marcus and Peter Nicholls, 2005.

Helpful treatments and surveys of English meter, rhyme, and stanza forms are Paul Fussell Jr., *Poetic Meter and Poetic Form*, rev. 1979; Donald Wesling, *The Chances of Rhyme: Device and Modernity*, 1980; Charles O. Hartman, *Free Verse: An Essay in Prosody*, 1983; John Hollander, *Rhyme's Reason: A Guide to English Verse*, rev. 1989; Derek Attridge, *Poetic Rhythm: An Introduction*, 1995; Robert Pinsky, *The Sounds of Poetry: A Brief Guide*, 1998; Mark Strand and Eavan Boland, eds., *The Making of a Poem: A Norton Anthology of Poetic Forms*, 2000; Helen Vendler, *Poems, Poets, Poetry*, 3rd ed., 2010; Virginia Jackson and Yopie Prins, eds., *The Lyric Theory Reader*, 2013; and Jonathan Culler, *Theory of the Lyric*, 2015.

On the development and functioning of the novel as a form, see Ian Watt, *The Rise of the Novel*, 1957; Gérard Genette, *Narrative Discourse: An Essay in Method*, 1980; *Theory of the Novel: A Historical Approach*, ed. Michael McKeon, 2000; McKeon, *The Origins of the English Novel, 1600–1740*, 15th anniversary ed., 2002; and *The Novel*, ed. Franco Moretti, 2 vols., 2006–07. *The Cambridge History of the English Novel*, eds. Robert L. Caserio and Clement Hawes, 2012; *A Companion to the English Novel*, eds. Stephen Arata et al., 2015; eight volumes have been published from *The Oxford History of the Novel in English*, 2011–16. On women novelists and readers, see Nancy Armstrong, *Desire and Domestic Fiction: A Political History of the Novel*, 1987; and Catherine Gallagher, *Nobody's Story: The Vanishing Acts of Women Writers in the Marketplace, 1670–1820*, 1994.

On the history of playhouse design, see Richard Leacroft, *The Development of the English Playhouse: An Illustrated Survey of Theatre Building in England from Medieval to Modern Times*, 1988. For a survey of the plays that have appeared on these and other stages, see Allardyce Nicoll, *British Drama*, rev. 1962; the eight-volume *Revels History of Drama in English*, gen. eds. Clifford Leech and T. W. Craik, 1975–83; and Alfred Harbage, *Annals of English Drama, 975–1700*, 3rd ed., 1989, rev. S. Schoenbaum and Sylvia Wagonheim; and the three volumes of *The Cambridge History of British Theatre*, eds. Jane Milling, Peter Thomson, and Joseph Donohue, 2004.

On some of the key intellectual currents that are at once reflected in and shaped by literature and contemporary literary criticism, Arthur O. Lovejoy's classic studies *The Great Chain of Being*, 1936, and *Essays in the History of Ideas*, 1948, remain valuable, along with such works as Georg Simmel, *The Philosophy of Money*, 1907; Lovejoy and George Boas, *Primitivism and Related Ideas in Antiquity*, 1935; Norbert Elias, *The Civilizing Process*, orig. pub. 1939, English trans. 1969; Simone de Beauvoir, *The Second Sex*, 1949; Frantz Fanon, *Black Skin, White Masks*, 1952, new trans. 2008; Ernst Cassirer, *The Philosophy of Symbolic Forms*, 4 vols., 1953–96; Ernst Kantorowicz, *The King's Two Bodies: A Study in Medieval Political Theology*, 1957, new ed. 1997; Hannah Arendt, *The Human Condition*, 1958; Richard Popkin, *The History of Skepticism from Erasmus to Descartes*, 1960; M. H. Abrams, *Natural Supernaturalism: Tradition and Revolution in Romantic Literature*, 1971; Michel Foucault, *Madness and Civilization: A History of Insanity in the Age of Reason*, Eng.

trans. 1965, and *The Order of Things: An Archaeology of the Human Sciences*, Eng. trans. 1970; Gaston Bachelard, *The Poetics of Space*, Eng. trans. 1969; Martin Jay, *The Dialectical Imagination: A History of the Frankfurt School and the Institute of Social Research, 1923–1950*, 1973, new ed. 1996; Hayden White, *Metahistory*, 1973; Roland Barthes, *The Pleasure of the Text*, Eng. trans. 1975; Jacques Derrida, *Of Grammatology*, Eng. trans. 1976, and *Dissemination*, Eng. trans. 1981; Richard Rorty, *Philosophy and the Mirror of Nature*, 1979; Gilles Deleuze and Félix Guattari, *A Thousand Plateaus*, 1980; Raymond Williams, *Keywords: A Vocabulary of Culture and Society*, rev. 1983; Pierre Bourdieu, *Distinction: A Social Critique of the Judgment of Taste*, Eng. trans. 1984; Michel de Certeau, *The Practice of Everyday Life*, Eng. trans. 1984; Hans Blumenberg, *The Legitimacy of the Modern Age*, Eng. trans. 1985; Jürgen Habermas, *The Philosophical Discourse of Modernity*, Eng. trans, 1987; Slavoj Žižek, *The Sublime Object of Ideology*, 1989; Homi Bhabha, *The Location of Culture*, 1994; Judith Butler, *The Psychic Life of Power: Theories in Subjection*, 1997; and Sigmund Freud, *Writings on Art and Literature*, ed. Neil Hertz, 1997.

Reference Works

The single most important tool for the study of literature in English is the *Oxford English Dictionary*, 2nd ed. 1989, 3rd ed. in process. The most current edition is available online to subscribers. The *OED* is written on historical principles: that is, it attempts not only to describe current word use but also to record the history and development of the language from its origins before the Norman conquest to the present. It thus provides, for familiar as well as archaic and obscure words, the widest possible range of meanings and uses, organized chronologically and illustrated with quotations. The *OED* can be searched as a conventional dictionary arranged a–z and also by subject, usage, region, origin, and timeline (the first appearance of a word). Beyond the *OED* there are many other valuable dictionaries, such as *The American Heritage Dictionary* (5th ed., 2016), *The Oxford Dictionary of Abbreviations*, *The Concise Oxford Dictionary of English Etymology*, *The Oxford Dictionary of English Grammar*, *A New Dictionary of Eponyms*, *The Oxford Essential Dictionary of Foreign Terms in English*, *The Oxford Dictionary of Idioms*, *The Concise Oxford Dictionary of Linguistics*, *The Oxford Guide to World English*, and *The Concise Oxford Dictionary of Proverbs*. Other valuable reference works include *The Cambridge Encyclopedia of the English Language*, 2nd ed., ed. David Crystal, 2003; *The Concise Oxford Companion to the English Language*; *Pocket Fowler's Modern English Usage*; and the numerous guides to specialized vocabularies, slang, regional dialects, and the like.

There is a steady flow of new editions of most major and many minor writers in English, along with a ceaseless outpouring of critical appraisals and scholarship. James L. Harner's *Literary Research Guide: An Annotated List of Reference Sources in English Literary Studies* (6th ed., 2009; online ed. available to subscribers at www.mlalrg.org/public) offers thorough, evaluative annotations of a wide range of sources. For the historical record of scholarship and critical discussion, *The New Cambridge Bibliography of English Literature*, ed. George Watson, 5 vols. (1969–77) and *The Cambridge Bibliography of English Literature*, 3rd ed., 5 vols. (1941–2000) are useful. The *MLA International Bibliography* (also online) is a key resource for following critical discussion of literatures in English. Ranging from 1926 to the present; it includes journal articles, essays, chapters from collections, books, and dissertations, and covers folklore, linguistics, and film. The *Annual Bibliography of English Language and Literature* (ABELL), compiled by the Modern Humanities Research Association, lists monographs, periodical articles, critical editions of literary works, book reviews, and collections of essays published anywhere in the world; unpublished doctoral dissertations are covered for the period 1920–99 (available online to subscribers and as part of Literature Online, http://literature. proquest.com/marketing/index.jsp).

For compact biographies of English authors, see the multivolume *Oxford Dictionary of National Biography* (DNB), ed. H. C. G. Matthew and Brian Harrison, 2004; since 2004 the *DNB* has been extended online with three annual updates. Handy reference books of authors, works, and various literary terms and allusions include many volumes in the *Cambridge Companion* and *Oxford Companion* series (e.g., *The Cambridge Companion to Narrative*, ed David Herman, 2007; *The Oxford Companion to English Literature*, ed. Dinah Birch, rev. 2016; *The Cambridge Companion to Allegory*, ed. Rita Copeland and Peter Struck, 2010; etc.). Likewise, *The Princeton Encyclopedia of Poetry and Poetics*, ed. Roland Greene and others, 4th ed., is available online to subscribers in ProQuest Ebook Central. Handbooks that define and illustrate literary concepts and terms are *The Penguin Dictionary of Literary Terms and Literary Theory*, ed. J. A. Cuddon and M. A. R. Habib, 5th ed., 2015; William Harmon, *A Handbook to Literature*, 12th ed., 2011; *Critical Terms for Literary Study*, ed. Frank Lentricchia and Thomas McLaughlin, rev. 1995; and M. H. Abrams and Geoffrey Harpham, *A Glossary of Literary Terms*, 11th ed., 2014. Also useful are Richard Lanham, *A Handlist of Rhetorical Terms*, 2nd ed., 2012; Arthur Quinn, *Figures of Speech: 60 Ways to Turn a Phrase*, 1995; and the *Barnhart Concise Dictionary of Etymology*, ed. Robert K. Barnhart, 1995; and George Kennedy, *A New History of Classical Rhetoric*, 2009.

On the Greek and Roman backgrounds, see *The Cambridge History of Classical Literature* (vol. 1: *Greek Literature*, 1982; vol. 2: *Latin Literature*, 1989), both available online; *The Oxford Companion to Classical Literature*, ed. M. C. Howatson, 3rd ed., 2011; Gian Biagio Conte, *Latin Literature: A History*, 1994; *The Oxford Classical Dictionary*, 4th ed., 2012; Richard Rutherford, *Classical Literature: A Concise History*, 2005; and Mark P. O. Morford, Robert J. Lenardon, and Michael Sham, *Classical Mythology*, 10th ed., 2013. The Loeb Classical Library of Greek and Roman texts is now available online to subscribers at www.loebclassics.com.

Digital resources in the humanities have vastly proliferated since the previous edition of *The Norton Anthology of English Literature* and are continuing to grow rapidly. The NAEL Archive (accessed at digital.wwnorton.com/englishlit10abc and digital .wwnorton.com/englishlit10def) is the gateway to an extensive array of annotated texts, images, and other materials especially gathered for the readers of this anthology. Among other useful electronic resources for the study of English literature are enormous digital archives, available to subscribers: Early English Books Online (EEBO), http://eebo.chadwyck.com/home; Literature Online, http://literature.proquest.com/ marketing/index.jsp; and Eighteenth Century Collections Online (ECCO), www.gale .com/primary-sources/eighteenth-century-collections-online. There are also numerous free sites of variable quality. Many of the best of these are period or author specific and hence are listed in the period/author bibiliographies in the NAEL Archive. Among the general sites, one of the most useful and wide-ranging is Voice of the Shuttle (http://vos.ucsb.edu), which includes in its aggregation links to Bartleby.com and Project Gutenberg.

Literary Criticism and Theory

Nine volumes of the *Cambridge History of Literary Criticism* have been published, 1989– : *Classical Criticism*, ed. George A. Kennedy; *The Middle Ages*, ed. Alastair Minnis and Ian Johnson; *The Renaissance*, ed. Glyn P. Norton; *The Eighteenth Century*, ed. H. B. Nisbet and Claude Rawson; *Romanticism*, ed. Marshall Brown; *The Nineteenth Century ca. 1830–1914*, ed. M. A. R. Habib; *Modernism and the New Criticism*, ed. A. Walton Litz, Louis Menand, and Lawrence Rainey; *From Formalism to Poststructuralism*, ed. Raman Selden; and *Twentieth-Century Historical, Philosoph-*

ical, and Psychological Perspectives, ed. Christa Knellwolf and Christopher Norris. See also M. H. Abrams, *The Mirror and the Lamp: Romantic Theory and the Critical Tradition,* 1953; William K. Wimsatt and Cleanth Brooks, *Literary Criticism: A Short History,* 1957; René Wellek, *A History of Modern Criticism: 1750–1950,* 9 vols., 1955–93; Frank Lentricchia, *After the New Criticism,* 1980; and J. Hillis Miller, *On Literature,* 2002. Raman Selden, Peter Widdowson, and Peter Brooker have written *A Reader's Guide to Contemporary Literary Theory,* 5th ed., 2015. Other useful resources include *The Johns Hopkins Guide to Literary Theory and Criticism,* 2nd ed., 2004; *Literary Theory, an Anthology,* eds. Julie Rivkin and Michael Ryan, 1998; and *The Norton Anthology of Theory and Criticism,* 3rd ed., gen. ed. Vincent Leitch, 2018.

Modern approaches to English literature and literary theory were shaped by certain landmark works: William Empson, *Seven Types of Ambiguity,* 1930, 3rd ed. 1953, *Some Versions of Pastoral,* 1935, and *The Structure of Complex Words,* 1951; F. R. Leavis, *Revaluation,* 1936, and *The Great Tradition,* 1948; Lionel Trilling, *The Liberal Imagination,* 1950; T. S. Eliot, *Selected Essays,* 3rd ed. 1951, and *On Poetry and Poets,* 1957; Erich Auerbach, *Mimesis: The Representation of Reality in Western Literature,* 1953; William K. Wimsatt, *The Verbal Icon,* 1954; Northrop Frye, *Anatomy of Criticism,* 1957; Wayne C. Booth, *The Rhetoric of Fiction,* 1961, rev. ed. 1983; and W. J. Bate, *The Burden of the Past and the English Poet,* 1970. René Wellek and Austin Warren, *Theory of Literature,* rev. 1970, is a useful introduction to the variety of scholarly and critical approaches to literature up to the time of its publication. Jonathan Culler's *Literary Theory: A Very Short Introduction,* 1997, discusses recurrent issues and debates.

Beginning in the late 1960s, there was a significant intensification of interest in literary theory as a specific field. Certain forms of literary study had already been influenced by the work of the Russian linguist Roman Jakobson and the Russian formalist Viktor Shklovsky and, still more, by conceptions that derived or claimed to derive from Marx and Engels, but the full impact of these theories was not felt until what became known as the "theory revolution" of the 1970s and '80s. For Marxist literary criticism, see Georg Lukács, *Theory of the Novel,* 1920, trans. 1971; *The Historical Novel,* 1937, trans. 1983; and *Studies in European Realism,* trans. 1964; Walter Benjamin's essays from the 1920s and '30s represented in *Illuminations,* trans. 1986, and *Reflections,* trans. 1986; Mikhail Bakhtin's essays from the 1930s represented in *The Dialogic Imagination,* trans. 1981, and *Rabelais and His World,* 1941, trans. 1968; *Selections from the Prison Notebooks of Antonio Gramsci,* ed. and trans. Quintin Hoare and Geoffrey Smith, 1971; Raymond Williams, *Marxism and Literature,* 1977; Tony Bennett, *Formalism and Marxism,* 1979; Fredric Jameson, *The Political Unconscious: Narrative as a Socially Symbolic Act,* 1981; and Terry Eagleton, *Literary Theory: An Introduction,* 3rd ed., 2008, and *The Ideology of the Aesthetic,* 1990.

Structural linguistics and anthropology gave rise to a flowering of structuralist literary criticism; convenient introductions include Robert Scholes, *Structuralism in Literature: An Introduction,* 1974, and Jonathan Culler, *Structuralist Poetics,* 1975. Poststructuralist challenges to this approach are epitomized in such influential works as Jacques Derrida, *Writing and Difference,* 1967, trans. 1978, and Paul de Man, *Blindness and Insight: Essays in the Rhetoric of Contemporary Criticism,* 1971, 2nd ed., 1983. Poststructuralism is discussed in Jonathan Culler, *On Deconstruction,* 1982; Slavoj Žižek, *The Sublime Object of Ideology,* 1989; Fredric Jameson, *Postmodernism; or the Cultural Logic of Late Capitalism,* 1991; John McGowan, *Postmodernism and Its Critics,* 1991; and *Beyond Structuralism,* ed. Wendell Harris, 1996. A figure who greatly influenced both structuralism and poststructuralism is Roland Barthes, in *Mythologies,* trans. 1972, and *S/Z,* trans. 1974. Among other influential contributions to literary theory are the psychoanalytic approach in Harold Bloom, *The Anxiety of*

Influence, 1973; and the reader-response approach in Stanley Fish, *Is There a Text in This Class?: The Authority of Interpretive Communities*, 1980. For a retrospect on the theory decades, see Terry Eagleton, *After Theory*, 2003.

Influenced by these theoretical currents but not restricted to them, modern feminist literary criticism was fashioned by such works as Patricia Meyer Spacks, *The Female Imagination*, 1975; Ellen Moers, *Literary Women*, 1976; Elaine Showalter, *A Literature of Their Own*, 1977; and Sandra Gilbert and Susan Gubar, *The Madwoman in the Attic*, 1979. Subsequent studies include Jane Gallop, *The Daughter's Seduction: Feminism and Psychoanalysis*, 1982; Luce Irigaray, *This Sex Which Is Not One*, trans. 1985; Gayatri Chakravorty Spivak, *In Other Worlds: Essays in Cultural Politics*, 1987; Sandra Gilbert and Susan Gubar, *No Man's Land: The Place of the Woman Writer in the Twentieth Century*, 3 vols., 1988–94; Barbara Johnson, *A World of Difference*, 1989; Judith Butler, *Gender Trouble*, 1990; and the critical views sampled in Elaine Showalter, *The New Feminist Criticism*, 1985; *The Hélène Cixous Reader*, ed. Susan Sellers, 1994; *Feminist Literary Theory: A Reader*, ed. Mary Eagleton, 3rd ed., 2010; and *Feminisms: An Anthology of Literary Theory and Criticism*, eds. Robyn R. Warhol and Diane Price Herndl, 2nd ed., 1997; *The Cambridge Companion to Feminist Literary Theory*, ed. Ellen Rooney, 2006; *Feminist Literary Theory and Criticism*, ed. Sandra Gilbert and Susan Gubar, 2007; and *Feminist Literary Theory: A Reader*, ed. Mary Eagleton, 3rd ed., 2011.

Just as feminist critics used poststructuralist and psychoanalytic methods to place literature in conversation with gender theory, a new school emerged placing literature in conversation with critical race theory. Comprehensive introductions include *Critical Race Theory: The Key Writings That Formed the Movement*, eds. Kimberlé Crenshaw et al.; *The Routledge Companion to Race and Ethnicity*, ed. Stephen Caliendo and Charlton McIlwain, 2010; and *Critical Race Theory: An Introduction*, ed. Richard Delgado and Jean Stefancic, 3rd ed., 2017. For an important precursor in cultural studies, see Stuart Hall et al., *Policing the Crisis*, 1978. Seminal works include Henry Louis Gates, Jr., *The Signifying Monkey: A Theory of African-American Literature*, 1988; Patricia Williams, *The Alchemy of Race and Rights*, 1991; Toni Morrison, *Playing the Dark: Whiteness and the Literary Imagination*, 1992; Cornel West, *Race Matters*, 2001; and Gene Andrew Jarrett, *Representing the Race: A New Political History of African American Literature*, 2011. Helpful anthologies and collections of essays have emerged in recent decades, such as *The Oxford Companion to African American Literature*, eds., William L. Andrews, Frances Smith Foster, and Trudier Harris, 1997; also their *Concise Companion*, 2001; *The Cambridge Companion to Jewish American Literature*, eds. Hana Wirth-Nesher and Michael P. Kramer, 2003; *The Routledge Companion to Anglophone Caribbean Literature*, eds. Michael A. Bucknor and Alison Donnell, 2011; *The Routledge Companion to Latino/a Literature*, eds. Suzanne Bost and Frances R. Aparicio, 2013; *A Companion to African American Literature*, ed. Gene Andrew Jarrett, 2013; *The Routledge Companion to Asian American and Pacific Islander Literature*, ed. Rachel Lee, 2014; *The Cambridge Companion to Asian American Literature*, eds. Crystal Parikh and Daniel Y. Kim, 2015; and *The Cambridge Companion to British Black and Asian Literature (1945–2010)*, ed. Deirdre Osborne, 2016.

Gay literature and queer studies are represented in *Inside/Out: Lesbian Theories, Gay Theories*, ed. Diana Fuss, 1991; *The Lesbian and Gay Studies Reader*, eds. Henry Abelove, Michele Barale, and David Halperin, 1993; *The Columbia Anthology of Gay Literature: Readings from Western Antiquity to the Present Day*, ed. Byrne R. S. Fone, 1998; and by such books as Eve Sedgwick, *Between Men: English Literature and Male Homosocial Desire*, 1985, and *Epistemology of the Closet*, 1990; Diana Fuss, *Essentially Speaking: Feminism, Nature, and Difference*, 1989; Terry Castle, *The Apparitional Lesbian: Female Homosexuality and Modern Culture*, 1993; Leo Bersani, *Homos*, 1995; Gregory Woods, *A History of Gay Literature: The Male Tradition*,

1998; David Halperin, *How to Do the History of Homosexuality*, 2002; Judith Halberstam, *In a Queer Time and Place: Transgender Bodies, Subcultural Lives*, 2005; Heather Love, *Feeling Backward: Loss and the Politics of Queer History*, 2009; *The Cambridge History of Gay and Lesbian Literature*, eds. E. L. McCallum and Mikko Tuhkanen, 2014; and *The Cambridge Companion to Lesbian Literature*, ed. Jodie Medd, 2015.

New historicism is represented in Stephen Greenblatt, *Learning to Curse*, 1990; in the essays collected in *The New Historicism Reader*, ed. Harold Veeser, 1993; in *New Historical Literary Study: Essays on Reproducing Texts, Representing History*, eds. Jeffrey N. Cox and Larry J. Reynolds, 1993; and in Catherine Gallagher and Stephen Greenblatt, *Practicing New Historicism*, 2000. The related social and historical dimension of texts is discussed in Jerome McGann, *Critique of Modern Textual Criticism*, 1983; and *Scholarly Editing: A Guide to Research*, ed. D. C. Greetham, 1995. Characteristic of new historicism is an expansion of the field of literary interpretation still further in cultural studies; for a broad sampling of the range of interests, see Lawrence Grossberg, Cary Nelson, and Paula Treichler, eds., *Cultural Studies*, 1992; *The Cultural Studies Reader*, ed. Simon During, 3rd ed., 2007; and *A Cultural Studies Reader: History, Theory, Practice*, eds. Jessica Munns and Gita Rajan, 1996.

This expansion of the field is similarly reflected in postcolonial studies: see Frantz Fanon, *Black Skin, White Masks*, 1952, new trans. 2008, and *The Wretched of the Earth*, 1961, new trans. 2004; Edward Said, *Orientalism*, 1978, and *Culture and Imperialism*, 1993; *The Post-Colonial Studies Reader*, 2nd ed., 2006; and such influential books as Homi Bhabha, ed., *Nation and Narration*, 1990, and *The Location of Culture*, 1994; Robert J. C. Young, *Postcolonialism: An Historical Introduction*, 2001; Bill Ashcroft, Gareth Griffiths, and Helen Tiffin, *The Empire Writes Back: Theory and Practice in Post-Colonial Literatures*, 2nd ed. 2002; Elleke Boehmer, *Colonial and Postcolonial Literature*, 2nd ed. 2005; and *The Cambridge History of Postcolonial Literature*, ed. Ato Quayson, 2011; *The Cambridge Companion to the Postcolonial Novel*, ed. Ato Quayson, 2015; and *The Cambridge Companion to Postcolonial Poetry*, ed. Jahan Ramazani, 2017.

In the wake of the theory revolution, critics have focused on a wide array of topics, which can only be briefly surveyed here. One current of work, focusing on the history of emotion, is represented in Brian Massumi, *Parables for the Virtual*, 2002; Sianne Ngai, *Ugly Feelings*, 2005; *The Affect Theory Reader*, eds. Melissa Gregg and Gregory J. Seigworth, 2010; and Judith Butler, *Senses of the Subject*, 2015. A somewhat related current, examining the special role of traumatic memory in literature, is exemplified in Cathy Caruth, *Trauma: Explorations in Memory*, 1995; and Dominic LaCapra, *Writing History, Writing Trauma*, 2000. Work on the literary implications of cognitive science may be glimpsed in *Introduction to Cognitive Cultural Studies*, ed. Lisa Zunshine, 2010. Interest in quantitative approaches to literature was sparked by Franco Moretti, *Graphs, Maps, Trees: Abstract Models for Literary History*, 2005. For the growing field of digital humanities, see also Moretti, *Distant Reading*, 2013; *Defining Digital Humanities: A Reader*, eds. Melissa Terras, Julianne Nyhan, and Edward Vanhoutte, 2014; and *A New Companion to Digital Humanities*, eds. Susan Schreibman, Ray Siemens, and John Unsworth, 2nd ed., 2016. There has also been a flourishing of ecocriticism, or studies of literature and the environment, including *The Ecocriticism Reader: Landmarks in Literary Ecology*, eds. Cheryll Glotfelty and Harold Fromm, 1996; *Writing the Environment*, eds. Richard Kerridge and Neil Sammells, 1998; Jonathan Bate, *The Song of the Earth*, 2002; Lawrence Buell, *The Future of Environmental Criticism: Environmental Crisis and Literary Imagination*, 2005; Timothy Morton, *Ecology Without Nature*, 2009; and *The Oxford Handbook of Ecocriticism*, ed. Greg Garrard, 2014. Related are the emerging fields of animal studies and posthumanism, where key works include

Bruno Latour, *We Have Never Been Modern*, 1993; Steve Baker, *Postmodern Animal*, 2000; Jacques Derrida, *The Animal That Therefore I Am*, trans. 2008; Cary Wolfe, *Animal Rites: American Culture, the Discourse of Species, and Posthumanist Theory*, 2003, and *What is Posthumanism?* 2009; Kari Weil, *Thinking Animals: Why Animal Studies Now?* 2012; and Aaron Gross and Anne Vallely, eds. *Animals and the Human Imagination: A Companion to Animal Studies*, 2012; and *Critical Animal Studies: Thinking the Unthinkable*, ed. John Sorenson, 2014. The relationship between literature and law is central to such works as *Interpreting Law and Literature: A Hermeneutic Reader*, eds. Sanford Levinson and Steven Mailloux, 1988; *Law's Stories: Narrative and Rhetoric in the Law*, eds. Peter Brooks and Paul Gerwertz, 1998; and *Literature and Legal Problem Solving: Law and Literature as Ethical Discourse*, Paul J. Heald, 1998. Ethical questions in literature have been usefully explored by, among others, Geoffrey Galt Harpham in *Getting It Right: Language, Literature, and Ethics*, 1997, and Derek Attridge in *The Singularity of Literature*, 2004. Finally, approaches to literature, such as formalism and literary biography, that seemed superseded in the theoretical ferment of the late twentieth century, have had a powerful resurgence. A renewed interest in form is evident in Susan Stewart, *Poetry and the Fate of the Senses*, 2002; *Reading for Form*, eds. Susan J. Wolfson and Marshall Brown, 2007; and Caroline Levine, *Forms: Whole, Rhythm, Hierarchy, Network*, 2015. Interest in the history of the book was spearheaded by D. F. McKenzie's *Bibliography and the Sociology of Texts*, 1986; Jerome McGann's *The Textual Condition*, 1991; and Roger Chartier's *The Order of Books: Readers, Authors, and Libraries in Europe Between the Fourteenth and Eighteenth Centuries*, 1994. See also *The Cambridge History of the Book in Britain*, 7 vols., 1998–2017; and *The Practice and Representation of Reading in England*, eds. James Raven, Helen Small, and Naomi Tadmor, 2007; *The Book History Reader*, eds. David Finkelstein and Alistair McCleery, 2nd ed., 2006; and *The Cambridge Companion to the History of the Book*, ed. Leslie Howsam, 2014.

Anthologies representing a range of recent approaches include *Modern Criticism and Theory*, ed. David Lodge, 1988; *Contemporary Literary Criticism*, ed. Robert Con Davis and Ronald Schlieffer, 4th ed., 1998; and *The Norton Anthology of Theory and Criticism*, gen. ed. Vincent Leitch, 3rd ed., 2018.

Literary Terminology*

Using simple technical terms can sharpen our understanding and streamline our discussion of literary works. Some terms, such as the ones in section A, help us address the internal style, structure, form, and kind of works. Other terms, such as those in section B, provide insight into the material forms in which literary works have been produced.

In analyzing what they called "rhetoric," ancient Greek and Roman writers determined the elements of what we call "style" and "structure." Our literary terms are derived, via medieval and Renaissance intermediaries, from the Greek and Latin sources. In the definitions that follow, the etymology, or root, of the word is given when it helps illuminate the word's current usage.

Most of the examples are drawn from texts in this anthology.

Words **boldfaced** within definitions are themselves defined in this appendix. Some terms are defined within definitions; such words are *italicized*.

A. Terms of Style, Structure, Form, and Kind

accent (synonym "stress"): a term of **rhythm.** The special force devoted to the voicing of one syllable in a word over others. In the noun "accent," for example, the accent, or stress, is on the first syllable.

act: the major subdivision of a play, usually divided into **scenes.**

aesthetics (from Greek, "to feel, apprehend by the senses"): the philosophy of artistic meaning as a distinct mode of apprehending untranslatable truth, defined as an alternative to rational enquiry, which is purely abstract. Developed in the late eighteenth century by the German philosopher Immanuel Kant especially.

Alexandrine: a term of **meter.** In French verse a line of twelve syllables, and, by analogy, in English verse a line of six stresses. See **hexameter.**

allegory (Greek "saying otherwise"): saying one thing (the "vehicle" of the allegory) and meaning another (the allegory's "tenor"). Allegories may be momentary aspects of a work, as in **metaphor** ("John is a lion"), or, through extended metaphor, may constitute the basis of narrative, as in Bunyan's *Pilgrim's Progress*: this second meaning is the dominant one. See also **symbol** and **type.** Allegory is one of the most significant **figures of thought.**

alliteration (from Latin "litera," alphabetic letter): a **figure of speech.** The repetition of an initial consonant sound or consonant cluster in consecutive or closely positioned words. This pattern is often an inseparable part of the meter in Germanic languages, where the tonic, or accented **syllable,** is usually the first syllable. Thus all Old English poetry and some varieties of Middle English poetry use alliteration as part of their basic metrical practice. *Sir Gawain and the Green Knight,* line 1: "Sithen the sege and the assaut was sesed at Troye" (see vol. A, p. 204). Otherwise used for local effects; Stevie Smith, "Pretty," lines 4–5: "And in the pretty pool the pike stalks / He stalks his prey . . ." (see vol. F, p. 733).

*This appendix was devised and compiled by James Simpson with the collaboration of all the editors. We especially thank Professor Lara Bovilsky of the University of Oregon at Eugene, for her help.

allusion: Literary allusion is a passing but illuminating reference within a literary text to another, well-known text (often biblical or **classical**). Topical allusions are also, of course, common in certain modes, especially **satire.**

anagnorisis (Greek "recognition"): the moment of **protagonist's** recognition in a narrative, which is also often the moment of moral understanding.

anapest: a term of **rhythm.** A three-syllable foot following the rhythmic pattern, in English verse, of two unstressed (uu) syllables followed by one stressed (/). Thus, for example, "Illinois."

anaphora (Greek "carrying back"): a **figure of speech.** The repetition of words or groups of words at the beginning of consecutive sentences, clauses, or phrases. Blake, "London," lines 5–8: "In every cry of every Man, / In every Infant's cry of fear, / In every voice, in every ban . . ." (see vol. D, p. 141); Louise Bennett, "Jamaica Oman," lines 17–20: "Some backa man a push, some side-a / Man a hole him han, / Some a lick sense eena him head, / Some a guide him pon him plan!" (see vol. F, p. 860).

animal fable: a **genre.** A short narrative of speaking animals, followed by moralizing comment, written in a low style and gathered into a collection. Robert Henryson, "The Preaching of the Swallow" (see vol. A, p. 523).

antithesis (Greek "placing against"): a **figure of thought.** The juxtaposition of opposed terms in clauses or sentences that are next to or near each other. Milton, *Paradise Lost* 1.777–80: "They but now who seemed / In bigness to surpass Earth's giant sons / Now less than smallest dwarfs, in narrow room / Throng numberless" (see vol. B, p. 1514).

apostrophe (from Greek "turning away"): a **figure of thought.** An address, often to an absent person, a force, or a quality. For example, a poet makes an apostrophe to a Muse when invoking her for inspiration.

apposition: a term of **syntax.** The repetition of elements serving an identical grammatical function in one sentence. The effect of this repetition is to arrest the flow of the sentence, but in doing so to add extra semantic nuance to repeated elements. This is an especially important feature of Old English poetic style. See, for example, Caedmon's *Hymn* (vol. A, p. 31), where the phrases "heaven-kingdom's Guardian," "the Measurer's might," "his mind-plans," and "the work of the Glory-Father" each serve an identical syntactic function as the direct objects of "praise."

assonance (Latin "sounding to"): a **figure of speech.** The repetition of identical or near identical stressed vowel sounds in words whose final consonants differ, producing half-rhyme. Tennyson, "The Lady of Shalott," line 100: "His broad clear brow in sunlight glowed" (see vol. E, p. 149).

aubade (originally from Spanish "alba," dawn): a **genre.** A lover's dawn song or lyric bewailing the arrival of the day and the necessary separation of the lovers; Donne, "The Sun Rising" (see vol. B, p. 926). Larkin recasts the genre in "Aubade" (see vol. F, p. 930).

autobiography (Greek "self-life writing"): a **genre.** A narrative of a life written by the subject; Wordsworth, *The Prelude* (see vol. D, p. 362). There are subgenres, such as the spiritual autobiography, narrating the author's path to conversion and subsequent spiritual trials, as in Bunyan's *Grace Abounding.*

ballad stanza: a **verse form.** Usually a **quatrain** in alternating **iambic tetrameter** and **iambic trimeter** lines, rhyming abcb. See "Sir Patrick Spens" (vol. D, p. 36); Louise Bennett's poems (vol. F, pp. 857–61); Eliot, "Sweeney among the Nightingales" (vol. F, p. 657); Larkin, "This Be The Verse" (vol. F, p. 930).

ballade: a **verse form** A form consisting usually of three stanzas followed by a four-line envoi (French, "send off"). The last line of the first stanza establishes a **refrain,** which is repeated, or subtly varied, as the last line of each stanza. The form was derived from French medieval poetry; English poets, from the fourteenth to the sixteenth centuries especially, used it with varying stanza forms. Chaucer, "Complaint to His Purse" (see vol. A, p. 363).

bathos (Greek "depth"): a **figure of thought.** A sudden and sometimes ridiculous descent of tone; Pope, *The Rape of the Lock* 3.157–58: "Not louder shrieks to pitying heaven are cast, / When husbands, or when lapdogs breathe their last" (see vol. C, p. 518).

beast epic: a **genre.** A continuous, unmoralized narrative, in prose or verse, relating the victories of the wholly unscrupulous but brilliant strategist Reynard the Fox over all adversaries. Chaucer arouses, only to deflate, expectations of the genre in *The Nun's Priest's Tale* (see vol. A, p. 344).

biography (Greek "life-writing"): a **genre.** A life as the subject of an extended narrative. Thus Izaak Walton, *The Life of Dr. Donne* (see vol. B, p. 976).

blank verse: a **verse form.** Unrhymed **iambic pentameter** lines. Blank verse has no stanzas, but is broken up into uneven units (verse paragraphs) determined by sense rather than form. First devised in English by Henry Howard, earl of Surrey, in his translation of two books of Virgil's *Aeneid* (see vol. B, p. 141), this very flexible verse type became the standard form for dramatic poetry in the seventeenth century, as in most of Shakespeare's plays. Milton and Wordsworth, among many others, also used it to create an English equivalent to **classical epic.**

blazon: strictly, a heraldic shield; in rhetorical usage, a **topos** whereby the individual elements of a beloved's face and body are singled out for **hyperbolic** admiration. Spenser, *Epithalamion*, lines 167–84 (see vol. B, p. 495). For an inversion of the **topos,** see Shakespeare, Sonnet 130 (vol. B, p. 736).

burlesque (French and Italian "mocking"): a work that adopts the **conventions** of a genre with the aim less of comically mocking the genre than of satirically mocking the society so represented (see **satire**). Thus Pope's *Rape of the Lock* (see vol. C, p. 507) does not mock **classical epic** so much as contemporary mores.

caesura (Latin "cut") (plural "caesurae"): a term of **meter.** A pause or breathing space within a line of verse, generally occurring between syntactic units; Louise Bennett, "Colonization in Reverse," lines 5–8: "By de hundred, by de tousan, / From country an from town, / By de ship-load, by de plane-load, / Jamaica is Englan boun" (see vol. F, p. 858), where the caesurae occur in lines 5 and 7.

canon (Greek "rule"): the group of texts regarded as worthy of special respect or attention by a given institution. Also, the group of texts regarded as definitely having been written by a certain author.

catastrophe (Greek "overturning"): the decisive turn in **tragedy** by which the plot is resolved and, usually, the **protagonist** dies.

catharsis (Greek "cleansing"): According to Aristotle, the effect of **tragedy** on its audience, through their experience of pity and terror, was a kind of spiritual cleansing, or catharsis.

character (Greek "stamp, impression"): a person, personified animal, or other figure represented in a literary work, especially in narrative and drama. The more a character seems to generate the action of a narrative, and the less he or she seems merely to serve a preordained narrative pattern, the "fuller," or more "rounded," a character is said to be. A "stock" character, common particularly in many comic genres, will perform a predictable function in different works of a given genre.

chiasmus (Greek "crosswise"): a **figure of speech**. The inversion of an already established sequence. This can involve verbal echoes: Pope, "Eloisa to Abelard," line 104, "The crime was common, common be the pain" (see vol. C, p. 529); or it can be purely a matter of syntactic inversion: Pope, *Epistle to Dr. Arbuthnot*, line 8: "They pierce my thickets, through my grot they glide" (see vol. C, p. 544).

classical, classicism, classic: Each term can be widely applied, but in English literary discourse, "classical" primarily describes the works of either Greek or Roman antiquity. "Classicism" denotes the practice of art forms inspired by classical antiquity, in particular the observance of rhetorical norms of **decorum** and balance, as opposed to following the dictates of untutored inspiration, as in Romanticism. "Classic" denotes an especially famous work within a given **canon.**

climax (Greek "ladder"): a moment of great intensity and structural change, especially in drama. Also a **figure of speech** whereby a sequence of verbally linked clauses is made, in which each successive clause is of greater consequence than its predecessor. Bacon, *Of Studies*: "Studies serve for pastimes, for ornaments, and for abilities. Their chief use for pastimes is in privateness and retiring; for ornament, is in discourse; and for ability, is in judgement" (see vol. B, p. 1223–24).

comedy: a **genre.** A term primarily applied to drama, and derived from ancient drama, in opposition to **tragedy.** Comedy deals with humorously confusing, sometimes ridiculous situations in which the ending is, nevertheless, happy. A comedy often ends in one or more marriages. Shakespeare, *Twelfth Night* (see vol. B, p. 741).

comic mode: Many genres (e.g., **romance, fabliau, comedy**) involve a happy ending in which justice is done, the ravages of time are arrested, and that which is lost is found. Such genres participate in a comic mode.

connotation: To understand connotation, we need to understand **denotation.** While many words can denote the same concept—that is, have the same basic meaning—those words can evoke different associations, or connotations. Contrast, for example, the clinical-sounding term "depression" and the more colorful, musical, even poetic phrase "the blues."

consonance (Latin "sounding with"): a **figure of speech.** The repetition of final consonants in words or stressed syllables whose vowel sounds are different. Herbert, "Easter," line 13: "Consort, both heart and lute . . ." (see vol. B, p. 1258).

convention: a repeatedly recurring feature (in either form or content) of works, occurring in combination with other recurring formal features, which constitutes a convention of a particular genre.

couplet: a **verse form.** In English verse two consecutive, rhyming lines usually containing the same number of stresses. Chaucer first introduced the **iambic pentameter** couplet into English (*Canterbury Tales*); the form was later used in many types of writing, including drama; imitations and translations of **classical epic** (thus *heroic couplet*); essays; and **satire** (see Dryden and Pope). The *distich* (Greek "two lines") is a couplet usually making complete sense; Aemilia Lanyer, *Salve Deus Rex Judaeorum*, lines 5–6: "Read it fair queen, though it defective be, / Your excellence can grace both it and me" (see vol. B, p. 981).

dactyl (Greek "finger," because of the finger's three joints): a term of **rhythm.** A three-syllable foot following the rhythmic pattern, in English verse, of one stressed followed by two unstressed syllables. Thus, for example, "Oregon."

decorum (Latin "that which is fitting"): a rhetorical principle whereby each formal aspect of a work should be in keeping with its subject matter and/or audience.

deixis (Greek "pointing"): relevant to **point of view.** Every work has, implicitly or explicitly, a "here" and a "now" from which it is narrated. Words that refer to or imply this point from which the voice of the work is projected (such as "here," "there," "this," "that," "now," "then") are examples of deixis, or "deictics." This technique is especially important in drama, where it is used to create a sense of the events happening as the spectator witnesses them.

denotation: A word has a basic, "prosaic" (factual) meaning prior to the associations it connotes (see **connotation**). The word "steed," for example, might call to mind a horse fitted with battle gear, to be ridden by a warrior, but its denotation is simply "horse."

denouement (French "unknotting"): the point at which a narrative can be resolved and so ended.

dialogue (Greek "conversation"): a **genre.** Dialogue is a feature of many genres, especially in both the **novel** and drama. As a genre itself, dialogue is used in philosophical traditions especially (most famously in Plato's *Dialogues*), as the representation of a conversation in which a philosophical question is pursued among various speakers.

diction, or **"lexis"** (from, respectively, Latin *dictio* and Greek *lexis*, each meaning "word"): the actual words used in any utterance—speech, writing, and, for our purposes here, literary works. The choice of words contributes significantly to the style of a given work.

didactic mode (Greek "teaching mode"): **Genres** in a didactic mode are designed to instruct or teach, sometimes explicitly (e.g., sermons, philosophical **discourses, georgic**), and sometimes through the medium of fiction (e.g., **animal fable, parable**).

diegesis (Greek for "narration"): a term that simply means "narration," but is used in literary criticism to distinguish one kind of story from another. In a *mimetic* story, the events are played out before us (see **mimesis**), whereas in diegesis someone recounts the story to us. Drama is for the most part *mimetic*, whereas the novel is for the most part diegetic. In novels the narrator is not, usually, part of the action of the narrative; s/he is therefore extradiegetic.

dimeter (Greek "two measure"): a term of **meter.** A two-stress line, rarely used as the meter of whole poems, though used with great frequency in single poems by Skelton, e.g., "The Tunning of Elinour Rumming" (see vol. B, p. 39). Otherwise used for single lines, as in Herbert, "Discipline," line 3: "O my God" (see vol. B, p. 1274).

discourse (Latin "running to and fro"): broadly, any nonfictional speech or writing; as a more specific genre, a philosophical meditation on a set theme. Thus Newman, *The Idea of a University* (see vol. E, p. 64).

dramatic irony: a feature of narrative and drama, whereby the audience knows that the outcome of an action will be the opposite of that intended by a **character.**

dramatic monologue (Greek "single speaking"): a **genre.** A poem in which the voice of a historical or fictional **character** speaks, unmediated by any narrator, to an implied though silent audience. See Tennyson, "Ulysses" (vol. E, p. 156); Browning, "The Bishop Orders His Tomb" (vol. E, p. 332); Eliot, "The Love Song of J. Alfred Prufrock" (vol. F, p. 654); Carol Ann Duffy, "Medusa" and "Mrs Lazarus" (vol. F, pp. 1211–13).

ecphrasis (Greek "speaking out"): a **topos** whereby a work of visual art is represented in a literary work. Auden, "Musée des Beaux Arts" (see vol. F, p. 815).

elegy: a **genre.** In **classical** literature elegy was a form written in elegiac **couplets** (a **hexameter** followed by a **pentameter**) devoted to many possible topics. In Ovidian elegy a lover meditates on the trials of erotic desire (e.g., Ovid's *Amores*). The **sonnet** sequences of both Sidney and Shakespeare exploit this genre, and, while it was still practiced in classical tradition by Donne ("On His Mistress" [see vol. B, p. 942]), by the later seventeenth century the term came to denote the poetry of loss, especially through the death of a loved person. See Tennyson, *In Memoriam* (vol. E, p. 173); Yeats, "In Memory of Major Robert Gregory" (vol. F, p. 223); Auden, "In Memory of W. B. Yeats" (see vol. F, p. 815); Heaney, "Clearances" (vol. F, p. 1104).

emblem (Greek "an insertion"): a **figure of thought.** A picture allegorically expressing a moral, or a verbal picture open to such interpretation. Donne, "A Hymn to Christ," lines 1–2: "In what torn ship soever I embark, / That ship shall be my emblem of thy ark" (see vol. B, p. 966).

end-stopping: the placement of a complete syntactic unit within a complete poetic line, fulfilling the metrical pattern; Auden, "In Memory of W. B. Yeats," line 42: "Earth, receive an honoured guest" (see vol. F, p. 817). Compare **enjambment.**

enjambment (French "striding," encroaching): The opposite of **end-stopping,** enjambment occurs when the syntactic unit does not end with the end of the poetic line and the fulfillment of the metrical pattern. When the sense of the line overflows its meter and, therefore, the line break, we have enjambment; Auden, "In Memory of W. B. Yeats," lines 44–45: "Let the Irish vessel lie / Emptied of its poetry" (see vol. F, p. 817).

epic (synonym, *heroic poetry*): a **genre.** An extended narrative poem celebrating martial heroes, invoking divine inspiration, beginning in medias res (see **order**), written in a high style (including the deployment of **epic similes;** on high style, see **register**), and divided into long narrative sequences. Homer's *Iliad* and Virgil's *Aeneid* were the prime models for English writers of epic verse. Thus Milton, *Paradise Lost* (see vol. B, p. 1495); Wordsworth, *The Prelude* (see vol. D, p. 362); and Walcott, *Omeros* (see vol. F, p. 947). With its precise repertoire of stylistic resources, epic lent itself easily to **parodic** and **burlesque** forms, known as **mock epic;** thus Pope, *The Rape of the Lock* (see vol. C, p. 507).

epigram: a **genre.** A short, pithy poem wittily expressed, often with wounding intent. See Jonson, *Epigrams* (see vol. B, p. 1089).

epigraph (Greek "inscription"): a **genre.** Any formal statement inscribed on stone; also the brief formulation on a book's title page, or a quotation at the beginning of a poem, introducing the work's themes in the most compressed form possible.

epistle (Latin "letter"): a **genre.** The letter can be shaped as a literary form, involving an intimate address often between equals. The *Epistles* of Horace provided a model for English writers from the sixteenth century. Thus Wyatt, "Mine own John Poins" (see vol. B, p. 131), or Pope, "An Epistle to a Lady" (vol. C, p. 655). Letters can be shaped to form the matter of an extended fiction, as the eighteenth-century epistolary **novel** (e.g., Samuel Richardson's *Pamela*).

epitaph: a **genre.** A pithy formulation to be inscribed on a funeral monument. Thus Ralegh, "The Author's Epitaph, Made by Himself" (see vol. B, p. 532).

epithalamion (Greek "concerning the bridal chamber"): a **genre.** A wedding poem, celebrating the marriage and wishing the couple good fortune. Thus Spenser, *Epithalamion* (see vol. B, p. 491).

epyllion (plural "epyllia") (Greek: "little epic"): a **genre.** A relatively short poem in the meter of epic poetry. See, for example, Marlowe, *Hero and Leander* (vol. B, p 660).

essay (French "trial, attempt"): a **genre**. An informal philosophical meditation, usually in prose and sometimes in verse. The journalistic periodical essay was developed in the early eighteenth century. Thus Addison and Steele, periodical essays (see vol. C, p. 462); Pope, *An Essay on Criticism* (see vol. C, p. 490).

euphemism (Greek "sweet saying"): a **figure of thought.** The figure by which something distasteful is described in alternative, less repugnant terms (e.g., "he passed away").

exegesis (Greek "leading out"): interpretation, traditionally of the biblical text, but, by transference, of any text.

exemplum (Latin "example"): an example inserted into a usually nonfictional writing (e.g., sermon or **essay**) to give extra force to an abstract thesis. Thus Johnson's example of "Sober" in his essay "On Idleness" (see vol. C, p. 732).

fabliau (French "little story," plural *fabliaux*): a **genre.** A short, funny, often bawdy narrative in low style (see **register**) imitated and developed from French models, most subtly by Chaucer; see *The Miller's Prologue and Tale* (vol. A, p. 282).

farce (French "stuffing"): a **genre.** A play designed to provoke laughter through the often humiliating antics of stock **characters.** Congreve's *The Way of the World* (see vol. C, p. 188) draws on this tradition.

figures of speech: Literary language often employs patterns perceptible to the eye and/or to the ear. Such patterns are called "figures of speech"; in classical rhetoric they were called "schemes" (from Greek *schema*, meaning "form, figure").

figures of thought: Language can also be patterned conceptually, even outside the rules that normally govern it. Literary language in particular exploits this licensed linguistic irregularity. Synonyms for figures of thought are "trope" (Greek "twisting," referring to the irregularity of use) and "conceit" (Latin "concept," referring to the fact that these figures are perceptible only to the mind). Be careful not to confuse **trope** with **topos** (a common error).

first-person narration: relevant to **point of view,** a narrative in which the voice narrating refers to itself with forms of the first-person pronoun ("I," "me," "my," etc., or possibly "we," "us," "our"), and in which the narrative is determined by the limitations of that voice. Thus Mary Wollstonecraft Shelley, *Frankenstein.*

frame narrative: Some narratives, particularly collections of narratives, involve a frame narrative that explains the genesis of, and/or gives a perspective on, the main narrative or narratives to follow. Thus Chaucer, *Canterbury Tales*; Mary Wollstonecraft Shelley, *Frankenstein*; or Conrad, *Heart of Darkness.*

free indirect style: relevant to **point of view,** a narratorial voice that manages, without explicit reference, to imply, and often implicitly to comment on, the voice of a **character** in the narrative itself. Virginia Woolf, "A Sketch of the Past," where the voice, although strictly that of the adult narrator, manages to convey the child's manner of perception: "—I begin: the first memory. This was of red and purple flowers on a black background—my mother's dress."

genre and mode: The **style**, structure, and, often, length of a work, when coupled with a certain subject matter, raise expectations that a literary work conforms to a certain **genre** (French "kind"). Good writers might upset these expectations, but they remain aware of the expectations and thwart them purposefully. Works in different genres may nevertheless participate in the same **mode,** a broader category designating the fundamental perspectives governing various genres of writing. For mode, see **tragic, comic, satiric,** and **didactic modes.** Genres are fluid, sometimes very fluid (e.g., the **novel**); the word "usually" should be added to almost every account of the characteristics of a given genre!

georgic (Greek "farming"): a **genre.** Virgil's *Georgics* treat agricultural and occasionally scientific subjects, giving instructions on the proper management of farms. Unlike **pastoral,** which treats the countryside as a place of recreational idleness among shepherds, the georgic treats it as a place of productive labor. For an English poem that critiques both genres, see Crabbe, "The Village" (vol. C, p. 1019).

hermeneutics (from the Greek god Hermes, messenger between the gods and humankind): the science of interpretation, first formulated as such by the German philosophical theologian Friedrich Schleiermacher in the early nineteenth century.

heroic poetry: see **epic.**

hexameter (Greek "six measure"): a term of **meter.** The hexameter line (a six-stress line) is the meter of **classical** Latin **epic;** while not imitated in that form for epic verse in English, some instances of the hexameter exist. See, for example, the last line of a Spenserian stanza, *Faerie Queene* 1.1.2: "O help thou my weake wit, and sharpen my dull tong" (vol. B, p. 253), or Yeats, "The Lake Isle of Innisfree," line 1: "I will arise and go now, and go to Innisfree" (vol. F, p. 215).

homily (Greek "discourse"): a **genre.** A sermon, to be preached in church; *Book of Homilies* (see vol. B, p. 165). Writers of literary fiction sometimes exploit the homily, or sermon, as in Chaucer, *The Pardoner's Tale* (see vol. A, p. 329).

homophone (Greek "same sound"): a **figure of speech.** A word that sounds identical to another word but has a different meaning ("bear" / "bare").

hyperbaton (Greek "overstepping"): a term of **syntax.** The rearrangement, or inversion, of the expected word order in a sentence or clause. Gray, "Elegy Written in a Country Churchyard," line 38: "If Memory o'er their tomb no trophies raise" (vol. C, p. 999). Poets can suspend the expected syntax over many lines, as in the first sentences of the *Canterbury Tales* (vol. A, p. 261) and of *Paradise Lost* (vol. B, p. 1495).

hyperbole (Greek "throwing over"): a **figure of thought.** Overstatement, exaggeration; Marvell, "To His Coy Mistress," lines 11–12: "My vegetable love should grow / Vaster than empires, and more slow" (see vol. B, p. 1347); Auden, "As I Walked Out One Evening," lines 9–12: "'I'll love you, dear, I'll love you / Till China and Africa meet / And the river jumps over the mountain / And the salmon sing in the street" (see vol. F, p. 813).

hypermetrical (adj.; Greek "over measured"): a term of **meter;** the word describes a breaking of the expected metrical pattern by at least one extra syllable.

hypotaxis, or **subordination** (respectively Greek and Latin "ordering under"): a term of **syntax.** The subordination, by the use of subordinate clauses, of different elements of a sentence to a single main verb. Milton, *Paradise Lost* 9.513–15: "As when a ship by skillful steersman wrought / Nigh river's mouth or foreland, where the wind / Veers oft, as oft so steers, and shifts her sail; So varied he" (vol. B, p. 1654). The contrary principle to **parataxis.**

iamb: a term of **rhythm.** The basic foot of English verse; two syllables following the rhythmic pattern of unstressed followed by stressed and producing a rising effect. Thus, for example, "Vermont."

imitation: the practice whereby writers strive ideally to reproduce and yet renew the **conventions** of an older form, often derived from **classical** civilization. Such a practice will be praised in periods of classicism (e.g., the eighteenth century) and repudiated in periods dominated by a model of inspiration (e.g., Romanticism).

irony (Greek "dissimulation"): a **figure of thought.** In broad usage, irony designates the result of inconsistency between a statement and a context that undermines the statement. "It's a beautiful day" is unironic if it's a beautiful day; if, however, the weather is terrible, then the inconsistency between statement and context is ironic. The effect is often amusing; the need to be ironic is sometimes produced by censorship of one kind or another. Strictly, irony is a subset of allegory: whereas allegory says one thing and means another, irony says one thing and means its opposite. For an extended example of irony, see Swift's "Modest Proposal." See also **dramatic irony.**

journal (French "daily"): a **genre.** A diary, or daily record of ephemeral experience, whose perspectives are concentrated on, and limited by, the experiences of single days. Thus Pepys, *Diary* (see vol. C, p. 86).

lai: a **genre.** A short narrative, often characterized by images of great intensity; a French term, and a form practiced by Marie de France (see vol. A, p. 160).

legend (Latin "requiring to be read"): a **genre.** A narrative of a celebrated, possibly historical, but mortal **protagonist.** To be distinguished from **myth.** Thus the "Arthurian legend" but the "myth of Proserpine."

lexical set: Words that habitually recur together (e.g., January, February, March, etc.; or red, white, and blue) form a lexical set.

litotes (from Greek "smooth"): a **figure of thought.** Strictly, understatement by denying the contrary; More, *Utopia*: "differences of no slight import" (see vol. B, p. 47). More loosely, understatement; Swift, "A Tale of a Tub": "Last week I saw a woman flayed, and you will hardly believe how much it altered her person for the worse" (see vol. C, p. 274). Stevie Smith, "Sunt Leones," lines 11–12: "And if the Christians felt a little blue— / Well people being eaten often do" (see vol. F, p. 729).

lullaby: a **genre.** A bedtime, sleep-inducing song for children, in simple and regular meter. Adapted by Auden, "Lullaby" (see vol. F, p. 809).

lyric (from Greek "lyre"): Initially meaning a song, "lyric" refers to a short poetic form, without restriction of meter, in which the expression of personal emotion, often by a voice in the first person, is given primacy over narrative sequence. Thus "The Wife's Lament" (see vol. A, p. 123); Yeats, "The Wild Swans at Coole" (see vol. F, p. 223).

masque: a **genre.** Costly entertainments of the Stuart court, involving dance, song, speech, and elaborate stage effects, in which courtiers themselves participated.

metaphor (Greek "carrying across," etymologically parallel to Latin "translation"): One of the most significant **figures of thought,** metaphor designates identification or implicit identification of one thing with another with which it is not literally identifiable. Blake, "London," lines 11–12: "And the hapless Soldier's sigh / Runs in blood down Palace walls" (see vol. D, p. 141).

meter: Verse (from Latin *versus*, turned) is distinguished from prose (from Latin *prorsus*, "straightforward") as a more compressed form of expression, shaped by metrical norms. **Meter** (Greek "measure") refers to the regularly recurring sound pattern of verse lines. The means of producing sound patterns across lines differ in different poetic traditions. Verse may be **quantitative,** or determined by the quantities of syllables (set patterns of long and short syllables), as in Latin and Greek poetry. It may be **syllabic,** determined by fixed numbers of syllables in the line, as in the verse of Romance languages (e.g., French and Italian). It may be **accentual,** determined by the number of accents, or stresses in the line, with variable numbers of syllables, as in Old English and some varieties of Middle English alliterative verse. Or it may be **accentual-syllabic,** determined by the numbers of accents, but possessing a regular pattern of stressed and unstressed syllables, so as to produce regular numbers of syllables per line. Since Chaucer, English verse has worked primarily within the many possibilities of accentual-syllabic meter. The unit of meter is the **foot.** In English verse the number of feet per line corresponds to the number of accents in a line. For the types and examples of different meters, see **monometer, dimeter, trimester, tetrameter, pentameter,** and **hexameter.** In the definitions below, "u" designates one unstressed syllable, and "/" one stressed syllable.

metonymy (Greek "change of name"): one of the most significant **figures of thought.** Using a word to **denote** another concept or other concepts, by virtue of habitual association. Thus "The Press," designating printed news media. Fictional names often work by associations of this kind. Closely related to **synecdoche.**

mimesis (Greek for "imitation"): A central function of literature and drama has been to provide a plausible imitation of the reality of the world beyond the literary work; mimesis is the representation and imitation of what is taken to be reality.

mise-en-abyme (French for "cast into the abyss"): Some works of art represent themselves in themselves; if they do so effectively, the represented artifact also represents itself, and so ad infinitum. The effect achieved is called *"mise-en-abyme."* Hoccleve's *Complaint*, for example, represents a depressed man reading about a depressed man. This sequence threatens to become a *mise-en-abyme.*

monometer (Greek "one measure"): a term of **meter.** An entire line with just one stress; *Sir Gawain and the Green Knight*, line 15, "most (u) grand (/)" (see vol. A, p. 204).

myth: a **genre.** The narrative of **protagonists** with, or subject to, superhuman powers. A myth expresses some profound foundational truth, often by accounting for the origin of natural phenomena. To be distinguished from **legend.** Thus the "Arthurian legend" but the "myth of Proserpine."

novel: an extremely flexible **genre** in both form and subject matter. Usually in prose, giving high priority to narration of events, with a certain expectation of length, novels are preponderantly rooted in a specific, and often complex, social world; sensitive to the realities of material life; and often focused on one **character** or a small circle of central characters. By contrast with chivalric **romance** (the main European narrative genre prior to the novel), novels tend to eschew the marvelous in favor of a recognizable social world and credible action. The novel's openness allows it to participate in all modes, and to be co-opted for a huge variety of subgenres. In English literature the novel dates from the late seventeenth century and has been astonishingly successful in appealing to a huge readership, particularly in the nineteenth and twentieth centuries. The English and Irish tradition of the novel includes, for example, Fielding, Austen, the Brontë sisters, Dickens, George Eliot, Conrad, Woolf, Lawrence, and Joyce, to name but a few very great exponents of the genre.

novella: a **genre.** A short **novel,** often characterized by imagistic intensity. Conrad, *Heart of Darkness* (see vol. F, p. 73).

occupatio (Latin "taking possession"): a **figure of thought.** Denying that one will discuss a subject while actually discussing it; also known as "praeteritio" (Latin "passing by"). See Chaucer, *Nun's Priest's Tale*, lines 414–32 (see vol. A, p. 353).

ode (Greek "song"): a **genre.** A **lyric** poem in elevated, or high style (see **register**), often addressed to a natural force, a person, or an abstract quality. The Pindaric ode in English is made up of **stanzas** of unequal length, while the Horatian ode has stanzas of equal length. For examples of both types, see, respectively, Wordsworth, "Ode: Intimations of Immortality" (vol. D, p. 348); and Marvell, "An Horatian Ode" (vol. B, p. 1356), or Keats, "Ode on Melancholy" (vol. D, p. 981). For a fuller discussion, see the headnote to Jonson's "Ode on Cary and Morison" (vol. B, p. 1102).

omniscient narrator (Latin "all-knowing narrator"): relevant to **point of view.** A narrator who, in the fiction of the narrative, has complete access to both the deeds and the thoughts of all **characters** in the narrative. Thus Thomas Hardy, "On the Western Circuit" (see vol. F, p. 36).

onomatopoeia (Greek "name making"): a **figure of speech.** Verbal sounds that imitate and evoke the sounds they denotate. Hopkins, "Binsey Poplars," lines 10–12 (about some felled trees): "O if we but knew what we do / When we delve [dig] or hew— / Hack and rack the growing green!" (see vol. E, p. 598).

order: A story may be told in different narrative orders. A narrator might use the sequence of events as they happened, and thereby follow what **classical** rhetoricians called the *natural order*; alternatively, the narrator might reorder the sequence of events, beginning the narration either in the middle or at the end of the sequence of events, thereby following an *artificial order*. If a narrator begins in the middle of events, he or she is said to begin *in medias res* (Latin "in the middle of the matter"). For a brief discussion of these concepts, see Spenser, *Faerie Queene*, "A Letter of the Authors" (vol. B, p. 249). Modern narratology makes a related distinction, between *histoire* (French "story") for the natural order that readers mentally reconstruct, and *discours* (French, here "narration") for the narrative as presented. See also **plot** and **story.**

ottava rima: a **verse form.** An eight-line stanza form, rhyming abababcc, using **iambic pentameter;** Yeats, "Sailing to Byzantium" (see vol. F, p. 230). Derived from the Italian poet Boccaccio, an eight-line stanza was used by fifteenth-century English poets for inset passages (e.g., Christ's speech from the Cross in Lydgate's *Testament*, lines 754–897). The form in this rhyme scheme was used in English poetry for long narrative by, for example, Byron (*Don Juan*; see vol. D, p. 669).

oxymoron (Greek "sharp blunt"): a **figure of thought.** The conjunction of normally incompatible terms; Milton, *Paradise Lost* 1.63: "darkness visible" (see vol. B, p. 1497).

panegyric: a **genre.** Demonstrative, or epideictic (Greek "showing"), rhetoric was a branch of **classical** rhetoric. Its own two main branches were the rhetoric of praise on the one hand and of vituperation on the other. Panegyric, or eulogy (Greek "sweet speaking"), or encomium (plural *encomia*), is the term used to describe the speeches or writings of praise.

parable: a **genre.** A simple story designed to provoke, and often accompanied by, **allegorical** interpretation, most famously by Christ as reported in the Gospels.

paradox (Greek "contrary to received opinion"): a **figure of thought.** An apparent contradiction that requires thought to reveal an inner consistency. Chaucer, "Troilus's Song," line 12: "O sweete harm so quainte" (see vol. A, p. 362).

parataxis, or **coordination** (respectively Greek and Latin "ordering beside"): a term of **syntax.** The coordination, by the use of coordinating conjunctions, of different main clauses in a single sentence. Malory, *Morte Darthur*: "So Sir Lancelot departed and took his sword under his arm, and so he walked in his mantel, that noble knight, and put himself in great jeopardy" (see vol. A, p. 539). The opposite principle to **hypotaxis.**

parody: a work that uses the **conventions** of a particular genre with the aim of comically mocking a **topos,** a genre, or a particular exponent of a genre. Shakespeare parodies the topos of **blazon** in Sonnet 130 (see vol. B, p. 736).

pastoral (from Latin *pastor,* "shepherd"): a **genre.** Pastoral is set among shepherds, making often refined **allusion** to other apparently unconnected subjects (sometimes politics) from the potentially idyllic world of highly literary if illiterate shepherds. Pastoral is distinguished from **georgic** by representing recreational rural idleness, whereas the georgic offers instruction on how to manage rural labor. English writers had classical models in the *Idylls* of Theocritus in Greek and Virgil's *Eclogues* in Latin. Pastoral is also called bucolic (from the Greek word for "herdsman"). Thus Spenser, *Shepheardes Calender* (see vol. B, p. 241).

pathetic fallacy: the attribution of sentiment to natural phenomena, as if they were in sympathy with human feelings. Thus Milton, *Lycidas,* lines 146–47: "With cowslips wan that hang the pensive head, / And every flower that sad embroidery wears" (see vol. B, p. 1472). For critique of the practice, see Ruskin (who coined the term), "Of the Pathetic Fallacy" (vol. E, p. 386).

pentameter (Greek "five measure"): a term of **meter.** In English verse, a five-stress line. Between the late fourteenth and the nineteenth centuries, this meter, frequently employing an iambic rhythm, was the basic line of English verse. Chaucer, Shakespeare, Milton, and Wordsworth each, for example, deployed this very flexible line as their primary resource; Milton, *Paradise Lost* 1.128: "O Prince, O Chief of many thronèd Powers" (see vol. B, p. 1499).

performative: Verbal expressions have many different functions. They can, for example, be descriptive, or constative (if they make an argument), or performative, for example. A performative utterance is one that makes something happen in the world by virtue of its utterance. "I hereby sentence you to ten years in prison," if uttered in the appropriate circumstances, itself performs an action; it makes something happen in the world. By virtue of its performing an action, it is called a "performative." See also **speech act.**

peripeteia (Greek "turning about"): the sudden reversal of fortune (in both directions) in a dramatic work.

periphrasis (Greek "declaring around"): a **figure of thought.** Circumlocution; the use of many words to express what could be expressed in few or one; Sidney, *Astrophil and Stella* 39.1–4 (vol. B, p. 593).

persona (Latin "sound through"): originally the mask worn in the Roman theater to magnify an actor's voice; in literary discourse persona (plural *personae*) refers to the narrator or speaker of a text, whose voice is coherent and whose person need have no relation to the person of the actual author of a text. Eliot, "The Love Song of J. Alfred Prufrock" (see vol. F, p. 654).

personification, or **prosopopoeia** (Greek "person making"): a **figure of thought.** The attribution of human qualities to nonhuman forces or objects; Keats, "Ode on a Grecian Urn," lines 1–2: "Thou still unvanish'd bride of quietness, / Thou foster-child of silence and slow time" (see vol. D, p. 979).

plot: the sequence of events in a story as narrated, as distinct from **story,** which refers to the sequence of events as we reconstruct them from the plot. See also **order.**

point of view: All of the many kinds of writing involve a point of view from which a text is, or seems to be, generated. The presence of such a point of view may be powerful and explicit, as in many novels, or deliberately invisible, as in much drama. In some genres, such as the **novel,** the narrator does not necessarily tell the story from a position we can predict; that is, the needs of a particular story, not the **conventions** of the genre, determine the narrator's position. In other genres, the narrator's position is fixed by convention; in certain kinds of love poetry, for example, the narrating voice is always that of a suffering lover. Not only does the point of view significantly inform the style of a work, but it also informs the structure of that work.

protagonist (Greek "first actor"): the hero or heroine of a drama or narrative.

pun: a figure of thought. A sometimes irresolvable doubleness of meaning in a single word or expression; Shakespeare, Sonnet 135, line 1: "Whoever hath her wish, thou hast thy *Will*" (see vol. B, p. 736).

quatrain: a verse form. A stanza of four lines, usually rhyming abcb, abab, or abba. Of many possible examples, see Crashaw, "On the Wounds of Our Crucified Lord" (see vol. B, p. 1296).

refrain: usually a single line repeated as the last line of consecutive stanzas, sometimes with subtly different wording and ideally with subtly different meaning as the poem progresses. See, for example, Wyatt, "Blame not my lute" (see vol. B, p. 128).

register: The register of a word is its stylistic level, which can be distinguished by degree of technicality but also by degree of formality. We choose our words from different registers according to context, that is, audience and/or environment. Thus a chemist in a laboratory will say "sodium chloride," a cook in a kitchen "salt." A formal register designates the kind of language used in polite society (e.g., "Mr. President"), while an informal or colloquial register is used in less formal or more relaxed social situations (e.g., "the boss"). In **classical** and medieval rhetoric, these registers of formality were called *high style* and *low style*. A *middle style* was defined as the style fit for narrative, not drawing attention to itself.

rhetoric: the art of verbal persuasion. **Classical** rhetoricians distinguished three areas of rhetoric: the forensic, to be used in law courts; the deliberative, to be used in political or philosophical deliberations; and the demonstrative, or epideictic, to be used for the purposes of public praise or blame. Rhetorical manuals covered all the skills required of a speaker, from the management of style and structure to delivery. These manuals powerfully influenced the theory of poetics as a separate branch of verbal practice, particularly in the matter of style.

rhyme: a figure of speech. The repetition of identical vowel sounds in stressed syllables whose initial consonants differ ("dead" / "head"). In poetry, rhyme often links the end of one line with another. *Masculine rhyme*: full rhyme on the final syllable of the line ("decays" / "days"). *Feminine rhyme*: full rhyme on syllables that are followed by unaccented syllables ("fountains" / "mountains"). *Internal rhyme*: full rhyme within a single line; Coleridge, *The Rime of the Ancient Mariner*, line 7: "The guests are met, the feast is set" (see vol. D, p. 448). *Rhyme riche*: rhyming on **homophones**; Chaucer, *General Prologue*, lines 17–18: "seeke" / "seke." *Off rhyme* (also known as *half rhyme, near rhyme*, or *slant rhyme*): differs from perfect rhyme in changing the vowel sound and/or the concluding consonants expected of perfect rhyme; Byron, "They say that Hope is Happiness," lines 5–7: "most" / "lost." *Pararhyme*: stressed vowel sounds differ but are flanked by identical or similar consonants; Owen, "Miners," lines 9–11: "simmer" / "summer" (see vol. F, p. 163).

rhyme royal: a verse form. A **stanza** of seven **iambic pentameter** lines, rhyming ababbcc; first introduced by Chaucer and called "royal" because the form was used by James I of Scotland for his *Kingis Quair* in the early fifteenth century. Chaucer, "Troilus's Song" (see vol. A, p. 362).

rhythm: Rhythm is not absolutely distinguishable from **meter.** One way of making a clear distinction between these terms is to say that rhythm (from the Greek "to flow") denotes the patterns of sound within the feet of verse lines and the combination of those feet. Very often a particular meter will raise expectations that a given rhythm will be used regularly through a whole line or a whole poem. Thus in English verse the pentameter regularly uses an iambic rhythm. Rhythm, however, is much more fluid than meter, and many lines within the same poem using a single meter will frequently exploit different rhythmic possibilities. For examples of different rhythms, see **iamb, trochee, anapest, spondee,** and **dactyl.**

romance: a **genre.** From the twelfth to the sixteenth century, the main form of European narrative, in either verse or prose, was that of chivalric romance. Romance, like the later **novel,** is a very fluid genre, but romances are often characterized by (i) a tripartite structure of social integration, followed by disintegration, involving moral tests and often marvelous events, itself the prelude to reintegration in a happy ending, frequently of marriage; and (ii) aristocratic social milieux. Thus *Sir Gawain and the Green Knight* (see vol. A, p. 204); Spenser's (unfinished) *Faerie Queene* (vol. B, p. 249). The immensely popular, fertile genre was absorbed, in both domesticated and undomesticated form, by the novel. For an adaptation of romance, see Chaucer, *Wife of Bath's Tale* (vol. A, p. 300).

sarcasm (Greek "flesh tearing"): a **figure of thought.** A wounding expression, often expressed ironically; Boswell, *Life of Johnson*: Johnson [asked if any man of the modern age could have written the **epic** poem *Fingal*] replied, "Yes, Sir, many men, many women, and many children" (see vol. C, p. 844).

satire (Latin for "a bowl of mixed fruits"): a **genre.** In Roman literature (e.g., Juvenal), the communication, in the form of a letter between equals, complaining of the ills of contemporary society. The genre in this form is characterized by a first-person narrator exasperated by social ills; the letter form; a high frequency of contemporary reference; and the use of invective in **low-style** language. Pope practices the genre thus in the *Epistle to Dr. Arbuthnot* (see vol. C, p. 543). Wyatt's "Mine own John Poins" (see vol. B, p. 131) draws ultimately on a gentler, Horatian model of the genre.

satiric mode: Works in a very large variety of genres are devoted to the more or less savage attack on social ills. Thus Swift's travel narrative *Gulliver's Travels* (see vol. C, p. 279), his **essay** "A Modest Proposal" (vol. C, p. 454), Pope's mock-**epic** *The Dunciad* (vol. C, p. 555), and Gay's *Beggar's Opera* (vol. C, p. 659), to look no further than the eighteenth century, are all within a satiric mode.

scene: a subdivision of an **act,** itself a subdivision of a dramatic performance and/ or text. The action of a scene usually occurs in one place.

sensibility (from Latin, "capable of being perceived by the senses"): as a literary term, an eighteenth-century concept derived from moral philosophy that stressed the social importance of fellow feeling and particularly of sympathy in social relations. The concept generated a literature of "sensibility," such as the sentimental **novel** (the most famous of which was Goethe's *Sorrows of the Young Werther* [1774]), or sentimental poetry, such as Cowper's passage on the stricken deer in *The Task* (see vol. C, p. 1024).

short story: a **genre.** Generically similar to, though shorter and more concentrated than, the **novel;** often published as part of a collection. Thus Mansfield, "The Daughters of the Late Colonel" (see vol. F, p. 698).

simile (Latin "like"): a **figure of thought.** Comparison, usually using the word "like" or "as," of one thing with another so as to produce sometimes surprising analogies. Donne, "The Storm," lines 29–30: "Sooner than you read this line did the gale, / Like shot, not feared till felt, our sails assail." Frequently used, in extended form, in **epic** poetry; Milton, *Paradise Lost* 1.338–46 (see vol. B, p. 1504).

soliloquy (Latin "single speaking"): a **topos** of drama, in which a **character,** alone or thinking to be alone on stage, speaks so as to give the audience access to his or her private thoughts. Thus Viola's soliloquy in Shakespeare, *Twelfth Night* 2.2.17–41 (vol. B, p. 758).

sonnet: a verse form. A form combining a variable number of units of rhymed lines to produce a fourteen-line poem, usually in rhyming **iambic pentameter** lines. In English there are two principal varieties: the Petrarchan sonnet, formed by an octave (an eight-line stanza, often broken into two **quatrains** having the same rhyme scheme, typically abba abba) and a sestet (a six-line stanza, typically cdecde or cdcdcd); and the Shakespearean sonnet, formed by three quatrains (abab cdcd efef) and a **couplet** (gg). The declaration of a sonnet can take a sharp turn, or "volta," often at the decisive formal shift from octave to sestet in the Petrarchan sonnet, or in the final couplet of a Shakespearean sonnet, introducing a trenchant counterstatement. Derived from Italian poetry, and especially from the poetry of Petrarch, the sonnet was first introduced to English poetry by Wyatt, and initially used principally for the expression of unrequited erotic love, though later poets used the form for many other purposes. See Wyatt, "Whoso list to hunt" (vol. B, p. 121); Sidney, *Astrophil and Stella* (vol. B, p. 586); Shakespeare, *Sonnets* (vol. B, p. 723); Wordsworth, "London, 1802" (vol. D, p. 357); McKay, "If We Must Die" (vol. F, p. 854); Heaney, "Clearances" (vol. F, p. 1104).

speech act: Words and deeds are often distinguished, but words are often (perhaps always) themselves deeds. Utterances can perform different speech acts, such as promising, declaring, casting a spell, encouraging, persuading, denying, lying, and so on. See also **performative.**

Spenserian stanza: a verse form. The stanza developed by Spenser for *The Faerie Queene*; nine **iambic** lines, the first eight of which are **pentameters,** followed by one **hexameter,** rhyming ababbcbcc. See also, for example, Shelley, *Adonais* (vol. D, p. 856), and Keats, *The Eve of St. Agnes* (vol. D, p. 961).

spondee: a term of meter. A two-syllable foot following the rhythmic pattern, in English verse, of two stressed syllables. Thus, for example, "Utah."

stanza (Italian "room"): groupings of two or more lines, though "stanza" is usually reserved for groupings of at least four lines. Stanzas are often joined by rhyme, often in sequence, where each group shares the same metrical pattern and, when rhymed, rhyme scheme. Stanzas can themselves be arranged into larger groupings. Poets often invent new **verse forms,** or they may work within established forms.

story: a narrative's sequence of events, which we reconstruct from those events as they have been recounted by the narrator (i.e., the **plot**). See also **order.**

stream of consciousness: usually a **first-person** narrative that seems to give the reader access to the narrator's mind as it perceives or reflects on events, prior to organizing those perceptions into a coherent narrative. Thus (though generated from a **third-person** narrative) Joyce, *Ulysses*, "Penelope" (see vol. F, p. 604).

style (from Latin for "writing instrument"): In literary works the manner in which something is expressed contributes substantially to its meaning. The expressions "sun," "mass of helium at the center of the solar system," "heaven's golden orb" all designate "sun," but do so in different manners, or styles, which produce different meanings. The manner of a literary work is its "style," the effect of which is its "tone." We often can intuit the tone of a text; from that intuition of tone we can analyze the stylistic resources by which it was produced. We can analyze the style of literary works through consideration of different elements of style; for example, **diction, figures of thought, figures of speech, meter and rhythm, verse form, syntax, point of view.**

sublime: As a concept generating a literary movement, the sublime refers to the realm of experience beyond the measurable, and so beyond the rational, produced especially by the terrors and grandeur of natural phenomena. Derived especially from the first-century Greek treatise *On the Sublime*, sometimes attributed to Longinus, the notion of the sublime was in the later eighteenth century a spur to Romanticism.

syllable: the smallest unit of sound in a pronounced word. The syllable that receives the greatest stress is called the *tonic* syllable.

symbol (Greek "token"): a **figure of thought.** Something that stands for something else, and yet seems necessarily to evoke that other thing. In Neoplatonic, and therefore Romantic, theory, to be distinguished from **allegory** thus: whereas allegory involves connections between vehicle and tenor agreed by convention or made explicit, the meanings of a symbol are supposedly inherent to it. For discussion, see Coleridge, "On Symbol and Allegory" (vol. D, p. 507).

synecdoche (Greek "to take with something else"): a **figure of thought.** Using a part to express the whole, or vice versa; e.g., "all hands on deck." Closely related to **metonymy.**

syntax (Greek "ordering with"): Syntax designates the rules by which sentences are constructed in a given language. Discussion of meter is impossible without some reference to syntax, since the overall effect of a poem is, in part, always the product of a subtle balance of meter and sentence construction. Syntax is also essential to the understanding of prose style, since prose writers, deprived of the full shaping possibilities of meter, rely all the more heavily on syntactic resources. A working command of syntactical practice requires an understanding of the parts of speech (nouns, verbs, adjectives, adverbs, conjunctions, pronouns, prepositions, and interjections), since writers exploit syntactic possibilities by using particular combinations and concentrations of the parts of speech.

taste (from Italian "touch"): Although medieval monastic traditions used eating and tasting as a metaphor for reading, the concept of taste as a personal ideal to be cultivated by, and applied to, the appreciation and judgment of works of art in general was developed in the eighteenth century.

tercet: a **verse form.** A stanza or group of three lines, used in larger forms such as **terza rima,** the **Petrarchan sonnet,** and the **villanelle.**

terza rima: a **verse form.** A sequence of rhymed **tercets** linked by rhyme thus: aba bcb cdc, etc. first used extensively by Dante in *The Divine Comedy*, the form was adapted in English **iambic pentameters** by Wyatt and revived in the nineteenth century. See Wyatt, "Mine own John Poins" (vol. B, p. 131); Shelley, "Ode to the West Wind" (vol. D, p. 806); and Morris, "The Defence of Guinevere" (vol. E, p. 560). For modern adaptations see Eliot, lines 78–149 (though unrhymed) of "Little Gidding" (vol. F, pp. 679–81); Heaney, "Station Island" (vol. F, p. 1102); Walcott, *Omeros* (vol. F, p. 947).

tetrameter (Greek "four measure"): a term of **meter.** A line with four stresses. Coleridge, *Christabel*, line 31: "She stole along, she nothing spoke" (see vol. D, p. 468).

theme (Greek "proposition"): In literary criticism the term designates what the work is about; the theme is the concept that unifies a given work of literature.

third-person narration: relevant to **point of view.** A narration in which the narrator recounts a narrative of **characters** referred to explicitly or implicitly by third-person pronouns ("he," she," etc.), without the limitation of a **first-person narration.** Thus Johnson, *The History of Rasselas.*

topographical poem (Greek "place writing"): a **genre.** A poem devoted to the meditative description of particular places. Thus Gray, "Ode on a Distant Prospect of Eton College" (see vol. C, p. 994).

topos (Greek "place," plural *topoi*): a commonplace in the content of a given kind of literature. Originally, in **classical** rhetoric, the topoi were tried-and-tested stimuli to literary invention: lists of standard headings under which a subject might be investigated. In medieval narrative poems, for example, it was commonplace to begin with a description of spring. Writers did, of course, render the commonplace uncommon, as in Chaucer's spring scene at the opening of *The Canterbury Tales* (see vol. A, p. 261).

tradition (from Latin "passing on"): A literary tradition is whatever is passed on or revived from the past in a single literary culture, or drawn from others to enrich a writer's culture. "Tradition" is fluid in reference, ranging from small to large referents: thus it may refer to a relatively small aspect of texts (e.g., the tradition of **iambic pentameter**), or it may, at the other extreme, refer to the body of texts that constitute a **canon.**

tragedy: a **genre.** A dramatic representation of the fall of kings or nobles, beginning in happiness and ending in catastrophe. Later transferred to other social milieux. The opposite of **comedy;** thus Shakespeare, *Othello* (see vol. B, p. 806).

tragic mode: Many genres (**epic** poetry, **legend**ary chronicles, **tragedy,** the **novel**) either do or can participate in a tragic mode, by representing the fall of noble **protagonists** and the irreparable ravages of human society and history.

tragicomedy: a **genre.** A play in which potentially tragic events turn out to have a happy, or **comic,** ending. Thus Shakespeare, *Measure for Measure.*

translation (Latin "carrying across"): the rendering of a text written in one language into another.

trimeter (Greek "three measure"): a term of **meter.** A line with three stresses. Herbert, "Discipline," line 1: "Throw away thy rod" (see vol. B, p. 1274).

triplet: a **verse form.** A **tercet** rhyming on the same sound. Pope inserts triplets among heroic **couplets** to emphasize a particular thought; see *Essay on Criticism,* 315–17 (vol. C, p. 497).

trochee: a term of **rhythm.** A two-syllable foot following the pattern, in English verse, of stressed followed by unstressed syllable, producing a falling effect. Thus, for example, "Texas."

type (Greek "impression, figure"): a **figure of thought.** In Christian allegorical interpretation of the Old Testament, pre-Christian figures were regarded as "types," or foreshadowings, of Christ or the Christian dispensation. *Typology* has been the source of much visual and literary art in which the parallelisms between old and new are extended to nonbiblical figures; thus the virtuous plowman in *Piers Plowman* becomes a type of Christ.

unities: According to a theory supposedly derived from Aristotle's *Poetics,* the events represented in a play should have unity of time, place, and action: that the play take up no more time than the time of the play, or at most a day; that the space of action should be within a single city; and that there should be no subplot. See Johnson, *The Preface to Shakespeare* (vol. C, p. 807).

vernacular (from Latin *verna*, "servant"): the language of the people, as distinguished from learned and arcane languages. From the later Middle Ages especially, the "vernacular" languages and literatures of Europe distinguished themselves from the learned languages and literatures of Latin, Greek, and Hebrew.

verse form: The terms related to **meter** and **rhythm** describe the shape of individual lines. Lines of verse are combined to produce larger groupings, called verse forms. These larger groupings are in the first instance **stanzas.** The combination of a certain meter and stanza shape constitutes the verse form, of which there are many standard kinds.

villanelle: a **verse form.** A fixed form of usually five **tercets** and a **quatrain** employing only two rhyme sounds altogether, rhyming aba for the tercets and abaa for the quatrain, with a complex pattern of two **refrains.** Derived from a French fixed form. Thomas, "Do Not Go Gentle into That Good Night" (see vol. F, p. 833).

wit: Originally a synonym for "reason" in Old and Middle English, "wit" became a literary ideal in the Renaissance as brilliant play of the full range of mental resources. For eighteenth-century writers, the notion necessarily involved pleasing expression, as in Pope's definition of true wit as "Nature to advantage dressed, / What oft was thought, but ne'er so well expressed" (*Essay on Criticism*, lines 297–98; see vol. C, p. 496–97). See also Johnson, *Lives of the Poets*, "Cowley," on "metaphysical wit" (see vol. C, p. 817). Romantic theory of the imagination deprived wit of its full range of apprehension, whence the word came to be restricted to its modern sense, as the clever play of mind that produces laughter.

zeugma (Greek "a yoking"): a **figure of thought.** A figure whereby one word applies to two or more words in a sentence, and in which the applications are surprising, either because one is unusual, or because the applications are made in very different ways; Pope, *Rape of the Lock* 3.7–8, in which the word "take" is used in two senses: "Here thou, great Anna! whom three realms obey, / Dost sometimes counsel take— and sometimes tea" (see vol. C, p. 515).

B: Publishing History, Censorship

By the time we read texts in published books, they have already been treated—that is, changed by authors, editors, and printers—in many ways. Although there are differences across history, in each period literary works are subject to pressures of many kinds, which apply before, while, and after an author writes. The pressures might be financial, as in the relations of author and patron; commercial, as in the marketing of books; and legal, as in, during some periods, the negotiation through official and unofficial censorship. In addition, texts in all periods undergo technological processes, as they move from the material forms in which an author produced them to the forms in which they are presented to readers. Some of the terms below designate important material forms in which books were produced, disseminated, and surveyed across the historical span of this anthology. Others designate the skills developed to understand these processes. The anthology's introductions to individual periods discuss the particular forms these phenomena took in different eras.

bookseller: In England, and particularly in London, commercial bookmaking and -selling enterprises came into being in the early fourteenth century. These were loose organizations of artisans who usually lived in the same neighborhoods (around St. Paul's Cathedral in London). A bookseller or dealer would coordinate the production of hand-copied books for wealthy patrons (see **patronage**), who would order books to be custom-made. After the introduction of **printing** in the late fifteenth century, authors generally sold the rights to their work to booksellers, without any further **royalties.** Booksellers, who often had their own shops, belonged to the **Stationers' Company.** This system lasted into the eighteenth century. In 1710, however, authors were for the first time granted **copyright,** which tipped the commercial balance in their favor, against booksellers.

censorship: The term applies to any mechanism for restricting what can be published. Historically, the reasons for imposing censorship are heresy, sedition, blasphemy, libel, or obscenity. External censorship is imposed by institutions having legislative sanctions at their disposal. Thus the pre-Reformation Church imposed the Constitutions of Archbishop Arundel of 1409, aimed at repressing the Lollard "heresy." After the Reformation, some key events in the history of censorship are as follows: 1547, when anti-Lollard legislation and legislation made by Henry VIII concerning treason by writing (1534) were abolished; the Licensing Order of 1643, which legislated that works be licensed, through the Stationers' Company, prior to publication; and 1695, when the last such Act stipulating prepublication licensing lapsed. Postpublication censorship continued in different periods for different reasons. Thus, for example, British publication of D. H. Lawrence's *Lady Chatterley's Lover* (1928) was obstructed (though unsuccessfully) in 1960, under the Obscene Publications Act of 1959. Censorship can also be international: although not published in Iran, Salman Rushdie's *Satanic Verses* (1988) was censored in that country, where the leader, Ayatollah Ruhollah Khomeini, proclaimed a fatwa (religious decree) promising the author's execution. Very often censorship is not imposed externally, however: authors or publishers can censor work in anticipation of what will incur the wrath of readers or the penalties of the law. Victorian and Edwardian publishers of **novels,** for example, urged authors to remove potentially offensive material, especially for serial publication in popular magazines.

codex: the physical format of most modern books and medieval manuscripts, consisting of a series of separate leaves gathered into quires and bound together, often with a cover. In late antiquity, the codex largely replaced the scroll, the standard form of written documents in Roman culture.

copy text: the particular text of a work used by a textual editor as the basis of an edition of that work.

copyright: the legal protection afforded to authors for control of their work's publication, in an attempt to ensure due financial reward. Some key dates in the history of copyright in the United Kingdom are as follows: 1710, when a statute gave authors the exclusive right to publish their work for fourteen years, and fourteen years more if the author were still alive when the first term had expired; 1842, when the period of authorial control was extended to forty-two years; and 1911, when the term was extended yet further, to fifty years after the author's death. In 1995 the period of protection was harmonized with the laws in other European countries to be the life of the author plus seventy years. In the United States no works first published before 1923 are in copyright. Works published since 1978 are, as in the United Kingdom, protected for the life of the author plus seventy years.

folio: the leaf formed by both sides of a single page. Each folio has two sides: a *recto* (the front side of the leaf, on the right side of a double-page spread in an open codex), and a *verso* (the back side of the leaf, on the left side of a double-page spread). Modern book pagination follows the pattern 1, 2, 3, 4, while medieval manuscript pagination follows the pattern 1r, 1v, 2r, 2v. "Folio" can also designate the size of a printed book. Books come in different shapes, depending originally on the number of times a standard sheet of paper is folded. One fold produces a large volume, a *folio* book; two folds produce a *quarto*, four an *octavo*, and six a very small *duodecimo*. Generally speaking, the larger the book, the grander and more expensive. Shakespeare's plays were, for example, first printed in quartos, but were gathered into a folio edition in 1623.

foul papers: versions of a work before an author has produced, if she or he has, a final copy (a "fair copy") with all corrections removed.

incunabulum (plural "incunabula"): any printed book produced in Europe before 1501. Famous incunabula include the Gutenberg Bible, printed in 1455.

manuscript (Latin, "written by hand"): Any text written physically by hand is a manuscript. Before the introduction of **printing** with moveable type in 1476, all texts in England were produced and reproduced by hand, in manuscript. This is an extremely labor-intensive task, using expensive materials (e.g., **vellum,** or **parchment**); the cost of books produced thereby was, accordingly, very high. Even after the introduction of printing, many texts continued to be produced in manuscript. This is obviously true of letters, for example, but until the eighteenth century, poetry written within aristocratic circles was often transmitted in manuscript copies.

paleography (Greek "ancient writing"): the art of deciphering, describing, and dating forms of handwriting.

parchment: animal skin, used as the material for handwritten books before the introduction of paper. See also **vellum.**

patronage, patron (Latin "protector"): Many technological, legal, and commercial supports were necessary before professional authorship became possible. Although some playwrights (e.g., Shakespeare) made a living by writing for the theater, other authors needed, principally, the large-scale reproductive capacities of **printing** and the security of **copyright** to make a living from writing. Before these conditions obtained, many authors had another main occupation, and most authors had to rely on patronage. In different periods, institutions or individuals offered material support, or patronage, to authors. Thus in Anglo-Saxon England, monasteries afforded the conditions of writing to monastic authors. Between the twelfth and the seventeenth centuries, the main source of patronage was the royal court. Authors offered patrons prestige and ideological support in return for financial support. Even as the conditions of professional authorship came into being at the beginning of the eighteenth century, older forms of direct patronage were not altogether displaced until the middle of the century.

periodical: Whereas journalism, strictly, applies to daily writing (from French *jour*, "day"), periodical writing appears at larger, but still frequent, intervals, characteristically in the form of the **essay.** Periodicals were developed especially in the eighteenth century.

printing: Printing, or the mechanical reproduction of books using moveable type, was invented in Germany in the mid-fifteenth century by Johannes Gutenberg; it quickly spread throughout Europe. William Caxton brought printing into England from the Low Countries in 1476. Much greater powers of reproduction at much lower prices transformed every aspect of literary culture.

publisher: the person or company responsible for the commissioning and publicizing of printed matter. In the early period of **printing,** publisher, printer, and bookseller were often the same person. This trend continued in the ascendancy of the **Stationers' Company,** between the middle of the sixteenth and the end of the seventeenth centuries. Toward the end of the seventeenth century, these three functions began to separate, leading to their modern distinctions.

quire: When medieval manuscripts were assembled, a few loose sheets of parchment or paper would first be folded together and sewn along the fold. This formed a quire (also known as a "gathering" or "signature"). Folded in this way, four large sheets of parchment would produce eight smaller manuscript leaves. Multiple quires could then be bound together to form a codex.

royalties: an agreed-upon proportion of the price of each copy of a work sold, paid by the publisher to the author, or an agreed-upon fee paid to the playwright for each performance of a play.

scribe: In **manuscript** culture, the scribe is the copyist who reproduces a text by hand.

scriptorium (plural "scriptoria"): a place for producing written documents and manuscripts.

serial publication: generally referring to the practice, especially common in the nineteenth century, of publishing novels a few chapters at a time, in periodicals.

Stationers' Company: The Stationers' Company was an English guild incorporating various tradesmen, including printers, publishers, and booksellers, skilled in the production and selling of books. It was formed in 1403, received its royal charter in 1557, and served as a means both of producing and of regulating books. Authors would sell the manuscripts of their books to individual stationers, who incurred the risks and took the profits of producing and selling the books. The stationers entered their rights over given books in the Stationers' Register. They also regulated the book trade and held their monopoly by licensing books and by being empowered to seize unauthorized books and imprison resisters. This system of licensing broke down in the social unrest of the Civil War and Interregnum (1640–60), and it ended in 1695. Even after the end of licensing, the Stationers' Company continued to be an intrinsic part of the **copyright** process, since the 1710 copyright statute directed that copyright had to be registered at Stationers' Hall.

subscription: An eighteenth-century system of bookselling somewhere between direct **patronage** and impersonal sales. A subscriber paid half the cost of a book before publication and half on delivery. The author received these payments directly. The subscriber's name appeared in the prefatory pages.

textual criticism: Works in all periods often exist in many subtly or not so subtly different forms. This is especially true with regard to manuscript textual reproduction, but it also applies to printed texts. Textual criticism is the art, developed from the fifteenth century in Italy but raised to new levels of sophistication from the eighteenth century, of deciphering different historical states of texts. This art involves the analysis of textual **variants,** often with the aim of distinguishing authorial from scribal forms.

variants: differences that appear among different manuscripts or printed editions of the same text.

vellum: animal skin, used as the material for handwritten books before the introduction of paper. See also **parchment.**

watermark: the trademark of a paper manufacturer, impressed into the paper but largely invisible unless held up to light.

Geographic Nomenclature

The British Isles refers to the prominent group of islands off the northwest coast of Europe, especially to the two largest, **Great Britain** and **Ireland**. At present these comprise two sovereign states: **the Republic of Ireland**, and **the United Kingdom of Great Britain and Northern Ireland**—known for short as the **United Kingdom** or the **U.K.** Most of the smaller islands are part of the **U.K.** but a few, like the **Isle of Man** and the tiny **Channel Islands,** are largely independent. The **U.K.** is often loosely referred to as "Britain" or "Great Britain" and is sometimes called simply, if inaccurately, "**England.**" For obvious reasons, the latter usage is rarely heard among the inhabitants of the other countries of the **U.K.**—**Scotland, Wales,** and **Northern Ireland** (sometimes called **Ulster**). England is by far the most populous part of the kingdom, as well as the seat of its capital, London.

From the first to the fifth century C.E. most of what is now **England** and **Wales** was a province of the Roman Empire called **Britain** (in Latin, **Britannia**). After the fall of Rome, much of the island was invaded and settled by peoples from northern Germany and Denmark speaking what we now call Old English. These peoples are collectively known as the Anglo-Saxons, and the word **England** is related to the first element of their name. By the time of the Norman Conquest (1066) most of the kingdoms founded by the Anglo-Saxons and subsequent Viking invaders had coalesced into the kingdom of **England,** which, in the latter Middle Ages, conquered and largely absorbed the neighboring Celtic kingdom of **Wales.** In 1603 James VI of **Scotland** inherited the island's other throne as James I of **England,** and for the next hundred years—except for the two decades of Puritan rule—**Scotland** (both its English-speaking **Lowlands** and its Gaelic-speaking **Highlands**) and **England** (with **Wales**) were two kingdoms under a single king. In 1707 the Act of Union welded them together as **the United Kingdom of Great Britain. Ireland,** where English rule had begun in the twelfth century and been tightened in the sixteenth, was incorporated by the 1800–1801 Act of Union into **the United Kingdom of Great Britain and Ireland**. With the division of Ireland and the establishment of **the Irish Free State** after World War I, this name was modified to its present form, and in 1949 **the Irish Free State** became **the Republic of Ireland,** or **Éire.** In 1999 **Scotland** elected a separate parliament it had relinquished in 1707, and **Wales** elected an assembly it lost in 1409; neither Scotland nor Wales ceased to be part of the **United Kingdom**.

The **British Isles** are further divided into counties, which in **Great Britain** are also known as shires. This word, with its vowel shortened in pronunciation, forms the suffix in the names of many counties, such as **Yorkshire, Wiltshire, Somersetshire**.

The Latin names **Britannia (Britain), Caledonia (Scotland),** and **Hibernia (Ireland)** are sometimes used in poetic diction; so too is **Britain's** ancient Celtic name, **Albion.** Because of its accidental resemblance to *albus* (Latin for "white"), **Albion** is especially associated with the chalk cliffs that seem to gird much of the English coast like defensive walls.

The **British Empire** took its name from **the British Isles** because it was created not only by the **English** but also by the **Irish, Scots,** and **Welsh,** as well as by civilians and servicemen from other constituent countries of the empire. Some of the empire's **overseas colonies**, or **crown colonies**, were populated largely by settlers of European origin and their descendants. These predominantly white **settler colonies,** such as **Canada, Australia,** and **New Zealand,** were allowed significant self-government in the nineteenth century and recognized as **dominions** in the early twentieth century. The white dominions became members of **the Commonwealth of Nations**, also called **the Commonwealth, the British Commonwealth**, and "**the Old Commonwealth**" at different times, an association of sovereign states under the symbolic leadership of the British monarch.

Other **overseas colonies** of the empire had mostly indigenous populations (or, in the Caribbean, the descendants of imported slaves, indentured servants, and others). These **colonies** were granted political independence after World War II, later than the **dominions**, and have often been referred to since as **postcolonial** nations. In South and Southeast Asia, **India** and **Pakistan** gained independence in 1947, followed by other countries including **Sri Lanka** (formerly **Ceylon**), **Burma** (now **Myanmar**), **Malaya** (now **Malaysia**), and **Singapore**. In West and East Africa, the **Gold Coast** was decolonized as **Ghana** in 1957, **Nigeria** in 1960, **Sierra Leone** in 1961, **Uganda** in 1962, **Kenya** in 1963, and so forth, while in southern Africa, the white minority government of **South Africa** was already independent in 1931, though majority rule did not come until 1994. In the Caribbean, **Jamaica** and **Trinidad and Tobago** won independence in 1962, followed by **Barbados** in 1966, and other islands of the British West Indies in the 1970s and '80s. Other regions with nations emerging out of British colonial rule included Central America (**British Honduras**, now **Belize**), South America (**British Guiana**, now **Guyana**), the Pacific islands (**Fiji**), and Europe (**Cyprus, Malta**). After decolonization, many of these nations chose to remain within a newly conceived **Commonwealth** and are sometimes referred to as "**New Commonwealth**" countries. Some nations, such as **Ireland, Pakistan**, and **South Africa,** withdrew from the **Commonwealth**, though **South Africa** and **Pakistan** eventually rejoined, and others, such as **Burma** (now **Myanmar**), gained independence outside the **Commonwealth**. Britain's last major overseas colony, **Hong Kong**, was returned to Chinese sovereignty in 1997, but while Britain retains only a handful of dependent territories, such as **Bermuda** and **Montserrat**, the scope of the **Commonwealth** remains vast, with 30 percent of the world's population.

British Money

One of the most dramatic changes to the system of British money came in 1971. In the system previously in place, the pound consisted of 20 shillings, each containing 12 pence, making 240 pence to the pound. Since 1971, British money has been calculated on the decimal system, with 100 pence to the pound. Britons' experience of paper money did not change very drastically: as before, 5- and 10-pound notes constitute the majority of bills passing through their hands (in addition, 20- and 50- pound notes have been added). But the shift necessitated a whole new way of thinking about and exchanging coins and marked the demise of the shilling, one of the fundamental units of British monetary history. Many other coins, still frequently encountered in literature, had already passed. These include the groat, worth 4 pence (the word "groat" is often used to signify a trifling sum); the angel (which depicted the archangel Michael triumphing over a dragon), valued at 10 shillings; the mark, worth in its day two-thirds of a pound or 13 shillings 4 pence; and the sovereign, a gold coin initially worth 22 shillings 6 pence, later valued at 1 pound, last circulated in 1932. One prominent older coin, the guinea, was worth a pound and a shilling; though it has not been minted since 1813, a very few quality items or prestige awards (like the purse in a horse race) may still be quoted in guineas. (The table below includes some other well-known, obsolete coins.) Colloquially, a pound was (and is) called a quid; a shilling a bob; sixpence, a tanner; a copper could refer to a penny, a half-penny, or a farthing (¼ penny).

Old Currency	New Currency
1 pound note	1 pound coin (or note in Scotland)
10 shilling (half-pound note)	50 pence
5 shilling (crown)	
2½ shilling (half crown)	20 pence
2 shilling (florin)	10 pence
1 shilling	5 pence
6 pence	
2½ pence	1 penny
2 pence	
1 penny	
½ penny	
¼ penny (farthing)	

Throughout its tenure as a member of the European Union, Britain contemplated but did not make the change to the EU's common currency, the Euro. Many Britons strongly identify their country with its rich commercial history and tend to view their currency patriotically as a national symbol. Now, with the planned withdrawal of the United Kingdom from the EU, the pound seems here to stay.

Even more challenging than sorting out the values of obsolete coins is calculating for any given period the purchasing power of money, which fluctuates over time by its very nature. At the beginning of the twentieth century, 1 pound was worth about 5 American dollars, though those bought three to four times what they now do. Now, the pound buys anywhere from $1.20 to $1.50. As difficult as it is to generalize, it is clear that money used to be worth much more than it is currently. In Anglo-Saxon times, the most valuable circulating coin was the silver penny: four would buy a sheep. Beyond long-term inflationary trends, prices varied from times of plenty to those marked by poor harvests; from peacetime to wartime; from the country to the metropolis (life in London has always been very expensive); and wages varied according to the availability of labor (wages would sharply rise, for instance, during the devastating Black Death in the fourteenth century). The following chart provides a glimpse of some actual prices of given periods and their changes across time, though all the variables mentioned above prevent them from being definitive. Even from one year to the next, an added tax on gin or tea could drastically raise prices, and a lottery ticket could cost much more the night before the drawing than just a month earlier. Still, the prices quoted below do indicate important trends, such as the disparity of incomes in British society and the costs of basic commodities. In the chart on the following page, the symbol £ is used for pound, s. for shilling, d. for a penny (from Latin *denarius*); a sum would normally be written £2.19.3, i.e., 2 pounds, 19 shillings, 3 pence. (This is Leopold Bloom's budget for the day depicted in Joyce's novel *Ulysses* [1922]; in the new currency, it would be about £2.96.)

circa	1390	1590	1650	1750	1815	1875	1950
food and drink	gallon (8 pints) of ale, 1.5d.	tankard of beer, .5d.	coffee, 1d. a dish	"drunk for a penny, dead drunk for two-pence" (gin shop sign in Hogarth print)	ounce of laudanum, 3d.	pint of beer, 3d.	pint of Guinness stout, 11d.
	gallon (8 pints) of wine, 3 to 4d.	pound of beef, 2s. 5d.	chicken, 1s. 4d.	dinner at a steakhouse, 1s.	ham and potato dinner for two, 7s.	dinner in a good hotel, 5s.	pound of beef, 2s. 2d.
	pound of cinnamon, 1 to 3s.	pound of cinnamon, 10s. 6d.	pound of tea, £3 10s.	pound of tea, 16s.	bottle of French claret, 12s.	pound of tea, 2s.	dinner on railway car, 7s. 6d.
entertainment	no cost to watch a cycle play	admission to public theater, 1 to 3d.	falcon, £11 5s.	theater tickets, 1 to 5s.	admission to Covent Garden theater, 1 to 7s.	theater tickets, 6d. to 7s.	admission to Old Vic theater, 1s. 6d. to 10s. 6d.
	contributory admission to professional troupe theater	cheap seat in private theater, 6d.	billiard table, £25	admission to Vauxhall Gardens, 1s.	annual subscription to Almack's (exclusive club), 10 guineas	admission to Madam Tussaud's waxworks, 1s.	admission to Odeon cinema, Manchester, 1s 3d.
	maintenance for royal hounds at Windsor, .75d. a day	"to see a dead Indian" (quoted in *The Tempest*), 1.25d. (ten "doits")	three-quarter length portrait painting, £31	lottery ticket, £20 (shares were sold)	Jane Austen's piano, 30 guineas	annual fees at a gentleman's club, 7 to 10 guineas	tropical fish tank, £4 4s.

circa	1390	1590	1650	1750	1815	1875	1950
reading	cheap romance, 1s.	play quarto, 6d.	pamphlet, 1 to 6d.	issue of The Gentleman's Magazine, 6d.	issue of Edinburgh Review, 6s.	copy of the Times, 3d.	copy of the Times, 3d.
	a Latin Bible, 2 to £4	Shakespeare's First Folio (1623), £1	student Bible, 6s.	cheap edition of Milton, 2s.	membership in circulating library (3rd class), £1 4s. a year	illustrated edition of Through the Looking-glass, 6s.	issue of Eagle comics, 4.5d.
	payment for illuminating a liturgical book, £22 9s.	Foxe's Acts and Monuments, 24s.	Hobbes's Leviathan, 8s.	Johnson's Dictionary, folio, 2 vols., £4 10s.	1st edition of Austen's Pride and Prejudice, 18s.	1st edition of Trollope's The Way We Live Now, 2 vols., £1 1s.	Orwell's Nineteen Eighty Four, paperback, 3s. 6d.
transportation	night's supply of hay for horse, 2d.	wherry (whole boat) across Thames, 1d.	day's journey, coach, 10s.	boat across Thames, 4d.	coach ride, outside, 2 to 3d. a mile; inside, 4 to 5d. a mile	15-minute journey in a London cab, 1s. 6d.	London tube fare, about 2d. a mile
	coach, £8	hiring a horse for a day, 12d.	coach horse, £30	coach fare, London to Edinburgh, £4 10s.	palanquin transport in Madras, 5s. a day	railway, 3rd class, London to Plymouth, 18s. 8d. (about 1d. a mile)	petrol, 3s. a gallon
	quality horse £10	hiring a coach for a day, 10s.	fancy carriage, £170	transport to America, £5	passage, Liverpool to New York, £10	passage to India, 1st class, £50	midsize Austin sedan, £449 plus £188 4s. 2d. tax
clothes	clothing allowance for peasant, 3s. a year	shoes with buckles, 8d.	footman's frieze coat, 15s.	working woman's gown, 6s. 6d.	checked muslin, 7s. per yard	flannel for a cheap petticoat, 1s. 3d. a yard	woman's sun frock, £3 13s. 10d.

labor/incomes

shoes for gentry wearer, 4d.	woman's gloves, £1 5s.	falconer's hat, 10s.	gentleman's suit, £8	hiring a dressmaker for a pelisse, 8s.	overcoat for an Eton schoolboy, £1 1s.	tweed sports jacket, £3 16s. 6d.
hat for gentry wearer, 10d.	fine cloak, £16	black cloth for mourning household of an earl, £100	very fine wig, £30	ladies silk stockings, 12s.	set of false teeth, £2 10s.	"Teddy boy" drape suit, £20
hiring a skilled building worker, 4d. a day	actor's daily wage during playing season, 1s.	agricultural laborer, 6s. 5d. a week	price of boy slave, £32	lowest-paid sailor on Royal Navy ship, 10s. 9d. a month	seasonal agricultural laborer, 14s. a week	minimum wage, agricultural laborer, £4 14s. per 47-hour week
wage for professional scribe, £2 3s. 4d. a year + cloak	household servant 2 to £5 a year + food, clothing	tutor to nobleman's children, £30 a year	housemaid's wage, £6 to £8 a year	contributor to Quarterly Review, 10 guineas per sheet	housemaid's wage, £10 to £25 a year	shorthand typist, £367 a year
minimum income to be called gentleman, £10 a year; for knighthood, 40 to £400	minimum income for eligibility for knighthood, £30 a year	Milton's salary as Secretary of Foreign Tongues, £288 a year	Boswell's allowance, £200 a year	minimum income for a "genteel" family, £100 a year	income of the "comfortable" classes, £800 and up a year	middle manager's salary, £1,480 a year
income from land of richest magnates, £3,500 a year	income from land of average earl, £4,000 a year	Earl of Bedford's income, £8,000 a year	Duke of Newcastle's income, £40,000 a year	Mr. Darcy's income, Pride and Prejudice, £10,000	Trollope's income, £4,000 a year	barrister's salary, £2,032 a year

The British Baronage

The English monarchy is in principle hereditary, though at times during the Middle Ages the rules were subject to dispute. In general, authority passes from father to eldest surviving son, to daughters in order of seniority if there is no son, to a brother if there are no children, and in default of direct descendants to collateral lines (cousins, nephews, nieces) in order of closeness. There have been breaks in the order of succession (1066, 1399, 1688), but so far as possible the usurpers have always sought to paper over the break with a legitimate, i.e., hereditary, claim. When a queen succeeds to the throne and takes a husband, he does not become king unless he is in the line of blood succession; rather, he is named prince consort, as Albert was to Victoria. He may father kings, but is not one himself.

The original Saxon nobles were the king's thanes, ealdormen, or earls, who provided the king with military service and counsel in return for booty, gifts, or landed estates. William the Conqueror, arriving from France, where feudalism was fully developed, considerably expanded this group. In addition, as the king distributed the lands of his new kingdom, he also distributed dignities to men who became known collectively as "the baronage." "Baron" in its root meaning signifies simply "man," and barons were the king's men. As the title was common, a distinction was early made between greater and lesser barons, the former gradually assuming loftier and more impressive titles. The first English "duke" was created in 1337; the title of "marquess," or "marquis" (pronounced "markwis"), followed in 1385, and "viscount" ("vyekount") in 1440. Though "earl" is the oldest title of all, an earl now comes between a marquess and a viscount in order of dignity and precedence, and the old term "baron" now designates a rank just below viscount. "Baronets" were created in 1611 as a means of raising revenue for the crown (the title could be purchased for about £1,000); they are marginal nobility and have never sat in the House of Lords.

Kings and queens are addressed as "Your Majesty," princes and princesses as "Your Highness," the other hereditary nobility as "My Lord" or "Your Lordship." Peers receive their titles either by inheritance (like Lord Byron, the sixth baron of that line) or from the monarch (like Alfred, Lord Tennyson, created 1st Baron Tennyson by Victoria). The children, even of a duke, are commoners unless they are specifically granted some other title or inherit their father's title from him. A peerage can be forfeited by act of attainder, as for example when a lord is convicted of treason; and, when forfeited, or lapsed for lack of a successor, can be bestowed on another family. Thus in 1605 Robert Cecil was made first earl of Salisbury in the third creation, the first creation dating from 1149, the second from 1337, the title having been in abeyance since 1539. Titles descend by right of succession and do not depend on tenure of land; thus, a title does not always indicate where a lord dwells or holds power. Indeed, noble titles do not always refer to a real place at all. At Prince Edward's marriage in 1999, the queen created him earl of Wessex, although the old kingdom of Wessex has had no political existence since the Anglo-Saxon period, and the name was all but forgotten until it was resurrected by Thomas Hardy as the setting of his novels. (This is perhaps but one of many ways in which the world of the aristocracy increasingly resembles the realm of literature.)

The king and queen	(These are all of the royal line.)
Prince and princess	
Duke and duchess	(These may or may not be of the royal
Marquess and marchioness	line, but are ordinarily remote from the succession.)
Earl and countess	
Viscount and viscountess	
Baron and baroness	
Baronet and lady	

Scottish peers sat in the parliament of Scotland, as English peers did in the parliament of England, till at the Act of Union (1707) Scottish peers were granted sixteen seats in the English House of Lords, to be filled by election. (In 1963, all Scottish lords were allowed to sit.) Similarly, Irish peers, when the Irish parliament was abolished in 1801, were granted the right to elect twenty-eight of their number to the House of Lords in Westminster. (Now that the Republic of Ireland is a separate nation, this no longer applies.) Women members (peeresses) were first allowed to sit in the House as nonhereditary Life Peers in 1958 (when that status was created for members of both genders); women first sat by their own hereditary right in 1963. Today the House of Lords still retains some power to influence or delay legislation, but its future is uncertain. In 1999, the hereditary peers (then amounting to 750) were reduced to 92 temporary members elected by their fellow peers. Holders of Life Peerages remain, as do senior bishops of the Church of England and high-court judges (the "Law Lords").

Below the peerage the chief title of honor is "knight." Knighthood, which is not hereditary, is generally a reward for services rendered. A knight (Sir John Black) is addressed, using his first name, as "Sir John"; his wife, using the last name, is "Lady Black"—unless she is the daughter of an earl or nobleman of higher rank, in which case she will be "Lady Arabella." The female equivalent of a knight bears the title of "Dame." Though the word *knight* itself comes from the Anglo-Saxon *cniht*, there is some doubt as to whether knighthood amounted to much before the arrival of the Normans. The feudal system required military service as a condition of land tenure, and a man who came to serve his king at the head of an army of tenants required a title of authority and badges of identity—hence the title of knighthood and the coat of arms. During the Crusades, when men were far removed from their land (or even sold it in order to go on crusade), more elaborate forms of fealty sprang up that soon expanded into orders of knighthood. The Templars, Hospitallers, Knights of the Teutonic Order, Knights of Malta, and Knights of the Golden Fleece were but a few of these companionships; not all of them were available at all times in England.

Gradually, with the rise of centralized government and the decline of feudal tenures, military knighthood became obsolete, and the rank largely honorific; sometimes, as under James I, it degenerated into a scheme of the royal government for making money. For hundreds of years after its establishment in the fourteenth century, the Order of the Garter was the only English order of knighthood, an exclusive courtly companionship. Then, during the late seventeenth, the eighteenth, and the nineteenth centuries, a number of additional orders were created, with names such as the Thistle, Saint Patrick, the Bath, Saint Michael, and Saint George, plus a number of special Victorian and Indian orders. They retain the terminology, ceremony, and dignity of knighthood, but the military implications are vestigial.

Although the British Empire now belongs to history, appointments to the Order of the British Empire continue to be conferred for services to that empire at home or abroad. Such honors (commonly referred to as "gongs") are granted by the monarch in her New Year's and Birthday lists, but the decisions are now made by the government in power. In recent years there have been efforts to popularize and democratize the dispensation of honors, with recipients including rock stars and actors. But this does not prevent large sectors of British society from regarding both knighthood and the peerage as largely irrelevant to modern life.

The Royal Lines of England and Great Britain

England

SAXONS AND DANES

Egbert, king of Wessex	802–839
Ethelwulf, son of Egbert	839–858
Ethelbald, second son of Ethelwulf	858–860
Ethelbert, third son of Ethelwulf	860–866
Ethelred I, fourth son of Ethelwulf	866–871
Alfred the Great, fifth son of Ethelwulf	871–899
Edward the Elder, son of Alfred	899–924
Athelstan the Glorious, son of Edward	924–940
Edmund I, third son of Edward	940–946
Edred, fourth son of Edward	946–955
Edwy the Fair, son of Edmund	955–959
Edgar the Peaceful, second son of Edmund	959–975
Edward the Martyr, son of Edgar	975–978 (murdered)
Ethelred II, the Unready, second son of Edgar	978–1016
Edmund II, Ironside, son of Ethelred II	1016–1016
Canute the Dane	1016–1035
Harold I, Harefoot, natural son of Canute	1035–1040
Hardecanute, son of Canute	1040–1042
Edward the Confessor, son of Ethelred II	1042–1066
Harold II, brother-in-law of Edward	1066–1066 (died in battle)

HOUSE OF NORMANDY

William I, the Conqueror	1066–1087
William II, Rufus, third son of William I	1087–1100 (shot from ambush)
Henry I, Beauclerc, youngest son of William I	1100–1135

HOUSE OF BLOIS

Stephen, son of Adela, daughter of William I	1135–1154

HOUSE OF PLANTAGENET

Henry II, son of Geoffrey Plantagenet by Matilda, daughter of Henry I	1154–1189
Richard I, Coeur de Lion, son of Henry II	1189–1199
John Lackland, son of Henry II	1199–1216
Henry III, son of John	1216–1272
Edward I, Longshanks, son of Henry III	1272–1307
Edward II, son of Edward I	1307–1327 (deposed)
Edward III of Windsor, son of Edward II	1327–1377
Richard II, grandson of Edward III	1377–1399 (deposed)

HOUSE OF LANCASTER

Henry IV, son of John of Gaunt, son of Edward III	1399–1413
Henry V, Prince Hal, son of Henry IV	1413–1422
Henry VI, son of Henry V	1422–1461 (deposed), 1470–1471 (deposed)

HOUSE OF YORK

Edward IV, great-great-grandson of Edward III	1461–1470 (deposed), 1471–1483
Edward V, son of Edward IV	1483–1483 (murdered)
Richard III, Crookback	1483–1485 (died in battle)

HOUSE OF TUDOR

Henry VII, married daughter of Edward IV	1485–1509
Henry VIII, son of Henry VII	1509–1547
Edward VI, son of Henry VIII	1547–1553
Mary I, "Bloody," daughter of Henry VIII	1553–1558
Elizabeth I, daughter of Henry VIII	1558–1603

HOUSE OF STUART

James I (James VI of Scotland)	1603–1625
Charles I, son of James I	1625–1649 (executed)

COMMONWEALTH & PROTECTORATE

Council of State	1649–1653
Oliver Cromwell, Lord Protector	1653–1658
Richard Cromwell, son of Oliver	1658–1660 (resigned)

HOUSE OF STUART (RESTORED)

Charles II, son of Charles I	1660–1685
James II, second son of Charles I	1685–1688

(INTERREGNUM, 11 DECEMBER 1688 TO 13 FEBRUARY 1689)

HOUSE OF ORANGE-NASSAU

William III of Orange, by	
Mary, daughter of Charles I	1689–1701
and Mary II, daughter of James II	–1694
Anne, second daughter of James II	1702–1714

Great Britain

HOUSE OF HANOVER

George I, son of Elector of Hanover and	
Sophia, granddaughter of James I	1714–1727
George II, son of George I	1727–1760
George III, grandson of George II	1760–1820
George IV, son of George III	1820–1830
William IV, third son of George III	1830–1837
Victoria, daughter of Edward, fourth son	
of George III	1837–1901

HOUSE OF SAXE-COBURG AND GOTHA

Edward VII, son of Victoria	1901–1910

HOUSE OF WINDSOR (NAME ADOPTED 17 JULY 1917)

George V, second son of Edward VII	1910–1936
Edward VIII, eldest son of George V	1936–1936 (abdicated)
George VI, second son of George V	1936–1952
Elizabeth II, daughter of George VI	1952–

Religions in Great Britain

In the late sixth century C.E., missionaries from Rome introduced Christianity to the Anglo-Saxons—actually, reintroduced it, since it had briefly flourished in the southern parts of the British Isles during the Roman occupation, and even after the Roman withdrawal had persisted in the Celtic regions of Scotland and Wales. By the time the earliest poems included in *The Norton Anthology of English Literature* were composed (i.e., the seventh century), therefore, there had been a Christian presence in the British Isles for hundreds of years. The conversion of the Germanic occupiers of England can, however, be dated only from 597. Our knowledge of the religion of pre-Christian Britain is sketchy, but it is likely that vestiges of Germanic polytheism assimilated into, or coexisted with, the practice of Christianity: fertility rites were incorporated into the celebration of Easter resurrection, rituals commemorating the dead into All-Hallows Eve and All Saints Day, and elements of winter solstice festivals into the celebration of Christmas. The most durable polytheistic remains are our days of the week, each of which except "Saturday" derives from the name of a Germanic pagan god, and the word "Easter," deriving, according to the Anglo-Saxon scholar Bede (d. 735), from the name of a Germanic pagan goddess, Eostre. In English literature such "folkloric" elements sometimes elicit romantic nostalgia. Geoffrey Chaucer's "Wife of Bath" looks back to a magical time before the arrival of Christianity in which the land was "fulfilled of fairye." Hundreds of years later, the seventeenth-century writer Robert Herrick honors the amalgamation of Christian and pagan elements in agrarian British culture in such poems as "Corinna's Gone A-Maying" and "The Hock Cart."

Medieval Christianity was fairly uniform, if complex, across Western Europe—hence called "catholic," or universally shared. The Church was composed of the so-called "regular" and "secular" orders, the regular orders being those who followed a rule in a community under an abbot or an abbess (i.e., monks, nuns, friars and canons), while the secular clergy of priests served parish communities under the governance of a bishop. In the unstable period from the sixth until the twelfth century, monasteries were the intellectual powerhouse of the Church. From the beginning of the thirteenth century, with the development of an urban Christian spirituality in Europe, friars dominated the recently invented institution of universities, as well as devoting themselves, in theory at least, to the urban poor.

The Catholic Church was also an international power structure. With its hierarchy of pope, cardinals, archbishops, and bishops, it offered a model of the centralized, bureaucratic state from the late eleventh century. That ecclesiastical power structure coexisted alongside a separate, often less centralized and feudal structure of lay authorities, with theoretically different and often competing spheres of social responsibilities. The sharing of lay and ecclesiastical authority in medieval England was sometimes a source of conflict. Chaucer's pilgrims are on their way to visit the memorial shrine to one victim of such exemplary struggle: Thomas à Becket, Archbishop of Canterbury, who opposed the policies of King Henry II, was assassinated by indirect suggestion of the king in 1170, and later made a saint. The Church, in turn, produced its own victims: Jews were subject to persecution in the late twelfth century in England, before being expelled in 1290. From the beginning of the fifteenth century, the English Church targeted Lollard heretics (see below) with capital punishment, for the first time.

As an international organization, the Church conducted its business in the universal language of Latin. Thus although in the period the largest segment of literate persons was made up of clerics, the clerical contribution to great literary writing in vernacular languages (e.g., French and English) was, so far as we know, relatively modest, with some great exceptions in the later Middle Ages (e.g., William Langland). Lay, vernacular writers of the period certainly reflect the importance of the Church as an institution and the pervasiveness of religion in the rituals that marked everyday life, as well as contesting institutional authority. From the late fourteenth century, indeed, England witnessed an active and articulate, proto-Protestant movement known as Lollardy, which attacked clerical hierarchy and promoted vernacular scriptures.

Beginning in 1517 the German monk Martin Luther, in Wittenberg, Germany, openly challenged many aspects of Catholic practice and by 1520 had completely repudiated the authority of the pope, setting in train the Protestant Reformation. Luther argued that the Roman Catholic Church had strayed far from the pattern of Christianity laid out in scripture. He rejected Catholic doctrines for which no biblical authority was to be found, such as the belief in Purgatory, and translated the Bible into German, on the grounds that the importance of scripture for all Christians made its translation into the vernacular tongue essential. Luther was not the first to advance such views— Lollard followers of the Englishman John Wycliffe had translated the Bible in the late fourteenth century. But Luther, protected by powerful German rulers, was able to speak out with impunity and convert others to his views, rather than suffer the persecution usually meted out to heretics. Soon other reformers were following in Luther's footsteps: of these, the Swiss Ulrich Zwingli and the French Jean Calvin would be especially influential for English religious thought.

At first England remained staunchly Catholic. Its king, Henry VIII, was so severe to heretics that the pope awarded him the title "Defender of the Faith," which British monarchs have retained to this day. In 1534, however, Henry rejected the authority of the pope to prevent his divorce from his queen, Catherine of Aragon, and his marriage to his mistress, Ann Boleyn. In doing so, Henry appropriated to himself ecclesiastical as well as secular authority. Thomas More, author of *Utopia*, was executed in 1535 for refusing to endorse Henry's right to govern the English church. Over the following six years, Henry consolidated his grip on the ecclesiastical establishment by dissolving the powerful, populous Catholic monasteries and redistributing their massive landholdings to his own lay followers. Yet Henry's church largely retained Catholic doctrine and liturgy. When Henry died and his young son, Edward, came to the throne in 1547, the English church embarked on a more Protestant path, a direction abruptly reversed when Edward died and his older sister Mary, the daughter of Catherine of Aragon, took the throne in 1553 and attempted to reintroduce Roman Catholicism. Mary's reign was also short, however, and her successor, Elizabeth I, the daughter of Ann Boleyn, was a Protestant. Elizabeth attempted to establish a "middle way" Christianity, compromising between Roman Catholic practices and beliefs and reformed ones.

The Church of England, though it laid claim to a national rather than pan-European authority, aspired like its predecessor to be the universal church of all English subjects. It retained the Catholic structure of parishes and dioceses and the Catholic hierarchy of bishops, though the ecclesiastical authority was now the Archbishop of Canterbury and the Church's "Supreme Governor" was the monarch. Yet disagreement and controversy persisted. Some members of the Church of England wanted to retain many of the ritual and liturgical elements of Catholicism. Others, the Puritans, advocated a more thoroughgoing reformation. Most Puritans remained within the Church of England, but a minority, the "Separatists" or "Congregationalists," split from the established church altogether. These dissenters no longer thought of the ideal church as an organization to which everybody belonged; instead, they conceived it as a more exclusive group of likeminded people, one not necessarily attached to a larger body of believers.

In the seventeenth century, the succession of the Scottish king James to the English throne produced another problem. England and Scotland were separate nations, and in the sixteenth century Scotland had developed its own national Presbyterian church, or "kirk," under the leadership of the reformer John Knox. The kirk retained fewer Catholic liturgical elements than did the Church of England, and its authorities, or "presbyters," were elected by assemblies of their fellow clerics, rather than appointed by the king. James I and his son Charles I, especially the latter, wanted to bring the Scottish kirk into conformity with Church of England practices. The Scots violently resisted these efforts, with the collaboration of many English Puritans, in a conflict that eventually developed into the English Civil War in the mid-seventeenth century. The effect of these disputes is visible in the poetry of such writers as John Milton, Robert Herrick, Henry Vaughan, and Thomas Traherne, and in the prose of Thomas Browne, Lucy Hutchinson, and Dorothy Waugh. Just as in the mid-sixteenth century, when a succession of monarchs with different religious commitments destabilized the church, so the seventeenth century endured spiritual whiplash. King Charles I's highly ritualistic Church of England was violently overturned by the Puritan victors in the Civil War—until 1660, after the death of the Puritan leader, Oliver Cromwell, when the Church of England was restored along with the monarchy.

The religious and political upheavals of the seventeenth century produced Christian sects that de-emphasized the ceremony of the established church and rejected as well its top-down authority structure. Some of these groups were ephemeral, but the Baptists (founded in 1608 in Amsterdam by the English expatriate John Smyth) and Quakers, or Society of Friends (founded by George Fox in the 1640s), flourished outside the established church, sometimes despite cruel persecution. John Bunyan, a Baptist, wrote the Christian allegory *Pilgrim's Progress* while in prison. Some dissenters, like the Baptists, shared the reformed reverence for the absolute authority of scripture but interpreted the scriptural texts differently from their fellow Protestants. Others, like the Quakers, favored, even over the authority of the Bible, the "inner light" or voice of individual conscience, which they took to be the working of the Holy Spirit in the lives of individuals.

The Protestant dissenters were not England's only religious minorities. Despite crushing fines and the threat of imprisonment, a minority of Catholics under Elizabeth and James openly refused to give their allegiance to the new church, and others remained secret adherents to the old ways. John Donne was brought up in an ardently Catholic family, and several other writers converted to Catholicism as adults—Ben Jonson for a considerable part of his career, Elizabeth Carey and Richard Crashaw permanently, and at profound personal cost. In the eighteenth century, Catholics remained objects of suspicion as possible agents of sedition, especially after the "Glorious Revolution" in 1688 deposed the Catholic James II in favor of the Protestant William and Mary. Anti-Catholic prejudice affected John Dryden, a Catholic convert, as well as the lifelong Catholic Alexander Pope. By contrast, the English colony of Ireland remained overwhelmingly Roman Catholic, the fervor of its religious commitment at least partly inspired by resistance to English occupation. Starting in the reign of Elizabeth, England shored up its own authority in Ireland by encouraging Protestant immigrants from Scotland to settle in the north of Ireland, producing a virulent religious divide the effects of which are still playing out today.

A small community of Jews had moved from France to London after 1066, when the Norman William the Conqueror came to the English throne. Although despised and persecuted by many Christians, they were allowed to remain as moneylenders to the Crown, until the thirteenth century, when the king developed alternative sources of credit. At this point, in 1290, the Jews were expelled from England. In 1655 Oliver Cromwell permitted a few to return, and in the late seventeenth and early eighteenth centuries the Jewish population slowly increased, mainly by immigration from Germany. In the mid-eighteenth century some prominent Jews had their children brought up as Christians so as to facilitate their full integration into English society: thus the nineteenth-century writer and politician Benjamin Disraeli, although he and his father were members of the Church of England, was widely considered a Jew insofar as his ancestry was Jewish.

In the late seventeenth century, as the Church of England reasserted itself, Catholics, Jews, and dissenting Protestants found themselves subject to significant legal restrictions. The Corporation Act, passed in 1661, and the Test Act, passed in 1673, excluded all who refused to take communion in the Church of England from voting, attending university, or working in government or in the professions. Members of religious minorities, as well as Church of England communicants, paid mandatory taxes in support of Church of England ministers and buildings. In 1689 the dissenters gained the right to worship in public, but Jews and Catholics were not permitted to do so.

During the eighteenth century, political, intellectual, and religious history remained closely intertwined. The Church of England came to accommodate a good deal of variety. "Low church" services resembled those of the dissenting Protestant churches, minimizing ritual and emphasizing the sermon; the "high church" retained more elaborate ritual elements, yet its prestige was under attack on several fronts. Many Enlightenment thinkers subjected the Bible to rational critique and found it wanting: the philosopher David Hume, for instance, argued that the "miracles" described therein were more probably lies or errors than real breaches of the laws of nature. Within the Church of England, the "broad church" Latitudinarians welcomed this rationalism, advocating theological openness and an emphasis on ethics rather than dogma. More radically, the Unitarian movement rejected the divinity of Christ while professing to accept his ethical teachings. Taking a different tack, the preacher John Wesley, founder of Methodism, responded to the rationalists' challenge with a newly fervent call to evangelism and personal discipline; his movement was particularly successful in Wales. Revolutions in America and France at the end of the century generated considerable millenarian excitement and fostered more new religious ideas, often in conjunction with a radical social agenda. Many important writers of the Romantic period were indebted to traditions of protestant dissent: Unitarian and rationalist protestant ideas influenced William Hazlitt, Anna Barbauld, Mary Wollstonecraft, and the young Samuel Taylor Coleridge. William Blake created a highly idiosyncratic poetic mythology loosely indebted to radical strains of Christian mysticism. Others were even more heterodox: Lord Byron and Robert Burns, brought up as Scots Presbyterians, rebelled fiercely, and Percy Shelley's writing of an atheistic pamphlet resulted in his expulsion from Oxford.

Great Britain never erected an American-style "wall of separation" between church and state, but in practice religion and secular affairs grew more and more distinct during the nineteenth century. In consequence, members of religious minorities no longer seemed to pose a threat to the commonweal. A movement to repeal the Test Act failed in the 1790s, but a renewed effort resulted in the extension of the franchise to dissenting Protestants in 1828 and to Catholics in 1829. The numbers of Roman Catholics in England were swelled by immigration from Ireland, but there were also some prominent English adherents. Among writers, the converts John Newman and Gerard Manley Hopkins are especially important. The political participation and social integration of Jews presented a thornier challenge. Lionel de Rothschild, repeatedly elected to represent London in Parliament during the 1840s and 1850s, was not permitted to take his seat there because he refused to take his oath of office "on the true faith of a Christian"; finally, in 1858, the Jewish Disabilities Act allowed him to omit these words. Only in 1871, however, were Oxford and Cambridge opened to non-Anglicans.

Meanwhile geological discoveries and Charles Darwin's evolutionary theories increasingly cast doubt on the literal truth of the Creation story, and close philological analysis of the biblical text suggested that its origins were human rather than divine. By the end of the nineteenth century, many writers were bearing witness to a world in which Christianity no longer seemed fundamentally plausible. In his poetry and prose, Thomas Hardy depicts a world devoid of benevolent providence. Matthew Arnold's poem "Dover Beach" is in part an elegy to lost spiritual assurance, as the "Sea of Faith" goes out like the tide: "But now I only hear / Its melancholy, long, withdrawing roar / Retreating." For Arnold, literature must replace religion as a source of spiritual truth, and intimacy between individuals substitute for the lost communal solidarity of the universal church.

The work of many twentieth-century writers shows the influence of a religious upbringing or a religious conversion in adulthood. T. S. Eliot and W. H. Auden embrace Anglicanism, William Butler Yeats spiritualism. James Joyce repudiates Irish Catholicism but remains obsessed with it. Yet religion, or lack of it, is a matter of individual choice and conscience, not social or legal mandate. In the past fifty years, church attendance has plummeted in Great Britain. Although 71 percent of the population still identified itself as "Christian" on the 2000 census, only about 7 percent of these regularly attend religious services of any denomination. Meanwhile, immigration from former British colonies has swelled the ranks of religions once uncommon in the British Isles—Muslim, Sikh, Hindu, Buddhist—though the numbers of adherents remain small relative to the total population.

PERMISSIONS ACKNOWLEDGMENTS

TEXT CREDITS

William Blake: Poems from THE COMPLETE POETRY AND PROSE OF WILLIAM BLAKE, edited by David V. Erdman, copyright © 1965, 1981, Doubleday & Company. Blake engravings: reproduced from the Lessing J. Rosenwald Collection, Library of Congress.

Robert Burns: Selections from THE POEMS AND SONGS OF ROBERT BURNS, edited by James Kinsley. Copyright 1968 by Oxford University Press. Reprinted by permission of Oxford University Press.

Lord Byron: Letters are reprinted by permission of the publisher from BYRON'S LETTERS AND JOURNALS, Volumes I–VII, edited by Leslie A. Marchand, Cambridge, Mass.: The Belknap Press of Harvard University Press: Copyright © Editorial 1975, 1976 Byron copyrighted material, John Murray. Reproduced by permission of Harvard University Press.

John Clare: "Mouse's Nest" and "Pastoral Poetry" from THE POEMS OF JOHN CLARE, edited by J. W. Tibble (J. M. Dent). Reprinted by permission Everyman's Library, London. "The Nightingale's Nest" from SELECTED POEMS AND PROSE OF JOHN CLARE, edited by Eric Robinson and Geoffrey Summerfield. Reproduced with permission of Curtis Brown Ltd., London, on behalf of Eric Robinson. Copyright © Eric Robinson 1984, 1967. All other poems from THE LATER POEMS OF JOHN CLARE 1837–1864, edited by Eric Robinson and David Powell. Reproduced with permission of Curtis Brown Ltd., London, on behalf of Eric Robinson. Copyright © Eric Robinson 1984, 1967. "The Badger" from JOHN CLARE: POEMS OF THE MIDDLE PERIOD 1822–1837, edited by Eric Robinson, David Powell, P.M.S. Dawson. Copyright © 2003 by Oxford University Press. Reprinted by permission of Oxford University Press.

John Keats: Reprinted by permission of the publisher from JOHN KEATS: COMPLETE POEMS, edited by Jack Stillinger, Cambridge, Mass.: The Belknap Press of Harvard University Press, copyright © 1978, 1982 by the President and Fellows of Harvard College. Reprinted by permission of the publisher from THE LETTERS OF JOHN KEATS 1814–1821, VOLUMES I and II, edited by Hyder Edward Rollins, Cambridge, Mass.: Harvard University Press, Copyright © 1958 by The President and Fellows of Harvard College. Copyright renewed 1986 by Herschel C. Baker.

Mary Prince: Republished with permission of University of Michigan Press, from THE HISTORY OF MARY PRINCE, A WEST INDIAN SLAVE, RELATED BY HERSELF by Mary Prince, edited by Moira Ferguson. Copyright © 1997 by University of Michigan Press. Permission conveyed through Copyright Clearance Center, Inc.

Percy Bysshe Shelley: Poems and *Prometheus Unbound* from SHELLEY'S POETRY AND PROSE, SECOND EDITION by Percy Bysshe Shelley, edited by Donald H. Reiman & Neil Fraistat. Copyright © 2002 by Donald H. Reiman, Neil Fraistat and Rebecca Thompson. Copyright © 1977 by Donald H. Reiman Sharon B. Powers. Reprinted by permission of W. W. Norton & Company, Inc.

Mary Wollstonecraft: Reprinted from LETTERS WRITTEN DURING A SHORT RESIDENCE IN SWEDEN, NORWAY, AND DENMARK by Mary Wollstonecraft, edited by Carol H. Poston, by permission of the University of Nebraska Press. Copyright © 1976 by the University of Nebraska Press. From A VINDICATION OF THE RIGHTS OF WOMAN: A NORTON CRITICAL EDITION, Second Edition, by Mary Wollstonecraft, edited by Carol H. Poston. Copyright © 1988, 1975 by W. W. Norton & Company, Inc. Reprinted by permission of W. W. Norton & Company, Inc.

Dorothy Wordsworth: Letter dated September 24, 1802 from THE GRASMERE JOURNALS, edited by Pamela Woof (1991). Reprinted by permission of Oxford University Press. "Grasmere—A Fragment" and "Thoughts on My Sick Bed" from DOROTHY WORDSWORTH AND ROMANTICISM. Reprinted by permission of The Wordsworth Trust, Dove Cottage, Grasmere.

William Wordsworth: Reprinted from William Wordsworth: THE RUINED COTTAGE AND THE PEDLAR. Edited by James A. Butler. Copyright © 1978 by Cornell University. Used by permission of the publisher, Cornell University Press. From THE PRELUDE 1799, 1805, 1850 by William Wordsworth: A Norton Critical Edition, edited by Jonathan Wordsworth, M. H. Abrams. Copyright © 1979 by W. W. Norton & Company, Inc. Used by permission of W. W. Norton & Company, Inc.

IMAGE CREDITS

Pp. 2–3: Tate Collection; p. 12 (left): The British Museum; p. 12 (right): The British Museum; p. 15: The Bardic Museum; p. 21: George Cruikshank / © Chetham's Library, Manchester, UK / The Bridgeman Art Library; p. 26: The British Museum; p. 55: Charlotte Smith, *Elegiac Sonnets*, 1788; p. 105: American School (18th century) / Private Collection / The Bridgeman Art Library; p. 128: Library of Congress / The Bridgeman Art Library; p. 135: Library of Congress / The Bridgeman Art Library; p. 139: Library of Congress / The Bridgeman Art Library; p. 142: William Blake (1757–1827) / Fitzwilliam Museum, University of Cambridge, UK / The Bridgeman Art Library; p. 143: Rogers Fund, 1917. Metropolitan Museum of Art.; p. 147: Library of Congress / The Bridgeman Art Library; p. 152: Library of Congress / The Bridgeman Art Library; p. 214: © Courtesy of Warden and Scholars of New College, Oxford / The Bridgeman Art Library; p. 215: British Library, London / © British Library Board. All Rights Reserved / The Bridgeman Art Library; p. 216: © Courtesy of Warden and Scholars of New College, Oxford / The Bridgeman Art Library; p. 217: Bibliotheque Nationale, Paris, France / Archives Charmet / Bridgeman Images; p. 532: Lilly Library / Indiana University; p. 746: 'John Bull's Progress', pub. by Hannah Humphrey, 1793 (etching) (b&w photo), Gillray, James (1757–1815) / British Museum, London, UK / Bridgeman Images; p. 804: The British Museum; p. 942: Artokoloro Quint Lox Limited / Alamy Stock Photo; p. 948: Preparation for a Suttee, or the Immolation of a Hindoo Widow, from Volume I of *Scenery, Costumes and Architecture of India*, etched by J. Willis and H. Melville, engraved by R. G. Reeve, pub., Smith, Elder and Company, 1826 (aquatint), Captain Robert M. Grindlay (1786–1877) (after) / Private Collection / The Stapleton Collection / Bridgeman Images.

COLOR INSERT CREDITS

Index